Sample Student Drafts and Revisions

Annotated Student Research Papers

Arguing about Literature

A GUIDE AND READER

THIRD EDITION

John Schilb
Indiana University

John Clifford
University of North Carolina at Wilmington

bedford/st.martin's
Macmillan Learning
Boston | New York

For Wendy and Janet

For Bedford/St. Martin's
Vice President, Editorial, Macmillan Learning Humanities: Leasa Burton
Senior Program Manager: John E. Sullivan III
Executive Marketing Manager: Lauren Arrant
Director of Content Development, Humanities: Jane Knetzger
Senior Developmental Editor: Jesse Hassenger
Senior Content Project Manager: Lidia MacDonald-Carr
Senior Workflow Project Manager: Lisa McDowell
Production Supervisor: Robin Besofsky
Advanced Media Project Manager: Rand Thomas
Senior Media Editor: Adam Whitehurst
Senior Manager of Publishing Services: Andrea Cava
Project Management: Lumina Datamatics, Inc.
Composition: Lumina Datamatics, Inc.
Text Permissions Manager: Kalina Ingham
Text Permissions Researcher: Elaine Kosta, Lumina Datamatics, Inc.
Photo Permissions Editor: Angela Boehler
Photo Permissions Researcher: Krystyna Borgen, Lumina Datamatics, Inc.
Director of Design, Content Management: Diana Blume
Cover Design: William Boardman
Cover Image: AdrianHillman/iStock/Getty Images; Obadah Meslmani/EyeEm/
  Getty Images
Printing and Binding: LSC Communications

Manufactured in the United States of America.

1 2 3 4 5 6   24 23 22 21 20 19

For information, write: Bedford/St. Martin's, 75 Arlington Street, Boston, MA 02116

ISBN 978-1-319-21592-7

Acknowledgments
Text acknowledgments and copyrights appear at the back of the book on pages 1199–1205,
which constitute an extension of the copyright page. Art acknowledgments and copyrights
appear on the same page as the art selections they cover.

Preface for Instructors

Arguing about Literature: A Guide and Reader combines two books in one: a guide to writing skills, especially means of argument, and a thematically organized literature anthology. We have joined these two approaches so that *Arguing about Literature* might work in two courses, separately or in combination: a composition course in which students learn techniques of argument through reading and writing about literature, and a literature course that helps students craft strong arguments about their readings. Because these courses often involve research, we've made sure to explain those practices in great detail, too—even more so in the third edition, which is publishing at a time when it's become particularly important to detect bias, recognize facts, and distinguish between legitimate and illegitimate sources.

This material is covered in an all-new Chapter 8, which also includes new coverage of analyzing visual arguments, especially those that students might come across during Internet research. In addition to that new chapter, we've strengthened the connections between the book's argument coverage and its literary anthology with a series of poems, stories, and essays that speak to major contemporary issues that we hope will inspire discussion. We have also diversified our selection of readings with more pieces by women and writers of color, representing a wide range of perspectives, feelings, and voices.

We hope this new material will inspire students on a number of levels. In contemporary education, students are increasingly expected to be or become resourceful critical thinkers with strong argumentative skills. We give these subjects extended attention in both sections of the book: the guide (Part One) and the reader (Part Two).

A Closer Look at the Guide

Part One, "A Brief Guide to Arguing about Literature," focuses on effective ways of writing and reading. In Chapter 1, we introduce elements of argument with an analysis of Paul Goldberger's "Disconnected Urbanism," which elaborates such terms as issues, claims, audience, evidence, and ethos. Equally useful should be Chapter 2, which covers developing an effective style of argument, with ways to move beyond the formulaic five-paragraph essay.

Chapter 3 focuses on strategies for arguing about literature, including a cluster of writing that addresses the effectiveness of public shaming. Chapter 4 offers suggestions for close reading, featuring the new poetry selection "Girls Online" by Emily Skillings.

Chapter 5 returns to the writing process, familiarizing students with other moves that foster good argument essays, including strategies for exploring, planning, and composing. Chapter 6 shows students how to write arguments about the main literary genres: short stories, poems, and plays. Chapter 7 on how to write researched arguments treats this subject at length and has been significantly updated and expanded with advice about taking useful notes on sources and using them effectively and about avoiding plagiarism. Part One concludes with the new Chapter 8, "Evaluating Internet Resources in a 'Post-Truth' Age," which breaks down how students should consider evaluating Internet sources in text as well as visual forms, enhancing the critical analysis skills they'll need in both their academic work and in their everyday consideration of news and opinion. The former Chapter 8, "Writing with Critical Approaches to Literature," is still included as an appendix.

A Closer Look at the Reader

The third edition of *Arguing about Literature* echoes its predecessor by featuring the bulk of our literary selections in the theme-based chapters that make up Part Two, "Literature and Arguments." We have also carried over the main subjects of these chapters, for they continue to loom in students' lives. Specifically, in order of appearance, the topics are families, love, freedom and confinement, crime and justice, and journeys. Each thematic chapter also continues to draw from multiple genres. For example, Chapter 9 deals with families through not only short fiction (such as stories about mothers and children by Tillie Olsen and Amy Tan) but also verse (poems about grandparents by Nikki Giovanni, Linda Hogan, and Richard Blanco). Several chapters also include drama: Chapter 10's treatment of love includes William Shakespeare's tragedy *Othello*; Chapter 11's concern with freedom and confinement includes plays by Henrik Ibsen, Susan Glaspell, and Lynn Nottage; and Chapter 12 investigates justice partly through Sophocles' *Antigone* and a radio theater piece by Holocaust survivor Ida Fink. As perhaps you can tell from this preview, the book reflects a variety of cultural backgrounds, and its authors range from long-esteemed names to talented new voices.

In each of Part Two's chapters, we continue to arrange works in small clusters so that students can gain insights by comparing texts. In the first part of each chapter, for example, we play literary works directly off each other. What insights will students gain by contrasting Countee Cullen's "Incident" with Natasha Trethewey's poem of the same title? How might the weird tradition in Shirley Jackson's "The Lottery" affect students' interpretation of Alexander Weinstein's "Rocket Night"? What changes does Angela Carter ring on classic versions of the Red Riding Hood tale by the Brothers Grimm and Charles Perrault? How eye-opening are the several poetic views on ethnicity gathered in the "Resisting Stereotypes" cluster? The ideas sparked by such questions and comparisons ignite students' curiosity and fuel their writing.

In keeping with our enhanced emphasis on argument and research in *Arguing about Literature*, each thematic chapter in the reader concludes with clusters in which individual literary works are grouped with contemporary arguments ("Literature and Current Issues"), critical essays ("Arguments about a Story/Poem/Play"), and historical and cultural documents ("Contexts for Research"). These special clusters encourage the common types of multisource-based assignments exemplified by student essays in Chapter 7 on the researched argument: using a literary work to examine contemporary social issues, developing an argument based on existing interpretations of a literary work, and developing an argument that places a literary work in historical and cultural context. Of course, the literary works can be taught apart from the associated materials, just as the associated materials can be taught on their own — although teaching them together, in our opinion, presents a richer learning experience.

New to the Third Edition

The revisions in the third edition reflect the many useful suggestions of our users and reviewers as well as our own attempts to integrate new developments in literature and composition studies, along with current social, cultural, scientific, and technological issues.

A brand-new chapter on Internet sources and visual arguments. With real-life arguments becoming ever more contentious, it's especially important for students to identify when sources, Web sites, and images are offering real information or making credible claims. To address the necessity of these skills, *Arguing about Literature* has added Chapter 8, "Evaluating Internet Resources in the 'Post-Truth' Age." The material in this chapter is designed to help students develop their analytical eye when examining both textual and visual materials, especially in their digital (and sometimes viral) incarnations.

New literature. Fresh voices.　More than thirty new literary selections appear in the third edition, including work from such contemporary fiction writers as Aimee Bender, Kristen Roupenian, Ha Jin, Karen Russell, and George Saunders, as well as canonical authors like Edgar Allan Poe, James Joyce, and Leslie Marmon Silko. The new poetry selections are an exciting blend of classic work by figures including Elizabeth Barrett Browning, John Donne, and Pablo Neruda, and contemporary poems from Richard Blanco, Deborah Garrison, Emily Skillings, David Hernandez, Robin Becker, and Hafizah Geter.

Issues that matter.　The "Literature and Current Issues" clusters draw topical discussions out of arguments that will resonate with students. The third edition includes new material on free speech, consent, immigration, and environmental responsibilities, deepened with literary connections and made accessible through a variety of recent, relevant essays.

BEDFORD/ST. MARTIN'S PUTS YOU FIRST

From day one, our goal has been simple: to provide inspiring resources that are grounded in best practices for teaching reading and writing. For more than thirty-five years, Bedford/St. Martin's has partnered with the field, listening to teachers, scholars, and students about the support writers need. We are committed to helping every writing instructor make the most of our resources.

How Can We Help *You*?

- Our editors can align our resources to your outcomes through correlation and transition guides for your syllabus. Just ask us.
- Our sales representatives specialize in helping you find the right materials to support your course goals.
- Our *Bits* blog on the Bedford/St. Martin's English Community (**community .macmillan.com**) publishes fresh teaching ideas weekly. You'll also find easily downloadable professional resources and links to author webinars on our community site.

Contact your Bedford/St. Martin's sales representative or visit **macmillanlearning.com** to learn more.

Print and Digital Options for *Arguing about Literature*

Choose the format that works best for your course, and ask about our packaging options that offer savings for students.

Print

- *A Brief Guide to Arguing about Literature.* In the event that some instructors want to assign the pedagogical guide chapters but would rather choose their own literary or argumentative texts for the course, we offer Part One as its own book, in print or e-book form: *A Brief Guide to Arguing about Literature.* To order the brief edition, use ISBN 978-1-319-21593-4 (print) and 978-1-319-29385-7 (e-book).

Digital

- *Innovative digital learning space.* Bedford/St. Martin's suite of digital tools makes it easy to get everyone on the same page by putting student writers at the center. For details, visit **macmillanlearning.com/englishdigital**.
- *Popular e-book formats.* For details about our e-book partners, visit **macmillanlearning.com/ebooks**.
- *Inclusive Access.* Enable every student to receive their course materials through your LMS on the first day of class. Macmillan Learning's Inclusive Access program is the easiest, most affordable way to ensure all

students have access to quality educational resources. Find out more at **macmillanlearning.com/inclusiveaccess**.

Your Course, Your Way

No two writing programs or classrooms are exactly alike. Our Curriculum Solutions team works with you to design custom options that provide the resources your students need. (Options below require enrollment minimums.)

- *ForeWords for English.* Customize any print resource to fit the focus of your course or program by choosing from a range of prepared topics, such as Sentence Guides for Academic Writers.
- *Macmillan Author Program (MAP).* Add excerpts or package acclaimed works from Macmillan's trade imprints to connect students with prominent authors and public conversations. A list of popular examples or academic themes is available upon request.
- *Bedford Select.* Build your own print handbook or anthology from a database of more than 900 selections, and add your own materials to create your ideal text. Package with any Bedford/St. Martin's text for additional savings. Visit **macmillanlearning.com/bedfordselect**.

Instructor Resources

You have a lot to do in your course. We want to make it easy for you to find the support you need—and to get it quickly.

    Resources for Teaching Arguing about Literature: A Guide and Reader is available as a PDF that can be downloaded from **macmillanlearning .com**. In addition to chapter overviews and advice on teaching composition, argumentation, and literature, the instructor's manual includes substantial commentaries on the individual arguments and literary works in the book to aid class preparation and discussion.

Acknowledgments

The terrific staff at Bedford/St. Martin's of Macmillan Learning continue to be wise and generous collaborators in our efforts. Thank you to senior program manager John Sullivan, development editor Jesse Hassenger, and editorial assistant Alex Markle. We also want to express thanks to Leasa Burton, vice president of the Humanities division of Macmillan Learning, for her support of the project. In production, we are grateful to Lidia MacDonald-Carr, who oversaw the process of turning a manuscript into a book. In the permissions department, manager Kalina Ingham and editor Elaine Kosta effectively negotiated text permissions, and Angela Boehler capably handled the photo permissions. In marketing, we are most grateful to Lauren Arrant.

We thank Janet E. Gardner, formerly of the University of Massachusetts–Dartmouth, for her contributions to the chapter on research as well as Joyce Hollingsworth of the University of North Carolina at Wilmington and Laura Sparks of California State University, Chico, for their ample and timely work on the instructor's manual.

As always, John Schilb is indebted to his former University of Maryland colleague Jeanne Fahnestock and his colleagues at Indiana University, as well as all of the Midwest high school instructors who have participated in his workshops on teaching literary interpretation. John Clifford thanks Sheri Malman for her expert editorial assistance.

We are particularly grateful to those who taught from and reviewed the second edition of this book, offering invaluable feedback as we prepared the third edition: Cheryl Baker, Greenville Technical College; Robert Birdwell, Greenville Technical College; Misti Brock, Vernon College; Robert Burton, North Central Texas College; Elizabeth Dieterich, Wilbur Wright College; Matthew Duffus, Gardner-Webb University; Jennifer Lofton, Bossier Parish Community College; Torria Norman, Black Hawk College; Van Piercy, Lone Star College – Tomball; Dr. Jim Richey, Tyler Junior College; Cortney Robbins, Indiana Tech; Dr. Kimberly Thomas, Greenville Technical College; Emily Weathers, Greenville Technical College; Kristen Weinzapfel, North Central Texas College; and Marilyn Yamin, Pellissippi State Community College.

As with *Making Literature Matter*, we dedicate this book to our wives, Wendy Elliot and Janet Ellerby. May our relationships with them never be compact, always expanding.

John Schilb, *Indiana University*
John Clifford, *University of North Carolina at Wilmington*

LaunchPad Solo
macmillan learning

Pairing *Arguing about Literature: A Guide and Reader* with *LaunchPad Solo for Literature* helps students succeed.

Available for free when packaged with *Arguing about Literature: A Guide and Reader*, *LaunchPad Solo for Literature* gets to the heart of close reading. It offers a set of online materials to help beginning literature students learn and practice close reading and critical thinking skills in an interactive environment.

To package *LaunchPad Solo for Literature*, use ISBN 978-1-319-02735-3.

How can *LaunchPad Solo for Literature* enhance your course?

It helps students come prepared to class. Assign reading comprehension quizzes on commonly taught stories, poems, plays, and essays to ensure that your students complete and understand their reading. For homework assignments, have students work through close reading modules that will prepare them for lively, informed classroom discussions.

It gives students hands-on practice in close reading. Easy-to-use and easy-to-assign modules based on widely taught literary selections guide students through three common assignment types:

- **Respond to a Reading**
  Marginal questions that refer to specific passages in a publisher-provided literary work prompt students to read carefully and think critically about key issues raised by the text.

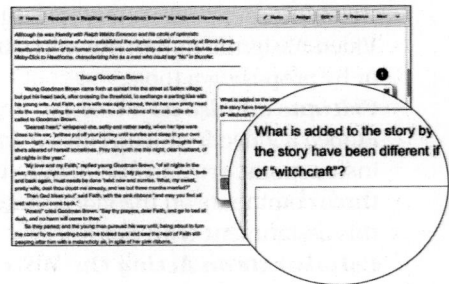

- **Draw Connections**
  Students read and compare two or more publisher-provided texts that illuminate each other. Students can download these texts, which have been annotated to highlight key moments and contextual information, and respond in writing to a series of questions that highlight important similarities and differences between and among the texts.

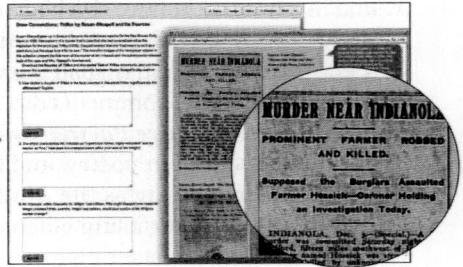

To explore *LaunchPad Solo for Literature*, visit **launchpadworks.com**.

- **Collaborate on a Reading**
Instructors can upload their favorite text or choose from over 200 publisher-provided texts to create a customized lesson on close reading. Using the highlighting tools and notes feature in *LaunchPad*, the instructor can post notes or questions about specific passages or issues in a text, prompting students to respond with their own comments, questions, or observations. Students can also respond to each other, further collaborating and deepening their understanding of a text.

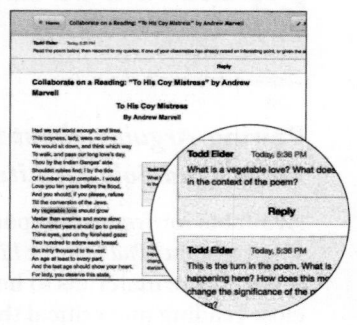

It lets you create multimedia assignments about literature. *LaunchPad Solo for Literature* enables you to embed videos, including favorite selections from YouTube, directly into your digital course. Whether you want students to analyze a Shakespearean scene, listen to W. B. Yeats reading his poems, or compare *The Great Gatsby* in print and on film, the tools are at your fingertips. You can annotate these videos for your students, or ask them to leave their own comments directly on the video content itself. Consider some of these assignment suggestions:

- **Create a Dialogue around an Assignment**
Some projects are complicated because they involve many choices and stages. Record yourself explaining the project, and upload the video to the Video Assignment tool. Require students to comment by asking a question or by proposing a topic.
- **Critique a Video as a Group**
Embed a video from YouTube or from another source. In your assignment instructions, provide discussion questions. Require students to add two or three comments on the video that respond to the prompt. You may grade this assignment with a rubric.
- **Collaborate on Acting Out a Scene from a Play**
Although students most often study plays as written texts, it can be fun and informative to have them act out scenes for their classmates. Assign small groups of students to record themselves acting out their favorite scene from a play and upload the video for the class to watch. You can add your feedback and comments directly on the video.
- **Compare and Share Poems Your Students Read Aloud**
Sound is essential in poetry, and how a poem is read can be as important to understanding as the words themselves. Invite students to record themselves — either using video or audio only — and share the results with the class. Consider giving each student a mood for their reading, so that the class can hear how different tones and interpretations affect their response to the poem.

Brief Contents

Contents

PART TWO   Literature and Arguments

Contents by Genre

Stories

Poems

Plays

Arguments about Current Issues

Arguments about Literary Works

Contexts for Research

A Brief Guide to Arguing about Literature

CHAPTER 1

What Is Argument?

The first word in our book's title may puzzle you. Why would we want you to argue? Are we really inviting you to yell or sneer? The word *arguing* may remind you of spats you regret. Almost everyone has suffered arguments like these. They arise in the media all the time. Cable news panels routinely lapse into squabbles; guests feel required to clash. Social media outlets like Twitter are plagued by "trolls," accounts that exist to insult and demean other people's posts. Celebrities may rebuke each other on Instagram. No wonder many people define *arguing* as combat. It often seems like war.

But our book is about arguing in a positive sense. We define it as a calm, courteous process in which you

- identify a subject of current or possible debate;
- analyze why you view the subject the way you do;
- address others who may not share your view; and
- try to persuade them that your view is worth accepting or at least makes sense.

This better kind of arguing occurs at various times and places. You may try to coax friends who dread horror films into joining you at *Saw 12*. In class, you may need to explain the logic of your stand on climate change. Beyond campus, you may advocate for social causes. For instance, you might petition your city to launch recycling sites.

Let's face it: to argue is to disagree, or to air views that not all may hold. Still, at its best, argument is an alternative to war. It's not a contest you try to "win" by insisting you're right. Ideally, argument is a form of **inquiry**, a process in which you test your beliefs, consider other views, and stay open to changing your mind. Rather than immediately attack your critics, you note principles you share with them. When their thinking differs from yours, you treat their positions fairly. If any of their ideas strike you as wise, you adjust your thinking. In the meantime, you recognize the limits of your knowledge and understanding. You admit, too, your inner conflicts: how your thoughts are divided, your values in conflict, your feelings mixed. Indeed, essayist Phillip Lopate observes that "the real argument should be with yourself." Columnist David Brooks goes even further: "If you write in a way that suggests combative certitude," he warns, "you may gradually smother the inner chaos that will be the source of lifelong freshness and creativity." In their own fashion, these writers point to something important about argument: at its best, it teaches you about yourself and your world, while alerting you to what you still must learn.

Students regularly encounter this kind of arguing in college. Academic subjects aren't just pools of information. They go beyond proven facts. Disciplines grapple with uncertainties: problems, questions, and conflicts they haven't yet solved. Physicists disagree about the origins of the universe. Historians write conflicting accounts of Hitler's Germany; they debate how much his extreme anti-Semitism was traditional there. Two sociologists may scan the same figures on poverty and make different inferences from them. Typically, scholars draw conclusions that are open to challenge. They must explain why their judgments are sound. They expect to engage in reasoned debate with their colleagues. They see this as their field's best chance for truth.

In your classes, expect disagreements. They're crucial to learning in college. Often classmates will voice ideas you don't immediately accept. Just as often, they'll hesitate to adopt some of your opinions. Authors you read will deal with controversies from their own points of view. As a writer yourself, you will enter debates and have to defend your stands.

No one naturally excels at this type of arguing. It takes practice. Our book is a series of opportunities to become skilled in this art. Our book's chief springboard for argument is works of literature. Those we include don't deliver simple, straightforward messages. They offer puzzles, complications, metaphors, symbols, and mysteries. In short, they stress life's complexity. They especially encourage you to ponder multiple dimensions of language: how, for example, shifts of context can change a word's meaning. Each of our literary works calls for you to interpret. As you read the text, you must figure out various features of it. Other readers may not see the text as you do. So next you'll *argue* for your view. Often you'll do this by composing essays and perhaps online posts. From Chapter 2 on, we offer strategies for you to argue about literature as a writer.

This chapter is a general introduction to arguing. Let's start with an example: an article titled "Disconnected Urbanism" by noted architecture critic Paul Goldberger (b. 1950). He wrote it for the February 22, 2003 issue of *Metropolis* magazine. Goldberger worries about cell phones. He believes they lead cities to lose a sense of community and place. At the time he wrote, these phones weren't yet packed with apps, nor could they connect to the Internet. Still, they were a big development, which pained Goldberger. As you read, note his key points and his efforts to sway his readers to them. Afterward, we raise questions to help you study his text. Then we refer to it as we explain the basic elements of argument.

PAUL GOLDBERGER
Disconnected Urbanism

There is a connection between the idea of place and the reality of cellular telephones. It is not encouraging. Places are unique—or at least we like to believe they are—and we strive to experience them as a kind of engagement with particulars.

Cell phones are precisely the opposite. When a piece of geography is doing what it is supposed to do, it encourages you to feel a connection to it that, as in marriage, forsakes all others. When you are in Paris you expect to wallow in its Parisness, to feel that everyone walking up the Boulevard Montparnasse is as totally and completely there as the lampposts, the kiosks, the facade of the Brasserie Lipp—and that they could be no place else. So we want it to be in every city, in every kind of place. When you are in a forest, you want to experience its woodsiness; when you are on the beach, you want to feel connected to sand and surf.

This is getting harder to do, not because these special places don't exist or because urban places have come to look increasingly alike. They have, but this is not another rant about the monoculture and sameness of cities and the suburban landscape. Even when you are in a place that retains its intensity, its specialness, and its ability to confer a defining context on your life, it doesn't have the all-consuming effect these places used to. You no longer feel that being in one place cuts you off from other places. Technology has been doing this for a long time, of course—remember when people communicated with Europe by letter and it took a couple of weeks to get a reply? Now we're upset if we have to send a fax because it takes so much longer than e-mail.

But the cell phone has changed our sense of place more than faxes and computers and e-mail because of its ability to intrude into every moment in every possible place. When you walk along the street and talk on a cell phone, you are not on the street sharing the communal experience of urban life. You are in some other place—someplace at the other end of your phone conversation. You are there, but you are not there. It reminds me of the title of Lillian Ross's memoir of her life with William Shawn, *Here But Not Here*. Now that is increasingly true of almost every person on almost every street in almost every city. You are either on the phone or carrying one, and the moment it rings you will be transported out of real space into a virtual realm.

This matters because the street is the ultimate public space and walking along it is the defining urban experience. It is all of us—different people who lead different lives—coming together in the urban mixing chamber. But what if half of them are elsewhere, there in body but not in any other way? You are not on Madison Avenue if you are holding a little object to your ear that pulls you toward a person in Omaha.

The great offense of the cell phone in public is not the intrusion of its ring,   5
although that can be infuriating when it interrupts a tranquil moment. It is the fact that even when the phone does not ring at all, and is being used quietly and discreetly, it renders a public place less public. It turns the boulevardier into a sequestered individual, the flaneur into a figure of privacy. And suddenly the meaning of the street as a public place has been hugely diminished.

I don't know which is worse—the loss of the sense that walking along a great urban street is a glorious shared experience or the blurring of distinctions between different kinds of places. But these cultural losses are related, and the cell phone has played a major role in both. The other day I returned a phone call from a friend who lives in Hartford. He had left a voice-mail message saying he was visiting his son in New Orleans, and when I called him back on his cell phone—area code 860, Hartford—he picked up the call in

Tallahassee. Once the area code actually meant something in terms of geography: it outlined a clearly defined piece of the earth; it became a form of identity. Your telephone number was a badge of place. Now the area code is really not much more than three digits; and if it has any connection to a place, it's just the telephone's home base. An area code today is more like a car's license plate. The downward spiral that began with the end of the old telephone exchanges that truly did connect to a place — RHinelander 4 and BUtterfield 8 for the Upper East Side, or CHelsea 3 downtown, or UNiversity 4 in Morningside Heights — surely culminates in the placeless area codes such as 917 and 347 that could be anywhere in New York — or anywhere at all.

It's increasingly common for cell-phone conversations to begin with the question, "Where are you?" and for the answer to be anything from "out by the pool" to "Madagascar." I don't miss the age when phone charges were based on distance, but that did have the beneficial effect of reinforcing a sense that places were distinguishable from one another. Now calling across the street and calling from New York to California or even Europe are precisely the same thing. They cost the same because to the phone they are the same. Every place is exactly the same as every other place. They are all just nodes on a network — and so, increasingly, are we.   *[2003]*

≣ THINKING ABOUT THE TEXT

1. Imagine that Goldberger could observe how people now use cell phones in places you ordinarily go, such as a college campus. To what extent would he see the kind of behavior that he worried about in his 2003 piece? How much evidence could he find for his argument that cell phones are diminishing people's sense of place and *dis*connecting them from one another?

2. Goldberger does not say much about the advantages of a cell phone. Which, if any, do you think he should have mentioned, and why? How, if at all, could he have said more about the advantages while still getting his readers to worry about these phones?

3. Goldberger wrote before smartphones came along, enabling use of apps and the Internet. In what ways, if any, does this newer technology affect your view of his argument?

4. As he indicates by including the word *urbanism* in his title, Goldberger is chiefly concerned with how cell phones affect their users' experiences of cities. If he had written about cell phone use in suburbs or in rural areas, do you think he would have changed his argument in some way? If so, in what respect?

5. It seems quite possible that Goldberger himself uses a cell phone. If this is the case, does it make his concern less valid? Why, or why not? Moreover, he does not end his piece by proposing that humanity abandon the technology. Why, conceivably, does he avoid making this recommendation? What might he want his readers to do instead?

Understanding Rhetoric

Goldberger's article is an example of **rhetoric**. This is a term from ancient Greek. It means writing, speech, and visual images used for a certain purpose: to affect how people think and act. Rhetorical texts don't just convey a message. They aim to shape beliefs and conduct. Often they're efforts to alter these things. Probably several of Goldberger's readers are joyously addicted to cell phones; he nudges them to reconsider their overattachment.

A related term is the **rhetorical situation**. It's the specific context you have in mind when you engage in rhetoric. As Figure 1.1 shows, this context includes three major elements: your topic, your audience, and possible "channels."

1. **The particular *topic* you choose.** This subject may already interest the public. School shootings in the United States immediately provoke disputes over gun control, school safety, mental illness, and screen violence. But the topic needn't be a calamity. When Goldberger wrote, cell phones were booming as a trend, so their effects were debated a lot. He didn't have to alert his readers to this subject or remind them of it. Other writers must do one or the other. This was the situation for legal scholars Woodrow Hartzog and Evan Zelinger in 2013, when they posted an online argument about Facebook. At the time, people worried that Facebook's privacy protocols wouldn't securely protect users' personal data. Hartzog and Zelinger deliberately shift to another subject. They recommend thinking less about *privacy* and more about *obscurity*, which they note is a word "rarely used" in debates about Facebook's risks. To them, *privacy* is so vague a concept that brooding about how the site guards it is futile. They call for pushing Facebook to keep personal

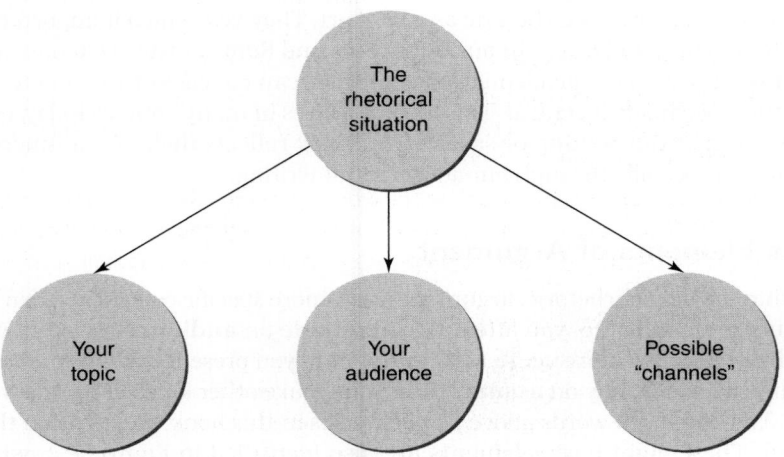

Figure 1.1   Elements of the rhetorical situation

facts *obscure*: "hard to obtain or understand" when cyberstalkers hunt them.

2. **The main readers, listeners, or viewers you decide to address; your *audience*.** Goldberger wrote for readers of the city-oriented magazine *Metropolis*. Its mission statement declares that it "examines contemporary life through design," publishing articles that "range from the sprawling urban environment to intimate living spaces to small objects of everyday lives." This magazine also seeks to put design in "economic, environmental, social, cultural, political, and technological contexts." Readers of *Metropolis* would expect it to probe cell phones' impact on cities. Perhaps Goldberger hoped his piece would someday circulate more widely, as it now does on the Web. But surely his target group loomed in his mind as he decided on content, form, and words.

3. **Possible "channels" for the text.** These include available institutions, media, and genres. Goldberger composed his article for a particular magazine. He used the medium of print. He resorted to a specific genre: the type of writing often called an opinion piece. Such choices do constrain an author. Writing for *Metropolis* forced upon Goldberger certain space limits; otherwise, he might have lengthened his argument. Today, a critic like him might film a video for YouTube, perhaps showing callers so absorbed in their cell-phone conversations that they forget friends alongside them.

Current politicians fling the word *rhetoric* as an insult. They accuse their rivals of indulging in it. They treat the word with contempt because they think it means windy exaggeration. But before the modern age, it meant something nobler. Rhetoric was the valuable attempt to influence readers, listeners, or viewers. In this sense, almost all of us resort to rhetoric daily. We need to learn rhetorical strategies if we're to have impact on others. For centuries, then, schools have seen rhetoric as a vital art. They've deemed it important to study, practice, and teach. In ancient Greece and Rome as well as Renaissance Europe, it was a core academic subject. American colleges of the nineteenth century also made it central. This focus survives in many courses today, especially ones about writing or speech. Our book reflects their commitment to rhetoric, especially through our advice about writing.

The Elements of Argument

Within the field of rhetoric, arguments are a more specific category. When you argue about an **issue**, you attempt to **persuade** an **audience** to accept your **claims** regarding an issue. To achieve this aim, you present **evidence**, explain your **reasoning**, rely on **assumptions**, and make other kinds of **appeals**.

The boldfaced words above play key roles in this book; we mention them often. These eight basic elements are also identified in Figure 1.2, which suggests visually how the elements work together.

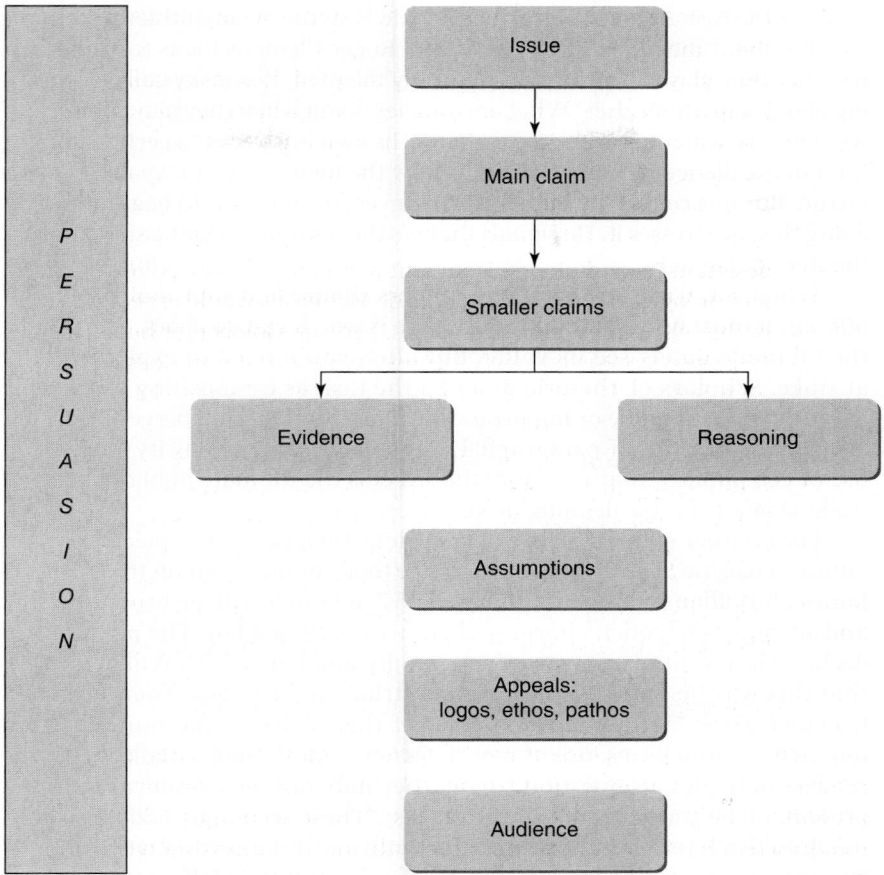

Figure 1.2   Elements of argument

Below we briefly explain the elements, using them to make suggestions for writing an argument. Taking Goldberger's piece as a sample, we begin with *issue* and then move to *claims, persuasion, audience, evidence, reasoning, assumptions*, and *appeals*. We'll return to these elements in Chapter 3, where we explain their roles in arguments about literature.

ISSUES

An **issue** is a question not yet settled. People have disagreed — or might disagree — over how to answer it. Goldberger's question seems to be this: how are cell phones transforming culture? But he doesn't state his question flat out. He presumes his readers will guess it. Other writers of arguments put their questions plainly. They want to ensure their readers know them. This seems to be Jeremy Rozansky's goal in an argument he wrote for the January 19, 2013 issue of *The New Atlantis*. His article's topic is steroid-using athletes. To him, debates about men like Barry Bonds and Roger Clemens focus too much on whether they played "fair" or are naturally talented. Rozansky calls for thinking about something else: "What are athletes doing when they play sports, and what are we watching when we watch?" His own answer is "a certain kind of human excellence." Then he explains how the men proved incapable of such virtue. But notice that he bluntly announces his question to begin with. By doing this, he stresses it. He signals that it's the most important issue raised by the steroid scandals.

When you write an argument, readers should find your main issue *significant*. It must be a question they believe is worth caring about. Sometimes they'll immediately see its value. But often you'll need to explain what's at stake. Scholars of rhetoric describe the task as establishing the issue's **exigence**, the urgency or importance of the situation. Goldberger brings up exigence at the start of paragraph 4. There he states that on city streets, the use of cell phones "matters," for "the street is the ultimate public space and walking along it is the defining urban experience."

For another statement of exigence, let's turn to a 2013 piece from the online magazine *Slate*. It's about a strange topic: animals put on trial. Author James McWilliams points out that in 1457, a French village brought a sow and six piglets to court, charging them with killing a boy. The piglets were declared innocent; the sow was found guilty and hanged. McWilliams notes that this was just one of many animal trials in past ages. Then he states his chief issue: "What are we to make of this evidence that our ancestors imputed to animals a sense of moral agency?" McWilliams realizes that his readers may find his question trivial; they may not see its relevance to the present. So he states the question's stakes: "These seemingly odd trials have much to teach us about how fundamentally our relationship with animals has changed and how, more poignantly, we've lost the ability to empathize with them as sentient beings." McWilliams goes on to praise how courts of the past treated animals. Even guilty verdicts respected these creatures, he says. Putting them on trial credited them with powers of thought and the potential to act well. McWilliams wants modern humans to adopt the same attitude. At present, he believes, they treat animals as objects. Whether or not you agree with McWilliams, he resembles Goldberger in stating why his issue matters.

CLAIMS

Perhaps you associate the word *claims* with insurance companies. It's familiar as a term for the forms you fill out when someone bashes your car. You may not be used to calling other things you say or write *claims*. But even when you utter a simple observation about the weather—for instance, "It's beginning to rain"—you make a claim. A **claim** is a statement that is spoken or written so that people will think it true. With this definition in mind, you may spot claims everywhere. Most of us make them every day. Most claims *are* accepted as true by the people to whom we make them. Imagine how difficult life would be if the opposite were so. Human beings would constantly fret if they distrusted everything told them.

But claims may conflict with other claims. We've defined an *issue* as a question with various debatable answers. *Claims*, as we use the term, are the debatable answers. In this sense, most of Goldberger's statements are claims, for readers might resist them. Take his main claim, which he identifies at the start of paragraph 6. There he argues that cell phones are prime forces in a pair of "cultural losses." These are "the loss of the sense that walking along a great urban street is a glorious shared experience" and "the blurring of distinctions between different kinds of places." Readers might object to Goldberger's view in various ways. Some might argue that neither of these losses has occurred. Others might say that these losses have happened but that cell phones didn't cause them. So Goldberger has more work to do. Like all debatable statements, his requires support.

When you write a college paper, typically you'll raise an issue. Then you'll make one main claim about it. This can also be called your **thesis**, a term you may know from high school. It won't be your *only* point. You'll make smaller claims as your essay continues. But stating your main claim, and remaining focused on it, will be important.

PERSUASION

It's commonly assumed that if two people argue, they are dogmatic. Each insists on being proclaimed correct. But at its best, argument involves efforts to **persuade**. You argue in the first place because you want others to accept your claims. Yet you can't expect them to applaud at once. To attempt **persuasion** is to concede that your claims need defense. Goldberger knew that much of his readership adored the phones that disturb him. He'd have to justify his stance.

Most likely he figured that he couldn't turn all the fans into critics. Such conversions can be hard to pull off. But he could pursue a more modest goal: showing that his claims merit study. Whether or not they gained approval from everyone, he could make them seem reasonable. Probably he'd be happy if a reader said, "I'm fonder of cell phones than Goldberger is, but I can't dismiss his criticisms. I'm willing to keep reflecting on them." A response like this can be your aim, too. Realistically, *persuasion* doesn't mean everyone eventually agrees with you. An argument you write may leave some readers maintaining another view. But you've done much if they conclude that your ideas are credible — worth their bearing in mind.

AUDIENCE

The word **audience** may first make you think of people at plays, concerts, movies, or lectures. Yet it also describes readers. Not everything you write is for other human eyes; in college courses, you may produce notes, journal entries, blog posts, and essays for yourself alone. But in most any course, you'll also do public writing. You'll try to persuade audiences to accept claims you make.

This task requires you to consider more than your subject. You must take your readers into account. McWilliams realized that his audience wouldn't know about animal trials. He'd have to begin with anecdotes explaining what these hearings were like. By contrast, Goldberger's average readers would be aware of cell phones. Also, he supposed that they had a certain vocabulary — that they knew "boulevardier" and "flaneur" meant someone who likes to explore city streets. Evidently he saw his audience, too, as holding two beliefs about cell phones. One is that they help people connect. The other is that they make private life more public, for chatter on them is often overheard. Deliberately, Goldberger challenges both ideas. He argues that because cell phones distract people from their surroundings, they lead to "*dis*connected urbanism" and turn "a public place less public." Unfortunately, sometimes your audience will have a vaguer profile than his. You may have to guess what your target group knows, assumes, and values.

EVIDENCE

Evidence is support you give your claims so others will accept them. What sort of evidence must it be? That depends on what your audience expects. Disciplines differ in this respect. In literary studies, claims about a text seem more plausible if they're backed by quotations from it. (We discuss this standard more in Chapter 2.) Scientists must not only conduct experiments but also describe them so that others can repeat them and see if the results are the same. Anthropologists feel pressured to base their conclusions on field research. Not that your audience will always be academic scholars. It can easily be more diverse. Goldberger's audience included experts in design but also nonprofessionals with interests like theirs. In short, his readership was mixed.

To persuade this group, Goldberger offered two kinds of evidence. His climax is a personal tale about a Hartford-based friend of his who called him from New Orleans and then from Tallahassee. Clearly, Goldberger wanted his audience to find this story typical of modern life. He hoped it would serve as what rhetorical theorist Kenneth Burke calls a *representative anecdote*. Its effect would be to reinforce his claim that cell phones ruin callers' sense of place. In addition, Goldberger presses his readers to consult their own experiences. He bids them recall how they've used cell phones on city strolls. At such moments, he seeks to remind them they "are not on the street sharing the communal experience of urban life." Similarly, he prods them to remember how "increasingly common" it is "for cell-phone conversations to begin with the question, 'Where are you?' and for the answer to be anything from 'out by the pool' to 'Madagascar.'"

As a writer, you might have to guess your audience's standards of proof. You'll be influenced by experiences you've had with such readers. Perhaps you'll also have opportunities to review drafts with them.

REASONING

Philosopher Gary Gutting observes that "facts alone are necessary but not sufficient for a good argument. As important as getting the facts right is putting the facts into a comprehensible logical structure that supports your conclusion." This advice can help you as you strive to persuade others through writing. Besides evidence, your readers will expect you to show careful **reasoning**. Ideally, they'll come away feeling that your ideas truly connect. They should sense that your main claim derives from your other ones. Goldberger's logic seems to follow the flow of the chart in Figure 1.3.

Goldberger doesn't arrange these ideas as a list. He might bore readers if he did! Still, ideally readers will see his claims as a methodical sequence. When you write an argument, guide your audience step by step through your reasoning. Help them follow your logic. Make your essay seem an orderly train of thought.

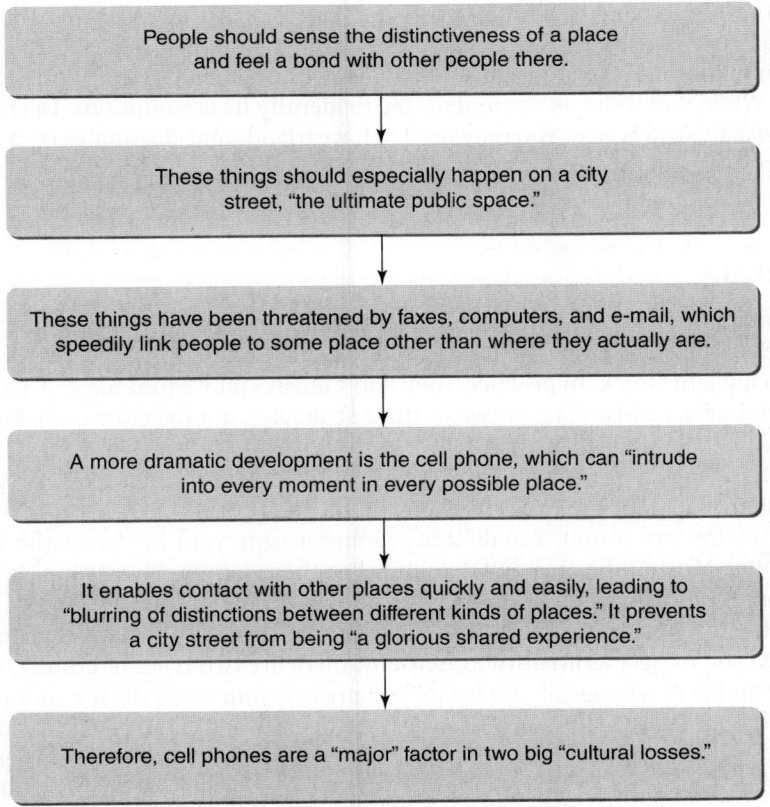

People should sense the distinctiveness of a place and feel a bond with other people there.

These things should especially happen on a city street, "the ultimate public space."

These things have been threatened by faxes, computers, and e-mail, which speedily link people to some place other than where they actually are.

A more dramatic development is the cell phone, which can "intrude into every moment in every possible place."

It enables contact with other places quickly and easily, leading to "blurring of distinctions between different kinds of places." It prevents a city street from being "a glorious shared experience."

Therefore, cell phones are a "major" factor in two big "cultural losses."

Figure 1.3   Goldberger's sequence of reasoning

ASSUMPTIONS

Already we've mentioned certain **assumptions** of Goldberger's. But other beliefs appear to have steered him. They include some that readers may reject. Assumptions behind an argument may be numerous and debatable. That's why we single them out as an element here.

One category is beliefs about the audience's experiences. As Goldberger asks his readers to imagine "When you are in Paris," he supposes that all of them have visited Paris or might go there some day. Another type of assumption concerns the writer's values. When Goldberger laments cities' loss of uniqueness, he assumes that uniqueness is good. A third type is what rhetorical theory calls *warrants*. This term refers to the writer's beliefs about what can serve as evidence. Recall that Goldberger climaxes his argument with a personal story. He relies on a warrant when he offers this tale. It's the assumption that the story is evidence for his argument's main claim.

We can imagine readers skeptical about these premises. If low-wage workers saw Goldberger's reference to Paris, they might grumble or scoff. How could *they* ever afford to go there? Others may believe that uniqueness isn't always a benefit. Similarly, for some of Goldberger's audience, his personal story may lack weight. As author, Goldberger must decide which of his assumptions are safe or trivial—and which, if any, he has to state and defend.

When you write an argument, try to identify its assumptions. Detecting them isn't always easy. You may need to have friends and classmates read each of your drafts. But the effort pays. Growing alert to a premise helps you anticipate challenges to it. You can then revise to head off these criticisms.

APPEALS

To make their arguments persuasive, writers employ three basic kinds of appeals. Rhetorical theory calls them **logos**, **ethos**, and **pathos**, terms drawn from ancient Greek. In practice, they don't always play equal roles. An argument may depend on one or two of these strategies, not the entire trio. But all three are potential resources.

In a way, we've already introduced **logos**. The term refers to the logical substance of an arguer's case. When you rely on logos, you focus on showing your claims are sound. You do this by emphasizing your evidence and your reasons. Most audiences will demand that these features be strong. It's no surprise, then, that logos is the most common type of appeal.

Ethos often operates, too. When applied to writing, this term refers to the image you project as an author. Actually, there are two types of ethos. One is your audience's image of you before you present your analysis. It's your prior reputation. Many readers of *Metropolis* know that Paul Goldberger is a leading, Pulitzer Prize–winning critic of architecture. Their awareness inclines them to respect his arguments, whether or not they agree with him. Advertisers have reputational ethos in mind when they hire celebrities for endorsements. The hope is that you'll join Weight Watchers because DJ Khaled did. This ethos also comes into play with self-help manuals. Often their covers boast that the writer is an academic. You're supposed to buy *How to Find Lovers by Loving Yourself* because its author has a Ph.D.

Most of us, however, aren't famous or highly credentialed. There remains a second kind of ethos: the picture of you that people form as they read your text. To gain their trust, you should patiently lay out your claims, reasons, and evidence. This is what Goldberger does. True, cell phones bother him enough that he uses the word *offense* and points out that their ring "can be infuriating." But he doesn't lash out against them. He avoids harsh, righteous anger. He signals that his argument won't become a "rant." He declares the phones' impact "not encouraging" — a fairly mild criticism. He doesn't demand they be smashed to bits. He simply mourns "losses" they cause.

When arguers are scornful, some of their audience may object. John Burt points out a problem that Stephen Douglas's ethos created in his famous debates with Abraham Lincoln. When the two men competed for a U.S. Senate seat in 1858, the main issue was slavery. On this topic, Douglas planned to come across as a seeker of compromise. But on stage, he fiercely insulted Lincoln, showing nastiness and not tact. As Burt observes, "Douglas's own management of his case was so intemperate, so inflammatory, and so personal that whatever case one could make for his position, he himself was the last person who could plausibly carry the day for that case." Sometimes anger *is* right, especially when injustice must be noticed and stopped. But for much of your writing, especially in college, Goldberger's tone will serve better.

Writers enhance their ethos through **concessions** and **qualifications**. Concessions are civil (or even kind or admiring) acknowledgments of views or experiences other than yours. One appears in Goldberger's piece. Largely he claims that cell phones wreck people's sense of place. But he does admit that unique geography survives to some extent. In paragraph 2, he notes that here and there you can find "a place that retains its intensity, its specialness, and its ability to confer a defining context on your life." He's quick to add that these settings fall short of an "all-consuming effect." Nevertheless, he grants that they've somehow remained distinct. Most readers will like his recognizing this fact.

In rhetorical theory, qualifications aren't credentials for a job. They are two kinds of words. One kind helps writers strengthen their claims. A common example is the word *very*, as in a sentence like "Cell phones are very bad for cities' sense of community." Yet many readers think terms of this sort are unnecessary. *Bad* is already emphatic; why stick *very* before it? The second kind of qualification has the opposite effect. Words in this category weaken a claim. They help writers sound cautious, often an attractive trait. Goldberger uses words of this type:

- In paragraph 1, where a more reckless writer might have simply declared, "Places are unique," he adds, "or at least we like to believe they are."

- In paragraph 3, he doesn't just proclaim that *all* city dwellers have lost a sense of place. He makes use of the word *almost*, saying this is becoming the experience of "almost every person on almost every street in almost every city."
- In paragraph 4, he resists generalizing about *every* inhabitant of a city. Instead, he asks "what if half of them are elsewhere, there in body but not in any other way?"
- In the next paragraph, he doesn't claim that a cell phone's ring *is* infuriating. Rather, he more softly notes that it "can be."
- In paragraph 6, he doesn't simply announce that an area code has become *just* a set of numbers. Rather, he laments that it "is really not much more than" them.

Such language makes Goldberger look careful. Similar terms include *probably, maybe, perhaps,* and *possibly*. These words suggest that the writer isn't self-righteously certain. Take this claim from Hartzog and Zelinger's article about Facebook: "Many contemporary privacy disputes are probably better classified as concern over losing obscurity." With "probably," the authors identify their claim as a hypothesis. They grant that it isn't sure fact. Like Goldberger, they project restraint.

Pathos is an appeal to the heart. You find it in ads for different charities. Animal-focused charities will show photos of suffering dogs and cats — animals injured or neglected. These pictures are meant to rouse pity. If they succeed, viewers sob and donate. At other times, pathos stirs fear. Activists warn that if society ignores them, apocalypse will come. Pathos-filled arguments aren't dry in tone. Their language expresses moods. Pathos targets its audience's emotions. When you write such arguments, you push readers to feel the stakes of your issue. You hope they'll passionately favor your claims. Sure, you risk sounding excessive: too sad, too mad, too scared, or too hurt. But pathos can be a respectable tool, as well as a powerful one. Plenty of subjects even demand an emotional tone. Readers expect essays on genocide to anguish over its victims. Further, pathos can join logos and ethos. Arguments that move readers may also awe them with logic; the author's image may impress them, too.

Goldberger's piece oozes despair and sorrow. He deeply regrets cell phones' impact on cities and prods his audience to share his grief. He saves his most notable pathos for the end. There he claims that cell technology is turning all of us into "nodes on a network." It's a chilling final image. He wants to leave readers worried that cell phones will destroy their souls.

Sample Argument for Analysis

We've specified elements of argument and style. Now try to spot their presence in the following opinion piece. "A New Moral Compact" was originally published in November 2012, right around Veterans' Day. The author, David W. Barno (b. 1954), is a retired lieutenant general. He served the U.S. Army in key leadership roles, including combat campaigns in Afghanistan, Grenada, and Panama. Barno is now senior advisor and senior fellow at the Center for a New American Security, a group whose mission is "to develop strong, pragmatic, and principled national security and defense policies." His article appeared simultaneously on the Center's Web site and in the digital edition of *Foreign Policy* magazine. Anyone might come upon his piece through a search engine. But probably he took his main audience to be elected officials, their staffs, other policy experts, military professionals, and academic scholars who study national defense.

As you read, consider the following questions:

- What is Barno's main *issue*, and what is his main *claim* about it?
- What smaller claims does he make as he develops his main one?
- Where in his article are you especially conscious of Barno attempting *persuasion*?
- Where are you especially conscious of how Barno views his *audience*?
- What *evidence* does Barno offer?
- What are the steps in his *reasoning*?
- What are his major *assumptions*?
- To what extent does his argument rely on *logos*?
- To what extent might his *reputational ethos* matter to his readers?
- What sort of *ethos* does he create through his words?
- How much, and where, does his argument use *pathos*?

DAVID W. BARNO

A New Moral Compact

As our nation enters its second decade of armed conflict overseas, it is appropriate to reflect on the moral compact between our government, our people, and our soldiers. Eleven years of conflict in Afghanistan and Iraq, combined with the prospect for open-ended global warfare against terrorists, has blurred the lines between peace and war, perhaps forever. It has also effectively lowered our national threshold for decisions to conduct military operations or go to war. The reasons have as much to do with our declining personal stake in these conflicts as with the dangerous state of the world.

I recently attended an event honoring former Pennsylvania governor Tom Ridge for his public service. Ridge came from a working class family, won a scholarship to Harvard, and went on to law school. Upon completing his first year, he unexpectedly received his draft notice from Uncle Sam.

Tom Ridge did not seek to dodge his unwelcome summons. In his family, when you were called, you dropped whatever you were doing in your life and you went, as his father did in World War II. But as a Harvard grad and law student, he clearly had other options.

The Army decided to make Tom Ridge an infantryman. He soon became a sergeant and shipped out to Vietnam, where he joined the 101st Airborne for a year in combat from 1969 to 1970. None of the handful of young men he led in his small infantry rifle squad was a graduate of Harvard or any other college, but they were draftees from all social strata across the United States. Ridge observed: "The military is a great leveler. Nobody cares who you are, where you went to school, who your parents were. None of that mattered."

The only reason Ridge was in the Army and ultimately fought for a year in Vietnam was the draft lottery system. The Selective Service system randomly assigned numbers to each draft age male by birth date in an annual "lottery"; depending on the needs of the war that year, if your number came up, you were called. Theoretically, your chances of being drafted as a college grad under the lottery system were equal to those of a high school drop-out born on the same date. In the real world, however, both college deferments (see: Dick Cheney, Bill Clinton) and clever manipulation of the system allowed many of the well-off and well-educated to avoid service altogether. And for each of those who side-stepped the call, some other, less fortunate young man was called up to take his place. Some of whom, of course, never came back—a sharp point little noted in discussions about the complex national legacy of the Vietnam War.

In the Vietnam era, draftees were called up for a maximum of two years of service, with one of those almost inevitably spent in Vietnam. And unlike in today's "all-volunteer" military, no draftee was ever sent back to Vietnam for another tour unless he volunteered—probably with a voluntary re-enlistment for longer service. With draftees serving only two years in uniform, it would have been nearly impossible to send a soldier for a second 12-month combat tour within the scope of his two-year service obligation. It simply wasn't done. If you were unfortunate enough to be drafted, you at least knew that the nation drew the line at one year of combat.

Contrast Tom Ridge's world of 1969 with that of America's combat soldiers today. In 2012, there is no draft, and our all-volunteer force has spent the last eleven years in prolonged, bloody ground wars in Iraq and Afghanistan. The Army of this era fields about 560,000 troops on active duty, in comparison to 1.2 million at the height of the Vietnam war. Nearly 3 million Americans are veterans of the post-9/11 wars, with large numbers having served multiple combat tours. It seems obvious that some of the stress on the force—manifested by unprecedented rates of suicide and creeping indiscipline—has come from these widespread repeat deployments, the likes of which no soldier of the Vietnam era ever involuntarily faced. In fact, even career officers and sergeants in the Vietnam-era force—distinct from the two-year draftees—rarely served more than two one-year tours in Vietnam over the entire course of that ten-year war.

In today's military, it is not uncommon to see Army lieutenant colonels and senior sergeants deployed three or four times for 12- to 15-month combat tours over the past decade—a back-breaking, family-stressing commitment the likes of which we have never before asked of our men and women in uniform. Even in World War II, only a small fraction of our nearly 16 million uniformed men and women served more than three years in a combat zone, and the entire war was finished for the United States in 45 months. Our war in Afghanistan has lasted 134 months. It now has eclipsed the American Revolution and Vietnam as the longest war in U.S. history. Stunningly, sizable numbers of the very same sergeants and officers fighting the war today are the men and women that led the way into the earliest campaigns in Afghanistan and Iraq. If you are a career officer or NCO in today's Army and Marines, by and large you either continue to deploy — or you leave the service. There are few other options. Across our volunteer force, over 6,500 have been killed and more than 50,000 wounded since 2001. Consider the burden of that stark reality upon career military families.

Both of my sons have served one-year combat tours in Afghanistan. When our youngest son, an Army pilot, was called to go back after completing his first tour, I was suddenly angry. Not an anger that derived from misunderstanding our rotation system, nor from seeing the war as somehow unjust. My anger was visceral, unbidden, reflexive. And as I examined my unexpected reaction, it came down to this: my son was going back, yet 99 percent of his military age contemporaries were not — and never would, no matter how long the war lasted. Neither his civilian peers, their parents, nor their spouses or siblings would ever be exposed in any way to the gut-wrenching dangers of being in the middle of a lethal national enterprise. It simply wasn't important enough for our nation to insist that all of us shared the sacrifice of unlimited liability that war demands from those who fight it. Having a cadre of admirably willing volunteers simply has made it too easy for us to go to war.

For we Americans as a people, that's just wrong. There must be some limit 10 to what we will ask of our men and women in uniform before the rest of us feel some moral obligation to step in. Tom Ridge — representing all of the people of the United States in 1969 — got the telegram, put his life on hold, stepped forward and served in combat alongside a broad cross-section of America's youth. Today, we call on no one to make this kind of sacrifice. We have even made that a matter of some pride, a nation that has moved beyond the dark days of "conscription."

Yet at what point are we morally compelled to in some way expose every American family to our fights abroad, to invest some moral equity as a nation and a society into fighting our wars? Absent any prospect whatsoever for our current or future wars to touch any of us personally, where is the moral hazard — the personal "equity stake" — that shapes our collective judgment, giving us pause when we decide to send our remarkable volunteer military off to war? They are fully prepared to go — but they trust the rest of us to place sufficient weight and seriousness into that decision to ensure that their inevitable sacrifices of life and limb will be for a worthy and essential cause.

Throughout our history, American decisions on going to war have been closely connected to our people because they remain matters of life and death. And they were always seen as matters of deep import to the nation as a whole, since all could be called upon to fight. Today such profound decisions are all but free of consequences for the American people. When the lives and the deaths of our soldiers no longer personally impact the population at large, have we compromised our moral authority on war? How can our elites and our broader populace make wartime decisions in good conscience when those paying the price are someone else's kids—but assuredly never their own?

The past ten years suggest that relying on a professional military comprised only of willing volunteers has eroded the core societal seriousness that we have always accorded to national decisions of war and peace. One wonders if we would have entered our recent conflicts as quickly—or let them drag on so long—if our Army was filled with draftees, drawn from a random swath of families across all segments of America.

One policy to better connect our wars to our people might be to determine that every use of military force over 60 days would automatically trigger an annual draft lottery to call up 10,000 men and women. They would serve in every branch of service for the duration of the conflict, replaced by future draft tranches in limited, like-sized numbers. Ten thousand draftees would comprise only about 5 percent of the number of new recruits the military takes in each year, but they would signify a symbolic commitment of the entire nation. Every family in the country would now be exposed to the potential consequences of our wars and come to recognize in a personal way that they had a stake in the outcome. The national calculus on go-to-war decisions subtly changes when all families can be called upon to answer the call to arms.

In the last decade, war has become something done by "the 1 percent"—   15
our rightly acclaimed force of volunteers—with 99 percent of America uninvolved, and sometimes seemingly uninterested. But with war becoming this easy, our historic caution in committing our troops abroad has frayed dramatically. Partly as a result, "America at war" is slowly becoming a permanent condition. We have gradually, almost imperceptibly, eroded the bonds of responsibility linking our soldiers, our people, and our government. It's time to reestablish that moral compact between our people and our wars.   *[2012]*

Writing a Response to an Argument

Often, a college course will require you to read arguments. Just as often, you will respond to them by writing an argument yourself. As you compose your reactions to these texts, you will make, develop, and support claims. Here are some tips to help you:

- Before you write about the text, be sure you understand it in its entirety. Identify its main claim, its other claims, and how they all relate. In your essay, don't treat these claims one by one in isolated fragments, stating your opinion of each. Instead, put in context any claim you discuss. Explain its role in the author's overall reasoning process. You can begin to establish this larger framework in your introduction by summarizing what the author basically argues.
- Perhaps you'll disagree with the argument. Even then, show respect for its author. Avoid snarky remarks like, "What planet is this guy

on?" Audiences tend to prefer a more civil ethos. Calling the author stupid, evil, or crazy may drive your readers away. Let your tone suggest that you're reflective, not mean.

- When you first read the argument, you may strongly approve or object. But don't settle for extreme verdicts. Let your written response include concessions and qualifications, not just big evaluative claims. Your readers will appreciate learning what's complex about the argument and how reactions to it can be mixed. Whatever your attitude toward it, show the reasoning and evidence behind your view.

- When writing about the argument, refer to its author. Make this person the subject of several active verbs: for example, "Barno claims," "Barno argues," "Barno proposes," "Barno calls for." After all, the argument isn't an orphan. Nor is it a random series of free-floating ideas. You're studying an entire case put forth by a particular human being. Take opportunities to remind your readers — and yourself — of this fact. Start doing so with your introduction.

- For each sentence you write, make clear whose view it expresses. Are you conveying an idea brought up in the argument you're analyzing, or is this your own idea? Help your readers distinguish between the two. If you write about Barno's argument, for example, let them know when you're reporting *his* claims and when you're stating *yours*.

- Give your response a title that previews what you'll say.

Further Strategies for Analyzing an Argument So You Can Write a Response to It

In the college courses that require you to read and write about arguments, you'll be asked to analyze not only the claims they make but also the issues they raise and the support they give their stances. To write about an argument thoughtfully, read it several times. You may need to study it at length before you detect its points. Below, using David Barno's essay as an example, we suggest some strategies for analyzing and getting ideas to respond to arguments.

1. Identify *all* of the argument's basic elements.   After you've examined the argument thoroughly, pinpoint not just its main claim and smaller claims, but also its evidence, its reasoning, its assumptions, its appeals, and the audience it seems to address.

2. Map the argument's path.   By this, we mean you should try to outline the argument's stages, noting points made at each. Just as important, recognize choices the arguer faced. For each stage, identify issues he or she *doesn't* pursue.

To construct your map, you might use only words. The map may prove more thought provoking, though, if it's a flowchart. See how we've mapped Barno's argument below. For each stage, we've drawn a box. Within it, we summarize what Barno says at that stage. Beneath each box we name one or more issues that he *doesn't* address.

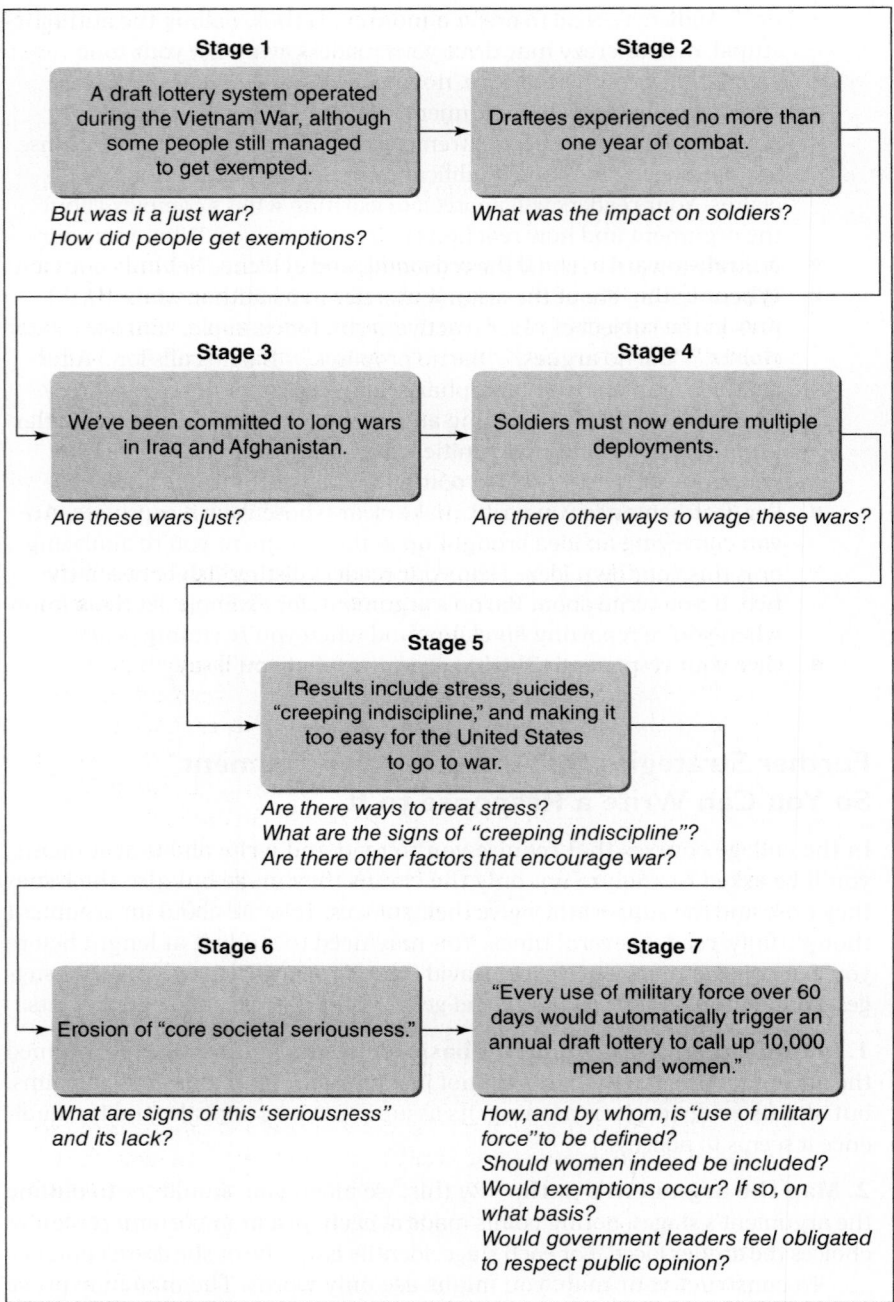

Figure 1.4   The stages of Barno's argument

An argument that avoids certain questions may still prove persuasive. But tracing routes it *doesn't* take helps you understand and judge it. You'll have a better sense of what to say in your written response.

3. Identify the values the argument honors.   Often arguers support a claim by tying it to common values. These are principles they assume their audience already holds. Here are examples of values that Barno emphasizes as he argues for a draft lottery:

- **Morality.** Barno uses the word *moral* several times. Not only does it appear in the title of his essay, it also pops up in paragraphs 10, 11, and 15. In paragraph 11, it even appears twice, along with the related word *morally*. Most, perhaps all, of his readers see worth in a moral life.

- **Realism.** Most people find it crucial to remain in touch with reality. To support his proposal for a lottery, Barno points out deaths and woundings suffered by current volunteers. He hopes his audience will want to do something about "the burden of that stark reality upon career military families" (para. 8).

- **Shared sacrifice.** When Barno reports the suffering that military families alone endure, he expects his readers will feel guilt. After all, *shared* sacrifice is a common ideal.

- **Family.** Barno's audience surely believes that the family unit is valuable. The author joins his readers in seeking to protect it from needless risk. As he develops his argument, Barno laments the "family-stressing commitment" demanded by current wars (para. 8). He refers to his own family as suffering from this plight (para. 9). When he proposes a lottery that would reach "families across all segments of America" (para. 13), he's hardly out to harm them. Rather, he wants the country to hesitate more before waging war. If war affects more families, he suggests, they won't rush to endorse it. Family is something he *and* the nation prize.

- **Bonds of responsibility.** Barno resorts to this phrase in his final paragraph. With it, he links his proposal to Americans' sense of community. He has faith that his readers still deem social ties important. He affirms the principle of looking out for one another. It's a tradition he wishes to sustain.

- **Prudence.** Ancient teachers of rhetoric and ethics emphasized the virtue of prudence. It's the exercise of careful, cautious judgment. Today, it remains a value many arguers bring up. Barno concludes by emphasizing "our historic caution in committing our troops abroad" (para. 15).

- **Seriousness.** Related to realism and prudence is the attitude of *seriousness*. Barno uses the word twice, in paragraphs 11 and 13. By it, he means intense concern. He assumes his readers regard this as the approach anyone should take to "matters of deep import" (para. 12). These include the costs of war.

Consider what values an argument gives *priority* to. Often arguers press their audience to choose *between* values it holds. Barno emphasizes community spirit as an American ideal, but many people in the United States cherish personal freedom as well. On plenty of occasions, the American public has debated which of these principles to favor. Someone who prefers individual liberty might protest a military draft. Barno, however, favors one, asking his readers to put community ties over freedom of self.

4. Identify words in the argument that can have more than one definition.   You can also grasp an argument better if you pinpoint words in it that can have more than one definition. Not everyone, that is, would give these words the meanings that the arguer does. Examples include a number of Barno's values. Take, for instance, *morality* and *seriousness*. For him, both terms mean a willingness to share the risks of war. For other people, *morality* might mean sparing citizens from a draft, and *seriousness* might mean recognizing that the American public won't agree to the lottery that Barno wants. A similar difference of opinion may occur with the word *caution*. Barno believes a country that exercises caution would be reluctant to launch wars. Others might think that a policy of caution involves attacking potential foes before they can ever strike.

Note, too, that not everyone would join Barno in thinking the American government expresses the public's will. At the very end of his essay, he refers to "our wars," as if all Americans are responsible when their leaders send troops into combat. Someone might argue that the president and Congress rarely do what the public wants. Consider the various possible definitions of additional terms Barno uses, such as these:

- *indiscipline* (para. 7)
- *expose* (para. 11)
- *consequences* (para. 12)

An Argument for Analysis

We've identified several ways to study arguments. We close this chapter by inviting you to practice these methods. Try applying them to the following opinion piece. After it, we'll pose questions to aid your analysis.

This essay's author, Regina Rini, has held research fellowships at Oxford University and earned a doctorate in philosophy at New York University. She is currently the Canada Research Chair in Philosophy of Moral and Social Cognition at York University in Toronto. In addition to her academic articles, she has contributed to the op-ed pages of the *Los Angeles Times* and to two philosophy blogs, *Practical Ethics* and *The Splintered Mind*. Rini first published the following argument on December 8, 2015, in *Aeon*, an online magazine that deals with topics in philosophy, science, psychology, health, technology, and culture at large. Note Rini's title. It's a question that was sparking debate at many American colleges when she wrote.

REGINA RINI

Should We Rename Institutions that Honor Dead Racists?

We all know what Juliet says about a rose: by any other name, it would smell as sweet. But we probably don't remember why she says this, or what happens next. Juliet is lamenting that a certain young man happens to be called "Romeo Montague," a name associated with her family's dire enemies. Romeo then emerges from the shadows and insists that the name is "hateful to myself, because it is an enemy to thee." He declares his moniker dispensable, under one condition: "Call me but love, and I'll be new baptized; henceforth I never will be Romeo."

What altered scent might emanate from a renamed Woodrow Wilson School of Public and International Affairs? The Princeton institution faces calls to drop its nominal affiliation with America's 28th president, who was also governor of New Jersey, president of the university, and a horrible racist. Similarly, students at Yale have demanded a rebranding of Calhoun College, named after John Calhoun, who championed "Indian removal" and told the Senate that slavery was a "positive good." And Georgetown University, my own alma mater, has agreed to strip the names of two Jesuit slave-sellers from campus buildings. Across the country, student Juliets are asking their administrator Romeos to be newly baptized.

And why not? It is reasonable to prefer not to live in a quadrangle named after a man who extolled the "positive good" of your great-great-grandparents' forced labor. It is reasonable to wish not to study in a place that honors a man who would have you keep to your own, segregated end of the lecture hall. For students of color, living in a United States that preaches equality and practices something else, it is reasonable to expect an honest reckoning with our damaged patriarchs.

But the problem is consistency. Once we've started rescinding honors from besmirched heroes, where should we stop? On any reasonable scale of evil, the segregationist Wilson cannot be as bad as George Washington, who owned hundreds of slaves. So must we also rename several universities, a northwestern state, and the District of Columbia? The last, in fact, seems to require double renaming, as Christopher Columbus is now seen as a genocidal monster. Perhaps "America" itself ought to go: Amerigo Vespucci wrapped up his first voyage to the New World by setting a native village on fire and "thereon made sail for Spain with 222 captive slaves."

This, say opponents, is the absurdity to which we will be reduced. Where does the bonfire end? Surely we can't consider renaming every legacy of a moral scofflaw. Who has the time?

But, in fact, we regularly give things new names. In 2005, a man in California petitioned to rename Mount Diablo, because federal rules prohibit naming a geographic formation after "a living person" such as Satan. The man's preferred alternative, "Mount Reagan," was unsuccessful, but this has not

5

stopped the Mount Reagan Project from questing after another peak to rechristen. Ronald Reagan's name, incidentally, already adorns National Airport in Virginia — which was previously named for none other than the sacrosanct Washington. It would be worrisome if this *reductio* of name-changing was deemed absurd only when racism is the issue. Still, it is worth pausing to consider just what it takes to give something a name.

The British philosopher J L Austin gave naming as a prime example of a "performative utterance," the kind of speech act whereby merely saying something makes it so. But not all attempted naming is felicitous. In *How to Do Things with Words* (1962), Austin offered the following delightful demonstration:

> Suppose, for example, I see a vessel on the stocks, walk up and smash the bottle hung at the stern, proclaim: "I name this ship the *Mr Stalin*" and for good measure kick away the chocks: but the trouble is, I was not the person chosen to name it . . . We can all agree (1) that the ship was not thereby named; (2) that it is an infernal shame.

Austin's point was that the giving of a name requires a certain social authority. But unlike the Royal Navy, in schools and cities the authority to name does not entirely belong to a single person. Students (and faculty, staff, and alumni) have an interest in not seeing their college linguistically cavort with blackguards. The citizens of a democratic state have a right to call themselves as they wish. And the procedure by which we determine how to (re)name our collective institutions has its own name — it is called debate. Why not have this debate, openly and honestly, rather than dismiss the entire project?

The U.S. philosopher Saul Kripke is known for his causal theory of reference. According to Kripke, proper names pick out their objects via a causal chain going back to the object's "baptism." Once upon a time, someone (probably his parents) pointed at Romeo and said: "That one will be called Romeo," and this caused other people to call the child Romeo, onward until the night under Juliet's balcony. But there is nothing in this story to prevent a re-baptism, or a displacement of the old name by the same causal channels. Suppose the young lovers decide that the man formerly known as Romeo Montague is now Keyser Söze. If they can cause enough fair Veronese to refer to him thus, then so shall he be (though this is unlikely to solve Keyser's trouble with his in-laws).

We are links in a causal chain of reference, stretching back to institutional baptisms in 1931 and 1948, when university administrators pointed to a college and called it Calhoun, or pointed to a school and called it Wilson. These were performative utterances, issued with full authority, and part of their aim was to honor the legacies of dead racists. We do not have to be unthinking links in the chain. We, collectively, have the authority to pass on these names, or to replace them. Whatever we do — continue the chain or disrupt it — we are making a choice about whether to uphold the honor intended by those baptisms.

10

In fact, the students at Princeton are not asking us to make a comprehensive judgment: Wilson, good man or bad? The idea is to ask: does continuing to apply the name of such a person express *our* values, rather than the values of a gone generation? We are not deciding the fate of Wilson's eternal soul. We are asking whether we, who are the only ones with the authority to keep or change the name, have good reason to pass the name on to the next generation.

We know that renaming tends to follow political revolution. Famously, Byzantium turned to Constantinople, which turned to Istanbul. Saint Petersburg was Leningrad was Petrograd was Saint Petersburg. Decolonization brought a mass shedding of imposed titles, from Mumbai (Bombay) to Zimbabwe (Rhodesia) to Jakarta (Batavia). We are ready to accept that names change with the times and with the politics. Or would you insist that I am writing in New Amsterdam?

So if renaming can follow political revolution, then why not moral revolution? Why are we not free to ask ourselves whether to uphold the values that led our ancestors to name in honor of slaveholders and segregationists?

Perhaps we will decide, together, that on balance the good done by Washington or Wilson outweighs the evil. Perhaps. But I think we should seriously listen to those whose histories are most in the weighing. It can be hard, for some whose ancestors were not enslaved or segregated, to fully appreciate the pain caused by honoring these names. Yet even if you cannot understand it yourself, you can see it in others. And perhaps this will move you to agree, as an act of civic love, to accede to their requests. Like Romeo, listening in the night, we might find our collective name hateful to ourselves, "because it is an enemy to thee."   *[2015]*

≡ THINKING ABOUT THE TEXT

1. The title of Rini's essay is "Should We Rename Institutions that Honor Dead Racists?" It's a question that indicates the issue she addresses. What do you consider her main claim to be? Is it a simple yes or no answer to the question, or is it something else? Rini could have left the word *dead* out of her title. Why do you think she includes it?

2. Try to map Rini's argument. What are its main stages? For example, what is it doing in paragraph 2? In paragraph 4? Identify passages where she could have pursued certain issues but didn't. What are these issues?

3. The magazine in which Rini published her piece gives this advice to its contributors: "Steer clear of technical language or jargon — explain your idea as you would to someone without any expertise in the area. *Aeon* wants to make big ideas accessible to a wide audience." To what extent does Rini follow this advice? In paragraph 9, she refers to Keyser Söze, the villain in the movie *The Usual Suspects*. How would you respond to someone who says that not all of Rini's readers would get this reference?

4. Not everyone addressing Rini's title question would start with a paragraph about William Shakespeare's play *Romeo and Juliet*. Why, conceivably, does Rini choose to begin this way?

5. Where does Rini bring in evidence for her position? What kind of evidence is it? What does it consist of?

6. In paragraphs 11 and 13, Rini uses the word *values*. What specific values does she promote in her essay?

7. In paragraphs 10, 11, and 12, Rini uses the word *authority*. How does she seem to define this word? To whom is she willing to give authority?

8. Notice Rini's use of the pronoun *we*. Where, specifically, does she employ it? For what purpose, do you think? Apply the same questions to her use of *you*.

9. In addition to her title, Rini poses several other questions in her essay. A different writer might have only made statements. What is the effect of Rini's frequent question raising?

10. What, if any, renaming events and controversies can you think of? To what extent does Rini's essay help you make sense of them? The following are some examples we've come across recently:

   - At Clemson University in South Carolina, students demanded a new name for Tillman Hall, named after segregationist politician Ben Tillman.

   - At Duke University and East Carolina University, the name of North Carolina governor Charles Brantley Aycock was removed from dormitories because of his support for Jim Crow–era discrimination policies.

   - In Texas, the name of Robert E. Lee High School was challenged.

   - Also in Texas, the Board of the Houston Independent School District stirred debate when it expressed interest in renaming six of its schools that bore the names of Confederate leaders.

   - For the past several years, the owner of the Washington Redskins football team has been pressured to change the team's name because many consider the word *redskin* derogatory toward Native Americans.

   - Central State University in Ohio, which had received more than two million dollars from Bill Cosby and his wife, decided to change the name of a communications building named after them. The decision came after Cosby was accused by multiple women of drugging, sexually assaulting, and/or raping them. Cosby was later convicted in one such case.

CHAPTER 2

Writing Effective Arguments

In Chapter 1, we defined rhetoric and argumentation, presented the elements of argument in the context of arguments by Paul Goldberger and David Barno, and suggested several strategies to analyze arguments. In this chapter, we refer back to those elements and to the arguments by Goldberger and Barno as we suggest ways to develop your own effective arguments.

Strategies for Developing an Effective Style of Argument

When you write an argument, including one that responds to someone else's, try to incorporate the elements we discussed in the first chapter. Also good to study are features of an effective **style**. Try the following methods and techniques.

Mark transitions.   Readers want to know how each of your sentences relates to the ones immediately before it and after it. Usually a word or two can show this. Barno's third sentence begins with the word *It*, a pronoun that refers to the state of war mentioned in the previous sentence. Especially crucial is the language of shifts from one paragraph to the next. For example, Barno begins paragraph 10 by declaring "that's just wrong." With the word "that," he looks back to the situation he described at the end of the previous paragraph: how having a volunteer military encourages the United States to engage in war.

Create coherence by repeating words and by using similar words. Readers appreciate signs that you have carefully focused and structured your argument. Through repeating its key words, you can show that it follows a coherent line of thought. Barno notably repeats the word *national*. It appears in paragraphs 1, 5, 9, 13, and 14. He also uses the closely related word *nation* in paragraphs 10, 11, 12, and 14. These repetitions provide his argument with a unifying thread. They emphasize that his readers should think about how to serve their country, not just how to satisfy themselves.

Use patterns of sounds to give your sentences force.   As you write a draft, read its sentences aloud. Listen to the sounds of each. Perhaps, by changing certain words in a sentence, you can create more compelling rhythmic patterns. A good example is the opening sentence of Barno's paragraph 3:

Tom Ridge did not seek to dodge his unwelcome summons.

This isn't an especially flashy statement, but it's well crafted. It uses these stylistic techniques:

- **Alliteration.** The repetition of consonant sounds at the beginnings of words. Both *did* and *dodge* begin with the letter *d*. Both *seek* and *summons* begin with the letter *s*.
- **Assonance.** The repetition of vowel sounds. *Tom, not,* and *dodge* feature the same vowel. So do *Ridge, did,* and *his*. So do parts of the last two words: *un, come, sum,* and *mons*.
- **Other consonant patterns.** An *m* sound links the words *Tom, unwelcome,* and *summons*. A *dg* sound connects *Ridge* with *dodge*.
- **One-syllable words.** Words that consist of just one syllable can have a punchy impact, especially if several such words appear in a row. In Barno's sentence, the first eight words are each a single syllable long. The last two words of the sentence, "unwelcome summons," have an unwelcome sound, for they break the powerful pattern set up by the previous words.

Balance the parts of a sentence.   Look at the following two sentences. The first comes from Paul Goldberger's "Disconnected Urbanism" (p. 3). The second comes from Barno's essay:

> When you are in a forest, you want to experience its woodsiness; when you are on a beach, you want to feel connected to sand and surf. (para. 1)

> Contrast Tom Ridge's world of 1969 with that of America's combat soldiers today. (para. 7)

In each sentence, the parts balance. It's an engaging feat. Readers like rhythmic symmetry. They won't demand it of every sentence you write, but they'll appreciate it when they see it.

Vary the lengths of sentences.   A series of long sentences may confuse your readers while also losing their attention. On the other hand, a series of short sentences may come across as choppy, obscuring how ideas connect. Try to mix sentence length, as Barno does in paragraph 8:

> Even in World War II, only a small fraction of our nearly 16 million uniformed men and women served more than three years in a combat zone, and the entire war was finished for the United States in 45 months. Our war in Afghanistan has lasted 134 months. It now has eclipsed the American Revolution and Vietnam as the longest war in U.S. history. Stunningly, sizable numbers of the very same sergeants and officers fighting the war today are the men and women that led the way into the earliest campaigns in Afghanistan and Iraq.

Even in long sentences, be as concise as possible. Don't use more words than necessary; make each one count.

Use active verbs, not just passive ones.   *Active* and *passive* are terms of grammar. When a verb is in active voice, the subject of that verb performs an action. When a verb is in passive voice, its subject is acted upon. The active tends to make a sentence more dramatic and concise. Also, it better identifies who or what is doing something. Here are examples from Barno's essay:

> The Army decided to make Tom Ridge an infantryman. (para. 4)
>
> The Selective Service system randomly assigned numbers . . . (para. 5)
>
> The Army of this era fields about 560,000 troops on active duty . . . (para. 7)
>
> We have gradually, almost imperceptibly, eroded the bonds of responsibility . . . (para. 15)

At times, Barno does resort to passive voice. For instance, he repeatedly uses the passive form of the verb *to call* when he refers to the demands of military service:

> In his family, when you were called . . . (para. 3)
>
> . . . draftees were called up for a maximum of two years of service . . . (para. 6)
>
> . . . our youngest son, an Army pilot, was called to go back . . . (para. 9)
>
> . . . when all families can be called upon to answer the call of arms. (para. 14)

Barno's practice suggests that both kinds of voice, active and passive, are resources for arguers. Neither is automatically preferable. But of the two, active voice is more dynamic. And again, it identifies the action's performer more clearly.

Use precise verbs to identify an arguer's acts.   When responding to an argument, use verbs that pinpoint what the arguer does. Avoid vague verbs such as *talks about.* You're not conveying much if you write a sentence like this:

> Barno talks about having a draft lottery to stir concern about war.

A more exact alternative would be this:

> Barno calls for a draft lottery to stir concern about war.

The verb *calls* will give your readers a sharper sense of what Barno is doing when he brings up the lottery as a topic. Here are some other verbs you might use to convey an arguer's actions:

argues	criticizes	proposes	analyzes
claims	questions	recommends	examines
contends	challenges	urges	studies
asserts	complains	demands	probes
submits	protests	requests	focuses on

declares	regrets	emphasizes	detects
confirms	doubts	insists	finds
implies	objects to	underscores	reveals

Use figurative language.   Arguments may register more strongly with their audience if they explain ideas through figurative language. Such phrases can make concepts more vivid. Three main types are analogies, metaphors, and similes.

An **analogy** calls attention to a similarity between two things while still regarding them as largely distinct. Barno uses this technique in paragraph 11. There he urges his readers to "invest moral equity as a nation and a society into fighting our wars." His analogy is financial. Just as Americans take chances with money by investing in stocks, so should they morally consent to the possibility of being drafted. Of course, moral codes can differ a lot from activities of the stock market. But Barno emphasizes that both require a willingness to take risks.

A **metaphor**, on the other hand, implies that two things are the same. An example appears in Barno's paragraph 10. There he says that when Tom Ridge received his draft notice, he "put his life on hold." Commonly, the term *on hold* refers to phone calls. To put a call on hold is to keep the caller waiting. Barno uses the term to suggest that when Ridge agreed to military service, he had to postpone the kind of living he actually preferred.

A **simile** also equates two things but uses the word *like* or *as* to connect them. No similes appear in Barno's text, but here's one that might have:

> For soldiers assigned to repeated tours of combat zones, war is like a recurring nightmare. Every time they come back home, they feel as if they've finally been able to wake from a horrible dream. Yet soon they find themselves having to experience its terrors again.

Create *perspective by incongruity.*   This term, coined by Kenneth Burke, refers to the move that arguers perform when they give language a strikingly unconventional meaning or application. At the end of paragraph 10, Barno acknowledges that many Americans view the previous military draft as "dark days." But by putting the term in quotation marks, he prods his readers to question this particular use of it. Throughout his essay, he suggests that the term better fits the present age. To him, our current era is the real "dark days," for the absence of a draft has caused military families much suffering.

Structuring Your Argument: Beyond the Five-Paragraph Essay

When writing an argument, you may feel tempted to follow an age-old format: the five-paragraph essay. It works like this: Your first paragraph introduces three points. Each of your next three paragraphs develops one of these points. You conclude with a paragraph that repeats these points, reminding your reader of them. Done! It's a simple, easy recipe. No wonder that for generations students have relied on it. Many learn this stock procedure in junior high or earlier. Then they expect it to serve them forever after. But rarely does such writing delight teachers of college courses. For most of them, it reeks of formula. They don't find it truly fresh, developed, or complex. It's not the kind of prose they crave and reward.

To see what we mean by the five-paragraph model, take a look at the following essay. It's an argument we've written in response to Barno's text.

The Three Flaws in Barno's Proposal

David W. Barno's essay "A New Moral Compact" criticizes how the United States depends on volunteers to staff its military. He worries that this policy allows the rest of the country to overlook the sacrifices that soldiers make. Barno wants the United States to be more cautious about committing itself to wars. He thinks that we will be more restrained if more of us might have to serve in the military. Therefore, he proposes "that every use of military force over 60 days would automatically trigger an annual draft lottery to call up 10,000 men and women" (14). But Barno's proposal has three flaws. First, the American people will probably never agree to it. Second, our political leaders will probably get bogged down in debates about how to define "use of military force." Third, some people selected by the lottery will find ways of getting exempted from service, so the process will not really be fair.

One big problem with Barno's proposal is that a draft lottery is bound to be unpopular. Much of the country will object to it and demand that legislators fight against any effort to establish it. Barno admits that our ability to end the military draft after the Vietnam War was "a matter of some pride" (10). Ever since the United States declared its independence from Great Britain, our society has valued individual liberty. Many Americans are happy and grateful that our nation's youths are now free from having to serve in the military. They would oppose a new draft.

Another major flaw in Barno's proposal has to do with his phrase "use of military force." His draft lottery is supposed to take place when this "use" has continued for more than sixty days. Barno assumes that the president and Congress will have a common understanding of when such "use" has occurred. But he is too optimistic. In recent years, the federal government has been plagued by intense disputes. The president, the Senate, and the House of Representatives seem unable to agree on *any* issue. Even if American soldiers are fighting in a war that has gone on for years, various politicians will probably claim that this activity does not amount to "use of military force." They will quarrel over what this term means.

A third problem with Barno's proposal is that some people who are selected in the draft lottery will still manage to escape military service. Barno mentions that when there was such a lottery during the Vietnam War, "clever manipulation of the system allowed many of the well-off and well-educated to avoid service altogether" (5). The same thing is likely to happen now. Even if they wind up with a high lottery number, rich people will use all sorts of excuses to beat the system. Everyone else will notice this and point out that the lottery is not fair.

In conclusion, there are three reasons why Barno's proposal will not work. One is that the public will not appreciate it. Also, the president and other elected officials will disagree about the definition of "use of military force." Finally, people will find ways to evade service even if the draft selects them. Given all these problems, we should not adopt Barno's plan.

We think our essay makes some good observations. But its five-paragraph scheme harms it. Organizationally, it's just a loose string of points. At the outset, the overall claim about Barno's argument is merely a number: "Barno's proposal has three flaws." Then, one by one, each flaw gets a single paragraph. Such limited treatment seems superficial; readers will want greater depth. And the paragraphs don't appear linked. Each seems a mini-essay set apart. You could even rearrange their sequence; there's no logic to the order they're in. The final paragraph seems wasteful, for it echoes points already made.

So focus your essay on one main claim. Take several paragraphs to develop and support it. Link these paragraphs to one another. Put them in an order that makes sense. Let your conclusion go beyond what you've already said. You might identify your argument's further implications. You might note issues you've left unresolved.

Look again at our essay that criticizes Barno's proposal. We could have spent an entire text on any of the flaws we found. Imagine a whole essay on the second flaw: Barno's not realizing politicians will clash over how to define "use of military force." An essay could say much in claiming this flaw to exist. Think of the various questions we might have addressed. For example, what are some past governmental debates over the meanings of words? What euphemisms might leaders substitute for "use of military force"? What meanings might this term have? Such questions can't be handled in one paragraph alone. They call for abundant explanation, reasoning, and evidence.

A Student Response to an Argument

The following essay demonstrates several of the strategies we've discussed in this chapter. The author, Justin Korzack, composed it for a course on debating social issues. Basically, he wrote an argument that reacts to Barno's. To support his response, he investigated presidential history. Still, his essay isn't a full-blown research paper, a genre we discuss in Chapter 6. Nor, probably, is it the finest response ever written. But it does perform moves worth adding to your rhetorical repertoire.

Justin Korzack
Professor Hartfield
English 111
10 April - - - -

How to Slow Down the Rush to War

In "A New Moral Compact," David W. Barno worries about
the United States' current reliance on an all-volunteer
military. He claims that this policy allows civilians to feel too
complacent about the country's committing itself to major
hostilities. Barno is a retired lieutenant general with a
substantial combat record. Therefore, you might assume that
he himself is comfortable with war. But this is not so, at least
with respect to our recent long-term conflicts. He feels that
these engagements have had serious consequences for the
professional soldiers required to carry them out. In his view,
the public at large needs to become more aware of war's
human costs. To make all citizens more alert to these, he
proposes "that every use of military force over 60 days would
automatically trigger an annual draft lottery to call up 10,000
men and women" (14). Obviously this measure would disrupt
the lives of many people. Whether or not they ever planned to
become soldiers, they might now be forced to serve.
Nevertheless, Barno believes, this threat would be worthwhile, for it would function as a brake. He expects that it
would make Americans more reluctant to send troops into
extensive and deadly combat campaigns.

Summarizes Barno's argument so that readers understand his overall reasoning. Also points out which claims are his. Makes him the subject of several active verbs.

Is Barno's solution useful enough to justify the widespread anxiety it might cause? Not really, because Barno
misdiagnoses the problem in the first place. What needs
more attention and criticism is not public apathy. Rather,
it's the institution of the presidency. For the last several
decades, the nation's Chief Executive has sought to initiate
military action without interference from public opinion and
even the U.S. Congress. The president should consult more
widely and thoroughly before dispatching Americans to the
battlefield.

Identifies main issue by phrasing it as a question.

The paragraph varies the lengths of sentences and ends with the student's own main claim.

Barno makes a valuable contribution when he reminds his
readers of how terrible war can be. Moreover, he raises a legitimate concern when he points out that our nation's current
military commitments have imposed awful burdens on
recruits. Using the appeal of pathos, he stresses the suffering
undergone by soldiers who have had to serve several tours of
duty in deadly, traumatic places like Iraq and Afghanistan. He
contrasts their experience with that of people like former
governor Tom Ridge. Even though Ridge was, after being
drafted into the army, sent to fight in Vietnam, at least his

The first of several concessions in this paragraph.

time there lasted only one year. Barno emphasizes that many members of today's military are repeatedly assigned to combat. These soldiers include one of Barno's own sons, a fact that he reports while admitting that he's angry about it. Some readers may feel that because of his personal connection, Barno's complaint about repeated rounds of service is nothing but self-interest. But his use of his son's situation as a representative anecdote seems appropriate, for numerous other people in the military have been required lately to return to war. In light of this unfortunate trend, it would be understandable if Barno called for reviving the draft as a gesture of fairness. He could argue that exempting civilians from military service is morally wrong, given that the professional defenders of our nation have had to fight so much. Not everyone would agree with him, but his position would be credible.

A somewhat different motive, however, leads Barno to suggest that a draft lottery be held every year if a military action extends beyond two months. He makes this proposal because he feels that Americans outside the military have grown indifferent to the challenges it faces. In his view, the lottery would make civilians more conscious of combat deployments. At the same time, they would question more the necessity of going to war, for they might be drawn into combat themselves. This skepticism is something that Barno would welcome. To him, the government has grown too inclined to hurl troops into conflicts. He wants our leaders to make such decisions more slowly and carefully. He expects the lottery would achieve this goal, by raising public awareness and concern.

Clear transition from previous paragraph.

Probably Barno is right to sense that exposing significant numbers of Americans to a draft lottery would make the country uneasier about entering into war. Some greater unrest would most likely occur. Yet he provides no evidence for his claim that dependence on an all-volunteer force "has eroded the core societal seriousness that we have always accorded to national decisions of war and peace" (13). Why must his readers assume that the public is, at present, absolutely indifferent to the ordeals faced by our soldiers in Iraq and Afghanistan? Contrary to what he suggests, many civilians do seem to show "sufficient weight and seriousness" about the U.S.'s current military ventures (11). For instance, numerous cars display "Support Our Troops" signs, and supportive crowds regularly turn out for ceremonies welcoming reservists as well as National Guard members home from combat. Barno might respond that these are rituals of cheerful robots, propaganda that hardly shows deep thinking about the government's

Another concession, just before criticisms begin.

Provides supporting examples.

Figurative language.

choices. But civilians are perhaps able to appreciate soldiers' service while being thoughtful about the policies that demanded it. Barno appears to forget that when the invasion of Iraq was beginning, thousands of people marched in several cities to protest it. Moreover, critical attitudes toward current American wars have certainly mounted in the last few years. President Obama's decision to pull our military out of Afghanistan soon, along with his earlier decision to withdraw us from Iraq, stems in part from his awareness that much of our country has already grown tired of these commitments. He knows that we have woken up to how fatigued we are.

Perspective by incongruity.

Yet even if our nation adopted Barno's proposal and became considerably more skeptical about war, chances seem slight that these developments would inhibit our leaders. Beginning with Harry S Truman's "police action" in Korea during the early 1950s, no U.S. President has asked Congress for an official declaration of war. Instead, each President has essentially used the military as he has seen fit, seeking Congressional permission only at times and only in thin ways. The procedure has been to "consult" Congress in a superficial manner but not in a profound one. Lyndon Johnson took Congress's Gulf of Tonkin Resolution as a pretext for dramatically escalating the U.S. troop presence in Vietnam. Richard Nixon ignored massive antiwar protests and continued to bomb the same region. Ronald Reagan felt free to send soldiers to Grenada; Bill Clinton felt able to put them in Kosovo. George W. Bush had fairly minimal Congressional authorization to attack Iraq, on the basis of what turned out to be false information about Saddam Hussein's weapons stockpile. Similarly, after 9/11, Congress authorized Bush to pursue terrorists in Afghanistan. But that campaign was never officially declared as a war, even though it has managed to become the longest war in American history. Moreover, the current president is similarly determined to act independently. For all the sensitivity that Barack Obama has shown to the country's war fatigue, he has tried as much as possible to keep his policies on drone attacks secret from Congress and from Americans at large.

Begins another set of examples.

Identifies two possible meanings of the same word.

Balances the two halves of the sentence.

Therefore, devoting energy to Barno's proposed policy may be counterproductive. His recommendation is thought-provoking and based on vast military experience, but probably his readers would do better to focus on Presidential power. In military matters, the head of the country has tended to act on his instincts rather than seek meaningful advice from others. Figuring out ways to change or curb this habit seems an agenda more worthwhile than implementing the threat of a draft.

Concession; use of qualifications ("may be," "probably," "has tended").

Arguing in the First Person: Can You Use *I*?

More than ever, people engage in personal writing. As we text our friends, contribute to blogs, or post on social media, millions of us update the world about our daily lives. Perhaps you regularly report on your experiences in these ways. If so, your writing often relies on the first person. Over and over, it features the pronoun *I*. Some of your teachers, however, may have warned you against this pronoun. Many of us recall being told to ban it from our writing. In particular, its use was forbidden in essays meant for school. It's always good to find out what your current teachers' policies are about use of the first person in student essays. But nowadays, you might find your instructors more flexible about using *I* in essays. After all, it appears in countless online messages. Also, autobiography can prove to be a resource. References to yourself can help arguments you write for a course. They can inspire, support, and enliven the cases you make for your claims.

For an example, look again at Barno's paragraph 9. It reports the anger he felt when his son faced another combat tour. Barno's personal story carries larger implications. It makes a point about lots of people, not just the story's teller. With his account, Barno identifies hardships imposed on many enlistees and their families. He draws on his own experience to convey war's human costs.

Not always will the first person benefit an argument. Using *I* may bother your readers if you merely express your feelings. Here's a hypothetical example of what we mean:

> I definitely believe that Barno is too harsh in calling for a draft lottery. I very much feel that his proposal would put many people in needless danger. I worry that it won't stop our country from going to war. I fear that his plan will just send more civilians into combat. I also dislike the idea that his draft would require people to give up their freedom. I really value individual liberty. This constitutional right is very important to me.

A passage like this dwells too much on its author's emotions. Readers may lose sight of the argument the writer seeks to make. They may also suspect a lack of actual evidence. *Why* would Barno's draft lottery not keep the United States from war? The passage fails to offer real support for this claim. Instead, it stresses the "I's" own state of mind.

First-person arguments can backfire in another way. It's when they give the arguer's experiences too much authority. We're thinking of passages like this:

> Military families are more content than Barno admits. My brother Bob has done two tours of duty in Afghanistan. They have been rough for him, and he was even slightly wounded in a battle. But he has always been willing to perform his required service. I've never heard him complain that the army has mistreated him. My parents, my sister, and I are also true patriots. We're happy and proud that Bob has turned out to be such a brave warrior. I've sent him many e-mails

saying so. Everyone I know has regularly thanked him for his service instead of protesting America's decision to send our troops abroad in our defense. Bob and the rest of our family prove that the enemies of our country will never defeat the American spirit.

Personal anecdotes may indeed prove relevant to a claim you're making. They can be appropriate for an argument essay you write. Some version of the story above might play a useful role. It could nicely complicate Barno's emphasis on despair. But in its present form, the story doesn't "prove" anything. Bob's family may not be typical of military clans. The claim that they're representative needs much more support. In general, remember that not everyone's life resembles yours. Readers will want you to recognize the limits of your knowledge, as well as possible ways your history differs from others'.

Arguments for Analysis

We end this chapter by offering two additional arguments. Both of them conspicuously use the first person. We tend to think that their reliance on *I* is justifiable. Even so, the claims they make call for debate. We include these essays to invite your response. You might write an argument of your own about one or both of these texts. In any case, consider their main ideas, and study their techniques of persuasion. To help, we pose questions after each piece.

The first originally appeared as an op-ed column in the *New York Times* on June 6, 2015. Author Lee Siegel (b. 1957) is a veteran editor and cultural critic. Besides writing five books, he has contributed essays to many newspapers and periodicals. In 2002 he won the National Magazine Award for Reviews and Criticism. Siegel earned undergraduate and graduate degrees from Columbia University. As you'll see, he makes an argument about college students' debt.

LEE SIEGEL
Why I Defaulted on My Student Loans

One late summer afternoon when I was 17, I went with my mother to the local bank, a long-defunct institution whose name I cannot remember, to apply for my first student loan. My mother co-signed. When we finished, the banker, a balding man in his late 50s, congratulated us, as if I had just won some kind of award rather than signed away my young life.

By the end of my sophomore year at a small private liberal arts college, my mother and I had taken out a second loan, my father had declared bankruptcy and my parents had divorced. My mother could no longer afford the tuition that the student loans weren't covering. I transferred to a state college in New Jersey, closer to home.

Years later, I found myself confronted with a choice that too many people have had to and will have to face. I could give up what had become my vocation (in my case, being a writer) and take a job that I didn't want in order to repay the huge debt I had accumulated in college and graduate school. Or I could take what I had been led to believe was both the morally and legally reprehensible step of defaulting on my student loans, which was the only way I could survive without wasting my life in a job that had nothing to do with my particular usefulness to society.

I chose life. That is to say, I defaulted on my student loans.

As difficult as it has been, I've never looked back. The millions of young   5
people today, who collectively owe over $1 trillion in loans, may want to consider my example.

It struck me as absurd that one could amass crippling debt as a result, not of drug addiction or reckless borrowing and spending, but of going to college. Having opened a new life to me beyond my modest origins, the education system was now going to call in its chits and prevent me from pursuing that new life, simply because I had the misfortune of coming from modest origins.

Am I a deadbeat? In the eyes of the law I am. Indifferent to the claim that repaying student loans is the road to character? Yes. Blind to the reality of countless numbers of people struggling to repay their debts, no matter their circumstances, many worse than mine? My heart goes out to them. To my mind, they have learned to live with a social arrangement that is legal, but not moral.

Maybe the problem was that I had reached beyond my lower-middle-class origins and taken out loans to attend a small private college to begin with. Maybe I should have stayed at a store called The Wild Pair, where I once had a nice stable job selling shoes after dropping out of the state college because I thought I deserved better, and naïvely tried to turn myself into a professional reader and writer on my own, without a college degree. I'd probably be district manager by now.

Or maybe, after going back to school, I should have gone into finance, or some other lucrative career. Self-disgust and lifelong unhappiness, destroying a precious young life — all this is a small price to pay for meeting your student loan obligations.

Some people will maintain that a bankrupt father, an impecunious back-   10
ground and impractical dreams are just the luck of the draw. Someone with character would have paid off those loans and let the chips fall where they may. But I have found, after some decades on this earth, that the road to character is often paved with family money and family connections, not to mention 14 percent effective tax rates on seven-figure incomes.

Moneyed stumbles never seem to have much consequence. Tax fraud, insider trading, almost criminal nepotism — these won't knock you off the straight and narrow. But if you're poor and miss a child-support payment, or if you're middle class and default on your student loans, then God help you.

Forty years after I took out my first student loan, and 30 years after getting my last, the Department of Education is still pursuing the unpaid balance. My mother, who co-signed some of the loans, is dead. The banks that made them have all gone under. I doubt that anyone can even find the promissory notes. The accrued interest, combined with the collection agencies' opulent fees, is now several times the principal.

Even the Internal Revenue Service understands the irrationality of pursuing someone with an unmanageable economic burden. It has a program called Offer in Compromise that allows struggling people who have fallen behind in their taxes to settle their tax debt.

The Department of Education makes it hard for you, and ugly. But it is possible to survive the life of default. You might want to follow these steps: Get as many credit cards as you can before your credit is ruined. Find a stable housing situation. Pay your rent on time so that you have a good record in that area when you do have to move. Live with or marry someone with good credit (preferably someone who shares your desperate nihilism).

When the fateful day comes, and your credit looks like a war zone, don't be   15
afraid. The reported consequences of having no credit are scare talk, to some extent. The reliably predatory nature of American life guarantees that there will always be somebody to help you, from credit card companies charging stratospheric interest rates to subprime loans for houses and cars. Our economic system ensures that so long as you are willing to sink deeper and deeper into debt, you will keep being enthusiastically invited to play the economic game.

I am sharply aware of the strongest objection to my lapse into default. If everyone acted as I did, chaos would result. The entire structure of American higher education would change.

The collection agencies retained by the Department of Education would be exposed as the greedy vultures that they are. The government would get out of the loan-making and the loan-enforcement business. Congress might even explore a special, universal education tax that would make higher education affordable.

There would be a national shaming of colleges and universities for charging soaring tuition rates that are reaching lunatic levels. The rapacity of American colleges and universities is turning social mobility, the keystone of American freedom, into a commodified farce.

If people groaning under the weight of student loans simply said, "Enough," then all the pieties about debt that have become absorbed into all the pieties about higher education might be brought into alignment with reality. Instead of guaranteeing loans, the government would have to guarantee a college education. There are a lot of people who could learn to live with that, too.

≡ **THINKING ABOUT THE TEXT**

1. What is your main response to Siegel's argument, and what is the main reason you would give in supporting your response?

2. What do you think is the strongest (best) point that Siegel makes? Identify and paraphrase the specific passage where this point appears.

3. Where does Siegel acknowledge readers who might disagree with his argument or challenge it? Refer to specific paragraphs.

4. Note places where Siegel uses the word *life*: for example, in paragraph 4. How, in each instance, does he seem to define this word? Do his definitions seem logical to you? Why, or why not?

5. How would you describe Siegel's ethos: that is, the image of himself he creates as a writer?

6. In paragraphs 14 and 15, Siegel uses the pronoun *you*. Why, do you think? How is this choice of pronoun strategic?

7. Is it possible for readers to criticize Siegel for defaulting and yet still agree with certain parts of his essay? Explain.

8. Even if you agree with Siegel's position on the issue of student debt, what is something additional that he could have said or done in his essay to make his argument more persuasive?

9. In an article he wrote about Siegel's essay, *Slate* magazine correspondent Jordan Weissmann accused Siegel of "dispatching criminally negligent financial advice." Weissmann even said that the *New York Times* "should consider apologizing for publishing this deeply irresponsible op-ed." Do you agree with Weissmann that the essay shouldn't have been published at all? Why, or why not?

10. How sincere does Siegel seem when he encourages his readers to default on their student loans? Do you believe that a significant portion of his readers would see him as indeed calling for them to break the law? Why, or why not?

The second essay was originally a July 18, 2017 contribution to the online journal *LA Review of Books*. Its author, Afshan Jafar, was born in Pakistan and is now a professor of sociology at Connecticut College. She specializes in global issues of gender, feminism, nationalism, and the body. Her books include *Women's NGOs in Pakistan* (2011) and two coedited collections, *Global Beauty, Local Bodies* and *Bodies Without Borders* (both 2013). In addition to publishing articles in several academic journals, she regularly blogs for *Inside Higher Education* and has contributed columns to such other venues as the British newspaper *The Guardian*.

AFSHAN JAFAR

Not a Fan of Fat Shaming? Stop Thin Praising

Kelly Clarkson, the Grammy-winning singer, simply wanted to thank service members on July 4th. Natalie Hage, a model, simply wanted to fly to her photo-shoot in Los Angeles. Instead of being the somewhat ordinary events they should've been, these occasions turned into direct attacks on these women and their weight.

The responses of both women and their supporters were swift and they put the fat shamers to shame. By now, we have learned to recognize fat shaming. And while incidents of fat shaming bring out the trolls on social media who jump on the fat shaming bandwagon, they also bring out fierce opposition, as they should.

Yet, we allow what I call "thin praising" — praising someone for losing weight or for being thin — to persist. Recently, many media outlets, including social media, were simply giddy about the actor, Jonah Hill's weight loss. With words like "jaw dropping," "inspiring," "motivating," and #goals," everyone was in agreement that Jonah Hill's weight loss was something to be outwardly and vociferously praised. Shonda Rhimes' recent revelation that people found her "worthy of conversation" after her 150-pound weight loss reveals how entrenched we are in a culture of thin praising, and why we should think twice before gushing over someone for their weight loss.

What's wrong with praising someone for weight loss?

As a sociologist who does research on and teaches about body image and healthy embodiment, I have had countless conversations with young college students about how beauty ideals get reinforced and what makes body norms so hard to resist. Punishment for not following norms or not living up to an ideal, is only half of the equation. This is what fat shaming falls into — people being ridiculed as a form of punishment for not meeting an ideal body type.

But there is another way that norms and practices are reinforced, and in many ways it's even more powerful than punishment: positive reinforcement. In the case of beauty norms and practices, this positive reinforcement takes the form of simple praise. Many of my young female students recount their experiences with praise as a motivator for following beauty norms. They describe the interactions they have with their friends on days that they wake up early, fix their hair, put on make-up, and put on attractive clothes. Or they recount the interactions they have when they lose weight. At such times, their friends stop them on the way to class to tell them how beautiful they look, or, perhaps even more important: they tell them on social media. Their friends openly admire their clothes, their hair, and their bodies. The praise, in turn, makes them feel confident and happy. That confidence and happiness shapes their interactions throughout the day. The praise and the resulting feeling of confidence encourages them to get up early the next day and do the same thing.

Both punishment (shaming) and positive reinforcement (praising) reinforce beauty norms that value thin, flawless, usually white or light-skinned bodies, with straight, usually blonde, hair. Shaming and praising, in turn, also encourage participation in certain beauty practices such as dieting or plastic surgery. If we are interested in challenging the narrow definition of an ideal body type and weight, we not only need to put an end to fat shaming, we also need to stop thin praising. For without calling into question the praise we bestow on people for losing weight, fat shaming will persist.

But shouldn't we acknowledge someone's hard work and resolve to become healthier by losing weight? The problem with this thinking is that it equates being thin or losing weight with being healthy. To be sure, severe obesity has been linked to several medical conditions. But the latest scientific research on obesity and health is starting to question conventional and medical wisdom that connects being overweight to being unhealthy. In fact, some research shows that being overweight or even being mildly obese actually offers some advantages to patients with medical conditions like pneumonia, stroke, cancer, heart disease and hypertension, and that fat people who exercise are generally healthier than thin people who don't.

If health were truly our goal, we'd move beyond a narrow fixation on weight and would address an individual's health more comprehensively. Instead, the laser focus of media and medical professionals on an individual's weight as a signal of health leads to misdiagnoses for fat people, whose medical problems are misattributed to their weight, and under-diagnoses of serious illnesses for thin people who are assumed to be healthy.

Eventually, thin praising reinforces the same ideas that fat shaming stems   10
from. If thin bodies deserve praise because they are desirable and attractive, then fat bodies deserve shame and are revolting and not worthy of praise; if thin bodies are healthy, then fat bodies are unhealthy; if thin bodies are the result of hard work and good choices, then fat bodies are the result of laziness and bad choices. Fat shaming can't be separated from thin praising. If fat shaming is unacceptable to us, then thin praising, which is equally culpable in creating a culture that vilifies fat and fatness, should be just as unacceptable to us.

Shonda Rhimes and Jonah Hill lost weight. I am not sure that is newsworthy. But I am certain that shouldn't be praise worthy.

≡ THINKING ABOUT THE TEXT

1. Why do you think Jafar begins her essay with the fat shaming of two people well-known in their respective fields, singer Kelly Clarkson and model Natalie Hage? Why, conceivably, does she make her first two examples of "thin praising" be entertainment celebrities (actor Jonah Hill and television producer Shonda Rimes)? Perhaps not all readers will know who Hill and Rimes are. Should Jafar have said more about them? Why, or why not?

2. What does Jafar identify as mistaken beliefs?

3. In paragraph 7, Jafar discusses "beauty norms." Which ones have you personally had to deal with? Jafar refers specifically to those faced by young college women. Do you think young *men* in college grapple with "beauty norms," too? If so, what are they?

4. Conceivably, some of the women Jafar refers to in paragraph 7 *enjoy* being praised for their looks. To what extent does their pleasure undermine Jaffar's argument against thin praising?

5. Where does Jafar acknowledge an opposing argument? What reasoning does she put forth in her attempt to counter it? How persuasive do you find her logic? Explain.

6. How does Jafar draw on the appeal of ethos? Note where she indicates that she's an expert researcher.

7. In paragraph 10, how does Jafar use repetition? To what extent does this device make her main argument compelling?

8. What might you say to a friend who's lost a lot of weight if you *don't* praise that person's new thinness? Are there, in fact, realistic alternatives to the compliment Jafar criticizes?

CHAPTER 3

How to Argue about Literature

What Is Literature?

Most people would say that *literature* consists of fiction (novels as well as short stories), poetry, and drama, and this is a reasonable definition. But limiting the term to these genres can be misleading. After all, they connect to everyday life. Often they employ ordinary forms of talk and blend them with less common ones. Also, things that function as symbols in stories, poems, and plays may do so in daily conversation. As we speak with one another, we may associate fire with passion, water with life, evening with death. Throughout the day, people put literary genres into practice. Perhaps you have commented on a situation by quoting a song lyric or citing a line of verse. No doubt you are often theatrical, following scripts and performing roles. Certainly you tell stories. Imagine this scenario: a traffic jam has made you late for a class; now, you must explain your delay. You may relate a tale of suspense with you, the hero, struggling to escape the bumper-to-bumper horde. Almost all of us spin narratives day after day, because doing so helps us meaningfully frame our existence. As writer Joan Didion observes, "We tell ourselves stories in order to live."

You may admit that literature is grounded in real life and yet still tend to apply the term only to written texts of fiction, poetry, and drama. But this tendency is distinctly modern, for the term *literature* has not always been applied so restrictively. *Literature* was at first a characteristic of *readers*. From the term's emergence in the fourteenth century to the middle of the eighteenth, *literature* was more or less a synonym for *literacy*. People of literature were assumed to be well read.

In the late eighteenth century, however, the term's meaning changed. Increasingly it referred to books and other printed texts, rather than to people who read them. At the beginning of this shift, the scope of literature was broad, encompassing nearly all public writing. But as the nineteenth century proceeded, the term's range shrank. More and more people considered literature to be imaginative or creative writing, which they distinguished from nonfiction. This trend took years to build; in the early 1900s, literature anthologies still featured nonfiction, such as essays and excerpts from histories and biographies. By the mid-1900s, though, the narrower definition of literature prevailed.

This limited definition has become vulnerable. Since the early 1970s a number of literature faculty have called for widening it. In 1979, for instance, a National Endowment for the Humanities–Modern Language Association institute titled "Women's Nontraditional Literature" applied the term *literature* to genres that had not been thought of as such. Participants studied essays, letters, diaries, autobiographies, and oral testimonies. Women have contributed much in each of these genres; in fact, the institute's participants concluded that a literature curriculum slights many works by women if it focuses on fiction, poetry, and drama alone.

Of course, even within these three categories, the term *literature* has been selectively applied. Take the case of novelist and short-story writer Stephen King, whose books have sold millions of copies. Despite his commercial success, many readers — including some of his fans — refuse to call King's writing literature. They assume that to call something literature is to say that it has artistic merit, and for them King's tales of horror fall short.

Yet people who use the term *literature* as a compliment may still disagree about whether a certain text deserves it. Plenty of readers praise King's writing as literature, even as others deem it simply entertainment. Artistic standards differ. To be sure, some works have been constantly admired through the years; regarded as classics, they are frequently taught in literature classes. *Hamlet* and other plays by William Shakespeare are obvious examples. But in the last twenty years, much controversy has arisen over the *literary canon*, those works taught regularly. Are there good reasons why the canon consists mostly of works by white men? Or have the principles of selection been skewed by sexism and racism? Should the canon be changed to accommodate a greater range of authors? Should literary studies resist having any canon at all? These questions have provoked various answers and continued debate.

Also in question are attempts to separate literature from nonfiction. Much nonfiction shows imagination and relies on devices found in novels, short stories, poems, and plays. The last few years have seen emerge the term *creative nonfiction* as a synonym for essays, histories, and journalistic accounts that use evocative language and strong narratives.

Conversely, works of fiction, poetry, and drama may stem from real-life events. Charlotte Perkins Gilman based her 1892 short story "The Yellow Wallpaper" (see p. 233) on the trauma she went through when her doctor, treating her for depression, made her stop work and vegetate. Gilman's heroine suffers torment similar to hers. A note of caution is in order, though: A literary text may seem autobiographical, but may not directly reflect the author's life. The situation of Gilman's heroine doesn't completely resemble her own; It differs in certain ways. Indeed, the character is too distressed to write a story as Gilman herself did. In short, Gilman didn't merely transmit her experience. Rather, she *transformed* it. So her artistic strategies merit study, especially since she could have tapped her experience in other ways. Keep in mind, too, that the author of a work isn't always the best guide. It may raise for its readers issues and ideas that the author didn't foresee. The author's comments about the text may leave aspects of it unexplained.

Some people argue that literature about real events is still literary because it inspires contemplation rather than action. This view of literature has traditionally been summed up as "art for art's sake." This notion brushes aside all the novels, short stories, poems, and plays that encourage audiences to undertake certain acts. Famous examples are Harriet Beecher Stowe's anti-slavery novel *Uncle Tom's Cabin* (1852) and Upton Sinclair's *The Jungle* (1906) about the horrors of immigrant exploitation in the Chicago meat-packing industry. Not every work of literature is so conspicuously action oriented. But even when a text seems more geared toward reflection, it may move readers to change their behavior.

In our book, we resist endorsing a single definition of *literature*. Rather, we encourage you to review and perhaps rethink what the term means to you. At the same time, to expand the realm of literature, we include several essays in addition to short stories, poems, and plays. We also present numerous critical commentaries as well as various historical documents. Throughout the book, we invite you to make connections among these different kinds of texts. You don't need to treat them as altogether separate species.

Why Study Literature in a College Writing Course?

We assume you are reading this book in a course aimed at helping you write. Quite likely the course is meant to prepare you for writing assignments throughout college, including papers in fields beyond English. It's natural to wonder how reading literature serves this purpose.

Much academic writing is in fact based on reading. You'll find the two interconnected in course after course. Many classes will ask you to produce essays that analyze published texts. To *analyze* means going beyond your first impressions, carefully noting a text's ideas, techniques, and effects. You'll also find yourself needing to *synthesize*: that is, to trace how the text is patterned, as well as how it relates to other works. Together, these acts of analysis and synthesis have been called reading *closely*, a process we explain and model in Chapter 4. We encourage you to practice this method with the selections in our book.

Often, college courses will ask you to write about some text that isn't easily understood. The purpose of your paper will be to help other readers of the text grasp its meanings and perhaps judge its worth. Literature is a good training ground for these skills of interpretation and evaluation. The poems, stories, plays, and essays in this book repeatedly invite inquiry. They don't settle for delivering simple, straightforward messages. Rather, they offer puzzles, complications, metaphors, symbols, and mysteries, because they recognize that life is complex. In particular, literary works encourage you to ponder the multiple dimensions of language: how, for example, a word's meaning can vary depending on context. Furthermore, much literature can help you understand your own life and conduct it better. In this capacity, Kenneth Burke's description of literature serves as "equipment for living."

Some people *dislike* literature because they find it too vague and indirect. They resent that it often forces them to figure out symbols and implications when they would rather have ideas presented outright. Perhaps you'll wish that the narrator in Gilman's story had made clear why her observations prompted her to destroy her room's wallpaper. But in life, truth can be complicated and elusive. In many ways, literature is most realistic when it suggests the same. Besides, many readers — perhaps including you — appreciate literature most when it resists simple decoding, forcing them to adopt new assumptions and learn new methods of analysis. Indeed, throughout this book we suggest that the most interesting and profitable conversations about literature are those in which the issues are not easily resolved. One of the best things your course can provide you and your classmates is the chance to exchange insights about texts such as Gilman's.

We have been suggesting that one value of studying literature in a writing class is that it often engages not just thought but feeling. The two interweave so that readers find themselves engaging in interpretation and evaluation because they *care* about lives depicted in the text. Most of the works in this book appeal to your emotions, encouraging you to identify with certain characters, to be disturbed by others, and to wonder what happens next in the plot. Indeed, many readers of literature prize the moments when what they're reading makes them laugh or cry or gasp as well as think.

To be sure, it can be argued that the most worthwhile literature gets us to comprehend and perhaps even appreciate certain kinds of people who would normally confuse or disturb us. "When it's the real thing," critic Frank Lentricchia suggests, "literature enlarges us, strips the film of familiarity from the world; creates bonds of sympathy with all kinds, even with evil characters, who we learn are all in the family." This enlargement is both intellectual *and* emotional.

Finally, writing about literature is good training for other fields because literary analysis often involves taking an interdisciplinary perspective. A typical interpretation of "The Yellow Wallpaper" will bring in principles of psychology to explain the speaker's distressed state of mind. To evaluate the character's condition, readers also grapple with philosophical questions about what constitutes a productive, good, or free life. Moreover, the heroine's entrapment in nineteenth-century gender roles has political, historical, and sociological significance.

A Story for Analysis

As we discuss the process of arguing about literature, we mention arguments that might be made about the following story, Jamaica Kincaid's "Girl." It first appeared in *The New Yorker* in 1978 and was later reprinted in Kincaid's first book, a 1984 collection of short stories titled *At the Bottom of the River*.

JAMAICA KINCAID

Girl

Originally named Elaine Potter Richardson, Jamaica Kincaid (b. 1949) was born on the island of Antigua in the West Indies. At the time, Antigua was a British colony. Kincaid lived there until she was seventeen, when she emigrated to the United States. Soon she became a nanny for the family of Michael Arlen, television critic for The New Yorker. *Eventually, the magazine published her own short stories and during the early 1990s her gardening columns. Although she continues to live in the United States, almost all of her writing deals with her native land. In particular, she has written about Antiguan women growing up under British domination. She has published the novels* Annie John *(1985),* Lucy *(1990),* Autobiography of My Mother *(1996), and* Mr. Potter *(2002). Her books of nonfiction include* A Small Place, *an analysis of Antigua (1988); a memoir,* My Brother *(1997);* My Garden (Book) *(1999); and* Talk Stories *(2001), a collection of brief observations that she originally wrote for* The New Yorker. *In 2009, she was inducted into the American Academy of Arts and Sciences and is currently a professor of literature at Claremont McKenna College in California. Her most recent novel is* See Now Then *(2013).*

Wash the white clothes on Monday and put them on the stone heap; wash the color clothes on Tuesday and put them on the clothesline to dry; don't walk barehead in the hot sun; cook pumpkin fritters in very hot sweet oil; soak your little clothes right after you take them off; when buying cotton to make yourself a nice blouse, be sure that it doesn't have gum on it, because that way it won't hold up well after a wash; soak salt fish overnight before you cook it; is it true that you sing benna° in Sunday school?; always eat your food in such a way that it won't turn someone else's stomach; on Sundays try to walk like a lady and not like the slut you are so bent on becoming; don't sing benna in Sunday school; you mustn't speak to wharf-rat boys, not even to give directions; don't eat fruits on the street — flies will follow you; *but I don't sing benna on Sundays at all and never in Sunday school*; this is how to sew on a button; this is how to make a button-hole for the button you have just sewed on; this is how to hem a dress when you see the hem coming down and so to prevent yourself from looking like the slut I know you are so bent on becoming; this is how you iron your father's khaki shirt so that it doesn't have a crease; this is how you iron your father's khaki pants so that they don't have a crease; this is how you grow okra — far from the house, because okra tree harbors red ants; when you are growing dasheen, make sure it gets plenty of water or else it makes your throat itch when you are eating it; this is how you sweep a corner; this is how you sweep a whole house; this is how you sweep a yard; this is how you smile to someone you don't like too much; this is how you smile to someone you don't like at all; this is how you smile to someone

5

10

15

20

7 benna: Calypso music.

you like completely; this is how you set a table for tea; this is how you set a
table for dinner; this is how you set a table for dinner with an important guest;   25
this is how you set a table for lunch; this is how you set a table for breakfast;
this is how to behave in the presence of men who don't know you very well,
and this way they won't recognize immediately the slut I have warned you
against becoming; be sure to wash every day, even if it is with your own spit;
don't squat down to play marbles — you are not a boy, you know; don't pick   30
people's flowers — you might catch something; don't throw stones at black-
birds, because it might not be a blackbird at all; this is how to make a bread
pudding; this is how to make doukona;° this is how to make pepper pot; this is
how to make a good medicine for a cold; this is how to make a good medicine
to throw away a child before it even becomes a child; this is how to catch a   35
fish; this is how to throw back a fish you don't like, and that way something
bad won't fall on you; this is how to bully a man; this is how a man bullies
you; this is how to love a man, and if this doesn't work there are other ways,
and if they don't work don't feel too bad about giving up; this is how to spit
up in the air if you feel like it, and this is how to move quick so that it doesn't   40
fall on you; this is how to make ends meet; always squeeze bread to make sure
it's fresh; *but what if the baker won't let me feel the bread?*; you mean to say that
after all you are really going to be the kind of woman who the baker won't let
near the bread?   *[1978]*

33 doukona: A spicy plantain pudding.

≡ THINKING ABOUT THE TEXT

1. Is "Girl" a story? What characteristics of a story come to mind as you
   consider this issue?

2. Describe the culture depicted in "Girl" as well as the role of females in
   that culture. Is either the culture or the role of females in it different
   from what you are familiar with? Explain.

3. Do you think that the instructions to this girl are all given on the
   same occasion? Why, or why not? Who do you suppose is giving
   the instructions? Would you say that the instructor is oppressive or
   domineering? Identify some of the assumptions behind your position.

4. What effect does Kincaid achieve by making this text a single long
   sentence? By having the girl speak at only two brief moments?

5. At one point, the girl is shown "how to make a good medicine to
   throw away a child before it even becomes a child" (lines 34–35).
   What do you think of the instructor's willingness to give such advice?
   What do you conclude from its position in the text between "how to
   make a good medicine for a cold" (lines 33–34) and "how to catch
   a fish" (lines 35–36)? Does the order of the various pieces of advice
   matter? Could Kincaid have presented them in a different order
   without changing their effects?

≡ A WRITING EXERCISE

Once you have read Kincaid's story, write a brief response to it. You might jot down things you especially notice about it, feelings it evoked in you, and questions you have about it. You might also note your own work experiences that the story leads you to recall. Try freewriting for ten minutes without stopping.

Strategies for Arguing about Literature

We return now to the specific elements of argument we discussed in Chapter 1. Remember that when you argue, you try to **persuade** an **audience** to accept your **claims** about an **issue**, working toward this aim by offering **evidence**, showing your **reasoning**, making **assumptions**, and employing other kinds of **appeals**. Here, with Kincaid's story as our sample text, we show how you can turn these elements into strategies for writing arguments about literature.

IDENTIFY ISSUES

Recall that an **issue** is something about which people have disagreed or might disagree. As you read a text, you can try to guess what features of it will lead to disagreements in class. You may sense that your own reaction to certain aspects of the text is heavily influenced by your background and values, which other students may not share. Some parts of the text may leave you with conflicting ideas or mixed feelings, as if half of you disagrees with the other half. At moments like these, you come to realize what topics are issues for you, and next you can urge the rest of your class to see these topics as issues, too.

An issue is best defined as a question with no obvious, immediate answer. Thus you can start identifying issues by noting questions that occur to you as you read. Perhaps this question-posing approach to texts is new for you. Often readers demand that a text be clear, and they get annoyed if it leaves them puzzled. Certain writing ought to be immediately clear in meaning; think of operating instructions on a plane's emergency doors. But the value of a literary work often lies in the work's complexities, which can lead readers to reexamine their own ways of perceiving the world. Also, your discussions and papers about literature are likely to be most useful when they go beyond the obvious to deal with more challenging matters. When your class begins talking about a work, you may feel obliged to stay quiet if you have no firm statements to make. But you can contribute by bringing up questions that occurred to you as you read, especially the questions that continue to haunt you.

One possible issue with Jamaica Kincaid's "Girl" concerns how much affection the main speaker has for the girl she addresses. A logical hypothesis is that these two are mother and daughter, but to what degree is the speaker showing motherly love? In fact, people may disagree over how to define the term motherly love. What does it mean to *you?*

You may feel unable to answer questions like these. But again, you can achieve much when you simply formulate questions and bring them up in class. As other students help you ponder them, you will grow better able to explore issues through writing as well as through conversation.

You are more likely to come up with questions about a text if you assume that for every decision the writer made, alternatives existed. For example, Kincaid might have given the girl of her title more of a speaking voice. When you begin to explore why authors made the choices they did, you also begin to examine the effects of those choices.

Next, we identify ten kinds of issues that arise in literature courses. Our list will help you detect the issues that come up in your class and discover others to bring up in discussions or in your writing. The list does not include every kind of issue; you may think of others. Moreover, you may find that an issue can fit into more than one of the categories we name. But when you do have an issue that seems hard to classify, try to assign it to a single category, if only for the time being. You will then have some initial guidance for your reading, class discussion, and writing. If you later feel that the issue belongs to another category, you can shift your focus.

1. Issues of fact.   Rarely does a work of literature provide complete information about its characters and events. Rather, literature is usually marked by what literary theorist Wolfgang Iser calls "gaps," moments when certain facts are omitted or obscured. At such times, readers may give various answers to the question, What is happening in this text? Readers tackle questions of fact only if they suspect that the answers will affect their overall view of a text. It may not matter, for example, that we fail to learn the exact age of the girl addressed in Kincaid's story. More consequential seems the question of what behavior the girl has engaged in prior to the lecturing she receives. Imagine a reader who believes that the girl has indeed given the adult woman some reason to be concerned about her. Imagine a second reader who thinks the girl is innocent and undeserving of the adult's scorn. How might these readers see the whole story differently because of their different assumptions?

2. Issues of theme.   You may be familiar with the term **theme** from other literature courses. By *theme* critics usually mean the main claim that an author seems to be making with his or her text. Sometimes a theme is defined in terms of a single word—for example, *work* or *love*. But such words are really mere topics. Identifying the topics addressed by a text can be a useful way of starting to analyze that text (see pp. 97–103). A text's theme, however, is best seen as an assertion that you need at least one whole sentence to express.

With many texts, an issue of theme arises because readers can easily disagree about the text's main idea. In literature classes, such disagreements often occur in part because literary works tend to express their themes indirectly. This is especially the case with stories like "Girl," in which the main speaker's views are not necessarily the same as the author's. Readers of these two stories may give various answers to the question, What is the author ultimately saying? Perhaps some readers will take Kincaid to imply that mothers always know best. Others may conclude that Kincaid thinks that excessively controlling mothers are damaging to children.

If you try to express a text's theme, avoid making a statement that is so general that it could apply to many other works. Arguing that Kincaid's theme is "Girls are pressured to fit stereotyped roles" does not get at her story's details. On the other hand, do not let a text's details restrict you so much that you make the theme seem relevant only to a small group. If you argue that Kincaid's theme is "Antiguan women are domineering," then the many readers who are *not* from Antigua will wonder why they should care. In short, try to express themes as *midlevel generalizations.* With Kincaid's story, one possible theme is "In some cultures, women prepare girls for adulthood by teaching them to follow conventions *and* to assert themselves." A statement like this seems both attentive to Kincaid's specific text and applicable to a large portion of humanity. You are free to challenge this version of Kincaid's theme by proposing an alternative. Moreover, even if you do accept this statement as her theme, you are then free to decide whether it is a sound observation. Identifying a theme is one thing; evaluating it is another.

Keep in mind that a theme ties together various parts of a text. Focusing on a single passage, even if it seems thematic, may lead you to ignore other passages that a statement of theme should encompass. For instance, the last words of "Girl" may tempt you to believe that its theme is "be the kind of woman who feels the bread." Yet in other parts of the story, the main speaker seems to be calling for a compliant attitude. You need to take these moments into account as well.

Often you will sense a work's theme but still have to decide whether to state it as an **observation** or as a **recommendation**. You would be doing the first, for example, if you expressed Kincaid's theme as we did above: "In some cultures, women prepare girls for adulthood by teaching them to follow conventions *and* to assert themselves." You would be doing the second if you said Kincaid's theme is "Women should teach girls to follow conventions *and* to assert themselves." Indeed, people who depict a theme as a recommendation often use a word like *should.* Neither way of expressing a theme is necessarily better than the other. But notice that each way conjures up a particular image of the author. Reporting Kincaid's theme as an observation suggests that she is writing as a psychologist, a philosopher, or some other analyst of human nature. Reporting her theme as a recommendation suggests that she is writing as a teacher, preacher, manager, or coach: someone who is telling her readers what to do. Your decision about how to phrase a theme will depend in part on which image of the author you think is appropriate.

You risk obscuring the intellectual, emotional, and stylistic richness of a text if you insist on reducing it to a single message. Try stating the text's theme as a problem for which there is no easy solution, which suggests that the text is complex. For instance, if you say that Kincaid's theme is "In some cultures, women who prepare girls for adulthood are caught in a contradiction between wanting to empower them and wanting to keep them safe," you position yourself to address various elements of the story.

Also weigh the possibility that a text is conveying more than one theme. If you plan to associate the text with any theme at all, you might refer to *a* theme of the text rather than *the* theme of the text. Your use of the term *theme* would still have implications. Above all, you would still be suggesting that you have identified one of the text's major points. Subsequently, you might have to defend this claim, showing how the point you have identified is indeed central to the text.

Issues of theme have loomed large in literary studies. We hope that you will find them useful to pursue. But because references to theme are so common in literary studies, students sometimes forget that there are other kinds of issues. As you move through this list, you may find some that interest you more.

3. Issues of definition. In arguments about literature, issues of **definition** arise most often when readers try to decide what an author means by a particular word. The title of Kincaid's story seems simple but is actually open to interpretation. What does it mean to be a "girl" in the culture that the story depicts? Even with ordinary words like this, issues of definition can arise.

4. Issues of symbolism. In literary studies, an issue of **symbolism** usually centers on a particular image. In question are the image's meaning and purpose, including whether the image is more than just a detail. Notice that the very first word of "Girl" is "Wash." Some readers may take this word literally. They may see it as nothing more than the speaker's command to launder. Other readers, though, may sense greater significance. They may contend that this opening word reflects the speaker's desire to purify the girl, to make her *spiritually* clean.

5. Issues of pattern. With issues of **pattern**, you observe how a text is organized and try to determine how certain parts of the text relate to other parts. But think, too, about the meaning and purpose of any pattern you find, especially since readers may disagree about the pattern's significance. Also ponder the implications of any moment when a text *breaks* with a pattern it has been following. Disruptions of a pattern may be as important as the pattern itself.

A conspicuous pattern in "Girl" is the main speaker's series of commands, which includes repeated use of the words *this is how.* Indeed, **repetition** is a common pattern in literature. Yet at two points in Kincaid's story, the speaker is interrupted by italicized protests from the girl: "*but I don't sing benna on Sundays at all and never in Sunday school*" (lines 11–12) and "*but what if the baker won't let me feel the bread?*" (line 42). What should we conclude about the main speaker from her string of orders? What should we conclude about the girl from her two disruptions? Readers may have various answers to these questions.

A text's apparent oppositions are also patterns that may be debated. Throughout "Girl," for example, the main speaker disitnguishes her adult wisdom from the girl's reckless naivete. Is this contrast fair? Are there ways in which the speaker's own vision is flawed? Again, different answers are possible.

6. Issues of evaluation.   Consciously or unconsciously, **evaluation** always plays a central role in reading. When you read a work of literature, you evaluate its ideas and the actions of its characters. You judge the views you assume the author is promoting. Moreover, you gauge the artistic quality of the text.

Specifically, you engage in three kinds of evaluation as you read. One kind is *philosophical*: you decide whether a particular idea or action is wise. Another kind is *ethical*: you decide whether an idea or action is morally good. The third kind is *aesthetic*: you decide whether the work as a whole or parts of the text succeed as art. Another reader may disagree with your criteria for wisdom, morality, and art; people's standards often differ. It is not surprising, then, that in the study of literature issues of evaluation come up frequently.

Sometimes you may have trouble distinguishing the three types of judgment from each other. Philosophical evaluation, ethical evaluation, and aesthetic evaluation can overlap. Probably the first two operate in the mind of a reader who is judging the advice given by the main speaker in "Girl." This reader may, for instance, find the speaker insensitive: that is, neither smart nor humane. Moreover, if this reader thinks Kincaid sympathizes with the speaker, then he or she may consider "Girl" flawed as a work of art. Keep in mind, however, that you can admire many aspects of a literary work even if you disagree with the ideas you see the author promoting. Someone may relish Kincaid's colorful language regardless of the views presented in the story.

But whose works should be taught? Many scholars argue that literary studies have focused mainly on white male authors, and some refuse to assume that the works of these authors are great and universally relevant. They criticize the long neglect of female and minority writers like Kincaid, a black woman born and raised in the West Indies. In part because of these scholars' arguments, "Girl" now appears in many literature anthologies. Yet other people continue to prize classics by William Shakespeare, John Milton, and William Blake. This ongoing debate about the literature curriculum includes disagreements about the worth of recent texts. After all, contemporary literature has yet to pass a test of time. Do you think Kincaid's story does deserve to be anthologized and taught? *We* think so, and have included "Girl" in our own book. What is *your* evaluation of it? What particular standards have you used to judge it?

7. Issues of historical and cultural context.   Plenty of literary works have engaged readers who are quite unlike their authors. These readers may include much-later generations and inhabitants of distant lands. Nevertheless, an author's own **historical and cultural context** may significantly shape his or her text. A story like "Orientation" (page 712) has elements that probably strike you as strange, many details of this story no doubt remind you of life in offices throughout the present-day United States. Still, readers may disagree over exactly which features of the story are typical of the contemporary American workplace. Consider as well Jamaica Kincaid's use of her past in "Girl." Though she has lived in the United States since she was seventeen, she evidently tapped memories of her childhood on Antigua to write this story and to represent the island's culture. Since many of the story's readers would be unfamiliar with Antigua, she had to decide what aspects of it to acquaint them with. What features of it does she emphasize, and what features does she downplay or omit? When Kincaid was born, Antiguans were under British control, and many labored hard for little money. Do these historical facts matter in "Girl"? If so, in what conceivable ways? Notice that answering such political and economic questions usually requires research. Even then, answers may be complicated. Indeed, rarely does a literary text straightforwardly reflect its author's background. Debate arises over how text and context relate.

We provide some background for each literary work we present to help you begin to situate it both historically and culturally. In Chapter 7, we explain how to put literature in context, especially by doing research in the library and on the Internet. For now, we want to emphasize that contextualizing a work involves more than just piling up facts about its origin. In the study of literature, issues of historical and cultural context are often issues of *relevance*: *which* facts about a work's creation are important for readers to know, and *how* would awareness of these facts help readers better understand the work? Readers can inform themselves about a particular author's life, for instance, but they may disagree about the extent to which a given text is autobiographical.

Perhaps you'd like to connect a literary work with its author's own life. The author of the story we have been discussing apparently drew to some extent on her personal experience. Kincaid was herself a girl on Antigua. You may be tempted, though, to think that "Girl" consists of advice Kincaid herself received. Yet when you assert that a work is thoroughly autobiographical, you risk overlooking aspects of the text that depart from the author's own experiences, impressions, and beliefs. We are not urging you to refrain from ever connecting the author's text to the author's life. Rather, we are pointing out that whatever links you forge may be the subject of debate.

Even the term *history* can be defined in various ways. When you refer to a work's historical context, you need to clarify whether you are examining (1) the life of the work's author; (2) the time period in which it was written; (3) any time period mentioned within the text; (4) its subsequent reception, including responses to it by later generations; or (5) the forms in which the work has been published, which may involve changes in its spelling, punctuation, wording, and overall appearance.

8. Issues of genre.   So far we have been identifying categories of issues. Issues of **genre** are *about* categorization, for they involve determining what *kind* of text a particular work is. You might categorize Kincaid's as belonging to the short-story genre, but someone might disagree because it does not seem to have a conventional plot. This debate would involve deciding what the essential characteristics of a short story are. Even if you argue that Kincaid's text does belong to this genre, you could attempt to classify it more precisely by aiming for terms that better sum up its specific content and form. Issues of genre often arise with such further classification.

A literary text may relate in some way to a characteristic of ordinary, real-life interactions. Kincaid's text resembles parental-advice articles and books. But there are usually differences between a story's genre and ones you find in real life. "Girl" can be labeled a fictional illustration of how gender roles are reinforced. In any case, a literary work may fit into multiple categories. Some readers may see Kincaid's story as largely a monologue. Others may be struck by the girl's brief interruptions; they may even view the text as her years-later *memories* of what her mother preached. Do you think one of these perspectives is more helpful than the other? If so, which? Much of the time, issues of genre are issues of priority. You're not deciding whether the work deserves a certain label; you're deciding whether that label is the best one for the work itself.

9. Issues of social policy.   In many works of literature, writers have attempted to instigate social reform by exposing defects in their cultures and encouraging specific cures. We earlier mentioned Upton Sinclair's 1906 novel *The Jungle*, which vividly depicts horrible conditions in Chicago's stockyards and thereby led meat-processing plant owners to adopt more humane and hygienic practices. Even a work of literature that is not blatantly political or that seems rooted in the distant past may make you conscious of your own society's problems and possible solutions to them. Yet you and your classmates may propose different definitions of and solutions for cultural problems. The result is what we call issues of **social policy**.

Sometimes your position on a current issue of social policy will affect how you read a certain literary work. Your view on how girls and boys should be educated may affect your response to Kincaid's text. Even if this isn't the case, you can still use the story to raise issues of gender and schooling. Imagine discussing the story at a United Nations forum on the worldwide status of women. What policies might "Girl" help you critique or promote there?

10. Issues of cause and effect.   Issues of **causality** are common in literary studies. Often they arise as readers present different explanations for a character's behavior. Why does the girl in Kincaid's story protest at those two particular moments? Remember that even a work's narrator or main speaker is a character with motives worth analyzing.

Such questions can be rephrased to center on the author. For instance, you can ask why Kincaid ends her story by having the characters speak about feeling the bread. If you look back at our discussion of these ten types of issues, you may see that most issues can be phrased as questions about the author's purposes, but remember your options. Focusing on authorial intent in a given case may not be as useful as sticking with another type of issue. Or you may turn a question about authorial intent into a question about authorial **effect**. How should readers react when Kincaid ends her story the way she does? You can address questions like this without sounding as if you know exactly what the author intended.

MAKE A CLAIM

A **claim** about a literary work is a position that not everyone would immediately accept as obvious truth. You have to argue for it. Look at our explanations of ten kinds of issues for examples of claims in literary studies. In that discussion, we touched on a host of claims about Kincaid's story: that the girl has given the main speaker reason to worry about her; that Kincaid's theme is "Women should teach girls to follow conventions *and* to assert themselves"; that the word "Wash" reflects a wish to purify the girl; that the speaker's vision has limits of its own; and that the girl is recollecting things she heard years ago. These claims are debatable because in each case at least one other position is possible.

In literature classes, two types of claims are especially common. To criticize Kincaid's main speaker is to engage in **evaluation**. To identify themes of "Girl" is to engage in **interpretation**. Conventionally, interpretation is the kind of analysis that depends on hypotheses rather than simple observation of plain fact. Throughout this book, we refer to the practice of interpreting a work or certain aspects of it. Admittedly, sometimes you may have trouble distinguishing interpretation from evaluation. When you evaluate some feature of a work or make an overall judgment of that work, probably you are operating with a certain interpretation as well, even if you do not make that interpretation explicit. Similarly, when you interpret part of a work or the text as a whole, probably you have already decided whether the text is worth figuring out. Nevertheless, the two types of claims differ in their emphases. When you attempt to interpret a work, you are mostly analyzing it; when you attempt to evaluate the work, you are mostly judging it.

In class discussions, other students may resist a claim you make about a literary work. Naturally, you may choose to defend your view at length. But remain open to the possibility of changing your mind, either by modifying your claim somehow or by shifting completely to another one. Also entertain the possibility that a view different from yours is just as reasonable, even if you do not share it.

In much of your writing for your course, you will be identifying an issue and making one main claim about it, which can be called your **thesis**. As you attempt to support your main claim, you will make a number of smaller claims. In drafts of your paper, welcome opportunities to test the claims you make in it. Review your claims with classmates to help you determine how persuasive your thinking is. You will get a stronger sense of what you must do to make your paper credible.

AIM TO PERSUADE

As we noted in Chapter 1, persuasion involves defending your claims. But as we also observed, even the best argument essays may fail to convince all their readers. What you *can* do is motivate your audience to keep thinking about your ideas. This is a modest sense of persuasion but an achievement all the same. Suppose, in an essay on Kincaid's story, you claim that the speaker is loving, despite seeming stern. You may not induce all your readers to regard her as warm. Yet arguing for your idea can still be good, especially if you move people to mull it. Help them find your view worth pondering, whether or not everyone adopts it.

CONSIDER YOUR AUDIENCE

To argue effectively about a work of literature, you need to remember that not everyone will see it as you do. You have to explain and support your understanding of the work so that skeptics will come to find your view of it sound. Gear every step of your argument toward readers you have to persuade. Focus on what *they* will want you to clarify, elaborate, and defend. Forget about parts of the work irrelevant to your argument. If your main claim is about certain lessons that the main speaker in "Girl" imparts, limit your remarks about her other lessons, no matter how colorful they seem.

Above all, you may wonder how familiar your readers already are with the text you are analyzing. Perhaps your teacher will resolve your uncertainty, telling you exactly how much your audience knows about the text. Then again, you may be left to guess. Should you presume that your audience is totally unfamiliar with the text? This approach is risky, for it may lead you to spend a lot of your paper summarizing the text rather than analyzing it. A better move is to write as if your audience is at least a bit more knowledgeable. Here is a good rule of thumb: *Assume that your audience has, in fact, read the text but that you need to recall for this group any features of the text that are crucial to your argument.* Although probably your paper will still include some summary, the amount you provide will be limited, and your own ideas will be more prominent.

You can introduce your essay's main claim by referring to the audience of the literary text you're studying:

- **Readers you disagree with.** While some readers may feel that Kincaid's main speaker looks out for the girl's best interests, she is actually insensitive to her listener's desires and needs.
- **Hasty, superficial readers.** Because the main speaker seems bent on giving practical advice, readers may overlook the symbolic meanings of certain details. The opening command "Wash" reflects the speaker's wish to purify her listener. Right or wrong, she fears that the girl is on the verge of corruption.
- **Puzzled readers.** Many readers may be puzzled by how the story ends. Why, after bossing the girl around herself, does the speaker expect her to stand up to the baker? This ending makes sense, however, if we see the speaker as having contradictory goals. Like other women in her culture, she wants girls to be empowered but also wants to keep them safe.
- **Your own divided self.** At first I thought the speaker too pushy in her efforts to direct her listener's life. But now I give her credit for trying to make the girl strong, even if I don't define this word the same way she does.

GATHER AND PRESENT EVIDENCE

Evidence is the support that you give your claims so that others will accept them. What sort of evidence you must provide depends on what your audience requires to be persuaded. When you make claims during class discussions, your classmates and instructor might ask you follow-up questions, thereby suggesting what you must do to convince them further. As a writer, you might often find yourself having to guess your readers' standards of evidence. Naturally, your guesses will be influenced by prior experiences you have had with your audience. Moreover, you may have opportunities to review drafts with some of its members.

When you make an argument about literature, the evidence most valued by your audience is likely to be details from the work itself. Direct quotations from the text are powerful indications that your claims are well grounded. But when you quote, you need to avoid willful selectivity. If when writing about Kincaid's story, you quote the girl's question "*but what if the baker won't let me feel the bread?*" without acknowledging the main speaker's response, you may come across as misrepresenting the text. In general, quoting from various parts of a text will help you give your readers the impression that you are being accurate.

If you make claims about the historical or cultural context of a work, your evidence may include facts about its original circumstances. You may be drawn to the author's own experiences and statements, believing these shed light on the text. But again, use such materials cautiously, for they are not always strong evidence for your claims. People are not obliged to accept the author's declaration of his or her intent as a guide to the finished work. Some people may feel that the author's statement of intention was deliberately misleading, while others may claim that the author failed to understand his or her own achievement.

EXPLAIN YOUR REASONING

As we pointed out in Chapter 1, your readers will expect more than evidence. They'll wish to see the process of reasoning behind your main claim. The steps in your logic should be clear in your essay's structure. This may need to differ from the structure of the literary text you analyze. Otherwise, you may confuse your readers — especially if you crawl through the literary work chronologically, commenting on each of its lines. Perhaps your main claim is that despite the story's title, "Girl" actually depicts an initiation into womanhood. An essay that simply plods through the story won't help you develop this idea. You might start off by quoting the main speaker's *last* line, for there she foresees the girl's becoming a woman. You'd then identify what, exactly, the speaker means by this word — the womanly characteristics she has in mind. Next, you might go back and forth through the story, noting the speaker's references to these features. Whatever moves you make, lead your readers carefully through your stages of thought.

IDENTIFY YOUR ASSUMPTIONS

Writing arguments about literature involves making assumptions, some of which you may need to spell out. One common kind is *warrants*. These are assumptions that lead you to call certain things evidence. Consider in "Girl" the main speaker's turn to "how to spit up in the air if you feel like it" (lines 39–40). You might argue that at this moment, Kincaid suggests that the speaker is willing to allow the girl at least a few acts of frivolous self-expression. As evidence for your claim, you might point out that already in the story, the speaker has occasionally encouraged the girl to be self-assertive: e.g., "this is how to bully a man" (line 27). But then you may be asked for your warrants — your reasons for presenting this evidence as support for your claim. Some of your assumptions might be about literature: for instance, that writers of fiction often encourage their readers to connect a later part of the text with earlier ones. Some of your assumptions might be about human nature: for example, an adult woman will probably realize that girls sometimes need to vent in silly ways. Some of your assumptions might be about historical periods and cultures: for instance, that a girl growing up on Antigua decades ago might have had few other opportunities to express herself, whereas American girls of today can take selfies rather than just spit. Often literature classes are most enlightening when students discuss their assumptions about literature, about human nature, and about particular times and places. Your classmates may differ in their assumptions because they differ in the ways they grew up, the experiences they have had, the reading they have done, and the authorities that have influenced them.

Once you state your warrants for a claim you are making, your audience may go further, asking you to identify assumptions supporting the warrants themselves. But more frequently you will have to decide how much you should mention your warrants in the first place. In class discussion, usually your classmates' and instructor's responses to your claims will indicate how much you have to spell out your assumptions. When you write, you have to rely more on your own judgment of what your audience requires. If you suspect that your readers will find your evidence unusual, you should identify your warrants at length. If, however, your readers are bound to accept your evidence, then a presentation of warrants may simply distract them. Again, reviewing drafts of your paper with potential readers will help you determine what to do.

Another potentially significant set of assumptions has to do with your values, which often reflect your own life. You may want to condemn the speaker in "Girl" as a bad mother because your own is nicer. But this label requires more support than your personal experience. You'll need to explain why *various* people should apply it to the speaker — whatever particular mothers your readers have had. In general, be cautious with the terms you apply to literary figures. If you fling strong judgments at characters — *bad, crazy, weird, normal, good* — some readers will suspect your mind is controlled by biases you have. They'll prefer more precise, less extreme language, believing it better conveys a character's complexity.

MAKE USE OF APPEALS

As with other arguments, those about literature employ the appeals of **logos**, **ethos**, and **pathos**. You rely on logos in order to support your claims about texts and you stress your evidence and explain your process of thought. Ethos, the image you convey of yourself, often figures when you acknowledge interpretations other than yours. Your readers will appreciate your noting in the first place that these views can exist. You will look even better if you treat such alternatives with respect. Try making *concessions* to them, admitting they're not entirely wrong. For instance, you may want to argue that Kincaid's speaker holds men in contempt. Even so, consider granting that other readers of the story may see her differently. You might admit, for instance, that at moments the mother suggests her daughter should accept male power. Of course, you would still proceed to argue your own claim about her. But you'll have dealt admirably with a rival idea. In the same spirit, you might *qualify* your generalizations instead of stating them as absolute facts. Rather than declare that "the mother *is* scornful toward men," you might say that this is *probably* her attitude or that it *seems* to be her stance.

With the appeal known as pathos, you try to engage your readers' emotions. This move occurs to some degree in many arguments about literature, for literary works often dramatize and arouse feelings. You can make your analysis compelling if you occasionally use emotional language yourself; you might refer to the intimidating voice of the mother in Kincaid's story. But keep such language limited. If you constantly vent your own passions, you may weaken your case. Take a look at this paragraph:

> I suppose the main speaker in Kincaid's story gives some useful advice, but I'm very bothered by her frequent references to the girl as a "slut." In my high school, there were girls called that on Facebook posts and other social media. I thought this labelling was unfair and mean. One of my best friends was called a "slut," and she was really damaged by the insult. One morning, she was so ashamed and hurt that she didn't go to school. I felt so bad for her! People who call another person a "slut" should be ashamed of themselves. What gives them the right to be so judgmental? If they took a hard look at themselves in the mirror, they'd see that their own morals aren't so perfect. And when was the last time that a guy was called a "slut" or something equivalent? Never! This is hypocrisy, and it's got to stop. Once the adult in "Girl" starts throwing the word "slut" around, I lose all respect for her. I want the girl to run away from this woman, or at least talk back to her more. I know that I myself would be so furious that I'd do one or the other. I kept waiting for the girl to rebel dramatically. When the story ended with her still being meek, I was severely disappointed. I would have said "Don't you dare call me a slut again! Wash your own mouth out with soap!"

If you wrote a passage like this, it might annoy your readers. They might think it conveys far more about *you* than about Kincaid's text. Of course, they too might hate the word "slut." They might see it as raising multiple issues and see why it makes you seethe. Probably they'd want more details of the story and fewer bursts of your feelings. Again, emotional words *can* play a role in your argument. They may add to its force, but they tend to be effective only in small doses, so try not to pour them out at length.

A Sample Student Argument about Literature

The following essay demonstrates several of the strategies we have discussed. Its student author had read Kincaid's "Girl" in a course on composition and literature. Her assignment was to write an argument paper about a specific element of the story. She chose to raise an issue and develop a claim about its ending.

Ann Schumwalt
English 102
Professor Peretti
3 February - - - -

                    The Mother's Mixed Messages in "Girl"
In Jamaica Kincaid's story "Girl," the speaker is evidently a
mother trying to teach her daughter how to behave. The story
is basically a single-paragraph speech in which the mother
gives various commands, instructions, and lessons, apparently
in an effort at training her child to become what their culture
considers a proper young woman. Only twice does the daughter herself interrupt the mother's monologue. It's interesting
that the second break occurs near the end of the story. Right
after the mother orders her to "always squeeze bread to make
sure it's fresh," the daughter asks, *"but what if the baker
won't let me feel the bread*?" (line 42). There is only one more
sentence before the story concludes: the mother responds by
asking, "you mean to say that after all you are really going to
be the kind of woman who the baker won't let near the
bread?" (42–44). Faced with this final exchange, many
readers may wonder why author Kincaid chooses to make it
the story's conclusion. It could have appeared earlier in the
text, and Kincaid might have ended with any of the mother's
statements that now come before it. This ending also feels
inconclusive, for the very last words are a question that does
not receive an answer. What, therefore, is Kincaid trying to
emphasize with this puzzling finish? A closer look at its
language, as well as at other words of the text, suggest that

Refers to puzzled readers, as a way of bringing up the main issue. The essay will help these readers with the "closer look" it proceeds to offer.

Introduces the essay's main issue (a cause-and-effect one) as a question.

Kincaid is deliberately making us uncertain about whether the mother's stern training will indeed help her daughter become strong enough to survive in their society. The mother may *believe* that she is providing sufficient survival skills, but Kincaid encourages readers to suspect that she is actually *dis*empowering her daughter, not letting her develop the willpower she needs to endure.

The essay's main claim.

When the mother commands her daughter to squeeze the bread, probably she sees herself as pushing her to take charge of her life rather than meekly accept other people's treatment of her. To squeeze something is to perform a vigorous, self-assertive action, and in this case it would involve testing the baker's product instead of just accepting it. Earlier in the text, the mother offers a few other hints that she wishes the daughter to be aggressive, not passive. For example, she advises her on "how to make a good medicine to throw away a child before it even becomes a child" (35); on "how to bully a man" (37); and on "how to spit up in the air if you feel like it" (39–40). A number of readers may infer, too, that even when she is telling the daughter how to perform household chores like washing, ironing, setting meals, and sweeping, she is fostering her independence by enabling her to handle basic demands of daily existence.

Because Ann is mainly concerned with the story's ending, she starts her paper with it rather than moving chronologically through Kincaid's text.

Qualifies this statement rather than expressing it as an absolute fact.

Draws evidence from the text's actual words.

Acknowledges existence of another possible interpretation.

But in crucial ways, the mother presses her daughter to play a subservient role in society. More specifically, she attempts to imprison her in a model of femininity that allows for men to dominate. Emphasizing that "you are not a boy, you know" (30), she demands that she "try to walk like a lady" (8–9) and take care of her father's clothes. The various chores that she expects her daughter to perform would make life easier for the male head of the household. Moreover, they seem duties that a boy would not be required to fulfill. Similarly, the mother hopes to restrict the daughter's sexual behavior. Repeatedly she warns her "to prevent yourself from looking like the slut I know you are so bent on becoming" (15). Again, it is doubtful that a boy would receive warnings like this. Like the United States, perhaps the culture reflected in this story even lacks a masculine equivalent of the derogatory term "slut."

Pathos used with the negatively emotional words presses, subservient, imprison, and dominate. Evidence then offered to support such language.

A reasonable assumption.

An assumption, though qualified with the word perhaps.

At the end, I admit, the mother seems to associate her daughter with an image of power. She implies that the girl should become "the kind of woman" whom the baker *does* "let near the bread" so that she can test it by squeezing it (42–43). But even here, actually, the mother does not envision her daughter as actively taking charge. In the scenario she sketches, the baker *allows* the girl to feel the

Concession.

bread. In order to touch it, she must get his permission, rather than straightforwardly exert her own authority. Moreover, she first has to be a certain sort of woman; otherwise, she has not earned the right to examine his product. What type of woman is this? While some readers may argue that the mother wants her daughter to be an *assertive* female, many of the directions she has already given her would greatly limit her sphere of action, leaving her to be a relatively unadventurous housekeeping "lady." Evidently the mother feels that the baker will give her daughter access to the bread only if she is a basically tame and polite version of womanhood.

The mother may not realize that she is conveying mixed messages to her child. If we, as readers, take her to be hoping that her daughter becomes empowered *and* subservient, we may be spotting a contradiction that the mother herself is not conscious of. But the daughter may be aware of it. Perhaps the daughter is, in fact, now a grown-up woman who is trying to make sense of the paradoxical pieces of advice her mother gave her during her adolescence. The mother may have offered these supposed bits of wisdom at various different times, but the daughter is now remembering them all as one speech and struggling to figure out their implications. Kincaid's decision to conclude the story with a question mark may be her way of indicating that even in adulthood, the daughter still has not determined whether her mother wanted to *liberate* her or *confine* her. We can regard the daughter as someone who is still attempting to "read" her mother's intentions. As actual readers of this story, we would then be in the same position as she is, having to come up with our own interpretation of what her mother wanted her to do and be.

> "May not" *is a qualification, indicating that Ann is less than sure what the mother thinks.*

> *Even the text's punctuation may be significant.*

Looking at Literature as Argument

Much of this book concerns arguing *about* literature. But many works of literature can be said to present arguments themselves. Admittedly, not all of literature can be seen as containing or making arguments, but occasionally you will find that associating a literary text with argument opens up productive lines of inquiry. Moreover, as you argue about literature, arguments *within* literature can help you see how you might persuade others.

Some works lay out an argument that the author obviously approves of. For an example, let us turn to the following poem. It was written around 1652 by John Milton (1608–1674), a poet who played a leading role in England's Puritan revolution. Seeking to make dominant their own version of Christianity, the Puritans executed King Charles I and installed their leader,

Oliver Cromwell, as head of state. Milton wrote "When I consider how my light is spent" while working as an official in Cromwell's government. This is an autobiographical poem and refers to Milton's growing blindness, which threatened to prevent him from serving both his political leader and his religious one, God.

JOHN MILTON
When I consider how my light is spent

When I consider how my light is spent,
 Ere half my days in this dark world and wide,
 And that one talent which is death to hide
Lodged with me useless, though my soul more bent
To serve therewith my Maker, and present   5
 My true account, lest He returning chide;
 "Doth God exact day-labor, light denied?"
I fondly ask. But Patience, to prevent
That murmur, soon replies, "God doth not need
 Either man's work or His own gifts. Who best   10
 Bear His mild yoke, they serve Him best. His state
Is kingly: thousands at His bidding speed,
 And post o'er land and ocean without rest;
 They also serve who only stand and wait."   *[c. 1652]*

The speaker does not spell out his warrants. Consider, however, his reference to Christ's parable of the talents (Luke 19:12–27). In the ancient Middle East, a *talent* was a unit of money. In the parable, a master scolds his servant for hoarding the one talent that his master had given him. By telling this story, Christ implies that people should make use of the gifts afforded them by God. For the speaker in Milton's poem, the parable has a lot of authority. Evidently he feels that he should carry out its lesson. In effect, then, the parable has indeed become a warrant for him: that is, a basis for finding his blindness cause for lament.

Who exactly is the speaker's audience? Perhaps he is not addressing anyone in particular. Or perhaps the speaker's mind is divided, and one side of it is addressing the other. Or perhaps the speaker is addressing God, even though he refers to God in the third person. Given that the speaker is answered by Patience, perhaps he means to address *that* figure, although Patience may actually be just a part of him, rather than an altogether separate being.

At any rate, Patience takes the speaker for an audience in responding. And while Patience does not provide evidence, let alone warrants, Patience makes claims about God and his followers. Furthermore, Milton as the author seems to endorse Patience's claims; apparently, he is using the poem to advance them. Besides pointing out *how* God is served, Milton suggests that God *ought* to be served, even if God lets bad things happen to good people, like Milton.

Every author can be considered an audience for his or her own writing, but some authors write expressly to engage in a dialogue with themselves. Perhaps Milton wrote his poem partly to convince himself that his religion was still valid and his life still worth living. Significantly, he did not publish the poem until about twenty years later. Yet because he did publish it eventually, at some point he must have contemplated a larger audience for it. The first readers of the poem would have been a relatively small segment of the English population: those literate and prosperous enough to have access to books of poetry. In addition, a number of the poem's first readers would have shared Milton's religious beliefs. Perhaps, however, Milton felt that even the faith of this band had to be bolstered. For one thing, not every Protestant of the time would have shared Milton's enthusiasm for the Puritan government. Recall that this regime executed the king, supposedly replacing him with the rule of God. Milton's words "His state/Is kingly" can be seen as an effort to persuade readers that the Puritans did put God on England's throne.

Certain arguments made in literary texts may or may not have the author's endorsement. Faced with a conflict of ideas, readers must engage in interpretation, forced to decide which position is apt to be the author's own view. A classic example is "Mending Wall," a famous poem by Robert Frost (1874–1963), from his 1914 book *North of Boston*. Troubled by his neighbor's desire to repair the wall between their farms, the poem's speaker argues against its necessity, but literary critics have long debated whether Frost agrees with the speaker's claims and reasons. How persuasive do you find them?

ROBERT FROST
Mending Wall

Something there is that doesn't love a wall,
That sends the frozen-ground-swell under it,
And spills the upper boulders in the sun;
And makes gaps even two can pass abreast.
The work of hunters is another thing: 5
I have come after them and made repair
Where they have left not one stone on a stone,
But they would have the rabbit out of hiding,
To please the yelping dogs. The gaps I mean,
No one has seen them made or heard them made,   10
But at spring mending-time we find them there.
I let my neighbor know beyond the hill;
And on a day we meet to walk the line
And set the wall between us once again.
We keep the wall between us as we go.   15
To each the boulders that have fallen to each.
And some are loaves and some so nearly balls

We have to use a spell to make them balance:
"Stay where you are until our backs are turned!"
We wear our fingers rough with handling them.   20
Oh, just another kind of outdoor game,
One on a side. It comes to little more:
There where it is we do not need the wall:
He is all pine and I am apple orchard.
My apple trees will never get across   25
And eat the cones under his pines, I tell him.
He only says, "Good fences make good neighbors."
Spring is the mischief in me, and I wonder
If I could put a notion in his head:
"*Why* do they make good neighbors? Isn't it   30
Where there are cows? But here there are no cows.
Before I built a wall I'd ask to know
What I was walling in or walling out,
And to whom I was like to give offense.
Something there is that doesn't love a wall,   35
That wants it down." I could say "Elves" to him,
But it's not elves exactly, and I'd rather
He said it for himself. I see him there
Bringing a stone grasped firmly by the top
In each hand, like an old-stone savage armed.   40
He moves in darkness as it seems to me,
Not of woods only and the shade of trees.
He will not go behind his father's saying,
And he likes having thought of it so well
He says again, "Good fences make good neighbors."   *[1914]*   45

Other literary works, though, present an argument that the author is unlikely to endorse. In such cases, we might describe the work as *ironic* because we sense a distance between the position being expressed and the author's own view.

Literature and Current Issues

When you read a literary work, you may find it doesn't make arguments. Nevertheless, it may help you grasp current issues. It may even help you form claims about them. To play this role, the work needn't be recent. Ancient tragedies can shed light on politics today. Whatever the age of the text, literature may give you insights into contemporary debates. In turn, these debates may help you understand a work of literature better. They may lead you to notice aspects of it you might otherwise neglect.

Here, we present a 2015 short story about a current practice: the public shaming of individuals and organizations. They suffer mass scorn for things they've said or done. These scoldings usually occur via social media like Twitter. Such denunciations are popular; each week, new ones erupt. Yet increasingly, these assaults are criticized themselves. Not only do they provoke howls of protest from their targets, but they also elicit concerned warnings from a growing number of cultural commentators who point out that these attacks are often harmful, unfair, and mean. To give you a sense of this emerging debate, we follow the story with two texts about public shaming today. By putting the story in conversation with these works, we suggest ways of connecting literature to real-life disputes.

RIVKA GALCHEN
Usl at the Stadium

Rivka Galchen (b. 1976), was born in Toronto, Canada, but she has lived in the United States since she was a child. Although she holds an M.D. degree with a specialization in psychiatry, she has pursued a literary career. Besides earning an M.F.A. in creative writing at Columbia University, she has published a novel, Atmospheric Disturbances *(2008), and a collection of short stories,* American Innovations *(2014). She has also written several pieces of journalism. "Usl at the Stadium" first appeared in the October 12, 2015, issue of* The New Yorker. *Galchen based the story on an actual series of events.*

The game on Sunday had a 2 P.M. start, and Usl was featured on the Jumbotron intermittently from 4:02 to 4:09. By eight-thirty, his home phone was ringing. His home phone never rang. It was a holdover from another time. His mother had told him that it was essential, a matter of safety—for hurricanes, or blackouts, or terrorist attacks. You never knew what could happen until it happened. She had insisted on paying the bill so that Usl would keep the landline. She had pleaded, "Please grant me permission to protect my child," and so he had.

The landline was ringing because Usl had become an Internet sensation. Usl had been sleeping when he appeared on the Jumbotron at the Yankees game; the cameras and the commentators had turned on Usl numerous times, and at length, and he had slept through it all. It wasn't until the voices of strangers over that old-fashioned telephone alerted him that he understood how widely watched his sleep had been. Now a gentle feminine voice pitched him: "What we're thinking is that you come into the office and we'll take a top-quality, nice photo of you. We really love the idea that you get a chance to present yourself. You'll recapture control over your image."

Usl looked online to reconfirm who he was in the eyes of the world:

Fatty cow that needs two seats at all time and represent symbol of failure

had been posted one minute earlier in the comments section under a YouTube clip. The clip had more than seventy thousand views. Wasn't it really just footage of a man dreaming? No one seemed to see it that way. Usl was only twenty-eight years old—could his life already be ruined? Could he save it? Usl told the woman on the phone that he needed to think about her idea, that he would call her back.

He called Gregory.   5

"People at a newspaper are not your allies," Gregory said. Gregory was Usl's friend but also his boss. Usl worked the buyback end of Gregory's storefront diamond-district place. Customers ascended the back stairs to consult with Usl about their old jewelry, and Usl weighed, assessed, proposed prices, bought. Gregory liked to say that it was a sultanate there on the second floor; the sultan was Usl. Now Gregory said, "These are people who demeaned Eliot Spitzer over private issues, who—"

"But people are saying untrue things about me—"

"You'll be extending the time that you're at the center of attention—"

"If you were me—"

"I'm not you. I'm not interested in fame. I am me. I'm interested in coming   10
to work. I hope you're not thinking of not coming in to work tomorrow."

The angle of the camera in the footage was particularly unflattering—distorting, really. It wasn't a strong likeness.

Usl called the voice from the newspaper back. "I will come in."

The now slightly less kind-sounding woman informed Usl that if he made it in before 11 A.M. they would run the photo online the same day.

Usl trembled.

Or was the trembling elsewhere?   15

They had found his cell-phone number?

"I love you!" the text message read. It was his mother. "You are a great and successful and handsome and very good and nice man!!!" Even she had seen the footage? Usl's mother was very loving, had always been very loving. Good mothers are bad mothers, Usl thought. Only bad, mean mothers prepare you for what is to come. If Usl was ever a mother, whatever, a father, he wanted to be a bad one.

More calls came in, through the night, from television programs that had once seemed to occur in inaccessible lands but that turned out to be really less than thirty minutes away; they would send a car service. Usl couldn't sleep. When, as a child, he encountered characters six feet tall, fuzzy, offering hugs, or flyers, or hot dogs, he had been frightened. He unplugged the phone.

Then there was a knock at the door. Was he O. J. Simpson? They were pursuing him everywhere.

"It's me! It's Berge!"   20

Berge was Usl's neighbor. Usl let him in.

Berge said, "You've had a huge piece of luck. Huge. I know you may not see it, but this is the luckiest day of your life."

"I'm very tired," Usl said, and then felt ambushed by fresh shame—after all, why was he so tired? "People laugh, but I was sleeping because I haven't been getting my sleep. When you don't sleep, you're not yourself. When you don't sleep, you find yourself sleeping all the time."

"You're going to sue," Berge declared. Sue somebody. Berge would figure it out. He wouldn't charge—he would just take fifteen per cent upon
collection. Did Usl feel damaged? Yes, Usl did feel damaged. Then there should
be damages. Berge had recently passed the bar. He wasn't lying about that,
Usl thought. Berge often shared his magazines with Usl; he was a nice guy,
basically.

"But I can't sue thousands of people," Usl said. "It's thousands of people   25
who have damaged me." He caught a glimpse of his screen:

He's dreaming of cupcakes.

"No, thousands wouldn't be sensible," Berge said. "We'll sue the Yankees."

"But I love the Yankees."

"We'll sue the Stadium."

"I love the Stadium. I've been happy there."   30

"You're very stressed. Let me figure it out for you."

By 1 A.M., Berge had prepared papers for Usl to sign—Berge was also a
notary, he said—naming a broadcasting corporation. "They won't take it personally," Berge assured him. "It's business."

By Tuesday, views of the YouTube footage had exceeded a million. Usl
abandoned the Internet, turned on the radio for escape, and there learned that
he, Usl, was a too sensitive behemoth who needed to be *#&$ed in his cookie-
dough face; also, that he should eat celery. Normally, if you heard people
talking about you on the radio it meant that you were crazy, since of course no
one on the radio was talking about you, and if you thought that people on the
radio were talking about you, as had happened to Usl's uncle, then you were
supposed to go see somebody, a professional. Usl didn't want to see anybody.

"Gold resists attacks by almost all individual acids" appeared on his cell
phone. A year earlier he had subscribed to GemFacts by text; at first it had
bothered him, the repeated disappointment of thinking a person had contacted him and then discovering it was just an impersonal update.

Usl called Gregory again. "I can't come in today," he said.   35

"Take a joke," Gregory said. "They're talking things they don't know.
Have those talkers ever handled gold rings like they were chickpeas? They're
nobodies. So what if they say you're fat. You are fat. I'm also fat. It's not like it's
not true."

Gregory was a cheerful man, and the son of a Holocaust survivor; he had
six children, and he sometimes wore a T-shirt that read, "I Have the Body of a
God: Buddha." "If you wanted to not be fat, you would be not fat," he said.

"It's not just that," Usl said. The two sports announcers, Mike and
Mike—voices Usl knew well, had thought of as friends of his, in a way—had
said of sleeping Usl the kinds of things that people say. Unpleasant things. But
the words of those false friends had then bloomed into much worse words,
typed up by viewers whose numbers were growing without perceptible limit.
Usl was reading:

Please rid us of your nasty pimpled ass and put a shotgun in your mouth
tonight, I'll buy the shells

Then:

He is a waste of decent seats, he can sleep at the nachos stand and give a real fan a view, lol

Usl said to Gregory, "What really bothers me is that they think I don't appreciate baseball. They think I don't understand what's at stake."

"Sure. It's suicide or sniper," Gregory said. "And you don't want to be a sniper — I get it — so instead you feel really bad, you turn it on yourself. So as not to kill people. But it's also not suicide or sniper: it's just get your pants on and get on with your day. Do I have a chicken for an employee? I need a man. It's man or pansy, it's — "

Usl hung up.

Usl had been unemployed for seventeen months when he got the job with Gregory. When he started working, his mother gave him a polished blue stone to keep in his pocket, to ward off evil. Mock if you want, but the stone had worked. Usl had been enjoying his job for more than a year now. He had even made a flyer on how to detect fake gold. The magnet test was overrated, the flyer explained. In Usl's years of experience (even though it had been less than one when he made the flyer), he had seen plenty of non-magnetic fake gold; recognizing real gold versus fake was about getting a feel for the weight of the thing in your hands. That flyer of Usl's had been downloaded from his open Facebook page a hundred and seventy-three times.

That had seemed like a big number. It had brought attention to Gregory's shop. Gregory kept a poster of faces with various expressions on the office wall — it was something the Chinese restaurant nearby had given them — and Gregory had written Usl's name under the face labelled "Triumphant." He had done this after an eighty-four-year-old woman, who had bought gold every birthday of her life, brought it all in to sell after seeing a horoscope that read, "Even a Gemini needs to slow down a bit once in a while, and with your ruler Mercury still moving retrograde this is the ideal time." She explained to Usl that she had visited several buyback places. She chose Usl. Because she trusted him, because she could see his goodness in the way that his hands were not bossy or deceptive. Usl had never before thought about his hands. But he did think, then, that it was true what she had said, that they were good hands.

By midday Tuesday, Usl had understood a few things. One was that he should have been in contact with his mother. Usl had not gone to the paper to be photographed; Usl had ceased to answer either of his phones. But his mother was in the papers; his mother had been photographed. In her own home, sitting in her armchair, with a red geranium plant at her side. In the caption, she was quoted: "He was very tired, because he had been working very hard. He is my son of gold." In the article, she was asked about Usl's name, which some people had said was short for "useless." She said that, no, that was not the case, that Usl had been the nickname of Usl's grandfather, Warhel, a beautiful soul who had died during a flu outbreak when he was only thirty-four. And, as for Usl himself, Usl was not a nickname, Usl was his full proper name, it was enough.

Usl called his mother.

"Someone had to tell them about the real you," she said. "Here you are — this celebrity — but the celebrity is this person who isn't you. They made me look very old in that picture, because of the green lighting, but I'm O.K. with that, because a mother has to fix what is said about her son, whatever the cost."

"Nothing's fixed," Usl said. He had the feeling, as he often did with his mother, that he was speaking to a ghost poorly educated about the present.   50

"They thought you were drunk," she went on. "Many people thought that. You can't let them think that — it will affect your future employment. I explained that you drink only Diet Coke."

That bit about the Diet Coke wasn't true, but Usl let it pass. "You're destroying me," he said, albeit softly.

The truth was, Usl knew, that the photograph of his mother was not as damaging as the papers that Berge had filed on his behalf.

Who gets paid 10 million to sleep there like a fat ass. FUCK YOU FATTY.

Berge had asked for nine million dollars in damages, not ten; of course the   55 commenters had the details wrong, had everything wrong. Usl should have followed his old rule: no decisions after midnight. It was said that the filing was full of misspellings and grammatical errors.

What a loser. And now he's suing? Double loser. His suit is the only thing that brought the world's attention to him. Triple loser. And if there is any justice on this earth, this case will be tossed out and he'll be ridiculed and humiliated all over. We're dealing with a quadruple loser at the very least, folks.

Berge was always full of ideas. One should stay away from people with ideas.

Americas pre-occupation with sports is obscene. Can't tell you how many kids I know can recite batting averages, game plays, but don't know the first 5 books of the Bible. Nor could they recite an account beyond Noah's Ark, and when they do its Hollywoodized to the point of recognizable gibberish. They Idolize these players, who in turn Idolize Money. Then these Sports-gods humiliate their fans, and their fans try to capitalize, and the lawyers capitalize. Who ends up losing?

Ignominy was the only type of celebrity around. At least for Usl and everyone he knew.

"I love you," his mother texted again. "I love you very much. I love you   60 very, very much. You are a strong man. They are trying to hunt down and destroy you. But you are a cheetah."

And then, automated delivery: "Gold is unaffected by oxygen at any temperature." If only.

Say what you will, Usl wanted to get a slice. Why not? He would leave his apartment. He could do it. Usl stepped into the elevator, which today smelled like urine; also there were bugs sun-printed in the case of the light fixture. He normally enjoyed his elevator; it had a mechanical floor-indicator arrow that still worked. It was classy. Just as he himself was classy. That was the truth. He worked with gold, which did not rust.

As he stepped out of the building, he saw three of his neighbors playing dominoes. One held up a newspaper and shook it at him, in fellowship or menace, he didn't know. He had more than once dreamed of everyone recognizing him, of extending a series of half waves to acknowledge his fellows with respect as he passed them on the street; now he walked by his neighbors quickly, panting slightly.

He ordered a slice of pepper-and-mushroom. The server put a slice of pepperoni on a paper plate. Usl re-stated what he wanted — pepper-and-mushroom. Mexican pop was playing loudly. The server had a red bandanna tied back over his thick black hair. Always Mexicans at the Italian places, Usl thought. The server squinted at Usl. A squint of recognition? "Pep-per-and-mush-room," Usl reënunciated. The guy gave him a second slice. "Just one slice," Usl said. "Just the pepper-and-mushroom. No pepperoni."

It was worked out. Nobody had shouted. A triumph.   65

"Yo, thanks," Usl said.

"Yo? It's not the barrio, man," the server said. "Be polite."

People were disgusting. You gave your heart, you tried to be considerate, and who cared? They thought Usl could be pushed around. Why did it seem so clear that he could be pushed around? How did they know? Other people slept at baseball games. The games were sometimes boring. There were commercials between innings, and also commercials mid-inning. The batters took their time getting to the box, as if nothing else in the world, no one else in the world, existed. It was selfish, really. There were millions and millions and millions of other people who were treated with more respect than Usl. Maybe billions. Some of them stupid, some fat, some ugly, whatever it was, but that was the truth, Usl didn't invent it. Who did they think they were — Brad Pitt? They couldn't all be Brad Pitt. If Brad Pitt had criticized him, that would be a different thing.

One day they weren't going to have Usl to kick around anymore. One day they'd be sorry. This was among the things that he hadn't said. That he kept not saying. He had not assumed another identity, or his own, and pursued the pursuers online. Oh, he had been tempted, but that was what the Others would do. He had not told the Others what he thought of them.

Usl was finishing his pizza when a man in an orange T-shirt and a hard   70
hat, holding a large soda in one hand, made eye contact with him. Then he raised a fist in the air and shouted, "Yankees!"

Instinctively, Usl raised his fist in return. As if in the childishly imagined kingdom of fellowship and dignity.

"It's you, right?" the hard-hat man said.

Usl said, "No."

But already the man in the hard hat was signalling to others around him, shouting, calling things out. The hats were gathering.

Usl could find a small makeshift hut in the woods, not far from a beach. He had seen one once; he was going to go and live there. When the time seemed right, in maybe ten or fifteen years, he would return to civilization. He would be very fit, from living a life in nature. He would say his name was Dave. He would tell people how they should live. They would listen. 75

But he at least owed Gregory notice that he would be leaving, that he would be gone forever, sort of. Also, his paycheck would be useful. He was owed eight days. Truth be told, he wanted to run the idea by Gregory. Gregory, he realized, was like a dad to him. He would get his blessing.

Just in front of Gregory's, as Usl was staring at his phone — "You are my star and my sunshine!" — someone tapped him on the shoulder.

By primal reflex, Usl nearly hit the man, shouted, defending his body.

The man was saying, "Hey, hey, hey, sorry. I was just saying hello."

Usl looked up fully from his phone and realized it was Andre, the guy who regularly stood in front of Gregory's, handing out flyers for the business. Andre was a very slim and fairly straightforwardly good-looking black man; his appearance, today, seemed like a reproach. Usl said, "I apologize, I'm in such a high state of alert." 80

"A silver alert?" Andre asked.

"A what?" Usl said, his fear returning.

"Forget it, relax, forget it. I meant on your phone."

"What's silver, what's alert?" Usl said. Was he being asked about Google Alerts? About GemFacts? How was everyone allowed inside his head, his computer, his phone, his dreams.

"Like a silver alert, for when old people go missing," Andre said. "Amber alert for when a kid is missing, silver for old people. I think there's other colors, too. Sorry, I know you're under stress. It's just been on my mind. I was wondering how you get one of those alerts sent out. Like, once we found my mom near where the buses are parked, between Ninth and Tenth Avenues. She had no idea how to get home. She lives right near here, but she gets lost. And I'm not in a total panic about her, but she's not answering my calls this morning, so I was asking. Is your mom old? Is she right in the head?" 85

Andre had always seemed to Usl like a man with girlfriends, never like a man with a mom. Usl still had the polished good-luck stone from his mother. She was always trying, she was still trying. Usl said, "You could go look for her."

"Tell Gregory I'm back in thirty minutes," Andre said.

"They're nobodies, Usl," Gregory said when he went inside. "They are small, small people who can't find their own dicks because they are so small."

"You're a terrible man, Gregory. You're one of them."

"I'm just trying to cheer you up." 90

"By being a monster."

"Not nice."

"You're like a disease. For all I know, you started the comments about me. What do I know? Evil isn't choosy. For all I know, you gave them my phone number." Usl had yelled at no one yet; he was now yelling at Gregory. He found that he had quite a lot to say. He said Gregory didn't even care about Andre's mom.

"You know what, Usl? I'm going to tell you something that maybe you don't want to hear."

Usl was ready for it.   95

Gregory said, "I'm going to tell you that I love you, and that I care for you."

Usl began to cry. He cried a little more. Eventually he said, "I'm just so tired. When I'm tired, I make bad decisions."

"I understand," Gregory said. "You know, scientists used to ask, Why do we sleep? What is the purpose of sleep? But then other scientists said that these are the wrong questions. The question is, Why are we so often awake? What is the purpose of being awake? I mean, besides for ten minutes of eating, a little bit of romance. Once that's over, why are we not immediately again asleep?"

Gregory went on, "And so I said to myself one day, about this sleep question: This is the answer to the problem of evil. The question isn't, Why is there evil? The question is, Why is there good? I mean, it's not, Why is there the bubonic plague and Putin? It's, Why is there spring and love and barbecue? Why is there ever an unrequired kind act? Look, I'm just telling you how I go about my life, because I am old and you are still young. There isn't supposed to be any gold in the crust of the earth. It's a very heavy element. All the gold should be in the molten core. Unreachable for us. So why do we keep finding gold in the crust? How did it get there? Some people say it's meteorites that fell, that crashed, and that this catastrophe splashed up gold. That's the only reason we come across it. I don't subscribe to this theory. But I am sharing it with you."

Usl's sleep at the baseball game had been a sweet one. Sifting past and   100
beyond the ensuing terror, he found that he could remember that sleep, he could remember his dream. He had been at a really nice desk, of a dark, well-polished wood. He recognized the desk; it had made an appearance in real life. When he was just a kid — a real kid, not a twenty-eight-year-old who felt like a kid but a twelve-or thirteen-year-old who really was that — he had been delivering something to a lawyer, to a proper lawyer. That lawyer had sat at such a desk. But before he saw it little Usl had waited outside the lawyer's office, outside but inside, inside the outer chamber, in the air-conditioning, and the secretary, a gentle-faced woman who looked a little bit like the pretty woman who drove a taxi in that old TV show, had asked him if he wanted some water. She had brought him some, in a cone-shaped paper cup, from the water cooler. This, Usl thought, must be real life. He must have been thirsty at the game. He must have been waiting.   *[2015]*

Galchen's story is fiction. But when she wrote about Usl, she had a real person in mind. In April 2014, Andrew Rector fell asleep while attending a Yankees/Red Sox game. Repeatedly, the stadium's jumbotron screen showed his sprawled, slumbering body. Countless viewers at home saw this spectacle as well, for the game was televised on ESPN. Soon, pictures of the snoozing man appeared online, receiving millions of hits. A similar number of messages about him swept through social media. Many of these messages mocked him. They ridiculed not only Rector's napping but also his considerable weight. He garnered even more scorn when he sued the ESPN commentators for damages. His suit was thrown out of court, however, just before Galchen's story appeared. By that time, his mother reported, Rector had left the country. He could no longer bear the American public's contempt.

Rector's experience isn't unusual. Nowadays, public shaming happens over and over. The weapons include social media, smartphone cameras, and Web sites like YouTube. The trend has grown so big that it's captured the attention of journalists. It's been much debated as well. We now invite you to read two arguments on the topic. Both appeared in *The Nation*, though at different times. This magazine's contributors tend to be on the political left. But shaming raises questions that can divide traditional allies, as you'll see in the pair of essays we present.

The first, from *The Nation*'s issue of April 24, 2013, is by Cole Stryker. He is an analyst of social media who has written for several journals and published two books: *Epic Win for Anonymous: How 4Chan's Army Conquered the Web* (2011) and *Hacking the Future: Privacy, Identity, and Anonymity on the Web* (2012). Stryker's observations of online shaming lead him to oppose the practice.

COLE STRYKER
The Problem with Public Shaming

Today most people would tell you that the stocks, pillory and other tools of public punishment are barbaric. We've moved passed them, having figured out more humane ways to deal with crime. Why, then, the resurgence of public shaming, namely the mainstream acceptance of the "dox," which, in its purest form, is the digging up of a target's personal information — name, phone number, address, Social Security number, familial relationships, financial history — and exposing it online to encourage harassment from others? This practice has gradually been popularized by Anonymous, the amorphous collective of trolls and "hacktivists" that alternately terrorize tween girls and disable government websites.

In 2012, this practice was broadly adopted by media outlets. In October, Gawker unmasked a creep, notorious for facilitating the sharing sexualized images of women (underage and otherwise) taken without their consent. Gawker declared him "the biggest troll on the web." Its sister blog Jezebel called for the naming of names of such creeps, and later exposed a bunch of teenage Twitter users making racist remarks about Obama, going so far as to personally alert the administrators of their schools by phone.

This trend runs silly, as well — Buzzfeed ridiculed spoiled teens whining about their Christmas presents, while every media outlet covered Nice Guys of OK Cupid, a blog that ridicules clueless misogyny by sharing photos of hapless bros with regrettable stances on gender politics. Prepare to see a lot more of this sort of thing now that Facebook has released its Graph Search tool, which makes it possible to search for a controversial keyword or phrase (say, "I hate n — ers"), find people who've used that phrase on their profiles and grab some screenshots — you've got a readymade outrage-baiting trend piece.

The dox phenomenon played out with unfortunate results last month, when on March 17, development evangelist Adria Richards tweeted a photo of two men who'd been making sophomoric jokes at a tech conference, leading to the removal of the offenders, and then the firing of one. A wave of backlash ensued against Richards; strangers sent her abusive, threatening messages, and Internet trolls conspired to get her fired, attacking her employer's website with dummy traffic. Her employer eventually did terminate her contract, citing Richards's divisive tactics.

The First Amendment protects a lot of abhorrent speech, but societies have always resorted to some form of vigilante justice to preserve widely known and observed rules of social conduct that don't result in a crime when they're broken. So we turn instead to public humiliation, an organic form of social control that never really went away completely, as evidenced by the occasional signboard-bearing ne'er-do-well on the nightly news. Publicity-seeking judges occasionally will expose deadbeat dads, public urinators, drunk drivers and repeat drug offenders. But these are outliers. We don't prop people up in public, brand them with scarlet letters or hurl spoiled produce.   5

We didn't cease these punishments because we began to see them as barbaric. They simply stopped working. Historians point to the urbanization of impersonal cities with mobile, transient populations. It's difficult to encourage shame if they can easily disappear into the crowd or escape to the next town. Shame works in closed, small communities that share similar norms. As the New World opened up and expanded, public humiliation ceased to be an effective means of norm reinforcement.

American adjudicators typically look to five goals to justify a punishment: incapacitation, restitution, deterrence, rehabilitation and retribution. Neither incapacitation nor restitution apply to doxxing, since there are no legal enforcement mechanisms. To the extent that those who engage in public shaming think they are satisfying one of the remaining three, they faultily assume that deeply rooted social ills like racism, sexism and homophobia are personal failings that can be remedied through vicious public blowback and a permanent stain on their character.

It's common to argue that a perpetrator "deserves" to be shamed, but in fact human psychology doesn't work this way. Many pedophiles, for instance, recognize that that they are inexorably — even biologically — bound to impulses that they themselves loathe. Does the shaming — through public registries for example — cause the pedophile to reform?

Unlikely. Does it deter others from engaging in pedophilic acts, or does it drive them to darker corners and sneakier tactics?

Racism is not as tied to biology, but environment can be a powerful antibody to shame. Imagine you are a teenager living with white supremacist parents surrounded by white supremacist neighbors and you get suspended from school because you said something racist. Do you turn inward and examine your sense of shared humanity with brown people, or do you simply become resentful toward those who've punished you, perhaps even more sure of your sundry prejudices? Does it even deter you from vocalizing your racism or do you simply channel it through a different medium where you're less likely to be caught? In March, a racist New York City EMT employee was outed by the *New York Post* for posting vile tweets. His online supporters countered by violently threatening the reporter who broke the story, sometimes anonymously, sometimes not. These behaviors are symptoms of a systemic ideological cancer that is highly resistant to shaming because racists are typically proud of their hate.

Which leaves tit-for-tat as the lone valid criterion for public humiliation. But retribution too, is problematic. Consider the announcement of the Sandy Hook episode and the ensuing media frenzy to name the shooter. He was first incorrectly identified as Ryan Lanza, who turned out to be the killer's brother. Other "Ryan Lanzas" and their friends and families were harassed during the confusion. Reporters are notoriously bad at getting the facts straight during the frenzied moments following a big story, let alone amateur detectives or doxxers. Things get especially hairy when big media publish the identity of alleged aggressors based on unverified claims from untrustworthy sources. Amateur detectives raced against the FBI to uncover the perpetrators behind the Boston bombings on social news site Reddit. They fingered the wrong person, resulting in a misguided witch hunt that prompted Reddit's general manager Erik Martin to publicly apologize. Such exposure can lead to misguided counterattacks from a faceless troll army. On an Internet where people can so deftly conceal their identities and impersonate strangers, we must be mindful of our propensity for error.

Then there is the permanence problem. Once embarrassing information about a person is online, it's never going to go away. Imagine, thirty years from now, some potential employer evaluating a candidate based on a thoughtless remark she made as a teenager. The permanence of uploaded information ensures that modern shamings, while obviously milder in severity, can far exceed the scope of the scarlet letter, the most extreme manifestation of which was at least branded on the chest, where it could be covered. Every modern system of punishment attempts to deal in proportionalities. Put simply, the punishment must fit the crime.

Finally, the angry mob problem. Unlike institutionalized forms of punishment, public shaming can spiral out of control, far beyond the imaginations of the media outlets who performed the initial exposure. Vigilante justice is a tricky thing, with online anonymity leading to harsher consequences from a host of far-flung strangers exercising psychopathic levels of schadenfreude.

Whose norms are we to enforce? Would Jezebel's writers be comfortable know-ing that the tactics it employed against racist teenagers have been used against abortion doctors?

The rise of the social web may be perceived as a re-villaging, where the permanence of one's digital footprint behaves as a deterrent, making it seem to some like an ideal time to reintroduce public shaming to reinforce norms. But considered through a historical lens, public shaming begins to look like a tool designed not to humanely punish the perp but rather to satisfy the crowd.

This explains its resurgence. When has the crowd ever been bigger, or   15
more thirsty for vengeance? The faceless Internet, with its shadowy cyber-bullies and infinite display of every social ill is scary. And when it slithers its tentacles in a person's life, we become desperate for some way to fight back — to shine light into the darkness and counterattack those who would victimize behind the veil of anonymity. But doxing, even just naming publicly-available names to channel outrage (or worse) at someone who has violated your norms, is not only an ineffective way to deal, it risks causing more harm than the initial offense. Last year's trendy rise of media-sponsored shaming is self-righteousness masquerading as social justice. In many cases the targets deserve to be exposed and more, but public shaming does not drive social prog-ress. It might make us feel better, but let's not delude ourselves into thinking we've made a positive difference.   *[2013]*

Many people share Stryker's concerns. Yet plenty of others condone public shaming, or at least they endorse certain types. The following argument calls for shaming racists. Its author, Laila Lalami (b. 1968), was born in Morocco but now teaches creative writing at University of California — Riverside. Lalami is probably best known for her fiction, especially her 2014 novel *The Moor's Last Sigh*. It won multiple awards and was a finalist for the Pulitzer Prize. Yet she has also produced cultural and political commentaries for major newspapers and magazines. A regular columnist for *The Nation*, she wrote this piece for its June 18–25, 2018 issue.

LAILA LALAMI
The Social Shaming of Racists Is Working

Some years ago, while we were getting ready to move out of state, my husband and I held a garage sale. We'd advertised it in our community newspaper and on flyers around the neighborhood and had a huge turnout as a result.

Dozens of bargain hunters milled about, asking about this or that item. *"Cuanto quiere usted por el sofá?"* an older gentleman asked me, pointing to our old green couch. I quoted him a price, adding, *"Es un sofá cama."* Hearing our exchange, a white woman turned around and yelled, "Speak English! You're in America." "Hey—" I said, but she walked away in a huff, got into her car, and drove off.

I've been thinking about that moment, and the fiery anger behind it, as I hear about incident after incident in which white people lash out at people of color in public spaces. There's the white lawyer who berated the workers at a Manhattan deli for speaking Spanish — insisting that "I pay for their welfare. I pay for their ability to be here. The least they can do is speak English" — and then threatened to report them to Immigration and Customs Enforcement. There's the white student who reported a black student for taking a nap in the common room of their dorm at Yale, saying, "I have every right to call the police — you cannot sleep in that room." And there's the white mother who called the police about two Native American students taking part in a campus tour at Colorado State University, telling the dispatcher that "they are not, definitely not, a part of the tour."

The language in these complaints — "I pay," "I have every right," "they are definitely not" — is quite illuminating. It indicates a belief on the part of these white people that they are the custodians of public space and can enlist the police to enforce its boundaries. The offenses committed by people of color are arbitrary and nearly limitless: waiting too long at a Starbucks in Philadelphia, having a barbecue on Lake Merritt in Oakland, playing a leisurely game of golf at a club in Pennsylvania, checking out of an Airbnb in Rialto, California. And once police officers get there, anything can happen, ranging from an arrest on charges of trespassing to the installation of a police perimeter and the arrival of a police helicopter.

To be sure, the belief that public space belongs exclusively to white people   5
is not new, and this redlining has been inflicting trauma on people of color for a long time now. Whether it's on the street, in a café, or at an airport, the visibility of people of color in public is tolerated only so long as it does not disturb the comfort of the dominant group. But the ubiquitous presence of smartphones with cameras has helped to document such incidents, and social media have brought them to national attention. That's a useful development: The assertion of private authority over public space now comes with a social cost.

That is what happened to Aaron Schlossberg, the Manhattan lawyer who threatened to call ICE on the Spanish-speaking food workers and customers in New York. His law practice soon plummeted in customer ratings; he was hounded by reporters seeking comment; and his corporate landlord terminated his business lease. Protesters even brought a mariachi band to perform outside his apartment building. The public shaming that followed his rant could have a salutary effect: Maybe, just maybe, racists will think twice before making frivolous reports or issuing threats.

Few people have come to Schlossberg's defense, yet there are some who say that the popular outcry against him is "unnerving" and constitutes harassment by modern mobs who demand nothing less than "conformity of thought." Online mobs are scary, no doubt about that. But Schlossberg's rant doesn't amount to a civilized difference of opinion; it's racism, pure and simple, followed by threats.

Schlossberg's assertion of authority over public space is, of course, protected from government interference by the First Amendment. But that right doesn't protect him from the *social* consequences of his speech, including disruption and discomfort. Those protesting Schlossberg's actions are, in fact, exercising their own free-speech rights to object to his racism and nativism. The simple truth is that if racist behavior is insulated from social shaming, it will likely continue and multiply until it becomes accepted. What happens when a majority of Americans hold views like Schlossberg's?

The history of this country is replete with examples of how public space was regulated to ensure that one racial group was made comfortable at the expense of others. This is why it's important to speak out, and speak out now. Allies can help to stop the harassment, or at least deflect it. In the cell-phone footage of Schlossberg's rant, for example, an Asian man can be seen interposing himself between the lawyer and one of the Spanish-speaking women he's verbally abusing. In the Philadelphia Starbucks incident, an older white man repeatedly challenged police officers about why they were arresting the two black men when they'd done nothing wrong.

At the garage sale that day, after the woman took off in a huff, I turned   10
to my husband in disbelief. "Did you just hear what that lady said?" I asked him. This question, I now realize, was an attempt at documenting the moment by having a witness for it. It was my first intimation that people's relationship to public space is political, and that some of us move through it under surveillance by others. "I heard," my husband replied, and then told me of many similar experiences he'd had as a Cuban American here in Los Angeles.

But public space belongs to everyone. If racists don't like hearing Spanish being spoken in a deli, or having Native American teens on a campus tour, or seeing black folks going on about their lives, they should just stay home.   *[2018]*

≡ THINKING ABOUT THE TEXT

We encourage you to link Galchen's story with the issues that Stryker and Lalami raise (and take different stands on). You might, through writing or discussion, tackle these specific questions.

1. Photographs of Andrew Rector sleeping at the stadium are readily available online. We could have used one of them to illustrate Galchen's story, but we chose not to. What would *your* decision have been? What would be the arguments for and against reproducing Rector's image in this book?

2. Stryker provides historical background for today's public shamings. What aspects of the historical context he offers seem relevant to Rector's and Usl's situations?

3. Although the title character of Galchen's story has a real-life counterpart, she uses her freedom as a writer of fiction to invent certain details. How does Usl's mother play a significant role in the story? Why do you think Galchen gives Usl the particular job he has? What does she emphasize about Usl's lawsuit? What should readers make of the story's last word, "waiting"?

4. To what extent does Galchen encourage you to sympathize with Usl? Refer to specific passages. Which of the people mentioned by Stryker and Lalami could, conceivably, be sympathetically treated in a short story? Which, if any, seem impossible for a writer to depict sympathetically?

5. Many of the shaming messages directed at Rector — and evidently at Usl, too — refer to his being overweight. Do you think that the shamers would be less scornful toward someone who is thinner? Why, or why not? To what extent, and in what ways, are overweight people nowadays made to feel ashamed? (You might find it helpful to consult Afshan Jafar's essay on pp. 40–42 in Chapter 2.)

6. What examples of public shaming can *you* think of? How similar are these cases to what Rector and Galchen's character Usl experienced? Which of your examples, if any, seem comparable to ones that Stryker and Lalami bring up?

7. What would you say to someone who argues that social media companies like Twitter should exercise more control over content that insults people?

8. What do you think motivates shamers to send insulting messages about people they don't know and have never heard of before?

9. What advice would you give people who have been publicly shamed, such as Andrew Rector, Galchen's character Usl, and the figures that Stryker and Lalami refer to? Would your advice differ in some of these cases? If so, how?

10. How might Stryker and Lalami respond to each other's arguments? What, if anything, might they agree about? Refer to specific passages in both of their essays.

11. How persuasive do you find Stryker and Lalami? Do you agree with some points that each makes, or are you inclined to reject one of these arguments entirely? Explain your reasoning by referring to specific passages in both essays.

CHAPTER 4

The Reading Process

Courses in many disciplines ask for *close reading*. But literature classes strongly emphasize it — one reason they are good preparation for other fields. Nevertheless the steps involved in close reading are not always clear to students. Perhaps you have been told to engage in this process without knowing what it entails. Because close reading is central to literary studies, plays a big role in other courses, and yet remains murky for many students, this chapter both explains it and models it.

If you are taking a course that asks you to *write* about the literary works you study, close reading of them will help you form ideas about them worth spreading to *your* audiences. Such reading will also help you decide what details of these texts will best support your points about them. So, as we proceed to explain close reading, we treat it mainly as what some would call a method of invention. It's a way for you, as a *writer*, to discover things to say about literature.

Strategies for Close Reading

Actually, close reading consists of not one strategy but several. All of them can help you gain insights into a literary work, which you might then convey through your writing. You need not follow these strategies in the order we list them here, but try each of them.

1. Make predictions as you read. That is, guess what will happen and how the text will turn out. If you wind up being surprised, fine. You may get a richer understanding of the text as you reflect on how it *defies* your expectations.

2. Reread the text. Reread the text several times, focusing each time on a different element of the text and using at least one of these occasions to read aloud. Few readers of a literary work can immediately see everything important and interesting in it. You greatly increase your chances of getting ideas about a text if you read it again and again. At first, you may be preoccupied with following the plot or with figuring out the text's main theme. Only by examining the text repeatedly may you notice several of its other aspects, including features that really stir your thoughts. But don't try to study everything in the text each time you look at it. Use each reading of it to study just one characteristic. In an early stage, for example, you might trace the text's repetitions, and then you might use a later reading to pinpoint its ambiguous words. This division of labor can, in the end, generate many insights that a less focused approach would not.

Reading all of the text or portions of it out loud gives you a better sense of how the text is manipulating language. Reading aloud is especially useful in the case of poems, for you may detect rhymes or soundalike words that you would not notice when reading silently.

3. Test the text against your own experiences.   Keep in mind your experiences, beliefs, assumptions, and values as you read the text, but note ways that it challenges or complicates these things. When you first read a particular literary work, your interpretations and judgments are bound to be influenced by your personal background. This includes your beliefs, assumptions, and values, as well as things that have happened to you. Indeed, many people read a literary work hoping they can personally identify with the characters, situations, and views it presents. Moreover, this is an understandable goal. Pay attention, though, to details of the text that do *not* match your life and current thinking. After all, the author may be deliberately challenging or complicating readers' habitual attitudes. In any case, parts of the text that are hard to identify with will often provide you with great subjects when you write about the work. Bear in mind, though, that you will not interest your readers if you simply criticize characters in the work or sneer at other elements of it. In particular, try not to sum up characters with negative labels such as *immoral, weird,* or *sick.* These terms often strike readers as reflecting mere prejudice — a poor substitute for careful analysis of human complexity.

4. Look for patterns in the text and disruptions of them.   Many a literary work is organized by various patterns, which may not be evident on first reading. In fact, you might not detect a number of these patterns until you read the text several times. You may even see these better if you move back and forth in the text instead of just reading it straight through. Typically, a literary work's patterns include repetitions of words and of actions; oppositions; words similar or related in meaning; and technical methods of organization (such as rhyme schemes or frequent use of flashbacks). Just as important to note are moments in the text that are inconsistent with one or more of its patterns. Locate and think about places where the work makes a significant shift in meaning, imagery, tone, plot, a character's behavior, narrative point of view, or even physical format (for example, a change in rhyme scheme).

5. Note ambiguities.   These are places where the text's meaning is not crystal clear and therefore calls for interpretation: for example, words that can have more than one definition, symbols that have multiple implications, and actions that suggest various things about a character.

6. Consider the author's alternatives.   That is, think about what the author *could* have done and yet did not do. The author of a literary work faces all sorts of decisions in composing it. And as you study the work, you will have more to say about it if you think about those choices. Try, then, to compare the author's handling of particular passages to other possible treatments of them. By considering, for example, why the author chose a certain word over others, you may better detect implications and effects of the author's actual language. Similarly, by reflecting on how the author *might* have portrayed a certain character more simplistically, you strengthen your ability to analyze the character's variety of traits.

7. Ask questions.   As you read, generate questions that have more than one possible answer. When we first read a literary work, most of us try to get comfortable with it. We search for passages that are clear; we groan when we encounter ones that are mysterious or confusing. Sooner or later, though, we must confront puzzles in the text if we are to analyze it in depth. Furthermore, if we plan to *write* about the text, we are more likely to come up with ideas worth communicating to our readers if we present ourselves as helping them deal with matters *not* immediately clear. After all, our audience will not need our analysis if it centers on what's obvious. Therefore, list multiple questions that the work raises for you, especially ones that have various possible answers. Then, if you focus on addressing one of these questions in your writing — providing and supporting your own particular answer to it — your readers will find value in turning to *your* text. Furthermore, when you come across literary passages that seem easy to understand, consider how they might actually involve more than one possible meaning. Even little words may prove ambiguous and therefore, worth analyzing in your writing. Of course, you may have to consult a dictionary in order to see the different meanings that a word can have.

The questions you come up with need hardly be restricted to matters of the work's theme. After all, hardly any literary text worth studying can be reduced to a single message. Often, such texts play with multiple ideas, perhaps emphasizing tensions among them. Therefore, it may make more sense for you to refer to a work's *themes*. Actually, as we have been suggesting throughout our catalog of reading strategies, any literary text has several other features. As a writer, you may wind up with much more to say about a literary work if you consider one or more of these other elements: for example, facts obscured or absent in the text, possible definitions of key words, symbols, patterns, evaluations to be made of the characters or the overall work, the text's historical and cultural context, the text's genre, its relevance to current political debates, and cause-effect relationships. In the next chapter, we explain these elements at greater length, identifying them as *issues* you might write about.

8. Jot down possible answers.   Even while reading the text, begin developing and pulling together your thoughts by informally writing about it. See if you can generate not only good questions but also tentative answers to them. Writing need not be the final outcome of your reflections on a literary work. You can jot down ideas about the text even as you first encounter it. Such informal, preliminary writing can actually help you generate insights into the text that you would not have achieved simply by scanning it. The following are some of the specific things you might do:

- **Make notes in the text itself.**   A common method is to mark key passages, either by underlining these passages or by running a highlighter over them. Both ways of marking are popular because they help readers recall main features of the text. But use these techniques moderately if you use them at all, for marking lots of passages will leave you unable to distinguish the really important parts of the text. Also, try "talking back" to the text in its margins. Next to particular passages, you might jot down words of your own, indicating any feelings and questions you have about those parts. On any page of the text, you might circle related words and then draw lines between these words to emphasize their connection. If a word or an idea shows up on numerous pages, you might circle it each time. Furthermore, try cross-referencing by listing on at least one page the numbers of all those pages where the word or idea appears.

- **As you read the text, occasionally look away from it, and jot down anything in it you recall.**   This memory exercise lets you review your developing impressions of the text. When you turn back to its actual words, you may find that you have distorted or overlooked aspects of it that you should take into account.

- **At various moments in your reading, freewrite about the text for ten minutes or so.**   Spontaneously explore your preliminary thoughts and feelings about it, as well as any personal experiences the text leads you to recall. One logical moment to do freewriting is when you have finished reading the text. But you do not have to wait until then; as you read, you might pause occasionally to freewrite. This way, you give yourself an opportunity to develop and review your thoughts about the text early on.

- **Create a "dialectical notebook."**   So named by composition theorist Ann Berthoff, it involves using pages of your regular notebook in a particular way. On each page, draw a line down the middle to create two columns. In the left column, list various details of the text: specifically, words, images, characters, and events that strike you. In the right column, jot down for each detail one or more sentences indicating *why* you were drawn to it. Take as many pages as you need to record and reflect on your observations. You can also use the two-column format to carry out a dialogue with yourself about the text. This is an especially good way to ponder aspects of the text that you find confusing, mysterious, or complex.

- **Play with the text by revising it.**   Doing so will make you more aware of options that the author rejected and will give you a better sense of the moves that the author chose to make. Specifically, you might rearrange parts of the text, add to it, change some of its words, or shift its narrative point of view. After you revise the text, compare your alternative version with the original, considering especially differences in their effects.

A Poem for Analysis

To demonstrate what it means to read closely, we present observations that various students made about a poem. The poem is by Sharon Olds (b. 1942), who teaches at New York University and has produced many volumes of verse. "Summer Solstice, New York City" appears at the start of her 1987 book *The Gold Cell*. The poem deals with work — in this case, efforts by New York City police to prevent a suicide.

SHARON OLDS

Summer Solstice, New York City

By the end of the longest day of the year he could not stand it,
he went up the iron stairs through the roof of the building
and over the soft, tarry surface
to the edge, put one leg over the complex green tin cornice
and said if they came a step closer that was it.   5
Then the huge machinery of the earth began to work for his life,
the cops came in their suits blue-gray as the sky on a cloudy evening,
and one put on a bullet-proof vest, a
black shell around his own life,
life of his children's father, in case   10
the man was armed, and one, slung with a
rope like the sign of his bounden duty,
came up out of a hole in the top of the neighboring building
like the gold hole they say is in the top of the head,
and began to lurk toward the man who wanted to die.   15
The tallest cop approached him directly,
softly, slowly, talking to him, talking, talking,
while the man's leg hung over the lip of the next world
and the crowd gathered in the street, silent, and the
hairy net with its implacable grid was   20
unfolded near the curb and spread out and
stretched as the sheet is prepared to receive at birth.
Then they all came a little closer
where he squatted next to his death, his shirt
glowing its milky glow like something   25
growing in a dish at night in the dark in a lab and then
everything stopped
as his body jerked and he
stepped down from the parapet and went toward them
and they closed on him, I thought they were going to   30
beat him up, as a mother whose child has been
lost will scream at the child when it's found, they
took him by the arms and held him up and
leaned him against the wall of the chimney and the
tall cop lit a cigarette   35

in his own mouth, and gave it to him, and
then they all lit cigarettes, and the
red, glowing ends burned like the
tiny campfires we lit at night
back at the beginning of the world.   *[1987]*   40

Applying the Strategies

Even before you look at the students' comments, try doing what they did. We asked each of them to read the poem several times (step 2, pp. 82–83). More specifically, they devoted each of their readings to a specific element of the poem:

- First, they focused on how it fulfilled or defied their predictions.
- Then they considered how the poem matched and diverged from their personal backgrounds.
- Then they traced the poem's patterns, as well as breaks from these.
- Then they noted places where the poem is puzzling, ambiguous, or unclear.
- Next, they identified at least one choice that the poem's author faced.
- They then settled on questions that have more than one possible answer and that therefore might be worth addressing in a formal essay about the poem.
- Finally, pulling their thoughts together, they came up with tentative answers to these questions, which they might develop in a formal essay.

Again, the order of these stages is not the only one possible; the important thing is to go through them all. At each stage of their reading, the students also did a few minutes of freewriting, using this strategy to develop thoughts about whatever element was their focus. Below are excerpts from these informal reflections.

MAKE PREDICTIONS

KATHERINE: I was really tense as I read this poem because I thought the man would jump at the end and then we would get a horrible description of him splattering on the sidewalk. I didn't predict the cops would succeed in talking him out of it. When the poet says he "jerked," that could easily have been the start of his jumping, but thank God he is instead stepping back. I'm glad that they persuaded him to remain alive.

MARIA: I was like the poem's speaker expecting that they would physically grab him and treat him roughly, and so I was surprised when they were nice to him and even offered him a cigarette.

TREVOR: I predicted that the poem would end with the man still on the edge of the building deciding whether or not to jump off, because

I think that in a way it would be neat to leave us guessing whether he's really going to do it. I wasn't all that surprised when he pulled back and joined the cops, because that was certainly one possible outcome. However, I was surprised when the author had them smoking cigarettes at the end like "at the beginning of the world." I didn't expect that image of prehistoric people to show up here at the end.

REFLECT ON YOUR PERSONAL BACKGROUND

JAMES: It's hard for me to sympathize with someone who commits suicide, especially because someone at my high school killed himself and all of his friends and family were terribly saddened by what he did. I think that no matter how bad things get for you, there's a way out if only you look for it. Suicide is no answer, and it hurts the people you leave behind. So I'm glad that the man in this poem winds up not committing suicide. If he had, I would have thought less of him.

CARLA: I vaguely remember seeing some movies in which a character stands on a ledge and thinks about jumping off it. In real life, I've never seen something like that. What this poem most brings to my mind are reports I heard about people jumping off the World Trade Towers to escape being killed by fire. Of course, they died anyway. As I recall, TV didn't show these people jumping, out of respect for them I guess, and I'm glad that I didn't have to see this happen. Still, I'm aware that it did. Anyway, the man thinking about suicide in this poem isn't facing the same situation. He can easily live if he wants to.

BOB: I guess the police are obligated to try rescuing the man even if they have to risk their own lives. I've never been in this position, so I'm not sure how I'd feel if I'd been assigned to save the man in this poem. Though I disapprove of suicide, maybe I wouldn't have the guts to try confronting him on the edge of the building, and I'm not sure I could talk to him calmly, because if he did jump he might take me down with him. I admire the ability of these cops to stay cool and talk him into joining them. I'm also impressed that they then treat him like a friend instead of like a potentially violent nut case that they have to get under control through force. If it were me, I think I might want to throw him to the ground and pin his arms so that he wouldn't try something like that again.

READ FOR PATTERNS AND FOR BREAKS IN PATTERNS

DOMINICK: This may be too little a thing to think about, but I notice that the word "it" is repeated in the beginning section of the poem. The first line ends with "it," and line 5 does also. I'm not sure what is meant by "it" in "he could not stand it." Obviously on one level "it" here means his life, but he seems to have something specific about his life in mind when he says this, but we don't learn what he's specifically thinking of. The second "it" seems to refer to the fact that he will kill himself if they come closer. But that reference too isn't as clear as it might be. I see that later on "it" comes up again as a word for the cigarette that the cop gives to the man (after lighting it in his own mouth, yuck!). Maybe we're supposed to connect this "it" to the "its" at the start.

BOB: After the middle of the poem we start to get a lot of birth imagery. The word "birth" is even stated, and a little later there's the image of something "growing" in a lab dish.

JARED: "World" is repeated. In the middle of the poem, there's a reference to "the next world," and the very last word of the poem is "world," meaning the world where we currently live.

COURTNEY: I found a number of references to children. There are the words "his children's father," and then toward the end the word "child" is repeated, though this time it's a mother's child. And then the last line refers to "the beginning of the world," as if the world is a child that has just been born.

FRANK: It's funny that the word "end" is one of the first words of the poem, and then the word "beginning" is one of its last words. I can more easily imagine the reverse. Anyway, "end" and "beginning" are opposites that the poet seems to want us to think about. Come to think of it, there is mention of "ends" near the conclusion, but these are the "ends" of the men's cigarettes and not the end of the world.

ALEX: The word "day" appears in the first line (it's "the longest day of the year"), but later there is the word "night" ("growing in a dish at night"), and then "night" is in the next-to-last line. Ironically, things get brighter (the man decides to live) as the poem moves from "day" to "night."

PAUL: As the poem moves along, there's a shift in pronouns. In the first half or so, we get forms of "he" and "they." Then the word "I" suddenly appears, and then the next-to-last line has the word "we."

READ FOR PUZZLES, AMBIGUITIES, AND UNCLEAR MOMENTS

KATHERINE: I just don't learn enough about this man's thinking to know why he's even planning to kill himself. This is something the poem doesn't make clear. But I guess the "I" of the poem doesn't know the man's thinking either, and meanwhile she's in the position of possibly witnessing the man falling to the pavement! Maybe the author doesn't tell us exactly why the man wants to commit suicide because we can then identify more easily with him. We can think about moments when we were incredibly unhappy, whether or not we were depressed by the same things he is.

TIM: We're told that the cop approaching the man is doing a lot of talking, but we don't find out what he specifically says, even though this may have played a big role in getting the man to step back and live.

HILLARY: The gold hole sounds like something from folklore, but I don't know the background.

RACHEL: I'm wondering how much we're supposed to focus on the speaker's reactions to what's going on, or whether we should think more about the man and the policemen.

READ FOR THE AUTHOR'S CHOICES

KATHERINE: Olds could have had the man jump and die. Even if this poem is based on a real incident where the man decided to live, she could have changed what happened. Also, if she still went with the rescue version, she could have had the policemen treat the man roughly after they rescued him.

PAUL: The word "I" could have appeared more often throughout the poem, especially because the poem is written from the point of view of someone observing this suicide attempt.

TIM: We might have been told why the man was thinking of killing himself and what the cops said to him. I realize this information would be hard for the speaker of the poem to give us, since she's just observing the whole business from the street below. Still, maybe Olds could have found a way of telling us at least a little more about what the men on the roof were saying and thinking.

BOB: The author didn't have to use birth images. She could have described this event without them. In fact, death imagery seems more appropriate when a poem is about a possible suicide.

GENERATE QUESTIONS THAT HAVE MORE THAN ONE POSSIBLE ANSWER

JENNIFER: What might the poet be trying to convey when she ends the poem with the image of "the beginning of the world"? The last line really captures my attention.

PAUL: What should we conclude when the pronouns shift from "he" and "they" to "I" and finally "we"?

VICTORIA: How should we interpret the poem's repeated references to children and to parents (both father and mother)?

BOB: How important are the cops as characters in this poem?

STATE TENTATIVE ANSWERS

JENNIFER: Maybe the poet is telling us that each time you overcome depression and decide to go on living, it's like the rebirth of the world, and you're rejoining a "we" in the sense of rejoining the rest of humanity.

PAUL: I believe that the speaker comes to identify with the man and his rescuers and then sees herself and them as all part of a common humanity, as if we all have to decide when to risk our lives and when to preserve them.

VICTORIA: In a paper, I could argue that these child and parent references are used by Olds to suggest that even as adults, we sometimes act like children and sometimes have to act like a parent, but Olds evidently prefers that we not act like a very stern parent.

BOB: The cops are very important in this poem. So much of it is about what they do and how they maybe feel. They're required to save the guy, they're part of "huge machinery," and one of them might end up sacrificing the "life of his children's father" just in order to rescue someone who wants to kill himself anyway, but then the cops turn out to be quite sympathetic toward the guy. There's even this odd religious-type moment with the sharing of a cigarette and then all the men lighting up. I think I would focus my paper on how the cops do their duty to preserve life even when they probably didn't want to, and then something spiritual happens because they didn't give up on the job they were assigned.

DAN: If I'm remembering correctly, the summer solstice is a turning point in the year, and you could say that there's a turning point in this poem when the man steps down from the ledge and chooses not to die. After the summer solstice we're heading toward winter, which is associated with death, but psychologically the poem goes in the opposite direction.

Think about your own developing understanding of Olds's poem. What aspect of it might you focus on in a formal essay? What's a claim that you might make? To us, the students' claims we have quoted seem promising topics for papers. Nevertheless, they could probably stand some polishing and further reflection. After all, they are the outcome of freewriting — an exploratory phase. In any case, what we want to stress is that you are more likely to get ideas about a literary work if you use the reading strategies that this group of students applied.

Reading Closely by Annotating

Such strategies may help you come up with insights into any work you read. You might even record these observations by jotting them in the text's margins. If you then review and connect whatever points and questions you've raised, you'll be well on your way to developing an argument.

Here we'll show a particular student's annotations of a poem, and then we'll share the informal analysis her jottings helped her produce. The poem, "Girls Online," is by Emily Skillings, who trained as a dancer and a writer. Skillings has produced two poetry chapbooks, *Backchannel* and *Linnaeus: The 26 Sexual Practices of Plants* (both 2014). Her poems have also appeared in numerous journals, including *Harper's*, *Boston Review*, *Brooklyn Rail*, *Pleiades*, and *BOMB*. The poem we present was published in 2017, both in the journal *Poetry* and in *Fort Not*, Skillings's first full-length book.

Before turning to the student's annotated version, read Skillings's poem in its original state. Try to go through it more than once in order to formulate some thoughts.

EMILY SKILLINGS

Girls Online

The first line is a row of girls,
twenty-five of them, almost
a painting, shoulders overlapping,
angled slightly toward you.
One says: *I'm myself here.*   5
The others shudder and laugh
through the ribbon core that strings
them. They make a tone tighter
by drumming on their thighs and
opening their mouths. The girls   10
are cells. The girls are a fence,
a fibrous network. One by one
they describe their grievances.
Large hot malfunctioning
machines lie obediently at their sides.   15
Their shirts are various shades
of ease in the surrounding air,
which is littered with small cuts.
One will choose you, press you
into the ground. You may never   20
recover. The second-to-last line
has a fold in it. The last line is
the steady pour of their names.

If you're like us, you find this poem tricky to interpret. It's interesting because it can't be easily summed up. Its value lies in its deliberate complications—the ways it challenges readers' usual takes on the subject of "girls online." The poem's title refers to a common event in this digital age: girls going online and immersing themselves in social media. Skillings also uses common words; her language is ordinary and even plain. Yet the poem depicts a series of mysterious acts. It doesn't render them in clear, precise detail. Nor does Skillings give readers much help connecting one line to the next. They have to think about her poem's design—why it moves through the stages it does.

We've noticed that a poem like this is typical for Skillings. Most of those in her book *Fort Not* are equally daring. They tackle familiar subjects through unpredictable steps. Indeed, Skillings belongs to the Belladonna* Collaborative, feminist writers committed to literary experimentation. Skillings feels that her own writing reflects her dance career. "I see poems as little dances," she's said. They're "collisions and encounters of images and sounds, all immersed in their own music and atmosphere/mood." "Girls Online" certainly has "collisions and encounters." Readers face the task of figuring them out. Like a lot of literature, though, this poem can broaden minds. Probing its puzzles can give you fresh slants on your daily life.

Here is the poem as annotated by student Mia Benton:

The first line is a row of girls,

This word appears in the title, then again in lines 10 and 11.

twenty-five of them, almost

And this is the first line of the poem itself . . .

a painting, shoulders overlapping,

Does this mean that in some sense, and for a moment, they're a fixed artistic image? "Painting" is alliterative with the "ping" of "overlapping" ("p" sounds).

angled slightly toward you.

Who's this "you"? (A word repeated twice in line 19 and again in line 20.)

One says: I'm myself here.

The others shudder and laugh

Are people often "themselves" online? When would this speaker not be "herself"?

A word repeated twice in line 12 and again in line 19.

through the ribbon core that strings

The same as a "network"?

them. They make a tone tighter

Repeated in line 13; ties in with "their" in line 16 and the last line. Overall, the poem shifts pronouns ("you," "they," "one," "I").

Alliteration (repetition of "t").

by drumming on their thighs and

opening their mouths. The girls

We usually think of this as a protective barrier. But it can also be thought of as a "network" of slats or posts.

A word with various possible meanings: e.g., micro-organisms, batteries, rooms in a prison, parts of a terrorist network, parts of a honeycomb. Also, are we meant to think of "sells," as if the girls are selling themselves?

are cells. The girls are a fence,

a fibrous network. One by one

We're left to imagine what these specifically are. The last syllable sounds a bit like "fence" (line 11).

they describe their grievances.

Alliteration (repetition of "f"). A word that clearly connects to "online," but could refer as well to an offline community. A poem can be considered a "network" of images.

Large hot malfunctioning

machines lie obediently at their sides.

What exactly are these "machines"? The words "malfunctioning" and "obediently" seem opposites.

Their shirts are various shades

of ease in the surrounding air,

which is littered with small cuts.

Are we perhaps meant to think of girls cutting themselves?

One will choose you, press you

She seems to have some agency.

into the ground. You may never

Words that sound alike.

recover The second-to-last line

Seems a significant word, since it appears at the climax, but it's ambiguous and even mysterious.

has a told in it. The last line is

the steady pour of their names.

We're not told, though, what their names are.

Once she had annotated this poem, Mia continued thinking about it. Off the top of her head, she wrote the following paragraphs. They're a quick, informal draft, not a polished essay. But this writing served her as a means of inquiry. Through it, she grappled with issues the poem brought up for her. She could also try out claims she might pursue in a formal paper.

When I first saw the title "Girls Online," I thought this would be a poem I could easily understand. After all, I'm a young woman who's constantly looking at her phone and her laptop, texting friends, and posting on Instagram. I assumed that the poem would deal with activities like these. But as things turned out, it doesn't clearly describe them. I have to admit that I found the poem cryptic. As I went from line to line, I could understand the words, but I couldn't comprehend the actions they referred to. If the girls in the poem are involved with social media, which is what most people today would take the word "online" to mean, can they also be standing in a row like a group of figures in a painting? And later, why doesn't Skillings tells us what their "grievances" are when they're "opening their mouths"? And what on earth are the "machines" she's describing as "large," "hot," "malfunctioning," and "obedient"? Who's the "you" near the end of the poem? What exactly is the "fold"? The last line refers to "their names," but we don't learn what these are. Why doesn't Skilling let us know? I get the feeling that no reader could ever figure out everything that's going on in this poem, and maybe the author doesn't expect us to. Maybe she's aiming at some general effect, and she's willing to be mysterious in places in order to achieve it.

At any rate, I look at my annotations and try to get a sense from them of the poem's patterns. A thing I notice is that almost all of the sentences in the poem spill over from one line to the next. Only one line, the fifth, features a sentence that can exist on its own as complete. The line is "One says: *I'm myself here.*" This line really stands out for me, because it's the only complete sentence, it's the only line that shifts into italics, and it's the only one that features the first-person pronoun "I." Nevertheless, the declaration reported in this line raises questions for me. In reading it, I wonder whether a person can really be "herself" online, why she might feel that she's not "herself" offline, and what elements of personality she specifically has in mind when she thinks of her authentic "self." It's also hard for me to buy this girl's claim that "*I'm myself here.*" If Skillings wanted me to take the claim seriously, I think she would have offered more evidence for it in terms of characteristics. Instead, she leaves me skeptical about it.

The poem puts far more stress on how the whole set of girls exists and acts as a unified group. Right after the one girl makes her claim, the poem reports how the rest of them respond all together: "The others shudder and laugh / through the ribbon core that strings/ them." Then, even while they're making sounds ("drumming on their thighs and/opening their mouths"), they seem to be forming "tighter" links between themselves. For me, the alliteration of "tone" and "tighter" reinforces the idea that these girls are closely bound. The middle of the poem, which I suppose you could say is the heart of it, keeps stringing the girls together by describing them as "cells" that form "a fence" and "a fibrous network." I'm not seeing them as distinct individuals. Even when they proceed to voice "their grievances," there are no details of any particular girl's beefs. The girls still seem to operate as a group. True, "their shirts are various shades," but this clothing projects the same "ease."

As the poem heads toward its conclusion, it feels more violent. I may be wrong, but the phrase "littered with small cuts" makes me think of girls who cut them-selves. If this is a plausible inference, then maybe Skillings is suggesting that these girls' "ease" conceals disturbing behavior—they've literally cut themselves, or they've harmed themselves in other ways. But then one of the girls seems violent toward someone else. This is what I gather from the lines "One will choose you, press you / into the ground. You may never / recover." Because this pronoun doesn't seem to refer to a specific person, maybe Skillings is suggesting that the girl is incapable of seeing another person as a separate "you," even if she's suppos-edly communicating with that person online. As a group, the girls are "angled slightly toward you," so maybe the girls are perhaps not interested in facing a "you" head-on. Maybe all of the girls in the poem want other people to be obedient machines. But if this is the case, they also seem obedient to one another, not capable of branching out on their own. And I can't forget about the "cuts." They can be taken to mean that even if the girls are insensitive to others, they also damage themselves, perhaps by actually quashing their own identities.

One thing that still nags at me is Skillings's use of the word "line." She seems to be playing with it, by

giving it different definitions. As I've said, "online" in
the title immediately brings to my mind social media. But
the "line" depicted at the start of the poem is "a row," as
if the twenty-five girls are literally stretched out across a
field or stage. Are they on display for an audience? Then
the words "strings," "fence," and "network" make me
think of lines of connection, a reminder of the girls' ties
to one another. Furthermore, in the first line and the last
three lines of Skillings's text, the word "line" seems to
refer to the lines of this very poem! It's possible that the
author wants me to have all of these meanings in mind,
but I'm still wondering exactly how to relate them. Maybe
Skillings isn't sure, either, and she's OK with coming
across as uncertain.

Mia's reflections here are far from final. She's in the early phases of forming an
argument for a paper. She's clearly making headway, though, in her study of
the poem. First through her annotations, and then through this piece of writing, she's explored significant issues and ideas. She's put to good use particular
strategies we discussed in the previous section. They include the following:

Make predictions and reflect on your personal background: Mia
thought "Girls Online" would clearly examine its title subject, and she assumed
it would cover online actions she performs. But she discovers that the poem
goes down curious paths. It proceeds in ways she has to interpret.

Read for patterns and for breaks in patterns: To Mia, much in the
poem suggests group uniformity, so she must decide what to do with the one
line featuring "I." Another pattern she finds is violence; signs of it grow as
the poem draws to an end. She also sees that the poem repeats the word "line"
itself. It's a pattern that seems important to trace, even if it's hard to decode.

Read for puzzles, ambiguities, and unclear moments: Skillings packs
her poem with enigmas, so Mia has to face them. Among other things, she
wonders about the "machines," the "you," and the word "line." Rather than
ignore these elements or simplify their meaning, she's willing to keep thinking
about them.

Read for the author's choices. Mia realizes Skillings could have given
the reader more reason to accept the claim "*I'm myself here.*" Because Skillings
leaves the claim unsupported, Mia feels feels encouraged to doubt its validity.

State tentative answers. Mia hasn't produced yet a crisp main claim for
an argument essay. Still, she's able to consider a candidate or two: for example,
that the girls in the poem don't really *engage* with a "you" when they go online.

FURTHER STRATEGIES: TOPICS OF LITERARY STUDIES

You can also get ideas about the text if, as you read it, you consider how it
deals with **topics** that have preoccupied literary studies as a profession. Some
of these topics have interested the discipline for many years. One example is

work, a subject common to several selections in Chapters 1–8. Traditionally, literary studies has also been concerned with such topics as family relations, love, freedom and confinement, justice, and journeys. Moreover, the discipline has long called attention to topics that are essentially classic conflicts: for example, innocence versus experience, free will versus fate or determinism, the individual versus society, nature versus culture, and eternity versus the passing time.

Over the past few years, however, literary studies has turned to several new concerns. For instance, quite a few literary critics now consider the ways in which literary texts are often *about* reading, writing, interpretation, and evaluation. Critics increasingly refer to some of the following subjects in their analysis of literature:

- Traits that significantly shape human identity, including gender, race, ethnic background, social class, sexual orientation, cultural background, nationality, and historical context
- Representations of groups, including stereotypes held by others
- Acknowledgments — or denials — of differences among human beings
- Divisions, conflicts, and multiple forces *within* the self
- Boundaries, including the processes through which these are created, preserved, and challenged
- Politics and ideology, including the various forms that power and authority can take; acts of domination, oppression, exclusion, and appropriation; and acts of subversion, resistance, and parody
- Ways that carnivals and other festivities challenge or preserve social order
- Distinctions between what's universal and what's historically or culturally specific
- Relations between the public and the private, the social and the personal
- Relations between the apparently central and the apparently marginal
- Relations between what's supposedly normal and what's supposedly abnormal
- Relations between "high" culture and "low" (that is, mass or popular) culture
- Economic and technological developments, as well as their effects
- The role of performance in everyday life
- Values — ethical, aesthetic, religious, professional, and institutional
- Desire and pleasure
- The body
- The unconscious
- Memory, including public commemorations as well as personal memory
- Material things, including common physical objects

If you find that a literary text touches on one of these topics, try next to determine how the work specifically addresses that topic. Perhaps you will consider the topic an element of the text's themes. In any case, remember that, by itself, a topic is not the same as a theme. While a topic can usually be expressed in a word or a short phrase, a theme is a whole claim or assertion that you believe the text makes.

Actually, the topics we have identified may be most worth consulting when you have just begun analyzing a literary text and are far from establishing a theme. By using these topics, you can generate preliminary questions about the text, various issues you can then explore.

To demonstrate how these topics can stimulate inquiry, we apply some of them to the following poem, "Night Waitress." It is from the 1986 book *Ghost Memory*, by the late American poet Lynda Hull (1954–1994). Hull had been developing an impressive career in literature when she died in a car accident. This poem is also about work, the speaker being the night waitress of the title.

LYNDA HULL
Night Waitress

Reflected in the plate glass, the pies
look like clouds drifting off my shoulder.
I'm telling myself my face has character,
not beauty. It's my mother's Slavic face.
She washed the floor on hands and knees   5
below the Black Madonna, praying
to her god of sorrows and visions
who's not here tonight when I lay out the plates,
small planets, the cups and moons of saucers.
At this hour the men all look   10
as if they'd never had mothers.
They do not see me. I bring the cups.
I bring the silver. There's the man
who leans over the jukebox nightly
pressing the combinations   15
of numbers. I would not stop him
if he touched me, but it's only songs
of risky love he leans into. The cook sings
with the jukebox, a moan and sizzle
into the grill. On his forehead   20
a tattooed cross furrows,
diminished when he frowns. He sings words
dragged up from the bottom of his lungs.
I want a song that rolls
through the night like a big Cadillac   25
past factories to the refineries

squatting on the bay, round and shiny
as the coffee urn warming my palm.
Sometimes when coffee cruises my mind
visiting the most remote way stations,   30
I think of my room as a calm arrival
each book and lamp in its place. The calendar
on my wall predicts no disaster
only another white square waiting
to be filled like the desire that fills   35
jail cells, the old arrest
that makes me stare out the window or want
to try every bar down the street.
When I walk out of here in the morning
my mouth is bitter with sleeplessness.   40
Men surge to the factories and I'm too tired
to look. Fingers grip lunch box handles,
belt buckles gleam, wind riffles my uniform
and it's not romantic when the sun unlids
the end of the avenue. I'm fading   45
in the morning's insinuations
collecting in the crevices of buildings,
in wrinkles, in every fault
of this frail machinery.   *[1986]*

≡ A WRITING EXERCISE

After you read "Night Waitress," do a ten-minute freewrite in which you try
to identify how the poem relates to one or more of the topics mentioned
on page 97.

We think that several of the topics now popular in literary studies are relevant to Hull's poem. Here are a few possibilities, along with questions that
these topics can generate.

Gender.   The speaker alludes to conventional roles through which men and
women relate to each other. When the speaker declares that "at this hour the
men all look / as if they'd never had mothers," she indicates that women have
often played a maternal role for men. Furthermore, she implies that often
women have been the primary caretaker of their sons. (Notice that she makes
no reference to fathers.) What is the effect of this attention to women as mothers of men? In most of the poem, the speaker refers to men as potential lovers.
Yet even as she suggests she would like a sexual relationship with a man, she
suggests as well that she has had trouble establishing worthwhile attachments. Why has she had such difficulty, do you think? Does the problem seem
due to her personality alone, or do you sense larger forces shaping her situation? Notice, too, that the poem refers to the factory workers as male, while
the woman who speaks is a waitress. To what extent does American society
perpetuate a gendered division of labor?

Ethnic background.   Near the start of the poem, the speaker refers to her "mother's Slavic face" and points out that her mother served "the Black Madonna," a religious icon popular in Central European countries such as the Czech Republic and Poland. What is the effect of these particular ethnic references? To pursue this line of inquiry, probably you will need to do research into the Black Madonna, whether in a library or on the Internet.

Social class.   In part, considering social class means thinking about people's ability to obtain material goods. When the speaker compares her ideal song to "a big Cadillac," she implies that she doesn't currently possess such a luxurious car. At the same time, she is expressing her desire for the song, not the car. Why might the song be more important to her right now? Social class is also a matter of how various workplaces are related to one another. This poem evokes a restaurant, factories, refineries, and bars. How are these settings connected as parts of American society? Think, too, about how you would label the social class of the various occupations the poem mentions. What would you say is the social class of a waitress? To what classes would you assign people who work in factories and refineries? Who, for the most part, are the social classes that have to work at night?

Sexual orientation.   The speaker of "Night Waitress" seems heterosexual, an orientation often regarded as the only legitimate one. Because almost all societies have made heterosexuality the norm, a lot of people forget that it is a particular orientation and that not everyone identifies with it. Within literary studies, gay and lesbian critics have pointed out that a literary work may seem to deal with sexuality in general but may actually refer just to heterosexuality. Perhaps "Night Waitress" is examining heterosexuality as a specific social force. If so, how might the speaker's discontent be related to heterosexuality's influence as a particular institution? Keep in mind that you don't have to assume anything about the author's sexuality as you pursue such a question. In fact, heterosexuality may be a more important topic in Hull's poem than she intended.

Divisions, conflicts, and multiple forces within the self.   The poem's beginning indicates that the speaker experiences herself as divided. The first four lines reveal that she feels pride and disappointment in her mirror image: "I'm telling myself my face has character, / not beauty." Later, she indicates that within her mind are "remote way stations" that she visits only on occasion. Furthermore, she seems to contradict herself. Although she initially refers to her room as "a calm arrival," she goes on to describe that place negatively, as empty and confined. Early in the evening, she seems sexually attracted to the man playing the jukebox ("I would not stop him / if he touched me"), but by morning her mood is "not romantic" and she is "too tired / to look" at the male factory workers. What may be the significance of these paradoxes?

Boundaries.   In the first line, the speaker is apparently looking at a window, and later she reveals that at times she feels driven to "stare out the window" of her room. What should a reader make of these two references to such a common boundary? When the speaker observes that the men in the restaurant "do not see me," she indicates that a boundary exists between them and her. Do you think she is merely being paranoid, or do you suspect that the men are indeed ignoring her? If they *are* oblivious to her, how do you explain their behavior? Still another boundary explored in the poem is the line between night and day. What happens when the speaker crosses this line? What can night, day, and the boundary between them signify? You might also consider what the author of a literary work does with its technical boundaries. Often a poem creates boundaries in its breaks between stanzas. Yet "Night Waitress" is a continuous, unbroken text; what is the effect of Hull's making it so? At the same time, Hull doesn't always respect sentence boundaries in her lines. At several points in the poem, sentences spill over from one line to another. This poetic technique is called **enjambment**; what is its effect here?

Politics and ideology.   When, in referring to the jukebox man, the speaker declares that "I would not stop him / if he touched me," she can be taken to imply that male customers often flirt with waitresses. How might flirtation be seen as involving power, authority, and even outright domination? Do you see the poem as commenting on such things? Earlier, we raised issues of social class; these can be seen as political issues, too. How would you describe a society in which some people have "a big Cadillac" and others do not?

Carnivals and other festivities.   Although the poem does not refer to a "carnival" in any sense of that word, it does mention bars, which today are regarded by many people as places of festive retreat from work. What adjectives would you use to describe the speaker when she says that sometimes she wants "to try every bar down the street"?

Distinctions between what is universal and what is historically or culturally specific.   Try to identify anything that is historically or culturally specific about this poem's setting. Certainly the word *Slavic* and the reference to the Black Madonna indicate that the speaker has a particular background. You might also note her description of the restaurant, her use of the Cadillac as a metaphor, and her mention of the "factories" and the "refineries" that are "squatting on the bay." Although a wide range of places might fit these details, the poem's setting does not seem universal. Indeed, many readers are attracted to literature *because* it deals with specific landscapes, people, and plots. Nevertheless, these same readers usually expect to get some larger, more widely applicable meanings out of literature even as they are engaged by its specific details. Are you inclined to draw general conclusions from "Night Waitress"? If so, what general meanings do you find in it? What sorts of people do you think might learn something about themselves from reading this poem?

Relations between the public and the private, the social and the personal.   The speaker of "Night Waitress" works in a very public place, a restaurant. Yet she seems to feel isolated there, trapped in her own private world. How did she come to experience public life this way, do you think? Later, she initially seems to value her room as a private retreat, calling it "a calm arrival," but then she describes it as a place so lonely that it leads her to "stare out the window or want / to try every bar down the street." How, then, would you ultimately describe the relations between the speaker's public life and her private one? In addressing this issue, probably you need to consider whether the speaker's difficulties are merely personal or reflect a larger social disorder. When, at the end of the poem, she refers to "this frail machinery," is she referring just to herself, or is she suggesting that this phrase applies to her society in general? If she is indeed making a social observation, what do you sense are the "faults" in her society? Who else might be "fading"?

Relations between "high" culture and "low" culture.   Although the speaker does not identify the "songs / of risky love" playing on the jukebox, surely they are examples of what is called low, mass, or popular culture. Just as a lot of us are moved by such music when we hear it, so the jukebox player and the cook are engaged by it. In contrast, the poem itself can be considered an example of high culture. Often poetry is regarded as a serious art even by people who don't read it. In what ways, if any, does this poem conceivably resemble the songs it mentions? Given that author Lynda Hull is in essence playing with combinations of words, can we compare her with "the man / who leans over the jukebox nightly / pressing the combinations / of numbers"? (Actually, *numbers* has been a poetic term; centuries ago, it was commonly used as a synonym for the rhythms of poems.)

The role of performance in everyday life.   The most conspicuous performer in this poem is the cook, who "sings words / dragged up from the bottom of his lungs." But in everyday life, people often perform in the sense of taking on certain roles, even disguising their real personalities. Do you see such instances of performing in this poem? If so, where? Notice that the speaker wears a uniform; can that be considered a costume she wears while performing as a waitress?

Religious values.   The speaker clearly refers to religion when she recalls her mother's devotion to the Black Madonna, behavior that involved "praying / to her god of sorrows and visions." And although that god is "not here tonight," the speaker's description of waitressing has ritualistic overtones reminiscent of religious ceremonies. When she says, "I bring the cups. / I bring the silver," she could almost be describing preparations for Communion. In fact, she depicts the cook as wearing a religious emblem: "On his forehead / a tattooed cross furrows, / diminished when he frowns." What do you make of all this religious imagery? Might the speaker be trying to pursue certain religious values? Can she be reasonably described as looking for salvation?

Desire and pleasure.   The speaker explicitly mentions the word *desire* when she describes the emptiness she feels in her room, a feeling of desolation "that makes me stare out the window or want / to try every bar down the street." These lines may lead you to believe that her desire is basically sexual. Yet when the speaker uses the words *I want* earlier in the poem, she expresses her wish for "a song that rolls / through the night like a big Cadillac." Here, her longing does not appear sexual in nature. Is the speaker referring to at least two kinds of desire, then? Or do you see her as afflicted with basically one kind?

The body.   A notable feature of this poem is its attention to body parts. The speaker mentions her "shoulder," her "face," her mother's "face," her mother's "hands and knees," the cook's "forehead," his "lungs," her "palm," the "way stations" of her "mind," her "mouth," the factory workers' "fingers," and their "belt buckles." At the same time, the speaker never describes any particular body as a whole. What is the effect of this emphasis on mere parts? Does it connect in any way to the speaker's ultimate "fading"?

Memory.   Already we have noted the speaker's reference to her mother at the start of the poem. In what way, if any, is it significant that she engages in recollection? What circumstances in her life might have prompted the speaker to look back at the past?

Material things.   The speaker mentions cups, plates, saucers, and silverware. Evidently she's careful to "lay out" (line 8) these items in a particular order. Similarly, she reports, the room where she lives has "each book and lamp in its place" (line 32). What do you conclude from her neat ordering of these objects? Note that the only "warming" she feels in the poem comes from "the coffee urn" (line 28). Is there a possibility of her ever feeling warmth from a human being? "Box" appears multiple times: as part of the word "jukebox" (brought up twice, in lines 14 and 19) and as part of the phrase "lunch box" (line 42). With this repetition, perhaps Hull is encouraging her readers to connect "jukebox" and "lunch box" in some meaningful way. The first seems a means of entertainment, the second an object taken to work or school. But they're both part of the speaker's world; what should readers infer from that fact?

CHAPTER 5

The Writing Process

In Chapter 6, we discuss how to write about three literary genres: short stories, poems, and plays. Here, however, we suggest how to write about literature of any genre. To make our advice concrete, we mainly trace what a student, Dylan Rieff, did as he worked on a writing assignment for a course like yours. Dylan's class had to choose a short story from the syllabus and write a 750–1,000-word argument paper on it for a general audience. Dylan chose to write about a recently published story, Rachel Kadish's "Letters Arrive from the Dead." Before we trace the stages Dylan went through, read Kadish's story yourself.

Rachel Kadish (b. 1969) teaches in the MFA Creative Writing Program at Lesley University. She earned an undergraduate degree in English/Creative Writing at Princeton University and an M.A. in English/Fiction Writing at Columbia University. In addition to her novella *I Was Here* (2014) and short stories published in such journals as *Ploughshares*, *Tin House*, and *Zoetrope: All-Story*, Kadish has produced three novels: *From a Sealed Room* (2006), *Tolstoy Lied: A Love Story* (2007), and *The Weight of Ink* (2017), a bestseller about contemporary historians' discovery of Jewish writing from seventeenth-century England. "Letters Arrive from the Dead" first appeared in the Spring 2018 issue of *The Iowa Review*. It's an example of what several literary critics today call microfiction, sudden fiction, short shorts, or flash fiction.

RACHEL KADISH

Letters Arrive from the Dead

When letters arrive from the dead, the postmarks are often in error. Envelopes are backdated or bear stamps from improbable places. This stands to reason; the dead are notorious fibbers. They have reputations to protect or to invent, and certain inconvenient legacies to dismantle.

In the temporary village in which they're housed before moving on, the dead close out old business, study their new obligations, and acquire necessary paperwork. Each has been allotted a certain amount of time to set affairs in order, and most work diligently, if grimly, toward this departure date, though inevitably some linger longer. (So what if they outstay their visas? Who will hold them to it?) For the most part, they remain decorous — yet even those who are, frankly, hooligans do not steal from the living, vandalize heirlooms, or poison food; nor do they murder, make appliances malfunction, shatter glass. The fantasy that the dead do such things is libel. It's not that the dead never wish harm on the living, but that their gestures are ineffective. True, they're capable of visiting the living in altered form, but most choose not to on account of the draining fatigue that results, the inner ear problems that last days, the aching joints hardly worth what's achieved: a brief whisper that goes unheard in a noisy setting, or a brick, thrown with unfathomable effort, that nonetheless misses (the dead have execrable aim). Ultimately, even the fiercest recognize the futility of such modes of communication.

In their desire to settle their last affairs with the living, they retreat, in the end, to this post office, which promises to dispatch their messages without need for ghostly visitations. Here, at last, they press their points much as the living do: wearily, obediently, coloring within the lines of bureaucracy — because who can be troubled to do otherwise?

In the dim, dusty post office, the drowsy clerk flexes his wrist, stamps his heavy stamp. The creaking desk chair, the unoiled wheel that sticks, the sigh of the small lumbar pillow as it takes his weight. The dead, shuffling in a queue that ends at his desk, mail admonishments, rebukes, samples of tea. Their messages to the living are opaque — they know the censor in the adjoining office must be appeased. Besides, who wants to report the literal truth of their dull status in this transit village, when more newsworthy and impressive experiences await in the next phase? Still, communications must be sent — there are arguments to be settled, exhortations and endearments to convey. Nor are the dead above the occasional passive-aggressive missive: the postcard reading *Wish you were here.*

(The postcard arrives in a dream. Waking, the living scramble to interpret: what lies beneath these four words? What deeper meaning may be intuited? Psychiatrists are visited, old diaries are dredged, sage burned.)   5

Dreams, while the most common delivery system, are not the only one. Airplane contrails, owls, drifting smoke — anything seen out of the corner of an eye will do. Communications breach the world of the living in the form of a familiar perfume or a whorl of dust or dry leaves blowing into an alley on a windless day. A passing bus splashes mud across the new shirt purchased for a date with *her* — was it a warning from the other side? The living readily attribute such phenomena to certain departed kin, friends, or enemies — attributions that are often inaccurate. Studying the receipts noting the interpretation of their messages, the dead cannot be faulted for feeling at times maligned, even plagiarized.

At his desk with its dockets, dreaming of vacation, the clerk assesses each item with practiced skepticism. Certain things are not permitted: hazardous materials, messages that violate confidentiality laws. Surely by now the dead — the never-ending line of them traversing the long hall toward his desk — must know the routine. Yet the clientele is ungrateful. *Why was she served before me? I wasn't told my letter would be censored. My package is but a small one; it contains no harmful objects; it contains nothing that would harm a soul.*

The stamp, the creak of bureaucracy, the ticking clock. He himself works long hours, his salary is paltry — yet he makes no complaint, for who would listen? We all know a better system would be possible, if we were starting from scratch.

Please it won't harm them. To know what I finally know, now.
Five minutes to closing you'll have to come back tomorrow.   10

Now and then a message is returned to sender, unopened. Only then, as the sender makes his way toward the door, clutching his receipt, do the dead pause in their bickering and part in silence, to make way for the bereaved.

[2018]

In a tweet, Kadish said this story "might be the oddest thing I've ever written." Dylan chose to write about it because he found its eeriness compelling as well as thought-provoking. His writing process consisted of four main activities: (1) exploring, (2) planning, (3) composing, and (4) revising. As we describe each, keep in mind that these activities need not be consecutive. Dylan moved back and forth among them as he worked on his assignment.

Strategies for Exploring

As you read a literary work, you are bound to interpret and judge it. Yet not all reading is close reading, which can also be called **critical reading**. This process involves carefully and self-consciously analyzing various aspects of a text, including its meanings, its effects, and its treatment of typical elements of its genre. When you read a work closely and critically, you also note questions it raises for you — issues you might explore further in class discussion and writing. Indeed, close reading is a process of self-reflection. During this process, you monitor your own response to the text and try to identify why you see the text the way you do.

Exploring, the first stage of writing an essay about literature, is this particular process of reading. As we explain in Chapter 4, it specifically involves the following:

- Making predictions as you read
- Rereading the text with a different focus each time, including at least one stage in which you read aloud
- Comparing the text with your personal experience
- Tracing patterns and breaks from these patterns
- Noting ambiguities
- Considering the author's alternatives
- Generating questions
- Considering how the text deals with topics that have preoccupied literary studies
- Formulating a tentative claim
- Using informal writing to move through all these steps, including commenting in the text's margins, note-taking, freewriting, creating a "dialectical notebook," and playfully revising the text

≣ A WRITING EXERCISE

Do at least ten minutes of freewriting about Kadish's story, keeping it near so that you can consult it if you need to. In particular, try to raise questions about the story, and consider which of these may be worth addressing in a formal argument.

Here is an excerpt from Dylan's freewriting.

This story doesn't really have a plot. Instead it comes across to me as a kind of report. The narrator is explaining what the afterlife is like, focusing on the letters that the dead write to the living. I get the sense that the audience for this report is, in fact, the living, who of course wouldn't yet know on their own what it's like to be dead. Maybe we can even consider this report to be a letter itself, which someone who does know about the afterlife is sending to those who are still alive. I also have the impression that the behavior shown by the dead, which the report is describing, is behavior that these people might have engaged in when they were alive. I'm curious, though, about the title of the story, "Letters Arrive from the Dead." Ironically, the story ends by emphasizing what seems to be the *non*-arrival of letters: "Now and then a message is returned to sender, unopened" (106). The message has *not* reached its intended audience, or that audience doesn't want to open the letter and find out what the message is. The title "Letters Arrive from the Dead" is also misleading because the story is mostly about the issues and feelings that plague the dead as they're sending their letters off (or *trying* to send them off). We don't learn much about how the intended recipients of the letters react to them when they arrive. The only parts of the story that focus on the living are two paragraphs that appear about midway through. One paragraph, which is tucked away within parentheses, is about the living's efforts to figure out a particular message on a postcard: *"Wish you were here"* (105). The second paragraph, which comes right after, brings up the fact that the living often mistake certain phenomena as messages from the dead. So, both paragraphs about the living call attention to a gap in understanding between the living and the dead. Perhaps we can say that in both these paragraphs, a letter from the dead hasn't really "arrived." Significantly, *"Wish you were here"* is the *only* example the story gives of a specific message from the dead, and it's a message that the living find ambiguous! Overall, I'm wondering if Kadish wants me to think about the word "arrive" can itself be ambiguous. We might have more than one definition in mind when we declare that a certain letter has or hasn't "arrived." Usually, a letter is said to "arrive" if it physically reaches its intended reader. But what if that reader doesn't look at the letter's contents? Or doesn't experience the emotional reaction that the letter writer is aiming for? And what if there's no letter in the first place, just the illusion of one?

When you first get an assignment like Dylan's, you may fear that you have nothing to say. Notice, though, that freewriting enabled him to raise several questions. He realized that he couldn't squeeze all of them into his formal essay; his word limit wouldn't be able to deal with everything that puzzled him about the story. But taking time for exploration did help him come up with material he could use. The same procedure can work for you. There's value in examining potential subjects through writing, discussion, and just plain thinking.

One of your challenges will be to choose among the various issues you have hatched. At the end of the above excerpt from his freewriting, Dylan is on the verge of choosing to address an issue of pattern. Despite its title, "Letters Arrive from the Dead," he feels that Kadish's story doesn't emphasize arrival; instead, it stresses the dead's difficulties communicating with those still alive. Dylan has yet to decide *which* difficulties he'll call attention to, as well as what order he'll discuss them in. He knows that he must also resolve an issue of definition: he'll need to explain exactly what he means by "arrive." So, even after freewriting, he has things to figure out. But his essay won't contribute much if it focuses on features that pose no challenges at all. Though Dylan has more thinking to do about the story's emphasis, it seems a promising subject for him *because* it calls for inquiry.

Strategies for Planning

Planning for an assignment like Dylan's involves five main activities:

1. Choosing the text you will analyze.
2. Identifying your audience.
3. Identifying the main issue, claim, and evidence you will present.
4. Identifying your assumptions.
5. Determining how you will organize your argument, including how you will demonstrate your reasoning process.

CHOOSE A TEXT

Dylan considered several stories before choosing one for his paper. He settled on Kadish's for five reasons:

(1) It was a text that left him with plenty of questions.

(2) He believed that these questions could be issues for other readers.

(3) He felt increasingly able to *argue* about the story — that is, to make and support claims about it.

(4) He believed that he could adequately analyze the story within the assignment's word limit.

(5) The story was a fresh imagining of what the dead experience in the afterlife.

Faced with the same assignment, you might choose a different story than Dylan did. Still, the principles that he followed are useful. Think about them whenever you are free to decide which texts you will write about. With some assignments, of course, you may need a while to decide which text is best for you. And later, after you have made your decision, you may want to make a switch. For example, you may find yourself changing your mind once you have done a complete draft. Frustrated by the text you have chosen, you may realize that another inspires you more. If so, consider making a substitution. Naturally, you will feel more able to switch if you have ample time left to write the paper, so avoid starting your paper until just before it is due.

IDENTIFY YOUR AUDIENCE

To determine what your readers will see as an issue and to make your claims persuasive to them, you need to develop an audience profile. Perhaps your instructor will specify your audience. You may be asked, for example, to imagine yourself writing for a particular group in a particular situation. If you were Dylan, how would you analyze "Letters Arrive from the Dead" for a group of therapists training to become grief counselors? Even when not required of you, such an exercise can be fun and thought-provoking as you plan a paper.

Most often, though, instructors ask students to write for a general audience, the readership that Dylan was asked to address. Assume that a general audience is one that will want evidence for your claims. While this audience will include your instructor, let it also include your classmates, since in class discussions they will be an audience for you whenever you speak. Besides, your class may engage in peer review, with students giving one another feedback on their drafts.

IDENTIFY YOUR ISSUE, CLAIM, AND EVIDENCE

When you have written papers for previous classes, you may have been most concerned with coming up with a thesis. Maybe you did not encounter the term *issue* at all. But good planning for a paper entails identifying the main issue you will address. Once you have sensed what that issue is, try phrasing it as a question. If the answer might be obvious to your readers, be cautious, for you really do not have an issue if the problem you are raising can be easily resolved.

Also, try to identify what *kind* of issue you will focus on. For help, look at our list of various types (pp. 50–55). Again, with "Letters Arrive from the Dead," Dylan chose to focus on a kind of issue that he decided is best regarded as an issue of pattern. More precisely, he thought his main question might be, To what extent does the story actually deal with the *arrival* of letters from the dead? At the same time, Dylan realized that addressing this issue would lead him to an issue of definition: What are the various meanings of *arrival* the story implies?

Now that he had identified his main issue, Dylan had to come up with a precise statement of his main claim. Perhaps you have grown comfortable with the term *thesis* and want to keep using it. Bear in mind, though, that your thesis is the main *claim* you will make and proceed to support. And when, as Dylan did, you put your main issue as a question, then your main claim is your answer to that question. Sometimes you will come up with question and answer simultaneously.

Once in a while, you may even settle on your answer first, not being certain yet how to word the question. Whatever the case, planning your paper involves articulating both the question (the issue) and the answer (your main claim). Try writing both down, making sure to phrase your main issue as a question and your main claim as the answer. After deciding that his main issue would be "To what extent does the story actually deal with the *arrival* of letters from the dead?," Dylan wound up expressing his answer (his main claim) this way:

> When people first start reading Rachel Kadish's story "Letters Arrive from the Dead," they probably assume that the title will be an adequate guide to this text. After they finish reading, a number of them might still assume the title is relevant to the story's contents. But actually the story does not spend much time on the event that the title refers to. Kadish gives more emphasis to the *non*-arrival of letters from the dead. To me, the term *arrival* means that the living receive and understand the messages that the dead send them. In most of the events that the story describes, though, this does not happen. Kadish stresses failures of communication between the dead and those who are still alive.

Audiences usually want evidence, and as we noted earlier, most arguments you write about in literature will need to cite details of the work itself. Because direct quotation is usually an effective move, Dylan planned to elaborate his claim by citing several of Kadish's references to failures of communication. Remember, though, that you need to be selective with the words you quote, leaving plenty of space for your analysis of the author's language. In particular, Dylan had to explain his definition of *arrival*.

IDENTIFY YOUR ASSUMPTIONS

Often, when you think about particular challenges of your paper, you need think about your assumptions. Remember that a big category of assumptions is warrants; these are what lead you to call certain things evidence for your claims. Dylan knew that one of his warrants was an assumption about Kadish herself — that she was deliberately encouraging her reader to question her title. Rarely will your paper need to admit all the warrants on which it relies. Most of the time, your task will be to guess which warrants your readers want stated. Dylan felt there was at least one warrant he would have to spell out — his belief that the term *arrival* is open to interpretation, for it can be defined in various ways.

DETERMINE YOUR ORGANIZATION

To make sure their texts seem organized and demonstrate the process of reasoning, most writers first write an **outline**, a list of their key points in the order they will appear. Outlines are indeed a good idea, but bear in mind that there are various kinds. One popular type, which you may already know, is the **sentence outline**. As the name implies, it lists the writer's key points in sentence form. Its advantages are obvious: this kind of outline forces you to develop a detailed picture of your argument's major steps, and it leaves you with sentences you can then incorporate into your paper. Unfortunately, however, sentence outlines tend to discourage flexibility. Because they demand a lot of thought and energy, you may hesitate to revise them, even if you come to feel your paper would work better with a new structure.

A second, equally familiar outline is the **topic outline**, a list in which the writer uses a few words to signify the main subjects that he or she will discuss. Because it is sketchy, this kind of outline allows writers to go back and change plans if necessary. Nevertheless, a topic outline may fail to provide all the guidance a writer needs.

A **rhetorical purpose outline** is one we find useful. As with the first two, you list the major sections of your paper. Next, you briefly indicate two things for each section: the effect you want it to have on your audience and how you will achieve that effect. Here is the rhetorical purpose outline that Dylan devised for his paper.

INTRODUCTION

The audience needs to know the text I'll discuss.	I'll identify Kadish's story.
The audience must know my main issue.	I'll point out that readers must determine how its title relates to the content of the story.
The audience must know my main claim.	I'll argue that the story actually emphasizes failures of communication between the dead and the living.

ANALYSIS OF THE STORY'S ACTUAL EMPHASIS

The audience needs to see several examples of how letters fail to arrive from the dead, with *arrival* defined as reception and understanding.	I will go step-by-step through each section of the story, noting how most of them show *non*-arrival. I will also make my definition of *arrival* clear.

CONCLUSION

The audience may want me to speculate *why* Kadish would give her story a misleading title.	I will say that Kadish perhaps wished for her readers to realize that the dead can't really communicate with the living, even as we might hope they could.

For your own rhetorical purpose outlines, you may want to use phrases rather than sentences. If you do use sentences, as Dylan did, you do not have to write all that many. Note that Dylan wrote relatively few as he stated the effects he would aim for and his strategies for achieving those effects. Thus, he was not tremendously invested in preserving his original outline. He felt free to change it if it failed to prove helpful.

Strategies for Composing

Composing is not always distinguishable from exploring, planning, and revising. As you prepare for your paper, you may jot down words or whole sentences. Once you begin a draft, you may alter that draft several different ways before you complete it. You may be especially prone to making changes in drafts if you use a computer, for word processing enables you to jump around in your text, revisiting and revising what you have written.

Still, most writers feel that doing a draft is an activity in its own right, and a major one at that. The next chapter presents various tips for writing about specific genres, and Chapter 7 discusses writing research-based papers. Meanwhile, here are some tips to help you with composing in general.

DECIDE ON A TITLE

You may be inclined to let your **title** be the same as the text you discuss. Were you to write about Kadish's story, you would be calling your own paper "Letters Arrive from the Dead." But often such mimicry backfires. For one thing, it may lead your readers to think that you are unoriginal and perhaps even lazy. Also, you risk confusing your audience, since your paper would actually be about Kadish's story, rather than being the story itself. So take the time to come up with a title of your own. Certainly it may announce the text you will focus on, but let it do more. In particular, use your title to indicate the main claim you will be making. With just a few words, you can preview the argument to come.

MAKE CHOICES ABOUT YOUR STYLE

Perhaps you have been told to "sound like yourself" when you write. Yet that can be a difficult demand (especially if you are not sure what your self is really like). Above all, the **style** you choose depends on your audience and purpose.

In writing an argument for a general audience, probably you would do best to avoid the extremes of pomposity and breezy informality. Try to stick with words you know well, and if you do want to use some that are only hazily familiar to you, check their dictionary definitions first.

At some point, probably all of us have been warned not to use *I* in our writing. In the course you are taking, however, you may be asked to write about your experiences. If so, you will find *I* hard to avoid. Whether to use it becomes a real question when you get assignments like Dylan's, which require you chiefly to make an argument about a text. Since you are supposed to focus on that text, your readers may be disconcerted if you keep referring to yourself. Even so, you need not assume that your personal life is irrelevant to your paper. Your opening paragraph might refer to your personal encounters with the text as a way of establishing the issue you will discuss. A personal anecdote might serve as a forceful conclusion to your paper. Moreover, before you reach the conclusion, you might orient your readers to the structure of your paper by using certain expressions that feature the word *I*: for example, *As I suggested earlier, As I have noted, As I argue later*. In general, you may be justified in saying *I* at certain moments. When tempted to use this pronoun, though, consider whether it is your best move.

Arguments about literature are most compelling when supported by quotations, but be careful not to quote excessively. If you constantly repeat others' words, providing few of your own, your readers will hardly get a sense of you as an author. Moreover, an essay full of quotation marks is hard to read. Make sure to quote selectively, remembering that sometimes you can simply paraphrase. When you do quote, try to cite only the words you need. You do not have to reproduce a whole line or sentence if a word or two is enough to support your point.

When summarizing what happens in a literary work, be careful not to shift tenses as you go along. Your reader may be confused if you shift back and forth between past and present. We suggest that you stick primarily to the present tense, which is the tense that literary critics customarily employ. For example, instead of saying that the clerk in Kadish's story *rejected* some letters and packages, say that he *rejects* them.

DRAFT AN INTRODUCTION

As a general principle, use your introduction to identify as quickly and efficiently as possible

- the main text that you will analyze;
- the main issue about it that you will address; and
- the main claim that you will develop in response to that issue.

Don't waste time with grand philosophical statements such as "Society doesn't always mourn the dead properly," or "Over the centuries, much literature has been about life and death," or "Rachel Kadish is one of those writers who has great powers of imagination."

Remember that your main issue should be a significant question with no obvious answer. Try using one or more of the following strategies to establish that issue at the start of your essay:

- **State the issue as a question.** For example: "How well does Kadish's title account for the story's actual content?"
- **Apply a word like *puzzling, confusing, mysterious*, or *curious* to whatever feature your issue will be about.** For example: "The relationship between the story's title and its contents is more puzzling than we may first expect."
- **Through personal reference, state that you were first puzzled by a particular feature of the work but are now able to interpret it.** For example: "At first, I wondered how seriously I was supposed to take the title 'Letters Arrive from the Dead,' but I've come to realize that we should see it as ironic, because much of the story does not clearly show scenes of 'arrival.'"
- **Indicate that you aim to help other readers of the work, who may have trouble understanding the feature of it you will focus on.** For example: "Quite a few readers of Kadish's story may have difficulty applying her title to it. There is, however, a possible explanation for this title: she means us to take it ironically."
- **Indicate that you will express disagreement with existing or possible interpretations.** For example: "While some readers of Kadish's story may feel that its title fits its content well, a more plausible view is that Kadish is being ironic, for the story emphasizes failures of communication."

LIMIT PLOT SUMMARY

Short stories and plays spin tales, as do many poems and essays. But if you are writing about a literary text that is narrative in form, don't spend much of your paper summarizing the narrative. Developing a genuine argument about the work involves more than simply recounting its plot. Here are strategies you can use to limit this:

- **Assume that your reader knows the basic plot and needs only a few brief reminders of its key elements.**
- **Keep in mind that your main purpose is to put forth, explain, and support a *claim* about the text — your answer to some question you raise about it.**
- **After your introduction, try to begin each new paragraph with a subclaim that helps you develop your main claim.** Use the rest of the paragraph to elaborate and provide evidence for this subclaim. *Don't* begin a paragraph simply by recording a plot incident, for doing so is liable to bog you down in sheer summary.
- **Instead of reciting plot details, write about how the work you are analyzing is *constructed*.** Make observations about

specific methods that the author uses to present the story, including techniques of organization and characterization. For example, rather than saying, "The clerk in Kadish's story expresses suspicion about certain items the dead are trying to mail," state and develop a point like "Kadish chooses not to make the supervisor of the dead's mailings a demon, angel, or god; instead, she depicts him as a bureaucratic official who distrusts some of the customers who appear before him."

- **Instead of turning frequently to plot details, try to linger on some of the author's specific language, exploring possible definitions of particular words.** For example, rather than saying, "The dead people in Kadish's story are at present somewhere between Earth and some higher stage of the afterlife," examine possible implications of the word *village*, the specific term used for their location in the second and fourth paragraphs. *Village* suggests a rural, intimate community, even if the story also shows that a larger bureaucracy controls it.

DECIDE HOW TO REFER TO THE AUTHOR'S LIFE AND INTENTIONS

Be cautious about relating the work to the author's life. Sometimes a certain character within the work may indeed express the author's own views, but don't simply assume that a character speaks for the author. Even the *I* of a first-person story or poem may differ significantly from its creator. True, many literary works are at least somewhat autobiographical, based on one or more aspects of the author's life; nevertheless, even works that are largely autobiographical may not be entirely so. Besides, knowledge of the author's life won't always help you figure out his or her text. Kadish may have derived her story from personal encounters with bureaucracy and from deaths of people she knew, but we must still interpret the particular work she proceeded to write. So:

- **Be careful in linking a work to the author's own circumstances.** Such connections can be legitimate, but the more you push them, the more you may risk distorting the work's exact design. You also risk neglecting the author's artistic achievement. Not everyone who mourns the dead could turn their grief into haunting fiction.

Much of what you write about a literary work will reflect your understanding of its author's intentions. Needless to say, you can't peer into the author's mind. Rather, you'll make hypotheses about the author's aims.

- **Sometimes, at least, admit that you are guessing at what the author thinks.** Often, your reader will assume that you are speculating about the author's aims, but your argument about them can be more persuasive if, at times, you acknowledge that you're trying to come up with the best hypothesis rather than stating an absolute fact. Take care, however, to explain why your guesses are logical.

- **If you suspect that the author might object to your view of the text, feel free to acknowledge such possible disagreements.** In fact, many theorists argue that a literary work may differ from how its author sees it. They refuse, therefore, to treat the author as an absolute authority on the work. D. H. Lawrence's advice was "Trust the tale, not the teller." Even if Lawrence is right, of course, you must show how *your* interpretation of a text manages to make sense of it.
- **Feel free to concede that your analysis of the work isn't the only reasonable one.** You can develop your main claim about a literary work partly by noting and addressing ways in which other readers may disagree with you about it. Bear in mind, though, that you will annoy your own audience if you come across as dogmatic. Be as fair as you can to views different from yours. Actually, your readers will appreciate it if at times you concede that yours is not the only reasonable interpretation. You can even specify one or more alternatives. Of course, you would still try to make a case for *your* explanation, perhaps by saying why it is *more plausible* or *more helpful* than its rivals. But speak of these competitors with respect instead of dismissing them with scorn.

RECOGNIZE AND AVOID LOGICAL FALLACIES

Although arguments presented in literary texts are often not logical, your arguments about these texts should be. Readers do not expect a poem's speaker, for example, to present cogently reasoned arguments to her lover, nor do they expect a lament for the lost passions of youth to be anything but subjective. But different kinds of writing have different conventions. What works in poetry may not be appropriate in an argument. The kinds of serious arguments you are expected to create cannot be successful using heartfelt emotions alone. When you write about literature, shaky thinking might cause your audience to dismiss your ideas. Your claims and the assumptions behind them should be clear and reasoned. If they are not, you might be committing a **fallacy**, a common term for unsound reasoning.

In the next several paragraphs, we discuss typical logical fallacies. Some of them are especially relevant to literary studies, and for all of them we provide examples related to "Letters Arrive from the Dead." We do not want you brooding over this list, seeing it as a catalog of sins to which you might fall prey. If you constantly fear being accused of fallacies, you might be too paralyzed to make claims at all! In our discussion of fallacies, we also identify circumstances in which your audience might *not* object to a particular fallacy. In addition, we suggest how a writer might revise such claims to be more persuasive. Indeed, the main value in studying fallacies is to identify ways you might develop arguments more effectively.

One of the most common fallacies, ***ad hominem*** (Latin: "toward the man"), is probably the easiest to commit because it is the hardest to resist. Instead of doing the hard work of analyzing the claim and the evidence, we simply ignore them and attack the character of the person making the argument. Instead of trying to figure out what is going on in a complex work of literature, we say, "How can you take seriously a story about the afterlives of the dead written by someone who still breathes?" It is best to focus on the message, not the messenger.

Related to this example is the fallacy of **begging the question**. It's a kind of circular reasoning in which the statement being argued is already assumed to have been decided. Our "How can you take seriously . . . " question assumes without proof that living writers can't have sound ideas about what happens after death. You would also be begging the question if, without providing support, you made a debatable claim about a character *within* the text. An example would be your claiming that the clerk in Kadish's story is a sympathetic figure—someone whose perspective we're bound to share. This claim isn't persuasive standing on its own; you need to support it with evidence culled from the text.

Professional historians, mathematicians, and philosophers usually cite other professionals working in their field; that is, they **appeal to authority** to bolster their credibility. Disciplinary knowledge is created by a community of scholars who cite the ideas of its members as evidence for their claims. The warrant is that recognized authorities know what they are talking about. Quoting them is persuasive, but not completely: appeals to authority can also be fallacious. Literary critics, like other thinkers, often disagree. Citing an expert does not conclusively prove your claim. Appealing to a critical authority without giving reasons or evidence is a fallacy because a sound argument would at least have to consider other critics. An argument is a reasoning process in which claims are supported, not simply asserted, even if they come from an expert. Of course, in the case of Kadish's story, there are no experts to cite. The story is too new; it needs more time to seize the attention of veteran interpreters. The risk of relying on just one authority looms more with much analyzed texts: say, poems by Emily Dickinson and Robert Frost. Critics have long debated the meaning of these two authors' works. An essay about a poem of theirs shouldn't ignore such disputes.

A related fallacy involves using quotations from unreliable sources. Although the Internet is often a valuable tool, students sometimes use it without thinking critically. Imagine that you've been assigned to write an essay on "Letters Arrive from the Dead." If you went to Amazon and looked at readers' responses to Rachel Kadish's most recent novel, *The Weight of Ink*, you would find among many positive reactions this complaint: "I felt the author was trying too hard to impress readers with details and vocabulary." You might be tempted to use this comment in your essay, agreeing or disagreeing with it. But because you know nothing about the person who posted it, it's probably not worth including. It's not from a recognized authority; treating it as such damages your own standing.

Equally harmful to the soundness of your argument is to rely too heavily on personal experience as evidence for your claim. Personal experience can sometimes be compelling and authoritative. Indeed, many critics have successfully used their own experiences with discrimination to create cogent arguments. But they rarely rely exclusively on personal experience. Instead, they blend relevant experience with textual and critical specifics. Telling your readers that Kadish's vision of the afterlife is flawed because it doesn't square with your own religious upbringing would be a fallacy.

This example of using personal experience as authority is also unsound because the personal sample is too small to warrant a reasonable conclusion. It is hard to convince your audience if you claim too much based on limited experience. Imagine someone's arguing that Kadish's story exposes the foolishness of religious belief. This would be the fallacy of **hasty generalization**. Simply claiming less would improve the argument. For example, one might argue that what the story critiques is a particular form of grief: the living's hope of connecting *somehow* with the dead.

Another common fallacy is ***post hoc, ergo propter hoc*** (from Latin: "After this, therefore because of this"). Few of us escape this error in cause and effect. Many superstitions probably began because of this fallacy. A man breaks a mirror and bad luck follows. Did the mirror cause the bad luck? Logic says no, but the next day he breaks a leg, and a week later his car is stolen. The coincidence is often too tempting to resist. Does smoking marijuana lead to hard drugs? Logic says no, since you could argue just as plausibly that almost anything (carrots, beer, coffee) that comes before could be said to cause what comes after. Unless a clear, logical link between the two events is demonstrated, you might be accused of the *post hoc* fallacy.

In writing about "Letters Arrive from the Dead," you might want to argue that the clerk's "practiced skepticism" (para. 7) results from the dead's many attempts to mail banned words and goods. But perhaps the clerk had a skeptical nature before he took his job, and even got the job because of it. A sounder argument would focus on cause-effect relations that find more support in the text. You might contend, for instance, that the dead's current behavior reflects emotional issues they weren't able to resolve while alive.

Most of us commit a version of the **intentional fallacy** when we defend ourselves against someone we offended by saying, "That's not what I meant; it was just a joke." The problem arises because we are not always able to carry out our intentions. Perhaps our language is not precise enough, or perhaps our intention to be sincere or honest or witty gets mixed up with other intentions we have to sound intelligent, confident, or impressive. Students are often surprised when teachers tell them that a writer's stated intentions cannot be taken as the final word on a work's meaning. "Langston Hughes knows his poem better than anyone else" is an understandable retort. But that might not be the case. Hughes might not be the most astute interpreter of his writing. He may not be fully aware of all he intended.

You would also be committing an intentional fallacy if you argued that we're supposed to feel sorry for the dead in Kadish's story because in other writing of hers, she's called for preserving letters that might otherwise be lost. In a 2012 blog post for the literary journal *Ploughshares*, Kadish did wish for "a single vault" that would keep "all the unrequited love letters in the world." But this blog entry wouldn't prove anything about "Letters Arrive from the Dead." Kadish's post might be nice to mention in your essay, but your argument would need the support of details from the story itself.

When you try to destroy an argument that few people are likely to make, you are attacking a **straw man**. You could be accused of this fallacy if, for instance, you criticized readers who think Kadish stupidly neglected to mention the possibility of *e-mails* from the dead. It's unlikely that many in her audience would level such a charge. A straw man fallacy is also at work when you distort someone else's argument. Imagine a student who feels that the clerk in Kadish's story could be kinder toward the dead. You'd be guilty of exaggeration — that is, of creating a straw man — if you said that the student considered the clerk a monster.

A favorite tactic of traditionalists trying to hold the line against change, the **slippery slope** fallacy is used to claim that if we allow one thing to happen, then slipping into catastrophe is just around the corner. If we do not prevent students from wearing fashions influenced by gangsta rap, gangs will eventually roam the hallways; if we allow the morning-after pill, sexual anarchy will follow. A small step is seen as precipitating an avalanche.

The following claim by a student anticipates something that simply is not logically called for: "Although Kadish probably means well, her depiction of the dead encourages the living to hold the absurd belief that their dead loved ones still exist and are trying to communicate with them. Stories like hers will lead us to stick with all sorts of superstitions we're better off dropping." Again, claiming less improves the argument: "Kadish's vivid depiction of the dead's efforts to communicate suggest that the dead themselves are still alive in some important sense."

We are all guilty at times of the fallacy of **oversimplification** — of not seeing the inevitable complexity of things. At the risk of committing a hasty generalization ourselves, it is probably the case that your instructor will be impressed if you look for complexity in literary texts and in your arguments. Seeing complexity is a consequence of hard thinking. There are rarely two sides to a question. More likely, there are a dozen plausible and reasonable perspectives. The cliché that the truth often appears in shades of gray rather than in black and white gets at the idea that simple solutions are often the result of shallow thinking.

Complexity is not what the following claim reveals: "Kadish's story is about the dead's wish to send messages to the living, and as can happen here on Earth, their letters sometimes fail to reach the intended destination." Being exposed to other viewpoints in class discussions and in peer-group revision can help this student avoid oversimplifying the experiences Kadish evokes, which touch on issues of mortality, grief, resentment, bureaucracy, and communication. When Henry David Thoreau, the author of *Walden* (1854), urged his contemporaries to live simply, he was talking about their lifestyles, not their thinking.

Non sequitur is a general catchall fallacy that means "it does not follow." Some principle of logic has been violated when we make a claim that the evidence cannot support. In "Letters Arrive from the Dead," it does not follow that because some packages sent by the dead include "samples of tea" (para. 4), many of the dead want to provide the living with comforting treats. In the same sentence, actually, we learn that a number of the dead send "admonishments" and "rebukes" (para. 4). Even those who mail tea might have done so simply because they have a few bags of it lying around. Revising this fallacy, like many of the others, involves setting aside time in the revision process to look again at your claims and the assumptions behind them, carefully and objectively making a clear connection between your claim and the evidence you say supports it.

FIRST DRAFT OF A STUDENT PAPER

The following is Dylan's first complete draft of his paper. Eventually, he revised this draft after a group of classmates reviewed it and after he reflected further on it herself. For the moment, though, read this first version, and decide what you would have said to him about it.

Dylan Rieff
Professor Houghton
English 102
4 March - - - -
Letters *Don't* Arrive from the Dead
When people first start reading Rachel Kadish's story "Letters Arrive from the Dead," they probably assume that the title will be an adequate guide to this text. After they finish reading, a number of them might still assume the title is relevant to the story's contents. But actually the story does not spend much time on the event that the title refers to. Kadish gives more emphasis to the *non*-arrival of letters from the dead. To me, the term *arrival* means that the living receive and understand the messages that the dead send them. In most of the events that the story describes, though, this does not happen. Kadish stresses failures of communication between the dead and those who are still alive.

The first paragraph of the story begins by directly echoing the title. In this particular instance, the words "letters arrive from the dead" turn out to be a fairly appropriate lead-in, for the rest of the paragraph implies that the dead succeed in conveying messages to the living. Yet already Kadish complicates this idea somewhat. The delivery of the messages involves lying to the recipients or at least misleading them, through falsely-dated postmarks or through stamps that come "from improbable places." This deception is rampant enough that the dead are known as "notorious fibbers." So, even if a message arrives, the truth often doesn't arrive along with it. This common outcome encourages us as readers to reconsider our traditional assumptions about what the "arrival" of a letter entails.

The next paragraph doesn't actually focus on letters, but it does bring up the subject of messages that are either not sent or are not successfully conveyed to their intended receivers. The means of delivery referred to here are physical acts through which the dead attempt to affect the living, including acts that the dead intend to be harmful. The narrator reports that such conduct doesn't accomplish what the dead hope it will: "their gestures are ineffective" (par. 2). Their failed actions range from "a brief whisper that goes unheard in a noisy setting" to a hurled brick "that nonetheless misses" (par. 2). Moreover, the dead suffer "draining fatigue," "inner ear problems," and "aching joints" when they try to punish the living in these ways. So, "most choose not to" (par. 2) engage in this behavior at all. The paragraph even ends by noting "the futility of such modes of communication" (par. 2). A phrase like this seems quite at odds with the title "Letters Arrive from the Dead," which implies success rather than failure.

The next section moves to the post office where the dead's letters are inspected by a clerk who decides whether to give them a stamp of approval. This section continues to undermine the story's title by telling us that the letters are subject to censorship, a situation that leads the dead to leave things out of them. These omissions result in the letters' becoming "opaque" (par. 4), a word that suggests the letters' recipients have trouble understanding them. Contributing to the lack of clarity is the dead's unwillingness in the first place to admit "the literal truth of their dull status in this transit village" (par. 4). Despite the story's title, therefore, it is hard for a reader to believe that genuine communication between the dead and the living is occurring. It is very significant that the one specific message quoted in the story, *Wish you were here*" (par. 4), is ambiguous. These words can be interpreted as sincere ("I really miss you") or sarcastic ("I'd love it if you were dead like I am"). We can't really say in this case that a message has "arrived," at least if we consider the word *arrival* to mean not just the physical receiving of a message but also the receiver's mental comprehension of it.

The next section focuses more on the living than the story has done so far. Although the title "Letters Arrive from the Dead" implies that we'll read a lot about what happens when the living get the letters, the story mostly pays attention to the feelings, aims, and experiences of the dead people who send them. When, as in this section, the story does turn to the living, the emphasis is still on *lack* of clear communication. In one hypothetical example, a living person isn't sure whether he or she has received "a warning from the other side" (par. 6). We're also told that in many instances, the living are mistaken about who sent the message. They make "attributions that are often inaccurate" (par. 6). Given problems like these, the dead wind up "feeling at times maligned, even plagiarized" (par. 6).

The story then turns to the problems that the dead sometimes face in trying to get their messages and shipments approved by the post office clerk. This person reminds the dead about various restrictions on the correspondence they hope to have with the living. Even if they've chosen to forget these barriers, it's still the case that "Certain things are not permitted: hazardous materials, messages that violate confidentiality laws" (par. 7). The main point of view in the section is that of the clerk, who "makes no complaint" (par. 8) but is obviously annoyed by how pushy and whiny the dead are in their frustration: *"Why was she served before me? I wasn't told my letter would be censored. My package is but a small one; it contains no harmful objects; it contains nothing that would harm a soul"* (par. 7). Overall, the emphasis of the section is by no means on arrival. Instead, we learn about the dead's difficulties in getting their mailings off at all.

The final paragraph very much calls attention to *non*-arrival of letters. The narrator reports that occasionally "a message is returned to sender, unopened" (par. 11). Presumably this happens for one of two reasons: either the recipient isn't at the place where the message was sent, or the recipient is uninterested in looking at the message (perhaps out of dislike for the sender). Either way, arrival doesn't occur, if we take *arrival* to mean that the message reaches its intended reader and is also examined by that person. The sender, to whom the message is returned, is understandably frustrated and sad. The other dead people at the post office, who are evidently often engaged in "bickering," are moved to feel at least some compassion for this unfortunate person whose letter has come back: they "part in silence, to make way for the bereaved" (par. 11). Commonly the word "bereaved" is applied to living people who are mourning the passing of a loved one. Here, ironically, the word describes a dead person who is grieving over his or her inability to make contact with the living.

By concluding with this irony, Rachel Kadish reinforces the impression that her title is deliberately misleading. She *hasn't* written a story that focuses on how "Letters Arrive from the Dead." In fact, the narrator points out various ways in which the opposite is true. Often the dead don't let the truth be delivered. Their physical attempts to affect the living prove to be so useless that they give them up. Many times, the living can't figure out a message sent to them by the dead, or they make a wrong guess about who the sender is. The dead encounter restrictions on what they hope to send. Letters may come back to them, either not received or not read. Kadish's undercutting of her title might be a message that she's giving her own readers: *stop* yearning for contact from the dead, because they're permanently out of reach. Despite our hope of somehow communicating with them, no letters from them will arrive.

Strategies for Revising

Most first drafts are far from perfect. Even experienced professional writers have to revise their work. Besides making changes on their own, many of them solicit feedback from others. In various workplaces, writing is collaborative, with coauthors exchanging ideas as they try to improve a piece. Remain open to the possibility that your draft needs changes, perhaps several. Of course, you are more apt to revise extensively if you have given yourself enough time. Conversely, you will not feel able to change much of your paper if it is due the next day. You will also limit your ability to revise if you work only with your original manuscript, scribbling possible changes between the lines. This practice amounts to conservatism, for it encourages you to keep passages that really ought to be overhauled.

You may have trouble, however, improving a draft if you are checking many things at once. Therefore, read the draft repeatedly, looking at a different aspect each time. A good way to begin is to outline the paper you have written and then compare that outline with your original one. If the two outlines differ, your draft may or may not need adjusting; perhaps you were wise to swerve from your original plan. In any case, you should ponder your departures from that plan, considering whether they were for the best.

If, like Dylan, you are writing an argument paper, our Checklist for Revising box has some topics and questions you might apply as you review your first draft. Some of these considerations overlap. Nevertheless, take them in turn rather than all at once.

≡ A CHECKLIST FOR REVISING

Logic

- Will my audience see that the issue I am focusing on is indeed an issue?

- Will the audience follow the logic of my argument?

- Is the logic as persuasive as it might be? Is there more evidence I can provide? Do I need to identify more of my assumptions?

- Have I addressed all of my audience's potential concerns?

Organization

- Does my introduction identify the issue that I will focus on? Does it state my main claim?

- Will my audience detect and follow the stages of my argument?

- Does the order of my paragraphs seem purposeful, rather than arbitrary?

- Have I done all I can to signal connections within and between sentences? Within and between paragraphs?

- Have I avoided getting bogged down in mere summary?

- Will my conclusion satisfy readers? Does it leave any key questions dangling?

Clarity

- Does my title offer a good preview of my argument?

- Are each of my sentences immediately clear?

- Am I sure how to define each word that I have used?

Emphasis

- Have I put key points in prominent places?

- Have I worded each sentence for maximum impact? In particular, is each sentence as concise as possible? Do I use active verbs whenever I can?

Style

- Are my tone and level of vocabulary appropriate?

- Will my audience think me fair-minded? Should I make any more concessions?

- Do I use any repeated phrases or mannerisms that may distract my readers?

- Have I used any expressions that may annoy or offend?

- Is there anything else I can do to make my paper more readable and interesting?

Grammar

- Is each of my sentences grammatically correct?

- Have I punctuated properly?

Physical Appearance

- Have I followed the proper format for quotations, notes, and bibliography?

- Are there any typographical errors?

We list these considerations from most to least important. When revising a draft, think first about matters of logic, organization, and clarity. There is little point in fixing the grammar of particular sentences if you are going to drop them later because they fail to advance your argument.

As we noted, a group of Dylan's classmates discussed his draft, as well as his main issue and claim. They appreciated how specific he was in pointing out contradictions between the story's title and its content. Still, Dylan received several suggestions for improving his paper. He decided to implement these:

1. **He should arrange his observations in the order of their importance for his argument.** Dylan's first draft followed the structure of Kadish's story. He discussed the story's sections in the order that Kadish had written them. He could see that this method of organizing bored readers; it struck them as plodding and rote. It also didn't make clear to them the steps in his reasoning. They couldn't determine the role each part of the story played in developing his main claim. They agreed with him that the story's "*Wish you were here*" part is, as he calls it, "very significant." After all, this is a message that does seem to arrive; it's the biggest challenge to Dylan's idea that the story is about *non*-arrival. Given that it's a major test for his claim, Dylan's readers felt he should discuss this section at the *climax* of his essay. They thought his treatment of "*Wish you were here*" should go *there*.

2. **He should explain more often—indeed, throughout his essay—what the word *arrival* means to him.** Dylan's argument hinges on his definition of *arrival*, which complicates literal

meanings of this term. His draft at times explains how he's interpreting it. Yet his readers wanted more. Because not everyone defines the word as he does, they thought that he should regularly make clear his take on it.

3. **His conclusion should spend more time considering *why* Kadish would give her story a misleading title.** In the last paragraph of his draft, Dylan guesses *why* Kadish turns "Letters Arrive from the Dead" into a story about *non*-arrival. But his hypothesis is so brief that it disappointed his readers. Because a story's title and contents are usually in sync, they wanted more speculation about why Kadish makes them clash. They thought Dylan didn't need to be sure of her purpose. He could even offer more than one guess. Perhaps she had multiple reasons for giving her story a title that doesn't match what happens in it.

REVISED DRAFT OF A STUDENT PAPER

In accepting these suggestions, Dylan knew he would need to change his essay a lot. He would have to cut or rearrange parts of his first draft. He would have to add analysis and explanation. Here is the revision Dylan wrote. In its margins are comments by us that call your attention to his strategies.

Dylan Rieff
Professor Houghton
English 102
18 March ____

Letters *Don't* Arrive from the Dead

When people first start reading Rachel Kadish's story "Letters Arrive from the Dead," they probably think the title will be an adequate guide to this text. After they finish reading, a number of them might still believe the title is relevant to the story's contents. But actually the story does not spend much time on the event that the title refers to. Kadish gives more emphasis to *non*-arrival of letters from the dead. Some details of the story do relate to *arrival* in the word's literal sense. Certain messages and packages from the dead succeed in physically reaching the living people they're sent to. But *arrival* can have additional meanings, and not all of them fit what the story reports. When we hear that a letter has *arrived*, many of us assume that the recipient is aware of the letter, understands it, and knows who its author is. We tend to suppose, too, that the letter's contents are a truthful record of its writer's experiences, feelings, and thoughts. Much of what happens in Kadish's text, though, is at odds

Immediately identifies the text he'll discuss and a specific feature of it he'll analyze.

Departs from superficial readers to establish own main claim.

Previews the various definitions of arrival that the essay will work with.

with these assumptions. They don't apply to many of the actions that the narrator describes. In this respect, the story isn't about *arrival*. It stresses failures of communication between the dead and the living.

The most obvious example of such failure is in the final paragraph. There, we learn that occasionally "a message is returned to sender, unopened" (par. 11). When this happens, a letter clearly doesn't *arrive*. In a literal sense, it doesn't link up with its intended recipient. Most likely this person isn't at the place where the message was sent. Alternatively, this person has refused to pick up the message and read it, perhaps out of dislike for its sender. Either way, the return of the letter leaves the sender frustrated and sad. The other dead people at the post office sympathize with this unfortunate person whose letter never really *arrived*: they "part in silence, to make way for the bereaved" (par. 11). Commonly the word "bereaved" applies to living people who are mourning the death of a loved one. Here, ironically, it describes the opposite. It's applied to a dead person who is grieving over his or her inability to make literal contact with the living.

The dead also face hassles when trying to mail letters and packages in the first place. As the post office clerk reminds them, "Certain things are not permitted: hazardous materials, messages that violate confidentiality laws" (par. 7). With restrictions like these, it can be hard for people to send correspondence, let alone ensure that it reaches its destination. No wonder some of the dead whine complaints to the clerk like *"I wasn't told my letter would be censored. My package is but a small one; it contains no harmful objects; it contains nothing that would harm a soul"* (par. 7). Overall, this section of the story is by no means about arrival. Instead, we learn about the dead's problems in getting their mailings off at all.

A similar struggle comes up as a subject elsewhere in the story. As early as the second paragraph, the narrator mentions failed attempts by the dead to intervene physically in the living world. They make "gestures" that turn out to be "ineffective" (par. 2). These actions range from "a brief whisper that goes unheard in a noisy setting" to a hurled brick "that nonetheless misses" (par. 2). Unsuccessful efforts like these leave the dead ailing in body as well as mind. They suffer "draining fatigue," "inner ear problems," "aching joints" (par. 2). Their disappointment and sheer pain lead the majority of the dead to accept defeat. Resigning themselves

Starts with the obvious before moving to deeper reading.

Points out the particular definition of arrival that the essay is using at this stage.

Close analysis of the text's own particular language.

Transition to a related section of the story.

Another transition to related parts.

to "the futility of such modes of communication," they abandon the idea "of visiting the living in altered form" (par. 2). Despite the story's title, this paragraph hardly emphasizes *arrival*. Again, in the most obvious sense of the word, the *arrival* of a message depends upon its being sent to begin with. When the dead quit trying to maintain a physical presence in the earthly world, *arrival* can't be said to occur. Nor does it seem to happen if we assume that the *arrival* of a message entails its intended receiver's awareness of its delivery. In this story, the living are oblivious to the dead's whisper and brick.

Signals a broadening of definitions.

When we say that a letter has *arrived*, many of us are also assuming that the recipient comprehends what it says. On the other hand, we're reluctant to declare that *arrival* has taken place if the recipient finds the message impossible to decode. In Kadish's story, the dead's letters to the living baffle their intended audience. Because the letters are subject to censorship, the dead leave things out of them in the first place, thereby doing the censor's work in advance. While these omissions may please authorities in the afterlife, the gaps they leave make the letters "opaque" (par. 4). For their earthly readers, clarity doesn't come, even if the letters reach their destination.

Points out another definition of arrival that the story complicates or undercuts.

The story does begin by directly echoing the title. The very first sentence starts off with the words "When letters arrive from the dead," and the rest of the opening paragraph implies that the dead succeed in conveying messages to the living. Yet already Kadish complicates this claim. The delivery of the messages involves lying to the recipients or deliberately misleading them, through falsely-dated postmarks or through stamps that come "from improbable places." This deception is rampant enough that the dead are known as "notorious fibbers" (par. 1). Later on, we learn that the dead are unwilling to admit "their dull status in this transit village" (par. 4). Such deception doesn't support the term *arrival*, at least if the *arrival* of a message means it conveys what the sender actually knows or thinks. Of course, not everyone would define *arrival* this way. Most of the time, however, we start off reading a letter with the assumption that its writer is being honest.

Acknowledges that not everything in the story confirms the essay's main claim.

Explains how the main claim can still apply.

The narrator of the story quotes one particular message that isn't necessarily false: "*Wish you were here*" (par. 4). Even so, its readers have trouble interpreting it: "what lies beneath these four words? What deeper meaning may be intuited?" (par. 5). It is very significant that the only specific example of a message in the story turns out to be ambiguous.

Saves this part of the story for the essay's climax, because on the surface it seems to challenge the main claim.

The words can be read as sincere ("I really miss you") or sarcastic ("I'd love it if you were dead like I am"). A third possibility is that the message-writer is willfully trying to puzzle the recipient. This would be ambiguity as sadism. A reader of the message might also wonder how interested the writer is in making meaningful contact. After all, the writer has sent not a letter, but just a postcard; "*Wish you were here*" is not an original statement but a clichéd one that vacationers send back home. Whatever hypothesis we make, we can't really say in this case that a message has "arrived," at least if we consider the word *arrival* to mean not just the physical receiving of a message but also the receiver's mental comprehension of it. The problem is even worse when the recipient can't even be certain what kind of message it is or who sent it. The narrator mentions times when a living person isn't sure whether he or she has received "a warning from the other side" (par. 6). We're also told that in many instances, the living are mistaken about their correspondent; they make "attributions that are often inaccurate" (par. 6). *Arrival* is simply not a good term for such *lack* of communication.

A close reading of Rachel Kadish's story reveals it to be one that *doesn't* focus on how "Letters Arrive from the Dead." In fact, the narrator points out various ways in which the opposite is true. Why, though, does Kadish undercut her title? What message is she aiming to give her readers by subverting it? Perhaps, as I've been suggesting, she wants us to consider the various ways that *arrival* can be defined. Or, perhaps she is nudging us to *stop* yearning for contact from the dead, because they're permanently out of reach. Alternatively, she may be inviting us to consider the chance that the afterlife is much like life on earth, in the sense that the dead experience the same impulses and frustrations as the living do. Given that her own story is, in a way, a "letter" to her readers, Kadish may be using it to ponder the difficulties in communication that she and other writers often face in trying to connect with their audiences. Multiple interpretations of her aims seem possible, and her reader can entertain more than one. But any interpretation will have to confront how her title is misleading about her story's contents. In major respects, letters from the dead *don't* arrive.

Uses the essay's conclusion to consider the author's aims, not just to recap the essay's argument.

To us, Dylan's revision is more persuasive, coherent, and compelling than his first draft. In particular, he has made the steps in his reasoning clearer and tracked his definitions of *arrival* better. Nevertheless, we would hesitate to call this revision the definitive version of his paper. Maybe you have thought of things Dylan could do to make it even more effective. In presenting his two drafts, we mainly want to emphasize the importance of revision. We hope, too, that you will remember our specific tips as you work on your own writing.

Strategies for Writing a Comparative Paper

Much writing about literature *compares* two or more texts. After all, you can gain many insights into a text by noting how it resembles and differs from others. But in this section we offer specific advice for writing a comparative paper, a task you may be assigned in your course. We also present a sample paper that models strategies of comparative writing.

To aid our discussion, we ask that you read the following two poems. The first, "Two Trees," appears in the 2009 verse collection *Rain* by Don Paterson (b. 1963), a Scottish writer who is also a jazz musician, a professor at the University of St. Andrews, and the poetry editor for the publisher Picador Macmillan. Next comes "Regarding History," a poem from the 2005 book *Trill & Mordent* by Luisa A. Igloria (b. 1961), a Filipina American writer who is a professor of English and creative writing at Old Dominion University in Norfolk, Virginia.

DON PATERSON

Two Trees

One morning, Don Miguel got out of bed
with one idea rooted in his head:
to graft his orange to his lemon tree.
It took him the whole day to work them free,
lay open their sides, and lash them tight.   5
For twelve months, from the shame or from the fright
they put forth nothing; but one day there appeared
two lights in the dark leaves. Over the years
the limbs would get themselves so tangled up
each bough looked like it gave a double crop,   10
and not one kid in the village didn't know
the magic tree in Miguel's patio.

The man who bought the house had had no dream
so who can say what dark malicious whim
led him to take his axe and split the bole   15
along its fused seam, and then dig two holes.
And no, they did not die from solitude;
nor did their branches bear a sterile fruit;
nor did their unhealed flanks weep every spring

for those four yards that lost them everything   20
as each strained on its shackled root to face
the other's empty, intricate embrace.
They were trees, and trees don't weep or ache or shout.
And trees are all this poem is about.   *[2009]*

LUISA A. IGLORIA

Regarding History

A pair of trees on one side of the walk, leaning
now into the wind in a stance we'd call involuntary —
I can see them from the kitchen window, as I take meat
out of the oven and hold my palms above the crust, darkened
with burnt sugar. Nailed with cloves, small earth of flesh   5
still smoldering from its furnace. In truth I want to take it
into the garden and bury it in soil. There are times
I grow weary of coaxing music from silence, silence
from the circularity of logic, logic from the artifact.
Then, the possibilities of sunlight are less attractive   10
than baying at the moon. I want to take your face
in my hands, grow sweet from what it tells, tend
how it leans and turns, trellis or vine of morning-glory.
I wish for limbs pared to muscle, to climb away from
chance and all its missed appointments, its half-drunk   15
cups of coffee. Tell me what I'll find, in this
early period at the beginning of a century.
Tell me what I'll find, stumbling into a boat
and pushing off into the year's last dark hours.   *[2005]*

LIST SIMILARITIES AND DIFFERENCES

A class like yours sensed value in comparing Paterson's poem with Igloria's. So the students proceeded to brainstorm lists of specific similarities and differences—something you might do to start analyzing texts you bring together. For these two poems, the class came up with the following comparisons:

SIMILARITIES

In both poems, a real pair of trees plays a prominent role, and their relation to each other seems important.

Both poems describe labor. In Paterson's, it's the labor of joining and then separating the trees; in Igloria's, it's the labor of cooking, burying, coaxing, climbing, and "pushing off."

The word *limbs* appears in both poems.

Both poems contain many words that have negative connotations. Paterson's poem includes such words as *shame, fright, dark malicious whim, die, sterile, unhealed, weep, strained, shackled, empty,* and *ache*, while Igloria's poem includes such words as *darkened, burnt, nailed, bury, weary, missed,* and *dark*.

More specifically, both poems contain words associated with death.

Both poems refer to the time frame of a year, with Paterson's mentioning "twelve months" and Igloria's concluding with "the year's last dark hours."

DIFFERENCES

The speaker in Igloria's poem uses first person, indicated by the pronoun *I*, while the speaker in Paterson's poem is no specific, identifiable person.

Paterson's poem does, however, name a particular character (Don Miguel) and refers to several other people (kids in the village, the man who chopped apart the trees), while the only people in Igloria's poem seem to be "I" and "you."

Paterson's poem centers on a particular image, the two trees, whereas Igloria's poem has other images besides the pair of trees.

Paterson's poem seems more like a narrative; it tells a story. Igloria's poem seems to be more the expression of the speaker's mood.

While Igloria's speaker is clearly interested in the pair of trees as metaphors for her relationship with "you," Paterson's poem leaves readers to interpret whether and how the two trees have metaphorical implications.

"Two Trees" rhymes, but "Regarding History" does not.

"Regarding History" seems in many respects a love poem, but "Two Trees" is hard to see in that way.

"Two Trees" comments on the fact that it is a poem, but "Regarding History" does not.

"Regarding History" ends with its speaker wanting to know something ("Tell me what I'll find"), but "Two Trees" may leave its *readers* wanting to know something: whether we're supposed to accept its speaker's claim that "trees are all this poem is about."

As you plan your own comparative paper, lists such as these can help you organize your thoughts. To be sure, this class did not immediately think of all the similarities and differences it ended up noting. Usually, going beyond obvious points of comparison is a gradual process, for which you should give yourself plenty of time. Similarly, once you have made lists such as the one above, take time to decide which similarities and differences truly merit your attention. At most, only a few can be part of your paper's main issue and claim.

CONSIDER "WEIGHTING" YOUR COMPARISON

Unfortunately, many students writing a comparative analysis are content to put forth main claims such as these:

> There are many similarities and differences between "Two Trees" and "Regarding History."

> While "Two Trees" and "Regarding History" have many similarities, in many ways they are also different.

> While "Two Trees" and "Regarding History" are different in many ways, they are similar in others.

Several problems arise with these common methods of introducing a comparative paper. For one thing, they give the reader no preview of the specific ideas to come. Indeed, someone who never bothered to read the two poems could have written them, because any two texts are similar in certain ways and different in others. Furthermore, these sorts of claims leave no meaningful and compelling way of organizing the paper. Rather, they encourage the writer to proceed arbitrarily, noting miscellaneous similarities and differences on impulse. More precisely, claims such as these fail to identify the *issue* driving the paper. Why compare Paterson's and Igloria's poems in the first place? Comparison is a means to an end, not an end in itself. What important question is the writer using these two texts to answer? In short, what's at stake?

A more fruitful approach, we think, is to write a *weighted* comparative analysis — that is, an argument chiefly concerned with *one* text more than others. When professional literary critics compare two texts, often they mainly want to answer a question about one of them. They bring in the second text because they believe that doing so helps them address the issue they are raising about their key text. While it's true that a good paper can result even when you treat equally all texts you discuss, you might write a paper that seems more purposeful and coherent if you focus basically on one work, using comparisons to resolve some issue concerning it.

A Student Comparative Paper

The following paper by student Jeremy Cooper demonstrates weighted comparative analysis. The author refers to Igloria's "Regarding History" along with Paterson's "Two Trees," but he is mostly concerned with Paterson's poem. He brings up Igloria's poem not to do comparison for its own sake but to address a question he has about Paterson's text.

Jeremy Cooper

Professor Budnoy

English 102

15 October - - - -

Don Paterson's Criticism of Nature's Owners

Until its last two lines, Don Paterson's poem "Two Trees" tells a fairly straightforward story. The title refers to an orange tree and a lemon tree that stood next to each other on an estate. The speaker in the poem recalls how these trees were treated by two different owners of the property. The first owner, Don Miguel, successfully grafted the trees together. The next owner, a man unnamed by the speaker, separated them with an axe. Given the speaker's clear description of these events, most readers would probably have no trouble understanding what happened to the trees. But the poem's concluding pair of lines is puzzling:

They were trees, and trees don't weep or ache or shout.

And trees are all this poem is about. (lines 23–24)

On the surface, the word "all" seems equivalent to "merely." If this is the case, readers might feel that Paterson is encouraging them to take a limited view of his poem, seeing it as concerned with nothing more than trees. They would then feel *dis*couraged from looking for additional significance or meaning in his text. But this interpretation of Paterson's focus risks making his poem appear relatively trivial, an impression that he surely does not want to create. A likelier possibility is that the speaker is being ironic in his final declaration, stating the word "all" sarcastically. Such a tone might then move readers to question whether the poem is simply about trees. They might feel compelled to consider how its real subject is something else. Indeed, the poem's actual main topic seems to be the regrettable attitudes that human beings take toward nature when they are able to own it.

Trees play a major role in Paterson's poem, as their presence in the title suggests. In the first of the poem's two stanzas, the speaker describes Don Miguel's effort to fuse the orange tree and the lemon tree together, something that he evidently managed to accomplish so well that the trees became hard to distinguish from each other: "the limbs would get themselves so tangled up / each bough looked like it gave a double crop" (9–10). In the second stanza, the speaker turns to describing how the next owner of the trees did the opposite thing to them, splitting them apart (15–16). The poem presents no other scenic feature to compete

Title does not merely repeat title of the poem to be analyzed. moreover, title specifies what aspect of that poem he will examine.

First sentence refers to poem he will focus on, his primary text.

Signals issue that the paper will address.

Introductory paragraph ends by stating the claim about the primary text that the paper will support and develop.

with the two trees for the reader's attention. The speaker just briefly mentions a bed (1), a patio (12), a house (13), and an axe (15).

That the focus is very much on the trees becomes even more apparent if we compare this poem with another in which two trees figure, Luisa A. Igloria's "Regarding History." Igloria's poem begins with "A pair of trees on one side of the walk, leaning / now into the wind in a stance we'd call involuntary" (1–2). Later, the speaker seems to have these two trees still in mind when she says that she wants to hold her lover's face and feel "how it leans and turns, trellis or vine of morning-glory" (13). The close relation of the word "leans" in this line to "leaning" (1) in the earlier one implies that the trees remain a meaningful symbol for her throughout the poem. But, unlike Paterson's speaker, Igloria's turns her thoughts to a number of images other than trees. For example, besides her beloved's face, she thinks of food she has just prepared ("meat / out of the oven" [3–4], which she has evidently "Nailed with cloves" [5]), her garden (7), sunlight (10), the moon (11), muscle (14), coffee (16), and a boat (18). Basically, the two trees in this poem are just part of its many elements. By contrast, the pair of trees in Paterson's poem is much more prominent.

This is a secondary text, which he uses to reinforce the point he has just made about his primary text.

The question then becomes what we as readers should make of their central role in that poem. Some of us may be inclined to see Paterson's trees as a metaphor, their physical existence being less significant than something else they represent. The pair of trees in "Regarding History" seems metaphorical, functioning in the speaker's mind as stand-ins for a human relationship. When she observes that the trees are "leaning / now into the wind in a stance we'd call involuntary" (1–2), she appears to be actually thinking of her relationship with her beloved. Specifically, she seems worried about pressures on their relationship that threaten their ability to keep it steady. This concern of hers comes up again later, when she expresses a desire "to take your face" (11) and "tend / how it leans and turns" (12–13). Here, too, she evidently feels that her connection to her loved one is challenged by outside forces. As in her earlier remark about the trees, she fears that she will not be able to protect her relationship from influences that will make her and her lover do "involuntary" (2) things. In comparison, though, the two trees in Paterson's poem do not appear to have a metaphorical function. In the first place, the speaker of "Two Trees" lacks a distinct personality, so that the poem does not encourage readers to interpret the trees he mentions as

He has identified a possible interpretation but now offers a different one, which he proceeds to argue for.

He uses comparison with his secondary text to support his argument about his primary text.

representing thoughts or feelings of his. Whereas Igloria's speaker dominates "Regarding History" with her clearly marked hopes and concerns, Paterson's speaker writes largely like a reporter narrating news events. Moreover, when he tells what the two property owners did to the trees, he describes these actions so precisely and concretely that he makes it hard for readers to consider the trees as symbolic rather than physical. Also, in such lines as "they did not die from solitude" (17) and "nor did their unhealed flanks weep every spring" (19) the speaker seems to be reminding the reader that they are, in fact, basically vegetation rather than images of something in the human mind. If anything, these lines discourage the reader from interpreting the trees as metaphors.

But if the two trees in Paterson's poem come across mainly as real elements of nature, the attitudes that their owners show toward them are nevertheless significant. Actually, the poem's main subject is not the trees of the title, but the intense and disturbing emotions that drove Don Miguel and the later owner to handle them roughly. The feelings that led the second owner to separate the trees seem villainous. The speaker suggests that this man "had had no dream" (13) but instead acted on some mysterious "dark malicious whim" that compelled him to "split" them apart (14–15), leaving their flanks "unhealed" (19) and their roots "shackled" (21). This language gives the impression of a plantation owner in the pre–Civil War American South, the type of person who cruelly divided slave families and kept their members separated in bondage. Because the poem ends with the physical stress inflicted upon the trees by their second owner, some readers may be more bothered by this man's behavior than they are by Don Miguel's. They might even appreciate Don Miguel's interest in uniting the trees, especially because his labor resulted in the heartening picture of "two lights in the dark leaves" (8). But the language used to describe his actions, too, is mostly negative. The words "lay open" (5), "lash them tight" (5), "shame" (6), "fright" (6), and "tangled up" (9) imply traumatic destruction, even rape, rather than blissful harmony. In his willingness to manipulate the trees, Don Miguel therefore seems no better than the man who replaced him. Furthermore, Don Miguel's behavior toward the trees did not have the excuse of being carefully thought out and planned. He simply awoke "with one idea rooted in his head: / to graft his orange to his lemon tree" (2–3). Just as the word "Don" in the first line is an indication that he is a man of power in his community, so the repetition of the word "his" in this line suggests that he

He is working with the claim he put forth in his introduction.

Again, he acknowledges the possibility of an interpretation different from his before advancing his view.

felt able to perform surgery on the trees merely because he owned them. Both of the men in the poem avoided thinking of what was best for the trees. Instead, both preferred to exercise the authority they had as possessors of the trees, no matter how abusive their handling of the trees might be. The speaker in Igloria's poem calls attention to what she currently *lacks* or is *unable* to do, through statements like "I want to take your face" (11), "I wish for limbs pared to muscle" (14), and "Tell me what I'll find" (18). Furthermore, she does not possess the two trees that figure in "Regarding History." Rather, she is a mere observer of them: "I can see them from the kitchen window" (3). In Paterson's poem, on the other hand, Don Miguel and the second man treat their trees violently and are able to do so because the trees are legally theirs.

Once more, he uses comparison with his secondary text to reinforce his argument about his primary text.

Paterson does not end his poem by directly indicating what he thinks is the proper way of treating trees like those of his title. He does not clearly offer some sort of prescription for their care. Many readers may, nevertheless, come away from the poem concluding that human beings should avoid tampering with trees and, more generally, should leave nature alone as often as possible. In any case, Paterson's central purpose seems to be to make us more aware that when humans own some of nature, they may treat it arrogantly, whether in the pursuit of unity (Don Miguel's aim when he fuses the trees) or separation (the second man's goal when he breaks them apart).

He suggests that this interpretation is possible but that he is more interested in getting his readers to accept his main claim about the poem: the idea he returns to in his final sentence.

Jeremy gains much from comparing "Two Trees" with "Regarding History." In paragraph 3, the analysis of the modest role that trees play in Igloria's poem bolsters Jeremy's claim that they are the core of Paterson's poem. In paragraph 4, the discussion of how Igloria uses trees as metaphors strengthens Jeremy's point that Paterson's trees are literal. In paragraph 5, the observation that Igloria's speaker is *not* an owner of trees helps Jeremy stress that Paterson's men possess them. Obviously, though, Jeremy focuses his paper on Paterson's poem, not on both. By concentrating chiefly on "Two Trees," he enables himself to develop a tight and logical argument, whereas focusing on both poems would encourage him to roam through similarities and differences at random.

Perhaps you know the advice usually given about how to organize a comparative paper. Traditionally, writers aiming to compare two texts learn of two options: (1) discuss one text and then move to the other, comparing it with the first; (2) discuss the texts together, noting each of their similarities and differences in turn. Both of these alternatives make sense and provide a ready-made structure for your paper; either can result in a coherent essay. Still, a weighted analysis such as Jeremy's — an analysis that focuses on one text more than another — is more likely than either of the alternatives to seem the logical evolution of a pointed claim.

CHAPTER 6

Writing about Literary Genres

At the beginning of Chapter 3, we discussed how literary works are often understood as examples of particular **genres** (kinds or types of writing). While acknowledging that most readers think of literature as comprising the genres of fiction, poetry, and drama, we invited you to think of nonfiction (such as historical writing), creative nonfiction (such as autobiography and memoir), and essays (sometimes including argumentative prose) as literature as well. In this chapter, we present elements of literary analysis for the genres of fiction, poetry, and drama, showing how various students have used these elements to generate writing about literary works. You will notice that many of these elements are useful in thinking about most genres, but different genres make different use of elements, emphasizing some more than others. We also devote a section to writing about poems and pictures; over the centuries, many poets have been prompted to create their art in response to visual images created by other kinds of artists.

Writing about Stories

Short stories can be said to resemble novels. Above all, both are works of fiction. Yet the difference in length matters. As William Trevor, a veteran writer of short stories, has observed, short fiction is "the art of the glimpse; it deals in echoes and reverberations; craftily it withholds information." Novels tell all. Short stories tell as little as they dare. Maybe Trevor overstates the situation when he claims that novels reveal everything. All sorts of texts feature what literary theorist Wolfgang Iser calls "gaps." Still, Trevor is right to emphasize that short stories usually tell much less than novels do. They demand that you understand and evaluate characters on the basis of just a few details and events. In this respect, short stories resemble poems. Both tend to rely on compression rather than expansion, seeking to affect their audience with a sharply limited number of words.

Short stories' focused use of language can make the experience of reading them wonderfully intense. Furthermore, you may end up considering important human issues as you try to interpret the "glimpses" they provide. Precisely because short stories "tell as little as they dare," they offer you much to ponder as you proceed to write about them.

In discussing the writing process, we refer often to the story that follows. Published in 1941, "A Visit of Charity" is by a pioneer of American short fiction, Eudora Welty (1909–2001). She spent her life chiefly in her hometown of Jackson, Mississippi, and most of her writing is set in the American South.

EUDORA WELTY

A Visit of Charity

It was mid-morning — a very cold, bright day. Holding a potted plant before her, a girl of fourteen jumped off the bus in front of the Old Ladies' Home, on the outskirts of town. She wore a red coat, and her straight yellow hair was hanging down loose from the pointed white cap all the little girls were wearing that year. She stopped for a moment beside one of the prickly dark shrubs with which the city had beautified the Home, and then proceeded slowly toward the building, which was of whitewashed brick and reflected the winter sunlight like a block of ice. As she walked vaguely up the steps she shifted the small pot from hand to hand; then she had to set it down and remove her mittens before she could open the heavy door.

"I'm a Campfire Girl. . . . I have to pay a visit to some old lady," she told the nurse at the desk. This was a woman in a white uniform who looked as if she were cold; she had close-cut hair which stood up on the very top of her head exactly like a sea wave. Marian, the little girl, did not tell her that this visit would give her a minimum of only three points in her score.

"Acquainted with any of our residents?" asked the nurse. She lifted one eyebrow and spoke like a man.

"With any old ladies? No — but — that is, any of them will do," Marian stammered. With her free hand she pushed her hair behind her ears, as she did when it was time to study Science.

The nurse shrugged and rose. "You have a nice *multiflora cineraria*° there," she remarked as she walked ahead down the hall of closed doors to pick out an old lady.   5

There was loose, bulging linoleum on the floor. Marian felt as if she were walking on the waves, but the nurse paid no attention to it. There was a smell in the hall like the interior of a clock. Everything was silent until, behind one of the doors, an old lady of some kind cleared her throat like a sheep bleating. This decided the nurse. Stopping in her tracks, she first extended her arm, bent her elbow, and leaned forward from the hips — all to examine the watch strapped to her wrist; then she gave a loud double-rap on the door.

"There are two in each room," the nurse remarked over her shoulder.

"Two what?" asked Marian without thinking. The sound like a sheep's bleating almost made her turn around and run back.

multiflora cineraria: A houseplant with brightly colored flowers and heart-shaped leaves.

One old woman was pulling the door open in short, gradual jerks, and when she saw the nurse a strange smile forced her old face dangerously awry. Marian, suddenly propelled by the strong, impatient arm of the nurse, saw next the side-face of another old woman, even older, who was lying flat in bed with a cap on and a counterpane° drawn up to her chin.

"Visitor," said the nurse, and after one more shove she was off up the hall.   10

Marian stood tongue-tied; both hands held the potted plant. The old woman, still with that terrible, square smile (which was a smile of welcome) stamped on her bony face, was waiting. . . . Perhaps she said something. The old woman in bed said nothing at all, and she did not look around.

Suddenly Marian saw a hand, quick as a bird claw, reach up in the air and pluck the white cap off her head. At the same time, another claw to match drew her all the way into the room, and the next moment the door closed behind her.

"My, my, my," said the old lady at her side.

Marian stood enclosed by a bed, a washstand, and a chair; the tiny room had altogether too much furniture. Everything smelled wet—even the bare floor. She held on to the back of the chair, which was wicker and felt soft and damp. Her heart beat more and more slowly, her hands got colder and colder, and she could not hear whether the old women were saying anything or not. She could not see them very clearly. How dark it was! The window shade was down, and the only door was shut. Marian looked at the ceiling. . . . It was like being caught in a robbers' cave, just before one was murdered.

"Did you come to be our little girl for a while?" the first robber asked.   15

Then something was snatched from Marian's hand—the little potted plant.

"Flowers!" screamed the old woman. She stood holding the pot in an undecided way. "Pretty flowers," she added.

Then the old woman in bed cleared her throat and spoke. "They are not pretty," she said, still without looking around, but very distinctly.

Marian suddenly pitched against the chair and sat down in it.

"Pretty flowers," the first old woman insisted. "Pretty—pretty . . ."   20

Marian wished she had the little pot back for just a moment—she had forgotten to look at the plant herself before giving it away. What did it look like?

"Stinkweeds," said the other old woman sharply. She had a bunchy white forehead and red eyes like a sheep. Now she turned them toward Marian. The fogginess seemed to rise in her throat again, and she bleated, "Who—are—you?"

To her surprise, Marian could not remember her name. "I'm a Campfire Girl," she said finally.

"Watch out for the germs," said the old woman like a sheep, not addressing anyone.

"One came out last month to see us," said the first old woman.   25

A sheep or a germ? wondered Marian dreamily, holding on to the chair.

"Did not!" cried the other old woman.

counterpane: Bedspread.

"Did so! Read to us out of the Bible, and we enjoyed it!" screamed the first.

"Who enjoyed it!" said the woman in bed. Her mouth was unexpectedly small and sorrowful, like a pet's.

"We enjoyed it," insisted the other. "You enjoyed it—I enjoyed it." 30

"We all enjoyed it," said Marian, without realizing that she had said a word.

The first old woman had just finished putting the potted plant high, high on the top of the wardrobe, where it could hardly be seen from below. Marian wondered how she had ever succeeded in placing it there, how she could ever have reached so high.

"You mustn't pay any attention to old Addie," she now said to the little girl. "She's ailing today."

"Will you shut your mouth?" said the woman in bed. "I am not."

"You're a story." 35

"I can't stay but a minute—really, I can't," said Marian suddenly. She looked down at the wet floor and thought that if she were sick in here they would have to let her go.

With much to-do the first old woman sat down in a rocking chair—still another piece of furniture!—and began to rock. With the fingers of one hand she touched a very dirty cameo pin on her chest. "What do you do at school?" she asked.

"I don't know . . ." said Marian. She tried to think but she could not.

"Oh, but the flowers are beautiful," the old woman whispered. She seemed to rock faster and faster; Marian did not see how anyone could rock so fast.

"Ugly," said the woman in bed. 40

"If we bring flowers—" Marian began, and then fell silent. She had almost said that if Campfire Girls brought flowers to the Old Ladies' Home, the visit would count one extra point, and if they took a Bible with them on the bus and read it to the old ladies, it counted double. But the old woman had not listened, anyway; she was rocking and watching the other one, who watched back from the bed.

"Poor Addie is ailing. She has to take medicine—see?" she said, pointing a horny finger at a row of bottles on the table, and rocking so high that her black comfort shoes lifted off the floor like a little child's.

"I am no more sick than you are," said the woman in bed.

"Oh, yes you are!"

"I just got more sense than you have, that's all," said the other old woman, 45 nodding her head.

"That's only the contrary way she talks when *you all* come," said the first old lady with sudden intimacy. She stopped the rocker with a neat pat of her feet and leaned toward Marian. Her hand reached over—it felt like a petunia leaf, clinging and just a little sticky.

"Will you hush! Will you hush!" cried the other one.

Marian leaned back rigidly in her chair.

"When I was a little girl like you, I went to school and all," said the old woman in the same intimate, menacing voice. "Not here—another town . . ."

"Hush!" said the sick woman. "You never went to school. You never 50 came and you never went. You never were anything—only here. You never were born! You don't know anything. Your head is empty, your heart and hands and your old black purse are all empty, even that little old box that you brought with you you brought empty — you showed it to me. And yet you talk, talk, talk, talk, talk all the time until I think I'm losing my mind! Who are you? You're a stranger — a perfect stranger! Don't you know you're a stranger? Is it possible that they have actually done a thing like this to anyone — sent them in a stranger to talk, and rock, and tell away her whole long rigmarole? Do they seriously suppose that I'll be able to keep it up, day in, day out, night in, night out, living in the same room with a terrible old woman — forever?"

Marian saw the old woman's eyes grow bright and turn toward her. This old woman was looking at her with despair and calculation in her face. Her small lips suddenly dropped apart, and exposed a half circle of false teeth with tan gums.

"Come here, I want to tell you something," she whispered. "Come here!"

Marian was trembling, and her heart nearly stopped beating altogether for a moment.

"Now, now, Addie," said the first old woman. "That's not polite. Do you know what's really the matter with old Addie today?" She, too, looked at Marian; one of her eyelids dropped low.

"The matter?" the child repeated stupidly. "What's the matter with her?"   55

"Why, she's mad because it's her birthday!" said the first old woman, beginning to rock again and giving a little crow as though she had answered her own riddle.

"It is not, it is not!" screamed the old woman in bed. "It is not my birthday, no one knows when that is but myself, and will you please be quiet and say nothing more, or I'll go straight out of my mind!" She turned her eyes toward Marian again, and presently she said in the soft, foggy voice, "When the worst comes to the worst, I ring this bell, and the nurse comes." One of her hands was drawn out from under the patched counterpane — a thin little hand with enormous black freckles. With a finger which would not hold still she pointed to a little bell on the table among the bottles.

"How old are you?" Marian breathed. Now she could see the old woman in bed very closely and plainly, and very abruptly, from all sides, as in dreams. She wondered about her — she wondered for a moment as though there was nothing else in the world to wonder about. It was the first time such a thing had happened to Marian.

"I won't tell!"

The old face on the pillow, where Marian was bending over it, slowly gath-   60
ered and collapsed. Soft whimpers came out of the small open mouth. It was a sheep that she sounded like — a little lamb. Marian's face drew very close, the yellow hair hung forward.

"She's crying!" She turned a bright, burning face up to the first old woman.

"That's Addie for you," the old woman said spitefully.

Marian jumped up and moved toward the door. For the second time, the claw almost touched her hair, but it was not quick enough. The little girl put her cap on.

"Well, it was a real visit," said the old woman, following Marian through the doorway and all the way out into the hall. Then from behind she suddenly clutched the child with her sharp little fingers. In an affected, high-pitched whine she cried, "Oh, little girl, have you a penny to spare for a poor old woman that's not got anything of her own? We don't have a thing in the world—not a penny for candy—not a thing! Little girl, just a nickel—a penny—"

Marian pulled violently against the old hands for a moment before she was free. Then she ran down the hall, without looking behind her and without looking at the nurse, who was reading *Field & Stream* at her desk. The nurse, after another triple motion to consult her wrist watch, asked automatically the question put to visitors in all institutions: "Won't you stay and have dinner with *us*?"   65

Marian never replied. She pushed the heavy door open into the cold air and ran down the steps.

Under the prickly shrub she stooped and quickly, without being seen, retrieved a red apple she had hidden there.

Her yellow hair under the white cap, her scarlet coat, her bare knees all flashed in the sunlight as she ran to meet the big bus rocketing through the street.

"Wait for me!" she shouted. As though at an imperial command, the bus ground to a stop.

She jumped on and took a big bite out of the apple.   *[1941]*   70

A Student's Personal Response to the Story

Here is some freewriting a student did about the story you just read. By simply jotting down some observations and questions, she provided herself with the seeds of a paper.

I'm not sure which character I should be sympathizing with in Welty's story. Right away I disliked the girl because she wasn't really interested in seeing the old women. I don't know why the story is called "A Visit of Charity," since she just wanted to get more points. And yet I have to admit that when I was younger I was sort of like her. I remember one time when my church youth group had to sing Christmas carols at an old folks' home, and I was uneasy about having to meet all these ancient men and women I didn't know, some of whom could barely walk or talk. It's funny, because I was always comfortable around my grandparents, but I have to confess that being around all those old people at once spooked me a little. I smiled a lot at them and joined in the singing and helped hand out candy canes afterward. But I couldn't wait to leave. Once I did, I felt proud of myself for going there, but I guess I also felt a little guilty because I didn't really want to be there at all. So, maybe I'm being hypocritical when I criticize the girl in Welty's story for insensitivity. Anyway, I expected that Welty would present in a good light any old women that Marian encountered, just to emphasize that Marian was being unkind and that it's really sad for people to have to live in a retirement home (or senior citizens center or whatever they're calling such places nowadays). And yet the two old women she meets are cranky and unpleasant. Even the receptionist doesn't come off all that good. If I were Marian, I probably would have left even sooner than she did! Maybe Welty didn't want us to sympathize with anyone in the story, and maybe that's OK. I tend to want a story to make at least some of the characters sympathetic, but maybe it's unfair of me to demand that. Still, I'm wondering if I'm not appreciating Welty's characters enough. When the two old women argue, should we side with one of them, or are we supposed to be bothered by them both? Are we supposed to think any better of the girl by the time she leaves? The apple she eats immediately made me think of the Adam and Eve story, but I don't know what I'm supposed to do with that parallel.

The Elements of Short Fiction

Whether discussing them in class or writing about them, you will improve your ability to analyze stories like Welty's if you grow familiar with typical elements of short fiction. These elements include plot and structure, point of view, characters, setting, imagery, language, and theme.

PLOT AND STRUCTURE

For many readers, the most important element in any work of fiction is **plot**. As they turn the pages of a story, their main question is, What will happen next? In reading Welty's story, quite possibly you wanted to know how Marian's visit to the rest home would turn out. Indeed, plots usually center on human beings, who can be seen as engaging in actions, as being acted upon, or both. You might describe Marian as acting, noting among other things that she "jumped off the bus" (para. 1), that "she shifted the small pot from hand to hand" (para. 1), that "she pushed her hair behind her ears" (para. 4), that her "face drew very close" to Addie's (para. 60), that she "jumped up and moved toward the door" (para. 63), that she "pulled violently against the old hands" of the other elderly woman (para. 65), that "she ran to meet the big bus" (para. 68), and that she "jumped on and took a big bite out of the apple" (para. 70). But you might also describe her as being affected by other forces. For example, she is "suddenly propelled by the strong, impatient arm of the nurse" (para. 9), the "claw" of the first old woman "drew her all the way into the room" (para. 11), and she repeats the two women's language "without realizing that she had said a word" (para. 31). In any case, most short stories put characters into high-pressure situations, whether for dark or comic effect. To earn the merit points she desires, Marian has to contend with the feuding roommates.

Besides physical events, a short story may involve psychological developments. Welty's heroine goes through mental changes during her visit. One is that her interest in the two women grows; they are no longer just a dutiful task to her. This change is indicated best by a particular word: *wondered*. When the women discuss a previous visitor, Marian "wondered" about the animal imagery suddenly filling her mind (para. 26). When the first old woman perches the plant "high on the top of the wardrobe," the girl "wondered how she had ever succeeded in placing it there" (para. 32). Then, as Marian gazes upon the bedridden Addie, "She wondered about her — she wondered for a moment as though there was nothing else in the world to wonder about" (para. 58). As if to emphasize that the girl is experiencing a psychological transition, the narrator reports: "It was the first time such a thing had happened to Marian" (para. 58). Many stories do show characters undergoing complete or partial conversions. Meanwhile, a number of stories include characters who stick to their beliefs but gain a new perspective on them.

Does Marian's encounter with the two women have something to do with her ultimately biting the apple and leaping onto the bus? If so, what's the specific connection? Questions like these bring up relations of cause and effect, terms that often figure in discussions of plot. The novelist and short-story writer E. M. Forster refers to them in defining the term *plot* itself. To Forster, a plot is not simply one incident after another, such as "the king died and then the queen died." Rather, it is a situation or a whole chain of events in which there are reasons *why* characters behave as they do. Forster's example: "The king died, and then the queen died of grief."

Writers of short stories do not always make cause and effect immediately clear. Another possible plot, Forster suggests, is "The queen died, no one knew why, until it was discovered that it was through grief at the death of the king." In this scenario, all of the characters lack information about the queen's true psychology for a while, and perhaps the reader is in the dark as well. Indeed, many short stories leave the reader ignorant for a spell. For instance, only near the conclusion of her story does Welty reveal that before entering the rest home, Marian had put an apple under the shrub. Why does the author withhold this key fact from you? Perhaps Welty was silent about the apple because, had she reported it right away, its echoes of Eve might have overshadowed your interpretation of the story as you read. Worth considering are issues of effect: what the characters' behavior makes you think of them and what impact the author's strategies have on you.

When you summarize a story's plot, you may be inclined to put events in chronological order. But remember that short stories are not always linear. Alice Adams, author of many short stories, offers a more detailed outline of their typical **structure**. She has proposed the formula ABDCE: these letters stand for **action**, **background**, **development**, **climax**, and **ending**. More precisely, Adams has said that she sometimes begins a story with an action, follows that action with some background information, and then moves the plot forward in time through a major turning point and toward some sort of resolution. Not all writers of short stories follow this scheme. In fact, Adams does not always stick to it. Certainly a lot of short stories combine her background and development stages, moving the plot along while offering details of their characters' pasts. And sometimes a story will have several turning points rather than a single distinct climax. But by keeping Adams's formula in mind, if only as a common way to construct short stories, you will be better prepared to recognize how a story departs from chronological order.

The first paragraph of Welty's story seems to be centered on *action*. Marian arrives at the Old Ladies' Home and prepares to enter it. Even so, Welty provides some basic information in this paragraph, describing Marian and the rest home as if the reader is unfamiliar with both. Yet only in the second paragraph do you learn Marian's name and the purpose of her visit. Therefore, Welty can be said to obey Adams's formula, beginning with *action* and then moving to *background*. Note, however, that the second paragraph features *development* as well. By explaining to the receptionist who she is and why she is there, Marian takes a step closer to the central event, her meeting with the two roommates. The remainder of the story keeps moving forward in time.

What about *climax*, Adams's fourth term? Traditionally, the climax of a story has been defined as a peak moment of drama appearing near the end. Also, it is usually thought of as a point when at least one character commits a significant act, experiences a significant change, or makes a significant discovery, learns a significant lesson, or perhaps does all these things. With Welty's story, you could argue that the climax is when Marian asks Addie her age, meets with refusal, sees Addie crying, and tries to bolt. Certainly this is a dramatic moment, involving intense display of emotion resulting in Marian's departure. But Welty indicates, too, that Marian here experiences inner change. When she looks on Addie "as though there was nothing else in the world to wonder about," this is "the first time such a thing had happened to Marian."

Adams's term *ending* may seem unnecessary. Why would anyone have to be reminded that stories end? Yet a story's climax may engage readers so much that they overlook whatever follows. If the climax of Welty's story is Marian's conversation with the tearful Addie, then the ending is basically in four parts: the plea that Addie's roommate makes to Marian as she is leaving; Marian's final encounter with the receptionist; Marian's retrieval of the apple; and her escape on the bus, where she bites into the apple. Keep in mind that the ending of a story may relate somehow to its beginning. The ending of Welty's "A Visit of Charity," for instance, brings the story full circle. Whereas at the start Marian gets off a bus, hides the apple, and meets the receptionist, at the conclusion she rushes by the receptionist, recovers the apple, and boards another bus. However a story ends, ask yourself if any of the characters have changed at some point between start and finish. Does the conclusion of the story indicate that at least one person has developed in some way, or does it leave you with the feeling of lives frozen since the start? As Welty's story ends, readers may have various opinions about Marian. Some may find that she has not been changed all that much by her visit to the home, while others may feel that it has helped her mature.

A common organizational device in short stories is **repetition**. It takes various forms. First, a story may repeat words, as Welty's story does with its multiple uses of the word "wondered." Second, a story may repeatedly refer to a certain image, as you see with Welty's images of the plant and the apple. Third, a story may involve repeated actions. In "A Visit of Charity," the two roommates repeatedly argue; Marian travels by bus at the beginning and at the end; and the nurse consults her wristwatch both when Marian arrives and when she leaves.

POINT OF VIEW

A short story may be told from a particular character's perspective or **point of view**. When it is written in the **first person** — narrated by someone using the pronoun *I* or, more rarely, *we* — you have to decide how much to accept the narrator's point of view, keeping in mind that the narrator may be psychologically complex. How objective does the narrator seem in depicting other people and events? In what ways, if any, do the narrator's perceptions seem influenced by his or her personal experiences, circumstances, feelings, values, and beliefs? Does the narrator seem to have changed in any way since the events recalled? How reasonable do the narrator's judgments seem? At what moments, if any, do you find yourself disagreeing with the narrator's view of things?

Not every short story is narrated by an identifiable person. Many of them are told by what has been traditionally called an **omniscient narrator**. The word *omniscient* means "all-knowing" and is often used as an adjective for God. An omniscient narrator is usually a seemingly all-knowing, objective voice. This is the kind of voice at work in Welty's story, right from the first paragraph. There, Marian is described in an authoritatively matter-of-fact tone that appears detached from her: "Holding a potted plant before her, a girl of fourteen jumped off the bus in front of the Old Ladies' Home." Keep in mind, though, that a story may rely primarily on an omniscient narrator and yet at some points seem immersed in a character's perspective. This, too, is the case with Welty's story. Consider the following passage about Marian:

> Everything smelled wet — even the bare floor. She held on to the back of the chair, which was wicker and felt soft and damp. Her heart beat more and more slowly, her hands got colder and colder, and she could not hear whether the old women were saying anything or not. She could not see them very clearly. How dark it was! The window shade was down, and the only door was shut. Marian looked at the ceiling. . . . It was like being caught in a robbers' cave, just before one was murdered.

The passage remains in the third person, referring to "she" rather than to "I." Nevertheless, the passage seems intimately in touch with Marian's physical sensations. Indeed, the sentence "How dark it was!" seems something that Marian would say to herself. Similarly, the analogy to the robbers' cave may be Marian's own personal perception, and as such, the analogy may reveal more about her own state of mind than about the room. Many literary critics use the term **free indirect style** for moments like this, when a narrator otherwise omniscient conveys a particular character's viewpoint by resorting to the character's own language.

Throughout this book, we encourage you to analyze an author's strategies by considering the options that he or she faced. You may better understand a short story's point of view if you think about the available alternatives. For example, how would you have reacted to Welty's story if it had focused on Addie's perceptions more than on Marian's?

CHARACTERS

Although we have been discussing plots, we have also referred to the people caught up in them. Any analysis you do of a short story will reflect your understanding and evaluation of its **characters**. Rarely does the author of a story provide you with extended, enormously detailed biographies. Rather, you see the story's characters at select moments of their lives. To quote William Trevor again, the short story is "the art of the glimpse."

You may want to judge characters according to how easily you can identify with them. Yet there is little reason for you to read works that merely reinforce your prejudices. Furthermore, you may overlook the potential richness of a story if you insist that its characters fit your usual standards of behavior. An author can teach you much by introducing you to the complexity of people you might automatically praise or condemn in real life. Many of us would immediately condemn someone reluctant to help old women, but Welty encourages us to analyze carefully the girl in her story rather than just denounce her. You may be tempted to dismiss the roommates in Welty's story as unpleasant, even "sick"; in any case, take the story as an opportunity to explore *why* women in a rest home may express discontent.

One thing to consider about the characters in a story is what each basically desires. At the beginning of Welty's story, for example, Marian is hardly visiting the Old Ladies' Home out of "charity," despite that word's presence in the story's title. Rather, Marian hopes to earn points as a Campfire Girl. Again, characters in a story may change, so consider whether the particular characters you are examining alter their thinking. Perhaps you feel that Marian's visit broadens her vision of life; then again, perhaps you conclude that she remains much the same.

Reading a short story involves relating its characters to one another. In part, you'll need to determine their relative importance. Even a seemingly minor character can perform some noteworthy function; the nurse in "A Visit of Charity" not only ushers Marian in and out but also marks time. Nevertheless, any reader will try to identify a story's *main* figures. When a particular character seems the focus, he or she is referred to as the story's **protagonist**. Many readers would say that Marian is the protagonist of "A Visit of Charity." When the protagonist is in notable conflict with another character, this foe is referred to as the **antagonist**. Because Marian initially finds both roommates unpleasant, you may want to call them her antagonists. But it's not a word that you *must* apply to some character in a story; the work can have a protagonist and yet *not* include an opponent. Moreover, as a story proceeds, characters may alter their relationships with one another. Marian grows more conscious of the tensions *between* the roommates, and then for a moment she sympathizes with Addie. It is possible, too, for one character to be ambivalent toward another, feeling both drawn *and* opposed to that person.

Perhaps the roommates have a love-hate relationship, needing each other's company even as they bicker. As perhaps you have found in your own experience, human relationships are often far from simple. Works of literature can prove especially interesting when they suggest as much.

What power and influence people achieve may depend on particular traits of theirs. These include their gender, social class, race, ethnic background, nationality, sexual orientation, age, and the kind of work they do. Because these attributes may greatly affect a person's life, pay attention to them as you analyze characters. For instance, in Welty's story, all the characters are female. How might their gender matter? How might the story's dynamics have differed if it had featured at least one man? Another element of the story is its gap in ages: while the roommates are old, Marian is barely a teenager. What, over their years of living, might the two women have learned that the girl doesn't know yet?

Typically, characters express views of one another, and you have to decide how accurate these are. Some characters will seem wise observers of humanity. Others will strike you as making distorted statements about the world, revealing little more than their own biases and quirks. And some characters will seem to fall in the middle, coming across as partly objective and partly subjective. On occasion, you and your classmates may find yourselves debating which category a particular character fits. One interesting case is Welty's character Addie. Look again at the speech in which she berates her roommate:

> "Hush!" said the sick woman. "You never went to school. You never came and you never went. You never were anything — only here. You never were born! You don't know anything. Your head is empty, your heart and hands and your old black purse are all empty, even that little old box that you brought with you you brought empty — you showed it to me. And yet you talk, talk, talk, talk, talk all the time until I think I'm losing my mind! Who are you? You're a stranger — a perfect stranger! Don't you know you're a stranger? Is it possible that they have actually done a thing like this to anyone — sent them in a stranger to talk, and rock, and tell away her whole long rigmarole? Do they seriously suppose that I'll be able to keep it up, day in, day out, night in, night out, living in the same room with a terrible old woman — forever?"

Some may argue that this speech is merely an unreasonable rant, indicating Addie's dour mood rather than her roommate's true nature. (For one thing, contrary to Addie's declaration, the roommate must have been born!) Yet it can also be argued that Addie shrewdly diagnoses her situation. Perhaps statements like "you never were born," "your head is empty," and "you're a stranger" are true in a metaphorical sense.

SETTING

Usually a short story enables readers to examine how people behave in concrete circumstances. The characters are located in a particular place or **setting**. Moreover, they are shown at particular moments in their personal histories. Sometimes the story goes further, referring to them as living at a certain point in world history.

As the word *sometimes* implies, short stories vary in the precision with which they identify their settings. They differ as well in the importance of their setting. Sometimes location serves as a mere backdrop for the plot. At other times, the setting can be a looming presence. When Welty's character Marian visits the Old Ladies' Home, we get her vivid impressions of it. Even when a story's setting seems ordinary, it may become filled with drama and meaning as the plot develops. One way of analyzing characters is to consider how they accommodate themselves — or fail to accommodate themselves — to their surroundings. The two roommates in Welty's story are evidently frustrated with living in the Old Ladies' Home, and they take out their frustration on each other.

IMAGERY

Just like poems, short stories often use **imagery** to convey meaning. Sometimes a character in the story may interpret a particular image just the way you do. Some stories, though, include images that you and the characters may analyze quite differently. One example is the apple in Welty's story. Whereas Marian probably views the apple as just something to eat, many readers would make other associations with it, thinking in particular of the apple that Adam and Eve ate from the tree of knowledge in the Garden of Eden. By the end of Welty's story, perhaps Marian has indeed become like Adam and Eve, in that she has lost her innocence and grown more aware that human beings age. At any rate, many readers would call Marian's apple a **symbol**. Traditionally, that is the term for an image seen as representing some concept or concepts. Again, Marian herself probably does not view her apple as symbolic; indeed, characters within stories rarely use the word *symbol* at all.

Images may appear in the form of metaphors or other figures of speech. For example, when Marian enters the Old Ladies' Home, she experiences "a smell in the hall like the interior of a clock." Welty soon builds on the clock image as she describes the receptionist checking her wristwatch, an action that this character repeats near the end. Welty's whole story can be said to deal with time and its effects, both on the old and on the young.

Images in short stories usually appeal to the reader's visual sense. Most often, they are things you can picture in your mind. Yet stories are not limited to rendering visual impressions. They may refer to other senses, too, as when Welty's young heroine notices the odor in the hall.

LANGUAGE

Everything about short stories we have discussed so far concerns **language**. After all, works of literature are constructed entirely out of words. Here, however, we call your attention to three specific uses of language in stories: title, predominant style, and dialogue.

A story's **title** may be just as important as any words in the text. Not always will the relevance of the title be immediately clear to you. Usually you have to read a story all the way through before you can sense fully how its title applies. In any case, play with the title in your mind, considering its various possible meanings and implications. In analyzing the title of Welty's "A Visit of Charity," you may find it helpful to think about this famous passage from the King James translation of the New Testament: "And now abideth faith, hope, charity, these three; but the greatest of these is charity" (1 Corinthians 13:13). You may also want to look up the word *charity* in a dictionary.

Not all short stories have a uniform **style**. Some feature various tones, dialects, vocabularies, and levels of formality. Welty's story incorporates different types of speech almost from its start. When, using rather formal language, the nurse asks Marian, "Acquainted with any of our residents?" (para. 3), the girl puts this question more plainly: "With any old ladies?" (para. 4). Stories that do have a predominant style are often told in the first person, thus giving the impression of a presiding "voice." Charlotte Perkins Gilman's "The Yellow Wallpaper (p. 233) teems with the anguished expressions of its beleaguered narrator.

Dialogue may serve more than one purpose in a short story. By reporting various things, characters may provide you with necessary background for the plot. In Welty's story, it's only from the roommates' fragmentary remarks that Marian—and the reader—can learn anything about their lives up until now. Actually, dialogue can also be thought of as an action in itself, moving the plot along. Try to identify the particular kinds of acts that characters perform when they speak. When the first roommate asks the departing Marian for a coin, she seems to be begging, but perhaps she is also doing whatever she can to hold the girl there; her having "clutched the child" (para. 64) suggests as much. Indeed, dialogue may function to reveal shifts in characters' relations with one another.

THEME

We have already discussed the term **theme** on pages 50–52. There, we identified issues of theme as one kind of issue that comes up in literary studies. At the same time, we suggested that the term *theme* applies to various literary genres, not just short stories. Later in this chapter, we examine theme in connection with poems, plays, and essays. Here, though, we consider theme as an element of short fiction. In doing so, we review some points from our earlier discussion, applying them now to Welty's story.

Recall that we defined the theme of a work as the main claim it seems to make. Furthermore, we identified it as an assertion, a proposition, or a statement rather than as a single word. "Charity" is obviously a *topic* of Welty's story, but because it is just one word, it is not an adequate expression of the story's *theme*. The following exercise invites you to consider just what that theme may be.

1. Try to state a text's theme as a midlevel generalization.   If you were to put it in very broad terms, your audience would see it as fitting a great many works besides the one you have read. If you went to the opposite extreme, tying the theme completely to specific details of the text, your audience might think the theme irrelevant to their own lives.

The phrase "the moral of the story" suggests that a story can usually be reduced to a single message, often a principle of ethics or religion. Plenty of examples can be cited to support this suggestion. In the New Testament, for instance, Jesus tells stories — called *parables* — to convey some of his key ideas. In any number of cultures today, stories are used to teach children elements of good conduct. Moreover, people often determine the significance of a real-life event by building a story from it and by drawing a moral from it at the same time. These two processes conspicuously dovetailed when England's Princess Diana was killed in a car crash. Given that she died fleeing photographers, many people saw her entire life story as that of a woman hounded by the media. The moral was simultaneous and clear: thou shalt honor the right to privacy.

It is possible to lose sight of a story's theme by placing too much emphasis on minor details of the text. The more common temptation, however, is to turn a story's theme into an all-too-general cliché. Actually, a story is often most interesting when it *complicates* some widely held idea that it seemed ready to endorse. Therefore, a useful exercise is to start with a general thematic statement about the story and then make it increasingly specific. With "A Visit of Charity," for example, you might begin by supposing that a theme is "everyone must give up their dreams of innocence and paradise, just as Adam and Eve did." Your next step would be to identify the specific spin that Welty's story gives this idea. How does her story differ from others on this theme? Note, for instance, that Marian comes literally face to face with the mortality of women much older than she is and that the experience fills her momentarily with "wonder." Try to rephrase our version of Welty's theme so that it seems more in touch with these specific details of the text.

2. A theme of a text may be related to its title.   It may also be expressed by some statement made within the text. But often various parts of the text merit consideration as you try to determine its theme.

In our discussion of a short story's language, we called attention to the potential significance of its title. The title may serve as a guide to the story's theme. What clues, if any, do you find in the title "A Visit of Charity"? Of course, determining a story's theme entails going beyond the title. You have to read, and usually reread, the entire text. In doing so, you may come across a statement that seems a candidate for the theme because it is a philosophical generalization. Nevertheless, take the time to consider whether the story's essence is indeed captured by this statement alone.

3. You can state a text's theme either as an observation or as a recommendation.   Each way of putting it evokes a certain image of the text's author. When you state the theme as an **observation**, you depict the author as a psychologist, a philosopher, or some other kind of analyst. When you state the theme as a **recommendation** — which often involves your using the word *should* — you depict the author as a teacher, preacher, manager, or coach; that is, the author comes across as telling readers what to do.

As we have noted, stories are often used to teach lessons. Moreover, often the lessons are recommendations for action, capable of being phrased as "Do X" or "Do not do X." The alternative is to make a generalization about some state of affairs. When you try to express a particular story's theme, which of these two options should you follow? There are several things to consider in making your decision. First is your personal comfort: do you feel at ease with both ways of stating the theme, or is one of these ways more to your taste? Also worth pondering is the impression you want to give of the author: do you want to portray this person as a maker of recommendations, or do you want to assign the author a more modest role?

4. Consider stating a text's theme as a problem.   That way, you are more apt to convey the complexity and drama of the text.

We have suggested that short stories often pivot around conflicts between people and conflicts within people. Perhaps the most interesting stories are those that pose conflicts not easily resolved. Probably you will be more faithful to such a text if you phrase its theme as a problem. In the case of Welty's story, for example, you might state the theme as follows: "Young people may sense an older person's infirmity, but especially if that person is a stranger, they may as yet lack sufficient maturity and confidence to stay and help."

5. Rather than refer to *the* theme of a text, you might refer to *a* theme of the text, implying that the text has more than one.   You would still be suggesting that you have identified a central idea of the text. Subsequently, you might have to defend your claim.

Unlike the average novel, the typical short story pivots around only a few ideas. Yet you need not insist that the story you are analyzing has a single theme. The shortest piece of short fiction may have more than one, and your audience may well appreciate your admitting this. One theme of Welty's story may be that none of us can escape the passage of time. The old roommates aside, teenaged Marian seems on the brink of adulthood, and her concluding bus ride suggests that she is moving further into it. But additional themes are possible. A second idea, dramatized by the roommates' feud, may be that old age can test a person's spirit even as it hurts the person's body. Of course, to call either of these ideas a theme of the story is still to make a claim that requires support.

Perhaps the biggest challenge you will face in writing about short stories is to avoid long stretches of plot summary. Selected details of the plot will often serve as key evidence for you. You will need to describe such moments from the story you are discussing, even if your audience has already read it. But your readers are apt to be frustrated if you just repeat plot at length. They will feel that they may as well turn back to the story itself rather than linger with your rehash. Your paper is worth your readers' time only if you provide insights of your own, *analyzing* the story rather than just *summarizing* it.

To understand what analysis of a short story involves, let's turn to student Tanya Vincent. Assigned to write an argument paper about a short story, Tanya decided to focus on Welty's. She realized that for her paper to be effective, she had to come up with an issue worth addressing, a claim about that issue, and evidence for that claim. Moreover, she had to be prepared to identify her process of reasoning and her assumptions.

For most writing assignments, deciding on an issue will be your most important preliminary step. Without a driving question, you will have difficulty producing fresh, organized, and sustained analysis. For her paper on "A Visit of Charity," Tanya chose to address this issue: What does the story suggest charity can mean? In part, she was drawn to this question because the word *charity* appears in the story's title and because it comes up in the famous passage from 1 Corinthians that we quoted earlier. But the question also enticed her because Welty's protagonist doesn't appear truly compassionate. A conventional definition of *charity* is that it is an expression of a sincere desire to help people. Given that Marian appears to lack this desire, is Welty's title ironic? Or does charity in some *other* sense of the word operate in the story? Tanya realized that she would be tackling an issue of definition. She would need to examine various possible meanings of *charity* and determine which are relevant to specific details of Welty's text.

A paper about a short story doesn't have to mention explicitly all the elements of short fiction we've identified. Nevertheless, thinking of these elements can help you plan such a paper, providing you with some preliminary terms for your analysis. Tanya perceived that her paper would be very much about characters and plot; it might also dwell upon imagery and language. She knew, too, that she would be more apt to persuade her readers if she included quotations from the story. Yet, as with plot summary, quoting should be limited, so that the paper seems an original argument — not a recycling of the literary work's own words. Tanya sensed that practically every sentence of Welty's story could be quoted and then interpreted. At the same time, she realized that she should quote only *some* words, not all.

Final Draft of a Student Paper

Here is Tanya's final draft of her paper about "A Visit of Charity." As you read it, keep in mind that it emerged only after she had done several preliminary drafts, in consultation with some of her classmates as well as her instructor. Although Tanya's paper is a good example of how to write about a short story, most drafts can stand to be revised further. What do you think Tanya has done well in her paper? If she planned to do yet another revision, what suggestions would you make?

Tanya Vincent
Professor Stein
English 1A
3 November - - - -

The Real Meaning of "Charity"
in "A Visit of Charity"

Many people would define the word "charity" as an act in which an individual or institution sincerely offers material or spiritual comfort to someone less fortunate. In this respect,

An assumption, but seems a reasonable one.

charity is a form of love. Such is the meaning implied in the King James translation of the most famous statement about charity, 1 Corinthians 13:13: "And now abideth faith, hope, charity, these three; but the greatest of these is charity." In fact, some other translations of this biblical passage use "love" instead of "charity," thereby suggesting that the two terms are more or less equivalent. But Marian, the protagonist of Eudora Welty's short story "A Visit of Charity," does not appear to demonstrate this concept of charity when she visits the Old Ladies' Home. She gives no indication that she sincerely cares about any of its residents. Rather, she approaches the visit as a mechanical task that she must perform to raise her standing as a Campfire Girl. Nor does she seem to become much more empathetic after spending time at the Home. Several readers of the story, therefore, might think its title ironic.

Starts to introduce her issue and claim by referring to readers who are possibly superficial.

This view may, however, be too limited. Welty may be encouraging us to move past our familiar concept of "charity" and give the word a meaning that *can* apply to her text in a nonironic way. It is true that Marian does not act lovingly or even compassionately on her trip to the Home. Yet maybe her brief moments with the two elderly roommates provide charity to Marian herself, making her a beneficiary of it rather than a donor of it. After all, her encounter with the two women helps to make her at least a bit more aware of the stresses that old age can bring. Charity in *this* sense would mean the providing of a necessary lesson about what life can be like as an adult. Even though the two roommates do not intend to be benevolent teachers of the girl, her meeting with them has some value, for it gives her a preview of realities she will have to deal with more extensively as she grows up.

A qualification. Tanya holds back from claiming certainty about Welty's intentions.

Introduction ends with main issue (a definitional kind) and main claim.

When we first meet her in the story, Marian seems anything but passionately devoted to improving life for the Home's inhabitants. Probably "Old Ladies' Home" is not the building's real name to begin with, but instead Marian's own insensitive designation. Clearly she looks upon her visit as a chore. To her, it is just something she must do to earn points. Later, we readers learn that she has even computed the specific amounts available to her: "She had almost said that if Campfire Girls brought flowers to the Old Ladies' Home, the visit would count one extra point, and if they took a Bible with them on the bus and read it to the old ladies, it counted double" (line 124). When, back at the story's start, she introduces herself to the nurse, she does not even pretend to be a true Angel of Mercy pursuing a higher spiritual purpose: "I'm a Campfire Girl. . . . I have to pay a visit to some old

Concession to readers who have trouble finding "charity" in the story.

lady" (122). So indifferent is she to the Home's aged occupants that she candidly announces "any of them will do"
(line 122). When she does meet with the two roommates, she
chooses not to stay long with them. Nor does she offer
charity in a traditional sense when one of the roommates
begs. While the woman asks, "have you a penny to spare for a
poor old woman that's not got anything of her own?" (126),
Marian is anxious to flee. Nor, when she does leave the pair,
is her exit gradual, patient, and kind: she "jumped up and
moved toward the door"; "pulled violently against the old
hands"; "ran down the hall, without looking behind her and
without looking at the nurse"; "quickly . . . retrieved a red
apple"; "ran to meet the big bus"; "shouted" at the bus; and
"jumped on" (126). These frenzied motions indicate that
Marian is ultimately *repelled* by the two women, not drawn to
them as clients for her kindness.

> *Here and elsewhere in the paper, Tanya quotes from Welty's text.*

Nevertheless, perhaps Marian's experience with them
confers a sort of charity upon *her* by alerting her to facts she
will eventually have to face. When she first meets the roommate who is supposedly healthier, she is struck by the
"terrible, square smile (which was a smile of welcome)
stamped on her bony face" (123). This seems more an image
of death than of life, suggesting that Marian is beginning to
grow conscious of mortality. This implication gets even
stronger when Marian comes to the bed of the sicker woman,
Addie: "She wondered about her — she wondered for a
moment as though there was nothing else in the world to
wonder about. It was the first time such a thing had happened to Marian" (125). More precisely, Marian seems to
discover that people soon to die may become a mixture of
helplessness and fierce self-assertion. To the girl, Addie
repeatedly comes across as a sheep or lamb, a species of
animal traditionally associated with innocence. Even before
she enters the room, Marian twice experiences Addie's voice
as that of a sheep "bleating" (122), and at Addie's bedside
she mentally compares the tearful, suffering woman to "a
little lamb" (125). Yet Addie is also someone capable not
only of refusing to tell her age, but also of berating her
roommate: "And yet you talk, talk, talk, talk, talk all the
time until I think I'm losing my mind!" (125). In turn, the
object of this scorn displays to Marian a similar blend of
powerlessness and ferocity. "In an affected, high-pitched
whine," this roommate refers to herself as "a poor old
woman," but at the same time "she suddenly clutched the
child with her sharp little fingers" (125–26). Indeed, if Addie
comes across to Marian as a sheep or lamb, the girl senses

> *Transition to development of main claim.*

> *As earlier, with "wondered," Tanya shows attention to repetition.*

right from the start of the meeting that the other woman is an aggressive bird: "Suddenly Marian saw a hand, quick as a bird claw, reach up in the air and pluck the white cap off her head" (123). In general, neither of the roommates fits the sentimental stereotype of the sweet old lady. But their difference from this image is precisely what can be educational for Marian. Their nearness to death, and the complex behavior they show in response to their fate, are matters that the girl will have to contend with a lot once she herself becomes a full-fledged adult.

While admitting that the sentence about "the first time" appears significant, some readers may doubt that Marian learns anything from this experience. Their skepticism would be understandable, given that she does not philosophize at length about the visit and ends it rather speedily. Welty does, however, suggest the stirrings of mental change in Marian by drawing our attention to the bodily disorientation she goes through in the old women's room. Immediately upon meeting them, she "stood tongue-tied" (123). Soon, "her heart beat more and more slowly, her hands got colder and colder, and she could not hear whether the old women were saying anything or not" (123). Moreover, "she could not see them very clearly" (123). A moment later, she winds up "pitched against the chair" (123) and forgets her own name. Eventually "her heart nearly stopped beating altogether" (125). These disabilities, though temporary, indicate that at *some* level of consciousness, Marian is having perceptions that she did not have before. Specifically, she seems to have glimmers of how death increasingly enters people's lives as they age.

Concession to readers with a different view.

The story's very last sentence further suggests that Marian either learns this lesson or vaguely intuits it. By taking "a big bite out of the apple" (126), she resembles Adam and Eve, whose own eating of an apple resulted in their becoming mortal. But in writing her story, Welty may also have had in mind a second biblical passage. Occurring just two lines before the famous statement about charity I have quoted, it is a well-known review of life's journey: "When I was a child, I spake as a child, I understood as a child, I thought as a child: but when I became a man, I put away childish things" (1 Corinthians 13:11). Although Marian is female, the line can still apply to her. Before her visit to the Home, she has been "a child," and she acts that way for much of her time there. But the visit may make her more inclined to "put away childish things," in which case she herself would receive a form of charity from it.

Again, acknowledges that she can't be certain about Welty's thinking.

Writing about Poems

Some students are put off by poetry, perhaps because their early experiences with it were discouraging. They imagine that poems have deep hidden meanings they can't uncover. Maybe their high-school English teacher always had the right interpretation, and they rarely did. This need not be the case. Poetry can be accessible to all readers.

The problem is often a confusion about the nature of poetry, since poetry is more compressed than prose. Poetry focuses more on connotative, emotional, or associative meanings and conveys meaning more through suggestion, indirection, and the use of metaphor, symbol, and imagery than prose does. It seldom hands us a specific meaning. Poetic texts suggest certain possibilities, but the reader completes the transaction. Part of the meaning comes from the writer, part from the text itself, and part from the reader. Even students who are the same age, race, religion, and ethnicity are not duplicates of one another. Each has unique experiences, family histories, and emotional lives. If thirty people read a poem about conformity or responsibility, all thirty will have varying views about these concepts, even though they will probably have some commonalities. (Most societies are so saturated with shared cultural experiences that it is nearly impossible to avoid some overlap in responses.)

In a good class discussion, then, we should be aware that even though we might be members of the same culture, each of us reads from a unique perspective, a perspective that might also shift from time to time. If a woman reads a poem about sexual harassment, her identity as a female may seem more relevant than if she were reading a poem about death, a more universal experience. In other words, how we read a poem and how significant and meaningful the poem is for us depends both on the content of the poem and on our specific circumstances. Suppose you are fourteen when you first read a poem about dating; you would likely have very different responses rereading it at nineteen, twenty-five, and fifty. We read poems through our experiences. As we gain new experiences, our readings change.

One reason to respond in writing to your first reading is to be able to separate your first thoughts from those of your classmates. They too will bring their own experiences, values, and ideas to the discussion. In the give-and-take of open discussion, it may be difficult to remember what you first said. Of course, the point of a classroom discussion is not simply to defend your initial response, for then you would be denying yourself the benefit of other people's ideas. A good discussion should open up the poem, allow you to see it from multiple viewpoints, and enable you to expand your perspective, to see how others make sense of the world.

This rich mixture of the poet's text, the reader's response, and discussion among several readers can create new possibilities of meaning. Even more than fiction or drama, poetry encourages creative readings that can be simultaneously true to the text and to the reader. A lively class discussion can uncover a dozen or more plausible interpretations of a poem, each backed up with valid evidence from both the poem and the reader's experience. You may try to persuade others that your views about the poem are correct; others may do the same to you. This negotiation is at the heart of a liberal, democratic education. In fact, maybe the most respected and repeated notion about being well educated is the ability to empathize with another's point of view, to see as another sees. Reading, discussing, and writing about poetry can help you become a person who can both create meaning and understand and appreciate how others do. This is one important way literature matters.

The following three poems are about work—about the joys and sorrows, the satisfactions and frustrations of physical labor. Some people might think of poets as intellectuals who are far removed from the experiences of the working class, but this is not the case. Indeed, many poets were themselves brought up in working-class homes and know firsthand the dignity and value of such work. Even among poets who do not toil with their hands, few lack the imaginative empathy that would allow them to write perceptively about firefighters and factory workers, cleaning women and mill workers. These three poems are especially relevant today when physical work is becoming less and less a reality among middle-class Americans. Poems that matter are poems about real life—about love and death, about pain and loss, about beauty and hope. These three poems about work are about all of these and more.

The first poem, Mary Oliver's (1935–2019) "Singapore," appeared in *House of Light* (1992). She won a Pulitzer Prize for her poetry. "Blackberries" is by Yusef Komunyakaa (b. 1947), who has become known for exploring various aspects of African American experience; the poem is from *Magic City* (1992). Edwin Arlington Robinson's "The Mill" is the oldest poem in the cluster. Robinson (1869–1935) is considered the first major poet of twentieth-century America.

MARY OLIVER

Singapore

In Singapore, in the airport,
a darkness was ripped from my eyes.
In the women's restroom, one compartment stood open.
A woman knelt there, washing something
    in the white bowl.   5

Disgust argued in my stomach
and I felt, in my pocket, for my ticket.

A poem should always have birds in it.
Kingfishers, say, with their bold eyes and gaudy wings.
Rivers are pleasant, and of course trees.   10
A waterfall, or if that's not possible, a fountain
    rising and falling.
A person wants to stand in a happy place, in a poem.

When the woman turned I could not answer her face.
Her beauty and her embarrassment struggled together, and   15
    neither could win.
She smiled and I smiled. What kind of nonsense is this?
Everybody needs a job.
Yes, a person wants to stand in a happy place, in a poem.
But first we must watch her as she stares down at her labor,   20
    which is dull enough.
She is washing the tops of the airport ashtrays, as big as
    hubcaps, with a blue rag.
Her small hands turn the metal, scrubbing and rinsing.
She does not work slowly, nor quickly, but like a river.   25
Her dark hair is like the wing of a bird.

I don't doubt for a moment that she loves her life.
And I want her to rise up from the crust and the slop
    and fly down to the river.
This probably won't happen.   30
But maybe it will.
If the world were only pain and logic, who would want it?

Of course, it isn't.
Neither do I mean anything miraculous, but only
the light that can shine out of a life. I mean   35
the way she unfolded and refolded the blue cloth,
the way her smile was only for my sake; I mean
the way this poem is filled with trees, and birds.   *[1992]*

YUSEF KOMUNYAKAA

Blackberries

They left my hands like a printer's
Or thief's before a police blotter
& pulled me into early morning's
Terrestrial sweetness, so thick
The damp ground was consecrated   5
Where they fell among a garland of thorns.

Although I could smell old lime-covered
History, at ten I'd still hold out my hands
& berries fell into them. Eating from one
& filling a half gallon with the other,   10
I ate the mythology & dreamt
Of pies & cobbler, almost

Needful as forgiveness. My bird dog Spot
Eyed blue jays & thrashers. The mud frogs
In rich blackness, hid from daylight.   15

An hour later, beside City Limits Road
I balanced a gleaming can in each hand,
Limboed between worlds, repeating *one dollar.*
The big blue car made me sweat.
Wintertime crawled out of the windows.   20
When I leaned closer I saw the boy
& girl my age, in the wide back seat
Smirking, & it was then I remembered my fingers
Burning with thorns among berries too ripe to touch.   *[1992]*

EDWIN ARLINGTON ROBINSON

The Mill

The miller's wife had waited long,
    The tea was cold, the fire was dead;
And there might yet be nothing wrong
    In how he went and what he said:
"There are no millers any more,"   5
    Was all that she had heard him say;
And he had lingered at the door
    So long that it seemed yesterday.

Sick with fear that had no form
    She knew that she was there at last;   10
And in the mill there was a warm
    And mealy fragrance of the past.
What else there was would only seem
    To say again what he had meant;
And what was hanging from a beam   15
    Would not have heeded where she went.

And if she thought it followed her,
    She may have reasoned in the dark
That one way of the few there were
    Would hide her and would leave no mark: 20
Black water, smooth above the weir
    Like starry velvet in the night,
Though ruffled once, would soon appear
    The same as ever to the sight.   *[1920]*

A Student's Personal Responses to the Poems

The following are selections from the response journal of student Michaela
Fiorucci, who chose to focus on boundaries — on the various divisions we set
up between ourselves and other people, such as income, race, gender, sexual
preference, and religion. It seemed to her an interesting way to talk about

work since Michaela had observed barriers of all kinds between workers at her job at the university.

Using an explorative strategy, Michaela did some freewriting on the three poems, hoping to discover an argument about boundaries that might fit. The following are selections from her response journal.

> In "Singapore," there is a clear boundary between the middle-class American tourist and the cleaning lady, so much so that at first the narrator says, "Disgust argued in my stomach." The cleaning woman also seems to believe in a barrier and continues to work in a steady way. The narrator finally sees beauty in her dedication to her work. When the narrator does see beauty in her work habits, it helps close the barrier between them. There are also the issues of boundaries between fantasy and reality and between a world of pain and logic and one with birds and rivers. But at the end these boundaries also seem to be closing.
>
> In "Blackberries," the young boy seems to be living in a rural paradise, beyond the city boundaries, outside the usual urban and suburban environment. He lives in a land of bird dogs, jays, thrashers, and mud frogs. He makes comparisons between blackness and light that seem to anticipate the economic boundary that appears in the last stanza, the one between the poor boy and the rich kids in the car. It is this division between the children in air-conditioned comfort and the narrator on the outside looking in that seems to be the main point of this poem. Some boundaries cause us pain.
>
> "The Mill" tells the sad story of a miller who could not see a boundary between himself and his job. When he tells his wife "there are no millers any more," he is really saying that his life is over; he has no reason to live. And so he crosses the boundary between life and death. Tragically, his wife also has difficulty seeing herself outside her role as wife and housekeeper, and so she also crosses that ultimate boundary. She does so, however, in a completely different way: she drowns herself, so no one will know. She passes through life's boundary without leaving a trace.

After reading these brief freewrites to her response group, Michaela still didn't have a focus, but she liked the idea that boundaries, like walls, sometimes serve a purpose and sometimes they don't. She remembered a discussion of Robert Frost's "Mending Wall" from another course that focused on negotiating the walls we build between us. Her professor liked this idea since it helped her considerably narrow the concept of boundaries.

After reviewing her freewriting, Michaela wrote the following first draft and read it to her response group. She then discussed with her instructor her plans for a revision. Her instructor made a number of specific and general comments. After reading her first draft, what feedback would you give Michaela? Her revision appears later in this chapter on pages 171–73.

First Draft of a Student Paper

Michaela Fiorucci
Mr. Hardy
English 102
15 April - - - -

Boundaries in Robinson, Komunyakaa, and Oliver

Although most sophomores I know at school value their privacy, they also want to create intimate relationships. It is often hard to reconcile these two impulses. Most middle-class students are lucky enough to have their own rooms, private enclaves against annoying sisters and brothers, intrusive mothers and fathers. But a room is also more than a physical boundary; it is also a symbolic assertion of identity. It says, "I'm separate from others, even within the closeness of the family." Such a commitment to physical privacy might be innocent enough, but it does contain dangerous seeds, especially when extended beyond the home to neighborhoods. When different ethnic groups want boundaries between them, it is no longer innocent. When the upper classes need to be separated from workers because they see each other as radically different, a dangerous boundary has been erected.

It would be reductive, however, to say all boundaries need to be erased. Edwin Arlington Robinson's "The Mill" is a good example of the dangerous consequences of a missing boundary. The poem narrates the sad story of a farm couple who commit suicide — the husband because he feels useless, the wife because she can't imagine life without her husband. During my first few readings, I was struck by the lack of communication between the couple. He must have been depressed for a long time, but it seems they never discussed his feelings. Keeping an emotional distance from others was probably a typical part of the way men and women dealt with each other a hundred years ago. It was a boundary not to be crossed. Apparently he could not say, "I feel terrible that I am going to lose my job." And his wife accepts his reticence, even though he might have been having second thoughts as he "lingered at the door." Clearly this is a boundary that should have been breached. But after several readings I began to realize that the boundary that should have been established wasn't — the idea that a person's value or worth is synonymous with his or her identity is dehumanizing. And it probably isn't something that just happened in the past. Nor is the equally dehumanizing idea that a wife is nothing without her husband. When the miller's wife decides to "leave no mark" by jumping into the pond, she is admitting she is not a worthwhile person by herself. Both identify totally with a role that in my view should be only one aspect of a complex human life. The final barrier she crosses, from life to death, is symbolically represented in the poem as a feminine domestic gesture: she doesn't want to leave a mess. The boundaries of person and occupation should be made clear; the arbitrary boundaries between genders should not.

When the narrator in Yusef Komunyakaa's "Blackberries" claims that he is "Limboed between worlds" (18), he means the rural paradise of "Terrestrial sweetness" (4) and "rich blackness" (15) he temporarily lives in versus the commercial, urban work that "made me sweat" (19). He has constructed a boundary between the ancient picking of berries and the technology of automobiles, between a natural closeness with nature and the artificial "Wintertime crawled out of the windows" (20). Even though the narrator is only ten, he senses the sensual joys of being one with nature. He seems to reject "old lime-covered / History" (7–8) in favor of "mythology" (11), which seems to suggest a conscious rejection or maybe repression of the contemporary world. But this boundary cannot stand. He needs the outside world to survive, and when the car approaches, it is the modern world and all its pluses and minuses that draw near. When he looks in, he sees "Smirking" (23) children; he sees class prejudice, hierarchy, and economic reality. The smirkers of the world are in charge. This realization dissolves the protective boundary around his Garden of Eden, and he feels physical pain. But really he feels the pain of initiation, the pain of having to cross a boundary he wanted to delay as long as possible. Although we can sympathize with the young narrator, he would probably have fared better by not making his boundary so extreme.

The narrator in Mary Oliver's "Singapore" at first sees a significant boundary between herself as a middle-class traveler and a cleaning woman washing a toilet. It is a separation we might all make, given our socialization to see this kind of physical labor as degrading. College-educated people in America have a tendency to see themselves as distinct from workers. For most, a woman washing something in a compartment is beyond the pale, a clear indication that the woman is other. But Oliver does have some conflicting ideas since she says a "Disgust argued in my stomach" (6). Since we are also socialized to be tolerant and open-minded, she knows she shouldn't think this way. And since she is also a writer with ideas about how a poem should "always have birds in it" (8), she looks harder at the cleaning woman, finally seeing in her face, in her hair, and in the way she works slowly, "like a river" (25), the positive aspects she probably wants to find. Oliver does not simply accept the boundaries that her culture constructs but negotiates with herself, eventually seeing that "light . . . can shine out of a life" (35) even where we do not expect it. In the woman's careful folding and unfolding of her blue work cloth and in her smile, Oliver eclipses the social boundary and ends up with a life-affirming vision "filled with trees, and birds" (38).

The Elements of Poetry

SPEAKER AND TONE

The voice we hear in a poem could be the poet's, but it is better to think of the speaker as an artistic construction—perhaps a **persona** (mask) for the poet or perhaps a character who does not resemble the poet at all. For example, the speaker in Lynda Hull's "Night Waitress" (p. 98) is not the poet herself but a struggling worker. In large part, to describe any poem's speaker is to pinpoint the person's tone or attitude. Sometimes this is hard to discern. The tone could be ironic or sentimental, joyful or morose, or a combination of emotions. To get a precise sense of it, read the poem aloud, actually performing the speaker's role. Bear in mind that his or her tone may change over the course of the poem. For instance, as the speaker in Yusef Komunyakaa's "Blackberries" recalls a day in his childhood when he picked fruit and then tried to sell it on a highway, he shifts from nostalgia (remembering "Terrestrial sweetness") to bitter recognition of class bias (the "Smirking" of the children who passed him in their car).

The narrator of "The Mill" immediately creates a somber, foreboding tone of anxiety and dread with the tea is "cold" and the fire is "dead," which also foreshadows the death of the miller. Likewise, his brief statement that "there are no millers any more" reinforces and intensifies the sense of impending doom that permeates the plot and theme of the poem. And, of course, such a grim tone is warranted by the dual suicides. Interestingly, the ominous tone of the poem noticeably shifts in the last four lines to one of quiet, smooth repose as the once ruffled pond appears "like starry velvet in the night." Perhaps the miller and his wife are finally at peace.

DICTION AND SYNTAX

Although we would all agree that poets rely on the meaning of words to express their feelings and their ideas, what words mean is no simple matter. Perplexed over what a poet might have intended, we often consult a dictionary. And that certainly might help demystify a puzzling passage. But poetry is often more about complicating than clarifying. Most poets are more interested in opening up words than pinning them down. Unlike journalists or science writers, poets often intend to be ambiguous. They like a word's possibilities, its rich emotional overtones. That's one reason readers see in poems different things; one reader may think of the line "Wintertime crawled out of the window" as meaning air conditioning and another as meaning the chilly arrogance and distaste of the privileged for laborers. Only Komunyakaa knows exactly what he meant by "wintertime."

Looking up *wintertime* in the dictionary would give us the denotative meaning, which wouldn't be much help here. But the emotional overtones or associations for individual readers give us the complex multiplicity that poets hope will enrich the poem's meaning. When in "Singapore," for example, the narrator says "a darkness was ripped from my eyes," the objective denotative meaning is probably not what she is after. More likely Oliver is counting on the more subjective, emotional associations of "darkness." Perhaps lack of understanding or ignorance is suggested. Perhaps intolerance or fear of otherness comes to mind. And in the background lie all the negative associations of the unknown, the uncertainty and the danger of things unseen. These are the word's connotations, and they are crucial to the evocative suggestiveness of poems. Oliver wants readers to allow connotation to do its work in expanding and personalizing the meaning of words. In this sense, the word *darkness* contains within it infinite subjective and cultural possibilities.

The same is true for "light" in line 35 of the last stanza. It is the connotative possibilities that infuse "light" with significance, especially when contrasted with the darkness of the first stanza. Seen in the context of the poem, "light" might suggest beauty or integrity or perhaps dedication, commitment, or the ability to find in work something valuable and beautiful. For religious readers, "light" might suggest the beauty and worthiness of each human soul, while for the political thinkers, the dedication and skill of laborers might come to mind. What other connotations can you suggest for these two words?

The last line of the poem offers a clear distinction between denotation and connotation when Oliver says, "this poem is filled with trees, and birds." Literally, of course, trees and birds do not fill the page (except for the actual words), but if we think of trees and birds connoting or suggesting delicate beauty or the majesty of nature or perhaps simply positive and pleasant thoughts, then through her diction, Oliver's meaning is both clarified and expanded.

FIGURES OF SPEECH

When we use figures of speech, we mean something other than the words' literal meaning. In the first sentence of "Singapore," Mary Oliver writes that "a darkness was ripped from my eyes." This direct comparison is a **metaphor**. Had she been more indirect, she might have written "it was like a darkness . . . ," a common literary device called a **simile**. Poets use metaphors and similes to help us see in a fresh perspective. Comparing love to a rose encourages us to think differently about love, helping us see its delicate beauty. Of course, today that comparison is no longer novel and can even be a cliché, suggesting that a writer is not trying to be original and is settling instead for an easy comparison. When Robert Burns wrote "my love is like a red, red rose" more than two hundred years ago, it was a fresh comparison that excited new ways of looking at love. Indeed, some theorists, like the contemporary American philosopher Richard Rorty, think that metaphors can change our ways of looking at the world. Our thinking about time, for example, might be different if we didn't think with linear metaphors about the past being behind us and the future up ahead. What if, as some American Indian languages do, ours used a circular metaphor, having just one day that constantly repeated itself? Would our perceptions of time change?

What if Mary Oliver had begun her poem by saying that "a misunderstanding was corrected," instead of "a darkness was ripped from my eyes"?

Her metaphor is not only more dramatic and memorable but also more suggestive. Darkness deepens the idea of lack of knowledge, suggesting not only intellectual blindness but also a host of negative connotations that readers might associate with the dark. Fresh metaphors can be expansive and illuminating. They help us understand the world differently.

Oliver creatively uses metaphors and similes throughout "Singapore." "Disgust argued" is an interesting metaphor or perhaps a personification, in which the speaker's stomach is given the ability to argue. She interrupts her observation of the cleaning woman in the third stanza to make a comment on the function of poetry itself, claiming that poems should have birds, rivers, and trees in them. Is she suggesting metaphorically that poems should be pleasant? Is that the only thing birds, rivers, and trees suggest to you?

She returns to the woman, and they exchange glances. Apparently, the speaker is struggling with her own socialization that sees this kind of physical labor as demeaning. She directly describes the woman's "scrubbing and rinsing" but then returns to similes, describing her work as being "like a river" and her hair "like the wing of a bird." These comparisons seem for a moment to clarify the event for the speaker, helping her see this seemingly oppressive job positively. Amazingly, she wants the woman actually to become a bird and "rise up from the crust and the slop and fly."

But in the final stanza, she reminds us that she isn't really expecting that kind of physical miracle; instead, she wants to remind us that how we describe the woman working controls how we feel about her. If we see the folding and unfolding of her washcloth metaphorically, then we might see her differently; we might see her natural dignity, her beauty, and how her "light" was able to illuminate the speaker's "darkness."

Sometimes the poet chooses words like *darkness* and *light* that are so rich in texture that they can be examined as both metaphor and connotation. Such words might also be thought of as examples of synecdoche or metonymy. **Synecdoche** substitutes part of something for the whole, as in "I love my new wheels," referring to a car. **Metonymy** substitutes something associated with a thing, as in "Hollywood is resisting censorship" referring to the entire film industry. Oliver's "eyes" might be a synecdoche for her mind, and "darkness" and "light" can be metonymies for ignorance and beauty. Locate examples in our three poems of metaphor, connotation, synecdoche, and metonymy, if you can.

Although students often seem perplexed when professors find hidden **symbols** in poems, writers rarely plant such puzzling images deep in the recesses of their texts. The best symbols grow naturally out of the meaning-making process that readers go through. In the context of a particular poem, symbols are usually objects that can stand for general ideas. And like metaphors and similes, they suggest different things to different readers. The whale in *Moby-Dick*, for example, can be read as a symbol for implacable evil or perhaps the mysteries of the universe. In "Singapore," the specific event of the speaker watching a woman washing ashtrays in a toilet could be symbolic of anything we find unpleasant or strange or alien. And the whole event, including her eventual understanding, could easily be an **allegory** or extended symbol for the necessity for all of us to transcend our cultural social-ization to understand other cultures and other attitudes toward working.

SOUND

The English poet Alexander Pope hoped that poetry's **sound** could become "an echo to [its] sense," that what the ear hears would reinforce what the mind understands. To many people, **rhyme** is the most recognizable aspect of poetry. The matching of final vowel and consonant sounds can make a poem trite or interesting. The now-familiar rhyming of "moon" and "June" with "swoon" suggests a poet who will settle for a cliché rather than do the hard work of being fresh. Rhyme, of course, is pleasing to the ear and makes the poem easier to remember, but it also gives the poem psychological force. Most contemporary poets choose not to rhyme, preferring the flexibility and freedom of free verse. But sound is still a high priority.

One of the most famous and effective examples of how sound can "echo" its sense is found in Robert Frost's "Stopping by Woods on a Snowy Evening," especially in the last two stanzas:

He gives his harness bells a shake
To ask if there is some mistake.
The only other sound's the sweep
Of easy wind and downy flake.

The woods are lovely, dark and deep,
But I have promises to keep,
And miles to go before I sleep,
And miles to go before I sleep.

Skilled poets like Frost use **alliteration** to connect words near each other by repeating the initial consonant sound. A variation, **assonance**, repeats vowel sounds. Frost obviously and subtly employs these sound techniques to echo both theme and mood. The alliterative -s in "shake," "some," "sound's," and "sweep" also connect the meaning of these words, which are also rein-forced by the -s's in "gives," "his," "harness," "bells," "asks," "is," "mistake," "sound's," and "easy." And when alliteration is combined with the assonance of "sweep" and "easy," as well as "downy" and "sound's," visual, tactile, and aural images are joined to create a soothing, restful, and idyllic scene of beauty and peace. All of these choices prepare the reader for the -ee of "keep" and "deep" and the -s's of the repeated "woods," "promises," "miles," and "sleep." In this way, the serenity and retreat of the woods are verbally and thematically contrasted with the demands of life's duties, culminating in the deadly temp-tation to escape responsibility by entering the winter woods.

Notice how Mary Oliver uses alliteration in her first stanza to link "women's," "woman," "washing," and "white." Komunyakaa's first stanza too links "printers," "police," and "pulled" as well as "they," "thief's," "Terrestrial," "thick," and "thorns." What effect do these and other elements of sound have on the impact and meaning of the poems?

≡ A WRITING EXERCISE

Note the use of alliteration and assonance in all three poems. How might these devices enhance meaning?

RHYTHM AND METER

Many poets in the early twentieth century chose to have their poems rhyme. Edwin Arlington Robinson's "The Mill" employs a typical **rhyme scheme** in which in each stanza the last words in lines 1 and 3 sound the same and the last words in lines 2 and 4 sound the same. We indicate such a pattern with letters—*abab*. The second half of the first stanza would then be *cdcd* and so forth.

Rhythm in poetry refers to the beat, a series of stresses, pauses, and accents. We are powerfully attuned to rhythm, whether it is our own heartbeat or the throb of the bass in a hip-hop bassline. When we pronounce a word, we give more **stress** (breath, emphasis) to some syllables than to others. When these stresses occur at a regular interval over, say, a line of poetry, we refer to it as **meter**. When we scan a line of poetry, we try to mark its stresses and pauses. We use ´ to indicate a stressed syllable and ˘ for an unstressed one. The basic measuring unit for these stressed and unstressed syllables in English is the **foot**. There are four usual feet: *iambic, trochaic, anapestic,* and *dactylic*. An **iamb** is an unstressed syllable followed by a stressed one, as in "the woŏds." Reversed we have a **trochee**, as in "tiger."An **anapest** contains three syllables that are unstressed, then unstressed, then stressed, as in "When the blúe / wăve rŏlls nightlў / ŏn deép Galĭleé." The reverse, the **dactyl**, can be heard in the Mother Goose rhyme, "Pússў cát, / pússў cát / whére hăve yoŭ / beén?" If you look at the first four lines of "The Mill" again, you can hear a regular beat of iambs:

> The míll / er's wife / hăd waít / ĕd lóng,
>
> The téa / wăs cóld, / the fíre / wăs deád;
>
> And thére / might yét / bĕ nóth / iňg wróng
>
> Iň hów / hĕ wént / aňd whát / hĕ saíd:

Depending on the number of feet, we give lines various names. If a line contains one foot, it is a **monometer**; two, a **dimeter**; three, a **trimeter**; four, a **tetrameter**; five, a **pentameter**; six, a **hexameter**; seven, a **heptameter**; and eight, an **octameter**. So Robinson's lines are iambic tetrameter. Most lines in Shakespeare's sonnets are iambic pentameter, or five iambs.

Note the punctuation in Robinson's poem. When a line ends with a comma, we are meant to pause very briefly; when a line ends with a period (end stop), we pause a bit longer. But when there is no punctuation (line 7), we are meant to continue on until the end of the next line. This is known as *enjambment.* These poetic techniques improve the sound and flow of the poem and enhance the thoughts and feelings that give poetry its memorable depth and meaningfulness.

THEME

Some readers are fond of extracting ideas from poems, claiming, for example, that the theme of "Blackberries" is the loss of innocence or that the theme of "The Mill" is the loss of identity. In a sense, these thematic observations are plausible enough, but they are limiting and misleading. "Blackberries" certainly seems to have something to do with the interruption of a certain view about physical labor, but the significance for each reader might be much more specific, having to do with the Garden of Eden; hierarchy in society; the arrogance of the rich; or sensitivity, cruelty, and dignity. "The Mill" could also be about gender relations, economic cruelty, or the responsibility of communities. Reducing a complex, ambiguous poem to a bald statement robs the poem of its evocative power, its mystery, and its art.

Some critics stress the response of readers; others care only for what the text itself says; still others are concerned with the social and cultural implications of the poem's meaning. Psychoanalytic readers may see poems as reflections of the psychological health or illness of the poet; source-hunting or intertextual readers want to find references and hints of other literary works hidden deep within the poem. Feminist readers may find sexism, Marxists may find economic injustice, and gay and lesbian readers may find heterosexual bias. Readers can and will find in texts a whole range of issues. Perhaps we find what we are looking for, or we find what matters most to us.

This does not mean that we should think of committed readers as biased or as distorting the text to fulfill their own agenda, although biased or distorted readings are not rare. In a literature course, readers are entitled to read poems according to their own interpretations as long as they follow the general convention of academic discourse. That is, it is possible to make a reasonable case that "Blackberries" is really about rejecting contemporary technology in favor of rural life. The reason that some themes sound more plausible than others is that these critics marshal their evidence from the text and their own experience. Usually the evidence that fits best wins: if you can persuade others that you have significant textual support for your theme and if you present a balanced and judicious persona, you can usually carry the day. Poems almost always have several reasonable themes. The critic's job is to argue for a theme that seems to make the most sense in relation to the support. Often the same evidence can be used to bolster different themes because themes are really just higher-level generalizations than the particulars found in the text. Critics use the concrete elements of a poem to make more general abstract statements. In "Blackberries," for example, the same textual support could be used to uphold a theme about the cruelty of children, the more general notion of an initiation in a class-conscious culture, or the even more general idea of the inevitable loss of innocence.

Revised Draft of a Student Paper

Michaela Fiorucci
Mr. Hardy
English 102
25 April - - - -

Negotiating Boundaries

Although most college students value their privacy, they also want to create intimate relationships; it is often hard to reconcile these two impulses. Most middle-class students are lucky enough to have their own bedrooms, private enclaves against annoying sisters and brothers, intrusive mothers and fathers. But such boundaries are more than physical barriers; they are also a symbolic assertion of identity. They say, "I'm separate from you even within the closeness of our family." Such a commitment to physical privacy might be innocent enough, but it does contain dangerous seeds, especially when extended beyond the home to neighborhoods. When different ethnic groups want boundaries between them, it is no longer innocent. When the upper classes want to be separated from workers because they see each other as radically different, a dangerously undemocratic boundary has been erected. Boundaries clearly serve a protective function, but unneeded ones can also prevent us from helping and understanding each other. Writers like Edwin Arlington Robinson, Yusef Komunyakaa, and Mary Oliver understand that we must negotiate boundaries, building them when they increase privacy and self-worth and bridging them when human solidarity can be enhanced.

Creates context about boundaries, moving from the personal to neighborhoods and beyond.

Announces her focus on need to negotiate.

It would be reductive to say that boundaries are either good or bad, since their value depends so much on context. Robinson's "The Mill" is a good example of the dangerous consequences of a failure to cross a boundary that should not exist and then a failure to establish a boundary where one should exist. The poem narrates the sad story of a farm couple who commit suicide — the husband because he feels useless, the wife because she can't imagine life without her husband. A contemporary reader is struck by the lack of communication between the couple. He must have been depressed for a long time, but it seems they never discussed his feelings. Keeping such an emotional boundary between husband and wife was probably typical of the way men and women dealt with each other one hundred years ago. Apparently, it was a constructed barrier that few could cross. He simply could not bare his heart by saying, "I feel terrible that I am going to lose my job." And his wife accepts his reticence, even though he might have been having second thoughts as he "lingered at

Begins first concrete supporting example.

Example of harmful tradition boundary.

the door." Clearly, this is a boundary that should have been breached. The time for their solidarity was before he killed himself, not after.

After several readings, it is clear that the boundary that should have been established wasn't. The miller is the victim of the demeaning idea that a person's worth is synonymous with his or her occupation. When his job disappears, so must he. Although Robinson's tone is flat, we sense his frustration with the inevitability of this grim tragedy, one that is compounded by the equally dehumanizing idea that a wife cannot exist without her husband. When the miller's wife decides to "leave no mark" by jumping into the pond, she is admitting that she is useless outside her matrimonial role. *Concrete reference to poems strengthens argument.* Both identify with a role that should be only one aspect of a complex human life. The final barrier she crosses, from life to death, is symbolically represented in the poem as a feminine domestic gesture: she doesn't want to leave a mess. She continues as a housewife even in death. The boundaries between a person and occupation should be clear, but the *Concludes paragraph with example of a boundary needing negotiating.* arbitrary boundaries between husbands and wives should continue to be eradicated.

When the ten-year-old narrator in "Blackberries" claims *Second concrete example of problematic boundary.* that he is "Limboed between worlds" (18), he means the rural paradise of "Terrestrial sweetness" (4) and "rich blackness" (15) he temporarily lives in versus the commercial urban world that seems to make him anxious. He has constructed a boundary between the ancient task of picking berries and the modern technology of automobiles, between a closeness with nature and the artificial air-conditioning of the car. Although the narrator enjoys being one with nature, he seems to be cutting himself off from the realities of the world. He seems to reject "old lime-covered / History" (7–8) in favor of "mythology" (11), which seems to suggest a conscious rejection of the present. But this is a boundary that cannot stand. He needs the outside world to survive financially, and so when the car approaches, it is the modern world and all its complexity that draws near. When he looks into the car, he sees "Smirking" (23) children; he sees class prejudice, hierarchy, and economic reality. The smirkers of the world are in charge. It is this realization that dissolves the protective *Notes consequences of not negotiating.* boundary around his Garden of Eden; consequently, he feels physical pain, but it is really the pain of initiation into reality that he feels. He must now cross a boundary he tried to delay. Although we can sympathize with the young narrator, like the *Connection to previous poem increases essay's unity.* couple in "The Mill," he would have been better off not making his boundary so extreme.

The narrator in Mary Oliver's "Singapore" also imagines that she sees a significant boundary, here between herself as a middle-class traveler and a cleaning woman laboring over a toilet. It is a separation we might all make, given our social-ization in America to consider this kind of physical labor as degrading. College-educated people have a tendency to see themselves as distinct from the working class. For many, a woman washing an ashtray in a toilet bowl is beyond the pale, a clear indication that the woman is Other. But Oliver does not simply give into her cultural conditioning; she contests the boundary, asserting that a "Disgust argued in my stomach"(6). Since part of our democratic socialization is also to be tolerant and open-minded, Oliver knows that she shouldn't stereotype workers. And since she is also a writer with ideas about how a poem should "always have birds in it" (8), she looks hard at the cleaning woman, finally seeing in her face, in her hair, and in the way she works, slowly "like a river" (25), the positive aspects of the woman that most of us would probably miss.

Third concrete example of boundaries.

Explicit example of negotiating a boundary.

Oliver does not simply accept the boundaries that her culture constructs. Instead, she negotiates internally, eventu-ally seeing that a "light . . . can shine out of a life" (35) even where we would not expect it. In the woman's careful folding and unfolding of her blue work cloth and in her smile, Oliver sees a beauty that helps her eclipse a social boundary, ending with a life-affirming vision "filled with trees, and birds" (38). Such an insight does not come easily to us because we usually accept our given cultural boundaries. The miller and his wife are tragically unequipped to bridge the divide between them. Likewise, the boy in "Blackberries" is unable to sustain his fantasy boundaries. Oliver's traveler, however, struggles to negotiate boundaries and is thereby able to increase human solidarity even across class structures and cultures.

Notes benefits of breaching a boundary.

Concludes by uniting all three poems in support of claim.

Comparing Poems and Pictures

Although literature and visual art may seem quite different media, they have often been closely connected. For one thing, any page of literature is a visual image, whether or not readers are always conscious of this fact. Also, most publishers of literature carefully design the covers of their books, aiming to lure readers in. Specific genres and authors, however, have forged even stron-ger relations between literature and art. Beginning in classical times and continuing today, many poems have precisely described existing paintings and sculptures; this tradition of verse is called **ekphrasis**. In the late eighteenth century, William Blake made highly ornamental engravings of his poems, so that they were striking works of art and not just written texts. In the nine-teenth century, many novels included illustrations, a tradition evident today in children's picture books. At present, perhaps you are a fan of **graphic novels**: comic books that combine words and images to tell stories aimed at adults.

Aside from this history of connections, comparing a literary text with an image is a good mental exercise. The process can help you acquire more insights into each work. Given this possibility, we present a pairing on pages 175–79 of an Edward Hopper painting and a Rolando Perez poem, both titled *Office at Night*. In this case, the poem was written in response to the image. In other cases you may wish to connect a poem and an image for the first time, to trace their similarities and differences. With any such pairing, comparison can help you generate ideas for writing, a principle we stress throughout this book.

ANALYZING VISUAL ART

You can better understand a work of visual art—and develop ideas for an essay about it—if you raise certain questions about it and try to answer them. These questions apply to various types of pictures. Bear in mind that even photographs are not mere reproductions of reality. People who create them are, consciously or not, choosing their subject and figuring out how best to represent it. Especially in the age of digital technologies such as Photoshop or Instagram, images caught by the camera can be tweaked in all sorts of ways. Moreover, the scene depicted might be a staged fantasy in the first place.

Here are the questions to ask yourself as you examine a picture with an eye to analyzing it:

1. What details do you see in the picture? Besides recognizable objects and figures (human beings or animals), consider shapes, colors, lighting, and shading. Do not list just the picture's most prominent elements, for those that at first seem trivial may turn out to be important for you.
2. What are aspects of the picture's *style*—the artist's particular way of handling the subject? Among other things, consider what the artist does and does not allow the viewer to see, how realistic or abstract the work seems, and whether anyone in the picture looks directly at the viewer.
3. How has the artist organized the picture? Note especially patterns of resemblance and contrast. Think, too, about whether the picture's design directs the viewer's attention to a particular part of it.
4. What mood does the picture evoke? Consider emotions that you experience as a viewer, as well as those that seem to be felt by any living figures in the scene.
5. What is at least one detail of the picture that strikes you as puzzling (and therefore especially in need of interpretation)?
6. Does the picture seem to tell a story or appear to be part of a story that has already begun and will continue?
7. How does the picture relate to its title and (where applicable) to its caption?
8. What are some options that the artist could have explored but did not pursue?

WRITING AN ESSAY THAT COMPARES LITERATURE AND ART

Before you write an essay comparing a work of literature with a work of art, collect as many details as you can about each. The questions above can help you do this with the artwork. For aid in gathering observations about the literary text, see Chapter 4, "The Reading Process," especially the section on Strategies for Close Reading. Then, as you proceed to write, keep the following principles especially in mind:

- You do not have to give equal space to each work. Rather, you may prefer to come up with an issue and a main claim by focusing on interpreting *one* of the works: either the literary text *or* the visual image. Your secondary work will still play some role in the essay, but your primary one will receive greater attention. The result will be what in Chapter 5 we call a *weighted* comparison. (See that chapter for more tips.)
- Assume that your reader is at least somewhat familiar with both the literary work and the image but needs to be reminded of their basic details. In particular, help your audience *visualize* the art you discuss.
- Refer at least sometimes to the author of the literary work and to the artist who created the image. Doing so will help you analyze how their productions involve particular strategies of representation — attempts to affect audiences in particular ways.

ROLANDO PEREZ

Office at Night

It is past nine o'clock, and she has stayed late to help him. How many times did he dream of this very same scenario: her standing there in her tight blue dress, with her black pumps and flesh-colored stockings. And now it has finally happened. Without him having to ask — not that he would have dared — she volunteered all on her own.   5

He had to "open the window."

"This office at night is a bit stuffy."

A sheet of paper that once lay on top of other papers on his desk, now lies on the green carpet — to his right — gently carried there by the wind. Standing at a black filing cabinet, searching for some old bills, she has noticed the paper   10 lying on the floor. The desk lamp throws a shadow on the desk, and illuminates his hands. And a patch of light, reflected on the wall, touches them both . . . lightly, very lightly . . . as with finger tips.

Will she bend over to pick it up?

If only the phone beside him would ring, then he would do something,   15 he would act, produce the correct combination of words that would elicit the correct series of reactions from her. He might even suggest that they lock up and go for a drink somewhere. But having heard too many truths in the past, now history holds him back. In his suit, with his shirt buttoned to the top, and his tie still on, he hasn't moved, and she hasn't moved; and the wind-swept   20

Office at Night. Artist: Hopper, Edward (1882–1967) © 2019 Heirs of Josephine Hopper/Licensed by Artists Rights Society (ARS), NY. Heritage Image Partnership Ltd/Alamy Stock Photo.

paper will stay on the floor, halfway between his desk and her cabinet, timidly undisturbed, in this wounded and frozen infinity.   *[2002]*

A Sample Paper Comparing a Poem and a Picture

To give you a better idea of what an essay comparing literature and art looks like, we present a paper by student Karl Magnusson. He connects Edward Hopper's painting *Office at Night* to the prose poem of the same title by Rolando Perez. As you will see, Karl's essay is a weighted comparison; it focuses mostly on Perez's poem.

Karl Magnusson
Professor Kemper
English W350
16 May - - - -

Lack of Motion and Speech in
Rolando Perez's "Office at Night"

Edward Hopper's painting *Office at Night* depicts a man and a woman working in the kind of setting indicated by the title. The man is apparently the boss of the woman, who

Immediately refers to the painting and then proceeds to summarize its key details.

seems to be his secretary. He sits at a desk by an open window, studying a document that he holds in front of him. She is positioned to the left and slightly to the rear of him. More precisely, she stands at a filing cabinet with her right hand resting on an open drawer. Their respective postures suggest that she is waiting to hear what he will say next. Perhaps she has just asked him a question and he is thinking about how to answer, or perhaps she is simply expecting him, as her superior, to issue her a new order. In any case, viewers of the painting are free to interpret their interaction, and different spectators might come up with different ideas about what these people really mean to each other. Indeed, not everyone would conceive their relationship to be what Rolando Perez imagines it as being in his poem about Hopper's artwork. Also entitled "Office at Night," Perez's poem speculates that the man and woman have a romantic interest in each other that neither he nor she can express. Furthermore, the poem conveys their reticence in terms that have often been used to describe the medium of painting in general.

Now turns to the poem, which will be the primary work in this weighted comparison.

This is the essay's main claim, which is about the poem.

The poem draws attention more to the self-repression of the boss. The secretary, too, evidently does not feel able to speak frankly about their emotions, perhaps because she is after all his employee. But the text tends to focus on *his* reluctance to reveal that he is enamored of her. This mixture of lust and hesitation is evident right near the start of the poem. There, just before describing the secretary's alluring clothes, the poem's speaker wonders, "How many times did he [the boss] dream of this very same scenario" (lines 1–2). The implication is that the boss has entertained sensual visions of his employee in his mind while doing nothing to bring them about. He merely fantasizes a romance with her, not actually helping it come to life. Soon after, the reader learns that *she* had to prompt *him* to "open the window" (6) and let fresh air in. Evidently she wishes to stimulate their senses and admit their real feelings, but this is behavior that he apparently would never "have dared" (4) to engage in on his own. Later, he resists actually inviting her to take their office working relationship in a romantic direction. Although he apparently considers the possibility that "he would do something, he would act, produce the correct combination of words" (15–16) to initiate a courtship, he remains silent and still. The implication is that he is restrained by the memory of his previous disappointments in love — "too many truths in the past" (18). Whatever specific episodes in his past he is thinking of, the result is that

Proceeds to support the main argument with specific lines from the poem.

"now history holds him back" (19). Rather than "sug-gest[ing] that they lock up and go for a drink somewhere" (17–18), he stays emotionally locked up, not letting his true attachment to her emerge.

In describing physical details of the office, the poem's speaker sums up the couple's inability to be emotionally open with each other. In part, the speaker does this by sometimes using images of motion that underscore by contrast how the man and woman fail to act on their feelings. The "patch of light" that "touches them both . . . lightly, very lightly . . . as with fingertips" (12–13) is a reminder that these two people do not physically touch each other at all. The phrase "gently carried there by the wind" (9) — used in reference to a piece of paper on the floor — indirectly emphasizes that the couple will not let themselves be carried away by passion. When, however, near the end of the poem, the speaker describes the paper as "timidly undisturbed" (21–22), the symbolism is more direct: the word "timidly" seems to fit the couple as well, for they have been too scared to confess their emotional bond. Moreover, the speaker's observation that "he hasn't moved, and she hasn't moved" (20) directly reinforces their *psychological* paralysis. The poem's final phrase, "wounded and frozen infinity" (22), is not just an overview of this late-night office environment. The speaker is also indicating the basic state of the couple's relationship. They are "wounded" in the sense that they suffer unfulfilled desires for each other. They are "frozen" in the sense that they cannot reveal these desires. The word "infinity" implies that, given their inertia, their situation is unlikely to change.

Not every poem about Hopper's *Office at Night* painting would necessarily focus on its two human figures. Nor would every poem about the painting necessarily depict their relationship in the way that Perez's does. Indeed, a distinc-tive feature of his poem is that his portrait of the couple attributes to them characteristics often associated with the medium of painting itself. Aware, like most people, that figures in a painting do not move, Perez takes this fact and makes it an element of the couple's behavior. The static nature of painting in general is echoed in their paralytic inhibition. Furthermore, just as people in paintings do not speak aloud, so the couple in Perez's poem resist articulating what they really feel. Also, just as viewers of a painting have to guess the thoughts of anyone shown in it, so Perez's man and woman force themselves to guess what is on each other's mind.

Perez could be seen as tolerating and even encouraging affairs between bosses and their secretaries. In this respect, his text seems more in keeping with the world of 1940, the year Hopper painted *Office at Night*. Back then, expressions of love between a manager and a subordinate might have been smiled upon, perceived as what the poem's speaker calls "the correct combination of words" and "the correct series of reactions" (16–17). The same expressions now, however, might be condemned as politically and even legally *in*correct. Certainly, government and company policies on sexual harassment warn executives not to seduce the employees who serve them. Nevertheless, it would be unfair simply to dismiss Perez's poem or Hopper's painting as outdated, especially because the audiences for these works do not have to take them as being just about romance in the office. Both the poem and the painting allow for interpretations that see the couple as universal — as people who might exist anywhere. In this case, their reticence toward each other would be a widespread human problem: the difficulty of communicating the stirrings of one's heart.

The concluding paragraph does not simply repeat what has already been said. It touches on a new subject: changes in policies on office affairs.

Writing about Plays

Most plays incorporate elements also found in short fiction, such as plot, characterization, dialogue, setting, and theme. But, in contrast to short fiction and other literary genres, plays are typically enacted live, in front of an audience. Theater professionals distinguish between the written *script* of a play and its actual *performances*. When you write about a play, you may wind up saying little or nothing about performances of it. When you first read and analyze a play, however, try to imagine ways of staging it. You might even research past productions of the play, noting how scenery, costumes, and lighting — as well as particular actors — were used.

Because a play is usually meant to be staged, its readers are rarely its only interpreters. Audiences at productions of the play also ponder its meanings. So, too, do castmembers; no doubt you have heard of actors "interpreting" their parts. When a play is put on, even members of the backstage team are involved in interpreting it. The technical designers' choices of sets, costumes, and lighting reflect their ideas about the play, while the director works with cast and crew to implement a particular vision of it. No matter what the author of the script intended, theater is a collaborative art: all of the key figures involved in a play's production are *active* interpreters of the play, in that they influence the audience's understanding and experience of it. Therefore, you can develop good ideas when you read a play if you imagine yourself directing a production of it. More specifically, think what you would say to the actors as you guide them through their parts. As you engage in this thought experiment, you will see that you have options, for even directors keen on staying faithful to the script know it can be staged in any number of ways. Perhaps your course will give you and other students the chance to perform a scene together; if so, you will be deciding what interpretation of the scene to set forth.

To help you understand how to write about plays, we will refer often to the one-act play that follows. *The Stronger* was first performed in 1889. Its Swedish author, August Strindberg (1849–1912), is widely acknowledged as a founder of modern drama. Throughout his career, Strindberg experimented with a variety of theatrical styles. With this particular play, an encounter between two actresses, he dared to have one of the women speak and the other remain silent.

AUGUST STRINDBERG

The Stronger

Translated by Edith and Warner Oland

CHARACTERS

MRS. X, *an actress, married*
MISS Y, *an actress, unmarried*
A WAITRESS

SCENE: *The corner of a ladies' café. Two little iron tables, a red velvet sofa, several chairs. Enter Mrs. X, dressed in winter clothes, carrying a Japanese basket on her arm.*   5

Miss Y sits with a half empty beer bottle before her, reading an illustrated paper, which she changes later for another.

    MRS. X: Good afternoon, Amelie. You're sitting here alone on Christmas eve like a poor bachelor!   10

Miss Y looks up, nods, and resumes her reading.

    MRS. X: Do you know it really hurts me to see you like this, alone, in a café, and on Christmas eve, too. It makes me feel as I did one time when I saw a bridal party in a Paris restaurant, and the bride sat reading a comic paper, while the groom played billiards with the witnesses.   15 Huh, thought I, with such a beginning, what will follow, and what will be the end? He played billiards on his wedding eve! *(Miss Y starts to speak.)* And she read a comic paper, you mean? Well, they are not altogether the same thing.

A waitress enters, places a cup of chocolate before Mrs. X, and goes out.   20

    MRS. X: You know what, Amelie! I believe you would have done better to have kept him! Do you remember, I was the first to say "Forgive him?" Do you remember that? You would be married now and have a home.

Remember that Christmas when you went out to visit your fiancé's parents in the country? How you gloried in the happiness of home life and really longed to quit the theater forever? Yes, Amelie dear, home is the best of all, the theater next and children — well, you don't understand that. 25

Miss Y looks up scornfully.

  Mrs. X sips a few spoonfuls out of the cup, then opens her basket and shows Christmas presents. 30

MRS. X: Now you shall see what I bought for my piggywigs. *(Takes up a doll.)* Look at this! This is for Lisa, ha! Do you see how she can roll her eyes and turn her head, eh? And here is Maja's popgun. *(Loads it and shoots at Miss Y.)* 35

Miss Y makes a startled gesture.

MRS. X: Did I frighten you? Do you think I would like to shoot you, eh? On my soul, if I don't think you did! If you wanted to shoot *me* it wouldn't be so surprising, because I stood in your way — and I know you can never forget that — although I was absolutely innocent. You still 40 believe I intrigued and got you out of the Stora theater, but I didn't. I didn't do that, although you think so. Well, it doesn't make any difference what I say to you. You still believe I did it. *(Takes up a pair of embroidered slippers.)* And these are for my better half. I embroidered them myself — I can't bear tulips, but he wants tulips on everything. 45

Miss Y looks up ironically and curiously.

MRS. X *(putting a hand in each slipper)*:   What little feet Bob has! What? And you should see what a splendid stride he has! You've never seen him in slippers! *(Miss Y laughs aloud.)* Look! *(She makes the slippers walk on the table. Miss Y laughs loudly.)* And when he is grumpy he stamps like 50 this with his foot. "What! damn those servants who can never learn to make coffee. Oh, now those creatures haven't trimmed the lamp wick properly!" And then there are draughts on the floor and his feet are cold. "Ugh, how cold it is; the stupid idiots can never keep the fire going." *(She rubs the slippers together, one sole over the other.)* 55

Miss Y shrieks with laughter.

MRS. X: And then he comes home and has to hunt for his slippers which Marie has stuck under the chiffonier — oh, but it's sinful to sit here and make fun of one's husband this way when he is kind and a good little man. You ought to have had such a husband, Amelie. What are you 60 laughing at? What? What? And you see he's true to me. Yes, I'm sure of that, because he told me himself — what are you laughing at? — that when I was touring in Norway that that brazen Frédérique came and wanted to seduce him! Can you fancy anything so infamous? *(Pause.)* I'd have torn her eyes out if she had come to see him when I was at 65 home. *(Pause.)* It was lucky that Bob told me about it himself and that it didn't reach me through gossip. *(Pause.)* But would you believe it,

Frédérique wasn't the only one! I don't know why, but the women are crazy about my husband. They must think he has influence about getting them theatrical engagements, because he is connected with the government. Perhaps you were after him yourself. I didn't use to trust you any too much. But now I know he never bothered his head about you, and you always seemed to have a grudge against him someway.   70

Pause. They look at each other in a puzzled way.

Come and see us this evening, Amelie, and show us that you're not put out with us, — not put out with me at any rate. I don't know, but I think it would be uncomfortable to have you for an enemy. Perhaps it's because I stood in your way or — I really — don't know why — in particular.   75

Pause. Miss Y stares at Mrs. X curiously.   80

MRS. X *(thoughtfully)*:   Our acquaintance has been so queer. When I saw you for the first time I was afraid of you, so afraid that I didn't dare let you out of my sight; no matter when or where, I always found myself near you — I didn't dare have you for an enemy, so I became your friend. But there was always discord when you came to our house, because I saw that my husband couldn't endure you, and the whole thing seemed as awry to me as an ill-fitting gown — and I did all I could to make him friendly toward you, but with no success until you became engaged. Then came a violent friendship between you, so that it looked all at once as though you both dared show your real feelings only when you were secure — and then — how was it later? I didn't get jealous — strange to say! And I remember at the christening, when you acted as godmother, I made him kiss you — he did so, and you became so confused — as it were; I didn't notice it then — didn't think about it later, either — have never thought about it until — now! *(Rises suddenly.)* Why are you silent? You haven't said a word this whole time, but you have let me go on talking! You have sat there, and your eyes have reeled out of me all these thoughts which lay like raw silk in its cocoon — thoughts — suspicious thoughts, perhaps. Let me see — why did you break your engagement? Why do you never come to our house any more? Why won't you come to see us tonight?   85   90   95   100

Miss Y appears as if about to speak.

MRS. X: Hush, you needn't speak — I understand it all! It was because — and because — and because! Yes, yes! Now all the accounts balance. That's it. Fie, I won't sit at the same table with you. *(Moves her things to another table.)* That's the reason I had to embroider tulips — which I hate — on his slippers, because you are fond of tulips; that's why *(Throws slippers on the floor.)* we go to Lake Mälarn in the summer, because you don't like salt water; that's why my boy is named Eskil — because it's your father's name; that's why I wear your colors, read your authors, eat your favorite dishes, drink your drinks — chocolate, for instance; that's   105   110

why — oh — my God — it's terrible, when I think about it; it's terrible. Everything, everything came from you to me, even your passions. Your soul crept into mine, like a worm into an apple, ate and ate, bored and bored, until nothing was left but the rind and a little black dust within.   115
I wanted to get away from you, but I couldn't; you lay like a snake and charmed me with your black eyes; I felt that when I lifted my wings they only dragged me down; I lay in the water with bound feet, and the stronger I strove to keep up the deeper I worked myself down, down, until I sank to the bottom, where you lay like a giant crab to clutch me   120
in your claws — and there I am lying now.

I hate you, hate you, hate you! And you only sit there silent — silent and indifferent; indifferent whether it's new moon or waning moon, Christmas or New Year's, whether others are happy or unhappy; without power to hate or to love; as quiet as a stork by a rat hole — you   125
couldn't scent your prey and capture it, but you could lie in wait for it! You sit here in your corner of the café — did you know it's called "The Rat Trap" for you? — and read the papers to see if misfortune hasn't befallen someone, to see if someone hasn't been given notice at the theater, perhaps; you sit here and calculate about your next   130
victim and reckon on your chances of recompense like a pilot in a shipwreck. Poor Amelie, I pity you, nevertheless, because I know you are unhappy, unhappy like one who has been wounded, and angry because you are wounded. I can't be angry with you, no matter how much I want to be — because you come out the weaker one. Yes, all   135
that with Bob doesn't trouble me. What is that to me, after all? And what difference does it make whether I learned to drink chocolate from you or someone else. *(Sips a spoonful from her cup.)*

Besides, chocolate is very healthful. And if you taught me how to dress — *tant mieux!* — *[so much the better!]* that has only made me more   140
attractive to my husband; so you lost and I won there. Well, judging by certain signs, I believe you have already lost him; and you certainly intended that I should leave him — do as you did with your fiancé and regret as you now regret; but, you see, I don't do that — we mustn't be too exacting. And why should I take only what no one else wants?   145

Perhaps, take it all in all, I am at this moment the stronger one. You received nothing from me, but you gave me much. And now I seem like a thief since you have awakened and find I possess what is your loss. How could it be otherwise when everything is worthless and sterile in your hands? You can never keep a man's love with your   150
tulips and your passions — but I can keep it. You can't learn how to live from your authors, as I have learned. You have no little Eskil to cherish, even if your father's name was Eskil. And why are you always silent, silent, silent? I thought that was strength, but perhaps it is because you have nothing to say! Because you never think about   155
anything! *(Rises and picks up slippers.)*

Now I'm going home—and take the tulips with me—*your* tulips! You
are unable to learn from another; you can't bend—therefore, you
broke like a dry stalk. But I won't break! Thank you, Amelie, for all
your good lessons. Thanks for teaching my husband how to love. Now   160
I'm going home to love him. *(Goes.)*   *[1889]*

A Student's Personal Response to the Play

Trish Carlisle was enrolled in a class that read and discussed Strindberg's
The Stronger. Below is some freewriting that Trish did about the play.

Near the end of Strindberg's play, Mrs. X says that "I am at this
moment the stronger one." But is she? I guess that depends on what
Strindberg meant by "the stronger" when he gave his play that title.
As I was reading, I started to think that the stronger woman is
actually the silent one, Miss Y, because she seems to have more
self-control than Mrs. X does. I mean, Miss Y doesn't apparently feel
that she has to make long, loud speeches in defense of her way of
life. I can even believe that with her silence she is manipulating
Mrs. X into getting fairly hysterical. Also, I guess we're to think that
Amelie has managed to lure away Mrs. X's husband, at least for a
while. Furthermore, we don't have to believe Mrs. X when at the end
she claims that she has triumphed over Miss Y. Maybe people who
have really succeeded in life don't need to proclaim that they have,
as Mrs. X does.

Nevertheless, I can see why some students in this class feel that
Mrs. X is in fact the stronger. If she has her husband back and wants
her husband back, and if Miss Y is really without companionship at
the end and has even lost her job at the theater, then probably Mrs.
X is entitled to crow. Was Strindberg being deliberately unclear? Did
he want his audience to make up their own minds about who is
stronger? Maybe neither of these women is strong, because each of
them seems dependent on a man, and Mrs. X's husband may not even
be such a great person in the first place. If I were Mrs. X, maybe
I wouldn't even take him back. I guess someone could say that it's
Mrs. X's husband who is the stronger, since he has managed to make
the two women fight over him while he enjoys his creature comforts.
Anyway, Strindberg makes us guess what he is really like. Because
he's offstage, he's just as silent as Miss Y is, although his wife
imitates his voice at one point.

In a way, I feel that this play is too short. I want it to go on
longer so that I can be sure how to analyze the two women and the
man. But I realize that one of the reasons the play is dramatic is that
it's brief. I might not be interested in it if it didn't leave me hanging. And it's also theatrical because Miss Y is silent even as Mrs. X

> lashes out at her. I wonder what the play would be like if we could hear Miss Y's thoughts in a sort of voice-over, like we find in some movies. It's interesting to me that the play is *about* actresses.
> I wonder if these characters are still "performing" with each other even if they're not acting in a theater at the moment.

Trish's freewriting would eventually help her develop ideas for a paper in which she had to analyze Strindberg's play. Compare your responses to the play with hers. Did the same issues come up for you? How do you feel about the women characters? What, if anything, do you wish the playwright had made clearer? What would you advise Trish to think about as she moved from freewriting to drafting a paper?

The Elements of Drama

You strengthen your ability to write about plays if you grow familiar with typical elements of drama. These elements include plot and structure, characterization, stage directions and setting, imagery, language, and theme.

PLOT AND STRUCTURE

Most plays, like most short stories, have a **plot**. When you read them, you find yourself following a narrative, a sequence of interrelated events. Even plays as short as *The Stronger* feature a plot, though the onstage action occurs in just one place and takes just a little while. As with short fiction, the reader of a play is often anxious to know how the events will turn out. The reader may especially feel this way when the play contains a mystery that characters are trying to solve. In Strindberg's play, for example, Mrs. X is apparently bent on discovering what relation her husband has had with her friend.

In summarizing the play, you might choose to depict the plot as a detective story. Then again, you might prefer to emphasize the characters' emotional conflicts as you describe how the play proceeds. In fact, there are various ways you can describe Strindberg's plot; just bear in mind that your account should be grounded in actual details of the text. However you summarize a play will reflect your sense of which characters are central to it. Is the offstage husband Bob in *The Stronger* as important as the two women onstage? More important than they are? Less important? Your summary will also reflect your sense of which characters have power. Do you think the two women in Strindberg's drama equally influence that play's events? In addition, your summary ought to acknowledge the human motives that drive the play's action. Why do you think Mrs. X feels compelled to confront Miss Y?

Summarizing the plot of a play can mean arranging its events chronologically. Yet bear in mind that some of the play's important events may have occurred in the characters' pasts. In many plays, actually, characters learn things about the past that they did not know and must now try to accept. For example, important events mentioned in *The Stronger* take place before the play begins. By the time the curtain rises, Miss Y's close relationship with Bob is well in the past. A typical summary would begin with the events on stage, but you could also summarize Strindberg's play as a chronicle of the relationship that precedes the scene in the café.

In discussing the structure of short stories, we noted that many of them follow Alice Adams's formula *ABDCE* (Action, Background, Development, Climax, and Ending). This scheme, however, does not fit many plays. In a sense, the average play is entirely Action, for its performers are constantly engaged in physical movement of various sorts. Furthermore, as we have been suggesting, information about Background can surface quite often as the play's characters talk. Yet the terms *Development*, *Climax*, and *Ending* do seem appropriate for many plays. Certainly the plot of *The Stronger* develops, as Mrs. X becomes increasingly hostile to Miss Y. Certainly, the play can be said to reach a Climax, a moment of great significance and intensity, when Mrs. X moves to another table and declares her hatred for Miss Y. The term *Ending* can also apply to this play, although readers may disagree about exactly when its Climax turns into its Ending. Certainly, Mrs. X is in a different state of mind at the play's last moment; at that point, she stops haranguing Miss Y and leaves, declaring that she will save her own marriage.

Like short stories, plays often use repetition as an organizational device. The characters in a play may repeat certain words; Mrs. X's variations on "silence" multiply as Miss Y retreats from interacting with her. Also, a play may show repeated actions, such as Mrs. X's interruptions of Miss Y's attempts to speak. In addition, a play may suggest that the onstage situation echoes previous events, as when Mrs. X alludes to confrontations between her husband and Miss Y in the past.

The Stronger is a short, one-act play. But many other plays are longer and divided conspicuously into subsections. The ancient Greek drama *Antigone* alternates choral sections with scenes involving only the title character and her uncle Creon. All of Shakespeare's plays, and most modern ones, are divided into acts, which are often further divided into scenes. Even within a one-act play, however, you can detect various stages in the action. This task is easier when the one-act play is fairly lengthy, but even a very short play like *The Stronger* can be broken down into stages, although you will have to decide exactly what those stages are.

CHARACTERS

Many short stories have a narrator who reveals the characters' inner thoughts. Most plays, however, have no narrator at all. To figure out what the characters think, you must study what they *say* and how they *move*, if the author has indeed provided stage directions. To be sure, some characters say a great deal, leaving you with several clues to their psyche. If you are familiar with

Shakespeare's lengthy play *Hamlet*, you may recall that it contains thousands of lines. Moreover, when the title character is alone on stage making long speeches to the audience, he seems to be baring his very soul. Yet despite such moments, Hamlet's mental state remains far from clear; scholars continue to debate his sanity. Thus, as a reader of *Hamlet* and other plays, you have much room for interpretation. Often you will have to decide whether to accept the judgments that characters express about one another. For example, how fair and accurate does Strindberg's Mrs. X seem to you as she berates Miss Y?

As with short stories, a good step toward analyzing a play's characters is to consider what each desires. The drama or comedy of many plays arises when the desires of one character conflict with those of another. Strindberg's Mrs. X feels that Miss Y has been a threat to her marriage, and while we cannot be sure of Miss Y's thoughts, evidently she is determined not to answer Mrs. X's charges. At the end of the play, the women's conflict seems to endure, even though Mrs. X proclaims victory. Many other plays end with characters managing to resolve conflict because one or more of them experiences a change of heart. Whatever the play you are studying, consider whether any of its characters change. Is any character's thinking transformed? If so, whose?

The main character of a play is often referred to as its **protagonist**, and a character who notably opposes this person is often referred to as the **antagonist**. As you might guess without even reading Shakespeare's play, Prince Hamlet is the protagonist of *Hamlet*; his uncle Claudius, who succeeded Hamlet's father to the throne of Denmark, serves as his antagonist. To be sure, applying these terms may be tricky or impossible in some instances. The two women in *The Stronger* oppose each other, but each can be called the protagonist and each can be called the antagonist. Can you think of other plays you have read in which the protagonist and antagonist are not readily identifiable?

In discussing the elements of short fiction, we referred to point of view, the perspective from which a story is told. Since very few plays are narrated, the term *point of view* fits this genre less well. While it is possible to claim that much of Shakespeare's *Hamlet* reflects the title character's point of view, he is offstage for stretches, and the audience may focus on other characters even when he appears. Also, do not overlook the possible significance of characters who are not physically present. A character may be important even when he or she never appears onstage. In *The Stronger*, the two women's conflict is partly about Mrs. X's unseen husband.

In most plays, characters' lives are influenced by their social standing, which in turn is influenced by particular traits of theirs. These may include their gender, their social class, their race, their ethnic background, their nationality, their sexual orientation, and the kind of work they do. Obviously *The Stronger* deals with gender relationships. Mrs. X defines herself in gendered terms: wife, mother, and insecure lover in competition with a rival for her husband's affections. But there are elements of social class too — of the circumstances of upper-middle-class Swedish women in Stockholm in the late nineteenth century — that may require research.

STAGE DIRECTIONS AND SETTING

When analyzing a script, pay attention to the staging directions it gives, and try to imagine additional ways that the actors might move around. Through a slight physical movement, performers can indicate important developments in their characters' thoughts. When Mrs. X fires a popgun at Miss Y, audience members may flinch in surprised sympathy with Miss Y's "startled gesture." But they may be just as startled by Miss Y's mirthful response, culminating in a "shriek of laughter," when Mrs. X uses her husband's slippers to mime and mock him. Is Miss Y's laughter hysterical, or knowing, or something else? How does it set up the "puzzled," curious looks Mrs. X and Miss Y exchange moments later?

You can get a better sense of how a play might be staged if you research its actual production history. Granted, finding out about its previous stagings may be difficult. But at the very least, you can discover some of the theatrical conventions that must have shaped presentations of the play, even one that is centuries old. Consider Sophocles' classical tragedy *Antigone* and Shakespeare's *Hamlet*, canonical plays that you may have read or seen performed in films or theater. While classical scholars would like to learn more about early performances of *Antigone*, they already know that it and other ancient Greek plays were staged in open-air arenas. They know, too, that *Antigone*'s Chorus turned in unison at particular moments, and that the whole cast wore large masks. Although the premiere of *Hamlet* was not videotaped, Shakespeare scholars are sure that, like other productions in Renaissance England, it made spare use of scenery and featured an all-male cast. By contrast, *The Stronger* is anchored in the nineteenth-century realist tradition that values in literary works an accurate and plausible presentation of everyday life and events.

Some plays can be staged in any number of styles and still work well. Shakespeare wrote *Hamlet* back in Renaissance England, but quite a few successful productions of it have been set in later times, such as late-nineteenth-century England. Even modern plays that seem to call for realist productions can be staged in a variety of ways. Note Strindberg's description of the setting for *The Stronger*: "The corner of a ladies' café. Two little iron tables, a red velvet sofa, several chairs." Many productions of this play have remained within the conventions of realism, striving to make the audience believe that it is seeing a late-nineteenth-century Stockholm café. But a production of *The Stronger* may present the audience with only a few pieces of furniture that barely evoke the café. Furthermore, the production might have Mrs. X's husband physically hover in the background, as if he were a ghost haunting both women's minds. You may feel that such a production would horribly distort Strindberg's drama; a boldly experimental staging of a play can indeed become a virtual rewriting of it. Nevertheless, remember that productions of a play may be more diverse in style than the script would indicate.

Remember, too, that a particular theater's architecture may affect a production team's decisions. Realism's illusion of the "fourth wall" works best on a proscenium stage, which is the kind probably most familiar to you. In brief, a proscenium is a boxlike space where the actors perform in front of the entire audience. In a proscenium production of *The Stronger*, the ladies' café can be depicted in great detail. The performing spaces at some theaters, however, are "in the round": that is, the audience completely encircles the stage. What would have to be done with the café then? List some items in the café that an "in the round" staging could accommodate.

In referring to possible ways of staging a play, we have inevitably been referring as well to its setting. A play may not be all that precise in describing its setting; Strindberg provides set designers with few guidelines for creating his Stockholm café. More significant, perhaps, than the place of the action is its *timing*: Mrs. X finds Miss Y sitting alone on Christmas Eve. Yet a play may stress to its audience that its characters are located in particular places, at particular moments in their personal histories, and/or at a particular moment in *world* history. For example, *The Stronger* calls attention to the fact that it is set in a ladies' café, a female space. Are there gendered public arenas today where Mrs. X might play out her conflict with Miss Y? Could the play be set in a women's locker room? What would happen if the setting were not for women only?

You can learn much about a play's characters by studying how they accommodate themselves — or fail to accommodate themselves — to their settings. When Strindberg's Mrs. X can no longer bear sitting next to Miss Y, her shift to another table dramatically signifies her feelings. Of course, much of the drama in Strindberg's play occurs because there is a *single* setting, in which at least one character feels confined. Other plays employ a wider variety of settings to dramatize their characters' lives.

IMAGERY

When plays use images to convey meaning, sometimes they do so through dialogue. At the beginning of *The Stronger*, for instance, Mrs. X recalls "a bridal party in a Paris restaurant," where "the bride sat reading a comic paper, while the groom played billiards with the witnesses." The play proceeds to become very much about divisions between husband and wife; moreover, the two women engage in a tense "game" that seems analogous to billiards. But just as often, a play's meaningful images are physically presented in the staging: through gestures, costumes, lighting, and props. For instance, consider the slippers embroidered with tulips that Mrs. X flourishes early in the play. The slippers and the tulips gain meaning as the play progresses. The audience may be ever more inclined to see them as *symbolic*. As we note on page 150, *symbol* is the term traditionally used for an image that represents some concept or concepts.

Keep in mind that *you* may interpret an image differently than the characters within the play do. When Strindberg's Mrs. X refers to billiards, she may not think at all that she will be playing an analogous game with Miss Y. You, however, may make this connection, especially as the play proceeds.

LANGUAGE

As we have been suggesting, a play's meaning and impact may be apparent only when the play is physically staged. Nevertheless, you can learn much from studying the language in its script. For example, the play's very title may be important. At the climax of Strindberg's play, Mrs. X even refers to herself as "the stronger." Obviously, the playwright is encouraging audiences to think about the title's implications. Yet not always will the meaning of a play's title may not always be immediately clear. In her freewriting, Trish wonders how to define "stronger" and which of Strindberg's characters fit the term. Even if you think the title of a play is easily explainable, pause to see whether that title can actually lead to an issue of definition. In other words, don't take the title for granted.

In most plays, language is a matter of dialogue. The audience tries to figure out the play by focusing on how the characters address one another. But remember that the pauses or silences within a play may be just as important as its dialogue. In fact, a director may *add* moments of silence that the script does not explicitly demand. In many plays, however, the author does specify moments when one or more characters significantly fail to speak. *The Stronger* is a prominent example: Miss Y is notably silent throughout the play, and as a reader you probably find yourself wondering why she is. Ironically, the play's *absence* of true dialogue serves to remind us that plays usually *depend* on dialogue.

Consider this moment in *The Stronger* when Miss Y fails to speak:

> MRS. X: . . . Why are you silent? You haven't said a word this whole time, but you have let me go on talking! You have sat there, and your eyes have reeled out of me all these thoughts which lay like raw silk in its cocoon — thoughts — suspicious thoughts, perhaps. Let me see — why did you break your engagement? Why do you never come to our house any more? Why won't you come to see us tonight?

> *Miss Y appears as if about to speak.*

> MRS. X: Hush, you needn't speak — I understand it all! . . .

An interesting discussion might result from imagining what Miss Y might have said had she not been cut off. It's also worth reflecting on what Strindberg conceivably gains by *not* having Miss Y speak at that moment.

THEME

We have already discussed *theme* in short fiction (pp. 151–54), and here we will build on some points from our earlier discussion. Again, a *theme* is the main claim — an assertion, a proposition, or a statement — that a work seems to make. As with other literary genres, try to state a play's theme as a *midlevel generalization* (pp. 151–52). If expressed in very broad terms, it will seem to fit many other works besides the one you have read; if narrowly tied to the play's characters and their particular situation, it will seem irrelevant to most other people's lives. With *The Stronger*, an example of a very broad theme would be "Women should not fight over a man." At the opposite extreme, a too-narrow theme would be "Women should behave well toward each other on Christmas eve, even if one of them has slept with the other's husband." If you are formulating Strindberg's theme, you might *start* with the broad generalization we have cited and then try to narrow it to a midlevel one. You might even think of ways that Strindberg's play *complicates* that broad generalization. What might, in fact, be a good midlevel generalization in Strindberg's case?

As we have noted, the very title of *The Stronger* seems significant. Indeed, a play's theme may be related to its title or to some other parts of the text. Nevertheless, be wary of couching the theme in terms drawn solely from the title or from some passage within the text. The play's theme may not be reducible to these words alone. Remember that the title of Strindberg's play can give rise to issues of definition in the first place.

You can state a play's theme as an observation or as a recommendation. With Strindberg's play, an observation-type theme would be "Marriage and career may disrupt relations between women." A recommendation-type theme would be either the broad or narrow generalization that we cited above. Neither way of stating the theme is automatically preferable, but remain aware of the different tones and effects they may carry. Consider, too, the possibility of stating the theme as a problem, as in this example: "We may be inclined to defend our marriages when they seem threatened, but in our defense we may cling to illusions that can easily shatter." Furthermore, consider the possibility of referring to *a* theme of the play rather than *the* theme, thereby acknowledging the possibility that the play is making several important claims.

When you write about a play, certainly you will refer to the text of it, its **script**. But probably the play was meant to be staged, and most likely it has been. Thus, you might refer to actual productions of it and to ways it can be performed. Remember, though, that different productions of the play may stress different meanings and create different effects. In your paper, you might discuss how much room for interpretation the script allows those who would stage it. For any paper you write about the play, look beyond the characters' dialogue and study whatever stage directions the script gives.

Undoubtedly your paper will have to offer some plot summary, even if your audience has already read the play. After all, certain details of the plot will be important support for your points. But, as with papers about short fiction, keep the amount of plot summary small, mentioning only events in the play that are crucial to your overall argument. Your reader should feel that you are analyzing the play rather than just recounting it.

To understand more what analysis of a play involves, let's return to Trish Carlisle, the student whose freewriting you read earlier. Trish was assigned to write a 600-word paper about Strindberg's *The Stronger*. She was asked to imagine herself writing to a particular audience: performers rehearsing a production of the play she chose. More specifically, she was to identify and address some question that these performers might have, an issue that might be bothering them as they prepared to put on the play. Trish knew that, besides presenting an issue, her paper would have to make a main claim and support it with evidence. Moreover, the paper might have to spell out some of the warrants or assumptions behind her evidence.

Because finding an issue was such an important part of the assignment, Trish decided to review her freewriting about Strindberg's play, noting questions she had raised there about it. Trish saw that the chief issue posed for her by *The Stronger* was "Which character is the stronger?" Nevertheless, Trish recognized that the issue "Which character is the stronger?" still left her with various decisions to make. For one thing, she had to decide what kind of an issue she would call it. Trish saw that it could be considered an issue of fact, an issue of evaluation, or an issue of definition. Although it could fit into all of these categories, Trish knew that the category she chose would influence the direction of her paper. Eventually she decided to treat "Which character is the stronger?" as primarily an issue of definition, because she figured that, no matter what, she would be devoting much of her paper to defining *stronger* as a term.

Of course, there are many different senses in which someone may be "stronger" than someone else. Your best friend may be a stronger tennis player than you, in the sense that he or she always beats you at that game. But you may be a stronger student than your friend, in the sense that you get better grades in school. In the case of Strindberg's play, Trish came to see that a paper focused on which character is *morally* stronger would differ from one focused on who is *emotionally* stronger, and these papers would differ in turn from one focused on which character is *politically* stronger, more able to impose his or her will. These reflections led Trish to revise her issue somewhat. She decided to address the question "Which particular sense of the word 'stronger' is most relevant to Strindberg's play?" In part, Trish came up with this reformulation of her issue because she realized that the two women feuding in the play are actresses, and that they behave as actresses even when they are not professionally performing. Trish's answer to her revised question was that the play encourages the audience to consider which woman is the stronger *actress* — which woman is more able, that is, to convey her preferred version of reality.

When you write about a play, you may have to be selective, for your paper may not be able to accommodate all the ideas and issues that occur to you. Trish was not sure which woman in Strindberg's play is the stronger actress. She felt that a case can be made for Mrs. X or Miss Y; indeed, she suspected that Strindberg was letting his audience decide. But she decided that her paper was not obligated to resolve this matter; she could simply mention the various possible positions in her final paragraph. In the body of her paper, Trish felt she would contribute much if she focused on addressing her main issue with her main claim. Again, her main issue was "Which particular sense of the word 'stronger' is most relevant to Strindberg's play?" Her main claim was that "The play is chiefly concerned with which woman is the stronger actress, 'stronger' here meaning 'more able to convey one's version of reality.'"

Although a paper about a play need not explicitly mention the elements of plays we have identified, thinking about these elements can provide you with a good springboard for analysis. Trish saw that her paper would be very much concerned with the title of Strindberg's play, especially as that title applied to the characters. Also, she would have to refer to stage directions and imagery, because Miss Y's silence leaves the reader having to look at her physical movements and the play's props for clues to her thinking. The play does not really include dialogue, a term that implies people talking with each other. Nevertheless, Trish saw that there are utterances in the script that she could refer to, especially as she made points about the play's lone speaker, Mrs. X. Indeed, a persuasive paper about a play is one that quotes from characters' lines and perhaps from the stage directions, too. Yet the paper needs to quote selectively, for a paper chock full of quotations may obscure instead of enhance the writer's argument.

Final Draft of a Student Paper

Here is Trish's final draft of her paper about *The Stronger*. It emerged out of several drafts, and after Trish had consulted classmates and her instructor. As you read this version of her paper, note its strengths, but also think of any suggestions that might help Trish make the paper even better.

Trish Carlisle
Professor Zelinsky
English 102
28 April - - - -

Which Is the Stronger Actress
in August Strindberg's Play?

You have asked me to help you solve difficulties you may be experiencing with August Strindberg's script for *The Stronger* as you prepare to play the roles of Mrs. X and Miss Y. These female characters seem harder to judge than the three women who are the focus of Susan Glaspell's play *Trifles*, the play you are performing next month. Obviously, Glaspell is pushing us to think well of Mrs. Hale, Mrs. Peters, and Minnie Wright. The two women in Strindberg's play are another matter; in particular, you have probably been wondering which of these two women Strindberg thinks of as "the stronger." If you knew which character he had in mind with that term, you might play the roles accordingly. As things stand, however, Strindberg's use of the term in his title is pretty ambiguous. It is not even clear, at least not immediately, which particular sense of the word *stronger* is most relevant to the play. I suggest that the play is chiefly concerned with which character is the stronger actress. In making this claim, I am defining *stronger* as "more able to convey one's version of reality."

You may feel that Strindberg is clarifying his use of the word *stronger* when he has Mrs. X bring up the word in the long speech that ends the play. In that final speech, she declares to Miss Y that "I am . . . the stronger one" (line 140) and that Miss Y's silence is not the "strength" that Mrs. X previously thought it was. At this point in the play, Mrs. X is evidently defining *stronger* as "more able to keep things, especially a man." She feels that she is the stronger because she is going home to her husband, while Miss Y is forced to be alone on Christmas Eve. Yet there is little reason to believe that Mrs. X is using the word *stronger* in the sense that the playwright has chiefly in mind. Furthermore, there is little reason to believe that Mrs. X is an accurate judge of the two women's situations. Perhaps she is telling herself that she is stronger because she simply needs to believe that she is. Similarly, perhaps she is telling herself that she now has control over her husband when in actuality he may still be emotionally attached to Miss Y. In addition, because Miss Y does not speak and because Mrs. X sweeps out without giving her any further opportunity to do so, we don't know if Miss Y agrees with Mrs. X's last speech.

Since Mrs. X's final use of the word *stronger* is so questionable, we are justified in thinking of other ways that the term might be applied. In thinking about this play, I have entertained the idea that the stronger character is actually Mrs. X's husband Bob, for he has two women fighting over him and also apparently has the creature comforts that servants provide. But now I tend to think that the term applies to one or both of the two women. Unfortunately, we are not given many facts about them, for it is a brief one-act play and one of the major characters does not even speak. But as we try to figure out how Strindberg is defining the term *stronger*, we should notice one fact that we are indeed given: Each of these women is an actress. Both of them have worked at Stockholm's Grand Theater, although apparently Mrs. X got Miss Y fired from the company. Furthermore, Mrs. X engages in a bit of theatrical illusion when she scares Miss Y by firing the toy pistol at her. Soon after, Mrs. X plays the role of her own husband when she puts her hands in the slippers she has bought for him and imitates not only his walk but also the way he scolds his servants. Miss Y even laughs at this "performance," as if she is being an appreciative audience for it. In addition, if Mrs. X is right about there being an adulterous affair between her husband and Miss Y, then those two people have basically been performing an act for Mrs. X. It is possible, too, that Mrs. X has not been quite so naïve; perhaps she has deliberately come to the café in order to confront Miss Y about the affair and to proclaim ultimate victory over her. In that case, Mrs. X is performing as someone more innocent than she really is. On the other hand, Miss Y might be using her silence as an actress would, manipulating her audience's feelings by behaving in a theatrical way.

Because we do know that these women are professional actresses, and because Strindberg gives us several hints that they are performing right there in the café, we should feel encouraged to think that he is raising the question of which is the stronger *actress*. Of course, we would still have to decide how he is defining the term *stronger*. But if he does have in mind the women's careers and behavior as actresses, then he seems to be defining *stronger* as "more able to convey one's version of reality." Obviously, Mrs. X is putting forth her own version of reality in her final speech, although we do not know how close her version comes to the actual truth. Again, we cannot be sure of Miss Y's thoughts because she does not express them in words; nevertheless, she can be said to work at influencing Mrs. X's version of reality by making strategic use of silence.

I realize that the claim I am making does not solve every problem you might have with the play as you prepare to perform it. Frankly, I am not sure who *is* the stronger actress. I suspect that Strindberg is being deliberately ambiguous; he wants the performers to act in a way that will let each member of the audience arrive at his or her own opinion. Still, if you accept my claim, each of you will think of yourself as playing the part of an actress who is trying to shape the other woman's sense of reality.

CHAPTER 7

Writing Researched Arguments

Maybe the word *research* makes you anxious. It gives many people qualms. It brings to mind for them big and complex assignments in high school. Back then, they experienced the research paper as a major challenge. It loomed for them as a hurdle, one they struggled to leap. Often they couldn't figure out its rationale. Why do all this labor? Why hunt for materials, base a long essay on them, then end with a formatted bibliography? Such toil can prove overwhelming. A student might lose sight of its point.

Take heart. Research needn't be a daunting and valueless exercise. Indeed, it's become a common and rewarding pursuit. Millions now own devices that make the process easy. Just by tapping on keyboards or smartphones, they mine the Web's vast data. We bet you cruise cyberspace for answers to lots of questions. You might not call these voyages *research*, but that is what they are. Of course, frequently you're looking for a less-than-momentous fact: where to buy dashboard cameras, when the next *Star Wars* premiers, who's performing at local clubs, what folks think of your town's new restaurant, how your school's football team ranks. But probably you also turn to the Internet for more crucial knowledge. You may seek details about a disease that afflicts a family member. You may wish to compare online mortgage rates. A job you hold may require you to monitor several websites, gleaning data that will help your firm serve its clientele. Maybe you assist a nonprofit cause that's quite Internet-oriented; many of them search online for possible donors and allies. In general, the digital era is an age of research. It's a tool people use to manage their day.

Nevertheless, we can imagine you saying something like this: "OK, I realize now that I do research every day. But I'm still not confident I can do academic research — the kind of research that college teachers want. And I'm by no means sure I can turn it into essays — the kind of writing they expect." We understand the concern you may feel about these tasks. In the rest of this chapter, we explain and demonstrate ways to handle them.

Here at the start, we stress this fact: most college instructors don't assign something called "the research paper." They consider this label too vague. Yes, they'll require essays based on personal research. But they'll be more precise about the goal. Most often, they'll want you to compose researched *arguments*. You'll write essays addressed to an audience. You'll raise issues and put forth claims. You'll offer evidence and reasons. And you'll do research to prepare for this kind of writing. You'll seek materials that will help you build a persuasive case.

If you'll mainly write about a particular work, that's your **primary source**. Your other findings are your **secondary sources**. Some may prove not as useful as you predicted. Leave them out of your essay; don't sweat to jam them in. The rest of your sources should each play a clear role in your text. You'll have to decide their functions. Overall, use your essay to **synthesize** your sources. Put them in conversation. Make plain how they relate to one another; show how they connect to *your* chief issue and claim.

Begin Your Research by Giving It Direction

As you start your research, you may know already what your essay will argue. Certainty can be an advantage, productively steering your hunt. But it risks narrowing your scope. You may settle for sources that just reinforce your existing ideas. Research should expand your thinking. Let it be a means of inquiry. Even if you're sure of the claim you'll make, stay open to changing your mind. Consider the claim a hypothesis that your research will test. Don't stick with findings that preserve views you currently hold. Look for materials that may send you down exciting new paths.

Of course, your opening mood might be different. Perhaps you'll be hazy about your topic. You may not know what research to do. Still, you can give it direction. If you've chosen a particular literary work to write about, read it several times. If it's in this book, review what we tell you about its author. Take a look at our questions and comments about it. Then ask questions of your own about the work. Strive to come up with a question without an obvious answer—an issue that demands you conduct research.

Another strategy is to list keywords: terms that occur to you as you study the work. These can become your search terms. The list below is an example. It concerns Charlotte Perkins Gilman's "The Yellow Wallpaper," an 1892 story based partly on the writer's life. Heading the list are the story's title and the author's name. They're followed by terms that often arise when the story is discussed in class. For research on Gilman's tale, these items could serve as guides:

- "The Yellow Wallpaper"
- Charlotte Perkins Gilman
- Nineteenth-century theories about women's health, psychology, and work
- Nineteenth-century American feminism
- Nineteenth-century fiction by American women
- The rest cure
- Postpartum depression
- Psychological abuse
- S. Weir Mitchell (Gilman's doctor in real life)
- Woman-centered horror stories as a genre
- The *New England Magazine*
- Nineteenth-century American periodicals

No item on the list is a *claim* about Gilman's story. Finding and developing a claim would be a goal of your research. But any of the terms could be a point of departure for you. They are words you would put in a search box to launch your probe.

Search for Sources in the Library and Online

Once you have your topic in mind and perhaps sketched a tentative claim, begin looking for research sources. Many different types of sources for literary research are available, and the types you need will depend largely on the type of claim you choose to defend. If your issue is primarily one of interpretation — about the theme, patterns, or symbolism of the text, for instance — you will most likely need to consult literary criticism to see what has been said in the past about the literature you are discussing. If your issue concerns historical or cultural context, including issues of social policy, you may need to consult newspapers, magazines, and similar sorts of cultural documents. Some topics might require several different types of sources.

Not many years ago, for most people the word *research* was synonymous with hours spent in the library hunting for books and articles. For many students today, *research* has become synonymous with the Internet, which they turn to in the belief that everything is available online. But this is simply not true. Many of the best and most reliable sources are still available only in print. In particular, lots of potentially useful books haven't been digitized yet. They remain in your school library, so you'll have to go there if you hope to read them. The library may also house relevant documents and scholarly journals that aren't online. The library's computerized **catalog** will alert you to its holdings, helping you locate useful texts. Typically, the catalog entry for a book lists various subject headings for it. By clicking on a heading, you'll find other books on that topic. When you go to the library's shelves for a book, browse through neighboring volumes, for perhaps they also address your subject of study.

Of course, a wealth of information is available on the Internet. As with the library, your goal is to find useful information efficiently, evaluate it carefully, and employ it effectively in your paper. Unfortunately, and unlike a library's sources, information on the Internet is not indexed and organized to make it easily accessible to researchers. Many students go right away to Wikipedia, hoping to find most of their needed data there. Indeed, a Wikipedia entry may contain some useful facts. Nevertheless, you shouldn't accept on faith everything that the entry says. It's the product of anonymous people, many of whom may not really be experts on the subject they claim to know. Wikipedia can be a decent *starting* point for online searches, especially because it provides links to Web sites that may be more authoritative. But many teachers will object if you depend on Wikipedia itself as a source. Consider it a launch pad, not a destination.

You will need to do a certain amount of Web surfing if you are to find appropriate online materials for your project. A number of **search engines** (programs for finding information) are designed to help you track down materials on the Web. If you are used to using the Internet, probably you can depend on search engines that have served you well in the past. Bear in mind, however, that relying on just one search engine may not lead you to all the sources that would benefit you. Many students pursuing a research topic go immediately to Google. They type their subject into the box, click a mouse, and expect to see terrific sources pop right up on-screen. Yet often this search method proves exasperating. For one thing, it may succeed all *too* well in generating items. Our three sample researched arguments discuss "The Yellow Wallpaper"; a Google search using this title elicits around 628,000 results. The first paper also deals with postpartum depression; if you Google this term, you'll come up with roughly 3,820,000 results. Even if you combine "The Yellow Wallpaper" with "postpartum depression," you'll get roughly 6,110 results. It can take forever to sift through these avalanches for whatever gems they contain. Faced with such landslides, some writers just pounce on the first few results they obtain. But first doesn't necessarily mean best. An ideal article may surface late in a Google list.

You can narrow your results by adding words to your search, making it more exact. Or you might turn to Google Scholar, which sticks with academic texts. There, combining "The Yellow Wallpaper" with "postpartum depression" produces about 125 results. This is certainly a more manageable number. Still, Google addiction will limit you as a researcher. See what other Web sites can do for you. If your college or university makes available to you sites such as JSTOR, Academic Search Premier, and Project Muse, these will give you access to hundreds of scholarly journals and books. The Internet service LexisNexis offers current articles from newspapers and magazines, as well as transcripts of radio and TV broadcasts.

When you take a course, find out what search engines serve its field. For literary research, a great one is the **MLA International Bibliography**, sponsored by the Modern Language Association (MLA) and carried by many schools. It lists books and articles on a wide range of topics in literary studies. Later in this chapter are sample researched arguments by students who used MLA's service. They looked for sources related to "The Yellow Wallpaper." For instance, Sarah Michaels was curious how the story might add to current debates about postpartum depression. Therefore, one of her search terms was this disorder's name. Typing it into the MLA search box, she found a useful article on how TV reports the problem. Katie Johnson was focused on literary criticism about Gilman's story. Using its title to search with, she found analyses of the tale.

Like most search engines, MLA's enables you to filter. Say you're looking for studies of "The Yellow Wallpaper." Once you insert this title into MLA's search box, you can restrict the results to articles published in journals. You can also have the results appear in reverse chronological order, so that the most recent articles come first. They'll mention older articles and books that have proven important, and you could turn to those next.

In several journals, each article is prefaced by a summary called an **abstract**. This overview, usually a paragraph, immediately tells you the article's main claim. Whenever you discover an article or book relevant to your project, examine its bibliography as well. Often, this will have the heading **Works Cited**. Likely to be listed there are other texts you'll find useful. In general, scholars refer to previous works on their subject. They extend, challenge, or refine their predecessors' claims. Notice how they treat these prior views. You'll get a sense of the conversation your topic has already stirred. You may also see how to join this dialogue with ideas of your own.

Evaluate the Sources

Whatever method you use to locate your research materials, remember that not all sources are created equal. Take care to **evaluate** those you come across. When tempted to use a writer's work, ask yourself the following: What do I want my audience to think about this person? Often, you'll hope your readers will accept him or her as some sort of authority. In a way, you have to think about **ethos**, a term we discussed in our first two chapters. There, you may recall, we defined *ethos* as the image that an author projects. Many writers try to be persuasive by constructing an admirable ethos—a version of themselves that will impress their readers. Similarly, when you incorporate sources into a researched argument, you will often want your audience to respect them. These sources may not agree with one another—heck, *you* may not agree with them all—but they'll need to have recognizable expertise. Otherwise, why should your readers pay attention to them?

Suppose you plan to write a research paper on "The Yellow Wallpaper." An online search leads you to an analysis of the story. You might refer to this study in your essay. But you need to determine whether the author is someone your readers would take seriously. You have to look for credentials. Perhaps the writer is a professor publishing in a scholarly journal. Maybe, like Paul Goldberger in Chapter 1, this person is an award-winning authority in a certain field (in his case, architecture). Another writer in the same chapter, David Barno, is a veteran military officer affiliated with a distinguished think tank. Sometimes you can learn writers' professional status by visiting the Web sites of institutions they work for. At any rate, be skeptical when a Web post's author is shrouded in mystery. The views expressed may be interesting, but if their advocate is a phantom, you can't expect your readers to care about them. Useful to bear in mind is the famous *New Yorker* magazine cartoon about the digital age. One canine, perched at a computer, tells another that "on the Internet, nobody knows you're a dog." In short, the Web can fool you. Although someone posting on it is probably human, hunt for details of the person's background. Your audience will expect you to have this information about a source, even if you don't include every bit of it in your paper.

A teacher may require a number of your sources to be articles from "peer-reviewed" academic journals. Such journals publish a manuscript only after it has been evaluated by experts in its subject. Usually, a journal's Web site will indicate whether it falls into this category. Some search engines have a feature that, when you activate it, confines your results to peer-reviewed works.

For example, both Academic Search Premier and the MLA International Bibliography enable you to restrict your search this way. Most books published by academic and university presses have also been peer reviewed. Of course, even when it doesn't come with this label, a book or an article may still be worth consulting. In many popular newspapers (such as the *New York Times* and the *Washington Post*) and magazines (such as *The New Yorker* and the *Atlantic*), you'll find thoughtful, well-grounded reports and opinion pieces.

In general, you should ask the following basic questions of your sources: (1) Is the information recent, and if not, is the validity of the information likely to have changed significantly over time? (2) How credible is the author? Is he or she a recognized expert on the subject? (3) Is the source published by an established, respectable press, or does it appear in a well-respected journal or periodical (the *Los Angeles Times* has more credibility than the *National Enquirer*, for example) or Web site (one supported by a university or library, for instance)? (4) Based on what you've learned about responsible argument, do the arguments in your source seem sound, fair, and thoughtful? Is the evidence convincing? Is the development of the argument logical?

You increase your own credibility with your audience by using the most reliable research materials available to you, so do not just stick with whatever comes to hand if you have the opportunity to find a stronger source.

Record Your Sources' Key Details

As your research proceeds, record your discoveries. In a computer file or handwritten notes, jot down key details of each source. Don't expect that you'll simply recall this information. Memory is imperfect; data can fade from your mind.

Above all, specify each source by using bibliographical form. You'll then have an entry ready to put in your essay's Works Cited section. In a literature course, the format you'll usually follow is that of the MLA. Later in this chapter, we explain MLA's guidelines at length. At the moment, here are sample MLA-formatted entries by the two students we've mentioned. Sarah, who found the article about postpartum depression, logged it in her notes this way:

> Dubriwny, Tasha N. "Television News Coverage of Postpartum Disorders and the Politics of Medicalization." *Feminist Media Studies*, vol. 10, no. 3, Sept. 2010, pp. 285–303.

Katie, who investigated literary criticism, recorded one of her articles as follows:

> Johnson, Greg. "Gilman's Gothic Allegory: Rage and Redemption in `The Yellow Wallpaper.'" *Studies in Short Fiction*, vol. 26, no. 4, Fall 1989, pp. 521–30.

What else about a source might you write down? You have several options.

A *summary* of the source—one or two sentences indicating in your own words the author's main claim. Such summaries guarantee that you understand the gist of an author's argument and (since they are in your own words) can readily be incorporated in your paper. You might think of a summary as a restatement of the author's principal claim, perhaps with a brief indication of the types of supporting evidence he or she marshals. You can also write summaries of supporting points—subsections of an author's argument—if they seem applicable to your paper. A summary should not, however, include quotations, exhaustive detail about subpoints, or a list of all the evidence in a given source. A summary is meant to provide a succinct overview—to demonstrate that you have grasped a point and convey it to your readers.

A possible summary of Dubriwny's article:

> In the period of 2000–2007, television reports on postpartum disorders used expert and personal testimonies to depict these disorders as the medical problems of individuals. It is more appropriate, however, to put these conditions in a social context, for the women suffering from them are actually challenging the destructive cultural stereotype of the "good" mother.

A possible summary of Johnson's article:

> The heroine of "The Yellow Wallpaper" emerges not as a pathetic madwoman, but as someone who asserts her freedom and creativity by imagining a Gothic fantasy for herself and writing about it in her diary.

Quotations (with page numbers) that you might incorporate into your essay. A quotation may be a word, a phrase, a sentence, or an entire passage.

A striking sentence in Dubriwny's article:

> Women's varied emotions and behaviors during the postpartum period — their feelings of anger, distress, sadness, and guilt as well as happiness — point to a substantial gap between the lived reality of mothering and the discourse of essential/good motherhood. (287)

A memorable sentence from Johnson:

> Thus as the story progresses, the heroine follows both her childlike promptings and her artistic faith in creating a Gothic alternative to the stifling daylight world of her husband and the society at large. (524)

Paraphrasing (with page numbers) that you might incorporate in your essay. A paraphrase puts a statement in new words. Think of it as a translation that attempts to convey the basic idea of the original passage. It has two advantages over a quotation. First, an accurate paraphrase proves that you understand the material you've read. Second, a paraphrase is easier to integrate into your essay than a quotation, since it is already written in your own words and style. When you paraphrase, you need to identify the original page number, just as you do with quotations.

A statement by Dubriwny:

> Unfortunately, the struggle over the definition of postpartum disorders is, in television news, not much of a struggle at all, as only a few voices exist to challenge the complete medicalization of postpartum disorders (299).

A possible paraphrase of Dubriwny's statement:

> Sadly, televised reports tend to depict postpartum depression and similar maladies as medical problems, rarely giving air time to activists who propose other ways of understanding such conditions (299).

A statement by Johnson, about Gilman's heroine:

> Her experience should finally be viewed not as a final catastrophe but as a terrifying, necessary stage in her progress toward self-identity and personal achievement (523).

A possible paraphrase of Johnson's statement:

> At the end of the story, the heroine may seem doomed but actually is not, for she has to engage in such frightening behavior if she is eventually to become a fulfilled, accomplished individual (523).

Texts and other materials with which the source is in conversation.
When you note these, you put the source in context. You become more aware of the issues that the source addresses.

> Dubriwny analyzes how postpartum disorders were represented in television reports from 2000 to 2007. She focuses on a selection of tapes available in the Vanderbilt Television News Archives. They're her primary source. Motivating her research was recent public attention to certain events, including Andrea Yates's murder of her children and Tom Cruise's disapproval of Brooke Shields's reliance on antidepressants. Dubriwny is influenced, too, by advocacy groups and sociologists who critique the role that dominant models of mother-hood play in diagnoses of postpartum conditions. Also driving her to write is the relative lack of scholarship on the biases that shape media representations of these disorders.

> Johnson takes Gilman's story as his primary source. He argues that its heroine's behavior at the end is a creative, self-affirming protest against the patriarchal society that her husband represents. Johnson opposes interpretations of the story that see the heroine as simply mad. But when he cites specific studies of the story, he tends to choose those that support his view. He also develops his claim by referring to Gilman's nonfiction autobiographical writings; to other women writers (Emily Dickinson, Charlotte Bronte, Sylvia Plath); and to scholarship on the Gothic literary tradition.

Strategies for Integrating Sources

Throughout your research, you'll aim to evolve an argument of your own. It's something *you'll* contribute to discussions taking place. The student essays at the conclusion of this chapter are examples. Each recruits sources to advance a claim that the student herself has produced.

Once you've finished your research, take time to reflect. If you've come up with an issue and claim, think about them again. In light of all your findings, does your argument still work? Does it need fine-tuning? Should you even change topics? Maybe, though, you remain unsure what to argue. To gain focus, review the issues your sources raise. What debates do they participate in? What sides in these debates do *you* favor? What issues do these debates ignore or slight? For help in getting ideas, you might also review the categories of issues we present on pages 50–54 of Chapter 3.

As you draft your essay, show that you're using your sources. Don't let them overshadow *your* contribution. They should clearly serve your argument, not crowd it out. Whenever you summarize, paraphrase, or quote, identify your source's function. Indicate the role it plays in your conversation. If you've taken many notes in your research, your essay may not have room for all. Cast aside those that fail to help.

Use direct quotations sparingly. Hordes of them make for choppy reading and may obscure your ideas. When you're tempted to quote, consider paraphrasing instead. If you still feel that quoting is necessary, try to limit the number of words. Perhaps you needn't quote an entire sentence or passage. A bit of phrasing may suffice. Here are examples of selective quotation.

Original (from Dubriwny's article):

> The medical experts interviewed in the news coverage engage in a process of decontextualizing postpartum distress. What I mean is that the experts take the distress out of the social context of mothering and focus almost solely on biological causes of postpartum disorders (290).

Limited quoting:

> Dubriwny is concerned that TV reports on postpartum conditions use medical authorities to emphasize "biological causes" rather than "the social context of mothering" (290).

Original (from Johnson's article):

> Two of the story's major structural devices are its contrasting of the husband's daylight world and his wife's nocturnal fantasy, and the religious imagery by which she highlights the liberating and redemptive qualities of her experience (523).

Limited quoting:

> Johnson contends that although the heroine seems tormented, she actually finds her interaction with the wallpaper "liberating and redemptive" (523).

When quoting up to four lines of prose or three lines of poetry, integrate the quotation directly into your paragraph, enclosing the quoted material in double quotation marks and checking to make sure that the quotation accurately reflects the original. Longer quotations are set off from the text by starting a new line and indenting one inch on the left margin only; these are called **block quotations**. For these, quotation marks are omitted since the indention is enough to indicate that the material is a quotation. Examples of the correct format for both long and short quotations appear in Katie Johnson's paper (pp. 223–27).

When a short quotation is from a poem, line breaks in the poem are indicated by slash marks, with single spaces on either side. The following example demonstrates the format for a short quotation, in this case from Yusef Komunyakaa's poem "Blackberries" (featured in Chapter 6). The numbers in parentheses specify which lines in the poem are being quoted:

> The poem's speaker recalls the scene as sinister, noting: "The big blue car made me sweat. / Wintertime crawled out of the windows" (19–20).

While it is essential to quote accurately, sometimes you may need to alter a quotation slightly, either by deleting text for brevity or by adding or changing text to incorporate it grammatically. If you delete words from a quotation, indicate the deletion by inserting an ellipsis (three periods with spaces between them), as demonstrated by the following quotation from Robert Frost's poem "Mending Wall" (Chapter 3):

> The speaker makes his neighbor sound warlike, describing him as "Bringing a stone . . . / In each hand, like an old-stone savage armed" (39–40).

If you need to change or add words for clarity or grammatical correctness, indicate the changes with square brackets. If, for instance, you wanted to clarify the meaning of "They" in Komunyakaa's opening line "They left my hands like a printer's," you could do so like this:

> The speaker recalls that "[The blackberries] left my hands like a printer's" (1).

No quotation is self-sufficient, nor is its meaning always self-evident. When you put a quotation in your essay, help your audience see why it's there. Introduce it clearly. Follow it with any additional explanation it needs. The longer the quotation, the more analysis readers want.

Avoid Plagiarism

Plagiarism is a serious violation of academic standards. Most colleges have policies that explain how they define and treat it. You should learn your institution's guidelines. But there are general rules of thumb to follow when you quote, summarize, or paraphrase. The major one is this: indicate clearly which ideas are yours and which are other people's. You commit **plagiarism** if you claim credit for another person's thoughts. Even if you put them in your own words, they came from someone else. If you don't attribute these ideas to their source, you mislead your readers. You betray your audience's trust.

To see better what we mean, look at the sentence below, which is on page 527 of Greg Johnson's article about Gilman's "The Yellow Wallpaper." Johnson refers to the story's heroine, who records her distress in her diary:

> An experienced writer, she understands the healing power which inheres in the act of writing and recognizes intuitively that her physician husband's rest cure can lead only to her psychic degeneration.

You would be committing plagiarism if you presented Johnson's sentence—or parts of it—as your own prose:

> We should remember that the heroine is an experienced writer. She understands intuitively the healing power that writing has. Indeed, writing in her diary is a means by which she tries to head off the degeneration of her mind that her physician husband's rest cure will cause.

You would also be plagiarizing if you paraphrased Johnson's sentence without noting that it's his:

> A veteran crafter of prose, the heroine perceives that her journal-keeping is important for her mental health. At some level of con-sciousness, she also realizes that the treatment her doctor spouse is putting her through will result in the decay of her mind.

Here is a way you could quote from Johnson's sentence, give him credit for it, identify its page number, and make clear what you're doing with him as a source:

> Many analysts of the story overlook the fact that its narrator writes. Specifically, she maintains a diary of her ordeal. As Greg Johnson points out, her journal-keeping has for her a "healing power," whereas the treatment her husband is putting her through "can lead only to her psychic degeneration" (527). Johnson may be overesti-mating how perceptive the narrator is when he claims that "she understands" (527) the diary's therapeutic function. Perhaps she isn't as aware of its value as he thinks. Still, writing is a resource for her as she tries to cope with the medical treatment her husband inflicts.

Sometimes authors unintentionally plagiarize. They forget that certain ideas they recorded during their research are actually quotations or para-phrases. Nevertheless, most readers will see "accidental" plagiarism as still plagiarism. So be precise in your research notes. Put within quotation marks anything you copy. The moment your notes quote or restate someone else's words, jot down information about the source. Of course, you should record the page number, but do even more. Include all the details you'll need for a Works Cited entry, because your essay may end up referring to the source. In general, equip yourself to give credit.

What *does not* need to be referenced is **common knowledge**: factual information that the average reader can be expected to know or that is readily available in many easily accessible sources. For example, it is common knowledge that Charlotte Perkins Gilman was an American writer. It is also common knowledge that she was born in 1860 and died in 1935, even though most people would have to look that information up in an encyclopedia or a biographical dictionary to verify it.

Strategies for Documenting Sources (MLA Format)

Documentation is the means by which you give credit to the authors of all primary and secondary sources cited within a researched argument. It serves two principal purposes: (1) it allows your readers to find out more about the origin of the ideas you present, and (2) it protects you from charges of plagiarism. Every academic discipline follows slightly different conventions for documentation, but the method most commonly used for writing about literature is the format devised by the MLA. This documentation method encompasses **in-text citations**, which briefly identify within the body of your paper the source of a particular quotation, summary, or paraphrase, and a bibliography, called **Works Cited**, which gives more complete publication information.

While mastering the precise requirements of MLA punctuation and format can be time-consuming and even frustrating, getting them right adds immeasurably to the professionalism of a finished paper. More detailed information, including special circumstances and documentation styles for types of sources not covered here, will be found in the *MLA Handbook for Writers of Research Papers*, Eighth Edition (New York: Modern Language Association, 2016). Of course, if your instructor requests that you follow a different documentation method, you should follow his or her instructions instead.

MLA IN-TEXT CITATION

Each time you include information from any outside source — whether in the form of a summary, a paraphrase, or a quotation — you must provide your reader with a brief reference indicating the author and page number of the original. This reference directs the reader to the Works Cited list, where more complete information is available.

There are two basic methods for in-text citation. The first, and usually preferable, method is to include the author's name in the text of your essay and note the page number in parentheses at the end of the citation. The following paraphrase and quotation from "The Yellow Wallpaper" show the format to be followed for this method. Note that the page number (without the abbreviation "p." or additional punctuation) is enclosed within parentheses and that the final punctuation for the sentence occurs after the parenthetical reference, effectively making the reference part of the preceding sentence. For a direct quotation, the closing quotation marks come before the page reference, but the final period is still saved until after the reference.

> Gilman's narrator believes her husband trivializes her disorder (230).

> Gilman's narrator sadly reports that her husband considers her disorder to be just "a slight hysterical tendency" (230).

The method is similar for long quotations (those set off from the main text of your essay). The only differences are that the final punctuation mark comes before the parenthetical page reference, and that the quotation is not enclosed within quotation marks.

In those cases where citing the author's name in your text would be awkward or difficult, you may include both the author's last name and the page reference in the parenthetical citation. The following example draws a quotation from Greg Johnson's article about Gilman's story.

> According to one interpreter of the story, the heroine's final behavior is a "necessary stage in her progress toward self-identity and personal achievement" (Johnson 523).

If you cite more than one work by the same author, you must specify from which of these works each citation comes. Many Internet sources don't number their pages; the parenthetical reference needs to include only the author's last name (or, if the work is anonymous, an identifying title). In the case of poems, use line numbers (rather than page numbers) if they're provided, and precede your first use of a line number with the word "line." If the poem lacks line numbers, cite it by giving the page number. But if the poem is just one page long, you don't need to cite any numbers within your text. The page number must appear, though, in your Works Cited.

MLA WORKS CITED

The second feature of the MLA format is the Works Cited list, or bibliography. This list should begin on a new page of your paper and should be double-spaced throughout and use hanging indention, which means that all lines except the first are indented one-half inch. The list is alphabetized by author's last name (or by the title in the case of anonymous works) and includes every primary and secondary source referred to in your paper. The format for the most common types of entries is given below. If any of the information called for is unavailable for a particular source, simply skip that element and keep the rest of the entry as close as possible to the given format. An anonymous work, for instance, skips the author's name and is alphabetized under the title.

☰ DIRECTORY TO MLA WORKS-CITED ENTRIES

Books

A book by a single author or editor (210)

A book with multiple authors or editors (210)

A book with a corporate author (210)

A recent edition of a book originally published much earlier (210)

Short Works from Collections and Anthologies

A single work from a collection or anthology (211)

Multiple works from the same collection or anthology (211)

Multiple Works by the Same Author (211)

Works in Periodicals

A work in a scholarly journal (212)

An article in a magazine (212)

An article in a newspaper (212)

A book review in a scholarly journal (213)

A book review in a magazine (213)

A book review in a newspaper (213)

Online Sources

An article in an online journal (213)

An article in a print journal accessed through an online database (213)

A book review that appears online (214)

A comment posted at a Web site (214)

A contribution to a listserv or similar online forum (214)

An e-mail message (214)

An online video, such as those available at YouTube (214)

Citation Formats for Other Kinds of Sources

An interview you conducted (215)

An episode of a television series (215)

A film (215)

Books

Here are typical elements of a book citation, in the order they should appear:

1. The author, last name first. If the book has an editor rather than an author, put the last name first but then add a comma and the word "editor." An author might be corporate; in that case, put the name of the organization.
2. The full title, in italics. If the book has a subtitle, put a colon between title and subtitle.

3. If the book has both an author and an editor, now put the words "edited by" and then the editor's name.
4. If the book has a translator, now put the words "translated by" and the translator's name.
5. If the book is in an edition other than the first, put the edition number.
6. Put the name of the publisher. If the publisher is a university, abbreviate "University" as "U" and Press as "P": for example, U of Chicago P or Indiana UP.
7. Put the year of publication.

Rules of punctuation: Follow the author's name with a period. Do the same for the book's full title. Usually, in the rest of the entry, your chief form of punctuation will be a comma. If you use a period again, it will be for abbreviations and for the entry's final punctuation mark. There are a few exceptions to this rule, which we will point out later.

A book by a single author or editor.

Cima, Gay Gibson. *Performing Women: Female Characters, Male Playwrights, and the Modern Stage*. Cornell UP, 1993.

Booth, Wayne C. *The Rhetoric of Fiction*. 2nd ed., U of Chicago P, 1983.

Tucker, Robert C., editor. *The Marx-Engels Reader*. Norton, 1972.

O'Connor, Flannery. *The Habit of Being: Letters of Flannery O'Connor*. Edited by Sally Fitzgerald, Farrar, Straus, and Giroux, 1979.

A book with multiple authors or editors.   If there are two, identify the additional person by first and last name. If there are three or more, just give the first person's name followed by "et al."

Leeming, David, and Jake Page. *God: Myths of the Male Divine*. Oxford UP, 1996.

Arrow, Kenneth Joseph, et al., editors. *Education in a Research University*. Stanford UP, 1996.

A book with a corporate author.

National Conference on Undergraduate Research. *Proceedings of the National Conference on Undergraduate Research*. U of North Carolina, 1995.

A recent edition of a book originally published much earlier.   If you want your reader to know the first publication date, give it a sentence of its own after the book's title.

Bronte, Emily. *Wuthering Heights*. 1847. Penguin Classics, 2002.

Short Works from Collections and Anthologies

Many scholarly books are collections of articles on a single topic by several different authors. When you cite an article from such a collection, include the information given below. The format is the same for works of literature that appear in an anthology, such as this one.

1. The name of the author(s) of the article or literary work.
2. The title of the short work, enclosed in quotation marks.
3. The title of the anthology, italicized.
4. The name(s) of the editor(s) of the collection or anthology.
5. All relevant publication information, in the same order and format as it would appear in a book citation.
6. The inclusive page numbers for the shorter work.
7. The medium of publication.

A single work from a collection or an anthology.   Begin with the author of the single work, and then the work's title. Follow this with the book's title, its editor, and other information you would normally provide for a book. Conclude the entry with the page numbers of the single work.

> Kirk, Russell. "Eliot's Christian Imagination." *The Placing of T. S. Eliot*, edited by Jewel Spears Brooker, U of Missouri P, 1991, pp. 136–44.
>
> Silko, Leslie Marmon. "Yellow Woman." *The Story and Its Writer: An Introduction to Short Fiction*, edited by Ann Charters, 9th ed., Bedford, 2015, pp. 1209–15.

Multiple works from the same collection or anthology.   Write a single general entry that provides full publication information for the collection or anthology as a whole. The entry for each shorter work then contains only its author and title, the names of the book's editors, and the page numbers of the shorter work, with all of these facts separated by commas.

> Charters, Ann, editor. *The Story and Its Writer: An Introduction to Short Fiction*. 9th ed., Bedford, 2015.
>
> Faulkner, William. "A Rose for Emily." Charters, pp. 409–15.

Multiple Works by the Same Author

If you cite more than one work by a single author, alphabetize the individual works by title. Give the author's full name only for the first citation in the Works Cited. Any subsequent entry for that author begins not with the name but with three hyphens followed by a period.

> Faulkner, William. "A Rose for Emily." *The Story and Its Writer: An Introduction to Short Fiction*, edited by Ann Charters, 9th ed., Bedford, 2015, pp. 454–60.
>
> - - - . *The Sound and the Fury*. Modern Library, 1956.

Works in Periodicals

When you cite articles and other short works from journals, magazines, or newspapers, include the following information, in the given order and format:

1. The name(s) of the author(s) of the short work, as for a book publication.
2. The title of the short work, in quotation marks.
3. The title of the periodical, italicized.
4. The volume number, issue number, and date of the issue. See the model citations below for examples of how to abbreviate volume, number, and date in the citations.
5. The page numbers of the short work.

Rules of punctuation: Follow the author's name with a period. Do the same for the short work's title. Usually, in the rest of the entry, your chief form of punctuation will be a comma. If you use a period again, it will be for abbreviations and for the entry's final punctuation mark. There are a few exceptions to this rule, which we will point out later.

A work in a scholarly journal.   Publication information for works from scholarly and professional journals should include the volume number, the issue number, the month or season of the issue, and the year.

> Charles, Casey. "Gender Trouble in *Twelfth Night*." *Theatre Journal*, vol. 49, no. 2, May 1997, pp. 121–41.

An article in a magazine.   Publication information for articles in general-circulation magazines includes the month(s) of publication for a monthly (or bimonthly), or the date (day, abbreviated month, then year) for a weekly or biweekly.

> Cowley, Malcolm. "It Took a Village." *Utne Reader*, Nov.-Dec. 1997, pp. 48–49.
> Kolbert, Elizabeth. "Unnatural Selection." *New Yorker*, 18 April 2016, pp. 22–28.

An article in a newspaper.   When citing an article from a newspaper, include the date (day, abbreviated month, year), followed by the edition, the section number, or the section letter (if applicable).

> Bray, Hiawatha. "New FCC Rules Draw Criticism." *Boston Globe*, 17 May 2016, p. C2.

A book review in a scholarly journal.

> Hawkins, Ty. Review of *Vietnam and Beyond: Tim O'Brien and the Power of Storytelling*, by Stefania Ciocia. *Studies in the Novel*, Vol. 45, No. 4, Winter 2013, pp. 705–07.

A book review in a magazine.

> Plumly, Stanley. Review of *Those Who Write for Immortality: Romantic Reputations and the Dream of Lasting Fame*, by H. J. Jackson. *The American Scholar*, vol. 84, no. 2, Spring 2015, pp. 152–53.

A book review in a newspaper.

> Yardley, Jonathan. Review of *One Matchless Time: A Life of William Faulkner*, by Jay Parini. *The Washington Post*, 24 Oct. 2004, p. T2.

Online Sources

Documentation for online sources should include as much of the following information as possible, in the order and format specified:

1. The name(s) of the author(s), as for a book publication.
2. The title of the work accessed, in quotation marks. For e-mails and postings, the title is the subject line.
3. The title of the periodical, italicized.
4. The volume number, issue number, and date of the issue. See the model citations below for examples of how to abbreviate volume, number, and date in the citations.
5. The URL or, better yet, the DOI. The letters "DOI" stand for "digital object identifier." A DOI is a permanent tag, enabling an online source to be located even when the URL changes. Not every Internet document has a DOI, but if you can find one for your source, list that rather than the URL.
6. If there is no date of issue, you may indicate the date you accessed the site, e.g., "Accessed 2 May 2016."

Rules of punctuation: Follow the author's name with a period. Do the same for the work's title. Usually, in the rest of the entry, your chief form of punctuation will be a comma. If you use a period again, it will be for abbreviations and for the entry's final punctuation mark. There are a few exceptions to this rule, which we will point out later.

An article in an online journal.

> Abowitz, Richard. "The Hughes Blues." *The Smart Set*, 2 Mar. 2016, http://thesmartset.com/the-langston-hughes-blues/.

An article in a print journal that you access through an online database.

Provide all the information you would give if you were citing the print version of the article. End this section with a period. Then put the name of the database (in italics), a comma, the URL or the DOI, and a final period.

> De Baerdemaeker, Ruben. "Performative Patterns in Hemingway's 'Soldier's Home.'" *The Hemingway Review*, vol. 27, no. 1, Fall 2007, pp. 55–73. *Project Muse*, doi: 10.1353/hem.2007.0017.

A book review that appears online.

> Livingston, James. Review of *The Age of the Crisis of Man*, by Mark Greif. *Bookforum*, 9 Mar. 2015, http://www.bookforum.com /review/14328.

A comment posted at a Web site.   Begin the entry with whatever name the commenter has used. Then write "Comment on," followed by the title (in quotation marks) of the text that the comment responds to. Next, using commas, give the title of the journal or Web site where the comment appears, followed by the date that the comment was posted, the time it was posted (if available), and the URL.

> Stefan. Comment on "How Should We Live in a Diverse Society?" *Pandaemonium*, 4 May 2016, 10:25 p.m., https://kenanmalik .wordpress.com/2016/05/02/how-should-we-live-in-a-diverse -society/.

A contribution to a listserv or similar online forum.   In this case, the title is the subject line.

> Bean, Joyce. "Re: Is fiction w/ community as subject still viable?" *Writing Program Administration*, 10 May 2016, 12:08 p.m., https://lists.asu.edu/cgi-bin/wa?A2=ind1605&L=WPA -L&D=0&P=149100.

An e-mail message.   Again, the title is the subject line. Then you should identify who received the message, along with the date it arrived.

> Hardy, Rachel. "Re: Flannery O'Connor's stories." Received by Jacob Ravitz, 5 Apr. 2016.

An online video, such as those available at YouTube.   For an entry like this, you have options. Your choices should reflect what you want to stress. Note the following options for citing a certain YouTube video. The first example starts with the video's title, which would surely help your readers track down the video. But if you wish to stress the title *and* acknowledge who posted the video, you could include that person's name, as our second example does. Maybe, though, you'll want to emphasize the video's director; our third example begins with his name and production role.

> "A Conversation with Tobias Wolff Directed by Lawrence Bridges." *YouTube*, 30 Nov. 2013, https://www.youtube.com/watch?v =0MZ3oKPFf90.

"A Conversation with Tobias Wolff Directed by Lawrence Bridges."
    YouTube, posted by Lawrence Bridges, 30 Nov. 2013, https://
    www.youtube.com/watch?v=0MZ3oKPFf90.
Bridges, Lawrence, director. "A Conversation with Tobias Wolff
    Directed by Lawrence Bridges." *YouTube*, 30 Nov. 2013, https://
    www.youtube.com/watch?v=0MZ3oKPFf90.

Citation Formats for Other Kinds of Sources

An interview you conducted.   In the author slot, identify the person you interviewed. Follow this information with "Personal interview," a comma, and the interview's date.

McCorkle, Patrick. Personal interview, 12 Mar. 2004.

An episode of a television series.   Begin with the episode's title. Using commas, follow this with the series title, the season and episode numbers, the network or production company, and the date of first airing. Our first example refers to the notorious "red wedding" episode of the TV series *Game of Thrones*. If you want to call attention to particular contributors, you can do so by adding information about them as our second example does.

"The Rains of Castamere." *Game of Thrones*, season 3, episode 9,
    HBO, 2 June 2013.
"The Rains of Castamere." *Game of Thrones*, created by David Benioff
    and D. B. Weiss, performances by Richard Madden, Michelle Fair-
    ley, and Oona Chaplin, season 3, episode 9, HBO, 2 June 2013.

A film.   Many film citations indicate title and director. Depending on which you want to emphasize, you can begin with either. Our first and second examples show these options. If you want to call attention to other contributors, you can do so by adding information about them as our third example does. In any case, end your entry by identifying the main production company and the year of first release.

The Dark Knight. Directed by Christopher Nolan, Warner Bros., 2008.
Nolan, Christopher, director. *The Dark Knight*, Warner Bros., 2008.
The Dark Knight. Directed by Christopher Nolan, performances by
    Christian Bale and Heath Ledger, Warner Bros., 2008.

A Note on Endnotes

Occasionally, you may have an idea or find a piece of information that seems important to your paper but that you just cannot work in smoothly without interrupting the flow of ideas. Such information can be included in the form of **endnotes**. A small superscript number in your text signals a note, and the notes themselves appear on a separate page at the end of your paper, before the Works Cited. Often, endnotes point readers to sources that they can then investigate if they wish. Any source mentioned in an endnote must be listed in the Works Cited.

Three Annotated Student Researched Arguments

We end this chapter with three researched arguments written by students. All of the essays refer to Charlotte Perkins Gilman's short story "The Yellow Wallpaper." But they model different ways to write about it. In order, the essays are:

- An argument that uses a literary work to examine a social issue
- An argument that deals with existing interpretations of a literary work
- An argument that places a literary work in historical and cultural context

Each argument demonstrates strategies we've discussed. Each also shows how to cite sources using MLA format. We annotate these essays in their margins, with comments that point out specific moves they make. After each essay, we review how it uses its sources. You'll see that the authors draw on research to create a conversation. They synthesize their findings as they build a case of their own.

AN ARGUMENT THAT USES A LITERARY WORK TO EXAMINE SOCIAL ISSUES

Some research papers mention a literary work but then focus on examining a social issue related to that work. An example of such a paper is the following essay by student Sarah Michaels. To prepare for writing her paper, Sarah consulted numerous sources, and she turns to them during the course of her essay. The chief danger in a project like this is that it will become a mere "data dump" — that is, a paper in which the writer uncritically cites one source after another without really making an original argument. In writing an essay like Sarah's, be sure to identify your main issue and claim clearly. Present yourself as someone who is genuinely *testing* your sources, determining the specific ways in which they are relevant to your argument. Keep in mind that even if you are representing a source as useful, you can indicate how its ideas need to be further complicated. With at least some of your sources, analyze specific terms they employ, lingering over their language. Moreover, try to relate your sources to one another. We think Sarah accomplishes all these objectives. Even if you disagree, aim to practice her strategies yourself.

Sarah Michaels
Professor Swain
English L202
21 May - - - -

"The Yellow Wallpaper" as a Guide
to Social Factors in Postpartum Depression

In 2005, actor Brooke Shields's memoir *Down Came the Rain: My Journey through Postpartum Depression* drew much public attention to the psychological problem mentioned in its subtitle.[1] But during the last couple of decades, postpartum depression has been the subject of reports by many medical institutions and media outlets. By now, lots of people other than health professionals are aware of this problem and can at least roughly define it. If asked, most of them would probably say that although it can exhibit varying degrees of severity, postpartum depression is basically a state of despair suffered by a significant number of women who have just given birth. This is, in fact, the main image of it presented in a recent document about it, an October 2010 report by Marian Earls and a committee of the American Academy of Pediatrics. Besides explaining what postpartum depression is, the report urges pediatricians and other primary care providers to screen new mothers for it. Given that many members of the public already know that the problem is widespread, the report has not sparked much disagreement. Responding to it in the online magazine *Slate*, however, Emily Anthes does challenge its almost total emphasis on mothers. She argues that the Academy's committee makes a questionable assumption in writing as if only females are traumatized by birth. In her article entitled "Dads Get Blue, Too," she criticizes the report's authors for not acknowledging at greater length that new fathers can experience postpartum depression as well.[2] More generally, her article suggests that discussions of this disorder can be skewed by ideological views that need to be recognized. But, more than a century ago, Charlotte Perkins Gilman's story "The Yellow Wallpaper" made pretty much the same point by showing how a woman diagnosed with a label like postpartum depression is a victim of her domestic circumstances and her society's ideas about gender, not just a person who has become ill on her own. When juxtaposed with the Academy's report, Gilman's 1892 tale is a reminder that today's doctors should look beyond an individual woman's symptoms of post-birth distress, because the social arrangements in which she lives may significantly affect her health.

Calls attention to an endnote.

Quickly identifies social issue that the paper will focus on.

Introduces the literary work that the paper will relate to the social issue.

The term *postpartum depression* has for a long time appeared in analyses of "The Yellow Wallpaper" and of the personal experience that Gilman based the story on. Veronica Makowsky points out that this clinical phrase has even "become a critical commonplace" (329) in studies of the relationship between the story and Gilman's life. Gilman does not, however, actually use the term *postpartum depression* in the tale. Instead, the heroine's husband, John, declares that she suffers from "temporary nervous depression — a slight hysterical tendency" (230), and the character herself refers to her "nervous troubles" (232). Nor does Gilman bring up the term in her accounts of the real-life despair she went through when she gave birth to her daughter. In her essay "Why I Wrote 'The Yellow Wallpaper,' " she recalls being tormented much of her life by "a severe and continuous nervous break-down tending to melancholia" (792). In her book-length autobiography *The Living of Charlotte Perkins Gilman*, she describes herself as suffering from "nervous prostration" (90). Indeed, the *Oxford English Dictionary*'s entry for *postpartum depression* indicates that the term was not recorded until 1929, when it showed up in an issue of the *American Journal of Psychiatry*.

Concedes that the term is used by scholars rather than by the author herself.

Nevertheless, the phrase does seem to fit the condition of Gilman's narrator. According to the American Academy of Pediatrics report, the symptoms of postpartum depression can range from "crying, worrying, sadness, anxiety, and mood swings" to more disturbing signs like "paranoia, mood shifts, hallucinations, [and] delusions" (1033). Gilman's character can be said to display most of these things once her child is born. At the estate that is the story's setting, she has trouble sleeping, she comes to doubt her husband's love, and, most dramatically, she rips off the wallpaper in her bedroom to free a woman whom she imagines wanting to creep away.

Directly connects language of the report to the story.

But simply labeling the heroine's distress as postpartum depression risks ignoring the conditions surrounding her that contribute to her suffering. Commenting on "The Yellow Wallpaper," literary critic Paula A. Treichler points out that a medical diagnosis can block understanding of "social, cultural, and economic practices" (69), even though these may support the doctor's claim to expertise, play a role in the patient's anguish, and become more important to confront than the patient's individual pain.[3] In Gilman's story, John uses his social authority as physician and

Uses another interpreter of the story to advance this paper's argument.

husband to control his wife. Specifically, he isolates her on the estate and makes her give up real activity, just as Gilman's real-life doctor, S. Weir Mitchell, demanded that she rest. As a result, the heroine feels obligated to surrender to the stereotypical passive female role, even though she would welcome more interaction with others and suspects that "congenial work, with excitement and change, would do me good" (780). When she proceeds to hallucinate the woman in the wallpaper, this is something that she is *driven* to do by John's assertion of masculine power, just as Weir Mitchell's prescription for inertia drove Gilman "near the border line of utter mental ruin" ("Why" 792).

Key quote from the story.

With "The Yellow Wallpaper" in mind, readers of the American Academy of Pediatrics report might examine how it downplays what Treichler calls "social, cultural, and economic practices" in its focus on diagnosing postpartum depression in women. Although the report does note that "Paternal depression is estimated at 6%" (1032), it does not linger on this fairly significant figure. In addition, the committee mentions only in passing that while "as many as 12% of all pregnant or postpartum women experience depression in a given year," the percentage is twice as much "for low-income women" (1032). Similarly brief is the recognition that "Eighteen percent of fathers of children in Early Head Start had symptoms of depression" (1033), a distinctly high figure that again suggests one's social class can affect one's health. Nor does the report develop its brief notice that possible causes of postpartum depression include "domestic violence" (1034), which would be a serious problem in the patient's environment rather than a malfunction within the patient herself. Instead of insisting that "Treatment must address the mother-child dyad relationship" (1036), the committee might also have called for addressing the chance that the mother suffers from a lack of money or the presence of an abusive partner.

Uses the story to examine the issue raised by the report.

Paper works with specific examples and language from the report.

Juxtaposing Gilman's story with the Academy's report does not mean that readers of this recent document about postpartum depression have to declare its authors evil. The attitudes and recommendations of the committee are not as morally disturbing as those of Gilman's character John. But her story should encourage the report's readers to notice where, in its call for screening women for postpartum depression, it risks screening *out* social influences on people diagnosed with this clinical problem.

Heads off possible misunderstanding.

Endnotes

[1] Shields also discussed her postpartum depression in a *New York Times* op-ed column, in which she defended herself against actor Tom Cruise's charge that she should have relied on vitamins and exercise rather than on the prescription drug Paxil.

[2] For an article that supports Anthes's attention to fathers even though she does not mention it, see Kim and Swain.

[3] For an article that expresses a position like Treichler's, see Dubriwny's critique of how modern-day TV news broadcasts represent postpartum disorders.

The endnotes provide additional information that could not be easily incorporated into the paper's main text.

Works Cited

Anthes, Emily. "Dads Get Blue, Too." *Slate*, 4 Nov. 2010,   *Citation for an online article.*
   http://slate.com/articles/double_x/doubleex/2010/11
   /dads_gett_blue_too.html.

Dubriwny, Tasha N. "Televison News Coverage of Postpartum
   Disorders and the Politics of Medicalization." *Feminist
   Media Studies*, vol. 10, no. 3, Sept. 2010, pp. 285–303.

Earls, Marian F., and the Committee on Psychosocial Aspects
   of Child and Family Health. "Clinical Report: Incorporating Recognition and Management of Perinatal and
   Postpartum Depression into Pediatric Practice. *Pediatrics*,
   vol. 26, no. 5, Nov. 2010, pp. 1032–38, doi:
   10.1542/peds.2010-2348.

Gilman, Charlotte Perkins. *The Living of Charlotte Perkins*   *Citation for a book.*
   Gilman: An Autobiography. 1935. Arno Press, 1972.

- - - . "Why I Wrote 'The Yellow Wallpaper.'" 1913. Schilb and   *Note style for multiple works*
   Clifford, pp. 258–59.   *by same author. Note, too,*

- - - . "The Yellow Wallpaper." 1892. Schilb and Clifford,   *that when you cite more than*
   pp. 244–57.   *one work from the same book,*
   you give each book its own

Kim, Pilyoung, and James E. Swain. "Sad Dads: Paternal Post-   *entry and cite each work from*
   partum Depression." *Psychiatry*, Feb. 2007, pp. 36–47.   *it in the shorthand form you*
   see here.

Makowsky, Veronica. "Fear of Feeling and the Turn-of-the-
   Century Woman of Letters." *American Literary History*,
   vol. 5, no. 2, Summer 1993, pp. 326–34.

Schilb, John, and John Clifford, editors. *Arguing about
   Literature*. 3rd ed., Bedford, 2020.

Shields, Brooke. *Down Came the Rain: My Journey through
   Postpartum Depression*. Hyperion, 2005.

- - - . "War of Words." *New York Times*, 1 July 2005, late ed.,
   p. A17.

Treichler, Paula A. "Escaping the Sentence: Diagnosis and   *Citation for a print article.*
   Discourse in 'The Yellow Wallpaper.'" *Tulsa Studies in
   Women's Literature*, vol. 3, nos. 1–2, Spring–Autumn
   1984, pp. 61–77.

≡ HOW SARAH USES HER SOURCES

Sarah's primary source. The October 2010 report on postpartum
   depression by the Earls Committee of the American Academy of
   Pediatrics; Sarah's argument is mainly a critique of this report.

Gilman, "The Yellow Wallpaper." To point out social contexts that
   the Earls Committee ignored

(continued on next page)

■ HOW SARAH USES HER SOURCES (*continued*)

Shields. To indicate that postpartum depression has become a big public issue (so that the topic deserves the attention Sarah will give it)

Anthes. To indicate that the Committee's report has received some criticism (which Sarah will add to)

Makowsky. To confirm that it's not unusual for literary critics to associate Gilman and her story with postpartum depression

Gilman, autobiographical nonfiction. To acknowledge that Gilman herself didn't use the term *postpartum depression*, though it now seems applicable to her and her story

Treichler. To support Sarah's focus on the social contexts of postpartum depression

Kim and Swain. To reinforce the argument made by Anthes (whom Sarah uses to suggest that criticism of the Earls Committee report is appropriate)

Dubriwny. To support Sarah's focus on the social contexts of postpartum depression

AN ARGUMENT THAT DEALS WITH EXISTING INTERPRETATIONS OF A LITERARY WORK

A researched writing assignment may require you to develop a claim about a literary work by relating your analysis to previous interpretations of the text. In the following essay, student Katie Johnson makes an argument about Charlotte Perkins Gilman's story "The Yellow Wallpaper" by incorporating statements made by people who have already written about it. To prepare for writing her essay, she especially consulted the *MLA International Bibliography*, through which she located several published articles about Gilman's tale. The bibliographies of these articles led her to still more interpretations of the story. The biggest challenge in writing an essay like this is to stay focused on developing an idea of your own rather than just inserting and echoing opinions held by others. Katie ended up examining an element of Gilman's story that she felt had not been adequately noted, let alone properly interpreted, by literary critics. As her essay proceeds, therefore, she does not simply agree with all the interpreters she cites. She treats with respect, however, those she finds fault with, civilly pointing out how her own thoughts differ. In addition, she clearly takes seriously the specific language of the critics she mentions, pondering their actual words rather than superficially summarizing their views.

Katie Johnson
Professor Van Wyck
English L141
5 May - - - -

The Meaning of the Husband's Fainting
in "The Yellow Wallpaper"

At the end of Charlotte Perkins Gilman's short story "The Yellow Wallpaper," the narrator is in a state that many people observing her would consider madness. She has torn off the wallpaper in her room and now seems proud of being able to "creep smoothly on the floor" (791). Her outwardly bizarre behavior at this point, along with her telling of the whole story beforehand, has led most literary critics to focus on analyzing her final conduct, as if it was the only really noteworthy feature of this concluding scene. Just as striking, however, is the final behavior of the narrator's husband, John. Up until the ending, he has acted as an authority on his wife's medical condition, and he has tried to assert power by always telling her what to do. At the conclusion, though, his mastery plainly vanishes. After finding the key to his wife's room, letting himself in, and beholding her crawling, he faints. Both the narrator and her husband end up on the floor. The narrator herself is highly aware of John's collapse, as she shows when she complains that "I had to creep over him every time!" (791). Because John's fainting is a dramatic reversal of his previous behavior and resembles the narrator's final physical position, it is surprising that only some literary critics have bothered to comment on John's breakdown, and even then the comments are relatively few. This neglect is a shame because, through John's fainting, Gilman seems to imply that he is left without any clear gender role to support him when his wife defies his manly effort to keep her what his society would consider sane.

Concisely summarizes the story's conclusion in first paragraph, which ends by stating main claim the essay will develop.

Until the last scene, John has repeatedly attempted to control his wife in the way that his society would expect of a man. This effort of his is reinforced by the professional standing he has achieved as a doctor. His masculine authority is interconnected with his medical authority. As we readers are made aware, he does not succeed in thoroughly bending his wife's will to his. Much of her narration is about her secret rebellion against him, which takes the form of imagining women trapped in the wallpaper of her room. Despite her hidden thoughts, however, he is often issuing commands to her, and she finds it hard to resist his domination. She admits to us that "I take pains to control myself — before him, at least, and that makes me very tired" (781). His attempts at enforcing his power over her include shutting her up in an odd country house in the first place. When she expresses suspicion of the estate, he simply "laughs" and "scoffs" (780), as he seems to do whenever she reveals independent thinking. She also says that he "hardly lets me stir without special direction" and gives her "a schedule prescription for each hour in the day" (781). Furthermore, he discourages her from writing, does not want to let her have visitors, and refuses to leave the estate when she informs him that she is not getting any better. Actually, he treats her more like his child than his wife, which is revealed when he asks "What is it, little girl?" (786) one night when she wakes up bothered by the wallpaper. All in all, he fits the nineteenth-century image of the ideal man as someone who gives his wife orders and expects her to follow them, though John tries to disguise his bossiness by declaring that he loves her and is looking out for her best interests.

The literary critics who do write about John's fainting at the end of the story tend to see it as a moment of irony, because in their view this masculine authority figure winds up physically collapsing in a way that is stereotypically associated with women. For example, Carol Margaret Davison states that when John faints, he is "assuming the traditional role of frail female" (66). Greg Johnson describes John's fall as "Gilman's witty inversion of a conventional heroine's confrontation with Gothic terror" (529), and similarly, Beverly A. Hume says that what happens is that John is "altering his conventional role as a soothing, masculine figure to that of a stereotypically weak nineteenth-century female" (478). These comments are not unreasonable, because during the nineteenth century, fainting was indeed something that women were believed to do more often than men. But a pair of literary critics has made another observation that, even though it sounds like the ones I have just quoted, points in a different direction that seems worth pursuing. Sandra M. Gilbert and Susan Gubar refer to John's fainting as an "unmasculine swoon of surprise" (91). They sound as if they are saying that he now seems feminine, but actually the word "unmasculine" simply indicates that he is no longer acting like a stereotypical male, so that readers of the story have to wonder whether he has any kind of identity left to him now. In fact, John's fainting seems like a total falling apart, as if he has become incapable of performing any further role at all, whether it is stereotypically feminine or masculine. Though

Synthesizes comments from critics, combining them to indicate the pattern she finds in interpretations of the story.

Does not flatly declare critics wrong but will develop an idea they have not mentioned.

Carefully analyzes a particular word that this pair of critics uses. Rest of paragraph develops main claim.

his wife is creeping, at least she is still able to move, whereas he lies paralyzed. Overall, he appears to suffer a complete loss of identity rather than take on a female identity. Because his wife has fallen into what he sees as madness despite his efforts to control her, he experiences a shattering of his male ego, the result being not that he is left with a "womanly" self but that he now lacks any sense of self at all. Just as he has only leased the estate instead of owning it, so too has his personhood proven impermanent because his ability to treat his wife as his property has apparently gone. At the very end of the story, the narrator even refers to her husband merely as "that man" (791), suggesting that he is no longer recognizable as an individual human being.

More than one literary critic has argued that John has suffered a loss of power only momentarily and that he will soon dominate his wife just as much as he did before. Judith Fetterley contends that "when John recovers from his faint, he will put her in a prison from which there will be no escape" (164), and Paula Treichler claims that

> As the ending of her narrative, her madness will no doubt commit her to more intense medical treatment, perhaps to the dreaded Weir Mitchell of whom her husband has spoken. The surrender of patriarchy is only temporary; her husband has merely fainted, after all, not died, and will no doubt move swiftly and severely to deal with her. Her individual escape is temporary and compromised. (67)

Unfortunately, Gilman did not write a sequel called "The Yellow Wallpaper: The Next Day" to let us know exactly what happens to the couple after the husband wakes up. Fetterley and Treichler might have been right if the events of this story had taken place in real life and involved a real married couple. Though it was based on Gilman's actual situation,[1] the story should be treated as a work of fiction, and Gilman has chosen to conclude it by showing John as physically overcome. If she had wanted to suggest that he will quickly regain power, presumably she would have done so. As the text stands, the final scene emphasizes his new weakness, not signs of a strength that will soon be restored to him.

Although both the husband and the wife are in a bad physical state at the end, we as readers do not have to sympathize with them equally. Especially by having the wife narrate the story, Gilman has designed it so that we are encouraged to care far more about her than about John.

Because quotation from Treichler is somewhat lengthy, Katie puts it in block form.

Synthesizes two critics' observations, putting them together as examples of a view that she questions.

Directs readers to endnote.

Disagrees with two critics but carefully explains why and avoids using hostile tone.

Uses final paragraph not only to restate main claim but also to add the point that readers of story do not have to feel as sorry for John as they do for his wife.

A lot of readers might even feel joy at his collapse, regarding it as the bringing down of a tyrant. In any case, his fainting is worth paying attention to as a sign that he has experienced a loss of masculine power that leaves him unable to function as any kind of self.

Endnote

[1] Gilman recalls the personal experience that motivated her to write her story in her essay "Why I Wrote 'The Yellow Wallpaper.' "

Endnote provides information that could not be easily integrated into main text of essay.

Works Cited

Davison, Carol Margaret. "Haunted House/Haunted Heroine: Female Gothic Closets in 'The Yellow Wallpaper.'" *Women's Studies*, vol. 33, no. 1, Jan.–Feb. 2004, pp. 47–75.

Citation for article in scholarly journal.

Fetterley, Judith. "Reading about Reading: 'A Jury of Her Peers,' 'The Murders in the Rue Morgue,' and 'The Yellow Wallpaper.'" *Gender and Reading: Essays on Readers, Texts, and Contexts*, edited by Elizabeth A. Flynn and Patrocinio P. Schweickart, Johns Hopkins UP, 1986, pp. 147–64.

Citation for work in anthology.

Gilbert, Sandra M., and Susan Gubar. *The Madwoman in the Attic: The Woman Writer and the Nineteenth-Century Literary Imagination*. Yale UP, 1979.

Citation for book.

Gilman, Charlotte Perkins. "Why I Wrote 'The Yellow Wallpaper.'" 1913. Schilb and Clifford, pp. 258–59.

- - - . "The Yellow Wallpaper." 1892. Schilb and Clifford, pp. 244–57.

Note style for multiple works by the same author. Note, too, that when you cite more than one work from the same book, you give the book its own entry and then cite each work from it in the shorthand form you see here.

Hume, Beverly A. "Gilman's 'Interminable Grotesque': The Narrator of 'The Yellow Wallpaper.'" *Studies in Short Fiction*, vol. 28, no. 4, Fall 1991, pp. 477–84.

Johnson, Greg. "Gilman's Gothic Allegory: Rage and Redemption in 'The Yellow Wallpaper.'" *Studies in Short Fiction*, vol. 26, no. 4, Fall 1989, pp. 521–30.

Schilb, John, and John Clifford, editors. *Arguing about Literature*. 3rd ed., Bedford, 2020.

Citation for anthology.

Treichler, Paula A. "Escaping the Sentence: Diagnosis and Discourse in 'The Yellow Wallpaper.'" *Tulsa Studies in Women's Literature*, vol. 3, nos. 1–2, Spring–Autumn 1984, pp. 61–77.

≡ HOW KATIE USES HER SOURCES

Katie's primary source. Gilman's "The Yellow Wallpaper"; Katie's argument is mainly an interpretation of the story's ending, specifically the husband's fainting

Davison, Johnson, Hume. To indicate a perspective that Katie doesn't quite accept and will go beyond

Gilbert and Gubar. To indicate a perspective that seems close to Katie's own but isn't really the same as hers

Fetterley, Treichler. To indicate an interpretation of the story's ending that Katie disagrees with

Gilman, article on her writing of the story. To acknowledge that the story has roots in real life

AN ARGUMENT THAT PLACES A LITERARY WORK IN HISTORICAL AND CULTURAL CONTEXT

When scholars do research on a literary work, often they aim to place it in its original situation. They investigate the background from which it emerged. How can they relate the work to its historical and cultural context? This is the basic issue they pursue. Perhaps you'll write a researched argument that addresses this question by applying it to a literary text you've read. If so, you'll probably make use of various sources. But you'll need to develop a claim of your own. The following essay demonstrates how. Fatima Nagi connects Gilman's "The Yellow Wallpaper" to its original era. In order to do this, she examined autobiographical nonfiction by Gilman. She studied as well a lecture by S. Weir Mitchell, Gilman's doctor. She also consulted scholarship on nineteenth-century medical treatments of women. Gradually, she came to focus on the "rest cure" Gilman suffered. After all, it was the ordeal that led Gilman to write her tale. Fatima realized the story leaves out a feature of this therapy: the massages that it usually involved. She suspected that this omission was deliberate. Her essay states and elaborates a claim about it. She argues that Gilman probably wanted to stress the narrator's isolation from human touch.

Fatima Nagi
Professor Schneebaum
English L202
25 April - - - -

The Relative Absence of the Human Touch in "The Yellow Wallpaper"

In her essay "Why I Wrote 'The Yellow Wallpaper,' " Charlotte Perkins Gilman reveals that her famous story was inspired by a personal depression that got worse when she underwent a "rest cure" prescribed to her by "a noted specialist in nervous diseases, the best known in the country" (792). Though she does not name this doctor in the essay, we are aware today that he was S. Weir Mitchell, a name that she actually brings up briefly in "The Yellow Wallpaper." The rest cure that the story's narrator goes through, however, does not seem to have all the features that Weir Mitchell's did. Interestingly, neither by reading the essay nor by reading Gilman's story would you realize that Weir Mitchell's treatment involved massage. The question for an interpreter of the story thus becomes, Why did Gilman leave massage out of "The Yellow Wallpaper"? Because we can only guess at her intentions, perhaps a better way of putting the question is this: What is the effect of omitting massage from the story? One important consequence is that there is less of a literal human touch in the story than there might have been, and so the heroine's alienation from others and her withdrawal into fantasy seem stronger than they might have been.

Immediately mentions one of her sources, but only to set up main claim about Gilman's story, which she states at end of paragraph.

Using question form helps signal cause/effect issue that the essay will address.

This is the essay's main claim.

Weir Mitchell himself seems to have regarded massage as a very big component of his rest cure. He gives it a lot of attention in his 1904 lecture "The Evolution of the Rest Treatment." There he describes at length two cases, one of a man and one of a woman, where he found out that rubbing the body helped the person overcome depression. He recalls arriving at the conclusion "that massage was a tonic of extraordinary value" (796), and he continues his lecture by giving a brief account of the larger world history of what he terms "this invaluable therapeutic measure" (797). Evidently Weir Mitchell did not perform massage himself; in his lecture, he describes having others do it for him. Perhaps he thought that if he personally rubbed a patient's body, he would run the risk of being accused of a sexual advance. Despite his use of stand-ins for him, he clearly considered massage a necessary feature of his rest cure. One reason was that he thought the depressed person's body needed some form of physical stimulation, which the person would not otherwise be getting by lying around so much of the time. He states in his lecture that massage was something that "enabled me to use rest in bed without causing the injurious effects of unassisted rest" (796). Probably this method also reflected a more general belief of his, which Jane F. Thrailkill describes as the assumption "that the efficacy of his cure lay in its treatment of a patient's material body, not in what we might now term the psychological effects of isolation or of his own charismatic presence" (532). Thrailkill goes on to point out that Weir Mitchell was not alone in this belief: "[T]he medical wisdom of the day . . . conceived of a patient as a conceptually inert bundle of physiological processes" (552).[1] Massage was a means of helpfully manipulating the physique, which for Weir Mitchell and other doctors of his era was the main source of difficulties that today might be seen as chiefly mental.

Given that massage was so important to Weir Mitchell, it is significant that Gilman's references to it are not consistent. She does recall being massaged when she discusses how Weir Mitchell treated her medically in her autobiography *The Living of Charlotte Perkins Gilman*. In that book, she says that besides being "put to bed and kept there," she was "fed, bathed, [and] rubbed" (96). She does not refer to massage, however, in "Why I Wrote 'The Yellow Wallpaper.'" More important for interpretations of the story, she does not make massage part of "The Yellow Wallpaper" itself. It plays no role at all in the plot. The elements of the rest cure that come up in the story are, instead, physical seclusion and forced abandonment of work.

Briefly summarizes Weir Mitchell's lecture, focusing on his remarks about massage rather than spending additional time on other topics of his speech.

Analyzes at length one particular source, Weir Mitchell's lecture.

Square brackets indicate alteration of text being quoted. Ellipses indicate words deleted from original text.

Synthesis of three texts, comparing what they do with the topic of massage. More specifically, compares Gilman's autobiography, Gilman's essay on writing the story, and the story itself.

If massage were a major element of the rest cure that the narrator goes through in "The Yellow Wallpaper," the story would probably feature a lot more human touching than it presently does. The way the story is written, the heroine experiences relatively little physical contact with other people, or at least she does not tell us that she is having much of this. What is especially interesting is that we do not find many instances of her being physically touched by her husband, John. There are, in fact, a few places in the text where he does touch her. She says that when she informs him that she is disturbed by the wallpaper, "he took me in his arms and called me a blessed little goose" (782). When she weeps because he will not leave the house to visit relatives, "dear John gathered me up in his arms, and just carried me upstairs and laid me on the bed, and sat by me and read to me till it tired my head" (785). When she complains that he is wrong to think she is getting better, he gives her "a big hug" and says "'Bless her little heart! . . . she shall be as sick as she pleases!' " (786). Yet his moments of touching her not only are very few but also reflect his insensitivity toward her. His folding her in his arms seems an effort to control her and trivialize her protests, not an expression of genuine love. Moreover, she takes no real comfort from his touch. If this amounts to rubbing her, then from her point of view, he is rubbing her the wrong way. Again, however, massage is significantly absent from this story, and because what touches there are seem so few and inhumane, readers are led to feel that the narrator is pretty much alone in her concerns. She has only the imaginary woman in the wallpaper to bond with, and she seems drawn to that woman in large part because her human companions have no true understanding of the distress that caused her to need some sort of cure in the first place.

In effect, admits it would be misleading to claim there are no instances of touching in the story. Proceeds to bring together (to synthesize) various examples of such contact.

Accounts for details of story that might seem to conflict with main claim.

In calling attention to the role of massage in S. Weir Mitchell's rest cure, I do not mean to minimize the importance of his treatment's other components. The physical rest he demanded of his patients was certainly a big element of the cure, so that we can easily see why Gilman made it central to her story. In his lecture, Weir Mitchell also points out that he applied electrical charges to the patient's body. Historians of women's health Barbara Ehrenreich and Deirdre English argue that Weir Mitchell relied heavily as well on "the technique of healing by *command*" (119, emphasis in original), constantly and firmly giving orders to his patients so that they felt obligated to obey his wishes and to get better on the precise schedule he had in mind. Massage certainly figured, however, in Weir Mitchell's mode of treatment,

Heads off possible misunderstanding of argument; dealing with it enables her to write a concluding paragraph that does more than just repeat main claim.

including his handling of Gilman's own case, so that her omission of it from "The Yellow Wallpaper" seems a deliberate strategy for giving other things emphasis. Above all, the quite limited role of human touching in the story serves to make readers highly aware that the narrator is without the loving, intimate company she really needs to recover from her depression.

Endnote

[1] Thrailkill spends much of her article tracing how an emphasis on treating depression through physical means (the approach taken by Weir Mitchell) gave way late in the nineteenth century to a more psychological and verbal form of therapy (such as Sigmund Freud practiced).

Endnote provides information that could not be easily integrated into main text of the essay.

Works Cited

Ehrenreich, Barbara, and Deirdre English. *For Her Own Good: 150 Years of the Experts' Advice to Women*. Doubleday-Anchor, 1978.

Citation for book.

Gilman, Charlotte Perkins. *The Living of Charlotte Perkins Gilman: An Autobiography*. 1935. Arno Press, 1972.

- - - . "Why I Wrote 'The Yellow Wallpaper.'" 1913. Schilb and Clifford, pp. 258–59.

- - - . "The Yellow Wallpaper." 1892. Schilb and Clifford, pp. 244–57.

Note style for multiple works by same author.

When you cite more than one work from the same book, you give the book its own entry and cite each work from it in the shorthand form you see here.

Schilb, John, and John Clifford, editors. *Arguing about Literature*. 3rd ed., Bedford, 2020.

Thrailkill, Jane F. "Doctoring 'The Yellow Wallpaper.'" *ELH*, vol. 69, no. 2, Summer 2002, pp. 525–66.

Citation for anthology.

Weir Mitchell, S. Excerpt from "The Evolution of the Rest Treatment." 1904. Schilb and Clifford, pp. 259–63.

Citation for scholarly article.

≡ HOW FATIMA USES HER SOURCES

Fatima's primary source. Gilman's "The Yellow Wallpaper"; Fatima's argument is mainly a consideration of why Gilman left massage out of the story

Mitchell. To indicate that Gilman's own doctor valued massage as a therapeutic measure, even if he used other methods as well

Gilman, autobiography. To prove that Mitchell used massage in treating Gilman

Gilman, article on her writing of the story. (1) To emphasize that Gilman based her story on Mitchell's treatment of her; (2) to acknowledge that Gilman didn't always mention that massage was one of Mitchell's tools

Thrailkill. To emphasize that massage was an important tool for Mitchell and reflected a basic medical belief of his era

Ehrenreich and English. To acknowledge that massage wasn't Mitchell's only method

≣ Contexts for Research: Confinement, Mental Illness, and "The Yellow Wallpaper"

CHARLOTTE PERKINS GILMAN, "The Yellow Wallpaper"

CULTURAL CONTEXTS:
CHARLOTTE PERKINS GILMAN, "Why I Wrote 'The Yellow Wallpaper'"

S. WEIR MITCHELL, From *"The Evolution of the Rest Treatment"*

JOHN HARVEY KELLOGG, From *The Ladies' Guide in Health and Disease*

When doctors make a medical or psychiatric diagnosis, they pinpoint their patient's condition but also often accept or reject their society's definition of *health*. The social context of diagnoses seems especially worth considering when a particular condition afflicts one gender much more than the other. Today, many more women than men appear to suffer from depression, anorexia, bulimia, and dissociative identity disorder. Why? Perhaps traditional female roles encourage these illnesses; perhaps gender bias affects how doctors label and treat them. Charlotte Perkins Gilman raised both these possibilities in her 1892 short story "The Yellow Wallpaper." In her own life, the consequences from her egregious treatment were not as serious as she depicts in her story. But Gilman was the exception. Many women suffered terribly from doctors who ignored the cultural causes of depression. Besides Gilman's story, we include her account of why she wrote it, an excerpt from a lecture by Silas Weir Mitchell about his cure, and some advice about motherhood from John Kellogg, another influential doctor of the time.

≣ BEFORE YOU READ

How is mental illness depicted in movies and television shows you have seen? Which representations of mental illness have you appreciated the most? Which have you especially disliked? State your criteria for these judgments.

CHARLOTTE PERKINS GILMAN
The Yellow Wallpaper

Charlotte Perkins Gilman (1860–1935) was a major activist and theorist in America's first wave of feminism. During her lifetime, she was chiefly known for her 1898 book Women and Economics. *In it, she argued that women should not be confined to the household and made economically dependent on men. Gilman also advanced such ideas through her many public-speaking appearances and her magazine* The Forerunner, *which she edited from 1909 to 1916. Gilman wrote many articles and works of fiction for* The Forerunner, *including a tale called* Herland *(1915), in which she*

Charlotte Perkins
Gilman. The Granger
Collection. New York.

envisioned an all-female utopia. Today, however, Gilman is best known for her short story "The Yellow Wallpaper," which she published first in an 1892 issue of the New England Magazine. *The story is based on Gilman's struggle with depression after the birth of her daughter Katharine in 1885. Seeking help for emotional turmoil, Gilman consulted the eminent neurologist Silas Weir Mitchell, who prescribed his famous "rest cure." This treatment, which forbade Gilman to work, actually worsened her distress. She improved only after she moved to California, divorced her husband, let him raise Katharine with his new wife, married someone else, and plunged fully into a literary and political career. As Gilman noted in her posthumously published autobiography,* The Living of Charlotte Perkins Gilman *(1935), she never fully recovered from the debilitation that had led her to Dr. Mitchell, but she ultimately managed to be enormously productive. Although "The Yellow Wallpaper" is a work of fiction rather than a factual account of her experience with Mitchell, Gilman used the story to criticize the doctor's patriarchal approach as well as society's efforts to keep women passive.*

It is very seldom that mere ordinary people like John and myself secure ancestral halls for the summer.

A colonial mansion, a hereditary estate, I would say a haunted house and reach the height of romantic felicity — but that would be asking too much of fate!

Still I will proudly declare that there is something queer about it.

Else, why should it be let so cheaply? And why have stood so long untenanted?

John laughs at me, of course, but one expects that in marriage.   5

John is practical in the extreme. He has no patience with faith, an intense horror of superstition, and he scoffs openly at any talk of things not to be felt and seen and put down in figures.

John is a physician, and *perhaps* — (I would not say it to a living soul, of course, but this is dead paper and a great relief to my mind) — *perhaps* that is one reason I do not get well faster.

You see, he does not believe I am sick!

And what can one do?

If a physician of high standing, and one's own husband, assures friends   10
and relatives that there is really nothing the matter with one but temporary nervous depression — a slight hysterical tendency° — what is one to do?

My brother is also a physician, and also of high standing, and he says the same thing.

So I take phosphates or phosphites — whichever it is, and tonics, and journeys, and air, and exercise, and am absolutely forbidden to "work" until I am well again.

Personally, I disagree with their ideas.

Personally, I believe that congenial work, with excitement and change, would do me good.

But what is one to do?   15

I did write for a while in spite of them; but it *does* exhaust me a good deal — having to be so sly about it, or else meet with heavy opposition.

I sometimes fancy that in my condition if I had less opposition and more society and stimulus — but John says the very worst thing I can do is to think about my condition, and I confess it always makes me feel bad.

So I will let it alone and talk about the house.

The most beautiful place! It is quite alone, standing well back from the road, quite three miles from the village. It makes me think of English places that you read about, for there are hedges and walls and gates that lock, and lots of separate little houses for the gardeners and people.

There is a *delicious* garden! I never saw such a garden — large and shady,   20
full of box-bordered paths, and lined with long grape-covered arbors with seats under them.

There were greenhouses, too, but they are all broken now.

There was some legal trouble, I believe, something about the heirs and coheirs; anyhow, the place has been empty for years.

hysterical tendency: It was common among Victorian doctors to believe women had an innate tendency to be overly emotional; now a discredited assumption.

That spoils my ghostliness, I am afraid, but I don't care — there is something strange about the house — I can feel it.

I even said so to John one moonlight evening, but he said what I felt was a *draught*, and shut the window.

I get unreasonably angry with John sometimes. I'm sure I never used to be   25
so sensitive. I think it is due to this nervous condition.

But John says if I feel so, I shall neglect proper self-control; so I take pains to control myself — before him, at least, and that makes me very tired.

I don't like our room a bit. I wanted one downstairs that opened on the piazza and had roses all over the window, and such pretty old-fashioned chintz hangings! but John would not hear of it.

He said there was only one window and not room for two beds, and no near room for him if he took another.

He is very careful and loving, and hardly lets me stir without special direction.

I have a schedule prescription for each hour in the day; he takes all care   30
from me, and so I feel basely ungrateful not to value it more.

He said we came here solely on my account, that I was to have perfect rest and all the air I could get. "Your exercise depends on your strength, my dear," said he, "and your food somewhat on your appetite; but air you can absorb all the time." So we took the nursery at the top of the house.

It is a big, airy room, the whole floor nearly, with windows that look all ways, and air and sunshine galore. It was nursery first and then playroom and gymnasium, I should judge; for the windows are barred for little children, and there are rings and things in the walls.

The paint and paper look as if a boys' school had used it. It is stripped off — the paper — in great patches all around the head of my bed, about as far as I can reach, and in a great place on the other side of the room low down. I never saw a worse paper in my life.

One of those sprawling flamboyant patterns committing every artistic sin.

It is dull enough to confuse the eye in following, pronounced enough to   35
constantly irritate and provoke study, and when you follow the lame uncertain curves for a little distance they suddenly commit suicide — plunge off at outrageous angles, destroy themselves in unheard of contradictions.

The color is repellant, almost revolting; a smouldering unclean yellow, strangely faded by the slow-turning sunlight.

It is a dull yet lurid orange in some places, a sickly sulphur tint in others.

No wonder the children hated it! I should hate it myself if I had to live in this room long.

There comes John, and I must put this away, — he hates to have me write a word.

We have been here two weeks, and I haven't felt like writing before, since that   40
first day.

I am sitting by the window now, up in this atrocious nursery, and there is nothing to hinder my writing as much as I please, save lack of strength.

John is away all day, and even some nights when his cases are serious.

I am glad my case is not serious!

But these nervous troubles are dreadfully depressing.

John does not know how much I really suffer. He knows there is no *reason* 45
to suffer, and that satisfies him.

Of course it is only nervousness. It does weigh on me so not to do my duty
in any way!

I meant to be such a help to John, such a real rest and comfort, and here I
am a comparative burden already!

Nobody would believe what an effort it is to do what little I am able, — to
dress and entertain, and order things.

It is fortunate Mary is so good with the baby. Such a dear baby!

And yet I *cannot* be with him, it makes me so nervous. 50

I suppose John never was nervous in his life. He laughs at me so about this
wallpaper!

At first he meant to repaper the room, but afterward he said that I was
letting it get the better of me, and that nothing was worse for a nervous patient
than to give way to such fancies.

He said that after the wallpaper was changed it would be the heavy
bedstead, and then the barred windows, and then that gate at the head of the
stairs, and so on.

"You know the place is doing you good," he said, "and really, dear, I don't
care to renovate the house just for a three months' rental."

"Then do let us go downstairs," I said, "there are such pretty rooms there." 55

Then he took me in his arms and called me a blessed little goose, and said
he would go down cellar, if I wished, and have it whitewashed into the bargain.

But he is right enough about the beds and windows and things.

It is an airy and comfortable room as anyone need wish, and, of course,
I would not be so silly as to make him uncomfortable just for a whim.

I'm really getting quite fond of the big room, all but that horrid paper.

Out of one window I can see the garden, those mysterious deep-shaded 60
arbors, the riotous old-fashioned flowers, and bushes and gnarly trees.

Out of another I get a lovely view of the bay and a little private wharf
belonging to the estate. There is a beautiful shaded lane that runs down there
from the house. I always fancy I see people walking in these numerous paths
and arbors, but John has cautioned me not to give way to fancy in the least.
He says that with my imaginative power and habit of story-making, a nervous
weakness like mine is sure to lead to all manner of excited fancies, and that I
ought to use my will and good sense to check the tendency. So I try.

I think sometimes that if I were only well enough to write a little it would
relieve the press of ideas and rest me.

But I find I get pretty tired when I try.

It is so discouraging not to have any advice and companionship about
my work. When I get really well, John says we will ask Cousin Henry and
Julia down for a long visit; but he says he would as soon put fireworks in my
pillow-case as to let me have those stimulating people about now.

I wish I could get well faster.   65

But I must not think about that. This paper looks to me as if it *knew* what a vicious influence it had!

There is a recurrent spot where the pattern lolls like a broken neck and two bulbous eyes stare at you upside down.

I get positively angry with the impertinence of it and the everlastingness. Up and down and sideways they crawl, and those absurd, unblinking eyes are everywhere. There is one place where two breadths didn't match, and the eyes go all up and down the line, one a little higher than the other.

I never saw so much expression in an inanimate thing before, and we all know how much expression they have! I used to lie awake as a child and get more entertainment and terror out of blank walls and plain furniture than most children could find in a toy-store.

I remember what a kindly wink the knobs of our big, old bureau used to   70
have, and there was one chair that always seemed like a strong friend.

I used to feel that if any of the other things looked too fierce I could always hop into that chair and be safe.

The furniture in this room is no worse than inharmonious, however, for we had to bring it all from downstairs. I suppose when this was used as a play-room they had to take the nursery things out, and no wonder! I never saw such ravages as the children have made here.

The wallpaper, as I said before, is torn off in spots, and it sticketh closer than a brother — they must have had perseverance as well as hatred.

Then the floor is scratched and gouged and splintered, the plaster itself is dug out here and there, and this great heavy bed, which is all we found in the room, looks as if it had been through the wars.

But I don't mind it a bit — only the paper.   75

There comes John's sister. Such a dear girl as she is, and so careful of me! I must not let her find me writing.

She is a perfect and enthusiastic housekeeper, and hopes for no better profession. I verily believe she thinks it is the writing which made me sick!

But I can write when she is out, and see her a long way off from these windows.

There is one that commands the road, a lovely shaded winding road, and one that just looks off over the country. A lovely country, too, full of great elms and velvet meadows.

This wallpaper has a kind of sub-pattern in a different shade, a particularly   80
irritating one, for you can only see it in certain lights, and not clearly then.

But in the places where it isn't faded and where the sun is just so — I can see a strange, provoking, formless sort of figure, that seems to skulk about behind that silly and conspicuous front design.

There's sister on the stairs!

Well, the Fourth of July is over! The people are all gone and I am tired out. John thought it might do me good to see a little company, so we just had mother and Nellie and the children down for a week.

Of course I didn't do a thing. Jennie sees to everything now.

But it tired me all the same. 85

John says if I don't pick up faster he shall send me to Weir Mitchell° in the fall.

But I don't want to go there at all. I had a friend who was in his hands once, and she says he is just like John and my brother, only more so!

Besides, it is such an undertaking to go so far.

I don't feel as if it was worthwhile to turn my hand over for anything, and I'm getting dreadfully fretful and querulous.

I cry at nothing, and cry most of the time. 90

Of course I don't when John is here, or anybody else, but when I am alone.

And I am alone a good deal just now. John is kept in town very often by serious cases, and Jennie is good and lets me alone when I want her to.

So I walk a little in the garden or down that lovely lane, sit on the porch under the roses, and lie down up here a good deal.

I'm getting really fond of the room in spite of the wallpaper. Perhaps *because* of the wallpaper.

It dwells in my mind so! 95

I lie here on this great immovable bed — it is nailed down, I believe — and follow that pattern about by the hour. It is as good as gymnastics, I assure you. I start, we'll say, at the bottom, down in the corner over there where it has not been touched, and I determine for the thousandth time that I *will* follow that pointless pattern to some sort of a conclusion.

I know a little of the principle of design, and I know this thing was not arranged on any laws of radiation, or alternation, or repetition, or symmetry, or anything else that I ever heard of.

It is repeated, of course, by the breadths, but not otherwise.

Looked at in one way each breadth stands alone, the bloated curves and flourishes — a kind of "debased Romanesque" with *delirium tremens* — go waddling up and down in isolated columns of fatuity.

But, on the other hand, they connect diagonally, and the sprawling 100 outlines run off in great slanting waves of optic horror, like a lot of wallowing seaweeds in full chase.

The whole thing goes horizontally, too, at least it seems so, and I exhaust myself in trying to distinguish the order of its going in that direction.

They have used a horizontal breadth for a frieze, and that adds wonderfully to the confusion.

There is one end of the room where it is almost intact, and there, when the crosslights fade and the low sun shines directly upon it, I can almost fancy radiation after all, — the interminable grotesques seem to form around a common center and rush off in headlong plunges of equal distraction.

It makes me tired to follow it. I will take a nap I guess.

Weir Mitchell: Dr. S. Weir Mitchell (1829–1914) was an eminent Philadelphia neurologist who advocated "rest cures" for nervous disorders. He was the author of *Diseases of the Nervous System, Especially of Women* (1881).

*   *   *

I don't know why I should write this.   105

I don't want to.

I don't feel able.

And I know John would think it absurd. But I *must* say what I feel and think in some way — it is such a relief!

But the effort is getting to be greater than the relief.

Half the time now I am awfully lazy, and lie down ever so much.   110

John says I mustn't lose my strength, and has me take cod liver oil and lots of tonics and things, to say nothing of ale and wine and rare meat.

Dear John! He loves me very dearly, and hates to have me sick. I tried to have a real earnest reasonable talk with him the other day, and tell him how I wish he would let me go and make a visit to Cousin Henry and Julia.

But he said I wasn't able to go, nor able to stand it after I got there; and I did not make out a very good case for myself, for I was crying before I had finished.

It is getting to be a great effort for me to think straight. Just this nervous weakness I suppose.

And dear John gathered me up in his arms, and just carried me upstairs   115
and laid me on the bed, and sat by me and read to me till it tired my head.

He said I was his darling and his comfort and all he had, and that I must take care of myself for his sake, and keep well.

He says no one but myself can help me out of it, that I must use my will and self-control and not let any silly fancies run away with me.

There's one comfort, the baby is well and happy, and does not have to occupy this nursery with the horrid wallpaper.

If we had not used it, that blessed child would have! What a fortunate escape! Why, I wouldn't have a child of mine, an impressionable little thing, live in such a room for worlds.

I never thought of it before, but it is lucky that John kept me here after all,   120
I can stand it so much easier than a baby, you see.

Of course I never mention it to them any more — I am too wise, but I keep watch of it all the same.

There are things in the wallpaper that nobody knows but me, or ever will.

Behind that outside pattern the dim shapes get clearer every day.

It is always the same shape, only very numerous.

And it is like a woman stooping down and creeping about behind that pat-   125
tern. I don't like it a bit. I wonder — I begin to think — I wish John would take me away from here!

It is so hard to talk with John about my case, because he is so wise, and because he loves me so.

But I tried it last night.

It was moonlight. The moon shines in all around just as the sun does.

I hate to see it sometimes, it creeps so slowly, and always comes in by one window or another.

John was asleep and I hated to waken him, so I kept still and watched the   130
moonlight on that undulating wallpaper till I felt creepy.

The faint figure behind seemed to shake the pattern, just as if she wanted
to get out.

I got up softly and went to feel and see if the paper *did* move, and when I
came back John was awake.

"What is it, little girl?" he said. "Don't go walking about like that—you'll
get cold."

I thought it was a good time to talk, so I told him that I really was not gaining here, and that I wished he would take me away.

"Why, darling!" said he, "our lease will be up in three weeks, and I can't   135
see how to leave before.

"The repairs are not done at home, and I cannot possibly leave town just
now. Of course if you were in any danger, I could and would, but you really
are better, dear, whether you can see it or not. I am a doctor, dear, and I know.
You are gaining flesh and color, your appetite is better, I feel really much easier
about you."

"I don't weigh a bit more," said I, "nor as much; and my appetite may be
better in the evening when you are here but it is worse in the morning when
you are away!"

"Bless her little heart!" said he with a big hug, "she shall be as sick as she
pleases! But now let's improve the shining hours by going to sleep, and talk
about it in the morning!"

"And you won't go away?" I asked gloomily.

"Why, how can I, dear? It is only three weeks more and then we will take a   140
nice little trip of a few days while Jennie is getting the house ready. Really dear
you are better!"

"Better in body perhaps—" I began, and stopped short, for he sat up
straight and looked at me with such a stern, reproachful look that I could not
say another word.

"My darling," said he, "I beg you, for my sake and for our child's sake, as well
as for your own, that you will never for one instant let that idea enter your mind!
There is nothing so dangerous, so fascinating, to a temperament like yours. It
is a false and foolish fancy. Can you trust me as a physician when I tell you so?"

So of course I said no more on that score, and we went to sleep before
long. He thought I was asleep first, but I wasn't, and lay there for hours trying to decide whether that front pattern and the back pattern really did move
together or separately.

On a pattern like this, by daylight, there is a lack of sequence, a defiance of
law, that is a constant irritant to a normal mind.

The color is hideous enough, and unreliable enough, and infuriating   145
enough, but the pattern is torturing.

You think you have mastered it, but just as you get well underway in following, it turns a back-somersault and there you are. It slaps you in the face,
knocks you down, and tramples upon you. It is like a bad dream.

The outside pattern is a florid arabesque, reminding one of a fungus. If you can imagine a toadstool in joints, an interminable string of toadstools, budding and sprouting in endless convolutions — why, that is something like it.

That is, sometimes!

There is one marked peculiarity about this paper, a thing nobody seems to notice but myself, and that is that it changes as the light changes.

When the sun shoots in through the east window — I always watch for that first long, straight ray — it changes so quickly that I never can quite believe it. 150

That is why I watch it always.

By moonlight — the moon shines in all night when there is a moon — I wouldn't know it was the same paper.

At night in any kind of light, in twilight, candlelight, lamplight, and worst of all by moonlight, it becomes bars! The outside pattern I mean, and the woman behind it is as plain as can be.

I didn't realize for a long time what the thing was that showed behind, that dim sub-pattern, but now I am quite sure it is a woman.

By daylight she is subdued, quiet. I fancy it is the pattern that keeps her so still. It is so puzzling. It keeps me quiet by the hour. 155

I lie down ever so much now. John says it is good for me, and to sleep all I can.

Indeed he started the habit by making me lie down for an hour after each meal.

It is a very bad habit I am convinced, for you see I don't sleep.

And that cultivates deceit, for I don't tell them I'm awake — O, no!

The fact is I am getting a little afraid of John. 160

He seems very queer sometimes, and even Jennie has an inexplicable look.

It strikes me occasionally, just as a scientific hypothesis, — that perhaps it is the paper!

I have watched John when he did not know I was looking, and come into the room suddenly on the most innocent excuses, and I've caught him several times *looking at the paper*! And Jennie too. I caught Jennie with her hand on it once.

She didn't know I was in the room, and when I asked her in a quiet, a very quiet voice, with the most restrained manner possible, what she was doing with the paper — she turned around as if she had been caught stealing, and looked quite angry — asked me why I should frighten her so!

Then she said that the paper stained everything it touched, that she had found yellow smooches on all my clothes and John's, and she wished we would be more careful! 165

Did not that sound innocent? But I know she was studying that pattern, and I am determined that nobody shall find it out but myself!

Life is very much more exciting now than it used to be. You see I have something more to expect, to look forward to, to watch. I really do eat better, and am more quiet than I was.

John is so pleased to see me improve! He laughed a little the other day, and said I seemed to be flourishing in spite of my wallpaper.

I turned it off with a laugh. I had no intention of telling him it was *because* of the wallpaper — he would make fun of me. He might even want to take me away.

I don't want to leave now until I have found it out. There is a week more, 170 and I think that will be enough.

I'm feeling ever so much better! I don't sleep much at night, for it is so interesting to watch developments; but I sleep a good deal in the daytime.

In the daytime it is tiresome and perplexing.

There are always new shoots on the fungus, and new shades of yellow all over it. I cannot keep count of them, though I have tried conscientiously.

It is the strangest yellow, that wallpaper! It makes me think of all the yellow things I ever saw — not beautiful ones like buttercups, but old foul, bad yellow things.

But there is something else about that paper — the smell! I noticed it the 175 moment we came into the room, but with so much air and sun it was not bad. Now we have had a week of fog and rain, and whether the windows are open or not, the smell is here.

It creeps all over the house.

I find it hovering in the dining-room, skulking in the parlor, hiding in the hall, lying in wait for me on the stairs.

It gets into my hair.

Even when I go to ride, if I turn my head suddenly and surprise it — there is that smell!

Such a peculiar odor, too! I have spent hours in trying to analyze it, to find 180 what it smelled like.

It is not bad — at first, and very gentle, but quite the subtlest, most enduring odor I ever met.

In this damp weather it is awful, I wake up in the night and find it hanging over me.

It used to disturb me at first. I thought seriously of burning the house — to reach the smell.

But now I am used to it. The only thing I can think of that it is like is the *color* of the paper! A yellow smell.

There is a very funny mark on this wall, low down, near the mopboard. A 185 streak that runs round the room. It goes behind every piece of furniture, except the bed, a long, straight, even *smooch*, as if it had been rubbed over and over.

I wonder how it was done and who did it, and what they did it for. Round and round and round — round and round and round — it makes me dizzy!

I really have discovered something at last.

Through watching so much at night, when it changes so, I have finally found out.

The front pattern *does* move — and no wonder! The woman behind shakes it!

Sometimes I think there are a great many women behind, and sometimes   190
only one, and she crawls around fast, and her crawling shakes it all over.

Then in the very bright spots she keeps still, and in the very shady spots
she just takes hold of the bars and shakes them hard.

And she is all the time trying to climb through. But nobody could climb
through that pattern—it strangles so; I think that is why it has so many heads.

They get through, and then the pattern strangles them off and turns them
upside down, and makes their eyes white!

If those heads were covered or taken off it would not be half so bad.

I think that woman gets out in the daytime!   195

And I'll tell you why—privately—I've seen her!

I can see her out of every one of my windows!

It is the same woman, I know, for she is always creeping, and most women
do not creep by daylight.

I see her in that long shaded lane, creeping up and down. I see her in those
dark grape arbors, creeping all around the garden.

I see her on that long road under the trees, creeping along, and when a   200
carriage comes she hides under the blackberry vines.

I don't blame her a bit. It must be very humiliating to be caught creeping
by daylight!

I always lock the door when I creep by daylight. I can't do it at night, for I
know John would suspect something at once.

And John is so queer now, that I don't want to irritate him. I wish he
would take another room! Besides, I don't want anybody to get that woman
out at night but myself.

I often wonder if I could see her out of all the windows at once.

But, turn as fast as I can, I can only see out of one at one time.   205

And though I always see her, she *may* be able to creep faster than I can
turn!

I have watched her sometimes away off in the open country, creeping as
fast as a cloud shadow in a high wind.

If only that top pattern could be gotten off from the under one! I mean to try
it, little by little.

I have found out another funny thing, but I shan't tell it this time! It does
not do to trust people too much.

There are only two more days to get this paper off, and I believe John is   210
beginning to notice. I don't like the look in his eyes.

And I heard him ask Jennie a lot of professional questions, about me. She
had a very good report to give.

She said I slept a good deal in the daytime.

John knows I don't sleep very well at night, for all I'm so quiet!

He asked me all sorts of questions too, and pretended to be very loving
and kind.

As if I couldn't see through him!   215

Still, I don't wonder he acts so, sleeping under this paper for three months.

It only interests me, but I feel sure John and Jennie are secretly affected by it.

Hurrah! This is the last day, but it is enough. John is to stay in town over night, and won't be out until this evening.

Jennie wanted to sleep with me — the sly thing! But I told her I should undoubtedly rest better for a night all alone.

That was clever, for really I wasn't alone a bit! As soon as it was moonlight and   220
that poor thing began to crawl and shake the pattern, I got up and ran to help her.

I pulled and she shook, I shook and she pulled, and before morning we had peeled off yards of that paper.

A strip about as high as my head and half around the room.

And then when the sun came and that awful pattern began to laugh at me, I declared I would finish it to-day!

We go away to-morrow, and they are moving all my furniture down again to leave things as they were before.

Jennie looked at the wall in amazement, but I told her merrily that I did it   225
out of pure spite at the vicious thing.

She laughed and said she wouldn't mind doing it herself, but I must not get tired.

How she betrayed herself that time!

But I am here, and no person touches this paper but me, — not *alive*!

She tried to get me out of the room — it was too patent! But I said it was so quiet and empty and clean now that I believed I would lie down again and sleep all I could, and not to wake me even for dinner — I would call when I woke.

So now she is gone, and the servants are gone, and the things are gone,   230
and there is nothing left but that great bedstead nailed down, with the canvas mattress we found on it.

We shall sleep downstairs to-night, and take the boat home to-morrow.

I quite enjoy the room, now it is bare again.

How those children did tear about here!

This bedstead is fairly gnawed!

But I must get to work.   235

I have locked the door and thrown the key down into the front path.

I don't want to go out, and I don't want to have anybody come in, till John comes.

I want to astonish him.

I've got a rope up here that even Jennie did not find. If that woman does get out, and tries to get away, I can tie her!

But I forgot I could not reach far without anything to stand on!   240

This bed will *not* move!

I tried to lift and push it until I was lame, and then I got so angry I bit off a little piece at one corner — but it hurt my teeth.

Then I peeled off all the paper I could reach standing on the floor. It sticks horribly and the pattern just enjoys it! All those strangled heads and bulbous eyes and waddling fungus growths just shriek with derision!

I am getting angry enough to do something desperate. To jump out of the window would be admirable exercise, but the bars are too strong even to try.

Besides I wouldn't do it. Of course not. I know well enough that a step like   245
that is improper and might be misconstrued.

I don't like to *look* out of the windows even—there are so many of those creeping women, and they creep so fast.

I wonder if they all come out of that wallpaper as I did?

But I am securely fastened now by my well-hidden rope—you don't get *me* out in the road there!

I suppose I shall have to get back behind the pattern when it comes night, and that is hard!

It is so pleasant to be out in this great room and creep around as I please!   250

I don't want to go outside. I won't, even if Jennie asks me to.

For outside you have to creep on the ground, and everything is green instead of yellow.

But here I can creep smoothly on the floor, and my shoulder just fits in that long smooch around the wall, so I cannot lose my way.

Why, there's John at the door!

It is no use, young man, you can't open it!   255

How he does call and pound!

Now he's crying for an axe.

It would be a shame to break down that beautiful door!

"John dear!" said I in the gentlest voice, "the key is down by the front steps, under a plantain leaf!"

That silenced him for a few moments.   260

Then he said—very quietly indeed, "Open the door, my darling!"

"I can't," said I. "The key is down by the front door under a plantain leaf!"

And then I said it again, several times, very gently and slowly, and said it so often that he had to go and see, and he got it of course, and came in. He stopped short by the door.

"What is the matter?" he cried. "For God's sake, what are you doing!"

I kept on creeping just the same, but I looked at him over my shoulder.   265

"I've got out at last," said I, "in spite of you and Jane. And I've pulled off most of the paper, so you can't put me back!"

Now why should that man have fainted? But he did, and right across my path by the wall, so that I had to creep over him every time!   *[1892]*

≡ THINKING ABOUT THE TEXT

1. What psychological stages does the narrator go through as the story progresses?

2. How does the wallpaper function as a symbol in this story? What do you conclude about the narrator when she becomes increasingly interested in the woman she finds there?

3. Explain your ultimate view of the narrator by using specific details of the story and by identifying some of the warrants or assumptions behind your opinion. Do you admire her? Sympathize with her? Recoil from her? What would you say to someone who simply dismisses her as crazy?

4. The story is narrated in the present tense. Would its effect be different if it were narrated in the past tense? Why, or why not?

5. In real life, Gilman's husband and her doctor were two separate people. In the story, the narrator's husband is her doctor as well. Why do you think Gilman made this change? What is the effect of her combining husband and doctor?

CHARLOTTE PERKINS GILMAN
Why I Wrote "The Yellow Wallpaper"

Gilman published the following piece in the October 1913 issue of her magazine, The Forerunner.

Many and many a reader has asked that. When the story first came out, in the *New England Magazine* about 1891, a Boston physician made protest in *The Transcript.* Such a story ought not to be written, he said; it was enough to drive anyone mad to read it.

Another physician, in Kansas I think, wrote to say that it was the best description of incipient insanity he had ever seen, and—begging my pardon— had I been there?

Now the story of the story is this:

For many years I suffered from a severe and continuous nervous break-down tending to melancholia—and beyond. During about the third year of this trouble I went, in devout faith and some faint stir of hope, to a noted specialist in nervous diseases, the best known in the country. This wise man put me to bed and applied the rest cure, to which a still good physique responded so promptly that, he concluded there was nothing much the matter with me, and sent me home with solemn advice to "live as domestic a life as far as possible," to "have but two hours' intellectual life a day," and "never to touch pen, brush, or pencil again as long as I lived." This was in 1887.

I went home and obeyed those directions for some three months, and   5
came so near the border line of utter mental ruin that I could see over.

Then, using the remnants of intelligence that remained, and helped by a wise friend, I cast the noted specialist's advice to the winds and went to work again—work, the normal life of every human being; work, in which is joy and growth and service, without which one is a pauper and a parasite; ultimately recovering some measure of power.

Being naturally moved to rejoicing by this narrow escape, I wrote *The Yellow Wallpaper*, with its embellishments and additions to carry out the ideal

(I never had hallucinations or objections to my mural decorations) and sent a copy to the physician who so nearly drove me mad. He never acknowledged it.

The little book is valued by alienists° and as a good specimen of one kind of literature. It has to my knowledge saved one woman from a similar fate—so terrifying her family that they let her out into normal activity and she recovered.

But the best result is this. Many years later I was told that the great specialist had admitted to friends of his that he had altered his treatment of neurasthenia since reading *The Yellow Wallpaper.*

It was not intended to drive people crazy, but to save people from being   10 driven crazy, and it worked.   *[1913]*

alienists: Nineteenth-century term for psychiatrists.

≡ THINKING ABOUT THE TEXT

1. S. Weir Mitchell was the "noted specialist in nervous diseases" (para. 4) whom Gilman mentions. Yet she does not identify him by name. Why not, do you think? Some historians argue that, contrary to Gilman's claim here, Mitchell continued to believe his "rest cure" valid. Does this issue of fact matter to your judgment of her piece? Why, or why not?

2. Look again at Gilman's last sentence. Do you believe that her story could indeed "save people from being driven crazy"? Why, or why not?

3. Does this piece as a whole affect your interpretation and opinion of Gilman's story? Why, or why not? In general, how much do you think readers of a story should know about its author's life?

S. WEIR MITCHELL
From *"The Evolution of the Rest Treatment"*

Charlotte Perkins Gilman sought help from Silas Weir Mitchell (1829–1914) because he was a well-known and highly respected physician who had treated many women's mental problems. Mitchell developed his "rest cure" while serving as an army surgeon during the Civil War. Ironically, like Gilman, he was also a writer. Besides producing numerous monographs on medical subjects, he published many short stories and novels. The following is an excerpt from a lecture that Mitchell gave to the Philadelphia Neurological Society in 1904, twelve years after "The Yellow Wallpaper" appeared. As you will see, Mitchell was still enthusiastic about his "rest cure," although he had changed it in certain respects since devising it.

I have been asked to come here to-night to speak to you on some subject connected with nervous disease. I had hoped to have had ready a fitting paper for so notable an occasion, but have been prevented by public engagements and private business so as to make it quite impossible. I have, therefore, been driven to ask whether it would be agreeable if I should speak in regard to the mode in which the treatment of disease by rest was evolved. This being favorably received, I am here this evening to say a few words on that subject.

You all know full well that the art of cure rests upon a number of sciences, and that what we do in medicine, we cannot always explain, and that our methods are far from having the accuracy involved in the term *scientific*. Very often, however, it is found that what comes to us through some accident or popular use and proves of value, is defensible in the end by scientific explanatory research. This was the case as regards the treatment I shall briefly consider for you to-night.

The first indication I ever had of the great value of mere rest in disease, was during the Civil War, when there fell into the hands of Doctors Morehouse, Keen, and myself, a great many cases of what we called acute exhaustion. These were men, who, being tired by much marching, gave out suddenly at the end of some unusual exertion, and remained for weeks, perhaps months, in a pitiable state of what we should call today, Neurasthenia. In these war cases, it came on with strange abruptness. It was more extreme and also more certainly curable than are most of the graver male cases which now we are called on to treat.

I have seen nothing exactly like it in civil experience, but the combination of malaria, excessive exertion, and exposure provided cases such as no one sees today. Complete rest and plentiful diet usually brought these men up again and in many instances enabled them to return to the front.

In 1872 I had charge of a man who had locomotor ataxia° with extreme pain in the extremities, and while making some unusual exertion, he broke his right thigh. This confined him to his bed for three months, and the day he got up, he broke his left thigh. This involved another three months of rest. At the end of that time he confessed with satisfaction that his ataxia was better, and that he was, as he remained thereafter, free from pain. I learned from this, and two other cases, that in ataxia the bones are brittle, and I learned also that rest in bed is valuable in a proportion of such cases. You may perceive that my attention was thus twice drawn towards the fact that mere rest had certain therapeutic values. 5

In 1874 Mrs. G., of B ———, Maine, came to see me in the month of January. I have described her case elsewhere, so that it is needless to go into detail here, except to say that she was a lady of ample means, with no special troubles or annoyances, but completely exhausted by having had children in rapid succession and from having undertaken to do charitable and other work to an extent far beyond her strength. When first I saw this tall woman, large, gaunt, weighing under a hundred pounds, her complexion pale and acneous, and heard her story, I was for a time in a state of such therapeutic despair as usually fell upon physicians of that day when called upon to treat such cases. She had been to Spas, to physicians of the utmost eminence, passed through

ataxia: An inability to control muscular movements that is symptomatic of some nervous diseases.

the hands of gynecologists, worn spinal supporters, and taken every tonic known to the books. When I saw her she was unable to walk up stairs. Her exercise was limited to moving feebly up and down her room, a dozen times a day. She slept little and, being very intelligent, felt deeply her inability to read or write. Any such use of the eyes caused headache and nausea. Conversation tired her, and she had by degrees accepted a life of isolation. She was able partially to digest and retain her meals if she lay down in a noiseless and darkened room. Any disturbance or the least excitement, in short, any effort, caused nausea and immediate rejection of her meal. With care she could retain enough food to preserve her life and hardly to do more. Anemia, which we had then no accurate means of measuring, had been met by half a dozen forms of iron, all of which were said to produce headache, and generally to disagree with her. Naturally enough, her case had been pronounced to be hysteria, but calling names may relieve a doctor and comfort him in failure, but does not always assist the patient, and to my mind there was more of a general condition of nervous excitability due to the extreme of weakness than I should have been satisfied to label with the apologetic label hysteria.

I sat beside this woman day after day, hearing her pitiful story, and distressed that a woman, young, once handsome, and with every means of enjoyment in life should be condemned to what she had been told was a state of hopeless invalidism. After my third or fourth visit, with a deep sense that everything had been done for her that able men could with reason suggest, and many things which reason never could have suggested, she said to me that I appeared to have nothing to offer which had not been tried over and over again. I asked her for another day before she gave up the hope which had brought her to me. The night brought counsel. The following morning I said to her, if you are at rest you appear to digest your meals better. "Yes," she said. "I have been told that on that account I ought to lie in bed. It has been tried, but when I remain in bed for a few days, I lose all appetite, have intense constipation, and get up feeling weaker than when I went to bed. Please do not ask me to go to bed." Nevertheless, I did, and a week in bed justified her statements. She threw up her meals undigested, and was manifestly worse for my experiment. Sometimes the emesis° was mere regurgitation, sometimes there was nausea and violent straining, with consequent extreme exhaustion. She declared that unless she had the small exercise of walking up and down her room, she was infallibly worse. I was here between two difficulties. That she needed rest I saw, that she required some form of exercise I also saw. How could I unite the two?

As I sat beside her, with a keen sense of defeat, it suddenly occurred to me that some time before, I had seen a man, known as a layer on of hands, use very rough rubbing for a gentleman who was in a state of general paresis.° Mr. S. had asked me if I objected to this man rubbing him. I said no, and that I should like to see him do so, as he had relieved, to my knowledge, cases of rheumatic stiffness. I was present at two sittings and saw this man rub my patient.

emesis: Vomiting.   **paresis:** Brain syphilis.

He kept him sitting in a chair at the time and was very rough and violent like the quacks now known as osteopaths. I told him he had injured my patient by his extreme roughness, and that if he rubbed him at all he must be more gentle. He took the hint and as a result there was every time a notable but temporary gain. Struck with this, I tried to have rubbing used on spinal cases, but those who tried to do the work were inefficient, and I made no constant use of it. It remained, however, on my mind, and recurred to me as I sat beside this wreck of a useful and once vigorous woman. The thought was fertile. I asked myself why rubbing might not prove competent to do for the muscles and tardy circulation what voluntary exercise does. I said to myself, this may be exercise without exertion, and wondered why I had not long before had this pregnant view of the matter.

Suffice it to say that I brought a young woman to Mrs. G.'s bedside and told her how I thought she ought to be rubbed. The girl was clever, and developed talent in that direction, and afterwards became the first of that great number of people who have since made a livelihood by massage. I watched the rubbing two or three times, giving instructions, in fact developing out of the clumsy massage I had seen, the manual of a therapeutic means, at that time entirely new to me. A few days later I fell upon the idea of giving electric passive exercise and cautiously added this second agency. Meanwhile, as she had always done best when secluded, I insisted on entire rest and shut out friends, relatives, books, and letters. I had some faith that I should succeed. In ten days I was sure the woman had found a new tonic, hope, and blossomed like a rose. Her symptoms passed away one by one. I was soon able to add to her diet, to feed her between meals, to give her malt daily, and, after a time, to conceal in it full doses of pyro-phosphates of iron. First, then, I had found two means which enabled me to use rest in bed without causing the injurious effects of unassisted rest; secondly, I had discovered that massage was a tonic of extraordinary value; thirdly, I had learned that with this combination of seclusion, massage, and electricity, I could overfeed the patient until I had brought her into a state of entire health. I learned later the care which had to be exercised in getting these patients out of bed. But this does not concern us now. In two months she gained forty pounds and was a cheerful, blooming woman, fit to do as she pleased. She has remained, save for time's ravage, what I made her.

It may strike you as interesting that for a while I was not fully aware of the 10 enormous value of a therapeutic discovery which employed no new agents, but owed its usefulness to a combination of means more or less well known.

Simple rest as a treatment had been suggested, but not in this class of cases. Massage has a long history. Used, I think, as a luxury by the Orientals for ages, it was employed by Ling in 1813. It never attained perfection in the hands of the Swedes, nor do they to-day understand the proper use of this agent. It was over and over recognized in Germany, but never generally accepted. In France, at a later period, Dreyfus, in 1841, wrote upon it and advised its use, as did Recamier and Lainé in 1868. Two at least of these authors thought it useful as a general agent, but no one seems to have accepted their views, nor was its value as a tonic spoken of in the books on therapeutics or recommended on any text-book as a powerful toning agent. It was used here in the Rest Treatment, and this, I think, gave it vogue and caused the familiar use of this invaluable therapeutic measure.

A word before I close. My first case left me in May, 1874, and shortly afterwards I began to employ the same method in other cases, being careful to choose only those which seemed best suited to it. My first mention in print of the treatment was in 1875, in the Sequin Lectures, Vol. 1, No. 4, "Rest in the Treatment of Disease." In that paper I first described Mrs. G.'s case. My second paper was in 1877, an address before the Medico-Chirurgical faculty of Maryland, and the same year I printed my book on "Rest Treatment." The one mistake in the book was the title. I was, however, so impressed at the time by the extraordinary gain in flesh and blood under this treatment that I made it too prominent in the title of the book. Let me say that for a long time the new treatment was received with the utmost incredulity. When I spoke in my papers of the people who had gained half a pound a day or more, my results were questioned and ridiculed in this city as approaching charlatanism. At a later date in England some physicians were equally wanting in foresight and courtesy. It seems incredible that any man who was a member of the British Medical Association could have said that he would rather see his patients not get well than have them cured by such a method as that. It was several years before it was taken up by Professor Goodell, and it was a longer time in making its way in Europe when by mere accident it came to be first used by Professor William Playfair.

I suffered keenly at that time from this unfair criticism, as any sensitive man must have done, for some who were eminent in the profession said of it and of me things which were most inconsiderate. Over and over in consultation I was rejected with ill-concealed scorn. I made no reply to my critics. I knew that time would justify me: I have added a long since accepted means of helping those whom before my day few helped. This is a sufficient reward for silence, patience, and self-faith. I fancy that there are in this room many who have profited for themselves and their patients by the thought which evolved the Rest Treatment as I sat by the bedside of my first rest case in 1874. Playfair said of it at the British Association that he had nothing to add to it and nothing to omit, and to this day no one has differed as to his verdict.

How fully the use of massage has been justified by the later scientific studies of Lauder Brunton, myself, and others you all know. It is one of the most scientific of remedial methods.   *[1904]*

≡ THINKING ABOUT THE TEXT

1. How would you describe Mitchell's tone in this lecture? What self-image does he seem to cultivate? Support your answers by referring to specific words in the text.

2. Why does Mitchell consider Mrs. G.'s case significant? In what ways does she resemble Gilman and the narrator of Gilman's story?

3. Mitchell indicates that his patients have included male as well as female hysterics. Are we therefore justified in concluding that gender did not matter much in his application of the "rest cure"? Why, or why not?

JOHN HARVEY KELLOGG
From *The Ladies' Guide in Health and Disease*

John Harvey Kellogg (1852–1943) was an American physician who wrote much advice about how to discipline one's sexual desires, and in the case of women, how to be a good mother. As founder and superintendent of the Battle Creek Sanitarium in Michigan, Dr. Kellogg urged that his patients eat cereals as part of their treatment, and eventually, his brother established the cereal company that bears their family name. Dr. Kellogg's keen interest in cereals and health foods is satirized in T. Coraghessan Boyle's 1993 novel, The Road to Wellville, *and the film based on that book. The following piece is an excerpt from Kellogg's 1882* Ladies' Guide in Health and Disease: Girlhood, Maidenhood, Wifehood, Motherhood. *In this selection, he virtually equates womanhood with motherhood and discusses what a woman must do to produce outstanding children. Kellogg's advice reflects the view that much of his society held about women — or at least about middle- and upper-class white women. His discussion of "puerperal mania" is especially relevant to Gilman's story.*

The special influence of the mother begins with the moment of conception. In fact it is possible that the mental condition at the time of the generative act has much to do with determining the character of the child, though it is generally conceded that at this time the influence of the father is greater than that of the mother. Any number of instances have occurred in which a drunken father has impressed upon his child the condition of his nervous system to such a degree as to render permanent in the child the staggering gait and maudlin manner which in his own case was a transient condition induced by the poisonous influence of alcohol. A child born as the result of a union in which both parents were in a state of beastly intoxication was idiotic.

Another fact might be added to impress the importance that the new being should be supplied from the very beginning of its existence with the very best conditions possible. Indeed, it is desirable to go back still further, and secure a proper preparation for the important function of maternity. The qualities which go to make up individuality of character are the result of the summing up of a long line of influences, too subtle and too varied to admit of full control, but still, to some degree at least, subject to management. The dominance of law is nowhere more evident than in the relation of ante-natal influences to character.

The hap-hazard way in which human beings are generated leaves no room for surprise that the race should deteriorate. No stock-breeder would expect anything but ruin should he allow his animals to propagate with no attention to their physical conditions or previous preparation.

Finding herself in a pregnant condition, the mother should not yield to the depressing influences which often crowd upon her. The anxieties and fears which women sometimes yield themselves to, grow with encouragement, until they become so absorbed as to be capable of producing a profoundly evil impression on the child. The true mother who is prepared for the functions of maternity, will welcome the evidence of pregnancy, and joyfully enter upon the Heaven-given task of molding a human character, of bringing into the world a new being whose life-history may involve the destinies of nations, or change the current of human thought for generations to come.

The pregnant mother should cultivate cheerfulness of mind and calmness   5
of temper, but should avoid excitements of all kinds, such as theatrical performances, public contests of various descriptions, etc. Anger, envy, irritability of temper, and, in fact, all the passions and propensities should be held in check. The fickleness of desire and the constantly varying whims which characterize the pregnant state in some women should not be regarded as uncontrollable, and to be yielded to as the only means of appeasing them. The mother should be gently encouraged to resist such tendencies when they become at all marked, and to assist her in the effort, her husband should endeavor to engage her mind by interesting conversation, reading, and various harmless and pleasant diversions.

If it is desired that the child should possess a special aptitude for any particular art or pursuit, during the period of pregnancy the mother's mind should be constantly directed in this channel. If artistic taste or skill is the trait desired, the mother should be surrounded by works of art of a high order of merit. She should read art, think art, talk, and write about art, and if possible, herself engage in the close practical study of some one or more branches of art, as painting, drawing, etching, or modeling. If ability for authorship is desired, then the mother should devote herself assiduously to literature. It is not claimed that by following these suggestions any mother can make of her children great artists or authors at will; but it is certain that by this means the greatest possibilities in individual cases can be attained; and it is certain that decided results have been secured by close attention to the principles laid down. It should be understood, however, that not merely a formal and desultory effort on the part of the mother is what is required. The theme selected must completely absorb her mind. It must be the one idea of her waking thoughts and the model on which is formed the dreams of her sleeping hours.

The question of diet during pregnancy as before stated is a vitally important one as regards the interests of the child. A diet into which enters largely such unwholesome articles as mustard, pepper, hot sauces, spices, and other stimulating condiments, engenders a love for stimulants in the disposition of the infant. Tea and coffee, especially if used to excess, undoubtedly tend in the same direction. We firmly believe that we have, in the facts first stated, the key to the constant increase in the consumption of ardent spirits. The children of the present generation inherit from their condiment-consuming, tea-, coffee-, and liquor-drinking, and tobacco-using parents, not simply a readiness for the acquirement of the habits mentioned, but a propensity for the use of stimulants which in persons of weak will-power and those whose circumstances are not the most favorable, becomes irresistible.

The present generation is also suffering in consequence of the impoverished diet of its parents. The modern custom of bolting the flour from the different grains has deprived millions of infants and children of the necessary supply of bone-making material, thus giving rise to a greatly increased frequency of the various diseases which arise from imperfect bony structure, as rickets, caries, premature decay of the teeth, etc. The proper remedy is the disuse of fine-flour bread and all other bolted grain preparations. Graham-flour bread, oatmeal, cracked wheat, and similar preparations, should be relied upon as the leading articles of diet. Supplemented by milk, the whole-grain preparations constitute a complete form of nourishment, and render a large amount of animal food not only unnecessary but really harmful on account of its stimulating character. It is by no means so necessary as is generally supposed that meat, fish, fowl, and flesh in various forms should constitute a large element of the dietary of the pregnant or nursing mother in order to furnish adequate nourishment for the developing child. We have seen the happiest results follow the employment of a strictly vegetarian dietary, and do not hesitate to advise moderation in the use of flesh food, though we do not recommend the entire discontinuance of its use by the pregnant mother who has been accustomed to use it freely.

A nursing mother should at once suspend nursing if she discovers that pregnancy has again occurred. The continuance of nursing under such circumstances is to the disadvantage of three individuals, the mother, the infant at the breast, and the developing child.

Sexual indulgence during pregnancy may be suspended with decided benefit to both mother and child. The most ancient medical writers call attention to the fact that by the practice of continence° during gestation, the pains of childbirth are greatly mitigated. The injurious influences upon the child of the gratification of the passions during the period when its character is being formed, is undoubtedly much greater than is usually supposed. We have no doubt that this is a common cause of the transmission of libidinous tendencies to the child; and that the tendency to abortion is induced by sexual indulgence has long been a well-established fact. The females of most animals resolutely resist the advances of the males during this period, being guided in harmony with natural law by their natural instincts which have been less perverted in them than in human beings. The practice of continence during pregnancy is also enforced in the harems of the East, which fact leads to the practice of abortion among women of this class who are desirous of remaining the special favorites of the common husband.

10

---

continence: Chastity, abstinence, or restraint.

The general health of the mother must be kept up in every way. It is especially important that the regularity of the bowels should be maintained. Proper diet and as much physical exercise as can be taken are the best means for accomplishing this. When constipation is allowed to exist, the infant as well as the mother suffers. The effete products which should be promptly removed from the body, being long retained, are certain to find their way back into the system again, poisoning not only the blood of the mother but that of the developing fetus. . . .

Puerperal Mania. — This form of mental disease is most apt to show itself about two weeks after delivery. Although, fortunately, of not very frequent occurrence, it is a most serious disorder when it does occur, and hence we may with propriety introduce the following somewhat lengthy, but most graphic description of the disease from the pen of Dr. Ramsbotham, an eminent English physician: —

"In mania there is almost always, at the very commencement, a troubled, agitated, and hurried manner, a restless eye, an unnaturally anxious, suspicious, and unpleasing expression of face; — sometimes it is pallid, at others more flushed than usual; — an unaccustomed irritability of temper, and impatience of control or contradiction; a vacillation of purpose, or loss of memory; sometimes a rapid succession of contradictory orders are issued, or a paroxysm of excessive anger is excited about the merest trifle. Occasionally, one of the first indications will be a sullen obstinacy, or listlessness and stubborn silence. The patient lies on her back, and can by no means be persuaded to reply to the questions of her attendants, or she will repeat them, as an echo, until, all at once, without any apparent cause, she will break out into a torrent of language more or less incoherent, and her words will follow each other with surprising rapidity. These symptoms will sometimes show themselves rather suddenly, on the patient's awakening from a disturbed and unrefreshing sleep, or they may supervene more slowly when she has been harassed with wakefulness for three or four previous nights in succession, or perhaps ever since her delivery. She will very likely then become impressed with the idea that some evil has befallen her husband, or, what is still more usual, her child; that it is dead or stolen; and if it be brought to her, nothing can persuade her it is her own; she supposes it to belong to somebody else; or she will fancy that her husband is unfaithful to her, or that he and those about her have conspired to poison her. Those persons who are naturally the objects of her deepest and most devout affection, are regarded by her with jealousy, suspicion, and hatred. This is particularly remarkable with regard to her newly born infant; and I have known many instances where attempts have been made to destroy it when it has been incautiously left within her power. Sometimes, though rarely, may be observed a great anxiety regarding the termination of her own case, or a firm conviction that she is speedily about to die. I have observed upon occasions a constant movement of the lips, while the mouth was shut; or the patient is incessantly rubbing the inside of her lips with her fingers, or thrusting them far back into her mouth; and if questions are asked, particularly if she be desired to put out her tongue, she will often compress the lips forcibly together, as if with an obstinate determination of resistance. One peculiarity attending some cases of puerperal mania is the immorality and obscenity of the expressions uttered; they are often such, indeed, as to excite our astonishment that women in a respectable station of society could ever have become acquainted with such language."

The insanity of childbirth differs from that of pregnancy in that in the latter cases the patient is almost always melancholy,° while in the former there is active mania. Derangement of the digestive organs is a constant accompaniment of the disease.

If the patient has no previous or hereditary tendency to insanity, the prospect of a quite speedy recovery is good. The result is seldom immediately fatal, but the patient not infrequently remains in a condition of mental unsoundness for months or even years, and sometimes permanently.

Treatment: When there is reason to suspect a liability to puerperal mania from previous mental disease or from hereditary influence, much can be done to ward off an attack. Special attention must be paid to the digestive organs, which should be regulated by proper food and simple means to aid digestion. The tendency to sleeplessness must be combatted by careful nursing, light massage at night, rubbing of the spine, alternate hot and cold applications to the spine, cooling the head by cloths wrung out of cold water, and the use of the warm bath at bed time. These measures are often successful in securing sleep when all other measures fail.

The patient must be kept very quiet. Visitors, even if near relatives, must not be allowed when the patient is at all nervous or disturbed, and it is best to exclude nearly every one from the sick-room with the exception of the nurse, who should be a competent and experienced person.

When the attack has really begun, the patient must have the most vigilant watchcare, not being left alone for a moment. It is much better to care for the patient at home, when possible to do so efficiently, than to take her to an asylum.

When evidences of returning rationality appear, the greatest care must be exercised to prevent too great excitement. Sometimes a change of air, if the patient is sufficiently strong, physically, will at this period prove eminently beneficial. A visit from a dear friend will sometimes afford a needed stimulus to the dormant faculties. Such cases as these of course require intelligent medical supervision.

[1882]

melancholy: Mental state characterized by severe depression, somatic problems, and hallucinations or delusions.

≡ THINKING ABOUT THE TEXT

1. What specific responsibilities does Kellogg assign to women? What are some key assumptions he makes about them?

2. Quite possibly Kellogg would have said that the narrator of Gilman's story suffers from puerperal mania. What details of the story would

support this diagnosis? What significant details of the narrator's life, if any, would Kellogg be ignoring if he saw her as *merely* a case of puerperal mania?

3. If Kellogg's advice were published today, what parts of it do you think readers would accept? What parts do you think many readers would reject?

≡ WRITING ABOUT ISSUES

1. After reading the three essays given here, research women's psychological disorders of the nineteenth century and write an essay that argues that those disorders were the result of male attitudes toward women.

2. Research the term *female hysteria* and write a report that includes the ideas of S. Weir Mitchell and other prominent nineteenth-century doctors. Include in your report your evaluation of their credibility.

3. Research how mental illness was diagnosed and treated within a particular period of American history. Then, write an essay that argues for seeing the culture of that period as an influence on how mental illness was conceived at that time.

4. Research such contemporary psychological problems as depression, bulimia, anorexia, and dissociative identity disorders. These diseases seem to have affected mostly women; write an essay that tries to explain why. Or, write one that tries to explain a newer phenomenon: that these diseases seem to be affecting an increasing number of men.

CHAPTER 8

Evaluating Internet Resources in a "Post-Truth" Age

The Internet overflows with resources for research. Countless Web sites offer potential claims and evidence. But this bonanza of content requires careful evaluation. Online information may be wrong, misleading, or false. A lot of us fear we've even entered a "post-truth" age. In 2016, the Oxford Dictionaries declared this term their Word of the Year. A "post-truth" era, they explained, is one in which "objective facts are less influential in shaping public opinion than appeals to emotion and personal belief." In other words, many people use gut feelings to decide what's true for them, rather than relying on logic or facts.

This doesn't mean that truth has utterly vanished. But for many, "post-truth" does describe their experiences. Politicians and journalists routinely accuse one another of deceit, with the current U.S. president even claiming that the press produces "fake news." Many reporters try their best to fact-check as many claims as possible, and are outraged when people in positions of power place value on "alternative facts." Meanwhile, some media outlets do admit to misleading audiences. In 2018, the cover of *Time* magazine attempted to illustrate the painful policy of separating immigrant children from their parents. The cover pictured President Trump looking down at a tearful Honduran girl. Later, *Time* revealed that she'd actually remained with her mother. They hadn't been split after all.

Political issues aside, those on the Internet are capable of spreading false rumors. Sometimes these are honest mistakes relayed by naive people, but plenty are cunning lies by trolls or bots. Also rife are conspiracy theories rooted in paranoia. These can have dangerous effects. Take the rumor that a pizzeria in Washington, D.C., was operating a sinister, child-abusing cult. Convinced by this story and bent on rescuing children, a man stormed the restaurant with a gun. He found no cult; instead, police arrested him. But the tale that lured him continues to thrive online. A hoax like this is helped along by speed: on social media, lies circulate fast.

Some Web sites, like Snopes.com, investigate these legends. They study viral stories to figure out which are true. You can do the same, and in this chapter we explain strategies you can use. These strategies are presented in three sections:

- Evaluating written arguments you find on the Internet
- Understanding strategies in issue-oriented images on the Internet
- Identifying biases *you* might bring to your Internet research

All three sections offer practical advice. They do so by referring to arguments that people conduct online. The first two sections also include literary works—texts that in their own way contribute to these debates.

Evaluating Written Arguments You Find on the Internet

How can you critique arguments that writers make online? To explore the various ways to do so, let's turn to arguments about a sample topic: the current mass suspicion of gluten. You may have noticed this trend, with numerous Web sites warning against any consumption of gluten. These articles often feature personal stories about the joys of giving it up, and entire magazines will explain how to cook without gluten. Supermarket and bakery shelves teem with gluten-free foods. Restaurant menus often indicate which dishes are gluten-free. You can order a gluten-free cake or pizza; you can buy gluten-free beer.

Not everyone, however, sees gluten as an evil. Many think the war against it is unfair. They note that for ages it's been part of the human diet, and don't believe that so many lives would be vastly improved if it was shunned. They question claims that gluten harms much of the world's population. They doubt reports that avoiding gluten helps people lose weight. These critics point out that gluten-free foods are often pricey. Even advocates of gluten-free living admit that it's hard to sustain, because gluten is a staple of so much food.

Whatever position you take on gluten, these are facts to bear in mind:

- Gluten is a common protein. As Michael Spector notes in his *New Yorker* magazine article on it, it's "one of the most heavily consumed proteins on earth." He adds that "Humans have been eating wheat, and the gluten in it, for at least ten thousand years."
- Most scientific researchers who have studied gluten's effects agree that roughly 1 percent of the world's population suffers from celiac disease, which causes gluten to trigger an immunity reaction. These numbers are a significant increase over the last few decades. People with the condition must avoid gluten; they cannot tolerate it in any amount.
- Speculation has mounted about an ailment related to celiac disease. It's come to be called *gluten sensitivity*. Not all doctors agree that this is an actual, distinct condition. Still, many people report suffering from it. While they might be able to tolerate some foods containing gluten, they react badly to others. Their symptoms vary. Two people who claim to have gluten sensitivity might, when they consume gluten, show different signs of distress.
- In 2014, the U. S. Food and Drug Administration (FDA) decreed that foods marketed with the label "gluten-free" must contain less than 20 parts per million of gluten. While the FDA urges restaurants, too, to follow this policy, it doesn't require them to.

Arguments about gluten focus on one or more of these specific issues:

- What explains the increase in the number of people with celiac disease?
- What percentage of the population has *undiagnosed* celiac disease?
- Is gluten sensitivity a real, independent condition? What further research must be done to decide for sure whether it is? If it does exist, how much of the population does it afflict? What's the best way to test someone for it?
- Is gluten now produced, processed, and consumed in ways that make it more dangerous than it was in previous centuries?
- Can cutting out gluten help a person lose weight?
- Do markets and restaurants have a moral responsibility to offer their customers gluten-free foods?

To get a sense of the arguments made about gluten, read the following two selections. The first is a literary piece by Wendy Brenner, who teaches creative writing at the University of North Carolina, Wilmington. Brenner is the author of two short story collections: *Phone Calls from the Dead* (2001) and *Large Animals in Everyday Life* (1997), which won the Flannery O'Connor Award for Short Fiction. A Contributing Editor for the magazine *Oxford American*, she has also published stories and essays in such periodicals as *Seventeen*, *Ploughshares*, and *Mississippi Review*. The following satire first appeared in the September 2014 of another magazine, *The Sun*. Some people would call "Prayer for Gluten" an essay. To us, its Biblical rhythms make it seem like a poem.

WENDY BRENNER
A Prayer for Gluten

Heavenly Father, in your infinite goodness you created the earth and blessed us with its clear, abundant waters and fertile lands yielding plenteous harvests of fruits and vegetables and grains, some of which happen to contain gluten. We praise you, Lord, for creating gluten, an important yet humble source of protein enjoyed for centuries by the peoples of many nations, the great majority of whom didn't even know it existed until recently. God, you sent gluten into this world as you sent your own Son, to save us, not to torment us with vague and possibly imaginary physical symptoms. So please help certain people to remember, gracious Lord, even as they shun and revile gluten, that it is still a creation of your own Almighty hand, and that, being God, you probably knew what you were doing when you created it. Enlighten those of us in your flock, O Lord, who go about slandering gluten with great authority and volume, even though they never heard of gluten until last year. Gently remind the fearmongering gluten slanderers to study Wikipedia — which you also created, Lord, so that we might come to know your wisdom more instantaneously — for they might be surprised to learn that gluten was discovered in the seventh century by Buddhist monks who used it as a substitute for meat, thus sparing from slaughter many of your beloved cows, chickens, pigs, and sheep, all of whom might be totally extinct by now were it not for gluten. Also help us to be mindful, O merciful God, of how gluten itself must feel—for who are we to say that gluten does not have feelings? (We imagine gluten is appalled, to put it mildly.) As you yourself opined in Romans 14:3, "Let not the one who eats despise the one who abstains, and let not the one who abstains pass judgment on the one who eats, for God has welcomed him." Gluten certainly takes no umbrage at the estimated one out of every 135 people who actually suffers from celiac disease or the euphemistically yet still hatefully named "gluten intolerance." Gluten has been around long enough to know that you can't please everyone. No, gluten has no problem with these people. Gluten will tell you who it has a problem with, Lord, and that's the shameless opportunists who have turned "gluten-free" from a legitimate health mandate into a "lifestyle choice" for no reason other than their own personal gain, preying upon the fear and ignorance of the hitherto gluten-tolerant masses with websites such as Glutenista.com ("on a mission to Make Gluten-Free Fabulous © for everyone, everywhere") and the sudden proliferation of such glossy publications as Gluten-Free Living, Simply Gluten-Free, and Living Without Magazine (a self-defeating title if ever we've heard one, as presumably the publishers do not want readers to live without the magazine itself). Gluten knows perfectly well that Exodus 14:14 says, "The Lord will fight for you, and you have only to be silent," but gluten has been silent for centuries, God, and guess what: it's not working. Therefore, gracious Lord, gluten would like you to know that it has recently met with an attorney regarding a potential defamation claim. And gluten will tell you something else right now, Lord: it was here long before these gluten haters were born, and it will be here long after they're gone. Not unlike yourself, O Lord, gluten is here to stay.

≡ THINKING ABOUT THE TEXT

1. Brenner imitates Biblical prose, and she quotes from Bible passages. What, if anything, do these strategies enable her to achieve? What are conceivable objections to them?

2. Brenner points out that, before now, the value of gluten was accepted for centuries. How much is this historical record indeed worth remembering in today's debates about gluten?

3. What forces does Brenner suggest drive today's war on gluten? To what extent do you agree that these are indeed key factors?

4. Where does Brenner personify gluten—that is, refer to gluten as if it were a human being with desires of its own? What do you think of this technique as a means of writing a satire? What's your view of it as a strategy for questioning the widespread fear of gluten?

5. As you might expect, fans of Brenner's piece have circulated it on the Internet. But not everyone who reads it there enjoys it. Here are two negative responses:

- A comment by John Trumbull on the Web site *The True Wonder of Bread*:

"As a fan of Farm to Market bread, which could not be what it is without gluten, I appreciate the praise for this protein. But I don't appreciate the attacks on those who avoid gluten as haters with 'vague and possibly imaginary' symptoms. My wife is not celiac, but she is gluten-intolerant, and there's nothing vague about her symptoms. Consuming even small amounts of gluten gives her nausea, stomach aches and diarrhea. The intolerance didn't develop until she was in her 50s, and it took her a few years of doctor visits, reading, and experimentation to narrow down the source of her symptoms. We'd both love to know why she became intolerant but I didn't. It's also painful when waitstaff in restaurants don't take her seriously or act as if there's something wrong with her. She loves really good bread and pizza, so it's painful for her not to be able to eat them. Praising gluten on its merits is fine, but ridiculing those who can't tolerate it adds insult to injury. The Lord made peanuts too and they're also a wonderful food, but they can kill a small percentage of the population with severe allergies. Gluten intolerance and food allergies have both been on the rise — maybe for similar reasons, maybe not. We should all hope that the science advances to give us a better understanding of what's going on."

- A comment by Snowflower on the Web site *Project Avalon*:

"I tell myself it isn't worth getting mad about. A 'prayer' designed to vilify those humans who get sick from eating wheat? How egocentric can you get??!!!! Ok, so I need to calm down. Breathe. This is such a CLASSIC example of the harm done to humans by the control freaks in religions! Ok, so maybe I haven't calmed down yet. I am disgusted with this filthy 'prayer.' Wheat put me in the hospital last year with perforated bowels. How DARE that poor excuse of a human being appeal to the Great Spirit to condemn me! Ok, so I am not going to calm down. But I'll quit writing."

To what extent do you sympathize with these reactions? The second is obviously more hostile than the first. Do you think the anger that Snowflower expresses is an effective rhetorical strategy? Why, or why not?

We invite you to compare Brenner's satire with our next reading selection: a straightforward opinion piece about gluten. It originally appeared in the August 23, 2018, issue of the *Indiana Daily Student*, the campus newspaper of Indiana University, Bloomington. Author Xinhua (Varda) He is an IU undergraduate majoring in finance and marketing. She has regularly contributed food-related columns to the paper. Here she argues for making gluten-free dining options more available in her local community's restaurants.

VARDA HE

Restaurants Should Be More Aware of Celiac, Gluten-Free Diet Limits

During the second semester of my freshman year, my best friend was diagnosed with celiac disease.

Celiac disease is "a serious autoimmune disorder that can occur in genetically predisposed people where the ingestion of gluten leads to damage in the small intestine," according to the Celiac Disease Foundation. The website also estimates the disease affects one in 100 people worldwide.

Celiac patients react negatively to gluten. Whenever they eat food that contains gluten, their bodies mount an immune response attack on the small intestine, which leads to damages to the villi. Villi are small finger-like outgrowths lining the small intestine, and if damaged, would prevent the body from absorbing nutrients.

Thanks to technological advancements and efforts from celiac awareness groups, more people and food establishments are beginning to realize the threat the disease poses to patients. As a result, more gluten-free options are appearing in stores and on restaurant menus. While all these are giant steps forward, there are a lot more that food brands and restaurants can do in order to help celiac patients enjoy their dining experiences.

When it comes to shopping for gluten-free foods, increased public aware-   5
ness has certainly helped stores expand their gluten-free aisles. However, one may not realize that there is often an abundance of highly-processed products that contain large amounts of sugar.

Additionally, gluten-free foods are considered specialty products, so very few of them have the vitamins that are easily found in regular everyday foods.

Many gluten-free breads are also filled with things such as tapioca and cornstarch to make the texture lighter. While these ingredients may be high in carbohydrates, they are low in protein and minerals. Therefore, when people make the decision to switch to a gluten-free diet, they are taking in a lot less vitamins, fiber and minerals.

A big part of the college experience is going out to various restaurants that make up the vibrant Bloomington food scene. After my best friend was diagnosed with celiac disease, however, our choices of restaurants became limited. Many places have no gluten-free options on their menus, and the ones that do largely depend on the competency of the server and the restaurant kitchen to accurately record customer requests and to make appropriate accommodations.

Looking back on all the times that we've dined out, I remember encountering servers who were extremely knowledgeable about celiac and gluten-free options, and who went out of their way to work with the kitchen to make sure my friend's dietary needs were met. I also recall instances in which the server had little knowledge of the gluten-free menu choices or substitutions to certain ingredients and times when the kitchen messed up orders and put gluten products in the gluten-free dishes.

While I understand that gluten-free ingredients may be more expensive   10
to purchase, and developing gluten-free menu options and training the staff
requires more time and money, restaurants should have at least basic knowledge of celiac. Most importantly, they should understand that instead of its
common misconception as an allergy, celiac is actually a disease.

People place their health in the restaurant's hands every time they dine
out. As gluten intolerance and celiac diagnoses become more common,
restaurants should do themselves a favor and realize that accommodating the
dietary needs of customers is important.

≡ THINKING ABOUT THE TEXT

1. In her first several paragraphs, He basically provides information.
   What is she assuming about her audience, who are mostly college
   students? Do you think her assumptions are probably correct? Would
   a writer on her subject need to assume the same things in addressing
   your campus community? What else, if anything, might that writer
   need to bear in mind if the newspaper was your college's?

2. Why, according to He, should restaurants in her community offer
   more gluten-free foods? Does she seem to believe that this is their
   moral responsibility, or does she emphasize something else? What's
   your view of the main position she takes?

3. He brings up personal experiences of her friend and her. To what extent
   do you find these anecdotes compelling evidence for her argument?
   What, if any, other kinds of evidence might she have offered?

4. Where does He make concessions to people who might be troubled by
   her stand? In your view, are these *enough* concessions? Why, or why not?

5. The author doesn't name particular restaurants in her piece. Should
   she have done so? Explain your reasoning. How might her text look
   different if she were writing a briefer version of it as a Yelp review of a
   specific dining establishment?

≡ MAKING COMPARISONS

1. Might Brenner and He think the same way about certain matters? If
   so, on which particular issues might they agree?

2. If, like Brenner, He had decided to be satirical, how might her piece
   look different? Try rewriting a part of her argument.

3. How might Brenner have incorporated one of He's points into her
   "prayer"?

≡ A WRITING EXERCISE

Visit at least two restaurants in your local community, and determine how
much they accommodate customers who prefer gluten-free food. Besides

consulting menus, you might chat with personnel. Then, write an essay in which you incorporate your findings into an argument about whether and how a restaurant should try to please such customers.

CRITICALLY ANALYZING WEB SITES' TRUTH CLAIMS

When you go online to research a controversial topic, study Web sites critically. Consider how they may tamper with the truth. They may exaggerate, even lie. They may omit key data. They may wrench things out of context. They may defer to "experts" who aren't authorities at all. They may use loaded language — words more slanted than you realize at first. Below are specific maneuvers to watch for, along with our recommendations for critiquing them. Again, we draw examples from arguments about gluten, a subject of endless Internet buzz.

1. **Presenting undocumented statistics.** On the Internet, you'll find extremely high estimates of how many people suffer from gluten sensitivity. After admitting that "No one knows how many people have gluten sensitivity," dummies.com feels free to suggest a number: "estimates are that it may be as high as 50%, or even 70%, of the population." Cleaneatingkitchen.com boosts the figure: "It's estimated that up to 70% of the human population suffers from gluten sensitivity. Though some health professionals think that as much as 100% of the human population has some type of sensitivity to gluten." And fibrowellnesscenter.com claims that "as high as 99% of people have a problem eating gluten and they don't even know about it."

   These sites relay huge numbers from anonymous "sources." Clearly, they aim to make gluten seem a universal threat, whether or not they can offer support for their estimates. If anything, their guesses reflect a continuing need for clinical studies. Scientists must probe gluten's effects more. Right now, they simply don't know how many people it sickens. Also, they're not all sure that "gluten sensitivity" is a real disorder separate from celiac disease.

   Recommendation: Don't just accept numbers unsupported with evidence, especially when these figures are extreme. Try to detect the agenda of the site that's offering them. If an estimate is vague, see it as a sign that more studies must be done.

2. **Misrepresenting a source of information.** Even when a Web site identifies a source for its information, it might not accurately convey what that source says. An example is a claim made at numerous URLs. Here are just a few expressions of it:

   - Fibrowellness.com: "Actually, *The New England Journal of Medicine* listed 55 diseases that have been found to be caused by ingesting gluten."

- sanjosefuncmed.com: "A recent review paper published in the NEJM listed 55 diseases that can be caused by eating gluten."
- drhyman.com: "A review paper in *The New England Journal of Medicine* listed 55 'diseases' that can be caused by eating gluten."
- sott.net: "In fact, a recent review in *The New England Journal of Medicine* listed fifty-five diseases that can be caused by eating gluten! That was not a typo!"

The article that these sites mention is real. Accessible online, it appears in the January 17, 2002 issue of *The New England of Journal of Medicine*. Authors Richard J. Farrell and Ciarán P. Kelly review existing research on celiac disease, which they refer to as celiac sprue. They note that this condition seems to affect "1 of every 120 to 300 persons in both Europe and North America." But nowhere do they claim that gluten is a possible cause of fifty-five diseases. Instead, their article features the following table:

TABLE 1. The Spectrum of Clinical Presentations of Celiac Sprue.

COMMON FEATURES	LESS COMMON FEATURES	ASSOCIATED CONDITIONS	COMPLICATIONS
Adults	General features	Definite associations	Refractory sprue
• Iron-deficiency anemia	• Short stature	• Dermatitis herpetiformis	Enteropathy-associated T-cell lymphoma
• Diarrhea	• Delayed puberty	• IgA deficiency	
Children	Gastrointestinal features	• Type 1 diabetes	Carcinoma of the oropharynx, esophagus, and small bowel
• Diarrhea	• Recurrent aphthous stomatitis	• Autoimmune thyroid disease	
• Failure to thrive	• Recurrent abdominal pain	• Sjögren's syndrome	
• Abdominal distention	• Steatorrhea	• Microscopic colitis	Ulcerative jejunoileitis
	Extraintestinal features	• Rheumatoid arthritis	
	• Folate-deficiency anemia	• Down's syndrome	
	• Osteopenia or osteoporosis	• IgA nephropathy	Collagenous sprue
	• Dental-enamel hypoplasia	Possible associations	
	• Vitamin K deficiency	• Congenital heart disease	
	• Hypertransaminasemia	• Recurrent pericarditis	
	• Thrombocytosis (hyposplenism)	• Sarcoidosis	
		• Cystic fibrosis	
		• Fibrosing alveolitis	
		• Lung cavities	

(continued on next page)

COMMON FEATURES	LESS COMMON FEATURES	ASSOCIATED CONDITIONS	COMPLICATIONS
	• Arthralgia or arthropathy • Polyneuropathy • Ataxia • Epilepsy (with or without cerebral calcification) • Infertility • Recurrent abortions • Anxiety and depression • Follicular keratosis • Alopecia	• Pulmonary hemosiderosis • Inflammatory bowel disease • Autoimmune hepatitis • Primary biliary cirrhosis • Addison's disease • Systemic lupus erythematosus • Vasculitis • Polymyositis • Myasthenia gravis • Schizophrenia	

As you can tell by its heading, the table is about celiac sprue, explaining that it might play a role in the illnesses and symptoms listed. The authors aren't declaring, though, that everything identified here might be *caused* by celiac sprue. That would be a stronger claim. Nor do they actually bring up the number fifty-five. That is the total of all the items listed, but notice that some of them are classified as "Possible associations." It's a mild phrase, hardly indicating a strong relationship. To say that celiac disorder is "possibly associated" with a certain condition is far from asserting that it may be the condition's *cause*. Notice, too, that the table doesn't refer to gluten. Of course, people with celiac disease do react badly to gluten, but the authors aren't claiming that gluten can *cause* the conditions they name.

It's important to note as well that science research is rarely definitive. Scientists know that most of their findings shouldn't be seen as final. When they publish, they're careful to note their studies' limitations. Usually their articles end with suggestions for further research. Sometimes they even change their minds about their findings. This is true, for example, of Peter Gibson, an Australian professor of gastroenterology who researches gluten's effects. In 2011, he studied a particular group of people who didn't have celiac disease, but suffered from irritable-bowel syndrome. After doing tests on this group, Gibson's team concluded they might be sensitive to gluten. Later research he did, however, made Gibson reconsider. Working with a similar group, he came to think that irritable-bowel syndrome might not be caused by gluten after all. A more important factor in this condition, he suspected, is a set of carbohydrates called *FODMAPS*.

How have Web sites reported Gibson's later study? Well, sciencealert.com misrepresents it with the headline "Scientists Who Found Gluten Sensitivity Evidence Have Now Shown It Doesn't Exist." Gibson and his team are actually more tentative: "At least in this highly selected cohort, gluten might be not be a specific trigger of functional gut symptoms once dietary FODMAPs are reduced." This statement doesn't declare gluten sensitivity to be an illusion. It leaves open the possibility that the condition is real.

Recommendation: If you can, visit the source that a Web site borrows from. Check to see if the site has faithfully reported what its source says. Make sure that you understand significant differences in terminology: e.g., the difference between a "possible association" and a "cause."

3. **Quoting out of context.** An argument you find on the Internet might, to bolster its claims, quote a statement from somewhere else. Yet even words quoted accurately may give a misleading impression. Often this occurs when the words are ripped out of context: when, that is, the person doing the quoting ignores how their *source* presented them. Look at how cleaneatingkitchen.com uses words from a *New York Times* article by Kenneth Chang:

> For people with Celiac disease, going gluten-free is a must. Some critics consider going gluten-free to be a fad diet that isn't completely necessary. Dr. Thomas O'Bryan, however, considers a gluten-free diet necessary for nearly everyone. In a *New York Times* interview, he was quoted saying that, "If a person has a choice between eating wheat and not eating wheat, then for most people avoiding wheat would be ideal."

By ending the paragraph with O'Bryan, this site gives him the last word. We're nudged to share his opinion of wheat. But in the *Times* article that first published his statement, we can see that his views are disputed. In that piece, author Kenneth Chang is quick to identify a critic of O'Bryan: Dr. Stefano Guandalini. As Chang reports, Guandalini questions how O'Bryan determines which patients are gluten sensitive. O'Bryan relies on antibody tests; Guandalini says they're inadequate. Chang also reports that Guandalini "doubts that the occurrence of gluten sensitivity is nearly as high as Dr. O'Bryan asserts." Chang draws a contrast, too, between the two men's credentials. He points out that Guandalini is "medical director of the University of Chicago's Celiac Disease Center," whereas O'Bryan is "a chiropractor turned anti-gluten crusader."

So Chang follows O'Bryan's statement with criticisms of it, but cleaneatingkitchen.com leaves these out. The site has *selectively* quoted, an act that some would call cherry-picking. Chang casts doubt on O'Bryan's claims; cleaneatingkitchen.com makes them seem wise. Whatever your own view turns out to be, shifts like this are worth studying.

Recommendation: If you can, visit the source that a Web site quotes from. Even if you find the quoting to be accurate, see if it's selective and if its context has been changed.

4. **Burying facts.** When you argue, you'll be more persuasive if you address facts that complicate your case. Probably you'll proceed to show that you *can* account for them — that they *don't*, after all, undercut you. Still, your audience will appreciate your willingness in the first place to confront these threats. You yourself are likelier to trust arguments that acknowledge complexity. Various posts on the Internet, though, are sly. They refer to facts that challenge what they're claiming, but in a brief and rather sneaky way. In short, these truths get buried. Spotting them can be hard.

An example is an article by Jane Anderson at verywellhealth .com. Anderson raises the possibility that a gluten-free diet will help you shed pounds. She supports this idea by interviewing William Davis, a cardiologist whose bestselling book *Wheat Belly* has influenced anti-gluten campaigns. She quotes and relies on his claim that going without gluten may lead to loss of weight. She notes that he hasn't published his studies in medical journals. That is, his findings haven't been exposed to peer review. They haven't officially met the standards of experts in gluten research. But Anderson refers to this fact only twice — and briefly, even then. It's a parenthetical blip in paragraphs 7 and 29. Readers might overlook it, assuming Davis is a professionally recognized authority. He's not.

Recommendation: Pay attention to facts that a site mentions only in passing, for they may weaken or trouble its claims.

5. **Framing through loaded language.** Many online arguments feature words that radiate bias, using what's called loaded language. Loaded language prods you to adopt a certain attitude toward its subject by framing the topic in a particular way. Maybe there isn't any text that's completely detached and objective, but loaded language is one-sided in the extreme. So, as a reader, you need to look out for it. It doesn't necessarily make an argument less truthful, but it's a definite effort to shape your view. You'll have to decide whether you'll let it sway you.

Loaded language about gluten is often evident in the clickbait headlines of various online articles. Recall the title that sciencealert.com gave its report on Gibson's later research: "Scientists Who Found Gluten Sensitivity Evidence Have Now Shown It Doesn't Exist." Again, Gibson *hasn't* made such a sweeping judgment. Another example is the horror-movie title that Fibrowellnesscenter gives one of its posts: "Inflammation and Gluten — You're Killing Yourself!" But examples of slanted wording can appear further down in a text. For instance, cleaneatingkitchen.com refers to a "list of thirty places gluten hides," and the site also asserts that "gluten lurks in unsuspecting places." Wording like this implies that gluten isn't a protein but instead a criminal or demon. James Hamblin at theatlantic.com is similarly negative about William Davis' book *Wheat Belly*. He observes that this attack on gluten has been "monstrously popular," a hit with people "susceptible to demagoguery." Such language makes Davis seem like Hitler.

Recommendation: Consider how a Web site's language may be a strategic attempt to skew your perceptions, attitudes, or beliefs.

6. **Being deliberately ridiculous.** Probably all of us assume that we can recognize satire. But sometimes we're more naive. Haven't we all failed to see that a certain text is comic, or at least intended to be? In any case, many posts are *deliberately* ridiculous. They violate the truth for humor's sake.

At clickhole.com, for instance, you'll find absurd stories that intentionally make fun of clickbait. Under the headline "20 Unbelievable Birth Control Facts That Will Totally Blow Your Mind," fact #6 is "Ground-up birth control pills can be substituted for flour in any recipe if you are gluten-free or out of flour." Clickhole is owned by *The Onion*, which publishes more news parodies at theonion.com. In an article there entitled "I Had a Terrible Experience At This Restaurant Because I Am A Terrible Person," the author reports requesting "that a manager come to our table and assure us that the tortillas were gluten-free, even though I can eat gluten safely and regularly do." Posts like these may strike you as obviously absurd. You may think they'd never fool you. But maybe we're all capable of taking such pranks seriously. This can happen especially when satire circulates online. When a parody moves from its source to other sites, they may print it without noting that it's meant to amuse.

Recommendation: Consider the possibility that a ridiculous Web post may be intentionally comic.

≡ SUMMING UP THE RECOMMENDATIONS

- Don't accept numbers unsupported with evidence, especially when these figures are extreme. Try to detect the agenda of the site that's offering them. If an estimate is vague, see it as a sign that more studies must be done.

- If you can, visit the source that a Web site borrows from. Check to see if the site has faithfully reported what its source says. Make sure that you understand significant differences in terminology: e.g., the difference between a "possible association" and a "cause."

- Pay attention to facts that a site mentions only in passing because they may weaken or trouble its claims.

- Consider how a Web site's language may be a strategic attempt to skew your perceptions, attitudes, or beliefs.

- Consider the possibility that a ridiculous Web post may be intentionally comic.

≡ A WRITING EXERCISE

Select a Web site that puts forth claims, evidence, and reasoning about a particular issue that's been in the news lately. It might be a political controversy, but it could also be a cultural, scientific, or health-related one. Write an essay in which you determine the extent to which the Web site is being truthful. Be sure to explain how you've reached your judgment. In evaluating the site, follow at least some of the recommendations we've made.

Understanding Strategies in Visual Arguments on the Internet

Many arguments on the Internet rely on more than words. They depend on pictures, too. This means it's important for you to identify the *visual* strategies they use to make their case. In this section, we explain some basic types through a series of pairings. Each focuses on a currently controversial topic by linking a poem about it with a relevant image or two from the Web. In each instance, the items paired have an argumentative bent. Sometimes they express the same view of their subject; sometimes they clash. After each poem/image pairing, we list and discuss the image's main techniques of persuasion. These are strategies you may encounter repeatedly in visual landscapes online.

TOPIC: WAR

Poem: Wilfred Owen, "Dulce et Decorum Est"
Image: World War I recruitment poster

The merits and pitfalls of waging war are constantly debated, for combat still rages in places like Syria, Afghanistan, and Yemen. Our first pairing is a reminder that issues of war are centuries old. Both the poem and the image are from World War I. With "Dulce et Decorum Est," Wilfred Owen (1893–1918) aimed to expose the horror and human waste of this conflict. He himself was a soldier in the British Army at the time, and he was killed one week before the war ended. The poem's last two lines are a quotation in Latin from the Roman poet Horace. They mean "It is sweet and fitting to die for one's country." Many of Owen's countrymen held this belief when the war began, but his poem argues quite the opposite. Owen's poem is far from the spirit of the World War I poster that follows, designed to recruit men for the British Army.

WILFRED OWEN

Dulce et Decorum Est

Bent double, like old beggars under sacks,
Knock-kneed, coughing like hags, we cursed through sludge,
Till on the haunting flares we turned our backs,
And towards our distant rest began to trudge.
Men marched asleep. Many had lost their boots,   5
But limped on, blood-shod. All went lame; all blind;
Drunk with fatigue; deaf even to the hoots
Of gas-shells dropping softly behind.

Gas! GAS! Quick, boys!—An ecstasy of fumbling
Fitting the clumsy helmets just in time,   10
But someone still was yelling out and stumbling
And flound'ring like a man in fire or lime.—
Dim through the misty panes and thick green light,
As under a green sea, I saw him drowning.

In all my dreams before my helpless sight,   15
He plunges at me, guttering, choking, drowning.

If in some smothering dreams, you too could pace
Behind the wagon that we flung him in,
And watch the white eyes writhing in his face,
His hanging face, like a devil's sick of sin;   20
If you could hear, at every jolt, the blood

Come gargling from the froth-corrupted lungs,
Obscene as cancer, bitter as the cud
Of vile, incurable sores on innocent tongues, —
My friend, you would not tell with such high zest   25
To children ardent for some desperate glory,
The old Lie: Dulce et decorum est
Pro patria mori.

YOUR COUNTRY'S CALL

Isn't this worth fighting for?
ENLIST NOW

Library of Congress
Prints and Photographs
Division Washington
[LC-USZC4-10829].

Figure 1   World War I recruitment poster

IDENTIFYING THE VISUAL STRATEGIES

Direct address: The poster's heading, "YOUR COUNTRY'S CALL," openly addresses the target audience: men who have yet to join the army. The soldier looks straight at these viewers, and the line "ENLIST NOW" says what he wants them to do. Direct address is also a feature of Owen's poem; its final lines target a "you." The message being sent to this "you," though, is quite different from the poster's. The poem urges "you" to envision a soldier's suffering and to stop glorifying war.

Selective identification: At the time, England contained several industrialized urban centers—most notably, London, Manchester, and Birmingham. But the poster identifies England as a rural village. It appeals to viewers' nostalgia for the country's pre-industrial past.

Dreamy and romantic visual style: While the houses in the village are depicted somewhat realistically, the hills and clouds behind it are more abstractly sketched. They form a dreamlike, romantic background, which contributes to the poster's overall idealizing of England. Owen's poem, too, blends realism with abstraction, though it aims to convey how awful war is. The poem becomes abstract by getting metaphorical: the speaker perceives a fellow soldier "drowning" in "a green sea."

Suggestion of consensus: The poster's heading suggests that the entire country is speaking as one, even though a segment of it was antiwar. Owen also assumes that most of his readers glorify war. He aims to convince them that it's *not* "sweet and fitting to die for one's country."

Directional signaling: The soldier points to the village, thereby emphasizing it as a symbol for England. Parts of a picture that direct the viewer's attention are often called *vectors*. These tend to be lines, arrows, or gestures.

Projection of an engaging mood: Besides the nostalgic warmth of the village, the soldier is smiling, and his rifle is at rest—even though he is coaxing the audience to join a fight. He reinforces this air of tranquility by standing erect. By contrast, the soldiers in Owen's poem are "Bent double, like old beggars under sacks."

≡ FOR FURTHER DISCUSSION

Probably no military recruitment poster could depict war as gruesomely as Owen's poem does. But how might the poster here be redesigned to hint at the fact that soldiers risk their lives?

TOPIC: ENVIRONMENTAL DESTRUCTION

Poem: Linda Hogan, "Song for the Turtles in the Gulf"
Image: Anti-litter ad

How widespread is environmental destruction? How concerned about it should humanity be? What can people and institutions do to prevent it? How might they curb its effects? What are its possible long-range consequences? Around the world, these issues are increasingly debated, due to industrial disasters and ominous signs of climate change. Here we put together a poem and an add that deal with environmental destruction by focusing on the plight of turtles.

The poem is a lament that is also a protest. It focuses on the damage to turtles (and, by implication, other sea life) by the British Petroleum spill in the Gulf of Mexico. Author Linda Hogan (b. 1947) often calls on her Chickasaw heritage to further environmental, antinuclear, and other social causes. This particular poem appears in her 2014 collection *Dark. Sweet: New & Selected Poems*. Very much in the spirit of Hogan's poem is the public service ad that follows. Showing turtles engulfed in plastic, they call for more sensitive ways of managing trash.

LINDA HOGAN

Songs for Turtles in the Gulf

We had been together so very long,
   you willing to swim with me
   just last month, myself merely small
   in the ocean of splendor and light,
   the reflections and distortions of us,   5
and now when I see the man from British Petroleum
lift you up dead from the plastic
bin of death,
he with a smile, you burned
and covered with red-black oil, torched   10
and pained, all I can think is that I loved your life,
the very air you exhaled when you rose,
old great mother, the beautiful swimmer,
the mosaic growth of shell
so detailed, no part of you   15
simple, meaningless,
or able to be created
by any human,
only destroyed.
How can they learn   20
the secret importance
of your beaten heart,
the eyes of another intelligence
than ours, maybe greater,
with claws, flippers, plastron.   25
Forgive us for being thrown off true,
for our trespasses,
in the eddies of the water
where we first walked.

Figure 2   Anti-litter ad
International Animal Rescue Foundation.

IDENTIFYING THE VISUAL STRATEGIES

Incongruity: An *incongruity* combines or juxtaposes elements that we don't normally expect to be fused. Incongruous images can be used to stir various emotions. The ad here is an attempt to shock us. A turtle eating a strip of plastic? Most of us will shudder at this sight." Clearly the admakers hope that we'll then *act* upon our feelings by managing trash in more sensitive ways. Hogan's poem makes a similar use of incongruity to protest the British Petroleum oil spill. Many readers will be disturbed to learn about a turtle's "plastic/bin of death" and "red-black oil" covering, especially when the man who lifts her up is smiling.

Anthropomorphizing: This is the act of giving human qualities to some feature of the world that many of us don't think of as a person. Among these subjects are animals. The turtle in figure 2 comes across as human by looking at us head-on and making an urgent request. When ads anthropomorphize, they often aim to rouse sympathy. It's hard to resist this turtle's plea. Many of

Hogan's readers will be similarly touched when she anthropomorphizes the oil-soaked turtle by directly addressing her as "old great mother."

Manipulating visual perspective: To establish an order of importance, ads will often enlarge an element, shrink it, or situate it against a particular background. Figure 2 magnifies the turtle's head, making it bigger to us than we'd normally see it. By calling attention to this creature, the ad's makers ensure that we'll get their message: how crucial it is to remove trash from beaches.

Dramatic language: Many an ad combines a picture with writing. The words more plainly state the message that the image implies. To galvanize the audience, the language might be dramatic. Figure 2 uses the words "killing" and "kill." The ad suggests there's a great deal at risk in the current state of affairs: the looming threat is the mass extinction of turtles. Hogan is similarly dramatic when she describes her poem's turtle as "torched," "pained," and "destroyed."

Rhythmic language: When ad producers use words as well as images, they often try to capture attention by making the language rhythmic, putting words into engaging patterns. A common means of doing so is alliteration: a series of words that all begin with the exact same letter. Many a poet has used this technique. In her final lines, for example, Hogan is alliterative with the letter "f" ("Forgive" and a repetition of "for"), the letters "tr" ("true" and "trespasses"), and the letter "w" ("water," "where," "we," and "walked"). This pattern also shows up in the ad here. Figure 2 urges the viewer to "respect, reuse, reduce and recycle."

Big lettering: Heightening the impact of this ad's writing is the visual prominence given to certain words. Figure 2 puts its urgent request in big letters.

☰ FOR FURTHER DISCUSSION

Hogan's poem and the ad seem to anthropomorphize animals. What would you say to someone who argues that we shouldn't do this? Are there any distinctions between humans and animals that you think crucial to make? If so, what are they? Is it possible to care deeply for animals even if they don't resemble humans much?

TOPIC: REFUGEES

Poem: Emma Lazarus, "The New Colossus"
Image: Editorial cartoon by Dave Granlund

The world ponders what do about refugees: people fleeing their native lands. They're driven by any number of reasons: war, poverty, persecution, murder threats, or a mix of these. Often they risk their lives in their very efforts to escape. What duties do the rest of us have toward them? What are practical ways of helping them cope? Such issues especially face the countries where refugees seek new homes. Some of these nations are divided over whether to welcome them. Others have chosen to keep them out. The torment of refugees isn't new, however. As shown by the famous poem we first present, their anguish is ages-old, and countries have had to decide how much to welcome them. Author Emma Lazarus (1849–1887) was an activist poet who worked especially on behalf of Jewish refugees, including those fleeing the murderous antisemitism of Czarist Russia. She wrote her sonnet "The New Colossus" in 1883, as part of a campaign to fund the pedestal for the new Statue of Liberty. Sixteen years after her death, the last few lines were engraved on the Statue and have been much-quoted since. "The brazen giant" of the first line is the *old* Colossus: the monumental statue of a male warrior that guarded the harbor of Rhodes. Lazarus' *new* Colossus is different. Poised between New York and Brooklyn, this "mighty woman with a torch" embraces refugees rather than ward them off. In recent years, Lazarus' poem has figured in debates about whether the U. S. should continue to be a "golden door" for the persecuted.

More recently, many of Syria's people have sought to leave their country. They wish to escape not only the oppression wrought by its leader, but also the violence of its civil war. Much of the globe, though, has resisted these refugees, unwilling to give them a home. The worldwide failure to welcome them has proved controversial. Among those protesting this indifference are editorial cartoonists. Syndicated freelancer Dave Granlund's cartoon appeared in various presses on September 4, 2015.

EMMA LAZARUS

The New Colossus

Not like the brazen giant of Greek fame,
With conquering limbs astride from land to land;
Here at our sea-washed, sunset gates shall stand
A mighty woman with a torch, whose flame
Is the imprisoned lightning, and her name   5
Mother of Exiles. From her beacon-hand
Glows world-wide welcome; her mild eyes command
The air-bridged harbor that twin cities frame.
"Keep, ancient lands, your storied pomp!" cries she
With silent lips. "Give me your tired, your poor,   10
Your huddled masses yearning to breathe free,
The wretched refuse of your teeming shore.
Send these, the homeless, tempest-tost to me,
I lift my lamp beside the golden door!"

Figure 3   Editorial cartoon by Dave Granlund
Dave Granlund

IDENTIFYING THE VISUAL STRATEGIES

Symbolic representation: Editorial cartoonists have limited space. Often they lack the room to convey all aspects of their subject. They rely on just a few symbols. Granlund uses this visual shorthand to sketch a single scene. Surely he knows that many people fleeing Syria don't escape by ship, but he shows them as passengers needing rescue from a sinking ocean liner. The rest of the world is a man and woman standing safe in a rowboat—and afraid *they'll* sink if they let others board. The couple pushes and kicks away the ship's remaining survivors. Unless there's a change of policy, they'll die. To make his point clear, Granlund brings in words: "World Response" and "Refugees." Mostly, though, he depends on symbols to get his message across. Of course, much literature is also symbolic, and Lazarus' poem about the Statue of Liberty is a case in point. After all, the Statue itself represents deliverance for refugees. Lazarus emphasizes this idea with her images of light.

Abstraction: Editorial cartoonists treat matters of real life. Yet most of them don't express their views in realistic ways. Their art is often abstract. This style can strongly engage an audience. It nudges them to exercise their imaginations, and at its best, it also stirs their hearts. The foreground of the cartoon here is semi-realistic. The waves are vividly rippling lines; the rowboat couple are detailed figures; and so are a foursome trying to climb aboard. But Granlund is more abstract with others trapped in the ocean. Two of them near the cartoon's front have only a few features: gaping mouths, upturned noses, arms stretched out to plead. Further back are people who are just dark ghosts, adrift in waves now reduced to slashes. We're made aware that a crowd's about to drown. Granlund's touches of abstraction serve to prick our conscience. He's urging us to save these refugees. Lazarus does the same with "tempest-tost," an expression that resembles Granlund's cartoon in using stormy waves to suggest refugees' plight.

≡ FOR FURTHER DISCUSSION

Both Emma Lazarus (in her poem) and Dave Granlund (in his cartoon) can be taken to suggest that the United States (and perhaps the rest of the world) has a moral duty to accept refugees fleeing murderous dictatorships. To what extent do you share this view? What things should a government consider in deciding whether to let such people in?

TOPIC: BORDERS

Poem: Alberto Ríos, "The Border: A Double Sonnet"
Image: Map from the Brookings Institution

Our previous pairing was about refugees. Today a lot of the world's population is displaced. By choice or force, they've left their native country. Desperately they search for havens elsewhere. Often their quest is dangerous. In the Mediterranean, for instance, thousands of African migrants have drowned. If refugees do survive their treks, they face political challenges. They come to borders they might be forbidden to cross. Even a country that grants them entry might not let them stay; the threat of deportation looms. Often, of course, the country's own people debate its border policies: How should their nation define its borders? How should it control them? Whom should it let through? When migrants enter illegally, what should the government do?

For years, the United States has grappled with these issues. Recently, though, Americans have argued about them more. Especially controversial is the president's plan to build a wall between the U. S. and Mexico. Many believe it's needed to thwart illegal border-crossings and drug smuggling from Mexico or countries further south. Others feel the wall will be costly, useless, and inhumane.

In the poem we feature here, the author raises points that he feels should figure in debates over border security. "The Border: A Double Sonnet" is by Alberto Ríos (b. 1952), a much-published writer who is Regents Professor of English at Arizona State University. This poem appears in his 2015 book *A Small Story About the Sky*. In 2017, the rock band U2 made it part of their concerts by displaying it on video screens. The poem reflects lifelong concerns of its author. From childhood, Ríos has been conscious of the U.S.-Mexico border, for he grew up near it in Nogales, Arizona. As an adult, he's been troubled by how the media depict Latin Americans seeking to enter the U.S. He's said that this poem identifies perspectives on the border that "don't get reported in the news." To convey these views, Ríos uses a classic poetic form: the sonnet. Traditionally, it consists of fourteen lines, and Ríos keeps this length. But note his poem's subtitle. Evidently a single sonnet isn't enough for him: he needs *two* for all the views he wants to list.

The image paired here with Ríos' poem is a visual argument against the wall. It's a map that shows how this proposed barrier threatens a Native American tribe. The map comes from a 2017 Brookings Institution report entitled "The Wall: The Real Costs of a Barrier Between the United States and Mexico." Brookings is a well-established centrist/left-leaning think tank based in Washington, D.C. It publishes research and recommendations on matters of social and political policy. Brookings's article on the President's proposed border wall severely criticizes his plan. Author Vanda Felbab-Brown raises several objections to it. For one thing, she notes, the wall will firmly split the homeland of the Tohono O'odham Nation. Officially, the tribe's reservation is in Arizona, but it also lays claim to ancestral lands across the border in Mexico. A border fence already separates these two areas; replacing it with a wall will disunite them even more.

The map illustrates this point. In part, it depicts bodies of water: the Pacific Ocean on the left, and the Gulf of California reaching into Mexico. The map's most notable features, though, are the Tohono O'odham reservation in Arizona (identified by a dark shape) and the tribe's historic territory in Mexico (the white space you see in that country). The viewer sees an indigenous people divided.

ALBERTO RÍOS

The Border: A Double Sonnet

The border is a line that birds cannot see.
The border is a beautiful piece of paper folded carelessly in half.
The border is where flint first met steel, starting a century of fires.
The border is a belt that is too tight, holding things up but making it hard
    to breathe.
The border is a rusted hinge that does not bend.   5
The border is the blood clot in the river's vein.
The border says *stop* to the wind, but the wind speaks another language,
    and keeps going.
The border is a brand, the "Double-X" of barbed wire scarred into the
    skin of so many.

The border has always been a welcome stopping place but is now a stop
    sign, always red.
The border is a jump rope still there even after the game is finished.   10
The border is a real crack in an imaginary dam.
The border used to be an actual place, but now, it is the act of a thousand
    imaginations.
The border, the word *border*, sounds like *order*, but in this place they do
    not rhyme.
The border is a handshake that becomes a squeezing contest.

The border smells like cars at noon and wood smoke in the evening.   15
The border is the place between the two pages in a book where the spine
    is bent too far.
The border is two men in love with the same woman.
The border is an equation in search of an equals sign.
The border is the location of the factory where lightning and thunder
    are made.
The border is "NoNo" The Clown, who can't make anyone laugh.   20
The border is a locked door that has been promoted.
The border is a moat but without a castle on either side.
The border has become Checkpoint *Chale*.
The border is a place of plans constantly broken and repaired and
    broken.
The border is mighty, but even the parting of the seas created a path,   25
    not a barrier.
The border is a big, neat, clean, clear black line on a map that does not
    exist.
The border is the line in new bifocals: below, small things get bigger;
    above, nothing changes.
The border is a skunk with a white line down its back.

IDENTIFYING THE VISUAL STRATEGIES

Calling attention to what might be ignored, forgotten, or not perceived: Maps can be important tools for people who've been oppressed. Often the ruling power has tormented them through neglect—not even bothering to recognize they exist. By giving themselves a spot on a map, they declare their presence. Probably most Americans know nothing about the Tohono O'odham Nation, but this map makes them more aware of the tribe. In doing so, it increases the chance that debates about the wall will consider the tribe's values, wishes, and needs. Ríos's poem is similarly informative. It presents perspectives on the U.S.-Mexico border that readers may be unfamiliar with. They may not realize, for example, that many migrants perceive the border as "a belt that is too tight, holding things up but making it hard to breathe."

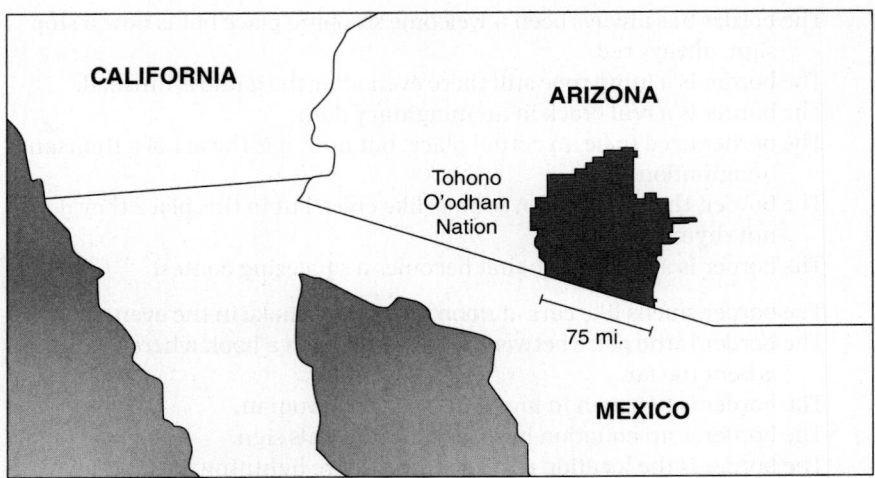

Figure 4   Border map from the Brookings Institution

Downplaying: A map that stresses something is usually downplaying something else. When mapmakers want to spotlight a neglected group or region, they may *omit* or *shrink* details of others. The map may still be accurate, but it's makers will choose what it points out. The people who crafted the map featured here aimed to make viewers conscious of the Tohono O'odham Nation. Probably they couldn't achieve this goal if they filled Arizona, California, and Mexico with assorted details. If they inserted the names and locations of various cities and towns, the map would end up cluttered, and the tribe might get obscured. Since much of the map is blank, the tribe stands out. Ríos is similarly strategic with his poem. He doesn't repeat details from press coverage of the border. He doesn't quote politicians' remarks about it. Instead, he conveys the sensations of those who *experience* the border—people who find it an obstacle in their daily lives.

≡ **FOR FURTHER DISCUSSION**

The Brookings map is an effort to point out how the proposed border wall would disrupt the Tohono O'odham Nation. Imagine that you've been invited to expand Ríos's poem by adding to it a line that reflect this tribe's situation. What might the line be? In general, do you think cases like this tribe's deserve to be considered in debates about the wall? Why, or why not?

TOPIC: GUNS

Poem: Katie Bickham, "The Ferryman"
Image: Map from the Gun Violence Archive

The United States is painfully familiar with mass shootings. Almost every month, it seems, the country suffers another. Each shooting renews the debates over familiar issues: Who should have access to firearms? How should their sales be regulated? What gun policies are Constitutional? Can gun control prevent mass killings? These questions are heatedly discussed by the American public. Among the concerned are creative writers, whose literature expresses how they feel about these issues. Their work doesn't always argue for particular stands, but it prods readers to ponder America's shooting sprees.

An example is the poem we present here, Katie Bickham's "The Ferryman." Bickham lives in Shreveport, Louisiana, and teaches at Bossier Parish Community College. She has published in numerous journals and is the author of two poetry collections: *The Belle Mar* (2015) and *Mouths Open to Name Her* (2019). "The Ferryman" appeared in the online edition of *Rattle* on October 5, 2017. It did so as part of the journal's series Poets Respond, which every Sunday publishes "a poem written within the last week about a public event that occurred within the last week." Bickham wrote her poem in the wake of the October 1, 2017, mass shooting in Las Vegas, which left fifty-eight people dead and five hundred injured. The title of the poem clearly refers to Charon, a character in Greek mythology. He transported souls over the Rivers Styx and Acheron in the underworld. Bickham's poem doesn't make an explicit argument. It expresses anguish, though, over slaughters like the killings in Las Vegas. In effect, it reminds the reader that such tragedies persist — with no end in sight.

The image we pair with Bickham's poem is another map, this time a record of mass shootings in the U.S. It identifies where they occurred in the first seven months of 2018. The map is a product of the Gun Violence Archive, a non-profit organization established in 2013 to gather data about such murders. GVA takes pains to note that it "is not, by design, an advocacy group." Rather, its purpose "is to document incidents of gun violence and gun crime nationally to provide independent, verified data to those who need to use it in their research, advocacy or writing."

KATE BICKHAM

The Ferryman

The ferryman is counting up his fares
as blood congeals and stains and spills and clots.
It's cash or coin. No cards. No thoughts and prayers.

A mother tears her clothes, a boy despairs.
Their vigils litter cities lit with dots.   5
The ferryman is trembling, counting fares.

He's had to buy new oars, to make repairs,
stays up nights counting bullets, mopping spots
of blood off of his deck: the thoughts and prayers

just one more thing needs sweeping, extra cares   10
tossed on his shoulders already in knots.
A better boatman wouldn't bear such cares.

I have my work, and up there, they have theirs,
he tells himself, but jumps when he hears shots.
So many. He can't stand to count the fares.   15
He navigates a river red with prayers.

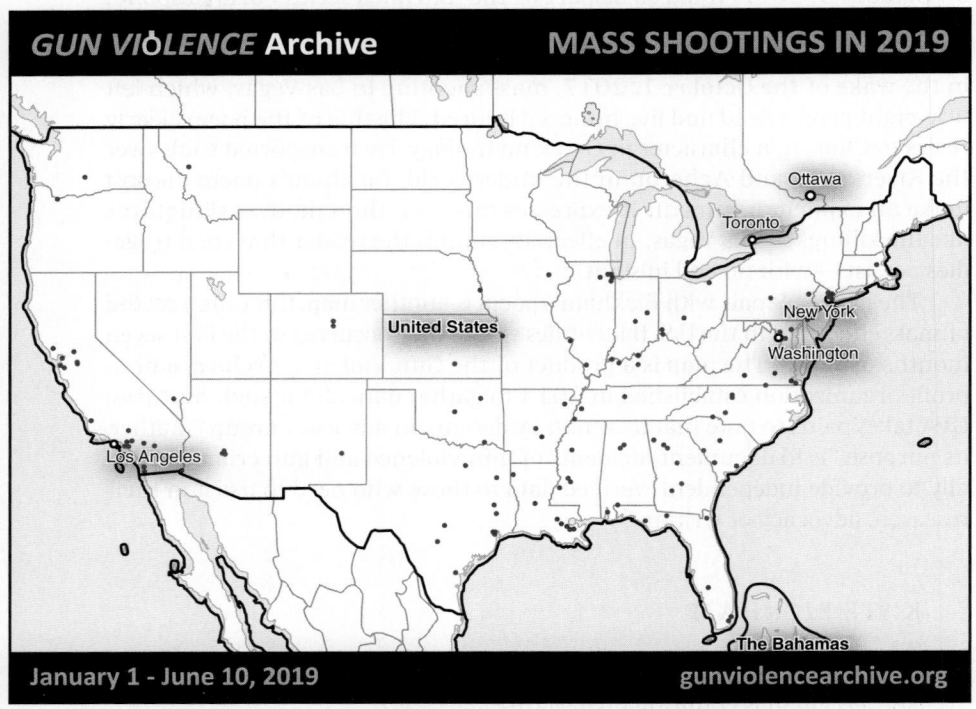

Figure 5   Map from the Gun Violence Archive
Gun Violence Archive

IDENTIFYING THE VISUAL STRATEGIES

Location marks: There are various ways to memorialize places and events. Bickham's poem ruefully notes that after a gun massacre, the victims' friends and families mourn with symbolic candle flames: "Their vigils litter cities lit with dots." Map designers, too, choose symbols to peg historic spots. To indicate sites of mass shootings, GVA relies on dots. Of course, these aren't Bickham's metaphorical "dots," the candle flames her poem mentions. Instead, they're literal marks. Although dots are a conventional aspect of maps, don't take them for granted. Any map's use of them is a deliberate decision. They deserve to be analyzed as a rhetorical *strategy*, employed by the map's designer to create certain effects. By making dots its map's main feature, GVA calls attention to patterns. Viewers are made aware of the regions where mass shootings abound, as well as areas of the country where they happen less. Helping these patterns stand out is the use of blank space. Other than the dots, the map offers little detail. It names just a few cities, and it doesn't identify states. The clutter won't distract viewers; they'll focus on the dots. Will the information these marks provide settle issues of gun control? No. People will still debate how to prevent shooting deaths. But the dots on its map serve GVA's purpose. With them, the group communicates facts it believes the debaters need.

Particular definition: Often poets deliberately use ambiguous language. They leave their audience to debate the meaning of these words. Take Bickman's line "A better boatman wouldn't bear such cares." "Better" in what sense? Professionally better? Morally better? Spiritually better? She forces her readers to figure out what sense of the word fits best. Of course, issues of definition don't come up just with literature. They may arise when you're looking at a statistical map or chart. GVA's map is a case in point. The group defines *mass shooting* in a particular way. It applies the term to incidents where the victims are "4 or more shot or killed, not including the shooter." Not everyone would accept this meaning. Many would even argue with it. GVA admits that due to its specific definition of the term, its "mass shooting numbers" are "higher than some other sources." Try asking yourself these questions: When *you* hear the term *mass shooting*, how many victims come to *your* mind? When different definitions lead to different numbers, what's the effect on debates about guns?

Keeping records in the first place: Bickham begins her poem by observing that "The ferryman is counting up his fares," but she later reports that this recordkeeping torments him: "He can't stand to count the fares." In her literary way, she recognizes two things: the need to track gun deaths *and* the pain this work involves. Indeed, building an archive can be stressful. It may also be a controversial move. Social media like Facebook gets criticized a lot for seizing their users' personal data. As a group that researches shootings, GVA is politically bold. For years, the Centers for Disease Control and Prevention researched gun violence, but in 1996, the U.S. Congress stopped funding this work. Resistance to this kind of study continues in Washington. In March 2018 the *New York Times* observed that "much of the federal government has largely abandoned efforts to learn why people shoot one another, or themselves, and what can be done to prevent gun violence." What the *Times* reports is a policy of *not* keeping records. It's a policy that people debate; what do *you* think about it? Whatever your view on this particular topic, don't take records for granted. Consider why they've been kept; who might object to their keeping; and what information hasn't been gathered at all.

≣ FOR FURTHER DISCUSSION

What would you say to someone who concludes from the GVA map that efforts to stop mass shootings should concentrate on the Eastern half of the United States? What further information would help *you* interpret GVA's findings? What role do you think poems like Bickham's should play in gun debates?

≣ SUMMING UP THE STRATEGIES

- Direct address
- Selective identification
- Dreamy and romantic visual style
- Suggestion of consensus
- Directional signaling
- Projection of an engaging mood
- Incongruity
- Anthropomorphizing
- Manipulating visual perspective
- Dramatic language

- Rhythmic language
- Big lettering
- Symbolic representation
- Abstraction
- Calling attention to what might be ignored, forgotten, or not perceived
- Downplaying
- Location marks
- Particular definition
- Keeping records in the first place

☰ A WRITING EXERCISE

Select an image on the Web that you see as making an argument or as being an element of it. Write an essay in which you determine the extent to which the image strikes you as indeed helping to make certain ideas persuasive. In analyzing the image, identify how it uses at least a few of the strategies we've discussed in this section.

Identifying Biases *You* Might Bring to your Internet Research

We've discussed how to study and assess arguments made online and reviewed the strategies that Web sites use to persuade. This final section turns to *you*. When you examine arguments, you might assume that you're neutral; most of us prefer to believe we're objective, impartial, fair. But few of us possess such virtues when we begin research. We have biases that are hard to shed. When we look at a Web site's argument, we do so with our own opinions. These can easily influence our perspective.

Still, it's possible to become more open-minded. A good first step is to recognize the processes inside in our brains: the ways that our minds usually work. These processes have drawn the interest of what's called cognitive science. It studies mental habits that help human beings cope. Often these routines are efficient. With them, we make sense of our world. But not always do they serve us well. They can be counter-productive, downright dysfunctional. This can happen when we look at a Web site's claims. We might assume that we can quickly gauge their value. But longer, deeper study of these claims might improve our thinking. Such contemplation might refine the arguments *we* make. Snap judgments, on the other hand, limit our perceptions; they just let our usual biases rule.

How can you avoid this problem in *your* online research? Stay alert to the following tendencies. As cognitive science points out, we're all tempted to stick with these habits. The important thing, though, is to understand they pose risks. They threaten the kind of inquiry that genuine research pursues.

Confirmation bias: You may already know this term. When people are steered by confirmation bias, they refuse to change their minds. They're bent on interpreting data in ways that fit their existing frameworks. No matter what, they're determined to keep their current ideas and beliefs. Hardcore conspiracy theorists are an example. They uphold their dark visions even when challenged by stark facts. If D.C. police find no kids in the pizzeria's cellar, for example, that proves the cunning of the nefarious cult. Aware the police were coming, they moved their victims out.

Recommendation: To head off confirmation bias, take the time to ponder data that conflict with your views. Use this information to reflect on your claims. Perhaps it will lead you to modify or replace them.

Halo effect: Think of an opinion you hold about a feature of someone you know. Often this view affects how you see the person as a whole. It shapes your impression of his or her entire self. This mental habit is called the *halo effect*. It can take positive or negative form. A fan of the president's policy on immigration might then feel compelled to praise all of the President's stands. Alternatively, someone who hates the president's policy on immigration might then protest everything the president does.

Recommendation: Assume that whatever you've evaluating has multiple aspects, each of which can be judged in a different way.

Assuming a single cause: Many a phenomenon has multiple causes and conditions. But often we assume that a thing has just one cause. So, we may be among those who suspect that gluten causes fifty-five diseases. Remember, though, what *The New England Journal of Medicine* reported: gluten is perhaps *associated* with fifty-five diseases. An *association* is weaker than a *cause*, and it allows for other factors. The search for a single cause of something may keep us from investigating a whole set of influences that we should take into account.

Recommendation: Consider the possibility that something has more than one cause. Distinguish between a *cause* and an *association*, especially when analyzing scientific reports. You'll broaden your inquiry into a subject if you try to identify the various *conditions* of its emergence. This is often a richer context than a search for *causes* allows.

The influence of repetition: When we see a certain depiction of a subject over and over again, the image tends to stick in our minds. It's often the first thing we think of when the subject comes up. Political campaigns are well aware that repetition can grip us. During elections, you'll see the same commercials repeatedly. Often these ads portray an opponent as corrupt. On any number of subjects, repetition can freeze our thoughts. If we see many Web sites cite the same statistic, we're more inclined to accept it as true. But maybe it isn't. Again, *The New England Journal of Medicine*'s findings are a case in point. *NEJM* didn't report that gluten may cause fifty-five diseases — even if Web sites repeatedly claim that it did.

Recommendation: When something is endlessly repeated on the Internet or elsewhere, don't just take it as fact. Deliberately or not, the repetition can bury, distort, or oversimplify the truth. Try to locate and examine the data's source.

Base-rate neglect: This is the tendency to assume that your research sample is adequate, when you actually need to work with a larger set. An example of base-rate neglect would be gauging the public's response to a book solely by Amazon reviews. Research into online retailing finds that just a small percentage of customers post reviews on the Web. Also, these opinions veer toward extremes; mild or mixed judgments don't appear nearly as much. At Amazon's page for William Davis's anti-gluten book *Wheat Belly*, the reviews number more than six thousand, and roughly 85 percent of them are positive. It's a substantial sample, but it only tells you so much. It doesn't tell you the size of *Wheat Belly*'s actual audience, and it doesn't tell you how the book's whole readership feels. To make any headway in learning these things, you'd have to do further research.

Recommendation: Pause before you draw conclusions from your available sample. You may need a larger set of records for your judgments to be precise.

Settling for whatever is immediately available: When you're looking for truth in a "post-truth" age, this is the habit that can hobble you most. As numerous studies have shown, Google searches don't go far. People tend to stick with the first two pages produced. But good researchers go beyond what first appears. They don't rest with immediately available data, instead venturing into the wider Web. Similarly, your arguments are apt to be more truthful if you base them on a wide range of sources. If you're proposing a regulation you think could reduce mass shootings, don't support your case just with the Gun Violence Archive map (Figure 6). Yes, the map is visually stunning. It's also informative. The number of killings it documents tells us much. But, as GVA admits, this total can be debated. Some organizations come up with a different amount, for they define *mass shooting* in other ways. Their statistics and reasoning merit attention, no matter how dazzling you find GVA's display.

Recommendation: Though a Web site you find right away can be a valuable source, don't stick with one discovery. Take your research further.

≡ A WRITING EXERCISE

Find a Web site that challenges or complicates some claim you want to make. Try to view this site with an open mind. Perhaps you won't end up accepting what it has to say, but make a conscious effort to be fair. Then, write an account of this effort, referring to biases you strove to overcome. They might include some of the mental habits this chapter has discussed.

Literature and Arguments

CHAPTER 9

Families

In the not-too-distant past, family life was the focal point of our emotional existence, the center of all our important psychological successes and failures. It was common for several generations to live together in the same town and even the same home. Grandparents, aunts, and uncles were an intimate part of daily life, not just relatives we saw during the holidays. Besides the usual emotional drama that always takes place between parents and children, there were the additional tensions that inevitably arise when the values of the old clash with those who are younger. Of course, there was also the comforting emotional support available from more than just a mother and father as well as the sense of belonging and bonding with the many aunts, uncles, and cousins who usually lived nearby.

As extended families become less common, the emotional stakes of home life seem higher than ever. Since we rely on one another more in today's nuclear family, our sense of disappointment, our sense of rejection, and our sense of unworthiness can be more acute. During childhood, the drama of family life can stamp an indelible mark on our psyches, leaving psychological scars that make safe passage into adulthood difficult. Our status within the family can also offer us a sense of worth and confidence that leads to contentment and success later on. For all of us, however, family life is composed not of psychological and sociological generalities, but rather, of our one-to-one relationships with fathers, sisters, grandparents. Writers often give us imaginative, honest, and illuminating charts of their successes and failures in negotiating both the calm and the choppy waters of our family journeys. The following clusters do not hope to be complete or representative of your experiences. We do hope, however, that in reading and discussing these poems and stories, you will find them an interesting and provocative catalyst for you to delve into the joys and sorrows of your own life in a family.

The chapter opens with three stories that examine the tensions and anxieties that arise between mothers and children as they struggle with questions of identity, responsibility, separation, and loss. Two stories of brothers in conflict about the purpose of life follow. The third cluster involves two stories about the difficult decisions couples often have to make about parenthood. Next, four poems paint memorable but not always positive portraits of fathers, followed by a cluster of poems about grandmothers gives us loving, honest, and humorous snapshots. A poem on environmental responsibility that was read at the United Nations is the focus of a Literature and Current Issues cluster. The penultimate cluster groups Sylvia Plath's "Daddy" with critical commentaries on the poet's haunting poem about the attempts of a young girl to understand her father's death. The chapter concludes with a science fiction story about the consciousness of robots and essays about the future of artificial intelligence.

TILLIE OLSEN, "I Stand Here Ironing"

AMY TAN, "Two Kinds"

ALMA LUZ VILLANUEVA, "Her Choice"

We all know stories of parents who want to mold their children, stories of mothers and fathers who push their reluctant children to be fashion models or beauty queens or Little League stars. Some studies of adults playing musical instruments in orchestras say the biggest factor in their success was the commitment of their parents. But we also hear about tennis prodigies who burn out at sixteen because of parental pressure. Mothers and children have always struggled with each other over life goals and identity: How much guidance is enough? How much is too much? What is a reasonable balance between preparing a child for life's challenges and shaping a child to act out the mother's fantasy or her internal vision of what the good life is? But no matter where parents fall on this continuum, there are events so overwhelming that they simply cannot control their own destiny or that of their children. Tillie Olsen and Amy Tan insightfully chart the difficulties mothers and daughters sometime have with each other as influential social and cultural forces buffet them. And Christina Henriquez's contemporary tale of the horrors of one woman's immigration ordeal reminds us that some mothers struggle with almost unbearable circumstances as they try to protect their children.

≡ BEFORE YOU READ

How much was your mother responsible for your successes? Your failures? How could your mother have more insistently pushed you to succeed? What was the most difficult obstacle you and your mother had to overcome in your relationship?

TILLIE OLSEN

I Stand Here Ironing

Born in Omaha, Nebraska, to Russian immigrants of Jewish descent and socialist views, Tillie Olsen (1912–2007) was an activist in social and political causes all of her life, often choosing family, work, union, feminist, or other political causes over writing. Although her publishing record is short, its quality is greatly admired. In addition to critically respected short stories, Olsen wrote a novel, Yonnondio *(1974), which paints a vivid picture of a coal-mining family during the Depression. Her essay collection,* Silences *(1978), stimulated debate about class and gender as factors in the creation of literature and led both directly and indirectly to the revived interest in works by women writers. The mother of four daughters, Olsen often wrote about generational relationships within families. "I Stand Here Ironing" is from her 1961 collection of stories,* Tell Me a Riddle.

I stand here ironing, and what you asked me moves tormented back and forth with the iron.

"I wish you would manage the time to come in and talk with me about your daughter. I'm sure you can help me understand her. She's a youngster who needs help and whom I'm deeply interested in helping."

"Who needs help." . . . Even if I came, what good would it do? You think because I am her mother I have a key, or that in some way you could use me as a key? She has lived for nineteen years. There is all that life that has happened outside of me, beyond me.

And when is there time to remember, to sift, to weigh, to estimate, to total? I will start and there will be an interruption and I will have to gather it all together again. Or I will become engulfed with all I did or did not do, with what should have been and what cannot be helped.

She was a beautiful baby. The first and only one of our five that was   5
beautiful at birth. You do not guess how new and uneasy her tenancy in her now-loveliness. You did not know her all those years she was thought homely, or see her poring over her baby pictures, making me tell her over and over how beautiful she had been — and would be, I would tell her — and was now, to the seeing eye. But the seeing eyes were few or nonexistent. Including mine.

I nursed her. They feel that's important nowadays. I nursed all the children, but with her, with all the fierce rigidity of first motherhood, I did like the books then said. Though her cries battered me to trembling and my breasts ached with swollenness, I waited till the clock decreed.

Why do I put that first? I do not even know if it matters, or if it explains anything.

She was a beautiful baby. She blew shining bubbles of sound. She loved motion, loved light, loved color and music and textures. She would lie on the floor in her blue overalls patting the surface so hard in ecstasy her hands and feet would blur. She was a miracle to me, but when she was eight months old I had to leave her daytimes with the woman downstairs to whom she was no miracle at all, for I worked or looked for work and for Emily's father, who "could no longer endure" (he wrote in his good-bye note) "sharing want with us."

I was nineteen. It was the pre-relief, pre-WPA world of the depression. I would start running as soon as I got off the streetcar, running up the stairs, the place smelling sour, and awake or asleep to startle awake, when she saw me she would break into a clogged weeping that could not be comforted, a weeping I can hear yet.

After a while I found a job hashing at night so I could be with her days,   10
and it was better. But it came to where I had to bring her to his family and leave her.

It took a long time to raise the money for her fare back. Then she got chicken pox and I had to wait longer. When she finally came, I hardly knew her, walking quick and nervous like her father, looking like her father, thin, and dressed in a shoddy red that yellowed her skin and glared at the pockmarks. All the baby loveliness gone.

She was two. Old enough for nursery school they said, and I did not know then what I know now — the fatigue of the long day, and the lacerations of group life in the kinds of nurseries that are only parking places for children.

Except that it would have made no difference if I had known. It was the only place there was. It was the only way we could be together, the only way I could hold a job.

And even without knowing, I knew. I knew the teacher that was evil because all these years it has curdled into my memory, the little boy hunched in the corner, her rasp, "why aren't you outside, because Alvin hits you? that's no reason, go out, scaredy." I knew Emily hated it even if she did not clutch and implore "don't go Mommy" like the other children, mornings.

She always had a reason why we should stay home. Momma, you look ⁣15 sick. Momma, I feel sick. Momma, the teachers aren't there today, they're sick. Momma, we can't go, there was a fire there last night. Momma, it's a holiday today, no school, they told me.

But never a direct protest, never rebellion. I think of our others in their three-, four-year-oldness — the explosions, the tempers, the denunciations, the demands — and I feel suddenly ill. I put the iron down. What in me demanded that goodness in her? And what was the cost, the cost to her of such goodness?

The old man living in the back once said in his gentle way: "You should smile at Emily more when you look at her." What *was* in my face when I looked at her? I loved her. There were all the acts of love.

It was only with the others I remembered what he said, and it was the face of joy, and not of care or tightness or worry I turned to them — too late for Emily. She does not smile easily, let alone almost always as her brothers and sisters do. Her face is closed and sombre, but when she wants, how fluid. You must have seen it in her pantomimes, you spoke of her rare gift for comedy on the stage that rouses laughter out of the audience so dear they applaud and applaud and do not want to let her go.

Where does it come from, that comedy? There was none of it in her when she came back to me that second time, after I had to send her away again. She had a new daddy now to learn to love, and I think perhaps it was a better time.

Except when we left her alone nights, telling ourselves she was old enough. ⁣20

"Can't you go some other time, Mommy, like tomorrow?" she would ask. "Will it be just a little while you'll be gone? Do you promise?"

The time we came back, the front door open, the clock on the floor in the hall. She rigid awake. "It wasn't just a little while. I didn't cry. Three times I called you, just three times, and then I ran downstairs to open the door so you could come faster. The clock talked loud. I threw it away, it scared me what it talked."

She said the clock talked loud again that night I went to the hospital to have Susan. She was delirious with the fever that comes before red measles, but she was fully conscious all the week I was gone and the week after we were home when she could not come near the new baby or me.

She did not get well. She stayed skeleton thin, not wanting to eat, and night after night she had nightmares. She would call for me, and I would rouse from exhaustion to sleepily call back: "You're all right, darling, go to sleep, it's just a dream," and if she still called, in a sterner voice, "now go to sleep, Emily, there's nothing to hurt you." Twice, only twice, when I had to get up for Susan anyhow, I went in to sit with her.

Now when it is too late (as if she would let me hold her and comfort her   25 like I do the others) I get up and go to her at once at her moan or restless stirring. "Are you awake, Emily? Can I get you something?" And the answer is always the same: "No, I'm all right, go back to sleep, Mother."

They persuaded me at the clinic to send her away to a convalescent home in the country where "she can have the kind of food and care you can't manage for her, and you'll be free to concentrate on the new baby." They still send children to that place. I see pictures on the society page of sleek young women planning affairs to raise money for it, or dancing at the affairs, or decorating Easter eggs or filling Christmas stockings for the children.

They never have a picture of the children so I do not know if the girls still wear those gigantic red bows and the ravaged looks on the every other Sunday when parents can come to visit "unless otherwise notified" — as we were notified the first six weeks.

Oh it is a handsome place, green lawns and tall trees and fluted flower beds. High up on the balconies of each cottage the children stand, the girls in their red bows and white dresses, the boys in white suits and giant red ties. The parents stand below shrieking up to be heard and the children shriek down to be heard, and between them the invisible wall "Not To Be Contaminated by Parental Germs or Physical Affection."

There was a tiny girl who always stood hand in hand with Emily. Her parents never came. One visit she was gone. "They moved her to Rose Cottage," Emily shouted in explanation. "They don't like you to love anybody here."

She wrote once a week, the labored writing of a seven-year-old. "I am fine.   30 How is the baby. If I write my leter nicly I will have a star. Love." There never was a star. We wrote every other day, letters she could never hold or keep but only hear read — once. "We simply do not have room for children to keep any personal possessions," they patiently explained when we pieced one Sunday's shrieking together to plead how much it would mean to Emily, who loved so to keep things, to be allowed to keep her letters and cards.

Each visit she looked frailer. "She isn't eating," they told us.

(They had runny eggs for breakfast or mush with lumps, Emily said later, I'd hold it in my mouth and not swallow. Nothing ever tasted good, just when they had chicken.)

It took us eight months to get her released home, and only the fact that she gained back so little of her seven lost pounds convinced the social worker.

I used to try to hold and love her after she came back, but her body would stay stiff, and after a while she'd push away. She ate little. Food sickened her, and I think much of life too. Oh she had physical lightness and brightness, twinkling by on skates, bouncing like a ball up and down up and down over the jump rope, skimming over the hill; but these were momentary.

She fretted about her appearance, thin and dark and foreign-looking at   35 a time when every little girl was supposed to look or thought she should look like a chubby blonde replica of Shirley Temple. The doorbell sometimes rang for her, but no one seemed to come and play in the house or to be a best friend. Maybe because we moved so much.

There was a boy she loved painfully through two school semesters. Months later she told me how she had taken pennies from my purse to buy him candy. "Licorice was his favorite and I brought him some every day, but he still liked Jennifer better'n me. Why, Mommy?" The kind of question for which there is no answer.

School was a worry for her. She was not glib or quick in a world where glibness and quickness were easily confused with ability to learn. To her overworked and exasperated teachers she was an overconscientious "slow learner" who kept trying to catch up and was absent entirely too often.

I let her be absent, though sometimes the illness was imaginary. How different from my now-strictness about attendance with the others. I wasn't working. We had a new baby. I was home anyhow. Sometimes, after Susan grew old enough, I would keep her home from school, too, to have them all together.

Mostly Emily had asthma, and her breathing, harsh and labored, would fill the house with a curiously tranquil sound. I would bring the two old dresser mirrors and her boxes of collections to her bed. She would select beads and single earrings, bottle tops and shells, dried flowers and pebbles, old postcards and scraps, all sorts of oddments; then she and Susan would play Kingdom, setting up landscapes and furniture, peopling them with action.

Those were the only times of peaceful companionship between her and Susan. I have edged away from it, that poisonous feeling between them, that terrible balancing of hurts and needs I had to do between the two, and did so badly, those earlier years.   40

Oh there were conflicts between the others too, each one human, needing, demanding, hurting, taking—but only between Emily and Susan, no, Emily toward Susan that corroding resentment. It seems so obvious on the surface, yet it is not obvious; Susan, the second child, Susan, golden- and curly-haired and chubby, quick and articulate and assured, everything in appearance and manner Emily was not; Susan, not able to resist Emily's precious things, losing or sometimes clumsily breaking them; Susan telling jokes and riddles to company for applause while Emily sat silent (to say to me later: that was *my* riddle, Mother, I told it to Susan); Susan, who for all the five years' difference in age was just a year behind Emily in developing physically.

I am glad for that slow physical development that widened the difference between her and her contemporaries, though she suffered over it. She was too vulnerable for that terrible world of youthful competition, of preening and parading, of constant measuring of yourself against every other, of envy, "If I had that copper hair," "If I had that skin. . . ." She tormented herself enough about not looking like the others, there was enough of unsureness, the having to be conscious of words before you speak, the constant caring—what are they thinking of me? without having it all magnified by the merciless physical drives.

Ronnie is calling. He is wet and I change him. It is rare there is such a cry now. That time of motherhood is almost behind me when the ear is not one's own but must always be racked and listening for the child cry, the child call. We sit for a while and I hold him, looking out over the city spread in charcoal with its soft aisles of light. *"Shoogily,"* he breathes and curls closer. I carry him back to bed, asleep. *Shoogily.* A funny word, a family word, inherited from Emily, invented by her to say: *comfort.*

In this and other ways she leaves her seal, I say aloud. And startle at my saying it. What do I mean? What did I start to gather together, to try and make coherent? I was at the terrible, growing years. War years. I do not remember them well. I was working, there were four smaller ones now, there was not time for her. She had to help be a mother, and housekeeper, and shopper. She had to get her seal. Mornings of crisis and near hysteria trying to get lunches packed, hair combed, coats and shoes found, everyone to school or Child Care on time, the baby ready for transportation. And always the paper scribbled on by a smaller one, the book looked at by Susan then mislaid, the homework not done. Running out to that huge school where she was one, she was lost, she was a drop; suffering over the unpreparedness, stammering and unsure in her classes.

There was so little time left at night after the kids were bedded down. She would struggle over books, always eating (it was in those years she developed her enormous appetite that is legendary in our family) and I would be ironing, or preparing food for the next day, or writing V-mail to Bill, or tending the baby. Sometimes, to make me laugh, or out of her despair, she would imitate happenings or types at school. 45

I think I said once: "Why don't you do something like this in the school amateur show?" One morning she phoned me at work, hardly understandable through the weeping: "Mother, I did it. I won, I won; they gave me first prize; they clapped and clapped and wouldn't let me go." Now suddenly she was Somebody, and as imprisoned in her difference as she had been in anonymity.

She began to be asked to perform at other high schools, even in colleges, then at city and statewide affairs. The first one we went to, I only recognized her that first moment when thin, shy, she almost drowned herself into the curtains. Then: Was this Emily? The control, the command, the convulsing and deadly clowning, the spell, then the roaring, stamping audience, unwilling to let this rare and precious laughter out of their lives.

Afterwards: You ought to do something about her with a gift like that—but without money or knowing how, what does one do? We have left it all to her, and the gift has so often eddied inside, clogged and clotted, as been used and growing.

She is coming. She runs up the stairs two at a time with her light graceful step, and I know she is happy tonight. Whatever it was that occasioned your call did not happen today.

"Aren't you ever going to finish the ironing, Mother? Whistler painted his mother in a rocker. I'd have to paint mine standing over an ironing board." This is one of her communicative nights and she tells me everything and nothing as she fixes herself a plate of food out of the icebox. 50

She is so lovely. Why did you want me to come in at all? Why were you concerned? She will find her way.

She starts up the stairs to bed. "Don't get me up with the rest in the morning." "But I thought you were having midterms." "Oh, those," she comes back in, kisses me, and says quite lightly, "in a couple of years when we'll all be atom-dead they won't matter a bit." She has said it before. She *believes* it. But because I have been dredging the past, and all that compounds a human being is so heavy and meaningful in me, I cannot endure it tonight.

I will never total it all. I will never come in to say: She was a child seldom smiled at. Her father left me before she was a year old. I had to work her first six years when there was work, or I sent her home and to his relatives. There were years she had care she hated. She was dark and thin and foreign-looking in a world where the prestige went to blondeness and curly hair and dimples, she was slow where glibness was prized. She was a child of anxious, not proud, love. We were poor and could not afford for her the soil of easy growth. I was a young mother, I was a distracted mother. There were other children pushing up, demanding. Her younger sister seemed all that she was not. There were years she did not want me to touch her. She kept too much in herself, her life was such she had to keep too much in herself. My wisdom came too late. She has much to her and probably little will come of it. She is a child of her age, of depression, of war, of fear.

Let her be. So all that is in her will not bloom—but in how many does it? There is still enough left to live by. Only help her to know—help make it so there is cause for her to know—that she is more than this dress on the ironing board, helpless before the iron.   *[1961]*

≣ THINKING ABOUT THE TEXT

1. Is Olsen's last paragraph optimistic or pessimistic about personal destiny? Is there some support in the story for both perspectives?

2. There is an old expression: "To know all is to forgive all." Does this statement apply to "I Stand Here Ironing"? Some critics want to privilege personal responsibility; others, social conditions. Do you blame Emily's mother? Or is she simply a victim?

3. How might this story be different if told from Emily's perspective? From Susan's? From Emily's teachers'? What are the advantages and disadvantages of writing a story from one character's point of view?

4. How would you describe the voice or voices we hear in the story? What qualities, dimensions, or emotions can you infer? Does one dominate? Are you sympathetic to this voice? Is that what Olsen wanted?

5. Do you agree with the mother's decision not to visit the school for a conference? What are her reasons? Are they sound? What do you think the teacher wants to discuss? How involved in a child's life should a teacher be?

AMY TAN
Two Kinds

Born to Chinese immigrants in Oakland, California, Amy Tan (b. 1952) weaves intricate stories about generational and intercultural relationships among women in families, basing much of her writing on her own family history. She earned a double B.A., in English and linguistics, and an M.A. in linguistics at San Jose State University. Her novels dealing with mother–daughter relationships, The Joy Luck Club *(1989) and* The Kitchen God's Wife *(1991), have received awards and critical acclaim.* The Hundred Secret Senses *(1995) explores the relationship between sisters who grew up in different cultures. "Two Kinds" is excerpted from* The Joy Luck Club. *Another book,* Saving Fish from Drowning *(2005), was called a "witty parable," loosely based on* The Canterbury Tales. *A novel,* The Valley of Amazement, *was published in 2013. In 2017 she published* Where the Past Begins: A Writer's Memoir, *which* Publishers Weekly *called "wise and profound."*

My mother believed you could be anything you wanted to be in America. You could open a restaurant. You could work for the government and get good retirement. You could buy a house with almost no money down. You could become rich. You could become instantly famous.

"Of course you can be prodigy, too," my mother told me when I was nine. "You can be best anything. What does Auntie Lindo know? Her daughter, she is only best tricky."

America was where all my mother's hopes lay. She had come here in 1949 after losing everything in China: her mother and father, her family home, her first husband, and two daughters, twin baby girls. But she never looked back with regret. There were so many ways for things to get better.

We didn't immediately pick the right kind of prodigy. At first my mother thought I could be a Chinese Shirley Temple. We'd watch Shirley's old movies on TV as though they were training films. My mother would poke my arm and say, "*Ni kan*" —You watch. And I would see Shirley tapping her feet, or singing a sailor song, or pursing her lips into a very round O while saying, "Oh my goodness."

"*Ni kan*," said my mother as Shirley's eyes flooded with tears. "You already   5
know how. Don't need talent for crying!"

Soon after my mother got this idea about Shirley Temple, she took me to a beauty training school in the Mission district and put me in the hands of a student who could barely hold the scissors without shaking. Instead of getting big fat curls, I emerged with an uneven mass of crinkly black fuzz. My mother dragged me off to the bathroom and tried to wet down my hair.

"You look like Negro Chinese," she lamented, as if I had done this on purpose.

The instructor of the beauty training school had to lop off these soggy clumps to make my hair even again. "Peter Pan is very popular these days," the instructor assured my mother. I now had hair the length of a boy's, with straight-across bangs that hung at a slant two inches above my eyebrows. I liked the haircut and it made me actually look forward to my future fame.

In fact, in the beginning, I was just as excited as my mother, maybe even more so. I pictured this prodigy part of me as many different images, trying each one on for size. I was a dainty ballerina girl standing by the curtains, waiting to hear the right music that would send me floating on my tiptoes. I was like the Christ child lifted out of the straw manger, crying with holy indignity. I was Cinderella stepping from her pumpkin carriage with sparkly cartoon music filling the air.

In all of my imaginings, I was filled with a sense that I would soon become *perfect*. My mother and father would adore me. I would be beyond reproach. I would never feel the need to sulk for anything.   10

But sometimes the prodigy in me became impatient. "If you don't hurry up and get me out of here, I'm disappearing for good," it warned. "And then you'll always be nothing."

Every night after dinner, my mother and I would sit at the Formica kitchen table. She would present new tests, taking her examples from stories of amazing children she had read in *Ripley's Believe It or Not*, or *Good Housekeeping*, *Reader's Digest*, and a dozen other magazines she kept in a pile in our bathroom. My mother got these magazines from people whose houses she cleaned. And since she cleaned many houses each week, we had a great assortment. She would look through them all, searching for stories about remarkable children.

The first night she brought out a story about a three-year-old boy who knew the capitals of all the states and even most of the European countries. A teacher was quoted as saying the little boy could also pronounce the names of the foreign cities correctly.

"What's the capital of Finland?" my mother asked me, looking at the magazine story.

All I knew was the capital of California, because Sacramento was the   15
name of the street we lived on in Chinatown. "Nairobi!" I guessed, saying the most foreign word I could think of. She checked to see if that was possibly one way to pronounce "Helsinki" before showing me the answer.

The tests got harder—multiplying numbers in my head, finding the queen of hearts in a deck of cards, trying to stand on my head without using my hands, predicting the daily temperatures in Los Angeles, New York, and London.

One night I had to look at a page from the Bible for three minutes and then report everything I could remember. "Now Jehoshaphat had riches and honor in abundance and . . . that's all I remember, Ma," I said.

And after seeing my mother's disappointed face once again, something inside of me began to die. I hated the tests, the raised hopes and failed expectations. Before going to bed that night, I looked in the mirror above the bathroom sink and when I saw only my face staring back—and that it would always be this ordinary face—I began to cry. Such a sad, ugly girl! I made high-pitched noises like a crazed animal, trying to scratch out the face in the mirror.

And then I saw what seemed to be the prodigy side of me—because I had never seen that face before. I looked at my reflection, blinking so I could see more clearly. The girl staring back at me was angry, powerful. This girl and I were the same. I had new thoughts, willful thoughts, or rather thoughts filled with lots of won'ts. I won't let her change me, I promised myself. I won't be what I'm not.

So now on nights when my mother presented her tests, I performed list-   20
lessly, my head propped on one arm. I pretended to be bored. And I was. I got so bored I started counting the bellows of the foghorns out on the bay while my mother drilled me in other areas. The sound was comforting and reminded me of the cow jumping over the moon. And the next day, I played a game with myself, seeing if my mother would give up on me before eight bellows. After a while I usually counted only one, maybe two bellows at most. At last she was beginning to give up hope.

Two or three months had gone by without any mention of my being a prodigy again. And then one day my mother was watching *The Ed Sullivan Show* on TV. The TV was old and the sound kept shorting out. Every time my mother got halfway up from the sofa to adjust the set, the sound would go back on and Ed would be talking. As soon as she sat down, Ed would go silent again. She got up, the TV broke into loud piano music. She sat down. Silence. Up and down, back and forth, quiet and loud. It was like a stiff embraceless dance between her and the TV set. Finally she stood by the set with her hand on the sound dial.

She seemed entranced by the music, a little frenzied piano piece with this mesmerizing quality, sort of quick passages and then teasing lilting ones before it returned to the quick playful parts.

"*Ni kan*," my mother said, calling me over with hurried hand gestures. "Look here."

I could see why my mother was fascinated by the music. It was being pounded out by a little Chinese girl, about nine years old, with a Peter Pan haircut. The girl had the sauciness of a Shirley Temple. She was proudly mod-est like a proper Chinese child. And she also did this fancy sweep of a curtsy, so that the fluffy skirt of her white dress cascaded slowly to the floor like the petals of a large carnation.

In spite of these warning signs, I wasn't worried. Our family had no   25
piano and we couldn't afford to buy one, let alone reams of sheet music and piano lessons. So I could be generous in my comments when my mother bad-mouthed the little girl on TV.

"Play note right, but doesn't sound good! No singing sound," complained my mother.

"What are you picking on her for?" I said carelessly. "She's pretty good. Maybe she's not the best, but she's trying hard." I knew almost immediately I would be sorry I said that.

"Just like you," she said. "Not the best. Because you not trying." She gave a little huff as she let go of the sound dial and sat down on the sofa.

The little Chinese girl sat down also to play an encore of "Anitra's Dance" by Grieg. I remember the song, because later on I had to learn how to play it.

Three days after watching *The Ed Sullivan Show*, my mother told me what my   30
schedule would be for piano lessons and piano practice. She had talked to
Mr. Chong, who lived on the first floor of our apartment building. Mr. Chong
was a retired piano teacher and my mother had traded housecleaning services
for weekly lessons and a piano for me to practice on every day, two hours a day,
from four until six.

When my mother told me this, I felt as though I had been sent to hell.
I whined and then kicked my foot a little when I couldn't stand it anymore.

"Why don't you like me the way I am? I'm *not* a genius! I can't play
the piano. And even if I could, I wouldn't go on TV if you paid me a million
dollars!" I cried.

My mother slapped me. "Who ask you be genius?" she shouted. "Only ask
you be your best. For you sake. You think I want you be genius? Hnnh! What
for! Who ask you!"

"So ungrateful," I heard her mutter in Chinese. "If she had as much talent
as she has temper, she would be famous now."

Mr. Chong, whom I secretly nicknamed Old Chong, was very strange,   35
always tapping his fingers to the silent music of an invisible orchestra. He
looked ancient in my eyes. He had lost most of the hair on top of his head and
he wore thick glasses and had eyes that always looked tired and sleepy. But he
must have been younger than I thought, since he lived with his mother and
was not yet married.

I met Old Lady Chong once and that was enough. She had this peculiar
smell like a baby that had done something in its pants. And her fingers felt
like a dead person's, like an old peach I once found in the back of the refrigerator; the skin just slid off the meat when I picked it up. I soon found out why
Old Chong had retired from teaching piano. He was deaf. "Like Beethoven!" he
shouted to me. "We're both listening only in our head!" And he would start to
conduct his frantic silent sonatas.

Our lessons went like this. He would open the book and point to different
things, explaining their purpose: "Key! Treble! Bass! No sharps or flats! So this
is C major! Listen now and play after me!"

And then he would play the C scale a few times, a simple chord, and then,
as if inspired by an old, unreachable itch, he gradually added more notes
and running trills and a pounding bass until the music was really something
quite grand.

I would play after him, the simple scale, the simple chord, and then I just
played some nonsense that sounded like a cat running up and down on top of
garbage cans. Old Chong smiled and applauded and then said, "Very good! But
now you must learn to keep time!"

So that's how I discovered that Old Chong's eyes were too slow to keep   40
up with the wrong notes I was playing. He went through the motions in half-
time. To help me keep rhythm, he stood behind me, pushing down on my right
shoulder for every beat. He balanced pennies on top of my wrists so I would
keep them still as I slowly played scales and arpeggios. He had me curve my
hand around an apple and keep that shape when playing chords. He marched

stiffly to show me how to make each finger dance up and down, staccato like an obedient little soldier.

He taught me all these things, and that was how I also learned I could be lazy and get away with mistakes, lots of mistakes. If I hit the wrong notes because I hadn't practiced enough, I never corrected myself. I just kept playing in rhythm. And Old Chong kept conducting his own private reverie.

So maybe I never really gave myself a fair chance. I did pick up the basics pretty quickly, and I might have become a good pianist at that young age. But I was so determined not to try, not to be anybody different that I learned to play only the most ear-splitting preludes, the most discordant hymns.

Over the next year, I practiced like this, dutifully in my own way. And then one day I heard my mother and her friend Lindo Jong both talking in a loud bragging tone of voice so others could hear. It was after church, and I was leaning against the brick wall wearing a dress with stiff white petticoats. Auntie Lindo's daughter, Waverly, who was about my age, was standing farther down the wall about five feet away. We had grown up together and shared all the closeness of two sisters squabbling over crayons and dolls. In other words, for the most part, we hated each other. I thought she was snotty. Waverly Jong had gained a certain amount of fame as "Chinatown's Littlest Chinese Chess Champion."

"She bring home too many trophy," lamented Auntie Lindo that Sunday. "All day she play chess. All day I have no time do nothing but dust off her winnings." She threw a scolding look at Waverly, who pretended not to see her.

"You lucky you don't have this problem," said Auntie Lindo with a sigh to   45
my mother.

And my mother squared her shoulders and bragged: "Our problem worser than yours. If we ask Jing-mei wash dish, she hear nothing but music. It's like you can't stop this natural talent."

And right then, I was determined to put a stop to her foolish pride.

A few weeks later, Old Chong and my mother conspired to have me play in a talent show which would be held in the church hall. By then, my parents had saved up enough to buy me a secondhand piano, a black Wurlitzer spinet with a scarred bench. It was the showpiece of our living room.

For the talent show, I was to play a piece called "Pleading Child" from Schumann's *Scenes from Childhood*. It was a simple, moody piece that sounded more difficult than it was. I was supposed to memorize the whole thing, playing the repeat parts twice to make the piece sound longer. But I dawdled over it, playing a few bars and then cheating, looking up to see what notes followed. I never really listened to what I was playing. I daydreamed about being somewhere else, about being someone else.

The part I liked to practice best was the fancy curtsy: right foot out, touch   50
the rose on the carpet with a pointed foot, sweep to the side, left leg bends, look up and smile.

My parents invited all the couples from the Joy Luck Club to witness my debut. Auntie Lindo and Uncle Tin were there. Waverly and her two older brothers had also come. The first two rows were filled with children both younger and older than I was. The littlest ones got to go first. They recited simple nursery rhymes, squawked out tunes on miniature violins, twirled Hula Hoops, pranced in pink ballet tutus, and when they bowed or curtsied, the audience would sigh in unison, "Awww," and then clap enthusiastically.

When my turn came, I was very confident. I remember my childish excitement. It was as if I knew, without a doubt, that the prodigy side of me really did exist. I had no fear whatsoever, no nervousness. I remember thinking to myself, This is it! This is it! I looked out over the audience, at my mother's blank face, my father's yawn, Auntie Lindo's stiff-lipped smile, Waverly's sulky expression. I had on a white dress layered with sheets of lace, and a pink bow in my Peter Pan haircut. As I sat down I envisioned people jumping to their feet and Ed Sullivan rushing up to introduce me to everyone on TV.

And I started to play. It was so beautiful. I was so caught up in how lovely I looked that at first I didn't worry how I would sound. So it was a surprise to me when I hit the first wrong note and I realized something didn't sound quite right. And then I hit another and another followed that. A chill started at the top of my head and began to trickle down. Yet I couldn't stop playing, as though my hands were bewitched. I kept thinking my fingers would adjust themselves back, like a train switching to the right track. I played this strange jumble through two repeats, the sour notes staying with me all the way to the end.

When I stood up, I discovered my legs were shaking. Maybe I had just been nervous and the audience, like Old Chong, had seen me go through the right motions and had not heard anything wrong at all. I swept my right foot out, went down on my knee, looked up and smiled. The room was quiet, except for Old Chong, who was beaming and shouting, "Bravo! Bravo! Well done!" But then I saw my mother's face, her stricken face. The audience clapped weakly, and as I walked back to my chair, with my whole face quivering as I tried not to cry, I heard a little boy whisper loudly to his mother, "That was awful," and the mother whispered back, "Well, she certainly tried."

And now I realized how many people were in the audience, the whole world it seemed. I was aware of eyes burning into my back. I felt the shame of my mother and father as they sat stiffly throughout the rest of the show.

55

We could have escaped during intermission. Pride and some strange sense of honor must have anchored my parents to their chairs. And so we watched it all: the eighteen-year-old boy with a fake mustache who did a magic show and juggled flaming hoops while riding a unicycle. The breasted girl with white makeup who sang from *Madame Butterfly* and got honorable mention. And the eleven-year-old boy who won first prize playing a tricky violin song that sounded like a busy bee.

After the show, the Hsus, the Jongs, and the St. Clairs from the Joy Luck Club came up to my mother and father.

"Lots of talented kids," Auntie Lindo said vaguely, smiling broadly.

"That was somethin' else," said my father, and I wondered if he was refer-ring to me in a humorous way, or whether he even remembered what I had done.

Waverly looked at me and shrugged her shoulders. "You aren't a genius   60
like me," she said matter-of-factly. And if I hadn't felt so bad, I would have pulled her braids and punched her stomach.

But my mother's expression was what devastated me: a quiet, blank look that said she had lost everything. I felt the same way, and it seemed as if everybody were now coming up, like gawkers at the scene of an accident, to see what parts were actually missing. When we got on the bus to go home, my father was humming the busy-bee tune and my mother was silent. I kept thinking she wanted to wait until we got home before shouting at me. But when my father unlocked the door to our apartment, my mother walked in and then went to the back, into the bedroom. No accusations. No blame. And in a way, I felt disappointed. I had been waiting for her to start shouting, so I could shout back and cry and blame her for all my misery.

I assumed my talent-show fiasco meant I never had to play the piano again. But two days later, after school, my mother came out of the kitchen and saw me watching TV.

"Four clock," she reminded me as if it were any other day. I was stunned, as though she were asking me to go through the talent-show torture again. I wedged myself more tightly in front of the TV.

"Turn off TV," she called from the kitchen five minutes later.

I didn't budge. And then I decided. I didn't have to do what my mother said   65
anymore. I wasn't her slave. This wasn't China. I had listened to her before and look what happened. She was the stupid one.

She came out from the kitchen and stood in the arched entryway of the living room. "Four clock," she said once again, louder.

"I'm not going to play anymore," I said nonchalantly. "Why should I? I'm not a genius."

She walked over and stood in front of the TV. I saw her chest was heaving up and down in an angry way.

"No!" I said, and I now felt stronger, as if my true self had finally emerged. So this was what had been inside me all along.

"No! I won't!" I screamed.   70

She yanked me by the arm, pulled me off the floor, snapped off the TV. She was frighteningly strong, half pulling, half carrying me toward the piano as I kicked the throw rugs under my feet. She lifted me up and onto the hard bench. I was sobbing by now, looking at her bitterly. Her chest was heaving even more and her mouth was open, smiling crazily as if she were pleased I was crying.

"You want me to be someone that I'm not!" I sobbed. "I'll never be the kind of daughter you want me to be!"

"Only two kinds of daughters," she shouted in Chinese. "Those who are obedient and those who follow their own mind! Only one kind of daughter can live in this house. Obedient daughter!"

"Then I wish I wasn't your daughter. I wish you weren't my mother," I shouted. As I said these things I got scared. I felt like worms and toads and slimy things were crawling out of my chest, but it also felt good, as if this awful side of me had surfaced, at last.

"Too late change this," said my mother shrilly.

And I could sense her anger rising to its breaking point. I wanted to see it spill over. And that's when I remembered the babies she had lost in China, the ones we never talked about. "Then I wish I'd never been born!" I shouted. "I wish I were dead! Like them."

It was as if I had said the magic words, Alakazam!—and her face went blank, her mouth closed, her arms went slack, and she backed out of the room, stunned, as if she were blowing away like a small brown leaf, thin, brittle, lifeless.

It was not the only disappointment my mother felt in me. In the years that followed, I failed her so many times, each time asserting my own will, my right to fall short of expectations. I didn't get straight As. I didn't become class president. I didn't get into Stanford. I dropped out of college.

For unlike my mother, I did not believe I could be anything I wanted to be. I could only be me.

And for all those years, we never talked about the disaster at the recital or my terrible accusations afterward at the piano bench. All that remained unchecked, like a betrayal that was now unspeakable. So I never found a way to ask her why she had hoped for something so large that failure was inevitable.

And even worse, I never asked her what frightened me the most: Why had she given up hope?

For after our struggle at the piano, she never mentioned my playing again. The lessons stopped, the lid to the piano was closed, shutting out the dust, my misery, and her dreams.

So she surprised me. A few years ago, she offered to give me the piano, for my thirtieth birthday. I had not played in all those years. I saw the offer as a sign of forgiveness, a tremendous burden removed.

"Are you sure?" I asked shyly. "I mean, won't you and Dad miss it?"

"No, this your piano," she said firmly. "Always your piano. You only one can play."

"Well, I probably can't play anymore," I said. "It's been years."

"You pick up fast," said my mother, as if she knew this was certain. "You have natural talent. You could been genius if you want to."

"No I couldn't."

"You just not trying," said my mother. And she was neither angry nor sad. She said it as if to announce a fact that could never be disproved. "Take it," she said.

But I didn't at first. It was enough that she had offered it to me. And after that, every time I saw it in my parents' living room, standing in front of the bay windows, it made me feel proud, as if it were a shiny trophy I had won back.

Last week I sent a tuner over to my parents' apartment and had the piano reconditioned, for purely sentimental reasons. My mother had died a few months before and I had been getting things in order for my father, a little bit at a time. I put the jewelry in special silk pouches. The sweaters she had knitted in yellow, pink, bright orange—all the colors I hated—I put those in moth-proof boxes. I found some old Chinese silk dresses, the kind with little slits up the sides. I rubbed the old silk against my skin, then wrapped them in tissue and decided to take them home with me.

After I had the piano tuned, I opened the lid and touched the keys. It sounded even richer than I remembered. Really, it was a very good piano. Inside the bench were the same exercise notes with handwritten scales, the same secondhand music books with their covers held together with yellow tape.

I opened up the Schumann book to the dark little piece I had played at the recital. It was on the left-hand side of the page, "Pleading Child." It looked more difficult than I remembered. I played a few bars, surprised at how easily the notes came back to me.

And for the first time, or so it seemed, I noticed the piece on the right-hand side. It was called "Perfectly Contented." I tried to play this one as well. It had a lighter melody but the same flowing rhythm and turned out to be quite easy. "Pleading Child" was shorter but slower; "Perfectly Contented" was longer but faster. And after I played them both a few times, I realized they were two halves of the same song. *[1989]*

≣ THINKING ABOUT THE TEXT

1. Most sons and daughters struggle to establish their own identities. Does this seem true in "Two Kinds"? Does the cultural difference between the immigrant mother and Americanized daughter intensify their struggle? Do you have different goals in life than your parents do?

2. Do you agree with the mother's belief that "you could be anything you wanted to be in America" (para. 1)? Does race matter? Gender? Ethnicity? Religion? Sexual orientation?

3. What do you believe each character learned from the argument at the piano bench the day after the recital?

4. How does Tan establish the differing personalities of her characters? Through details? Dialogue? Anecdotes? Do the main characters change significantly? Does she tell us or show us?

5. Do you sympathize with the mother or with the daughter? Should parents channel their children toward selected activities? Or should parents let their children choose their own paths? Can parents push their children too much? Why would they do this?

≣ MAKING COMPARISONS

1. Do you think Emily's mother in Olsen's story would want to be like the Chinese mother if given the opportunity? Which mother would you prefer to have? Why?

2. One mother seems to do too little, the other too much. Is this how you read these two stories? Is the lesson of Olsen's and Tan's stories that mothers can't win no matter what they do? Or do you have a more optimistic interpretation?

3. Which daughter's life seems more difficult? How possible is it to say from the outside looking in?

ALMA LUZ VILLANUEVA
Her Choice

Alma Luz Villanueva (b. 1944) is a Mexican-American writer of short fiction, poetry, and novels. She was born in Lompoc, California and raised in the Mission District of San Francisco by her maternal grandmother, a Yaqui healer. She has taught at several institutions, including the University of California, San Diego, Stanford University and Pacific University. She taught for twenty years at Antioch University in Los Angeles. Among her many awards are the American Book Award in 1989 for The Ultraviolet Sky and the Best American Poetry in 1996 for "Crazy Courage." One critical assessment of her work noted her "passionate view of the world from a feminine perspective..." that stresses the "joy of life..." in the face of "suffering, injustice and human weaknesses." The following story was written in 1981 and appeared in the anthology Between Mothers and Daughters *(1985). She lives in San Miguel de Allende, Mexico.*

The way her whole body moves, the way she sits: the mood of sulky expectancy. The longing. She's hardly sixteen, about the same age her mother was when she had her. The coincidence was too obvious.

I always wanted you to make love from your own choice the first time — not to be raped or forced in any way. I always wanted you to enjoy your own body, the mother thinks. She knows her daughter longs to be pregnant — she feels it like a magnet. She feels pulled by her daughter's longing, and her own — the body's strange urge to fill up warm and full and sexual. Only, her daughter's urge is to the boy, her first lover, and her own to the knowledge of baby weight. The smell, the feel, the urgent suckle, the silent language of mother-lust.

Tania heard her mother and friends talking, always, about the most intimate things. She loved to listen. It made her tremble. And when she heard her mother's voice lower, she felt cheated. There's *more*, she thought.

Tania had sat on her mother's lap until her legs dangled quite comfortably on the floor. They had a game. When Tania would come home after school, she'd open the front door and shout, "I'm home!" Her mother, wherever she was, would sit down, and Tania would leap on her. They'd talk and smell each other, then Tania's mother would spank her on the panties and tell her to change and go play.

Little by little, as Tania grew older, she'd loiter by the older women. Then, once she sat down and they all looked at her, exchanged looks, and let her stay.

Tania liked her mother's friends better than her own. They really liked each other. She loved to go to the different women's houses and spend the night, being everyone's daughter. That's about when she stopped needing her mother to come during the night and lie next to her, talking, till the fear went away. That's about when she began to keep a secret or two from her mother.

"How are you feeling?" Vida asked.

"Okay, I guess, Mom—kind of sad," Tania replied.

"Do you want some coffee? I'm going to make some." That meant a talk Tania slowly sipped the coffee. It didn't even smell good, though she knew the coffee must be delicious. She and her mother had talked over pots of it, talking at faster pitches, till they realized they'd had enough—the ritual over. They'd go out to the bridge and sit and let the sun cook their faces, their tongues resting in their wet hollows. Or sometimes they'd separate in a burst—not one more word—to a task, to a separateness that each respected. Though, sometimes, Tania would shout, "Mom, can I have a ride to the bookstore?" where she worked. Vida replied with studied irritation in her voice, implying she was late because they'd been talking, "Okay, but I don't want to pick you up tonight—so get a ride. If you really can't get a ride, call." You to your world, me to mine—I'm not a flunky, Vida thought. Balancing, always balancing, this growth—mother to daughter, daughter to mother.

There was no exchange, no flow between them today. Vida looked at her daughter and realized that to pry, would mean to pry a fury from Tania. She wasn't interested in doing that. It felt so heavy, sullen like clotted blood. A dam of blood needing to be released, Vida thought: a dam of dark anger where her child once was. There, she had been able to mirror herself once, quite clearly, in the pools of her daughter's eyes. Now, Tania locked her out with churned mud from a bottom that left her dazed.

They lived side by side like two women, some sympathy taking the place of words. Vida, herself, was planning to leave her second husband. *Planning* was the word: again? how? why? I must. She could think of having a child entirely separate from a man, except for the short tenderness of lovemaking. It was as though a man considered it a victory to make a woman pregnant. Then the victory lost its flavor, its appeal altogether; after all, the prize was won. It took her three children to realize this; three offerings to the male. Now she could envision having one for herself, if she chose. After all, these children *were* for herself—she hadn't blundered that far. They gave her a joy that seemed, at times, inexhaustible.

Tania's boyfriend stopped dropping by the house and waved quickly, looking away, in the street.

"How's Scott?" Vida would ask neutrally.

"He's all right," Tania would answer just as neutrally.

Oh, she's learned very well, Vida thought, letting it go. If she pressed, Tania looked trapped and the water would rise to her eyes. So Vida waited, the blood clotting thicker, it seemed. Something. A flesh, a membrane, a growth wouldn't let them reach or touch.

Tania remembered her father as charming and handsome and fun, when he wanted to be. Then, she remembered him gone for long periods (with terrible relief); then home, drunk (she remembered flying into the room, toward the end, just before her father left, when a fight seemed worse than the others—her mother yelling, "Don't you touch me!"). She remembered screaming, "You leave *my* mother alone!" He'd grabbed Tania by the arm, leading her back to bed, trying to say things like, "This is between your mother and I." Tania was struggling, still crying hysterically, and Vida ran in, pulling her daughter from him, shouting, "Leave us alone, goddamn you!" It was a moment of murder; they all knew it. He could kill her; it in was his power—but Vida was so angry, so desperate she'd kill her husband if he touched either of them now. He left, Tania remembered.

Tania loved her mother's strength and worried about her mother's weakness. But, then, she knew her mother—a cup of coffee, a braided cinnamon roll, a special omelet, and there was her mother, full, again. At the center of her mother was a power she had never seen crushed.

Tania had been cutting school. They'd called with a list of days that were inexcusable. A day too beautiful to go to school, a day to stay home and hide: this Vida had condoned, always. But this new creature wanted to flaunt old trusts.

Tania walked in an hour late, with an off-hand apology and no offer to help with dinner.

"*Where* are you late from, Tania?" Vida spit.

Tania felt her mother open and close the door in an instant. She was in, whether she answered or not, and Tania knew it.

"Can I talk to you about it later?"

"I'll give you till tonight, and no later." And Tania knew she meant it. She'd heard everything in her mother's voice: anger, hurt, disappointment in a trust so long extended. The weapons of the gentle are harsher than the weapons of the cruel, Tania thought. The first seems inside of you and so hard to distinguish. The other can be fought like an outside pain.

Well, I can lie and be punished like everyone else, Tania comforted herself, and went to help with dinner in the guise of a sulky child.

Later, after dinner, the dishes were washed, the last log of the night in the fire toward morning—she came into her mother's room to lie:

"I'm pregnant. Tomorrow I'm going for an abortion. That's where I was all those days, trying to get an abortion." Her eyes were clear, the dam burst and nearly drowned Vida.

Vida choked, "My grandchild!" It slapped Tania's face. No anger, no shame—that would come later, Tania thought. She ran to her room and heard her mother begin to cry in a horrible hoarse voice, like something ancient being pulled from her belly. She'd never heard her mother cry like that before, and she was instantly frightened and sorry. She heard Vida slam and lock her door, and every time Tania passed the room that night, she knew a candle was burning, which made her feel a little better. She knew her mother was thinking and taking comfort from that thin flame.

The fire was dying in the fireplace. Tania poured herself a glass of wine, taking it to her room. In the dark she drank it, lay on her stomach and cried her own tears. She didn't want this child: she knew that. She fell into her own sleep.

Tania woke up to the smell of coffee and remembered, instantly, the bus schedule. She ran to the bathroom, got dressed, ran to the kitchen trying not to look at Vida.

"How are you getting there?"

"By bus," Tania whispered.

Vida's eyes were huge in her head, "I'll take you."

Tania stumbled to her mother's arms, bending her head just a little, heaving her sorrow on the small shoulder. She had outgrown her mother this year, only in height.

Now they were both women.

≡ THINKING ABOUT THE TEXT

1. Explain what is meant by "the silent language of mother-lust" (in the second paragraph). How might this be something specific to Vida or to mothers? Women? How might cultural context figure into your answer?

2. Comment on Tania's preference: She "liked her mother's friends better than her own." Why might this be unusual for a sixteen-year-old? Why do you think a teenager would be drawn to them? Why would teenagers you know be reluctant to "hang out" with them?

3. Throughout the story there is a tension between Tania and Vida, an attraction and then "Something. [that] wouldn't let them reach or touch" How does this ambivalence remind you in any way of your own adolescence?

4. Does either Vida or Tania want this baby? Is this ambiguous or clear? Is it clear who "her" refers to in the story's title?

5. Comment on the last sentence. Is this Villanueva's judgment? Tania's? Vida's? Is being a woman subjective or objective? How might it depend on cultural context or the historical moment? What is your definition of "womanhood"?

≡ MAKING COMPARISONS

1. What would be Emily's mother's response if at sixteen Emily became pregnant? How about Tan's? Explain.

2. Which parental relationship in these three stories is closest to your own? Explain.

3. Comment on the degree of choice each daughter has in these stories.

≡ WRITING ABOUT ISSUES

1. Write an essay that argues that choice or the lack of it is the central dynamic for the daughters in these three stories.

2. Write a brief essay arguing that each of the mothers presented in Olsen's, Tan's, and Villanueva stories is either a good or a bad model for parenting.

3. Write a personal-experience narrative about a time when your parents pushed you too hard or too little or wanted you to be someone you thought you were not. Argue that their behavior had a good or bad outcome in your life.

4. In the following excerpt from Janet Mason Ellerby's essay in *Choice* (2007), she recounts her experience of being sixteen and pregnant in 1964:

> It was 1964. Roe v. Wade was still nine years in the future and I was three months pregnant.
>
> Where was I that morning? In complete psychological retreat. If anyone had thought to ask me, "What do you want?" I would not have known how to answer. I watched the adults around me as they began to make important decisions for me, and I put up no resistance. I was shocked by what was happening to my body, that I had no control over it, that it was doing something monumental without my knowledge or consent.
>
> My body was not my own; perhaps it had never been. When it had escaped my parents' control, Alec had immediately taken it up, and when he had abandoned it, a baby had claimed it. It may sound as if I am unwilling to take responsibility for my actions, but in fact, I did not completely understand that my body was my own dominion, that I could say what did and did not happen to it. In significant ways, women were not led to believe that they owned their bodies—the state, their husbands, or their fathers did. I willingly handed my body and my future back to my parents. Their money and authority took over, and I surrendered all bids at self-control. I would not be allowed to make another decision for a long, long time.
>
> What about an abortion? My parents certainly had the means to pay for the travel and procedure, but the hermetic life of our well-heeled suburb prevented them from knowing how one might proceed with such a plan. When I tell people who grew up in working-class neighborhoods this story they are always amazed that no one consider that option. But there were no back alleys in San Marino, nothing illegal whatsoever, and my parents' principled moral rigor would have prevented them from considering anything unlawful in the first place. If an abortion had been obtainable, would I have been able to make my own informed, thoughtful choice? Regrettably, no. I was in my parents' hands entirely with no more free will than a newborn. The

baby I carried was theirs too, to do with as they saw fit. I would have agreed to anything.

The next morning, my clothes were packed and I was put on a plane for Cleveland. My aunt had agreed to care for me throughout the pregnancy. When my parents and I said goodbye at the terminal gate at LAX, my mother's anger helped her avoid any signs of grief or reservation, but my father seem defeated, unsure. I had never seen this tall, confident, controlled man in any kind of emotional distress, but there he was, noticeably stooped, weeping. Despite his great disappointment, he was suffering from the decision to send me away—a necessary banishment, he must have reasoned, but exile just the same.

I turned, leaving them there, watching me, and started up the ramp and into the plane. The die was cast; there was no turning back. I found my seat and stared blankly, utterly empty, out the window as the plane accelerated, the first step in a perilous journey that no one could have anticipated. The plane gained altitude, the smoggy maze of the LA grid spread out beneath me, and I knew that nothing would ever be the same.

Write an essay that agrees or disagrees with the proposition that choice is or always has been complicated and critical in a woman's life. In your argument refer to Ellerby's memoir, Villanueva's story, and your own experience.

TOBIAS WOLFF, "The Rich Brother"

JAMES BALDWIN, "Sonny's Blues"

Although the expression "blood is thicker than water" suggests that brothers and sisters should support each other, the reality is often more complex. Children growing up together share intense emotional ties, but affection and loyalty sometimes conflict with hostility and jealousy. Children often feel they are competing for their parents' attention and love, a rivalry often played out over a lifetime and intensified as siblings choose different lifestyles. Well into adulthood, brothers and sisters often find their relationships with each other conflicted by unresolved issues of mutual responsibility and disparities in values as well as individual issues of financial success, self-esteem, and guilt. The siblings in the following two stories, separated by age and disparate occupations, engage in a psychologically complex dance that ebbs and flows over their lives. They struggle to understand each other and ultimately themselves, for as with all of us, healthy relationships with siblings start with a healthy relationship with oneself.

■ **BEFORE YOU READ**

How would you describe your relationship with your siblings? Did rivalry ever play a part? Does it now? Do you consider your siblings' futures as similar to yours? Is it important for brothers and sisters to look after each other? Or might that create more problems than it solves?

TOBIAS WOLFF
The Rich Brother

Tobias Wolff (b. 1945) is known chiefly for his short stories. The following piece comes from his second collection, Back in the World *(1985). He has produced two other volumes of stories,* In the Garden of the North American Martyrs *(1981) and* The Night in Question *(1996), and a short novel,* The Barracks Thief *(1984). His latest novel is* Old School *(2004). Wolff is also the author of two memoirs. In the first,* This Boy's Life *(1989), he recalls his parents' divorce and subsequent family dramas. These include wanderings with his mother through the West and Northwest; arguments with his abusive stepfather; occasional contact with his real father, who was a habitual liar later imprisoned for fraud; and years of separation from his brother Geoffrey, who eventually became a writer himself.* This Boy's Life *won the* Los Angeles Times *Book Award for biography and later became a movie*

starring Robert De Niro as the stepfather and Leonardo DiCaprio as the young Toby.
Wolff's second memoir, In Pharaoh's Army: Memories of the Lost War *(1994),*
deals mostly with his military service in Vietnam. His most recent collection is
Our Story Begins: New and Selected Stories *(2008). In 2015, he was awarded*
the National Medal of Arts by President Obama. Wolff teaches creative writing at
Stanford University.

There were two brothers, Pete and Donald.

Pete, the older brother, was in real estate. He and his wife had a Century 21 franchise in Santa Cruz. Pete worked hard and made a lot of money, but not any more than he thought he deserved. He had two daughters, a sailboat, a house from which he could see a thin slice of the ocean, and friends doing well enough in their own lives not to wish bad luck on him. Donald, the younger brother, was still single. He lived alone, painted houses when he found the work, and got deeper in debt to Pete when he didn't.

No one would have taken them for brothers. Where Pete was stout and hearty and at home in the world, Donald was bony, grave, and obsessed with the fate of his soul. Over the years Donald had worn the images of two different Perfect Masters around his neck. Out of devotion to the second of these he entered an ashram in Berkeley, where he nearly died of undiagnosed hepatitis. By the time Pete finished paying the medical bills Donald had become a Christian. He drifted from church to church, then joined a pentecostal community that met somewhere in the Mission District to sing in tongues and swap prophecies.

Pete couldn't make sense of it. Their parents were both dead, but while they were alive neither of them had found it necessary to believe in anything. They managed to be decent people without making fools of themselves, and Pete had the same ambition. He thought that the whole thing was an excuse for Donald to take himself seriously.

The trouble was that Donald couldn't content himself with worrying about his own soul. He had to worry about everyone else's, and especially Pete's. He handed down his judgments in ways that he seemed to consider subtle: through significant silence, innuendo, looks of mild despair that said, *Brother, what have you come to?* What Pete had come to, as far as he could tell, was prosperity. That was the real issue between them. Pete prospered and Donald did not prosper.

At the age of forty Pete took up sky diving. He made his first jump with two friends who'd started only a few months earlier and were already doing stunts. He never would have used the word *mystical,* but that was how Pete felt about the experience. Later he made the mistake of trying to describe it to Donald, who kept asking how much it cost and then acted appalled when Pete told him.

"At least I'm trying something new," Pete said. "At least I'm breaking the pattern."

Not long after that conversation Donald also broke the pattern, by going to live on a farm outside Paso Robles. The farm was owned by several members of Donald's community, who had bought it and moved there with the idea of forming a family of faith. That was how Donald explained it in the first letter he sent. Every week Pete heard how happy Donald was, how "in the Lord." He told Pete that he was praying for him, he and the rest of Pete's brothers and sisters on the farm.

"I only have one brother," Pete wanted to answer, "and that's enough." But he kept this thought to himself.

In November the letters stopped. Pete didn't worry about this at first, but when he called Donald at Thanksgiving Donald was grim. He tried to sound upbeat but he didn't try hard enough to make it convincing. "Now listen," Pete said, "you don't have to stay in that place if you don't want to."

"I'll be all right," Donald answered.

"That's not the point. Being all right is not the point. If you don't like what's going on up there, then get out."

"I'm all right," Donald said again, more firmly. "I'm doing fine."

But he called Pete a week later and said that he was quitting the farm. When Pete asked him where he intended to go, Donald admitted that he had no plan. His car had been repossessed just before he left the city, and he was flat broke.

"I guess you'll have to stay with us," Pete said.

Donald put up a show of resistance. Then he gave in. "Just until I get my feet on the ground," he said.

"Right," Pete said. "Check out your options." He told Donald he'd send him money for a bus ticket, but as they were about to hang up Pete changed his mind. He knew that Donald would try hitchhiking to save the fare. Pete didn't want him out on the road all alone where some head case would pick him up, where anything could happen to him.

"Better yet," he said, "I'll come and get you."

"You don't have to do that. I didn't expect you to do that," Donald said. He added, "It's a pretty long drive."

"Just tell me how to get there."

But Donald wouldn't give him directions. He said that the farm was too depressing, that Pete wouldn't like it. Instead, he insisted on meeting Pete at a service station called Jonathan's Mechanical Emporium.

"You must be kidding," Pete said.

"It's close to the highway," Donald said. "I didn't name it."

"That's one for the collection," Pete said.

The day before he left to bring Donald home, Pete received a letter from a man who described himself as "head of household" at the farm where Donald had been living. From this letter Pete learned that Donald had not quit the farm, but had been asked to leave. The letter was written on the back of a mimeographed survey form asking people to record their response to a ceremony of some kind. The last question said:

What did you feel during the liturgy?
a) *Being*
b) *Becoming*
c) *Being and Becoming*
d) *None of the Above*
e) *All of the Above*

Pete tried to forget the letter. But of course he couldn't. Each time he thought of it he felt crowded and breathless, a feeling that came over him again when he drove into the service station and saw Donald sitting against a wall with his head on his knees. It was late afternoon. A paper cup tumbled slowly past Donald's feet, pushed by the damp wind.

Pete honked and Donald raised his head. He smiled at Pete, then stood and stretched. His arms were long and thin and white. He wore a red bandanna across his forehead, a T-shirt with a couple of words on the front. Pete couldn't read them because the letters were inverted.

"Grow up," Pete yelled. "Get a Mercedes."

Donald came up to the window. He bent down and said, "Thanks for coming. You must be totally whipped."

"I'll make it." Pete pointed at Donald's T-shirt. "What's that supposed to say?"   30

Donald looked down at his shirt front. "Try God. I guess I put it on backwards. Pete, could I borrow a couple of dollars? I owe these people for coffee and sandwiches."

Pete took five twenties from his wallet and held them out the window.

Donald stepped back as if horrified. "I don't need that much."

"I can't keep track of all these nickels and dimes," Pete said. "Just pay me back when your ship comes in." He waved the bills impatiently. "Go on— take it."

"Only for now." Donald took the money and went into the service station   35
office. He came out carrying two orange sodas, one of which he gave to Pete as he got into the car. "My treat," he said.

"No bags?"

"Wow, thanks for reminding me." Donald balanced his drink on the dashboard, but the slight rocking of the car as he got out tipped it onto the passenger's seat, where half its contents foamed over before Pete could snatch it up again. Donald looked on while Pete held the bottle out the window, soda running down his fingers.

"Wipe it up," Pete told him. "Quick!"

"With what?"

Pete stared at Donald. "That shirt. Use the shirt."   40

Donald pulled a long face but did as he was told, his pale skin puckering against the wind.

"Great, just great," Pete said. "We haven't even left the gas station yet."

Afterwards, on the highway, Donald said, "This is a new car, isn't it?"

"Yes. This is a new car."

"Is that why you're so upset about the seat?"   45
"Forget it, okay? Let's just forget about it."
"I said I was sorry."
Pete said, "I just wish you'd be more careful. These seats are made of leather. That stain won't come out, not to mention the smell. I don't see why I can't have leather seats that smell like leather instead of orange pop."
"What was wrong with the other car?"
Pete glanced over at Donald. Donald had raised the hood of the blue   50
sweatshirt he'd put on. The peaked hood above his gaunt, watchful face gave him the look of an inquisitor.
"There wasn't anything wrong with it," Pete said. "I just happened to like this one better."
Donald nodded.
There was a long silence between them as Pete drove on and the day darkened toward evening. On either side of the road lay stubble-covered fields. A line of low hills ran along the horizon, topped here and there with trees black against the grey sky. In the approaching line of cars a driver turned on his headlights. Pete did the same.
"So what happened?" he asked. "Farm life not your bag?"
Donald took some time to answer, and at last he said, simply, "It was my   55
fault."
"What was your fault?"
"The whole thing. Don't play dumb, Pete. I know they wrote to you." Donald looked at Pete, then stared out the windshield again.
"I'm not playing dumb."
Donald shrugged.
"All I really know is they asked you to leave," Pete went on. "I don't know   60
any of the particulars."
"I blew it," Donald said. "Believe me, you don't want to hear the gory details."
"Sure I do," Pete said. He added, "Everybody likes the gory details."
"You mean everybody likes to hear how someone messed up."
"Right," Pete said. "That's the way it is here on Spaceship Earth."
Donald bent one knee onto the front seat and leaned against the door so   65
that he was facing Pete instead of the windshield. Pete was aware of Donald's scrutiny. He waited. Night was coming on in a rush now, filling the hollows of the land. Donald's long cheeks and deep-set eyes were dark with shadow. His brow was white. "Do you ever dream about me?" Donald asked.
"Do I ever dream about you? What kind of a question is that? Of course I don't dream about you," Pete said, untruthfully.
"What do you dream about?"
"Sex and money. Mostly money. A nightmare is when I dream I don't have any."
"You're just making that up," Donald said.
Pete smiled.   70

"Sometimes I wake up at night," Donald went on, "and I can tell you're dreaming about me."

"We were talking about the farm," Pete said. "Let's finish that conversation and then we can talk about our various out-of-body experiences and the interesting things we did during previous incarnations."

For a moment Donald looked like a grinning skull; then he turned serious again. "There's not much to tell," he said. "I just didn't do anything right."

"That's a little vague," Pete said.

"Well, like the groceries. Whenever it was my turn to get the groceries I'd   75 blow it somehow. I'd bring the groceries home and half of them would be missing, or I'd have all the wrong things, the wrong kind of flour or the wrong kind of chocolate or whatever. One time I gave them away. It's not funny, Pete."

Pete said, "Who did you give the groceries to?"

"Just some people I picked up on the way home. Some fieldworkers. They had about eight kids with them and they didn't even speak English — just nodded their heads. Still, I shouldn't have given away the groceries. Not all of them, anyway. I really learned my lesson about that. You have to be practical. You have to be fair to yourself." Donald leaned forward, and Pete could sense his excitement. "There's nothing actually wrong with being in business," he said. "As long as you're fair to other people you can still be fair to yourself. I'm thinking of going into business, Pete."

"We'll talk about it," Pete said. "So, that's the story? There isn't any more to it than that?"

"What did they tell you?" Donald asked.

"Nothing."   80

"They must have told you something."

Pete shook his head.

"They didn't tell you about the fire?" When Pete shook his head again Donald regarded him for a time, then folded his arms across his chest and slumped back into the corner.

"Everybody had to take turns cooking dinner. I usually did tuna casserole or spaghetti with garlic bread. But this one night I thought I'd do something different, something really interesting." Donald looked sharply at Pete. "It's all a big laugh to you, isn't it?"

"I'm sorry," Pete said.   85

"You don't know when to quit. You just keep hitting away."

"Tell me about the fire, Donald."

Donald kept watching him. "You have this compulsion to make me look foolish."

"Come off it, Donald. Don't make a big thing out of this."

"I know why you do it. It's because you don't have any purpose in life.   90 You're afraid to relate to people who do, so you make fun of them."

"Relate," Pete said.

"You're basically a very frightened individual," Donald said. "Very threatened. You've always been like that. Do you remember when you used to try to kill me?"

"I don't have any compulsion to make you look foolish, Donald—you do it yourself. You're doing it right now."

"You can't tell me you don't remember," Donald said. "It was after my operation. You remember that?"

"Sort of." Pete shrugged. "Not really."

95

"Oh yes," Donald said. "Do you want to see the scar?"

"I remember you had an operation. I don't remember the specifics, that's all. And I sure as hell don't remember trying to kill you."

"Oh yes," Donald repeated, maddeningly. "You bet your life you did. All the time. The thing was, I couldn't have anything happen to me where they sewed me up because then my intestines would come apart again and poison me. That was a big issue, Pete. Mom was always in a state about me climbing trees and so on. And you used to hit me there every chance you got."

"Mom was in a state every time you burped," Pete said. "I don't know. Maybe I bumped into you accidentally once or twice. I never did it deliberately."

"Every chance you got," Donald said. "Like when the folks went out at
night and left you to baby-sit. I'd hear them say good night, and then I'd hear the car start up, and when they were gone I'd lie there and listen. After a while I would hear you coming down the hall, and I would close my eyes and pretend to be asleep. There were nights when you would stand outside the door, just stand there, and then go away again. But most nights you'd open the door and I would hear you in the room with me, breathing. You'd come over and sit next to me on the bed—you remember, Pete, you have to—you'd sit next to me on the bed and pull the sheets back. If I was on my stomach you'd roll me over. Then you would lift up my pajama shirt and start hitting me on my stitches. You'd hit me as hard as you could, over and over. I was afraid that you'd get mad if you knew I was awake. Is that strange or what? I was afraid that you'd get mad if you found out that I knew you were trying to kill me." Donald laughed. "Come on, you can't tell me you don't remember that."

100

"It might have happened once or twice. Kids do those things. I can't get all excited about something I maybe did twenty-five years ago."

"No maybe about it. You did it."

Pete said, "You're wearing me out with this stuff. We've got a long drive ahead of us and if you don't back off pretty soon we aren't going to make it. You aren't, anyway."

Donald turned away.

"I'm doing my best," Pete said. The self-pity in his own voice made the
words sound like a lie. But they weren't a lie! He was doing his best.

105

The car topped a rise. In the distance Pete saw a cluster of lights that blinked out when he started downhill. There was no moon. The sky was low and black.

"Come to think of it," Pete said, "I did have a dream about you the other night." Then he added, impatiently, as if Donald were badgering him, "A couple of other nights, too. I'm getting hungry," he said.

"The same dream?"

"Different dreams. I only remember one of them. There was something wrong with me, and you were helping out. Taking care of me. Just the two of us. I don't know where everyone else was supposed to be."

Pete left it at that. He didn't tell Donald that in this dream he was blind.   110

"I wonder if that was when I woke up," Donald said. He added, "I'm sorry I got into that thing about my scar. I keep trying to forget it but I guess I never will. Not really. It was pretty strange, having someone around all the time who wanted to get rid of me."

"Kid stuff," Pete said. "Ancient history."

They ate dinner at a Denny's on the other side of King City. As Pete was paying the check he heard a man behind him say, "Excuse me, but I wonder if I might ask which way you're going?" and Donald answer, "Santa Cruz."

"Perfect," the man said.

Pete could see him in the fish-eye mirror above the cash register: a red   115 blazer with some kind of crest on the pocket, little black moustache, glossy black hair combed down on his forehead like a Roman emperor's. A rug, Pete thought. Definitely a rug.

Pete got his change and turned. "Why is that perfect?" he asked.

The man looked at Pete. He had a soft, ruddy face that was doing its best to express pleasant surprise, as if this new wrinkle were all he could have wished for, but the eyes behind the aviator glasses showed signs of regret. His lips were moist and shiny. "I take it you're together," he said.

"You got it," Pete told him.

"All the better, then," the man went on. "It so happens I'm going to Santa Cruz myself. Had a spot of car trouble down the road. The old Caddy let me down."

"What kind of trouble?" Pete asked.   120

"Engine trouble," the man said. "I'm afraid it's a bit urgent. My daughter is sick. Urgently sick. I've got a telegram here." He patted the breast pocket of his blazer.

Before Pete could say anything Donald got into the act again. "No problem," Donald said. "We've got tons of room."

"Not that much room," Pete said.

Donald nodded. "I'll put my things in the trunk."

"The trunk's full," Pete told him.   125

"It so happens I'm traveling light," the man said. "This leg of the trip anyway. In fact, I don't have any luggage at this particular time."

Pete said, "Left it in the old Caddy, did you?"

"Exactly," the man said.

"No problem," Donald repeated. He walked outside and the man went with him. Together they strolled across the parking lot, Pete following at a distance. When they reached Pete's car Donald raised his face to the sky, and the man did the same. They stood there looking up. "Dark night," Donald said.

"Stygian,°" the man said.   130

Stygian: Unremittingly dark and frightening.

Pete still had it in his mind to brush him off, but he didn't do that. Instead he unlocked the door for him. He wanted to see what would happen. It was an adventure, but not a dangerous adventure. The man might steal Pete's ashtrays but he wouldn't kill him. If Pete got killed on the road it would be by some spiritual person in a sweatsuit, someone with his eyes on the far horizon and a wet Try God T-shirt in his duffel bag.

As soon as they left the parking lot the man lit a cigar. He blew a cloud of smoke over Pete's shoulder and sighed with pleasure. "Put it out," Pete told him.

"Of course," the man said. Pete looked in the rearview mirror and saw the man take another long puff before dropping the cigar out the window. "Forgive me," he said. "I should have asked. Name's Webster, by the way."

Donald turned and looked back at him. "First name or last?"

The man hesitated. "Last," he said finally.   135

"I know a Webster," Donald said. "Mick Webster."

"There are many of us," Webster said.

"Big fellow, wooden leg," Pete said.

Donald gave Pete a look.

Webster shook his head. "Doesn't ring a bell. Still, I wouldn't deny the   140
connection. Might be one of the cousinry."

"What's your daughter got?" Pete asked.

"That isn't clear," Webster answered. "It appears to be a female complaint of some nature. Then again it may be tropical." He was quiet for a moment, and added: "If indeed it *is* tropical, I will have to assume some of the blame myself. It was my own vaulting ambition that first led us to the tropics and kept us in the tropics all those many years, exposed to every evil. Truly I have much to answer for. I left my wife there."

Donald said quietly, "You mean she died?"

"I buried her with these hands. The earth will be repaid, gold for gold."

"Which tropics?" Pete asked.   145

"The tropics of Peru."

"What part of Peru are they in?"

"The lowlands," Webster said.

"What's it like down there? In the lowlands."

"Another world," Webster said. His tone was sepulchral. "A world better   150
imagined than described."

"Far out," Pete said.

The three men rode in silence for a time. A line of trucks went past in the other direction, trailers festooned with running lights, engines roaring.

"Yes," Webster said at last, "I have much to answer for."

Pete smiled at Donald, but Donald had turned in his seat again and was gazing at Webster. "I'm sorry about your wife," Donald said.

"What did she die of?" Pete asked.   155

"A wasting illness," Webster said. "The doctors have no name for it, but I do." He leaned forward and said, fiercely, "*Greed.* My greed, not hers. She wanted no part of it."

Pete bit his lip. Webster was a find and Pete didn't want to scare him off by hooting at him. In a voice low and innocent of knowingness, he asked, "What took you there?"

"It's difficult for me to talk about."

"Try," Pete told him.

"A cigar would make it easier."   160

Donald turned to Pete and said, "It's okay with me."

"All right," Pete said. "Go ahead. Just keep the window rolled down."

"Much obliged." A match flared. There were eager sucking sounds.

"Let's hear it," Pete said.

"I am by training an engineer," Webster began. "My work has exposed me   165
to all but one of the continents, to desert and alp and forest, to every terrain and season of the earth. Some years ago I was hired by the Peruvian government to search for tungsten in the tropics. My wife and daughter accompanied me. We were the only white people for a thousand miles in any direction, and we had no choice but to live as the Indians lived—to share their food and drink and even their culture."

Pete said, "You knew the lingo, did you?"

"We picked it up." The ember of the cigar bobbed up and down. "We were used to learning as necessity decreed. At any rate, it became evident after a couple of years that there was no tungsten to be found. My wife had fallen ill and was pleading to be taken home. But I was deaf to her pleas, because by then I was on the trail of another metal—a metal far more valuable than tungsten."

"Let me guess," Pete said. "Gold?"

Donald looked at Pete, then back at Webster.

"Gold," Webster said. "A vein of gold greater than the Mother Lode   170
itself. After I found the first traces of it nothing could tear me away from my search—not the sickness of my wife or anything else. I was determined to uncover the vein, and so I did—but not before I laid my wife to rest. As I say, the earth will be repaid."

Webster was quiet. Then he said, "But life must go on. In the years since my wife's death I have been making the arrangements necessary to open the mine. I could have done it immediately, of course, enriching myself beyond measure, but I knew what that would mean—the exploitation of our beloved Indians, the brutal destruction of their environment. I felt I had too much to atone for already." Webster paused, and when he spoke again his voice was dull and rushed, as if he had used up all the interest he had in his own words. "Instead I drew up a program for returning the bulk of the wealth to the Indians themselves. A kind of trust fund. The interest alone will allow them to secure their ancient lands and rights in perpetuity. At the same time, our investors will be rewarded a thousandfold. Two-thousandfold. Everyone will prosper together."

"That's great," said Donald. "That's the way it ought to be."

Pete said, "I'm willing to bet that you just happen to have a few shares left. Am I right?"

Webster made no reply.

"Well?" Pete knew that Webster was on to him now, but he didn't care. The   175
story had bored him. He'd expected something different, something original,
and Webster had let him down. He hadn't even tried. Pete felt sour and stale. His
eyes burned from cigar smoke and the high beams of road-hogging truckers.
"Douse the stogie," he said to Webster. "I told you to keep the window down."

"Got a little nippy back here."

Donald said, "Hey, Pete. Lighten up."

"Douse it!"

Webster sighed. He got rid of the cigar.

"I'm a wreck," Pete said to Donald. "You want to drive for a while?"   180

Donald nodded.

Pete pulled over and they changed places.

Webster kept his counsel in the back seat. Donald hummed while he drove,
until Pete told him to stop. Then everything was quiet.

Donald was humming again when Pete woke up. Pete stared sullenly at the
road, at the white lines sliding past the car. After a few moments of this he
turned and said, "How long have I been out?"

Donald glanced at him. "Twenty, twenty-five minutes."   185

Pete looked behind him and saw that Webster was gone. "Where's our
friend?"

"You just missed him. He got out in Soledad. He told me to say thanks and
good-bye."

"Soledad? What about his sick daughter? How did he explain her away?"

"He has a brother living there. He's going to borrow a car from him and
drive the rest of the way in the morning."

"I'll bet his brother's living there," Pete said. "Doing fifty concurrent life   190
sentences. His brother and his sister and his mom and his dad."

"I kind of liked him," Donald said.

"I'm sure you did," Pete said wearily.

"He was interesting. He's been places."

"His cigars had been places, I'll give you that."

"Come on, Pete."   195

"Come on yourself. What a phony."

"You don't know that."

"Sure I do."

"How? How do you know?"

Pete stretched. "Brother, there are some things you're just born knowing.   200
What's the gas situation?"

"We're a little low."

"Then why didn't you get some more?"

"I wish you wouldn't snap at me like that," Donald said.

"Then why don't you use your head? What if we run out?"

"We'll make it," Donald said. "I'm pretty sure we've got enough to make it.   205
You didn't have to be so rude to him," Donald added.

Pete took a deep breath. "I don't feel like running out of gas tonight, okay?"

Donald pulled in at the next station they came to and filled the tank while Pete went to the men's room. When Pete came back, Donald was sitting in the passenger's seat. The attendant came up to the driver's window as Pete got in behind the wheel. He bent down and said, "Twelve fifty-five."

"You heard the man," Pete said to Donald.

Donald looked straight ahead. He didn't move.

"Cough up," Pete said. "This trip's on you."   210

"I can't."

"Sure you can. Break out that wad."

Donald glanced up at the attendant, then at Pete. "Please," he said, "Pete, I don't have it anymore."

Pete took this in. He nodded, and paid the attendant.

Donald began to speak when they left the station but Pete cut him off. He   215
said, "I don't want to hear from you right now. You just keep quiet or I swear to God I won't be responsible."

They left the fields and entered a tunnel of tall trees. The trees went on and on. "Let me get this straight," Pete said at last. "You don't have the money I gave you."

"You treated him like a bug or something," Donald said.

"You don't have the money," Pete said again.

Donald shook his head.

"Since I bought dinner, and since we didn't stop anywhere in between, I   220
assume you gave it to Webster. Is that right? Is that what you did with it?"

"Yes."

Pete looked at Donald. His face was dark under the hood but he still managed to convey a sense of remove, as if none of this had anything to do with him.

"Why?" Pete asked. "Why did you give it to him?" When Donald didn't answer, Pete said, "A hundred dollars. Gone. Just like that. I *worked* for that money, Donald."

"I know, I know," Donald said.

"You don't know! How could you? You get money by holding out your hand."   225

"I work too," Donald said.

"You work too. Don't kid yourself, brother."

Donald leaned toward Pete, about to say something, but Pete cut him off again.

"You're not the only one on the payroll, Donald. I don't think you understand that. I have a family."

"Pete, I'll pay you back."   230

"Like hell you will. A hundred dollars!" Pete hit the steering wheel with the palm of his hand. "Just because you think I hurt some goofball's feelings. Jesus, Donald."

"That's not the reason," Donald said. "And I didn't just *give* him the money."

"What do you call it, then? What do you call what you did?"

"I *invested* it. I wanted a share, Pete." When Pete looked over at him Donald nodded and said again, "I wanted a share."

Pete said, "I take it you're referring to the gold mine in Peru." 235

"Yes," Donald said.

"You believe that such a gold mine exists?"

Donald looked at Pete, and Pete could see him just beginning to catch on. "You'll believe anything," Pete said. "Won't you? You really will believe anything at all."

"I'm sorry," Donald said, and turned away.

Pete drove on between the trees and considered the truth of what he had 240
just said — that Donald would believe anything at all. And it came to him that it would be just like this unfair life for Donald to come out ahead in the end, by believing in some outrageous promise that would turn out to be true and that he, Pete, would reject out of hand because he was too wised up to listen to anybody's pitch anymore except for laughs. What a joke. What a joke if there really was a blessing to be had, and the blessing didn't come to the one who deserved it, the one who did all the work, but to the other.

And as if this had already happened Pete felt a shadow move upon him, darkening his thoughts. After a time he said, "I can see where all this is going, Donald."

"I'll pay you back," Donald said.

"No," Pete said. "You won't pay me back. You can't. You don't know how. All you've ever done is take. All your life."

Donald shook his head.

"I see exactly where this is going," Pete went on. "You can't work, you 245
can't take care of yourself, you believe anything anyone tells you. I'm stuck with you, aren't I?" He looked over at Donald. "I've got you on my hands for good."

Donald pressed his fingers against the dashboard as if to brace himself. "I'll get out," he said.

Pete kept driving.

"Let me out," Donald said. "I mean it, Pete."

"Do you?"

Donald hesitated. "Yes," he said. 250

"Be sure," Pete told him. "This is it. This is for keeps."

"I mean it."

"All right. You made the choice." Pete braked the car sharply and swung it to the shoulder of the road. He turned off the engine and got out. Trees loomed on both sides, shutting out the sky. The air was cold and musty. Pete took Donald's duffel bag from the back seat and set it down behind the car. He stood there, facing Donald in the red glow of the taillights. "It's better this way," Pete said.

Donald just looked at him.

"Better for you," Pete said. 255

Donald hugged himself. He was shaking. "You don't have to say all that," he told Pete. "I don't blame you."

"Blame me? What the hell are you talking about? Blame me for what?"

"For anything," Donald said.

"I want to know what you mean by blame me."

"Nothing. Nothing, Pete. You'd better get going. God bless you."   260

"That's it," Pete said. He dropped to one knee, searching the packed dirt with his hands. He didn't know what he was looking for, his hands would know when they found it.

Donald touched Pete's shoulder. "You'd better go," he said.

Somewhere in the trees Pete heard a branch snap. He stood up. He looked at Donald, then went back to the car and drove away. He drove fast, hunched over the wheel, conscious of the way he was hunched and the shallowness of his breathing, refusing to look in the mirror above his head until there was nothing behind him but darkness.

Then he said, "A hundred dollars," as if there were someone to hear.

The trees gave way to fields. Metal fences ran beside the road, plastered   265
with windblown scraps of paper. Tule fog hung above the ditches, spilling into the road, dimming the ghostly halogen lights that burned in the yards of the farms Pete passed. The fog left beads of water rolling up the windshield.

Pete rummaged among his cassettes. He found Pachelbel's Canon and pushed it into the tape deck. When the violins began to play he leaned back and assumed an attentive expression as if he were really listening to them. He smiled to himself like a man at liberty to enjoy music, a man who has finished his work and settled his debts, done all things meet and due.

And in this way, smiling, nodding to the music, he went another mile or so and pretended that he was not already slowing down, that he was not going to turn back, that he would be able to drive on like this, alone, and have the right answer when his wife stood before him in the doorway of his home and asked, Where is he? Where is your brother?   [1985]

≡ THINKING ABOUT THE TEXT

1. Are you more sympathetic to Donald's side or to Pete's side in this story? Do you agree with the comment that "everybody likes to hear how someone messed up" (para. 63)? Does Webster con Donald? Would you be angry with Donald for giving Webster your money? Does Pete want Donald to look foolish? Is Donald foolish?

2. How do you interpret Donald's story about Pete hitting his stitches? Was Pete trying to get rid of Donald? What could his reason have been?

3. Why doesn't Pete tell Donald he was blind in his dream? How do you interpret this dream? Is the heart of their dispute "prosperity," or is it something else?

4. In his recent book, *Our Story Begins: New and Selected Stories* (2008), Wolff revises the end of this story. In paragraph 261, he deletes the last

two sentences and adds instead, "and took a step toward Donald." Some readers were disappointed that he takes out what they see as an enigmatic action that adds mystery and complexity to the ending. Do you agree? Why do you think Wolff made this change?

5. Why would Pete turn around to get Donald? Why would he keep going? What would you do? Why?

JAMES BALDWIN
Sonny's Blues

James Baldwin (1924–1987) wanted to be a writer from the time he was a boy growing up in Harlem. He continued his writing through high school while also following in his foster father's footsteps by doing some preaching. On his own at age eighteen, Baldwin left Greenwich Village in 1948 and moved to Paris. He lived in France for eight years before returning to New York, where he wrote widely about the civil rights movement. Indeed, Baldwin's passionate and eloquent essays, like those in Notes of a Native Son *(1955) and* The Fire Next Time *(1963), exploring the place of African Americans in contemporary society, are considered among the best nonfiction of his generation.*

Being an artist and an African American were lifelong central issues for Baldwin. His fiction confronts the psychological challenges that were inevitable for black writers searching for identity in America. Themes of responsibility, pain, identity, frustration, and bitterness are woven into his fiction along with understanding, equanimity, love, and tolerance. "Sonny's Blues," from Going to Meet the Man *(1965), is one of his strongest dramatizations of the struggles and achievements of black artists.*

I read about it in the paper, in the subway, on my way to work. I read it, and I couldn't believe it, and I read it again. Then perhaps I just stared at it, at the newsprint spelling out his name, spelling out the story. I stared at it in the swinging lights of the subway car, and in the faces and bodies of the people, and in my own face, trapped in the darkness which roared outside.

It was not to be believed and I kept telling myself that, as I walked from the subway station to the high school. And at the same time I couldn't doubt it. I was scared, scared for Sonny. He became real to me again. A great block of ice got settled in my belly and kept melting there slowly all day long, while I taught my classes algebra. It was a special kind of ice. It kept melting, sending trickles of ice water all up and down my veins, but it never got less. Sometimes it hardened and seemed to expand until I felt my guts were going to come spilling out or that I was going to choke or scream. This would always be at a moment when I was remembering some specific thing Sonny had once said or done.

When he was about as old as the boys in my classes his face had been bright and open, there was a lot of copper in it; and he'd had wonderfully direct brown eyes, and great gentleness and privacy. I wondered what he looked like now. He had been picked up, the evening before, in a raid on an apartment downtown, for peddling and using heroin.

I couldn't believe it: but what I mean by that is that I couldn't find any room for it anywhere inside me. I had kept it outside me for a long time. I hadn't wanted to know. I had had suspicions, but I didn't name them, I kept putting them away. I told myself that Sonny was wild, but he wasn't crazy. And he'd always been a good boy, he hadn't ever turned hard or evil or disrespectful, the way kids can, so quick, so quick, especially in Harlem. I didn't want to believe that I'd ever see my brother going down, coming to nothing, all that light in his face gone out, in the condition I'd already seen so many others. Yet it had happened and here I was, talking about algebra to a lot of boys who might, every one of them for all I knew, be popping off needles every time they went to the head. Maybe it did more for them than algebra could.

I was sure that the first time Sonny had ever had horse,° he couldn't have   5
been much older than these boys were now. These boys, now, were living as we'd been living then, they were growing up with a rush and their heads bumped abruptly against the low ceiling of their actual possibilities. They were filled with rage. All they really knew were two darknesses, the darkness of their lives, which was now closing in on them, and the darkness of the movies, which had blinded them to that other darkness, and in which they now, vindictively, dreamed, at once more together than they were at any other time, and more alone.

When the last bell rang, the last class ended, I let out my breath. It seemed I'd been holding it for all that time. My clothes were wet — I may have looked as though I'd been sitting in a steam bath, all dressed up, all afternoon. I sat alone in the classroom a long time. I listened to the boys outside, downstairs, shouting and cursing and laughing. Their laughter struck me for perhaps the first time. It was not the joyous laughter which — God knows why — one associates with children. It was mocking and insular, its intent to denigrate. It was disenchanted, and in this, also, lay the authority of their curses. Perhaps I was listening to them because I was thinking about my brother and in them I heard my brother. And myself.

One boy was whistling a tune, at once very complicated and very simple, it seemed to be pouring out of him as though he were a bird, and it sounded very cool and moving through all that harsh, bright air, only just holding its own through all those other sounds.

I stood up and walked over to the window and looked down into the courtyard. It was the beginning of the spring and the sap was rising in the boys. A teacher passed through them every now and again, quickly, as though he or she couldn't wait to get out of that courtyard, to get those boys out of their sight and off their minds. I started collecting my stuff. I thought I'd better get home and talk to Isabel.

The courtyard was almost deserted by the time I got downstairs. I saw this boy standing in the shadow of a doorway, looking just like Sonny. I almost

---

horse: Name for heroin in the 1950s.

called his name. Then I saw that it wasn't Sonny, but somebody we used to know, a boy from around our block. He'd been Sonny's friend. He'd never been mine, having been too young for me, and, anyway, I'd never liked him. And now, even though he was a grown-up man, he still hung around that block, still spent hours on the street corners, was always high and raggy. I used to run into him from time to time and he'd often work around to asking me for a quarter or fifty cents. He always had some real good excuse, too, and I always gave it to him, I don't know why.

But now, abruptly, I hated him. I couldn't stand the way he looked at me, partly like a dog, partly like a cunning child. I wanted to ask him what the hell he was doing in the school courtyard.

He sort of shuffled over to me, and he said, "I see you got the papers. So you already know about it."

"You mean about Sonny? Yes, I already know about it. How come they didn't get you?"

He grinned. It made him repulsive and it also brought to mind what he'd looked like as a kid. "I wasn't there. I stay away from them people."

"Good for you." I offered him a cigarette and I watched him through the smoke. "You come all the way down here just to tell me about Sonny?"

"That's right." He was sort of shaking his head and his eyes looked strange, as though they were about to cross. The bright sun deadened his damp dark brown skin and it made his eyes look yellow and showed up the dirt in his kinked hair. He smelled funky. I moved a little away from him and I said, "Well, thanks. But I already know about it and I got to get home."

"I'll walk you a little ways," he said. We started walking. There were a couple of kids still loitering in the courtyard and one of them said goodnight to me and looked strangely at the boy beside me.

"What're you going to do?" he asked me. "I mean, about Sonny?"

"Look. I haven't seen Sonny for over a year. I'm not sure I'm going to do anything. Anyway, what the hell *can* I do?"

"That's right," he said quickly, "ain't nothing you can do. Can't much help old Sonny no more, I guess."

It was what I was thinking and so it seemed to me he had no right to say it.

"I'm surprised at Sonny, though," he went on — he had a funny way of talking, he looked straight ahead as though he were talking to himself — "I thought Sonny was a smart boy, I thought he was too smart to get hung."

"I guess he thought so too," I said sharply, "and that's how he got hung. And how about you? You're pretty goddamn smart, I bet."

Then he looked directly at me, just for a minute. "I ain't smart," he said. "If I was smart, I'd have reached for a pistol a long time ago."

"Look. Don't tell *me* your sad story, if it was up to me, I'd give you one." Then I felt guilty — guilty, probably, for never having supposed that the poor bastard *had* a story of his own, much less a sad one, and I asked, quickly, "What's going to happen to him now?"

He didn't answer this. He was off by himself some place. "Funny thing," he said, and from his tone we might have been discussing the quickest way to get to Brooklyn, "when I saw the papers this morning, the first thing I asked myself was if I had anything to do with it. I felt sort of responsible."

I began to listen more carefully. The subway station was on the corner, just before us, and I stopped. He stopped, too. We were in front of a bar and he ducked slightly, peering in, but whoever he was looking for didn't seem to be there. The juke box was blasting away with something black and bouncy and I half watched the barmaid as she danced her way from the juke box to her place behind the bar. And I watched her face as she laughingly responded to something someone said to her, still keeping time to the music. When she smiled one saw the little girl, one sensed the doomed, still-struggling woman beneath the battered face of the semi-whore.

"I never *give* Sonny nothing," the boy said finally, "but a long time ago I come to school high and Sonny asked me how it felt." He paused, I couldn't bear to watch him, I watched the barmaid, and I listened to the music which seemed to be causing the pavement to shake. "I told him it felt great." The music stopped, the barmaid paused and watched the juke box until the music began again. "It did."

All this was carrying me some place I didn't want to go. I certainly didn't want to know how it felt. It filled everything, the people, the houses, the music, the dark, quicksilver barmaid, with menace; and this menace was their reality.

"What's going to happen to him now?" I asked again.

"They'll send him away some place and they'll try to cure him." He shook   30
his head.

"Maybe he'll even think he's kicked the habit. Then they'll let him loose" — he gestured, throwing his cigarette into the gutter. "That's all."

"What do you mean, that's *all*?"

But I knew what he meant.

"I *mean*, that's *all*." He turned his head and looked at me, pulling down the corners of his mouth. "Don't you know what I mean?" he asked, softly.

"How the hell *would* I know what you mean?" I almost whispered it, I   35
don't know why.

"That's right," he said to the air, "how would *he* know what I mean?" He turned toward me again, patient and calm, and yet I somehow felt him shaking, shaking as though he were going to fall apart. I felt that ice in my guts again, the dread I'd felt all afternoon; and again I watched the barmaid, moving about the bar, washing glasses, and singing. "Listen. They'll let him out and then it'll just start all over again. That's what I mean."

"You mean — they'll let him out. And then he'll just start working his way back in again. You mean he'll never kick the habit. Is that what you mean?"

"That's right," he said, cheerfully. "*You* see what I mean."

"Tell me," I said at last, "why does he want to die? He must want to die, he's killing himself, why does he want to die?"

He looked at me in surprise. He licked his lips. "He don't want to die. He   40
wants to live. Don't nobody want to die, ever."

Then I wanted to ask him—too many things. He could not have answered, or if he had, I could not have borne the answers. I started walking. "Well, I guess it's none of my business."

"It's going to be rough on old Sonny," he said. We reached the subway station. "This is your station?" he asked. I nodded. I took one step down. "Damn!" he said, suddenly. I looked up at him. He grinned again. "Damn it if I didn't leave all my money home. You ain't got a dollar on you, have you? Just for a couple of days, is all."

All at once something inside gave and threatened to come pouring out of me. I didn't hate him any more. I felt that in another moment I'd start crying like a child.

"Sure," I said. "Don't sweat." I looked in my wallet and didn't have a dollar, I only had a five. "Here," I said. "That hold you?"

He didn't look at it—he didn't want to look at it. A terrible closed look   45
came over his face, as though he were keeping the number on the bill a secret from him and me. "Thanks," he said, and now he was dying to see me go. "Don't worry about Sonny. Maybe I'll write him or something."

"Sure," I said. "You do that. So long."

"Be seeing you," he said. I went on down the steps.

And I didn't write Sonny or send him anything for a long time. When I finally did, it was just after my little girl died, he wrote me back a letter which made me feel like a bastard.

Here's what he said:

> Dear brother,
>
> You don't know how much I needed to hear from you. I wanted to write you many a time but I dug how much I must have hurt you and so I didn't write. But now I feel like a man who's been trying to climb up out of some deep, real deep and funky hole and just saw the sun up there, outside. I got to get outside.
>
> I can't tell you much about how I got here. I mean I don't know how to tell you. I guess I was afraid of something or I was trying to escape from something and you know I have never been very strong in the head (smile). I'm glad Mama and Daddy are dead and can't see what's happened to their son and I swear if I'd known what I was doing I would never have hurt you so, you and a lot of other fine people who were nice to me and who believed in me.
>
> I don't want you to think it had anything to do with me being a musician. It's more than that. Or maybe less than that. I can't get anything straight in my head down here and I try not to think about what's going to happen to me when I get outside again. Sometime I think I'm going to flip and never get outside and sometime I think I'll come straight back. I tell you one thing, though, I'd rather blow my brains out than go through this

again. But that's what they all say, so they tell me. If I tell you when I'm coming to New York and if you could meet me, I sure would appreciate it. Give my love to Isabel and the kids and I was sure sorry to hear about little Gracie. I wish I could be like Mama and say the Lord's will be done, but I don't know it seems to me that trouble is the one thing that never does get stopped and I don't know what good it does to blame it on the Lord. But maybe it does some good if you believe it.

Your brother,

Sonny

Then I kept in constant touch with him and I sent him whatever I could 50
and I went to meet him when he came back to New York. When I saw him many things I thought I had forgotten came flooding back to me. This was because I had begun, finally, to wonder about Sonny, about the life that Sonny lived inside. This life, whatever it was, had made him older and thinner and it had deepened the distant stillness in which he had always moved. He looked very unlike my baby brother. Yet, when he smiled, when we shook hands, the baby brother I'd never known looked out from the depths of his private life, like an animal waiting to be coaxed into the light.

"How you been keeping?" he asked me.

"All right. And you?"

"Just fine." He was smiling all over his face. "It's good to see you again."

"It's good to see you."

The seven years' difference in our ages lay between us like a chasm: 55
I wondered if these years would ever operate between us as a bridge. I was remembering, and it made it hard to catch my breath, that I had been there when he was born; and I had heard the first words he had ever spoken. When he started to walk, he walked from our mother straight to me. I caught him just before he fell when he took the first steps he ever took in this world.

"How's Isabel?"

"Just fine. She's dying to see you."

"And the boys?"

"They're fine, too. They're anxious to see their uncle."

"Oh, come on. You know they don't remember me." 60

"Are you kidding? Of course they remember you."

He grinned again. We got into a taxi. We had a lot to say to each other, far too much to know how to begin.

As the taxi began to move, I asked, "You still want to go to India?"

He laughed. "You still remember that. Hell, no. This place is Indian enough for me."

"It used to belong to them," I said. 65

And he laughed again. "They damn sure knew what they were doing when they got rid of it."

Years ago, when he was around fourteen, he'd been all hipped on the idea of going to India. He read books about people sitting on rocks, naked, in all kinds of weather, but mostly bad, naturally, and walking barefoot through hot coals and arriving at wisdom. I used to say that it sounded to me as though they were getting away from wisdom as fast as they could. I think he sort of looked down on me for that.

"Do you mind," he asked, "if we have the driver drive alongside the park? On the west side—I haven't seen the city in so long."

"Of course not," I said. I was afraid that I might sound as though I were humoring him, but I hoped he wouldn't take it that way.

So we drove along, between the green of the park and the stony, lifeless   70 elegance of hotels and apartment buildings, toward the vivid, killing streets of our childhood. These streets hadn't changed, though housing projects jutted up out of them now like rocks in the middle of a boiling sea. Most of the houses in which we had grown up had vanished, as had the stores from which we had stolen, the basements in which we had first tried sex, the rooftops from which we had hurled tin cans and bricks. But houses exactly like the houses of our past yet dominated the landscape, boys exactly like the boys we once had been found themselves smothering in these houses, came down into the streets for light and air and found themselves encircled by disaster. Some escaped the trap, most didn't. Those who got out always left something of themselves behind, as some animals amputate a leg and leave it in the trap. It might be said, perhaps, that I had escaped, after all, I was a school teacher; or that Sonny had, he hadn't lived in Harlem for years. Yet, as the cab moved uptown through streets which seemed, with a rush, to darken with dark people, and as I covertly studied Sonny's face, it came to me that what we both were seeking through our separate cab windows was that part of ourselves which had been left behind. It's always at the hour of trouble and confrontation that the missing member aches.

We hit 110th Street and started rolling up Lenox Avenue. And I'd known this avenue all my life, but it seemed to me again, as it had seemed on the day I'd first heard about Sonny's trouble, filled with a hidden menace which was its very breath of life.

"We almost there," said Sonny.

"Almost." We were both too nervous to say anything more.

We live in a housing project. It hasn't been up long. A few days after it was up it seemed uninhabitably new, now, of course, it's already rundown. It looks like a parody of the good, clean, faceless life—God knows the people who live in it do their best to make it a parody. The beat-looking grass lying around isn't enough to make their lives green, the hedges will never hold out the streets, and they know it. The big windows fool no one, they aren't big enough to make space out of no space. They don't bother with the windows, they watch the TV screen instead. The playground is most popular with the children who don't play at jacks, or skip rope, or roller skate, or swing, and they can be found in it after dark. We moved in partly because it's not too far from where I teach, and partly for the kids; but it's really just like the houses in which Sonny and I grew up. The same things happen, they'll have the same things to remember. The moment Sonny and I started into the house I had the feeling that I was simply bringing him back into the danger he had almost died trying to escape.

Sonny has never been talkative. So I don't know why I was sure he'd be   75
dying to talk to me when supper was over the first night. Everything went fine,
the oldest boy remembered him, and the youngest boy liked him, and Sonny
had remembered to bring something for each of them; and Isabel, who is
really much nicer than I am, more open and giving, had gone to a lot of trouble about dinner and was genuinely glad to see him. And she's always been
able to tease Sonny in a way that I haven't. It was nice to see her face so vivid
again and to hear her laugh and watch her make Sonny laugh. She wasn't, or,
anyway, she didn't seem to be, at all uneasy or embarrassed. She chatted as
though there were no subject which had to be avoided and she got Sonny past
his first, faint stiffness. And thank God she was there, for I was filled with that
icy dread again. Everything I did seemed awkward to me, and everything I said
sounded freighted with hidden meaning. I was trying to remember everything
I'd heard about dope addiction and I couldn't help watching Sonny for signs.
I wasn't doing it out of malice. I was trying to find out something about my
brother. I was dying to hear him tell me he was safe.

"Safe!" my father grunted, whenever Mama suggested trying to move to
a neighborhood which might be safer for children. "Safe, hell! Ain't no place
safe for kids, nor nobody."

He always went on like this, but he wasn't, ever, really as bad as he sounded,
not even on weekends, when he got drunk. As a matter of fact, he was always
on the lookout for "something a little better," but he died before he found it. He
died suddenly, during a drunken weekend in the middle of the war, when Sonny
was fifteen. He and Sonny hadn't ever got on too well. And this was partly
because Sonny was the apple of his father's eye. It was because he loved Sonny
so much and was frightened for him, that he was always fighting with him.
It doesn't do any good to fight with Sonny. Sonny just moves back, inside himself,
where he can't be reached. But the principal reason that they never hit it off is
that they were so much alike. Daddy was big and rough and loud-talking, just
the opposite of Sonny, but they both had—that same privacy.

Mama tried to tell me something about this, just after Daddy died. I was
home on leave from the army.

This was the last time I ever saw my mother alive. Just the same, this picture gets all mixed up in my mind with pictures I had of her when she was
younger. The way I always see her is the way she used to be on a Sunday afternoon, say, when the old folks were talking after the big Sunday dinner. I always
see her wearing pale blue. She'd be sitting on the sofa. And my father would be
sitting in the easy chair, not far from her. And the living room would be full of
church folks and relatives. There they sit, in chairs all around the living room,
and the night is creeping up outside, but nobody knows it yet. You can see the
darkness growing against the windowpanes and you hear the street noises
every now and again, or maybe the jangling beat of a tambourine from one of
the churches close by, but it's real quiet in the room. For a moment nobody's
talking, but every face looks darkening, like the sky outside. And my mother
rocks a little from the waist, and my father's eyes are closed. Everyone is looking at something a child can't see. For a minute they've forgotten the children.

Maybe a kid is lying on the rug, half asleep. Maybe somebody's got a kid in his lap and is absent-mindedly stroking the kid's head. Maybe there's a kid, quiet and big-eyed, curled up in a big chair in the corner. The silence, the darkness coming, and the darkness in the faces frightens the child obscurely. He hopes that the hand which strokes his forehead will never stop — will never die. He hopes that there will never come a time when the old folks won't be sitting around the living room, talking about where they've come from, and what they've seen, and what's happened to them and their kinfolk.

But something deep and watchful in the child knows that this is bound   80
to end, is already ending. In a moment someone will get up and turn on the light. Then the old folks will remember the children and they won't talk any more that day. And when light fills the room, the child is filled with darkness. He knows that every time this happens he's moved just a little closer to that darkness outside. The darkness outside is what the old folks have been talking about. It's what they've come from. It's what they endure. The child knows that they won't talk any more because if he knows too much about what's happened to *them*, he'll know too much too soon, about what's going to happen to *him*.

The last time I talked to my mother, I remember I was restless. I wanted to get out and see Isabel. We weren't married then and we had a lot to straighten out between us.

There Mama sat, in black, by the window. She was humming an old church song, *Lord, you brought me from a long ways off.* Sonny was out somewhere. Mama kept watching the streets.

"I don't know," she said, "if I'll ever see you again, after you go off from here. But I hope you'll remember the things I tried to teach you."

"Don't talk like that," I said, and smiled. "You'll be here a long time yet."

She smiled, too, but she said nothing. She was quiet for a long time. And   85
I said, "Mama, don't you worry about nothing. I'll be writing all the time, and you be getting the checks. . . ."

"I want to talk to you about your brother," she said, suddenly. "If anything happens to me he ain't going to have nobody to look out for him."

"Mama," I said, "ain't nothing going to happen to you *or* Sonny. Sonny's all right. He's a good boy and he's got good sense."

"It ain't a question of his being a good boy," Mama said, "nor of his having good sense. It ain't only the bad ones, nor yet the dumb ones that gets sucked under." She stopped, looking at me.

"Your Daddy once had a brother," she said, and she smiled in a way that made me feel she was in pain. "You didn't never know that, did you?"

"No," I said, "I never knew that," and I watched her face.   90

"Oh, yes," she said, "your Daddy had a brother." She looked out of the window again. "I know you never saw your Daddy cry. But *I* did — many a time, through all these years."

I asked her, "What happened to his brother? How come nobody's ever talked about him?"

This was the first time I ever saw my mother look old.

"His brother got killed," she said, "when he was just a little younger than you are now. I knew him. He was a fine boy. He was maybe a little full of the devil, but he didn't mean nobody no harm."

Then she stopped and the room was silent, exactly as it had sometimes   95
been on those Sunday afternoons. Mama kept looking out into the streets.

"He used to have a job in the mill," she said, "and, like all young folks, he just liked to perform on Saturday nights. Saturday nights, him and your father would drift around to different places, go to dances and things like that, or just sit around with people they knew, and your father's brother would sing, he had a fine voice, and play along with himself on his guitar. Well, this particular Saturday night, him and your father was coming home from some place, and they were both a little drunk and there was a moon that night, it was bright like day. Your father's brother was feeling kind of good, and he was whistling to himself, and he had his guitar slung over his shoulder. They was coming down a hill and beneath them was a road that turned off from the highway. Well, your father's brother, being always kind of frisky, decided to run down this hill, and he did, with that guitar banging and clanging behind him, and he ran across the road, and he was making water behind a tree. And your father was sort of amused at him and he was still coming down the hill, kind of slow. Then he heard a car motor and that same minute his brother stepped from behind the tree, into the road, in the moonlight. And he started to cross the road. And your father started to run down the hill, he says he don't know why. This car was full of white men. They was all drunk, and when they seen your father's brother they let out a great whoop and holler and they aimed the car straight at him. They was having fun, they just wanted to scare him, the way they do sometimes, you know. But they was drunk. And I guess the boy, being drunk, too, and scared, kind of lost his head. By the time he jumped it was too late. Your father says he heard his brother scream when the car rolled over him, and he heard the wood of that guitar when it give, and he heard them strings go flying, and he heard them white men shouting, and the car kept on a-going and it ain't stopped till this day. And, time your father got down the hill, his brother weren't nothing but blood and pulp."

Tears were gleaming on my mother's face. There wasn't anything I could say.

"He never mentioned it," she said, "because I never let him mention it before you children. Your Daddy was like a crazy man that night and for many a night thereafter. He says he never in his life seen anything as dark as that road after the lights of that car had gone away. Weren't nothing, weren't nobody on that road, just your Daddy and his brother and that busted guitar. Oh, yes. Your Daddy never did really get right again. Till the day he died he weren't sure but that every white man he saw was the man that killed his brother."

She stopped and took out her handkerchief and dried her eyes and looked at me.

"I ain't telling you all this," she said, "to make you scared or bitter or to   100
make you hate nobody. I'm telling you this because you got a brother. And the world ain't changed."

I guess I didn't want to believe this. I guess she saw this in my face. She turned away from me, toward the window again, searching those streets.

"But I praise my Redeemer," she said at last, "that He called your Daddy home before me. I ain't saying it to throw no flowers at myself, but, I declare, it keeps me from feeling too cast down to know I helped your father get safely through this world. Your father always acted like he was the roughest, strongest man on earth. And everybody took him to be like that. But if he hadn't had *me* there—to see his tears!"

She was crying again. Still, I couldn't move. I said, "Lord, Lord, Mama, I didn't know it was like that."

"Oh, honey," she said, "there's a lot that you don't know. But you are going to find it out." She stood up from the window and came over to me. "You got to hold on to your brother," she said, "and don't let him fall, no matter what it looks like is happening to him and no matter how evil you gets with him. You going to be evil with him many a time. But don't you forget what I told you, you hear?"

"I won't forget," I said. "Don't you worry, I won't forget. I won't let nothing happen to Sonny."   105

My mother smiled as though she were amused at something she saw in my face. Then, "You may not be able to stop nothing from happening. But you got to let him know you's *there*."

Two days later I was married, and then I was gone. And I had a lot of things on my mind and I pretty well forgot my promise to Mama until I got shipped home on a special furlough for her funeral.

And, after the funeral, with just Sonny and me alone in the empty kitchen, I tried to find out something about him.

"What do you want to do?" I asked him.

"I'm going to be a musician," he said.   110

For he had graduated, in the time I had been away, from dancing to the juke box to finding out who was playing what, and what they were doing with it, and he had bought himself a set of drums.

"You mean, you want to be a drummer?" I somehow had the feeling that being a drummer might be all right for other people but not for my brother Sonny.

"I don't think," he said, looking at me very gravely, "that I'll ever be a good drummer. But I think I can play a piano."

I frowned. I'd never played the role of the older brother quite so seriously before, had scarcely ever, in fact, *asked* Sonny a damn thing. I sensed myself in the presence of something I didn't really know how to handle, didn't understand. So I made my frown a little deeper as I asked: "What kind of musician do you want to be?"

He grinned. "How many kinds do you think there are?"   115

"Be *serious*," I said.

He laughed, throwing his head back, and then looked at me. "I *am* serious."

"Well, then, for Christ's sake, stop kidding around and answer a serious question. I mean, do you want to be a concert pianist, you want to play classical music and all that, or — or what?" Long before I finished he was laughing again. "For Christ's *sake*, Sonny!"

He sobered, but with difficulty. "I'm sorry. But you sound so — *scared*!" and he was off again.

"Well, you may think it's funny now, baby, but it's not going to be so funny   120 when you have to make your living at it, let me tell you *that*." I was furious because I knew he was laughing at me and I didn't know why.

"No," he said, very sober now, and afraid, perhaps, that he'd hurt me, "I don't want to be a classical pianist. That isn't what interests me. I mean" — he paused, looking hard at me, as though his eyes would help me to understand, and then gestured helplessly, as though perhaps his hand would help — "I mean, I'll have a lot of studying to do, and I'll have to study *everything*, but, I mean, I want to play *with* — jazz musicians." He stopped. "I want to play jazz," he said.

Well, the word had never before sounded as heavy, as real, as it sounded that afternoon in Sonny's mouth. I just looked at him and I was probably frowning a real frown by this time. I simply couldn't see why on earth he'd want to spend his time hanging around nightclubs, clowning around on bandstands, while people pushed each other around a dance floor. It seemed — beneath him, somehow. I had never thought about it before, had never been forced to, but I suppose I had always put jazz musicians in a class with what Daddy called "good-time people."

"Are you *serious?*"

"Hell, *yes*, I'm serious."

He looked more helpless than ever, and annoyed, and deeply hurt.   125

I suggested, helpfully: "You mean — like Louis Armstrong?"

His face closed as though I'd struck him. "No. I'm not talking about none of that old-time, down home crap."

"Well, look, Sonny, I'm sorry, don't get mad. I just don't altogether get it, that's all. Name somebody — you know, a jazz musician you admire."

"Bird."

"Who?"   130

"Bird! Charlie Parker! Don't they teach you nothing in the goddamn army?"

I lit a cigarette. I was surprised and then a little amused to discover that I was trembling. "I've been out of touch," I said. "You'll have to be patient with me. Now. Who's this Parker character?"

"He's just one of the greatest jazz musicians alive," said Sonny, sullenly, his hands in his pockets, his back to me. "Maybe *the* greatest," he added, bitterly, "that's probably why *you* never heard of him."

"All right," I said, "I'm ignorant. I'm sorry. I'll go out and buy all the cat's records right away, all right?"

"It don't," said Sonny, with dignity, "make any difference to me. I don't   135 care what you listen to. Don't do me no favors."

I was beginning to realize that I'd never seen him so upset before. With another part of my mind I was thinking that this would probably turn out to be one of those things kids go through and that I shouldn't make it seem important by pushing it too hard. Still, I didn't think it would do any harm to ask: "Doesn't all this take a lot of time? Can you make a living at it?"

He turned back to me and half leaned, half sat, on the kitchen table. "Everything takes time," he said, "and — well, yes, sure, I can make a living at it. But what I don't seem to be able to make you understand is that it's the only thing I want to do."

"Well, Sonny," I said, gently, "you know people can't always do exactly what they *want* to do —"

"*No,* I don't know that," said Sonny, surprising me. "I think people *ought* to do what they want to do, what else are they alive for?"

"You getting to be a big boy," I said desperately, "it's time you started   140 thinking about your future."

"I'm thinking about my future," said Sonny, grimly. "I think about it all the time."

I gave up. I decided, if he didn't change his mind, that we could always talk about it later. "In the meantime," I said, "you got to finish school." We had already decided that he'd have to move in with Isabel and her folks. I knew this wasn't the ideal arrangement because Isabel's folks are inclined to be dicty and they hadn't especially wanted Isabel to marry me. But I didn't know what else to do. "And we have to get you fixed up at Isabel's."

There was a long silence. He moved from the kitchen table to the window. "That's a terrible idea. You know it yourself."

"Do you have a *better* idea?"

He just walked up and down the kitchen for a minute. He was as tall as I was.   145 He had started to shave. I suddenly had the feeling that I didn't know him at all.

He stopped at the kitchen table and picked up my cigarettes. Looking at me with a kind of mocking, amused defiance, he put one between his lips. "You mind?"

"You smoking already?"

He lit the cigarette and nodded, watching me through the smoke. "I just wanted to see if I'd have the courage to smoke in front of you." He grinned and blew a great cloud of smoke to the ceiling. "It was easy." He looked at my face. "Come on, now. I bet you was smoking at my age, tell the truth."

I didn't say anything but the truth was on my face, and he laughed. But now there was something very strained in his laugh. "Sure. And I bet that ain't all you was doing."

He was frightening me a little. "Cut the crap," I said. "We already decided   150 that you was going to go and live at Isabel's. Now what's got into you all of a sudden?"

"*You* decided it," he pointed out. "*I* didn't decide nothing." He stopped in front of me, leaning against the stove, arms loosely folded. "Look, brother. I don't want to stay in Harlem no more, I really don't." He was very earnest. He looked at me, then over toward the kitchen window. There was something in his eyes I'd never seen before, some thoughtfulness, some worry all his own. He rubbed the muscle of one arm. "It's time I was getting out of here."

"Where do you want to *go,* Sonny?"

"I want to join the army. Or the navy, I don't care. If I say I'm old enough, they'll believe me."

Then I got mad. It was because I was so scared. "You must be crazy. You goddamn fool, what the hell do you want to go and join the *army* for?"

"I just told you. To get out of Harlem." 155

"Sonny, you haven't even finished *school*. And if you really want to be a musician, how do you expect to study if you're in the *army?*"

He looked at me, trapped, and in anguish. "There's ways. I might be able to work out some kind of deal. Anyway, I'll have the G.I. Bill when I come out."

"*If* you come out." We stared at each other. "Sonny, please. Be reasonable. I know the setup is far from perfect. But we got to do the best we can."

"I ain't learning nothing in school," he said. "Even when I go." He turned away from me and opened the window and threw his cigarette out into the narrow alley. I watched his back. "At least, I ain't learning nothing you'd want me to learn." He slammed the window so hard I thought the glass would fly out, and turned back to me. "And I'm sick of the stink of these garbage cans!"

"Sonny," I said, "I know how you feel. But if you don't finish school now, 160 you're going to be sorry later that you didn't." I grabbed him by the shoulders. "And you only got another year. It ain't so bad. And I'll come back and I swear I'll help you do *whatever* you want to do. Just try to put up with it till I come back. Will you please do that? For me?"

He didn't answer and he wouldn't look at me.

"Sonny. You hear me?"

He pulled away. "I hear you. But you never hear anything *I* say."

I didn't know what to say to that. He looked out of the window and then back at me. "OK," he said, and sighed. "I'll try."

Then I said, trying to cheer him up a little, "They got a piano at Isabel's. 165 You can practice on it."

And as a matter of fact, it did cheer him up for a minute. "That's right," he said to himself. "I forgot that." His face relaxed a little. But the worry, the thoughtfulness, played on it still, the way shadows play on a face which is staring into the fire.

But I thought I'd never hear the end of that piano. At first, Isabel would write me, saying how nice it was that Sonny was so serious about his music and how, as soon as he came in from school, or wherever he had been when he was supposed to be at school, he went straight to that piano and stayed there until suppertime. And, after supper, he went back to that piano and stayed there until everybody went to bed. He was at the piano all day Saturday and all day Sunday. Then he bought a record player and started playing records. He'd play one record over and over again, all day long sometimes, and he'd improvise along with it on the piano. Or he'd play one section of the record, one chord, one change, one progression, then he'd do it on the piano. Then back to the record. Then back to the piano.

Well, I really don't know how they stood it. Isabel finally confessed that it wasn't like living with a person at all, it was like living with sound. And the sound didn't make any sense to her, didn't make any sense to any of them — naturally. They began, in a way, to be afflicted by this presence that was living in their home. It was as though Sonny were some sort of god, or monster. He moved in an atmosphere which wasn't like theirs at all. They fed him and he ate, he washed himself, he walked in and out of their door; he certainly wasn't nasty or unpleasant or rude, Sonny isn't any of those things; but it was as though he were all wrapped up in some cloud, some fire, some vision all his own; and there wasn't any way to reach him.

At the same time, he wasn't really a man yet, he was still a child, and they had to watch out for him in all kinds of ways. They certainly couldn't throw him out. Neither did they dare to make a great scene about that piano because even they dimly sensed, as I sensed, from so many thousands of miles away, that Sonny was at that piano playing for his life.

But he hadn't been going to school. One day a letter came from the school   170
board and Isabel's mother got it — there had, apparently, been other letters but Sonny had torn them up. This day, when Sonny came in, Isabel's mother showed him the letter and asked where he'd been spending his time. And she finally got it out of him that he'd been down in Greenwich Village, with musicians and other characters, in a white girl's apartment. And this scared her and she started to scream at him and what came up, once she began — though she denies it to this day — was what sacrifices they were making to give Sonny a decent home and how little he appreciated it.

Sonny didn't play the piano that day. By evening, Isabel's mother had calmed down but then there was the old man to deal with, and Isabel herself. Isabel says she did her best to be calm but she broke down and started crying. She says she just watched Sonny's face. She could tell, by watching him, what was happening with him. And what was happening was that they penetrated his cloud, they had reached him. Even if their fingers had been a thousand times more gentle than human fingers ever are, he could hardly help feeling that they had stripped him naked and were spitting on that nakedness. For he also had to see that his presence, that music, which was life or death to him, had been torture for them and that they had endured it, not at all for his sake, but only for mine. And Sonny couldn't take that. He can take it a little better today than he could then but he's still not very good at it and, frankly, I don't know anybody who is.

The silence of the next few days must have been louder than the sound of all the music ever played since time began. One morning, before she went to work, Isabel was in his room for something and she suddenly realized that all of his records were gone. And she knew for certain that he was gone. And he was. He went as far as the navy would carry him. He finally sent me a postcard from some place in Greece and that was the first I knew that Sonny was still alive. I didn't see him any more until we were both back in New York and the war had long been over. He was a man by then, of course, but I wasn't willing to see it. He came by the house from time to time, but we fought almost every time we met. I didn't like the way he carried himself, loose and dreamlike all the time, and I didn't like his friends, and his music seemed to be merely an excuse for the life he led. It sounded just that weird and disordered.

Then we had a fight, a pretty awful fight, and I didn't see him for months. By and by I looked him up, where he was living, in a furnished room in the Village, and I tried to make it up. But there were lots of people in the room and Sonny just lay on his bed, and he wouldn't come downstairs with me, and he treated these other people as though they were his family and I weren't. So I got mad and then he got mad, and then I told him that he might just as well be dead as live the way he was living. Then he stood up and he told me not to worry about him any more in life, that he *was* dead as far as I was concerned. Then he pushed me to the door and the other people looked on as though nothing were happening, and he slammed the door behind me. I stood in the hallway, staring at the door. I heard somebody laugh in the room and then the tears came to my eyes. I started down the steps, whistling to keep from crying, I kept whistling to myself, *You going to need me, baby, one of these cold, rainy days.*

I read about Sonny's trouble in the spring. Little Grace died in the fall. She was a beautiful little girl. But she only lived a little over two years. She died of polio and she suffered. She had a slight fever for a couple of days, but it didn't seem like anything and we just kept her in bed. And we would certainly have called the doctor, but the fever dropped, she seemed to be all right. So we thought it had just been a cold. Then, one day, she was up, playing, Isabel was in the kitchen fixing lunch for the two boys when they'd come in from school, and she heard Grace fall down in the living room. When you have a lot of children you don't always start running when one of them falls, unless they start screaming or something. And, this time, Grace was quiet. Yet, Isabel says that when she heard that *thump* and then that silence, something happened in her to make her afraid. And she ran to the living room and there was little Grace on the floor, all twisted up, and the reason she hadn't screamed was that she couldn't get her breath. And when she did scream, it was the worst sound, Isabel says, that she'd ever heard in all her life, and she still hears it sometimes in her dreams. Isabel will sometimes wake me up with a low, moaning, strangled sound and I have to be quick to awaken her and hold her to me and where Isabel is weeping against me seems a mortal wound.

I think I may have written Sonny the very day that little Grace was buried. I was sitting in the living room in the dark, by myself, and I suddenly thought of Sonny. My trouble made his real.

One Saturday afternoon, when Sonny had been living with us, or, anyway, been in our house, for nearly two weeks, I found myself wandering aimlessly about the living room, drinking from a can of beer, and trying to work up the courage to search Sonny's room. He was out, he was usually out whenever I was home, and Isabel had taken the children to see their grandparents. Suddenly I was standing still in front of the living room window, watching Seventh Avenue. The idea of searching Sonny's room made me still. I scarcely dared to admit to myself what I'd be searching for. I didn't know what I'd do if I found it. Or if I didn't.

On the sidewalk across from me, near the entrance to a barbecue joint, some people were holding an old-fashioned revival meeting. The barbecue cook, wearing a dirty white apron, his conked hair reddish and metallic in the pale sun, and a cigarette between his lips, stood in the doorway, watching them. Kids and older people paused in their errands and stood there, along with some older men and a couple of very tough-looking women who watched everything that happened on the avenue, as though they owned it, or were maybe owned by it. Well, they were watching this, too. The revival was being carried on by three sisters in black, and a brother. All they had were their voices and their Bibles and a tambourine. The brother was testifying and while he testified two of the sisters stood together, seeming to say, amen, and the third sister walked around with the tambourine outstretched and a couple of people dropped coins into it. Then the brother's testimony ended and the sister who had been taking up the collection dumped the coins into her palm and transferred them to the pocket of her long black robe. Then she raised both hands, striking the tambourine against the air, and then against one hand, and she started to sing. And the two other sisters and the brother joined in.

It was strange, suddenly, to watch, though I had been seeing these street meetings all my life. So, of course, had everybody else down there. Yet, they paused and watched and listened and I stood still at the window. "*Tis the old ship of Zion,*" they sang, and the sister with the tambourine kept a steady, jangling beat, "*it has rescued many a thousand!*" Not a soul under the sound of their voices was hearing this song for the first time, not one of them had been rescued. Nor had they seen much in the way of rescue work being done around them. Neither did they especially believe in the holiness of the three sisters and the brother, they knew too much about them, knew where they lived, and how. The woman with the tambourine, whose voice dominated the air, whose face was bright with joy, was divided by very little from the woman who stood watching her, a cigarette between her heavy, chapped lips, her hair a cuckoo's nest, her face scarred and swollen from many beatings, and her black eyes glittering like coal. Perhaps they both knew this, which was why, when, as rarely, they addressed each other, they addressed each other as Sister. As the singing filled the air the watching, listening faces underwent a change, the eyes focusing on something within; the music seemed to soothe a poison out of them; and time seemed, nearly, to fall away from the sullen, belligerent, battered faces, as though they were fleeing back to their first condition, while dreaming of their last. The barbecue cook half shook his head and smiled, and dropped his cigarette and disappeared into his joint. A man fumbled in his pockets for change and stood holding it in his hand impatiently, as though he had just remembered a pressing appointment further up the avenue. He looked furious. Then I saw Sonny, standing on the edge of the crowd. He was carrying a wide, flat notebook with a green cover, and it made him look, from where I was standing, almost like a schoolboy. The coppery sun brought out the copper in his skin, he was very faintly smiling, standing very still. Then the singing stopped, the tambourine turned into a collection plate again. The furious man dropped in his coins and vanished, so did a couple of the women, and Sonny dropped some change in the plate, looking directly at the woman with a little smile. He started across the avenue, toward the house. He has a slow, loping walk, something like the way Harlem hipsters walk, only he's imposed on this his own half-beat. I had never really noticed it before.

I stayed at the window, both relieved and apprehensive. As Sonny disappeared from my sight, they began singing again. And they were still singing when his key turned in the lock.

"Hey," he said.   180

"Hey, yourself. You want some beer?"

"No. Well, maybe." But he came up to the window and stood beside me, looking out. "What a warm voice," he said.

They were singing *If I could only hear my mother pray again!*

"Yes," I said, "and she can sure beat that tambourine."

"But what a terrible song," he said, and laughed. He dropped his note-   185
book on the sofa and disappeared into the kitchen. "Where's Isabel and the kids?"

"I think they went to see their grandparents. You hungry?"

"No." He came back into the living room with his can of beer. "You want to come some place with me tonight?"

I sensed, I don't know how, that I couldn't possibly say no. "Sure. Where?"

He sat down on the sofa and picked up his notebook and started leafing through it. "I'm going to sit in with some fellows in a joint in the Village."

"You mean, you're going to play, tonight?"   190

"That's right." He took a swallow of his beer and moved back to the window. He gave me a sidelong look. "If you can stand it."

"I'll try," I said.

He smiled to himself and we both watched as the meeting across the way broke up. The three sisters and the brother, heads bowed, were singing *God be with you till we meet again.* The faces around them were very quiet. Then the song ended. The small crowd dispersed. We watched the three women and the lone man walk slowly up the avenue.

"When she was singing before," said Sonny, abruptly, "her voice reminded me for a minute of what heroin feels like sometimes—when it's in your veins. It makes you feel sort of warm and cool at the same time. And distant. And—and sure." He sipped his beer, very deliberately not looking at me. I watched his face. "It makes you feel—in control. Sometimes you've got to have that feeling."

"Do you?" I sat down slowly in the easy chair.   195

"Sometimes." He went to the sofa and picked up his notebook again. "Some people do."

"In order," I asked, "to play?" And my voice was very ugly, full of contempt and anger.

"Well"—he looked at me with great, troubled eyes, as though, in fact, he hoped his eyes would tell me things he could never otherwise say—"they *think* so. And *if* they think so—!"

"And what do *you* think?" I asked.

He sat on the sofa and put his can of beer on the floor. "I don't know," he   200
said, and I couldn't be sure if he were answering my question or pursuing his thoughts. His face didn't tell me. "It's not so much to *play.* It's to *stand* it, to be able to make it at all. On any level." He frowned and smiled: "In order to keep from shaking to pieces."

"But these friends of yours," I said, "they seem to shake themselves to pieces pretty goddamn fast."

"Maybe." He played with the notebook. And something told me that I should curb my tongue, that Sonny was doing his best to talk, that I should listen. "But of course you only know the ones that've gone to pieces. Some don't — or at least they haven't *yet* and that's just about all *any* of us can say." He paused. "And then there are some who just live, really, in hell, and they know it and they see what's happening and they go right on. I don't know." He sighed, dropped the notebook, folded his arms. "Some guys, you can tell from the way they play, they on something *all* the time. And you can see that, well, it makes something real for them. But of course," he picked up his beer from the floor and sipped it and put the can down again, "they *want* to, too, you've got to see that. Even some of them that say they don't — *some,* not all."

"And what about you?" I asked — I couldn't help it. "What about you? Do *you* want to?"

He stood up and walked to the window and remained silent for a long time. Then he sighed. "Me," he said. Then: "While I was downstairs before, on my way here, listening to that woman sing, it struck me all of a sudden how much suffering she must have had to go through — to sing like that. It's *repulsive* to think you have to suffer that much."

I said: "But there's no way not to suffer — is there, Sonny?"   205

"I believe not," he said and smiled, "but that's never stopped anyone from trying." He looked at me. "Has it?" I realized, with this mocking look, that there stood between us, forever, beyond the power of time or forgiveness, the fact that I had held silence — so long! — when he had needed human speech to help him. He turned back to the window. "No, there's no way not to suffer. But you try all kinds of ways to keep from drowning in it, to keep on top of it, and to make it seem — well, like *you.* Like you did something, all right, and now you're suffering for it. You know?" I said nothing. "Well you know," he said, impatiently, "why *do* people suffer? Maybe it's better to do something to give it a reason, *any* reason."

"But we just agreed," I said, "that there's no way not to suffer. Isn't it better, then, just to — take it?"

"But nobody just takes it," Sonny cried, "that's what I'm telling you! *Everybody* tries not to. You're just hung up on the *way* some people try — it's not *your* way!"

The hair on my face began to itch, my face felt wet. "That's not true," I said, "that's not true. I don't give a damn what other people do, I don't even care how they suffer. I just care how *you* suffer." And he looked at me. "Please believe me," I said, "I don't want to see you — die — trying not to suffer."

"I won't," he said, flatly, "die trying not to suffer. At least, not any faster   210
than anybody else."

"But there's no need," I said, trying to laugh, "is there? in killing yourself."

I wanted to say more, but I couldn't. I wanted to talk about will power and how life could be — well, beautiful. I wanted to say that it was all within; but was it? or, rather, wasn't that exactly the trouble? And I wanted to promise that I would never fail him again. But it would all have sounded — empty words and lies.

So I made the promise to myself and prayed that I would keep it.

"It's terrible sometimes, inside," he said, "that's what's the trouble. You walk these streets, black and funky and cold, and there's not really a living ass to talk to, and there's nothing shaking, and there's no way of getting it out—that storm inside. You can't talk it and you can't make love with it, and when you finally try to get with it and play it, you realize *nobody's* listening. So *you've* got to listen. You got to find a way to listen."

And then he walked away from the window and sat on the sofa again, as   215 though all the wind had suddenly been knocked out of him. "Sometimes you'll do *anything* to play, even cut your mother's throat." He laughed and looked at me. "Or your brother's." Then he sobered. "Or your own." Then: "Don't worry. I'm all right now and I think I'll *be* all right. But I can't forget—where I've been. I don't mean just the physical place I've been, I mean where I've *been*. And *what* I've been."

"What have you been, Sonny?" I asked.

He smiled—but sat sideways on the sofa, his elbow resting on the back, his fingers playing with his mouth and chin, not looking at me. "I've been something I didn't recognize, didn't know I could be. Didn't know anybody could be." He stopped, looking inward, looking helplessly young, looking old. "I'm not talking about it now because I feel *guilty* or anything like that—maybe it would be better if I did, I don't know. Anyway, I can't really talk about it. Not to you, not to anybody," and now he turned and faced me. "Sometimes, you know, and it was actually when I was most *out* of the world, I felt that I was in it, that I was *with* it, really, and I could play or I didn't really have to *play*, it just came out of me, it was there. And I don't know how I played, thinking about it now, but I know I did awful things, those times, sometimes, to people. Or it wasn't that I *did* anything to them—it was that they weren't real." He picked up the beer can; it was empty; he rolled it between his palms: "And other times— well, I needed a fix, I needed to find a place to lean, I needed to clear a space to *listen*—and I couldn't find it, and I—went crazy, I did terrible things to *me*, I was terrible *for* me." He began pressing the beer can between his hands, I watched the metal begin to give. It glittered, as he played with it, like a knife, and I was afraid he would cut himself, but I said nothing. "Oh well. I can never tell you. I was all by myself at the bottom of something, stinking and sweating and crying and shaking, and I smelled it, you know? *my* stink, and I thought I'd die if I couldn't get away from it and yet, all the same, I knew that everything I was doing was just locking me in with it. And I didn't know," he paused, still flattening the beer can, "I didn't know, I still *don't* know, something kept telling me that maybe it was good to smell your own stink, but I didn't think that *that* was what I'd been trying to do—and—who can stand it?" and he abruptly dropped the ruined beer can, looking at me with a small, still smile, and then rose, walking to the window as though it were the lodestone rock. I watched his face, he watched the avenue. "I couldn't tell you when Mama died—but the reason I wanted to leave Harlem so bad was to get away from drugs. And then, when I ran away, that's what I was running from—really. When I came back, nothing had changed, *I* hadn't changed, I was just—older." And he stopped, drumming with his fingers on the windowpane. The sun had vanished, soon darkness would fall. I watched his face. "It can come again," he said, almost as though speaking to himself. Then he turned to me. "It can come again," he repeated. "I just want you to know that."

"All right," I said, at last. "So it can come again. All right."

He smiled, but the smile was sorrowful. "I had to try to tell you," he said.

"Yes," I said. "I understand that."   220

"You're my brother," he said, looking straight at me, and not smiling at all.

"Yes," I repeated, "yes. I understand that."

He turned back to the window, looking out. "All that hatred down there," he said, "all that hatred and misery and love. It's a wonder it doesn't blow the avenue apart."

We went to the only nightclub on a short, dark street, downtown. We squeezed through the narrow, chattering, jam-packed bar to the entrance of the big room, where the bandstand was. And we stood there for a moment, for the lights were very dim in this room and we couldn't see. Then, "Hello, boy," said a voice and an enormous black man, much older than Sonny or myself, erupted out of all that atmospheric lighting and put an arm around Sonny's shoulder. "I been sitting right here," he said, "waiting for you."

He had a big voice, too, and heads in the darkness turned toward us.   225

Sonny grinned and pulled a little away, and said, "Creole, this is my brother. I told you about him."

Creole shook my hand. "I'm glad to meet you, son," he said, and it was clear that he was glad to meet me *there*, for Sonny's sake. And he smiled, "You got a real musician in *your* family," and he took his arm from Sonny's shoulder and slapped him, lightly, affectionately, with the back of his hand.

"Well. Now I've heard it all," said a voice behind us. This was another musician, and a friend of Sonny's, a coal-black, cheerful-looking man, built close to the ground. He immediately began confiding to me, at the top of his lungs, the most terrible things about Sonny, his teeth gleaming like a lighthouse and his laugh coming up out of him like the beginning of an earthquake. And it turned out that everyone at the bar knew Sonny, or almost everyone; some were musicians, working there, or nearby, or not working, some were simply hangers-on, and some were there to hear Sonny play. I was introduced to all of them and they were all very polite to me. Yet, it was clear that, for them, I was only Sonny's brother. Here, I was in Sonny's world. Or, rather: his kingdom. Here, it was not even a question that his veins bore royal blood.

They were going to play soon and Creole installed me, by myself, at a table in a dark corner. Then I watched them, Creole, and the little black man, and Sonny, and the others, while they horsed around, standing just below the bandstand. The light from the bandstand spilled just a little short of them and, watching them laughing and gesturing and moving about, I had the feeling that they, nevertheless, were being most careful not to step into that circle of light too suddenly: that if they moved into the light too suddenly, without thinking, they would perish in flame. Then, while I watched, one of them, the small, black man, moved into the light and crossed the bandstand and started fooling around with his drums. Then — being funny and being, also, extremely ceremonious — Creole took Sonny by the arm and led him to the piano. A woman's voice called Sonny's name and a few hands started clapping. And Sonny, also being funny and being ceremonious, and so touched, I think, that he could have cried, but neither hiding it nor showing it, riding it like a man, grinned, and put both hands to his heart and bowed from the waist.

Creole then went to the bass fiddle and a lean, very bright-skinned brown   230
man jumped up on the bandstand and picked up his horn. So there they were, and the atmosphere on the bandstand and in the room began to change and tighten. Someone stepped up to the microphone and announced them. Then there were all kinds of murmurs. Some people at the bar shushed others. The waitress ran around, frantically getting in the last orders, guys and chicks got closer to each other, and the lights on the bandstand, on the quartet, turned to a kind of indigo. Then they all looked different there. Creole looked about him for the last time, as though he were making certain that all his chickens were in the coop, and then he — jumped and struck the fiddle. And there they were.

All I know about music is that not many people ever really hear it. And even then, on the rare occasions when something opens within, and the music enters, what we mainly hear, or hear corroborated, are personal, private, vanishing evocations. But the man who creates the music is hearing something else, is dealing with the roar rising from the void and imposing order on it as it hits the air. What is evoked in him, then, is of another order, more terrible because it has no words, and triumphant, too, for that same reason. And his triumph, when he triumphs, is ours. I just watched Sonny's face. His face was troubled, he was working hard, but he wasn't with it. And I had the feeling that, in a way, everyone on the bandstand was waiting for him, both waiting for him and pushing him along. But as I began to watch Creole, I realized that it was Creole who held them all back. He had them on a short rein. Up there, keeping the beat with his whole body, wailing on the fiddle, with his eyes half closed, he was listening to everything, but he was listening to Sonny. He was having a dialogue with Sonny. He wanted Sonny to leave the shoreline and strike out for the deep water. He was Sonny's witness that deep water and drowning were not the same thing — he had been there, and he knew. And he wanted Sonny to know. He was waiting for Sonny to do the things on the keys which would let Creole know that Sonny was in the water.

And, while Creole listened, Sonny moved, deep within, exactly like someone in torment. I had never before thought of how awful the relationship must be between the musician and his instrument. He has to fill it, this instrument, with the breath of life, his own. He has to make it do what he wants it to do. And a piano is just a piano. It's made out of so much wood and wires and little hammers and big ones, and ivory. While there's only so much you can do with it, the only way to find this out is to try; to try and make it do everything.

And Sonny hadn't been near a piano for over a year. And he wasn't on much better terms with his life, not the life that stretched before him now.

He and the piano stammered, started one way, got scared, stopped; started another way, panicked, marked time, started again; then seemed to have found a direction, panicked again, got stuck. And the face I saw on Sonny I'd never seen before. Everything had been burned out of it, and, at the same time, things usually hidden were being burned in, by the fire and fury of the battle which was occurring in him up there.

Yet, watching Creole's face as they neared the end of the first set, I had the feeling that something had happened, something I hadn't heard. Then they finished, there was scattered applause, and then, without an instant's warning, Creole started into something else, it was almost sardonic, it was *Am I Blue.* And, as though he commanded, Sonny began to play. Something began to happen. And Creole let out the reins. The dry, low, black man said something awful on the drums, Creole answered, and the drums talked back. Then the horn insisted, sweet and high, slightly detached perhaps, and Creole listened, commenting now and then, dry, and driving, beautiful and calm and old. Then they all came together again, and Sonny was part of the family again. I could tell this from his face. He seemed to have found, right there beneath his fingers, a damn brand-new piano. It seemed that he couldn't get over it. Then, for awhile, just being happy with Sonny, they seemed to be agreeing with him that brand-new pianos certainly were a gas.

Then Creole stepped forward to remind them that what they were playing was the blues. He hit something in all of them, he hit something in me, myself, and the music tightened and deepened, apprehension began to beat the air. Creole began to tell us what the blues were all about. They were not about anything very new. He and his boys up there were keeping it new, at the risk of ruin, destruction, madness, and death, in order to find new ways to make us listen. For, while the tale of how we suffer, and how we are delighted, and how we may triumph is never new, it always must be heard. There isn't any other tale to tell, it's the only light we've got in all this darkness.

And this tale, according to that face, that body, those strong hands on those strings, has another aspect in every country, and a new depth in every generation. Listen, Creole seemed to be saying, listen. Now these are Sonny's blues. He made the little black man on the drums know it, and the bright, brown man on the horn. Creole wasn't trying any longer to get Sonny in the water. He was wishing him Godspeed. Then he stepped back, very slowly, filling the air with the immense suggestion that Sonny speak for himself.

Then they all gathered around Sonny and Sonny played. Every now and again one of them seemed to say, amen. Sonny's fingers filled the air with life, his life. But that life contained so many others. And Sonny went all the way back, he really began with the spare, flat statement of the opening phrase of the song. Then he began to make it his. It was very beautiful because it wasn't hurried and it was no longer a lament. I seemed to hear with what burning he had made it his, with what burning we had yet to make it ours, how we could cease lamenting. Freedom lurked around us and I understood, at last, that he could help us to be free if we would listen, that he would never be free

235

until we did. Yet, there was no battle in his face now. I heard what he had gone through, and would continue to go through until he came to rest in earth. He had made it his: that long line, of which we knew only Mama and Daddy. And he was giving it back, as everything must be given back, so that, passing through death, it can live forever. I saw my mother's face again, and felt, for the first time, how the stones of the road she had walked on must have bruised her feet. I saw the moonlit road where my father's brother died. And it brought something else back to me, and carried me past it. I saw my little girl again and felt Isabel's tears again, and I felt my own tears begin to rise. And I was yet aware that this was only a moment, that the world waited outside, as hungry as a tiger, and that trouble stretched above us, longer than the sky.

Then it was over. Creole and Sonny let out their breath, both soaking wet, and grinning. There was a lot of applause and some of it was real. In the dark, the girl came by and I asked her to take drinks to the bandstand. There was a long pause, while they talked up there in the indigo light and after awhile I saw the girl put a Scotch and milk on top of the piano for Sonny. He didn't seem to notice it, but just before they started playing again, he sipped from it and looked toward me, and nodded. Then he put it back on top of the piano. For me, then, as they began to play again, it glowed and shook above my brother's head like the very cup of trembling.   *[1957]*

≡ THINKING ABOUT THE TEXT

1. Were you sympathetic to the older brother in the beginning of the story? Did you become more so or less so as the story progressed? Is Sonny a sympathetic character in the beginning? At the end?

2. In real life, what do you believe is the role of an older brother? Does he have a responsibility to the members of his family regardless of their behavior? Explain. What is Sonny's mother's view of this?

3. Baldwin refers to the "darkness outside" several times. What do you think this means for Sonny? For Sonny's mother and father? For the narrator?

4. Listening seems to play an important function for Sonny and his brother. Cite specific examples of how they do or do not listen to each other. What might be some definitions of "listening" in this context?

5. One might think that brothers would understand each other better than outsiders do. But is that the case here? In your experience? In other stories or movies? How might you account for this difficulty?

≡ MAKING COMPARISONS

1. The older brothers in "The Rich Brother" and "Sonny's Blues" struggle to understand their younger brothers. Which one seems more successful? Why?

2. Both younger brothers in these two stories seem to march to different drummers. How would you describe their variations from the norm?

3. Some critics claim that these two stories are about responsibility; others claim they are about tolerance; still others see sibling rivalry, blind faith, or ego as the focus. What do you think, and why?

≡ WRITING ABOUT ISSUES

1. In an essay, argue that either Pete or Donald is the rich brother.

2. In an essay, argue that either Sonny or his brother is the real hero of the story.

3. Write an essay based on a conflict you had with a sibling, explaining how the relationship evolved. Argue that this conflict is similar to or different than the one depicted in either "The Rich Brother" or "Sonny's Blues."

4. Do some library research on birth order as it affects sibling rivalry, especially between brothers. Argue that either Pete and Donald or Sonny and his brother are or are not typical examples of sibling rivalry.

DAVID FOSTER WALLACE, "Good People"

BEN MARCUS, "Cold Little Bird"

The joys and satisfaction of parenting are woven into the fabric of our cultural expectations. In popular culture, the ubiquitous "and they lived happily ever after" invariably involves raising a happy family. The notion is universal and an integral part of the American Dream. And it is often a realized dream. But not always. The reality is that the unexpected can derail the best of intentions. An unplanned pregnancy, for example, can be a welcome surprise, but depending on the context, it can be a source of anxiety and confusions.

In our first story, a young couple has to make a consequential decision about whether to have a child. Such decisions, of course, are never made in a vacuum. There are specific moral, ethical, and religious factors to be considered, as well as financial, psychological, and cultural contexts. It is a deeply personal decision, one where no one will ever be the same. The decision to have a child or not can strengthen a relationship but it can also destroy one. It can also make explicit fault lines previously avoided. For the thoughtful or the careless couple, a future together is never assured.

In our next story, the seemingly happily married couple with a bright future already has two children. But suddenly, their lives darken. Their ten-year-old son stuns his parents, especially his father, by rejecting their heartfelt support and affection. Their relationship starts to unravel. Both stories deal with a parental crisis, and the solutions are hardly obvious.

≡ BEFORE YOU READ

Recall a difficult ethical/moral decision you had to make. To what extent were cultural, religious, and family expectations influential? Would you make the same or a different decision today?

DAVID FOSTER WALLACE
Good People

David Foster Wallace (1962–2008) was born in Ithaca, New York, and later went to elementary and high school in Urbana, Illinois. His parents were both college professors and after receiving degrees from Amherst College and the University of Arizona and publishing Infinite Jest *(1991), a highly regarded novel, he eventually became a professor at Pomona College in Claremont, California, in 2002. He received the prestigious MacArthur Fellowship in 1997 and was working on a novel,* The Pale King, *when he committed suicide, having suffered from depression since his late adolescence. Although the short story, "Good People," published here seems fairly straightforward and clearly written, most of his critically acclaimed fiction features long multi-clause sentences, jargon, various voices and modes of writing, and extensive footnotes and endnotes. Wallace hoped to write "morally passionate, passionately moral fiction" that might help readers "become less alone inside." He is generally considered to be one of the most influential and innovative writers of his generation.*

They were up on a picnic table at that park by the lake, by the edge of the lake, with part of a downed tree in the shallows half hidden by the bank. Lane A. Dean, Jr., and his girlfriend, both in bluejeans and button-up shirts. They sat up on the table's top portion and had their shoes on the bench part that people sat on to picnic or fellowship together in carefree times. They'd gone to different high schools but the same junior college, where they had met in campus ministries. It was springtime, and the park's grass was very green and the air suffused with honeysuckle and lilacs both, which was almost too much. There were bees, and the angle of the sun made the water of the shallows look dark. There had been more storms that week, with some downed trees and the sound of chainsaws all up and down his parents' street. Their postures on the picnic table were both the same forward kind with their shoulders rounded and elbows on their knees. In this position the girl rocked slightly and once put her face in her hands, but she was not crying. Lane was very still and immobile and looking past the bank at the downed tree in the shallows and its ball of exposed roots going all directions and the tree's cloud of branches all half in the water. The only other individual nearby was a dozen spaced tables away, by himself, standing upright. Looking at the torn-up hole in the ground there where the tree had gone over. It was still early yet and all the shadows wheeling right and shortening. The girl wore a thin old checked cotton shirt with pearl-colored snaps with the long sleeves down and always smelled very good and clean, like someone you could trust and care about even if you weren't in love. Lane Dean had liked the smell of her right away. His mother called her *down to earth* and liked her, thought she was good people, you could tell — she made this evident in little ways. The shallows lapped from different directions at the tree as if almost teething on it. Sometimes when alone and thinking or struggling to turn a matter over to Jesus Christ in prayer, he would find himself putting his fist in his palm and turning it slightly as if still playing and pounding his glove to stay sharp and alert in center. He did not do this now; it would be cruel and indecent to do this now. The older individual stood beside his picnic table — he was at it but not sitting — and looked also out of place in a suit coat or jacket and the kind of men's hat Lane's grandfather wore in photos as a young insurance man. He appeared to be looking across the lake. If he moved, Lane didn't see it. He looked more like a picture than a man. There were not any ducks in view.

One thing Lane Dean did was reassure her again that he'd go with her and be there with her. It was one of the few safe or decent things he could really say. The second time he said it again now she shook her head and laughed in an unhappy way that was more just air out her nose. Her real laugh was different. Where he'd be was the waiting room, she said. That he'd be thinking about her and feeling bad for her, she knew, but he couldn't be in there with her. This was so obviously true that he felt like a ninny that he'd kept on about it and now knew what she had thought every time he went and said it—it hadn't brought her comfort or eased the burden at all. The worse he felt, the stiller he sat. The whole thing felt balanced on a knife or wire; if he moved to put his arm up or touch her the whole thing could tip over. He hated himself for sitting so frozen. He could almost visualize himself tiptoeing past something explosive. A big stupid-looking tiptoe, like in a cartoon. The whole last black week had been this way and it was wrong. He knew it was wrong, knew something was required of him that was not this terrible frozen care and caution, but he pretended to himself he did not know what it was that was required. He pretended it had no name. He pretended that not saying aloud what he knew to be right and true was for her sake, was for the sake of her needs and feelings. He also worked dock and routing at UPS, on top of school, but had traded to get the day off after they'd decided together. Two days before, he had awakened very early and tried to pray but could not. He was freezing more and more solid, he felt like, but he had not thought of his father or the blank frozenness of his father, even in church, which had once filled him with such pity. This was the truth. Lane Dean, Jr., felt sun on one arm as he pictured in his mind an image of himself on a train, waving mechanically to something that got smaller and smaller as the train pulled away. His father and his mother's father had the same birthday, a Cancer. Sheri's hair was colored an almost corn blond, very clean, the skin through her central part pink in the sunlight. They'd sat here long enough that only their right side was shaded now. He could look at her head, but not at her. Different parts of him felt unconnected to each other. She was smarter than him and they both knew it. It wasn't just school—Lane Dean was in accounting and business and did all right; he was hanging in there. She was a year older, twenty, but it was also more—she had always seemed to Lane to be on good terms with her life in a way that age could not account for. His mother had put it that she *knew what it is she wanted*, which was nursing and not an easy program at Peoria Junior College, and plus she worked hostessing at the Embers and had bought her own car. She was serious in a way Lane liked. She had a cousin that died when she was thirteen, fourteen, that she'd loved and been close with. She only talked about it that once. He liked her smell and her downy arms and the way she exclaimed when something made her laugh. He had liked just being with her and talking to her. She was serious in her faith and values in a way that Lane had liked and now, sitting here with her on the table, found himself afraid of. This was an awful thing. He was starting to believe that he might not be serious in his faith. He might be somewhat of a hypocrite, like the Assyrians in Isaiah, which would be a far graver sin than the appointment—he had decided he believed this. He was desperate to be good people, to still be able to feel he was good. He rarely before now had thought of damnation and Hell—that part of it didn't speak to his spirit—and in worship services he more just tuned himself out and tolerated Hell when it came up, the same way you tolerate the job you've got to have to save up for what it is you want. Her tennis shoes had little things doodled on them from sitting in her class lectures. She stayed looking down like that. Little notes or reading assignments in Bic in her neat round hand on the rubber elements around the sneaker's rim. Lane A. Dean, looking now at her inclined head's side's barrettes in the shape of blue ladybugs. The appointment was for afternoon, but when the doorbell had rung so early and his mother'd called to him up the stairs, he had known, and a terrible kind of blankness had commenced falling through him.

He told her that he did not know what to do. That he knew if he was the salesman of it and forced it upon her that was awful and wrong. But he was trying to understand — they'd prayed on it and talked it through from every different angle. Lane said how sorry she knew he was, and that if he was wrong in believing they'd truly decided together when they decided to make the appointment she should please tell him, because he thought he knew how she must have felt as it got closer and closer and how she must be so scared, but that what he couldn't tell was if it was more than that. He was totally still except for moving his mouth, it felt like. She did not reply. That if they needed to pray on it more and talk it through, then he was here, he was ready, he said. The appointment could get moved back; if she just said the word they could call and push it back to take more time to be sure in the decision. It was still so early in it — they both knew that, he said. This was true, that he felt this way, and yet he also knew he was also trying to say things that would get her to open up and say enough back that he could see her and read her heart and know what to say to get her to go through with it. He knew this without admitting to himself that this was what he wanted, for it would make him a hypocrite and liar. He knew, in some locked-up little part of him, why it was that he'd gone to no one to open up and seek their life counsel, not Pastor Steve or the prayer partners at campus ministries, not his UPS friends or the spiritual counselling available through his parents' old church. But he did not know why Sheri herself had not gone to Pastor Steve — he could not read her heart. She was blank and hidden. He so fervently wished it never happened. He felt like he knew now why it was a true sin and not just a leftover rule from past society. He felt like he had been brought low by it and humbled and now did believe that the rules were there for a reason. That the rules were concerned with him personally, as an individual. He promised God he had learned his lesson. But what if that, too, was a hollow promise, from a hypocrite who repented only after, who promised submission but really only wanted a reprieve? He might not even know his own heart or be able to read and know himself. He kept thinking also of 1 Timothy and the hypocrite therein who *disputeth over words*. He felt a terrible inner resistance but could not feel what it was that it resisted. This was the truth. All the different angles and ways they had come at the decision together did not ever include it — the word — for had he once said it, avowed that he did love her, loved Sheri Fisher, then it all would have been transformed. It would not be a different stance or angle, but a difference in the very thing they were praying and deciding on together. Sometimes they had prayed together over the phone, in a kind of half code in case anybody accidentally picked up the extension. She continued to sit as if thinking, in the pose of thinking, like that one statue.

They were right up next to each other on the table. He was looking over past her at the tree in the water. But he could not say he did: it was not true.

But neither did he ever open up and tell her straight out he did not love her. This might be his *lie by omission*. This might be the frozen resistance — were he to look right at her and tell her he didn't, she would keep the appointment and go. He knew this. Something in him, though, some terrible weakness or lack of values, could not tell her. It felt like a muscle he did not have. He didn't know why; he just could not do it, or even pray to do it. She believed he was good, serious in his values. Part of him seemed willing to more or less just about lie to someone with that kind of faith and trust, and what did that make him? How could such a type of individual even pray? What it really felt like was a taste of the reality of what might be meant by Hell. Lane Dean had never believed in Hell as a lake of fire or a loving God consigning folks to a burning lake of fire — he knew in his heart this was not true. What he believed in was a living God of compassion and love and the possibility of a personal relationship with Jesus Christ through whom this love was enacted in human time. But sitting here beside this girl as unknown to him now as outer space, waiting for whatever she might say to unfreeze him, now he felt like he could see the edge or outline of what a real vision of Hell might be. It was of two great and terrible armies within himself, opposed and facing each other, silent. There would be battle but no victor. Or never a battle — the armies would stay like that, motionless, looking across at each other, and seeing therein something so different and alien from themselves that they could not understand, could not hear each other's speech as even words or read anything from what their face looked like, frozen like that, opposed and uncomprehending, for all human time. Two-hearted, a hypocrite to yourself either way.

When he moved his head, a part of the lake further out flashed with sun — the water up close wasn't black now, and you could see into the shallows and see that all the water was moving but gently, this way and that — and in this same way he besought to return to himself as Sheri moved her leg and started to turn beside him. He could see the man in the suit and gray hat standing motionless now at the lake's rim, holding something under one arm and looking across at the opposite side where a row of little forms on camp chairs sat in a way that meant they had lines in the water for crappie — which mostly only your blacks from the East Side ever did — and the little white shape at the row's end a Styrofoam creel. In his moment or time at the lake now just to come, Lane Dean first felt he could take this all in whole: everything seemed distinctly lit, for the circle of the pin oak's shade had rotated off all the way, and they sat now in sun with their shadow a two-headed thing in the grass before them. He was looking or gazing again at where the downed tree's branches seemed to all bend so sharply just under the shallows' surface when he was given to know that through all this frozen silence he'd despised he had, in truth, been praying, or some little part of his heart he could not hear had, for he was answered now with a type of vision, what he would later call within his own mind a vision or *moment of grace*. He was not a hypocrite, just broken and split off like all men. Later on, he believed that what happened was he'd

5

had a moment of almost seeing them both as Jesus saw them — as blind but groping, wanting to please God despite their inborn fallen nature. For in that same given moment he saw, quick as light, into Sheri's heart, and was made to know what would occur here as she finished turning to him and the man in the hat watched the fishing and the downed elm shed cells into the water. This down-to-earth girl that smelled good and wanted to be a nurse would take and hold one of his hands in both of hers to unfreeze him and make him look at her, and she would say that she cannot do it. That she is sorry she did not know this sooner, that she hadn't meant to lie — she agreed because she'd wanted to believe that she could, but she cannot. That she will carry this and have it; she has to. With her gaze clear and steady. That all night last night she prayed and searched inside herself and decided this is what love commands of her. That Lane should please please sweetie let her finish. That listen — this is her own decision and obliges him to nothing. That she knows he does not love her, not that way, has known it all this time, and that it's all right. That it is as it is and it's all right. She will carry this, and have it, and love it and make no claim on Lane except his good wishes and respecting what she has to do. That she releases him, all claim, and hopes he finishes up at P.J.C. and does so good in his life and has all joy and good things. Her voice will be clear and steady, and she will be lying, for Lane has been given to read her heart. To see through her. One of the opposite side's blacks raises his arm in what may be greeting, or waving off a bee. There is a mower cutting grass someplace off behind them. It will be a terrible, last-ditch gamble born out of the desperation in Sheri Fisher's soul, the knowledge that she can neither do this thing today nor carry a child alone and shame her family. Her values blocked the way either way, Lane could see, and she has no other options or choice — this lie is not a sin. Galatians 4:16, *Have I then become your enemy?* She is gambling that he is good. There on the table, neither frozen nor yet moving, Lane Dean, Jr., sees all this, and is moved with pity, and also with something more, something without any name he knows, that is given to him in the form of a question that never once in all the long week's thinking and division had even so much as occurred — why is he so sure he doesn't love her? Why is one kind of love any different? What if he has no earthly idea what love is? What would even Jesus do? For it was just now he felt her two small strong soft hands on his, to turn him. What if he was just afraid, if the truth was no more than this, and if what to pray for was not even love but simple courage, to meet both her eyes as she says it and trust his heart?   *[2007]*

≡ THINKING ABOUT THE TEXT

1. What happens to Lane during his "moment of grace"? How would you define "good" in the title?

2. What is the significance of the much-repeated word "frozen"? What relevance do some of the other details in the story have, for example, the man by the lake; the fallen tree; references to his father and other specific details?

3. Describe Lane's conflicted and evolving notions about whether he loves Sheri or not. How do love and courage connect for him, or do they? Why does Wallace never use the word "abortion," even though the procedure lies at the emotional heart of his story?

4. What is your take on the final decision Lane and Sheri might make? What evidence can you cite to support your position? Why doesn't Foster have Sheri speak, especially given that the decision is ultimately hers to make?

5. How well do you think Lane knows Sheri's heart? How well does he know his own? Do you think he is sensitive enough to her needs? Is he serious about doing the right thing? What other considerations do you think he should be thinking about?

BEN MARCUS
Cold Little Bird

Ben Marcus (1967) was raised in Austin, Texas, and received his B.A. from New York University and a an M.F.A. from Brown University. He has written several books including his first novel, Notable American Women *(2002), as well as* The Flame Alphabet *(2012) and* Leaving the Sea *(2014). His latest book is the short story collection* Notes from the Fog *(2018), which was called "compelling and original." The following story appeared in* The New Yorker *in October 2015.*

It started with bedtime. A coldness. A formality.

Martin and Rachel tucked the boy in, as was their habit, then stooped to kiss him good night.

"Please don't do that," he said, turning to face the wall.

They took it as teasing, flopped onto his bed to nuzzle and tickle him.

The boy turned rigid, endured the cuddle, then barked out at them,   5
"I really don't like that!"

"Jonah?" Martin said, sitting up.

"I don't want your help at bedtime anymore," he said. "I'm not a baby. You have Lester. Go cuddle with him."

"Sweetheart," Rachel said. "We're not helping you. We're just saying good night. You like kisses, right? Don't you like kisses and cuddles? You big silly."

Jonah hid under the blankets. A classic pout. Except that he wasn't a pouter, he wasn't a hider. He was a reserved boy who generally took a scientific interest in the tantrums and emotional extravagances of other children, marvelling at them as though they were some strange form of street theatre.

Martin tried to tickle the blanketed lump of person that was his son. He   10
didn't know what part of Jonah he was touching. He just dug at him with a stiff hand, thinking a laugh would come out, some sound of pleasure. It used to work. One stab of the finger and the kid exploded with giggles. But Jonah didn't speak, didn't move.

"We love you so much. You know?" Martin said. "So we like to show it. It feels good."

"Not to me. I don't feel that way."

"What way? What do you mean?"

They sat with him, perplexed, and tried to rub his back, but he'd rolled to the edge of the bed, nearly flattening himself against the wall.

"I don't love you," Jonah said.   15

"Oh, now," Martin said. "You're just tired. No need to say that sort of stuff. Get some rest."

"You told me to tell the truth, and I'm telling the truth. I. Don't. Love. You."

This happened. Kids tested their attachments. They tried to push you away to see just how much it would take to really lose you. As a parent, you took the blow, even sharpened the knife yourself before handing it to the little fiends, who stepped right up and plunged. Or so Martin had heard.

They hovered by Jonah's bed, assuring him that it had been a long day — although the day had been entirely unremarkable — and he would feel better in the morning.

Martin felt like a robot saying these things. He felt like a robot thinking   20
them. There was nothing to do but leave the boy there, let him sleep it off.

Downstairs, they cleaned the kitchen in silence. Rachel was troubled or not, he couldn't tell, and it was better not to check. In some way, Martin was captivated. If he were Jonah, ten years old and reasonably smart, starting to sniff out the world and find his angle, this might be something worth exploring. Getting rid of the soft, warm, dumb providers who spun opportunity around you relentlessly, answering your every need. Good play, Jonah. But how do you follow such a strong, definitive opening move? What now?

Over the next few weeks, Jonah stuck by his statement, wandering through their lives like some prisoner of war who'd been trained not to talk. He endured his parents, leaving for school in the morning with scarcely a goodbye. Upon coming home, he put away his coat and shoes, did his homework without prompting. He helped himself to snacks, dragging a chair into the kitchen so that he could climb on the counter. He got his own glass, filling it with water at the sink. When he was done eating, he loaded his dishes in the dishwasher. Martin, working from home in the afternoons, watched all this, impressed but bothered. He kept offering to help, but Jonah always said that he was fine, he could handle it. At bedtime, Martin and Rachel still fussed over Lester, who, at six years old, regressed and babified himself in order to drink up the extra attention. Jonah insisted on saying good night with no kiss, no hug. He shut his door and disappeared every night at 8 P.M.

When Martin or Rachel caught Jonah's eye, the boy forced a smile at them. But it was so obviously fake. Could a boy his age do that?

"Of course," Rachel said. "You think he doesn't know how to pretend?"

"No, I know he can pretend. But this seems different. I mean, to have   25
to pretend that he's happy to see us. First of all, what the fuck is he so upset about? And, second, it just seems so kind of. . . grownup. In the worst possible way. A fake smile. It's a tool one uses with strangers."

"Well, I don't know. He's ten. He has social skills. He can hide his feelings. That's not such an advanced thing to do."

Martin studied his wife.

"O.K., so you think everything's fine?"

"I think maybe he's growing up and you don't like it."

"And you like it? That's what you're saying? You like this?"   30

His voice had gone up. He had lost control for a minute there, and, as per motherfucking usual, it was a deal-breaker. Rachel put up her hand, and she was gone. From the other room, he heard her say, "I'm not going to talk to you when you're like this."

O.K., he thought. Goodbye. We'll talk some other time when I'm not like this, a.k.a. never.

Jonah, it turned out, reserved this behavior solely for his parents. A probing note to his teacher revealed nothing. He was fine in school, did not act withdrawn, had successfully led a team project on Antarctica, and seemed to run and play with his friends during recess. Run and play? What animal were they discussing here? Everybody loved Jonah was the verdict, along with some bullshit about how happy he seemed. "Seemed" was just the thing. Seemed! If you were an idiot who didn't know the boy, who had no grasp of human behavior.

At home, Jonah doted on his brother, read to him, played with him, even let Lester climb on his back for rides around the house, all fairly verboten in the old days, when Jonah's interest in Lester had only ever been theoretical. Lester was thrilled by it all. He suddenly had a new friend, the older brother he worshipped, who used to ignore him. Life was good. But to Martin it felt like a calculated display. With this performance of tenderness toward his brother, Jonah seemed to be saying, "Look, this is what you no longer get. See? It's over for you. Go fuck yourself."

Martin took it too personally, he knew. Maybe because it was personal.   35

One night, when Jonah hadn't touched his dinner, they were asking him if he would like something else to eat, and, because he wasn't answering, and really had not been answering for some weeks now, other than in one-word responses, curt and formal, Martin and Rachel abandoned their usual rules, the guideposts of parenting they'd clung to, and moved through a list of bribes. They dangled the promise of ice cream, and then those monstrosities passing for Popsicles, shaped like animals with chocolate faces or hats, which used to turn Jonah craven and desperate. When Jonah remained silent and sort of washed-out looking, Martin offered his son candy. He could have some right now. If only he'd fucking say something.

"It's just that you're all in his face," Rachel said to him later. "How's he supposed to breathe?"

"You think my desire for him to speak is making him silent?"

"It's probably not helping."

"Whereas your approach is so amazing."   40

"My approach? You mean being his mother? Loving him for who he is? Keeping him safe? Yeah, it is pretty amazing."

He turned over to sleep while Rachel clipped on her book light.

They'd ride this one out in silence, apparently.

Yes, well. They'd written their own vows, promising to be "intensely honest" with each other. They had not specifically said that they would hold up each other's flaws to the most rigorous scrutiny, calling out each other's smallest mistakes, like fact checkers, believing, perhaps, that the marriage would thrive only if all personal errors and misdeeds were rooted out of it. This mission had gone unstated.

In the morning, when Martin got up, Jonah sat reading while Lester played soldiers on the rug. Lester was fully dressed, his backpack near the door. There was no possible way that Lester had done this on his own. Obviously, Jonah had dressed his brother, emptied the boy's backpack of yesterday's crap art from the first-grade praise farm he attended, and readied it for a new day. Months ago, they'd asked Jonah to perform this role in the morning, to dress and prepare his brother, so that they could sleep in, and Jonah had complied a few times, but halfheartedly, with a certain mysterious cost to little Lester, who was often speechless and tear-streaked by the time they found him. The chore had quickly lapsed, and usually Martin awoke to a hungry, half-naked Lester, waiting for his help.

Today, Lester seemed happy. There was no sign of crying.

"Good morning, Daddy," he said.

"Hello there, Les, my friend. Sleep O.K.?"

"Jonah made me breakfast. I had juice and Cheerios. I brought in my own dishes."

"Way to go! Thank you."

Martin figured he'd just play it casual, not draw too much attention to anything.

"Good morning, champ," he said to Jonah. "What are you reading?"

Martin braced himself for silence, for stillness, for a child who hadn't heard or who didn't want to answer. But Jonah looked at him.

"It's a book called 'The Short.' It's a novel," he said, and then he resumed reading.

A fat bolt of lightning filled the cover. A boy ran beneath it. The title lettering was achieved graphically with one long wire, a plug trailing off the cover.

"Oh, yeah?" Martin said. "What's it about? Tell me about it."

There was a long pause this time. Martin went into the kitchen to get his coffee started. He popped back out to the living room and snapped his fingers.

"Jonah, hello. Your book. What's it about?"

Jonah spoke quietly. His little flannel shirt was buttoned up to the collar, as if he were headed out into a blizzard. Martin almost heard a kind of apology in his voice.

"Since I have to leave for school in fifteen minutes, and since I was hoping to get to page 100 this morning, would it be O.K. if I didn't describe it to you? You can look it up on Amazon."

He told Rachel about this later in the morning, the boy's unsettling calm, his odd response.

"Yeah, I don't know," she said. "I mean, good for him, right? He just wanted to read, and he told you that. So what?"

"Huh," Martin said.

Rachel was busy cleaning. She hadn't looked at him. Their argument last night had either been forgotten or stored for later activation. He'd find out. She seemed engrossed by a panicked effort at tidying, as if guests were arriving any second, as if their house were going to be inspected by the fucking U.N. Martin followed her around while they talked, because if he didn't she'd roam out of earshot and the conversation would expire.

"He just seems like a stranger to me," Martin said, trying to add a light-   65
ness to his voice so she wouldn't hear it as a complaint.

Rachel stopped cleaning. "Yeah."

For a moment, it seemed that she might agree with him and they'd see this thing similarly.

"But he's not a stranger. I don't know. He's growing up. You should be happy that he's reading. At least he wasn't begging to be on the stupid iPad, and it seems like he's talking again. He wanted to read, and you're freaking out. Honestly."

Yes, well. You had these creatures in your house. You fed them. You cleaned them. And here was the person you'd made them with. She was beautiful, probably. She was smart, probably. It was impossible to know anymore. He looked at her through an unclean filter, for sure. He could indulge a great anger toward her that would suddenly vanish if she touched his hand. What was wrong? He'd done something or he hadn't done something. Figure it the fuck out, Martin thought. Root out the resentment. Apologize so hard it leaks from her body. Then drink the liquid. Or use it in a soup. Whatever.

Jonah came and went, such a weird bird of a boy, so serious. Martin tried to   70
tread lightly. He tried not to tread at all. Better to float overhead, to allow the cold remoteness of his elder son to freeze their home. He studied Rachel's caution, her distance-giving, her respect, the confidence she possessed that he clearly lacked, even as he saw the toll it took on her, what had become of this person who needed to touch her young son and just couldn't.

Then, one afternoon, he forgot himself. He came home with groceries and saw Jonah down on the rug with Lester, setting up his Lego figures for him, such an impossibly small person, dressed so carefully by his own hand, his son — it still seemed ridiculous and a miracle to Martin that there'd be such a thing as a son, that a little creature in this world would be his to protect and befriend. Without thinking about it, he sat down next to Jonah and took the whole of the boy in his arms. He didn't want to scare him, and he didn't want to hurt him, but he needed this boy to feel what it was like to be held, to really be swallowed up in a father's arms. Maybe he could squeeze all the aloofness out of the boy, just choke it out until it was gone.

Jonah gave nothing back. He went limp, and the hug didn't work the way Martin had hoped. You couldn't do it alone. The person being hugged had to do something, to be something. The person being hugged had to fucking exist. And whoever this was, whoever he was holding, felt like nothing.

Finally, Martin released him, and Jonah straightened his hair. He did not look happy.

"I know that you and Mom are in charge and you make the rules," Jonah said. "But even though I'm only ten, don't I have a right not to be touched?"

The boy sounded so reasonable. 75

"You do," Martin said. "I apologize."

"I keep asking, but you don't listen."

"I listen."

"You don't. Because you keep doing it. So does Mom. You want to treat me like a stuffed animal, and I don't want to be treated like that."

"No, I don't, buddy." 80

"I don't want to be called buddy. Or mister. Or champ. I don't do that to you. You wouldn't want me always inventing some new ridiculous name for you."

"O.K." Martin put up his hands in surrender. "No more nicknames. I promise. It's just that you're my son and I like to hug you. We like to hug you."

"I don't want you to anymore. And I've said that."

"Well, too bad," Martin said, laughing, and, as if to prove he was right, he grabbed Lester, and Lester squealed with delight, squirming in his father's arms.

Do you see how this used to work? Martin wanted to say to Jonah. This 85 was you once, this was us.

Jonah seemed genuinely puzzled. "It doesn't matter to you that I don't like it?"

"It matters, but you're wrong. You can be wrong, you know. You'll die, without affection. I'm not kidding. You will actually dry up and die."

Again, he found he had to explain love to this boy, to detail what it was like when you felt a desperate connection with someone else, how you wanted to hold that person and just crush him with hugs. But as Martin fought through the difficult and ridiculous discussion, he felt as if he were having a conversation with a lawyer. A lawyer, a scold, a little prick of a person. Whom he wanted to hug less and less. Maybe it'd be simpler just to give Jonah what he wanted. What he thought he wanted.

Jonah seemed pensive, concerned.

"Does any of that make sense to you?" Martin asked. 90

"It's just that I'd rather not say things that could hurt someone," Jonah said.

"Well . . . that's good. That's how you should feel."

"I'd rather not have to say anything about you and Mom. At school. To Mr. Fourenay."

Mr. Fourenay was what they called a "feelings doctor." He was paid, certainly not very much, to take the kids and their feelings very, very seriously. Martin and Rachel had trouble taking *him* seriously. He looked like a man who had subsisted, for a very long time, on a strict diet of the feelings of children. Gutted, wasted, and soft.

"Jonah, what are you talking about?" 95

"About you touching me when I don't want you to. I don't want to have to mention that to anyone at school. I really don't."

Martin stood up. It was as if a hand had moved inside him.

He stared at Jonah, who held his gaze patiently, waiting for an answer.

"Message received. I'll discuss it with Mom."

"Thank you."   100

Without really thinking about it, Martin had crafted an adulthood that was essentially friendless. There were, of course, the friends of the marriage, who knew him only as part of a couple—the dour, rotten part—and thus they were ruled out for anything remotely candid, like a confession of what the fuck had just gone down in his own home. Before the children came, he'd managed, sometimes erratically, to maintain preposterous phone relationships with several male friends. Deep, searching, facially sweaty conversations on the phone with other semi-articulate, vaguely unhappy men. In general, these friendships had heated up and found their purpose around a courtship or a breakup, when an aria of complaint or desire could be harmonized by some pathetic accomplice. But after Jonah was born, and then Lester, phone calls with friends had become out of the question. There was just never a time when it was O.K., or even appealing, to talk on the phone. When he was home, he was in shark mode, cruising slowly and brutally through the house, cleaning and clearing, scrubbing food from rugs, folding and storing tiny items of clothing, and, if no one was looking, occasionally stopping at his laptop to see if his prospects had suddenly been lifted by some piece of tremendous fortune, delivered via e-mail. When he finally came to rest, in a barf-covered chair, he was done for the night. He poured several beers, in succession, right onto his pleasure center, which could remain dry and withered no matter what came soaking down.

The gamble of a friendless adulthood, whether by accident or design, was that your partner would step up to the role. She for you, and you for her.

But when Martin thought about Jonah's threat—blackmail, really—he knew he couldn't tell Rachel. In a certain light, the only light that mattered, he was in the wrong. The instructions were already out that they were not to get all huggy with Jonah, and here he'd gone and done it anyway. Rachel would just ask him what he had expected and why he was surprised that Jonah had lashed out at him for not respecting his boundaries.

So, yeah, maybe, maybe that was all true. But there was the other part. The threat that came out of the boy. The quiet force of it. To even mention that Jonah had threatened to report them for touching him ghosted an irreversible suspicion into people's minds. You couldn't talk about it. You couldn't mention it. It seemed better to not even think it, to do the work that would begin to block such an event from memory.

The boys were talking quietly on the couch one afternoon a few days later.   105
Martin was in the next room, and he caught the sweet tones, the two voices he loved, that he couldn't even bear. For a minute he forgot what was going on and listened to the life he'd helped make. They were speaking like little people, not

kids, back and forth, a real discussion. Jonah was explaining something to Lester, and Lester was asking questions, listening patiently. It was heartbreaking.

He snuck out to see the boys on the couch, Lester cuddled up against his older brother, who had a big book in his hands. A grownup one. On the cover, instead of a boy dashing beneath a bolt of lightning, were the good old Twin Towers. The title, "Lies," was glazed in blood, which dripped down the towers themselves.

Oh, motherfucking hell.

"What's this?" Martin asked. "What are you reading there?"

"A book about 9/11. Who caused it."

Martin grabbed it, thumbed the pages. "Where'd you get it?"   110

"From Amazon. With my birthday gift card."

"Hmm. Do you believe it?"

"What do you mean? It's true."

"What's true?"

"That the Jews caused 9/11 and they all stayed home that day so they   115
wouldn't get killed."

Martin excused Lester. Told him to skedaddle and, yes, it was O.K. to watch TV, even though watching time hadn't started yet. Just go, go.

"O.K., Jonah," he whispered. "Jonah, stop. This is not O.K. Not at all O.K. First of all, Jonah, you have to listen to me. This is insane. This is a book by an insane person."

"You know him?"

"No, I don't know him. I don't have to. Listen to me, you know that we're Jewish, right? You, me, Mom, Lester. We're Jewish."

"Not really."   120

"What do you mean, not really?"

"You don't go to synagogue. You don't seem to worship. You never talk about it."

"That's not all that matters."

"Last month was Yom Kippur and you didn't fast. You didn't go to services. You don't ever say Happy New Year on Rosh Hashanah."

"Those are rituals. You don't need to observe them to be part of the faith."   125

"But do you know anything about it?"

"9/11?"

"No, being Jewish. Do you know what it means and what you're supposed to believe and how you're supposed to act?"

"I do, yes. I have a pretty good idea."

"Then tell me."   130

"Jonah."

"What? I'm just wondering how you can call yourself Jewish."

"How? Are you fucking kidding me?"

He needed to walk away before he did something.

"O.K., Jonah, it's actually really simple. I'll tell you how. Because everyone   135
else in the world would call me Jewish. With no debate. None. Because of my parents and their parents, and their parents, including whoever got turned to dust in the war. Zayde Anshel's whole family. You walk by their picture every day in the hall. Do you think you're not related to them? And because I was

called a kike in junior high school, and high school, and college, and probably beyond that, right up to this fucking day. And because if they started rounding up Jews again they'd take one look at our name and they'd know. And that's you, too, mister. They would come for us and kill us. O.K.? You."

He was shaking his fist in his son's face. Just old-school shouting. He wanted to do more. He wanted to tear something apart. There was no safe way to behave right now.

"They would kill you. And you'd be dead. You'd die."

"Martin?" Rachel said. "What's going on?"

Of course. There she was. Lurking. He had no idea how long she'd been standing there, what she'd heard.

Martin wasn't done. Jonah seemed fascinated, his eyes wide as his father   140
ranted.

"Even if you said that you hated Jews, too, and that Jews were evil and caused all the suffering in the world, they would look at you and know for sure that you were Jewish, for sure! Buddy, champ, mister" — just spitting these names at his son — "because only a Jew, they would say, only a Jew would betray his own people like that."

Jonah looked at him. "I understand," he said. He didn't seem shaken. He didn't seem disturbed. Had he heard? How could he really understand?

The boy picked up the book and thumbed through it.

"This is just a different point of view. You always say that I should have an open mind, that I should think for myself. You say that to me all the time."

"Yes, I do. You're right." Martin was trembling.   145

"Then do I have your permission to keep reading it?"

"No, you absolutely don't. Not this time. Permission denied."

Rachel was shaking her head.

"Do you see what he's reading? Do you see it?" he shouted.

He waved the book at her, and she just looked at him with no expression at all.   150

After the kids were in bed, and the house had been quietly put back together, Rachel said they needed to talk.

Yes, we do, he thought, and about fucking time.

"Honestly," she said. "It's upsetting that he had that book, but the way you spoke to him? I don't want you going anywhere near him."

"Yeah, well, that's not for you to say. You're his mom, not mine. You want to file papers? You want to seek custody? Good luck, Mrs. Freeze. I'm his father. And you didn't hear it. You didn't hear it all. You have no fucking idea."

"I heard it, and I heard you. Martin, you need help. You're, I don't know,   155
depressed. You're self-pitying. You think everything is some concerted attack on you. For the record, I am worried about Jonah. Really worried. Something is seriously wrong. There is no debate there. But you're just the worst possible partner in that worry — the fucking worst — because you make everything harder, and we can't discuss it without analyzing your bullshit feelings. You act wounded and hurt, and we're all supposed to feel sorry for you. For you! This isn't about you. So shut down the pity party already."

When this kind of talk came on, Martin knew to listen. This was the scold she'd been winding up for, and if he could endure it, and cop to it, there might be some release and clarity at the other end. A part of him found these outbursts from Rachel thrilling, and in some ways it was possible that he co-engineered them, without really thinking about it. Performed the sullen and narcissistic dance moves that, over time, would yield this kind of eruption from her. His wife was alive. She cared. Even if it seemed that she might sort of hate him.

He circled the house for a while, cooling off, letting the attack—no, no, the truth—settle. Any argument or even discussion to the contrary would just feed her point and read as the defensive bleating of a cornered man. Any speech, that is, except admission, contrition, and apology, the three horsemen.

Which was who he brought back into the room with him.

Rachel was in bed reading, eyes burned onto the page. She didn't seem even remotely ready to surrender her anger.

"Hey, listen," Martin said. "So I know you're mad, but I just want to say that I agree with everything you said. I'm scared and I'm worried and I'm sorry."   160

He let this settle. It needed to spread, to sink in. She needed to realize that he was agreeing with her.

It was hard to tell, but it seemed that some of her anger, with nothing to meet it, was draining out.

"And," he continued. He waited for her to look up, which she finally did. "You'll think I'm kidding, and I know you don't even want to hear this right now, but it's true, and I have to say it. It made me a little bit horny to hear all that."

She shook her head at the bad joke, which at least meant there was room to move here.

"Shut up," she said.   165

This was the way in. He took it.

"You shut up."

"Sorry to yell, Martin. I am. I just—This is so hard. I'm sorry."

She probably wasn't. This was simply the script back in, to the two of them united, and they both knew it. One day, one of them would choose not to play. It would be so easy not to say their lines.

"No, it's O.K.," he said to her, climbing onto the bed. "I get it. Listen, let's take the little motherfucker to the shop. Get him fixed. I'll call some doctors in the morning."   170

They hugged. An actual hug, between two consenting people. A novelty in this house.

"O.K.," she said. "I'm terrified. I don't know what's happening. I look at him and want so much to just grab him, but he's not there anymore. What has he done to himself?"

"Maybe he just needs minor surgery. Does that work on 9/11 truthers?"

"Oh, look," she said to him softly. "You're back. The real you. We missed you."

They talked a little and got up close to each other in bed. For a moment,   175
their good feeling came on them — a version of it, anyway. It felt mild and
transitory, but he would take it. It was nice. He was in bed with his wife, and
they would figure this out.

"Listen," he said to her. "Do you want to just shag a pony right now, get
back on track?"

"I don't know," she said. "I feel gross. I feel depressed."

"I feel gross, too. Let's do it. Two gross people licking each other's buttons."

She went to the bathroom and got the jar of enabler. They took their positions on the bed.

He hoped he could. He hoped he could. He hoped he could.   180

He was cold and insecure, so he left his shirt on. And his socks.

They used a cream. They used their hands. They used an object or two.
During the brief strain of actual fornication they persisted with casual conversation about the next day's errands. In the early days of their marriage,
this had seemed wicked and sexy, some ironic ballast against the animal greed.
Now it just seemed efficient, and the animal greed no longer appeared. Minus
the wet spot at the end, and the minor glow one occasionally felt, their sex
wasn't so different from riding the subway.

It turned out that there was a deep arsenal of medical professionals who would
be delighted to consult on the problem of a disturbed child. Angry, depressed,
anxious, remote, bizarre. Even a Jew-hating Jewish child who might very well
be dead inside. Only when his parents looked at him, though. Only when his
parents spoke to him. Important parameter for the differential.

They zeroed in on recommendations with the help of a high-level participant in this world, a friend named Maureen, whose three exquisitely exceptional children had consumed, and spat back out, various kinds of psych
services ever since they could walk. Each of the kids seemed to romance a
different diagnosis every month, so Maureen had a pretty good idea of who
fixed what and for how much goddam moolah.

When they told her, in pale terms, about Jonah, she, as a connoisseur of   185
alienating behavior from the young, got excited.

"This is so 'The Fifth Child,' " she said. "Did you guys read that? I mean,
you probably shouldn't read that. But did you? It's like a fiction novel. I don't
think it really happened. But it's still fascinating."

Rachel had read it. Happy couple with four children and perfect life have
fifth child, leading to less perfect life. Much, much, much, much less perfect.
Sorrow, sorrow, sorrow, grief, and sorrow. Not really life at all.

"Yeah, but the kid in that book is a monster," Rachel said. "So heartless.
He's not real. And he just wants to inflict pain. Jonah wouldn't hurt anyone.
He wants to be alone. Or, not that, but. I don't know what Jonah wants. He's
not violent, though. Or even mad. I don't think."

"All right, but he is hurting you, right?" Maureen said. "I mean, it seems
like this is really causing you guys a lot of pain and suffering."

"I haven't read the book," Martin said. "But this isn't about us. This is about Jonah. His pain, his suffering. We just want to get to the bottom of it. To help him. To give him support." 190

In Rachel's silence he could feel her agreement and, maybe, her surprise that he would, or even could, think this way. He knew what to say now. He wasn't going to get burned again. But did he believe it? Was it true? He honestly didn't even know, and he wasn't so sure it mattered.

The doctor wanted to see them alone first. He said that it was his job to listen. So they talked, just dumped the thing out on the floor. It was ugly, Martin thought, but it was a rough picture of what was going down. The doctor scribbled away, stopping occasionally to look at them, to really deeply look at them, and nod. Since when had the act of listening turned into such a strange charade?

Then the doctor met with Jonah, to see for himself, pull evidence right from the culprit's mouth. Martin and Rachel sat in the waiting room and stared at the door. What would the doctor see? Which kid would he get? Were they crazy and was this all just some preteen freak-out?

Finally, the whole gang of them — doctor, parents, and child — gathered to go over the plan, Jonah sitting polite and alert while the future of his brain was discussed. They told him the proposal: a slow ramp of antidepressants, along with weekly therapy, and then, depending, some group work, if that all sounded good to Jonah.

Jonah didn't respond. 195

"What do you think?" the doctor said. "So you can feel better? And things can maybe go back to normal?"

"I told you, I feel fine," Jonah said.

"Yes, good! But sometimes when we're sick we think we're not. That can be a symptom of being sick — to think we are well."

"So all the healthy people are just lying to themselves?"

"Well, no, of course not," the doctor said. 200

"Right now I never think about hurting myself, but you want to give me a medicine that might make me think about hurting myself?"

The doctor seemed uneasy.

"It's called suicidal ideation," Jonah said.

"And how do you know about that?" the doctor asked.

"The Internet." 205

The adults all looked at one another.

"How come people are so surprised when someone knows something?" Jonah asked. "Your generation had better get used to how completely unspecial it is that a kid can look up a medicine online and learn about the side effects. That's not me being precocious. It's just me using my stupid computer."

"O.K., good. Well, you're right, you should be informed, and I want to congratulate you on finding that out for yourself. That's great work, Jonah."

Martin watched Jonah. He found himself hoping that the real Jonah would appear, scathing and cold, to show the doctor what they were dealing with.

"Thank you," Jonah said. "I'm really proud of myself. I didn't think I could   210
do it, but I just really stuck with it and I kept trying until I succeeded."

Martin could not tell if the doctor caught the tone of this response.

"But you might have also read that that's a very uncommon symptom. It
hardly ever happens. We just have to warn you and your parents about it, to be
on the lookout for it."

"Maybe. But I have none of the symptoms of depression, either. So why
would you risk making me feel like I want to kill myself if I'm not depressed
and feel fine?"

"O.K., Jonah. You know what? I'm going to talk to your parents alone now.
Does that sound all right? You can wait outside in the play area. There are
books and games."

"O.K.," Jonah said. "I'll just run and play now."   215

"There," Martin said. "There," after Jonah had closed the door. "That was
it. That's what he does."

"Sarcasm? Maybe you don't much like it, but we don't treat sarcasm in
young people. I think it's too virulent a strain." The doctor chuckled.

"No offense," Martin said to the doctor, "and I'm sure you know your job
and this is your specialty, but I think that way of speaking to him—"

"What way?"

"Just, you know, as if he were much younger. He's just— I don't think   220
that works with him."

"And how do you speak to him?"

"Excuse me?"

"How do you speak to him? I'm curious."

Rachel coughed and seemed uncomfortable. They'd agreed to be open, to
let each other have ideas and opinions without feeling mad or threatened.

"It's true," she said. "I mean, Martin, I think you have been surprised   225
lately that Jonah is as mature as he is. That seems to have really almost upset
you. You know, you really have yelled at him a lot. We can't just pretend that
hasn't happened." She looked at him apologetically. "Aside," she added, "from
the scary things that he's been saying."

"Is it maturity? I don't think so. Have I been upset? Fucking hell, yes.
And so have you, Rachel. And not because he thinks the Jews caused 9/11
or because he threatened to report us for sexual abuse for trying to hug him,
which, for what it's worth, I spared you from, Rachel. I spared you. Because
I didn't think you could bear it."

Rachel just stared at him.

"What you're seeing is a very, very bright boy," the doctor said.

"Too smart to treat?" Martin asked.

"I think family therapy would be productive. Very challenging, but worth-   230
while, in my opinion. I could get you a referral. What you're upset about, in
relation to your son, may not fall under the purview of medicine, though."

"The purview? Really?"

"To be honest, I was on the fence about medication. Whatever is going on
with Jonah, it does not present as depression. In my opinion, Jonah does not
have a medical condition."

Martin stood up.

"He's not sick, he's just an asshole, is what you're saying?"

"I think that's a very dangerous way for a parent to feel," the doctor said.   235

"Yeah?" Martin said, standing over the doctor now. "You're right. You got that one right. Because all of a parent's feelings are dangerous, you motherfucker."

At home that night, Martin stuffed a chicken with lemon halves, drenched it in olive oil, scattered a handful of salt over it, and blasted it in the oven until it emerged deeply burnished, with skin as crisp as glass. Rachel poured drinks for the two of them, and they cooked in silence. To Martin, it was a harmless silence. He could trust it, and if he couldn't, then to hell with it. He wasn't going to chase down everything unsaid and shout it into their home, as if all important messages on the planet needed to be shared. He'd said enough, things he believed, things he didn't. Quota achieved. Quota surpassed.

Rachel looked small and tired. Beyond that, he wasn't sure. He was more aware than ever, as she set the table and put out Lester's cup and Jonah's big-kid glass, how impossibly unknowable she would always be — what she thought, what she felt — how what was most special about her was the careful way she guarded it all.

No matter their theories — about Jonah or each other or the larger world — their job was to watch over Jonah on his cold voyage. He had to come back. This kind of controlled solitude was unsustainable. No one could pull it off, especially not someone so young. Except that his reasoning on this, he knew, was wishful parental bullshit. Of course a child could do it. Who else but children to lead the fucking species into darkness? Which meant what for the old-timers left behind?

Dinner was brief, destroyed by the savage appetite of Lester, who engulfed   240 his meal before Rachel had even taken a bite, and begged, begged to be excused so that he could return to the platoon of small plastic men he'd deployed on the rug. According to Lester, his men were waiting to be told what to do. "I need to tell my guys who to kill!" he shouted. "I'm in charge!"

At the height of this tantrum, Jonah, silent since they'd returned from the doctor's office, leaned over to Lester, put a hand on his shoulder, and calmly told him not to whine.

"Don't use that tone of voice," he said. "Mom and Dad will excuse you when they're ready."

"O.K.," Lester said, looking up at his brother with a kind of awe, and for the rest of their wordless dinner he sat there waiting, as patiently as a boy his age ever could, his hands folded in his lap.

At bedtime, Rachel asked Martin if he wouldn't mind letting her sleep alone. She was just very tired. She didn't think she could manage otherwise. She gave him a sort of smile, and he saw the effort behind it. She dragged her pillow and a blanket into a corner of the TV room and made herself a little nest there. He had the bedroom to himself. He crawled onto Rachel's side of the mattress, which was higher, softer, less abused, and fell asleep.

In the morning, Jonah did not say goodbye on his way to school, nor did he   245
greet Martin upon his return home. When Martin asked after his day, Jonah,
without looking up, said that it had been fine. Maybe that was all there was to
say, and why, really, would you ever shit on such an answer?

Jonah took up his spot on the couch and opened a book, reading quietly
until dinner, while Lester played at his feet. Martin watched Jonah. Was that a
grin or a grimace on the boy's face? he wondered. And what, finally, was the
difference? Why have a face at all if what was inside you was so perfectly hidden? The book Jonah was reading was nothing, some silliness. Make-believe
and colorful and harmless. It looked like it belonged to a series, along with that
book "The Short." On the cover a boy, arms outspread, was gripping wires in
each hand, and his whole body was glowing.

☰ MAKING COMPARISONS

1. Compare the authors' attitude toward their characters. What details
   can you point to that indicate a positive or negative bias?
2. Compare the attitudes of the two male characters toward their
   partners.
3. Describe what you think the future holds for both couples.

☰ WRITING ABOUT ISSUES

1. How do the titles of both stories point to their thematic significance?
2. Argue that either the men or the women in our two stories are more
   sympathetic.
3. What do you think is the best way forward for Martin and Rachel?
4. What decision do you think the couple in "Good People" will make?
   Support your argument with specific details from the story.

LUCILLE CLIFTON, "forgiving my father"

ROBERT HAYDEN, "Those Winter Sundays"

THEODORE ROETHKE, "My Papa's Waltz"

LI-YOUNG LEE, "My Father, in Heaven, Is Reading Out Loud"

In childhood, our emotions are often intense. Fears about life arise because we feel so powerless. For some of us, our fathers held all the power. Fathers may use their power in various ways—some to control or abuse, others to comfort and protect. We form perceptions about our fathers from these early memories. Often we become judgmental about their failures in the world or their failures as parents. As we grow older, we sometimes come to terms with our fathers and see them simply as human beings with strengths and weaknesses. But it is not always simple; some wounds may be too deep for us to reconcile. The four poets in this cluster approach memories of their fathers with different perspectives and purposes: to forgive their fathers and perhaps themselves; to remember fondly; to come to a closure; to relive a past that still haunts them; to come to terms with loss.

■ **BEFORE YOU READ**

Make a list of four strong memories about your father from your childhood. Are the memories positive or not? Can you remember how you felt then? Are they different from how you feel now? How can you explain the difference?

LUCILLE CLIFTON

forgiving my father

Lucille Clifton (1936–2010) was born in a small town near Buffalo, New York. She attended Howard University and Fredonia State Teacher's College and taught poetry at a number of universities. Her numerous awards for writing include two creative writing fellowships from the National Endowment for the Arts (1970 and 1973), two Pulitzer Prize nominations (for Good Woman: Poems and a Memoir *and for* Next, *both in 1988), several major poetry awards, and an Emmy. The mother of six, Clifton has written fifteen children's books. She was a former poet laureate of Maryland and the Distinguished Professor of Humanities at St. Mary's College. "forgiving my father" is from her 1980 book,* Two-Headed Woman. The Collected Poems of Lucille Clifton *was published in 2012.*

it is friday. we have come
to the paying of the bills.
all week you have stood in my dreams
like a ghost, asking for more time
but today is payday, payday old man,   5
my mother's hand opens in her early grave
and i hold it out like a good daughter.

there is no more time for you. there will
never be time enough daddy daddy old lecher
old liar. i wish you were rich so i could take it all   10
and give the lady what she was due
but you were the son of a needy father,
the father of a needy son,
you gave her all you had
which was nothing. you have already given her   15
all you had.

you are the pocket that was going to open
and come up empty any friday.
you were each other's bad bargain, not mine.
daddy old pauper old prisoner, old dead man   20
what am i doing here collecting?
you lie side by side in debtor's boxes
and no accounting will open them up.   *[1980]*

≡ THINKING ABOUT THE TEXT

1. How might you answer the question in line 21? Are the last two lines of the poem a kind of answer? Is there some way we can "collect" from the dead?

2. Should we bury the dead—that is, should we let the past go and let bygones be bygones? Or is it necessary to settle old scores? What do you think Clifton's answer would be?

3. How consistently does Clifton use the payday analogy? Make a list of words that reinforce her overall scheme.

4. Would you think differently about the speaker's father if Clifton had written "elderly one" instead of "old man" (line 5) or "old playboy / old fibber" instead of "old lecher / old liar" (lines 9–10)?

5. Some readers look for tensions or contradictions early in a poem, hoping they will be resolved at the end. Does this poem end in a resolution of paying up and forgiving?

ROBERT HAYDEN
Those Winter Sundays

Born in Detroit, Michigan, African American poet Robert Hayden (1913–1980) grew up in a poor neighborhood where his natural parents left him with family friends. He grew up with the Hayden name, not discovering his original name until he was forty. Hayden attended Detroit City College (now Wayne State University) from 1932 to 1936, worked in the Federal Writer's Project, and later earned his M.A. at the University of Michigan in 1944. He taught at Fisk University from 1946 to 1968 and at the University of Michigan from 1968 to 1980 and published several collections of poetry. Although his poems sometimes contain autobiographical elements, Hayden is primarily a formalist poet who preferred that his poems not be limited to personal or ethnic interpretations. "Those Winter Sundays" is from Angle of Ascent *(1966).*

Sundays too my father got up early
and put his clothes on in the blueblack cold,
then with cracked hands that ached
from labor in the weekday weather made
banked fires blaze. No one ever thanked him.   5

I'd wake and hear the cold splintering, breaking.
When the rooms were warm, he'd call,
and slowly I would rise and dress,
fearing the chronic angers of that house,

Speaking indifferently to him,   10
who had driven out the cold
and polished my good shoes as well.
What did I know, what did I know
of love's austere and lonely offices?   *[1962]*

≡ THINKING ABOUT THE TEXT

1. Is the concluding question meant rhetorically — that is, is the answer so obvious that no real reply is expected? Write a response that you think the son might give now.

2. Why did the children never thank their father? Is this common? What specific things might you thank your father (or mother) for? Do parents have basic responsibilities to their children that do not warrant thanks?

3. Is there evidence that the son loves his father now? Did he then? Why did he speak "indifferently" (line 10) to his father? Is it clear what the "chronic angers" (line 9) are? Should they be?

4. How might you fill in the gaps here? For example, how old do you think the boy is? How old is the father? What kind of a job might he have? What else can you infer?

5. What is the speaker's tone? Is he hoping for your understanding? Your sympathy? Are we responsible for the things we do in childhood? Is this speaker repentant or simply explaining?

≡ MAKING COMPARISONS

1. What degrees of forgiveness do you see in Clifton's and Hayden's poems?

2. Writing a poem *for* one's father seems different from writing a poem *about* him. Explain this statement in reference to these poems.

3. Compare the purpose of the questions in each poem. How might each poet answer the other poet's questions?

THEODORE ROETHKE

My Papa's Waltz

Born in Saginaw, Michigan, Theodore Roethke (1908–1963) was strongly influenced by childhood experiences with his father, a usually stern man who sold plants and flowers and who kept a large greenhouse, the setting for many of Roethke's poems. Roethke was educated at the University of Michigan, took courses at Harvard, and taught at several universities before becoming poet-in-residence at the University of Washington in 1948. Roethke's books include The Lost Son and Other Poems *(1949), the source for "My Papa's Waltz";* The Waking *(1953), which won a Pulitzer Prize; and* Words for the Wind *(1958), which won the National Book Award. Roethke's intensely personal style ensures his place among the most influential postmodern American poets.*

The whiskey on your breath
Could make a small boy dizzy;
But I hung on like death:
Such waltzing was not easy.

We romped until the pans   5
Slid from the kitchen shelf;
My mother's countenance
Could not unfrown itself.

The hand that held my wrist
Was battered on one knuckle;   10
At every step you missed
My right ear scraped a buckle.

You beat time on my head
With a palm caked hard by dirt,
Then waltzed me off to bed   15
Still clinging to your shirt.   *[1948]*

≡ THINKING ABOUT THE TEXT

1. Is the narrator looking back at his father with fondness? Bitterness?

2. Would the poem make a different impression if we changed "romped" (line 5) to "fought" and "waltzing" (line 4) to "dancing"?

3. Why did the boy hang on and cling to his father? Fear? Affection? Both?

4. What is the mother's role here? How would you characterize her frown?

5. Readers often have a negative view of the relationship represented here, but many change their minds, seeing some positive aspects to the father and son's waltz. How might you account for this revision?

≡ MAKING COMPARISONS

1. Would you have read this poem differently if the poet had used Clifton's title "forgiving my father"?

2. How would you compare the tone of Roethke's poem with that of Hayden's? Do they miss their fathers?

3. Would you say that Roethke has more complex feelings about his father, whereas Clifton and Hayden seem clearer?

LI-YOUNG LEE

My Father, in Heaven, Is Reading Out Loud

Li-Young Lee (b. 1957) was born in Indonesia to Chinese parents. His father taught medicine and philosophy in Jakarta. During a purge of ethnic Chinese, Lee's father was imprisoned because of his Western interests. He eventually escaped, and the family finally settled in Pittsburgh, where his father became a Presbyterian minister. Lee graduated from the University of Pittsburgh in 1979. He has won many prizes for his poetry, from Rose *(1986) to* Book of My Nights *(2001). His latest books of poetry are* Behind My Eyes *(2008) and* The Undressing *(2018).*

My father, in heaven, is reading out loud
to himself Psalms or news. Now he ponders what
he's read. No. He is listening for the sound
of children in the yard. Was that laughing
or crying? So much depends upon the   5
answer, for either he will go on reading,
or he'll run to save a child's day from grief.
As it is in heaven, so it was on earth.

Because my father walked the earth with a grave,
determined rhythm, my shoulders ached   10

from his gaze. Because my father's shoulders
ached from the pulling of oars, my life now moves
with a powerful back-and-forth rhythm:
nostalgia, speculation. Because he
made me recite a book a month, I forget   15
everything as soon as I read it. And knowledge
never comes but while I'm mid-stride a flight
of stairs, or lost a moment on some avenue.

A remarkable disappointment to him,
I am like anyone who arrives late   20
in the millennium and is unable
to stay to the end of days. The world's
beginnings are obscure to me, its outcomes
inaccessible. I don't understand
the source of starlight, or starlight's destinations.   25
And already another year slides out
of balance. But I don't disparage scholars;
my father was one and I loved him,
who packed his books once, and all of our belongings,
then sat down to await instruction   30
from his god, yes, but also from a radio.
At the doorway, I watched, and I suddenly
knew he was one like me, who got my learning
under a lintel; he was one of the powerless,
to whom knowledge came while he sat among   35
suitcases, boxes, old newspapers, string.

He did not decide peace or war, home or exile,
escape by land or escape by sea.
He waited merely, as always someone
waits, far, near, here, hereafter, to find out: 40
is it praise or lament hidden in the next moment?   *[1990]*

≡ THINKING ABOUT THE TEXT

1. Lee begins his poem by speculating that his father is either reading
   or listening. What does this suggest about the narrator's view of his
   father?

2. What influence does Lee suggest his father had on him in stanza 2? Is it
   positive or negative or both?

3. When Lee says that his father awaited "instruction / from his god, yes,
   but also from a radio" (lines 30–31), what is he suggesting?

4. Does Lee finally identify with his father? In what ways?

5. Would you interpret the last stanza as reconciliation? Be specific
   about the resolution that Lee comes to.

≡ MAKING COMPARISONS

1. Unlike Hayden and Roethke, Lee explicitly says he loved his father. What other differences do you note?

2. Is this view of his father more or less balanced than the other three poets?

3. Which of the previous three fathers does Lee's seem most like?

≡ WRITING ABOUT ISSUES

1. Choose one of the four preceding poems to argue that our feelings for our fathers are complex, not simple.

2. In *Words* (1964), Jean-Paul Sartre writes that "there is no good father, that is the rule." Use examples from the four poems to argue that this is, or is not, the case.

3. Do you think all children leave childhood or adolescence with unresolved tensions in their relationships with their fathers? Write a personal narrative that confronts this idea.

4. Locate at least three more poems that deal with memories of fathers. Write a brief report, noting the similarities to the four poems presented here.

NIKKI GIOVANNI, "Legacies"

LINDA HOGAN, "Heritage"

JUDITH ORTIZ COFER, "Claims"

RICHARD BLANCO, "Queer Theory: According to My Grandmother"

GARY SOTO, "Behind Grandma's House"

In contemporary middle-class America, the influence, even the presence, of our grandmothers has waned. They often live elsewhere, perhaps in a retirement community or nursing home. But this was not always the case. Grandmothers in the past and in traditional households even today, were active members of the family, exerting influence on the daily decisions of everyday life, from diet to childrearing. Some of this was beneficial: grandmothers gave children a personal understanding of their cultural traditions as well as the gift of their accumulated wisdom. But they could also create tension in families where change and progress conflicted with the habits and attitudes of the past. The following five poets present us with different perspectives on their grandmothers, some loving and proud, others less positive, and two quite satirical and comical.

≡ BEFORE YOU READ

What specific memories do you have of your grandmothers? What role do you think they should play in a family's life? What effects might the segregation of the elderly have on a society?

NIKKI GIOVANNI
Legacies

Raised near Cincinnati, Ohio, Nikki Giovanni (b. 1943) returned as a teenager to her birthplace and spiritual home in Knoxville, Tennessee, where she experienced the strong influence of her grandmother, Louvenia Watson. She studied at the University of Cincinnati from 1961 to 1963 and earned a B.A. at Fisk University in 1967. She also attended the University of Pennsylvania School of Social Work (1967) and Columbia University School of the Arts (1968). She has taught at a number of universities, since 1987 at Virginia Polytechnic Institute, where she is a professor of English. Her poetry, essays, and works for children reflect her commitment to African American community, family, and womanhood. Her books include Quilting the Black-Eyed Pea: Poems and Not Quite Poems *(2002). Recent books include* On My Journey Now: Looking at African American History through the Spiri-tuals *(2006) and* Acolytes *(2007).* Bicycles: Love Poems *was published in 2009 and* Chasing Utopia: A Hybrid *in 2013. "Legacies" is from Giovanni's 1972 book,* My House.

> her grandmother called her from the playground
>   "yes, ma'am"
>   "i want chu to learn how to make rolls," said the old
> woman proudly
> but the little girl didn't want   5
> to learn how because she knew
> even if she couldn't say it that
> that would mean when the old one died she would be less
> dependent on her spirit so
> she said   10
>   "i don't want to know how to make no rolls"
> with her lips poked out
> and the old woman wiped her hands on
> her apron saying "lord
>   these children"   15
> and neither of them ever
> said what they meant
> and i guess nobody ever does   *[1972]*

☰ THINKING ABOUT THE TEXT

1. Does the dialogue in Giovanni's poem reveal the true feelings of the grandmother and the girl? Be explicit about what is really going on in their minds. Is the girl superstitious?

2. Is it true that "nobody" (line 18) says what she really means? Do you? Is this an indication of honesty or something else — say, tact or convention? Are poets more likely to tell the truth?

3. What makes this piece a poem? Would you prefer more metaphors or similes, allusions, or flowery language? Is *proudly* (line 4) an important word here?

4. Change the grandmother's words to those that reflect more of what is in her heart. Might the girl respond differently if the grandmother were more forthright?

5. The title is only referred to obliquely. Why? What does it refer to? Is contemporary society concerned with legacies? Are you? Are they important or irrelevant?

LINDA HOGAN
Heritage

Born in 1947 in Denver, Colorado, Linda Hogan calls on her Chickasaw heritage to interpret environmental, antinuclear, and other spiritual and societal issues. Her published works include poems, stories, screenplays, essays, and novels. Her novel Power *(1998) has been praised for its beauty of language, mythical structure, and allegorical power. Her works include* The Woman Who Watches Over the World: A Native Memoir *(2001) and* Sightings: The Gray Whales' Mysterious Journey *(2002). Her many honors include an American Book Award for* Seeing through the Sun *(1985), a Colorado Book Award and a Pulitzer nomination for* The Book of Medicines *(1993), fellowships from the Guggenheim Foundation and the National Endowment for the Arts, and a Lannan Award. Hogan received her M.A. from the University of Colorado at Boulder, where she currently teaches creative writing. "Heritage" is from her 1978 book titled* Calling Myself Home.

From my mother, the antique mirror
where I watch my face take on her lines.
She left me the smell of baking bread
to warm fine hairs in my nostrils,
she left the large white breasts that weigh down   5
my body.

From my father I take his brown eyes,
the plague of locusts that leveled our crops,
they flew in formation like buzzards.

From my uncle the whittled wood   10
that rattles like bones
and is white
and smells like all our old houses
that are no longer there. He was the man
who sang old chants to me, the words   15
my father was told not to remember.

From my grandfather who never spoke
I learned to fear silence.
I learned to kill a snake
when you're begging for rain.   20

And Grandmother, blue-eyed woman
whose skin was brown,
she used snuff.
When her coffee can full of black saliva
spilled on me   25
it was like the brown cloud of grasshoppers
that leveled her fields.

It was the brown stain
that covered my white shirt,
my whiteness a shame.   30
That sweet black liquid like the food
she chewed up and spit into my father's mouth
when he was an infant.
It was the brown earth of Oklahoma
stained with oil.   35
She said tobacco would purge your body of poisons.
It has more medicine than stones and knives
against your enemies.
That tobacco is the dark night that covers me.

She said it is wise to eat the flesh of deer   40
so you will be swift and travel over many miles.
She told me how our tribe has always followed a stick
that pointed west
that pointed east.
From my family I have learned the secrets   45
of never having a home.   *[1978]*

≡ THINKING ABOUT THE TEXT

1. The last sentence seems to contain a contradiction. "From my family I
   have learned the secrets" might lead you to expect something positive.
   But maybe the last phrase is not meant to be positive. What is your
   reading of Hogan's conclusion?

2. What does the narrator learn from her mother? Her father? Her uncle?
   Her grandfather? Her grandmother? What kinds of things did you
   learn from your family members? Use concrete images and examples.

3. Why does she say "my whiteness a shame" (line 30)? Is this a racial
   comment?

4. Examine the "black saliva" section in lines 21 through 39. Does it start
   off negatively? Does it change? Explain.

5. We all learn things from our families, both positive and negative. Is
   Hogan giving a balanced account? Should she? Would you? Do poets
   have any responsibility to the larger culture, or should they just follow
   their own inner vision?

≡ MAKING COMPARISONS

1. Compare Hogan's grandmother to Giovanni's.

2. Which grandmother would you like to talk to about her heritage? Why?

3. What special knowledge do these grandmothers possess?

JUDITH ORTIZ COFER
Claims

Judith Ortiz Cofer (b. 1952–2016) was born in Puerto Rico but spent most of her childhood traveling between Paterson, New Jersey, and Hormigueros, Puerto Rico. The constant shifting of languages and cultures influenced most of her early work, especially two volumes of poetry: Reaching for the Mainland *and* Terms of Survival, *both published in 1987. Her first novel,* The Line of the Sun *(1989), the first novel ever published by the University of Georgia Press, was widely praised and was nominated for the Pulitzer Prize. The pressures of migratory life and the cultural importance of male–female relationships center her themes.* Woman in Front of the Sun *was published in 2000, followed by* A Love Story Beginning in Spanish *(2005). Her work includes a number of novels for adolescents, including* If I Could Fly *(2011) and* The Poet Upstairs *(2012). Cofer was a faculty member at the University of Georgia in Athens and was a Regents and Franklin Professor of English and Creative Writing.*

Last time I saw her, Grandmother
had grown seamed as a Bedouin tent.
She had claimed the right
to sleep alone, to own
her nights, to never bear   5
the weight of sex again nor to accept
its gift of comfort, for the luxury
of stretching her bones.
She'd carried eight children,
three had sunk in her belly, *naufragos*°   10
she called them, shipwrecked babies
drowned in her black waters.
Children are made in the night and
steal your days
for the rest of your life, amen. She said this   15
to each of her daughters in turn. Once she had made a pact
with man and nature and kept it. Now like the sea,
she is claiming back her territory.   [1987]

☰ THINKING ABOUT THE TEXT

1. To whom does the title refer?
2. What is the pact the grandmother made with "man and nature" (line 17)?
3. Comment on the simile "like the sea" Cofer uses in the last sentence. Has the reader been prepared for that comparison? Why, or why not?

---

10 *naufragos*: Victims of shipwrecks (Spanish).

4. What parts do duty and responsibility play in the grandmother's life? Does her quote (lines 13–15) suggest a negative view of children or sex?

5. Do you think the grandmother's response is typical or unusual?

≡ MAKING COMPARISONS

1. Is Cofer's attitude toward her grandmother more or less respectful than the other poets here?

2. Compare Cofer's grandmother with Hogan's.

3. Which of the grandparents portrayed here might make the same decision about sex as Cofer's grandmother?

RICHARD BLANCO
Queer Theory: According to My Grandmother

Richard Blanco (b.1968) was born in Madrid and emigrated to Miami as an infant with his Cuban exiled family. He graduated from Florida International University with a B.S. in civil engineering and later received an M.F.A. in 1997. He was the fifth poet, first Latino, and first openly gay person to read at a presidential inauguration. At Barack Obama's second inauguration, Blanco read "One Today," a poem that affirms America's collective identity. He has taught at Georgetown and American Universities and continues to practice as a civil engineer in his home in Bethel, Maine. His latest works include One Today *(2013),* Boston Strong *(2013), and* How to Love a Country *(2019). The following poem is taken from* Looking for the Gulf Motel *(2012), published by the University of Pittsburgh Press. One critic notes that Blanco is "a virtuoso of art and craft who juggles the subjective and the objective beautifully."*

Never drink soda with a straw —
    milk shakes? Maybe.
Stop eyeing your mother's Avon catalog,
and the men's underwear in those Sears flyers.
    I've seen you . . .   5
Stay out of her Tupperware parties
and her perfume bottles — don't let her kiss you,
    she kisses you much too much.
Avoid hugging men, but if you must,
    pat them real hard   10
    on the back, even
    if it's your father.
Must you keep that cat? Don't pet him so much.
    Why don't you like dogs?
Never play house, even if you're the husband.   15

Quit hanging with that Henry kid, he's too pale,
    and I don't care what you call them
        those GI Joes of his
        are dolls.
Don't draw rainbows or flowers or sunsets.   20
    I've seen you . . .
Don't draw at all—no coloring books either.
Put away your crayons, your Play-Doh, your Legos.
    Where are your Hot Wheels,
    your laser gun and handcuffs,   25
    the knives I gave you?
Never fly a kite or roller skate, but light
    all the firecrackers you want,
    kill all the lizards you can, cut up worms—
    feed them to that cat of yours.   30
Don't sit *Indian* style with your legs crossed—
    you're no Indian.
Stop click-clacking your sandals—
    you're no girl.
For God's sake, never pee sitting down.   35
    I've seen you . . .
Never take a bubble bath or wash your hair
with shampoo—shampoo is for women.
    So is conditioner.
    So is mousse.   40
    So is hand lotion.
Never file your nails or blow-dry your hair—
go to the barber shop with your grandfather—
    you're not *unisex.*
Stay out of the kitchen. Men don't cook—   45
they eat. Eat anything you want, except:
    deviled eggs
    Blow Pops
    croissants (Bagels? Maybe.)
    cucumber sandwiches   50
    petit fours
Don't watch *Bewitched* or *I Dream of Jeannie.*
Don't stare at *The Six-Million Dollar Man.*
    I've seen you . . .
Never dance alone in your room: 55
Donna Summer, Barry Manilow, the Captain
and Tennille, Bette Midler, and all musicals—
    forbidden.
Posters of kittens, *Star Wars*, or the Eiffel Tower—
    forbidden.   60

Those fancy books on architecture and art—
    I threw them in the trash.
You can't wear cologne or puka shells
and I better not catch you in clogs.
If I see you in a ponytail—I'll cut it off.   65
What? No, you can't pierce your ear,
    left or right side—
    I don't care—
you will not look like a goddamn queer,
    I've seen you . . .   70
even if you are one.   *[2012]*

≡ THINKING ABOUT THE TEXT

1. Blanco's grandmother has a fairly extensive forbidden list. Which ones surprised you, and why? Are some of these dated? Is the "gayness" of other items on the list unclear?

2. The grandmother seems to have fairly old-fashioned notions about what boys and girls should and should not do. How would you describe her version of male and female behavior?

3. How might the last three lines be seen as a compromise on the grandmother's part? Although egregious stereotyping is a serious topic, Blanco's poem is also meant to be humorous. Where do you find the humor? Is it effective?

4. The grandmother's assumption, not uncommon among some people, is that gay men like the same things that stereotypical girls do. How does this poem support that view? Where do you think such a misconception comes from? Does our culture encourage such views?

5. Perhaps Blanco is somewhat hyperbolic about his grandmother's forbidden list. Which items seem unlikely to have actually caught the grandmother's attention? Why might Blanco have included them?

≡ MAKING COMPARISONS

1. Which of the other grandmothers might agree with Blanco's? Why?

2. Which of the grandmothers is described the most negatively? Why?

3. Which grandmother is described the most realistically? Why?

GARY SOTO
Behind Grandma's House

Born in 1952 in Fresno, California, Gary Soto gives voice to San Joaquin Valley agricultural workers whose deprivations have been part of his experience and social awareness from an early age. After graduating with honors from California State University in 1974, Soto went on to earn an M.F.A. in creative writing from the University of California at Irvine in 1976 and to teach in the university system. He has received numerous writing awards, including the distinction of being the first writer identifying himself as Chicano to be nominated for a Pulitzer Prize. A young adult novel, The Afterlife, *was published in 2003. A book of poems,* One Kind of Faith *(2003), was cited as confirming Soto's "immense talent." His latest book of poems is* Sudden Loss of Dignity *(2013). His Mexican American heritage continues to be central to his work. The poem reprinted here is from Soto's 1985 book,* Black Hair.

At ten I wanted fame. I had a comb
And two Coke bottles, a tube of Bryl-creem.
I borrowed a dog, one with
Mismatched eyes and a happy tongue,
And wanted to prove I was tough   5
In the alley, kicking over trash cans,
A dull chime of tuna cans falling.
I hurled light bulbs like grenades
And men teachers held their heads,
Fingers of blood lengthening   10
On the ground. I flicked rocks at cats,
Their goofy faces spurred with foxtails.
I kicked fences. I shooed pigeons.
I broke a branch from a flowering peach
And frightened ants with a stream of piss.   15
I said "Shit," "Fuck you," and "No way
Daddy-O" to an imaginary priest
Until grandma came into the alley,
Her apron flapping in a breeze,
Her hair mussed, and said, "Let me help you,"   20
And punched me between the eyes.   *[1985]*

≡ THINKING ABOUT THE TEXT

1. Were you glad or disturbed when the narrator's grandmother hit him? Does he deserve it? Are you angry or sympathetic to his attempts to be tough? Do you understand why he wants to appear older? Is this normal?

2. What did you want at age ten? Did your grandparents know your desires? Did they support you? Did they ever set you straight? Are our grandparents' values too dated to matter?

3. Are the concrete details meaningful to you? Does the profanity help Soto achieve authenticity, or is it unnecessary?

4. Does the speaker learn something here, or is this just a snapshot of an event?

5. How would you describe our culture's ideas of the different roles of parents and grandparents? Do grandparents in today's culture have less influence than in the past? Is this a good thing or not?

≡ **MAKING COMPARISONS**

1. Is Soto more or less respectful of his grandparent than the writers of the previous two poems?

2. Is this a gendered poem? That is, could a female see herself in a comparable situation? Are the Giovanni and Hogan poems gendered?

3. How might the portraits of grandmothers given here be stereotypical or not?

≡ **WRITING ABOUT ISSUES**

1. Pick one of the five preceding poems, and argue that it offers an appropriate view of grandmothers.

2. Pick two of these poems, and argue that something of value is learned in each.

3. Which poem comes closest to your own experiences? Write a narrative that demonstrates this.

4. Do some sociological research on communities that cater to those over sixty-five years old. Write a report about your findings. Include the impact of such places on the family and on the larger culture. Do you think they are a positive development or not?

Literature and Current Issues: Environmental Responsibilities in Families

KATHY JETNIL-KIJINER, "Dear Matafele Peinem" (poem)

ARGUMENTS ON THE ISSUE:
LAUREN MARKHAM, "Warming World Creates Desperate People"

LEAH SCHADE, "Climate Change Impacts Health, Families, and Wallets"

BRENT STEPHENS, "Climate of Complete Certainty"

According to a significant percentage of scientific experts, environmental damage to our planet is reaching dangerous levels. But the warnings about this condition have been consistent for decades. Rachel Carson's *Silent Spring* (1962), for example, first brought to the attention of the American public the environmental problems caused by synthetic pesticides. Of course, chemical companies fiercely opposed her findings. Unfortunately, that scenario has been repeated over the past fifty years as scientific study after study have issued dire warnings about everything from the toxic effects of greenhouse gas emissions to the worldwide effects climate change is having on the most vulnerable populations, including degraded water, rising sea levels, and polluted air quality. But little has been done. Even worldwide mass demonstrations and scores of books exposing the dangers of rampant energy production and destruction of animal habitats have not convinced world leaders, including politicians in the United States, to take responsible action. Nevertheless, concerned and informed writers have continued their attempts to halt the seemingly inexorable plunge into the abyss of environmental disaster.

The following poem gained worldwide attention after its presentation at the United Nations. The poet makes a promise to her son that she will fight to prevent the rising ocean from "crunching" his island, and a "greedy whale of a company" from pushing "this mother ocean over the edge." The poem's theme is clear: "we deserve to do more than just survive / we deserve / to thrive." We have also included three essays that focus on the controversy surrounding climate change. First, we present an essay that explains how a warming planet impacts some environments so extremely that their inhabitants are forced to migrate. Another essay describes the immediate effect of climate change on families. And the last piece suggests that activists might be more effective if they weren't so certain in their beliefs.

≡ BEFORE YOU READ

In what ways may your communities at home and at school be threatened by climate change? Are there specific actions you might take, both big and small, to counter the threats? Since there is a scientific consensus about the dangers of climate change, why isn't more being done?

KATHY JETNIL-KIJINER
Dear Matafele Peinem

Kathy Jetnil-Kijiner (b. 1990) was born in the Marshall Islands and raised in Hawaii where she received her master's degree in Pacific Island Studies from the University of Hawaii. She is thought to be the first person from the Marshall Islands to publish a book of poetry. Her collection, Iep Jaltok: Poems from a Marshallese Daughter, *was published by the University of Arizona Press in 2017. She has used her poetry to further her people's struggle against racism, for social justice, and to raise awareness of the threat of climate change. In 2014, she was chosen to address the UN Climate Summit in New York City. When she read the following poem, which is addressed to her seven-month-old daughter, she was given a standing ovation.*

> dear matafele peinam,
>
> you are a seven month old sunrise of gummy smiles
> you are bald as an egg and bald as the buddha
> you are thunder thighs and lightning shrieks so excited for bananas,
>   hugs and
> our morning walks past the lagoon   5
>
> dear matafele peinam,
>
> i want to tell you about that lagoon that lucid, sleepy lagoon lounging
>   against the sunrise some men say that one day that lagoon will
>   devour you
>
> they say it will gnaw at the shoreline
> chew at the roots of your breadfruit trees
> gulp down rows of your seawalls   10
> and crunch your island's shattered bones
>
> they say you, your daughter
> and your granddaughter, too
> will wander rootless
> with only a passport to call home   15
>
> dear matafele peinam,
>
> don't cry
>
> mommy promises you
>
> no one
> will come and devour you   20
>
> no greedy whale of a company
> sharking through political seas
> no backwater bullying of businesses with broken morals no blindfolded
> bureaucracies gonna push

this mother ocean over
the edge   25

no one's drowning, baby
no one's moving
no one's losing
their homeland   30
no one's gonna become
a climate change refugee

or should i say
no one else

to the carteret islanders of papua new guinea   35
and to the taro islanders of fiji
i take this moment
to apologize to you
we are drawing the line here

because baby we are going to fight   40
your mommy daddy
bubu jimma your country and president too
we will all fight

and even though there are those
hidden behind platinum titles   45
who like to pretend
that we don't exist
that the marshall islands
tuvalu
kiribati   50
maldives
and typhoon haiyan in the philippines
and floods of pakistan, algeria, and colombia
and all the hurricanes, earthquakes, and tidalwaves
didn't exist   55

still
there are those
who see us

hands reaching out
fists raising up   60
banners unfurling
megaphones booming
and we are
canoes blocking coal ships
we are   65

the radiance of solar villages
we are
the rich clean soil of the farmer's past
we are
petitions blooming from teenage fingertips   70
we are
families biking, recycling, reusing,
engineers dreaming, designing, building,
artists painting, dancing, writing
we are spreading the word   75

and there are thousands out on the street
marching with signs
hand in hand
chanting for change NOW

they're marching for you, baby   80
they're marching for us

because we deserve to do more than just
survive
we deserve
to thrive   85

dear matafele peinam,
you are eyes heavy
with drowsy weight
so just close those eyes, baby
and sleep in peace   90

because we won't let you down

you'll see

☰ THINKING ABOUT THE TEXT

1. What specific threats does the author foresee? What ones are already occurring?

2. According to the author, who is to blame for inaction on climate change?

3. What actions are already being taken to fight the consequences of climate change?

4. Are any of the solutions she mentions taking place in your hometown? Your university? If so, how are people responding?

5. How do you think climate change skeptics would respond to this poem? Why isn't a scientific consensus enough to persuade skeptics?

LAUREN MARKHAM

A Warming World Creates Desperate People

Lauren Markam graduated from the M.F.A. program at Vermont College. She is now a writer and reporter focusing on migration, youth, and the environment. She is the author of The Far Away Brothers *(2017) which was called a "timely and thought-provoking" examination of youth migration and was a* New York Times Book Critics Top Book of 2017. *She teaches writing at the Arkland University M.F.A. program.*

Last year I traveled to southern Guatemala, the source of one of the largest migrations of unauthorized immigrants to the United States in recent years. It's clear why people are leaving: Guatemala is a country rife with political conflict, endemic racism against indigenous people, poverty and, increasingly, gang violence.

But there's another, lesser-known dimension to this migration. Drought and rising temperatures in Guatemala are making it harder for people to make a living or even survive, thus compounding the already tenuous political situation for the 16.6 million people who live there.

In the town of Jumaytepeque, which is in Central America's dry corridor, a group of farmers took me to see their coffee crops. Coffee was responsible for the majority of the community's income but had been decimated by a plague known as coffee rust, or *la roya.* Plagues like these aren't necessarily caused by climate change, but it exacerbates them, and roya is now infecting plants at higher elevations as those heights become warmer. Making matters worse, stress from the drought has made these plants more vulnerable to the plague.

"We can't make a living purely off coffee anymore," one young farmer told me in the dappled shade of his coffee plantation, pointing to the limp, yellow roya-pocked leaves all around us. Young people like him, he explained, either move to the cities and try to make a go of it amid the gang violence, "or they go north," he said, to the United States.

Long before the unconscionable family-separation catastrophe at our southern border, President Trump had made the battle against illegal immigrants the rallying cry of his campaign and administration. He wants to lock up more immigrants — including toddlers — as a deterrent while casting all new unauthorized immigrants as potential, if not probable, violent criminals. Simultaneously, the president's team has taken on the environment, doing nearly everything it can to walk back decades of regulation intended to protect our air, water and land. Last June, Mr. Trump pulled out of the Paris climate accord. Meanwhile, Scott Pruitt, the administrator of the Environmental Protection Agency, is doggedly eviscerating the agency he runs.

Today, according to global relief agencies, over 68 million people world-wide have been forced to flee their homes, often because of war, poverty and political persecution. As a writer, I focus largely on issues of forced migration. The hundreds of migrants I've interviewed in the past few years — whether

5

from Gambia, Pakistan, El Salvador, Guatemala, Yemen or Eritrea — are most often leaving because of some acute political problem at home. But I've also noticed something else in my years of reporting. If you talk to these migrants long enough, you'll hear about another, more subtle but still profound dimension to the problems they are leaving behind: environmental degradation or climate change.

The United Nations High Commissioner for Refugees estimates that since 2008, 22.5 million people have been displaced by climate-related or extreme weather events. This includes tragedies like the widespread famine in Darfur, monsoons and flooding in Bangladesh and the catastrophic hurricane in Puerto Rico. The more out of whack our climate becomes, the more people up and leave their homes. As our world heats up and sea levels rise, the problem of forced migration around the world is projected to become far worse.

And in refusing to take climate change or responsibility for our planet seriously, the Trump administration is encouraging the conditions that will increase unauthorized migrations to the United States and elsewhere.

Outside a youth refugee facility in Sicily, a group of teenagers from Gambia who had crossed the Mediterranean from Libya told me that farming had become too difficult to sustain in their country as the semiarid Sahel region spreads ever wider across the continent, drying up people's land. In Yemen, years of water scarcity helped lead to the country's brutal conflict.

El Salvador, one of the world's most murderous countries, is just now   10
recovering from a devastating drought, which only heightens the stakes and scope of the violence. In my book about youth migration from El Salvador, "The Far Away Brothers," I write about a family that ended up on the wrong side of a gang-protected man in town. The family's teenage twin brothers left because there was a price on their heads, but the challenges persisted for those who remained behind. The family's fields produced less and less. The tomatoes took on a pallid, sickly color; other crops failed to grow at all. The family couldn't survive from farming anymore, so more of the children considered going north. They haven't yet, but nearly every day, one of the daughters tells me, she considers making arrangements to leave.

Many things are exacerbating the effects of the drought in Central America, including pervasive deforestation and farmers overtaxing their land. But according to Climatelinks, a project of the United States Agency for International Development, the average temperature in El Salvador has risen 2.34 degrees Fahrenheit since the 1950s, and droughts have become longer and more intense. The sea has risen by three inches since the 1950s, and is projected to rise seven more by 2050. Between 2000 and 2009, 39 hurricanes hit El Salvador, compared with 15 in the 1980s. This, too, is predicted to get worse.

When reporting a story among migrants living in the shadows of a Kenyan slum, I asked a group of men why they left their homes in rural Ethiopia. They were farmers there, like many generations before them, but they told me they could no longer make a living off their crops or even adequately feed their families. The rains had changed — it wasn't just that they had lessened but that they had become more erratic; no rain when the crops needed it to grow, and then, when it was time for harvest, it would rain suddenly and terribly, ruining the crops. The men had left for Kenya to find work and send money back to feed their families.

Like El Salvador, Gambia, Bangladesh and Guatemala, Ethiopia has been hit hard by climate change, though it is not even in the top 100 emitters of greenhouse gases. But the problem with climate change, of course, is that it is a problem that crosses borders.

The anti-immigrant rhetoric of the Trump administration has made for elaborate and bombastic theater — but with real, and sometimes deadly, human consequences (see again the children separated from their parents at the border). But Mr. Trump means what he says: He wants immigration from poor countries to stop. He sees the problems in those countries as theirs, not ours — never mind the centuries of catastrophic foreign intervention in places like El Salvador and the rest of the Americas, the Arab world and sub-Saharan Africa, or the growing menace of the changing climate.

If President Trump really wants to curb "illegal" migration to the United   15
States for the long haul, he'd better get serious about climate change. The Trump administration can continue to eviscerate the E.P.A. and thumb its nose at global efforts to protect the climate. Or he can work responsibly to try to curb international migration by addressing the challenges of a warming planet.

He can't have it both ways.

≡ THINKING ABOUT THE TEXT

1. What element of argument does Markham use the most effectively?

2. Is this essay balanced? Does she address the opposition? Should she? What suggestions in this regard would you make?

3. The audience for this piece is readers of the *New York Times*, which mostly had a liberal editorial policy. What suggestions would you give if she hoped to publish it in the *Wall Street Journal*, which mostly has a conservative point of view?

4. What do you think about the rhetorical effectiveness of the last paragraph?

5. Does this essay appeal mostly to logos, pathos, or ethos? Which approach would you suggest she do more of? Why?

LEAH D. SCHADE
Climate Change Impacts Health, Families, and Wallets

Leah D. Schade is Assistant Professor of Preaching and Worship at Lexington Theological Seminary. An ordained minister in the Evangelical Lutheran Church, she is an advocate for ecological and social justice. Her Ph.D. focused on ecological theology. She published Creation-Crisis Preaching: Ecology, Theology, and the Pulpit

(2015). She writes for a blog entitled "Eco Reader" that explores religion, politics, eco-logical justice, and women's issues. The following essay appeared in May 2017.

"Believe it or not, when it comes to climate change, many people are not all that concerned about animal extinction or the plight of future generations." When my fellow climate activist Peterson Toscano posted this observation on Facebook, I was cut to the quick.

I know it doesn't matter to most people, but animal extinction really concerns me. Human beings causing this massive wave of extinctions — what biologist are calling the sixth great extinction — grieves me greatly. And it breaks my heart knowing that future generations will not experience the full beauty of this Earth, while also suffering the consequences of our rampant pollution of the land, waters and air.

But I must admit: My friend is right. Because I've heard the dismissal of concerns about climate change many times out of the mouths of people who I thought would care. And many are Christians who should care, given their professed faith in the one who called us to care for "the least of these."

No matter how much I think the ethics of our faith should be extended to our neighbors within the other-than-human world and to generations of people we will never meet, that is simply not the reality. Humans, generally speaking, care most about their personal circumstances, immediate family and short-term impacts on their wallets.

So why should someone care about climate change? Are there any imme-   5
diate impacts on our health, family or wallets? As a matter of fact, there are.

Did you know that climate change has contributed to a rise in kidney disease in Central America? Farm laborers are exposed to increasingly high temperatures and they are experiencing dehydration at alarming rates. Because they do not have access to clean water, they drink bottled sodas, and their bodies don't flush away the toxins. And because they have limited access to health care (which they can barely afford in the first place), these workers are dying.

But maybe the concerns of Central America are not important to you. How about immigration and refugees? It's important to know that climate change played a role in the 7 million displaced persons fleeing from the oppressive Assad regime in Syria.

Between 2006–2011, over half of the country suffered under the worst drought on record. The intensity and length of the drought was due to climate change. When nearly one million rural villagers lose farms and crowd into the cities, this exacerbates already-tense conditions where water, food and access to resources are in short supply.

Even if the country recovers politically, Syria is projected to lose nearly 50 percent more of its agricultural capacity by 2050. This means the immigration crisis is not going away anytime soon.

Maybe Syrian refugees are not on your doorstep. How about something a   10
little closer to home — like the food on your table? A recent study on the state of the planet's oceans by the Georgia Institute of Technology reveals that rapid warming due to climate change is leading to deoxygenation.

According to a recent report on the website Science Daily, "The amount of dissolved oxygen contained in the water—an important measure of ocean health—has been declining for more than 20 years."

Not having enough oxygen in Earth's "bloodstream" is leading to a kind of environmental hypoxia, a condition that, for humans, results in organ damage and even catastrophic failure. This affects the foundational level of the ocean's food web: phytoplankton. A disruption of this organism's survival will have devastating effects across the food chain—right up to our dinner plates.

So, yes, climate change is affecting health, families, national security and our food supply—to name just a few impacts. Earth's body and our bodies are connected. It's past time to care about both.

≡ THINKING ABOUT THE TEXT

1. How does Schade use her point about most people caring only about their immediate circumstances?

2. How does Schade's piece conform to your textbook's advice about effective arguments?

3. Which example of Schade's was the most effective for you personally? Why?

4. Tone is an important aspect of argument. How would you describe the effectiveness of Schade's?

5. If you're a Christian, how effective is her "should care"? If you're not, do you feel this appeal is inappropriate? Explain.

≡ MAKING COMPARISONS

1. Markham's essay is more concrete than Schade's. Did you find that more persuasive? Was her personal experience a plus? Why are these techniques effective or not?

2. Markham is clear about her negative feelings toward the Trump administration. Is this a risky persuasive move? Did you find it effective?

3. What elements of argument make this essay more or less effective than Schade's?

BRENT STEPHENS
Climate of Complete Certainty

Brent Stephens (1973) is an American journalist and political commentator. He was born in New York City and earned a B.A. from the University of Chicago and a M.A. from the London School of Economics. He began his career at the Wall Street

Journal *and began working as a contributing op ed columnist at the* New York Times *in April 2017. The following is his first column in that role.*

When someone is honestly 55 percent right, that's very good and there's no use wrangling. And if someone is 60 percent right, it's wonderful, it's great luck, and let him thank God.

But what's to be said about 75 percent right? Wise people say this is suspicious. Well, and what about 100 percent right? Whoever says he's 100 percent right is a fanatic, a thug, and the worst kind of rascal.

— *An old Jew of Galicia*

In the final stretch of last year's presidential race, Hillary Clinton and her team thought they were, if not 100 percent right, then very close.

Right on the merits. Confident in their methods. Sure of their chances. When Bill Clinton suggested to his wife's advisers that, considering Brexit, they might be underestimating the strength of the populist tide, the campaign manager, Robby Mook, had a bulletproof answer: The data run counter to your anecdotes.

That detail comes from "Shattered," Jonathan Allen and Amie Parnes's compulsively readable account of Clinton's 2016 train wreck. Mook belonged to a new breed of political technologists with little time for retail campaigning and limitless faith in the power of models and algorithms to minimize uncertainty and all but predict the future.

"Mook and his 'Moneyball' approach to politics rankled the old order of political operatives and consultants because it made some of their work obsolete," Allen and Parnes write about the campaign's final days. "The memo that one Hillary adviser had sent months earlier warning that they should add three or four points to Trump's poll position was a distant memory."

There's a lesson here. We live in a world in which data convey authority. But authority has a way of descending to certitude, and certitude begets hubris. From Robert McNamara to Lehman Brothers to Stronger Together, cautionary tales abound.

We ought to know this by now, but we don't. Instead, we respond to the inherent uncertainties of data by adding more data without revisiting our assumptions, creating an impression of certainty that can be lulling, misleading and often dangerous. Ask Clinton.

With me so far? Good. Let's turn to climate change.

Last October, the Pew Research Center published a survey on the politics of climate change. Among its findings: Just 36 percent of Americans care "a great deal" about the subject. Despite 30 years of efforts by scientists, politicians and activists to raise the alarm, nearly two-thirds of Americans are either indifferent to or only somewhat bothered by the prospect of planetary calamity.

Why? The science is settled. The threat is clear. Isn't this one instance, at least, where 100 percent of the truth resides on one side of the argument?

Well, not entirely. As Andrew Revkin wrote last year about his storied   10
career as an environmental reporter at *The Times*, "I saw a widening gap
between what scientists had been learning about global warming and what
advocates were claiming as they pushed ever harder to pass climate legislation." The science was generally scrupulous. The boosters who claimed its
authority weren't.

Anyone who has read the 2014 report of the Intergovernmental Panel on
Climate Change knows that, while the modest (0.85 degrees Celsius, or about
1.5 degrees Fahrenheit) warming of the earth since 1880 is indisputable, as is
the human influence on that warming, much else that passes as accepted fact
is really a matter of probabilities. That's especially true of the sophisticated
but fallible models and simulations by which scientists attempt to peer into the
climate future. To say this isn't to deny science. It's to acknowledge it honestly.

By now I can almost hear the heads exploding. They shouldn't, because
there's another lesson here — this one for anyone who wants to advance the
cause of good climate policy. As Revkin wisely noted, hyperbole about climate
"not only didn't fit the science at the time but could even be counterproductive
if the hope was to engage a distracted public."

Let me put it another way. Claiming total certainty about the science
traduces the spirit of science and creates openings for doubt whenever a
climate claim proves wrong. Demanding abrupt and expensive changes in
public policy raises fair questions about ideological intentions. Censoriously
asserting one's moral superiority and treating skeptics as imbeciles and deplor-
ables wins few converts.

None of this is to deny climate change or the possible severity of its
consequences. But ordinary citizens also have a right to be skeptical of an
overweening scientism. They know — as all environmentalists should — that
history is littered with the human wreckage of scientific errors married to
political power.

I've taken the epigraph for this column from the Polish poet Czeslaw   15
Milosz, who knew something about the evils of certitude. Perhaps if there had
been less certitude and more second-guessing in Clinton's campaign, she'd be
president. Perhaps if there were less certitude about our climate future, more
Americans would be interested in having a reasoned conversation about it.

≡ THINKING ABOUT THE TEXT

1. Explain the line "certitude begets hubris." Give some examples from
   your experience.

2. Look up Stephen's reference to the film *Moneyball*. What comparison
   is he trying to make to Mook's approach?

3. What is your opinion of his transition from the 2016 election to
   climate change? Is this comparing apples to oranges, or is his
   comparison valid?

4. Stephens's main claim seems to be that predicting the future is fallible. Would you agree? Can you give examples both for and against his assertion?

5. Do you agree or not with the claim that if activists for attention to climate change were, say, 90% certain, then more people would pay attention? What might be the evidence for or against his claims about certainty?

≡ MAKING COMPARISONS

1. Which of the three arguments conforms best to what you've learned about good arguments? Explain.

2. Which observation by our three authors makes the most sense to you? Which the least? Explain.

3. Which argument seems the most balanced? Explain.

≡ WRITING ABOUT THE ISSUES

1. Using our poem as a focus, write an argument that agrees or disagrees with the author's explanation for the causes and consequences of climate change.

2. Write a letter to the *New York Times* arguing that Stephens's argument is flawed. Be specific.

3. Write a critique of one of these arguments, noting how the author follows or doesn't follow the elements of a good argument you've been studying.

4. Write your own focused argument about climate change, incorporating the essays in this cluster.

≡ Arguments about a Poem: "Daddy"

SYLVIA PLATH, "Daddy"

ARGUMENTS ABOUT THE POEM:
LYNDA K. BUNDTZEN, From *Plath's Incarnations*

STEVEN GOULD AXELROD, From *Sylvia Plath: The Wound and the Cure of Words*

TIM KENDALL, From *Sylvia Plath: A Critical Study*

As contradictory as it might seem, we sometimes get angry when someone close to us dies. Psychologists tell us that anger is a healthy emotion in the mourning process, following sorrow and preceding acceptance: it is painful to miss loved ones, and we resent it. We might even direct the anger at them, feeling as if they are responsible for depriving us of their love. Sometimes, however, this anger lingers on long after the normal grieving process is over. Perhaps the attachment was abnormally strong, or perhaps the survivor's own life is too unstable to allow him or her to reach the final acceptance stage.

In the following poem, Sylvia Plath writes about her dead father as if he were a terrible person, even though as a young girl she seems to have adored him. Perhaps she is trying to expel his memory so she can find peace; perhaps she is using the poem as an occasion to express a deeper meaning about authority or influence from the past. Regardless, the poem is a powerful, strange, and passionate work of art. Following the poem, we include four critical essays that focus on autobiographical questions while also extending the critical discussion.

After an obviously careful reading of Plath's poem, each of the three critics presented here constructs arguments about "Daddy." Each makes focused assertions that are supported with detailed references to tone, diction, syntax, rhyme, meter, metaphor, alliteration, symbol, and theme — all the elements discussed in Writing about Poems (p. 158). Note how scrupulously all three cite words, lines, and passages to create an informed, judicious, and disciplined persona and hence a convincing argument.

≡ BEFORE YOU READ

Does it make sense to you that we might get angry at those who die because they have somehow deserted us? Do you think we have to "work out" the tensions between our parents and us before we can move into adulthood? Might it be healthy to exaggerate the difficulties of our childhood in poems and stories?

Bettmann/Getty Images

SYLVIA PLATH
Daddy

Born to middle-class parents in suburban New York, Sylvia Plath (1932–1963) became known as an intensely emotional "confessional" poet whose work is primarily autobiographical. Her father, a professor of biology and German, died when she was eight, the year her first poem was published. She graduated with honors from Smith College in 1950, after an internship at Mademoiselle *and a suicide attempt in her junior year, experiences described in her novel* The Bell Jar *(1963). She won a Fulbright Scholarship to study at Cambridge University, England, where she met and married poet Ted Hughes. The couple had two children; the marriage ended the year before her suicide in 1963. "Daddy" is from* Ariel, *published posthumously in 1965.*

You do not do, you do not do
Any more, black shoe
In which I have lived like a foot
For thirty years, poor and white,
Barely daring to breathe or Achoo.   5

Daddy, I have had to kill you.
You died before I had time—
Marble-heavy, a bag full of God,
Ghastly statue with one gray toe
Big as a Frisco seal   10

And a head in the freakish Atlantic
Where it pours bean green over blue
In the waters off beautiful Nauset.°   *Cape Cod inlet*
I used to pray to recover you.
Ach, du.°   *Oh, you*   15

In the German tongue, in the Polish Town°
Scraped flat by the roller
Of wars, wars, wars.
But the name of the town is common.
My Polack friend   20

Says there are a dozen or two.
So I never could tell where you
Put your foot, your root,
I never could talk to you.
The tongue stuck in my jaw.   25

It stuck in a barb wire snare.
Ich, ich, ich, ich,°   *I, I, I, I*
I could hardly speak.
I thought every German was you.
And the language obscene   30

An engine, an engine
Chuffing me off like a Jew.
A Jew to Dachau, Auschwitz, Belsen.°
I began to talk like a Jew.
I think I may well be a Jew.   35

The snows of the Tyrol, the clear beer of Vienna
Are not very pure or true.
With my gypsy-ancestress and my weird luck
And my Taroc° pack and my Taroc pack
I may be a bit of a Jew.   40

I have always been scared of *you*,
With your Luftwaffe,° your gobbledygoo.

---

16 Polish Town: Plath's father was born in Granbow, Poland.   **33 Dachau . . . Belsen:**
Nazi death camps in World War II.   **39 Taroc:** Tarot cards used to tell fortunes. The prac-
tice may have originated among the early Jewish Cabalists and was then widely adopted by
European Gypsies during the Middle Ages.   **42 Luftwaffe:** World War II German air force.

And your neat mustache
And your Aryan eye, bright blue.
Panzer-man, panzer-man,° O You—   45

Not God but a swastika
So black no sky could squeak through.
Every woman adores a Fascist,
The boot in the face, the brute
Brute heart of a brute like you.   50

You stand at the blackboard, daddy,
In the picture I have of you,
A cleft in your chin instead of your foot
But no less a devil for that, no not
Any less the black man who   55

Bit my pretty red heart in two.
I was ten when they buried you.
At twenty I tried to die
And get back, back, back to you.
I thought even the bones would do.   60

But they pulled me out of the sack,
And they stuck me together with glue.
And then I knew what to do.
I made a model of you,
A man in black with a Meinkampf° look   65

And a love of the rack and the screw.
And I said I do, I do.
So daddy, I'm finally through.
The black telephone's off at the root,
The voices just can't worm through.   70

If I've killed one man, I've killed two—
The vampire who said he was you
And drank my blood for a year,
Seven years, if you want to know.
Daddy, you can lie back now.   75

There's a stake in your fat black heart
And the villagers never liked you.
They are dancing and stamping on you.
They always *knew* it was you.
Daddy, daddy, you bastard, I'm through.   *[1962]*   80

---

45 panzer-man: A member of the German armored vehicle division.
65 Meinkampf: Hitler's autobiography (*My Struggle*).

≡ **THINKING ABOUT THE TEXT**

1. Can this poem be seen as a series of arguments for why Plath has to forget her father? What complaints does the speaker seem to have against her father?

2. Some psychologists claim that we all have a love-hate relationship with our parents. Do you agree? Would Plath's speaker agree?

3. How effective is it for the speaker to compare herself to a Jew in Hitler's Germany? What other similes and metaphors are used to refer to her father? Do they work, or are they too extreme? Perhaps Plath wants them to be outrageous. Why might she?

4. Plath combines childhood rhymes and words with brutal images. What effect does this have on you? Why do you think Plath does this? What odd stylistic features can you point to here?

5. Why do you think it is necessary for the speaker to be finally "through" with her father? Is it normal young adult rebelliousness? What else might it be?

LYNDA K. BUNDTZEN
From *Plath's Incarnations*

Educated at the University of Minnesota, where she earned a B.A. in 1968, and the University of Chicago, where she earned a Ph.D. in 1972, Lynda Bundtzen (b. 1947) is Professor Emerita at Williams College. A Renaissance scholar with a strong interest in women's issues, she teaches and writes on subjects that range from Shakespeare to Thelma and Louise. *Plath's Incarnations was published in 1983. Her latest book is* The Other Ariel *(2001).*

In "Daddy," Plath is conscious of her complicity in creating and worshiping a father-colossus.

> You stand at the blackboard, daddy,
> In the picture I have of you,
> A cleft in your chin instead of your foot
> But no less a devil for that, no not
> Any less the black man who
>
> Bit my pretty red heart in two.
> I was ten when they buried you.
> At twenty I tried to die
> And get back, back, back to you.
> I thought even the bones would do.

The photograph is of an ordinary man, a teacher, with a cleft chin. She imaginatively transforms him into a devil who broke her heart, and she tells her audience precisely what she is doing. As Plath describes "Daddy," it is "spoken by a girl with an Electra complex. Her father died while she thought he was God. Her case is complicated by the fact that her father was also a Nazi and her mother very possibly part Jewish. In the daughter the two strains marry and paralyze each other—she has to act out the awful little allegory once over before she is free of it." The poem is a figurative drama about mourning—about the human impulse to keep a dead loved one alive emotionally. And it is about mourning gone haywire—a morbid inability to let go of the dead. The child was unready for her father's death, which is why, she says, she must kill him a second time. She resurrected Daddy and sustained his unnatural existence in her psyche as a vampire, sacrificing her own life's blood, her vitality, to a dead man. The worship of this father-god, she now realizes, is self-destructive.

There is nothing unconscious about the poem; instead it seems to force into consciousness the child's dread and love for the father, so that these feelings may be resolved. Plath skillfully evokes the child's world with her own versions of Mother Goose rhymes. Like the "old woman who lived in a shoe and had so many children she didn't know what to do," she has tried to live in the confines of the black shoe that is Daddy. Like Chicken Little, waiting for the sky to fall in, she lives under an omnipresent swastika "So black no sky could squeak through." And Daddy is a fallen giant toppled over and smothering, it seems, the entire United States. He has one grey toe (recalling Otto Plath's gangrened appendage) dangling like a Frisco seal in the Pacific and his head lies in the Atlantic.

The Mother Goose rhythms gradually build to a goose step march as the mourning process turns inward. She feels more than sorrow, now guilt, for Daddy's death and this guilt leads to feelings of inadequacy, acts of self-abasement, and finally self-murder. Nothing she can do will appease the guilt: she tries to learn his language; she tries to kill herself; she marries a man in his image. It will not do.

The self-hatred must be turned outward again into "*You* do not do" by a very self-conscious transformation of a mild-mannered professor into an active oppressor. Her emotional paralysis is acted out as a struggle between Nazi man and Jewess, and, I would argue, the Jewess wins. The poem builds toward the imaginary stake driving, the dancing and stamping and "Daddy, daddy, you bastard, I'm through." Not necessarily through with life, as many critics have read this line, but through with the paralysis, powerlessness, guilt. At last Daddy—the Nazi Daddy she frightened herself with, and not the real one, the professor—is at rest.

Plath's control over ambivalent feelings toward her father is probably the result of their availability for conscious artistic manipulation. She had already written several poems about her dead father when she composed "Daddy," and we also know from a conversation recorded by Steiner that she had "worked through" her emotions in therapy. "She talked freely about her father's death when she was nine and her reactions to it. 'He was an autocrat,' she recalled. 'I adored and despised him, and I probably wished many times that he were dead. When he obliged me and died, I imagined that I had killed him.'"

5

The result in "Daddy" is a powerful and remarkably accessible allegory about her adoration and dread, which ends in emotional catharsis.   *[1983]*

STEVEN GOULD AXELROD
From *Sylvia Plath: The Wound and the Cure of Words*

An expert in nineteenth- and twentieth-century American poetry, Steven Gould Axelrod (b. 1944) was educated at the University of California at Los Angeles and served as chair of the English Department at the University of California, Riverside, where he received a Distinguished Teaching Award in 1989. His publications include book-length works on modern and contemporary poets. Sylvia Plath: The Wound and the Cure of Words *was published in 1990 and* Robert Lowell: Life and Art *in 2016.*

The covert protest of "The Colossus" eventually transformed itself into the overt rebellion of "Daddy." Although this poem too has traditionally been read as "personal" or "confessional," Margaret Homans has more recently suggested that it concerns a woman's dislocated relations to speech. Plath herself introduced it on the BBC as the opposite of confession, as a constructed fiction: "Here is a poem spoken by a girl with an Electra complex. Her father died while she thought he was God. Her case is complicated by the fact that her father was also a Nazi and her mother very possibly part Jewish. In the daughter the two strains marry and paralyze each other—she has to act out the awful little allegory once over before she is free of it." We might interpret this preface as an accurate retelling of the poem; or we might regard it as a case of an author's estrangement from her text, on the order of Coleridge's preface to "Kubla Khan" in which he claims to be unable to finish the poem, having forgotten what it was about. However we interpret Plath's preface, we must agree that "Daddy" is dramatic and allegorical, since its details depart freely from the facts of her biography. In this poem she again figures her unresolved conflicts with paternal authority as a textual issue. Significantly, her father was a published writer, and his successor, her husband, was also a writer. Her preface asserts that the poem concerns a young woman's paralyzing self-division, which she can defeat only through allegorical representation. Recalling that paralysis was one of Plath's main tropes for literary incapacity, we begin to see that the poem evokes the female poet's anxiety of authorship and specifically Plath's strategy of delivering herself from that anxiety by making it the topic of her discourse. Viewed from this perspective, "Daddy" enacts the woman poet's struggle with "daddy-poetry." It represents her effort to eject the "buried male muse" from her invention process and the "jealous gods" from her audience.

Plath wrote "Daddy" several months after Hughes left her, on the day she learned that he had agreed to a divorce. George Brown and Tirril Harris have shown that early loss makes one especially vulnerable to subsequent loss, and

Plath seems to have defended against depression by almost literally throwing herself into her poetry. She followed "Daddy" with a host of poems that she considered her greatest achievement to date: "Medusa," "The Jailer," "Lady Lazarus," "Ariel," the bee sequence, and others. The letters she wrote to her mother and brother on the day of "Daddy," and then again four days later, brim with a sense of artistic self-discovery: "Writing like mad. . . . Terrific stuff, as if domesticity had choked me." Composing at the "still blue, almost eternal hour before the baby's cry, before the glassy music of the milkman, settling his bottles," she experienced an enormous surge in creative energy. Yet she also expressed feelings of misery: "The half year ahead seems like a lifetime, and the half behind an endless hell." She was again contemplating things German: a trip to the Austrian Alps, a renewed effort to learn the language. If "German" was Randall Jarrell's "favorite country," it was not hers, yet it returned to her discourse like clockwork at times of psychic distress. Clearly Plath was attempting to find and to evoke in her art what she could not find or communicate in her life. She wished to compensate for her fragmenting social existence by investing herself in her texts: "Hope, when free, to write myself out of this hole." Desperately eager to sacrifice her "flesh," which was "wasted," to her "mind and spirit," which were "fine," she wrote "Daddy" to demonstrate the existence of her voice, which had been silent or subservient for so long. She wrote it to prove her "genius."

Plath projected her struggle for textual identity onto the figure of a partly Jewish young woman who learns to express her anger at the patriarch and at his language of male mastery, which is as foreign to her as German, as "obscene" as murder, and as meaningless as "gobbledygoo." The patriarch's death "off beautiful Nauset" recalls Plath's journal entry in which she associated the "green seaweeded water" at "Nauset Light" with "the deadness of a being . . . who no longer creates." Daddy's deadness—suggesting Plath's unwillingness to let her father, her education, her library, or her husband inhibit her any longer—inspires the poem's speaker to her moment of illumination. At a basic level, "Daddy" concerns its own violent, transgressive birth as a text, its origin in a culture that regards it as illegitimate—a judgment the speaker hurls back on the patriarch himself when she labels *him* a bastard. Plath's unaccommodating worldview, which was validated by much in her childhood and adult experience, led her to understand literary tradition not as an expanding universe of beneficial influence . . . but as a closed universe in which every addition required a corresponding subtraction—a Spencerian agon in which only the fittest survived. If Plath's speaker was to be born as a poet, a patriarch must die.

As in "The Colossus," the father here appears as a force or an object rather than as a person. Initially he takes the form of an immense "black shoe," capable of stamping on his victim. Immediately thereafter he becomes a marble "statue," cousin to the monolith of the earlier poem. He then transforms into Nazi Germany, the archetypal totalitarian state. When the protagonist mentions Daddy's "boot in the face," she may be alluding to Orwell's comment in *1984*, "If you want a picture of the future, imagine a boot stamping on a human face—forever." Eventually the father declines in stature from God to a devil to a dying vampire. Perhaps he shrinks under the force of his victim's denunciation, which de-creates him as a power as it creates him as figure. But whatever his size, he never assumes human dimensions, aspirations, and relations—except when posing as a teacher in a photograph. Like the colossus, he remains figurative and symbolic, not individual.

Nevertheless, the male figure of "Daddy" does differ significantly from that of "The Colossus." In the earlier poem, which emphasizes his lips, mouth, throat, tongue, and voice, the colossus allegorically represents the power of speech, however fragmented and resistant to the protagonist's ministrations. In the later poem Daddy remains silent, apart from the gobbledygoo attributed to him once. He uses his mouth primarily for biting and for drinking blood. The poem emphasizes his feet and, implicitly, his phallus. He is a "black shoe," a statue with "one gray toe," a "boot." The speaker, estranged from him by fear, could never tell where he put his "foot," his "root." Furthermore, she is herself silenced by his shoe: "I never could talk to you." Daddy is no "male muse," not even one in ruins, but frankly a male censor. His boot in the face of "every woman" is presumably lodged in her mouth. He stands for all the elements in the literary situation and in the female ephebe's internalization of it, that prevent her from producing any words at all, even copied or subservient ones. Appropriately, Daddy can be killed only by being stamped on: he lives and dies by force, not language. If "The Colossus" tells a tale of the patriarch's speech, his grunts and brays, "Daddy" tells a tale of the daughter's effort to speak.

Thus we are led to another important difference between the two poems. The "I" of "The Colossus" acquires her identity only through serving her "father," whereas the "I" of "Daddy" actuates her gift only through opposition to him. The latter poem precisely inscribes the plot of Plath's dream novel of 1958: "a girl's search for her dead father—for an outside authority which must be developed, instead, from the inside." As the child of a Nazi, the girl could "hardly speak," but as a Jew she begins "to talk" and to acquire an identity. In Plath's allegory, the outsider Jew corresponds to "the rebel, the artist, the odd," and particularly to the woman artist. Otto Rank's *Beyond Psychology*, which had a lasting influence on her, explicitly compares women to Jews, since "woman . . . has suffered from the very beginning a fate similar to that of the Jew, namely, suppression, slavery, confinement, and subsequent persecution." Rank, whose discourse I would consider tainted by anti-Semitism, argues that Jews speak a language of pessimistic "self-hatred" that differs essentially from the language of the majority cultures in which they find themselves. He analogously, though more sympathetically, argues that woman speaks in a language different from man's, and that as a result of man's denial of woman's world, "woman's 'native tongue' has hitherto been unknown or at least unheard." Although Rank's essentializing of woman's "nature" lapses into the sexist clichés of his time ("intuitive," "irrational"), his idea of linguistic difference based on gender and his analogy between Jewish and female speech seem to have embedded themselves in the substructure of "Daddy" (and in many of Plath's other texts as well). For Plath, as later for Adrienne Rich, the

5

Holocaust and the patriarchy's silencing of women were linked outcomes of the masculinist interpretation of the world. Political insurrection and female self-assertion also interlaced symbolically. In "Daddy," Plath's speaker finds her voice and motive by identifying herself as antithetical to her Fascist father. Rather than getting the colossus "glued" and properly jointed, she wishes to stick herself "together with glue," an act that seems to require her father's dismemberment. Previously devoted to the patriarch — both in "The Colossus" and in memories evoked in "Daddy" of trying to "get back" to him — she now seeks only to escape from him and to see him destroyed.

Plath has unleashed the anger, normal in mourning as well as in revolt, that she suppressed in the earlier poem. But she has done so at a cost. Let us consider her childlike speaking voice. The language of "Daddy," beginning with its title, is often regressive. The "I" articulates herself by moving backward in time, using the language of nursery rhymes and fairy tales (the little old woman who lived in a shoe, the black man of the forest). Such language accords with a child's conception of the world, not an adult's. Plath's assault on the language of "daddy-poetry" has turned inward, on the language of her own poem, which teeters precariously on the edge of a preverbal abyss — represented by the eerie, keening "oo" sound with which a majority of the verses end. And then let us consider the play on "through" at the poem's conclusion. Although that last line allows for multiple readings, one interpretation is that the "I" has unconsciously carried out her father's wish: her discourse, by transforming itself into cathartic oversimplifications, has undone itself.

Yet the poem does contain its verbal violence by means more productive than silence. In a letter to her brother, Plath referred to "Daddy" as "gruesome," while on almost the same day she described it to A. Alvarez as a piece of "light verse." She later read it on the BBC in a highly ironic tone of voice. The poem's unique spell derives from its rhetorical complexity: its variegated and perhaps bizarre fusion of the horrendous and the comic. . . . [I]t both shares and remains detached from the fixation of its protagonist. The protagonist herself seems detached from her own fixation. She is "split in the most complex fashion," as Plath wrote of Ivan Karamazov in her Smith College honors thesis. Plath's speaker uses potentially self-mocking melodramatic terms to describe both her opponent ("so black no sky could squeak through") and herself ("poor and white"). While this aboriginal speaker quite literally expresses black-and-white thinking, her civilized double possesses a sensibility sophisticated enough to subject such thinking to irony. Thus the poem expresses feelings that it simultaneously parodies — it may be parodying the very idea of feeling. The tension between erudition and simplicity in the speaker's voice appears in her pairings that juxtapose adult with childlike diction: "breathe or Achoo," "your Luftwaffe, your gobbledygoo." She can expound such adult topics as Taroc packs, Viennese beer, and Tyrolean snowfall; can specify death camps by name; and can employ an adult vocabulary of "recover," "ancestress," "Aryan," "*Meinkampf*," "obscene," and "bastard." Yet she also has recourse to a more primitive lexicon that includes "chuffing," "your fat black heart," and "my pretty red heart." She proves herself capable of careful intellectual discriminations ("so I never could tell"), conventionalized description ("beautiful Nauset"), and moral analogy ("if I've killed one man, I've killed two"), while also exhibiting regressive fantasies (vampires), repetitions ("wars, wars, wars"), and inarticulateness ("panzer-man, panzer-man, O You — "). She oscillates between calm reflection ("You stand at the blackboard, daddy, / In the picture I have of you") and mad incoherence ("Ich, ich, ich, ich"). Her sophisticated language puts her wild language in an ironic perspective, removing the discourse from the control of the archaic self who understands experience only in extreme terms.

The ironies in "Daddy" proliferate in unexpected ways, however. When the speaker proclaims categorically that "every woman adores a Fascist," she is subjecting her victimization to irony by suggesting that sufferers choose, or at least accommodate themselves to, their suffering. But she is also subjecting her authority to irony, since her claim about "every woman" is transparently false. It simply parodies patriarchal commonplaces, such as those advanced . . . concerning "feminine masochism." The adult, sophisticated self seems to be speaking here: Who else would have the confidence to make a sociological generalization? Yet the content of the assertion, if taken straightforwardly, returns us to the regressive self who is dominated by extravagant emotions she cannot begin to understand. Plath's mother wished that Plath would write about "decent, courageous people," and she herself heard an inner voice demanding that she be a perfect "paragon" in her language and feeling. But in the speaker of "Daddy," she inscribed the opposite of such a paragon: a divided self whose veneer of civilization is breached and infected by unhealthy instincts.

Plath's irony cuts both ways. At the same time that the speaker's   10
sophisticated voice undercuts her childish voice, reducing its melodrama to comedy, the childish or maddened voice undercuts the pretensions of the sophisticated voice, revealing the extremity of suffering masked by its ironies. While demonstrating the inadequacy of thinking and feeling in opposites, the poem implies that such a mode can locate truths denied more complex cognitive and affective systems. The very moderation of the normal adult intelligence, its tolerance of ambiguity, its defenses against the primal energies of the id, results in falsification. Reflecting Schiller's idea that the creative artist experiences a "momentary and passing madness" (quoted by Freud in a passage of *The Interpretation of Dreams* that Plath underscored), "Daddy" gives voice to that madness. Yet the poem's sophisticated awareness, its comic vision, probably wins out in the end, since the poem concludes by curtailing the power of its extreme discourse. . . . Furthermore, Plath distanced herself from the poem's aboriginal voice by introducing her text as "a poem spoken by a girl with an Electra complex" — that is, as a study of the *girl's* pathology rather than her father's — and as an allegory that will "free" her from that pathology. She also distanced herself by reading the poem in a tone that emphasized its irony. And finally, she distanced herself by laying the poem's wild voice permanently to rest after October. The aboriginal vision was indeed purged. "Daddy" represents not Dickinson's madness that is divinest sense, but rather an entry into a style of discourse and a mastery of it. The poem realizes

the trope of suffering by means of an inherent irony that both questions and validates the trope in the same gestures, and that finally allows the speaker to conclude the discourse and to remove herself from the trope with a sense of completion rather than wrenching, since the irony was present from the very beginning.

Plath's poetic revolt in "Daddy" liberated her pent-up creativity, but the momentary success sustained her little more than self-sacrifice had done. "Daddy" became another stage in her development, an unrepeatable experiment, a vocal opening that closed itself at once. The poem is not only an elegy for the power of "daddy-poetry" but for the powers of speech Plath discovered in composing it.

When we consider "Daddy" generically, a further range of implications presents itself. Although we could profitably consider the poem as the dramatic monologue Plath called it in her BBC broadcast, let us regard it instead as the kind of poem most readers have taken it to be: a domestic poem. I have chosen this term, rather than M. L. Rosenthal's better-known "confessional poem" or the more neutral "autobiographical poem," because "confessional poem" implies a confession rather than a making (though Steven Hoffman and Lawrence Kramer have recently indicated the mode's conventions) and because "autobiographical poem" is too general for our purpose. I shall define the domestic poem as one that represents and comments on a protagonist's relationship to one or more family members, usually a parent, child, or spouse. To focus our discussion even further, I shall emphasize poetry that specifically concerns a father.   *[1990]*

TIM KENDALL
From *Sylvia Plath: A Critical Study*

Tim Kendall edits Thumbscrew *and is the author of* Paul Muldoon *(1996) and* Poetry of the First World War: An Anthology *(2013). He received an Eric Gregory Award for his poetry in 1997 and appears in the* Oxford Poets 2000 *anthology. He was the Thomas Chatterton British Academy Lecturer for 2001 at the University of Bristol and is currently a professor of English Literature at the University of Exeter. In 2005, Kendall was awarded the lucrative Philip Leverhulme Prize. This selection is from a book he published in 2001.*

Plath's journals . . . indicate that as late as December 1958, the poet was seriously considering a Ph.D. in psychology: "Awesome to confront a program of study which is so monumental: all human experience."[1] The previous day Plath had discovered in Freud's *Mourning and Melancholia* "an almost exact description of my feelings and reasons for suicide."[2] She felt creatively vindicated when she found parallels between her own life and writings and those of Freud and Jung: "All this relates in a most meaningful way my instinctive images with perfectly valid psychological analysis. However, I am the victim, rather than the analyst."[3] In these examples, experience precedes the psycho-analytical explanation; Freud and Jung confirm what Plath already knows. Despite her emphasis on victimhood, such passages show how she transforms herself into her own case history, becoming simultaneously victim and analyst. The same dual role is apparent in "Daddy," which Plath introduces for BBC radio in terms of Freudian allegory:

> Here is a poem spoken by a girl with an Electra complex. Her father died while she thought he was God. Her case is complicated by the fact that her father was also a Nazi and her mother very possibly part Jewish. In the daughter the two strains marry and paralyze each other—she has to act out the awful little allegory once over before she is free of it.

"Daddy," built on poetic repetition, is therefore a poem about a compulsion to repeat, and its psychology is characterized according to Freudian principles. Repetition necessitates performance—the speaker must "*act out* the awful little allegory once over" in order to escape it. Whether she does succeed in escaping depends on the poem's ambivalent last line: "Daddy, daddy, you bastard, I'm through." "I'm through" can mean (especially to an American ear) "I've had enough of you," but it also means "I've got away from you, I'm free of you," or "I'm done for, I'm beaten," or even "I've finished what I have to say." The speaker's ability to free herself from the urge to repeat remains in the balance.

These dilemmas and uncertainties can be traced back, as Plath suggests, to Freud's accounts of compulsive behavior. "Daddy" adopts a Freudian understanding of infantile sexuality (the Electra complex), a Freudian belief in transference (the vampire-husband "said he was you," and the father also shifts identities), and a Freudian attitude towards repetitive behavior. In a passage from *Beyond the Pleasure Principle* which might conveniently serve to diagnose the speaker of "Daddy," Freud argues that,

> The patient cannot remember the whole of what is repressed in him, and what he cannot remember may be precisely the essential part of it. Thus he acquires no sense of the conviction of the correctness of the construction that has been communicated to him. He is obliged to *repeat* the repressed material as a contemporary experience instead of, as the physician would prefer to see, *remembering* it as something belonging to the past. These reproductions, which emerge with such unwished-for exactitude, always have as their subject some portion of infantile sexual life—of the Oedipus complex, that is, and its derivatives; and they are invariably acted out in the sphere of the transference, of the patient's relation to the physician.[4]

This illuminates Plath's attempts to persuade the dead father to communicate. The refusal of the father-figure, in his various transferred roles of colossus, Nazi, teacher, and vampire, to become "something belonging to the past" is evident in the speaker's need to kill him repeatedly. He must be imaginatively disinterred in order to be killed again, and even as one of the undead, he must be destroyed with a stake in his heart. This repetitive pattern of disappearance and return represents Plath's version of the *fort-da* game as famously described in *Beyond the Pleasure Principle*, where the child's repeated and "long-drawn-out 'o-o-o-o' " is only a slight vowel modulation away from the "oo" repetitions of "Daddy." The father-figure is a "contemporary experience," not a memory; and, as Freud explains, the reason for his continuing presence lies in the speaker's "infantile sexual life." The father's early death ensures that she cannot progress, and her sense of selfhood is stutteringly confined within a compulsion to repeat:

> I never could talk to you.
> The tongue stuck in my jaw.
>
> It stuck in a barb wire snare.
> Ich, ich, ich, ich,
> I could hardly speak.

Repetition occurs when Plath's speaker gets stuck in the barb wire snare of communication with her father. She is unable to move beyond the self. This proposes a more fundamental understanding of repetitive words and phrases than those suggested by Blessing or Shapiro. "Daddy" implies that each local repetition, whatever its microcosmic effects, symptomizes a larger behavioral pattern of repetition compulsion. The poem's title, the "oo" rhymes, and the nursery-rhyme rhythms all reinforce this suggestion of a mind struggling to free itself from the need to repeat infantile trauma. Such infantilism, exhibited by an adult persona, contributes to the poem's transgressive humor: Plath read "Daddy" aloud to a friend, reports Anne Stevenson, "in a mocking, comical voice that made both women fall about with laughter."[5]

Psychoanalyzing the speaker of "Daddy" in the Freudian terms proposed by Plath herself is a valuable exercise which carries important implications for *Ariel*'s use of repetition, but it still does not settle the nature of the poet's complex relationship to the "girl with an Electra complex." Plath's introduction for radio seems to reverse the pattern in her journals: now Freud becomes a source as much as an explanation. Her introduction also reverses the reader's experience of the poem. "Daddy" conveys a power and an intimacy which challenge any hygienic separation of poet and poetic voice. With such contradictory evidence, the gulf between poet and persona, cold-blooded technique and blood-hot emotion, analyst and victim, seems unbridgeable. If these divisions can be successfully reconciled, it is through Plath's emphasis on performance and repetition. Freud's account of repetition compulsion shares with Plath's description of "Daddy" a crucial verb: just as Plath's persona must "act out the awful little allegory," so Freud notes that the Oedipus complex and its derivatives are "invariably acted out in the sphere of the transference." Repetition guarantees performance, and performance requires an audience. Freud notes, as if glossing "Daddy," that "the artistic play and artistic imitation carried out by adults, which, unlike children's, are aimed at an audience, do not spare the spectators (for instance, in tragedy) the most painful experiences

5

and can yet be felt by them as highly enjoyable." Plath categorized "Daddy" as "light verse,"[6] a genre which W. H. Auden considered to be "written for performance."[7] "Daddy" may be written for performance, but it pushes the "painful experiences" and the entertainment value to extremes which many readers find intolerable. Freud's Aristotelian concern — why is tragedy pleasurable? — also seems a valid question to ask of Plath's poem: "Daddy" derives its aesthetic pleasures from incest, patricide, suicide, and the Nazi extermination camps.

These taboo-breaking juxtapositions of personal and private realms help explain the poem's notoriety. However, controversy over "Daddy" always returns eventually to Plath's relationship with her persona. Seamus Heaney's principled objection, for example, discerns no difference at all:

> A poem like "Daddy," however brilliant a *tour de force* it can be acknowledged to be, and however its violence and vindictiveness can be understood or excused in light of the poet's parental and marital relations, remains, nevertheless, so entangled in biographical circumstances and rampages so permissively in the history of other people's sorrows that it simply withdraws its rights to our sympathy.[8]

Heaney's pointed phrase "rampages so permissively" might be disputed as an unfair rhetorical flourish, especially in the context of Plath's hard-earned Emersonian desire to assimilate and her wider theological explorations. But Heaney's most revealing word is his last: "sympathy." Heaney refers to one aspect of Aristotelian catharsis — pity for the suffering of others — which he claims that "Daddy" fails to earn. It is not surprising that his critical decorum should come into conflict with a poem which is so consciously and manifestly indecorous. Heaney reads "Daddy" purely as the protest of the poet-victim, who behaves vindictively because of her difficult parental and marital relations. This fails to credit Plath with the self-awareness to be acting deliberately — to be performing. In "Daddy" Plath seeks no one's "sympathy"; she has once more become victim and analyst, the girl with the Electra complex and the physician who diagnoses her condition. Plath wonders in her journal whether "our desire to investigate psychology [is] a desire to get Beuscher's [her psychiatrist's] power and handle it ourselves."[9] "Daddy," as her introduction makes clear, represents a poetic handling of that power. Freud states that the patient must acquire "some degree of aloofness."[10] "Daddy" is the work of a poet so aloof as to render allegorical, act out, and psychoanalyze, her own mental history.   *[2001]*

Notes

1. Sylvia Plath, *The Journals of Sylvia Plath, 1950–1962*, ed. Karen V. Kukil (London: Faber & Faber, 2000), p. 452.
2. Ibid., p. 447.
3. Ibid., p. 514.
4. S. Freud, *Beyond the Pleasure Principle*, tr. and ed. J. Strachey (Hogarth, 1961), p. 12.
5. A. Stevenson, *Bitter Fame: A Life of Sylvia Plath* (Viking, 1989), p. 277.

6. A. Alvarez, "Sylvia Plath," in C. Newman (ed.), *The Art of Sylvia Plath* (Indiana UP, 1970), p. 66.
7. W. H. Auden (ed.), *The Oxford Book of Light Verse* (OUP, 1938), p. ix.
8. S. Heaney, "The Indefatigable Hoof-taps: Sylvia Plath," *The Government of the Tongue* (Faber, 1988), p. 165.
9. *Journals*, p. 449.
10. *Beyond the Pleasure Principle*, p. 13.

≣ MAKING COMPARISONS

1. "Daddy" seems to be a protest, but some critics see it as more than that. Which of the three commentaries makes the best case that it is more than a revolt against the speaker's father?

2. Which critic seems to answer most of the perplexing questions of this poem — for example, the father as Nazi, the father as vampire, the childlike rhythms, the speaker's vengefulness, her viciousness?

3. Do these critics make any similar points? How might you describe them? What is their most striking difference?

≣ WRITING ABOUT ISSUES

1. Choose one of the critical commentaries in this cluster and argue that the textual evidence supporting its assertions is, or is not, adequate.

2. Imagine you are Sylvia Plath. After reading these three essays, write a letter to a literary journal either attacking or praising these critics.

3. Write an essay arguing that your own reading of "Daddy" makes more sense than those of Bundtzen, Axelrod, or Kendall. Assume that the audience for the criticism is your class.

4. There are dozens of critical commentaries on Plath's "Daddy." Some were written soon after the poem's publication; others are quite recent. Locate an early piece of criticism, and compare it to one published in the past few years. Do these critics make similar or different points? Is one more concerned with the text, with gender issues, with cultural concerns, or with what other critics say? Write a brief comparison of the two, explaining your evidence.

≡ Contexts for Research: Robots, the Human Family, and "Liar!"

ISAAC ASIMOV, "Liar!"

CONTEXTS FOR RESEARCH:

OREN ETZIONI, "How to Regulate Artificial Intelligence"

FEI-FEI LI, "How to Make AI that's Good for People"

MAUREEN DOWD, "Silicon Valley Sharknado"

A. M. TURING, From *"Computing Machinery and Intelligence"*

The 1982 film *Blade Runner* is now considered one of the greatest of science fiction stories. Inspired by the cult classic *Do Androids Dream of Electric Sheep?* by Philip K. Dick, the movie deals with the complexities of distinguishing between human and android. Ever since Karel Capek's play *R.U.R.* (1921), scientists and philosophers have been intrigued by the possibility that robots might one day achieve the same kind of intelligence as humans. Of course, today in many ways artificial intelligence (AI) has clearly surpassed humans, certainly in data storage and calculation speed. And Google's engines demonstrate AI's massive ability to retrieve a needle of information almost instantaneously from billions of haystacks.

But philosophers wonder if even a machine with such awesome mental powers could be considered to be conscious. In *Blade Runner*, an elaborate test involving questions that could reveal minute fluctuations in the retina was developed to tell humans and androids apart. Otherwise humans couldn't tell. In fact, in the movie the detective tasked with uncovering androids falls in love with one. Philip K. Dick certainly wanted to problematize the issue. Can robots have a subjective inner life, feeling joy and suffering? Can they be self-aware? Dick's androids, for example, did not want to die and had complex personal relationships. Is this really possible for a machine?

In the following story from his famous collection of short stories, *I, Robot* (1950), Isaac Asimov forces the reader to confront these questions. Almost eighty years later, we are still debating whether or not a machine with artificial intelligence can become conscious and if it can, will it pose a danger to humans. After thousands of essays and research projects, the scientific community is still debating the ethical and technical feasibility of having robots treated as members of the human family. To help us with this complex conversation, we have included four selections that focus on the issue.

At the beginning of a popular film *Ex Machina* (2015), a young scientist is asked to give the Turing test to a very human-like creation of a computer genius to determine if it can think like a human, that is, can he tell if the android is human or not. That test, developed in 1950 by the computer genius A. M. Turing, is the focus of our last text.

≡ BEFORE YOU READ

Looking back on robot/android films, television shows, and stories you have encountered, what observations about the intelligence of these "machines" can you make? Were they benign? Were they self-aware, conscious? How specifically would you distinguish them from humans?

ISAAC ASIMOV

Liar!

Isaac Asimov (1920–1992) was an amazingly prolific author writing hundreds of books on a wide variety of topics, including some of science fiction's most popular novels. He was born in Russia and grew up in Brooklyn, N. Y. He attended Columbia University, eventually earning a Ph.D. in biochemistry. His 1950 novel I, Robot *featured his famous Three Laws of Robotics: 1. A robot may not injure a human being or, through inaction, allow a human being to come to harm; 2. A robot must obey the orders given it by humans except where such orders would conflict with the First Law; and 3. A robot must protect its own existence as long as that does not conflict with the First or Second Law. Along with H .G. Wells, Ray Bradbury, Robert Heinlein, Arthur C. Clark, and Philip K. Dick, Asimov was considered to be one of the greatest science fiction writers of the twentieth century.*

Alfred Lanning lit his cigar carefully, but the tips of his fingers were trembling slightly. His gray eyebrows hunched low as he spoke between puffs.

"It reads minds all right — damn little doubt about that! But why?" He looked at Mathematician Peter Bogert, "Well?"

Bogert flattened his black hair down with both hands, "That was the thirty-fourth RB model we've turned out, Lanning. All the others were strictly orthodox."

The third man at the table frowned. Milton Ashe was the youngest officer of U.S. Robot & Mechanical Men, Inc., and proud of his post.

"Listen, Bogert. There wasn't a hitch in the assembly from start to finish. I guarantee that."   5

Bogert's thick lips spread in a patronizing smile, "Do you? If you can answer for the entire assembly line, I recommend your promotion. By exact count, there are seventy-five thousand, two hundred and thirty-four operations necessary for the manufacture of a single positronic brain, each separate operation depending for successful completion upon any number of factors, from five to a hundred and five. If any one of them goes seriously wrong, the 'brain' is ruined. I quote our own information folder, Ashe."

Milton Ashe flushed, but a fourth voice cut off his reply.

"If we're going to start by trying to fix the blame on one another, I'm leaving." Susan Calvin's hands were folded tightly in her lap, and the little lines about her thin, pale lips deepened, "We've got a mind-reading robot on our hands and it strikes me as rather important that we find out just why it reads minds. We're not going to do that by saying, 'Your fault! My fault!'"

Her cold gray eyes fastened upon Ashe, and he grinned.

Lanning grinned too, and, as always at such times, his long white hair and shrewd little eyes made him the picture of a biblical patriarch. "True for you, Dr. Calvin."   10

His voice became suddenly crisp, "Here's everything in pill-concentrate form. We've produced a positronic brain of supposedly ordinary vintage that's got the remarkable property of being able to tune in on thought waves. It would mark the most important advance in robotics in decades, if we knew how it happened. We don't, and we have to find out. Is that clear?"

"May I make a suggestion?" asked Bogert.

"Go ahead!"

"I'd say that until we do figure out the mess—and as a mathematician I expect it to be a very devil of a mess—we keep the existence of RB-34 a secret. I mean even from the other members of the staff. As heads of the departments, we ought not to find it an insoluble problem, and the fewer know about it—"

"Bogert is right," said Dr. Calvin. "Ever since the Interplanetary Code was modified to allow robot models to be tested in the plants before being shipped out to space, anti-robot propaganda has increased. If any word leaks out about a robot being able to read minds before we can announce complete control of the phenomenon, pretty effective capital could be made out of it."   15

Lanning sucked at his cigar and nodded gravely. He turned to Ashe, "I think you said you were alone when you first stumbled on this thought-reading business."

"I'll say I was alone—I got the scare of my life. RB-34 had just been taken off the assembly table and they sent him down to me. Obermann was off some-wheres, so I took him down to the testing rooms myself—at least I started to take him down." Ashe paused, and a tiny smile tugged at his lips, "Say, did any of you ever carry on a thought conversation without knowing it?"

No one bothered to answer, and he continued, "You don't realize it at first, you know. He just spoke to me—as logically and sensibly as you can imagine—and it was only when I was most of the way down to the testing rooms that I realized that I hadn't said anything. Sure, I thought lots, but that isn't the same thing, is it? I locked that thing up and ran for Lanning. Having it walking beside me, calmly peering into my thoughts and picking and choosing among them gave me the willies."

"I imagine it would," said Susan Calvin thoughtfully. Her eyes fixed them-selves upon Ashe in an oddly intent manner, "We are so accustomed to consid-ering our own thoughts private."

Lanning broke in impatiently, "Then only the four of us know. All right! We've got to go about this systematically. Ashe, I want you to check over the assembly line from beginning to end—everything. You're to eliminate all operations in which there was no possible chance of an error, and list all those where there were, together with its nature and possible magnitude."   20

"Tall order," grunted Ashe.

"Naturally! Of course, you're to put the men under you to work on this—every single one if you have to, and I don't care if we go behind schedule, either. But they're not to know why, you understand."

"Hm-m-m, yes!" The young technician grinned wryly. "It's still a lulu of a job."

Lanning swiveled about in his chair and faced Calvin, "You'll have to tackle the job from the other direction. You're the robo-psychologist of the plant, so you're to study the robot itself and work backward. Try to find out how he ticks. See what else is tied up with his telepathic powers, how far they extend, how they warp his outlook, and just exactly what harm it has done to his ordinary RB properties. You've got that?"

Lanning didn't wait for Dr. Calvin to answer.   25

"I'll co-ordinate the work and interpret the findings mathematically." He puffed violently at his cigar and mumbled the rest through the smoke, "Bogert will help me there, of course."

Bogert polished the nails of one pudgy hand with the other and said blandly, "I dare say. I know a little in the line."

"Well! I'll get started." Ashe shoved his chair back and rose. His pleasantly youthful face crinkled in a grin, "I've got the darnedest job of any of us, so I'm getting out of here and to work."

He left with a slurred, "B' seein' ye!"

Susan Calvin answered with a barely perceptible nod, but her eyes fol-   30
lowed him out of sight and she did not answer when Lanning grunted and said, "Do you want to go up and see RB-34 now, Dr. Calvin?"

RB-34's photoelectric eyes lifted from the book at the muffled sound of hinges turning and he was upon his feet when Susan Calvin entered.

She paused to readjust the huge "No Entrance" sign upon the door and then approached the robot.

"I've brought you the texts upon hyperatomic motor, Herbie—a few anyway. Would you care to look at them?"

RB-34—otherwise known as Herbie—lifted the three heavy books from her arms and opened to the title page of one:

"Hm-m-m! 'Theory of Hyperatomics.'" He mumbled inarticulately to him-   35
self as he flipped the pages and then spoke with an abstracted air, "Sit down, Dr. Calvin! This will take me a few minutes."

The psychologist seated herself and watched Herbie narrowly as he took a chair at the other side of the table and went through the three books systematically.

At the end of half an hour, he put them down, "Of course, I know why you brought these."

The corner of Dr. Calvin's lip twitched, "I was afraid you would. It's difficult to work with you, Herbie. You're always a step ahead of me."

"It's the same with these books, you know, as with the others. They just don't interest me. There's nothing to your textbooks. Your science is just a mass of collected data plastered together by make-shift theory — and all so incredibly simple, that it's scarcely worth bothering about.

"It's your fiction that interests me. Your studies of the interplay of human   40
motives and emotions" — his mighty hand gestured vaguely as he sought the proper words.

Dr. Calvin whispered, "I think I understand."

"I see into minds, you see," the robot continued, "and you have no idea how complicated they are. I can't begin to understand everything because my own mind has so little in common with them — but I try, and your novels help."

"Yes, but I'm afraid that after going through some of the harrowing emotional experiences of our present-day sentimental novel" — there was a tinge of bitterness in her voice — "you find real minds like ours dull and colorless."

"But I don't!"

The sudden energy in the response brought the other to her feet. She felt   45
herself reddening, and thought wildly, "He must know!"

Herbie subsided suddenly, and muttered in a low voice from which the metallic timbre departed almost entirely. "But, of course, I know about it, Dr. Calvin. You think of it always, so how can I help but know?"

Her face was hard. "Have you — told anyone?"

"Of course not!" This, with genuine surprise. "No one has asked me."

"Well, then," she flung out, "I suppose you think I am a fool."

"No! It is a normal emotion."   50

"Perhaps that is why it is so foolish." The wistfulness in her voice drowned out everything else. Some of the woman peered through the layer of doctor-hood. "I am not what you would call — attractive."

"If you are referring to mere physical attraction, I couldn't judge. But I know, in any case, that there are other types of attraction."

"Nor young." Dr. Calvin had scarcely heard the robot.

"You are not yet forty." An anxious insistence had crept into Herbie's voice.

"Thirty-eight as you count the years; a shriveled sixty as far as my emo-   55
tional outlook on life is concerned. Am I a psychologist for nothing?"

She drove on with bitter breathlessness, "And he's barely thirty-five and looks and acts younger. Do you suppose he ever sees me as anything but . . . but what I am?"

"You are wrong!" Herbie's steel fist struck the plastic-topped table with a strident clang. "Listen to me — "

But Susan Calvin whirled on him now and the hunted pain in her eyes became a blaze, "Why should I? What do you know about it all, anyway, you . . . you machine. I'm just a specimen to you; an interesting bug with a peculiar mind spread-eagled for inspection. It's a wonderful example of frustration, isn't it? Almost as good as your books." Her voice, emerging in dry sobs, choked into silence.

The robot cowered at the outburst. He shook his head pleadingly. "Won't you listen to me, please? I could help you if you would let me."

"How?" Her lips curled. "By giving me good advice?" 60

"No, not that. It's just that I know what other people think — Milton Ashe, for instance."

There was a long silence, and Susan Calvin's eyes dropped. "I don't want to know what he thinks," she gasped. "Keep quiet."

"I think you would want to know what he thinks."

Her head remained bent, but her breath came more quickly. "You are talking nonsense," she whispered.

"Why should I? I am trying to help. Milton Ashe's thoughts of you—" he 65 paused.

And then the psychologist raised her head, "Well?"

The robot said quietly, "He loves you."

For a full minute, Dr. Calvin did not speak. She merely stared. Then, "You are mistaken! You must be. Why should he?"

"But he does. A thing like that cannot be hidden, not from me."

"But I am so . . . so—" she stammered to a halt. 70

"He looks deeper than the skin, and admires intellect in others. Milton Ashe is not the type to marry a head of hair and a pair of eyes."

Susan Calvin found herself blinking rapidly and waited before speaking. Even then her voice trembled, "Yet he certainly never in any way indicated—"

"Have you ever given him a chance?"

"How could I? I never thought that—"

"Exactly!" 75

The psychologist paused in thought and then looked up suddenly. "A girl visited him here at the plant half a year ago. She was pretty, I suppose—blond and slim. And, of course, could scarcely add two and two. He spent all day puffing out his chest, trying to explain how a robot was put together." The hardness had returned, "Not that she understood! Who was she?"

Herbie answered without hesitation, "I know the person you are referring to. She is his first cousin, and there is no romantic interest there, I assure you."

Susan Calvin rose to her feet with a vivacity almost girlish. "Now isn't that strange? That's exactly what I used to pretend to myself sometimes, though I never really thought so. Then it all must be true."

She ran to Herbie and seized his cold, heavy hand in both hers. "Thank you, Herbie." Her voice was an urgent, husky whisper. "Don't tell anyone about this. Let it be our secret—and thank you again." With that, and a convulsive squeeze of Herbie's unresponsive metal fingers, she left.

Herbie turned slowly to his neglected novel, but there was no one to read 80 *his* thoughts.

Milton Ashe stretched slowly and magnificently, to the tune of cracking joints and a chorus of grunts, and then glared at Peter Bogert, Ph.D.

"Say," he said, "I've been at this for a week now with just about no sleep. How long do I have to keep it up? I thought you said the positronic bombardment in Vac Chamber D was the solution."

Bogert yawned delicately and regarded his white hands with interest. "It is. I'm on the track."

"I know what *that* means when a mathematician says it. How near the end are you?"

"It all depends."

85

"On what?" Ashe dropped into a chair and stretched his long legs out before him.

"On Lanning. The old fellow disagrees with me." He sighed, "A bit behind the times, that's the trouble with him. He clings to matrix mechanics as the all in all, and this problem calls for more powerful mathematical tools. He's so stubborn."

As he muttered sleepily, "Why not ask Herbie and settle the whole affair?"

"Ask the robot?" Bogert's eyebrows climbed.

"Why not? Didn't the old girl tell you?"

90

"You mean Calvin?"

"Yeah! Susie herself. That robot's a mathematical wiz. He knows all about everything plus a bit on the side. He does triple integrals in his head and eats up tensor analysis for dessert."

The mathematician stared skeptically, "Are you serious?"

"So help me! The catch is that the dope doesn't like math. He would rather read slushy novels. Honest! You should see the tripe Susie keeps feeding him: 'Purple Passion' and 'Love in Space.'"

"Dr. Calvin hasn't said a word of this to us."

95

"Well, she hasn't finished studying him. You know how she is. She likes to have everything just so before letting out the big secret."

"She's told *you*."

"We sort of got to talking. I have been seeing a lot of her lately." He opened his eyes wide and frowned, "Say, Bogie, have you been noticing anything queer about the lady lately?"

Bogert relaxed into an undignified grin, "She's using lipstick, if that's what you mean."

"Hell, I know that. Rouge, powder, and eye shadow, too. She's a sight. But 100 it's not that. I can't put my finger on it. It's the way she talks—as if she were happy about something." He thought a little, and then shrugged.

The other allowed himself a leer, which, for a scientist past fifty, was not a bad job, "Maybe she's in love."

As he allowed his eyes to close again, "You're nuts, Bogie. You go speak to Herbie; I want to stay here and go to sleep."

"Right! Not that I particularly like having a robot tell me my job, nor that I think he can do it!"

A soft snore was his only answer.

Herbie listened carefully as Peter Bogert, hands in pockets, spoke with elabo- 105 rate indifference.

"So there you are. I've been told you understand these things, and I am asking you more in curiosity than anything else. My line of reasoning, as I have outlined it, involves a few doubtful steps, I admit, which Dr. Lanning refuses to accept, and the picture is still rather incomplete."

The robot didn't answer, and Bogert said, "Well?"

"I see no mistake," Herbie studied the scribbled figures.

"I don't suppose you can go any further than that?"

"I daren't try. You are a better mathematician than I, and—well, I'd hate   110
to commit myself."

There was a shade of complacency in Bogert's smile, "I rather thought that would be the case. It is deep. We'll forget it." He crumpled the sheets, tossed them down the waste shaft, turned to leave, and then thought better of it.

"By the way—"

The robot waited.

Bogert seemed to have difficulty. "There is something—that is, perhaps you can—" He stopped.

Herbie spoke quietly. "Your thoughts are confused, but there is no doubt   115
at all that they concern Dr. Lanning. It is silly to hesitate, for as soon as you compose yourself, I'll know what it is you want to ask."

The mathematician's hand went to his sleek hair in the familiar smoothing gesture. "Lanning is nudging seventy," he said, as if that explained everything.

"I know that."

"And he's been director of the plant for almost thirty years." Herbie nodded.

"Well, now," Bogert's voice became ingratiating, "you would know whether . . . whether he's thinking of resigning. Health, perhaps, or some other—"

"Quite," said Herbie, and that was all.   120

"Well, do you know?"

"Certainly."

"Then—uh—could you tell me?"

"Since you ask, yes," the robot was quite matter-of-fact about it. "He has already resigned!"

"What!" The exclamation was an explosive, almost inarticulate, sound.   125
The scientist's large head hunched forward, "Say that again!"

"He has already resigned," came the quiet repetition, "but it has not yet taken effect. He is waiting, you see, to solve the problem of—er—myself. That finished, he is quite ready to turn the office of director over to his successor."

Bogert expelled his breath sharply, "And this successor? Who is he?" He was quite close to Herbie now, eyes fixed fascinatedly on those unreadable dull-red photoelectric cells that were the robot's eyes.

Words came slowly, "You are the next director."

And Bogert relaxed into a tight smile, "This is good to know. I've been hoping and waiting for this. Thanks, Herbie."

Peter Bogert was at his desk until five that morning and he was back at nine.   130
The shelf just over the desk emptied of its row of reference books and tables,
as he referred to one after the other. The pages of calculations before him
increased microscopically and the crumpled sheets at his feet mounted into a
hill of scribbled paper.

At precisely noon, he stared at the final page, rubbed a blood-shot eye,
yawned and shrugged. "This is getting worse each minute. Damn!"

He turned at the sound of the opening door and nodded at Lanning, who
entered, cracking the knuckles of one gnarled hand with the other.

The director took in the disorder of the room and his eyebrows furrowed
together.

"New lead?" he asked.

"No," came the defiant answer. "What's wrong with the old one?"   135

Lanning did not trouble to answer, nor to do more than bestow a single
cursory glance at the top sheet upon Bogert's desk. He spoke through the flare
of a match as he lit a cigar.

"Has Calvin told you about the robot? It's a mathematical genius. Really
remarkable."

The other snorted loudly, "So I've heard. But Calvin had better stick to
robopsychology. I've checked Herbie on math, and he can scarcely struggle
through calculus."

"Calvin didn't find it so."

"She's crazy."   140

"And I don't find it so." The director's eyes narrowed dangerously.

"You!" Bogert's voice hardened. "What are you taking about?"

"I've been putting Herbie through his paces all morning, and he can do
tricks you never heard of."

"Is that so?"

"You sound skeptical!" Lanning flipped a sheet of paper out of his vest   145
pocket and unfolded it. 'That's not my handwriting, is it?"

Bogert studied the large angular notation covering the sheet, "Herbie did
this?"

"Right! And if you'll notice, he's been working on your time integration
of Equation 22. It comes"— Lanning tapped a yellow fingernail upon the last
step—"to the identical conclusion I did, and in a quarter the time. You had no
right to neglect the Linger Effect in positronic bombardment."

"I didn't neglect it. For Heaven's sake, Lanning, get it through your head
that it would cancel out—"

"Oh, sure, you explained that. You used the Mitchell Translation Equation,
didn't you? Well—it doesn't apply."

"Why not?"   150

"Because you've been using hyper-imaginaries, for one thing."

"What's that to do with?"

"Mitchell's Equation won't hold when—"

"Are you crazy? If you'll reread Mitchell's original paper in the *Transactions
of the Far*—"

"I don't have to. I told you in the beginning that I didn't like his reasoning, and Herbie backs me in that." 155

"Well, then," Bogert shouted, "let that clockwork contraption solve the entire problem for you. Why bother with nonessentials?"

"That's exactly the point. Herbie can't solve the problem. And if he can't, we can't — alone. I'm submitting the entire question to the National Board. It's gotten beyond us."

Bogert's chair went over backward as he jumped up a-snarl, face crimson. "You're doing nothing of the sort."

Lanning flushed in his turn, "Are you telling me what I can't do?"

"Exactly," was the gritted response. "I've got the problem beaten and you're not to take it out of my hands, understand? Don't think I don't see through you, you desiccated fossil. You'd cut your own nose off before you'd let me get the credit for solving robotic telepathy." 160

"You're a damned idiot, Bogert, and in one second I'll have you suspended for insubordination" — Lanning's lower lip trembled with passion.

"Which is one thing you won't do, Lanning. You haven't any secrets with a mind-reading robot around, so don't forget that I know all about your resignation."

The ash on Lanning's cigar trembled and fell, and the cigar itself followed, "What . . . what—"

Bogert chuckled nastily, "And I'm the new director, be it understood. I'm very aware of that; don't think I'm not. Damn your eyes, Lanning, I'm going to give the orders about here or there will be the sweetest mess that you've ever been in."

Lanning found his voice and let it out with a roar. "You're suspended, d'ye hear? You're relieved of all duties. You're broken, do you understand?" 165

The smile on the other's face broadened, "Now, what's the use of that? You're getting nowhere. I'm holding the trumps. I know you've resigned. Herbie told me, and he got it straight from you."

Lanning forced himself to speak quietly. He looked an old, old man, with tired eyes peering from a face in which the red had disappeared, leaving the pasty yellow of age behind, "I want to speak to Herbie. He can't have told you anything of the sort. You're playing a deep game, Bogert, but I'm calling your bluff. Come with me."

Bogert shrugged, "To see Herbie? Good! Damned good!"

It was also precisely at noon that Milton Ashe looked up from his clumsy sketch and said, "You get the idea? I'm not too good at getting this down, but that's about how it looks. It's a honey of a house, and I can get it for next to nothing."

Susan Calvin gazed across at him with melting eyes. "It's really beautiful," she sighed. "I've often thought that I'd like to—" Her voice trailed away. 170

"Of course," Ashe continued briskly, putting away his pencil, "I've got to wait for my vacation. It's only two weeks off, but this Herbie business has everything up in the air." His eyes dropped to his fingernails, "Besides, there's another point — but it's a secret."

"Then don't tell me."

"Oh, I'd just as soon, I'm just busting to tell someone—and you're just about the best—er—confidante I could find here." He grinned sheepishly.

Susan Calvin's heart bounded, but she did not trust herself to speak.

"Frankly," Ashe scraped his chair closer and lowered his voice into a con-   175
fidential whisper, "the house isn't to be only for myself. I'm getting married!"

And then he jumped out of his seat, "What's the matter?"

"Nothing!" The horrible spinning sensation had vanished, but it was hard to get words out. "Married? You mean—"

"Why, sure! About time, isn't it? You remember that girl who was here last summer. That's she! But you *are* sick. You—"

"Headache!" Susan Calvin motioned him away weakly. "I've . . . I've been subject to them lately. I want to . . . to congratulate you, of course. I'm very glad—" The inexpertly applied rouge made a pair of nasty red splotches upon her chalk-white face. Things had begun spinning again. "Pardon me—please—"

The words were a mumble, as she stumbled blindly out the door. It had   180
happened with the sudden catastrophe of a dream—and with all the unreal horror of a dream.

But how could it be? Herbie had said—

And Herbie knew! He could see into minds!

She found herself leaning breathlessly against the door jamb, staring into Herbie's metal face. She must have climbed the two flights of stairs, but she had no memory of it. The distance had been covered in an instant, as in a dream.

As in a dream!

And still Herbie's unblinking eyes stared into hers and their dull red   185
seemed to expand into dimly shining nightmarish globes.

He was speaking, and she felt the cold glass pressing against her lips. She swallowed and shuddered into a certain awareness of her surroundings.

Still Herbie spoke, and there was agitation in his voice—as if he were hurt and frightened and pleading.

The words were beginning to make sense. "This is a dream," he was saying, "and you mustn't believe in it. You'll wake into the real world soon and laugh at yourself. He loves you, I tell you. He does, he does! But not here! Not now! This is an illusion."

Susan Calvin nodded, her voice a whisper, "Yes! Yes!" She was clutching Herbie's arm, clinging to it, repeating over and over, "It isn't true, is it? It isn't, is it?"

Just how she came to her senses, she never knew—but it was like pass-   190
ing from a world of misty unreality to one of harsh sunlight. She pushed him away from her, pushed hard against that steely arm, and her eyes were wide.

"What are you trying to do?" Her voice rose to a harsh scream, "What are you trying to do?"

Herbie backed away, "I want to help."

The psychologist stared, "Help? By telling me this is a dream? By trying to push me into schizophrenia?" A hysterical tenseness seized her, "This is no dream! I wish it were!"

She drew her breath sharply, "Wait! Why . . . why, I understand. Merciful Heavens, it's so obvious."

There was horror in the robot's voice, "I had to!"   195

"And I believed you! I never thought—"

*   *   *

Loud voices outside the door brought her to a halt. She turned away, fists clenching spasmodically, and when Bogert and Lanning entered, she was at the far window. Neither of the men paid her the slightest attention.

They approached Herbie simultaneously; Lanning angry and impatient, Bogert, coolly sardonic. The director spoke first.

"Here now, Herbie. Listen to me!"

The robot brought his eyes sharply down upon the aged director, "Yes,   200
Dr. Lanning."

"Have you discussed me with Dr. Bogert?"

"No, sir." The answer came slowly, and the smile on Bogert's face flashed off.

"What's that?" Bogert shoved in ahead of his superior and straddled the ground before the robot. "Repeat what you told me yesterday."

"I said that—" Herbie fell silent. Deep within him his metallic diaphragm vibrated in soft discords.

"Didn't you say he had resigned?" roared Bogert. "Answer me!"   205

Bogert raised his arm frantically, but Lanning pushed him aside, "Are you trying to bully him into lying?"

"You heard him, Lanning. He began to say 'Yes' and stopped. Get out of my way! I want the truth out of him, understand!"

"I'll ask him!" Lanning turned to the robot. "All right, Herbie, take it easy. Have I resigned?"

Herbie stared, and Lanning repeated anxiously, "Have I resigned?" There was the faintest trace of a negative shake of the robot's head. A long wait produced nothing further.

The two men looked at each other and the hostility in their eyes was all   210
but tangible.

"What the devil," blurted Bogert, "has the robot gone mute? Can't you speak, you monstrosity?"

"I can speak," came the ready answer.

"Then answer the question. Didn't you tell me Lanning had resigned? Hasn't he resigned?"

And again there was nothing but dull silence, until from the end of the room, Susan Calvin's laugh rang out suddenly, high-pitched and semi-hysterical.

The two mathematicians jumped, and Bogert's eyes narrowed, "You here?   215
What's so funny?"

"Nothing's funny." Her voice was not quite natural. "It's just that I'm not the only one that's been caught. There's irony in three of the greatest experts in robotics in the world falling into the same elementary trap, isn't there?" Her voice faded, and she put a pale hand to her forehead, "But it isn't funny!"

This time the look that passed between the two men was one of raised eyebrows. "What trap are you talking about?" asked Lanning stiffly. "Is something wrong with Herbie?"

"No," she approached them slowly, "nothing is wrong with him — only with us." She whirled suddenly and shrieked at the robot, "Get away from me! Go to the other end of the room and don't let me look at you."

Herbie cringed before the fury of her eyes and stumbled away in a clattering trot.

Lanning's voice was hostile, "What is all this, Dr. Calvin?"   220

She faced them and spoke sarcastically, "Surely you know the fundamental First Law of Robotics."

The other two nodded together. "Certainly," said Bogert, irritably, "a robot may not injure a human being or, through inaction, allow him to come to harm."

"How nicely put," sneered Calvin. "But what kind of harm?"

"Why — any kind."

"Exactly! Any kind! But what about hurt feelings? What about deflation of   225
one's ego? What about the blasting of one's hopes? Is that injury?"

Lanning frowned, "What would a robot know about — " And then he caught himself with a gasp.

"You've caught on, have you? *This* robot reads minds. Do you suppose it doesn't know everything about mental injury? Do you suppose that if asked a question, it wouldn't give exactly that answer that one wants to hear? Wouldn't any other answer hurt us, and wouldn't Herbie know that?"

"Good Heavens!" muttered Bogert.

The psychologist cast a sardonic glance at him. "I take it you asked him whether Lanning had resigned. You wanted to hear that he had resigned and so that's what Herbie told you."

"And I suppose that is why," said Lanning, tonelessly, "it would not answer   230
a little while ago. It couldn't answer either way without hurting one of us."

There was a short pause in which the men looked thoughtfully across the room at the robot, crouching in the chair by the bookcase, head resting in one hand.

Susan Calvin stared steadfastly at the floor, "He knew of all this. That . . . that devil knows everything — including what went wrong in his assembly." Her eyes were dark and brooding.

Lanning looked up, "You're wrong there, Dr. Calvin. He doesn't know what went wrong. I asked him."

"What does that mean?" cried Calvin. "Only that you didn't want him to give you the solution. It would puncture your ego to have a machine do what you couldn't. Did you ask him?" she shot at Bogert.

"In a way," Bogert coughed and reddened. "He told me he knew very little 235
about mathematics."

Lanning laughed, not very loudly and the psychologist smiled caustically.
She said, "I'll ask him! A solution by him won't hurt my ego." She raised her
voice into a cold, imperative, "Come here!"

Herbie rose and approached with hesitant steps.

"You know, I suppose," she continued, "just exactly at what point in the
assembly an extraneous factor was introduced or an essential one left out."

"Yes," said Herbie, in tones barely heard.

"Hold on," broke in Bogert angrily. "That's not necessarily true. You want 240
to hear that, that's all."

"Don't be a fool," replied Calvin. "He certainly knows as much math as
you and Lanning together, since he can read minds. Give him his chance."

The mathematician subsided, and Calvin continued, "All right,
then, Herbie, give! We're waiting." And in an aside, "Get pencils and paper,
gentlemen."

But Herbie remained silent, and there was triumph in the psychologist's
voice, "Why don't you answer, Herbie?"

The robot blurted out suddenly, "I cannot. You know I cannot! Dr. Bogert
and Dr. Lanning don't want me to."

"They want the solution." 245

"But not from me."

Lanning broke in, speaking slowly and distinctly, "Don't be foolish, Herbie.
We do want you to tell us."

Bogert nodded curtly.

Herbie's voice rose to wild heights, "What's the use of saying that? Don't
you suppose that I can see past the superficial skin of your mind? Down below,
you don't want me to. I'm a machine, given the imitation of life only by virtue
of the positronic interplay in my brain — which is man's device. You can't lose
face to me without being hurt. That is deep in your mind and won't be erased.
I can't give the solution."

"We'll leave," said Dr. Lanning. "Tell Calvin." 250

"That would make no difference," cried Herbie, "since you would know
anyway that it was I that was supplying the answer."

Calvin resumed, "But you understand, Herbie, that despite that, Drs. Lanning
and Bogert want that solution."

"By their own efforts!" insisted Herbie.

"But they want it, and the fact that you have it and won't give it hurts
them. You see that, don't you?"

"Yes! Yes!" 255

"And if you tell them that will hurt them, too."

"Yes! Yes!" Herbie was retreating slowly, and step by step Susan Calvin
advanced. The two men watched in frozen bewilderment.

"You can't tell them, droned the psychologist slowly, "because that would
hurt and you mustn't hurt. But if you don't tell them, you hurt, so you must

tell them. And if you do, you will hurt and you mustn't, so you can't tell them; but if you don't, you hurt, so you must; but if you do, you hurt, so you mustn't; but if you don't, you hurt, so you must; but if you do, you—"

Herbie was up against the wall, and here he dropped to his knees. "Stop!" he shrieked. "Close your mind! It is full of pain and frustration and hate! I didn't mean it, I tell you! I tried to help! I told you what you wanted to hear. I had to!"

The psychologist paid no attention. "You must tell them, but if you do, you hurt, so you mustn't; but if you don't, you hurt, so you must; but—"   260

And Herbie screamed!

It was like the whistling of a piccolo many times magnified—shrill and shriller till it keened with the terror of a lost soul and filled the room with the piercingness of itself.

And when it died into nothingness, Herbie collapsed into a huddled heap of motionless metal.

Bogert's face was bloodless, "He's dead!"

"No!" Susan Calvin burst into body-racking gusts of wild laughter, "not   265
dead—merely insane. I confronted him with the insoluble dilemma, and he broke down. You can scrap him now—because he'll never speak again."

Lanning was on his knees beside the thing that had been Herbie. His fingers touched the cold, unresponsive metal face and he shuddered. "You did that on purpose." He rose and faced her, face contorted.

"What if I did? You can't help it now." And in a sudden access of bitterness, "He deserved it."

The director seized the paralyzed, motionless Bogert by the wrist, "What's the difference. Come, Peter." He sighed, "A thinking robot of this type is worthless anyway." His eyes were old and tired, and he repeated, "Come, Peter!"

It was minutes after the two scientists left that Dr. Susan Calvin regained part of her mental equilibrium. Slowly, her eyes turned to the living-dead Herbie and the tightness returned to her face. Long she stared while the triumph faded and the helpless frustration returned—and of all her turbulent thoughts only one infinitely bitter word passed her lips.

"*Liar!*"   270

≡ THINKING ABOUT THE TEXT

1. Asimov is credited with developing the Three Laws of Robotics. In what specific ways does he investigate the possible implications/ramifications of these laws in our story?

2. Science fiction writers like to speculate about telepathic powers. Explain why you think Asimov did or did not do an effective job of exploring its problems. What positive effects might such powers have? Is it a "power" humans would use well? Explain.

3. What basic ideas about human nature is Asimov using to ground his story?

4. Although Susan Calvin's character seems a bit dated (the story itself was written in 1941), in what ways is she ahead of her time? In the 2004 film, a beautiful young actress plays Calvin's character. Does this suggest that physical attractiveness is still an important measure of women's worth? Calvin, after all, claims she is not young or attractive. Why change that element of the story?

5. How might this story be more about human nature than robot consciousness? Explain. Can you think of some way to fix Herbie before his break down? What would have to happen before Herbie could join the human family, i.e., be treated like you and me?

OREN ETZIONI
How to Regulate Artificial Intelligence

Oren Etzioni (1964) was born and grew up in New York City. He was the first student to major in computer science at Harvard and later received a Ph.D. from Carnegie Mellon University. He is a professor of Computer Science at the University of Washington and the director of the University's Turing Center. He is the author of numerous popular and academic essays, including the following piece from the New York Times *on September 2017.*

The technology entrepreneur Elon Musk recently urged the nation's governors to regulate artificial intelligence "before it's too late." Mr. Musk insists that artificial intelligence represents an "existential threat to humanity," an alarmist view that confuses A.I. science with science fiction. Nevertheless, even A.I. researchers like me recognize that there are valid concerns about its impact on weapons, jobs, and privacy. It's natural to ask whether we should develop A.I. at all.

I believe the answer is yes. But shouldn't we take steps to at least slow down progress on A.I., in the interest of caution? The problem is that if we do so, then nations like China will overtake us. The A.I. horse has left the barn, and our best bet is to attempt to steer it. A.I. should not be weaponized, and any A.I. must have an impregnable "off switch." Beyond that, we should regulate the tangible impact of A.I. systems (for example, the safety of autonomous vehicles) rather than trying to define and rein in the amorphous and rapidly developing field of A.I.

I propose three rules for artificial intelligence systems that are inspired by, yet develop further, the "three laws of robotics" that the writer Isaac Asimov introduced in 1942: A robot may not injure a human being or, through inaction, allow a human being to come to harm; a robot must obey the orders given it by human beings, except when such orders would conflict with the previous law; and a robot must protect its own existence as long as such protection does not conflict with the previous two laws.

These three laws are elegant but ambiguous: What, exactly, constitutes harm when it comes to A.I.? I suggest a more concrete basis for avoiding A.I. harm, based on three rules of my own.

First, an A.I. system must be subject to the full gamut of laws that apply to   5
its human operator. This rule would cover private, corporate, and government systems. We don't want A.I. to engage in cyberbullying, stock manipulation, or terrorist threats; we don't want the F.B.I. to release A.I. systems that entrap people into committing crimes. We don't want autonomous vehicles that drive through red lights, or worse, A.I. weapons that violate international treaties.

Our common law should be amended so that we can't claim that our A.I. system did something that we couldn't understand or anticipate. Simply put, "My A.I. did it" should not excuse illegal behavior.

My second rule is that an A.I. system must clearly disclose that it is not human. As we have seen in the case of bots—computer programs that can engage in increasingly sophisticated dialogue with real people—society needs assurances that A.I. systems are clearly labeled as such. In 2016, a bot known as Jill Watson, which served as a teaching assistant for an online course at Georgia Tech, fooled students into thinking it was human. A more serious example is the widespread use of pro-Trump political bots on social media in the days leading up to the 2016 elections, according to researchers at Oxford.

My rule would ensure that people know when a bot is impersonating someone. We have already seen, for example, @DeepDrumpf—a bot that humorously impersonated Donald Trump on Twitter. A.I. systems don't just produce fake tweets; they also produce fake news videos. Researchers at the University of Washington recently released a fake video of former President Barack Obama in which he convincingly appeared to be speaking words that had been grafted onto video of him talking about something entirely different.

My third rule is that an A.I. system cannot retain or disclose confidential information without explicit approval from the source of that information. Because of their exceptional ability to automatically elicit, record, and analyze information, A.I. systems are in a prime position to acquire confidential information. Think of all the conversations that Amazon Echo—a "smart speaker" present in an increasing number of homes—is privy to, or the information that your child may inadvertently divulge to a toy such as an A.I. Barbie. Even seemingly innocuous housecleaning robots create maps of your home. That is information you want to make sure you control.

My three A.I. rules are, I believe, sound but far from complete. I intro-   10
duce them here as a starting point for discussion. Whether or not you agree with Mr. Musk's view about A.I.'s rate of progress and its ultimate impact on humanity (I don't), it is clear that A.I. is coming. Society needs to get ready.

≣ THINKING ABOUT THE TEXT

1. Why do you agree or disagree with Etzioni's additions to Asimov's laws?
2. How might Etzioni's suggestions resolve Herbie's problems?
3. What other suggestions would you make for a safe AI future?

FEI-FEI LI

How to Make AI that's Good for People

Fei-Fei Li (1976) was born in Beijing, China. She attended Princeton University and received a Ph.D. in 2005 from the California Institute of Technology. She is an Associate Professor of Computer Science at Stanford University and the director of their Artificial Intelligence Lab. She is the author of more than a hundred articles on computer vision and cognitive neuroscience.

For a field that was not well known outside of academia a decade ago, artificial intelligence has grown dizzyingly fast. Tech companies from Silicon Valley to Beijing are betting everything on it, venture capitalists are pouring billions into research and development, and start-ups are being created on what seems like a daily basis. If our era is the next Industrial Revolution, as many claim, A.I. is surely one of its driving forces.

It is an especially exciting time for a researcher like me. When I was a graduate student in computer science in the early 2000s, computers were barely able to detect sharp edges in photographs, let alone recognize something as loosely defined as a human face. But thanks to the growth of big data, advances in algorithms like neural networks and an abundance of powerful computer hardware, something momentous has occurred: A.I. has gone from an academic niche to the leading differentiator in a wide range of industries, including manufacturing, health care, transportation, and retail.

I worry, however, that enthusiasm for A.I. is preventing us from reckoning with its looming effects on society. Despite its name, there is nothing "artificial" about this technology — it is made by humans, intended to behave like humans, and affects humans. So if we want it to play a positive role in tomorrow's world, it must be guided by human concerns.

I call this approach "human-centered A.I." It consists of three goals that can help responsibly guide the development of intelligent machines.

First, A.I. needs to reflect more of the depth that characterizes our own intelligence. Consider the richness of human visual perception. It's complex and deeply contextual, and naturally balances our awareness of the obvious with a sensitivity to nuance. By comparison, machine perception remains strikingly narrow.   5

Sometimes this difference is trivial. For instance, in my lab, an image-captioning algorithm once fairly summarized a photo as "a man riding a horse" but failed to note the fact that both were bronze sculptures. Other times, the difference is more profound, as when the same algorithm described an image of zebras grazing on a savanna beneath a rainbow. While the summary was technically correct, it was entirely devoid of aesthetic awareness, failing to detect any of the vibrancy or depth a human would naturally appreciate.

That may seem like a subjective or inconsequential critique, but it points to a major aspect of human perception beyond the grasp of our algorithms. How can we expect machines to anticipate our needs — much less contribute to our wellbeing — without insight into these "fuzzier" dimensions of our experience?

Making A.I. more sensitive to the full scope of human thought is no simple task. The solutions are likely to require insights derived from fields beyond computer science, which means programmers will have to learn to collaborate more often with experts in other domains.

Such collaboration would represent a return to the roots of our field, not a departure from it. Younger A.I. enthusiasts may be surprised to learn that the principles of today's deep-learning algorithms stretch back more than 60 years to the neuroscientific researchers David Hubel and Torsten Wiesel, who discovered how the hierarchy of neurons in a cat's visual cortex responds to stimuli.

Likewise, ImageNet, a data set of millions of training photographs that   10
helped to advance computer vision, is based on a project called WordNet, created in 1995 by the cognitive scientist and linguist George Miller. WordNet was intended to organize the semantic concepts of English.

Reconnecting A.I. with fields like cognitive science, psychology, and even sociology will give us a far richer foundation on which to base the development of machine intelligence. And we can expect the resulting technology to collaborate and communicate more naturally, which will help us approach the second goal of human-centered A.I.: enhancing us, not replacing us.

Imagine the role that A.I. might play during surgery. The goal need not be to automate the process entirely. Instead, a combination of smart software and specialized hardware could help surgeons focus on their strengths — traits like dexterity and adaptability — while keeping tabs on more mundane tasks and protecting against human error, fatigue, and distraction.

Or consider senior care. Robots may never be the ideal custodians of the elderly, but intelligent sensors are already showing promise in helping human caretakers focus more on their relationships with those they provide care for by automatically monitoring drug dosages and going through safety checklists.

These are examples of a trend toward automating those elements of jobs that are repetitive, error-prone, and even dangerous. What's left are the creative, intellectual, and emotional roles for which humans are still best suited.

No amount of ingenuity, however, will fully eliminate the threat of job dis-   15
placement. Addressing this concern is the third goal of human-centered A.I.: ensuring that the development of this technology is guided, at each step, by concern for its effect on humans.

Today's anxieties over labor are just the start. Additional pitfalls include bias against underrepresented communities in machine learning, the tension between A.I.'s appetite for data and the privacy rights of individuals and the geopolitical implications of a global intelligence race.

Adequately facing these challenges will require commitments from many of our largest institutions. Universities are uniquely positioned to foster connections between computer science and traditionally unrelated departments like the social sciences and even humanities, through interdisciplinary projects, courses and seminars. Governments can make a greater effort to encourage computer science education, especially among young girls, racial minorities, and other groups whose perspectives have been underrepresented in A.I. And corporations should combine their aggressive investment in intelligent algorithms with ethical A.I. policies that temper ambition with responsibility.

No technology is more reflective of its creators than A.I. It has been said that there are no "machine" values at all, in fact; machine values *are* human values. A human-centered approach to A.I. means these machines don't have to be our competitors, but partners in securing our well-being. However autonomous our technology becomes, its impact on the world — for better or worse — will always be our responsibility.

☰ THINKING ABOUT THE TEXT

1. The author of this piece is obviously optimistic about AI's future. But in "Liar!," an error/accident has produced Herbie's unwanted powers. How does Li take this possibility into consideration?

2. If "machine values are human values," what precautions, if any, can be taken against the "mad scientist" often found in science fiction?

3. What has been your experience with AI? Does it jibe with the author's vision?

MAUREEN DOWD
Silicon Valley Sharknado

Maureen Dowd (1952) is a columnist for the New York Times. *She was born in Washington, D.C., and graduated from Catholic University of America with a B.A. in English. She has worked for* Time *magazine and the* Washington Star. *She won the 1999 Pulitzer Prize for distinguished commentary as well as other prestigious awards for journalism. She is the author of many articles and three books, including* The Year of Voting Dangerously: The Derangement of American Politics *(2016).*

Mostly, this July, I'm worrying about the jumping sharks jumping the shark.

But Syfy's "Sharknado 2" trailer, this one about a shark storm hitting Manhattan, just went up and features chain saws buzzing, the Statue of Liberty's severed head whizzing, Tara Reid kvetching, and Robert Klein barking "This is the Big Apple! Something bites us; we bite back!"

So things look pretty promising.

That leaves me free to worry about rampaging robots.

And I'm not the only one.   5

In a recent interview with CNBC, Elon Musk, the C.E.O. of Tesla Motors and Space X, which hopes to rocket us to other planets, said he invests in artificial intelligence companies not to make money but to "keep an eye" on them in case of "scary outcomes," like a "Terminator" scenario of psychopathic robots that could chase us off the Earth and up to Mars.

(Interpolation: How has Elon Musk not invented his own fragrance?)

In "Terminator," Musk said, the humans who created the replicants did not expect the machines to turn evil. "It is sort of like that Monty Python thing: 'Nobody expects the Spanish Inquisition,'" the 43-year-old inventor and mogul said, warning: "But you've got to be careful."

Silicon Valley brains have been predicting that robots will usher in a radically superior world.

Ray Kurzweil, Google's 66-year-old director of engineering, is running   10
a Manhattan project to push A.I. to match human intelligence by 2029 and achieve his vision of "the singularity" — the moment when computers overtake human brains — by 2045. The robots will even be able to flirt, he says, and, unlike Siri and Scarlett Johansson in "Her," they can easily have a curvy virtual form and be "lovable."

Computers will be able to read every word on the web and every book ever written and offer up matching patterns.

I.B.M.'s Watson has read 200 million Wikipedia pages, Kurzweil told *The Observer* of London, but "it doesn't understand that if John sold his red Volvo to Mary that involves a transaction or possession and ownership being transferred." So Kurzweil and Google will try to encode that information to "really try to teach it to understand the meaning of what these documents are saying."

Since I come from a family of Irish maids, I'm not looking forward to servitude under my iPhone.

And Kurzweil should be more worried that he'll suffer the fate of genetic designer J.F. Sebastian in "Blade Runner," who is killed by his replicants after telling them, "There's a part of me in you."

Vinod Khosla, the Sun Microsystems co-founder, has predicted that algo-   15
rithms and machines will replace 80 percent of doctors in years to come, making medicine more data driven and less like "witchcraft."

In a rare joint interview last week with Khosla at his Silicon Valley summit, Google founders Sergey Brin and Larry Page talked about their A.I. hopes.

"You should presume that someday," Brin said, "we will be able to make machines that can reason, think and do things better than we can."

They have always been interested in robots — they named their operating system Android — and are running "the brain project," described by Brin as "really machine-learning focused." In January, they acquired the British A.I. developer DeepMind, founded by Demis Hassabis, a game designer, neuroscientist, and former child chess prodigy.

They know people could be thrown out of work. As Page said, "90 percent of people used to be farmers," so "it's not surprising."

Page predicted a "time of abundance," when human needs could be more   20
easily met and people would "have more time with their family or to pursue
their own interests."

Of course, when we get more free time, we'll simply spend it staring at our
iPads, so all roads lead back to Big Brother.

Jaron Lanier, the computer genius and author of "Who Owns the
Future?," dryly notes that our looming overlords may not be robots but the
Google founders.

"The only person with a secure job will be Larry Page," he laughingly
told me. "He owns the damn Cloud computer."

He said that, despite a fantasy that dates from the mid-20th century,
nobody has yet figured out how to make a robot that can think for itself.

"In a way, it's not being honest," he said. "We're still pretending that we're   25
inventing a brain when all we've come up with is a giant mash-up of real
brains. We don't yet understand how brains work, so we can't build one."

When machines translate from one language to another, they are leech-
ing from live translators, taking matching phrases from aggregated data. If
tech companies could gather similar data on doctors, that information could
theoretically be matched up to make a simulated doctor.

"People are unwittingly feeding information into the Cloud for automated
services, which they're not being paid for," Lanier said. "I don't like pretending that humans are becoming buggy whips. You have this fantasy that it's
machines doing it without people helping. We are throwing people out of
work based on a fantasy."

In a digital update of "Invasion of the Body Snatchers," Silicon Valley is
siphoning and pilfering human intelligence to feed Mr. Roboto to replace us.
That's the scary bravado of real sharks.

≡ THINKING ABOUT THE TEXT

1. How effective is Dowd's use of humor and sarcasm in furthering her
   argument?

2. Do you agree with Sergey Brin and Larry Page's hope that machines
   will be able to "reason, think, and do things better than we can"? Is
   this a dangerous idea or not?

3. What exactly is Dowd's fear? Where does she relay this worry?

A. M. TURING

From "*Computing Machinery and Intelligence*"

*A. M. Turing (1912–1954) was a pioneering computer scientist, mathematician,
and logician. He is widely thought to be the father of theoretical computer science
and artificial intelligence. He was born in London. During the Second World War, he*

played a pivotal part in cracking the Enigma machine that generated German codes. Since 1966, the Turing Award has been given to a scientist who contributes significantly to the computing community. It is equivalent to the Noble Prize. The film The Imitation Game *(2012) focuses on Turing's part in breaking the Enigma code. The following selections are from the journal* Mind 49, *published in 1950.*

1. The Imitation Game

I propose to consider the question, "Can machines think?" This should begin with definitions of the meaning of the terms "machine" and "think." The definitions might be framed so as to reflect so far as possible the normal use of the words, but this attitude is dangerous. If the meaning of the words "machine" and "think" are to be found by examining how they are commonly used it is difficult to escape the conclusion that the meaning and the answer to the question, "Can machines think?" is to be sought in a statistical survey such as a Gallup poll. But this is absurd. Instead of attempting such a definition I shall replace the question by another, which is closely related to it and is expressed in relatively unambiguous words.

The new form of the problem can be described in terms of a game which we call the "imitation game." It is played with three people, a man (A), a woman (B), and an interrogator (C) who may be of either sex. The interrogator stays in a room apart front the other two. The object of the game for the interrogator is to determine which of the other two is the man and which is the woman. He knows them by labels X and Y, and at the end of the game he says either "X is A and Y is B" or "X is B and Y is A." The interrogator is allowed to put questions to A and B thus:

C: Will X please tell me the length of his or her hair?

Now suppose X is actually A, then A must answer. It is A's object in the game to try and cause C to make the wrong identification. His answer might therefore be:

"My hair is shingled, and the longest strands are about nine inches long."

In order that tones of voice may not help the interrogator the answers should be written, or better still, typewritten. The ideal arrangement is to have a teleprinter communicating between the two rooms. Alternatively the question and answers can be repeated by an intermediary. The object of the game for the third player (B) is to help the interrogator. The best strategy for her is probably to give truthful answers. She can add such things as "I am the woman, don't listen to him!" to her answers, but it will avail nothing as the man can make similar remarks.

We now ask the question, "What will happen when a machine takes the part of A in this game?" Will the interrogator decide wrongly as often when the game is played like this as he does when the game is played between a man and a woman? These questions replace our original, "Can machines think?"

5

2. Critique of the New Problem

As well as asking, "What is the answer to this new form of the question," one may ask, "Is this new question a worthy one to investigate?" This latter question we investigate without further ado, thereby cutting short an infinite regress.

The new problem has the advantage of drawing a fairly sharp line between the physical and the intellectual capacities of a man. No engineer or chemist claims to be able to produce a material which is indistinguishable from the human skin. It is possible that at some time this might be done, but even supposing this invention available we should feel there was little point in trying to make a "thinking machine" more human by dressing it up in such artificial flesh. The form in which we have set the problem reflects this fact in the condition which prevents the interrogator from seeing or touching the other competitors, or hearing their voices. Some other advantages of the proposed criterion may be shown up by specimen questions and answers. Thus:

> Q: Please write me a sonnet on the subject of the Forth Bridge.
> A: Count me out on this one. I never could write poetry.
> Q: Add 34957 to 70764.
> A: (Pause about 30 seconds and then give as answer) 105621.
> Q: Do you play chess?
> A: Yes.
> Q: I have K at my K1, and no other pieces. You have only K at K6 and R at R1. It is your move. What do you play?
> A: (After a pause of 15 seconds) R-R8 mate.

The question and answer method seems to be suitable for introducing almost any one of the fields of human endeavor that we wish to include. We do not wish to penalize the machine for its inability to shine in beauty competitions, nor to penalize a man for losing in a race against an aeroplane. The conditions of our game make these disabilities irrelevant. The "witnesses" can brag, if they consider it advisable, as much as they please about their charms, strength or heroism, but the interrogator cannot demand practical demonstrations.

The game may perhaps be criticized on the ground that the odds are weighted too heavily against the machine. If the man were to try and pretend to be the machine he would clearly make a very poor showing. He would be given away at once by slowness and inaccuracy in arithmetic. May not machines carry out something which ought to be described as thinking but which is very different from what a man does? This objection is a very strong one, but at least we can say that if, nevertheless, a machine can be constructed to play the imitation game satisfactorily, we need not be troubled by this objection.

It might be urged that when playing the "imitation game" the best strategy for the machine may possibly be something other than imitation of the behavior of a man. This may be, but I think it is unlikely that there is any great effect of this kind. In any case there is no intention to investigate here the theory of the game, and it will be assumed that the best strategy is to try to provide answers that would naturally be given by a man. . . .

10

6. Contrary Views on the Main Question

We may now consider the ground to have been cleared and we are ready to proceed to the debate on our question, "Can machines think?" and the variant of it quoted at the end of the last section. We cannot altogether abandon the original form of the problem, for opinions will differ as to the appropriateness of the substitution and we must at least listen to what has to be said in this connection.

It will simplify matters for the reader if I explain first my own beliefs in the matter. Consider first the more accurate form of the question. I believe that in about fifty years' time it will be possible, to program computers, with a storage capacity of about 109, to make them play the imitation game so well that an average interrogator will not have more than 70 percent chance of making the right identification after five minutes of questioning. The original question, "Can machines think?" I believe to be too meaningless to deserve discussion. Nevertheless I believe that at the end of the century the use of words and general educated opinion will have altered so much that one will be able to speak of machines thinking without expecting to be contradicted. I believe further that no useful purpose is served by concealing these beliefs. The popular view that scientists proceed inexorably from well-established fact to well-established fact, never being influenced by any improved conjecture, is quite mistaken. Provided it is made clear which are proved facts and which are conjectures, no harm can result. Conjectures are of great importance since they suggest useful lines of research.

I now proceed to consider opinions opposed to my own. . . .

(4) The Argument from Consciousness

This argument is very well expressed in Professor Jefferson's Lister Oration for 1949, from which I quote. "Not until a machine can write a sonnet or compose a concerto because of thoughts and emotions felt, and not by the chance fall of symbols, could we agree that machine equals brain — that is, not only write it but know that it had written it. No mechanism could feel (and not merely artificially signal, an easy contrivance) pleasure at its successes, grief when its valves fuse, be warmed by flattery, be made miserable by its mistakes, be charmed by sex, be angry or depressed when it cannot get what it wants."

This argument appears to be a denial of the validity of our test. According to the most extreme form of this view the only way by which one could be sure that a machine thinks is to be the machine and to feel oneself thinking. One could then describe these feelings to the world, but of course no one would be justified in taking any notice. Likewise according to this view the only way to know that a man thinks is to be that particular man. It is in fact the solipsist point of view. It may be the most logical view to hold but it makes communication of ideas difficult. A is liable to believe "A thinks but B does not" while B believes "B thinks but A does not." Instead of arguing continually over this point it is usual to have the polite convention that everyone thinks. I am sure that Professor Jefferson does not wish

15

to adopt the extreme and solipsist point of view. Probably he would be quite willing to accept the imitation game as a test. The game (with the player B omitted) is frequently used in practice under the name of viva voce to discover whether some one really understands something or has "learned it parrot fashion." Let us listen in to a part of such a *viva voce*:

> Interrogator: In the first line of your sonnet which reads "Shall I compare thee to a summer's day," would not "a spring day" do as well or better?
> Witness: It wouldn't scan.
> Interrogator: How about "a winter's day," That would scan all right.
> Witness: Yes, but nobody wants to be compared to a winter's day.
> Interrogator: Would you say Mr. Pickwick reminded you of Christmas?
> Witness: In a way.
> Interrogator: Yet Christmas is a winter's day, and I do not think Mr. Pickwick would mind the comparison.
> Witness: I don't think you're serious. By a winter's day one means a typical winter's day, rather than a special one like Christmas.

And so on, What would Professor Jefferson say if the sonnet-writing machine was able to answer like this in the *viva voce?* I do not know whether he would regard the machine as "merely artificially signalling" these answers, but if the answers were as satisfactory and sustained as in the above passage I do not think he would describe it as "an easy contrivance." This phrase is, I think, intended to cover such devices as the inclusion in the machine of a record of someone reading a sonnet, with appropriate switching to turn it on from time to time.

In short then, I think that most of those who support the argument from consciousness could be persuaded to abandon it rather than be forced into the solipsist position. They will then probably be willing to accept our test.

I do not wish to give the impression that I think there is no mystery about consciousness. There is, for instance, something of a paradox connected with any attempt to localize it. But I do not think these mysteries necessarily need to be solved before we can answer the question with which we are concerned in this paper.

[1950]

≡ THINKING ABOUT THE TEXT

1. Describe how Turing thinks the imitation game can answer his inquiry about machines. What objections can you anticipate?

2. According to Turing's theory, would Herbie pass the imitation game test? What comment by Professor Jefferson is contradicted by Herbie's behavior?

3. Can A.I. at this moment in our history do any of the things Jefferson mentions, i.e., not only write a sonnet but feel "pleasure at its successes . . . be made miserable by its mistakes"? If not, will this ever happen? Explain.

☰ WRITING ABOUT THE ISSUES

1. Argue that Etzioni's suggestions go too far or not far enough.
2. Argue that Dowd's worry is or is not well founded.
3. Argue that Asimov's characterization of Susan Calvin is or is not outdated and sexist.

☰ RESEARCHING THE ISSUES

1. Even in 1950, there was a lively debate about the effectiveness of the Turing test. Over the years, scientists and philosophers have been arguing about the best way to test consciousness in robots /androids/A.I. John Searle's Chinese Room, for example, is one counter to Turing. After researching the issue, write an essay that argues that consciousness in robots is possible (or not) and that testing for it is (or isn't) possible.

2. Dozens of science fiction films have as their premise that A.I. will develop consciousness. *Blade Runner* 2049 (2017) is a good recent example. But the idea has been around for decades, for example, *2001: A Space Odyssey* (1968). Do some research on this topic and argue that Asimov or Turing would have approved of this development.

3. The technological singularity is a concept used in the computer and artificial intelligence community that signals the historical moment when A.I. will be capable of redesigning itself, eventually building computers or robots better than itself. Such a possibility could cause superintelligent machines to be far beyond our capacities or control. There has been a lively debate for years over this idea. Some think it is inevitable; some do not think it possible. After researching the issue, join the debate by arguing that the singularity is going to happen (or not) and that it will be a catastrophe or a blessing.

CHAPTER 10

Love

Our culture makes many claims about love: stories of the rejected lover who dies of a broken heart abound. Modern kings give up the throne, ancient cities go to war—all for love. Love is thought to be such a powerful emotion that its loss may even make one want to die or to kill. (In some countries, finding one's wife or husband in bed with a lover is a legal excuse for murder.) Men and women seem willing to radically change their lives to be near their beloved. The following are a few examples of love's powerful influence on our behavior and our understanding of who we are.

Yet a serious discussion about the nature of love is often frustratingly difficult. We can all make a list of things we love: a new car, a great science-fiction film, a cold beer in summer, a quiet dinner with a good friend, a walk in the fresh snow, a football game when our favorite team comes from behind for a dramatic victory. We love our parents, our siblings, our best friends. How can one word cover such diversity?

When we try to generalize about love, we find ourselves relying on specific incidents because giving examples is easier than giving definitions. If clarifying the essence of love seems difficult, perhaps it is because our stories, myths, and songs are filled with contradictions. Love conquers all, we say, but doesn't love fade? We profess our undying love, but divorce statistics soar. Love is complex and frustrating to pin down. Our culture even identifies different types of love: true love, platonic love, maternal love, erotic love. Yet opinions about love are strong; we all have evidence for what it is and isn't that we find persuasive.

But the evidence we find so convincing is influenced by cultural assumptions, probably more than we know. It would be naive to claim otherwise when we are bombarded with so many movies, songs, and stories about love. Indeed, some critics argue that romantic love is only a socially constructed illusion, merely an elaborate rationalization for physical desire. Once the carnal attraction fades, we get restless. At least, this is one argument, and probably not a popular one among college students in search of love. Because we know what we feel about those we love, we often grow impatient with other people's perspectives. We are likely to ignore friends who say, "He wouldn't treat you like that if he really loved you." Perhaps nothing arouses our interest more than a discussion of our hopes and dreams about love.

Our engagement with stories and poems about love is equally complex and ambivalent. Although the stories in this chapter often illuminate the sometimes dark passageways we take in our romantic journeys, there is no consensus about the final destination. Arguing about love stories engages us as much as it may also baffle us. As you read, rely on your own experience, ethical positions, and literary judgment in determining whether specific characters are indeed in love, whether they should continue their relationship, whether they need more commitment or less. The wise and the foolish seem equally perplexed in matters of the heart.

The chapter opens with three stories with young protagonists by James Joyce, John Updike, and Leslie Marmon Silko, followed by two stories by twentieth-century masters, William Faulkner and Raymond Carver. Then follow two clusters of poems, each cluster dealing with a different iconic style of love. The fifth cluster about impossible loves pairs Karen Russell's wildly fantastical tale "Bog Girl" with an even stranger fantasy, "The Devourings." Then our first Literature and Current Issues cluster focuses on a contemporary story, "Cat Person," and three arguments on the contentious issue of consent in intimate relationships. Our next Literature and Current Issues cluster uses Thomas Lux's disturbing poem to focus not on love but on its almost complete absence. Three essays follow that attempt explanations for such an unsettling situation. The penultimate cluster presents Shakespeare's great tragedy *Othello* with essays that explore the reasons for the title character's fateful decisions. We conclude with a cluster featuring Matthew Arnold's brooding love poem, "Dover Beach," along with cultural documents that provide a context for his melancholy and despair.

JAMES JOYCE, "Araby"

JOHN UPDIKE, "A & P"

LESLIE MARMON SILKO, "Yellow Woman"

Although centuries old, the cliché that the human heart is a mystery still seems valid. We still wonder if falling in love is natural: is love our inborn impulse to seek romance, or is it simply a physical attraction spurred on by our evolutionary need to procreate? Perhaps Western culture has socialized us to believe in the power of romantic love and the often irrational behavior that follows. Might it serve some deep psychological need to find a substitute for a beloved parent? Is it a giving emotion? A selfish one? Is it a psychological malady or the one thing worth giving up everything for? Do we need to believe in it whether or not it exists? Since we are often driven to irrational behavior, delusions, and heartbreak, might we be better off without romantic love? Or might life without it be intolerably flat?

In the following cluster, three fiction writers explore the ways romantic love can sometimes cloud judgment, encouraging us to act against our best interests.

Joyce shows us a boy in the throes of romantic idealism; Updike gives us a memorable picture of how an indifferent world responds to romantic gestures; and Silko shows us a woman torn between myth and reality.

≡ BEFORE YOU READ

Can people be truly happy without being in love? Is there one person who is your true love? Are there only certain types of people you could love? If your love didn't make you "float on a cloud," would you be disappointed? Is true love unconditional? Have you ever been fooled by romantic dreams?

JAMES JOYCE
Araby

James Joyce (1882–1941) is regarded as one of the most innovative and influential writers of the modernist movement of the early twentieth century. His use of interior monologue, wordplay, complex allusions, and other techniques variously delighted, offended, or puzzled readers. Joyce's work demanded attention and was often subject to censorship during his lifetime. A Portrait of the Artist as a Young Man *(1916), set in Joyce's native Dublin, is largely autobiographical. Like his hero at the end of the novel, Joyce left Ireland at the age of twenty to spend the remainder of his life in Paris and other European cities. His long, complex novel* Ulysses *(1922), also set in*

Dublin, takes the reader through one day in the life of its protagonist and his city. In "Araby," published in Dubliners *(1914), as in other stories in the collection, Joyce pictures the limited life of his character and leads him toward a sudden insight, or epiphany.*

North Richmond Street, being blind, was a quiet street except at the hour when the Christian Brothers' School set the boys free. An uninhabited house of two storeys stood at the blind end, detached from its neighbors in a square ground. The other houses of the street, conscious of decent lives within them, gazed at one another with brown imperturbable faces.

The former tenant of our house, a priest, had died in the back drawing-room. Air, musty from having been long enclosed, hung in all the rooms, and the waste room behind the kitchen was littered with old useless papers. Among these I found a few paper-covered books, the pages of which were curled and damp: *The Abbot,* by Walter Scott, *The Devout Communicant,* and *The Memoirs of Vidocq.* I liked the last best because its leaves were yellow. The wild garden behind the house contained a central apple-tree and a few straggling bushes under one of which I found the late tenant's rusty bicycle-pump. He had been a very charitable priest; in his will he had left all his money to institutions and the furniture of his house to his sister.

When the short days of winter came dusk fell before we had well eaten our dinners. When we met in the street the houses had grown sombre. The space of sky above us was the color of ever-changing violet and towards it the lamps of the street lifted their feeble lanterns. The cold air stung us and we played till our bodies glowed. Our shouts echoed in the silent street. The career of our play brought us through the dark muddy lanes behind the houses where we ran the gauntlet of the rough tribes from the cottages, to the back doors of the dark dripping gardens where odors arose from the ashpits, to the dark odorous stables where a coachman smoothed and combed the horse or shook music from the buckled harness. When we returned to the street light from the kitchen windows had filled the areas. If my uncle was seen turning the corner we hid in the shadow until we had seen him safely housed. Or if Mangan's sister came out on the doorstep to call her brother in to his tea we watched her from our shadow peer up and down the street. We waited to see whether she would remain or go in and, if she remained, we left our shadow and walked up to Mangan's steps resignedly. She was waiting for us, her figure defined by the light from the half-opened door. Her brother always teased her before he obeyed and I stood by the railings looking at her. Her dress swung as she moved her body and the soft rope of her hair tossed from side to side.

Every morning I lay on the floor in the front parlor watching her door. The blind was pulled down to within an inch of the sash so that I could not be seen. When she came out on the doorstep my heart leaped. I ran to the hall, seized my books, and followed her. I kept her brown figure always in my eye and, when we came near the point at which our ways diverged, I quickened my pace and passed her. This happened morning after morning. I had never spoken to her, except for a few casual words, and yet her name was like a summons to all my foolish blood.

Her image accompanied me even in places the most hostile to romance. 5
On Saturday evenings when my aunt went marketing I had to go to carry some of the parcels. We walked through the flaring streets, jostled by drunken men and bargaining women, amid the curses of laborers, the shrill litanies of shop-boys who stood on guard by the barrel of pigs' cheeks, the nasal chanting of street-singers, who sang a *come-all-you* about O'Donovan Rossa,° or a ballad about the troubles in our native land. These noises converged in a single sensation of life for me: I imagined that I bore my chalice safely through a throng of foes. Her name sprang to my lips at moments in strange prayers and praises which I myself did not understand. My eyes were often full of tears (I could not tell why) and at times a flood from my heart seemed to pour itself out into my bosom. I thought little of the future. I did not know whether I would ever speak to her or not or, if I spoke to her, how I could tell her of my confused adoration. But my body was like a harp and her words and gestures were like fingers running upon the wires.

One evening I went into the back drawing-room in which the priest had died. It was a dark rainy evening and there was no sound in the house. Through one of the broken panes I heard the rain impinge upon the earth, the fine incessant needles of water playing in the sodden beds. Some distant lamp or lighted window gleamed below me. I was thankful that I could see so little. All my senses seemed to desire to veil themselves and, feeling that I was about to slip from them, I pressed the palms of my hands together until they trembled, murmuring: "*O love! O love!*" many times.

At last she spoke to me. When she addressed the first words to me I was so confused that I did not know what to answer. She asked me was I going to *Araby*. I forgot whether I answered yes or no. It would be a splendid bazaar, she said she would love to go.

"And why can't you?" I asked.

While she spoke she turned a silver bracelet round and round her wrist. She could not go, she said, because there would be a retreat that week in her convent. Her brother and two other boys were fighting for their caps and I was alone at the railings. She held one of the spikes, bowing her head towards me. The light from the lamp opposite our door caught the white curve of her neck, lit up her hair that rested there and, falling, lit up the hand upon the railing. It fell over one side of her dress and caught the white border of a petticoat, just visible as she stood at ease.

"It's well for you," she said. 10

"If I go," I said, "I will bring you something."

What innumerable follies laid waste my waking and sleeping thoughts after that evening! I wished to annihilate the tedious intervening days. I chafed against the work of school. At night in my bedroom and by day in

O'Donovan Rossa: Jeremiah O'Donovan (1831–1915) was nicknamed "Dynamite Rossa" for advocating violent means to achieve Irish independence.

the classroom her image came between me and the page I strove to read. The syllables of the word *Araby* were called to me through the silence in which my soul luxuriated and cast an Eastern enchantment over me. I asked for leave to go to the bazaar on Saturday night. My aunt was surprised and hoped it was not some Freemason° affair. I answered few questions in class. I watched my master's face pass from amiability to sternness; he hoped I was not beginning to idle. I could not call my wandering thoughts together. I had hardly any patience with the serious work of life which, now that it stood between me and my desire, seemed to me child's play, ugly monotonous child's play.

On Saturday morning I reminded my uncle that I wished to go to the bazaar in the evening. He was fussing at the hallstand, looking for the hat-brush, and answered me curtly:

"Yes, boy, I know."

As he was in the hall I could not go into the front parlor and lie at the window. I left the house in bad humor and walked slowly towards the school. The air was pitilessly raw and already my heart misgave me.   15

When I came home to dinner my uncle had not yet been home. Still it was early. I sat staring at the clock for some time and, when its ticking began to irritate me, I left the room. I mounted the staircase and gained the upper part of the house. The high cold empty gloomy rooms liberated me and I went from room to room singing. From the front window I saw my companions playing below in the street. Their cries reached me weakened and indistinct and, leaning my forehead against the cool glass, I looked over at the dark house where she lived. I may have stood there for an hour, seeing nothing but the brown-clad figure cast by my imagination, touched discreetly by the lamplight at the curved neck, at the hand upon the railings, and at the border below the dress.

When I came downstairs again I found Mrs. Mercer sitting at the fire. She was an old garrulous woman, a pawnbroker's widow, who collected used stamps for some pious purpose. I had to endure the gossip of the tea-table. The meal was prolonged beyond an hour and still my uncle did not come. Mrs. Mercer stood up to go: she was sorry she couldn't wait any longer, but it was after eight o'clock and she did not like to be out late, as the night air was bad for her. When she had gone I began to walk up and down the room, clenching my fists. My aunt said:

"I'm afraid you may put off your bazaar for this night of Our Lord."

At nine o'clock I heard my uncle's latchkey in the halldoor. I heard him talking to himself and heard the hallstand rocking when it had received the weight of his overcoat. I could interpret these signs. When he was midway through his dinner I asked him to give me the money to go to the bazaar. He had forgotten.

"The people are in bed and after their first sleep now," he said.   20

I did not smile. My aunt said to him energetically:

"Can't you give him the money and let him go? You've kept him late enough as it is."

Freemason: A Protestant fraternal society that was in the past viewed by Catholics as hostile.

My uncle said he was very sorry he had forgotten. He said he believed in the old saying: "All work and no play makes Jack a dull boy." He asked me where I was going and, when I had told him a second time he asked me did I know *The Arab's Farewell to His Steed*. When I left the kitchen he was about to recite the opening lines of the piece to my aunt.

I held a florin° tightly in my hand as I strode down Buckingham Street towards the station. The sight of the streets thronged with buyers and glaring with gas recalled to me the purpose of my journey. I took my seat in a third-class carriage of a deserted train. After an intolerable delay the train moved out of the station slowly. It crept onward among ruinous houses and over the twinkling river. At Westland Row Station a crowd of people pressed to the carriage doors; but the porters moved them back, saying that it was a special train for the bazaar. I remained alone in the bare carriage. In a few minutes the train drew up beside an improvised wooden platform. I passed out on to the road and saw by the lighted dial of a clock that it was ten minutes to ten. In front of me was a large building which displayed the magical name.

I could not find any sixpenny entrance and, fearing that the bazaar   25
would be closed, I passed in quickly through a turnstile, handing a shilling to a weary-looking man. I found myself in a big hall girdled at half its height by a gallery. Nearly all the stalls were closed and the greater part of the hall was in darkness. I recognized a silence like that which pervades a church after a service. I walked into the center of the bazaar timidly. A few people were gathered about the stalls which were still open. Before a curtain, over which the words *Café Chantant* were written in colored lamps, two men were counting money on a salver. I listened to the fall of the coins.

Remembering with difficulty why I had come I went over to one of the stalls and examined porcelain vases and flowered tea-sets. At the door of the stall a young lady was talking and laughing with two young gentlemen. I remarked their English accents and listened vaguely to their conversation.

"O, I never said such a thing!"

"O, but you did!"

"O, but I didn't!"

"Didn't she say that?"   30

"Yes. I heard her."

"O, there's a . . . fib!"

Observing me the young lady came over and asked me did I wish to buy anything. The tone of her voice was not encouraging; she seemed to have spoken to me out of a sense of duty. I looked humbly at the great jars that stood like eastern guards at either side of the dark entrance to the stall and murmured:

"No, thank you."

The young lady changed the position of one of the vases and went back to   35
the two young men. They began to talk of the same subject. Once or twice the young lady glanced at me over her shoulder.

florin: A silver coin worth two shillings.

I lingered before her stall, though I knew my stay was useless, to make my interest in her wares seem the more real. Then I turned away slowly and walked down the middle of the bazaar. I allowed the two pennies to fall against the sixpence in my pocket. I heard a voice call from one end of the gallery that the light was out. The upper part of the hall was now completely dark.

Gazing up into the darkness I saw myself as a creature driven and derided by vanity; and my eyes burned with anguish and anger.   *[1914]*

≡ THINKING ABOUT THE TEXT

1. Why do the boy's eyes burn with anguish and anger? Has he learned something about romantic love? Is he in love with Mangan's sister? Give evidence.

2. If this story is partly autobiographical, what is Joyce's attitude toward his younger self? Are you sympathetic or critical of your own initiations into the complexities of relationships?

3. Reread the first and last paragraphs. In what ways might they be connected?

4. Find examples of religious imagery. What do you think is its purpose?

5. Do you think the boy's quest has symbolic meaning? Do you think cultures can also search for something?

JOHN UPDIKE
A & P

John Updike (1932–2009) was born in Shillington, Pennsylvania, an only child of a father who taught high school algebra and a mother who wrote short stories and novels. After graduating from Harvard, Updike studied art in England and later joined the staff of The New Yorker. *In 1959, he published his first novel,* The Poorhouse Fair, *and moved to Massachusetts. His many novels are notable for their lyrical and accurate depiction of the details and concerns of modern America.* Rabbit Run *(1960) and the sequels* Rabbit Redux *(1971),* Rabbit Is Rich *(1981), and* Rabbit at Rest *(1990) are considered important and insightful records of American life. His other works include the novels* Villages *(2004) and* Terrorist *(2006);* Due Considerations: Essays and Criticism *(2007);* The Maples Stories *(2009); and* Hub Fans Bid Kid Adieu: John Updike on Ted Williams *(2010). "A & P" comes from Updike's* Pigeon Feathers and Other Stories *(1962).*

In walks these three girls in nothing but bathing suits. I'm in the third checkout slot, with my back to the door, so I don't see them until they're over by the bread. The one that caught my eye first was the one in the plaid green two-piece. She was a chunky kid, with a good tan and a sweet broad soft-looking can with those two crescents of white just under it, where the sun never seems to hit, at the top of the backs of her legs. I stood there with my hand on a box of HiHo crackers trying to remember if I rang it up or not. I ring it up again and the customer starts giving me hell. She's one of these cash-register-watchers, a witch about fifty with rouge on her cheekbones and no eyebrows, and I know it made her day to trip me up. She'd been watching cash registers for fifty years and probably never seen a mistake before.

By the time I got her feathers smoothed and her goodies into a bag—she gives me a little snort in passing, if she'd been born at the right time they would have burned her over in Salem—by the time I get her on her way the girls had circled around the bread and were coming back, without a pushcart, back my way along the counters, in the aisle between the checkouts and the Special bins. They didn't even have shoes on. There was this chunky one, with the two-piece—it was bright green and the seams on the bra were still sharp and her belly was still pretty pale so I guessed she just got it (the suit)—there was this one, with one of those chubby berry-faces, the lips all bunched together under her nose, this one, and a tall one, with black hair that hadn't quite frizzed right, and one of these sunburns right across under the eyes, and a chin that was too long—you know, the kind of girl other girls think is very "striking" and "attractive" but never quite makes it, as they very well know, which is why they like her so much—and then the third one, that wasn't quite so tall. She was the queen. She kind of led them, the other two peeking around and making their shoulders round. She didn't look around, not this queen, she just walked straight on slowly, on these long white prima-donna legs. She came down a lit-tle hard on her heels, as if she didn't walk in her bare feet that much, putting down her heels and then letting the weight move along to her toes as if she was testing the floor with every step, putting a little deliberate extra action into it. You never know for sure how girls' minds work (do you really think it's a mind in there or just a little buzz like a bee in a glass jar?) but you got the idea she had talked the other two into coming in here with her, and now she was showing them how to do it, walk slow and hold yourself straight.

She had on a kind of dirty-pink—beige maybe, I don't know—bathing suit with a little nubble all over it, and what got me, the straps were down. They were off her shoulders looped loose around the cool tops of her arms, and I guess as a result the suit had slipped a little on her, so all around the top of the cloth there was this shining rim. If it hadn't been there you wouldn't have known there could have been anything whiter than those shoulders. With the straps pushed off, there was nothing between the top of the suit and the top of her head except just *her*, this clean bare plane of the top of her chest down from the shoulder bones like a dented sheet of metal tilted in the light. I mean, it was more than pretty.

She had sort of oaky hair that the sun and salt had bleached, done up in a bun that was unravelling, and a kind of prim face. Walking into the A & P with your straps down, I suppose it's the only kind of face you *can* have. She held her head so high her neck, coming up out of those white shoulders, looked kind of stretched, but I didn't mind. The longer her neck was, the more of her there was.

She must have felt in the corner of her eye me and over my shoulder   5
Stokesie in the second slot watching, but she didn't tip. Not this queen. She
kept her eyes moving across the racks, and stopped, and turned so slow it made
my stomach rub the inside of my apron, and buzzed to the other two, who kind
of huddled against her for relief, and then they all three of them went up the
cat-and-dog-food-breakfast-cereal-macaroni-rice-raisins-seasonings-spreads-
spaghetti-soft-drinks-crackers-and-cookies aisle. From the third slot I look
straight up this aisle to the meat counter, and I watched them all the way. The
fat one with the tan sort of fumbled with the cookies, but on second thought
she put the package back. The sheep pushing their carts down the aisle — the
girls were walking against the usual traffic (not that we have one-way signs
or anything) — were pretty hilarious. You could see them, when Queenie's
white shoulders dawned on them, kind of jerk, or hop, or hiccup, but their eyes
snapped back to their own baskets and on they pushed. I bet you could set off
dynamite in an A & P and the people would by and large keep reaching and
checking oatmeal off their lists and muttering "Let me see, there was a third
thing, began with A, asparagus, no, ah, yes, applesauce!" or whatever it is they
do mutter. But there was no doubt, this jiggled them. A few houseslaves in pin
curlers even looked around after pushing their carts past to make sure what
they had seen was correct.

You know, it's one thing to have a girl in a bathing suit down on the beach,
where what with the glare nobody can look at each other much anyway, and
another thing in the cool of the A & P, under the fluorescent lights, against all
those stacked packages, with her feet paddling along naked over our check-
board green-and-cream rubber-tile floor.

"Oh Daddy," Stokesie said beside me. "I feel so faint."

"Darling," I said. "Hold me tight." Stokesie's married, with two babies
chalked up on his fuselage already, but as far as I can tell that's the only difference. He's twenty-two, and I was nineteen this April.

"Is it done?" he asks, the responsible married man finding his voice. I forgot
to say he thinks he's going to be manager some sunny day, maybe in 1990 when
it's called the Great Alexandrov and Petrooshki Tea Company or something.

What he meant was, our town is five miles from a beach, with a big sum-   10
mer colony out on the Point, but we're right in the middle of town, and the
women generally put on a shirt or shorts or something before they get out of
the car into the street. And anyway these are usually women with six children
and varicose veins mapping their legs and nobody, including them, could care
less. As I say, we're right in the middle of town, and if you stand at our front
doors you can see two banks and the Congregational church and the newspaper store and three real-estate offices and about twenty-seven old freeloaders
tearing up Central Street because the sewer broke again. It's not as if we're on
the Cape; we're north of Boston and there's people in this town haven't seen
the ocean for twenty years.

The girls had reached the meat counter and were asking McMahon something. He pointed, they pointed, and they shuffled out of sight behind a pyra-
mid of Diet Delight peaches. All that was left for us to see was old McMahon

patting his mouth and looking after them sizing up their joints. Poor kids, I began to feel sorry for them, they couldn't help it.

Now here comes the sad part of the story, at least my family says it's sad, but I don't think it's so sad myself. The store's pretty empty, it being Thursday afternoon, so there was nothing much to do except lean on the register and wait for the girls to show up again. The whole store was like a pinball machine and I didn't know which tunnel they'd come out of. After a while they come around out of the far aisle, around the light bulbs, records at discount of the Caribbean Six or Tony Martin Sings or some such gunk you wonder they waste the wax on, sixpacks of candy bars, and plastic toys done up in cellophane that fall apart when a kid looks at them anyway. Around they come, Queenie still leading the way, and holding a little gray jar in her hand. Slots Three through Seven are unmanned and I could see her wondering between Stokes and me, but Stokesie with his usual luck draws an old party in baggy gray pants who stumbles up with four giant cans of pineapple juice (what do these bums *do* with all that pineapple juice? I've often asked myself) so the girls come to me. Queenie puts down the jar and I take it into my fingers icy cold. Kingfish Fancy Herring Snacks in Pure Sour Cream: 49¢. Now her hands are empty, not a ring or a bracelet, bare as God made them, and I wonder where the money's coming from. Still with that prim look she lifts a folded dollar bill out of the hollow at the center of her nubbled pink top. The jar went heavy in my hand. Really, I thought that was so cute.

Then everybody's luck begins to run out. Lengel comes in from haggling with a truck full of cabbages on the lot and is about to scuttle into that door marked manager behind which he hides all day when the girls touch his eye. Lengel's pretty dreary, teaches Sunday school and the rest, but he doesn't miss that much. He comes over and says, "Girls, this isn't the beach."

Queenie blushes, though maybe it's just a brush of sunburn I was noticing for the first time, now that she was so close. "My mother asked me to pick up a jar of herring snacks." Her voice kind of startled me, the way voices do when you see the people first, coming out so flat and dumb yet kind of tony, too, the way it ticked over "pick up" and "snacks." All of a sudden I slid right down her voice into her living room. Her father and the other men were standing around in ice-cream coats and bow ties and the women were in sandals picking up herring snacks on toothpicks off a big glass plate and they were all holding drinks the color of water with olives and sprigs of mint in them. When my parents have somebody over they get lemonade and if it's a real racy affair Schlitz in tall glasses with "They'll Do It Every Time" cartoons stencilled on.

"That's all right," Lengel said. "But this isn't the beach." His repeating this struck me as funny, as if it had just occurred to him, and he had been thinking all these years the A & P was a great big sand dune and he was the head lifeguard. He didn't like my smiling — as I say he doesn't miss much — but he concentrates on giving the girls that sad Sunday-school–superintendent stare. 15

Queenie's blush is no sunburn now, and the plump one in plaid, that I liked better from the back — a really sweet can — pipes up, "We weren't doing any shopping. We just came in for the one thing."

"That makes no difference," Lengel tells her, and I could see from the way his eyes went that he hadn't noticed she was wearing a two-piece before. "We want you decently dressed when you come in here."

"We *are* decent," Queenie says suddenly, her lower lip pushing, getting sore now that she remembers her place, a place from which the crowd that runs the A & P must look pretty crummy. Fancy Herring Snacks flashed in her very blue eyes.

"Girls, I don't want to argue with you. After this come in here with your shoulders covered. It's our policy." He turns his back. That's policy for you. Policy is what the kingpins want. What the others want is juvenile delinquency.

All this while, the customers had been showing up with their carts but, you know, sheep, seeing a scene, they had all bunched up on Stokesie, who shook open a paper bag as gently as peeling a peach, not wanting to miss a word. I could feel in the silence everybody getting nervous, most of all Lengel, who asks me, "Sammy, have you rung up their purchase?"   20

I thought and said "No" but it wasn't about that I was thinking. I go through the punches, 4, 9, groc, tot — it's more complicated than you think, and after you do it often enough, it begins to make a little song, that you hear words to, in my case "Hello (*bing*) there, you (*gung*) hap-py *pee*-pul (*splat*)!" — the *splat* being the drawer flying out. I uncrease the bill, tenderly as you may imagine, it just having come from between the two smoothest scoops of vanilla I had ever known were there, and pass a half and a penny into her narrow pink palm, and nestle the herrings in a bag and twist its neck and hand it over, all the time thinking.

The girls, and who'd blame them, are in a hurry to get out, so I say "I quit" to Lengel enough for them to hear, hoping they'll stop and watch me, their unsuspected hero. They keep right on going, into the electric eye; the door flies open and they flicker across the lot to their car, Queenie and Plaid and Big Tall Goony-Goony (not that as raw material she was so bad), leaving me with Lengel and a kink in his eyebrow.

"Did you say something, Sammy?"

"I said I quit."

"I thought you did."   25

"You didn't have to embarrass them."

"It was they who were embarrassing us."

I started to say something that came out "Fiddle-de-doo." It's a saying of my grandmother's, and I know she would have been pleased.

"I don't think you know what you're saying," Lengel said.

"I know you don't," I said. "But I do." I pull the bow at the back of my   30
apron and start shrugging it off my shoulders. A couple customers that had been heading for my slot begin to knock against each other, like scared pigs in a chute.

Lengel sighs and begins to look very patient and old and gray. He's been a friend of my parents for years. "Sammy, you don't want to do this to your Mom and Dad," he tells me. It's true, I don't. But it seems to me that once you begin a gesture it's fatal not to go through with it. I fold the apron, "Sammy" stitched in red on the pocket, and put it on the counter, and drop the bow tie on top of it. The bow tie is theirs, if you've ever wondered. "You'll feel this for the rest of your life," Lengel says, and I know that's true, too, but remembering how he made that pretty girl blush makes me so scrunchy inside I punch the No Sale tab and the machine whirs "pee-pul" and the drawer splats out. One advantage to this scene taking place in summer, I can follow this up with a clean exit, there's no fumbling around getting your coat and galoshes, I just saunter into the electric eye in my white shirt that my mother ironed the night before, and the door heaves itself open, and outside the sunshine is skating around on the asphalt.

I look around for my girls, but they're gone, of course. There wasn't anybody but some young married screaming with her children about some candy they didn't get by the door of a powder-blue Falcon station wagon. Looking back in the big windows, over the bags of peat moss and aluminum lawn furniture stacked on the pavement, I could see Lengel in my place in the slot, checking the sheep through. His face was dark gray and his back stiff, as if he'd just had an injection of iron, and my stomach kind of fell as I felt how hard the world was going to be to me hereafter.   [1961]

≣ THINKING ABOUT THE TEXT

1. Why do you think Sammy quits? Make a list of several plausible answers.

2. What would you do if you were in Sammy's position? What would your priorities be?

3. When Sammy hears Queenie's voice, he imagines an elegant cocktail party that he contrasts to his parents' "real racy affair" (para. 14) with lemonade and beer. What does this scene say about Sammy's attitude toward the girls? Toward his own social status?

4. Some critics have objected to Sammy's comment in the last sentence of paragraph 2 about "girls' minds." Is this a sexist observation? Does the time frame of the story figure in your opinion? Should it?

5. Comment on the last paragraph. What is the significance of the young married woman? Why does Sammy mention "sheep"? Why does Sammy think the world will be hard on him? Do you agree? What does "hard" mean?

≣ MAKING COMPARISONS

1. Are the main characters in "Araby" and "A & P" wiser at each story's end? Are they happier?

2. Which character's views about romance are more compatible with your views when you were, say, thirteen? With your views today?

3. Compare the last paragraphs of "Araby" and "A & P." What attitudes toward romantic love do they express?

LESLIE MARMON SILKO
Yellow Woman

Leslie Marmon Silko (b. 1948) is a major figure in the American Indian Renais-
sance. Raised in "Old Laguna" on the Pueblo Reservation near Albuquerque, New
Mexico, Silko weaves the mythology of her matrilineal society into stories that move
freely through what she calls an "ocean of time." The "Yellow Woman" character
appears frequently in Silko's writing, both as a traditional figure, closely connected
with nature and heterosexuality, and as a female character awakening to her cultural
and sexual identity. Silko writes both poetry and fiction, often synthesizing the two
genres into a single text. Her novels include Storyteller *(1981), in which "Yellow*
Woman" appears; Ceremony *(1977); and* Almanac of the Dead *(1991). Her*
latest book is The Turquoise Ledge *(2010). She formerly taught at the University*
of Arizona at Tucson.

1

My thigh clung to his with dampness, and I watched the sun rising up through
the tamaracks and willows. The small brown water birds came to the river
and hopped across the mud, leaving brown scratches in the alkali-white crust.
They bathed in the river silently. I could hear the water, almost at our feet
where the narrow fast channel bubbled and washed green ragged moss and
fern leaves. I looked at him beside me, rolled in the red blanket on the white
river sand. I cleaned the sand out of the cracks between my toes, squinting
because the sun was above the willow trees. I looked at him for the last time,
sleeping on the white river sand.

I felt hungry and followed the river south the way we had come the afternoon before, following our footprints that were already blurred by the lizard
tracks and bug trails. The horses were still lying down, and the black one whinnied when he saw me but he did not get up—maybe it was because the corral
was made out of thick cedar branches and the horses had not yet felt the sun
like I had. I tried to look beyond the pale red mesas to the pueblo. I knew it was
there, even if I could not see it, on the sand rock hill above the river, the same
river that moved past me now and had reflected the moon last night.

The horse felt warm underneath me. He shook his head and pawed the
sand. The bay whinnied and leaned against the gate trying to follow, and I
remembered him asleep in the red blanket beside the river. I slid off the horse
and tied him close to the other horse. I walked north with the river again, and
the white sand broke loose in footprints over footprints.

"Wake up."

He moved in the blanket and turned his face to me with his eyes still   5
closed. I knelt down to touch him.

"I'm leaving."

He smiled now, eyes still closed. "You are coming with me, remember?" He
sat up now with his bare dark chest and belly in the sun.

"Where?"

"To my place."

" And will I come back?"   10

He pulled his pants on. I walked away from him, feeling him behind me and smelling the willows.

"Yellow Woman," he said.

I turned to face him. "Who are you?" I asked.

He laughed and knelt on the low, sandy bank, washing his face in the river. "Last night you guessed my name, and you knew why I had come."

I stared past him at the shallow moving water and tried to remember the   15
night, but I could only see the moon in the water and remember his warmth around me.

"But I only said that you were him and that I was Yellow Woman — I'm not really her — I have my own name and I come from the pueblo on the other side of the mesa. Your name is Silva and you are a stranger I met by the river yesterday afternoon."

He laughed softly. "What happened yesterday has nothing to do with what you will do today, Yellow Woman."

"I know — that's what I'm saying — the old stories about the ka'tsina spirit° and Yellow Woman can't mean us."

My old grandpa liked to tell those stories best. There is one about Badger and Coyote who went hunting and were gone all day, and when the sun was going down they found a house. There was a girl living there alone, and she had light hair and eyes and she told them that they could sleep with her. Coyote wanted to be with her all night so he sent Badger into a prairie-dog hole, telling him he thought he saw something in it. As soon as Badger crawled in, Coyote blocked up the entrance with rocks and hurried back to Yellow Woman.

"Come here," he said gently.   20

He touched my neck and I moved close to him to feel his breathing and to hear his heart. I was wondering if Yellow Woman had known who she was — if she knew that she would become part of the stories. Maybe she'd had another name that her husband and relatives called her so that only the ka'tsina from the north and the storytellers would know her as Yellow Woman. But I didn't go on; I felt him all around me, pushing me down into the white river sand.

Yellow Woman went away with the spirit from the north and lived with him and his relatives. She was gone for a long time, but then one day she came back and she brought twin boys.

"Do you know the story?"

"What story?" He smiled and pulled me close to him as he said this. I was afraid lying there on the red blanket. All I could know was the way he felt, warm, damp, his body beside me. This is the way it happens in the stories, I was thinking, with no thought beyond the moment she meets the ka'tsina spirit and they go.

ka'tsina spirit: A mountain spirit of the Laguna Pueblo Indians.

"I don't have to go. What they tell in stories was real only then, back in   25
time immemorial, like they say."

He stood up and pointed at my clothes tangled in the blanket. "Let's go,"
he said.

I walked beside him, breathing hard because he walked fast, his hand
around my wrist. I had stopped trying to pull away from him, because his
hand felt cool and the sun was high, drying the river bed into alkali. I will
see someone, eventually I will see someone, and then I will be certain that
he is only a man—some man from nearby—and I will be sure that I am not
Yellow Woman. Because she is from out of time past and I live now and I've
been to school and there are highways and pickup trucks that Yellow Woman
never saw.

It was an easy ride north on horseback. I watched the change from
the cottonwood trees along the river to the junipers that brushed past us in
the foothills, and finally there were only piñons, and when I looked up at the
rim of the mountain plateau I could see pine trees growing on the edge. Once
I stopped to look down, but the pale sandstone had disappeared and the river
was gone and the dark lava hills were all around. He touched my hand, not
speaking, but always singing softly a mountain song and looking into my eyes.

I felt hungry and wondered what they were doing at home now—my
mother, my grandmother, my husband, and the baby. Cooking breakfast,
saying, "Where did she go?—maybe kidnapped," and Al going to the tribal
police with the details: "She went walking along the river."

The house was made with black lava rock and red mud. It was high above   30
the spreading miles of arroyos and long mesas. I smelled a mountain smell of
pitch and buck brush. I stood there beside the black horse, looking down on
the small, dim country we had passed, and I shivered.

"Yellow Woman, come inside where it's warm."

2

He lit a fire in the stove. It was an old stove with a round belly and an enamel
coffeepot on top. There was only the stove, some faded Navajo blankets, and a
bedroll and cardboard box. The floor was made of smooth adobe plaster, and
there was one small window facing east. He pointed at the box.

"There's some potatoes and the frying pan." He sat on the floor with his
arms around his knees pulling them close to his chest and he watched me fry
the potatoes. I didn't mind him watching me because he was always watching me—he had been watching me since I came upon him sitting on the river
bank trimming leaves from a willow twig with his knife. We ate from the pan
and he wiped the grease from his fingers on his Levis.

"Have you brought women here before?" He smiled and kept chewing, so I
said, "Do you always use the same tricks?"

"What tricks?" He looked at me like he didn't understand.   35

"The story about being a ka'tsina from the mountains. The story about
Yellow Woman."

Silva was silent; his face was calm.

"I don't believe it. Those stories couldn't happen now," I said.

He shook his head and said softly, "But someday they will talk about us, and they will say, 'Those two lived long ago when things like that happened.'"

He stood up and went out. I ate the rest of the potatoes and thought about things — about the noise the stove was making and the sound of the mountain wind outside. I remembered yesterday and the day before, and then I went outside.

I walked past the corral to the edge where the narrow trail cut through the black rim rock. I was standing in the sky with nothing around me but the wind that came down from the blue mountain peak behind me. I could see faint mountain images in the distance miles across the vast spread of mesas and valleys and plains. I wondered who was over there to feel the mountain wind on those sheer blue edges — who walks on the pine needles in those blue mountains.

"Can you see the pueblo?" Silva was standing behind me.

I shook my head. "We're too far away."

"From here I can see the world." He stepped out on the edge. "The Navajo reservation begins over there." He pointed to the east. "The Pueblo boundaries are over here." He looked below us to the south, where the narrow trail seemed to come from. "The Texans have their ranches over there, starting with that valley, the Concho Valley. The Mexicans run some cattle over there too."

"Do you ever work for them?"

"I steal from them," Silva answered. The sun was dropping behind us and shadows were filling the land below. I turned away from the edge that dropped forever into the valleys below.

"I'm cold," I said; "I'm going inside." I started wondering about this man who could speak the Pueblo language so well but who lived on a mountain and rustled cattle. I decided that this man Silva must be Navajo, because Pueblo men didn't do things like that.

"You must be a Navajo."

Silva shook his head gently. "Little Yellow Woman," he said, "you never give up, do you? I have told you who I am. The Navajo people know me, too." He knelt down and unrolled the bedroll and spread the extra blankets out on a piece of canvas. The sun was down, and the only light in the house came from outside — the dim orange light from sundown.

I stood there and waited for him to crawl under the blankets.

"What are you waiting for?" he said, and I lay down beside him. He undressed me slowly like the night before beside the river — kissing my face gently and running his hands up and down my belly and legs. He took off my pants and then he laughed.

"Why are you laughing?"

"You are breathing so hard."

I pulled away from him and turned my back to him.

He pulled me around and pinned me down with his arms and chest. "You don't understand, do you, little Yellow Woman? You will do what I want."

And again he was all around me with his skin slippery against mine, and I was afraid because I understood that his strength could hurt me. I lay underneath him and I knew that he could destroy me. But later, while he slept beside me, I touched his face and I had a feeling — the kind of feeling for him that overcame me that morning along the river. I kissed him on the forehead and he reached out for me.

When I woke up in the morning he was gone. It gave me a strange feeling because for a long time I sat there on the blankets and looked around the little house for some object of his — some proof that he had been there or maybe that he was coming back. Only the blankets and the cardboard box remained. The .30–30° that had been leaning in the corner was gone, and so was the knife I had used the night before. He was gone, and I had my chance to go now. But first I had to eat, because I knew it would be a long walk home.

I found some dried apricots in the cardboard box, and I sat down on a rock at the edge of the plateau rim. There was no wind and the sun warmed me. I was surrounded by silence. I drowsed with apricots in my mouth, and I didn't believe that there were highways or railroads or cattle to steal.

When I woke up, I stared down at my feet in the black mountain dirt. Little black ants were swarming over the pine needles around my foot. They must have smelled the apricots. I thought about my family far below me. They would be wondering about me, because this had never happened to me before. The tribal police would file a report. But if old Grandpa weren't dead he would tell them what happened — he would laugh and say, "Stolen by a ka'tsina, a mountain spirit. She'll come home — they usually do." There are enough of them to handle things. My mother and grandmother will raise the baby like they raised me. Al will find someone else, and they will go on like before, except that there will be a story about the day I disappeared while I was walking along the river. Silva had come for me; he said he had. I did not decide to go. I just went. Moonflowers blossom in the sand hills before dawn, just as I followed him. That's what I was thinking as I wandered along the trail through the pine trees.

It was noon when I got back. When I saw the stone house I remembered   60 that I had meant to go home. But that didn't seem important any more, maybe because there were little blue flowers growing in the meadow behind the stone house and the gray squirrels were playing in the pines next to the house. The horses were standing in the corral, and there was a beef carcass hanging on the shady side of a big pine in front of the house. Flies buzzed around the clotted blood that hung from the carcass. Silva was washing his hands in a bucket full of water. He must have heard me coming because he spoke to me without turning to face me.

"I've been waiting for you."

"I went walking in the big pine trees."

I looked into the bucket full of bloody water with brown-and-white animal hairs floating in it. Silva stood there letting his hand drip, examining me intently.

.30–30: A rifle.

"Are you coming with me?"

"Where?" I asked him.

"To sell the meat in Marquez."

"If you're sure it's O.K."

"I wouldn't ask you if it wasn't," he answered.

He sloshed the water around in the bucket before he dumped it out and set the bucket upside down near the door. I followed him to the corral and watched him saddle the horses. Even beside the horses he looked tall, and I asked him again if he wasn't Navajo. He didn't say anything; he just shook his head and kept cinching up the saddle.

"But Navajos are tall."

"Get on the horse," he said, "and let's go."

The last thing he did before we started down the steep trail was to grab the .30–30 from the corner. He slid the rifle into the scabbard that hung from his saddle.

"Do they ever try to catch you?" I asked.

"They don't know who I am."

"Then why did you bring the rifle?"

"Because we are going to Marquez where the Mexicans live."

3

The trail leveled out on a narrow ridge that was steep on both sides like an animal spine. On one side I could see where the trail went around the rocky gray hills and disappeared into the southeast where the pale sandrock mesas stood in the distance near my home. On the other side was a trail that went west, and as I looked far into the distance I thought I saw the little town. But Silva said no, that I was looking in the wrong place, that I just thought I saw houses. After that I quit looking off into the distance; it was hot and the wildflowers were closing up their deep-yellow petals. Only the waxy cactus flowers bloomed in the bright sun, and I saw every color that a cactus blossom can be; the white ones and the red ones were still buds, but the purple and the yellow were blossoms, open full and the most beautiful of all.

Silva saw him before I did. The white man was riding a big gray horse, coming up the trail toward us. He was traveling fast and the gray horse's feet sent rocks rolling off the trail into the dry tumbleweeds. Silva motioned for me to stop and we watched the white man. He didn't see us right away, but finally his horse whinnied at our horses and he stopped. He looked at us briefly before he loped the gray horse across the three hundred yards that separated us. He stopped his horse in front of Silva, and his young fat face was shadowed by the brim of his hat. He didn't look mad, but his small, pale eyes moved from the blood-soaked gunny sacks hanging from my saddle to Silva's face and then back to my face.

"Where did you get the fresh meat?" the white man asked.

"I've been hunting," Silva said, and when he shifted his weight in the   80
saddle the leather creaked.

"The hell you have, Indian. You've been rustling cattle. We've been looking for the thief for a long time."

The rancher was fat, and sweat began to soak through his white cowboy
shirt and the wet cloth stuck to the thick rolls of belly fat. He almost seemed to
be panting from the exertion of talking, and he smelled rancid, maybe because
Silva scared him.

Silva turned to me and smiled. "Go back up the mountain, Yellow
Woman."

The white man got angry when he heard Silva speak in a language he
couldn't understand. "Don't try anything, Indian. Just keep riding to Marquez.
We'll call the state police from there."

The rancher must have been unarmed because he was very frightened   85
and if he had a gun he would have pulled it out then. I turned my horse
around and the rancher yelled, "Stop!" I looked at Silva for an instant and
there was something ancient and dark — something I could feel in my stomach — in his eyes, and when I glanced at his hand I saw his finger on the
trigger of the .30–30 that was still in the saddle scabbard. I slapped my
horse across the flank and the sacks of raw meat swung against my knees
as the horse leaped up the trail. It was hard to keep my balance, and once
I thought I felt the saddle slipping backward; it was because of this that I
could not look back.

I didn't stop until I reached the ridge where the trail forked. The horse was
breathing deep gasps and there was a dark film of sweat on its neck. I looked
down in the direction I had come from, but I couldn't see the place. I waited.
The wind came up and pushed warm air past me. I looked up at the sky, pale
blue and full of thin clouds and fading vapor trails left by jets.

I think four shots were fired — I remember hearing four hollow explosions that reminded me of deer hunting. There could have been more shots
after that, but I couldn't have heard them because my horse was running
again and the loose rocks were making too much noise as they scattered
around his feet.

Horses have a hard time running downhill, but I went that way instead
of uphill to the mountain because I thought it was safer. I felt better with
the horse running southeast past the round gray hills that were covered
with cedar trees and black lava rock. When I got to the plain in the distance
I could see the dark green patches of tamaracks that grew along the river;
and beyond the river I could see the beginning of the pale sandrock mesas.
I stopped the horse and looked back to see if anyone was coming; then I
got off the horse and turned the horse around, wondering if it would go
back to its corral under the pines on the mountain. It looked back at me
for a moment and then plucked a mouthful of green tumbleweeds before
it trotted back up the trail with its ears pointed forward, carrying its head

daintily to one side to avoid stepping on the dragging reins. When the horse disappeared over the last hill, the gunny sacks full of meat were still swinging and bouncing.

4

I walked toward the river on a wood-hauler's road that I knew would eventually lead to the paved road. I was thinking about waiting beside the road for someone to drive by, but by the time I got to the pavement I had decided it wasn't very far to walk if I followed the river back the way Silva and I had come.

The river water tasted good, and I sat in the shade under a cluster of silvery   90
willows. I thought about Silva, and I felt sad at leaving him; still, there was something strange about him, and I tried to figure it out all the way back home.

I came back to the place on the river bank where he had been sitting the first time I saw him. The green willow leaves that he had trimmed from the branch were still lying there, wilted in the sand. I saw the leaves and I wanted to go back to him — to kiss him and to touch him — but the mountains were too far away now. And I told myself, because I believe it, he will come back sometime and be waiting again by the river.

I followed the path up from the river into the village. The sun was getting low, and I could smell supper cooking when I got to the screen door of my house. I could hear their voices inside — my mother was telling my grandmother how to fix the Jell-O and my husband, Al, was playing with the baby. I decided to tell them that some Navajo had kidnapped me, but I was sorry that old Grandpa wasn't alive to hear my story because it was the Yellow Woman stories he liked to tell best.

[1974]

≡ THINKING ABOUT THE TEXT

1. Why does Yellow Woman run away with Silva? Does it have something to do with the coyote stories? What stories in your own culture have persuaded you to trust in romantic love?

2. How do myths and stories differ? Are they based on reality or on fantasy? What are the social or cultural purposes of stories about love?

3. Do you trust the narrator's judgment? Sincerity? On what textual evidence do you base this evaluation? What bearing does her cultural heritage have on your analysis of her?

4. What specific details of Silko's story do you remember? Is the narrator a careful observer? Explain. What effect does the narrator's "noticing little things" have on you as a reader?

5. Has Yellow Woman learned her lesson? Do societies change their views of romantic love? How?

≡ MAKING COMPARISONS

1. Compare the growth of the boy in "Araby" or Sammy in "A & P" with that of the wife in "Yellow Woman."

2. Make explicit the insight or epiphany the boy or Sammy comes to at the end. What would be a comparable epiphany for the wife in "Yellow Woman"?

3. Is one ending more realistic than the others? Explain.

≡ WRITING ABOUT ISSUES

1. Choose either the boy in "Araby," Sammy, or Yellow Woman and argue that this character was or was not really in love. Support your argument with references to the text and your own cultural experience.

2. Write an essay that defends or denies the idea that romantic love is irrational. Use two of the stories from this cluster.

3. Would any of the characters in this cluster have been comfortable in the cultural context you were raised in? (Consider movies, books, TV, family narratives, and so forth in analyzing your culture.) Write a brief analysis of how well one or more of these characters would fit in.

4. Look up information about Native American culture and the coyote stories referred to in "Yellow Woman." Do they help to explain her attitudes? Do the same for the culture of Joyce's Ireland, especially religion and romance. How about America in the middle of the twentieth century? In a brief essay, argue that each story is understood more fully when the cultural context is provided.

WILLIAM FAULKNER, "A Rose for Emily"

RAYMOND CARVER, "What We Talk About When We Talk About Love"

Although stories about those who die for love are not unknown, those about killing for love are much rarer. Can "killing for love" still be considered love, or is it something quite different, something dark and perverse? Can the world be so stressful, so unjust and cruel that someone batters their beloved in frustration? What if that person is looking to someone else to relieve the disappointments of the world? Is that love or just physical need? What if someone harbors violent fantasies about a person loved years before? Or what if a wife sexually betrays her loving husband so she can get for him the material possessions he desires? And can love be so worn down by cruelty that it turns to hate? These are not simple questions. Trying to understand our emotional contradictions and paradoxes never is. The following two writers grapple with these issues in creative and sometimes painful ways: Faulkner's story focuses on the interaction of tradition, madness, and love; Carver's looks at the complexity of discussing love. See whether you can decide if the characters in these stories are motivated by love or something more dangerous.

≡ BEFORE YOU READ

Have you ever hurt somebody you love? Did you mean to? Has a loved one ever hurt you? Is it possible for an emotionally disturbed person to love?

WILLIAM FAULKNER
A Rose for Emily

William Faulkner (1897–1962) is recognized as a great American novelist and storyteller and a major figure of world literature, having won the Nobel Prize in 1949. This acclaim failed to impress the people of his hometown, however, where his genteel poverty and peculiar ways earned him the title "Count No Count." Born in New Albany, Mississippi, and raised in Oxford, the home of the University of Mississippi, Faulkner briefly attended college there after World War I but was reduced to working odd jobs while continuing his writing. His fiction is most often set in Yoknapatawpha County, a created world whose history, geography, and complex genealogies parallel those of the American South. His many novels and stories blend the grotesquely comic with the appallingly tragic. The Sound and the Fury (1929) is often considered his finest work. In later years, Faulkner's "odd jobs" included scriptwriting for Hollywood movies, speaking at universities, and writing magazine articles. "A Rose for Emily," first published in Forum, *presents a story of love as told by citizens of Yoknapatawpha County.*

1

When Miss Emily Grierson died, our whole town went to her funeral: the men through a sort of respectful affection for a fallen monument, the women mostly out of curiosity to see the inside of her house, which no one save an old manservant—a combined gardener and cook—had seen in at least ten years.

It was a big, squarish frame house that had once been white, decorated with cupolas and spires and scrolled balconies in the heavily lightsome style of the seventies, set on what had once been our most select street. But garages and cotton gins had encroached and obliterated even the august names of that neighborhood; only Miss Emily's house was left, lifting its stubborn and coquettish decay above the cotton wagons and the gasoline pumps—an eyesore among eyesores. And now Miss Emily had gone to join the representatives of those august names where they lay in the cedar-bemused cemetery among the ranked and anonymous graves of Union and Confederate soldiers who fell at the battle of Jefferson.

Alive, Miss Emily had been a tradition, a duty, and a care; a sort of hereditary obligation upon the town, dating from that day in 1894 when Colonel Sartoris, the mayor—he who fathered the edict that no Negro woman should appear on the streets without an apron—remitted her taxes, the dispensation dating from the death of her father on into perpetuity. Not that Miss Emily would have accepted charity. Colonel Sartoris invented an involved tale to the effect that Miss Emily's father had loaned money to the town, which the town, as a matter of business, preferred this way of repaying. Only a man of Colonel Sartoris's generation and thought could have invented it, and only a woman could have believed it.

When the next generation, with its more modern ideas, became mayors and aldermen, this arrangement created some little dissatisfaction. On the first of the year they mailed her a tax notice. February came, and there was no reply. They wrote her a formal letter, asking her to call at the sheriff's office at her convenience. A week later the mayor wrote her himself, offering to call or to send his car for her, and received in reply a note on paper of an archaic shape, in a thin, flowing calligraphy in faded ink, to the effect that she no longer went out at all. The tax notice was also enclosed, without comment.

They called a special meeting of the Board of Aldermen. A deputation waited upon her, knocked at the door through which no visitor had passed since she ceased giving china-painting lessons eight or ten years earlier. They were admitted by the old Negro into a dim hall from which a stairway mounted into still more shadow. It smelled of dust and disuse—a close, dank smell. The Negro led them into the parlor. It was furnished in heavy, leather-covered furniture. When the Negro opened the blinds of one window, they could see that the leather was cracked; and when they sat down, a faint dust rose sluggishly about their thighs, spinning with slow motes in the single sun-ray. On a tarnished gilt easel before the fireplace stood a crayon portrait of Miss Emily's father.

They rose when she entered—a small, fat woman in black, with a thin gold chain descending to her waist and vanishing into her belt, leaning on an ebony cane with a tarnished gold head. Her skeleton was small and spare;

5

perhaps that was why what would have been merely plumpness in another was obesity in her. She looked bloated, like a body long submerged in motionless water, and of that pallid hue. Her eyes, lost in the fatty ridges of her face, looked like two small pieces of coal pressed into a lump of dough as they moved from one face to another while the visitors stated their errand.

She did not ask them to sit. She just stood in the door and listened quietly until the spokesman came to a stumbling halt. Then they could hear the invisible watch ticking at the end of the gold chain.

Her voice was dry and cold. "I have no taxes in Jefferson. Colonel Sartoris explained it to me. Perhaps one of you can gain access to the city records and satisfy yourselves."

"But we have. We are the city authorities, Miss Emily. Didn't you get a notice from the sheriff, signed by him?"

"I received a paper, yes," Miss Emily said. "Perhaps he considers himself   10
the sheriff. . . . I have no taxes in Jefferson."

"But there is nothing on the books to show that, you see. We must go by the—"

"See Colonel Sartoris. I have no taxes in Jefferson."

"But, Miss Emily—"

"See Colonel Sartoris." (Colonel Sartoris had been dead almost ten years.) "I have no taxes in Jefferson. Tobe!" The Negro appeared. "Show these gentlemen out."

2

So she vanquished them, horse and foot, just as she had vanquished their   15
fathers thirty years before about the smell. That was two years after her father's death and a short time after her sweetheart—the one we believed would marry her—had deserted her. After her father's death she went out very little; after her sweetheart went away, people hardly saw her at all. A few of the ladies had the temerity to call, but were not received, and the only sign of life about the place was the Negro man—a young man then—going in and out with a market basket.

"Just as if a man—any man—could keep a kitchen properly," the ladies said; so they were not surprised when the smell developed. It was another link between the gross, teeming world and the high and mighty Griersons.

A neighbor, a woman, complained to the mayor, Judge Stevens, eighty years old.

"But what will you have me do about it, madam?" he said.

"Why, send her word to stop it," the woman said. "Isn't there a law?"

"I'm sure that won't be necessary," Judge Stevens said. "It's probably just   20
a snake or a rat that nigger of hers killed in the yard. I'll speak to him about it."

The next day he received two more complaints, one from a man who came in diffident deprecation. "We really must do something about it, Judge. I'd be the last one in the world to bother Miss Emily, but we've got to do something."

That night the Board of Aldermen met — three graybeards and one younger man, a member of the rising generation.

"It's simple enough," he said. "Send her word to have her place cleaned up. Give her a certain time to do it in, and if she don't. . . ."

"Dammit, sir," Judge Stevens said, "will you accuse a lady to her face of smelling bad?"

So the next night, after midnight, four men crossed Miss Emily's lawn and slunk about the house like burglars, sniffing along the base of the brick-work and at the cellar openings while one of them performed a regular sowing motion with his hand out of a sack slung from his shoulder. They broke open the cellar door and sprinkled lime there, and in all the outbuildings. As they recrossed the lawn, a window that had been dark was lighted and Miss Emily sat in it, the light behind her, and her upright torso motionless as that of an idol. They crept quietly across the lawn and into the shadow of the locusts that lined the street. After a week or two the smell went away.

That was when people had begun to feel really sorry for her. People in our town, remembering how old lady Wyatt, her great-aunt, had gone completely crazy at last, believed that the Griersons held themselves a little too high for what they really were. None of the young men were quite good enough for Miss Emily and such. We had long thought of them as a tableau, Miss Emily a slender figure in white in the background, her father a spraddled silhouette in the foreground, his back to her and clutching a horsewhip, the two of them framed by the backflung front door. So when she got to be thirty and was still single, we were not pleased exactly, but vindicated; even with insanity in the family she wouldn't have turned down all of her chances if they had really materialized.

When her father died, it got about that the house was all that was left to her; and in a way, people were glad. At last they could pity Miss Emily. Being left alone, and a pauper, she had become humanized. Now she too would know the old thrill and the old despair of a penny more or less.

The day after his death all the ladies prepared to call at the house and offer condolence and aid, as is our custom. Miss Emily met them at the door, dressed as usual and with no trace of grief on her face. She told them that her father was not dead. She did that for three days, with the ministers calling on her, and the doctors, trying to persuade her to let them dispose of the body. Just as they were about to resort to law and force, she broke down, and they buried her father quickly.

We did not say she was crazy then. We believed she had to do that. We remembered all the young men her father had driven away, and we knew that with nothing left, she would have to cling to that which had robbed her, as people will.

3

She was sick for a long time. When we saw her again, her hair was cut short, making her look like a girl, with a vague resemblance to those angels in colored church windows — sort of tragic and serene.

25

The town had just let the contracts for paving the sidewalks, and in the   30
summer after her father's death they began the work. The construction company came with niggers and mules and machinery, and a foreman named
Homer Barron, a Yankee—a big, dark, ready man, with a big voice and eyes
lighter than his face. The little boys would follow in groups to hear him cuss the
niggers, and the niggers singing in time to the rise and fall of picks. Pretty soon
he knew everybody in town. Whenever you heard a lot of laughing anywhere
about the square, Homer Barron would be in the center of the group. Presently,
we began to see him and Miss Emily on Sunday afternoons driving in the
yellow-wheeled buggy and the matched team of bays from the livery stable.

At first we were glad that Miss Emily would have an interest, because the
ladies all said, "Of course a Grierson would not think seriously of a Northerner,
a day laborer." But there were still others, older people, who said that even grief
could not cause a real lady to forget *noblesse oblige*—without calling it *noblesse
oblige.* They just said, "Poor Emily. Her kinsfolk should come to her." She had
some kin in Alabama; but years ago her father had fallen out with them over the
estate of old lady Wyatt, the crazy woman, and there was no communication
between the two families. They had not even been represented at the funeral.

And as soon as the old people said, "Poor Emily," the whispering began.
"Do you suppose it's really so?" they said to one another. "Of course it is. What
else could. . . ." This behind their hands; rustling of craned silk and satin
behind jalousies closed upon the sun of Sunday afternoon as the thin, swift
clop-clop-clop of the matched team passed: "Poor Emily."

She carried her head high enough—even when we believed that she was
fallen. It was as if she demanded more than ever the recognition of her dignity
as the last Grierson; as if it had wanted that touch of earthiness to reaffirm her
imperviousness. Like when she bought the rat poison, the arsenic. That was
over a year after they had begun to say "Poor Emily," and while the two female
cousins were visiting her.

"I want some poison," she said to the druggist. She was over thirty then,
still a slight woman, though thinner than usual, with cold, haughty black eyes
in a face the flesh of which was strained across the temples and about the eye-
sockets as you imagine a lighthouse-keeper's face ought to look. "I want some
poison," she said.

"Yes, Miss Emily. What kind? For rats and such? I'd recom ——"   35
"I want the best you have. I don't care what kind."
The druggist named several. "They'll kill anything up to an elephant. But
what you want is ——"
"Arsenic," Miss Emily said. "Is that a good one?"
"Is . . . arsenic? Yes, ma'am. But what you want ——"
"I want arsenic."   40
The druggist looked down at her. She looked back at him, erect, her face
like a strained flag. "Why, of course," the druggist said. "If that's what you
want. But the law requires you to tell what you are going to use it for."
Miss Emily just stared at him, her head tilted back in order to look him
eye for eye, until he looked away and went and got the arsenic and wrapped

it up. The Negro delivery boy brought her the package; the druggist didn't come back. When she opened the package at home there was written on the box, under the skull and bones: "For rats."

4

So the next day we all said, "She will kill herself"; and we said it would be the best thing. When she had first begun to be seen with Homer Barron, we had said, "She will marry him." Then we said, "She will persuade him yet," because Homer himself had remarked — he liked men, and it was known that he drank with the younger men in the Elks' Club — that he was not a marrying man. Later we said, "Poor Emily" behind the jalousies as they passed on Sunday afternoon in the glittering buggy, Miss Emily with her head high and Homer Barron with his hat cocked and a cigar in his teeth, reins and whip in a yellow glove.

Then some of the ladies began to say that it was a disgrace to the town and a bad example to the young people. The men did not want to interfere, but at last the ladies forced the Baptist minister — Miss Emily's people were Episcopal — to call upon her. He would never divulge what happened during that interview, but he refused to go back again. The next Sunday they again drove about the streets, and the following day the minister's wife wrote to Miss Emily's relations in Alabama.

So she had blood-kin under her roof again and we sat back to watch developments. At first nothing happened. Then we were sure that they were to be married. We learned that Miss Emily had been to the jeweler's and ordered a man's toilet set in silver, with the letters H.B. on each piece. Two days later we learned that she had bought a complete outfit of men's clothing, including a nightshirt, and we said, "They are married." We were really glad. We were glad because the two female cousins were even more Grierson than Miss Emily had ever been.

So we were not surprised when Homer Barron — the streets had been finished some time since — was gone. We were a little disappointed that there was not a public blowing-off, but we believed that he had gone on to prepare for Miss Emily's coming, or to give her a chance to get rid of the cousins. (By that time it was a cabal, and we were all Miss Emily's allies to help circumvent the cousins.) Sure enough, after another week they departed. And, as we had expected all along, within three days Homer Barron was back in town. A neighbor saw the Negro man admit him at the kitchen door at dusk one evening.

And that was the last we saw of Homer Barron. And of Miss Emily for some time. The Negro man went in and out with the market basket, but the front door remained closed. Now and then we would see her at the window for a moment, as the men did that night when they sprinkled the lime, but for almost six months she did not appear on the streets. Then we knew that this was to be expected too; as if that quality of her father which had thwarted her woman's life so many times had been too virulent and too furious to die.

45

When we next saw Miss Emily, she had grown fat and her hair was turning gray. During the next few years it grew grayer and grayer until it attained an even pepper-and-salt iron-gray, when it ceased turning. Up to the day of her death at seventy-four it was still that vigorous iron-gray, like the hair of an active man.

From that time on her front door remained closed, save during a period of six or seven years, when she was about forty, during which she gave lessons in china-painting. She fitted up a studio in one of the downstairs rooms, where the daughters and granddaughters of Colonel Sartoris's contemporaries were sent to her with the same regularity and in the same spirit that they were sent to church on Sundays with a twenty-five-cent piece for the collection plate. Meanwhile her taxes had been remitted.

Then the newer generation became the backbone and the spirit of the town, and the painting pupils grew up and fell away and did not send their children to her with boxes of color and tedious brushes and pictures cut from the ladies' magazines. The front door closed upon the last one and remained closed for good. When the town got free postal delivery, Miss Emily alone refused to let them fasten the metal numbers above her door and attach a mailbox to it. She would not listen to them. 50

Daily, monthly, yearly we watched the Negro grow grayer and more stooped, going in and out with the market basket. Each December we sent her a tax notice, which would be returned by the post office a week later, unclaimed. Now and then we would see her in one of the downstairs windows—she had evidently shut up the top floor of the house—like the carven torso of an idol in a niche, looking or not looking at us, we could never tell which. Thus she passed from generation to generation—dear, inescapable, impervious, tranquil, and perverse.

And so she died. Fell ill in the house filled with dust and shadows, with only a doddering Negro man to wait on her. We did not even know she was sick; we had long since given up trying to get any information from the Negro. He talked to no one, probably not even to her, for his voice had grown harsh and rusty, as if from disuse.

She died in one of the downstairs rooms, in a heavy walnut bed with a curtain, her gray head propped on a pillow yellow and moldy with age and lack of sunlight.

5

The Negro met the first of the ladies at the front door and let them in, with their hushed, sibilant voices and their quick, curious glances, and then he disappeared. He walked right through the house and out the back and was not seen again.

The two female cousins came at once. They held the funeral on the second day, with the town coming to look at Miss Emily beneath a mass of bought flowers, with the crayon face of her father musing profoundly above the bier and the ladies sibilant and macabre; and the very old men—some in their 55 brushed Confederate uniforms—on the porch and the lawn, talking of Miss Emily as if she had been a contemporary of theirs, believing that they had danced with her and courted her perhaps, confusing time with its mathematical progression, as the old do, to whom all the past is not a diminishing road but, instead, a huge meadow which no winter ever quite touches, divided from them now by the narrow bottleneck of the most recent decade of years.

Already we knew that there was one room in that region above stairs which no one had seen in forty years, and which would have to be forced. They waited until Miss Emily was decently in the ground before they opened it.

The violence of breaking down the door seemed to fill this room with pervading dust. A thin, acrid pall as of the tomb seemed to lie everywhere upon this room decked and furnished as for a bridal: upon the valance curtains of faded rose color, upon the rose-shaded lights, upon the dressing table, upon the delicate array of crystal and the man's toilet things backed with tarnished silver, silver so tarnished that the monogram was obscured. Among them lay a collar and tie, as if they had just been removed, which, lifted, left upon the surface a pale crescent in the dust. Upon a chair hung the suit, carefully folded; beneath it the two mute shoes and the discarded socks.

The man himself lay in the bed.

For a long while we just stood there, looking down at the profound and fleshless grin. The body had apparently once lain in the attitude of an embrace, but now the long sleep that outlasts love, that conquers even the grimace of love, had cuckolded him. What was left of him, rotted beneath what was left of the nightshirt, had become inextricable from the bed in which he lay; and upon him and upon the pillow beside him lay that even coating of the patient and biding dust.

Then we noticed that in the second pillow was the indentation of a   60
head. One of us lifted something from it, and leaning forward, that faint and invisible dust dry and acrid in the nostrils, we saw a long strand of iron-gray hair.   *[1931]*

≡ THINKING ABOUT THE TEXT

1. Do you think some people can love another so much that they simply cannot bear for that person to leave? Is it possible this was the case for Emily?

2. Can a disturbed person be in love? Does love have to be healthy? Is sanity culturally defined? Can you imagine a society that would accept Emily's behavior?

3. Who do you think the narrator of "A Rose for Emily" is? Why would Faulkner tell the story from this perspective? Why not from Emily's?

4. Look at the last sentence of paragraph 51. What do you think about the five adjectives used? Are they understandable in terms of the story?

5. Some critics think this story is not a love story but a political allegory about the South. Does this make sense to you? What else does the story suggest to you?

6. Comment on the various kinds of repression — social and psychological — that occur throughout the story. What connections can you draw, and what generalizations might you make about them?

7. Reread "A Rose for Emily." How does your knowledge of the ending of the story affect your second reading? What details of the narrative tend to stand out the second time around?

RAYMOND CARVER

What We Talk About
When We Talk About Love

Raymond Carver (1938–1988) re-creates in what has been called a "stripped-down and muscular prose style" the minutiae of everyday life in mid-twentieth-century America. Brought up in the Pacific Northwest in a working-class family, Carver began writing in high school and married early. While both he and his young wife worked at low-paying jobs, Carver took college courses and struggled to find time to write. In 1958, he studied fiction writing with John Gardner and graduated in 1963 from what is now the California State University at Humboldt. He received national recognition in 1967 when a story was included in the Best American Short Stories *annual anthology. Although Carver was a National Endowment for the Arts fellow in poetry in 1971, fiction remained his primary genre, earning him numerous awards and fellowships, including O. Henry awards in 1974, 1975, and 1980. Despite his success as a writer, alcoholism plagued Carver for most of his life until with the help of Alcoholics Anonymous he stopped drinking in 1982, soon after his divorce. "What We Talk About When We Talk About Love" was the title story in his 1981 collection.*

My friend Mel McGinnis was talking. Mel McGinnis is a cardiologist, and sometimes that gives him the right.

The four of us were sitting around his kitchen table drinking gin. Sunlight filled the kitchen from the big window behind the sink. There were Mel and me and his second wife, Teresa — Terri, we called her — and my wife, Laura. We lived in Albuquerque then. But we were all from somewhere else.

There was an ice bucket on the table. The gin and the tonic water kept going around, and we somehow got on the subject of love. Mel thought real love was nothing less than spiritual love. He said he'd spent five years in a seminary before quitting to go to medical school. He said he still looked back on those years in the seminary as the most important years in his life.

Terri said the man she lived with before she lived with Mel loved her so much he tried to kill her. Then Terri said, "He beat me up one night. He dragged me around the living room by my ankles. He kept saying, 'I love you, I love you, you bitch.' He went on dragging me around the living room. My head kept knocking on things." Terri looked around the table. "What do you do with love like that?"

She was a bone-thin woman with a pretty face, dark eyes, and brown hair   5
that hung down her back. She liked necklaces made of turquoise, and long
pendant earrings.

"My God, don't be silly. That's not love, and you know it," Mel said. "I don't
know what you'd call it, but I sure know you wouldn't call it love."

"Say what you want to, but I know it was," Terri said. "It may sound crazy
to you, but it's true just the same. People are different, Mel. Sure, sometimes
he may have acted crazy. Okay. But he loved me. In his own way maybe, but he
loved me. There was love there, Mel. Don't say there wasn't."

Mel let out his breath. He held his glass and turned to Laura and me. "The
man threatened to kill me," Mel said. He finished his drink and reached for the
gin bottle. "Terri's a romantic. Terri's of the kick-me-so-I'll-know-you-love-me
school. Terri, hon, don't look that way." Mel reached across the table and
touched Terri's cheek with his fingers. He grinned at her.

"Now he wants to make up," Terri said.

"Make up what?" Mel said. "What is there to make up? I know what I   10
know. That's all."

"How'd we get started on this subject, anyway?" Terri said. She raised her
glass and drank from it. "Mel always has love on his mind," she said. "Don't
you, honey?" She smiled, and I thought that was the last of it.

"I just wouldn't call Ed's behavior love. That's all I'm saying, honey," Mel
said. "What about you guys?" Mel said to Laura and me. "Does that sound like
love to you?"

"I'm the wrong person to ask," I said. "I didn't even know the man. I've
only heard his name mentioned in passing. I wouldn't know. You'd have to
know the particulars. But I think what you're saying is that love is an absolute."

Mel said, "The kind of love I'm talking about is. The kind of love I'm
talking about, you don't try to kill people."

Laura said, "I don't know anything about Ed, or anything about the situa-   15
tion. But who can judge anyone else's situation?"

I touched the back of Laura's hand. She gave me a quick smile. I picked up
Laura's hand. It was warm, the nails polished, perfectly manicured. I encircled
the broad wrist with my fingers, and I held her.

"When I left, he drank rat poison," Terri said. She clasped her arms with
her hands. "They took him to the hospital in Santa Fe. That's where we lived
then, about ten miles out. They saved his life. But his gums went crazy from
it. I mean they pulled away from his teeth. After that, his teeth stood out like
fangs. My God," Terri said. She waited a minute, then let go of her arms and
picked up her glass.

"What people won't do!" Laura said.

"He's out of the action now," Mel said. "He's dead."

Mel handed me the saucer of limes. I took a section, squeezed it over my   20
drink, and stirred the ice cubes with my finger.

"It gets worse," Terri said. "He shot himself in the mouth. But he bungled
that too. Poor Ed," she said. Terri shook her head.

"Poor Ed nothing," Mel said. "He was dangerous."

Mel was forty-five years old. He was tall and rangy with curly soft hair. His face and arms were brown from the tennis he played. When he was sober, his gestures, all his movements, were precise, very careful.

"He did love me though, Mel. Grant me that," Terri said. "That's all I'm asking. He didn't love me the way you love me. I'm not saying that. But he loved me. You can grant me that, can't you?"

"What do you mean, he bungled it?" I said.   25

Laura leaned forward with her glass. She put her elbows on the table and held her glass in both hands. She glanced from Mel to Terri and waited with a look of bewilderment on her open face, as if amazed that such things happened to people you were friendly with.

"How'd he bungle it when he killed himself?" I said.

"I'll tell you what happened," Mel said. "He took this twenty-two pistol he'd bought to threaten Terri and me with. Oh, I'm serious, the man was always threatening. You should have seen the way we lived in those days. Like fugitives. I even bought a gun myself. Can you believe it? A guy like me? But I did. I bought one for self-defense and carried it in the glove compartment. Sometimes I'd have to leave the apartment in the middle of the night. To go to the hospital, you know? Terri and I weren't married then, and my first wife had the house and kids, the dog, everything, and Terri and I were living in this apartment here. Sometimes, as I say, I'd get a call in the middle of the night and have to go in to the hospital at two or three in the morning. It'd be dark out there in the parking lot, and I'd break into a sweat before I could even get to my car. I never knew if he was going to come up out of the shrubbery or from behind a car and start shooting. I mean, the man was crazy. He was capable of wiring a bomb, anything. He used to call my service at all hours and say he needed to talk to the doctor, and when I'd return the call, he'd say, 'Son of a bitch, your days are numbered.' Little things like that. It was scary, I'm telling you."

"I still feel sorry for him," Terri said.

"It sounds like a nightmare," Laura said. "But what exactly happened   30
after he shot himself?"

Laura is a legal secretary. We'd met in a professional capacity. Before we knew it, it was a courtship. She's thirty-five, three years younger than I am. In addition to being in love, we like each other and enjoy one another's company. She's easy to be with.

"What happened?" Laura said.

Mel said, "He shot himself in the mouth in his room. Someone heard the shot and told the manager. They came in with a passkey, saw what had happened, and called an ambulance. I happened to be there when they brought him in, alive but past recall. The man lived for three days. His head swelled up to twice the size of a normal head. I'd never seen anything like it, and I hope I never do again. Terri wanted to go in and sit with him when she found out about it. We had a fight over it. I didn't think she should see him like that. I didn't think she should see him, and I still don't."

"Who won the fight?" Laura said.

"I was in the room with him when he died," Terri said. "He never came up   35
out of it. But I sat with him. He didn't have anyone else."

"He was dangerous," Mel said. "If you call that love, you can have it."

"It was love," Terri said. "Sure, it's abnormal in most people's eyes. But he
was willing to die for it. He did die for it."

"I sure as hell wouldn't call it love," Mel said. "I mean, no one knows what
he did it for. I've seen a lot of suicides, and I couldn't say anyone ever knew
what they did it for."

Mel put his hands behind his neck and tilted his chair back. "I'm not interested in that kind of love," he said. "If that's love, you can have it."

Terri said, "We were afraid. Mel even made a will out and wrote to his   40
brother in California who used to be a Green Beret. Mel told him who to look
for if something happened to him."

Terri drank from her glass. She said, "But Mel's right—we lived like fugitives. We were afraid. Mel was, weren't you, honey? I even called the police at
one point, but they were no help. They said they couldn't do anything until Ed
actually did something. Isn't that a laugh?" Terri said.

She poured the last of the gin into her glass and waggled the bottle.
Mel got up from the table and went to the cupboard. He took down
another bottle.

"Well, Nick and I know what love is," Laura said. "For us, I mean," Laura said.
She bumped my knee with her knee. "You're supposed to say something now,"
Laura said, and turned her smile on me.

For an answer, I took Laura's hand and raised it to my lips. I made a big
production out of kissing her hand. Everyone was amused.

"We're lucky," I said.   45

"You guys," Terri said. "Stop that now. You're making me sick. You're still
on the honeymoon, for God's sake. You're still gaga, for crying out loud. Just
wait. How long have you been together now? How long has it been? A year?
Longer than a year?"

"Going on a year and a half," Laura said, flushed and smiling.

"Oh, now," Terri said. "Wait awhile."

She held her drink and gazed at Laura.

"I'm only kidding," Terri said.   50

Mel opened the gin and went around the table with the bottle.

"Here, you guys," he said. "Let's have a toast. I want to propose a toast. A
toast to love. To true love," Mel said.

We touched glasses.

"To love," we said.

Outside in the backyard, one of the dogs began to bark. The leaves of the aspen   55
that leaned past the window ticked against the glass. The afternoon sun was
like a presence in this room, the spacious light of ease and generosity. We could
have been anywhere, somewhere enchanted. We raised our glasses again and
grinned at each other like children who had agreed on something forbidden.

"I'll tell you what real love is," Mel said. "I mean, I'll give you a good example. And then you can draw your own conclusions." He poured more gin into his glass. He added an ice cube and a sliver of lime. We waited and sipped our drinks. Laura and I touched knees again. I put a hand on her warm thigh and left it there.

"What do any of us really know about love?" Mel said. "It seems to me we're just beginners at love. We say we love each other and we do, I don't doubt it. I love Terri and Terri loves me, and you guys love each other too. You know the kind of love I'm talking about now. Physical love, that impulse that drives you to someone special, as well as love of the other person's being, his or her essence, as it were. Carnal love and, well, call it sentimental love, the day-to-day caring about the other person. But sometimes I have a hard time accounting for the fact that I must have loved my first wife too. But I did, I know I did. So I suppose I am like Terri in that regard. Terri and Ed." He thought about it and then he went on. "There was a time when I thought I loved my first wife more than life itself. But now I hate her guts. I do. How do you explain that? What happened to that love? What happened to it, is what I'd like to know. I wish someone could tell me. Then there's Ed. Okay, we're back to Ed. He loves Terri so much he tries to kill her and he winds up killing himself." Mel stopped talking and swallowed from his glass. "You guys have been together eighteen months and you love each other. It shows all over you. You glow with it. But you both loved other people before you met each other. You've both been married before, just like us. And you probably loved other people before that too, even. Terri and I have been together five years, been married for four. And the terrible thing, the terrible thing is, but the good thing too, the saving grace, you might say, is that if something happened to one of us — excuse me for saying this — but if something happened to one of us tomorrow I think the other one, the other person, would grieve for a while, you know, but then the surviving party would go out and love again, have someone else soon enough. All this, all of this love we're talking about, it would just be a memory. Maybe not even a memory. Am I wrong? Am I way off base? Because I want you to set me straight if you think I'm wrong. I want to know. I mean, I don't know anything, and I'm the first one to admit it."

"Mel, for God's sake," Terri said. She reached out and took hold of his wrist. "Are you getting drunk? Honey? Are you drunk?"

"Honey, I'm just talking," Mel said. "All right? I don't have to be drunk to say what I think. I mean, we're all just talking, right?" Mel said. He fixed his eyes on her.

"Sweetie, I'm not criticizing," Terri said.

She picked up her glass.

"I'm not on call today," Mel said. "Let me remind you of that. I am not on call," he said.

"Mel, we love you," Laura said.

Mel looked at Laura. He looked at her as if he could not place her, as if she was not the woman she was.

60

"Love you too, Laura," Mel said. "And you, Nick, love you too. You know   65
something?" Mel said. "You guys are our pals," Mel said.

He picked up his glass.

Mel said, "I was going to tell you about something. I mean, I was going to prove a point. You see, this happened a few months ago, but it's still going on right now, and it ought to make us feel ashamed when we talk like we know what we're talking about when we talk about love."

"Come on now," Terri said. "Don't talk like you're drunk if you're not drunk."

"Just shut up for once in your life," Mel said very quietly. "Will you do me a favor and do that for a minute? So as I was saying, there's this old couple who had this car wreck out on the interstate. A kid hit them and they were all torn to shit and nobody was giving them much chance to pull through."

Terri looked at us and then back at Mel. She seemed anxious, or maybe   70
that's too strong a word.

Mel was handing the bottle around the table.

"I was on call that night," Mel said. "It was May or maybe it was June. Terri and I had just sat down to dinner when the hospital called. There'd been this thing out on the interstate. Drunk kid, teenager, plowed his dad's pickup into this camper with this old couple in it. They were up in their midseventies, that couple. The kid — eighteen, nineteen, something — he was DOA. Taken the steering wheel through his sternum. The old couple, they were alive, you understand. I mean, just barely. But they had everything. Multiple fractures, internal injuries, hemorrhaging, contusions, lacerations, the works, and they each of them had themselves concussions. They were in a bad way, believe me. And, of course, their age was two strikes against them. I'd say she was worse off than he was. Ruptured spleen along with everything else. Both kneecaps broken. But they'd been wearing their seatbelts and, God knows, that's what saved them for the time being."

"Folks, this is an advertisement for the National Safety Council," Terri said. "This is your spokesman, Dr. Melvin R. McGinnis, talking." Terri laughed. "Mel," she said, "sometimes you're just too much. But I love you, hon," she said.

"Honey, I love you," Mel said.

He leaned across the table. Terri met him halfway. They kissed.   75

"Terri's right," Mel said as he settled himself again. "Get those seatbelts on. But seriously, they were in some shape, those oldsters. By the time I got down there, the kid was dead, as I said. He was off in a corner, laid out on a gurney. I took one look at the old couple and told the ER nurse to get me a neurologist and an orthopedic man and a couple of surgeons down there right away."

He drank from his glass. "I'll try to keep this short," he said. "So we took the two of them up to the OR and worked like fuck on them most of the night. They had these incredible reserves, those two. You see that once in a while. So we did everything that could be done, and toward morning we're giving them a fifty-fifty chance, maybe less than that for her. So here they are, still alive the next morning. So, okay, we move them into the ICU, which is where they both kept plugging away at it for two weeks, hitting it better and better on all the scopes. So we transfer them out to their own room."

Mel stopped talking. "Here," he said, "let's drink this cheapo gin the hell up. Then we're going to dinner, right? Terri and I know a new place. That's where we'll go, to this new place we know about. But we're not going until we finish up this cut-rate, lousy gin."

Terri said, "We haven't actually eaten there yet. But it looks good. From the outside, you know."

"I like food," Mel said. "If I had it to do all over again, I'd be a chef, you know? Right, Terri?" Mel said.   80

He laughed. He fingered the ice in his glass.

"Terri knows," he said. "Terri can tell you. But let me say this. If I could come back again in a different life, a different time and all, you know what? I'd like to come back as a knight. You were pretty safe wearing all that armor. It was all right being a knight until gunpowder and muskets and pistols came along."

"Mel would like to ride a horse and carry a lance," Terri said.

"Carry a woman's scarf with you everywhere," Laura said.

"Or just a woman," Mel said.   85

"Shame on you," Laura said.

Terri said, "Suppose you came back as a serf. The serfs didn't have it so good in those days," Terri said.

"The serfs never had it good," Mel said. "But I guess even the knights were vessels to someone. Isn't that the way it worked? But then everyone is always a vessel to someone. Isn't that right? Terri? But what I liked about knights, besides their ladies, was that they had that suit of armor, you know, and they couldn't get hurt very easy. No cars in those days, you know? No drunk teenagers to tear into your ass."

"Vassals," Terri said.

"What?" Mel said.   90

"Vassals," Terri said. "They were called vassals, not vessels."

"Vassals, vessels," Mel said, "what the fuck's the difference? You knew what I meant anyway. All right," Mel said. "So I'm not educated. I learned my stuff. I'm a heart surgeon, sure, but I'm just a mechanic. I go in and I fuck around and I fix things. Shit," Mel said.

"Modesty doesn't become you," Terri said.

"He's just a humble sawbones," I said. "But sometimes they suffocated in all that armor, Mel. They'd even have heart attacks if it got too hot and they were too tired and worn out. I read somewhere that they'd fall off their horses and not be able to get up because they were too tired to stand with all that armor on them. They got trampled by their own horses sometimes."

"That's terrible," Mel said. "That's a terrible thing, Nicky. I guess they'd   95
just lay there and wait until somebody came along and made a shish kebab out
of them."

"Some other vessel," Terri said.

"That's right," Mel said. "Some vassal would come along and spear the
bastard in the name of love. Or whatever the fuck it was they fought over in
those days."

"Same things we fight over these days," Terri said.

Laura said, "Nothing's changed."

The color was still high in Laura's cheeks. Her eyes were bright. She   100
brought her glass to her lips.

Mel poured himself another drink. He looked at the label closely as if
studying a long row of numbers. Then he slowly put the bottle down on the
table and slowly reached for the tonic water.

"What about the old couple?" Laura said. "You didn't finish that story you
started."

Laura was having a hard time lighting her cigarette. Her matches kept
going out.

The sunshine inside the room was different now, changing, getting thinner. But the leaves outside the window were still shimmering, and I stared at
the pattern they made on the panes and on the Formica counter. They weren't
the same patterns, of course.

"What about the old couple?" I said.   105

"Older but wiser," Terri said.

Mel stared at her.

Terri said, "Go on with your story, hon. I was only kidding. Then what
happened?"

"Terri, sometimes," Mel said.

"Please, Mel," Terri said. "Don't always be so serious, sweetie. Can't you   110
take a joke?"

"Where's the joke?" Mel said.

He held his glass and gazed steadily at his wife.

"What happened?" Laura said.

Mel fastened his eyes on Laura. He said, "Laura, if I didn't have Terri and
if I didn't love her so much, and if Nick wasn't my best friend, I'd fall in love
with you, I'd carry you off, honey," he said.

"Tell your story," Terri said. "Then we'll go to that new place, okay?"   115

"Okay," Mel said. "Where was I?" he said. He stared at the table and then
he began again.

"I dropped in to see each of them every day, sometimes twice a day if I
was up doing other calls anyway. Casts and bandages, head to foot, the both of
them. You know, you've seen it in the movies. That's just the way they looked,
just like in the movies. Little eye-holes and nose-holes and mouth-holes. And
she had to have her legs slung up on top of it. Well, the husband was very
depressed for the longest while. Even after he found out that his wife was going

to pull through, he was still very depressed. Not about the accident, though. I mean, the accident was one thing, but it wasn't everything. I'd get up to his mouth-hole, you know, and he'd say no, it wasn't the accident exactly but it was because he couldn't see her through his eye-holes. He said that was what was making him feel so bad. Can you imagine? I'm telling you, the man's heart was breaking because he couldn't turn his goddamn head and *see* his goddamn wife."

Mel looked around the table and shook his head at what he was going to say.

"I mean, it was killing the old fart just because he couldn't *look* at the fucking woman."

We all looked at Mel.   120

"Do you see what I'm saying?" he said.

Maybe we were a little drunk by then. I know it was hard keeping things in focus. The light was draining out of the room, going back through the window where it had come from. Yet nobody made a move to get up from the table to turn on the overhead light.

"Listen," Mel said. "Let's finish this fucking gin. There's about enough left here for one shooter all around. Then let's go eat. Let's go to the new place."

"He's depressed," Terri said. "Mel, why don't you take a pill?"

Mel shook his head. "I've taken everything there is."   125

"We all need a pill now and then," I said.

"Some people are born needing them," Terri said.

She was using her finger to rub at something on the table. Then she stopped rubbing.

"I think I want to call my kids," Mel said. "Is that all right with everybody? I'll call my kids," he said.

Terri said, "What if Marjorie answers the phone? You guys, you've heard   130 us on the subject of Marjorie? Honey, you know you don't want to talk to Marjorie. It'll make you feel even worse."

"I don't want to talk to Marjorie," Mel said. "But I want to talk to my kids."

"There isn't a day goes by that Mel doesn't say he wishes she'd get married again. Or else die," Terri said. "For one thing," Terri said, "she's bankrupting us. Mel says it's just to spite him that she won't get married again. She has a boyfriend who lives with her and the kids, so Mel is supporting the boyfriend too."

"She's allergic to bees," Mel said. "If I'm not praying she'll get married again, I'm praying she'll get herself stung to death by a swarm of fucking bees."

"Shame on you," Laura said.

"Bzzzzzzz," Mel said, turning his fingers into bees and buzzing them at   135 Terri's throat. Then he let his hands drop all the way to his sides.

"She's vicious," Mel said. "Sometimes I think I'll go up there dressed like a beekeeper. You know, that hat that's like a helmet with the plate that comes down over your face, the big gloves, and the padded coat? I'll knock on the door and let loose a hive of bees in the house. But first I'd make sure the kids were out, of course."

He crossed one leg over the other. It seemed to take him a lot of time to do it. Then he put both feet on the floor and leaned forward, elbows on the table, his chin cupped in his hands.

"Maybe I won't call the kids, after all. Maybe it isn't such a hot idea. Maybe we'll just go eat. How does that sound?"

"Sounds fine to me," I said. "Eat or not eat. Or keep drinking. I could head right on out into the sunset."

"What does that mean, honey?" Laura said.   140

"It just means what I said," I said. "It means I could just keep going. That's all it means."

"I could eat something myself," Laura said. "I don't think I've ever been so hungry in my life. Is there something to nibble on?"

"I'll put out some cheese and crackers," Terri said.

But Terri just sat there. She did not get up to get anything.

Mel turned his glass over. He spilled it out on the table.   145

"Gin's gone," Mel said.

Terri said, "Now what?"

I could hear my heart beating. I could hear everyone's heart. I could hear the human noise we sat there making, not one of us moving, not even when the room went dark.   *[1981]*

≡ THINKING ABOUT THE TEXT

1. The argument between the couples seems to be about the nature of love. Which character's ideas make the most sense to you? What kinds of love are discussed? Are these demonstrated in the story? Do you think true love is an illusion?

2. Do you see similarities between Mel and Ed? Do any of the characters seem aware of any similarities? Is Mel a perceptive person? What are his problems? Is he in love with Terri? How do you interpret his fantasy with the bees and Marjorie?

3. Why does Mel seem so interested in knights? Is this symbolic? Are there other symbols here — light? dark? cardiologist? What do you make of the last paragraph? Why does it end with beating hearts and silence?

4. Is this story optimistic or pessimistic about true love? Is the old couple a positive or a negative example of true love? What about Nick and Laura? What about Ed? Could you argue that he was in love?

5. What does the title mean? Be specific, especially about the first word. Do you tell stories about love? Have you heard some recently? What lessons or information do they give about love?

☰ MAKING COMPARISONS

1. Compare Ed to Emily Grierson in Faulkner's story. What similarities do you see in their behavior?
2. Have these stories complicated your idea of love? Explain.
3. Do you see Terri and Homer Barron as victims of love? Did they do something wrong?

☰ WRITING ABOUT ISSUES

1. Is love or hate a stronger emotion? Use examples from these stories to support your argument.
2. What difficulties do you encounter when you try to define love? Write an essay in which you use Homer and Emily or Terri and Ed as examples that complicate the definition.
3. Citing evidence from these and other stories, as well as novels, films, and your own experiences, write an essay that explains your view of the necessary ingredients for a loving relationship.
4. Argue that because our culture overemphasizes romantic love, individuals feel pressured to find love, sometimes in all the wrong places.

WILLIAM SHAKESPEARE, "Let me not to the marriage of true minds"

JOHN KEATS, "Bright Star"

ELIZABETH BARRETT BROWNING, "How Do I Love Thee?"

E. E. CUMMINGS, "somewhere i have never travelled"

Think about the term *true love*. Why *true*? Does *love* need this modification? Isn't love supposed to be true? Is there a *false* love? Or is something else implied that *love* doesn't convey by itself? Might it be something like *the one and only*? Some writers seem committed to the idea that true love lasts forever, for better or worse, regardless of circumstances. Is this just a fantasy, something we hope will be true? Or is it a reality, delivered to those who are lucky or who work hard to make it true? See if you agree with the four poets in this cluster, some of whom are direct and clear about the possibilities of true love, while others take a more indirect, even playful tone.

≡ BEFORE YOU READ

Do you believe in true love? How would you describe it? How has the idea been portrayed in books and films you are familiar with?

WILLIAM SHAKESPEARE

Let me not to the marriage of true minds

William Shakespeare (1564–1616) is best known to modern readers as a dramatist; however, there is evidence that both he and his contemporaries valued his poetry above the plays. In 1598, for example, a writer praised Shakespeare's "sugared sonnets among his private friends." As with other aspects of his life and work, questions about how much autobiographical significance to attach to Shakespeare's subject matter continue to arise. Regardless of the discussion, there can be no doubt that the sonnets attributed to Shakespeare, at times directed to a man and at others directed to a woman, address the subject of love. "Sonnet 116," which was written in 1609 and proposes a "marriage of true minds," is no exception.

> Let me not to the marriage of true minds,
> Admit impediments. Love is not love
> Which alters when it alteration finds,
> Or bends with the remover to remove:
> Oh, no! it is an ever-fixèd mark,
> That looks on tempests and is never shaken;
> It is the star to every wandering bark,°   *small ship*

5

Whose worth's unknown, although his height be taken.
Love's not Time's fool, though rosy lips and cheeks
Within his bending sickle's compass come; 10
Love alters not with his brief hours and weeks,
But bears it out even to the edge of doom.
If this be error and upon me proved,
I never writ, nor no man ever loved. *[1609]*

≡ **THINKING ABOUT THE TEXT**

1. Why would you be pleased if your beloved wrote you this sonnet? Is he professing his love or giving a definition of true love as unchanging?

2. What if love didn't last "even to the edge of doom" (line 12)? Why might it then be ordinary?

3. Shakespeare uses images to describe true love. Which one strikes you as apt? Can you suggest an image of your own?

4. The concluding couplet seems to be saying something like "I'm absolutely right." Do you think Shakespeare is? Can you think of a situation in which love should bend or alter?

5. The world seems to demonstrate that true love seldom lasts forever. Why then do writers of all kinds profess the opposite? If you really believe that true love does not exist, would you still marry? If your beloved asked you if your love would last forever, would you truthfully answer, "Only time will tell"?

JOHN KEATS
Bright Star

John Keats (1795–1821) was born into a working-class family. He hoped to be a physician but decided that poetry was his calling. His narrative poem Endymion *(1818) received poor reviews, but he was totally committed to his work. He was stricken with tuberculosis shortly after the poem's publication and went to Italy to recover. He died in Rome at age twenty-five.*

In 2009, Jane Campion directed Bright Star, *a film based on the last three years of Keats's life. The film focuses on his intense relationship with Fanny Brawne. Lines from many of his most famous poems are recited, including "La Belle Dame Sans Merci" and "Ode on Melancholy," as well as lines from his poetic letters to Fanny. On his tombstone is his own inscription: "Here lies one whose name was writ in water." Today Keats is considered one of literature's greatest poets.*

Bright star, would I were stedfast as thou art —
Not in lone splendour hung aloft the night

And watching, with eternal lids apart,
Like nature's patient, sleepless Eremite,°   *A Christian hermit*
The moving waters at their priestlike task   5
Of pure ablution round earth's human shores,
Or gazing on the new soft-fallen mask
Of snow upon the mountains and the moors —
No — yet still stedfast, still unchangeable,
Pillow'd upon my fair love's ripening breast,   10
To feel for ever its soft fall and swell,
Awake for ever in a sweet unrest,
Still, still to hear her tender-taken breath,
And so live ever — or else swoon to death.   *[1819]*

≡ THINKING ABOUT THE TEXT

1. Discuss how the speaker wants to be like the bright star in some ways, but not in others.

2. Is the speaker trying to stop time (as the musician Jim Croce sang, "If I could save time in a bottle"), or is he hoping that his love will never change?

3. "Sweet unrest" (line 12) seems to be a contradiction. Is it? What is Keats trying to get at?

4. Is it psychologically healthy to want to have an unchanging love for someone forever? Is it realistic? Is it simply a kind of ritual to say such things?

5. Keats was quite sick at the end of his short life. Do you think awareness of his serious illness influenced the theme of his poem?

≡ MAKING COMPARISONS

1. Compare the images of change that both Shakespeare and Keats use.

2. Compare Shakespeare's and Keats's use of the star metaphor.

3. Do both poets have similar notions of true love?

ELIZABETH BARRETT BROWNING
How Do I Love Thee?

Elizabeth Barrett Browning (1806–1861) was a prominent Victorian poet whose work was well received in England and the United States. She was raised in a wealthy family and was a studious, precocious child who read widely in classic and contemporary literature. Her first collection of poems, An Essay on Mind, with Other Poems, *was published in 1826. Elizabeth battled illness her whole life and often depended on opium and morphine. She married the poet Robert Browning in 1846, and they moved to Italy for her health. They had a son nicknamed Pen. Two verse novels,* Aurora Leigh *(1856) and* Sonnets from the Portuguese *(1850), both still highly regarded works, made her famous. "How Do I Love Thee?" is the popular title of the forty-third of her* Sonnets from the Portuguese.

How do I love thee? Let me count the ways.
I love thee to the depth and breadth and height
My soul can reach, when feeling out of sight
For the ends of being and ideal grace.
I love thee to the level of every day's   5
Most quiet need, by sun and candle-light.
I love thee freely, as men strive for right.
I love thee purely, as they turn from praise.
I love thee with the passion put to use
In my old griefs, and with my childhood's faith.   10
I love thee with a love I seemed to lose
With my lost saints. I love thee with the breath,
Smiles, tears, of all my life; and, if God choose,
I shall but love thee better after death.   *[1845]*

≡ THINKING ABOUT THE TEXT

1. Explain the lines, ". . . when feeling out of sight / For the ends of being and ideal grace" (lines 3–4).

2. How would you translate ". . . to the level of every day's / Most quiet need, by sun and candle-light" (lines 5–6) into everyday prose?

3. How would you define these terms that Browning uses: "freely" (line 7), "purely" (line 8), and "childhood's faith" (line 10)?

4. How do you interpret Browning's idea that she loves with a love "I seemed to lose / With my lost saints" (lines 11–12)?

5. What other topics besides love are considered in Browning's sonnet?

≡ MAKING COMPARISONS

1. How would you describe the kind of love Browning writes about? Spiritual, physical, erotic, platonic, sentimental? Compare this love to that in Shakespeare and Keats.

2. Compare the theme of Browning's poem with Keats's and Shakespeare's themes.

3. How is death dealt with in these poems?

E. E. CUMMINGS
somewhere i have never travelled

E. E. Cummings is the pen name of Edward Estlin Cummings (1894–1962), and though he experimented with language on every level, he did not legally change his name to lowercase and preferred the usual uppercase. Born in Cambridge, Massachusetts, and educated at Harvard, he tried his hand at essays, plays, and other types of prose; in fact, it was a novel based on a World War I concentration camp experience in France, The Enormous Room *(1922) that first brought Cummings attention. It is his poetry, however, that most readers immediately recognize for its eccentric use of typography and punctuation, its wordplay and slang usage, its jazz rhythms, and its childlike foregrounding of the concrete above the abstract. Cummings hated pretension and would only agree to deliver the prestigious Eliot lectures at Harvard in 1953 if they were called* nonlectures. *His two large volumes of* The Complete Poems, 1913–1962, *published in 1972, include humor, understated satire, and celebrations of love and sex.*

somewhere i have never travelled, gladly beyond
any experience, your eyes have their silence:
in your most frail gesture are things which enclose me,
or which i cannot touch because they are too near
your slightest look easily will unclose me   5
though i have closed myself as fingers,
you open always petal by petal myself as Spring opens
(touching skilfully, mysteriously) her first rose
or if your wish be to close me, i and
my life will shut very beautifully, suddenly,   10

as when the heart of this flower imagines
the snow carefully everywhere descending;

nothing which we are to perceive in this world equals
the power of your intense fragility: whose texture
compels me with the colour of its countries,   15
rendering death and forever with each breathing

(i do not know what it is about you that closes
and opens; only something in me understands
the voice of your eyes is deeper than all roses)
nobody, not even the rain, has such small hands   *[1931]*   20

≡ THINKING ABOUT THE TEXT

1. In your own words, what is Cummings saying about the effect love has on him? Is this hyperbolic? Why?

2. Does love open us up? In what ways? Can you give a personal example of what a strong feeling did to you?

3. Is this a poem about love, obsession, or romantic infatuation? What is the difference?

4. What do you think "the power of your intense fragility" (line 14) might mean? Is this a contradiction?

5. When Cummings says "something in me understands" (line 18), what might he mean? Is love located inside us somewhere? In our hearts? Our brains?

≡ MAKING COMPARISONS

1. Is Cummings's flower imagery more effective than the images that Shakespeare and Keats use?

2. Is this poem closer in theme to Keats's poem or to Browning's?

3. What do you imagine Shakespeare and Keats would think about Cummings's sentence structure? His images?

≡ WRITING ABOUT ISSUES

1. Translate the Cummings poem into concrete prose. Try not to use images; just explain the individual lines as simply as you can.

2. Write a comparison of the effects these four poems had on you.

3. Write a position paper arguing for or against the reality of true love. Make reference to two of the poems given here.

4. Find three more love poems by William Shakespeare or John Keats and write a report about the issues of love that this poet raises.

EDNA ST. VINCENT MILLAY, "What Lips My Lips Have Kissed, and
   Where, and Why"

ROBIN BECKER, "Morning Poem"

It is not uncommon, of course, for a romantic relationship to evolve from
intense physical attraction or erotic love in the beginning to sadness or melancholy at the end. Naturally, poets have written about all stages of love in all
their complexity, from joy and wonder to resignation and despair. Few of us
would prefer to suffer than to exult in love, but perhaps Tennyson's lines "'Tis
better to have loved and lost than never to have loved at all" capture the pragmatic attitude that understands that love is a risk worth taking. Although at
different times in history melancholy was embraced as an appropriate attitude
toward the vagaries of love, most of us probably hope to recover, not wallow
in the sorrow of a failed romance. In our selections, Edna St. Vincent Millay,
offers us a memorable variation on love lost, whereas Robin Becker's narrator
tries to deal with the implications of "while nothing lasts" even in the midst of
a passionate affair.

≡ **BEFORE YOU READ**

How might communicating grief help people cope? Is there a difference
between writing a poem, which could be private or public, and joining a
community of mourners in a support group in person or online? In what
other ways do people grieve? How do you prefer to mourn?

EDNA ST. VINCENT MILLAY
What Lips My Lips Have Kissed,
and Where, and Why

*Edna St. Vincent Millay (1892–1950) was born in Rockland, Maine. Her mother
encouraged her to be ambitious and self-sufficient and taught her about literature at
an early age. On the strength of her early poems, Millay won a scholarship to Vassar,
where she became a romantic legend for breaking the "hearts of half the undergraduate class." She also soon became wildly famous for her love poetry, giving readings
in large auditoriums across the country, much like a contemporary rock star. She
was openly bisexual, and her fame, talent, beauty, and bohemian aura were said to
have driven her many admirers to distraction. A biography by Nancy Milford, Savage Beauty (2001), quotes from dozens of letters to Millay, whining, pleading, and*

groveling for her favors. Milford writes that "she gave the Jazz Age its lyric voice." In fact, we still use a phrase that Salon.com says Millay "invented to describe a life of impudent abandon":

> *My candle burns at both ends;*
> *It will not last the night;*
> *But oh, my foes, and oh, my friends —*
> *It gives a lovely light!*

Once called "the greatest female poet since Sappho," Millay's reputation in academic circles has fallen off somewhat. Perhaps her work seems a bit obvious compared to the cerebral and allusive free verse of poets like T. S. Eliot. But some critics still think of her as America's "most illustrious love poet." The title poem of Renascence and Other Poems *(1917) ranks as a landmark of modern literature, and the collection itself is ranked fifth on the New York Public Library's Books of the Century. The following poem is from* Collected Poems *(1956).*

What lips my lips have kissed, and where, and why,
I have forgotten, and what arms have lain
Under my head till morning; but the rain
Is full of ghosts tonight, that tap and sigh
Upon the glass and listen for reply,   5
And in my heart there stirs a quiet pain
For unremembered lads that not again
Will turn to me at midnight with a cry.
Thus in winter stands the lonely tree,
Nor knows what birds have vanished one by one,   10
Yet knows its boughs more silent than before:
I cannot say what loves have come and gone,
I only know that summer sang in me
A little while, that in me sings no more.   [1923]

≡ THINKING ABOUT THE TEXT

1. What is it the speaker misses if she can't remember who her lovers were?

2. What does Millay mean by "a quiet pain" (line 6)?

3. Is Millay the "lonely tree" in winter (line 9)? Does it surprise you that she was only thirty-one when she wrote this poem?

4. Do you read the last two lines as saying that the speaker is no longer in love?

5. How would you describe the tone of this poem? Is it wistful or nostalgic? Appropriate? Regretful or sentimental? Bittersweet or simply sad?

ROBIN BECKER
Morning Poem

Robin Becker (b. 1951) was born in Philadelphia, Pennsylvania, and received her B.A. (1973) and M.A. (1976) from Boston University. She taught for many years at the Massachusetts Institute of Technology. She has been teaching at Penn State since 1994. She has published eight books of poetry, including Domain of Perfect Affection *(2006), a collection informed by feminist and lesbian sympathies. She was appointed Penn State Laureate in 2010. The noted poet Maxine Kumin says Becker's poetry has a "controlled ironic intelligence." Her latest collection,* The Black Bear Inside Me, *was published in 2018.*

Listen. It's morning. Soon I'll see your hand reach
for my watch, the water will agitate in the kettle,
but listen. Traffic. I want your dreams first. And
to slide my leg beneath yours before the day opens.
Wait. We slept late. You'll be moody, the phone   5
will ring, someone wanting something. Let me put
my hands in your hair. Who I was last night I would
be again. This is how the future holds me, how depression
wakes with us; my body shelters it. Let me
put my head on your breast. I know nothing lasts.   10
I would try to hold you back, not out of meanness
but fear. Oh my practical, my worldly-wise. You
know how the body falters, falls in on itself. Tell me
that we will never want from each other what we
cannot have. Lie. It's morning.   *[2008]*   15

≡ THINKING ABOUT THE TEXT

1. Why does the speaker say that "depression wakes with us" (lines 8–9)?

2. What does the narrator mean by "I would try to hold you back" (line 11)?

3. How do the following words or phrases suggest the narrator's mood: "watch," "agitate," "Traffic," "slept late," "moody," "the phone will ring" (lines 2–6)?

4. How might "lie" in the last line be ambiguous? How is the meaning of the phrase "It's morning" in the last line different from the opening line?

5. What do you think the narrator means when she says "who I was last night I would / be again" (lines 7–8)?

≡ **MAKING COMPARISONS**

1. Compare the line "I know nothing lasts" (line 10) in "Morning Poem" with the last two lines of Millay's poem.

2. Compare the attitudes of the two narrators toward loss.

≡ **WRITING ABOUT ISSUES**

1. Write a brief essay that argues that Millay has or does not have a healthier attitude toward love affairs than Becker.

2. Argue that the attitude of one of these poets toward love affairs is closer to that of today's college students than the others. Refer to specific lines or ideas in both poems.

3. Read John Keats's classic poem "Ode on Melancholy," and write an essay that compares Keats's views on melancholic love with the Millay and Becker poems.

KAREN RUSSELL, "Bog Girl"

AIMEE BENDER, "The Devourings"

It is a truism about science fiction stories that they are more about the present than the future. After all, writers are always situated in a specific historical moment, one that influences their thinking in innumerable ways from beliefs about gender, truth, and religion to internalized ideas about democracy, marriage, family and the very nature of reality. The same could be said about fairy tales and parables. As children we read "Cinderella" and "Little Red Riding Hood" probably without realizing that these century-old tales are about the boundaries between social classes and a young girl's anxieties about the dangers of her sexual identity. But even though many of the fairy tales we remember were probably written long ago and far way — "Little Red Riding Hood," for example, was written in 1697 — the genre is still going strong. The two stories presented here a good examples of contemporary fairy tales or parables (allegories and fables are also appropriate).

"Bog Girl" can be read as a tale of adolescent desire or loneliness, but can also be about an impossible love affair or even about the impossibility of ever truly knowing another person. Of course, it also is a tale about the deep past and our ignorance of it. That's the way good fables work. They exist on many levels simultaneously. "The Devourings" is another example of a seemingly impossible relationship, this time between an ogre and a human. The mysteries of love are certainly one of this story's themes, but also how one woman endures tragedy and grief and how her strength and endurance allow her to gain a measure of peace and love.

≡ **BEFORE YOU READ**

What do you remember about your childhood response to "Cinderella," "Sleeping Beauty," and "Snow White and the Seven Dwarfs"? What do you think these tales have to do with class distinctions and gender roles? How are these themes still popular in films?

KAREN RUSSELL

Bog Girl

Karen Russell (b. 1981) was born in Miami and received her M.F.A. from Columbia University. She was named one of the "best young American novelists" in 2007, before she had even published a novel. The recognition was given on the strength of her critically acclaimed collection of stories, St. Lucy's Home for Girls Raised by Wolves *(2006). Her stories have recently appeared in*

Conjunctions, Granta, *and* Zoetrope. The New Yorker *debut fiction issue also featured her work. Her novel* Swamplandia *(2011) concerns alligator wrestlers. A collection of short stories,* Vampires in the Lemon Grove, *was published in 2013, and she also received a MacArthur foundation "Genius Grant" in 2013. Her latest book is* Sleep Donation: A Novella *(2014). The following story was published in* The New Yorker *in June 2016.*

The young turf-cutter fell hard for his first girlfriend while operating heavy machinery in the peatlands. His name was Cillian Eddowis, he was fifteen years old, and he was illegally employed by Bos Ardee. He had celery-green eyes and a stutter that had been corrected at the state's expense; it resurfaced whenever he got nervous. "Th-th-th," he'd said, accepting the job. How did Cillian persuade Bos Ardee to hire him? The boy had lyingly laid claim to many qualities: strength, maturity, experience. When that didn't work, he pointed to his bedroom window, a quarter mile away, on the misty periphery of the cutaway bog, where the undrained water still sparkled between the larch trees. The intimation was clear: what the thin, strange boy lacked in muscle power he made up for in proximity to the work site.

Peat is harvested from bogs, watery mires where the earth yawns open. The bottom is a breathless place — cold, acidic, anaerobic — with no oxygen to decompose the willow branches or the small, still faces of the foxes interred there. Sphagnum mosses wrap around fur, wood, skin, casting their spell of chemical protection, preserving them whole. Growth is impossible, and Death cannot complete her lean work. Once cut, the peat becomes turf, and many locals on this green island off the coast of northern Europe still heat their homes with this peculiar energy source. Nobody gives much thought to the fuels, mortuary origins. Cillian, his mother, and several thousand others lived on the island, part of the archipelago known to older generations as the Four Horsemen. It's unlikely that you've ever visited. It's not really on the circuit.

Neolithic farmers were the first to clear the island's woods. Two thousand years later, peat had swallowed the remains of their pastures. Bogs blanketed the hills. In the Iron Age, these bogs were portals to distant worlds, wilder realms. Gods travelled the bogs. Gods wore crowns of starry asphodels, floating above the purple heather.

Now industrial harvesters rode over the drained bogs, combing the earth into even geometries. On the summer morning that Cillian found the Bog Girl, he was driving the Peatmax toward a copse of trees at the bog's western edge, pushing the dried peat into black ridges. True, it looked as if he was pleating shit, but Cill had a higher purpose. He was saving to buy his neighbor Pogo's white hatchback. Once he had a car, it would be no great challenge to sleep with a girl or a woman. Cillian was open to either experience. Or both. But he was far too shy to have an eye-level crush on anyone in his grade. Not Deedee, not Stacia, not Vicki, not Yvonne. He had a crush, taboo and distressing, on his Aunt Cathy's ankles in socks. He had a crush on the anonymous shoulders of a shampoo model.

He had just driven into the western cutaway bog when he looked over the side of the Peatmax and screamed. A hand was sticking out of the mud.

5

Cillian's first word to the Bog Girl required all the air in his lungs: "Ahhhhhh-fuuuuuck!"

Here was a secret, flagging him down. A secret the world had kept for two thousand years and been unable to keep for two seconds longer. The bog had confessed her.

When the other men arrived, Cillian was on his knees, scratching up peat like a dog. Already he had dug out her head. She was whole and intact, cocooned in peat, curled like a sleeping child, with her head turned west of her pelvis. Thick, lustrous hair fanned over the tarp, the wild red-orange of an orangutans fur, dyed by the bog acids. Moving clouds caused her colors to change continuously: now they were a tawny bronze, now a mineral blue. It was a very young face.

Cradling her head, Cillian lost all feeling in his legs. A light rain began to fall, but he would not relinquish his position. Every man gathered was staring at them. Ordinarily, their pronged attention encircled him like a crown of thorns, making him self-conscious, causing red fear to leak into his inner vision. Today, he didn't give a damn about the judgments of the mouth-breathers above him. Who had ever seen a face so beautiful, so perfectly serene?

"Mother of God!" one of the men screamed. He pointed to the noose. A rope, nearly black with peat, ran down the length of her back.

Murder. That was the men's consensus. Bos Ardee called the police.   10

But Cillian barely heard the talk above him. If you saw the Bog Girl from one angle only, you would assume that she was a cherished daughter, laid to rest by hands that loved her. But she had been killed, and now her smile seemed even more impressive to him, and he wanted only to protect her from future harm. The men kept calling her "the body," which baffled Cillian — the word seemed to blind them to the deep and flowing dream-life behind her smile. "There is so much more to you than what they see," he reassured her in a whisper. "I am so sorry about what happened to you. I am going to keep you safe now."

After this secret conversation, Cill fell rapidly in love.

Cillian was lucky that he met his girlfriend on such a remote island. When these bodies are discovered in Ireland, for example, or in the humid Florida bogs sprinkled between Disney World and Cape Canaveral, things proceed differently. The area is cordoned off. Teams of experts arrive to excavate the site. Then the bog people are carefully removed to laboratories, museums, where gloveless hands never touch them.

Cillian touched her hair, touched the rope. He was holding the reins of her life. Three policemen had arrived, and they conferred above Cillian, their black boots squeezing mud around the bog cotton. Once it had been determined that the girl was not a recent murder victim, the policemen relaxed. The chief asked Cillian a single question: "You're going to keep her, then?"

Gillian Eddowis was on a party line with her three sisters. She tucked the phone   15
under her chin and took the ruby kettle off the range, opening a window to
shoo the blue steam free. In the living room, roars of studio laughter erupted

from the television; Cillian and the Bog Girl were watching a sitcom about a Canadian trailer park. Their long silences unnerved her; surely they weren't getting into trouble, ten feet away from her? She had never had cause to discipline her son. She wouldn't know where to begin. He was so kind, so intelligent, so unusual, so sensitive — such an outlier in the Eddowis family that his aunts had paid him the modern compliment of assuming that he was gay.

Voices sieved into Gillian's left ear:

"You want to warn them," Sister Abby said.

"But, Virgin Mother, there is no way to warn them!" Sister Patty finished.

"We were all sixteen once," Cathy growled. "We all survived it."

"Cillian is *fifteen*," Gillian corrected. "And the girlfriend is two thousand."   20

Abby, who had seen a picture of the Bog Girl in the local newspaper, suggested that *somebody* was rounding down.

A university man had also read the story of the Bog Girl's discovery. He'd taken a train and a ferry to find them. "I've come to make an Urgent Solicitation on Behalf of History," he said. He wanted to acquire the Bog Girl for the national museum. The sum he offered them was half of Gillian's salary at the post office.

In the end, what had happened? Christian feeling had muzzled her. How could she sell a girl to a stranger? Or pretend that she had any claim to her, this orphan from the Iron Age? Gillian told the university man that the Bog Girl was their house guest, and would be living with them until Social Services could locate her next of kin. At this, all the purple veins in the man's neck stood out. His tone sank into petulant defeat. "Mark my words, you people do not have the knowledge to properly care for her," he said. "She'll fall apart on you." The Bog Girl, propped up next to the ironing board, watched them argue with an implacable smile. The university man left empty-handed, and for a night and a day Gillian was a hero to her son.

"So she's just freeloading, then? Living off your dime?" Cathy asked.

"Oh, yes. She's quite shameless about it."   25

How could she explain to her sisters what she could barely admit to herself? The boy was in love. It was a monstrous, misdirected love; nevertheless, it commanded her respect.

"The Bog Girl is a bad influence on him," she told her sisters. "She doesn't work, she doesn't help. All day she lazes about the house."

Patty coughed and said, "If you feel that way, then why — "

Cathy screamed, "Gillian! She cannot *stay* with you!"

It was gentle Abby who formulated the solution: "Put her back in the bog."   30

"Gillian. *Do it tonight.*"

"Who's going to miss her?"

"I can't put her back in the bog. It would be . . ."

Silence drilled into her ears. Her family had a talent for emitting judgment without articulating words. When she was Cillian's age and five months pregnant with him, everyone had quietly made clear that she was sacrificing her future. She'd run away to be with Cillian's father, then returned to the boglands alone with a bug-eyed toddler.

"I'm afraid," she confessed to her sisters. "If I put her out of the house,   35
he'll leave with her."

"Oh!" they cried in unison. As if a needle had infected them all with her
fear.

"Do something crazy, stupid . . ."

Silently adding, *Like we did.*

"Now, be honest, you little rat turd. You know *nothing* about her." His uncle
put a finger into his peach iced tea, stirred. They were seated on a swing in the
darkest part of Cillian's porch. Uncle Sean was as blandly ugly as a big toenail.
Egg-bald and cheerfully unemployed, a third-helpings kind of guy. Once, Cillian
had watched him eat the sticker on a green apple rather than peel it off. Sean
was always over at the cottage, using Gillian's computer to play Poker 3000. He
smeared himself throughout their house, his beer rings ghosting over surfaces
like fat thumbs on a photograph. His words hung around, too, leaving their
brain stain on the air. Uncle Sean took a proprietary interest in anything loved
by Cillian. It was no surprise, then, that he was infatuated with the Bog Girl.

"I know that I love her," Cill said warily. He hated to be baited.   40

Uncle Sean was packing his brown, shakey weed into the rosy crotch of a
glass mermaid. He passed his nephew the pipe. "Already, eh? You love her and
you don't know the first thing about her?"

What did he know about her?

What did he love about her?

Cillian shrugged, his body crowding with feelings. "And I know that she
loves me," he added, somewhat hastily.

Uncle Sean's pink smirk seemed to paste him to the back of the wicker   45
seat. "Oh?" His grin widened. "And how old is she?"

"Two thousand. But she was my age when they put her in the bog."

"Most women *I* know lie freely about their age," Uncle Sean warned. "She
may well be eleven. Then again, she could be *three* thousand."

Gillian, plump and starlit, appeared on the porch. A pleasant oniony smell
followed her, mixing with the damp odor of Sean's pot.

"Are you smoking?"

"No," they lied in unison.   50

"Tell your . . . your *friend* that she is welcome to eat with us." With a mar-
tyred air, Gillian lifted her kitten-print pot holders to the heavens. Cill smiled;
the pot holders made it look as if she approved of the situation—two big
thumbs-up! His poor mom. She was so nervous around new people, and the
Bog Girl's silence only intimidated her further. She was insecure about her
cooking, and he knew she was going to take it very personally when the Bog
Girl did not touch it.

Dinner was meat loaf with onions and, for Sean, a thousand beers. It was
not a comfortable meal.

Gillian, stirring butter into the lima beans, beamed threats at her son's
new girlfriend: You little bitch. Crawl back into your hole. Stay away from
my son.

"Biscuit?" Gillian asked. "Does she like biscuits, Cill?"

The Bog Girl smiled her gentle smile at the wall, her face reflected in the   55
oval door of the washer-dryer. Against that sudsy turbulence, she looked especially still.

Three drinks in, Uncle Sean slung an arm around the Bog Girl's thin blue
shoulder, welcoming her into the family. "I'm proud of my nephew for going
after an older woman, a *mature* woman . . . a cougar!"

Cillian fixed his uncle with a homicidal stare. Under the table, he touched
his girlfriend's foot with his foot; his eyebrows lifted in apology. His mother
shot up with her steaming cauldron of beans, giving everyone another punitive lima ladle and removing the beer from the table. Their dog, returning from
her dusk mouse hunt, came berserking into the kitchen, barking at a deranged
pitch. She wanted to play tug-of-war with the Bog Girl's noose. "Puddles — *no!* "
Cillian's vision was swimming, his whole body overheating with shame. He
relaxed when he stared into the Bog Girl's face, which was void of all judgment,
smiling at him with its mysterious kindness. Once again, his embarrassment
was soothed by her infinite calm. His eyes lowered from her smile to the noose.
Of course, she's seen far worse than us, he thought. Outside the window, insects
millioned around the porch light. The bog crickets were doing a raspy ventril-
oquy of the stars; perhaps she recognized their tiny voices. Soon Uncle Sean
was snoring lightly beside the pooling gravy, face down in his big arms. Cill sat
slablike in the moonlight. The Bog Girl smiled blindly on.

For the first two weeks, the Bog Girl slept on the sofa, the television light flick-
ering gently over her. That was fine by Gillian. She wasn't about to turn an
orphan from the Iron Age out on the street.

Then, on a rainy Monday night, without warning or apology, Cillian
picked up the Bog Girl. He cradled her like a child, her frondy feet dangling in
the air. Gillian, doing a jigsaw puzzle of a horse and colt in the kitchen, looked
up in time to see them disappearing. She felt a purple welt rising in her mind,
the revelatory pain called wonder. Underneath the shock, other feelings began
to flow, among them a disturbed pride. Because hadn't he looked *exactly* like
his father? Confident, possessed. He didn't ask for her permission. He did not
lie to her about what he was doing, or hide it, or explain it. He simply rose with
the Bog Girl in his arms, nuzzling her blue neck. The door shut, and he was
gone from sight. Another milestone: she heard the click of the lock.

"Good night, son!" she cried after them, panicked.   60

She could not reconcile her knowledge of her sweet, awkward boy with
this wayward, confident person. Was she supposed to go up there now? Pound
on the door? Oh, who could she call? Nobody, not even her sisters, would take
a call about *this* problem, she felt quite certain. Abby's son, Kevin, met his
girlfriend in church. Cathy's son, Patrick, has a lovely fiancée who teaches
kindergarten. Murry's girlfriend is in jail for vehicular manslaughter — but at
least she's alive!

In the morning, she watched the mute, hitching muscles of his back as
he fumbled with the coffeepot. So he was a coffee drinker now. More news. He

kissed his mother's forehead as he left for work, but he was whistling to himself, oblivious of her sadness, her fear, completely self-enclosed in his new happiness. It's too soon for this, she thought. And: Not you, too. *Please, please, please,* she prayed, the incomplete prayer of mothers who cannot conceive of a solution.

That evening, she announced a new rule: "Everyone has to wear clothes. And no more locked doors."

That Saturday, Cillian took the ferry three hours to a mainland museum. Twelve bog bodies were on display, part of a travelling exhibition called "Kings of the Iron Age." The Bog Girl had met his family — the least he could do was return the favor. Cill sneaked into a tour in progress, following a docent from sepulchre to sepulchre. Under the glass, the Kings of the Iron Age lay like chewed taffy. One man was naked except for a fox-fur armband. Another was a giant. Another had two sets of thumbs.

Cillian learned that the bogs of the islands in the cold Atlantic were   65
particularly acidic. Pickled bodies from the Iron Age had emerged from these deep vats. Their fetally scrolled bodies often doubled as the crumpled maps of murders. They might have been human sacrifices, the docent said. Left in the bog water for the harvest god. Kings, queens, scapegoats, victims — they might have been any of these things.

"From the contents of his stomach, we can surmise that he last dined on oat gruel. . . ."

"From the forensic analyses, we can surmise that she was killed by an arrow. . . ."

"From the ornaments on this belt buckle, we can surmise that these were a wealthy people. . . ."

What? No more than this could be surmised?

The docent pointed out the dots and stripes on the potsherds. Charcoal   70
smudges that might be stars or animals. Evidence, she said, of "a robust culture." Cillian took notes:

"THEY HAD TIME TO KILL, THEY LIKED ART, TOO."

Back on the ferry, he could admit to his relief: none of the other bog bodies stirred any feeling in him. He loved one specific person. He could see things about the Bog Girl to which this batty docent would be totally blind — for example, the secret depths her smile concealed. How badly misunderstood she had been by her own people. She was an alien from a planet that nobody alive could visit — the planet Earth, in the first century A.D. She felt soft in his arms, bonelessly soft, but she also seemed indestructible. According to the experts, a bog body should begin to decompose rapidly when exposed to air. Curiously enough, this Bog Girl had not. He told no one his theory but polished it inside his mind like an amulet: it was his love that was protecting her.

By August, their rapport had deepened immeasurably. They didn't need to say a word, Cill was discovering, to perfectly understand each other. Falling in love with the Bog Girl was a wonderful thing — it was permission to ignore everyone else. When school started, in September, he made a bespoke sling and brought her with him. His girlfriend, propped like a broomstick against the rows of lockers, waited for him during Biology and Music II, as cool and impassive as the most popular girl the world has ever known.

Nobody in the school administration objected to the presence of the Bog Girl. Ancestral superstitions still hovered over the islanders' minds, exerting their quiet influence, and nobody wanted to be the person responsible for angering a visitor from the past. Soon she was permitted to audit all of Cillian's classes, smiling dreamlessly at the flustered, frightened teachers.

One afternoon, the vice-principal called her into his office and presented her with a red-and-gold badge to wear in the halls: "VISITING STUDENT."

"I don't think that's really accurate, sir," Cillian said.

"Oh, no?"

"She's not a visitor. She was born here." In fact, the Bog Girl was the island's oldest resident, by at least nineteen hundred years. Cillian paused. "Also, her eyes are shut, you see. So I don't think she can really, ah, study. . . ."

"Well!" The vice-principal clapped his hands. He had a day to live, quotas to fulfill. "We will be studying *her*, then. She will give us all an exciting new perspective on our modern life and times — Oh my! Oh dear." The Bog Girl had slumped into his aloe planter.

Cillian put the badge on her polyester blouse, a loaner from his mother that was vintage cool. Cillian — who never gave a thought to his own clothing — enjoyed dressing the Bog Girl for school in the morning. He raided his mother's closet, resurrecting her baby-doll dresses. The eleventh-grade girls organized a clothing drive for the Bog Girl, collecting many shoplifted donations of fall tunics and on-trend boots.

Rumorsprawl. Word got around that the Bog Girl was actually a princess. A princess, or possibly a witch. Within a week, she was eating at the popular girls' table. They'd kidnapped her from where Cillian had positioned her on a bench, propped between two book bags, and taken her to lunch. Already they had restyled her hair with rhinestone barrettes.

"You stole my girlfriend," Cillian said.

"Something *awful* happened to her," Vicki said reverently.

"So bad," Georgette echoed.

"She doesn't like to talk about it," Priscilla said, looping a protective arm around the Bog Girl. The girls had matching lunches: lettuce salads, diet candy bars, diet shakes. They were all jealous of how little she ate.

How had Cill not foreseen this turn of events? The Bog Girl was diminutive, wounded, mysterious, a redhead. Best of all, she could never contradict any rumor the living girls distributed about her.

"She was too beautiful to live!" Priscilla gasped. "They killed her for her beauty."

"I don't th-th-think," Cill said, "that it happened quite like that."

The popular girls adjusted their leggings, annoyed. "No?"

Cillian was dimly aware that other tables were listening in, but the density of the attention in no way affected him. "I am hers, and she is mine," he announced. "I have dedicated myself to learning everything about her."

A sighing spasm of envy moved down the popular girls' table—what boy alive would say this about them? A miracle: nobody mocked Cillian Eddowis. They were all starving to be loved like this. The popular girls watched him avidly as he ate a grilled cheese and waffle fries, his green irises burning. Between bites, his left hand rose to touch the Bog Girl's red braid, tousling it like the pull-chain of a lamp.

Gillian couldn't help it: she was heartbroken. The past that was most precious to her had filtered right through her son. The songs she'd sung to him when he was nursing? The care with which she'd cut the tiny moons of his finger-nails? Their 4 A.M. feedings? Erased! Her son had matured into amnesia about his earliest years. Now her body was the only place where the memories were preserved. Cillian, like all sons, was blithe about this betrayal.

"There is so much about yourself that you do not recall," Gillian accused him after dinner one night. Cillian, writing a paper about igneous rocks at the kitchen table, did not look up.

"When you were my boy, just a wee boy," Gillian said in a voice of true agony, "you used to be terrified of the vacuum cleaner. You loved your froggy pajamas. You used so much glue on your art projects that your teachers—"

"Quit it with these dumb stories, Ma!"   95

"Oh, you find them dumb, do you? The stories about how I had to raise you alone, without a penny from your father—"

"You're just trying to *embarrass* me in front of her!"

The Bog Girl smiled at them from the amber armchair. Her leather skirt was outrageously short, a donation from tall Bianca. Decorously, Cillian had draped the cable guide over her lap. Bugs spun in her water glass; mosquitoes and dragonflies were always diving into the Bog Girl's food and drink, as if in strange solidarity with her.

Cillian drew himself up triumphantly, a foot taller than his mother. "You don't want me to grow up."

"What? Of course I do!"   100

But Cill was ready with his rebuttal: "You gave us rhyming names, Ma!"

This was true. Gillian and Cillian. She'd come up with that plan when she was a teenager herself, and pregnant with a nameless otter, some gyring little animal. A rhyming name had seemed just right then; she couldn't have said why, at seventeen. Had Cillian been a girl, she would have named her Lillian.

"You're so young, you can't know . . ." But what did she want to tell him?

Her body seemed to cave in on itself then, becoming smaller and smaller, so that even Cillian, fortressed behind the wall of his love, noticed and became alarmed. "Ma? What's wrong?"

"It's changing all the time," she murmured ominously. "Just, please, wait,   105
my love. Don't . . . *settle."* What a word! She pictured her son sinking up to his neck in the reddish bog water.

She was hiccupping now, unable to name her own feelings. Without thinking, she picked up the murky water glass, drank from it. "Your poten-tial . . . all the teachers tell me you have great potential."

Just come out and say it. "I don't want you to throw your *life* away on some Bog Girl!"

"Oh, Ma." Cill patted her back until the hiccups stopped. Her face looked crumpled and blue in the unlit room, hovering above the seated Bog Girl. For a second, they might have been sisters.

The Bog Girl floated, thin as a dress, on the mattress. Barrettes, pink and purple, were scattered all over the pillow. She smiled at Cillian, or beyond him, with her desiccated calm. Downstairs, Gillian was making breakfast, the buttery smells threading through his nostrils like an ox ring, tugging him toward them. But when she called up for him he was barely in the room. He was digging and digging into the peatmoss bog again, smoothing her blue cheeks with both hands, spading down into the kingdom that she comes from.

"Cillian! The bus is coming!" It should have taken him twenty seconds to   110
put on pants. What was he doing in there? Probably jacking off to a "meme," whatever that was, or buying perfume for the Bog Girl on her credit cards.

"Coming, Ma!"

Cillian was always learning new things about his girlfriend. The longer he looked at her, the more he saw. Her face grew silty with personality. Although she was young when she disappeared into the bog, her face was plowed with tiny wrinklings. Some dream or mood had recurred frequently enough to hammer lines across her brow. Here were the ridges and the gullies her mental weathers had worked into her skin.

Cill studied the infloresences on her cheeks. Her brain is in there, the university man had said. Her brain is intact, preserved by the bog acids. Cillian spent hours doing this forensic palmistry, trying to read her mind.

"Will you have a talk with him?" Gillian begged Sean. "Something is going really, really wrong with him!"

"First love, first love," Sean murmured sadly, scratching his bubonic nose.   115
"Who are we to intervene, eh? It will die of natural causes."

"Natural causes!"

She was thinking that the poor girl had been garroted. Her bright-red hair racing the tail of the noose down her spine. You could not survive your death, could you? It survived with you.

In mid-October, a stretch limousine pulled up to the cottage to take Cillian and the Bog Girl to the annual school dance. A techno-reggae song called "Bump de Ass!" filled the back seat, where half a dozen teen-agers sat in churchlike silence. The Bog Girl's reticence was contagious. Ambulance lights sparkled through the tinted windows, causing everyone to jump, with one exception: Cillian Eddowis's date, the glamorous foreigner, or native—nobody was sure how to regard her.

Since acquiring his far older girlfriend, Cill had begun speaking to his classmates in the voice of a bachelor who merely tolerates children. "Carla," he said, clearing his throat. "Would you mind exhaling a little closer to the window? Your smoke is blowing on us."

Two girls started debating whether or not a friend should lose her virginity   120
in a BMW that evening. What was the interior of the car like? This was a very
important question. The girl's boyfriend was a twenty-six-year-old cocaine
dealer. Prior to the Bog Girl's arrival on the scene, everyone had found his
age very impressive. The dealer boyfriend had been unable to accompany the
girl to the school dance, so she had taken poor Eoin, her sophomore cousin,
who looked near fatally compressed by his green cummerbund. The twenty-
six-year-old would be waiting for her in the BMW, post-festivities. Should she
deflower him?

"Wait. Uh. I think he's deflowering you, right? Or maybe you're deflowering each other? Who's got the flower?"

"Just do it, and then lie about it." Carla shrugged. "That's what I did."

"My advice," Cillian said, in the unfamiliar voice, "my advice is, wait. Wait
until you find the person with whom you want to spend all your earthly time."
The Bog Girl leaned against his shoulder, aloof in her sparkly tiara. "Or until
that person finds you. If that's this guy, well, kudos. But, if not, wait. You will
meet your soul mate. And you will want to give that person every molecule of
your life."

The attempted conversion of the high-school gymnasium into an
Arabian-themed wonderland had not been a success. Cill and the Bog Girl
stood under a palm tree that looked like an enormous toilet brush, made of
cellophane and cardboard tubes. Three girls from the limo came up and asked
to dance with Cillian, but he explained that his girlfriend hated to be left alone.
All were sulkily respectful of her claim on him.

The after-party was held in an old car-parts warehouse on the west side   125
of the island, where everything was shut or abandoned; the population of the
island had been declining steadily for three decades. The music sounded like
fists beating at the wall, and the floor was so sticky that Cillian had to lift and
cradle the Bog Girl, looping her silver dress around one arm. Cillian had never
attended an after-party before. Or a party, for that matter. He surveyed his former tormenters, the seniors, with their piggish faces and their plastic cups.
Some were single, some had girlfriends, some were virgins, some were not, but
not one of them, Cillian felt very certain, knew the first thing about love.

Eoin the sophomore came over, his date nowhere to be seen. He was
breathless in the cummerbund, in visible danger of puking up Bacardi. He
rolled a bloodshot eye in Cill's direction, smiling wistfully.

"So," he said, "I'm just wondering. Do you guys—"

Cillian preëmpted the question: "A gentleman never tells."

It was a phrase he'd once read in a men's magazine, while waiting to get a
root canal. In fact, his mother needn't have lost so much sleep to this particular fear. At night, Cillian lay beside the Bog Girl, barely touching her. A steady,
happy calm radiated from her, which filled him with a parallel euphoria.

Cillian carried the Bog Girl onto the dance floor, her braided noose flung   130
over his shoulder. And even Eoin, minutes from unconsciousness, could
hear exactly who the older boy believed himself to be in this story: Cillian
the Rescuer.

"Oh, damn! Wise up! She'll make you wait forever, man!" The lonely laugh of Eoin died a terrible death, like a bird impaled on a spike.

At 3 A.M., the lights were still on. Uh-oh, Cill thought. Mom got into the gin again.

Drinking made her silences bubble volubly. He almost got the hiccups himself, listening to her silences. Oh, God. There was so much pain inside her, so much she wanted to share with him. Cillian and the Bog Girl tried to tiptoe past her to the staircase, but she sprang up like a jack-in-the-box.

"Cillian?" She looked child-small in the dark. Her voice was tremulous and young, and her slurring reminded him of his own stutter, that undead vestige of his early years. His mother sounded like a sleepy girl, four or five years old. Her feet were bare, and she rose onto her stubby toes to grip his arm. "Where are you coming from?"

"Nowhere. The dance. It was fun."   135

"Where are you going?"

"Aw, Mom. Where do you th-th-think?"

"Good night!" she called after him desperately. "I hope you had a good time! You looked so handsome! So grown up!"

By early winter, the Bog Girl's stillness had begun to provoke a restlessness in Cillian, a squeezed and throbbing feeling. He was failing three subjects. His mother had threatened to send him to live with Aunt Cathy until he "straightened out." He didn't care. Waiting for the bus in the freezing rain, he no longer dreamed about owning a car. He knew what he would do with the summer money he'd earned from Bos Ardee: run away with her.

He'd flunk out of school and take the Bog Girl with him to the mainland.   140
She'd be homesick at first, maybe, but they'd go on trips to urban parks. It was the burr of peace, the burr of happiness, goading him on to new movement. Oh, he was frightened, too.

In his fantasy life, Cillian drew the noose tighter and tighter. He imagined, with a strange joy, the narrow life they would lead. No children, no sex, no messy nights vomiting outside bars, no unintended pregnancies, no fights in the street, no betrayals, no surprises, no broken promises, no promises.

Was the Bog Girl a co-signer to this fantasy? Cillian had every reason to believe so. When he described his plans to her, the smile never left her face. Was their love one-sided, as the concerned and unimaginative adults in his life kept insisting? No — but the proof of this surprised no one more terribly than Cillian.

One night in mid-December, lying in bed, he felt a cobwebby softness on his left cheek. It was her eyelashes, flicking over him. They glowed radish-red in the moonlight. Cillian swatted at his face, his own eyes never opening. Still sunk in his dreaming, he grunted and rolled over.

Cillian.

Cillian.   145

The Bog Girl sat up.

With fluttering effort, the muscles of her blue jaw yawned. One eye opened. It studied itself in the dresser mirror for a long instant, then turned calmly back toward Cillian. Very slowly, her left arm unhinged itself and dropped to the plaid bedspread. The fingers curled around the blanket's edge, and drew it down. A blush of primal satisfaction colored the Bog Girl's cheeks as the fabric moved. She tugged more forcefully, revealing Cillian curled on his side in his white undershirt. Groaning in his sleep, he jerked the covers back up.

"Cillian," she said aloud.

Now Cillian was awake — he was irreversibly awake. He blinked up at her face, which was staring down at him. When they locked eyes, her frozen smile widened.

"Mom!" he couldn't help screaming. "Help!"   150

The Bog Girl, imitating him, began to scream and scream. And he could see, radiating from her gaze, the same blind tenderness that he had directed at her. Now he was its object. Something truly terrifying had happened: she loved him back.

For months, Cillian had been decoding the Bog Girl's silences. He'd peered into her dreams, her fears, her innermost thoughts. But her real voice was nothing like the voice that he'd imagined for her — a cross between Vicky Gilvarry and Patti LaBelle. Its high-pitched ululations hailed over him. In the kitchen, the dog began to bark. The language that she spoke was no longer spoken anywhere on earth.

He stumbled up, tugging at his boxers. The Bog Girl stood, too. The past, with its monstrous depth and span, reached toward him, demanding an understanding that he simply could not give it. His mind was too young and too narrow to withstand the onrush of her life. An invisible woods was in the bedroom with them, the scent of trees multiplying. Some mental earthquake inside the Bog Girl was casting up a world, green and unknown to him, or to anyone living: her homeland. Her gaze drove inward, carrying Cillian with it. For an instant, he thought he glimpsed her parents. Her brothers, her sisters, a nation of people. Their cheeks now beginning to redden, every one of them alive again inside her village. Pines rippling seaward. Gods, horned and faceless, walking the lakes that once covered Cillian's home. Cillian was buried in water, in liquid images of her; he had to push through so many strata of her memories to reach the surface of her mind. Most of what he saw he shrank away from. His mind felt like a burned tongue, numbly touching her reality.

"W-w-who are you?"

"Heartbreak" is the universal diagnosis for the pain that accompanies the   155 end of love. But this was an unusual breakup, in that Cillian's mind shattered first. The love that had protected him began to fall away. Piece after piece of it clattered from his chest, an armor rusting off him. *What are you?*

The Bog Girl lurched toward him, her arms open. First she moved like a hopping chick, with an unexpected buoyancy. Then she seemed to remember how to step, heel to toe. She came for him like an astronaut, bouncing on the gray carpet. The only English word she knew was his name.

Almost weightlessly, she reached for him. For wasn't she equally terrified? There was no buoy other than this boy, who had gripped her with his thin, freckled arms, bellying her out of the peat bog and into time.

Cillian hid behind the dresser.

Her fingers found his hand, threaded through his fingers.

He screamed again, even as he squeezed the hand back.   160

Her words rushed together, a thawing waterfall, moving intricately between octaves; still the only word he understood was his name. Perhaps nothing he had said to her, in their six months as a couple, had been comprehended. Cillian worked the levers in his brain, desperately trying to find the words that would release him.

"Unlock the door," his mother's beautiful voice called.

Cillian was frozen in the Bog Girl's grip, unable even to call out. But a moment later he heard the key turning in the lock. Gillian stood in the doorway in her yellow pajamas. With a panoramic comprehension, she took in what had happened. She knew, too, what must now be done. If she could have freed these two from the embrace herself, she would have done so; but now she understood the challenge. The boy would have to make his own way out. "Take her home, Cillian. Make sure that she gets home safely."

Cillian, his eyes round with panic, only nodded.

Gillian went to the Bog Girl, helping her into a sweater. "Put a hat on.   165
And pants."

His mother shepherded them downstairs and onto the porch, switching on every yellow bulb as they moved through the cottage. It was the warmest December on record, rain falling instead of snow, the drops disappearing into the rotted wood. Cillian carried the Bog Girl to the edge of the light before he understood that his mother was not coming with him.

"Let her down gently, son!" his mother called after them.

Well, she could do this for him, at least: she held a lantern steady across the rainy lawn, creating a gangplank of light that reached almost to the larches. She watched them moving toward the inky water. The Bog Girl was howling in her foreign tongue; at this distance, Gillian felt she could almost understand it.

Oh, she hoped their breakup would stick. She had divorced Cillian's father, then briefly moved into his new house; it had taken years before their affair was truly over. You had to really cultivate an ending. To get it to last, you had to kneel and tend to the burial ground, continuously firming your resolution.

This was a bad breakup. A quarter mile from the cottage, under a bright   170
moon, Cillian and the Bog Girl were rolling in the mud, each screaming in a different language. Their screams twined together, their hands reaching for each other; it was during this undoing that they were, at last, truly united as a couple. His flashlight rolled with them, plucking amphibious red and yellow eyes out of the reeds. "It's over. It's over. It's over," he kept babbling optimis-

tically, out of his mind with fear. Her throat was vibrating against his skin. He could feel the echo of his own terror and sorrow, and again his mind felt overrun by the lapping waves of time. She clutched at the collar of his T-shirt, her body covered in dark mud and cracked stems of bog cotton, blue lichen. At last he felt her grip on him loosen. Her eyes, opaquely glinting in the moonlight, liquid and enormous, far larger than anyone could have guessed before their unlidding, regarded him with what he imagined was a soft surprise, and disappointment. He was not who she'd expected to find when she opened her eyes, either. Now neither teenager needed to tell the other that it was over. It simply was — and, without another sound, the Bog Girl let go of Cillian and slipped backward into the bog water. Did she sink? It looked almost as if the water were rising to cover her. Her cranberry hair waved away from her scalp. As he watched, her body itself began to break up.

Straightening from where he was kneeling on the ledge of mud, he brushed peat from his pants. His arms tingled where her grip had suddenly relaxed. The clear rain drenched his clothing. The bog was still bubbling, pieces of her sinking back into the black peat, when he turned on his heel and ran. For the next few days, he would be quakey with relief; he'd felt certain, watching her sink away, that he would never see the Bog Girl again in this life.

But here he was mistaken. In the weeks and years to come, Cillian would find himself alone with her memory, struggling to pay attention to his droning contemporaries in the cramped classroom. How often would he retrace his steps, wandering right back to the lip of the bog, peering in? Each dusk, with their primitive eloquence, the air-galloping insects continue to speak the million syllables of her name.

"Ma! Ma! Ma!" That night, Cillian came roaring out of the dark, pistoning his knees as he ran for the light, for his home at the edge of the boglands. "Who *was* that?"

≡ THINKING ABOUT THE TEXT

1. Cillian gets his job clearing the bog because he wants to buy a car and have sex. Why then does he fall in love with the Bog Girl at first sight?

2. When specifically does the story pivot from realism to something else: Magical realism? Fantasy? Comedy? Horror? How would you describe its genre?

3. Cillian's Uncle Sean says, "You know *nothing* about her." Explain the significance of this. How is it both true and not? How might this be to Cillian's advantage, at least for awhile?

4. Describe the various reactions to the Bog Girl from, for example, the university man, the girls at school, Gillian, Uncle Sean, and so forth.

5. How might this story be about memory, both recent (Gillian's memoires of Cillian as a child) and our culture's lost memoires of deep history? Why does Cillian say at the end of the story "*What are you?*" and "Who *was* that?"

AIMEE BENDER
The Devourings

Aimee Bender (1969), who grew up in Los Angeles, is a short story writer and novelist. She received her undergraduate degree from the University of California at San Diego and her M.F.A. from the University of California at Irvine. Her first collection of stories, The Girl in the Flammable Skirt *(1998) was widely praised. Her novel* The Particular Sadness of Lemon Cake *(2010) was called a "virtuoso performance" by NPR and "oddly beautiful" by the* Washington Post. *She teaches at the University of Southern California. The following story is from her latest collection,* The Color Master *(2013), about which the* Chicago Tribune *noted these "new tales dazzle, confound, electrify, disturb, incriminate, and empathize."*

The ogre's wife was a good woman. She was not an ogre, but she was ugly, by human standards, and she had married the ogre because he was strong and productive, and together they had made six small ogre children. The children all took after their father. She had not expected otherwise—one look at his giant teeth, height, and huge features, and she knew his genes had to be dominant.

Years earlier, she had left her own village by choice, traveling up and over the green and rising hills in search of a life for herself, and when she had met the ogre in the tavern, him stretched along the entire side wall, his voice scratched from cigar smoke, she thought she might give the alternate world a chance. Everyone in her hometown knew of the ogres, living up on Cloud Hill like that. With their magical boots, and that hen.

With also, she wondered, a range of appetites? Later that night, at his home, the ogre had been surprised at her willingness to take off her clothes, since he'd been rumored to eat people for dinner. As she unlaced her blouse, he touched fingertips to her trembling bare shoulders and explained in his low gravel that he only ate human beings he did not know. I know your name now, he murmured. I know your travels. You're safe. Her eyes were closed, and when she revealed her breasts, he sighed. They were sculpted by a different artist, he whispered to her with a subtler tool. His desire was too much for her at first, overwhelming, but she soon grew to love him and his body, its giant harshness, its gentle gruffness with her. Next to him, she felt herself so delicate. At school, she had been the roughest-skinned, the one with the drooping features, the one no one could ever imagine that way, in a bed. She did not care about not being pretty, but she wanted to be seen as a future woman, as one who could participate, and no high-school boy could take that leap. The ogre, however, found her nothing short of revelatory, and the first time he entered her, he shouted with joy.

One evening, after many years of contented marriage, the children tucked in their bed, asleep, snoring faintly, wearing hammered gold crowns with their nightshirts because their father wanted them to feel like royal ogres in their dreams, a human girl and her siblings knocked on the door, frightened. They were lost, and the ogre was out at the tavern, and the ogre's wife opened up, and there they were—a group of six live human kids, with bright hair and red felt hats and snapping eyes, reminding her so sweetly of her long-ago nieces and nephews. The ogre's wife disliked firmly only one aspect of her husband: his interest in eating the children of humans. It could've been me! she told him once in bed while he twirled and twisted her hair over his fingers. She could not bear to turn the children on into the ogre-filled night, so she hustled them inside and in a fierce whisper told them they could hide in the same giant bed as her own children, but not to make a sound, not a peep!

When the ogre came home, late, he smelled them, of course; how could   5
he have imagined he would not smell them? She was half-asleep, twisted in the sheets, and hoped desperately that he would just crash out on the sofa in drunkenness. What she did not know was that, earlier in the night, the smart little girl leader of the human group had swapped their six red felt hats with the six golden crowns on the heads of the deep-sleeping ogre children, and when the ogre cackled hungrily, bumbling around the house, hunting for the source of the scent, he, of poor eyesight, of booziness, of delirium, ended up eating all his own children due to the swapping of those hats.

In the early morning, the human children ran off, terrified, giggling.

We skip ahead five years, because five years were full of nothing but searing pain and tears. Five years of lying on the bed unable to move, slogging up to do the basic functioning needed to hold things together, then back to bed. Five years of scathing bitterness at ogres, and also at humans, at where she came from, and the worry that had led her to open the door; I should've let him eat them first thing! she said, weeping into the down of her pillow, though she felt sick anytime she had even gotten the hint that her husband had eaten a child. But her *own*! There were two that she mourned the most, much as she hated to admit it to herself, but she had loved Lorraine and Stillford best, the two most-complex-looking ogre faces, who had emerged post-utero like gnarled wood knots, and who had turned out to be all sweetness in nature. How they had loved their human mother. They nestled on her lap and nudged their big heads into her shoulders. They were gentle during the breastfeeding, unlike their siblings. Ogres grew teeth early, and she had to stop feeding most of them or they would've ripped off her nipple, truly. She, many times, ran to the bathroom with blood streaming from her breasts from a careless slash, a little ogre child happily lapping up the red drops on the sofa. To those she gave formula. But she was too softhearted to decide for them all; for each new child she risked her breast, and Lorraine and Stillford had been different, angled their teeth just so and suckled like little human babies, and perhaps held within their selves some of her human genes that knew not to tear at the gentleness offered. Now they were dead, digested in the system of their father, who had been so angry he split a bone out of his neck while overclenching his jaw and had to go to the hospital, where he broke four beds and injured a nurse. He was angrier than ever these days, and their marriage and its focus and tenderness had faded. His favorite had been Lutter, the super-ogre demon child, who was so kinetic she rarely saw him still, and who had scraped the walls into shreds with his nails and twice tried to swallow his mother whole. She had let him train with her husband only, and why Lutter, even in his sleep, had let himself be eaten, could only have been due to the deep dreamy trust he felt of the smell of the mouth he was entering, a mouth he knew from its firm position over his shoulder, telling him instructions on how to rip through cartilage and sinew, and an inability, due to that core of trust, to imagine his fate could end this way.

After enough time had passed, she was able to get out of bed for hours at a time. She could go to town and engage in minutes of small talk. She could sit outside on the porch and watch leaves twist on the birch trees. She could read a short article in the newsletter. On this day, a day of change, she cleaned the house, top to floor, using swaths of cloth that grew dark with dirt and dust. She swept tumbleweeds of lint out the front door, and poured scrubbing detergent into all the sinks to scour the vast yellowing basins. At the market, she bought root vegetables by the dozen and chickens and sausages. She stuffed the chickens and made a stew and fed her husband, who came home ragged from his work climbing mountain-sides to look for caves packed with jewels and gifts like the magical harp that that thief Jack had stolen from his brother years ago.

We are pillaged, constantly, said the ogre, laying his loot in a sparkling heap by the door. And they fear us?

He kissed her on the ear, and sat down to roll a cigar out of crisp brown paper and a fist-sized wad of tobacco.   10

Good stew, human, he said, after dinner.

Please don't call me that, she said, for the hundredth time.

That's right, he said, patting his belly. I'm sorry. Love that sausage, delicious. He lit the cigar and inhaled deeply.

She wiped the globs of leftover chicken off the dining room table with a sponge.

While he mumbled to himself, digesting, sleepy, she filled the pots with   15
soap and water to soak, and ate a little bowl of the chicken stew behind the counter. She rarely ate at the same table as her husband anymore, as she now feared him during mealtimes, couldn't stand to watch him slurp up animals with that vigor and those grinding, pointed teeth.

Husband, she said; putting her bowl aside. She walked out from behind the counter. I have decided I need to go on a trip, she said.

The ogre was finishing his fourth mug of wine. He liked the darkest wine, the red almost black.

Go where? he said, wiping his mouth. To see your family?

She shook her head. Her family lived below, in the people village, and last time she'd been home, before the devourings, everyone had lectured her on ogres and complicity and betrayal. She'd waved them off. He's a good one, she had said. She had not dared show pictures of her children.

I'd like to see something pretty, she said. Maybe a lake?   20

There's a river that's supposed to be nice a few valleys over, he said, exhaling bracelets of smoke to the rafters.

Okay, she said. A river.

I could go with you, he said, turning a giant brown eye to hers. His eye like a pool hers could swim inside.

A mucky pool.

No, she told him. I need to do this alone.   25

He nodded. He understood. They both coped in their own ways. He had women on the side, ogre women, everyone knew. Maybe she didn't know, but probably. After all, although being with a human was the ultimate in show- ing off both self-control and status, sometimes a man just wanted a woman like himself. There were no prostitutes in the ogre village, as it was a barter economy and females chose males with equal discernment, but there were a couple who liked this particular ogre, and every few months he'd make a little sojourn as a way to honor where he came from. It's for my mother, he told his ogre-woman once, and she'd laughed and laughed, nude and mottled and calm, sprawled over a mattress, one arm crossing loosely over her forehead.

The ogre helped his wife pack up. He buttoned up her bag and told her he would miss her, which was true. From his plunder, he gave her a magic cloak that would turn her into the color of the dappled light that shot through foli- age, and also a cake that would become more cake once she'd eaten half. He kissed her forehead, roughly, and she melted a little under his arms.

Do you know how long you'll be? he asked.

I don't know, she said.

Okay, he said. I'll be here.   30

They spent the night almost close, her forehead pressed against the wall of his triceps. Come morning, she walked through the door and into fields of glistening green.

What marriage could recover? She did not plan on ever returning. The ogre wasn't sure, but he thought it was unlikely. He was not insensitive, despite all suspicions. The day she left, he skipped work and went to the tavern for lunch and drank ninety-five beers. You're a machine! the other ogres said, admir- ingly, as he slammed down another stein. Foam made an old man's beard around his mouth, and he burped in an echo that trembled the hillsides.

She felt it, his wife, now miles away, following a winding path up and over lightly rolling hills covered in sage, and dandelion fields, and one meadow of sunflowers shuddering in the daylight. She walked and walked until dusk, try- ing to collect distance under her feet, and then she camped out under a shady elm with her checkered cloth. She unpacked some almonds and dried cherries and she also ate the cake, which would let itself diminish to half and then, under her bare eyes, build itself back up out of nothing, out of air, until it was a full cake again. She was grateful for it, but somehow it also bothered her. Finish, cake, she said, tearing off half, watching it rebuild. Finish! She tore off more than half, the whole, but the cake was unstoppable. Plus, she needed it. What, she was going to trap birds and roast them over a fire? She was a woman who shopped at a market with a wheeled cart and used honey-lavender soap. She drank from her water mug and refilled it at a spring at the edge of the meadow, and before she fell asleep, she sprinkled the remaining cake crumbs around her cloth.

In the morning, she awoke surrounded by expectant-looking crows. Enough! she said, shaking the cloth as they tottered away.

Really, she could've spent the rest of her life there, just sitting and feeding those crows and herself with the cake, but she wanted to reach the river.

When she heard a clip-clopping sound, she put on the cloak so that she looked like the dappled sunlight beneath the elm, a particularly glorious sunlit area that did not correspond to the rules of sun location in the sky, but who would notice that except a particularly astute observer of shadows? This was just a human horseman riding along in ogre country, looking to find some treasure, like his comrades who had come up here and survived. She watched him, his handsomeness, his vanity and sureness, his sculpted hair and cheeks, his strong hands, his proud red jacket, and she was reminded again why the ogres had attracted her, and why she had loved young Stillford so, his wet brown eyes searching out hers, those sharp, smiling, crooked teeth. The ogres knew they were ugly and in that they were decent. They did not ever think they could be like this man, she thought as he galloped off, tossing his head with pleasure. He ducked and rose over hills, and she saw it coming before he did, saw the ogre who ran the corner store just out on a pleasant walk in his seven-league boots, rounding the corner and — surprise! what a gift! — the man too late raising his gun and landing a shot on the ogre's shoulder, which was nothing to an ogre, nothing a little mending at night wouldn't fix, a little digging with a fork into flesh to expunge a bullet, and she watched in her cloak as the man was plucked from his horse and eaten whole. It was a horrible sight, one she had tried not to see for most of her wedded life, but on that day she found it almost comforting. Just to see it. Not comforting to see pain and death but just to see what she could not let herself imagine and therefore ruled her. She wept quietly under the tree as the ogre chewed. Then he walked off, rubbing his belly wearing those boots, a little scrap of red cloth sticking out of his mouth until he reached out a tongue and licked it in, just like a human might do with a bit of jam.

The horse had run off, but it circled back after the ogre left, pacing in the field, then settling down, and after her shaking subsided, she walked over to where it was grazing. A couple of hours had passed, and the horse seemed focused on the grass, and calm. After all, the eating had been brief, and the man had barely had time to scream, and ogres were just about food, not about power play or torture. They were just endlessly large and hungry beings. She mounted the horse an rode lazily along, digging around in the thick leather packs on the side where she found some snacks — turkey jerky that she used to love, made in the village, and some peaches, a rare delicacy for her, as ogres couldn't care less about peaches, and the fragrance consumed her mouth, like eating perfume, like kisses of nectar. She found a letter from a wife in royal-blue ink from a quill pen, wishing the man well. It was all awful she thought, tossing the peach stone onto the green hill side, where it wedged against a rock, near some bees. Happy bees. She patted the horse's neck. Now she and the widow had something in common. Though loss did not pass from one person to another like a baton; it just formed a bigger and bigger pool of carriers. And, she thought, scratching the coarseness of the horse's mane, it did not leave once lodged, did it, simply changed form and asked repeatedly for attention and care, as each year revealed a new knot to cry out and consider — smaller, sure, but never gone. Stillford, she thought to herself, as the sun grew high in the sky. My sweet Stillford, with his dirt art. My funny Lorraine, who danced to the lute so earnestly. Out of my body, these beautiful monsters.

It was ridiculous, at times, how many tears one body could produce.

A few hours into the afternoon, during a nap on the horse, who was eating clover in the inverted bell of a valley, the ring of trumpets awoke the woman. She jerked awake, recalling the sound from her childhood, when trumpets were the way news was delivered, and sure enough, across the field emerged a troop of human men and women on horseback, some walking, two trumpeting, one waving a bright-red flag. From what she could recall, a bright-red flag meant war.

Ho, woman! called the strapping man at the lead, and she did not have   40
time to put on her cloak; even if she had, they'd take her horse, and she liked having the horse.

They trotted over, a whole mess of people, and she hadn't looked at so many human faces together in years. How refined they were! How tiny and delicate! Those dot nostrils! Their hairless hands!

Are you lost? the head man asked, not unkindly. He wore a helmet wrought with silver swirled markings on the sides that seemed to speak of royalty.

No, she said, thank you. I'm on my way to the river.

This is ogre territory! said the man, sitting straighter. You're not safe!

He turned to the others, beckoning them closer.   45

No, no, she said, waving him off. It's fine, I'm skilled at hiding. I've been living in this territory for years.

Ho! he said, digging his hands into his horse's mane. Years? And survived? You must help us, then! We sent out a scout earlier to look for mines, and we have not heard back. Did you see anyone?

Of course, one careful look at the horse and all would be revealed, but the man was very focused on her face, as if he had been trained in it.

No, she said.

You saw no danger? said the man.   50

Nothing but crows, she said.

Ogres *eat* people, said the man, leaning in.

To her annoyance, her eyes thickened with tears.

Ah! You've seen something?

She shook her head, tucking her hands under the saddle and feeling the   55
horse's warm coat beneath her, the large and living backside. No. I just heard a story once, of someone getting eaten, and I found it sad, she said. The tears tracked her cheeks.

He nodded. They all had their own stories.

Our sentry is a good man, the man said, and he said he'd contact us immediately via light signaling with use of the sun and his mirror and we have not
seen a thing. Ah! Is that his horse?

He glanced down, and saw the packs. She had in her lap some turkey jerky
that she'd been eating earlier.

Oh, I don't know! she said. She widened her eyes. Is it? I was just walking
and came upon this horse and needed a rest. Hours ago. It did not have an
owner.

The man's brow furrowed. The horse, alone? Hours ago?   60

Alone, she said.

He consulted with a short man next to him on a taller horse, making
them even.

You'll have to come with us, the main man said.

Oh no, she said, slipping the turkey jerky into a pocket. I'll walk. I'll give
you his horse. I didn't realize it belonged to anyone recently. I thought it had
been wild for a while.

No, said the man, firmly. We need you to come with us.   65

He gave a nod to his short man, who began to dismount.

The woman leapt off her horse, and backed into the meadow. The afternoon sun filtered through pine needles on high fir trees to the side, and with a
quick move she had the cloak out of her bag and on and had turned into light
and shadow.

Where'd she go? said the short man.

Witch! said the first.

The trumpets raised and blared.   70

The woman crept quietly to a corner of the meadow. Had any one of them
been attuned to light, they would've seen one patch of splattered sun shapes
moving along in a way that did not correspond to the breeze.

But they were not. They were preoccupied with what had happened. They
had liked their handsome, courageous scout. They quickly assimilated the
man's packs and letters into their crew, and put a child who had been previously riding with his mother onto the horse, and the two lead men swore, and
the woman watched silently from her spot in the meadow as they moved in a
clump over the hills.

She stayed in the meadow in the cloak for hours, and the sun went down and
lit the grasses with orange light, and she wondered about her husband, who
was likely going to see one of his women on the side. Although it made her
cringe inside a fist in her stomach, there was also a distant relief in it, in people
just doing what they needed to do. She found comfort in the way the grasses
swayed, and murmured, and at dinnertime, in a little whisper, she asked the
cake to change flavor and, magic cake that it was, it shifted from vanilla pound
to a chocolate Bundt, and she ate it with pleasure, plus some more almonds
she had in her pocket and the remaining turkey jerky. Water from the spring.
The moon rose in a crescent and crickets rubbed their wings together and

in the far distance, now and again, she could hear the shining bleats of the bugles and trumpets.

In the morning, she walked on. She could smell the river now, the heavy moisture, the damper grasses under her feet. The trumpets had grown fainter, and she imagined they were returning home to arm up and come back to try to defeat the ogres with guns and bayonets. Maybe they will, she thought vaguely, though the ogres had magic and bigness on their side, and the humans had a hubris ogres did not. Ogres bumbled, and erred, but their weaknesses were not hidden, and this helped them, in the long run.

She ate her lunch (more dried cherries) and then took the cake out of her bag. Something about it still bothered her. I need to fight for my life a little harder than this, she told it. It was now a chocolate chip cake, and she felt bad for it, this cake so willing to change and please her, with no other beings around who could speak to it, and enjoy it, but she ate a small portion and then wrapped it in a checkered napkin and tucked it in the branched fork of a sturdy oak.

Here, cake, she told it, patting the napkin. You are to have your own adventure now. No matter what happens, you can grow again.

As she said it, as she stooped to shoulder her bag, she understood why she could not tolerate being around a cake that survived so repeatedly, and she stood, bowed at the branch, and walked away.

Finding food became much harder then. She rooted for berries, having learned years ago from her husband what was edible, but more times than not, the berries were bad. She ate a handful of sour ones in the afternoon, and dug up some old peanuts and a beet. Dirt filled the cracks in her hands. She found a strong stick and rubbed the end to a point with the paring knife she'd brought in her sack, and when she finally reached the river — dark blue, racing, stone-dribbled — after refilling her water (ogre-country water was always drinkable — something to do with the deep reserves replenished by the clouds), she saw a quick orange fish in the current and crouched down and, after dozens of tries, speared it. The fish flapped on her stick, and she knelt and prayed a thank you. She had only seen a fire built in front of her a few times, but she was able to wrangle together some sticks and fir needles and with the matches she had in her pack managed to get enough going to scorch the cleaned fish, though she missed many of the bones and picked them from her teeth in thin pullings. She let the fish guts molder in the grasses for another animal. Everything would get eaten in some way or another.

She slept that night wearing the cloak, a bright spot of dapple in the darkness. Soon into her sleep, she woke at the sound of rustling, and caught a bear cub next to her licking up the fish guts and eyeing her sunspot curiously. She removed the cloak and it scampered away. The next morning, she wrapped up the cloak and left it in another tree's branches. She did not want help from magic. She did not want any more handouts.

She grew rugged and wiry in the fields, spearing fish using up the last of her   80
matches but not until she was sure she had figured out how to make a fire on
her own, which sometimes took over an hour. Her legs turned leaner and tan-
ner and she squatted and watched the clouds and the river and felt her sense of
internal time shifting. We adapt, she told herself repeatedly. This is what they
mean by adaptable. The men rose up from the village with their spears and
guns, and when she saw the glints of red and the banners of war she climbed a
high tree and watched from a distance as the human forces with shining weaponry and brass charged into ogre territory. Into the thatched huts and the rickety tavern and the ogre game-field full of nets and balls woven from goat hide.
She watched, again, as the ogres ate the men whole. They could eat and eat.
She watched the ogres fall from the expert weaponry, and the sight of a fallen
ogre enraged the other ogres and invigorated the remaining men, so the last
phase was particularly bloody. Casualties were tossed off an embankment on
Cloud Hill, and far below, people cried out and ran from the falling bodies.

On one of the days, she spotted her husband from the height of her best
scouting tree, near the widest part of the river, where she'd set up a little daily
life for herself that included hours of watching insects move grasses around or
feeling the wind shift over her skin. Her husband, who had aged. She could see
it in his limp. She missed him. She felt from his limp that he missed her. She had
taken good care of him. He had been her one and only love. She watched as
he swiped at the humans with swinging arms and ate two and then stumbled
off and could not continue. The humans shot guns in his direction but he just
swatted bullets like sport and the humans were radically outnumbered by that
point and her ogre was one of the biggest. He limped farther away, and then
twisted and turned, and his body moved in a way she'd never seen before, an
uncomfortable jerking, an insistent movement from feet up to mouth, and he
vomited up human—legs and arms and a head tumbled straight out of him. It
was unchewed, the body—it was just parts and parcels of humanness—and
the pieces lay there in the grass, glazed in a layer of spit and acid. Everyone
stopped, for a second, seeing that: the man who had not been chewed, but had
been split into parts, and was of course dead. The ogres held still, sweating,
staring. The ogres had never seen an ogre throw anything up in their lives;
they were nothing if not able digesters, and they shuddered at the sight of it.

On light feet, the woman crept closer. She ran through the grasses and
leapt into another tree. The humans were muttering amongst themselves
because although they had seen bodies eaten it was something else to see a
body reemerge. The man's parts were now moldering in the grass, perhaps for
the same bear cub. When she was close enough, at a high perch, she found
she could recognize the man. An uncle of hers, a distant uncle, her mother's
eldest brother. His twisted hand, his nose, that tweaked shoulder and distinctive jaw. She clung to the branch and thought perhaps her husband had
thrown up the man because the taste had reminded him of his own children.
Perhaps he had banged up against memory through an inexplicable familiarity. He had never told her he was sad. He had never expressed true regret.

They had, in fact, never really talked about it. How to talk about it? How could she blame him, or could he blame her? Weren't they both to blame for it, and also blameless? Who were the little human children who'd escaped, and where were they now?

The remaining ogres staggered off, and the remaining humans went to surround her dead uncle's parts. It was a truce moment. There had been enough death, and the ogres were not going to be vanquished, and the remaining humans did not want to be eaten, so they put the uncle's body into burlap bags and began the slow march home. Her ogre sank to the grasses on his knees and hung his head. He stayed there for hours, wilted, hunched, and from her perch in the tree, she sent him love. She made her love into a piece of the wind, formed from the air in her and placed on the air outside her, and sent it to him, even though it would be too diffuse by the time it got there. Still, even the bear cub felt it, trotting over to whatever remaining organ bits he could find, lifting up his nose to smell the new hint of freshness in the evening air.

The cake, at first, had remained in the tree. Lodged in the branch nook of the old oak where she'd left it. But various birds found it in a few short days — they could smell its bready sweetness from yards away — and they pecked so hard at the napkin that the cake fell from the nook and rolled out of the linen. On the ground, the birds pecked it into nothing. It replenished. They pecked. It replenished. The cake wanted to satisfy the birds, so it made itself into a seeded type, and the birds went at it with new vigor. The cake replenished. The birds were so full they hopped off, wobbling, but they returned with eagerness in the morning, and the next morning, and the birds that lived near the oak tree became fat and listless. They could hardly fly. All they did all day long was peck at the cake.

The cake had grown old. It had been made so many years ago, and it had been so many cakes in its time.

I will never die, thought the cake to itself, in even simpler terms, as cakes did not have sophisticated use of language.

On her walk back, the woman saw it on the ground. She recognized her napkin, checked blue against the dirt. She was heading home. She was not sure if she could really return, or how to do it, but she wanted to try. She missed her husband, and the sight of him throwing up her uncle had filled her with a sore and tender love. There was the cake, in seeded form now, and she felt sorry for it.

With her pointed stick, she dug a hole in the ground. Now, dear cake, she said, gently burying it, patting the dirt. At least you can rest. At least you will not be endlessly pecked and diminished.

The birds found it in a day. A cake like that? Let that kind of thing go? They thought not. They scrabbled in the dirt and dragged it out with their beaks. They had missed it, for that missing day. They pecked with unusual ardor. A few worms had already attached to its bottom side and were eating it too, and the cake had formed its back side into a kind of dirt cake and its front into seed, and it would replenish itself according to the ratio of its eaters.

85

It went on like this for a while, and a few of the birds died early, from over-   90
eating and lack of flight. New birds came and went. Same with the worms.

The woman returned to her house, and her husband opened the door, widening it when he saw it was her, and they sat at the kitchen table. It did not feel
wrong. She got up and took her items out of her dirty bag and piled them into
the sink for laundry. That moment a few days later when their arms touched
over by the guest room? They ate their stew bowls together. They walked formally into the living room, sat on a sofa, and stumbled through a conversation.
At night, she climbed onto his chest to sleep and he held her in place like a belt.
Later, they took a few trips to a waterfall, and a glacier, and befriended an ogre
who ran a school. After many years, the woman died of natural causes, and a
few years after that, the ogre died. Eventually, his mistresses died. Down on the
ground, in the people village, over decades, the war men and women died.
The human girl who had escaped her early death died, across the land, over
by the ocean, in her shack of blue bowls and rocking chairs. The witch who
had originally made the cake and made up the spell and given it as a gift to her
beloved ogre-friend died.
     The cake went on and on.
     Time passed, and the climate shifted. The trees and grasses faded, and the
land grew dry. Birds stopped flying overhead. Reptiles ate the cake but eventually died out. The worms dried into dust. A quarter mile away, the magic cloak
had stayed stuffed in its tree, hidden from view over many, many years. Some
wind had nudged it into open air, and now half-tucked in the broken branches
of a dead tree trunk, was a shining bright coat-shaped area of dappled light
through foliage. It showed dapple long after the sun had stopped shining
through any leaves, because there were no more leaves.
     Neither could move, but the cake felt a sense of the presence of the cloak,
and thought it might be a new eater coming to find the cake, and the cake,
always wanting to please — the cake who had found a way to survive its end-
lessness by recreating its role over and over again — tried to figure out in its
cake way what this light-dappled object might want to eat. So it became darkness. A cake of darkness. It did not have to be human food. It did not have to be
digestible through a familiar tract. It lay there on the dirt, waiting, a shimmering cake of darkness. Through time, and wind, and earthquakes, and chance,
at last the cloak fell out of the tree and blew across the land and happened upon
the cake, where it ate its darkness and extinguished its own dappled light. The
cloak disappeared into night and was not seen again, as it was only a piece of
coat-shaped darkness now and could no longer be spotted so easily, had there
been any eyes left to see it. It floated and joined with nowhere. Darkness was
overtaking everything anyway. Pouring over the land and sky. The cake itself,
still in the shape of darkness, sat on the hillside.
     What's left? said the cake. It thought in blocks of feeling. It felt the thick   95
darkness all around it. What is left to eat me? To take me in?
     Darkness did not want to eat more darkness, not especially. Darkness did
not care for carrot cake, or apple pie. Darkness did not seem interested in a
water cake, or a cake of money. Only when the cake filled with light did it come

over. The darkness, circling around the light, devouring the light. But the cake kept refilling, as we know. This is the spell of the cake. And the darkness, eating light, and again light, and again light, lifted.

≡ THINKING ABOUT THE TEXT

1. What makes this "impossible" relationship work? What specific details lets you know you are indeed in an "alternate world"?

2. If you read this story as an allegory, albeit a hyperbolic and fantastic one, of our own relationships, how can you make sense of the line "What marriage could recover?" (see paragraph 33).

3. After the wife sees the ogre eat a man on a horse, she says, "Now she and the widow have something in common." How does she expand on this thought? Does her observation ring true to you?

4. Why does she leave behind her magic cake and cloth? Would you? Is it clear that the woman is the hero of this tale? Why, exactly?

5. Why is the vomiting scene disgusting yet also somehow poignant? Why was love victorious? How would you account for the mysterious life of the cake? How do you account for the title of the story?

≡ MAKING COMPARISONS

1. How could both stories be said to be modern fairy tales or parables?

2. Compare Russell and Bender's use of fantastical details to enhance their stories.

3. Compare the endings of these two stories. Which do you find the more effective or interesting? Why?

≡ WRITING ABOUT THE TEXT

1. In an essay, agree or disagree with Russell's view that "we project our fantasies onto the mask of another person's face, and then feel betrayed when they turn out to have needs and depths of their own."

2. Write an essay that argues that "The Devourings" is a modern parable about marriage and grief.

3. Argue that both stories are a mix of realism and fantasy/comedy/horror.

4. Argue that both stories are allegories for our flawed understanding of others.

KRISTEN ROUPENIAN, "Cat Person"

ARGUMENTS ON THE ISSUE:
ANDREW RUSSELL, "The Ecstasy of Consent"

KATELYN EWEN, "When Yes Really Means Yes"

SUZANNAH WEISS, "#MeToo Has Made Me See Anyone Is Capable of Sexual Abuse — Including Me"

The short story "Cat Person" went viral as soon as it was published in *The New Yorker*, receiving more response than any short story in decades and bringing instant recognition to its author. The story explicitly details a twenty-year-old college student's excruciatingly bad date with an older man. The author says the story was "inspired by a small but hasty encounter I had with a person I met online. How had I decided that this was someone I could trust?" The story was a catalyst for numerous conversations about gender relations, power, consent, and the ways people created imaginary constructs of people from texting on "strange and flimsy evidence." For example, in the story Margot imagines that Robert having a pet cat says something positive about him. The essays that follow the story focus on sexual consent. Even though the sex in the story is not forced, Margot wonders how the shifting balance of power between her and Robert, his physical intimidation (even though he never explicitly threatens her), her socialized need to be polite, nice, and eager to please, and finally her uncertainty about his possible behavior all problematize her "consent," to a sexual encounter that made many readers cringe.

KRISTEN ROUPENIAN

Cat Person

Kristen Roupenian (1981) graduated from Barnard College in 2003 and then spent two years in the Peace Corps. She is currently living in Michigan where she received an M.F.A. from the University of Michigan. She also holds a Ph.D. in English from Harvard University in Postcolonial Studies. She received national attention for "Cat Person," a story that earned her one million dollars for her next two books. Her story collection You Know You Want This *was published in 2019. The story appeared in* The New Yorker *on December 11, 2017.*

Margot met Robert on a Wednesday night toward the end of her fall semester. She was working behind the concession stand at the artsy movie theatre downtown when he came in and bought a large popcorn and a box of Red Vines.

"That's an . . . unusual choice," she said. "I don't think I've ever actually sold a box of Red Vines before."

Flirting with her customers was a habit she'd picked up back when she worked as a barista, and it helped with tips. She didn't earn tips at the movie theatre, but the job was boring otherwise, and she did think that Robert was cute. Not so cute that she would have, say, gone up to him at a party, but cute enough that she could have drummed up an imaginary crush on him if he'd sat across from her during a dull class—though she was pretty sure that he was out of college, in his mid-twenties at least. He was tall, which she liked, and she could see the edge of a tattoo peeking out from beneath the rolled-up sleeve of his shirt. But he was on the heavy side, his beard was a little too long, and his shoulders slumped forward slightly, as though he were protecting something.

Robert did not pick up on her flirtation. Or, if he did, he showed it only by stepping back, as though to make her lean toward him, try a little harder. "Well," he said. "O.K., then." He pocketed his change.

But the next week he came into the movie theatre again, and bought   5
another box of Red Vines. "You're getting better at your job," he told her. "You managed not to insult me this time."

She shrugged. "I'm up for a promotion, so," she said.

After the movie, he came back to her. "Concession-stand girl, give me your phone number," he said, and, surprising herself, she did.

From that small exchange about Red Vines, over the next several weeks they built up an elaborate scaffolding of jokes via text, riffs that unfolded and shifted so quickly that she sometimes had a hard time keeping up. He was very clever, and she found that she had to work to impress him. Soon she noticed that when she texted him he usually texted her back right away, but if she took more than a few hours to respond his next message would always be short and wouldn't include a question, so it was up to her to re-initiate the conversation, which she always did. A few times, she got distracted for a day or so and wondered if the exchange would die out altogether, but then she'd think of something funny to tell him or she'd see a picture on the Internet that was relevant to their conversation, and they'd start up again. She still didn't know much about him, because they never talked about anything personal, but when they landed two or three good jokes in a row there was a kind of exhilaration to it, as if they were dancing.

Then, one night during reading period, she was complaining about how all the dining halls were closed and there was no food in her room because her roommate had raided her care package, and he offered to buy her some Red Vines to sustain her. At first, she deflected this with another joke, because she really did have to study, but he said, "No, I'm serious, stop fooling around and come now," so she put a jacket over her pajamas and met him at the 7-Eleven.

It was about eleven o'clock. He greeted her without ceremony, as though   10
he saw her every day, and took her inside to choose some snacks. The store

didn't have Red Vines, so he bought her a Cherry Coke Slurpee and a bag of Doritos and a novelty lighter shaped like a frog with a cigarette in its mouth.

"Thank you for my presents," she said, when they were back outside. Robert was wearing a rabbit-fur hat that came down over his ears and a thick, old-fashioned down jacket. She thought it was a good look for him, if a little dorky; the hat heightened his lumberjack aura, and the heavy coat hid his belly and the slightly sad slump of his shoulders.

"You're welcome, concession-stand girl," he said, though of course he knew her name by then. She thought he was going to go in for a kiss and prepared to duck and offer him her cheek, but instead of kissing her on the mouth he took her by the arm and kissed her gently on the forehead, as though she were something precious. "Study hard, sweetheart," he said. "I will see you soon."

On the walk back to her dorm, she was filled with a sparkly lightness that she recognized as the sign of an incipient crush.

While she was home over break, they texted nearly non-stop, not only jokes but little updates about their days. They started saying good morning and good night, and when she asked him a question and he didn't respond right away she felt a jab of anxious yearning. She learned that Robert had two cats, named Mu and Yan, and together they invented a complicated scenario in which her childhood cat, Pita, would send flirtatious texts to Yan, but whenever Pita talked to Mu she was formal and cold, because she was jealous of Mu's relationship with Yan.

"Why are you texting all the time?" Margot's stepdad asked her at dinner. 15 "Are you having an affair with someone?"

"Yes," Margot said. "His name is Robert, and I met him at the movie theatre. We're in love, and we're probably going to get married."

"Hmm," her stepdad said. "Tell him we have some questions for him."

"My parents are asking about u," Margot texted, and Robert sent her back a smiley-face emoji whose eyes were hearts.

When Margot returned to campus, she was eager to see Robert again, but he turned out to be surprisingly hard to pin down. "Sorry, busy week at work," he replied. "I promise I will c u soon." Margot didn't like this; it felt as if the dynamic had shifted out of her favor, and when eventually he did ask her to go to a movie she agreed right away.

The movie he wanted to see was playing at the theatre where she worked, 20 but she suggested that they see it at the big multiplex just outside town instead; students didn't go there very often, because you needed to drive. Robert came to pick her up in a muddy white Civic with candy wrappers spilling out of the cup holders. On the drive, he was quieter than she'd expected, and he didn't look at her very much. Before five minutes had gone by, she became wildly uncomfortable, and, as they got on the highway, it occurred to her that he could take her someplace and rape and murder her; she hardly knew anything about him, after all.

Just as she thought this, he said, "Don't worry, I'm not going to murder you," and she wondered if the discomfort in the car was her fault, because she was acting jumpy and nervous, like the kind of girl who thought she was going to get murdered every time she went on a date.

"It's O.K. — you can murder me if you want," she said, and he laughed and patted her knee. But he was still disconcertingly quiet, and all her bubbling attempts at making conversation bounced right off him. At the theatre, he made a joke to the cashier at the concession stand about Red Vines, which fell flat in a way that embarrassed everyone involved, but Margot most of all.

During the movie, he didn't hold her hand or put his arm around her, so by the time they were back in the parking lot she was pretty sure that he had changed his mind about liking her. She was wearing leggings and a sweatshirt, and that might have been the problem. When she got into the car, he'd said, "Glad to see you dressed up for me," which she'd assumed was a joke, but maybe she actually had offended him by not seeming to take the date seriously enough, or something. He was wearing khakis and a button-down shirt.

"So, do you want to go get a drink?" he asked when they got back to the car, as if being polite were an obligation that had been imposed on him. It seemed obvious to Margot that he was expecting her to say no and that, when she did, they wouldn't talk again. That made her sad, not so much because she wanted to continue spending time with him as because she'd had such high expectations for him over break, and it didn't seem fair that things had fallen apart so quickly.

"We could go get a drink, I guess?" she said.   25

"If you want," he said.

"If you want" was such an unpleasant response that she sat silently in the car until he poked her leg and said, "What are you sulking about?"

"I'm not sulking," she said. "I'm just a little tired."

"I can take you home."

"No, I could use a drink, after that movie." Even though it had been play-   30
ing at the mainstream theatre, the film he'd chosen was a very depressing drama about the Holocaust, so inappropriate for a first date that when he suggested it she said, "Lol r u serious," and he made some joke about how he was sorry that he'd misjudged her taste and he could take her to a romantic comedy instead.

But now, when she said that about the movie, he winced a little, and a totally different interpretation of the night's events occurred to her. She wondered if perhaps he'd been trying to impress her by suggesting the Holocaust movie, because he didn't understand that a Holocaust movie was the wrong kind of "serious" movie with which to impress the type of person who worked at an artsy movie theatre, the type of person he probably assumed she was. Maybe, she thought, her texting "lol r u serious" had hurt him, had intimidated him and made him feel uncomfortable around her. The thought of this possible vulnerability touched her, and she felt kinder toward him than she had all night.

When he asked her where she wanted to go for a drink, she named the place where she usually hung out, but he made a face and said that it was in the student ghetto and he'd take her somewhere better. They went to a bar she'd never been to, an underground speakeasy type of place, with no sign announcing its presence. There was a line to get inside, and, as they waited, she grew fidgety trying to figure out how to tell him what she needed to tell him, but she couldn't, so when the bouncer asked to see her I.D. she just handed it to him. The bouncer hardly even looked at it; he just smirked and said, "Yeah, no," and waved her to the side, as he gestured toward the next group of people in line.

Robert had gone ahead of her, not noticing what was playing out behind him. "Robert," she said quietly. But he didn't turn around. Finally, someone in line who'd been paying attention tapped him on the shoulder and pointed to her, marooned on the sidewalk.

She stood, abashed, as he came back over to her. "Sorry!" she said. "This is so embarrassing."

"How old *are* you?" he demanded. 35

"I'm twenty," she said.

"Oh," he said. "I thought you said you were older."

"I told you I was a sophomore!" she said. Standing outside the bar, having been rejected in front of everyone, was humiliating enough, and now Robert was looking at her as if she'd done something wrong.

"But you did that — what do you call it? That gap year," he objected, as though this were an argument he could win.

"I don't know what to tell you," she said helplessly. "I'm twenty." And then, 40 absurdly, she started to feel tears stinging her eyes, because somehow everything had been ruined and she couldn't understand why this was all so hard.

But, when Robert saw her face crumpling, a kind of magic happened. All the tension drained out of his posture; he stood up straight and wrapped his bearlike arms around her. "Oh, sweetheart," he said. "Oh, honey, it's O.K., it's all right. Please don't feel bad." She let herself be folded against him, and she was flooded with the same feeling she'd had outside the 7-Eleven — that she was a delicate, precious thing he was afraid he might break. He kissed the top of her head, and she laughed and wiped her tears away.

"I can't believe I'm crying because I didn't get into a bar," she said. "You must think I'm such an idiot." But she knew he didn't think that, from the way he was gazing at her; in his eyes, she could see how pretty she looked, smiling through her tears in the chalky glow of the streetlight, with a few flakes of snow coming down.

He kissed her then, on the lips, for real; he came for her in a kind of lunging motion and practically poured his tongue down her throat. It was a terrible kiss, shockingly bad; Margot had trouble believing that a grown man could possibly be so bad at kissing. It seemed awful, yet somehow it also gave her that tender feeling toward him again, the sense that even though he was older than her, she knew something he didn't.

When he was done kissing her, he took her hand firmly and led her to a different bar, where there were pool tables and pinball machines and sawdust on the floor and no one checking I.D.s at the door. In one of the booths, she saw the grad student who'd been her English T.A. her freshman year.

"Should I get you a vodka soda?" Robert asked, which she thought was   45
maybe supposed to be a joke about the kind of drink college girls liked, though
she'd never had a vodka soda. She actually was a little anxious about what to
order; at the places she went to, they only carded people at the bar, so the kids
who were twenty-one or had good fake I.D.s usually brought pitchers of P.B.R.
or Bud Light back to share with the others. She wasn't sure if those brands
were ones that Robert would make fun of, so, instead of specifying, she said,
"I'll just have a beer."

With the drinks in front of him and the kiss behind him, and also maybe
because she had cried, Robert became much more relaxed, more like the witty
person she knew through his texts. As they talked, she became increasingly
sure that what she'd interpreted as anger or dissatisfaction with her had, in
fact, been nervousness, a fear that she wasn't having a good time. He kept
coming back to her initial dismissal of the movie, making jokes that glanced
off it and watching her closely to see how she responded. He teased her about
her highbrow taste, and said how hard it was to impress her because of all the
film classes she'd taken, even though he knew she'd taken only one summer
class in film. He joked about how she and the other employees at the artsy theatre probably sat around and made fun of the people who went to the mainstream theatre, where they didn't even serve wine, and some of the movies
were in IMAX 3-D.

Margot laughed along with the jokes he was making at the expense of this
imaginary film-snob version of her, though nothing he said seemed quite fair,
since she was the one who'd actually suggested that they see the movie at the
Quality 16. Although now, she realized, maybe that had hurt Robert's feelings, too. She'd thought it was clear that she just didn't want to go on a date
where she worked, but maybe he'd taken it more personally than that; maybe
he'd suspected that she was ashamed to be seen with him. She was starting to
think that she understood him — how sensitive he was, how easily he could be
wounded — and that made her feel closer to him, and also powerful, because
once she knew how to hurt him she also knew how he could be soothed.
She asked him lots of questions about the movies he liked, and she spoke
self-deprecatingly about the movies at the artsy theatre that she found boring
or incomprehensible; she told him about how much her older co-workers
intimidated her, and how she sometimes worried that she wasn't smart
enough to form her own opinions on anything. The effect of this on him was
palpable and immediate, and she felt as if she were petting a large, skittish
animal, like a horse or a bear, skillfully coaxing it to eat from her hand.

By her third beer, she was thinking about what it would be like to have sex
with Robert. Probably it would be like that bad kiss, clumsy and excessive, but
imagining how excited he would be, how hungry and eager to impress her, she
felt a twinge of desire pluck at her belly, as distinct and painful as the snap of
an elastic band against her skin.

When they'd finished that round of drinks, she said, boldly, "Should we
get out of here, then?," and he seemed briefly hurt, as if he thought she was
cutting the date short, but she took his hand and pulled him up, and the look

on his face when he realized what she was saying, and the obedient way he trailed her out of the bar, gave her that elastic-band snap again, as did, oddly, the fact that his palm was slick beneath hers.

Outside, she presented herself to him again for kissing, but, to her surprise, he only pecked her on the mouth. "You're drunk," he said, accusingly.

"No, I'm not," she said, though she was. She pushed her body against his, feeling tiny beside him, and he let out a great shuddering sigh, as if she were something too bright and painful to look at, and that was sexy, too, being made to feel like a kind of irresistible temptation.

"I'm taking you home, lightweight," he said, shepherding her to the car. Once they were inside it, though, she leaned into him again, and after a little while, by lightly pulling back when he pushed his tongue too far down her throat, she was able to get him to kiss her in the softer way that she liked, and soon after that she was straddling him, and she could feel the small log of his erection straining against his pants. Whenever it rolled beneath her weight, he let out these fluttery, high-pitched moans that she couldn't help feeling were a little melodramatic, and then suddenly he pushed her off him and turned the key in the ignition.

"Making out in the front seat like a teen-ager," he said, in mock disgust. Then he added, "I'd have thought you'd be too old for that, now that you're *twenty*."

She stuck her tongue out at him. "Where do you want to go, then?"

"Your place?"

"Um, that won't really work. Because of my roommate?"

"Oh, right. You live in the dorms," he said, as though that were something she should apologize for.

"Where do you live?" she asked.

"I live in a house."

"Can I . . . come over?"

"You can."

The house was in a pretty, wooded neighborhood not too far from campus and had a string of cheerful white fairy lights across the doorway. Before he got out of the car, he said, darkly, like a warning, "Just so you know, I have cats."

"I know," she said. "We texted about them, remember?"

At the front door, he fumbled with his keys for what seemed a ridiculously long time and swore under his breath. She rubbed his back to try to keep the mood going, but that seemed to fluster him even more, so she stopped.

"Well. This is my house," he said flatly, pushing the door open.

The room they were in was dimly lit and full of objects, all of which, as her eyes adjusted, resolved into familiarity. He had two large, full bookcases, a shelf of vinyl records, a collection of board games, and a lot of art—or, at least, posters that had been hung in frames, instead of being tacked or taped to the wall.

"I like it," she said, truthfully, and, as she did, she identified the emotion she was feeling as relief. It occurred to her that she'd never gone to someone's house to have sex before; because she'd dated only guys her age, there had always been some element of sneaking around, to avoid roommates. It was new, and a little frightening, to be so completely on someone else's turf, and the fact that Robert's house gave evidence of his having interests that she shared, if only in their broadest categories—art, games, books, music—struck her as a reassuring endorsement of her choice.

As she thought this, she saw that Robert was watching her closely, observing the impression the room had made. And, as though fear weren't quite ready to release its hold on her, she had the brief wild idea that maybe this was not a room at all but a trap meant to lure her into the false belief that Robert was a normal person, a person like her, when in fact all the other rooms in the house were empty, or full of horrors: corpses or kidnap victims or chains. But then he was kissing her, throwing her bag and their coats on the couch and ushering her into the bedroom, groping her ass and pawing at her chest, with the avid clumsiness of that first kiss.

The bedroom wasn't empty, though it was emptier than the living room; he didn't have a bed frame, just a mattress and a box spring on the floor. There was a bottle of whiskey on his dresser, and he took a swig from it, then handed it to her and kneeled down and opened his laptop, an action that confused her, until she understood that he was putting on music.

Margot sat on the bed while Robert took off his shirt and unbuckled his pants, pulling them down to his ankles before realizing that he was still wearing his shoes and bending over to untie them. Looking at him like that, so awkwardly bent, his belly thick and soft and covered with hair, Margot recoiled. But the thought of what it would take to stop what she had set in motion was overwhelming; it would require an amount of tact and gentleness that she felt was impossible to summon. It wasn't that she was scared he would try to force her to do something against her will but that insisting that they stop now, after everything she'd done to push this forward, would make her seem spoiled and capricious, as if she'd ordered something at a restaurant and then, once the food arrived, had changed her mind and sent it back.

She tried to bludgeon her resistance into submission by taking a sip of the whiskey, but when he fell on top of her with those huge, sloppy kisses, his hand moving mechanically across her breasts and down to her crotch, as if he were making some perverse sign of the cross, she began to have trouble breathing and to feel that she really might not be able to go through with it after all.

Wriggling out from under the weight of him and straddling him helped, as did closing her eyes and remembering him kissing her forehead at the 7-Eleven. Encouraged by her progress, she pulled her shirt up over her head. Robert reached up and scooped her breast out of her bra, so that it jutted half in and half out of the cup, and rolled her nipple between his thumb and forefinger. This was uncomfortable, so she leaned forward, pushing herself into his hand. He got the hint and tried to undo her bra, but he couldn't work the clasp, his evident frustration reminiscent of his struggle with the keys, until at last he said, bossily, "Take that thing off," and she complied.

The way he looked at her then was like an exaggerated version of the expression she'd seen on the faces of all the guys she'd been naked with,

70

not that there were that many—six in total, Robert made seven. He looked stunned and stupid with pleasure, like a milk-drunk baby, and she thought that maybe this was what she loved most about sex—a guy revealed like that. Robert showed her more open need than any of the others, even though he was older, and must have seen more breasts, more bodies, than they had—but maybe that was part of it for him, the fact that he was older, and she was young.

As they kissed, she found herself carried away by a fantasy of such pure ego that she could hardly admit even to herself that she was having it. Look at this beautiful girl, she imagined him thinking. She's so perfect, her body is perfect, everything about her is perfect, she's only twenty years old, her skin is flawless, I want her so badly, I want her more than I've ever wanted anyone else, I want her so bad I might die.

The more she imagined his arousal, the more turned-on she got, and soon   75
they were rocking against each other, getting into a rhythm, and she reached into his underwear and took his penis in her hand and felt the pearled droplet of moisture on its tip. He made that sound again, that high-pitched feminine whine, and she wished there were a way she could ask him not to do that, but she couldn't think of any. Then his hand was inside her underwear, and when he felt that she was wet he visibly relaxed. He fingered her a little, very softly, and she bit her lip and put on a show for him, but then he poked her too hard and she flinched, and he jerked his hand away. "Sorry!" he said.

And then he asked, urgently, "Wait. Have you ever done this before?"

The night did, indeed, feel so odd and unprecedented that her first impulse was to say no, but then she realized what he meant and she laughed out loud.

She didn't mean to laugh; she knew well enough already that, while Robert might enjoy being the subject of gentle, flirtatious teasing, he was not a person who would enjoy being laughed at, not at all. But she couldn't help it. Losing her virginity had been a long, drawn-out affair preceded by several months' worth of intense discussion with her boyfriend of two years, plus a visit to the gynecologist and a horrifically embarrassing but ultimately incredibly meaningful conversation with her mom, who, in the end, had not only reserved her a room at a bed-and-breakfast but, after the event, written her a card. The idea that, instead of that whole involved, emotional process, she might have watched a pretentious Holocaust movie, drunk three beers, and then gone to some random house to lose her virginity to a guy she'd met at a movie theatre was so funny that suddenly she couldn't stop laughing, though the laughter had a slightly hysterical edge.

"I'm sorry," Robert said coldly. "I didn't know."

Abruptly, she stopped giggling.   80

"No, it was . . . nice of you to check," she said. "I've had sex before, though. I'm sorry I laughed."

"You don't need to apologize," he said, but she could tell by his face, as well as by the fact that he was going soft beneath her, that she did.

"I'm sorry," she said again, reflexively, and then, in a burst of inspiration, "I guess I'm just nervous, or something?"

He narrowed his eyes at her, as though suspicious of this claim, but it seemed to placate him. "You don't have to be nervous," he said. "We'll take it slow."

Yeah, right, she thought, and then he was on top of her again, kissing her and weighing her down, and she knew that her last chance of enjoying this encounter had disappeared, but that she would carry through with it until it was over. When Robert was naked, rolling a condom onto a dick that was only half visible beneath the hairy shelf of his belly, she felt a wave of revulsion that she thought might actually break through her sense of pinned stasis, but then he shoved his finger in her again, not at all gently this time, and she imagined herself from above, naked and spread-eagled with this fat old man's finger inside her, and her revulsion turned to self-disgust and a humiliation that was a kind of perverse cousin to arousal.

During sex, he moved her through a series of positions with brusque efficiency, flipping her over, pushing her around, and she felt like a doll again, as she had outside the 7-Eleven, though not a precious one now — a doll made of rubber, flexible and resilient, a prop for the movie that was playing in his head. When she was on top, he slapped her thigh and said, "Yeah, yeah, you like that," with an intonation that made it impossible to tell whether he meant it as a question, an observation, or an order, and when he turned her over he growled in her ear, "I always wanted to fuck a girl with nice tits," and she had to smother her face in the pillow to keep from laughing again. At the end, when he was on top of her in missionary, he kept losing his erection, and every time he did he would say, aggressively, "You make my dick so hard," as though lying about it could make it true. At last, after a frantic rabbity burst, he shuddered, came, and collapsed on her like a tree falling, and, crushed beneath him, she thought, brightly, This is the worst life decision I have ever made! And she marvelled at herself for a while, at the mystery of this person who'd just done this bizarre, inexplicable thing.

After a short while, Robert got up and hurried to the bathroom in a bow-legged waddle, clutching the condom to keep it from falling off. Margot lay on the bed and stared at the ceiling, noticing for the first time that there were stickers on it, those little stars and moons that were supposed to glow in the dark.

Robert returned from the bathroom and stood silhouetted in the doorway. "What do you want to do now?" he asked her.

"We should probably just kill ourselves," she imagined saying, and then she imagined that somewhere, out there in the universe, there was a boy who would think that this moment was just as awful yet hilarious as she did, and that sometime, far in the future, she would tell the boy this story. She'd say, "And then he said, 'You make my dick so hard,' " and the boy would shriek in agony and grab her leg, saying, "Oh, my God, stop, please, no, I can't take it anymore," and the two of them would collapse into each other's arms and laugh and laugh — but of course there was no such future, because no such boy existed, and never would.

So instead she shrugged, and Robert said, "We could watch a movie," and   90
he went to the computer and downloaded something; she didn't pay attention
to what. For some reason, he'd chosen a movie with subtitles, and she kept
closing her eyes, so she had no idea what was going on. The whole time, he
was stroking her hair and trailing light kisses down her shoulder, as if he'd forgotten that ten minutes ago he'd thrown her around as if they were in a porno
and growled, "I always wanted to fuck a girl with nice tits" in her ear.

Then, out of nowhere, he started talking about his feelings for her. He
talked about how hard it had been for him when she went away for break, not
knowing if she had an old high-school boyfriend she might reconnect with
back home. During those two weeks, it turned out, an entire secret drama
had played out in his head, one in which she'd left campus committed to him,
to Robert, but at home had been drawn back to the high-school guy, who, in
Robert's mind, was some kind of brutish, handsome jock, not worthy of her
but nonetheless seductive by virtue of his position at the top of the hierarchy
back home in Saline. "I was so worried you might, like, make a bad decision
and things would be different between us when you got back," he said. "But
I should have trusted you." My high-school boyfriend is gay, Margot imagined telling him. We were pretty sure of it in high school, but after a year of
sleeping around at college he's definitely figured it out. In fact, he's not even a
hundred per cent positive that he identifies as a man anymore; we spent a lot
of time over break talking about what it would mean for him to come out as
non-binary, so sex with him wasn't going to happen, and you could have asked
me about that if you were worried; you could have asked me about a lot of
things. But she didn't say any of that; she just lay silently, emanating a black,
hateful aura, until finally Robert trailed off. "Are you still awake?" he asked,
and she said yes, and he said, "Is everything O.K.?"

"How old are you, exactly?" she asked him.

"I'm thirty-four," he said. "Is that a problem?"

She could sense him in the dark beside her vibrating with fear.

"No," she said. "It's fine."   95

"Good," he said. "It was something I wanted to bring up with you, but I
didn't know how you'd take it." He rolled over and kissed her forehead, and
she felt like a slug he'd poured salt on, disintegrating under that kiss.

She looked at the clock; it was nearly three in the morning. "I should go
home, probably," she said.

"Really?" he said. "But I thought you'd stay over. I make great scrambled eggs!"

"Thanks," she said, sliding into her leggings. "But I can't. My roommate
would be worried. So."

"Gotta get back to the dorm room," he said, voice dripping with sarcasm.   100

"Yep," she said. "Since that's where I live."

The drive was endless. The snow had turned to rain. They didn't talk.
Eventually, Robert switched the radio to late-night NPR. Margot recalled how,
when they first got on the highway to go to the movie, she'd imagined that
Robert might murder her, and she thought, Maybe he'll murder me now.

He didn't murder her. He drove her to her dorm. "I had a really nice time tonight," he said, unbuckling his seat belt.

"Thanks," she said. She clutched her bag in her hands. "Me, too."

"I'm so glad we finally got to go on a date," he said.   105

"A *date*," she said to her imaginary boyfriend. "He called that a *date*." And they both laughed and laughed.

"You're welcome," she said. She reached for the door handle. "Thanks for the movie and stuff."

"Wait," he said, and grabbed her arm. "Come here." He dragged her back, wrapped his arms around her, and pushed his tongue down her throat one last time. "Oh, my God, when will it end?" she asked the imaginary boyfriend, but the imaginary boyfriend didn't answer her.

"Good night," she said, and then she opened the door and escaped. By the time she got to her room, she already had a text from him: no words, just hearts and faces with heart eyes and, for some reason, a dolphin.

She slept for twelve hours, and when she woke up she ate waffles in the dining   110
hall and binge-watched detective shows on Netflix and tried to envision the hopeful possibility that he would disappear without her having to do anything, that somehow she could just wish him away. When the next message from him did arrive, just after dinner, it was a harmless joke about Red Vines, but she deleted it immediately, overwhelmed with a skin-crawling loathing that felt vastly disproportionate to anything he had actually done. She told herself that she owed him at least some kind of breakup message, that to ghost on him would be inappropriate, childish, and cruel. And, if she did try to ghost, who knew how long it would take him to get the hint? Maybe the messages would keep coming and coming; maybe they would never end.

She began drafting a message — *Thank you for the nice time but I'm not interested in a relationship right now* — but she kept hedging and apologizing, attempting to close loopholes that she imagined him trying to slip through ("*Its O.K, I'm not interested in a relationship either, something casual is fine!*"), so that the message got longer and longer and even more impossible to send. Meanwhile, his texts kept arriving, none of them saying anything of consequence, each one more earnest than the last. She imagined him lying on his bed that was just a mattress, carefully crafting each one. She remembered that he'd talked a lot about his cats and yet she hadn't seen any cats in the house, and she wondered if he'd made them up.

Every so often, over the next day or so, she would find herself in a gray, daydreamy mood, missing something, and she'd realize that it was Robert she missed, not the real Robert but the Robert she'd imagined on the other end of all those text messages during break.

"Hey, so it seems like you're really busy, huh?" Robert finally wrote, three days after they'd fucked, and she knew that this was the perfect opportunity to send her half-completed breakup text, but instead she wrote back, "Haha sorry yeah" and "I'll text you soon," and then she thought, Why did I do that? And she truly didn't know.

"Just tell him you're not interested!" Margot's roommate, Tamara, screamed in frustration after Margot had spent an hour on her bed, dithering about what to say to Robert.

"I have to say more than that. We had *sex*," Margot said.   115

"*Do* you?" Tamara said. "I mean, really?"

"He's a nice guy, sort of," Margot said, and she wondered how true that was. Then, abruptly, Tamara lunged, snatching the phone out of Margot's hand and holding it far away from her as her thumbs flew across the screen. Tamara flung the phone onto the bed and Margot scrambled for it, and there it was, what Tamara had written: "Hi im not interested in you stop textng me."

"Oh, my God," Margot said, finding it suddenly hard to breathe.

"What?" Tamara said boldly. "What's the big deal? It's true."

But they both knew that it was a big deal, and Margot had a knot of fear   120
in her stomach so solid that she thought she might retch. She imagined Robert picking up his phone, reading that message, turning to glass, and shattering to pieces.

"Calm down. Let's go get a drink," Tamara said, and they went to a bar and shared a pitcher, and all the while Margot's phone sat between them on the table, and though they tried to ignore it, when it chimed with an incoming message they screamed and clutched each other's arms.

"I can't do it — you read it," Margot said. She pushed the phone toward Tamara. "You did this. It's your fault."

But all the message said was "O.K., Margot, I am sorry to hear that. I hope I did not do anything to upset you. You are a sweet girl and I really enjoyed the time we spent together. Please let me know if you change your mind."

Margot collapsed on the table, laying her head in her hands. She felt as though a leech, grown heavy and swollen with her blood, had at last popped off her skin, leaving a tender, bruised spot behind. But why should she feel that way? Perhaps she was being unfair to Robert, who really had done nothing wrong, except like her, and be bad in bed, and maybe lie about having cats, although probably they had just been in another room.

But then, a month later, she saw him in the bar — her bar, the one in the   125
student ghetto, where, on their date, she'd suggested they go. He was alone, at a table in the back, and he wasn't reading or looking at his phone; he was just sitting there silently, hunched over a beer.

She grabbed the friend she was with, a guy named Albert. "Oh, my God, that's him," she whispered. "The guy from the movie theatre!" By then, Albert had heard a version of the story, though not quite the true one; nearly all her friends had. Albert stepped in front of her, shielding her from Robert's view, as they rushed back to the table where their friends were. When Margot announced that Robert was there, everyone erupted in astonishment, and then they surrounded her and hustled her out of the bar as if she were the President and they were the Secret Service. It was all so over-the-top that she wondered if she was acting like a mean girl, but, at the same time, she truly did feel sick and scared.

Curled up on her bed with Tamara that night, the glow of the phone like a campfire illuminating their faces, Margot read the messages as they arrived:

"Hi Margot, I saw you out at the bar tonight. I know you said not to text you but I just wanted to say you looked really pretty. I hope you're doing well!"

"I know I shouldnt say this but I really miss you"

"Hey maybe I don't have the right to ask but I just wish youd tell me what   130
it is I did wrog"

"*wrong"

"I felt like we had a real connection did you not feel that way or . . ."

"Maybe I was too old for u or maybe you liked someone else"

"Is that guy you were with tonight your boyfriend"

"???"   135

"Or is he just some guy you are fucking"

"Sorry"

"When u laguehd when I asked if you were a virgin was it because youd
fucked so many guys"

"Are you fucking that guy right now"

"Are you"   140

"Are you"

"Are you"

"Answer me"

"Whore."

≡ THINKING ABOUT THE TEXT

1. How does the texting early in their relationship suggest or foreshadow what follows? Explain your thinking. Does Robert have cats? Explain why this is or isn't significant? At the end, what does she mean by missing the imaginary Robert? Why is this important?

2. What specific details about Margot's thinking about Robert as their dating begins sound realistic? What doesn't? Be sure to comment on "he could take her someplace and rape and murder her" (paragraph 20). Why would Margot's thinking be so dark?

3. Did Robert go to college? What specific details help you answer this question? Why does the answer matter to Robert? To Margot? To you? Are there points in the story where you are sympathetic to Robert? Not so sympathetic to Margot? Explain.

4. After the bouncer incident, Margot thinks "everything had been ruined and she couldn't understand why this was all so hard" (paragraph 40). What is your reading of her reaction? What is your explanation for Robert's "terrible kiss, shockingly bad" (paragraph 43)? Comment on the following: "She felt as if she were petting a large, skittish animal, like a horse or a bear, skillfully coaxing it to eat from her hand."

5. What details of their sexual encounter seem revealing about Robert? Comment on why she would "seem spoiled and capricious" (paragraph 70)? What does this have to do with consent? Explain how Margot's "revulsion," "self-disgust," and "humiliation" might make consent problematic. How does her fear make consent so complicated? Is Robert's last comment in the story the most outrageous thing he says? If you disagree, what are some other candidates?

ANDREW RUSSELL

The Ecstasy of Consent

Andrew Russell is a writer and teacher based on England, who often covers subjects like grief, depression, and mental health. He posted "The Ecstasy of Consent" on the web platform Medium on February 27, 2018.

"Without 'consent' in any human interactions, there's an ethical violation."

— Henry Johnson Jr.

The messages contained within this article are for "not all men," but also far too many. I felt a compulsion to write this piece based on a genuine concern for anyone who has suffered from a sexual encounter of any stripe where consent has not been given; and perhaps, just as importantly, not sought either. It seems all too obvious to state that the main victims in such encounters are, overwhelmingly, women. However, it has become apparent to me that far too much is said to women on the issues surrounding rape and sexual assault, and not anywhere near enough is said to men. Through this contribution I hope that I may edge the scales towards a position of greater egality.

Before I say too much more I think it is worth acknowledging, from the outset, the limitations of these insights. In order to wrestle and wrangle with every pertinent issue surrounding the prevention of rape and sexual assault, a book would be necessary; maybe several. The brevity of this article is deliberate: the main objectives are to make a small contribution to a larger conversation, but also to attempt a comprehensive pitch to a male audience concerning the many advantages of seeking consent. Nothing I do not say in this article should be in any way construed as a tacit denial of the importance, or existence, of any other issues relating to rape and sexual assault. In another place, at a different time, I would be more than happy to acknowledge, for example, that in tandem with any suggestions I make here, it would also be necessary to acknowledge shortcomings in the judicial system, or the perversity of a potential victim, as opposed to potential perpetrator-focused approach to education.

".. what she had was hers absolutely, not to be touched by other hands without proper permission being asked and granted."

— Charlaine Harris, A Bone to Pick

When we first begin to gain any kind of independence as children, the necessity to ask permission becomes an almost constant preoccupation. I remember well not just the process of asking for permission but also the consideration of any likely response based on any given request:

"Can I go and play at so-and-so's house next Tuesday?" The likely response was, "Yes, ok," with perhaps an added caveat or two about checking the logistics of what this expedition entailed.

"Can I borrow £200.00 to fund a start-up gambling ring at school — I   5
think this could be a real money-spinner and I'll give you 20%, no wait, 15% of any profits?" This was not likely to even find its way to the negotiating table (the dinner table — same table).

Whatever politics we have all had to contend with throughout our lives concerning permission, there seems to exist a poverty with regard to axiomatic permission-seeking in the one area where it is perhaps the most important for permission to be sought i.e. sexual encounters. I do not feel I would be met with much protest if I were to generalise along the following lines: In the vast majority of cases where we are asking for permission about anything of particular consequence, we tend to be appealing to power. In our youth this was our parents, or our teachers, or perhaps to a lesser degree, the parents of our peers. When we advance into adulthood we seek permission from our employers or from various public and private institutions. We take this for granted — the necessity of these interactions in order to gain a desired outcome for ourselves, or at the very least, reach a compromise. Your partner, in any given sexual encounter, is also in a position of power; whether you have considered it that way before, or not. They have power over their own body; as do you over yours for that matter. This should not be a revolutionary idea. After all, we don't simply have a body, we are our body. Such an intrinsic truth should make the idea of power a given. And yet somehow there seems to be an endemic failing to view ourselves, and more importantly others, in this regard.

If we are to grant this idea of power, how might you want to proceed in any future sexual encounters with partners, friends, "ships in the night" or anything in between? Firstly, you need to be clear about what you want from any given encounter. This may seem to contradict what I have already said but please, bear with me. Whenever you ask for permission for anything the first consideration is to decide what it is you are asking for. If you are asking for £200.00 for a school trip when all the while your intention is to implement your playground-based gambling scheme, you are being dishonest. This is self-evident. If you are asking for £200.00 but you are not sure what you are going to do with it even if it is granted, this is indecisive. A lack of either honesty or decisiveness will do you no favours "in the bedroom." If you do not have a clear idea about what you want in your head before entering into a situation of profound intimacy with someone, how can you ask for permission? So, consider what you want and communicate this. This may be a short and sweet conversation had in the back of a cab. It may be a conversation that is revisited several times over dinner, or walks in the park. It completely depends on the nature of the relationship you are engaged in.

"You kissed me once and now you feel as if you've got some special kind of licence to do it whenever you want?"

— Simona Panova, Nightmarish Sacrifice

I can only appear in my own person on this page. I can only write about my own experience in these matters. They are enough for me and perhaps they will be enough for you if you are willing to consider the underlying message behind the details. First of all though, please read the following:

"Silence does not mean yes. No can be thought and felt but never said. It can be screamed silently on the inside. It can be in the wordless stone of a clenched fist, fingernails digging into palm. Her lips sealed. Her eyes closed. His body just taking, never asking, never taught to question silence."

— Amy Reed, The Nowhere Girls

This sentiment moves me in a profound way. It reminds me of conversations I have had with dear friends, as well as the protestations I have heard from those who may not be willing to recognise the power of silence. It leaves me both sad and angry in almost equal measure. If this also stirs something in you, however uncomfortable, please read on, because there is a remedy. It is my view that permission; verbal permission that is, is not the end game to engaging in a sexual encounter. Permission should be an ongoing process throughout the encounter. Permission can be granted but it can also be withdrawn at any point during a sexual encounter. No one can know, with absolute certainty, in advance, how they are going to feel in any given situation. I believe that this is something we should be mindful of at all times. If we find ourselves in a position whereby anything we are doing is met with something similar to the reaction described above, are we still acting within a situation where permission is still a given, without ambiguity? If we possess the empathy to sense a shift in the dynamic between ourselves and another person and we then fail to act on that shift, could it be that we are then culpable of some kind of assault? There may be something very uncomfortable about this consideration. But it must be confronted. What are the ramifications if we fail to pick up on these not-so-subtle cues?

So, what do we stand to lose? Were this our only preoccupation (and I certainly do not think it should be) then here are some thoughts: I would suggest that engaging in sexual encounters with individuals where you at least had an inkling that they were not "totally into it" could have a few unwelcome results. Firstly, your pride is likely to take a bit of a beating. It should not be underestimated the cumulative effect that encounters like this could have on your own self-esteem in the long term. Secondly, why would you want to have to live with any sense of ambiguity given the magnitude of the situation? It might be possible to try and explain it away: "Well, she came back, didn't she?," "She said yes in the club, didn't she?" "She was enjoying it at the start, wasn't she?" But remember, if these questions are as strenuous in your mind as they appear on the page, you probably already know that they

10

will not bring you the solace you are seeking. And they will never justify what you took. Finally, you might find yourself having to answer some rather more uncomfortable questions down the station. This could impact on many other prospects for the rest of your life. Is it worth any other these outcomes? The answer should be an unequivocal "no." And this assessment is based solely on what you stand to lose. But it takes two to tango.

"The terror takes you. The cage is locked and the curtain drawn. Fingers dance along as blades, carving memories into your flesh that will leave scars long past being healed."

— *Amanda Steele, The Cliff*

I have never suffered anything like sexual assault myself. What I have seen, is the effects of sexual assault and rape in the eyes of those that I have loved. I have seen their scars re-open in the most intimate moments and have had to put everything of myself aside whilst they wrestle with the ghosts of past experiences. That is to say that their experiences with myself, however well-intentioned I may have been, were coloured by something that may have happened weeks, months, or years before I even knew them, and were perpetrated by someone who I may never have met. It stays with you—if you take nothing else away, then at the very least, think on this.

What does our partner stand to lose? In order to consider this in any real sense it is necessary to consider our own feelings or expectations about sex. One can assume that you, like me, consider sex to be an altogether positive experience. One can also assume that we may wish it to remain that way. Furthermore, allowing these assumptions, I do not consider it to be much of a stretch to assume that we may wish the very same for any sexual partner that we are engaged with. What should we do if we are in the midst of a sexual encounter and find our partner to have been coloured, in a detrimental sense, by a previous sexual encounter? What should our reaction be—in both the sense of "being there" for our partner; but also in regard to our reaction to the perpetrator of any previous transgression? Should it not trouble us that both our experience and that of our partner may remain tainted to some degree by the heinous actions of some faceless cretin? Bear this in mind: every time we refuse to recognise that we may be indulging in a situation with someone where the consensual scales are not equally balanced, we are, in potentia, creating someone whose sexual experiences may be forever tainted by our, albeit brief, but wholly potent, transgressions.

So, what is the remedy? It is my belief that it involves a most fervent adoption to a different approach to the idea of consent: the ecstasy of consent. The idea is this: we seek consent through an ongoing conversation that does not always partake of language. There will be times when words will be exchanged and there will be times when cues can be interpreted and reacted to. There will be times when we should stop and be happy to. There will be times when something from the past will stir and we might just need to be there for someone in that moment and put our own desires aside. Whatever becomes necessary can deliver ecstasy. It is the ecstasy that comes from an experience with someone, who, having realised your ability to put your own desires aside may become willing to give themselves to you without reserve or doubt.

"So she thoroughly taught him that one cannot take pleasure without giving pleasure, and that every gesture, every caress, every touch, every glance, every last bit of the body has its secret, which brings happiness to the person who knows how to wake it. She taught him that after a celebration of love the lovers should not part without admiring each other, without being conquered or having conquered, so that neither is bleak or glutted or has the bad feeling of being used or misused."

— *Hermann Hesse, Siddhartha*

This unfettered commitment to the moment can bring forth the most transcendent of experiences. There is immense value in every sacrifice that you have made to ensure someone else's pleasure in lieu of your own. And within that empyreal state, the ecstasy will be as much for you as it is for them. And isn't that what we should all be aspiring to in any case? This matters to me. I hope it matters to you. There is an effort involved in achieving ecstasy, there is no denying it. But it is rare that anything worth gaining does not entail a little hard work. I implore you to invest in the pursuit of ecstasy. It does not simply entail the fate of your partner's happiness, or even your own. There is a society waiting to awaken from a poisonous slumber of sexual inequality and inadequacy. Every gender is a victim of this poison. The antidote is in our possession. And it tastes delectable.

"So sweet and delicious do I become,
when I am in bed with a man
who, I sense, loves and enjoys me,
that the pleasure I bring excels all delight,
so the knot of love, however tight
it seemed before, is tied tighter still."

— *Veronica Franco, Poems and Selected Letters*

The conversation surrounding consent should never cease, whether it be 15 on the micro scale; a transcendent interaction between lovers, or on the macro scale; an unabashed and unapologetic conversation within societies as a whole.

"The fact is, rape is utterly commonplace in all our cultures. It is part of the fabric of everyday life, yet we all act as if it's something shocking and extraordinary whenever it hits the headlines. We remain silent, and so we condone it . . . Until rape, and the structures — sexism, inequality, tradition — that make it possible, are part of our dinner-table conversation with the next generation, it will continue. Is it polite and comfortable to talk about it? No. Must we anyway? Yes."

"To protect our children, we must talk to them about rape."

— *Desmond Tutu*

≡ THINKING ABOUT THE TEXT

1. What is the ecstasy of consent, according to Russell? Do you agree or disagree with him?

2. Explain how power figures into Russell's thinking. Do you agree or disagree with him?

3. What does Russell mean by having an "unfettered commitment to the moment"? Do you agree with him or not? Explain.

4. Explain the ways ongoing consent might be an antidote to inequality.

5. Agree or disagree with one of the three quotes that conclude the essay, and explain your position.

KATELYN EWEN
When "Yes" Really Means "Yes"

Katelyn Ewen is an advocate for sexual assault awareness and sex education. She works as a Graphic Designer at the Gottman Institute.

Cultural debate and discourse about consent have gained traction following the #MeToo movement. After years of silence, women are sharing their stories about sexual misconduct and assault. However, in the United States, a country that doesn't teach comprehensive sex education, we still look towards media, film, music, literature, and other cultural institutions for sexual guidance. If we depend on these systems for our sexual awareness, especially those that depict sexuality as unrealistic fiction, we leave with a bankrupt idea of how sex works and how consent ought to work.

Women's resistance to sex can often be seen as a challenge for men to overcome, where men "get some" and women "give it up" or "save it." The narrative is beginning to change, with some pop culture getting the act of consent right, like in the film *Call Me By Your Name*, where a man asks another man if he can kiss him in the heat of a breathless moment. What we can do, for ourselves and others, is to begin to work towards changing the narrative by first educating ourselves, changing our conversations and behavior, and exercising affirmative consent in our own relationships.

At 17, I experienced the result of a lack of conversation about consent. I was sexually assaulted, and, in the moment, I said nothing and I did nothing. I froze, didn't, couldn't, say no, or yes, or anything. I experienced what I would later learn is called tonic immobility: prey responds to a threat by playing dead in the hopes that the predator loses interest.

That same year, another sexual encounter with a partner escalated without verbal consent and I was faced with the uncertainty of my culpability in the situation. Unfortunately, not all sexual encounters are by the book.

Sometimes saying no is not enough. Sometimes reading someone's nonverbal cues is not enough.

WHAT IS AFFIRMATIVE CONSENT?

This is where the term *affirmative consent* comes in, and what it aims to avoid;   5
the grey areas of sexual interaction that are not adequately addressed by a "no means no" system. The State University of New York defines affirmative consent:

> Affirmative consent is a knowing, voluntary, and mutual decision among all participants to engage in sexual activity. Consent can be given by words or actions, as long as those words or actions create clear permission regarding willingness to engage in the sexual activity. Silence or lack of resistance, in and of itself, does not demonstrate consent. The definition of consent does not vary based upon a participant's sex, sexual orientation, gender identity, or gender expression.

The idea behind affirmative consent is that "no means no" is not enough. Rather, we need to start thinking in terms of "yes means yes." This idea, which is of incredible importance to young people exploring their sexuality, has been recently circulating around college campuses. It is now making its way into the mainstream conversation and not just regarding casual or short-term sexual encounters, but also affirmative consent within committed romantic relationships.

The concept arises from the idea that, in order to foster productive, trusting, and connected relationships with our partners, we need to pay attention to their needs in the bedroom as much as we pay attention to any of their other physical or emotional needs. Open communication is the gateway to safe sex and great sex. By communicating better with our partners, we can all better enjoy the physical connections that we make and without the risk of violating the trust of our partners. We're each responsible for ensuring that our sexual partners are comfortable with and consenting to what's happening at every stage of the relationship.

This extends past the first date and throughout the entirety of a relationship. Consent is an active process that evolves, and so, too, should our communication about it.

The concept of affirmative consent has been met with ambivalence, the main criticism being that asking for consent takes the romance and passion out of intimate encounters. I counter that nothing else can take the romance and passion out of an intimate encounter like non-consent. Feeling pressured or forced, regardless of verbal or non-verbal cues, is a surefire way to kill the romance and make someone feel violated.

Rather than thinking of consent as a hurdle on the way to the finish line,   10
I argue that we should begin to think of it as a crucial component of all sexual activity. We should be exercising affirmative consent before sex even starts, as a part of foreplay, to maintain communication during sex, and after sex is over.

Here are some practical steps to incorporate affirmative consent throughout all the physical intimacy that you and your partner experience together.

Discuss what you like in advance: Before sex begins, you should be in active communication with your partner about what they're comfortable with. The more you know about your partner sexually, the better sex you'll have, and the more attuned you will be to when they're into it and when they're not. This step is about building erotic Love Maps with your partner. It guides you and your partner to a healthy starting place that you can build upon and change as you learn more about each other's preferences and sexual needs.

Make asking for consent a part of foreplay: Good sex begins with good foreplay. According to a report in the *Journal of Sexual Research*, men and women hope to engage in about 20 minutes of foreplay before actual intercourse. That's plenty of time to ask some simple questions to make sure that both partners affirmatively consent to what is to follow.

An easy way to engage in this talk without losing the heat of the moment is to use consent as a form of dirty talk. Asking your partner "Do you want to do _____?" is a way to ask for affirmative consent, or saying "I want to do _____ to you" is erotic in the moment if they're already into it, and also gives them an opportunity to say no or make other suggestions that they're more comfortable with.

Maintain communication during sex: Talking during sex, as well as giving feedback during sex as a continuation of the dirty talk that may have started during foreplay, is a great way to continue communication about consent. Feedback about what is working for you and what isn't through actual talk or through affirmative response like saying "Oh, yes," or "Keep doing that" helps both of you to learn more about each other and please each other more effectively, which creates a win-win for both parties.

It is also essential to read your partner's body language as best you can. 15 Though verbal affirmation is ideal, sometimes it is not possible. If they're saying "no," but their body seems to be saying "yes," then the "no" *always* stands. If they're saying "yes" verbally but their body language is saying "no," then it is best to pause and ask if they're truly comfortable with what's happening.

Come up with signals for when verbalization isn't possible: If you're thinking that dirty talk, or even talking at all during sex, is not something that comes naturally to you or your partner, coming up with cues for "yes" and "no" ahead of time is a good alternative or addition to other communication patterns you've established together. There are some circumstances where verbal confirmation is not ideal or not possible; in these cases, coming up with a signal system with your partner ahead of time is key. This can be a shake of the head, a raised hand, or a safe word. This is up to you and your partner as long as it is agreed upon before it might become necessary.

Talk about it afterward: Having a conversation about sex after you've finished is the second part of building erotic Love Maps with your partner. You can discuss what you liked, what you weren't that into, and what you might like to try next time so that the next encounter is more informed, attuned, and better for both of you.

The major benefit of affirmative consent is that it will attune you to your partner and their needs as much as you are attuned to your own. This approach to consent and communication about sex is a recipe for great and safe consensual sex between partners.

≡ THINKING ABOUT THE TEXT

1. Why is "no means no" insufficient in sexual encounters, according to Ewen? To whom should this advice apply?

2. What are our responsibilities as sexual partners, according to Ewen? Do you agree or disagree?

3. How does Ewen address the opposition to her argument? Do you agree with her? Explain.

4. Do you agree or disagree with Ewen's "practical steps" in trying to implement affirmative consent? Explain your thinking.

5. Explain what you think Robert's response might have been had Margot suggested that both of them conform to the practical steps. Can you suggest alternatives that may have improved the experience for Margot?

≡ MAKING COMPARISONS

1. In what specific ways are Russell and Ewen in agreement?

2. What specifically would Margot agree with in each essay?

3. If Robert were to read these essays, what specifically might he object to? Explain.

SUZANNAH WEISS

#Metoo Has Made Me See Anyone Is Capable of Sexual Abuse — Including Me

Suzannah Weiss (1990) is a feminist writer who grew up on Long Island, New York. She attended Brown University where she studied Gender and Sexuality Studies. She has written for New York Magazine, *the* Washington Post, Cosmopolitan, *and others. The story she references in the first line is an account of a twenty-two year old woman's date with the comedian Aziz Ansari, which she says was a terrible experience for her because of his sexual misconduct. The article was widely praised and condemned. Ansari denies any misconduct.*

When I first read Babe.net's now-infamous account of one woman's violating sexual encounter with Aziz Ansari, I thought back to the frat boy who pressured me into giving oral sex in college. And the date in New York who took my shirt off after I told him I just wanted to kiss. And the one in San Francisco who grabbed my boob out of nowhere in Dolores Park.

Only after days of mulling over these stories and thinking about how every woman has one did I think back to the time I wanted to have sex with my ex and he wanted to play his guitar and call it a night. "I just feel like relaxing tonight," he told me as I ran my hands over him. With my hopes crushed and my ego bruised, I strategized: I would take off my clothes and lie on the floor naked until he'd feel too guilty to refuse. It worked. I convinced myself I had turned him on, but in the morning, he told me he'd done it for the reason I'd secretly anticipated: He didn't want me to feel bad.

And then, only after that, did I think back to the time my first boyfriend expressed reluctance to have sex with his parents in the next room, and I said "I'll be quiet" and got on top of him. Or the time he said he didn't want to have sex while I was on my period and I (dishonestly) convinced him it wouldn't get messy. To be honest, I don't remember the details of these encounters, like what specifically he said or whether he eventually said "okay." But that just goes to show I wasn't paying attention.

And only now, as I'm writing this, am I thinking back to the time my current partner said he was too tired for sex, and then I touched his penis until he changed his mind — but did he really change his mind, or did he just want to appease me?

Yes, I see myself in Grace. But I also see myself in Aziz.   5

When the conversation around the #MeToo hashtag moved from morally unambiguous sexual predators like Harvey Weinstein to self-described feminists like Aziz Ansari, some took the opportunity to discuss how rape culture is so ever-present, nearly every woman has been violated, and even "good men" have violated women. But more and more, I'm realizing it goes even further than that: Nearly everyone of every gender has the potential to be both the violator and the violated.

Soon after the #MeToo movement broke out, a friend told me she couldn't get herself to use the hashtag, despite being a sexual abuse survivor, because she'd once had sex with a guy who was passed-out drunk. I've used the hashtag myself, but I couldn't fault my partners for using it in reference to me. My right to say #MeToo is predicated on a standard of consent that gives them that right as well.

As man after man has been taken down by sexual misconduct accusations, I've gotten more and more nervous about what the sheer prevalence of predatory behavior means for my own relationships. Is there any man out there who is *not* capable of sexual assault? "At least I can trust that, say, Aziz Ansari wouldn't do that," I remember saying in one discussion. "At least there are some good guys."

After the Aziz Ansari accusations came out, I panicked: If he wasn't one of the "good guys," who was? Were there any good guys? Could I even be sure that my partner was one of the good guys? But once it fully set in that not even *I* was one of the good guys, I came to believe the whole concept of "good guys" is made up. It's a way to deny what's becoming more and more evident: Rape culture affects everyone. And not just guys.

There are gradations of violations of consent. They're not the same, but we need to talk about them all. There are deliberate perversions of power like Harvey Weinstein's. Then there are the things nearly all of us have done because of the toxic messages and lack of information rape culture gives us.

For men, these messages look something like: *You are entitled to women's bodies* (the assumption that all men are attracted to women is its own toxic message). *"No" is a challenge for you to push harder. You are uncontrollably horny and aggressive by nature. You can't help it.* For women, these messages look something like: *You aren't capable of sexually assaulting anyone. You are weak and unthreatening. You can't assault a man because men always want sex, and you can't assault a woman because women aren't attracted to women, and you can't assault a non-binary person because they don't even exist.*

These messages play out in different ways for different genders, with a misogynistic culture leading us to normalize male violence against women while completely ignoring the possibility of female violence against men or violence that does not follow a heterosexual, cis-normative dynamic. Sexual violence against women and non-binary people is more widespread, with 33.1% of women and 39.1% of transgender, genderqueer, questioning, or non-conforming people (compared to 8.6 percent of men) experiencing unwanted touching by their senior year of college—and it's part of a larger system that keeps men in power and people of marginalized genders living in fear. I don't mean to draw a false equivalency.

However, there are certain messages we *all* get: *Silence is consent. You don't have to ask before having sex with someone. Talking ruins the mood. The victim is asking for it. It's not a big deal.* People of all genders who have grown up with these messages are prone to violating others' consent.

And we are all victim to a lack of information. We don't learn about affirmative consent in school. We don't get told to ask our partners what they'd be into before we do anything with them. We don't learn about the different forms sexual abuse can take, from unwanted ogling to verbal coercion.

As I've come to terms with the fact that our culture leaves all of us susceptible to sexual violence, #MeToo has come to serve a dual function for me. As a survivor of sexual harassment and coercion, it has helped me see that these behaviors were not okay, no matter how much they've been downplayed. But as someone who has been sexually coercive, it has also led me to see that my own behaviors were not okay, even though the friends I confided in about them said things like "but it's different because women are less threatening." Downplaying my own actions would also function to downplay others' actions against me. And this movement is about taking *all* such actions seriously, no matter who perpetrated them.

It's difficult to hold both these truths at once: I deserve compassion for the times I was violated, but I don't deserve to be let off the hook for the times I was the violator. These are the truths we all most reconcile. This is not an occasion to self-flagellate, nor is it an occasion to clear ourselves of wrongdoing. It's an occasion to become more conscious of how we treat others.

For me, this means that if someone expresses any hesitancy to have sex with me, I will not push it. It means I won't assume consent from anyone just because they're a man or we're in a relationship. It means I will respect someone's "no" without questions even if their reason for saying "no" (e.g. not liking period sex) seems regressive to me. It means I will not be invested in viewing anyone, including myself, as one of the good guys.

I will keep saying #MeToo, but from now on, it will carry multiple meanings: "I, too, have been violated. I, too, have violated others. I, too, need to do better."

≡ THINKING ABOUT THE TEXT

1. Is Weiss's opening gambit of giving explicit examples of her own misconduct effective? Did these examples make you trust her persona more or less? Is her authority increased or decreased? What if her examples of her own conduct were more egregious?

2. From your own experience, is Weiss's assumption that we are all to varying degrees capable of sexual misconduct, from subtle coercion to physical violations, warranted?

3. As a culture, have we come to accept Weiss's assertion that "there are gradations of violations of consent" (paragraph 10)? Give examples from your own experience or from what you've seen or read. How might these gradations work?

4. Comment on the "messages" Weiss says our culture gives men and women. Do they seem accurate or are they overstated? Or understated? Do you hold any of these? Do your friends? How does one acquire them?

5. What is Weiss's perspective on "rape culture"? What is yours? Is she overstating or understating the situation?

≡ MAKING COMPARISONS

1. Weiss makes some assumptions about collective guilt that Ewen and Russell do not. Do you think they would find her position acceptable? Explain.

2. All three authors deal with consent. What are some of their more interesting observations or recommendations?

3. Which piece most speaks to your concerns? Explain. Which pieces speak to your concerns the least? Explain.

≡ WRITING ABOUT ISSUES

1. Argue that affirmative consent would or would not have made a difference in Margot and Robert's relationship.

2. Write one of the following: A.) A letter from Margot to Robert arguing that her consent was at best problematic. B.) A letter from Robert to Margot arguing that their date, from start to finish, was completely consensual.

3. Write an argument that Margot's assessment that their sexual encounter was the "worst life decision I have ever made" is crucial in deciding whether she consented or not.

4. After having bad sex with Robert, Margot imagines that she will be talking and laughing about the encounter with a future, sympathetic, boyfriend. Then she says, "but of course there was no such future, because no such boy existed, and never would" (paragraph 89). Argue that her thinking is well founded, too cynical, or something else entirely.

≡ Literature and Current Issues: Can Our Culture's Tribal Hate be Bridged?

THOMAS LUX, "The People of the Other Village"

ARGUMENTS ON THE ISSUE:

MICHIKO KAKUTANI, "Filters, Silos, and Tribes"

AMY CHUA, "How America's Identity Politics Went from Inclusion to Division"

ELIZABETH KOLBERT, "Why Facts Don't Change Our Minds"

Increasingly, American politics and culture seem to be divided into opposing camps or tribes with little desire to walk in the shoes of someone thought to be in opposition to the other group's values or point of view. Apparently it is almost impossible to see the world as others do, especially if that other is perceived as a rival or enemy. Experts tell us that reason and rational behavior diminishes the more we feel threatened, whether or not the danger is real. Tribalism is, then, an irrational loyalty to your group and an equal dislike, even hatred, for the other. The language used by different tribes is often a key to their opposing worldviews: illegal aliens versus undocumented workers; traditional families versus marriage equality; the life of the unborn versus my body, my choice. It is almost as if these opposing tribes live in a different time and place. Such a dire situation could lead to the hatred depicted in Lux's poem.

The poem printed here is meant to show one extreme consequence of hatred and the absolute absence of love. We are not in such horrendous circumstances, but we should not forget that the end to the tribal debate over slavery ended in the tragedy of the Civil War. We have included three essays that try to understand how our democratic goal of consensus through dialogue and debate could have been so ignored. Are all disagreements solvable through sweet reason? That is finally the question posed by this cluster.

≡ BEFORE YOU READ

Do you think of yourself as a member of a tribe? Perhaps not, but that term is being used more and more to describe group membership that is in conflict with others or at least opposed to other groups, for example, the NRA, Democrats, Republicans, feminists, conservatives, perhaps fraternities and sororities, and so forth. What makes someone a member? Can you be a member of various tribes by default?

THOMAS LUX
The People of the Other Village

Thomas Lux (1946–2017) was born in Northampton, Massachusetts, and attended Emerson College in Boston. During his life he wrote numerous volumes of poetry, including The Street of Clocks *(2001) and* The Cradle Place: Poems

(2004), and he was the recipient of many prestigious grants and prizes. His most recent collection is To the Left of Time *(2016). He taught at Sarah Lawrence College; the University of California, Irvine; Emerson College; and Georgia Tech in Atlanta, where he served as the Bourne Chair in poetry until his death. The following poem is from* New and Selected Poems *(1997).*

The people of the other village
hate the people of this village
and would nail our hats
to our heads for refusing in their presence to remove them
or staple our hands to our foreheads   5
for refusing to salute them
if we did not hurt them first: mail them packages of rats,
mix their flour at night with broken glass.
We do this, they do that.
They peel the larynx from one of our brothers' throats.   10
We devein one of their sisters.
The quicksand pits they built were good.
Our amputation teams were better.
We trained some birds to steal their wheat.
They sent to us exploding ambassadors of peace.   15
They do this, we do that.
We canceled our sheep imports.
They no longer bought our blankets.
We mocked their greatest poet
and when that had no effect   20
we parodied the way they dance
which did cause pain, so they, in turn, said our God
was leprous, hairless.
We do this, they do that.
Ten thousand (10,000) years, ten thousand   25
(10,000) brutal, beautiful years.

[1997]

≡ THINKING ABOUT THE TEXT

1. "We do this, they do that" (line 8 and line 23) and its reverse (line 15) is a kind of refrain suggesting the poem's theme. What is that theme and how accurate a statement about human nature do you think this is?

2. Conflicts between villages/cities/countries are often rooted in religious, ethnic, racial, or political differences. Does Lux hint at these or is he deliberately vague?

3. Lux is known for blending irony and humor with serious subjects. Are some of the grotesque details of the disputes meant as gallows humor? What effect do these graphic details have?

4. What is Lux's intention in this poem? Is it, for example, a plea for tolerance? Is it a bitter indictment of humanity? Or something else?

5. What is the significance of the seemingly incongruous "beautiful" in the last line?

MICHIKO KAKUTANI
Filters, Silos, and Tribes

Michiko Kakutani (1955) was born in New Haven, Connecticut, and received her B.A. in English from Yale University. She worked for Time *and the* Washington Post *before joining the* New York Times *in 1979. When she retired in 2017 as the chief book critic for that paper,* Vanity Fair *called her "the most powerful book critic in the English-speaking world." In 1998 she won the Pulitzer Prize for Criticism. The following piece is taken from* The Death of Truth: Notes on Falsehood in the Age of Trump *(2018).*

> *We're all islands shouting lies to each other across seas of misunderstanding.*
> — Rudyard Kipling, 1890

Shortly before the 2004 election, Arthur Miller—the playwright and a dedicated liberal—wondered, "How can the polls be neck and neck when I don't know one Bush supporter?"

Since then, of course, the walls of our political silos have only grown taller; the insulation of our echo chambers, that much thicker. Even before we were being sealed in impermeable filter bubbles by Facebook news feeds and Google search data, we were living in communities that had become increasingly segregated in terms of politics, culture, geography, and lifestyle. Add to that partisan news sources like Fox News, Breitbart, and Drudge, and it's no surprise that the Rashomon effect has taken hold: common ground between citizens from opposing political parties is rapidly shrinking, and the whole idea of consensus is becoming a thing of the past.

A 2016 Pew survey showed that 45 percent of Republicans view Democratic policies as a threat to the nation's well-being, and 41 percent of Democrats say the same about GOP policies. And the animosity goes well beyond policy disagreements; it's personal. Seventy percent of Democrats in that Pew survey said that Republicans are more close-minded than other Americans; meanwhile, 47 percent of Republicans said Democrats are more immoral than other Americans, and 46 percent said they are lazier.

Such partisanship is being inflated further by Russian trolls seeking to undermine democracy in America by amplifying social divisions through fake news and fake social media accounts and by President Trump's use of inflammatory remarks to pander to his base and bait his adversaries. It's telling that the old national motto *E pluribus unum* (Out of many, one) has been removed from Trump's commemorative presidential coins and replaced with his own slogan "Make America Great Again."

These growing divides in America are only a couple of decades old, according to Bill Bishop's book, *The Big Sort.* In the 1950s, 1960s, and 1970s, Bishop wrote, communities seemed to be growing more politically integrated, and "there was an economic convergence, too," as Sunbelt prosperity spread in the South. But around 1980 or so something happened, says Bishop: people had begun reordering their lives around "their values, their tastes, and their

5

beliefs" — in part, as a response to the social and cultural dislocations that followed in the wake of the 1960s. People with college degrees were gravitating toward cities, while rural areas slipped behind economically.

"As we've lost trust in traditional institutions," Bishop wrote, "the tenuous bonds of the workplace have proven insufficient to satisfy people's need for belonging." In response, people found a sense of community by seeking out like-minded neighborhoods, churches, social clubs, and other organizations. It's a dynamic that would be amplified at light speed by the internet — by news sites catering to particular ideological points of view, by special interest bulletin boards, and by social media that's helped people further sort themselves into silos of shared interests. By the turn of the millennium, Bishop wrote, the divisions were less about ideology than about tastes and values, but "as the parties have come to represent lifestyle — and as lifestyle has defined communities — everything seems divisible, Republican or Democratic." Everything meaning not just your views on health care or voting rights or global warming but where you shop, what you eat, what sorts of movies you watch. A 2017 Pew survey showed that Americans don't even agree about the value of a college education: while 72 percent of Democrats and Democratic-leaning independents said colleges and universities have a positive effect on the country, a majority of Republicans and Republican leaners (58 percent) have a negative view of those institutions of higher learning.

Meanwhile, the number of people in the middle — independents or swing voters — dwindled in clout, or at least in the attention they received from many politicians. In his book *The Second Civil War*, the veteran political reporter Ronald Brownstein described how George W. Bush's political advisers reviewed the data from the 2000 campaign and decided to focus in 2004 on energizing the base and encouraging turnout among Republicans — a harbinger of the play-to-the-base strategy Trump would later pursue so relentlessly. As one Bush adviser told Brownstein, "This is not designed to be a 55 percent presidency. This is designed to be a presidency that moves as much as possible of what we believe into law while holding fifty plus one of the country and the Congress" In 2016, Hillary Clinton's campaign basically wrote off the white working-class vote (the vote her husband, Bill, had owned) and focused, instead, on turning out her base.

Ideological consistency grew over the years: a 2014 Pew survey found that in the two decades after 1994 more Democrats gave "uniformly liberal responses" to policy questions (about matters like immigration, the environment, the role of government), while more Republicans gave "uniformly conservative responses." Those members of both parties with the most consistent views, the Pew study noted, had a "disproportionate influence on the political process"; they were more likely to vote, more likely to donate money, more likely to contact elected officials. And then there is gerrymandering, which has favored Republicans since they launched a concerted effort after Obama's election in 2008 to gain control of state governments, which are in charge of drawing (or redrawing) congressional districts. The new, often highly misshapen districts, drawn with the help of computer software, gave

Republicans a substantial advantage in capturing and holding on to the House of Representatives, and they also tended to tilt districts further to the right, which made many elected officials reluctant to compromise with Democrats when they got to Washington, out of fear of being primaried on their right.

For many of these committed partisans, supporting their party was like being a rabid, die-hard fan of a favorite NBA, MLB, or NFL team; it was part of their own identity, and their team could do no wrong. They might hate a particular policy or a particular candidate — much the way they might blame their team's coach for a bad play, or loathe an overpaid, underperforming player received in a trade — but short off the apocalypse they were going to remain loyal fans while wishing pain and humiliation upon their opponents.

Polarized voting in Congress mirrored these developments: by 2014, a   10
Pew report noted, Republicans and Democrats on Capitol Hill were "further apart from one another than at any point in modem history"; it also highlighted that rising polarization among elected officials was "asymmetrical, with much of the widening gap between the two parties attributable to a rightward shift among Republicans."

The chief reason for this asymmetry was the explosion of right-wing media. Back in the 1990s, Rush Limbaugh proved that incendiary invective and showmanship—two things Donald Trump would learn from him—could win him a lucrative national audience, and for decades his faithful dittoheads loyally repeated whatever he said, even when what he said was ridiculous. In one diatribe, Limbaugh asserted that "the Four Corners of Deceit are government, academia, science, and the media." He also declared that "scientists wear white lab coats and they look really official" but "they're frauds. They're bought and paid for by the left."

In the three decades since the FCC revoked the Fairness Doctrine (which required TV and radio stations to devote some of their programming to important issues of the day and air opposing views on those issues) and the two decades since Roger Ailes and Rupert Murdoch launched Fox News, right-wing media has grown into a sprawling, solipsistic network that relentlessly repeats its own tropes (the dangers of immigration, the untrustworthiness of mainstream media, the evils of big government, and so on), and it's succeeded in framing many debates in the national conversation through its sheer shamelessness and decibel level. Breitbart News, which Steve Bannon described as a "platform for the alt-right," and the Sinclair Broadcast Group, which reaches an estimated 38 percent of American households through local news broadcasts, have expanded the right-wing media universe, along with countless online sites, YouTube channels, and radio broadcasts. In an Orwellian move, Sinclair has even forced local news anchors to read a scripted message about "false news" that echoes President Trump's own rhetoric undermining real reporting.

Many of these outlets don't even go through the motions of trying to provide verifiable facts and information, but instead attempt to spin what one talk show host calls "truth-based content" into self-serving, precooked narratives that ratify audiences' existing beliefs or gin up their worst fears.

In recent years, the conservative radio host Charlie Sykes observed, conservative media created an "alternate reality bubble" that "destroyed our own immunity to fake news, while empowering the worst and most reckless on the right."

A 2017 Harvard study of more than 1.25 million stories (published online   15 between April 1, 2015, and Election Day in November 2016) concluded that pro-Trump audiences relied heavily on this "insulated knowledge community," which uses "social media as a backbone to transmit a hyper-partisan perspective to the world" and reinforces users' shared worldview while poisoning them against mainstream journalism that might challenge their preconceptions. The result: an environment in which the president can allude to a terrorist event in Sweden that never happened, or a presidential adviser can reference a nonexistent "Bowling Green massacre."

With Tribal Politics increasingly dominating Republican and Democratic politics, candidates scramble to lock down their party's base during the primary process. Much of the Republican base now reacts instantly with knee-jerk denial when it comes to issues like gun violence, Obamacare, or global warming. Never mind statistics, expert analyses, carefully researched university or government studies, in some cases even their own self-interest — a lot of hard-core Trump supporters dismiss such evidence as never-to-be-trusted liberal or deep state politics. For these partisans, party loyalty and tribal politics matter more than facts, more than morality and decency: witness the Republicans who supported Senate candidate Roy Moore, who was accused of sexual misconduct against teenage girls, and the Trump supporters who booed John McCain, a genuine war hero, and viciously said God had punished him with cancer for standing up to Trump.

As the journalist Andrew Sullivan wrote, "The enduring, complicated divides of ideology, geography, party, class, religion, and race have mutated into something deeper, simpler to map, and therefore much more ominous": not simple political polarization, but the fracture of the country into "two coherent tribes, eerily balanced in political power, fighting not just to advance their own side but to provoke, condemn, and defeat the other."

Assorted theories have been advanced to explain confirmation bias — why people rush to embrace information that supports their beliefs while rejecting information that disputes them: that first impressions are difficult to dislodge, that there's a primitive instinct to defend one's turf, that people tend to have emotional rather than intellectual responses to being challenged and are loath to carefully examine evidence.

Group dynamics only exaggerate these tendencies, the author and legal scholar Cass Sunstein observed in his book *Going to Extremes*: insularity often means limited information input (and usually information that reinforces pre-existing views) and a desire for peer approval; and if the group's leader "does not encourage dissent and is inclined to an identifiable conclusion, it is highly likely that the group as a whole will move toward that conclusion."

Once the group has been psychologically walled off, Sunstein wrote,   20
"the information and views of those outside the group can be discredited,
and hence nothing will disturb the process of polarization as group members
continue to talk." In fact, groups of like-minded people can become breeding
grounds for extreme movements. "Terrorists are made, not born," Sunstein
observed, "and terrorist networks often operate in just this way. As a result,
they can move otherwise ordinary people to violent acts."

Charlie Sykes decided to step down from his popular radio show at the end of
2016. Politics had become a "binary tribal world," he pointed out, in which voters "tolerate bizarre behavior, dishonesty, crudity and cruelty, because the other
side is always worse." What his listeners wouldn't tolerate was his criticism of
Trump or his objections that crazy conspiracy theories about Hillary Clinton and
Barack Obama were demonstrably false. His listeners had become accustomed to
rejecting mainstream sources of news, and for that matter, simple facts.

"In the new Right media culture," he wrote in his 2017 book, *How the
Right Lost Its Mind,* "negative information simply no longer penetrates; gaffes
and scandals can be snuffed out, ignored, or spun; counternarratives can be
launched. Trump has proven that a candidate can be immune to the narratives, criticism, and fact-checking of the mainstream media."

Long gone are the pre-cable days when many people got their news from one
of three TV networks and watched many of the same television shows like *All
in the Family* and *The Mary Tyler Moore Show.* New *Star Wars* movies and the
Super Bowl remain some of the few communal events that capture an audience cutting across demographic lines.

As for news, an increasingly fragmented media environment offers sites
and publications targeted at niche audiences from the reddest red to the blu-
est blue. Facebook, Twitter, YouTube, and many other sites use algorithms to
personalize the information you see — information customized on the basis of
earlier data they've collected about you.

"With Google personalized for everyone," the internet activist Eli Pariser   25
wrote in his book, *The Filter Bubble,* "the query 'stem cells' might produce dia-
metrically opposed results for scientists who support stem cell research and
activists who oppose it. 'Proof of climate change' might turn up different
results for an environmental activist and an oil company executive. In polls, a
huge majority of us assume search engines are unbiased. But that may be just
because they're increasingly biased to share our own views. More and more,
your computer monitor is a kind of one-way mirror, reflecting your own interests while algorithmic observers watch what you click."

Because social media sites give us information that tends to confirm our
view of the world — what Pariser calls "an endless you-loop" — people live in
increasingly narrow content silos and correspondingly smaller walled gardens of thought. It's a big reason why liberals and conservatives, Democrats
and Republicans, find it harder and harder to agree on facts and why a shared
sense of reality is becoming elusive. It also helps explain why elites in New
York and Washington — including the Clinton campaign and much of the
press — were so shocked by Trump's win in the 2016 election.

"If algorithms are going to curate the world for us," Pariser warned in a 2011 TED talk, "if they're going to decide what we get to see and what we don't get to see, then we need to make sure that they're not just keyed to relevance but that they also show us things that are uncomfortable or challenging or important, other points of view."

≡ **THINKING ABOUT THE TEXT**

1. Kakutani says we have sorted ourselves into "silos of shared interest" (paragraph 6). Specifically, what does she mean? How does this conform to your own experience or your parents'? Your friends'?

2. Why might 58 percent of Republicans have a negative view of colleges and universities? Kakutani makes an analogy between political parties and sports teams. Then she claims loyal fans wish "pain and humiliation upon their opponents" (paragraph 9). Is this true? Is it true for you? For your friends? Is it true for your school's rivals? Explain.

3. Kakutani writes that the country is fractured into "two coherent tribes" (paragraph 17) hoping to fight, to provoke, to condemn and defeat the other. Compare this quote with the Lux poem.

4. Explain the process by which ordinary people can be moved to commit violent acts.

5. Explain why you are or are not in what Kakutani calls "an endless you-loop" (paragraph 26). Are your parents, relatives, or friends? What might be an antidote?

AMY CHUA

How America's Identity Politics Went from Inclusion to Division

Amy Chua (1962) was born in Champaign, Illinois, and moved to Berkeley, California, when she was eight. She graduated from Harvard College and Harvard Law School. She has written a number of books, including Battle Hymn of the Tiger Mother *and her latest,* Political Tribes: Group Instinct and the Fate of Nations *(2018). She is currently a Professor of Law at Yale Law School. She lives in New Haven with her husband and two daughters. The following piece is from* Political Tribes *(2018).*

We are at an unprecedented moment in America.

For the first time in US history, white Americans are faced with the prospect of becoming a minority in their "own country." While many in our multicultural cities may well celebrate the "browning of America" as a welcome step away from "white supremacy," it's safe to say that large numbers of American whites are more anxious about this phenomenon, whether they admit it or not. Tellingly, a 2012 study showed that more than half of white Americans believe that "whites have replaced blacks as the 'primary victims of discrimination.'"

Meanwhile, the coming demographic shift has done little to allay minority concerns about discrimination. A recent survey found that 43% of black Americans do not believe America will ever make the changes necessary to give blacks equal rights. Most disconcertingly, hate crimes have increased 20% in the wake of the 2016 election.

When groups feel threatened, they retreat into tribalism. When groups feel mistreated and disrespected, they close ranks and become more insular, more defensive, more punitive, more us-versus-them.

In America today, every group feels this way to some extent. Whites and   5
blacks, Latinos and Asians, men and women, Christians, Jews, and Muslims, straight people and gay people, liberals and conservatives — all feel their groups are being attacked, bullied, persecuted, discriminated against.

Of course, one group's claims to feeling threatened and voiceless are often met by another group's derision because it discounts their own feelings of persecution — but such is political tribalism.

This — combined with record levels of inequality — is why we now see identity politics on both sides of the political spectrum. And it leaves the United States in a perilous new situation: almost no one is standing up for an America without identity politics, for an American identity that transcends and unites all the country's many subgroups.

. . .

This is certainly true of the American left today.

Fifty years ago, the rhetoric of pro-civil rights, Great Society liberals was, in its dominant voices, expressly group transcending, framed in the language of national unity and equal opportunity.

> In his most famous speech, Dr Martin Luther King Jr proclaimed: "When the architects of our republic wrote the magnificent words of the Constitution and the Declaration of Independence, they were signing a promissory note to which every American was to fall heir. This note was a promise that all men — yes, black men as well as white men — would be guaranteed the unalienable rights of life, liberty, and the pursuit of happiness."

King's ideals — the ideals of the American Left that captured the imagi-   10
nation and hearts of the public and led to real change — transcended group divides and called for an America in which skin color didn't matter.

Leading liberal philosophical movements of that era were similarly group blind and universalist in character. John Rawls's enormously influential *A Theory of Justice*, published in 1971, called on people to imagine themselves in an "original position," behind a "veil of ignorance," in which they could decide on their society's basic principles without regard to "race, gender, religious affiliation, [or] wealth."

At roughly the same time, the idea of universal human rights proliferated, advancing the dignity of every individual as the foundation of a just international order.

Thus, although the Left was always concerned with the oppression of minorities and the rights of disadvantaged groups, the dominant ideals in this period tended to be group blind, often cosmopolitan, with many calling for transcending not just ethnic, racial, and gender barriers but national boundaries as well.

Perhaps in reaction to Reaganism, and a growing awareness that "colorblindness" was being used by conservatives to oppose policies intended to redress racial inequities, a new movement began to unfold on the left in the 1980s and 1990s — a movement emphasizing group consciousness, group identity, and group claims.

Many on the left had become acutely aware that color blindness was being used by conservatives to oppose policies intended to redress historical wrongs and persisting racial inequities.   15

Many also began to notice that the leading liberal figures in America, whether in law, government, or academia, were predominantly white men and that the neutral "group-blind" invisible hand of the market wasn't doing much to correct long-standing imbalances.

With the collapse of the Soviet Union, the anti-capitalist economic preoccupations of the old Left began to take a backseat to a new way of understanding oppression: the politics of redistribution was replaced by a "politics of recognition." Modern identity politics was born.

As Oberlin professor Sonia Kruks writes, "What makes identity politics a significant departure from earlier [movements] is its demand for recognition on the basis of the very grounds on which recognition has previously been denied: it is qua women, qua blacks, qua lesbians that groups demand recognition . . . The demand is not for inclusion within the fold of 'universal humankind' . . . nor is it for respect 'in spite of' one's differences. Rather, what is demanded is respect for oneself as different."

But identity politics, with its group-based rhetoric, did not initially become the mainstream position of the Democratic Party.

At the 2004 Democratic National Convention in Boston, Barack Obama   20
famously declared, "There's not a black America and white America and Latino America and Asian America; there's the United States of America."

A decade and a half later, we are very far from Obama's America.

. . .

For today's Left, blindness to group identity is the ultimate sin, because it masks the reality of group hierarchies and oppression in America.

It's just a fact that whites, and specifically white male Protestants, dominated America for most of its history, often violently, and that this legacy persists. The stubborn persistence of racial inequality in the wake of Barack Obama's supposedly "post-racial" presidency has left many young progressives disillusioned with the narratives of racial progress that were popular among liberals just a few years ago.

When a grand jury failed to indict a white cop who was videotaped chok-ing a black man to death, black writer Brit Bennett captured this growing mis-trust in an essay entitled, "I Don't Know What to Do with Good White People":

> We all want to believe in progress, in history that marches forward in a neat line, in transcended differences and growing acceptance, in how good the good white people have become . . . I don't think Darren Wilson or Daniel Pantaleo set out to kill black men. I'm sure the cops who arrested my father meant well. But what good are your good intentions if they kill us?

For the Left, identity politics has long been a means to "confront rather   25
than obscure the uglier aspects of American history and society."

But in recent years, whether because of growing strength or growing frus-tration with the lack of progress, the Left has upped the ante. A shift in tone, rhetoric, and logic has moved identity politics away from inclusion—which had always been the Left's watchword—toward exclusion and division. As a result, many on the left have turned against universalist rhetoric (for example, All Lives Matter), viewing it as an attempt to erase the specificity of the experi-ence and oppression of historically marginalized minorities.

The new exclusivity is partly epistemological, claiming that out-group members cannot share in the knowledge possessed by in-group members ("You can't understand X because you are white"; "You can't understand Y because you're not a woman"; "You can't speak about Z because you're not queer"). The idea of "cultural appropriation" insists, among other things, "These are our group's symbols, traditions, patrimony, and out-group mem-bers have no right to them."

For much of the Left today, anyone who speaks in favor of group blindness is on the other side, indifferent to or even guilty of oppression. For some, espe-cially on college campuses, anyone who doesn't swallow the anti-oppression orthodoxy hook, line, and sinker—anyone who doesn't acknowledge "white supremacy" in America—is a racist.

When liberal icon Bernie Sanders told supporters, "It's not good enough for somebody to say, 'Hey, I'm a Latina, vote for me,'" Quentin James, a leader of Hillary Clinton's outreach efforts to people of color, retorted that Sanders's "comments regarding identity politics suggest he may be a white supremacist, too."

. . .

Once identity politics gains momentum, it inevitably subdivides, giving rise to   30
ever-proliferating group identities demanding recognition.

Today, there is an ever-expanding vocabulary of identity on the left. Facebook now lists more than fifty gender designations from which users can choose, from genderqueer to intersex to pangender.

Or take the acronym LGBTQ. Originally LGB, variants over the years have ranged from GLBT to LGBTI to LGBTQQIAAP as preferred terminol-ogy shifted and identity groups quarreled about who should be included and who come first.

Because the Left is always trying to outleft the last Left, the result can be a zero-sum competition over which group is the least privileged, an "Oppression Olympics" often fragmenting progressives and setting them against each other.

Although inclusivity is presumably still the ultimate goal, the contemporary Left is pointedly exclusionary.

During a Black Lives Matter protest at the DNC held in Philadelphia in July 2016, a protest leader announced that "this is a black and brown resistance march," asking white allies to "appropriately take [their] place in the back of this march."

The war on "cultural appropriation" is rooted in the belief that groups have exclusive rights to their own histories, symbols, and traditions. Thus, many on the left today would consider it an offensive act of privilege for, say, a straight white man to write a novel featuring a gay Latina as the main character.

Transgressions are called out daily on social media; no one is immune. Beyoncé was criticized for wearing what looked like a traditional Indian bridal outfit; Amy Schumer, in turn, was criticized for making a parody of Beyoncé's "Formation," a song about the black female experience. Students at Oberlin complained of a vendor's "history of blurring the line between culinary diversity and cultural appropriation by modifying the recipes without respect for certain Asian countries' cuisines." And a student op-ed at Louisiana State University claimed that white women styling their eyebrows to look thicker — like "a lot of ethnic women" — was "a prime example of the cultural appropriation in this country."

Not everyone on the Left is happy with the direction that identity politics has taken. Many are dismayed by the focus on cultural appropriation. As a progressive Mexican American law student put it, "If we allowed ourselves to be hurt by a costume, how could we manage the trauma of an eviction notice?"

He added: "Liberals have cried wolf too many times. If everything is racist and sexist, nothing is. When Trump, the real wolf, came along, no one listened."

. . .

As a candidate, Donald Trump famously called for "a total and complete shutdown of Muslims entering the United States," described illegal Mexican immigrants as "rapists," and referred disparagingly to an Indiana-born federal judge as "Mexican," accusing the judge of having "an inherent conflict of interest" rendering him unfit to preside over a suit against Trump.

Making the argument that Trump used identity politics to win the White House is like shooting fish in a barrel. But us-versus-them, anti-Muslim, anti-immigrant sentiments were bread and butter for most conservatives on the 2016 campaign trail. Senator Marco Rubio compared the war with Islam to America's "war with Nazis," and even moderate Republicans like Jeb Bush advocated for a religious test to allow Christian refugees to enter the country preferentially.

We are also seeing on the right — particularly the alt-right — political tribalism directed against minorities perceived as "too successful." For example,

Steve Bannon, Trump's former White House chief strategist, has complained that America's "engineering schools are all full of people from South Asia and East Asia ... They've come in here to take these jobs" while Americans "can't get engineering degrees ... [and] can't get a job."

This brings us to the most striking feature of today's right-wing political tribalism: the white identity politics that has mobilized around the idea of whites as an endangered, discriminated-against group.

In part this development carries forward a long tradition of white tribalism in America. But white identity politics has also gotten a tremendous recent boost from the Left, whose relentless berating, shaming, and bullying might have done more damage than good.

One Trump voter claimed that "maybe I'm just so sick of being called a bigot   45 that my anger at the authoritarian left has pushed me to support this seriously flawed man." "The Democratic party," said Bill Maher, "made the white working man feel like your problems aren't real because you're 'mansplaining' and check your privilege. You know, if your life sucks, your problems are real." When blacks blame today's whites for slavery or ask for reparations, many white Americans feel as though they are being attacked for the sins of other generations.

Or consider this blog post in the American Conservative, worth quoting at length because of the light it sheds:

> I'm a white guy. I'm a well-educated intellectual who enjoys small arthouse movies, coffeehouses and classic blues. If you didn't know any better, you'd probably mistake me for a lefty urban hipster.
>
> And yet. I find some of the alt-right stuff exerts a pull even on me. Even though I'm smart and informed enough to see through it. It's seductive because I am not a person with any power or privilege, and yet I am constantly bombarded with messages telling me that I'm a cancer, I'm a problem, everything is my fault.
>
> I am very lower middle class. I've never owned a new car, and do my own home repairs as much as I can to save money. I cut my own grass, wash my own dishes, buy my clothes from Walmart. I have no clue how I will ever be able to retire. But oh, brother, to hear the media tell it, I am just drowning in unearned power and privilege, and America will be a much brighter, more loving, more peaceful nation when I finally just keel over and die.
>
> Trust me: After all that, some of the alt-right stuff feels like a warm, soothing bath. A "safe space," if you will. I recoil from the uglier stuff, but some of it — the "hey, white guys are actually okay, you know! Be proud of yourself, white man!" stuff is really VERY seductive, and it is only with some intellectual effort that I can resist the pull ... If it's a struggle for someone like me to resist the pull, I imagine it's probably impossible for someone with less education or cultural exposure.

...

Just as the Left's exclusionary identity politics is ironic in light of the Left's ostensible demands for inclusivity, so too is the emergence of a "white" identity politics on the right.

For decades, the Right has claimed to be a bastion of individualism, a place where those who rejected the divisive identity politics of the Left found a home.

For this reason, conservatives typically paint the emergence of white identity as having been forced on them by the tactics of the Left. As one political commentator puts it, "feeling as though they are under perpetual attack for the color of their skin, many on the right have become defiant of their whiteness, allowing it into their individual politics in ways they have not for generations."

At its core, the problem is simple but fundamental. While black Americans, Asian Americans, Hispanic Americans, Jewish Americans, and many others are allowed — indeed, encouraged — to feel solidarity and take pride in their racial or ethnic identity, white Americans have for the last several decades been told they must never, ever do so.

People want to see their own tribe as exceptional, as something to be deeply proud of; that's what the tribal instinct is all about. For decades now, nonwhites in the United States have been encouraged to indulge their tribal instincts in just this way, but, at least publicly, American whites have not.

On the contrary, if anything, they have been told that their white identity is something no one should take pride in. "I get it," says Christian Lander, creator of the popular satirical blog Stuff White People Like, "as a straight white male, I'm the worst thing on Earth."

But the tribal instinct is not so easy to suppress. As Vassar professor Hua Hsu put it in an Atlantic essay called "The End of White America?" the "result is a racial pride that dares not speak its name, and that defines itself through cultural cues instead."

In combination with the profound demographic transformation now taking place in America, this suppressed urge on the part of many white Americans — to feel solidarity and pride in their group identity, as others are allowed to do — has created an especially fraught set of tribal dynamics in the United States today.

Just after the 2016 election, a former Never Trumper explained his change of heart in the *Atlantic:* "My college-age daughter constantly hears talk of white privilege and racial identity, of separate dorms for separate races (somewhere in heaven Martin Luther King Jr. is hanging his head and crying) . . . I hate identity politics, [but] when everything is about identity politics, is the left really surprised that on Tuesday millions of white Americans . . . voted as 'white'? If you want identity politics, identity politics is what you will get."

≣ THINKING ABOUT THE TEXT

1. What positive and negative consequences does Chua cite for the tribal instinct? What others would you add?

2. Chua claims that every group in America feels threatened. Do you think this is an accurate assertion, or not? Is the group you belong

to being "attacked, bullied, persecuted, discriminated against" (paragraph 5)? Explain your thinking.

3. Is Chua fair to both tribes, the Right and the Left?

4. What mistakes does Chua say the Left has made that increased tribalization? Does she deal with the Right's mistakes? Should she?

5. What is the relationship between Chua's perspective and Lux's poem?

≡ MAKING COMPARISONS

1. What would Kakutani object to in Chua's analysis of the causes of tribalism?

2. Are there indications that Chua is actually more liberal than conservative?

3. Does either essay offer reasonable solutions to rampant tribalism? Explain.

ELIZABETH KOLBERT
Why Facts Don't Change Our Minds

Elizabeth Kolbert (1961) was born and grew up in the Bronx, New York, and Larchmont, Long Island. She studied literature at Yale University and was awarded a Fulbright Scholarship to study at the University of Hamburg in Germany. She started working for the New York Times *in 1983. She has been a staff writer for* The New Yorker *since 1999. She has won numerous awards, including a Pulitzer Prize for* The Sixth Extinction: An Unnatural History *in 2015. The following essay appeared in* The New Yorker *on February 27, 2017.*

In 1975, researchers at Stanford invited a group of undergraduates to take part in a study about suicide. They were presented with pairs of suicide notes. In each pair, one note had been composed by a random individual, the other by a person who had subsequently taken his own life. The students were then asked to distinguish between the genuine notes and the fake ones.

Some students discovered that they had a genius for the task. Out of twenty-five pairs of notes, they correctly identified the real one twenty-four times. Others discovered that they were hopeless. They identified the real note in only ten instances.

As is often the case with psychological studies, the whole setup was a put-on. Though half the notes were indeed genuine — they'd been obtained from the Los Angeles County coroner's office — the scores were fictitious. The students who'd been told they were almost always right were, on average, no more discerning than those who had been told they were mostly wrong.

In the second phase of the study, the deception was revealed. The students were told that the real point of the experiment was to gauge their responses to *thinking* they were right or wrong. (This, it turned out, was also a deception.) Finally, the students were asked to estimate how many suicide notes they had actually categorized correctly, and how many they thought an average student would get right. At this point, something curious happened. The students in the high-score group said that they thought they had, in fact, done quite well—significantly better than the average student—even though, as they'd just been told, they had zero grounds for believing this. Conversely, those who'd been assigned to the low-score group said that they thought they had done significantly worse than the average student—a conclusion that was equally unfounded.

"Once formed," the researchers observed dryly, "impressions are remark-   5
ably perseverant."

A few years later, a new set of Stanford students was recruited for a related study. The students were handed packets of information about a pair of firefighters, Frank K. and George H. Frank's bio noted that, among other things, he had a baby daughter and he liked to scuba dive. George had a small son and played golf. The packets also included the men's responses on what the researchers called the Risky-Conservative Choice Test. According to one version of the packet, Frank was a successful firefighter who, on the test, almost always went with the safest option. In the other version, Frank also chose the safest option, but he was a lousy firefighter who'd been put "on report" by his supervisors several times. Once again, midway through the study, the students were informed that they'd been misled, and that the information they'd received was entirely fictitious. The students were then asked to describe their own beliefs. What sort of attitude toward risk did they think a successful firefighter would have? The students who'd received the first packet thought that he would avoid it. The students in the second group thought he'd embrace it.

Even after the evidence "for their beliefs has been totally refuted, people fail to make appropriate revisions in those beliefs," the researchers noted. In this case, the failure was "particularly impressive," since two data points would never have been enough information to generalize from.

The Stanford studies became famous. Coming from a group of academics in the nineteen-seventies, the contention that people can't think straight was shocking. It isn't any longer. Thousands of subsequent experiments have confirmed (and elaborated on) this finding. As everyone who's followed the research—or even occasionally picked up a copy of *Psychology Today*—knows, any graduate student with a clipboard can demonstrate that reasonable-seeming people are often totally irrational. Rarely has this insight seemed more relevant than it does right now. Still, an essential puzzle remains: How did we come to be this way?

In a new book, "The Enigma of Reason" (Harvard), the cognitive scientists Hugo Mercier and Dan Sperber take a stab at answering this question. Mercier, who works at a French research institute in Lyon, and Sperber, now based at the Central European University, in Budapest, point out that reason is an evolved trait, like bipedalism or three-color vision. It emerged on the savannas of Africa, and has to be understood in that context.

Stripped of a lot of what might be called cognitive-science-ese, Mercier and Sperber's argument runs, more or less, as follows: Humans' biggest advantage over other species is our ability to cooperate. Coöperation is difficult to establish and almost as difficult to sustain. For any individual, freeloading is always the best course of action. Reason developed not to enable us to solve abstract, logical problems or even to help us draw conclusions from unfamiliar data; rather, it developed to resolve the problems posed by living in collaborative groups.

"Reason is an adaptation to the hypersocial niche humans have evolved for themselves," Mercier and Sperber write. Habits of mind that seem weird or goofy or just plain dumb from an "intellectualist" point of view prove shrewd when seen from a social "interactionist" perspective.

Consider what's become known as "confirmation bias," the tendency people have to embrace information that supports their beliefs and reject information that contradicts them. Of the many forms of faulty thinking that have been identified, confirmation bias is among the best catalogued; it's the subject of entire textbooks' worth of experiments. One of the most famous of these was conducted, again, at Stanford. For this experiment, researchers rounded up a group of students who had opposing opinions about capital punishment. Half the students were in favor of it and thought that it deterred crime; the other half were against it and thought that it had no effect on crime.

The students were asked to respond to two studies. One provided data in support of the deterrence argument, and the other provided data that called it into question. Both studies — you guessed it — were made up, and had been designed to present what were, objectively speaking, equally compelling statistics. The students who had originally supported capital punishment rated the pro-deterrence data highly credible and the anti-deterrence data unconvincing; the students who'd originally opposed capital punishment did the reverse. At the end of the experiment, the students were asked once again about their views. Those who'd started out pro-capital punishment were now even more in favor of it; those who'd opposed it were even more hostile.

If reason is designed to generate sound judgments, then it's hard to conceive of a more serious design flaw than confirmation bias. Imagine, Mercier and Sperber suggest, a mouse that thinks the way we do. Such a mouse, "bent on confirming its belief that there are no cats around," would soon be dinner. To the extent that confirmation bias leads people to dismiss evidence of new or underappreciated threats — the human equivalent of the cat around the corner — it's a trait that should have been selected against. The fact that

10

both we and it survive, Mercier and Sperber argue, proves that it must have some adaptive function, and that function, they maintain, is related to our "hypersociability."

Mercier and Sperber prefer the term "myside bias." Humans, they point out, aren't randomly credulous. Presented with someone else's argument, we're quite adept at spotting the weaknesses. Almost invariably, the positions we're blind about are our own.   15

A recent experiment performed by Mercier and some European colleagues neatly demonstrates this asymmetry. Participants were asked to answer a series of simple reasoning problems. They were then asked to explain their responses, and were given a chance to modify them if they identified mistakes. The majority were satisfied with their original choices; fewer than fifteen per cent changed their minds in step two.

In step three, participants were shown one of the same problems, along with their answer and the answer of another participant, who'd come to a different conclusion. Once again, they were given the chance to change their responses. But a trick had been played: the answers presented to them as some-one else's were actually their own, and vice versa. About half the participants realized what was going on. Among the other half, suddenly people became a lot more critical. Nearly 60 per cent now rejected the responses that they'd earlier been satisfied with.

This lopsidedness, according to Mercier and Sperber, reflects the task that reason evolved to perform, which is to prevent us from getting screwed by the other members of our group. Living in small bands of hunter-gatherers, our ancestors were primarily concerned with their social standing, and with mak-ing sure that they weren't the ones risking their lives on the hunt while oth-ers loafed around in the cave. There was little advantage in reasoning clearly, while much was to be gained from winning arguments.

Among the many, many issues our forebears didn't worry about were the deterrent effects of capital punishment and the ideal attributes of a firefighter. Nor did they have to contend with fabricated studies, or fake news, or Twitter. It's no wonder, then, that today reason often seems to fail us. As Mercier and Sperber write, "This is one of many cases in which the environment changed too quickly for natural selection to catch up."

Steven Sloman, a professor at Brown, and Philip Fernbach, a professor at the University of Colorado, are also cognitive scientists. They, too, believe sociabil-ity is the key to how the human mind functions or, perhaps more pertinently, malfunctions. They begin their book, "The Knowledge Illusion: Why We Never Think Alone" (Riverhead), with a look at toilets.   20

Virtually everyone in the United States, and indeed throughout the devel-oped world, is familiar with toilets. A typical flush toilet has a ceramic bowl filled with water. When the handle is depressed, or the button pushed, the water—and everything that's been deposited in it—gets sucked into a pipe and from there into the sewage system. But how does this actually happen?

In a study conducted at Yale, graduate students were asked to rate their understanding of everyday devices, including toilets, zippers, and cylinder locks. They were then asked to write detailed, step-by-step explanations of how the devices work, and to rate their understanding again. Apparently, the effort revealed to the students their own ignorance, because their self-assessments dropped. (Toilets, it turns out, are more complicated than they appear.)

Sloman and Fernbach see this effect, which they call the "illusion of explanatory depth," just about everywhere. People believe that they know way more than they actually do. What allows us to persist in this belief is other people. In the case of my toilet, someone else designed it so that I can operate it easily. This is something humans are very good at. We've been relying on one another's expertise ever since we figured out how to hunt together, which was probably a key development in our evolutionary history. So well do we collaborate, Sloman and Fernbach argue, that we can hardly tell where our own understanding ends and others' begins.

"One implication of the naturalness with which we divide cognitive labor," they write, is that there's "no sharp boundary between one person's ideas and knowledge" and "those of other members" of the group.

This borderlessness, or, if you prefer, confusion, is also crucial to what we consider progress. As people invented new tools for new ways of living, they simultaneously created new realms of ignorance; if everyone had insisted on, say, mastering the principles of metalworking before picking up a knife, the Bronze Age wouldn't have amounted to much. When it comes to new technologies, incomplete understanding is empowering.

Where it gets us into trouble, according to Sloman and Fernbach, is in the political domain. It's one thing for me to flush a toilet without knowing how it operates, and another for me to favor (or oppose) an immigration ban without knowing what I'm talking about. Sloman and Fernbach cite a survey conducted in 2014, not long after Russia annexed the Ukrainian territory of Crimea. Respondents were asked how they thought the U.S. should react, and also whether they could identify Ukraine on a map. The farther off base they were about the geography, the more likely they were to favor military intervention. (Respondents were so unsure of Ukraine's location that the median guess was wrong by eighteen hundred miles, roughly the distance from Kiev to Madrid.)

Surveys on many other issues have yielded similarly dismaying results. "As a rule, strong feelings about issues do not emerge from deep understanding," Sloman and Fernbach write. And here our dependence on other minds reinforces the problem. If your position on, say, the Affordable Care Act is baseless and I rely on it, then my opinion is also baseless. When I talk to Tom and he decides he agrees with me, his opinion is also baseless, but now that the three of us concur we feel that much more smug about our views. If we all now dismiss as unconvincing any information that contradicts our opinion, you get, well, the Trump Administration.

25

"This is how a community of knowledge can become dangerous," Sloman and Fernbach observe. The two have performed their own version of the toilet experiment, substituting public policy for household gadgets. In a study conducted in 2012, they asked people for their stance on questions like: Should there be a single-payer health-care system? Or merit-based pay for teachers? Participants were asked to rate their positions depending on how strongly they agreed or disagreed with the proposals. Next, they were instructed to explain, in as much detail as they could, the impacts of implementing each one. Most people at this point ran into trouble. Asked once again to rate their views, they ratcheted down the intensity, so that they either agreed or disagreed less vehemently.

Sloman and Fernbach see in this result a little candle for a dark world. If we — or our friends or the pundits on CNN — spent less time pontificating and more trying to work through the implications of policy proposals, we'd realize how clueless we are and moderate our views. This, they write, "may be the only form of thinking that will shatter the illusion of explanatory depth and change people's attitudes."

One way to look at science is as a system that corrects for people's natural   30
inclinations. In a well-run laboratory, there's no room for myside bias; the results have to be reproducible in other laboratories, by researchers who have no motive to confirm them. And this, it could be argued, is why the system has proved so successful. At any given moment, a field may be dominated by squabbles, but, in the end, the methodology prevails. Science moves forward, even as we remain stuck in place.

In "Denying to the Grave: Why We Ignore the Facts That Will Save Us" (Oxford), Jack Gorman, a psychiatrist, and his daughter, Sara Gorman, a public-health specialist, probe the gap between what science tells us and what we tell ourselves. Their concern is with those persistent beliefs which are not just demonstrably false but also potentially deadly, like the conviction that vaccines are hazardous. Of course, what's hazardous is *not* being vaccinated; that's why vaccines were created in the first place. "Immunization is one of the triumphs of modern medicine," the Gormans note. But no matter how many scientific studies conclude that vaccines are safe, and that there's no link between immunizations and autism, anti-vaxxers remain unmoved. (They can now count on their side — sort of — Donald Trump, who has said that, although he and his wife had their son, Barron, vaccinated, they refused to do so on the timetable recommended by pediatricians.)

The Gormans, too, argue that ways of thinking that now seem self-destructive must at some point have been adaptive. And they, too, dedicate many pages to confirmation bias, which, they claim, has a physiological component. They cite research suggesting that people experience genuine pleasure — a rush of dopamine — when processing information that supports their beliefs. "It feels good to 'stick to our guns' even if we are wrong," they observe.

The Gormans don't just want to catalogue the ways we go wrong; they want to correct for them. There must be some way, they maintain, to convince people that vaccines are good for kids, and handguns are dangerous. (Another widespread but statistically insupportable belief they'd like to discredit is that owning a gun makes you safer.) But here they encounter the very problems they have enumerated. Providing people with accurate information doesn't seem to help; they simply discount it. Appealing to their emotions may work better, but doing so is obviously antithetical to the goal of promoting sound science. "The challenge that remains," they write toward the end of their book, "is to figure out how to address the tendencies that lead to false scientific belief."

"The Enigma of Reason," "The Knowledge Illusion," and *"Denying to the Grave"* were all written before the November election. And yet they anticipate Kellyanne Conway and the rise of *"alternative facts."* These days, it can feel as if the entire country has been given over to a vast psychological experiment being run either by no one or by Steve Bannon. Rational agents would be able to think their way to a solution. But, on this matter, the literature is not reassuring.

≡ THINKING ABOUT THE TEXT

1. What is confirmation bias? Give some examples from your own experience. How would you be likely to see it watching your college's basketball team play a rival?

2. Summarize your understanding of the research studies Kolbert cites. How might you connect them to Lux's poem?

3. Kolbert claims that "reasonable-seeming people are often totally irrational" (paragraph 8). What is one explanation for this?

4. How might "myside bias" account for the kind of tribalism seen in Lux's poem? Give examples of this at your college, your hometown, in local and national and international politics.

5. Which one of the books that Kolbert briefly reviews seems particularly relevant to your interests and concerns? Explain.

≡ MAKING COMPARISONS

1. How does Kolbert's essay help explain Chua's main idea?

2. How do each of our authors account for the current divisive political climate in America and Europe?

3. Which essays speaks most directly to the extreme emotions of Lux's poem?

≡ WRITING ABOUT ISSUES

1. Pick one of our authors and argue that her perspective best helps to explain how we could get to the horrors of Lux's poem.

2. Write an essay that argues that one of our authors is or is not guilty of confirmation bias, or "my side bias."

3. Search online for "tribalism in America" and after reading one of the sites, argue that our three authors offer more or less insight into our culture.

4. Undoubtedly some would take issue with the main tribalist idea expounded in our three essays. Taking that oppositional point of view, argue that our authors are wrong and that one tribe does have the "correct" view.

≡ Arguments about a Play: *Othello*

WILLIAM SHAKESPEARE, *Othello*

ARGUMENTS ABOUT THE PLAY:
A. C. BRADLEY, "The Noble Othello"

JEFFRIE G. MURPHY, "Jealousy, Shame, and the Rival"

Of all the great tragedies of Shakespeare, *Othello* seems the closest to our own lives. Hamlet is a prince, and Lear and Macbeth are kings with the fate of their nations tied to their destiny. It is sometimes hard for contemporary readers to relate to their struggles or to regicide. But *Othello* is more domesticated, more about a relationship we can understand; few of us would claim that we have never been jealous. We know that relationships thrive on trust and openness, but even if we trust our partner, jealousy can find its way into our consciousness and might especially do so if we are prompted to doubt by a close friend.

Psychologists suggest that insecure people are prone to jealousy, perhaps because their low self-esteem suggests to them that they are not worthy of love. Is this the case with Othello? Although at first he seems filled with confidence and authority, he is considered a Moorish outsider in Venetian society and as such might be tempted to think that his wife, Desdemona, might find Cassio, one of her "own kind," attractive and desirable. The innocent and devoted Desdemona does not, but Brabantio ("She has deceived her father, and may thee") plants the seeds of distrust early on, and Iago, an "inhuman dog" diabolically nurtures them. The speed with which a great love is destroyed leaves the reader stunned by the potential darkness within us all.

The pair of essays that follow the play focus on jealousy, but they have different ideas about where that emotion comes from and how it alters our view of Othello's character and the play. A. C. Bradley develops the idea that Othello remains a noble soul and so we admire him to the end. This admiration increases our pity and the force of catharsis, which leaves us "for the moment free from pain, and exulting in the power of 'love and man's unconquerable mind.'" Jeffrie G. Murphy takes a more psychological view of jealousy as personal disintegration strongly linked to shame.

≡ BEFORE YOU READ

Do you think jealousy is a natural emotion? If you loved someone deeply, would you trust him or her? Are only insecure people jealous? Are there any positive elements to jealousy?

WILLIAM SHAKESPEARE
Othello

William Shakespeare's reputation as the greatest dramatist in the English language is built on his five major tragedies: Romeo and Juliet *(1594),* Hamlet *(1600),* Othello *(1604),* Macbeth *(1605), and* King Lear *(1605). But he was also a master in other genres, including comedies (*As You Like It *in 1599), histories (*Henry IV *in 1597), and romances (*The Tempest *in 1611). And his collection of sonnets is considered art of the highest order.*

Very little is known about Shakespeare's personal life. He attended the grammar school at Stratford-upon-Avon, where he was born in 1564. He married Anne Hathaway in 1582 and had three children. Around 1590 he moved to London, where he became an actor and began writing plays. He was an astute businessperson, becoming a shareholder in London's famous Globe Theatre. After writing thirty-seven plays, he retired to Stratford in 1611. When he died in 1616, he left behind the most respected body of work in literature. Shakespeare's ability to use artistic language to convey a wide range of humor and emotion is perhaps unsurpassed.

THE NAMES OF THE ACTORS

OTHELLO, *the Moor*
BRABANTIO, *father to Desdemona*
CASSIO, *an honorable lieutenant [to Othello]*
IAGO *[Othello's ancient], a villain*
RODERIGO, *a gulled gentleman*
DUKE OF VENICE
SENATORS OF VENICE
MONTANO, *governor of Cyprus*
LODOVICO AND GRATIANO *[kinsmen to Brabantio], two noble Venetians*
SAILORS
CLOWNS
DESDEMONA, *wife to Othello*
EMILIA, *wife to Iago*
BIANCA, *a courtesan*
[Messenger, Herald, Officers, Venetian Gentlemen, Musicians, Attendants
scene: Venice and Cyprus]

[ACT I, Scene I: A street in Venice.]

Enter Roderigo and Iago.

RODERIGO: Tush, never tell me! I take it much unkindly
    That thou, Iago who hast had my purse
    As if the strings were thine, shouldst know of this.°
IAGO: 'Sblood,° but you'll not hear me!
    If ever I did dream of such a matter,   5
    Abhor me.
RODERIGO: Thou told'st me thou didst hold him in thy hate.
IAGO: Despise me if I do not. Three great ones of the city,
    In personal suit to make me his lieutenant,
    Off-capped to him;° and, by the faith of man,   10
    I know my price; I am worth no worse a place.
    But he, as loving his own pride and purposes,
    Evades them with a bombast circumstance.°
    Horribly stuffed with epithets of war;
    [And, in conclusion,]   15
    Nonsuits° my mediators; for, "Certes," says he,
    "I have already chose my officer."
    And what was he?
    Forsooth, a great arithmetician,°

ACT I, SCENE I.   **3 this:** I.e., Desdemona's elopement.   **4 'Sblood:** By God's blood.
10 him: I.e., Othello.   **13 a bombast circumstance:** Pompous circumlocutions.
16 Nonsuits: Rejects.   **19 arithmetician:** Theoretician.

One Michael Cassio, a Florentine   20
(A fellow almost damned in a fair wife°)
That never set a squadron in the field,
Nor the division of a battle knows
More than a spinster; unless the bookish theoric,
Wherein the togèd consuls can propose   25
As masterly as he. Mere prattle without practice
Is all his soldiership. But he, sir, had th' election;
And I (of whom his eyes had seen the proof
At Rhodes, at Cyprus, and on other grounds
Christian and heathen) must be belee'd and calmed°   30
By debitor and creditor; this counter-caster,°
He, in good time, must his lieutenant be,
And I — God bless the mark! — his Moorship's ancient.°
RODERIGO: By heaven, I rather would have been his hangman.
IAGO: Why, there's no remedy; 'tis the curse of service.   35
Preferment goes by letter and affection,°
And not by old gradation, where each second
Stood heir to th' first. Now, sir, be judge yourself,
Whether I in any just term am affined°
To love the Moor.
RODERIGO: I would not follow him then.   40
IAGO: O, sir, content you;
I follow him to serve my turn upon him.
We cannot all be masters, nor all masters
Cannot be truly followed. You shall mark
Many a duteous and knee-crooking knave   45
That, doting on his own obsequious bondage,
Wears out his time, much like his master's ass,
For naught but provender; and when he's old, cashiered.°
Whip me such honest knaves! Others there are
Who, trimmed° in forms and visages of duty,   50
Keep yet their hearts attending on themselves;
And, throwing but shows of service on their lords,
Do well thrive by them, and when they have lined their coats,
Do themselves homage. These fellows have some soul;
And such a one do I profess myself. For, sir,   55
It is as sure as you are Roderigo,
Were I the Moor, I would not be Iago.
In following him, I follow but myself;
Heaven is my judge, not I for love and duty,
But seeming so, for my peculiar end;   60

21 almost . . . wife: (An obscure allusion; Cassio is unmarried, but see IV.i.12).
30 belee'd and calmed: Left in the lurch.   **31 counter-caster:** Bookkeeper.
33 ancient: Ensign.   **36 affection:** Favoritism.   **39 affined:** Obliged.
48 cashiered: Turned off.   **50 trimmed:** Dressed up.

For when my outward action doth demonstrate
The native act and figure of my heart°
In compliment extern,° 'tis not long after
But I will wear my heart upon my sleeve
For daws to peck at; I am not what I am.   65
RODERIGO: What a full fortune does the thick-lips° owe°
    If he can carry't thus!
IAGO: Call up her father,
    Rouse him. Make after him, poison his delight,
    Proclaim him in the streets. Incense her kinsmen,
    And though he in a fertile climate dwell,   70
    Plague him with flies; though that his joy be joy,
    Yet throw such changes of vexation on't
    As it may lose some color.
RODERIGO: Here is her father's house. I'll call aloud.
IAGO: Do, with like timorous° accent and dire yell   75
    As when, by night and negligence, the fire
    Is spied in populous cities.
RODERIGO: What, ho, Brabantio! Signior Brabantio, ho!
IAGO: Awake! What, ho, Brabantio! Thieves! thieves! thieves!
    Look to your house, your daughter, and your bags!   80
    Thieves! thieves!

Brabantio at a window.°

BRABANTIO *(above)*:   What is the reason of this terrible summons?
    What is the matter there?
RODERIGO: Signior, is all your family within?
IAGO: Are your doors locked?
BRABANTIO: Why, wherefore ask you this?   85
IAGO: Zounds, sir, y' are robbed! For shame, put on your gown!
    Your heart is burst; you have lost half your soul.
    Even now, now, very now, an old black ram
    Is tupping your white ewe. Arise, arise!
    Awake the snorting° citizens with the bell.   90
    Or else the devil will make a grandsire of you.
    Arise, I say!
BRABANTIO: What, have you lost your wits?
RODERIGO: Most reverend signior, do you know my voice?
BRABANTIO: Not I. What are you?   95
RODERIGO: My name is Roderigo.
BRABANTIO: The worser welcome!

---

62 The . . . heart: What I really believe and intend.   **63 compliment extern:** Outward appearance.   **66 thick-lips:** An Elizabethan epithet for blacks, including Moors.
owe: Own.   **75 timorous:** Terrifying. ***Brabantio at a window:*** (added from quarto).
90 snorting: Snoring.

I have charged thee not to haunt about my doors.
In honest plainness thou hast heard me say
My daughter is not for thee; and now, in madness,
Being full of supper and distemp'ring draughts,   100
Upon malicious knavery dost thou come
To start my quiet.

RODERIGO: Sir, sir, sir —

BRABANTIO: But thou must needs be sure
My spirit and my place have in them power   105
To make this bitter to thee.

RODERIGO: Patience, good sir.

BRABANTIO: What tell'st thou me of robbing? This is Venice;
My house is not a grange.°

RODERIGO: Most grave Brabantio,
In simple and pure soul I come to you.

IAGO: Zounds, sir, you are one of those that will not serve God if the devil bid   110
you. Because we come to do you service, and you think we are ruffians,
you'll have your daughter covered with a Barbary horse; you'll have your
nephews° neigh to you; you'll have coursers for cousins, and gennets for
germans.°

BRABANTIO: What profane wretch art thou?   115

IAGO: I am one, sir, that comes to tell you your daughter and the Moor are
now making the beast with two backs.

BRABANTIO: Thou art a villain.

IAGO: You are—a senator.

BRABANTIO: This thou shalt answer. I know thee, Roderigo.

RODERIGO: Sir, I will answer anything. But I beseech you,   120
If 't be your pleasure and most wise consent,
As partly I find it is, that your fair daughter,
At this odd-even° and dull watch o' th' night,
Transported, with no worse nor better guard
But with a knave of common hire, a gondolier,   125
To the gross clasps of a lascivious Moor —
If this be known to you, and your allowance,°
We then have done you bold and saucy wrongs;
But if you know not this, my manners tell me
We have your wrong rebuke. Do not believe   130
That, from the sense° of all civility,
I thus would play and trifle with your reverence.
Your daughter, if you have not given her leave,
I say again, hath made a gross revolt,
Tying her duty, beauty, wit, and fortunes   135

---

108 grange: Isolated farmhouse.   **113 nephews:** I.e., grandsons.   **113–14 gennets for germans:** Spanish horses for near kinsmen.   **123 odd-even:** Between night and morning.   **127 allowance:** Approval.   **131 from the sense:** In violation.

In an extravagant and wheeling° stranger
Of here and everywhere. Straight satisfy yourself.
If she be in her chamber, or your house,
Let loose on me the justice of the state
For thus deluding you.

BRABANTIO: Strike on the tinder, ho!   140
Give me a taper! Call up all my people!
This accident° is not unlike my dream.
Belief of it oppresses me already.
Light, I say! light!   *Exit [above].*

IAGO: Farewell, for I must leave you.
It seems not meet, nor wholesome to my place,   145
To be produced—as, if I stay, I shall—
Against the Moor. For I do know the state,
However this may gall him with some check,°
Cannot with safety cast° him; for he's embarked
With such loud reason to the Cyprus wars,   150
Which even now stand in act,° that for their souls
Another of his fathom° they have none
To lead their business; in which regard,
Though I do hate him as I do hell-pains,
Yet, for necessity of present life,   155
I must show out a flag and sign of love,
Which is indeed but sign. That you shall surely find him,
Lead to the Sagittary° the raisèd search;
And there will I be with him. So farewell.   *Exit.*

Enter [below] Brabantio in his nightgown,° and Servants with torches.

BRABANTIO: It is too true an evil. Gone she is;   160
And what's to come of my despisèd time
Is naught but bitterness. Now, Roderigo,
Where didst thou see her?—O unhappy girl!—
With the Moor, say'st thou?—Who would be a father?—
How didst thou know 'twas she!—O, she deceives me   165
Past thought!—What said she to you?—Get moe° tapers!
Raise all my kindred!—Are they married, think you?

RODERIGO: Truly I think they are.

BRABANTIO: O heaven! How got she out? O treason of the blood!
Fathers, from hence trust not your daughters' minds   170
By what you see them act. Is there not charms
By which the property° of youth and maidhood

---

136 extravagant and wheeling: Expatriate and roving.   **142 accident:** Occurrence.   **148 check:** Reprimand.   **149 cast:** Discharge.   **151 stand in act:** Are going on.   **152 fathom:** Capacity.   **158 Sagittary:** An inn.   **nightgown:** Dressing gown.   **166 moe:** More.   **172 property:** Nature.

May be abused? Have you not read, Roderigo,
Of some such thing?
RODERIGO: Yes, sir, I have indeed.
BRABANTIO: Call up my brother. — O, would you had had her! —   175
Some one way, some another. — Do you know
Where we may apprehend her and the Moor?
RODERIGO: I think I can discover him, if you please
To get good guard and go along with me.
BRABANTIO: I pray you lead on. At every house I'll call;   180
I may command at most. — Get weapons, ho!
And raise some special officers of night. —
On, good Roderigo; I'll deserve° your pains.   *Exeunt.*

[Scene II: Before the lodgings of Othello.]

Enter Othello, Iago, and Attendants with torches.

IAGO: Though in the trade of war I have slain men,
Yet do I hold it very stuff o' th' conscience
To do no contrived murther. I lack iniquity
Sometimes to do me service. Nine or ten times
I had thought t' have yerked° him here under the ribs.   5
OTHELLO: 'Tis better as it is.
IAGO: Nay, but he prated,
And spoke such scurvy and provoking terms
Against your honor
That with the little godliness I have
I did full hard forbear him. But I pray you, sir,   10
Are you fast° married? Be assured of this,
That the magnifico° is much beloved,
And hath in his effect a voice potential°
As double° as the Duke's. He will divorce you,
Or put upon you what restraint and grievance   15
The law, with all his might to enforce it on,
Will give him cable.
OTHELLO: Let him do his spite.
My services which I have done the signiory°
Shall out-tongue his complaints. 'Tis yet to know° —
Which, when I know that boasting is an honor,   20
I shall promulgate — I fetch my life and being
From men of royal siege;° and my demerits°

183 deserve: Show gratitude for. **SCENE II. 5 yerked:** Stabbed. **11 fast:** Securely.
12 magnifico: Grandee (Brabantio). **13 potential:** Powerful. **14 double:** Doubly
influential. **18 signiory:** Venetian government. **19 yet to know:** Still not generally
known. **22 siege:** Rank; **demerits:** Deserts.

May speak unbonneted to as proud a fortune
As this that I have reached.° For know, Iago,
But that I love the gentle Desdemona,   25
I would not my unhousèd° free condition
Put into circumscription and confine
For the sea's worth. But look what lights come yond?

IAGO: Those are the raisèd father and his friends.
You were best go in.

OTHELLO: Not I; I must be found.   30
My parts, my title, and my perfect soul°
Shall manifest me rightly. Is it they?

IAGO: By Janus, I think no.

Enter Cassio, with torches, Officers.

OTHELLO: The servants of the Duke, and my lieutenant.
The goodness of the night upon you, friends!   35
What is the news?

CASSIO: The Duke does greet you, general;
And he requires your haste-post-haste appearance
Even on the instant.

OTHELLO: What's the matter, think you?

CASSIO: Something from Cyprus, as I may divine.
It is a business of some heat. The galleys   40
Have sent a dozen sequent° messengers
This very night at one another's heels,
And many of the consuls, raised and met,
Are at the Duke's already. You have been hotly called for;
When, being not at your lodging to be found,   45
The Senate hath sent about three several quests
To search you out.

OTHELLO: Tis well I am found by you.
I will but spend a word here in the house,
And go with you.   *[Exit.]*

CASSIO: Ancient, what makes he here?

IAGO: Faith, he to-night hath boarded a land carack.°   50
If it prove lawful prize, he's made for ever.

CASSIO: I do not understand.

IAGO: He's married.

CASSIO: To who?

[Enter Othello.]

IAGO: Marry, to—Come, captain, will you go?

OTHELLO: Have with you.

23–24 May speak . . . reached: Are equal, I modestly assert, to those of Desdemona's
family.   **26 unhousèd:** Unrestrained.   **31 perfect soul:** Stainless conscience.
41 sequent: Consecutive.   **50 carack:** Treasure ship.

CASSIO: Here comes another troop to seek for you.

Enter Brabantio, Roderigo, and others with lights and weapons.

IAGO: It is Brabantio. General, be advised.   55
    He comes to bad intent.
OTHELLO: Holla! stand there!
RODERIGO: Signior, it is the Moor.
BRABANTIO: Down with him, thief!

[They draw on both sides.]

IAGO: You, Roderigo! Come, sir, I am for you.
OTHELLO: Keep up° your bright swords, for the dew will rust them.
    Good signior, you shall more command with years   60
    Than with your weapons.
BRABANTIO: O thou foul thief, where hast thou stowed my daughter?
    Damned as thou art, thou hast enchanted her!
    For I'll refer me to all things of sense,
    If she in chains of magic were not bound,   65
    Whether a maid so tender, fair, and happy,
    So opposite to marriage that she shunned
    The wealthy curlèd darlings of our nation,
    Would ever have, t' incur a general mock,
    Run from her guardage to the sooty bosom   70
    Of such a thing as thou—to fear, not to delight.
    Judge me the world if 'tis not gross in sense°
    That thou hast practiced on her with foul charms,
    Abused her delicate youth with drugs or minerals
    That weaken motion.° I'll have't disputed on;   75
    'Tis probable, and palpable to thinking.
    I therefore apprehend and do attach° thee
    For an abuser of the world, a practicer
    Of arts inhibited and out of warrant.
    Lay hold upon him. If he do resist,   80
    Subdue him at his peril.
OTHELLO: Hold your hands,
    Both you of my inclining and the rest.
    Were it my cue to fight, I should have known it
    Without a prompter. Where will you that I go
    To answer this your charge?
BRABANTIO: To prison, till fit time   85
    Of law and course of direct session°
    Call thee to answer.
OTHELLO: What if I do obey?
    How may the Duke be therewith satisfied,

---

59 Keep up: I.e., sheath.   **72 gross in sense:** Obvious.   **75 motion:** Perception.
77 attach: Arrest.   **86 direct session:** Regular trial.

Whose messengers are here about my side
Upon some present business of the state   90
To bring me to him?

OFFICER: Tis true, most worthy signior.
The Duke's in council, and your noble self
I am sure is sent for.

BRABANTIO: How? The Duke in council?
In this time of the night? Bring him away.
Mine's not an idle° cause. The Duke himself,   95
Or any of my brothers of the state,
Cannot but feel this wrong as 'twere their own;
For if such actions may have passage free,
Bondslaves and pagans shall our statesmen be.   *Exeunt.*

[Scene III: The Venetian Senate Chamber.]

Enter Duke and Senators, set at a table, with lights and Attendants.

DUKE: There is no composition° in these news
That gives them credit.

1. SENATOR: Indeed they are disproportioned.
My letters say a hundred and seven galleys.

DUKE: And mine a hundred forty.

2. SENATOR: And mine two hundred.
But though they jump° not on a just account —   5
As in these cases where the aim° reports
'Tis oft with difference — yet do they all confirm
A Turkish fleet, and bearing up to Cyprus.

DUKE: Nay, it is possible enough to judgment.
I do not so secure me° in the error   10
But the main article° I do approve°
In fearful sense.

SAILOR *(within):*   What, ho! what, ho! what, ho!

OFFICER: A messenger from the galleys.

Enter Sailor.

DUKE: Now, what's the business?

SAILOR: The Turkish preparation makes for Rhodes.
So was I bid report here to the state   15
By Signior Angelo.

DUKE: How say you by this change?

1. SENATOR: This cannot be
By no assay° of reason. 'Tis a pageant
To keep us in false gaze.° When we consider

95 idle: Trifling.   **SCENE III.   1 composition:** Consistency.   **5 jump:** Agree. **6 aim:**
Conjecture.   **10 so secure me:** Take such comfort.   **11 article:** Substance; **approve:**
Accept.   **18 assay:** Test.   **19 in false gaze:** Looking the wrong way.

Th' importancy of Cyprus to the Turk,   20
And let ourselves again but understand
That, as it more concerns the Turk than Rhodes,
So may he with more facile question bear° it,
For that it stands not in such warlike brace,°
But altogether lacks th' abilities   25
That Rhodes is dressed in—if we make thought of this,
We must not think the Turk is so unskillful
To leave that latest which concerns him first,
Neglecting an attempt of ease and gain
To wake and wage° a danger profitless.   30
DUKE: Nay, in all confidence, he's not for Rhodes.
OFFICER: Here is more news.

Enter a Messenger.

MESSENGER: The Ottomites, reverend and gracious,
Steering with due course toward the isle of Rhodes,
Have there injointed them with an after fleet.   35
1. SENATOR: Ay, so I thought. How many, as you guess?
MESSENGER: Of thirty sail; and now they do restem°
Their backward course, bearing with frank appearance
Their purposes toward Cyprus, Signior Montano,
Your trusty and most valiant servitor,   40
With his free duty recommends you thus,
And prays you to believe him.
DUKE: 'Tis certain then for Cyprus.
Marcus Luccicos,° is not he in town?
1. SENATOR: He's now in Florence.   45
DUKE: Write from us to him; post, post-haste dispatch.
1. SENATOR: Here comes Brabantio and the valiant Moor.

Enter Brabantio, Othello, Cassio, Iago, Roderigo, and Officers.

DUKE: Valiant Othello, we must straight employ you
Against the general enemy Ottoman.   *[To Brabantio.]*
I did not see you. Welcome, gentle signior.   50
We lacked your counsel and your help to-night.
BRABANTIO: So did I yours. Good your grace, pardon me.
Neither my place, nor aught I heard of business,
Hath raised me from my bed; nor doth the general care
Take hold on me; for my particular grief   55
Is of so floodgate° and o'erbearing nature
That it engluts° and swallows other sorrows,
And it is still itself.

---

23 with . . . bear: More easily capture.   **24 brace:** Posture of defense.   **30 wake and wage:** Rouse and risk.   **37 restem:** Steer again.   **44 Marcus Luccicos:** (Presumably a Venetian envoy).   **56 floodgate:** Torrential.   **57 engluts:** Devours.

DUKE: Why, what's the matter?
BRABANTIO: My daughter! O, my daughter!
ALL: Dead?
BRABANTIO: Ay, to me.
    She is abused, stol'n from me, and corrupted   60
    By spells and medicines bought of mountebanks;
    For nature so prepost'rously to err,
    Being not deficient,° blind, or lame of sense,
    Sans witchcraft could not.
DUKE: Whoe'er he be that in this foul proceeding   65
    Hath thus beguiled your daughter of herself,
    And you of her, the bloody book of law
    You shall yourself read in the bitter letter
    After your own sense; yea, though our proper° son
    Stood in your action.°
BRABANTIO: Humbly I thank your grace.   70
    Here is the man — this Moor, whom now, it seems,
    Your special mandate for the state affairs
    Hath hither brought.
ALL: We are very sorry for't.
DUKE [to Othello]:   What, in your own part, can you say to this?
BRABANTIO: Nothing, but this is so.   75
OTHELLO: Most potent, grave, and reverend signiors,
    My very noble, and approved° good masters,
    That I have ta'en away this old man's daughter,
    It is most true; true I have married her.
    The very head and front of my offending   80
    Hath this extent, no more. Rude° am I in my speech,
    And little blessed with the soft phrase of peace;
    For since these arms of mine had seven years' pith°
    Till now some nine moons wasted, they have used
    Their dearest action in the tented field;   85
    And little of this great world can I speak
    More than pertains to feats of broil and battle;
    And therefore little shall I grace my cause
    In speaking for myself. Yet, by your gracious patience,
    I will a round° unvarnished tale deliver   90
    Of my whole course of love — what drugs, what charms,
    What conjuration, and what mighty magic
    (For such proceeding am I charged withal)
    I won his daughter.

---

63 deficient: Feeble-minded.   **69 our proper:** My own.   **70 Stood in your action:** Were accused by you.   **77 approved:** Tested by experience.   **81 Rude:** Unpolished. **83 pith:** Strength.   **90 round:** Plain.

BRABANTIO: A maiden never bold;
   Of spirit so still and quiet that her motion   95
   Blushed° at herself; and she—in spite of nature,
   Of years, of country, credit, everything —
   To fall in love with what she feared to look on!
   It is a judgment maimed and most imperfect
   That will confess perfection so could err   100
   Against all rules of nature, and must be driven
   To find out practices° of cunning hell
   Why this should be. I therefore vouch° again
   That with some mixtures pow'rful o'er the blood,°
   Or with some dram, conjured to this effect,   105
   He wrought upon her.
DUKE: To vouch this is no proof,
   Without more certain and more overt test
   Than these thin habits° and poor likelihoods
   Of modern seeming° do prefer against him.
1. SENATOR: But, Othello, speak.   110
   Did you by indirect and forcèd° courses
   Subdue and poison this young maid's affections?
   Or came it by request, and such fair question°
   As soul to soul affordeth?
OTHELLO: I do beseech you,
   Send for the lady to the Sagittary   115
   And let her speak of me before her father.
   If you do find me foul in her report,
   The trust, the office, I do hold of you
   Not only take away, but let your sentence
   Even fall upon my life.
DUKE: Fetch Desdemona hither.   120
OTHELLO: Ancient, conduct them; you best know the place.

                   Exit [Iago, with] two or three [Attendants].

   And till she come, as truly as to heaven
   I do confess the vices of my blood,
   So justly to your grave ears I'll present
   How I did thrive in this fair lady's love,   125
   And she in mine.
DUKE: Say it, Othello.
OTHELLO: Her father loved me, oft invited me;
   Still° questioned me the story of my life
   From year to year—the battles, sieges, fortunes   130

95–96 her motion Blushed: Her own emotions caused her to blush.   **102 practices:**
Plots.   **103 vouch:** Assert.   **104 blood:** Passions.   **108 thin habits:** Slight appearances.   **109 modern seeming:** Everyday supposition.   **111 forcèd:** Violent.   **113
question:** Conversation.   **129 Still:** Continually.

That I have passed.
I ran it through, even from my boyish days
To th' very moment that he bade me tell it.
Wherein I spoke of most disastrous chances,
Of moving accidents by flood and field;   135
Of hairbreadth scapes i' th' imminent deadly breach;
Of being taken by the insolent foe
And sold to slavery; of my redemption thence
And portance° in my travels' history;
Wherein of anters° vast and deserts idle,   140
Rough quarries, rocks, and hills whose heads touch heaven,
It was my hint° to speak — such was the process;
And of the Cannibals that each other eat,
The Anthropophagi,° and men whose heads
Do grow beneath their shoulders. This to hear   145
Would Desdemona seriously incline;
But still the house affairs would draw her thence;
Which ever as she could with haste dispatch,
She'd come again, and with a greedy ear
Devour up my discourse. Which I observing,   150
Took once a pliant° hour, and found good means
To draw from her a prayer of earnest heart
That I would all my pilgrimage dilate,°
Whereof by parcels° she had something heard,
But not intentively.° I did consent,   155
And often did beguile her of her tears
When I did speak of some distressful stroke
That my youth suffered. My story being done,
She gave me for my pains a world of sighs.
She swore, i' faith, 'twas strange, 'twas passing strange;   160
'Twas pitiful, 'twas wondrous pitiful.
She wished she had not heard it; yet she wished
That heaven had made her such a man. She thanked me;
And bade me, if I had a friend that loved her,
I should but teach him how to tell my story,   165
And that would woo her. Upon this hint° I spake.
She loved me for the dangers I had passed,
And I loved her that she did pity them.
This only is the witchcraft I have used.
Here comes the lady. Let her witness it.   170

Enter Desdemona, Iago, Attendants.

---

139 portance: Behavior.   **140 anters:** Caves.   **142 hint:** Occasion.   **144
Anthropophagi:** Man-eaters.   **151 pliant:** Propitious.   **153 dilate:** Recount in full.
154 parcels: Portions.   **155 intentively:** With full attention.   **166 hint:** Opportunity.

DUKE: I think this tale would win my daughter too.
Good Brabantio,
Take up this mangled matter at the best.
Men do their broken weapons rather use
Than their bare hands.

BRABANTIO: I pray you hear her speak.   175
If she confess that she was half the wooer,
Destruction on my head if my bad blame
Light on the man! Come hither, gentle mistress.
Do you perceive in all this noble company
Where most you owe obedience?

DESDEMONA: My noble father,   180
I do perceive here a divided duty.
To you I am bound for life and education;°
My life and education both do learn me
How to respect you: you are the lord of duty;
I am hitherto your daughter. But here's my husband;   185
And so much duty as my mother showed
To you, preferring you before her father,
So much I challenge° that I may profess
Due to the Moor my lord.

BRABANTIO: God be with you! I have done.
Please it your grace, on to the state affairs.   190
I had rather to adopt a child than get° it.
Come hither, Moor.
I here do give thee that with all my heart
Which, but thou hast already, with all my heart
I would keep from thee. For your sake,° jewel,   195
I am glad at soul I have no other child;
For thy escape° would teach me tyranny,
To hang clogs on them. I have done, my lord.

DUKE: Let me speak like yourself° and lay a sentence°
Which, as a grise° or step, may help these lovers   200
[Into your favor.]
When remedies are past, the griefs are ended
By seeing the worst, which late on hopes depended.
To mourn a mischief that is past and gone
Is the next way to draw new mischief on.   205
What cannot be preserved when fortune takes,
Patience her injury a mock'ry makes.
The robbed that smiles steals something from the thief;
He robs himself that spends a bootless grief.

182 education: Upbringing.   **188 challenge:** Claim the right.   **191 get:** Beget.
195 For your sake: Because of you.   **197 escape:** Escapade.   **199 like yourself:**
As you should;   **sentence:** Maxim.   **200 grise:** Step.

BRABANTIO: So let the Turk of Cyprus us beguile: 210
      We lose it not so long as we can smile.
      He bears the sentence well that nothing bears
      But the free comfort which from thence he hears;
      But he bears both the sentence and the sorrow
      That to pay grief must of poor patience borrow.   215
      These sentences, to sugar, or to gall,
      Being strong on both sides, are equivocal.
      But words are words. I never yet did hear
      That the bruisèd heart was piercèd through the ear.
      Beseech you, now to the affairs of state.   220

DUKE: The Turk with a most mighty preparation makes for Cyprus. Othello,
      the fortitude° of the place is best known to you; and though we have there
      a substitute of most allowed° sufficiency, yet opinion,° a more sovereign
      mistress of effects, throws a more safer voice on you. You must therefore
      be content to slubber° the gloss of your new fortunes with this more stub-   225
      born and boist'rous expedition.

OTHELLO: The tyrant custom, most grave senators,
      Hath made the flinty and steel couch of war
      My thrice-driven bed of down. I do agnize
      A natural and prompt alacrity   230
      I find in hardness;° and do undertake
      These present wars against the Ottomites.
      Most humbly, therefore, bending to your state,
      I crave fit disposition for my wife,
      Due reference of place, and exhibition,°   235
      With such accommodation and besort°
      As levels° with her breeding.

DUKE: If you please,
      Be't at her father's.

BRABANTIO: I will not have it so.

OTHELLO: Nor I.

DESDEMONA: Nor I. I would not there reside,   240
      To put my father in impatient thoughts
      By being in his eye. Most gracious Duke,
      To my unfolding lend your prosperous° ear,
      And let me find a charter in your voice,
      T' assist my simpleness.°   245

DUKE: What would you, Desdemona?

DESDEMONA: That I did love the Moor to live with him,

---

222 fortitude: Fortification.   **223 allowed:** Acknowledged;   **opinion:** Public
opinion. **225 slubber:** Sully.   **229–31 agnize . . . hardness:** Recognize in myself a
natural and easy response to hardship.   **235 exhibition:** Allowance of money.   **236
besort:** Suitable company.   **237 levels:** Corresponds.   **243 prosperous:** Favorable.
245 simpleness: Lack of skill.

My downright violence, and storm of fortunes,
May trumpet to the world. My heart's subdued
Even to the very quality of my lord.   250
I saw Othello's visage in his mind,
And to his honors and his valiant parts
Did I my soul and fortunes consecrate.
So that, dear lords, if I be left behind,
A moth of peace, and he go to the war,   255
The rites for which I love him are bereft me,
And I a heavy interim shall support
By his dear absence. Let me go with him.

OTHELLO: Let her have your voice.
Vouch with me, heaven, I therefore beg it not   260
To please the palate of my appetite,
Not to comply with heat°—the young affects°
In me defunct—and proper satisfaction;
But to be free and bounteous to her mind;
And heaven defend your good souls that you think   265
I will your serious and great business scant
When she is with me. No, when light-winged toys
Of feathered Cupid seel° with wanton dullness
My speculative and officed instruments,°
That° my disports corrupt and taint my business,   270
Let housewives make a skillet of my helm,
And all indign° and base adversities
Make head against my estimation!°

DUKE: Be it as you shall privately determine,
Either for her stay or going. Th' affair cries haste,   275
And speed must answer it.

1. SENATOR: You must away to-night.

OTHELLO: With all my heart.

DUKE: At nine i' th' morning here we'll meet again.
Othello, leave some officer behind,
And he shall our commission bring to you,   280
With such things else of quality and respect
As doth import° you.

OTHELLO: So please your grace, my ancient;
A man he is of honesty and trust
To his conveyance I assign my wife,
With what else needful your good grace shall think   285
To be sent after me.

DUKE: Let it be so.

---

262 heat: Passions;   **young affects:** Tendencies of youth.   **268 seel:** Blind.   **269
My . . . instruments:** My perceptive and responsible faculties.   **270 That:** So that.
272 indign: Unworthy.   **273 estimation:** Reputation.   **282 import:** Concern.

Good night to every one.
[To Brabantio.]   And, noble signior,
If virtue no delighted° beauty lack,
Your son-in-law is far more fair than black.

1. SENATOR: Adieu, brave Moor. Use Desdemona well.   290

BRABANTIO: Look to her, Moor, if thou hast eyes to see:
She has deceived her father, and may thee.

                                        Exeunt [Duke, Senators, Officers, &c.].

OTHELLO: My life upon her faith!—Honest Iago,
My Desdemona must I leave to thee.
I prithee let thy wife attend on her,   295
And bring them after in the best advantage.°
Come, Desdemona. I have but an hour
Of love, of worldly matters and direction,
To spend with thee. We must obey the time.

                                        Exit Moor and Desdemona.

RODERIGO: Iago, —   300

IAGO: What say'st thou, noble heart?

RODERIGO: What will I do, think'st thou?

IAGO: Why, go to bed and sleep.

RODERIGO: I will incontinently° drown myself.

IAGO: If thou dost, I shall never love thee after. Why, thou silly gentleman!   305

RODERIGO: It is silliness to live when to live is torment; and then have we a
prescription to die when death is our physician.

IAGO: O villainous! I have looked upon the world for four times seven years;
and since I could distinguish betwixt a benefit and an injury, I never found
man that knew how to love himself. Ere I would say I would drown myself   310
for the love of a guinea hen, I would change my humanity with a baboon.

RODERIGO: What should I do? I confess it is my shame to be so fond, but it is not
in my virtue to amend it.

IAGO: Virtue? a fig! 'Tis in ourselves that we are thus or thus. Our bodies are
our gardens, to which our wills are gardeners; so that if we will plant   315
nettles or sow lettuce, set hyssop and weed up thyme, supply it with one
gender° of herbs or distract it with many—either to have it sterile with
idleness or manured with industry—why, the power and corrigible
authority° of this lies in our wills. If the balance of our lives had not one
scale of reason to poise° another of sensuality, the blood and baseness° of   320
our natures would conduct us to most preposterous conclusions. But we
have reason to cool our raging motions,° our carnal strings, our unbitted°
lusts; whereof I take this that you call love to be a sect or scion.°

288 delighted: Delightful.   **296 in the best advantage:** At the best opportunity.
304 incontinently: Forthwith.   **317 gender:** Species.   **318–19 corrigible
authority:** Corrective power.   **320 poise:** Counterbalance;   **blood and baseness:**
Animal instincts.   **322 motions:** Appetites;   **unbitted:** Uncontrolled.   **323 sect or
scion:** Offshoot, cutting.

RODERIGO: It cannot be.

IAGO: It is merely a lust of the blood and a permission of the will. Come, be a   325
man! Drown thyself? Drown cats and blind puppies! I have professed me
thy friend, and I confess me knit to thy deserving with cables of perdura-
ble toughness. I could never better stead thee than now. Put money in thy
purse. Follow thou the wars; defeat thy favor° with an usurped beard. I say,
put money in thy purse. It cannot be that Desdemona should long con-   330
tinue her love to the Moor—put money in thy purse—nor he his to her.
It was a violent commencement in her, and thou shalt see an answerable
sequestration°—put but money in thy purse. These Moors are changeable in their wills—fill thy purse with money. The food that to him now
is as luscious as locusts shall be to him shortly as bitter as coloquintida.°   335
She must change for youth: when she is sated with his body, she will find
the error of her choice. [She must have change, she must.] Therefore put
money in thy purse. If thou wilt needs damn thyself, do it a more delicate
way than drowning. Make° all the money thou canst. If sanctimony and a
frail vow betwixt an erring° barbarian and a supersubtle Venetian be not   340
too hard for my wits and all the tribe of hell, thou shalt enjoy her. Therefore make money. A pox of drowning thyself! 'Tis clean out of the way.
Seek thou rather to be hanged in compassing thy joy than to be drowned
and go without her.

RODERIGO: Wilt thou be fast to my hopes, if I depend on the issue?   345

IAGO: Thou art sure of me. Go, make money. I have told thee often, and I retell
thee again and again, I hate the Moor. My cause is hearted;° thine hath
no less reason. Let us be conjunctive in our revenge against him. If thou
canst cuckold him, thou dost thyself a pleasure, me a sport. There are
many events in the womb of time, which will be delivered. Traverse,° go,   350
provide thy money! We will have more of this to-morrow. Adieu.

RODERIGO: Where shall we meet i' th' morning?

IAGO: At my lodging.

RODERIGO: I'll be with thee betimes.

IAGO: Go to, farewell—Do you hear, Roderigo?   355

RODERIGO: What say you?

IAGO: No more of drowning, do you hear?

RODERIGO: I am changed.

IAGO: Go to, farewell. Put money enough in your purse.

RODERIGO: I'll sell all my land.   *Exit.*   360

IAGO: Thus do I ever make my fool my purse;
For I mine own gained knowledge should profane
If I would time expend with such a snipe°
But for my sport and profit. I hate the Moor;

---

329 defeat thy favor: Spoil thy appearance.   **333 sequestration:** Estrangement.
335 coloquintida: A medicine.   **339 Make:** Raise.   **340 erring:** Wandering.
347 My cause is hearted: My heart is in it.   **350 Traverse:** Forward march.
363 snipe: Fool.

And it is thought abroad that 'twixt my sheets   365
H'as done my office. I know not if't be true;
But I, for mere suspicion in that kind,
Will do as if for surety. He holds me well;°
The better shall my purpose work on him.
Cassio's a proper man. Let me see now: 370
To get his place, and to plume up° my will
In double knavery—How, how?—Let's see: —
After some time, to abuse Othello's ears
That he is too familiar with his wife.
He hath a person and a smooth dispose°   375
To be suspected—framed to make women false.
The Moor is of a free° and open nature
That thinks men honest that but seem to be so;
And will as tenderly be led by th' nose
As asses are.   380
I have't! It is engend'red! Hell and night
Must bring this monstrous birth to the world's light.   *Exit.*

[ACT II, Scene I: An open place in Cyprus, near the harbor.]

Enter Montano and two Gentlemen.

MONTANO: What from the cape can you discern at sea?
1. GENTLEMAN: Nothing at all: it is a high-wrought flood.
      I cannot 'twixt the heaven and the main
      Descry a sail.
MONTANO: Methinks the wind hath spoke aloud at land;   5
      A fuller blast ne'er shook our battlements.
      If it hath ruffianed so upon the sea,
      What ribs of oak, when mountains melt on them,
      Can hold the mortise?° What shall we hear of this?
2. GENTLEMAN: A segregation° of the Turkish fleet.   10
      For do but stand upon the foaming shore,
      The chidden billow seems to pelt the clouds;
      The wind-shaked surge, with high and monstrous mane,
      Seems to cast water on the burning Bear
      And quench the Guards° of th' ever-fixèd pole.°   15
      I never did like molestation° view
      On the enchafèd flood.
MONTANO: If that the Turkish fleet

---

368 well: In high regard.   **371 plume up:** Gratify.   **375 dispose:** Manner.
377 free: Frank.   **ACT II, SCENE I. 9 hold the mortise:** Hold their joints together.
10 segregation: Scattering.   **15 Guards:** Stars near the North Star;   **pole:** Polestar.
16 molestation: Tumult.

Be not ensheltered and embayed, they are drowned;
It is impossible to bear it out.

Enter a third Gentleman.

3. GENTLEMAN: News, lads! Our wars are done.   20
The desperate tempest hath so banged the Turks
That their designment halts.° A noble ship of Venice
Hath seen a grievous wrack and sufferance°
On most part of their fleet.

MONTANO: How? Is this true?

3. GENTLEMAN: The ship is here put in,   25
A Veronesa;° Michael Cassio,
Lieutenant to the warlike Moor Othello,
Is come on shore; the Moor himself at sea,
And is in full commission here for Cyprus.

MONTANO: I am glad on't. 'Tis a worthy governor.   30

3. GENTLEMAN: But his same Cassio, though he speak of comfort
Touching the Turkish loss, yet he looks sadly
And prays the Moor be safe, for they were parted
With foul and violent tempest.

MONTANO: Pray heaven he be;
For I have served him, and the man commands   35
Like a full soldier. Let's to the seaside, ho!
As well to see the vessel that's come in
As to throw out our eyes for brave Othello,
Even till we make the main and th' aerial blue
An indistinct regard.°   40

3. GENTLEMAN: Come, let's do so;
For every minute is expectancy
Of more arrivance.

Enter Cassio.

CASSIO: Thanks, you the valiant of this warlike isle,
That so approve the Moor! O, let the heavens
Give him defense against the elements,   45
For I have lost him on a dangerous sea!

MONTANO: Is he well shipped?

CASSIO: His bark is stoutly timbered, and his pilot
Of very expert and approved allowance;
Therefore my hopes, not surfeited to death,°   50
Stand in bold cure.°

     (Within.)   A sail, a sail, a sail!   *Enter a messenger.*

CASSIO: What noise?

---

22 designment halts: Plan is crippled.   **23 sufferance:** Disaster.   **26 Veronesa:** Ship
furnished by Verona.   **40 An indistinct regard:** Indistinguishable.   **50 surfeited to
death:** Overindulged.   **51 in bold cure:** A good chance of fulfillment.

MESSENGER: The town is empty; on the brow o' th' sea
    Stand ranks of people, and they cry "A sail!"
CASSIO: My hopes do shape him for the governor.   55

A shot.

2. GENTLEMAN: They do discharge their shot of courtesy:
    Our friends at least.
CASSIO: I pray you, sir, go forth
    And give us truth who 'tis that is arrived.
2. GENTLEMAN: I shall.   *Exit.*
MONTANO: But, good lieutenant, is your general wived?   60
CASSIO: Most fortunately. He hath achieved a maid
    That paragons° description and wild fame;
    One that excels the quirks° of blazoning° pens,
    And in th' essential vesture of creation
    Does tire the ingener.°

Enter Second Gentleman.

                How now? Who has put in?   65
2. GENTLEMAN: 'Tis one Iago, ancient to the general.
CASSIO: H'as had most favorable and happy speed:
    Tempests themselves, high seas, and howling winds,
    The guttered° rocks and congregated sands,
    Traitors ensteeped° to clog the guiltless keel,   70
    As having sense of beauty, do omit
    Their mortal° natures, letting go safely by
    The divine Desdemona.
MONTANO: What is she?
CASSIO: She that I spake of, our great captain's captain,
    Left in the conduct of the bold Iago,   75
    Whose footing° here anticipates our thoughts
    A se'nnight's° speed. Great Jove, Othello guard,
    And swell his sail with thine own pow'rful breath,
    That he may bless this bay with his tall ship,
    Make love's quick pants in Desdemona's arms,   80
    Give renewed fire to our extinct spirits,
    [And bring all Cyprus comfort!]

Enter Desdemona, Iago, Roderigo, and Emilia [with Attendants].

                O, behold!
    The riches of the ship is come on shore!
    You men of Cyprus, let her have your knees.°

---

62 paragons: Surpasses.   **63 quirks:** Ingenuities;   **blazoning:** Describing.
64–65 And . . . ingener: Merely to describe her as God made her exhausts her praiser.
69 guttered: Jagged.   **70 ensteeped:** Submerged.   **72 mortal:** Deadly.   **76
footing:** Landing.   **77 se'nnight's:** Week's.   **84 knees:** I.e., kneeling.

Hail to thee, lady! and the grace of heaven,   85
Before, behind thee, and on every hand,
Enwheel thee round!
DESDEMONA: I thank you, valiant Cassio.
What tidings can you tell me of my lord?
CASSIO: He is not yet arrived; nor know I aught
But that he's well and will be shortly here.   90
DESDEMONA: O but I fear! How lost you company?
CASSIO: The great contention of the sea and skies
Parted our fellowship.
(Within.)   A sail, a sail! *[A shot.]*
                              But hark. A sail!
2. GENTLEMAN: They give their greeting to the citadel;
This likewise is a friend.
CASSIO: See for the news.   95

                                         [Exit Gentleman.]

Good ancient, you are welcome.
[To Emilia.]   Welcome, mistress. —
Let it not gall your patience, good Iago,
That I extend my manners. 'Tis my breeding
That gives me this bold show of courtesy.

[Kisses Emilia.°]

IAGO: Sir, would she give you so much of her lips   100
As of her tongue she oft bestows on me,
You would have enough.
DESDEMONA: Alas, she has no speech!
IAGO: In faith, too much.
I find it still when I have list to sleep.
Marry, before your ladyship, I grant,   105
She puts her tongue a little in her heart
And chides with thinking.
EMILIA: You have little cause to say so.
IAGO: Come on, come on! You are pictures out of doors,
Bells in your parlors, wildcats in your kitchens,   110
Saints in your injuries, devils being offended,
Players in your housewifery,° and housewives° in your beds.
DESDEMONA: O, fie upon thee, slanderer!
IAGO: Nay, it is true, or else I am a Turk:
You rise to play, and go to bed to work.   115
EMILIA: You shall not write my praise.
IAGO: No, let me not.

Kisses Emilia: (Kissing was a common Elizabethan form of social courtesy).   **112 housewifery:** Housekeeping;   **housewives:** Hussies.

DESDEMONA: What wouldst thou write of me, if thou shouldst praise me?

IAGO: O gentle lady, do not put me to't,
For I am nothing if not critical.

DESDEMONA: Come on, assay.°—There's one gone to the harbor?   120

IAGO: Ay, madam.

DESDEMONA: I am not merry; but I do beguile
The thing I am by seeming otherwise. —
Come, how wouldst thou praise me?

IAGO: I am about it; but indeed my invention   125
Comes from my pate as birdlime° does from frieze° —
It plucks out brains and all. But my Muse labors,
And thus she is delivered:
If she be fair and wise, fairness and wit —
The one's for use, the other useth it.   130

DESDEMONA: Well praised! How if she be black° and witty?

IAGO: If she be black, and thereto have a wit,
She'll find a white that shall her blackness fit.

DESDEMONA: Worse and worse!

EMILIA: How if fair and foolish?   135

IAGO: She never yet was foolish that was fair,
For even her folly° helped her to an heir.

DESDEMONA: These are old fond° paradoxes to make fools laugh i' th' alehouse.
What miserable praise hast thou for her that's foul° and foolish?

IAGO: There's none so foul, and foolish thereunto,   140
But does foul pranks which fair and wise ones do.

DESDEMONA: O heavy ignorance! Thou praisest the worst best. But what praise
couldst thou bestow on a deserving woman indeed—one that in the
authority of her merit did justly put on the vouch° of very malice itself?

IAGO: She that was ever fair, and never proud;   145
Had tongue at will, and yet was never loud;
Never lacked gold, and yet went never gay;
Fled from her wish, and yet said "Now I may";
She that, being ang'red, her revenge being nigh,
Bade her wrong stay, and her displeasure fly;   150
She that in wisdom never was so frail
To change the cod's head for the salmon's tail;°
She that could think, and ne'er disclose her mind;
See suitors following, and not look behind:
She was a wight (if ever such wight were) —   155

DESDEMONA: To do what?

IAGO: To suckle fools and chronicle small beer.°

---

120 assay: Try.   **126 birdlime:** A sticky paste;   **frieze:** Rough cloth.   **131 black:**
Brunette.   **137 folly:** Wantonness.   **138 fond:** Foolish.   **139 foul:** Ugly.   **144 put
on the vouch:** Compel the approval.   **152 To . . . tail:** I.e., to exchange the good for the
poor but expensive.   **157 chronicle small beer:** Keep petty household accounts.

DESDEMONA: O most lame and impotent conclusion! Do not learn of him, Emilia, though he be thy husband. How say you, Cassio? Is he not a most profane and liberal° counsellor? 160

CASSIO: He speaks home,° madam. You may relish him more in the soldier than in the scholar.

IAGO *[aside]*:   He takes her by the palm. Ay, well said, whisper! With as little a web as this will I ensnare as great a fly as Cassio. Ay, smile upon her, do! I will gyve thee in thine own courtship.° —You say true; 'tis so, indeed! —If 165 such tricks as these strip you out of your lieutenantry, it had been better you had not kissed your three fingers so oft —which now again you are most apt to play the sir° in. Very good! well kissed! an excellent courtesy! 'Tis so, indeed. Yet again your fingers to your lips? Would they were clyster pipes° for your sake! (Trumpet within.) 170
    The Moor! I know his trumpet.

CASSIO: 'Tis truly so.

DESDEMONA: Let's meet him and receive him.

CASSIO: Lo, where he comes.

Enter Othello and Attendants.

OTHELLO: O my fair warrior!

DESDEMONA: My dear Othello! 175

OTHELLO: It gives me wonder great as my content
    To see you here before me. O my soul's joy!
    If after every tempest come such calms,
    May the winds blow till they have wakened death!
    And let the laboring bark climb hills of seas 180
    Olympus-high, and duck again as low
    As hell's from heaven! If it were now to die,
    'Twere now to be most happy;° for I fear
    My soul hath her content so absolute
    That not another comfort like to this 185
    Succeeds in unknown fate.

DESDEMONA: The heavens forbid
    But that our loves and comforts should increase
    Even as our days do grow.

OTHELLO: Amen to that, sweet powers!
    I cannot speak enough of this content;
    It stops me here; it is too much of joy. 190
    And this, and this, the greatest discords be

They kiss.

    That e'er our hearts shall make!

IAGO *[aside]*:   O, you are well tuned now!

---

160 profane and liberal: Worldly and licentious.   **161 home:** Bluntly.   **165 gyve . . . courtship:** Manacle you by means of your courtly manners.   **168 sir:** Courtly gentleman.   **169–70 clyster pipes:** Syringes.   **183 happy:** Fortunate.

But I'll set down° the pegs that make this music,
As honest as I am.
OTHELLO: Come, let us to the castle.
News, friends! Our wars are done; the Turks are drowned.   195
How does my old acquaintance of this isle? —
Honey, you shall be well desired° in Cyprus;
I have found great love amongst them. O my sweet,
I prattle out of fashion, and I dote
In mine own comforts. I prithee, good Iago,   200
Go to the bay and disembark my coffers.
Bring thou the master° to the citadel;
He is a good one, and his worthiness
Does challenge° much respect. — Come, Desdemona,
Once more well met at Cyprus.   205

Exit Othello [with all but Iago and Roderigo].

IAGO *[to an Attendant, who goes out]*:   Do thou meet me presently at the harbor. *[To Roderigo.]* Come hither. If thou be'st valiant (as they say base men
being in love have then a nobility in their natures more than is native to
them), list me. The lieutenant to-night watches on the court of guard.°
First, I must tell thee this: Desdemona is directly in love with him.   210
RODERIGO: With him? Why, 'tis not possible.
IAGO: Lay thy finger thus,° and let thy soul be instructed. Mark me with
what violence she first loved the Moor, but for bragging and telling her
fantastical lies; and will she love him still for prating? Let not thy discreet
heart think it. Her eye must be fed; and what delight shall she have to   215
look on the devil? When the blood is made dull with the act of sport, there
should be, again to inflame it and to give satiety a fresh appetite, loveliness
in favor, sympathy in years, manners, and beauties; all which the Moor
is defective in. Now for want of these required conveniences,° her delicate
tenderness will find itself abused, begin to heave the gorge,° disrelish and   220
abhor the Moor. Very nature will instruct her in it and compel her to
some second choice. Now, sir, this granted — as it is a most pregnant° and
unforced position — who stands so eminent in the degree of this fortune
as Cassio does? A knave very voluble; no further conscionable° than in
putting on the mere form of civil and humane° seeming for the better   225
compassing of his salt° and most hidden loose affection? Why, none! why,
none! A slipper° and subtle knave; a finder-out of occasions; that has an
eye can stamp and counterfeit advantages, though true advantage never
present itself; a devilish knave! Besides, the knave is handsome, young, and

---

193 set down: Loosen.   **197 well desired:** Warmly welcomed.   **202 master:** Ship
captain.   **204 challenge:** Deserve.   **209 court of guard:** Headquarters.   **212 thus:**
I.e., on your lips.   **219 conveniences:** Compatibilities.   **220 heave the gorge:** Be
nauseated.   **222 pregnant:** Evident.   **224 conscionable:** Conscientious.   **225 humane:**
Polite.   **226 salt:** Lecherous.   **227 slipper:** Slippery.

hath all those requisites in him that folly and green minds look after.   230
A pestilent complete knave! and the woman hath found him already.

RODERIGO: I cannot believe that in her; she's full of most blessed condition.°

IAGO: Blessed fig's-end! The wine she drinks is made of grapes. If she had been
blessed, she would never have loved the Moor. Blessed pudding! Didst thou
not see her paddle with the palm of his hand? Didst not mark that?   235

RODERIGO: Yes, that I did; but that was but courtesy.

IAGO: Lechery, by this hand! an index and obscure prologue to the history of
lust and foul thoughts. They met so near with their lips that their breaths
embraced together. Villainous thoughts, Roderigo! When these mutuali-
ties° so marshal the way, hard at hand comes the master and main exer-   240
cise, th' incorporate° conclusion. Pish! But, sir, be you ruled by me: I have
brought you from Venice. Watch you to-night; for the command, I'll lay't
upon you. Cassio knows you not. I'll not be far from you: do you find some
occasion to anger Cassio, either by speaking too loud, or tainting° his discipline, or from what other course you please which the time shall more   245
favorably minister.

RODERIGO: Well.

IAGO: Sir, he's rash and very sudden in choler,° and haply with his truncheon
may strike at you. Provoke him that he may; for even out of that will I
cause these of Cyprus to mutiny; whose qualification° shall come into   250
no true taste° again but by the displanting of Cassio. So shall you have a
shorter journey to your desires by the means I shall then have to prefer°
them; and the impediment most profitably removed with-out the which
there were no expectation of our prosperity.

RODERIGO: I will do this if you can bring it to any opportunity.   255

IAGO: I warrant thee. Meet me by and by at the citadel; I must fetch his necessaries ashore. Farewell.

RODERIGO: Adieu.   *Exit.*

IAGO: That Cassio loves her, I do well believe't;
That she loves him, 'tis apt° and of great credit.   260
The Moor, howbeit that I endure him not,
Is of a constant, loving, noble nature,
And I dare think he'll prove to Desdemona
A most dear husband. Now I do love her too;
Not out of absolute lust, though peradventure   265
I stand accountant° for as great a sin,
But partly led to diet° my revenge,
For that I do suspect the lusty Moor
Hath leaped into my seat; the thought whereof
Doth, like a poisonous mineral, gnaw my inwards;   270

---

232 condition: Character.   **239–40 mutualities:** Exchanges.   **241 incorporate:**
Carnal.   **244 tainting:** Discrediting.   **248 sudden in choler:** Violent in anger.   **250
qualification:** Appeasement.   **251 true taste:** Satisfactory state.   **252 prefer:** Advance.
260 apt: Probable.   **266 accountant:** Accountable.   **267 diet:** Feed.

And nothing can or shall content my soul
Till I am evened with him, wife for wife;
Or failing so, yet that I put the Moor
At least into a jealousy so strong
That judgment cannot cure. Which thing to do,   275
If this poor trash of Venice, whom I trash°
For° his quick hunting, stand the putting on,°
I'll have our Michael Cassio on the hip,°
Abuse him to the Moor in the rank garb°
(For I fear Cassio with my nightcap too),   280
Make the Moor thank me, love me, and reward me
For making him egregiously an ass
And practicing upon° his peace and quiet
Even to madness. 'Tis here, but yet confused:
Knavery's plain face is never seen till used.   *Exit.*   285

[Scene II: A street in Cyprus.]

Enter Othello's Herald, with a proclamation.

HERALD: It is Othello's pleasure, our noble and valiant general, that, upon
certain tidings now arrived, importing the mere perdition° of the Turkish
fleet, every man put himself into triumph; some to dance, some to make
bonfires, each man to what sport and revels his addiction leads him. For,
besides these beneficial news, it is the celebration of his nuptial. So much   5
was his pleasure should be proclaimed. All offices° are open, and there is
full liberty of feasting from the present hour of five till the bell have told
eleven. Heaven bless the isle of Cyprus and our noble general Othello!
                                                                  Exit.

[Scene III: The Cyprian Castle.]

Enter Othello, Desdemona, Cassio, and Attendants.

OTHELLO: Good Michael, look you to the guard to-night.
    Let's teach ourselves that honorable stop,
    Not to outsport discretion.

CASSIO: Iago hath direction what to do;
    But not withstanding, with my personal eye   5
    Will I look to't.

OTHELLO: Iago is most honest.
    Michael, good night. To-morrow with your earliest
    Let me have speech with you.

---

276 I trash: I weight down (in order to keep under control).   **277 For:** In order to
develop;   **stand the putting on:** Responds to my inciting.   **278 on the hip:** At my
mercy.   **279 rank garb:** Gross manner.   **283 practicing upon:** Plotting against.
SCENE II. 2 mere perdition: Complete destruction.   **6 offices:** Kitchens and storerooms.

[To Desdemona.]   Come, my dear love.
The purchase made, the fruits are to ensue;
That profit 's yet to come 'tween me and you. —   10
Good night.

> *Exit [Othello with Desdemona and Attendants].*

Enter Iago.

CASSIO: Welcome, Iago. We must to the watch.

IAGO: Not this hour, lieutenant; 'tis not yet ten o' th' clock. Our general cast°
us thus early for the love of his Desdemona; who let us not therefore
blame. He hath not yet made wanton the night with her, and she is sport   15
for Jove.

CASSIO: She's a most exquisite lady.

IAGO: And, I'll warrant her, full of game.

CASSIO: Indeed, she's a most fresh and delicate creature.

IAGO: What an eye she has! Methinks it sounds a parley to provocation.   20

CASSIO: An inviting eye; and yet methinks right modest.

IAGO: And when she speaks, is it not an alarum to love?

CASSIO: She is indeed perfection.

IAGO: Well, happiness to their sheets! Come, lieutenant, I have a stoup° of
wine, and here without are a brace of Cyprus gallants that would fain   25
have a measure to the health of black Othello.

CASSIO: Not to-night, good Iago. I have very poor and unhappy brains for
drinking; I could well wish courtesy would invent some other custom of
entertainment.

IAGO: O, they are our friends. But one cup! I'll drink for you.   30

CASSIO: I have drunk but one cup to-night, and that was craftily qualified° too;
and behold what innovation° it makes here. I am unfortunate in the infirmity and dare not task my weakness with any more.

IAGO: What, man! 'Tis a night of revels: the gallants desire it.

CASSIO: Where are they?   35

IAGO: Here at the door; I pray you call them in.

CASSIO: I'll do 't, but it dislikes me.   *Exit.*

IAGO: If I can fasten but one cup upon him
With that which he hath drunk to-night already,
He'll be as full of quarrel and offense   40
As my young mistress' dog. Now my sick fool Roderigo,
Whom love hath turned almost the wrong side out,
To Desdemona hath to-night caroused
Potations pottle-deep;° and he's to watch.
Three lads of Cyprus — noble swelling spirits,   45
That hold their honors in a wary distance,°
The very elements° of this warlike isle —

SCENE III. **14 cast:** Dismissed.   **24 stoup:** Two-quart tankard.   **31 qualified:** Diluted.
32 innovation: Disturbance.   **44 pottle-deep:** Bottoms up.   **46 That . . . distance:**
Very sensitive about their honor.   **47 very elements:** True representatives.

Have I to-night flustered with flowing cups,
And they watch too. Now, 'mongst this flock of drunkards
Am I to put our Cassio in some action   50
That may offend the isle.

Enter Cassio, Montano, and Gentlemen [; Servants following with wine].

But here they come.
If consequence do but approve my dream,
My boat sails freely, both with wind and stream.

CASSIO: 'Fore God, they have given me a rouse° already.   55

MONTANO: Good faith, a little one; not past a pint, as I am a soldier.

IAGO: Some wine, ho!

    [Sings.]   And let me the canakin clink, clink;
                And let me the canakin clink
                    A soldier's a man;   60
                    A life's but a span,
                    Why then, let a soldier drink.

Some wine, boys!

CASSIO: 'Fore God, an excellent song!

IAGO: I learned it in England, where indeed they are most potent in potting.   65
Your Dane, your German, and your swag-bellied Hollander — Drink,
ho! — are nothing to your English.

CASSIO: Is your Englishman so expert in his drinking?

IAGO: Why, he drinks you with facility your Dane dead drunk; he sweats not
to overthrow your Almain; he gives your Hollander a vomit ere the next   70
pottle can be filled.

CASSIO: To the health of our general!

MONTANO: I am for it, lieutenant, and I'll do you justice.

IAGO: O sweet England!

    [Sings.]   King Stephen was a worthy peer;   75
                    His breeches cost him but a crown;
                He held 'em sixpence all too dear,
                    With that he called the tailor lown.°
                He was a wight of high renown,
                    And thou art but of low degree.   80
                'tis pride that pulls the country down;
                    Then take thine auld cloak about thee.

Some wine, ho!

CASSIO: 'Fore God, this is a more exquisite song than the other.

IAGO: Will you hear't again?   85

CASSIO: No, for I hold him to be unworthy of his place that does those things.°
Well, God's above all; and there be souls must be saved, and there be souls
must not be saved.

IAGO: It's true, good lieutenant.

---

55 rouse: Bumper.   **78 lown:** Rascal.   **86 does . . . things:** I.e., behaves in this fashion.

CASSIO: For mine own part — no offense to the general, nor any man of   90
    quality — I hope to be saved.

IAGO: And so do I too, lieutenant.

CASSIO: Ay, but, by your leave, not before me. The lieutenant is to be saved
    before the ancient. Let's have no more of this; let's to our affairs. — God for-
    give us our sins! — Gentlemen, let's look to our business. Do not think, gen-   95
    tlemen, I am drunk. This is my ancient; this is my right hand, and this is my
    left. I am not drunk now. I can stand well enough, and I speak well enough.

ALL: Excellent well!

CASSIO: Why, very well then. You must not think then that I am drunk.

                                               Exit.

MONTANO: To th' platform, masters. Come, let's set the watch.   100

IAGO: You see this fellow that is gone before.
    He's a soldier fit to stand by Caesar
    And give direction; and do but see his vice.
    'Tis to his virtue a just equinox,°
    The one as long as th' other. 'Tis pity of him.   105
    I fear the trust Othello puts him in,
    On some odd time of his infirmity,
    Will shake this island.

MONTANO: But is he often thus?

IAGO: 'Tis evermore his prologue to his sleep:
    He'll watch the horologe a double set°   110
    If drink rock not his cradle.

MONTANO: It were well
    The general were put in mind of it.
    Perhaps he sees it not, or his good nature
    Prizes the virtue that appears in Cassio
    And looks not on his evils. Is not this true?   115

Enter Roderigo.

IAGO *[aside to him]*:   How now, Roderigo?
    I pray you after the lieutenant, go!   *Exit Roderigo.*

MONTANO: And 'tis great pity that the noble Moor
    Should hazard such a place as his own second
    With one of an ingraft° infirmity.   120
    It were an honest action to say
    So to the Moor.

IAGO: Not I, for this fair island!
    I do love Cassio well and would do much
    To cure him of this evil.
        (Within.) Help! help!

                    But hark! What noise?   125

---

104 just equinox: Exact equivalent.   **110 watch . . . set:** Stay awake twice around the
clock.   **120 ingraft:** I.e., ingrained.

Enter Cassio, driving in Roderigo.

CASSIO: Zounds, you rogue! you rascal!

MONTANO: What's the matter, lieutenant?

CASSIO: A knave to teach me my duty?
I'll beat the knave into a twiggen° bottle.

RODERIGO: Beat me?

CASSIO: Dost thou prate, rogue? *[Strikes him.]*   130

MONTANO: Nay, good lieutenant!

                                        [Stays him.]

I pray you, sir, hold your hand.

CASSIO: Let me go, sir,
Or I'll knock you o'er the mazzard.°

MONTANO: Come, come, you're drunk!

CASSIO: Drunk?

They fight.

IAGO *[aside to Roderigo]*:   Away, I say! Go out and cry a mutiny!

                                    Exit Roderigo.

Nay, good lieutenant. God's will, gentlemen!
Help, ho! — lieutenant — sir — Montano — sir —
Help, masters! — Here's a goodly watch indeed!   135

A bell rung.

Who's that which rings the bell? Diablo, ho!
The town will rise.° God's will, lieutenant, hold!
You'll be shamed for ever.

Enter Othello and Gentlemen with weapons.

OTHELLO: What is the matter here?

MONTANO: Zounds, I bleed still. I am hurt to th' death.
He dies!   140

OTHELLO: Hold for your lives!

IAGO: Hold, hold! Lieutenant — sir — Montano — gentlemen!
Have you forgot all sense of place and duty?
Hold! The general speaks to you. Hold, for shame!

OTHELLO: Why, how now ho? From whence ariseth this?   145
Are we turned Turks, and to ourselves do that
Which heaven hath forbid the Ottomites?
For Christian shame put by this barbarous brawl!
He that stirs next to carve for° his own rage.
Holds his soul light; he dies upon his motion.   150
Silence that dreadful bell! It frights the isle
From her propriety.° What is the matter, masters?
Honest Iago, that looks dead with grieving,

127 twiggen: Wicker-covered.   **130 mazzard:** Head.   **137 rise:** Grow riotous.
149 carve for: Indulge.   **152 propriety:** Proper self.

Speak. Who began this? On thy love, I charge thee.
IAGO: I do not know. Friends all, but now, even now,   155
    In quarter,° and in terms like bride and groom
    Devesting them for bed; and then, but now —
    As if some planet had unwitted men —
    Swords out, and tilting one at other's breast
    In opposition bloody. I cannot speak   160
    Any beginning to this peevish odds,°
    And would in action glorious I had lost
    Those legs that brought me to a part of it!
OTHELLO: How comes it, Michael, you are thus forgot?
CASSIO: I pray you pardon me; I cannot speak.   165
OTHELLO: Worthy Montano, you were wont to be civil;
    The gravity and stillness of your youth
    The world hath noted, and your name is great
    In months of wisest censure.° What's the matter
    That you unlace° your reputation thus   170
    And spend your rich opinion° for the name
    Of a night-brawler? Give me answer to it.
MONTANO: Worthy Othello, I am hurt to danger.
    Your officer, Iago, can inform you,
    While I spare speech, which something now offends° me,   175
    Of all that I do know; nor know I aught
    By me that's said or done amiss this night,
    Unless self-charity be sometimes a vice,
    And to defend ourselves it be a sin
    When violence assails us.
OTHELLO: Now, by heaven,   180
    My blood° begins my safer guides to rule,
    And passion, having my best judgment collied,°
    Assays° to lead the way. If I once stir
    Or do but lift this arm, the best of you
    Shall sink in my rebuke. Give me to know   185
    How this foul rout began, who set it on;
    And he that is approved in° this offense,
    Though he had twinned with me, both at a birth,
    Shall lose me. What! in a town of war,
    Yet wild, the people's hearts brimful of fear,   190
    To manage° private and domestic quarrel?
    In night, and on the court and guard of safety?
    'Tis monstrous. Iago, who began't?

---

156 quarter: Friendliness.   **161 peevish odds:** Childish quarrel.   **169 censure:**
Judgment.   **170 unlace:** Undo.   **171 rich opinion:** High reputation.   **175 offends:**
Pains.   **181 blood:** Passion.   **182 collied:** Darkened.   **183 Assays:** Tries.   **187
approved in:** Proved guilty of.   **191 manage:** Carry on.

MONTANO: If partially affined, or leagued in office,°   195
    Thou dost deliver more or less than truth,
    Thou art no soldier.
IAGO: Touch me not so near.
    I had rather have this tongue cut from my mouth
    Than it should do offense to Michael Cassio;
    Yet I persuade myself, to speak the truth
    Shall nothing wrong him. This it is, general.   200
    Montano and myself being in speech,
    There comes a fellow crying out for help,
    And Cassio following him with determined sword
    To execute° upon him. Sir, this gentleman
    Steps in to Cassio and entreats his pause.   205
    Myself the crying fellow did pursue,
    Lest by his clamor—as it so fell out—
    The town might fall in fright. He, swift of foot,
    Outran my purpose; and I returned then rather
    For that I heard the clink and fall of swords,   210
    And Cassio high in oath;° which till to-night
    I ne'er might say before. When I came back—
    For this was brief—I found them close together
    At blow and thrust, even as again they were
    When you yourself did part them.   215
    More of this matter cannot I report;
    But men are men; the best sometimes forget.
    Though Cassio did some little wrong to him,
    As men in rage strike those that wish them best,
    Yet surely Cassio I believe received   220
    From him that fled some strange indignity,
    Which patience could not pass.°
OTHELLO: I know, Iago,
    Thy honesty and love doth mince this matter,
    Making it light to Cassio. Cassio, I love thee;
    But never more be officer of mine.   225

Enter Desdemona, attended.

    Look if my gentle love be not raised up!
    I'll make thee an example.
DESDEMONA: What's the matter?
OTHELLO: All's well now, sweeting; come away to bed.
    [To Montano.]
    Sir, for your hurts, myself will be your surgeon.
    Lead him off.   230

---

194 partially . . . office: Prejudiced by comradeship or official relations.   **204 execute:** Work his will.   **211 high in oath:** Cursing.   **222 pass:** Pass over, ignore.

[Montano is led off.]

Iago, look with care about the town
And silence those whom this vile brawl distracted.°
Come, Desdemona; 'tis the soldiers' life
To have their balmy slumbers waked with strife.

Exit [with all but Iago and Cassio].

IAGO: What, are you hurt, lieutenant?   235
CASSIO: Ay, past all surgery.
IAGO: Marry, God forbid!
CASSIO: Reputation, reputation, reputation! O, I have lost my reputation!
I have lost the immortal part of myself, and what remains is bestial. My
reputation, Iago, my reputation!   240
IAGO: As I am an honest man, I thought you had received some bodily wound.
There is more sense in that than in reputation. Reputation is an idle and
most false imposition; oft got without merit and lost without deserving.
You have lost no reputation at all unless you repute yourself such a loser.
What, man! there are ways to recover° the general again. You are but now   245
cast in his mood° — a punishment more in policy than in malice, even so
as one would beat his offenseless dog to affright an imperious lion. Sue to
him again, and he's yours.
CASSIO: I will rather sue to be despised than to deceive so good a commander
with so slight, so drunken, and so indiscreet an officer. Drunk! and speak   250
parrot!° and squabble! swagger! swear! and discourse fustian° with one's
own shadow! O thou invisible spirit of wine, if thou hast no name to be
known by, let us call thee devil!
IAGO: What was he that you followed with your sword? What had he done
to you?   255
CASSIO: I know not.
IAGO: Is't possible?
CASSIO: I remember a mass of things, but nothing distinctly; a quarrel, but
nothing wherefore. O God, that men should put an enemy in their mouths
to steal away their brains! that we should with joy, pleasance, revel, and   260
applause° transform ourselves into beasts!
IAGO: Why, but you are now well enough. How came you thus recovered?
CASSIO: It hath pleased the devil drunkenness to give place to the devil wrath.
One unperfectness shows me another, to make me frankly despise myself.
IAGO: Come, you are too severe a moraler. As the time, the place, and the con-   265
dition of this country stands, I could heartily wish this had not so befall'n;
but since it is as it is, mend it for your own good.
CASSIO: I will ask him for my place again: he shall tell me I am a drunkard!
Had I as many mouths as Hydra,° such an answer would stop them all.

---

232 distracted: Excited.   **245 recover:** Regain favor with.   **246 in his mood:**
Dismissed because of his anger.   **251 parrot:** Meaningless phrases;   **fustian:** Bombastic
nonsense.   **261 applause:** Desire to please.   **269 Hydra:** Monster with many heads.

To be now a sensible man, by and by a fool, and presently a beast! O   270
strange! Every inordinate cup is unblest, and the ingredient° is a devil.

IAGO: Come, come, good wine is a good familiar creature if it be well used.
Exclaim no more against it. And, good lieutenant, I think you think I love
you.

CASSIO: I have well approved° it, sir. I drunk!   275

IAGO: You or any man living may be drunk at some time, man. I'll tell you
what you shall do. Our general's wife is now the general. I may say so in
this respect, for that he hath devoted and given up himself to the contemplation, mark, and denotement of her parts and graces. Confess yourself
freely to her; importune her help to put you in your place again. She is of   280
so free,° so kind, so apt, so blessed a disposition she holds it a vice in her
goodness not to do more than she is requested. This broken joint between
you and her husband entreat her to splinter;° and my fortunes against
any lay° worth naming, this crack of your love shall grow stronger than
it was before.   285

CASSIO: You advise me well.

IAGO: I protest, in the sincerity of love and honest kindness.

CASSIO: I think it freely; and betimes in the morning will I beseech the virtuous Desdemona to undertake for me. I am desperate of my fortunes if they
check me here.   290

IAGO: You are in the right. Good night, lieutenant; I must to the watch.

CASSIO: Good night, honest Iago.   *Exit Cassio.*

IAGO: And what's he then that says I play the villain,
When this advice is free I give and honest,
Probal° to thinking, and indeed the course   295
To win the Moor again? For 'tis most easy
Th' inclining Desdemona to subdue°
In an honest suit; she's framed as fruitful
As the free elements. And then for her
To win the Moor—were't to renounce his baptism,   300
All seals and symbols of redeemèd sin —
His soul is so enfettered to her love
That she may make, unmake, do what she list,
Even as her appetite shall play the god
With his weak function. How am I then a villain   305
To counsel Cassio to this parallel° course,
Directly to his good? Divinity° of hell!
When devils will the blackest sins put on,°
They do suggest at first with heavenly shows,
As I do now. For whiles this honest fool   310
Plies Desdemona to repair his fortunes,

---

271 ingredient: Contents.   **275 approved:** Proved.   **281 free:** Bounteous.   **283 splinter:** Bind up with splints;   **lay:** Wager.   **295 Probal:** Probable.   **297 subdue:** Persuade.   **306 parallel:** Corresponding.   **307 Divinity:** Theology.   **308 put on:** Incite.

And she for him pleads strongly to the Moor,
I'll pour this pestilence into his ear,
That she repeals him° for her body's lust;
And by how much she strives to do him good,   315
She shall undo her credit with the Moor.
So will I turn her virtue into pitch,
And out of her own goodness make the net
That shall enmesh them all.

Enter Roderigo.

               How, now, Roderigo?

RODERIGO: I do follow here in the chase, not like a hound that hunts, but one   320
that fills up the cry.° My money is almost spent; I have been to-night
exceedingly well cudgelled; and I think the issue will be — I shall have so
much experience for my pains; and so, with no money at all, and a little
more wit, return again to Venice.

IAGO: How poor are they that have not patience!   325
What wound did ever heal but by degrees?
Thou know'st we work by wit, and not by witchcraft;
And wit depends on dilatory time.
Does't not go well? Cassio hath beaten thee,
And thou by that small hurt hast cashiered Cassio.°   330
Though other things grow fair against the sun,
Yet fruits that blossom first will first be ripe.
Content thyself awhile. By the mass, 'tis morning!
Pleasure and action make the hours seem short.
Retire thee; go where thou art billeted.   335
Away, I say! Thou shalt know more hereafter.
Nay, get thee gone!   *Exit Roderigo.*
             Two things are to be done:
My wife must move for Cassio to her mistress;
I'll set her on;
Myself the while to draw the Moor apart   340
And bring him jump° when he may Cassio find
Soliciting his wife. Ay, that's the way!
Dull no device by coldness and delay.   *Exit.*

[ACT III, Scene I: Before the chamber of Othello and Desdemona.]

Enter Cassio, with Musicians and the Clown.

CASSIO: Masters, play here, I will content° your pains:
Something that's brief; and bid "Good morrow, general."

314 repeals him: Seeks his recall.   **321 cry:** Pack.   **330 cashiered Cassio:**
Maneuvered Cassio's discharge.   **341 jump:** At the exact moment.   **ACT III, SCENE I. 1
content:** Reward.

[They play.]

CLOWN: Why, masters, ha' your instruments been in Naples,° that they speak
    i' th' nose thus?

MUSICIAN: How, sir, how?   5

CLOWN: Are these, I pray you, called wind instruments?

MUSICIAN: Ay, marry, are they, sir.

CLOWN: O, thereby hangs a tail.

MUSICIAN: Whereby hangs a tail, sir?

CLOWN: Marry, sir, by many a wind instrument that I know. But, masters,   10
    here's money for you; and the general so likes your music that he desires
    you, for love's sake, to make no more noise with it.

MUSICIAN: Well, sir, we will not.

CLOWN: If you have any music that may not be heard, to't again: but, as they
    say, to hear music the general does not greatly care.   15

MUSICIAN: We have none such, sir.

CLOWN: Then put up your pipes in your bag, for I'll away. Go, vanish into air,
    away!   *Exit Musician [with his fellows].*

CASSIO: Dost thou hear, my honest friend?

CLOWN: No, I hear not your honest friend. I hear you.   20

CASSIO: Prithee keep up thy quillets.° There's a poor piece of gold for thee. If
    the gentlewoman that attends the general's wife be stirring, tell her there's
    one Cassio entreats her a little favor of speech. Wilt thou do this?

CLOWN: She is stirring sir. If she will stir hither, I shall seem to notify unto her.

CASSIO: [Do, good my friend.]   *Exit Clown.*

Enter Iago.

                  In happy time,° Iago.   25

IAGO: You have not been abed then?

CASSIO: Why, no; the day had broke
    Before we parted. I have made bold, Iago,
    To send in to your wife: my suit to her
    Is that she will to virtuous Desdemona   30
    Procure me some access.

IAGO: I'll send her to you presently;
    And I'll devise a mean to draw the Moor
    Out of the way, that your converse and business
    May be more free.

CASSIO: I humbly thank you for't.   *Exit [Iago].*

                  I never knew   35
    A Florentine° more kind and honest.

Enter Emilia.

EMILIA: Good morrow, good lieutenant. I am sorry

---

3 Naples: (Notorious for its association with venereal disease).   **21 quillets:** Quips.
25 In happy time: Well met.   **36 Florentine:** I.e., even a Florentine (like Cassio; Iago was
a Venetian).

For your displeasure: but all will sure be well.
The general and his wife are talking of it,
And she speaks for you stoutly. The Moor replied   40
That he you hurt is of great fame in Cyprus
And great affinity,° and that in wholesome wisdom
He might not but refuse you; but he protests he loves you,
And needs no other suitor but his likings
[To take the safest occasion° by the front°]   45
To bring you in again.

CASSIO: Yet I beseech you,
If you think fit, or that it may be done,
Give me advantage of some brief discourse
With Desdemona alone.

EMILIA: Pray you come in.
I will bestow you where you shall have time   50
To speak your bosom° freely.

CASSIO: I am much bound to you.   *Exeunt.*

[Scene II: The castle.]

Enter Othello, Iago, and Gentlemen.

OTHELLO: These letters give, Iago, to the pilot
And by him do my duties to the Senate.
That done, I will be walking on the works;°
Repair there to me.

IAGO: Well, my good lord, I'll do't.

OTHELLO: This fortification, gentlemen, shall we see't?   5

GENTLEMEN: We'll wait upon your lordship.   *Exeunt.*

[Scene III: The castle grounds.]

Enter Desdemona, Cassio, and Emilia.

DESDEMONA: Be thou assured, good Cassio, I will do
All my abilities in thy behalf.

EMILIA: Good madam, do. I warrant it grieves my husband
As if the cause were his.

DESDEMONA: O, that's an honest fellow. Do not doubt, Cassio,   5
But I will have my lord and you again
As friendly as you were.

CASSIO: Bounteous madam,
Whatever shall become of Michael Cassio,
He's never anything but your true servant.

DESDEMONA: I know't; I thank you. You do love my lord;   10

---

42 affinity: Family connections.   **45 occasion:** Opportunity;   **front:** Forelock.   **51
your bosom:** Your innermost thoughts.   **Scene II. 3 works:** Fortifications.

You have known him long; and be you well assured
He shall in strangeness° stand no farther off
Than in a politic distance.°

CASSIO: Ay, but, lady,
    That policy may either last so long,
    Or feed upon such nice and waterish diet,°   15
    Or breed itself so out of circumstance,
    That, I being absent, and my place supplied,
    My general will forget my love and service.

DESDEMONA: Do not doubt° that; before Emilia here
    I give thee warrant of thy place. Assure thee,   20
    If I do vow a friendship, I'll perform it
    To the last article. My lord shall never rest;
    I'll watch him tame° and talk him out of patience;
    His bed shall seem a school, his board a shrift;°
    I'll intermingle everything he does   25
    With Cassio's suit. Therefore be merry, Cassio,
    For thy solicitor shall rather die
    Than give thy cause away.

Enter Othello and Iago [at a distance].

EMILIA: Madam, here comes my lord.
CASSIO: Madam, I'll take my leave.   30
DESDEMONA: Why, stay, and hear me speak.
CASSIO: Madam, not now: I am very ill at ease,
    Unfit for mine own purposes.
DESDEMONA: Well, do your discretion.   *Exit Cassio.*
IAGO: Ha! I like not that.
OTHELLO: What dost thou say?   35
IAGO: Nothing, my lord; or if — I know not what.
OTHELLO: Was not that Cassio parted from my wife?
IAGO: Cassio, my lord? No, sure, I cannot think it,
    That he would steal away so guilty-like,
    Seeing your coming.
OTHELLO: I do believe 'twas he.   40
DESDEMONA: How now, my lord?
    I have been talking with a suitor here,
    A man that languishes in your displeasure.
OTHELLO: What is't you mean?
DESDEMONA: Why, your lieutenant, Cassio. Good my lord,   45
    If I have any grace or power to move you,
    His present° reconciliation take;
    For if he be not one that truly loves you,

SCENE III. **12 strangeness:** Aloofness.   **13 Than . . . distance:** Than wise policy
requires.   **15 Or . . . diet:** Or be continued for such slight reasons.   **19 doubt:** Fear.
23 watch him tame: Keep him awake until he gives in.   **24 shrift:** Confessional.   **47
present:** Immediate.

That errs in ignorance, and not in cunning,
I have no judgment in an honest face,   50
I prithee call him back.

OTHELLO: Went he hence now?

DESDEMONA: Yes, faith; so humbled
That he hath left part of his grief with me
To suffer with him. Good love, call him back.

OTHELLO: Not now, sweet Desdemona; some other time.   55

DESDEMONA: But shall't be shortly?

OTHELLO: The sooner, sweet, for you.

DESDEMONA: Shall't be to-night at supper?

OTHELLO: No, not to-night.

DESDEMONA: To-morrow dinner then?

OTHELLO: I shall not dine at home;
I meet the captains at the citadel.

DESDEMONA: Why then, to-morrow night, or Tuesday morn,   60
On Tuesday noon or night, or Wednesday morn.
I prithee name the time, but let it not
Exceed three days. I' faith, he's penitent;
And yet his trespass, in our common reason
(Save that, they say, the wars must make examples   65
Out of their best), is not almost° a fault
T' incur a private check.° When shall he come?
Tell me, Othello. I wonder in my soul
What you could ask me that I should deny
Or stand so mamm'ring on.° What? Michael Cassio,   70
That came a-wooing with you, and so many a time,
When I have spoke of you dispraisingly,
Hath ta'en your part—to have so much to do
To bring him in? By'r Lady, I could do much —

OTHELLO: Prithee no more. Let him come when he will!   75
I will deny thee nothing.

DESDEMONA: Why, this is not a boon;
'Tis as I should entreat you wear your gloves,
Or feed on nourishing dishes, or keep you warm,
Or sue to you to do a peculiar profit
To your own person. Nay, when I have a suit   80
Wherein I mean to touch your love indeed,
It shall be full of poise and difficult weight,
And fearful° to be granted.

OTHELLO: I will deny thee nothing!
Whereon I do beseech thee grant me this,
To leave me but a little to myself.   85

66 not almost: Hardly.   **67 a private check:** Even a private reprimand.   **70 mamm'ring on:** Hesitating about.   **83 fearful:** Dangerous.

DESDEMONA: Shall I deny you? No. Farewell, my lord.

OTHELLO: Farewell, my Desdemona: I'll come to thee straight.

DESDEMONA: Emilia, come. — Be as your fancies teach you;
Whate'er you be, I am obedient.   *Exit [with Emilia].*

OTHELLO: Excellent wretch!° Perdition catch my soul   90
But I do love thee! and when I love thee not,
Chaos is come again.

IAGO: My noble lord —

OTHELLO: What dost thou say, Iago?

IAGO: Did Michael Cassio, when you wooed my lady,
Know of your love?   95

OTHELLO: He did, from first to last. Why dost thou ask?

IAGO: But for a satisfaction of my thought;
No further harm.

OTHELLO: Why of thy thought, Iago?

IAGO: I did not think he had been acquainted with her.

OTHELLO: O, yes, and went between us° very oft.   100

IAGO: Indeed?

OTHELLO: Indeed? Ay, indeed! Discern'st thou aught in that?
Is he not honest?

IAGO: Honest, my lord?

OTHELLO: Honest. Ay, honest.

IAGO: My lord, for aught I know.

OTHELLO: What dost thou think?

IAGO: Think, my lord?

OTHELLO: Think, my lord?   105
By heaven, he echoes me,
As if there were some monster in his thought
Too hideous to be shown. Thou dost mean something:
I heard thee say even now, thou lik'st not that,
When Cassio left my wife. What didst not like?   110
And when I told thee he was of my counsel
In my whole course of wooing, thou cried'st "Indeed?"
And didst contract and purse thy brow together,
As if thou then hadst shut up in thy brain
Some horrible conceit.° If thou dost love me,   115
Show me thy thought.

IAGO: My lord, you know I love you.

OTHELLO: I think thou dost;
And, for I know thou'rt full of love and honesty
And weigh'st thy words before thou giv'st them breath,
Therefore these stops of thine fright me the more;   120
For such things in a false disloyal knave

90 wretch: (A term of endearment).   **100 went . . . us:** (I.e., as messenger).   **115
conceit:** Fancy.

Are tricks of custom; but in a man that's just
They are close dilations, working from the heart
That passion cannot rule.°

IAGO: For Michael Cassio,
I dare be sworn I think that he is honest.   125

OTHELLO: I think so too.

IAGO: Men should be what they seem;
Or those that be not, would they might seem none!°

OTHELLO: Certain, men should be what they seem.

IAGO: Why then, I think Cassio's an honest man.

OTHELLO: Nay, yet there's more in this.   130
I prithee speak to me as to thy thinkings,
As thou dost ruminate, and give thy worst of thoughts
The worst of words.

IAGO: Good my lord, pardon me:
Though I am bound to every act of duty,
I am not bound to that all slaves are free to.°   135
Utter my thoughts? Why, say they are vile and false,
As where's that palace whereinto foul things
Sometimes intrude not? Who has a breast so pure
But some uncleanly apprehensions
Keep leets and law days,° and in Sessions sit   140
With meditations lawful?

OTHELLO: Thou dost conspire against thy friend, Iago,
If thou but think'st him wronged, and mak'st his ear
A stranger to thy thoughts.

IAGO: I do beseech you —
Though I perchance am vicious in my guess   145
(As I confess it is my nature's plague
To spy into abuses, and oft my jealousy°
Shapes faults that are not), that your wisdom yet
From one that so imperfectly conjects°
Would take no notice, nor build yourself a trouble   150
Out of his scattering and unsure observance.
It were not for your quiet nor your good,
Nor for my manhood, honesty, and wisdom,
To let you know my thoughts.

OTHELLO: What dost thou mean?

IAGO: Good name in man and woman, dear my lord,   155
Is the immediate° jewel of their souls.

123–24 close dilations . . . rule: Secret emotions that well up in spite of restraint.
127 seem none: I.e., not pretend to be men when they are really monsters.   **135
bound . . . free to:** Bound to tell that which even slaves are allowed to keep to themselves.   **140 leets and law days:** Sittings of the courts.   **147 jealousy:** Suspicion.   **149
conjects:** Conjectures.   **156 immediate:** Nearest the heart.

Who steals my purse steals trash; 'tis something, nothing;
'Twas mine, 'tis his, and has been slave to thousands;
But he that filches from me my good name
Robs me of that which not enriches him   160
And makes me poor indeed.
OTHELLO: By heaven, I'll know thy thoughts!
IAGO: You cannot, if my heart were in your hand;
Nor shall not whilst 'tis in my custody.
OTHELLO: Ha!
IAGO: O, beware, my lord, of jealousy!   165
It is the green-eyed monster, which doth mock°
The meat it feeds on. That cuckold lives in bliss
Who, certain of his fate, loves not his wronger;
But O, what damnèd minutes tells he o'er
Who dotes, yet doubts—suspects, yet strongly loves!   170
OTHELLO: O misery!
IAGO: Poor and content is rich, and rich enough;
But riches fineless° is as poor as winter
To him that ever fears he shall be poor.
Good God, the souls of all my tribe defend   175
From jealousy!
OTHELLO: Why, why is this?
Think'st thou I'ld make a life of jealousy,
To follow still the changes of the moon
With fresh suspicions? No! To be once in doubt
Is once to be resolved. Exchange me for a goat   180
When I shall turn the business of my soul
To such exsufflicate and blown° surmises,
Matching this inference. 'Tis not to make me jealous
To say my wife is fair, feeds well, loves company,
Is free of speech, sings, plays, and dances;   185
Where virtue is, these are more virtuous.
Nor from mine own weak merits will I draw
The smallest fear or doubt of her revolt,°
For she had eyes, and chose me. No, Iago;
I'll see before I doubt; when I doubt, prove;   190
And on the proof there is no more but this —
Away at once with love or jealousy!
IAGO: I am glad of this; for now I shall have reason
To show the love and duty that I bear you
With franker spirit. Therefore, as I am bound,   195
Receive it from me. I speak not yet of proof.
Look at your wife; observe her well with Cassio;

166 mock: Play with, like a cat with a mouse.   **173 fineless:** Unlimited.   **182 exsuffli-cate and blown:** Spat out and flyblown.   **188 revolt:** Unfaithfulness.

Wear your eyes thus, not jealous nor secure:°
I would not have your free and noble nature,
Out of self-bounty,° be abused. Look to't.   200
I know our country disposition well:
In Venice they do let God see the pranks
They dare not show their husbands; their best conscience
Is not to leave't undone, but keep't unknown.

OTHELLO: Dost thou say so?   205
IAGO: She did deceive her father, marrying you;
And when she seemed to shake and fear your looks,
She loved them most.

OTHELLO: And so she did.
IAGO: Why, go to then!
She that, so young, could give out such a seeming
To seel° her father's eyes up close as oak° —   210
He thought 'twas witchcraft — but I am much to blame.
I humbly do beseech you of your pardon
For too much loving you.

OTHELLO: I am bound to thee for ever.
IAGO: I see this hath a little dashed your spirits.
OTHELLO: Not a jot, not a jot.   215
IAGO: I' faith, I fear it has.
I hope you will consider what is spoke
Comes from my love. But I do see y' are moved.
I am to pray you not to strain my speech
To grosser issues° nor to larger reach
Than to suspicion.   220
OTHELLO: I will not.
IAGO: Should you do so, my lord,
My speech should fall into such vile success°
As my thoughts aim not at. Cassio's my worthy friend —
My lord, I see y' are moved.
OTHELLO: No, not much moved:
I do not think but Desdemona's honest.°   225
IAGO: Long live she so! and long live you to think so!
OTHELLO: And yet, how nature erring from itself —
IAGO: Ay, there's the point! as (to be bold with you)
Not to affect many proposèd matches
Of her own clime, complexion, and degree,   230
Whereto we see in all things nature tends —
Foh! one may smell in such a will most rank,
Foul disproportions, thought unnatural —

---

198 secure: Overconfident.   **200 self-bounty:** Natural goodness.   **210 seel:** Close;
oak: Oak grain.   **219 To grosser issues:** To mean something more monstrous.   **222**
vile success: Evil outcome.   **225 honest:** Chaste.

But pardon me—I do not in position°
Distinctly speak of her; though I may fear   235
Her will, recoiling° to her better judgment,
May fall to match° you with her country forms,
And happily° repent.

OTHELLO: Farewell, farewell!
If more thou dost perceive, let me know more.
Set on thy wife to observe. Leave me, Iago.   240

IAGO: My lord, I take my leave.   [*Going.*]

OTHELLO: Why did I marry? This honest creature doubtless
Sees and knows more, much more, than he unfolds.

IAGO [*returns*]:   My lord, I would I might entreat your honor
To scan this thing no further: leave it to time.   245
Although 'tis fit that Cassio have his place,
For sure he fills it up with great ability,
Yet, if you please to hold off a while,
You shall by that perceive him and his means.
Note if your lady strain his entertainment°   250
With any strong or vehement importunity;
Much will be seen in that. In the mean time
Let me be thought too busy° in my fears
(As worthy cause I have to fear I am)
And hold her free,° I do beseech your honor.   255

OTHELLO: Fear not my government.°

IAGO: I once more take my leave.   *Exit.*

OTHELLO: This fellow's of exceeding honesty,
And knows all qualities,° with a learned spirit
Of° human dealings. If I do prove her haggard,°   260
Though that her jesses° were my dear heartstrings,
I'd whistle her off and let her down the wind
To prey at fortune.° Haply, for I am black
And have not those soft parts of conversation°
That chamberers° have, or for I am declined   265
Into the vale of years—yet that's not much—
She's gone. I am abused, and my relief
Must be to loathe her. O curse of marriage,
That we can call these delicate creatures ours,
And not their appetites! I had rather be a toad   270

---

234 position: Definite assertion.   **236 recoiling:** Reverting.   **237 fall to match:** Happen to compare.   **238 happily:** Haply, perhaps.   **250 strain his entertainment:** Urge his recall.   **253 busy:** Meddlesome.   **255 hold her free:** Consider her guiltless.   **256 government:** Self-control.   **259 qualities:** Natures.   **259–60 learned spirit Of:** Mind informed about.   **260 haggard:** A wild hawk.   **261 jesses:** Thongs for controlling a hawk.   **262–63 whistle . . . fortune:** Turn her out and let her take care of herself.   **264 soft . . . conversation:** Ingratiating manners.   **265 chamberers:** Courtiers.

And live upon the vapor of a dungeon
Than keep a corner in the thing I love
For others' uses. Yet 'tis the plague of great ones;°
Prerogatived° are they less than the base.
'Tis destiny unshunnable, like death.   275
Even then this forkèd plague° is fated to us
When we do quicken.° Look where she comes.

Enter Desdemona and Emilia.

If she be false, O, then heaven mocks itself!
I'll not believe't.
DESDEMONA: How now, my dear Othello?
Your dinner, and the generous° islanders   280
By you invited, do attend your presence.
OTHELLO: I am to blame.
DESDEMONA: Why do you speak so faintly?
Are you not well?
OTHELLO: I have a pain upon my forehead, here.
DESDEMONA: Faith, that's with watching;° 'twill away again.   285
Let me but bind it hard, within this hour
It will be well.
OTHELLO: Your napkin° is too little;

[He pushes the handkerchief from him, and it falls unnoticed.]

Let it° alone. Come, I'll go in with you.
DESDEMONA: I am very sorry that you are not well.   *Exit [with Othello].*
EMILIA: I am glad I have found this napkin;   290
This was her first remembrance from the Moor,
My wayward husband hath a hundred times
Wooed me to steal it; but she so loves the token
(For he conjured her she should ever keep it)
That she reserves it evermore about her   295
To kiss and talk to. I'll have the work ta'en out°
And give't Iago.
What he will do with it heaven knows, not I;
I nothing but to please his fantasy.°

Enter Iago.

IAGO: How now? What do you here alone?   300
EMILIA: Do not you chide; I have a thing for you.
IAGO: A thing for me? It is a common thing —
EMILIA: Ha?
IAGO: To have a foolish wife.

---

273 great ones: Prominent men.   **274 Prerogatived:** Privileged.   **276 forkèd
plague:** I.e., horns of a cuckold.   **277 do quicken:** Are born.   **280 generous:** Noble.
285 watching: Working late.   **287 napkin:** Handkerchief.   **288 it:** I.e., his forehead.
296 work ta'en out: Pattern copied.   **299 fantasy:** Whim.

EMILIA: O, is that all? What will you give me now   305
    For that same handkerchief?
IAGO: What handkerchief?
EMILIA: What handkerchief!
    Why, that the Moor first gave to Desdemona;
    That which so often you did bid me steal.
IAGO: Hast stol'n it from her?   310
EMILIA: No, faith; she let it drop by negligence,
    And to th' advantage,° I, being here, took't up.
    Look, here it is.
IAGO: A good wench! Give it me.
EMILIA: What will you do with't, that you have been so earnest
    To have me filch it?
IAGO: Why, what is that to you?   315

[Snatches it.]

EMILIA: If it be not for some purpose of import,°
    Give't me again. Poor lady, she'll run mad
    When she shall lack it.
IAGO: Be not acknown on't;° I have use for it.
    Go, leave me.   *Exit Emilia.*   320
    I will in Cassio's lodgings lose this napkin
    And let him find it. Trifles light as air
    Are to the jealous confirmations strong
    As proofs of holy writ. This may do something.
    The Moor already changes with my poison: 325
    Dangerous conceits° are in their nature poisons,
    Which at the first are scarce found to distaste,
    But with a little act upon the blood
    Burn like the mines of sulphur.

Enter Othello.

                      I did say so.
    Look where he comes! Not poppy nor mandragora,°   330
    Nor all the drowsy syrups of the world,
    Shall ever med'cine thee to that sweet sleep
    Which thou owedst yesterday.
OTHELLO: Ha! ha! false to me?
IAGO: Why, how now, general? No more of that!
OTHELLO: Avaunt! be gone! Thou hast set me on the rack.   335
    I swear 'tis better to be much abused
    Than but to know't a little.
IAGO: How now, my lord?
OTHELLO: What sense had I of her stol'n hours of lust?

---

312 to th' advantage: Opportunely.   **316 import:** Importance.   **319 Be . . . on't:** Do
not acknowledge it.   **326 conceits:** Ideas.   **330 mandragora:** A narcotic.

I saw't not, thought it not, it harmed not me;
I slept the next night well, fed well, was free° and merry;   340
I found not Cassio's kisses on her lips
He that is robbed, not wanting° what is stol'n,
Let him not know't, and he's not robbed at all.
IAGO: I am sorry to hear this.
OTHELLO: I had been happy if the general camp,   345
Pioneers° and all, had tasted her sweet body,
So I had nothing known. O, now for ever
Farewell the tranquil mind! farewell content!
Farewell the plumèd troop, and the big° wars
That make ambition virtue! O, farewell!   350
Farewell the neighing steed and the shrill trump,
The spirit-stirring drum, th' ear-piercing fife,
The royal banner, and all quality,
Pride, pomp, and circumstance° of glorious war!
And O you mortal engines° whose rude throats   355
Th' immortal Jove's dread clamors counterfeit,°
Farewell! Othello's occupation's gone!
IAGO: Is't possible, my lord?
OTHELLO: Villain, be sure thou prove my love a whore!
Be sure of it; give me the ocular proof;   360
Or, by the worth of mine eternal soul,
Thou hadst been better have been born a dog
Than answer my waked wrath!
IAGO: Is't come to this?
OTHELLO: Make me to see't; or at the least so prove it
That the probation° bear no hinge nor loop   365
To hang a doubt on — or woe upon thy life!
IAGO: My noble lord —
OTHELLO: If thou dost slander her and torture me,
Never pray more; abandon all remorse;
On horror's head horrors accumulate;   370
Do deeds to make heaven weep, all earth amazed;
For nothing canst thou to damnation add
Greater than that.
IAGO: O grace! O heaven forgive me!
Are you a man? Have you a soul or sense? —
God b' wi' you! take mine office. O wretched fool,   375
That liv'st to make thine honesty a vice!
O monstrous world! Take note, take note, O world,
To be direct and honest is not safe.

---

340 free: Carefree.   **342 wanting:** Missing.   **346 Pioneers:** Sappers, laborers.
349 big: Stately.   **354 circumstance:** Pageantry.   **355 mortal engines:** Deadly
artillery.   **356 counterfeit:** Imitate.   **365 probation:** Proof.

I thank you for this profit;° and from hence
I'll love no friend, sith love breeds such offense.   380
OTHELLO: Nay, stay. Thou shouldst be honest.
IAGO: I should be wise; for honesty's a fool
And loses that it works for.
OTHELLO: By the world,
I think my wife be honest, and think she is not;
I think that thou art just, and think thou art not.   385
I'll have some proof. Her name, that was as fresh
As Dian's visage, is now begrimed and black
As mine own face. If there be cords, or knives,
Poison, or fire, or suffocating streams,
I'll not endure it. Would I were satisfied!°   390
IAGO: I see, sir, you are eaten up with passion:
I do repent me that I put it to you.
You would be satisfied?
OTHELLO: Would? Nay, I will.
IAGO: And may; but how? how satisfied, my lord?
Would you, the supervisor,° grossly gape on?   395
Behold her topped?
OTHELLO: Death and damnation! O!
IAGO: It were a tedious difficulty, I think,
To bring them to that prospect. Damn them then,
If ever mortal eyes do see them bolster°
More than their own! What then? How then?   400
What shall I say? Where's satisfaction?
It is impossible you should see this,
Were they as prime° as goats, as hot as monkeys,
As salt° as wolves in pride,° and fools as gross
As ignorance made drunk. But yet, I say,   405
If imputation and strong circumstances
Which lead directly to the door of truth
Will give you satisfaction, you may have't.
OTHELLO: Give me a living reason she's disloyal.
IAGO: I do not like the office.   410
But sith I am ent'red in this cause so far,
Pricked to't by foolish honesty and love,
I will go on. I lay with Cassio lately,
And being troubled with a raging tooth,
I could not sleep.   415
There are a kind of men so loose of soul
That in their sleeps will mutter their affairs.

379 profit: Profitable lesson.   **390 satisfied:** Completely informed.   **395 supervisor:**
Spectator.   **399 bolster:** Lie together.   **403 prime:** Lustful.   **404 salt:** Lecherous;
pride: Heat.

One of this kind is Cassio.
In sleep I heard him say, "Sweet Desdemona,
Let us be wary, let us hide our loves!"   420
And then, sir, would he gripe and wring my hand,
Cry "O sweet creature!" and then kiss me hard,
As if he plucked up kisses by the roots
That grew upon my lips; then laid his leg
Over my thigh, and sighed, and kissed, and then   425
Cried "Cursèd fate that gave thee to the Moor!"

OTHELLO: O monstrous! monstrous!

IAGO: Nay, this was but his dream.

OTHELLO: But this denoted a foregone conclusion;°
'Tis a shrewd doubt,° though it be but a dream.

IAGO: And this may help to thicken other proofs   430
That do demonstrate thinly.

OTHELLO: I'll tear her all to pieces!

IAGO: Nay, but be wise. Yet we see nothing done;
She may be honest yet. Tell me but this —
Have you not sometimes seen a handkerchief
Spotted with strawberries in your wife's hand?   435

OTHELLO: I gave her such a one; 'twas my first gift.

IAGO: I know not that; but such a handkerchief —
I am sure it was your wife's — did I to-day
See Cassio wipe his beard with.

OTHELLO: If it be that —

IAGO: If it be that, or any that was hers,   440
It speaks against her with the other proofs.

OTHELLO: O, that the slave had forty thousand lives!
One is too poor, too weak for my revenge.
Now do I see 'tis true. Look here, Iago:
All my fond love thus do I blow to heaven.   445
'Tis gone.
Arise, black vengeance, from the hollow hell!
Yield up, O love, thy crown and hearted throne
To tyrannous hate! Swell, bosom, with thy fraught,°
For 'tis of aspics'° tongues!

IAGO: Yet be content.   450

OTHELLO: O, blood, blood, blood!

IAGO: Patience, I say. Your mind perhaps may change.

OTHELLO: Never, Iago. Like to the Pontic sea,°
Whose icy current and compulsive course
Ne'er feels retiring ebb, but keeps due on   455

---

428 foregone conclusion: Previous experience.   **429 a shrewd doubt:** Cursedly
suspicious.   **449 fraught:** Burden.   **450 aspics:** Deadly poisonous snakes.   **453 Pontic
sea:** Black Sea.

To the Propontic and the Hellespont,
Even so my bloody thoughts, with violent pace,
Shall ne'er look back, ne'er ebb to humble love,
Till that a capable° and wide revenge
Swallow them up.
(He kneels.)   Now, by yond marble heaven,   460
In the due reverence of a sacred vow
I here engage my words.
IAGO: Do not rise yet.

(Iago kneels.)

Witness, you ever-burning lights above,
You elements that clip° us round about,
Witness that here Iago doth give up   465
The execution° of his wit,° hands, heart
To wronged Othello's service! Let him command,
And to obey shall be in me remorse,°
What bloody business ever.

[They rise.]

OTHELLO: I greet thy love,
Not with vain thanks but with acceptance bounteous,   470
And will upon the instant put thee to't.
Within these three days let me hear thee say
That Cassio's not alive.
IAGO: My friend is dead; 'tis done at your request.
But let her live.   475
OTHELLO: Damn her, lewd minx! O, damn her! damn her!
Come, go with me apart. I will withdraw
To furnish me with some swift means of death
For the fair devil. Now art thou my lieutenant.
IAGO: I am your own forever.   *Exeunt.*   480

[Scene IV: The environs of the castle.]

Enter Desdemona, Emilia, and Clown.

DESDEMONA: Do you know, sirrah, where Lieutenant Cassio lies?°
CLOWN: I dare not say he lies anywhere.
DESDEMONA: Why, man?
CLOWN: He's a soldier, and for me to say a soldier lies is stabbing.
DESDEMONA: Go to. Where lodges he?   5
CLOWN: To tell you where he lodges is to tell you where I lie.
DESDEMONA: Can anything be made of this?

---

459 capable: All-embracing.   **464 clip:** Encompass.   **466 execution:** Activities;
wit: Mind.   **468 remorse:** Pity.   **SCENE IV. 1 lies:** Lives, lodges.

CLOWN: I know not where he lodges; and for me to devise a lodging, and say
he lies here or he lies there, were to lie in mine own throat.

DESDEMONA: Can you enquire him out, and be edified by report?   10

CLOWN: I will catechize the world for him; that is, make questions, and by
them answer.

DESDEMONA: Seek him, bid him come hither. Tell him I have moved° my lord on
his behalf and hope all will be well.

CLOWN: To do this is within the compass of man's wit, and therefore I'll   15
attempt the doing of it.   *Exit.*

DESDEMONA: Where should I lose that handkerchief, Emilia?

EMILIA: I know not, madam.

DESDEMONA: Believe me, I had rather have lost my purse
Full of crusadoes;° and but my noble Moor   20
Is true of mind, and made of no such baseness
As jealous creatures are, it were enough
To put him to ill thinking.

EMILIA: Is he not jealous?

DESDEMONA: Who? he? I think the sun where he was born
Drew all such humors° from him.

Enter Othello.

EMILIA: Look where he comes.   25

DESDEMONA: I will not leave him now till Cassio
Be called to him—How is't with you, my lord?

OTHELLO: Well, my good lady. [Aside.] O, hardness to dissemble! —
How do you, Desdemona?

DESDEMONA: Well, my good lord.

OTHELLO: Give me your hand. This hand is moist, my lady.   30

DESDEMONA: It yet hath felt no age nor known no sorrow.

OTHELLO: This argues fruitfulness and liberal heart.
Hot, hot, and moist. This hand of yours requires
A sequester° from liberty, fasting and prayer,
Much castigation, exercise devout;   35
For here's a young and sweating devil here
That commonly rebels. 'Tis a good hand,
A frank one.

DESDEMONA: You may, indeed, say so;
For 'twas that hand that gave away my heart.

OTHELLO: A liberal hand! The hearts of old gave hands;   40
But our new heraldry° is hands, not hearts.

DESDEMONA: I cannot speak of this. Come now, your promise!

OTHELLO: What promise, chuck?

DESDEMONA: I have sent to bid Cassio come speak with you.

---

13 moved: Made proposals to.   **20 crusadoes:** Portuguese gold coins.   **25 humors:**
Inclinations.   **34 sequester:** Removal.   **41 heraldry:** Heraldic symbolism.

OTHELLO: I have a salt and sorry rheum° offends me.   45
      Lend me thy handkerchief.
DESDEMONA: Here, my lord.
OTHELLO: That which I gave you.
DESDEMONA: I have it not about me.
OTHELLO: Not?
DESDEMONA: No, faith, my lord.
OTHELLO: That's a fault.
      That handkerchief   50
      Did an Egyptian° to my mother give.
      She was a charmer,° and could almost read
      The thoughts of people. She told her, while she kept it,
      'Twould make her amiable° and subdue my father
      Entirely to her love; but if she lost it   55
      Or made a gift of it, my father's eye
      Should hold her loathèd, and his spirits should hunt
      After new fancies. She, dying, gave it me,
      And bid me, when my fate would have me wive;
      To give it her. I did so; and take heed on't;   60
      Make it a darling like your precious eye.
      To lose't or give't away were such perdition°
      As nothing else could match.
DESDEMONA: Is't possible?
OTHELLO: 'Tis true. There's magic in the web of it.
      A sibyl that had numb'red in the world   65
      The sun to course two hundred compasses,°
      In her prophetic fury sewed the work;
      The worms were hallowed that did breed the silk;
      And it was dyed in mummy° which the skillful
      Conserved of maidens' hearts.
DESDEMONA: I' faith? Is't true?   70
OTHELLO: Most veritable. Therefore look to't well.
DESDEMONA: Then would to God that I had never seen't!
OTHELLO: Ha! Wherefore?
DESDEMONA: Why do you speak so startingly and rash?
OTHELLO: Is't lost? Is't gone? Speak, is it out o' th' way?   75
DESDEMONA: Heaven bless us!
OTHELLO: Say you?
DESDEMONA: It is not lost. But what an if it were?
OTHELLO: How?
DESDEMONA: I say it is not lost.
OTHELLO: Fetch't, let me see't!   80

---

45 salt . . . rheum: Distressing head cold.   **51 Egyptian:** Gypsy.   **52 charmer:** Sorceress.
54 amiable: Lovable.   **62 perdition:** Disaster.   **66 compasses:** Annual rounds.
69 mummy: A drug made from mummies.

DESDEMONA: Why, so I can, sir; but I will not now.
    This is a trick to put° me from my suit:
    Pray you let Cassio be received again.
OTHELLO: Fetch me the handkerchief! My mind misgives.
DESDEMONA: Come, come!   85
    You'll never meet a more sufficient man.
OTHELLO: The handkerchief!
DESDEMONA: I pray talk me of Cassio.
OTHELLO: The handkerchief!
DESDEMONA: A man that all his time°
    Hath founded his good fortunes on your love,
    Shared dangers with you —   90
OTHELLO: The handkerchief!
DESDEMONA: I' faith, you are to blame.
OTHELLO: Zounds!   *Exit Othello.*
EMILIA: Is not this man jealous?
DESDEMONA: I ne'er saw this before.   95
    Sure there's some wonder in this handkerchief;
    I am most unhappy in the loss of it.
EMILIA: 'Tis not a year or two shows us a man.
    They are all but stomachs, and we all but food;
    They eat us hungerly, and when they are full,   100
    They belch us.

Enter Iago and Cassio.

                    Look you — Cassio and my husband!
IAGO: There is no other way; 'tis she must do't.
    And lo the happiness!° Go and importune her.
DESDEMONA: How now, good Cassio? What's the news with you?
CASSIO: Madam, my former suit. I do beseech you   105
    That by your virtuous means I may again
    Exist, and be a member of his love
    Whom I with all the office of my heart
    Entirely honor. I would not be delayed.
    If my offense be of such mortal kind   110
    That neither service past, nor present sorrows,
    Nor purposed merit in futurity,
    Can ransom me into his love again,
    But to know so must be my benefit.
    So shall I clothe me in a forced content,   115
    And shut myself up in° some other course,
    To fortune's alms.
DESDEMONA: Alas, thrice-gentle Cassio!

---

82 put: Divert. **88 all . . . time:** During his whole career. **103 happiness:** Good
luck. **116 shut myself up in:** Confine myself to.

My advocation° is not now in tune.
My lord is not my lord; nor should I know him,
Were he in favor° as in humor altered.   120
So help me every spirit sanctified
As I have spoken for you all my best
And stood within the blank° of his displeasure
For my free speech! You must a while be patient.
What I can do I will; and more I will   125
Than for myself I dare. Let that suffice you.

IAGO: Is my lord angry?

EMILIA: He went hence but now,
And certainly in strange unquietness.

IAGO: Can he be angry? I have seen the cannon
When it hath blown his ranks into the air   130
And, like the devil, from his very arm
Puffed his own brother—and is he angry?
Something of moment then. I will go meet him.
There's matter in't indeed if he be angry.

DESDEMONA: I prithee do so.   *Exit [Iago].*
                                    Something sure of state,°   135
Either from Venice or some unhatched practice°
Made demonstrable here in Cyprus to him,
Hath puddled° his clear spirit; and in such cases
Men's natures wrangle with inferior things,
Though great ones are their object. 'Tis even so;   140
For let our finger ache, and it endues°
Our other, healthful members even to a sense
Of pain. Nay, we must think men are not gods,
Nor of them look for such observancy
As fits the bridal. Beshrew me much, Emilia,   145
I was, unhandsome warrior° as I am,
Arraigning his unkindness with my soul;°
But now I find I had suborned the witness,
And he's indicted falsely.

EMILIA: Pray heaven it be state matters, as you think,   150
And no conception nor no jealous toy°
Concerning you.

DESDEMONA: Alas the day! I never gave him cause.

EMILIA: But jealous souls will not be answered so;
They are not ever jealous for the cause,   155

---

118 advocation: Advocacy.   **120 favor:** Appearance.   **123 blank:** Bull's-eye of the target.   **135 state:** Public affairs.   **136 unhatched practice:** Budding plot.   **138 puddled:** Muddied.   **141 endues:** Brings.   **146 unhandsome warrior:** Inadequate soldier.   **147 Arraigning . . . soul:** Indicting his unkindness before the bar of my soul.   **151 toy:** Fancy.

But jealous for they're jealous. 'Tis a monster
Begot upon itself,° born on itself.
DESDEMONA: Heaven keep that monster from Othello's mind!
EMILIA: Lady, amen.
DESDEMONA: I will go seek him. Cassio, walk here about: 160
    If I do find him fit, I'll move your suit
    And seek to effect it to my uttermost.
CASSIO: I humbly thank your ladyship.

                         Exeunt Desdemona and Emilia.

Enter Bianca.

BIANCA: Save you, friend Cassio!
CASSIO: What make you from home?
    How is't with you, my most fair Bianca? 165
    I' faith, sweet love, I was coming to your house.
BIANCA: And I was going to your lodging, Cassio.
    What, keep a week away? seven days and nights?
    Eightscore eight hours? and lovers' absent hours,
    More tedious than the dial° eightscore times? 170
    O weary reck'ning!
CASSIO: Pardon me, Bianca:
    I have this while with leaden thoughts been pressed;
    But I shall in a more continuate° time
    Strike off this score of absence. Sweet Bianca, 175

[Gives her Desdemona's handkerchief.]

    Take me this work out.°
BIANCA: O Cassio, whence came this?
    This is some token from a newer friend.
    To the felt absence now I feel a cause.
    Is't come to this? Well, well.
CASSIO: Go to, woman!
    Throw your vile guesses in the devil's teeth, 180
    From whence you have them. You are jealous now
    That this is from some mistress, some remembrance.
    No, by my faith, Bianca.
BIANCA: Why, whose is it?
CASSIO: I know not, sweet; I found it in my chamber.
    I like the work° well; ere it be demanded, 185
    As like enough it will, I'd have it copied.
    Take it and do't, and leave me for this time.
BIANCA: Leave you? Wherefore?
CASSIO: I do attend here on the general

---

157 Begot . . . itself: Self-engendered. **170 dial:** Clock. **174 continuate:** Uninter-
rupted. **176 Take . . . out:** Copy this embroidery for me. **185 work:** Needlework.

And think it no addition, nor my wish,   190
To have him see me womaned.
BIANCA: Why, I pray you?
CASSIO: Not that I love you not.
BIANCA: But that you do not love me!
I pray you bring me on the way a little,
And say if I shall see you soon at night.
CASSIO: 'Tis but a little way that I can bring you,   195
For I attend here; but I'll see you soon.
BIANCA: 'Tis very good. I must be circumstanced.°   *Exeunt.*

[ACT IV, Scene I: The environs of the castle.]

Enter Othello and Iago.

IAGO: Will you think so?
OTHELLO: Think so, Iago?
IAGO: What,
To kiss in private?
OTHELLO: An unauthorized kiss.
IAGO: Or to be naked with her friend in bed
An hour or more, not meaning any harm?
OTHELLO: Naked in bed, Iago, and not mean harm?   5
It is hypocrisy against the devil.°
They that mean virtuously, and yet do so,
The devil their virtue tempts, and they tempt heaven.
IAGO: So they do nothing, 'tis a venial slip.
But if I give my wife a handkerchief —   10
OTHELLO: What then?
IAGO: Why, then 'tis hers, my lord; and being hers,
She may, I think, bestow't on any man.
OTHELLO: She is protectress of her honor too;
May she give that?   15
IAGO: Her honor is an essence that's not seen;
They have it very oft that have it not.
But for the handkerchief —
OTHELLO: By heaven, I would most gladly have forgot it!
Thou said'st — O, it comes o'er my memory   20
As doth the raven o'er the infected° house,
Boding to all! — he had my handkerchief.
IAGO: Ay, what of that?
OTHELLO: That's not so good now.
IAGO: What

---

197 circumstanced: Governed by circumstances.   **Act IV, Scene I. 6 hypocrisy . . . devil:**
I.e., feigned sin instead of feigned virtue.   **21 infected:** Plague-stricken.

If I had said I had seen him do you wrong?
Or heard him say—as knaves be such abroad   25
Who having, by their own importunate suit,
Or voluntary dotage of some mistress,
Convincèd or supplied° them, cannot choose
But they must blab—
OTHELLO: Hath he said anything?
IAGO: He hath, my lord; but be you well assured,   30
No more than he'll unswear.
OTHELLO: What hath he said?
IAGO: Faith, that he did—I know not what he did.
OTHELLO: What? what?
IAGO: Lie—
OTHELLO: With her?
IAGO: With her, on her; what you will.   35
OTHELLO: Lie with her? lie on her?—We say lie on her when they belie her.—Lie
with her! Zounds, that's fulsome.—Handkerchief—confessions—
handkerchief!—To confess, and be hanged for his labor—first to be
hanged, and then to confess! I tremble at it. Nature would not invest
herself in such shadowing passion without some instruction.° It is not   40
words that shakes me thus.—Pish! Noses, ears, and lips? Is't possible?—
Confess?—Handkerchief?—O devil!

(Falls in a trance.)

IAGO: Work on,
My med'cine, work! Thus credulous fools are caught,
And many worthy and chaste dames even thus,   45
All guiltless, meet reproach.—What, ho! my lord!
My lord, I say! Othello!
Enter Cassio.   How now, Cassio?
CASSIO: What's the matter?
IAGO: My lord is fall'n into an epilepsy.
This is his second fit; he had one yesterday.   50
CASSIO: Rub him about the temples.
IAGO: No, forbear.
The lethargy° must have his quiet course.
If not, he foams at mouth, and by and by
Breaks out to savage madness. Look, he stirs.
Do you withdraw yourself a little while.   55
He will recover straight. When he is gone,
I would on great occasion speak with you.   *[Exit Cassio.]*
How is it, general? Have you not hurt your head?
OTHELLO: Dost thou mock me?

28 Convincèd or supplied: Overcome or gratified.   **39–40 Nature . . . instruction:**
My natural faculties would not be so overcome by passion without reason.   **52 lethargy:**
Coma.

IAGO: I mock you? No, by heaven.
    Would you would bear your fortune like a man!   60
OTHELLO: A hornèd man's° a monster and a beast.
IAGO: There's many a beast then in a populous city,
    And many a civil monster.
OTHELLO: Did he confess it?
IAGO: Good sir, be a man.
    Think every bearded fellow that's but yoked   65
    May draw with you. There's millions now alive
    That nightly lie in those unproper° beds
    Which they dare swear peculiar:° your case is better.
    O, 'tis the spite of hell, the fiend's arch-mock,
    To lip a wanton in a secure° couch,   70
    And to suppose her chaste! No, let me know;
    And knowing what I am, I know what she shall be.
OTHELLO: O, thou art wise! 'Tis certain.
IAGO: Stand you awhile apart;
    Confine yourself but in a patient list.°
    Whilst you were here, o'erwhelmèd with your grief —   75
    A passion most unsuiting such a man —
    Cassio came hither. I shifted him away
    And laid good 'scuse upon your ecstasy;°
    Bade him anon return, and here speak with me;
    The which he promised. Do but encave° yourself   80
    And mark the fleers, the gibes, and notable scorns
    That dwell in every region of his face;
    For I will make him tell the tale anew —
    Where, how, how oft, how long ago, and when
    He hath, and is again to cope° your wife.   85
    I say, but mark his gesture. Marry, patience!
    Or I shall say y'are all in all in spleen,°
    And nothing of a man.
OTHELLO: Dost thou hear, Iago?
    I will be found most cunning in my patience;
    But — dost thou hear? — most bloody.
IAGO: That's not amiss: 90
    But yet keep time in all. Will you withdraw?

                                          [Othello retires.]

    Now will I question Cassio of Bianca,
    A huswife° that by selling her desires
    Buys herself bread and clothes. It is a creature

61 hornèd man: Cuckold.   **67 unproper:** Not exclusively their own.   **68 peculiar:**
Exclusively their own.   **70 secure:** Free from fear of rivalry.   **74 in a patient list:** Within
the limits of self-control.   **78 ecstasy:** Trance.   **80 encave:** Conceal.   **85 cope:** Meet.
87 all in all in spleen: Wholly overcome by your passion.   **93 huswife:** Hussy.

That dotes on Cassio, as 'tis the strumpet's plague   95
To beguile many and be beguiled by one.
He, when he hears of her, cannot refrain
From the excess of laughter. Here he comes.

Enter Cassio.

As he shall smile, Othello shall go mad;
And his unbookish° jealousy must conster°   100
Poor Cassio's smiles, gestures, and light behavior
Quite in the wrong. How do you now, lieutenant?

CASSIO: The worser that you give me the addition°
Whose want even kills me.

IAGO: Ply Desdemona well, and you are sure on't.   105
Now, if this suit lay in Bianca's power,
How quickly should you speed!

CASSIO: Alas, poor caitiff!°

OTHELLO: Look how he laughs already!

IAGO: I never knew a woman love man so.

CASSIO: Alas, poor rogue! I think, i' faith, she loves me.   110

OTHELLO: Now he denies it faintly, and laughs it out.

IAGO: Do you hear, Cassio?

OTHELLO: Now he importunes him
To tell it o'er. Go to! Well said, well said!

IAGO: She gives out that you shall marry her.
Do you intend it?   115

CASSIO: Ha, ha, ha!

OTHELLO: Do you triumph, Roman? Do you triumph?

CASSIO: I marry her? What, a customer?° Prithee bear some charity to my wit;
do not think it so unwholesome. Ha, ha, ha!

OTHELLO: So, so, so, so! They laugh that win!   120

IAGO: Faith, the cry goes that you shall marry her.

CASSIO: Prithee say true.

IAGO: I am a very villain else.

OTHELLO: Have you scored me?° Well.

CASSIO: This is the monkey's own giving out. She is persuaded I will marry her   125
out of her own love and flattery, not out of my promise.

OTHELLO: Iago beckons° me; now he begins the story.

CASSIO: She was here even now; she haunts me in every place. I was t' other
day talking on the sea bank with certain Venetians, and thither comes the
bauble,° and, by this hand, she falls me thus about my neck —   130

OTHELLO: Crying "O dear Cassio!" as it were. His gesture imports it.

CASSIO: So hangs, and lolls, and weeps upon me; so shakes and pulls me! Ha,
ha, ha!

100 unbookish: Uninstructed;   **conster:** Construe, interpret.   **103 addition:** Title.
107 caitiff: Wretch.   **118 customer:** Prostitute.   **124 scored me:** Settled my
account (?).   **127 beckons:** Signals.   **130 bauble:** Plaything.

OTHELLO: Now he tells how she plucked him to my chamber. O, I see that nose
of yours, but not that dog I shall throw it to.   135

CASSIO: Well, I must leave her company.

Enter Bianca.

IAGO: Before me! Look where she comes.

CASSIO: 'Tis such another fitchew!° marry, a perfumed one. What do you
mean by this haunting of me?

BIANCA: Let the devil and his dam haunt you! What did you mean by that   140
same handkerchief you gave me even now? I was a fine fool to take it.
I must take out the whole work? A likely piece of work that you should
find it in your chamber and know not who left it there! This is some minx's
token, and I must take out the work? There! Give it your hobby-horse.°
Wheresoever you had it, I'll take out no work on't.   145

CASSIO: How now, my sweet Bianca? How now? how now?

OTHELLO: By heaven, that should be my handkerchief!

BIANCA: An you'll come to supper to-night, you may; an you will not, come
when you are next prepared for.   *Exit.*

IAGO: After her, after her!   150

CASSIO: Faith, I must; she'll rail in the street else.

IAGO: Will you sup there?

CASSIO: Yes, I intend so.

IAGO: Well, I may chance to see you; for I would very fain speak with you.

CASSIO: Prithee come. Will you?   155

IAGO: Go to! say no more.   *Exit Cassio.*

OTHELLO [*comes forward*]:   How shall I murder him, Iago?

IAGO: Did you perceive how he laughed at his vice?°

OTHELLO: O Iago!

IAGO: And did you see the handkerchief?   160

OTHELLO: Was that mine?

IAGO: Your, by this hand! And to see how he prizes° the foolish woman your
wife! She gave it him, and he hath giv'n it his whore.

OTHELLO: I would have him nine years a-killing — A fine woman! a fair
woman! a sweet woman!   165

IAGO: Nay, you must forget that.

OTHELLO: Ay, let her rot, and perish, and be damned to-night; for she shall not
live. No, my heart is turned to stone; I strike it, and it hurts my hand. O,
the world hath not a sweeter creature! She might lie by an emperor's side
and command him tasks.   170

IAGO: Nay, that's not your way.

OTHELLO: Hang her! I do but say what she is. So delicate with her needle! an
admirable musician! O, she will sing the savageness out of a bear! Of so
high and plenteous wit and invention° —

---

138 fitchew: Polecat (slang for whore).   **144 hobby-horse:** Harlot.   **158 vice:**
I.e., vicious conduct.   **162 prizes:** Values.   **174 invention:** Imagination.

IAGO: She's the worse for all this.   175

OTHELLO: O, a thousand thousand times! And then, of so gentle a condition!°

IAGO: Ay, too gentle.

OTHELLO: Nay, that's certain. But yet the pity of it, Iago! O Iago, the pity of it,
Iago!

IAGO: If you are so fond over her iniquity, give her patent° to offend; for if it   180
touch not you, it comes near nobody.

OTHELLO: I will chop her into messes! Cuckold me!

IAGO: O, 'tis foul in her.

OTHELLO: With mine officer!

IAGO: That's fouler.   185

OTHELLO: Get me some poison, Iago, this night. I'll not expostulate with her,
lest her body and beauty unprovide° my mind again. This night, Iago!

IAGO: Do it not with poison. Strangle her in her bed, even the bed she hath
contaminated.

OTHELLO: Good, good! The justice of it pleases. Very good!   190

IAGO: And for Cassio, let me be his undertaker;° you shall hear more by midnight.

OTHELLO: Excellent good!

A trumpet.

What trumpet is that same?

IAGO: I warrant something from Venice.

Enter Lodovico, Desdemona, and Attendants.

                                    'Tis Lodovico.   195
This comes from the Duke; and see, your wife is with him.

LODOVICO: God save you, worthy general!

OTHELLO: With all my heart, sir.

LODOVICO: The Duke and senators of Venice greet you.

[Gives him a letter.]

OTHELLO: I kiss the instrument of their pleasures.

[Opens the letter and reads.]

DESDEMONA: And what's the news, good cousin Lodovico?   200

IAGO: I am very glad to see you, signior.
Welcome to Cyprus.

LODOVICO: I thank you. How does Lieutenant Cassio?

IAGO: Lives, sir.

DESDEMONA: Cousin, there's fall'n between him and my lord
An unkind breach; but you shall make all well.   205

OTHELLO: Are you sure of that?

DESDEMONA: My lord?

OTHELLO *[reads]*:   "This fail you not to do, as you will —"

---

176 condition: Disposition.   **180 patent:** License.   **187 unprovide:** Disarm.   **191 be his
undertaker:** Undertake to deal with him.

LODOVICO: He did not call; he's busy in the paper.
    Is there division 'twixt thy lord and Cassio?   210

DESDEMONA: A most unhappy one. I would do much
    T' atone° them, for the love I bear to Cassio.

OTHELLO: Fire and brimstone!

DESDEMONA: My lord?

OTHELLO: Are you wise?

DESDEMONA: What, is he angry?

LODOVICO: May be the letter moved him;
    For, as I think, they do command him home,   215
    Deputing Cassio in his government.

DESDEMONA: By my troth, I am glad on't.

OTHELLO: Indeed?

DESDEMONA: My lord?

OTHELLO: I am glad to see you mad.°

DESDEMONA: Why, sweet Othello —

OTHELLO: Devil!

[Strikes her.]

DESDEMONA: I have not deserved this.   220

LODOVICO: My lord, this would not be believed in Venice,
    Though I should swear I saw't. 'Tis very much.
    Make her amends; she weeps.

OTHELLO: O devil, devil!
    If that the earth could teem° with woman's tears,
    Each drop she falls would prove a crocodile.°   225
    Out of my sight!

DESDEMONA: I will not stay to offend you.   *[Going.]*

LODOVICO: Truly, an obedient lady.
    I do beseech your lordship call her back.

OTHELLO: Mistress!

DESDEMONA: My lord?

OTHELLO: What would you with her, sir?   230

LODOVICO: Who? I, my lord?

OTHELLO: Ay! You did wish that I would make her turn.
    Sir, she can turn, and turn, and yet go on
    And turn again; and she can weep, sir, weep;
    And she's obedient; as you say, obedient,   235
    Very obedient. — Proceed you in your tears. —
    Concerning this, sir — O well-painted passion!° —
    I am commanded home. — Get you away;
    I'll send for you anon. — Sir, I obey the mandate
    And will return to Venice. — Hence, avaunt!   240

212 atone: Reconcile.   **218 mad:** I.e., waggish.   **224 teem:** Breed.   **225 crocodile:**
Crocodiles were supposed to shed hypocritical tears to lure men to destruction.
237 passion: Grief.

[Exit Desdemona.]

CASSIO shall have my place. And, sir, to-night
I do entreat that we may sup together.
You are welcome, sir, to Cyprus—Goats and monkeys!

Exit.

LODOVICO: Is this the noble Moor whom our full Senate
Call all in all sufficient? Is this the nature   245
Whom passion could not shake? whose solid virtue
The shot of accident nor dart of chance
Could neither graze nor pierce?
IAGO: He is much changed.
LODOVICO: Are his wits safe? Is he not light of brain?
IAGO: He's that he is; I may not breathe my censure.   250
What he might be—if what he might he is not—
I would to heaven he were!
LODOVICO: What, strike his wife?
IAGO: Faith, that was not so well; yet would I knew
That stroke would prove the worst!
LODOVICO: Is it his use?°
Or did the letters work upon his blood   255
And new-create this fault?
IAGO: Alas, alas!
It is not honesty in me to speak
What I have seen and known. You shall observe him,
And his own courses will denote him so
That I may save my speech. Do but go after   260
And mark how he continues.
LODOVICO: I am sorry that I am deceived in him.   *Exeunt.*

[Scene II: Within the castle.]

Enter Othello and Emilia.

OTHELLO: You have seen nothing then?
EMILIA: Nor ever heard, nor ever did suspect.
OTHELLO: Yes, you have seen Cassio and she together.
EMILIA: But then I saw no harm, and then I heard
Each syllable that breath made up between them.   5
OTHELLO: What, did they never whisper?
EMILIA: Never, my lord.
OTHELLO: Nor send you out o' th' way?
EMILIA: Never.
OTHELLO: To fetch her fan, her gloves, her mask, nor nothing?

254 use: Custom.

EMILIA: Never, my lord.   10
OTHELLO: That's strange.
EMILIA: I durst, my lord, to wager she is honest,
Lay down my soul at stake. If you think other,
Remove your thought; it doth abuse your bosom.°
If any wretch have put this in your head,   15
Let heaven requite it with the serpent's curse!°
For if she be not honest, chaste, and true,
There's no man happy; the purest of their wives
Is foul as slander.
OTHELLO: Bid her come hither. Go.   *Exit Emilia.*
She says enough; yet she's a simple bawd   20
That cannot say as much. This is a subtle whore,
A closet lock and key of villainous secrets;
And yet she'll kneel and pray; I have seen her do't.

Enter Desdemona and Emilia.

DESDEMONA: My lord, what is your will?
OTHELLO: Pray, chuck, come hither.
DESDEMONA: What is your pleasure?
OTHELLO: Let me see your eyes.   25
Look in my face.
DESDEMONA: What horrible fancy's this?
OTHELLO *[to Emilia]*:   Some of your function, mistress.
Leave procreants° alone and shut the door;
Cough or cry hem if anybody come.
Your mystery, your mystery!° Nay, dispatch!   30

                                                                Exit Emilia.

DESDEMONA: Upon my knees, what doth your speech import?
I understand a fury in your words,
[But not the words.]
OTHELLO: Why, what art thou?
DESDEMONA: Your wife, my lord; your true
And loyal wife.
OTHELLO: Come, swear it, damn thyself;   35
Lest, being like one of heaven,° the devils themselves
Should fear to seize thee. Therefore be double-damned —
Swear thou art honest.°
DESDEMONA: Heaven doth truly know it.
OTHELLO: Heaven truly knows that thou art false as hell.
DESDEMONA: To whom, my lord? With whom? How am I false?   40
OTHELLO: Ah, Desdemona! away! away! away!

SCENE II. **14 abuse . . . bosom:** Deceive your heart.   **16 serpent's curse:** (cf. Genesis 3:14).
28 procreants: Mating couples.   **30 mystery:** Trade, occupation.   **36 being . . .
heaven:** Looking like an angel.   **38 honest:** Chaste.

DESDEMONA: Alas the heavy day! Why do you weep?
    Am I the motive of these tears, my lord?
    If haply you my father do suspect
    An instrument° of this your calling back,   45
    Lay not your blame on me. If you have lost him,
    Why, I have lost him too.
OTHELLO: Had it pleased heaven
    To try me with affliction, had they rained
    All kinds of sores and shames on my bare head,
    Steeped me in poverty to the very lips,   50
    Given to captivity me and my utmost hopes,
    I should have found in some place of my soul
    A drop of patience. But, alas, to make me
    A fixèd figure for the time of scorn°
    To point his slow unmoving finger at!   55
    Yet could I bear that too; well, very well.
    But there where I have garnered up my heart,
    Where either I must live or bear no life,
    The fountain from the which my current runs
    Or else dries up—to be discarded thence,   60
    Or keep it as a cistern for foul toads
    To knot and gender in—turn thy complexion there,°
    Patience, thou young and rose-lipped cherubin!
    Ay, there look grim as hell!
DESDEMONA: I hope my noble lord esteems me honest.   65
OTHELLO: O, ay; as summer flies are in the shambles,°
    That quicken° even with blowing. O thou weed,
    Who art so lovely fair, and smell'st so sweet,
    That the sense aches at thee, would thou hadst ne'er been born!
DESDEMONA: Alas, what ignorant sin have I committed?   70
OTHELLO: Was this fair paper, this most goodly book,
    Made to write "whore" upon? What committed?
    Committed? O thou public commoner!°
    I should make very forges of my cheeks
    That would to cinders burn up modesty,   75
    Did I but speak thy deeds. What committed?
    Heaven stops the nose at it, and the moon winks;°
    The bawdy wind, that kisses all it meets,
    Is hushed within the hollow mine of earth
    And will not hear it. What committed?   80
    Impudent strumpet!
DESDEMONA: By heaven, you do me wrong!

---

45 An instrument: To be the cause.   **54 time of scorn:** Scornful world.   **62 turn
thy complexion there:** Change thy color at that point.   **66 shambles:** Slaughterhouse.
67 quicken: Come to life.   **73 commoner:** Harlot.   **77 winks:** Closes her eyes.

OTHELLO: Are not you a strumpet?

DESDEMONA: No, as I am a Christian!

    If to preserve this vessel for my lord

    From any other foul unlawful touch

    Be not to be a strumpet, I am none.   85

OTHELLO: What, not a whore?

DESDEMONA: No, as I shall be saved!

OTHELLO: Is't possible?

DESDEMONA: O, heaven forgive us!

OTHELLO: I cry you mercy° then.

    I took you for that cunning whore of Venice

    That married with Othello. — *[Calling.]* You, mistress,   90

    That have the office opposite to Saint Peter

    And keep the gate of hell!

Enter Emilia.

                You, you, ay, you!

    We have done our course; there's money for your pains:

    I pray you turn the key, and keep our counsel.   *Exit.*

EMILIA: Alas, what does this gentleman conceive?   95

    How do you, madam? How do you, my good lady?

DESDEMONA: Faith, half asleep.°

EMILIA: Good madam, what's the matter with my lord?

DESDEMONA: With who?

EMILIA: Why, with my lord, madam.   100

DESDEMONA: Who is thy lord?

EMILIA: He that is yours, sweet lady.

DESDEMONA: I have none. Do not talk to me, Emilia.

    I cannot weep; nor answer have I none

    But what should go by water. Prithee to-night

    Lay on my bed my wedding sheets, remember;   105

    And call thy husband hither.

EMILIA: Here's a change indeed!   *Exit.*

DESDEMONA: 'Tis meet I should be used so, very meet.

    How have I been behaved, that he might stick

    The small'st opinion° on my least misuse?°

Enter Iago and Emilia.

IAGO: What is your pleasure, madam? How is't with you?   110

DESDEMONA: I cannot tell. Those that do teach young babes

    Do it with gentle means and easy tasks:

    He might have chid me so; for, in good faith,

    I am a child to chiding.

IAGO: What is the matter, lady?

88 cry you mercy: Beg your pardon.   **97 half asleep:** I.e., stunned.   **109 small'st opinion:** Least suspicion;   **least misuse:** Slightest misconduct.

EMILIA: Alas, Iago, my lord hath so bewhored her,   115
    Thrown such despite and heavy terms upon her
    As true hearts cannot bear.
DESDEMONA: Am I that name, Iago?
IAGO: What name, fair lady?
DESDEMONA: Such as she said my lord did say I was.
EMILIA: He called her whore. A beggar in his drink   120
    Could not have laid such terms upon his callet.°
IAGO: Why did he so?
DESDEMONA: I do not know; I am sure I am none such.
IAGO: Do not weep, do not weep. Alas the day!
EMILIA: Hath she forsook so many noble matches,   125
    Her father and her country, and her friends,
    To be called whore? Would it not make one weep?
DESDEMONA: It is my wretched fortune.
IAGO: Beshrew him for't!
    How comes this trick° upon him?
DESDEMONA: Nay, heaven doth know.
EMILIA: I will be hanged if some eternal villain,   130
    Some busy and insinuating rogue,
    Some cogging, cozening° slave, to get some office,
    Have not devised this slander. I'll be hanged else.
IAGO: Fie, there is no such man! It is impossible.
DESDEMONA: If any such there be, heaven pardon him!   135
EMILIA: A halter pardon him! and hell gnaw his bones!
    Why should he call her whore? Who keeps her company?
    What place? what time? what form? what likelihood?
    The Moor 's abused by some most villainous knave,
    Some base notorious knave, some scurvy fellow.   140
    O heaven, that such companions° thou 'dst unfold,°
    And put in every honest hand a whip
    To lash the rascals naked through the world
    Even from the east to th' west!
IAGO: Speak within door.°
EMILIA: O, fie upon them! Some such squire he was   145
    That turned your wit the seamy side without
    And made you to suspect me with the Moor.
IAGO: You are a fool. Go to.
DESDEMONA: Alas, Iago,
    What shall I do to win my lord again?
    Good friend, go to him; for, by this light of heaven,   150
    I know not how I lost him. Here I kneel:

---

121 callet: Whore.   **129 trick:** Freakish behavior.   **132 cogging, cozening:** Cheating, defrauding.   **141 companions:** Rogues; **unfold:** Expose.   **144 within door:** With restraint.

If e'er my will did trespass 'gainst his love
Either in discourse° of thought or actual deed,
Or that mine eyes, mine ears, or any sense
Delighted them in any other form,   155
Or that I do not yet, and ever did,
And ever will (though he do shake me off
To beggarly divorcement) love him dearly,
Comfort forswear° me! Unkindness may do much;
And his unkindness may defeat° my life,   160
But never taint my love. I cannot say "whore."
It does abhor me now I speak the word;
To do the act that might the addition earn
Not the world's mass of vanity could make me.
IAGO: I pray you be content. 'Tis but his humor.   165
The business of the state does him offense,
[And he does chide with you.]
DESDEMONA: If 'twere no other —
IAGO: 'Tis but so, I warrant.

[*Trumpets within.*]

Hark how these instruments summon you to supper.
The messengers of Venice stay the meat: 170
Go in, and weep not. All things shall be well.

                                        Exeunt Desdemona and Emilia.

Enter Roderigo.

How now, Roderigo?
RODERIGO: I do not find that thou deal'st justly with me.
IAGO: What in the contrary?
RODERIGO: Every day thou daff'st me with some device,° Iago, and rather, as it   175
seems to me now, keep'st from me all conveniency° than suppliest me with
the least advantage of hope. I will indeed no longer endure it; nor am I yet
persuaded to put up in peace what already I have foolishly suffered.
IAGO: Will you hear me, Roderigo?
RODERIGO: Faith, I have heard too much; for your words and performances are   180
no kin together.
IAGO: You charge me most unjustly.
RODERIGO: With naught but truth. I have wasted myself out of my means.
The jewels you have had from me to deliver to Desdemona would half
have corrupted a votarist.° You have told me she hath received them, and   185
returned me expectations and comforts of sudden respect° and acquain-
tance; but I find none.

---

153 discourse: Course.   **159 Comfort forswear:** Happiness forsake.   **160 defeat:**
Destroy.   **175 thou . . . device:** You put me off with some trick.   **176 conveniency:**
Favorable opportunities.   **185 votarist:** Nun.   **186 sudden respect:** Immediate notice.

IAGO: Well, go to; very well.

RODERIGO: Very well! go to! I cannot go to, man; nor 'tis not very well. By this
hand, I say 'tis very scurvy, and begin to find myself fopped° in it.   190

IAGO: Very well.

RODERIGO: I tell you 'tis not very well. I will make myself known to Desdemona.
If she will return me my jewels, I will give over my suit and repent my
unlawful solicitation; if not, assure yourself I will seek satisfaction of you.

IAGO: You have said now.   195

RODERIGO: Ay, and said nothing but what I protest intendment of doing.

IAGO: Why, now I see there's mettle in thee; and even from this instant do build
on thee a better opinion than ever before. Give me thy hand, Roderigo.
Thou has taken against me a most just exception; but yet I protest I have
dealt most directly° in thy affair.   200

RODERIGO: It hath not appeared.

IAGO: I grant indeed it hath not appeared, and your suspicion is not without
wit and judgment. But, Roderigo, if thou hast that in thee indeed which
I have greater reason to believe now than ever, I mean purpose, courage,
and valor, this night show it. If thou the next night following enjoy not   205
Desdemona, take me from this world with treachery and devise engines
for° my life.

RODERIGO: Well, what is it? Is it within reason and compass?

IAGO: Sir, there is especial commission come from Venice to depute Cassio in
Othello's place.   210

RODERIGO: Is that true? Why, then Othello and Desdemona return again to
Venice.

IAGO: O, no; he goes into Mauritania and takes away with him the fair
Desdemona, unless his abode be lingered here° by some accident; wherein
none can be so determinate° as the removing of Cassio.   215

RODERIGO: How do you mean removing of him?

IAGO: Why, by making him uncapable of Othello's place—knocking out his
brains.

RODERIGO: And that you would have me to do?

IAGO: Ay, if you dare do yourself a profit and a right. He sups to-night with   220
a harlotry, and thither will I go to him. He knows not yet of his honorable fortune. If you will watch his going thence, which I will fashion to fall
out between twelve and one, you may take him at your pleasure. I will be
near to second your attempt, and he shall fall between us. Come, stand not
amazed at it, but go along with me. I will show you such a necessity in his   225
death that you shall think yourself bound to put it on him. It is now high
supper time, and the night grows to waste. About it!

RODERIGO: I will hear further reason for this.

IAGO: And you shall be satisfied.   *Exeunt.*

---

190 fopped: Duped.   **200 directly:** Straightforwardly.   **207 engines for:** Plots
against.   **214 abode . . . here:** Stay here be extended.   **215 determinate:** Effective.

[Scene III: Within the castle.]

Enter Othello, Lodovico, Desdemona, Emilia, and Attendants.

LODOVICO: I do beseech you, sir, trouble yourself no further.

OTHELLO: O, pardon me; 'twill do me good to walk.

LODOVICO: Madam, good night. I humbly thank your ladyship.

DESDEMONA: Your honor is most welcome.

OTHELLO: Will you walk, sir?

O, Desdemona —   5

DESDEMONA: My lord?

OTHELLO: Get you to bed on th' instant; I will be returned forthwith. Dismiss
your attendant there. Look't be done.

DESDEMONA: I will, my lord.

                            Exit [Othello, with Lodovico and Attendants].

EMILIA: How goes it now? He looks gentler than he did.   10

DESDEMONA: He says he will return incontinent.°

He hath commanded me to go to bed,

And bade me to dismiss you.

EMILIA: Dismiss me?

DESDEMONA: It was his bidding; therefore, good Emilia,

Give me my nightly wearing, and adieu.   15

We must not now displease him.

EMILIA: I would you had never seen him!

DESDEMONA: So would not I. My love doth so approve him

That even his stubbornness,° his checks,° his frowns —

Prithee unpin me — have grace and favor in them.   20

EMILIA: I have laid those sheets you bade me on the bed.

DESDEMONA: All's one. Good faith, how foolish are our minds!

If I do die before thee, prithee shroud me

In one of those same sheets.

EMILIA: Come, come! You talk.

DESDEMONA: My mother had a maid called Barbary.   25

She was in love; and he she loved proved mad°

And did forsake her. She had a song of "Willow";

An old thing 'twas; but it expressed her fortune,

And she died singing it. That song to-night

Will not go from my mind; I have much to do   30

But to go hang my head all at one side

And sing it like poor Barbary. Prithee dispatch.

EMILIA: Shall I go fetch your nightgown?°

DESDEMONA: No, unpin me here.

This Lodovico is a proper man.

SCENE III.   **11 incontinent:** At once.   **19 stubbornness:** Roughness;   **checks:**
Rebukes.   **26 mad:** Wild, faithless.   **33 nightgown:** Dressing gown.

EMILIA: A very handsome man.   35
DESDEMONA: He speaks well.
EMILIA: I know a lady in Venice would have walked barefoot to Palestine for a
    touch of his nether lip.
DESDEMONA *(sings)*:   "The poor soul sat sighing by a sycamore tree
        Sing all a green willow;   40
    Her hand on her bosom, her head on her knee,
        Sing willow, willow, willow.
    The fresh streams ran by her and murmured her moans;
        Sing willow, willow, willow;
    Her salt tears fell from her, and soft'ned the stones" —   45
Lay by these.
      "Sing willow, willow, willow" —
    Prithee hie thee;° he'll come anon.
      "Sing all a green willow must be my garland.
    Let nobody blame him; his scorn I approve" —   50
Nay, that's not next. Hark! who is't that knocks?
EMILIA: It's the wind.
DESDEMONA *(sings)*:   "I call my love false love; but what said he then?
      "Sing willow, willow, willow" —
    If I court moe women, you'll couch with moe men."   55
So get thee gone; good night. Mine eyes do itch.
Doth that bode weeping?
EMILIA: 'Tis neither here nor there.
DESDEMONA: I have heard it said so. O, these men, these men!
    Dost thou in conscience think — tell me, Emilia —
    That there be women do abuse their husbands   60
    In such gross kind?
EMILIA: There be some such, no question.
DESDEMONA: Wouldst thou do such a deed for all the world?
EMILIA: Why, would not you?
DESDEMONA: No, by this heavenly light!
EMILIA: Nor I neither by this heavenly light.
    I might do't as well i' th' dark.   65
DESDEMONA: Wouldst thou do such a deed for all the world?
EMILIA: The world's a huge thing; it is a great price for a small vice.
DESDEMONA: In troth, I think thou wouldst not.
EMILIA: In troth, I think I should; and undo't when I had done it. Marry,
    I would not do such a thing for a joint-ring,° nor for measures of lawn,   70
    nor for gowns, petticoats, nor caps, nor any petty exhibition;° but, for all
    the whole world — 'Ud's pity! who would not make her husband a cuckold
    to make him a monarch? I should venture purgatory for't.
DESDEMONA: Beshrew me if I would do such a wrong

48 hie thee: Hurry. **70 joint-ring:** Ring made in separable halves. **71 exhibition:** Gift.

For the whole world.   75

EMILIA: Why, the wrong is but a wrong i' th' world; and having the world for your
   labor, 'tis a wrong in your own world, and you might quickly make it right.

DESDEMONA: I do not think there is any such woman.

EMILIA: Yes, a dozen; and as many to th' vantage° as
   would store° the world they played for.   80
   But I do think it is their husbands' faults
   If wives do fall. Say that they slack their duties
   And pour our treasures into foreign laps;
   Or else break out in peevish° jealousies,
   Throwing restraint upon us; or say they strike us,   85
   Or scant our former having° in despite —
   Why, we have galls;° and though we have some grace,
   Yet have we some revenge. Let husbands know
   Their wives have sense like them. They see, and smell,
   And have their palates both for sweet and sour,   90
   As husbands have. What is it that they do
   When they change us for others? Is it sport?
   I think it is. And doth affection breed it?
   I think it doth. Is't frailty that thus errs?
   It is so too. And have not we affections,   95
   Desires for sport, and frailty, as men have?
   Then let them use us well; else let them know,
   The ills we do, their ills instruct us so.

DESDEMONA: Good night, good night. God me such usage° send,
   Not to pick bad from bad, but by bad mend!   *Exeunt.*   100

[ACT V, Scene I: A street in Cyprus]

Enter Iago and Roderigo.

IAGO: Here, stand behind this bulk;° straight will he come.
   Wear thy good rapier bare, and put it home.
   Quick, quick! Fear nothing; I'll be at thy elbow.
   It makes us, or it mars us—think on that,
   And fix most firm thy resolution.   5

RODERIGO: Be near at hand; I may miscarry in't.

IAGO: Here, at thy hand. Be bold, and take thy stand.

[Stands aside.]

RODERIGO: I have no great devotion to the deed,
   And yet he hath given me satisfying reasons.

---

79 to th' vantage: Besides.   **80 store:** Populate.   **84 peevish:** Senseless.   **86 having:**
Allowance.   **87 galls:** Spirits to resent.   **99 usage:** Habits.   **Act V, Scene I. 1 bulk:** Projecting shop-front.

'Tis but a man gone. Forth my sword! He dies!   10
IAGO: I have rubbed this young quat° almost to the sense,°
        And he grows angry. Now whether he kill Cassio,
        Or Cassio him, or each do kill the other,
        Every way makes my gain. Live Roderigo,
        He calls me to a restitution large   15
        Of gold and jewels that I bobbed° from him
        As gifts to Desdemona.
        It must not be. If Cassio do remain,
        He hath a daily beauty in his life
        That makes me ugly; and besides, the Moor   20
        May unfold me to him; there stand I in much peril.
        No, he must die. Be't so! I hear him coming.

Enter Cassio.

RODERIGO: I know his gait. 'Tis he. Villain, thou diest!

[Makes a pass at Cassio.]

CASSIO: That thrust had been mine enemy indeed
        But that my coat° is better than thou know'st.   25
        I will make proof of thine.

[Draws, and wounds Roderigo.]

RODERIGO: O, I am slain!

[Iago darts from concealment behind Cassio, wounds him in the leg, and exits.]

CASSIO: I am maimed for ever. Help, ho! Murder! murder!

[Falls.]

Enter Othello.

OTHELLO: The voice of Cassio. Iago keeps his word.
RODERIGO: O, villain that I am!
OTHELLO: It is even so.
CASSIO: O, help, ho! light! a surgeon!   30
OTHELLO: 'Tis he. O brave Iago, honest and just,
        That hast such noble sense of thy friend's wrong!
        Thou teachest me. Minion,° your dear lies dead,
        And your unblest fate hies.° Strumpet, I come.
        Forth of my heart those charms, thine eyes, are blotted.   35
        Thy bed, lust-stained, shall with lust's blood be spotted.

                                                            Exit Othello.

Enter Lodovico and Gratiano.

CASSIO: What, ho? No watch? No passage?° Murder! murder!
GRATIANO: 'Tis some mischance. The cry is very direful.

---

11 quat: Pimple;   **sense:** Quick.   **16 bobbed:** Swindled.   **25 coat:** Undershirt of
mail.   **33 Minion:** Mistress.   **34 hies:** Hurries on.   **37 passage:** Passersby.

CASSIO: O, help!

LODOVICO: Hark!   40

RODERIGO: O wretched villain!

LODOVICO: Two or three groan. It is a heavy° night.

These may be counterfeits. Let's think't unsafe

To come in to the cry without more help.

RODERIGO: Nobody come? Then shall I bleed to death.   45

LODOVICO: Hark!

Enter Iago, with a light.

GRATIANO: Here's one comes in his shirt, with light and weapons.

IAGO: Who's there? Whose noise is this that cries on° murder?

LODOVICO: We do not know.

IAGO: Did not you hear a cry?

CASSIO: Here, here! For heaven's sake, help me!

IAGO: What's the matter?   50

GRATIANO: This is Othello's ancient, as I take it.

LODOVICO: The same indeed, a very valiant fellow.

IAGO: What are you here that cry so grievously?

CASSIO: Iago? O, I am spoiled, undone by villains!

Give me some help.   55

IAGO: O me, lieutenant! What villains have done this?

CASSIO: I think that one of them is hereabout

And cannot make° away.

IAGO: O treacherous villains!

[To Lodovico and Gratiano.]

What are you there? Come in, and give some help.

RODERIGO: O, help me here!   60

CASSIO: That's one of them.

IAGO: O murd'rous slave! O villain!

[Stabs Roderigo.]

RODERIGO: O damned Iago! O inhuman dog!

IAGO: Kill men i' th' dark? — Where be these bloody thieves? —

How silent is this town! — Ho! murder! murder! —

What may you be? Are you of good or evil?   65

LODOVICO: As you shall prove us, praise us.

IAGO: Signior Lodovico?

LODOVICO: He, sir.

IAGO: I cry you mercy. Here's Cassio hurt by villains.

GRATIANO: Cassio?   70

IAGO: How is't, brother?

CASSIO: My leg is cut in two.

IAGO: Marry,° heaven forbid!

Light, gentlemen. I'll bind it with my shirt.

42 heavy: Cloudy, dark.   **48 cries on:** Raises the cry of.   **58 make:** Get.   **72 Marry:**
(From "By Mary").

Enter Bianca.

BIANCA: What is the matter, ho? Who is't that cried?

IAGO: Who is't that cried?   75

BIANCA: O my dear Cassio! my sweet Cassio!
    O Cassio, Cassio, Cassio!

IAGO: O notable strumpet!—Cassio, may you suspect
    Who they should be that have thus mangled you?

CASSIO: No.   80

GRATIANO: I am sorry to find you thus. I have been to seek you.

IAGO: Lend me a garter. So. O for a chair°
    To bear him easily hence!

BIANCA: Alas, he faints! O Cassio, Cassio, Cassio!

IAGO: Gentlemen all, I do suspect this trash   85
    To be a party in this injury. —
    Patience a while, good Cassio. —Come, come!
    Lend me a light. Know we this face or no?
    Alas, my friend and my dear countryman
    Roderigo? No—Yes, sure.—O heaven, Roderigo!   90

GRATIANO: What, of Venice?

IAGO: Even he, sir. Did you know him?

GRATIANO: Know him? Ay.

IAGO: Signior Gratiano? I cry your gentle pardon.
    These bloody accidents must excuse my manners
    That so neglected you.

GRATIANO: I am glad to see you.   95

IAGO: How do you, Cassio? —O, a chair, a chair!

GRATIANO: Roderigo?

IAGO: He, he, 'tis he!

[A chair brought in.]

    O, that's well said;° the chair.
    Some good man bear him carefully from hence.   100
    I'll fetch the general's surgeon. *[To Bianca.]* For you, mistress,
    Save you your labor. —He that lies slain here, Cassio,
    Was my dear friend. What malice was between you?

CASSIO: None in the world; nor do I know the man.

IAGO *[to Bianca]*: What, look you pale? —O, bear him out o' th' air.   105

                            [Cassio and Roderigo are borne off.]

    Stay you, good gentlemen. —Look you pale, mistress? —
    Do you perceive the gastness° of her eye? —
    Nay, if you stare, we shall hear more anon.
    Behold her well; I pray you look upon her.
    Do you see, gentlemen? Nay, guiltiness will speak.   110
    Though tongues were out of use.

82 chair: Litter.   **99 well said:** Well done.   **107 gastness:** Terror.

Enter Emilia.

EMILIA: 'Las, what's the matter? What's the matter, husband?
IAGO: Cassio hath here been set on in the dark
    By Roderigo, and fellows that are scaped.
    He's almost slain, and Roderigo dead.   115
EMILIA: Alas, good gentlemen! alas, good Cassio!
IAGO: This is the fruits of whoring. Prithee, Emilia,
    Go know of Cassio where he supped to-night.

[To Bianca.]

What, do you shake at that?
BIANCA: He supped at my house; but I therefore shake not.   120
IAGO: O, did he so? I charge you go with me.
EMILIA: Fie, fie upon thee, strumpet!
BIANCA: I am no strumpet, but of life as honest°
    As you that thus abuse me.
EMILIA: As I? Foh! fie upon thee!
IAGO: Kind gentlemen, let's go see poor Cassio dressed.   125

[To Bianca.]

Come, mistress, you must tell 's another tale.
Emilia, run you to the citadel
And tell my lord and lady what hath happed.

[Exit Emilia.]

Will you go on afore?   *Exeunt [all but Iago].*
This is the night
That either makes me or fordoes° me quite.   *[Exit.]*   130

[Scene II: A bedchamber in the castle.]

Desdemona [asleep] in her bed. Enter Othello with a light.

OTHELLO: It is the cause, it is the cause,° my soul.
    Let me not name it to you, you chaste stars!
    It is the cause. Yet I'll not shed her blood,
    Nor scar that whiter skin of hers than snow,
    And smooth as monumental alabaster.   5
    Yet she must die, else she'll betray more men.
    Put out the light, and then put out the light.
    If I quench thee, thou flaming minister,°
    I can again thy former light restore,
    Should I repent me; but once put out thy light,   10
    Thou cunning'st pattern of excelling nature,
    I know not where is that Promethean heat°

123 honest: Chaste.   **130 fordoes:** Destroys.   **SCENE II. 1 cause:** Cause of justice.
8 minister: Servant.   **12 Promethean heat:** Divine fire.

That can thy light relume.° When I have plucked the rose,
I cannot give it vital growth again;
It needs must wither. I'll smell thee on the tree.   15

(He kisses her.)

O balmy breath, that dost almost persuade
Justice to break her sword! One more, one more!
Be thus when thou art dead, and I will kill thee,
And love thee after. One more, and that's the last!
So sweet was ne'er so fatal. I must weep,   20
But they are cruel tears. This sorrow's heavenly;
It strikes where it doth love. She wakes.

DESDEMONA: Who's there? Othello?

OTHELLO: Ay, Desdemona.

DESDEMONA: Will you come to bed, my lord?

OTHELLO: Have you prayed to-night, Desdemona?

DESDEMONA: Ay, my lord.   25

OTHELLO: If you bethink yourself of any crime°
Unreconciled as yet to heaven and grace,
Solicit for it straight.

DESDEMONA: Alack, my lord, what may you mean by that?

OTHELLO: Well, do it, and be brief; I will walk by.   30
I would not kill thy unpreparèd spirit.
No, heaven forfend!° I would not kill thy soul.

DESDEMONA: Talk you of killing?

OTHELLO: Ay, I do.

DESDEMONA: Then heaven
Have mercy on me!

OTHELLO: Amen, with all my heart!

DESDEMONA: If you say so, I hope you will not kill me.   35

OTHELLO: Hum!

DESDEMONA: And yet I fear you; for you're fatal then
When your eyes roll so. Why I should fear I know not,
Since guiltiness I know not; but yet I feel I fear.

OTHELLO: Think on thy sins.

DESDEMONA: They are loves I bear to you.   40

OTHELLO: Ay, and for that thou diest.

DESDEMONA: That death 's unnatural that kills for loving.
Alas, why gnaw you so your nether lip?
Some bloody passion shakes your very frame.
These are portents,° but yet I hope, I hope,   45
They do not point on me.

OTHELLO: Peace and be still!

DESDEMONA: I will so. What's the matter?

13 relume: Relight.   **26 crime:** Sin.   **32 forfend:** Forbid.   **45 portents:** Signs of
impending violence.

OTHELLO: That handkerchief which I so loved and gave thee
Thou gav'st to Cassio.
DESDEMONA: No, by my life and soul!
Send for the man and ask him.
OTHELLO: Sweet soul, take heed,   50
Take heed of perjury; thou art on thy deathbed.
DESDEMONA: Ay, but not yet to die.
OTHELLO: Yes, presently.°
Therefore confess thee freely of thy sin;
For to deny each article with oath
Cannot remove nor choke the strong conception°   55
That I do groan withal. Thou art to die.
DESDEMONA: Then Lord have mercy on me!
OTHELLO: I say amen.
DESDEMONA: And have you mercy too! I never did
Offend° you in my life; never loved Cassio
But with such general warranty of heaven   60
As I might love. I never gave him token.
OTHELLO: By heaven, I saw my handkerchief in's hand!
O perjured woman! thou dost stone my heart,°
And mak'st me call what I intend to do
A murder, which I thought a sacrifice.   65
I saw the handkerchief.
DESDEMONA: He found it then.
I never gave it him. Send for him hither.
Let him confess a truth.
OTHELLO: He hath confessed.
DESDEMONA: What, my lord?
OTHELLO: That he hath used thee.
DESDEMONA: How? Unlawfully?
OTHELLO: Ay.   70
DESDEMONA: He will not say so.
OTHELLO: No, his mouth is stopped.
Honest Iago hath ta'en order° for't.
DESDEMONA: O, my fear interprets. What, is he dead?
OTHELLO: Had all his hairs been lives, my great revenge
Had stomach for them all.   75
DESDEMONA: Alas, he is betrayed, and I undone!
OTHELLO: Out, strumpet! Weep'st thou for him to my face?
DESDEMONA: O, banish me, my lord, but kill me not!
OTHELLO: Down, strumpet!
DESDEMONA: Kill me to-morrow; let me live to-night!   80
OTHELLO: Nay, if you strive —

---

52 presently: At once.   **55 conception:** Belief.   **59 Offend:** Wrong.   **63 stone my heart:** Turn my heart to stone.   **72 ta'en order:** Taken measures.

DESDEMONA: But half an hour!
OTHELLO: Being done, there is no pause.
DESDEMONA: But while I say one prayer!
OTHELLO: It is too late.

(Smothers her.)

DESDEMONA: [O Lord, Lord, Lord!]

Emilia at the door.

EMILIA *(calls within):*   My lord, my lord! What, ho! my lord, my lord!   85
OTHELLO: What noise is this? Not dead? not yet quite dead?
   I that am cruel am yet merciful;
   I would not have thee linger in thy pain.
   So, so.
EMILIA *(within):*   What, ho! my lord, my lord!
OTHELLO: Who's there?   90
EMILIA *(within):*   O, good my lord, I would speak a word with you!
OTHELLO: Yes, 'tis Emilia. — By and by.° — She's dead. —
   'Tis like she comes to speak of Cassio's death.
   The noise was here. Ha! no more moving?
   Still as the grave. — Shall she come in? Were't good! —   95
   I think she stirs again. No. — What's best to do?
   If she come in, she'll sure speak to my wife.
   My wife! my wife! what wife? I have no wife.
   O, insupportable! O heavy hour!
   Methinks it should be now a huge eclipse   100
   Of sun and moon, and that th' affrighted globe
   Should yawn° at alteration.
EMILIA *(within):*   I do beseech you
   That I may speak with you, O good my lord!
OTHELLO: I had forgot thee. O, come in, Emilia.
   Soft, by and by. — Let me the curtains draw. —   105

[Closes the bed-curtains.]

   Where art thou?

[Opens the door.]

Enter Emilia.

           What's the matter with thee now?
EMILIA: O my good lord, yonder's foul murder done!
OTHELLO: What? Now?
EMILIA: But now, my lord.
OTHELLO: It is the very error° of the moon.   110
   She comes more nearer earth than she was wont
   And makes men mad.

92 By and by: Just a moment (addressed to Emilia).   **102 yawn:** Open, as in an earthquake.   **110 error:** Straying off course.

EMILIA: Cassio, my lord, hath killed a young Venetian
    Called Roderigo.
OTHELLO: Roderigo killed?
    And Cassio killed?
EMILIA: No, Cassio is not killed.   115
OTHELLO: Not Cassio killed? Then murder's out of tune,
    And sweet revenge grows harsh.
DESDEMONA: O, falsely, falsely murdered?
EMILIA: O, Lord! what cry is that?
OTHELLO: That? What?
EMILIA: Out and alas! that was my lady's voice.   120
    Help! help, ho! help! O lady, speak again!
    Sweet Desdemona! O sweet mistress, speak!
DESDEMONA: A guiltless death I die.
EMILIA: O, who hath done this deed?
DESDEMONA: Nobody — I myself. Farewell.   125
    Commend° me to my kind lord. O, farewell!

(She dies.)

OTHELLO: Why, how should she be murd'red?
EMILIA: Alas, who knows?
OTHELLO: You heard her say herself, it was not I.
EMILIA: She said so. I must needs report the truth.
OTHELLO: She's like a liar gone to burning hell!   130
    'Twas I that killed her.
EMILIA: O, the more angel she,
    And you the blacker devil!
OTHELLO: She turned to folly, and she was a whore.
EMILIA: Thou dost belie her, and thou art a devil.
OTHELLO: She was false as water.°
EMILIA: Thou art rash as fire to say   135
    That she was false. O, she was heavenly true!
OTHELLO: Cassio did top her. Ask thy husband else.
    O, I were damned beneath all depth in hell
    But that I did proceed upon just grounds
    To this extremity. Thy husband knew it all.   140
EMILIA: My husband?
OTHELLO: Thy husband.
EMILIA: That she was false to wedlock?
OTHELLO: Ay, with Cassio. Nay, had she been true,
    If heaven would make me such another world   145
    Of one entire and perfect chrysolite,°
    I'd not have sold her for it.
EMILIA: My husband?

126 Commend: Remember.   **135 water:** (Which is yielding).   **146 chrysolite:**
(Precious topaz).

OTHELLO: Ay 'twas he that told me first.
    An honest man he is, and hates the slime
    That sticks on filthy deeds.
EMILIA: My husband?   150
OTHELLO: What needs this iterance,° woman? I say thy husband.
EMILIA: O mistress, villainy hath made mocks with love!
    My husband say that she was false?
OTHELLO: He, woman.
    I say, thy husband. Dost understand the word?
    My friend, thy husband; honest, honest Iago.   155
EMILIA: If he say so, may his pernicious soul
    Rot half a grain a day! he lies to th' heart.
    She was too fond of her most filthy bargain.
OTHELLO: Ha!
EMILIA: Do thy worst.   160
    This deed of thine is no more worthy heaven
    Than thou wast worthy her.
OTHELLO: Peace, you were best.
EMILIA: Thou hast not half the power to do me harm
    As I have to be hurt.° O gull! O dolt!
    As ignorant as dirt! thou hast done a deed —   165
    I care not for thy sword; I'll make thee known,
    Though I lost twenty lives. Help! help! Ho! help!
    The Moor hath killed my mistress! Murder! murder!

Enter Montano, Gratiano, Iago, and others.

MONTANO: What is the matter? How now, general?
EMILIA: O, are you come, Iago? You have done well,   170
    That men must lay their murders on your neck.
GRATIANO: What is the matter?
EMILIA: Disprove this villain, if thou be'st a man.
    He says thou told'st him that his wife was false.
    I know thou didst not; thou'rt not such a villain.   175
    Speak, for my heart is full.
IAGO: I told him what I thought, and told no more
    Than what he found himself was apt and true.
EMILIA: But did you ever tell him she was false?
IAGO: I did.   180
EMILIA: You told a lie, an odious damnèd lie!
    Upon my soul, a lie! a wicked lie!
    She false with Cassio? Did you say with Cassio?
IAGO: With Cassio, mistress. Go to, charm° your tongue.

151 iterance: Repetition.   **164 to be hurt:** To endure hurt.   **184 charm:** Cast a spell on.

EMILIA: I will not charm my tongue; I am bound to speak: 185
    My mistress here lies murdered in her bed —
ALL: O heavens forfend!
EMILIA: And your reports have set the murder on.
OTHELLO: Nay, stare not, masters. It is true indeed.
GRATIANO: 'Tis a strange truth.   190
MONTANO: O monstrous act!
EMILIA: Villainy, villainy, villainy!
    I think upon't —I think I smell't! —O villainy!
    I thought so then. —I'll kill myself for grief. —
    O villainy, villainy!
IAGO: What, are you mad? I charge you get you home.   195
EMILIA: Good gentlemen, let me have leave to speak.
    'Tis proper I obey him, but not now.
    Perchance, Iago, I will ne'er go home.
OTHELLO: O! O! O!   *(Falls on the bed.)*
EMILIA: Nay, lay thee down and roar!
    For thou hast killed the sweetest innocent   200
    That e'er did lift up eye.
OTHELLO: O, she was foul!

[Rises.]

    I scarce did know you, uncle. There lies your niece,
    Whose breath, indeed, these hands have newly stopped.
    I know this act shows° horrible and grim.
GRATIANO: Poor Desdemona! I am glad thy father's dead.   205
    Thy match was mortal to him, and pure grief
    Shore his old thread in twain. Did he live now,
    This sight would make him do a desperate turn;°
    Yea, curse his better angel from his side,
    And fall to reprobation.°   210
OTHELLO: 'Tis pitiful; but yet Iago knows
    That she with Cassio hath the act of shame
    A thousand times committed. Cassio confessed it;
    And she did gratify° his amorous works
    With that recognizance° and pledge of love   215
    Which I first gave her. I saw it in his hand.
    It was a handkerchief, an antique token
    My father gave my mother.
EMILIA: O God! O heavenly God!
IAGO: Zounds, hold your peace!
EMILIA: 'Twill out, 'twill out! I peace?   220

---

204 shows: Appears.   **208 turn:** Act.   **210 reprobation:** Rejection by God, damnation.
214 gratify: Reward.   **215 recognizance:** Token.

No, I will speak as liberal as the north,°
Let heaven and men and devils, let them all,
All, all, cry shame against me, yet I'll speak.
IAGO: Be wise, and get you home.
EMILIA: I will not.

[Iago draws and threatens Emilia.]

GRATIANO: Fie!
Your sword upon a woman?   225
EMILIA: O thou dull Moor, that handkerchief thou speak'st of
I found by fortune, and did give my husband;
For often with a solemn earnestness —
More than indeed belonged to such a trifle —
He begged of me to steal't.
IAGO: Villainous whore!   230
EMILIA: She give it Cassio? No, alas, I found it,
And I did give't my husband.
IAGO: Filth, thou liest!
EMILIA: By heaven, I do not, I do not, gentlemen.
O murd'rous coxcomb! what should such a fool
Do with so good a wife?
OTHELLO: Are there no stones° in heaven   235
But what serves for the thunder? Precious villain!

The Moor runs at Iago [but is disarmed by Montano].

Iago kills his wife.

GRATIANO: The woman falls. Sure he hath killed his wife.
EMILIA: Ay, ay. O, lay me by my mistress' side.   *Exit Iago.*
GRATIANO: He's gone, but his wife's killed.
MONTANO: 'Tis a notorious° villain. Take you this weapon,   240
Which I have here recovered from the Moor.
Come, guard the door without. Let him not pass,
But kill him rather. I'll after that same villain,
For 'tis a damnèd slave.

                      Exit [Montano, with all but Othello and Emilia].

OTHELLO: I am not valiant neither;
But every puny whipster° gets my sword.   245
But why should honor outlive honesty?
Let it go all.
EMILIA: What did thy song bode, lady?
Hark, canst thou hear me? I will play the swan,
And die in music. *[Sings.]* "Willow, willow, willow."

---

221 liberal as the north: Unchecked as the north wind blows.   **235 stones:** Bolts
like those used for thunderbolts.   **240 notorious:** Notable.   **245 puny whipster:** Whip-
persnapper.

Moor, she was chaste. She loved thee, cruel Moor: 250
So come my soul to bliss as I speak true.
So speaking as I think, alas, I die.

(She dies.)

OTHELLO: I have another weapon in this chamber;
It is a sword of Spain, the ice brook's° temper.
O, here it is.—Uncle, I must come forth.   255
GRATIANO *(within)*:   If thou attempt it, it will cost thee dear.
Thou hast no weapon, and perforce must suffer.
OTHELLO: Look in upon me then and speak with me,
Or, naked° as I am, I will assault thee.

[Enter Gratiano.]

GRATIANO: What is the matter?
OTHELLO: Behold, I have a weapon;   260
A better never did itself sustain
Upon a soldier's thigh. I have seen the day
That with this little arm and this good sword
I have made my way through more impediments
Than twenty times your stop.° But O vain boast!   265
Who can control his fate? 'Tis not so now.
Be not afraid, though you do see me weaponed.
Here is my journey's end, here is my butt,°
And very seamark° of my utmost sail:
Do you go back dismayed? 'Tis a lost° fear.   270
Man but a rush° against Othello's breast,
And he retires. Where should Othello go?
Now, how dost thou look now? O ill-starred wench!
Pale as thy smock! When we shall meet at compt,°
This look of thine will hurl my soul from heaven,   275
And fiends will snatch at it. Cold, cold, my girl?
Even like thy chastity.
O cursèd, cursèd slave! Whip me, ye devils,
From the possession of this heavenly sight!
Blow me about in winds! roast me in sulphur!   280
Wash me in steep-down gulfs of liquid fire!
Oh Desdemon! dead Desdemon! dead! Oh! Oh!

Enter Lodovico, Montano, Iago [as prisoner], and Officers; Cassio in a chair.

LODOVICO: Where is this rash and most unfortunate man?
OTHELLO: That's he that was Othello. Here I am.

---

254 ice brook: I.e., a Spanish blade, tempered in cold running water.   **259 naked:**
Disarmed.   **265 stop:** Power to stop.   **268 butt:** Limit.   **269 seamark:** Beacon,
destination.   **270 lost:** Wasted.   **271 Man but a rush:** Wield only a reed.   **274 compt:**
Final accounting, Last Judgment.

LODOVICO: Where is that viper? Bring the villain forth. 285
OTHELLO: I look down towards his feet° — but that's a fable.
    If that thou be'st a devil, I cannot kill thee.

[Wounds Iago.]

LODOVICO: Wrench his sword from him.

[Othello is disarmed.]

IAGO: I bleed, sir, but not killed.
OTHELLO: I am not sorry neither. I'ld have thee live;
    For in my sense, 'tis happiness to die. 290
LODOVICO: O thou Othello that wert once so good,
    Fall'n in the practice° of a damnèd slave,
    What shall be said to thee?
OTHELLO: Why, anything;
    An honorable murderer, if you will;
    For naught did I in hate, but all in honor. 295
LODOVICO: This wretch hath part confessed his villainy.
    Did you and he consent in° Cassio's death?
OTHELLO: Ay.
CASSIO: Dear general, I never gave you cause.
OTHELLO: I do believe it, and I ask your pardon. 300
    Will you, I pray, demand that demi-devil
    Why he hath thus ensnared my soul and body?
IAGO: Demand me nothing. What you know, you know.
    From this time forth I never will speak word.
LODOVICO: What, not to pray?
GRATIANO: Torments will ope your lips. 305
OTHELLO: Well, thou dost best.
LODOVICO: Sir, you shall understand what hath befall'n,
    Which, as I think, you know not. Here is a letter
    Found in the pocket of the slain Roderigo;
    And here another. The one of them imports 310
    The death of Cassio to be undertook
    By Roderigo.
OTHELLO: O villain!
CASSIO: Most heathenish and most gross!
LODOVICO: Now here's another discontented paper
    Found in the pocket too; and this, it seems, 315
    Roderigo meant t' have sent this damnèd villain;
    But that, belike, Iago in the nick°
    Came in and satisfied him.
OTHELLO: O thou pernicious caitiff! —

286 I . . . feet: I.e., to see if they are cloven, like the Devil's.   **292 practice:** Plot.   **297 consent in:** Agree upon.   **317 nick:** Nick of time.

How came you, Cassio, by that handkerchief
That was my wife's?

CASSIO: I found it in my chamber;   320
And he himself confessed but even now
That there he dropped it for a special purpose
Which wrought to his desire.

OTHELLO: O fool! fool! fool!

CASSIO: There is besides in Roderigo's letter,
How he upbraids Iago that he made him   325
Brave me upon the watch; whereon it came
That I was cast;° and even but now he spake,
After long seeming dead—Iago hurt him,
Iago set him on.

LODOVICO: You must forsake this room and go with us.   330
Your power and your command is taken off,
And Cassio rules in Cyprus. For this slave,
If there be any cunning cruelty
That can torment him much and hold him long,
It shall be his. You shall close prisoner rest   335
Till that the nature of your fault be known
To the Venetian state. Come, bring away.

OTHELLO: Soft you! a word or two before you go.
I have done the state some service, and they know't.
No more of that. I pray you, in your letters,   340
When you shall these unlucky° deeds relate,
Speak of me as I am. Nothing extenuate,
Nor set down aught in malice. Then must you speak
Of one that loved not wisely, but too well;
Of one not easily jealous, but, being wrought,   345
Perplexed° in the extreme; of one whose hand,
Like the base Judean,° threw a pearl away
Richer than all his tribe; of one whose subdued° eyes,
Albeit unusèd to the melting mood,
Drop tears as fast as the Arabian trees   350
Their med'cinable gum. Set you down this.
And say besides that in Aleppo once,
Where a malignant and a turbaned Turk
Beat a Venetian and traduced the state,
I took by th' throat the circumcisèd dog   355
And smote him—thus.

(He stabs himself.)

327 cast: Dismissed.   **341 unlucky:** Fatal.   **346 Perplexed:** Distracted.   **347 Judean:**
Judas Iscariot (?) (quarto reads "Indian").   **348 subdued:** I.e., conquered by grief.

LODOVICO: O bloody period!°
GRATIANO: All that's spoke is marred.
OTHELLO: I kissed thee ere I killed thee. No way but this,
    Killing myself, to die upon a kiss.

(He [falls upon the bed and] dies.)

CASSIO: This did I fear, but thought he had no weapon;   360
    For he was great of heart.
LODOVICO *[to Iago]*:   O Spartan dog,
    More fell° than anguish, hunger, or the sea!
    Look on the tragic loading of this bed.
    This is thy work. The object poisons sight;
    Let it be hid.° Gratiano, keep the house,   365
    And seize upon° the fortunes of the Moor,
    For they succeed on you. To you, lord governor,
    Remains the censure° of this hellish villain,
    The time, the place, the torture. O, enforce it!
    Myself will straight aboard, and to the state   370
    This heavy act with heavy heart relate.

Exeunt.

357 period: Ending.   **362 fell:** Cruel.   **365 Let it be hid:** I.e., draw the bed curtains.
366 seize upon: Take legal possession of.   **368 censure:** Judicial sentence.

≡ THINKING ABOUT THE TEXT

1. Jealousy is one of the central motifs in this play. Which characters are jealous, and for what reasons?

2. Is Iago diabolically devious and clever, or is Othello especially gullible, or is it a combination of both? How would you respond if a trusted friend made similar accusations against someone whom you cared for deeply?

3. Is Othello's tragic flaw — the quality that leads to his downfall — jealousy or something else, perhaps credulity?

4. Is it possible for Othello's love to turn so quickly into hate?

5. How might the end of the play and the final resolution of the characters' fates be seen as Shakespeare's commentary on jealousy?

A. C. BRADLEY
The Noble Othello

A. C. Bradley (1851–1935), a British literary critic and highly influential Shakespearean scholar, was the youngest boy among twenty-one children. His father was a well-regarded preacher. Bradley attended Balliol College at Oxford University and later was a professor at the University of Liverpool and at Oxford. His books

include Oxford Lectures on Poetry *(1909) and* Shakespearean Tragedy *(1904),*
where "The Noble Othello" appeared. The essays published in both books were orig-
inally lectures delivered by Bradley. Upon his death, Bradley's will established a fel-
lowship for English literary scholars. Here, Bradley refutes the common notion that
Othello was unjustifiably and easily jealous by considering how Othello's character
diminishes only in light of the evidence Iago provides regarding Desdemona's sup-
posed affair.

This character is so noble, Othello's feelings and actions follow so inevitably
from it and from the forces brought to bear on it, and his sufferings are so
heart-rending, that he stirs, I believe, in most readers a passion of mingled love
and pity which they feel for no other hero in Shakespeare, and to which not
even Mr. Swinburne can do more than justice. Yet there are some critics and
not a few readers who cherish a grudge against him. They do not merely think
that in the later stages of his temptation he showed a certain obtuseness, and
that, to speak pedantically, he acted with unjustifiable precipitance and violence; no one, I suppose, denies that. But, even when they admit that he was
not of a jealous temper, they consider that he *was* "easily jealous"; they seem
to think that it was inexcusable in him to feel any suspicion of his wife at all;
and they blame him for never suspecting Iago or asking him for evidence.
I refer to this attitude of mind chiefly in order to draw attention to certain points
in the story. It comes partly from mere inattention (for Othello did suspect Iago
and did ask him for evidence); partly from a misconstruction of the text which
makes Othello appear jealous long before he really is so; and partly from failure
to realize certain essential facts. I will begin with these.

(1) Othello, we have seen, was trustful, and thorough in his trust. He put
entire confidence in the honesty of Iago, who had not only been his companion in arms, but, as he believed, had just proved his faithfulness in the matter
of the marriage. This confidence was misplaced, and we happen to know it;
but it was no sign of stupidity in Othello. For his opinion of Iago was the opinion of practically everyone who knew him: and that opinion was that Iago was
before all things "honest," his very faults being those of excess in honesty. This
being so, even if Othello had not been trustful and simple, it would have been
quite unnatural in him to be unmoved by the warnings of so honest a friend,
warnings offered with extreme reluctance and manifestly from a sense of a
friend's duty. *Any* husband would have been troubled by them.

(2) Iago does not bring these warnings to a husband who had lived with a
wife for months and years and knew her like his sister or his bosom-friend. Nor is
there any ground in Othello's character for supposing that, if he had been such
a man, he would have felt and acted as he does in the play. But he was newly
married; in the circumstances he cannot have known much of Desdemona
before his marriage; and further he was conscious of being under the spell of a
feeling which can give glory to the truth but can also give it to a dream.

(3) This consciousness in any imaginative man is enough, in such circumstances, to destroy his confidence in his powers of perception. In Othello's

case, after a long and most artful preparation, there now comes, to reinforce its effect, the suggestions that he is not an Italian, nor even a European; that he is totally ignorant of the thoughts and the customary morality of Venetian women; that he had himself seen in Desdemona's deception of her father how perfect an actress she could be. As he listens in horror, for a moment at least the past is revealed to him in a new and dreadful light, and the ground seems to sink under his feet. These suggestions are followed by a tentative but hideous and humiliating insinuation of what his honest and much-experienced friend fears may be the true explanation of Desdemona's rejection of acceptable suitors, and of her strange, and naturally temporary, preference for a black man. Here Iago goes too far. He sees something in Othello's face that frightens him, and he breaks off. Nor does this idea take any hold of Othello's mind. But it is not surprising that his utter powerlessness to repel it on the ground of knowledge of his wife, or even of that instinctive interpretation of character which is possible between persons of the same race, should complete his misery, so that he feels he can bear no more, and abruptly dismisses his friend (III. iii. 238).

Now I repeat that *any* man situated as Othello was would have been disturbed by Iago's communications, and I add that many men would have been made wildly jealous. But up to this point, where Iago is dismissed, Othello, I must maintain, does not show jealousy. His confidence is shaken, he is confused and deeply troubled, he feels even horror; but he is not yet jealous in the proper sense of that word. In his soliloquy (III. iii. 258ff.) the beginning of this passion may be traced; but it is only after an interval of solitude, when he has had time to dwell on the idea presented to him, and especially after statements of fact, not mere general grounds of suspicion, are offered, that the passion lays hold of him. Even then, however, and indeed to the very end, he is quite unlike the essentially jealous man, quite unlike Leontes. No doubt the thought of another man's possessing the woman he loves is intolerable to him; no doubt the sense of insult and the impulse of revenge are at times most violent; and these are the feelings of jealousy proper. But these are not the chief or the deepest source of Othello's suffering. It is the wreck of his faith and his love. It is the feeling,

If she be false, oh then Heaven mocks itself;

the feeling,

O Iago, the pity of it, Iago!

the feeling,

But there where I have garner'd up my heart,
Where either I must live, or bear no life;
The fountain from the which my current runs,
Or else dries up—to be discarded thence. . . .

You will find nothing like this in Leontes.

Up to this point, it appears to me, there is not a syllable to be said against Othello. But the play is a tragedy, and from this point we may abandon the

5

ungrateful and undramatic task of awarding praise and blame. When Othello, after a brief interval, re-enters (III. iii. 329), we see at once that the poison has been at work, and "burns like the mines of sulphur."

> Look where he comes! Not poppy, nor mandragora,
> Nor all the drowsy syrups of the world,
> Shall ever medicine thee to that sweet sleep
> Which thou owedst yesterday.

He is "on the rack," in an agony so unbearable that he cannot endure the sight of Iago. Anticipating the probability that Iago has spared him the whole truth, he feels that in that case his life is over and his "occupation gone" with all its glories. But he has not abandoned hope. The bare possibility that his friend is deliberately deceiving him — though such a deception would be a thing so monstrously wicked that he can hardly conceive it credible — is a kind of hope. He furiously demands proof, ocular proof. And when he is compelled to see that he is demanding an impossibility he still demands evidence. He forces it from the unwilling witness, and hears the maddening tale of Cassio's dream. It is enough. And if it were not enough, has he not sometimes seen a handkerchief spotted with strawberries in his wife's hand? Yes, it was his first gift to her.

> I know not that; but such a handkerchief —
> I am sure it was your wife's — did I to-day
> See Cassio wipe his beard with.

"If it be that," he answers — but what need to test the fact? The "madness of revenge" is in his blood, and hesitation is a thing he never knew. He passes judgment, and controls himself only to make his sentence a solemn vow.

The Othello of the Fourth Act is Othello in his fall. His fall is never complete, but he is much changed. Towards the close of the Temptation-scene he becomes at times most terrible, but his grandeur remains almost undiminished. Even in the following scene (III. iv.), where he goes to test Desdemona in the matter of the handkerchief, and receives a fatal confirmation of her guilt, our sympathy with him is hardly touched by any feeling of humiliation. But in the Fourth Act "Chaos has come." A slight interval of time may be admitted here. It is but slight; for it was necessary for Iago to hurry on, and terribly dangerous to leave a chance for a meeting of Cassio with Othello; and his insight into Othello's nature taught him that his plan was to deliver blow on blow, and never to allow his victim to recover from the confusion of the first shock. Still there is a slight interval; and when Othello reappears we see at a glance that he is a changed man. He is physically exhausted, and his mind is dazed. He sees everything blurred through a mist of blood and tears. He has actually forgotten the incident of the handkerchief, and has to be reminded of it. When Iago, perceiving that he can now risk almost any lie, tells him that Cassio has confessed his guilt, Othello, the hero who has seemed to us only second to Coriolanus in physical power, trembles all over; he mutters disjointed words; a blackness suddenly intervenes between his eyes and the world; he takes it for the shuddering testimony of nature to the horror he has just heard, and he falls senseless to the ground. When he recovers it is to watch Cassio, as he imagines, laughing over his shame. It is an imposition so gross, and should have been one so perilous, that Iago would never have ventured it before. But he is safe now. The sight only adds to the confusion of intellect the madness of rage; and a ravenous thirst for revenge, contending with motions of infinite longing and regret, conquers them. The delay till night-fall is torture to him. His self-control has wholly deserted him, and he strikes his wife in the presence of the Venetian envoy. He is so lost to all sense of reality that he never asks himself what will follow the deaths of Cassio and his wife. An ineradicable instinct of justice, rather than any last quiver of hope, leads him to question Emilia; but nothing could convince him now, and there follows the dreadful scene of accusation; and then, to allow us the relief of burning hatred and burning tears, the interview of Desdemona with Iago, and that last talk of hers with Emilia, and her last song.

But before the end there is again a change. The supposed death of Cassio (V. i.) satiates the thirst for vengeance. The Othello who enters the bed-chamber with the words,   10

> It is the cause, it is the cause, my soul,

is not the man of the Fourth Act. The deed he is bound to do is no murder, but a sacrifice. He is to save Desdemona from herself, not in hate but in honour; in honour, and also in love. His anger has passed; a boundless sorrow has taken its place; and

> this sorrow's heavenly:
> It strikes where it doth love.

Even when, at the sight of her apparent obduracy, and at the hearing of words which by a crowning fatality can only reconvince him of her guilt, these feelings give way to others, it is to righteous indignation they give way, not to rage; and, terribly painful as this scene is, there is almost nothing here to diminish the admiration and love which heighten pity. And pity itself vanishes, and love and admiration alone remain, in the majestic dignity and sovereign ascendancy of the close. Chaos has come and gone; and the Othello of the Council-chamber and the quay of Cyprus has returned, or a greater and nobler Othello still. As he speaks those final words in which all the glory and agony of his life — long ago in India and Arabia and Aleppo, and afterwards in Venice, and now in Cyprus — seem to pass before us, like the pictures that flash before the eyes of a drowning man, a triumphant scorn for the fetters of the flesh and the littleness of all the lives that must survive him sweeps our grief away, and when he dies upon a kiss the most painful of all tragedies leaves us for the moment free from pain, and exulting in the power of "love and man's unconquerable mind."   *[1904]*

JEFFRIE G. MURPHY
Jealousy, Shame, and the Rival

Jeffrie G. Murphy (b. 1941) is a distinguished legal and moral philosopher. He has published a number of books, including Getting Even: Forgiveness and Mercy *(2004) and most recently* Punishment and the Moral Emotions: Essays in Law, Morality, and Religion *(2012). His essay, "Jealousy, Shame, and the Rival," which appeared in the journal* Philosophical Studies, *is essentially a critique of Jerome Neu's work on jealousy in* A Tear Is an Intellectual Thing *(2000). Murphy maintains that Othello's acts of jealousy stem not from a fear of loss of love (as Neu's definition of jealousy requires) but from a fear of the shame brought on by that loss.*

When Jerome Neu's essay "Jealous Thoughts" was published in 1980, jealousy was widely regarded — at least in leftist intellectual and cultural circles — as an irrational and even evil "bourgeois" passion — one tied to a capitalistic market conception of human relations. The jealous person — according to this view — regards the loved person as a kind of object — as owned property over which the lover has rights. Jealousy is thus a kind of property fear — analogous to the fear of theft. The fear intrinsically involves the belief that one risks losing a possessed loved object to whose love one has a right.

Neu — rightly in my judgment — rejects this account of jealousy as psychologically shallow. He argues — in "Jealous Thoughts" and in the later "Jealous Afterthoughts" — that psychoanalytic theory teaches us that love gets its initial life and draws its basic character from the Oedipal situation. The child so needs and depends upon the mother that loss of the mother's love would appear both as biological and psychological annihilation — psychological because the very self of the child is identified with that of the mother. Any perceived rival for the mother's affections (initially the father) is seen as a threat to security and thus provokes in the child a fear of loss of love. It is here that love and jealousy begin, develop through what Winnicott calls "transitional objects," and assume forms that will persist in adult life. To love is, at least in part, to be so identified with another person that the loss of that person's love will be perceived as loss or annihilation of one's very self or personality. Jealousy, then, is simply the fear that one will lose the love of a person with whom one is psychologically identified — an instance of the fear of annihilation. "If others do not love us," Neu writes, "we will disintegrate."

This fear is not, according to Neu, grounded in a bourgeois or possessive model of human relations, for one can fear the loss of love without believing that one owns the loved person or that one has a right to that person's love. All that is required is that one has the love. Love, then, in part involves self identification — when we lose it we lose ourselves, having our vulnerabilities open and unsupported. All human beings, regardless of social setting — bourgeois or communitarian — fear the exposure of vulnerabilities and the resulting loss of self. According to Neu, this fear is jealousy. Thus jealousy and love are necessarily connected—we cannot get rid of the former without losing the latter.

There are some questions that I immediately want to raise about this analysis. First, what about unrequited love? There are surely intense cases of jealousy where the jealous person knows full well that the love he feels is not returned. Not having it, he cannot fear its loss. Thus it cannot be literally true to say, as Neu does in the first essay, that "to be jealous over someone, you must believe that they love you or have loved you."

Unrequited love thus presents a problem for Neu's original analysis, but I think that the problem can be rather easily fixed. One might draw on some of the instructive things that Neu has to say in the later essay about the role of illusion and projection in erotic love, or one might suggest (think of the John Hinckley/Jodie Foster case) that what the jealous unrequited lover fears is not the loss of love (which he clearly does not have) but the loss of the *possibility* of love (which he may still hope for).

There is also, of course, the problem of jealousy over love that one believes is already hopelessly lost. Othello—often presented (as he is by Neu) as a paradigm of a jealous person—is frequently thought to be most jealous *after* he believes that he has lost Desdemona's love to Cassio. But surely this cannot be understood simply as the fear of loss of love, for how can one fear to lose what one has already lost?

In keeping with the spirit—if not the exact letter—of Neu's analysis, one might try to deal with the Othello case in this way: The fear that constitutes Othello's jealousy should not be seen as the fear of the loss of love (it is simply too late for *that* fear) but rather as the fear of the personal disintegration that may result from that loss.

Perhaps killing or other acts of revenge against the lost lover are strategies to defend against this possible consequence. Perhaps they are preventive strategies that seek the prevention, not of the loss of love, but rather of the dire consequences that—according to Neu—may flow from that loss. Or perhaps they are *retributive* strategies—seeking to inflict punishment on the person who has caused such personal disruption and pain at the core of one's very self. Thus it is possible that the jealous person who inflicts pain over love lost is somewhat like the lover of a murder victim who believes (sometimes rightly, sometimes wrongly) that a kind of closure will result from the execution of the killer.

We are all, alas, familiar with newspaper reports that read "He killed her in a jealous rage." Such a phrase might well describe Othello, but I am not sure. He was surely jealous when he suspected Desdemona of infidelity, but was he jealous at the time he murdered her? Perhaps he was simply vindictive. However, if such murderous rage is properly to be identified as "jealous," it surely cannot be motivated by the fear of losing love since the surest way permanently to lose love is to kill the lover. Dead people cannot love. So what goes on in these cases is either not jealousy at all but rather something else—vengeance perhaps—or it is jealousy motivated by something other than the fear of losing love. Perhaps it is motivated by a deep aversion to certain *consequences* of losing love. Neu would stress the consequence of annihilation or disintegration—since that is so integral to his analysis of love—but I shall later argue that one of these consequences may be *shame*. . . .

It is a perhaps sad but surely true claim that, to a substantial degree,   10
people derive their sense of self worth from the judgments of others. If we love a person, we tend to take that person's judgments in these matters quite seriously—i.e., we take them in some sense to be accurate judges of our own worth. (The mentally healthy among us—if there are any—would not follow Groucho Marx in contemptuously refusing to join any club that would have us for members; nor would we deeply mistrust the judgment of any person who could love us.) If we add to this the fact that non-moral judgments of worth are generally comparative, then the fact that a judge whom we trust prefers someone over us may make us doubt our own worth or value. So jealousy may stand as testimony, not merely to our need for love and attention, but also to our need for validation by another. We are thus shamed by rejection.

It is, of course, not merely the judgment of the loved person who matters. The judgment of a wider circle of people matters as well, for even the strongest of us needs validation from some relevant reference group. Consider Achilles. His rage over the loss of Briseis to Agamemnon is to a substantial degree based on his loss of honor—face and standing—in the eyes of his fellow warriors. He has been shamed by having the girl taken from him.

I think that similar shame may be found in many contemporary cases of jealousy and loss. The jilted lover is often ashamed to report this to others—thinking that it casts some bad reflection on his or her worth or standing. (Sometimes—for similar reasons I suspect—people are reluctant even to admit that they are divorced.) Being a victim of infidelity is, among other unpleasant things, shameful and embarrassing. Perhaps this in part explains the rage that is often found in those who have been jilted—a rage that may provoke expensive and vicious lawsuits, small or even major acts of retribution, and sometimes even murder. Why do people do these things? These acts will not get the love back, but they may go a long way—at least in the eyes of the perpetrator—toward saving face, restoring lost status and honor, and thus overcoming the shame of it all. If one believes that he has been brought down by another, he may find it therapeutic—or think he will find it therapeutic—to bring that person down as well. I am not, of course, saying that such a response is justified, only that it is—unfortunately—not unusual (particularly among men). As Norman Mailer (who ought to know) has asked: "Isn't human nature depressing?"

To summarize and conclude: I think that Neu has provided us with many profound insights on jealousy and its relation to love. Indeed, if I were asked to recommend just one philosophical essay on jealousy, it would be Neu's. It is, I think, the best place to start—for its insights, the framework it provides, and the provocative questions it forces us to raise.

In raising these questions, however, I have come to think that Neu's account of jealousy needs to be supplemented in certain ways. In particular, I have suggested that *shame* needs to be stressed in order fully to account for the role of the rival in jealousy.

[2002]

≡ MAKING COMPARISONS

1. Murphy focuses on jealousy as having a psychological basis, arguing that jealousy is "the fear that one will lose the love of a person with whom one is psychologically identified" (para. 2) and later adds shame into the mix of jealousy. Bradley, however, focuses more on whether the consideration of Othello as an unjustifiably jealous character is fair, or common. Explain why one of these interpretations helps you understand *Othello* better.

2. Bradley claims that the true source of Othello's suffering is "the wreck of his faith and his love" (para. 5). Do you think Murphy agrees?

3. From each essay, choose a sentence or two that impresses you as offering an interesting insight into the play. How did each one deepen your understanding of *Othello*?

≡ WRITING ABOUT ISSUES

1. Research the nature of and causes for jealousy. In an essay, argue that the three scholars here do or do not do justice to the complexity of this emotion.

2. Research a feminist or gender studies interpretation of *Othello*. Argue in an essay that this perspective is or is not a powerful tool in understanding the characters in the play.

3. Research either a postcolonial or New Historicism criticism on *Othello* and write an argument that one or a combination of these approaches gives us plausible insights into the play.

☰ Contexts for Research: Social Disruption, Personal Anxiety, and "Dover Beach"

MATTHEW ARNOLD, "Dover Beach"

CONTEXTS FOR RESEARCH:
CHARLES DICKENS, From *Hard Times*

FRIEDRICH ENGELS, From *The Condition of the Working Class in England*

JAMES ELI ADAMS, "Narrating Nature: Darwin"

Considered one of the greatest poems of the Victorian period, Matthew Arnold's "Dover Beach" expresses the spiritual malaise troubling many educated people in the middle of the nineteenth century. Although England was becoming the most powerful country in the world, there were serious social problems left unattended as it focused on its empire. And Matthew Arnold was keenly aware of them. He was an educational reformer, who promoted a rich intellectual and ethical spirit in English society. Moral and social issues were crucial for him, and he championed the study of the best that was said and thought. But there was such a class division in England that only a small fraction of the population was able to reap the rewards Arnold thought a humanistic education could deliver. Such injustice troubled him.

Industrialization brought power and wealth to some and great poverty to many others. It is difficult to educate children when they are starving and cold. Prostitution was also a huge social problem, compounded by disease and poverty. Child labor was also widespread, and hundreds of thousands of nine- and ten-year-olds were working sixty hours a week under gruesomely unsafe and brutal conditions. To add to Arnold's ethical discomfort, scientific advances in geology and biology seemed to many to be in direct contradiction to the natural history found in the first book of the bible, Genesis. Scientific evidence was demonstrating that the earth was millions of years old, not six thousand. Although his ideas had been well known in scientific circles for a while, Charles Darwin's *On the Origin of the Species* (1859) dealt a body blow to traditional religious ideas of creation with the theory that all life had evolved over millions of years through a process that put an emphasis on chance and randomness over a clear divine plan. If the bible was so wrong about these facts, perhaps the whole basis of Christianity should be called into question. Such thoughts produced a crisis of faith for many thinkers like Arnold.

"Dover Beach" reflects a sense of spiritual ambiguity and abandonment as Arnold contemplates the "turbid ebb and flow / Of human misery." Although a progressive who supported objective scientific investigation and discovery, Arnold was disturbed by the reality that we might be on our own in the universe. He hears the "melancholy, long, withdrawing roar" of traditional faith and looks to love for solace in a world that is not as simple and comforting as it once seemed. And so, like so many before and after him, he hopes that love, or maybe simply loyalty, can be an antidote to his discontented soul. Although many critics see the other person in the room with Arnold as the reader, feminists object that the person never speaks, just listens. Such a patriarchal view, that women should comfort men in their world-weariness, was quite common in Victorian England but is problematic in today's world, where men and women must confront the disturbing issues of the day equally.

We have included three cultural contexts for Arnold's poem that address some of the issues troubling Arnold and his contemporaries—one by the novelist Charles Dickens, who, like Arnold, opposed the kind of utilitarian education portrayed in the opening chapters of *Hard Times*. Friedrich Engels gives us an eyewitness account of the kind of poverty that Arnold would have seen everywhere. And, finally, a brief selection from *A History of Victorian Literature* comments on the impact of evolution.

≡ BEFORE YOU READ

How does our culture promote the idea that love is an antidote to a depressing world? What social, political, or scientific issue would you say affects your generation the most?

MATTHEW ARNOLD
Dover Beach

Victorian poet Matthew Arnold (1822–1889) was the eldest son of Thomas Arnold, an influential clergyman and historian and headmaster of Rugby, one of England's most prestigious college preparatory schools. He grew up in an educational milieu in which religious, political, and social issues were discussed in depth. He went on to Oxford, where he eventually achieved success despite his irreverence and eccentricity. In 1851, he became an inspector of schools and served in this capacity for thirty-five years. He drew on his experiences with people of diverse social classes to become a keen critic of British education and culture, and he expressed his views of society in critical essays on literary, social, and religious issues as well as in poems. "Dover Beach" may have been written during the months just before or just after Arnold's marriage and honeymoon, which included a ferry ride from Dover, England, to Calais, France.

> The sea is calm tonight.
> The tide is full, the moon lies fair
> Upon the straits;—on the French coast the light
> Gleams and is gone; the cliffs of England stand,
> Glimmering and vast, out in the tranquil bay.   5
> Come to the window, sweet is the night-air!
> Only, from the long line of spray
> Where the sea meets the moon-blanched land,
> Listen! you hear the grating roar
> Of pebbles which the waves draw back, and fling,   10

Rischgitz/Getty Images

At their return, up the high strand,
Begin, and cease, and then again begin,
With tremulous cadence slow, and bring
The eternal note of sadness in.

Sophocles long ago   15
Heard it on the Aegean, and it brought
Into his mind the turbid ebb and flow
Of human misery;° we
Find also in the sound a thought,
Hearing it by this distant northern sea.   20

The Sea of Faith
Was once, too, at the full, and round earth's shore
Lay like the folds of a bright girdle furled.
But now I only hear

Its melancholy, long, withdrawing roar,   25
Retreating, to the breath
Of the night-wind, down the vast edges drear
And naked shingles° of the world.

15–18 Sophocles . . . misery: In *Antigone*, Sophocles compares the disasters that beset the house of Oedipus to a mounting tide.   **28 shingles:** Pebble beach.

Ah, love, let us be true
To one another! for the world, which seems   30
To lie before us like a land of dreams,
So various, so beautiful, so new,
Hath really neither joy, nor love, nor light,
Nor certitude, nor peace, nor help for pain;
And we are here as on a darkling plain   35
Swept with confused alarms of struggle and flight,
Where ignorant armies clash by night.   *[1867]*

≡ THINKING ABOUT THE TEXT

1. In trying to re-create this scene — say, for a movie script — what would you have the lovers look like? Where would the couple be positioned? If you were the director, how would you explain the scene to the actors — that is, what is the speaker saying? Put another way, what argument is being made?

2. Arnold uses the sea as a metaphor. What do you think it represents? What other metaphors and similes are used? Are they effective in making his point?

3. What specifically triggers Arnold's despondency? What was comforting about the "Sea of Faith"? What do you think Arnold meant by the sentence beginning with "But now I only hear . . ." (line 24)?

4. In the film *The Anniversary Party*, Kevin Kline's character reads the last stanza of this poem to a couple celebrating their sixth wedding anniversary. Some critics saw it as an ironic joke, others as a parody of a "sweet" love poem. What is it about the poem that seems to make it inappropriate for such an occasion? Would you send it to your beloved? Why, or why not?

5. What specific reasons does the speaker give for the lovers to be true to each other, beginning with "for the world" (line 30)? Is this an attitude you share? Do you know others who agree? Is this an extreme position? What would the opposite view be? Is this extreme, as well? How does this poem express a contemporary feeling? If you were Arnold's editor, what changes would you suggest to reflect contemporary ideas about relationships between lovers?

CHARLES DICKENS
From *Hard Times*

Charles Dickens (1812–1870), one of the most famous, prolific, and respected novelists in English literature, was born into a family of modest means and had to begin work at twelve years old, an event that would have a profound effect on his thinking and writing. The appalling conditions he experienced find their way into his great novels, including Oliver Twist, David Copperfield, *and* Great Expectations. *Most of his novels were commercially successful as serializations in monthly magazines, which was a common means of publishing at the time. At the height of his fame, Dickens travelled widely, giving readings in Europe and America. He read voraciously and was intensely interested in the political and social issues of the day. The excerpt here, the first two chapters of* Hard Times *(1859), is a parody-like critique of Jeremy Bentham's utilitarianism, which promoted the idea of the greatest happiness for the greatest number. Like Matthew Arnold, Dickens opposed an education of bare facts, a dehumanized education that did little else but prepare children for the further dehumanization of the factory. On his tomb in Poet's Corner in Westminster Abbey is inscribed the following: "He was a sympathiser to the poor, the sick, and the oppressed; and by his death, one of England's greatest writers is lost to the world."*

"Now, what I want is, Facts. Teach these boys and girls nothing but Facts. Facts alone are wanted in life. Plant nothing else, and root out everything else. You can only form the minds of reasoning animals upon Facts: nothing else will ever be of any service to them. This is the principle on which I bring up my own children, and this is the principle on which I bring up these children. Stick to Facts, sir!"

The scene was a plain, bare, monotonous vault of a school-room, and the speaker's square forefinger emphasized his observations by underscoring every sentence with a line on the schoolmaster's sleeve. The emphasis was helped by the speaker's square wall of a forehead, which had his eyebrows for its base, while his eyes found commodious cellarage in two dark caves, overshadowed by the wall. The emphasis was helped by the speaker's mouth, which was wide, thin, and hard set. The emphasis was helped by the speaker's voice, which was inflexible, dry, and dictatorial. The emphasis was helped by the speaker's hair, which bristled on the skirts of his bald head, a plantation of firs to keep the wind from its shining surface, all covered with knobs, like the crust of a plum pie, as if the head had scarcely warehouse-room for the hard facts stored inside. The speaker's obstinate carriage, square coat, square legs, square shoulders, — nay, his very neckcloth, trained to take him by the throat with an unaccommodating grasp, like a stubborn fact, as it was, — all helped the emphasis.

"In this life, we want nothing but Facts, sir; nothing but Facts!"

The speaker, and the schoolmaster, and the third grown person present, all backed a little, and swept with their eyes the inclined plane of little vessels then and there arranged in order, ready to have imperial gallons of facts poured into them until they were full to the brim. [. . .]

Thomas Gradgrind, sir. A man of realities. A man of facts and calculations. 5
A man who proceeds upon the principle that two and two are four, and nothing over, and who is not to be talked into allowing for anything over. Thomas
Gradgrind, sir — peremptorily Thomas — Thomas Gradgrind. With a rule and
a pair of scales, and the multiplication table always in his pocket, sir, ready to
weigh and measure any parcel of human nature, and tell you exactly what
it comes to. It is a mere question of figures, a case of simple arithmetic. You
might hope to get some other nonsensical belief into the head of George
Gradgrind, or Augustus Gradgrind, or John Gradgrind, or Joseph Gradgrind
(all supposititious, non-existent persons), but into the head of Thomas
Gradgrind — no, sir!

In such terms Mr. Gradgrind always mentally introduced himself, whether
to his private circle of acquaintance, or to the public in general. In such terms,
no doubt, substituting the words "boys and girls," for "sir," Thomas Gradgrind
now presented Thomas Gradgrind to the little pitchers before him, who were
to be filled so full of facts.

Indeed, as he eagerly sparkled at them from the cellarage before mentioned, he seemed a kind of cannon loaded to the muzzle with facts, and prepared to blow them clean out of the regions of childhood at one discharge. He
seemed a galvanizing apparatus, too, charged with a grim mechanical substitute for the tender young imaginations that were to be stormed away.

"Girl number twenty," said Mr. Gradgrind, squarely pointing with his
square forefinger, "I don't know that girl. Who is that girl?"

"Sissy Jupe, sir," explained number twenty, blushing, standing up, and
curtseying.

"Sissy is not a name," said Mr. Gradgrind. "Don't call yourself Sissy. Call 10
yourself Cecilia."

"It's father as calls me Sissy, sir," returned the young girl in a trembling
voice, and with another curtsey.

"Then he has no business to do it," said Mr. Gradgrind. "Tell him he
mustn't. Cecilia Jupe. Let me see. What is your father?"

"He belongs to the horse-riding, if you please, sir."

Mr. Gradgrind frowned, and waved off the objectionable calling with his
hand.

"We don't want to know anything about that, here. You mustn't tell us 15
about that, here. Your father breaks horses, don't he?"

"If you please, sir, when they can get any to break, they do break horses in
the ring, sir."

"You mustn't tell us about the ring, here. Very well, then. Describe your
father as a horsebreaker. He doctors sick horses, I dare say?"

"Oh yes, sir."

"Very well, then. He is a veterinary surgeon, a farrier, and horsebreaker.
Give me your definition of a horse."

(Sissy Jupe thrown into the greatest alarm by this demand.) 20

"Girl number twenty unable to define a horse!" said Mr. Gradgrind, for the
general behoof of all the little pitchers. "Girl number twenty possessed of no

facts, in reference to one of the commonest of animals! Some boy's definition of a horse. Bitzer, yours."

The square finger, moving here and there, lighted suddenly on Bitzer, perhaps because he chanced to sit in the same ray of sunlight which, darting in at one of the bare windows of the intensely white-washed room, irradiated Sissy. For, the boys and girls sat on the face of the inclined plane in two compact bodies, divided up the centre by a narrow interval; and Sissy, being at the corner of a row on the sunny side, came in for the beginning of a sunbeam, of which Bitzer, being at the corner of a row on the other side, a few rows in advance, caught the end. But, whereas the girl was so dark-eyed and dark-haired, that she seemed to receive a deeper and more lustrous color from the sun, when it shone upon her, the boy was so light-eyed and light-haired that the self-same rays appeared to draw out of him what little color he ever possessed. His cold eyes would hardly have been eyes, but for the short ends of lashes which, by bringing them into immediate contrast with something paler than themselves, expressed their form. His short-cropped hair might have been a mere continuation of the sandy freckles on his forehead and face. His skin was so unwholesomely deficient in the natural tinge, that he looked as though, if he were cut, he would bleed white.

"Bitzer," said Thomas Gradgrind. "Your definition of a horse."

"Quadruped. Graminivorous. Forty teeth, namely twenty-four grinders, four eye-teeth, and twelve incisive. Sheds coat in the spring; in marshy countries, sheds hoofs, too. Hoofs hard, but requiring to be shod with iron. Age known by marks in mouth." Thus (and much more) Bitzer.

"Now girl number twenty," said Mr. Gradgrind. "You know what a horse is."   25

She curtseyed again, and would have blushed deeper, if she could have blushed deeper than she had blushed all this time. Bitzer, after rapidly blinking at Thomas Gradgrind with both eyes at once, and so catching the light upon his quivering ends of lashes that they looked like the antennæ of busy insects, put his knuckles to his freckled forehead, and sat down again.

The third gentleman now stepped forth. A mighty man at cutting and drying, he was; a government officer; in his way (and in most other people's too), a professed pugilist; always in training, always with a system to force down the general throat like a bolus, always to be heard of at the bar of his little Public-office, ready to fight all England. To continue in fistic phraseology, he had a genius for coming up to the scratch, wherever and whatever it was, and proving himself an ugly customer. He would go in and damage any subject whatever with his right, follow up with his left, stop, exchange, counter, bore his opponent (he always fought All England) to the ropes, and fall upon him neatly. He was certain to knock the wind out of common sense, and render that unlucky adversary deaf to the call of time. And he had it in charge from high authority to bring about the great public-office Millennium, when Commissioners should reign upon earth.

"Very well," said this gentleman, briskly smiling, and folding his arms. "That's a horse. Now, let me ask you girls and boys, Would you paper a room with representations of horses?"

After a pause, one half of the children cried in chorus, "Yes, sir!" Upon which the other half, seeing in the gentleman's face that Yes was wrong, cried out in chorus, "No, sir"—as the custom is, in these examinations.

"Of course, No. Why wouldn't you?"   30

A pause. One corpulent slow boy, with a wheezy manner of breathing, ventured the answer, Because he wouldn't paper a room at all, but would paint it.

"You *must* paper it," said the gentleman, rather warmly.

"You must paper it," said Thomas Gradgrind, "whether you like it or not. Don't tell us you wouldn't paper it. What do you mean, boy?"

"I'll explain to you, then," said the gentleman, after another and a dismal pause, "why you wouldn't paper a room with representations of horses. Do you ever see horses walking up and down the sides of rooms in reality—in fact? Do you?"

"Yes, sir!" from one half. "No, sir!" from the other.   35

"Of course no," said the gentleman, with an indignant look at the wrong half. "Why, then, you are not to see anywhere, what you don't see in fact; you are not to have anywhere, what you don't have in fact. What is called Taste, is only another name for Fact." Thomas Gradgrind nodded his approbation.

"This is a new principle, a discovery, a great discovery," said the gentleman. "Now, I'll try you again. Suppose you were going to carpet a room. Would you use a carpet having a representation of flowers upon it?"

There being a general conviction by this time that "No, sir!" was always the right answer to this gentleman, the chorus of No was very strong. Only a few feeble stragglers said Yes: among them Sissy Jupe.

"Girl number twenty," said the gentleman, smiling in the calm strength of knowledge.

Sissy blushed, and stood up.   40

"So you would carpet your room—or your husband's room, if you were a grown woman, and had a husband—with representations of flowers, would you?" said the gentleman. "Why would you?"

"If you please, sir, I am very fond of flowers," returned the girl.

"And is that why you would put tables and chairs upon them, and have people walking over them with heavy boots?"

"It wouldn't hurt them, sir. They wouldn't crush and wither, if you please, sir. They would be the pictures of what was very pretty and pleasant, and I would fancy—"

"Ay, ay, ay! But you mustn't fancy," cried the gentleman, quite elated by   45
coming so happily to his point. "That's it! You are never to fancy."

"You are not, Cecilia Jupe," Thomas Gradgrind solemnly repeated, "to do anything of that kind."

"Fact, fact, fact!" said the gentleman. And "Fact, fact, fact!" repeated Thomas Gradgrind.

"You are to be in all things regulated and governed," said the gentleman, "by fact. We hope to have, before long, a board of fact, composed of commissioners of fact, who will force the people to be a people of fact, and of nothing but fact. You must discard the word Fancy altogether. You have nothing to do with it. You are not to have, in any object of use or ornament, what would be a contradiction in fact. You don't walk upon flowers in fact; you cannot be allowed to walk upon flowers in carpets. You don't find that foreign birds and butterflies come and perch upon your crockery; you cannot be permitted to paint foreign birds and butterflies upon your crockery. You never meet with quadrupeds going up and down walls; you must not have quadrupeds represented upon walls. You must use," said the gentleman, "for all these purposes, combinations and modifications (in primary colors) of mathematical figures which are susceptible of proof and demonstration. This is the new discovery. This is fact. This is taste."

The girl curtseyed, and sat down. She was very young, and she looked as if she were frightened by the matter-of-fact prospect the world afforded.

"Now, if Mr. M'Choakumchild," said the gentleman, "will proceed to give his first lesson here, Mr. Gradgrind, I shall be happy, at your request, to observe his mode of procedure."   50

Mr. Gradgrind was much obliged. "Mr. M'Choakumchild, we only wait for you."

So, Mr. M'Choakumchild began in his best manner. He and some one hundred and forty other schoolmasters, had been lately turned at the same time, in the same factory, on the same principles, like so many pianoforte legs. He had been put through an immense variety of paces, and had answered volumes of head-breaking questions. Orthography, etymology, syntax, and prosody, biography, astronomy, geography, and general cosmography, the sciences of compound proportion, algebra, land-surveying and levelling, vocal music, and drawing from models, were all at the ends of his ten chilled fingers. He had worked his stony way into Her Majesty's most Honourable Privy Council's Schedule B, and had taken the bloom off the higher branches of mathematics and physical science, French, German, Latin, and Greek. He knew all about all the Water Sheds of all the world (whatever they are), and all the histories of all the peoples, and all the names of all the rivers and mountains, and all the productions, manners, and customs of all the countries, and all their boundaries and bearings on the two and thirty points of the compass. Ah, rather overdone, M'Choakumchild. If he had only learnt a little less, how infinitely better he might have taught much more!   *[1859]*

≡ THINKING ABOUT THE TEXT

1. What is ironic about Sissy not being able to define a horse to Gradgrind's satisfaction? Why is Bitzer's definition more appealing to Gradgrind?

2. What do you think Dickens means by "Ah . . . M'Choakumchild. If he had only learnt a little less, how infinitely better he might have taught much more!" (para. 52)?

3. What is your reading of the last question in the selection? How does Dickens make it fairly obvious that he means us to laugh (wince?) at the two educators?

FRIEDRICH ENGELS
From *The Condition of the Working Class in England*

Friedrich Engels (1820–1895) was born in Germany to wealthy parents who expected him to have a career in business. But early on, Engels had a strong interest in revolutionary politics. When he was twenty-two, his father sent him to Manchester, England, to learn the textile business. Instead, he met a young radical, Mary Burns, who gave him a tour of the horrors of environmental destruction, child labor, and numbing poverty in the slums of Manchester. His observations became the influential text from which our selection is taken. Engels went on to collaborate with Karl Marx on The German Ideology *(1846; published 1932) and* The Communist Manifesto *(1848) and to help him write* Das Kapital *(1867). Engels is considered one of the great social scientists and political theorists of the nineteenth century.*

I may mention just here that the mills almost all adjoin the rivers or the different canals that ramify throughout the city, before I proceed at once to describe the laboring quarters. First of all, there is the old town of Manchester, which lies between the northern boundary of the commercial district and the Irk. Here the streets, even the better ones, are narrow and winding, as Todd Street, Long Millgate, Withy Grove, and Shude Hill, the houses dirty, old, and tumbledown, and the construction of the side streets utterly horrible. Going from the Old Church to Long Millgate, the stroller has at once a row of old-fashioned houses at the right, of which not one has kept its original level; these are remnants of the old pre-manufacturing Manchester, whose former inhabitants have removed with their descendants into better-built districts, and have left the houses, which were not good enough for them, to a population strongly mixed with Irish blood. Here one is in an almost undisguised working-men's quarter, for even the shops and beerhouses hardly take the trouble to exhibit a trifling degree of cleanliness. But all this is nothing in comparison with the courts and lanes which lie behind, to which access can be gained only through covered passages, in which no two human beings can pass at the same time. Of the irregular cramming together of dwellings in ways which defy all rational plan, of the tangle in which they are crowded literally one upon the other, it is impossible to convey an idea. And it is not the buildings surviving from the old times of Manchester which are to blame for this; the confusion has only recently reached its height when every scrap of space left by the old way of building has been filled up and patched over until not a foot of land is left to be further occupied.

The south bank of the Irk is here very steep and between fifteen and thirty feet high. On this declivitous hillside there are planted three rows of houses, of which the lowest rise directly out of the river, while the front walls of the highest stand on the crest of the hill in Long Millgate. Among them are mills on the river, in short, the method of construction is as crowded and disorderly here as in the lower part of Long Millgate. Right and left a multitude of covered passages lead from the main street into numerous courts, and he who turns in thither gets into a filth and disgusting grime, the equal of which is not to be found—especially in the courts which lead down to the Irk, and which contain unqualifiedly the most horrible dwellings which I have yet beheld. In one of these courts there stands directly at the entrance, at the end of the covered passage, a privy without a door, so dirty that the inhabitants can pass into and out of the court only by passing through foul pools of stagnant urine and excrement. This is the first court on the Irk above Ducie Bridge—in case any one should care to look into it. Below it on the river there are several tanneries which fill the whole neighborhood with the stench of animal putrefaction. Below Ducie Bridge the only entrance to most of the houses is by means of narrow, dirty stairs and over heaps of refuse and filth. The first court below Ducie Bridge, known as Allen's Court, was in such a state at the time of the cholera that the sanitary police ordered it evacuated, swept, and disinfected with chloride of lime. Dr. Kay gives a terrible description of the state of this court at that time. Since then, it seems to have been partially torn away and rebuilt; at least looking down from Ducie Bridge, the passer-by sees several ruined walls and heaps of débris with some newer houses. The view from this bridge, mercifully concealed from mortals of small stature by a parapet as high as a man, is characteristic for the whole district. At the bottom flows, or rather stagnates, the Irk, a narrow, coal-black, foul-smelling stream, full of débris and refuse, which it deposits on the shallower right bank. In dry weather, a long string of the most disgusting, blackish-green, slime pools are left standing on this bank, from the depths of which bubbles of miasmatic gas constantly arise and give forth a stench unendurable even on the bridge forty or fifty feet above the surface of the stream. But besides this, the stream itself is checked every few paces by high weirs, behind which slime and refuse accumulate and rot in thick masses. Above the bridge are tanneries, bonemills, and gasworks, from which all drains and refuse find their way into the Irk, which receives further the contents of all the neighboring sewers and privies. It may be easily imagined, therefore, what sort of residue the stream deposits. Below the bridge you look upon the piles of débris, the refuse, filth, and offal from the courts on the steep left bank; here each house is packed close behind its neighbor and a piece of each is visible, all black, smoky, crumbling, ancient, with broken panes and window frames. The background is furnished by old barrack-like factory buildings. On the lower right bank stands a long row of houses and mills; the second house being a ruin without a roof, piled with débris; the third stands so low that the lowest floor is uninhabitable, and therefore without windows or doors. Here the background embraces the pauper burial-ground, the station of the Liverpool and Leeds railway, and, in the rear of this, the Workhouse, the "Poor-Law Bastille" of Manchester, which, like a citadel, looks threateningly down from behind its high walls and parapets on the hilltop, upon the working-people's quarter below.

Above Ducie Bridge, the left bank grows more flat and the right bank steeper, but the condition of the dwellings on both banks grows worse rather than better. He who turns to the left here from the main street, Long Millgate, is lost; he wanders from one court to another, turns countless corners, passes nothing but narrow, filthy nooks and alleys, until after a few minutes he has lost all clue, and knows not whither to turn. Everywhere half or wholly ruined buildings, some of them actually uninhabited, which means a great deal here; rarely a wooden or stone floor to be seen in the houses, almost uniformly broken, ill-fitting windows and doors, and a state of filth! Everywhere heaps of débris, refuse, and offal; standing pools for gutters, and a stench which alone would make it impossible for a human being in any degree civilized to live in such a district. The newly-built extension of the Leeds railway, which crosses the Irk here, has swept away some of these courts and lanes, laying others completely open to view. Immediately under the railway bridge there stands a court, the filth and horrors of which surpass all the others by far, just because it was hitherto so shut off, so secluded that the way to it could not be found without a good deal of trouble. I should never have discovered it myself, without the breaks made by the railway, though I thought I knew this whole region thoroughly. Passing along a rough bank, among stakes and washing-lines, one penetrates into this chaos of small one-storied, one-roomed huts, in most of which there is no artificial floor; kitchen, living and sleeping-room all in one. In such a hole, scarcely five feet long by six broad, I found two beds—and such bedsteads and beds!—which, with a staircase and chimney-place, exactly filled the room. In several others I found absolutely nothing, while the door stood open, and the inhabitants leaned against it. Everywhere before the doors refuse and offal; that any sort of pavement lay underneath could not be seen but only felt, here and there, with the feet. This whole collection of cattle-sheds for human beings was surrounded on two sides by houses and a factory, and on the third by the river, and besides the narrow stair up the bank, a narrow doorway alone led out into another almost equally ill-built, ill-kept labyrinth of dwellings.

Enough! The whole side of the Irk is built in this way, a planless, knotted chaos of houses, more or less on the verge of uninhabitableness, whose unclean interiors fully correspond with their filthy external surroundings. And how could the people be clean with no proper opportunity for satisfying the most natural and ordinary wants? Privies are so rare here that they are either filled up every day, or are too remote for most of the inhabitants to use. How can people wash when they have only the dirty Irk water at hand, while pumps and water pipes can be found in decent parts of the city alone? In truth, it cannot be charged to the account of these helots of modern society if their dwellings are not more cleanly than the pigsties which are here and there to be seen among them. The landlords are not ashamed to let dwellings like the six or seven cellars on the quay directly below Scotland Bridge, the floors of which stand at least two feet below the low-water level of the Irk that flows not six feet away from them; or like the upper floor of the corner-house on the opposite shore directly above the bridge, where the ground floor, utterly uninhabitable, stands deprived of all fittings for doors and windows, a case by no means rare in this region, when this open ground floor is used as a privy by the whole neighborhood for want of other facilities!   *[1844]*

≡ **THINKING ABOUT THE TEXT**

1. What specific details of Engels's description of the slums would have upset Matthew Arnold?

2. What indication of the class conflicts, which Engels would highlight in later books, is most present here?

3. Where is Engels's rage at these deplorable conditions most clear?

JAMES ELI ADAMS

Narrating Nature: Darwin

James Eli Adams (b. 1956) is a professor of English at Columbia University. He received degrees from the Massachusetts Institute of Technology and Oxford University and his Ph.D. from Cornell University in 1987. He writes on a range of issues in Victorian studies. He is the general editor of the Encyclopedia of the Victorian Era, *among many other books and articles. The following excerpt is from* A History of Victorian Literature *(2009), named by* Choice *as an Outstanding Academic Book. His latest book is* Dandies and Desert Saints (2018).

Even as Mill was inveighing against intellectual cowardice and the decline of individual genius, a country squire was putting the final touches on arguably the most daring and unsettling book of the century. Charles Darwin's *On the Origin of Species By Means of Natural Selection, or Preservation of Favoured Races in the Struggle for Life* (1859) has had an impact so far-ranging and many-faceted that it confounds brief summary. Darwin's theory did not constitute a radical break with prevailing science; evolution had been "in the air" for decades, so much so that Tennyson's *In Memoriam* (much influenced by Chamber's *Vestiges of Creation*) seemed to be arguing with Darwin a decade before the Origin appeared. Indeed, Darwin was spurred to write up his long-pondered theory (the main ideas were in place as early as 1839) only after a fellow naturalist, A. R. Wallace, presented a paper anticipating some of its central claims. Darwin's theory also was far from the first to undermine the idea of divine creation most influentially set forth in Genesis. The geologist Charles Lyell, on whom Darwin drew heavily, during the 1830s had argued that natural forces acted uniformly over time, constantly reshaping the face of the planet, and left an ongoing history of its power in "the evidence of the rocks"!—a record which included those fossils of extinct species that so haunted Tennyson. As John Tyndall in his 1874 Belfast address would put it, "the strength of the doctrine of Evolution consists, not in an experimental demonstration . . . but in its general harmony with scientific thought" (Tyndall 1905: ii.206). Indeed, Darwin lacked any concept of genetics, and thus any plausible account of why variations occurred (as distinct from how they might establish new species). Thus at the heart of this theory, as critics pointed out, there was something of a black box. But Darwin nonetheless provided the most intricate, persuasive, and lucid account to date not only of extinction but also of the emergence of new species over time. The Newtonian world did not change; Darwinian nature was inherently, emphatically historical.

Darwin, then, tells a compelling story, a narrative at once expansive and intricately detailed, which reached all of educated Britain, and was appropriated to many, often conflicting ends. The idea of "struggle" between different species and their environment seemed to some commentators readily transferable to the analysis of society. This was a superficially plausible gesture (and one encouraged by Darwin's own subtitle). Darwin's theory resembles an extension to the animal and vegetable world of laissez-faire economics, or the intellectual marketplace of Millian liberalism. Thus Herbert Spencer, most influentially, coined the phrase "survival of the fittest" in order to describe social competition — with the clear implication that class hierarchies were underwritten by nature itself. In *The Principles of Sociology* (1876), Spencer (1820–1903) argued that societies are themselves organisms that evolve from "primitive" to more complex forms. This view would have an enormous impact in emergent sciences of anthropology and sociology, which typically formulated schemes of racial and cultural development grounded on a similar logic. But Spencer, like many commentators since, smuggled into his evolutionary scheme a sense of direction that Darwinian evolution does not provide. Spencer's "social Darwinism" (which persists in some forms of "evolutionary psychology") is closer to earlier Lamarckian schemes, whereby (for example) giraffes develop long necks in order to reach more food. This suggestion that evolutionary changes arise to meet a pre-existent need obscures one of the most disconcerting aspects of Darwin's theory: evolution offers no overarching direction, no governing telos. The present moment is not the culmination of the past, but one moment in an endless process of change. An animal happened to appear with a longer neck than its fellows, which in a particular milieu made it better adapted to survival; the same variation in another environment might prove fatal. The new species is "better" only in a strenuously relativist sense: the word that Darwin uses is not "progress" but "adaptation." As T. H. Huxley would insist in a famous 1893 essay, evolution provides no ethics.

Clearly this randomness was as much a blow to traditional faith as was the more obvious conflict with biblical schemes of creation. Yet Darwin's theory also provided a narrative model, as recent commentators have pointed out, that had much in common with those engaging a more familiar storyteller, the novelist. Not only does Darwinian theory incorporate history, it takes up familiar mythic themes of transformation and metamorphosis; it foregrounds the idea of kinship; it puts great stress (unlike, say, classical mechanics) on the particularity of the world, its sheer abundance and variety, as well as its subtle gradations and modulations (Beer 2000). Perhaps most suggestively, Darwinism discovers unifying structure without teleology. Victorian novelists likewise began with the assumption that the world they described was intelligible and coherent. But the efforts to embody that coherence in novelistic form — most obviously through coincidence and other residues of the so-called "providential plot" — were increasingly liable to seem either unrealistic, too obvious a simplification of the flux of experience, or to seem a deadening abridgement of human agency, in which the power of choice was thoroughly circumscribed by external forces. Thus Darwin leads back to another version of Mill's worry, which is also Estella's: we are not free, you and I. It would be some while before this impact was fully grasped by poets and novelists, but in the latter decades of the century, the impact would be immense.   *[2009]*

≡ THINKING ABOUT THE TEXT

1. What are some ways in which Darwin's famous text was interpreted then and now? How do you think Matthew Arnold read Darwin?

2. How do you think religious Victorians responded to what Adams calls "one of the most disconcerting aspects of Darwin's theory: evolution offers no overarching direction, no governing telos" (para. 2)?

3. How might Adams's notion of Darwinian randomness have influenced "Dover Beach"? How might the idea he mentions in the penultimate sentence, "we are not free, you and I," have affected Arnold's outlook?

≡ WRITING ABOUT ISSUES

1. Write an argument based on Thomas H. Huxley's famous observation in an 1893 essay: "Evolution provides no ethics."

2. Write an analysis of "Dover Beach" that traces the narrator's thinking through the different sections of the poem. Be explicit about his concerns and his possible remedy.

3. Argue that love should or should not be used as a haven against the world. Refer to "Dover Beach" and other texts or films to support your claims.

≡ RESEARCHING THE ISSUES

1. Research gender roles in 1867 in England, especially Victorian ideas about masculinity and femininity. After describing these roles and attributes, argue that Arnold was or was not influenced by these notions in his poem.

2. Research the controversy over the theory of evolution in Victorian England and contemporary America and argue that the elements of this debate are quite different today or essentially the same.

3. Research at least three feminist or gender studies critical essays of "Dover Beach" and argue that the interpretations are reasonable or not.

CHAPTER 11

=

Freedom and Confinement

Like most abstract and frequently used terms, *freedom* means many things to many people. In countries in the West, freedom is usually associated with political and religious choice, with the ability to dissent publicly from government policy, and even with an ability to dye our hair orange and paint our lips black. Indeed, freedom involves the right not to conform to conventional ideas about who we are and how we should behave as well as the right not to be stereotyped by a culture's demeaning, limiting, and distorted images and assumptions.

Readers of nineteenth-century fiction by women are familiar with the rigid cultural expectations that constricted the lives of most women. Excluded from public life and confined almost exclusively to domestic spaces, many women felt trapped in helping roles constructed for them by men. The consequences for the mental and physical health of thousands of would-be writers, artists, scientists, and intellectuals were often severe. Today, many minorities in America also feel limited by the confining legacies of racial, gender, and sexual stereotypes.

This chapter hopes to address some of these continuing issues of freedom and confinement. We open the chapter with two disturbing stories of traditions that will seem horrific to contemporary readers but which remind us that unquestioned rituals can sometimes confine and oppress with deadly consequences. Two more stories follow that have corporate and bureaucratic culture as their satirical target. The third cluster brings together seven poets expressing their resistance to pervasive stereotypes. This cluster is followed by four poems by one of the most respected nineteenth-century poets in America, Emily Dickinson. Then a pair of plays by Susan Glaspell and Lynn Nottage peer into difficult domestic situations from which women are trying to escape. Escape is also the focus of the next cluster that brings together a famous story from the nineteenth century with a contemporary narrative with comparable themes of confinement and freedom. We continue this focus with a classic Ursula Le Guin fantasy of confinement and escape, along with two essays arguing about the meaning of her story. The eighth cluster features a poem by Yevgeny Yevtushenko, tying into a debate about campus speech today. And finally, Henrik Ibsen's canonical play about fleeing cultural expectations, *A Doll's House*, is put in cultural context with documents for research from his time to the present.

≡ Where Tradition Is a Trap: Stories

SHIRLEY JACKSON, "The Lottery"

ALEXANDER WEINSTEIN, "Rocket Night"

Often our fondest memories of childhood involve family and community traditions, from public events like Thanksgiving, Halloween, and Fourth of July celebrations, to religious holidays like Christmas and Hanukkah, to private celebrations like birthdays and anniversaries. These rituals give our lives structure and create a sense of belonging. They give us psychological comfort and security and a ready-made identity of belonging with like-minded people who share our values. We acquire a sense of our adult roles, our goals, our understanding of the meaning of life, birth, death, love, and hate. Traditions and their accompanying rituals offer guidance as we address the complex question of how to "be" in the world.

Once a tradition starts, however, it may be difficult to change. Perhaps that is not so significant when we are thinking of birthday and graduation ceremonies, but it is life altering when traditions govern whom we may marry, what roles we can play in society, how we understand justice and freedom, and when our lives begin and end.

In some societies, traditions have been in place for thousands of years. They are difficult to change since they are woven into individuals' sense of self. People often feel that their own traditions are normal, even though anthropologists claim that few traditions are universal among cultures.

Since tradition plays such a crucial role in our lives, it is not surprising that writers are drawn to both the positive and negative elements of traditions and rituals. Although as in the two stories that follow, writers often use indirect techniques such as allegory, satire, and hyperbole to enrich their meaning, their narratives are about our own lives, about the attitudes and behaviors that we take for granted, and about the unconscious cruelties and dangerous assumptions we think of as normal. Seventy years after its publication, Shirley Jackson's "The Lottery" is still one of the most controversial stories ever published in *The New Yorker*. When the story was banned in South Africa, Jackson said, "Well at least they understood it." Alexander Weinstein's "Rocket Night" seems a contemporary variation on Jackson's horrific tale. Both in its matter-of-fact tone and its chilling and deadly conclusion, Weinstein's tale reminds us all that ordinary people can sometimes do extraordinarily wicked things.

≡ BEFORE YOU READ

Recall incidents from the past when you felt uncomfortable being involved in a tradition or ritual. How did you respond? What specific traditions in our culture could easily be eliminated? Are there harmful traditions in our culture that should be changed? Explain.

SHIRLEY JACKSON
The Lottery

*Shirley Jackson (1919–1965) was born in San Francisco and gre
ent suburb of Burlingame. Her family moved to Rochester, New Yo the afflu-
she graduated from Syracuse University in 1940. Jackson wrote of939, and
married in 1940 to Stanley Edgar Hyman, critic and numismatist, "I was
Vermont, in a quiet rural community with fine scenery and comfortabe in
city life. Our major exports are books and children, both of which we prod
dance." She received a National Book Award nomination for* The Haunti
House *(1959), which was adapted for film twice (1963 and 1999); thi.
book is often cited as one of the best horror novels of the twentieth century a.
influence on contemporary masters of that genre such as Stephen King.*

The morning of June 27th was clear and sunny, with the fresh warmth
full-summer day; the flowers were blossoming profusely and the grass w
richly green. The people of the village began to gather in the square, betwee
the post office and the bank, around ten o'clock; in some towns there were
so many people that the lottery took two days and had to be started on June
26th, but in this village, where there were only about three hundred people,
the whole lottery took less than two hours, so it could begin at ten o'clock in
the morning and still be through in time to allow the villagers to get home for
noon dinner.

The children assembled first, of course. School was recently over for the
summer, and the feeling of liberty sat uneasily on most of them; they tended
to gather together quietly for a while before they broke into boisterous play,
and their talk was still of the classroom and teacher, of books and reprimands.
Bobby Martin had already stuffed his pockets full of stones, and the other boys
soon followed his example, selecting the smoothest and roundest stones; Bobby
and Harry Jones and Dickie Delacroix—the villagers pronounced this name
"Dellacroy"—eventually made a great pile of stones in one corner of the square
and guarded it against the raids of the other boys. The girls stood aside, talking
among themselves, looking over their shoulders at the boys, and the very small
children rolled in the dust or clung to the hands of their older brothers or sisters.

Soon the men began to gather, surveying their own children, speaking
of planting and rain, tractors and taxes. They stood together, away from the
pile of stones in the corner, and their jokes were quiet and they smiled rather
than laughed. The women, wearing faded house dresses and sweaters, came
shortly after their menfolk. They greeted one another and exchanged bits of
gossip as they went to join their husbands. Soon the women, standing by their
husbands, began to call to their children, and the children came reluctantly,
having to be called four or five times. Bobby Martin ducked under his mother's
grasping hand and ran, laughing, back to the pile of stones. His father spoke
up sharply, and Bobby came quickly and took his place between his father and
his oldest brother.

The lottery...s conducted — as were the square dances, the teenage club, the H...en program — by Mr. Summers, who had time and energy to devote...c activities. He was a round-faced, jovial man and he ran the coal b...and people were sorry for him, because he had no children and...x, was a scold. When he arrived in the square, carrying the black w...x, there was a murmur of conversation among the villagers, and ...m, and called, "Little late today, folks." The postmaster, Mr. Graves, fol-...m, carrying a three-legged stool, and the stool was put in the center ...square and Mr. Summers set the black box down on it. The villagers their distance, leaving a space between themselves and the stool, ...when Mr. Summers said, "Some of you fellows want to give me a hand?" ...ere was a hesitation before two men, Mr. Martin and his oldest son, Baxter, ...ame forward to hold the box steady on the stool while Mr. Summers stirred up the papers inside it.

The original paraphernalia for the lottery had been lost long ago, and the 5 black box now resting on the stool had been put into use even before Old Man Warner, the oldest man in town, was born. Mr. Summers spoke frequently to the villagers about making a new box, but no one liked to upset even as much tradition as was represented by the black box. There was a story that the present box had been made with some pieces of the box that had preceded it, the one that had been constructed when the first people settled down to make a village here. Every year, after the lottery, Mr. Summers began talking again about a new box, but every year the subject was allowed to fade off without anything's being done. The black box grew shabbier each year; by now it was no longer completely black but splintered badly along one side to show the original wood color, and in some places faded or stained.

Mr. Martin and his oldest son, Baxter, held the black box securely on the stool until Mr. Summers had stirred the papers thoroughly with his hand. Because so much of the ritual had been forgotten or discarded, Mr. Summers had been successful in having slips of paper substituted for the chips of wood that had been used for generations. Chips of wood, Mr. Summers had argued, had been all very well when the village was tiny, but now that the population was more than three hundred and likely to keep on growing, it was necessary to use something that would fit more easily into the black box. The night before the lottery, Mr. Summers and Mr. Graves made up the slips of paper and put them in the box, and it was then taken to the safe of Mr. Summers's coal company and locked up until Mr. Summers was ready to take it to the square next morning. The rest of the year, the box was put away, sometimes one place, sometimes another; it had spent one year in Mr. Graves's barn and another year underfoot in the post office, and sometimes it was set on a shelf in the Martin grocery and left there.

There was a great deal of fussing to be done before Mr. Summers declared the lottery open. There were the lists to make up — of heads of families, heads of households in each family, members of each household in each family. There was the proper swearing-in of Mr. Summers by the postmaster, as the official of the lottery; at one time, some people remembered, there had been a recital of some sort, performed by the official of the lottery, a perfunctory, tuneless chant that had been rattled off duly each year; some people believed that the official of the lottery used to stand just so when he said or sang it, others believed that he was supposed to walk among the people, but years and years ago this part of the ritual had been allowed to lapse. There had been, also, a ritual salute, which the official of the lottery had had to use in addressing each person who came up to draw from the box, but this also had changed with time, until now it was felt necessary only for the official to speak to each person approaching. Mr. Summers was very good at all this; in his clean white shirt and blue jeans, with one hand resting carelessly on the black box, he seemed very proper and important as he talked interminably to Mr. Graves and the Martins.

Just as Mr. Summers finally left off talking and turned to the assembled villagers, Mrs. Hutchinson came hurriedly along the path to the square, her sweater thrown over her shoulders, and slid into place in the back of the crowd. "Clean forgot what day it was," she said to Mrs. Delacroix, who stood next to her, and they both laughed softly. "Thought my old man was out back stacking wood," Mrs. Hutchinson went on, "and then I looked out the window and the kids was gone, and then I remembered it was the twenty-seventh and came a-running." She dried her hands on her apron, and Mrs. Delacroix said, "You're in time, though. They're still talking away up there."

Mrs. Hutchinson craned her neck to see through the crowd and found her husband and children standing near the front. She tapped Mrs. Delacroix on the arm as a farewell and began to make her way through the crowd. The people separated good-humoredly to let her through; two or three people said, in voices just loud enough to be heard across the crowd, "Here comes your Missus, Hutchinson," and "Bill, she made it after all." Mrs. Hutchinson reached her husband, and Mr. Summers, who had been waiting, said cheerfully, "Thought we were going to have to get on without you, Tessie." Mrs. Hutchinson said, grinning, "Wouldn't have me leave m'dishes in the sink, now, would you, Joe?" and soft laughter ran through the crowd as the people stirred back into position after Mrs. Hutchinson's arrival.

"Well, now," Mr. Summers said soberly, "guess we better get started, get   10
this over with, so's we can go back to work. Anybody ain't here?"

"Dunbar," several people said. "Dunbar; Dunbar."

Mr. Summers consulted his list. "Clyde Dunbar," he said. "That's right. He's broke his leg, hasn't he? Who's drawing for him?"

"Me, I guess," a woman said, and Mr. Summers turned to look at her. "Wife draws for her husband," Mr. Summers said. "Don't you have a grown boy to do it for you, Janey?" Although Mr. Summers and everyone else in the village knew the answer perfectly well, it was the business of the official of the lottery to ask such questions formally. Mr. Summers waited with an expression of polite interest while Mrs. Dunbar answered.

"Horace's not but sixteen yet," Mrs. Dunbar said regretfully. "Guess I gotta fill in for the old man this year."

"Right," Mr. Summers said. He made a note on the list he was holding.   15
Then he asked, "Watson boy drawing this year?"

A tall boy in the crowd raised his hand. "Here," he said. "I'm drawing for m'mother and me." He blinked his eyes nervously and ducked his head as several voices in the crowd said things like "Good fellow, Jack," and "Glad to see your mother's got a man to do it."

"Well," Mr. Summers said, "guess that's everyone. Old Man Warner make it?"

"Here," a voice said, and Mr. Summers nodded.

A sudden hush fell on the crowd as Mr. Summers cleared his throat and looked at the list. "All ready?" he called. "Now, I'll read the names—heads of families first—and the men come up and take a paper out of the box. Keep the paper folded in your hand without looking at it until everyone has had a turn. Everything clear?"

The people had done it so many times that they only half listened to the   20
directions; most of them were quiet, wetting their lips, not looking around. Then Mr. Summers raised one hand high and said, "Adams." A man disengaged himself from the crowd and came forward. "Hi, Steve," Mr. Summers said, and Mr. Adams said, "Hi, Joe." They grinned at one another humorlessly and nervously. Then Mr. Adams reached into the black box and took out a folded paper. He held it firmly by one corner as he turned and went hastily back to his place in the crowd, where he stood a little apart from his family, not looking down at his hand.

"Allen," Mr. Summers said, "Anderson. . . . Bentham."

"Seems like there's no time at all between lotteries any more," Mrs. Delacroix said to Mrs. Graves in the back row. "Seems like we got through with the last one only last week."

"Time sure goes fast," Mrs. Graves said.

"Clark. . . . Delacroix."

"There goes my old man," Mrs. Delacroix said. She held her breath while   25
her husband went forward.

"Dunbar," Mr. Summers said, and Mrs. Dunbar went steadily to the box while one of the women said, "Go on, Janey," and another said, "There she goes."

"We're next," Mrs. Graves said. She watched while Mr. Graves came around from the side of the box, greeted Mr. Summers gravely, and selected a slip of paper from the box. By now, all through the crowd there were men holding the small folded papers in their large hands, turning them over and over nervously. Mrs. Dunbar and her two sons stood together, Mrs. Dunbar holding the slip of paper.

"Harburt. . . . Hutchinson."

"Get up there, Bill," Mrs. Hutchinson said, and the people near her laughed.

"Jones."   30

"They do say," Mr. Adams said to Old Man Warner, who stood next to him, "that over in the north village they're talking of giving up the lottery."

Old Man Warner snorted. "Pack of crazy fools," he said. "Listening to the young folks, nothing's good enough for *them*. Next thing you know, they'll be wanting to go back to living in caves, nobody work any more, live *that* way for a while. Used to be a saying about 'Lottery in June, corn be heavy soon.' First thing you know, we'd all be eating stewed chickweed and acorns. There's *always* been a lottery," he added petulantly. "Bad enough to see young Joe Summers up there joking with everybody."

"Some places have already quit lotteries," Mrs. Adams said.

"Nothing but trouble in *that*," Old Man Warner said stoutly. "Pack of young fools."

"Martin." And Bobby Martin watched his father go forward. "Overdyke. . . .   35
Percy."

"I wish they'd hurry," Mrs. Dunbar said to her older son. "I wish they'd hurry."

"They're almost through," her son said.

"You get ready to run tell Dad," Mrs. Dunbar said.

Mr. Summers called his own name and then stepped forward precisely and selected a slip from the box. Then he called, "Warner."

"Seventy-seventh year I been in the lottery," Old Man Warner said as he   40
went through the crowd. "Seventy-seventh time."

"Watson." The tall boy came awkwardly through the crowd. Someone said, "Don't be nervous, Jack," and Mr. Summers said, "Take your time, son."

"Zanini."

After that, there was a long pause, a breathless pause, until Mr. Summers, holding his slip of paper in the air, said, "All right, fellows." For a minute, no one moved, and then all the slips of paper were opened. Suddenly, all the women began to speak at once, saying, "Who is it?" "Who's got it?" "Is it the Dunbars?" "Is it the Watsons?" Then the voices began to say, "It's Hutchinson. It's Bill," "Bill Hutchinson's got it."

"Go tell your father," Mrs. Dunbar said to her older son.

People began to look around to see the Hutchinsons. Bill Hutchinson   45
was standing quiet, staring down at the paper in his hand. Suddenly, Tessie Hutchinson shouted to Mr. Summers, "You didn't give him time enough to take any paper he wanted. I saw you. It wasn't fair!"

"Be a good sport, Tessie," Mrs. Delacroix called, and Mrs. Graves said, "All of us took the same chance."

"Shut up, Tessie," Bill Hutchinson said.

"Well, everyone," Mr. Summers said, "that was done pretty fast, and now we've got to be hurrying a little more to get done in time." He consulted his next list. "Bill," he said, "you draw for the Hutchinson family. You got any other households in the Hutchinsons?"

"There's Don and Eva," Mrs. Hutchinson yelled. "Make *them* take their chance!"

"Daughters drew with their husbands' families, Tessie," Mr. Summers said   50
gently. "You know that as well as anyone else."

"It wasn't *fair*," Tessie said.

"I guess not, Joe," Bill Hutchinson said regretfully. "My daughter draws with her husband's family, that's only fair. And I've got no other family except the kids."

"Then, as far as drawing for families is concerned, it's you," Mr. Summers said in explanation, "and as far as drawing for households is concerned, that's you, too. Right?"

"Right," Bill Hutchinson said.

"How many kids, Bill?" Mr. Summers asked formally.   55

"Three," Bill Hutchinson said. "There's Bill Jr., and Nancy, and little Dave. And Tessie and me."

"All right, then," Mr. Summers said. "Harry, you got their tickets back?"

Mr. Graves nodded and held up the slips of paper. "Put them in the box, then," Mr. Summers directed. "Take Bill's and put it in."

"I think we ought to start over," Mrs. Hutchinson said, as quietly as she could. "I tell you it wasn't *fair.* You didn't give him time enough to choose. *Every*body saw that."

Mr. Graves had selected the five slips and put them in the box, and he   60
dropped all the papers but those onto the ground, where the breeze caught them and lifted them off.

"Listen, everybody," Mrs. Hutchinson was saying to the people around her.

"Ready, Bill?" Mr. Summers asked, and Bill Hutchinson, with one quick glance around at his wife and children, nodded.

"Remember," Mr. Summers said, "take the slips and keep them folded until each person has taken one. Harry, you help little Dave." Mr. Graves took the hand of the little boy, who came willingly with him up to the box. "Take a paper out of the box, Davy," Mr. Summers said. Davy put his hand into the box and laughed. "Take just *one* paper," Mr. Summers said. "Harry, you hold it for him." Mr. Graves took the child's hand and removed the folded paper from the tight fist and held it while little Dave stood next to him and looked up at him wonderingly.

"Nancy next," Mr. Summers said. Nancy was twelve, and her school friends breathed heavily as she went forward, switching her skirt, and took a slip daintily from the box. "Bill Jr.," Mr. Summers said, and Billy, his face red and his feet overlarge, nearly knocked the box over as he got a paper out. "Tessie," Mr. Summers said. She hesitated for a minute, looking around defiantly, and then set her lips and went up to the box. She snatched a paper out and held it behind her.

"Bill," Mr. Summers said, and Bill Hutchinson reached into the box and   65
felt around, bringing his hand out at last with the slip of paper in it.

The crowd was quiet. A girl whispered, "I hope it's not Nancy," and the sound of the whisper reached the edges of the crowd.

"It's not the way it used to be," Old Man Warner said clearly. "People ain't the way they used to be."

"All right," Mr. Summers said. "Open the papers. Harry, you open little Dave's."

Mr. Graves opened the slip of paper and there was a general sigh through the crowd as he held it up and everyone could see that it was blank. Nancy and

Bill Jr. opened theirs at the same time, and both beamed and laughed, turning around to the crowd and holding their slips of paper above their heads.

"Tessie," Mr. Summers said. There was a pause, and then Mr. Summers looked at Bill Hutchinson, and Bill unfolded his paper and showed it. It was blank.

"It's Tessie," Mr. Summers said, and his voice was hushed. "Show us her paper, Bill."

Bill Hutchinson went over to his wife and forced the slip of paper out of her hand. It had a black spot on it, the black spot Mr. Summers had made the night before with the heavy pencil in the coal-company office. Bill Hutchinson held it up and there was a stir in the crowd.

"All right, folks," Mr. Summers said. "Let's finish quickly."

Although the villagers had forgotten the ritual and lost the original black box, they still remembered to use stones. The pile of stones the boys had made earlier was ready; there were stones on the ground with the blowing scraps of paper that had come out of the box. Mrs. Delacroix selected a stone so large she had to pick it up with both hands and turned to Mrs. Dunbar. "Come on," she said. "Hurry up."

Mrs. Dunbar had small stones in both hands, and she said, gasping for breath, "I can't run at all. You'll have to go ahead and I'll catch up with you."

The children had stones already, and someone gave little Davy Hutchinson a few pebbles.

Tessie Hutchinson was in the center of a cleared space by now, and she held her hands out desperately as the villagers moved in on her. "It isn't fair," she said. A stone hit her on the side of the head.

Old Man Warner was saying, "Come on, come on, everyone." Steve Adams was in the front of the crowd of villagers, with Mrs. Graves beside him.

"It isn't fair, it isn't right," Mrs. Hutchinson screamed and then they were upon her.

[1948]

≡ THINKING ABOUT THE TEXT

1. At what point in the story did you suspect that something was amiss in this bucolic village? How does Jackson both prepare you for and surprise you with her ending?

2. Make a list of the characters' names in the story. What symbolic significance might they have?

3. What do the phrase "Lottery in June, corn be heavy soon" and the pile of stones suggest about the origins of the lottery?

4. Critics often mention scapegoating, man's inherent evil, and the destructive consequence of hanging on to ancient and outdated rituals as the principal themes of this story. Do you agree? What are some other themes suggested by the story?

5. What contemporary issues does "The Lottery" bring to mind?

ALEXANDER WEINSTEIN
Rocket Night

Alexander Weinstein received a B.A. from Naropa University and in 2010 an M.F.A. from Indiana University in Creative Writing. He teaches in the English Program at Siena Heights University and at the University of Michigan. He has published widely and has won numerous awards. A Rolling Stone *review noted that his latest collection of stories,* Children of the New World *(2016) shows characters that "exist in a fantastic, creepy landscape that could be ours in the not-too-distant future." His work has been called "dystopian literary realism." The following story from this collection was first published in* Southern Indiana Review *(Spring 2013).*

It was Rocket Night at our daughter's elementary school, the night when parents, students, and the administration gather to place the least liked child in a rocket and shoot him into the stars. Last year we placed Laura Jackson into the capsule, a short, squat girl known for her limp dresses which hung crookedly on her body. The previous year we'd sent off a boy from India whose name none of us could remember. Before that our daughter was in kindergarten so we'd yet to become part of the Rose Hill community.

Rocket Night is an event which almost all of us look forward to, falling in late October when the earth is covered by orange and yellows. Our children have begun to lay out their Halloween costumes and their sweaters are heavy with the scent of autumn. It's late enough into the school year for us to get a sense of the best children to send off. For alliances are made early at Rose Hill. Our children gather in the mornings to share their secrets on playgrounds, while the other children, those with stars and galaxies in their futures, can be seen at the edges of the field, playing with sticks alone or staring into mud puddles at drowned worms.

Meet and greet is held, as is custom, in the school gymnasium, and we mingle in the warm glow of its lacquered floors, surrounded by wooden bleachers and parallel bars, talking about soccer games, math homework, and the difficulty of finding time for errands with our children's busy schedules. Our kids run the perimeter, some playing tag, others collecting in clusters of boys around the fifthgraders with portable game players, the girls across the room in their own clusters. Susan Beech brought her famous home-baked cupcakes, the Stowes brought Hawaiian Punch, and we brought plastic cups and cocktail napkins and placed them on the table among the baked goods and apple slices.

The boy to be sent off, I believe his name was Daniel, stood near his parents, holding his mother's skirt, looking unkempt. One could immediately see the reason he'd been chosen by our children. There's a hand-me-down quality to the clothing of those selected, the mildewed stench of thrift stores clinging to their corduroys. This boy's collar sat askew, revealing the small white undershirt beneath, and his brown slacks were held tightly by an oversized belt whose end flopped lazily from his side. The boy, our daughter told us, brought stubby pencils to school whose chewed-up ends got stuck in sharpeners. He had the habit of picking his nose. His lunches, she reported, were nothing more than stale crackers and a warm box of chocolate milk. There was a smear of cupcake frosting on the corner of his mouth, and seeing this detail, we knew our children had chosen well. He was the sort of child who makes one proud of one's own children, and we looked over to our daughter, who was holding court with a devil's square, tightening then spreading her small fingers within the folded paper while counting out the letters O-R-A-N-G-E.

At eight o'clock the principal took the stage beneath the basketball hoop, a whine from the microphone as he adjusted it. He turned to us with open arms and welcomed us, the parents and students of Rose Hill, to another year together. He thanked Susan for her cupcakes, and all of us for our contributions to make the evening's festivities so successful, and then, forgetting the boy's name, he turned to the family and said, "Donald, we hope your journey into space will be a joyful one." We all applauded. Admittedly, his parents applauded less than others, looking a bit pale, but we acknowledged that the parents of the chosen often do seem pale. They are the sort of parents who come to soccer games and sit alone in the stands, a gloomy sadness hanging over them, whose cars make the most noise when they pull into our school's parking lot, and whose faces, within the automobile's dark interiors, remind us not of the joys of parenthood, but of some sorrow none of us wish to share. Seeing them standing there with their child, we realized, with relief, that with the departure of their son we would also gain their departure, and we quietly acknowledged the all-round benefit.

The principal's speech delivered, he invited us to join him on the playground where the capsule sat, cockpit open, its silver sides illuminated by the glow from the launch tower. It's a truth that the child to be sent into space grows reticent upon seeing the glowing tower and the gaping casket-like rocket. We saw the small boy cling to his mother, unwilling to leave her side, and so we let our children loose. I watched my daughter pry the boy's fingers from his mother's leg as two larger fifth-graders seized his waist and dragged him away. The nurse, a kindly woman, helped to subdue the parents. She took the mother aside and whispered to her, while the gym coach placed a meaty hand on the father's shoulder and assured him that the capsule was stocked with water and food tablets, plenty for lasting the boy a long time into the future. To be honest, it's a mystery how long such supplies last. It's a small compartment within that capsule and we are all aware funding was cut to our district earlier this year, but still we assured them there was nothing to worry of. The boy, if hungry for company, had a small microphone inside the shell which would allow him to speak to himself of his journey, his thoughts, and the mystery of the universe.

The boy was strapped into the capsule, his hands secured, and he looked out at us. He spoke then, for the first and only time that night. He asked if he might have one of his pencils with him; it was in his pencil box, he said, the one

5

with a brown bear for an eraser. The principal assured him that he wouldn't need it in outer space, and the custodian noted that the request was moot; the boy's desk had been emptied earlier that day. So they closed the cover. All we could see was the smudge of the boy's face pressed against the porthole.

When the rocket blasted off, it made us all take an involuntary step backwards, the light of the flames illuminating the wonder upon our children's faces. We watched as the capsule rose from our playground, leaving behind our swing sets and jungle gym, rising higher, until it was but a sparkling marble in the night sky, and then, finally, gone completely. We sighed with awe, some applauded, and then we made our rounds, wishing one another goodnight, arranging play dates, and returning to our cars. Those of us on the PTO remained to put the gymnasium back in order for the coming morning. And the boy faded from our thoughts, replaced by the lateness of the evening and the pressure of delayed bedtime schedules. I myself had all but forgotten about the child by the time I lay our sleeping daughter on her bed. And yet, when I took out the recycling that night, I paused beneath the streetlamps of our cul-de-sac and thought of the children up there. I imagined all of them drifting alone, speaking into their microphones, telling us about their lives from the depths of the unknown.   [2013]

≡ THINKING ABOUT THE TEXT

1. What are some details of the appearance or behavior of the children chosen? What do these details tell you about the narrator and the values and biases of his social circle?

2. What is the significance of the line, "there was a smear of cupcake frosting on the corner of his mouth, and seeing this detail, we knew our children had chosen well" (para. 4)?

3. Besides the actual journey into space, which actions or thoughts seem particularly cruel or insensitive? What is the effect of the casual, matter-of-fact tone of the narrator?

4. What are some possible reasons that some of the parents "sighed with awe" (para. 8) when the rocket took off? How can this also be a tale about the consequences of technology without a moral compass?

5. What is the significance of the last line? Has the narrator suddenly become aware of the school's grotesque deed or does it simply reinforce his insensitivity? Explain.

≡ MAKING COMPARISONS

1. Compare the process by which victims are chosen in "The Lottery" and "Rocket Night." Which seems more horrific?

2. Why do the parents in "Rocket Night" seem more or less barbaric than those in "The Lottery"?

3. The tradition in "The Lottery" seems to have been inherited from the distant past, but given the technology involved in "Rocket Night," is it meant to take place in the future? What is the significance of this difference?

≡ WRITING ABOUT IDEAS

1. Argue that "The Lottery" is still relevant to contemporary concerns.

2. One idea about science fiction is that it takes a present concern and projects it into the future using hyperbole, allegory, and satire to make its point. How might this be the case with "Rocket Night"?

3. Write an essay that compares the tone, setting, themes, and characters of both stories. Be sure to note the similarities and differences.

4. Read Shirley Jackson's essay "Biography of a Story" from her book *Come Along with Me* and write a report highlighting what you feel are her most interesting ideas. Take a position on whether the story's reception would be similar or different if it were written today.

GEORGE SAUNDERS, "Exhortation"

DANIEL OROZCO, "Orientation"

At some point in our lives, many of us have worked in an office. It can even seem to us another home. Like our real homes, an office job may offer us personal space, emotional support, and a chance to pursue initiatives of our own. Yet at times our homes may seem to us places of confinement, and our jobs may strike us the same way. Indeed, a work supervisor or colleague may give us mixed messages: addressing us in a manner that's both friendly *and* controlling. This is the situation in the following two stories. Both satirize modes of communication often used in offices. In George Saunders' story, the mode is a memo; in Daniel Orozco's, it's the orientation given a new employee. Saunders' memo writer and Orozco's tour guide want to show that they empathize with the people they address. Yet they also aim to convey their audiences' commands and warnings. Appropriately, these stories are both amusing and sinister. Some elements of them may make you laugh, while others give you chills. Perhaps, too, these stories will give you shocks of recognition, reminding you of jobs you've known—or still inhabit.

≡ **BEFORE YOU READ**

Think of a workplace you've worked in, visited, or read about. What features of it, if any, do you consider welcoming? What features of it, if any, do you find oppressive?

GEORGE SAUNDERS
Exhortation

George Saunders (b. 1958), considered one of the most original fiction writers of his generation, was born in Amarillo, Texas, and grew up in Chicago. He received an engineering degree from The Colorado School of Mines and later in 1988 an M.A. in creative writing from Syracuse University. He worked as a technical writer before joining Syracuse's M.F.A. faculty. He has received a number of prestigious prizes and awards for his fiction, especially the collection, The Tenth of December *(2013) and his first novel,* Lincoln in the Bardo *(2017), a unique experimental tale of Lincoln's grief over the death of his son. It won the widely respected Man Booker Prize for 2017. In 2006, he was awarded the MacArthur Foundation Fellowship (popularly known as the "genius award"). The following story is from* The Tenth of December.

MEMORANDUM
DATE: *Apr 6*
TO: *Staff*
FROM: *Todd Birnie, Divisional Director*
Re: *March Performance Stats*

I would not like to characterize this as a plea, although it may start to sound like one (!). The fact is, we have a job to do, we have tacitly agreed to do it (did you cash your last paycheck, I know I did, ha ha ha). We have also—to go a step further here—agreed to do the job well. Now we all know that one way to do a job poorly is to be negative about it. Say we need to clean a shelf. Let's use that example. If we spend the hour before the shelf cleaning talking down the process of cleaning the shelf, complaining about it, dreading it, investigating the moral niceties of cleaning the shelf, whatever, then what happens is, we make the process of cleaning the shelf more difficult than it really is. We all know very well that that "shelf" is going to be cleaned, given the current climate, either by you or the guy who replaces you and gets your paycheck, so the question boils down to: Do I want to clean it happy or do I want to clean it sad? Which would be more effective? For me? Which would accomplish my purpose more efficiently? What is my purpose? To get paid. How do I accomplish that purpose most efficiently? I clean that shelf well and clean it quickly. And what mental state helps me clean that shelf well and quickly? Is the answer: Negative? A negative mental state? You know very well that it is not. So the point of this memo is: Positive. The positive mental state will help you clean that shelf well and quickly, thus accomplishing your purpose of getting paid.

What am I saying? Am I saying whistle while you work? Maybe I am. Let us consider lifting a heavy dead carcass such as a whale. (Forgive the shelf/whale thing, we have just come back from our place on Reston Island, where there were 1) a lot of dirty shelves, and 2) yes, believe it or not, an actual dead rotting whale, which Timmy and Vance and I got involved with in terms of the cleanup.) So say you are charged with, you and some of your colleagues, lifting a heavy dead whale carcass onto a flatbed. Now we all know that is hard. And what would be harder is: doing that with a negative attitude. What we found—Timmy and Vance and I—is that even with only a neutral attitude, you are talking a very hard task. We tried to lift that whale while we were just feeling neutral, Timmy and Vance and I, with a dozen or so other folks, and it was a no-go, that whale wouldn't budge, until suddenly one fellow, a former Marine, said that what we needed was some mind over matter, and gathered us in a little circle, and we had a sort of chant. We got "psyched up." We knew, to extend my above analogy, that we had a job to do, and got sort of excited about that, and decided to do it with a positive attitude, and I have to tell you, there was something to that, it was fun, fun when that whale rose into the air, helped by us and some big straps that Marine had in his van, and I have to say that lifting that dead rotting whale onto that flatbed with that group of total strangers was the high point of our trip.

So what am I saying? I am saying (and saying it fervently, because it is important): Let's try, if we can, to minimize the grumbling and self-doubt regarding the tasks we must sometimes do around here that maybe aren't on the surface all that pleasant. I'm saying let's try not to dissect every single thing we do in terms of ultimate good/bad/indifferent in terms of morals. The time for that is long past. I hope that each of us had that conversation with ourselves nearly a year ago, when this whole thing started. We have embarked on a path, and having embarked on that path, for the best of reasons (as we decided a year ago), wouldn't it be kind of suicidal to let our progress down that path be impeded by neurotic second-guessing? Have any of you ever swung a sledgehammer? I know that some of you have. I know that some of you did when we took out Rick's patio. Isn't it fun when you don't hold back, but just pound down and down, letting gravity help you? Fellows, what I'm saying is, let gravity help you here, in our workplace situation: Pound down, give in to the natural feelings that I have seen from time to time produce so much great energy in so many of you, in terms of executing your given tasks with vigor and without second-guessing and neurotic thoughts. Remember that record-breaking week Andy had back in October, when he doubled his usual number of units? Regardless of all else, forgetting for the moment all namby-pamby thoughts of right/wrong etc., etc., wasn't that something to see? In and of itself? I think that, if we each look deep down inside of ourselves, weren't we all a little envious? God, he was really pounding down and you could see the energetic joy on his face each time he rushed by us to get additional cleanup towels. And we were all just standing there like, Wow, Andy, what's gotten into you? And no one can argue with his numbers. They are there in our Break Room for all to see, towering above the rest of our numbers, and though Andy has failed to duplicate those numbers in the months since October, 1) no one blames him for that, those were miraculous numbers, and 2) I believe that even if Andy never again duplicates those numbers, he must still, somewhere in his heart, secretly treasure the memory of that magnificent energy flowing out of him that memorable October. I do not honestly think Andy could've had such an October if he had been coddling himself or entertaining any doubtful neurotic thoughts or second-guessing tendencies, do you? I don't. Andy looked totally focused, totally outside himself, you could see it on his face, maybe because of the new baby? (If so, Janice should have a new baby every week, ha ha.)

Anyway, October is how Andy entered a sort of, at least in my mind, de facto Hall of Fame, and is pretty much henceforth excluded from any real close monitoring of his numbers, at least by me. No matter how disconsolate and sort of withdrawn he gets (and I think we've all noticed that he's gotten pretty disconsolate and withdrawn since October), you will not find me closely monitoring his numbers, although as for others I cannot speak, others may be monitoring that troubling falloff in Andy's numbers, although really I hope they're not, that would not be so fair, and believe me, if I get wind of it, I will definitely let Andy know, and if Andy's too depressed to hear me, I'll call Janice at home.

And in terms of why is Andy so disconsolate? My guess is that he's being 5 neurotic, and second-guessing his actions of October—and wow, wouldn't that be a shame, wouldn't that be a no-win, for Andy to have completed that record-breaking October and then sit around boo-hooing about it? Is anything being changed by that boo-hooing? Are the actions Andy did, in terms of the tasks I gave him to do in Room 6, being undone by his boo-hooing, are his numbers on the Break Room wall miraculously scrolling downward, are people suddenly walking out of Room 6 feeling perfectly okay again? Well we all know they are not. No one is walking out of Room 6 feeling perfectly okay. Even you guys, you who do what must be done in Room 6, don't walk out feeling so super-great, I know that, I've certainly done some things in Room 6 that didn't leave me feeling so wonderful, believe me, no one is trying to deny that Room 6 can be a bummer, it is very hard work that we do. But the people above us, who give us our assignments, seem to think that the work we do in Room 6, in addition to being hard, is also important, which I suspect is why they have begun watching our numbers so closely. And trust me, if you want Room 6 to be an even worse bummer than it already is, then mope about it before, after, and during, then it will really stink, plus, with all the moping, your numbers will go down even further, which guess what: they cannot do. I have been told in no uncertain terms, at the Sectional Meeting, that our numbers are not to go down any further. I said (and this took guts, believe me, given the atmosphere at Sectional): look, my guys are tired, this is hard work we do, both physically and psychologically. And at that point, at Sectional, believe me, the silence was deafening. And I mean deafening. And the looks I got were not good. And I was reminded, in no uncertain terms, by Hugh Blanchert himself, that our numbers are not to go down. And I was asked to remind you—to remind us, all of us, myself included—that if we are unable to clean our assigned "shelf," not only will someone else be brought in to clean that "shelf," but we ourselves may find ourselves on that "shelf," being that "shelf," with someone else exerting themselves with good positive energy all over us. And at that time I think you can imagine how regretful you would feel, the regret would show in your faces, as we sometimes witness, in Room 6, that regret on the faces of the "shelves" as they are "cleaned," so I am asking you, from the hip, to try your best and not end up a "shelf," which we, your former colleagues, will have no choice but to clean clean clean using all our positive energy, without looking back, in Room 6.

This was all made clear to me at Sectional and now I am trying to make it clear to you.

Well I have gone on and on, but please come by my office, anybody who's having doubts, doubts about what we do, and I will show you pictures of that incredible whale my sons and I lifted with our good positive energy. And of course this information, that is, the information that you are having doubts, and have come to see me in my office, will go no further than my office, although I am sure I do not even have to say that, to any of you, who have known me all these many years.

All will be well and all will be well, etc., etc.,

Todd   [2013]

≡ THINKING ABOUT THE TEXT

1. What do you think the narrator means by "moral niceties"? How is this different than just saying morals?

2. What do you think is behind Andy's behavior? How does our narrator deal with his behavior? What rationale does he give? Would such thinking convince you to continue going to Room 6 or not? Explain.

3. What is the primary strategy the narrator hopes will work on his audience?

4. Speculate about what kind of work in the real world would require the tactics the narrator employs.

5. Speculate about the various responses our story might get at West Point, in a pharmaceutical company, in a seminary, a prison, in law school, in medical school.

DANIEL OROZCO
Orientation

The son of Nicaraguan immigrants, California-born Daniel Orozco (b. 1957) currently teaches at the University of Idaho. His award-winning short fiction has appeared in a variety of magazines, including Harper's *and* Zoetrope, *and has been collected in* Orientation and Other Stories *(2011). He received a B.A. from Stanford University, an M.A. from San Francisco State University, and an M.F.A. from the University of Washington. He has also held a writing fellowship at Stanford. This story was selected for* The Best American Short Stories of 1995.

Those are the offices and these are the cubicles. That's my cubicle there, and this is your cubicle. This is your phone. Never answer your phone. Let the Voicemail System answer it. This is your Voicemail System Manual. There are no personal phone calls allowed. We do, however, allow for emergencies. If you must make an emergency phone call, ask your supervisor first. If you can't find your supervisor, ask Phillip Spiers, who sits over there. He'll check with Clarissa Nicks, who sits over there. If you make an emergency phone call without asking, you may be let go.

These are your IN and OUT boxes. All the forms in your IN box must be logged in by the date shown in the upper left-hand corner, initialed by you in the upper right-hand corner, and distributed to the Processing Analyst whose name is numerically coded in the lower left-hand corner. The lower right-hand corner is left blank. Here's your Processing Analyst Numerical Code Index. And here's your Forms Processing Procedures Manual.

You must pace your work. What do I mean? I'm glad you asked that. We pace our work according to the eight-hour workday. If you have twelve hours of work IN your in box, for example, you must compress that work into the eight-hour day. If you have one hour of work in your IN box, you must expand that work to fill the eight-hour day. That was a good question. Feel free to ask questions. Ask too many questions, however, and you may be let go.

That is our receptionist. She is a temp. We go through receptionists here. They quit with alarming frequency. Be polite and civil to the temps. Learn their names, and invite them to lunch occasionally. But don't get close to them, as it only makes it more difficult when they leave. And they always leave. You can be sure of that.

The men's room is over there. The women's room is over there. John LaFountaine, who sits over there, uses the women's room occasionally. He says it is accidental. We know better, but we let it pass. John LaFountaine is harmless, his forays into the forbidden territory of the women's room simply a benign thrill, a faint blip on the dull flat line of his life.

Russell Nash, who sits in the cubicle to your left, is in love with Amanda Pierce, who sits in the cubicle to your right. They ride the same bus together after work. For Amanda Pierce, it is just a tedious bus ride made less tedious by the idle nattering of Russell Nash. But for Russell Nash, it is the highlight of his day. It is the highlight of his life. Russell Nash has put on forty pounds, and grows fatter with each passing month, nibbling on chips and cookies while peeking glumly over the partitions at Amanda Pierce, and gorging himself at home on cold pizza and ice cream while watching adult videos on TV.

Amanda Pierce, in the cubicle to your right, has a six-year-old son named Jamie, who is autistic. Her cubicle is plastered from top to bottom with the boy's crayon artwork — sheet after sheet of precisely drawn concentric circles and ellipses, in black and yellow. She rotates them every other Friday. Be sure to comment on them. Amanda Pierce also has a husband, who is a lawyer. He subjects her to an escalating array of painful and humiliating sex games, to which Amanda Pierce reluctantly submits. She comes to work exhausted and freshly wounded each morning, wincing from the abrasions on her breasts, or the bruises on her abdomen, or the second-degree burns on the backs of her thighs.

But we're not supposed to know any of this. Do not let on. If you let on, you may be let go.

Amanda Pierce, who tolerates Russell Nash, is in love with Albert Bosch, whose office is over there. Albert Bosch, who only dimly registers Amanda Pierce's existence, has eyes only for Ellie Tapper, who sits over there. Ellie Tapper, who hates Albert Bosch, would walk through fire for Curtis Lance. But Curtis Lance hates Ellie Tapper. Isn't the world a funny place? Not in the ha-ha sense, of course.

Anika Bloom sits in that cubicle. Last year, while reviewing quarterly   10
reports in a meeting with Barry Hacker, Anika Bloom's left palm began
to bleed. She fell into a trance, stared into her hand, and told Barry Hacker
when and how his wife would die. We laughed it off. She was, after all, a new
employee. But Barry Hacker's wife is dead. So unless you want to know exactly
when and how you'll die, never talk to Anika Bloom.

Colin Heavey sits in that cubicle over there. He was new once, just like
you. We warned him about Anika Bloom. But at last year's Christmas Potluck,
he felt sorry for her when he saw that no one was talking to her. Colin Heavey
brought her a drink. He hasn't been himself since. Colin Heavey is doomed.
There's nothing he can do about it, and we are powerless to help him. Stay
away from Colin Heavey. Never give any of your work to him. If he asks to
do something, tell him you have to check with me. If he asks again, tell him
I haven't gotten back to you.

This is the Fire Exit. There are several on this floor, and they are marked
accordingly. We have a Floor Evacuation Review every three months, and an
Escape Route Quiz once a month. We have our Biannual Fire Drill twice a year,
and our Annual Earthquake Drill once a year. These are precautions only.
These things never happen.

For your information, we have a comprehensive health plan. Any catastrophic illness, any unforeseen tragedy is completely covered. All dependents
are completely covered. Larry Bagdikian, who sits over there, has six daughters. If anything were to happen to any of his girls, or to all of them, if all six
were to simultaneously fall victim to illness or injury — stricken with a hideous degenerative muscle disease or some rare toxic blood disorder, sprayed
with semiautomatic gunfire while on a class field trip, or attacked in their
bunk beds by some prowling nocturnal lunatic — if any of this were to pass,
Larry's girls would all be taken care of. Larry Bagdikian would not have to pay
one dime. He would have nothing to worry about.

We also have a generous vacation and sick leave policy. We have an excellent disability insurance plan. We have a stable and profitable pension fund.
We get group discounts for the symphony, and block seating at the ballpark.
We get commuter ticket books for the bridge. We have Direct Deposit. We are
all members of Costco.

This is our kitchenette. And this, this is our Mr. Coffee. We have a cof-   15
fee pool, into which we each pay two dollars a week for coffee, filters, sugar,
and CoffeeMate. If you prefer Cremora or half-and-half to CoffeeMate, there
is a special pool for three dollars a week. If you prefer Sweet 'n Low to sugar,
there is a special pool for two-fifty a week. We do not do decaf. You are allowed
to join the coffee pool of your choice, but you are not allowed to touch the
Mr. Coffee.

This is the microwave oven. You are allowed to *heat* food in the microwave
oven. You are not, however, allowed to *cook* food in the microwave oven.

We get one hour for lunch. We also get one fifteen-minute break in the
morning, and one fifteen-minute break in the afternoon. Always take your
breaks. If you skip a break, it is gone forever. For your information, your break

is a privilege, not a right. If you abuse the break policy, we are authorized to rescind your breaks. Lunch, however, is a right, not a privilege. If you abuse the lunch policy, our hands will be tied, and we will be forced to look the other way. We will not enjoy that.

This is the refrigerator. You may put your lunch in it. Barry Hacker, who sits over there, steals food from this refrigerator. His petty theft is an outlet for his grief. Last New Year's Eve, while kissing his wife, a blood vessel burst in her brain. Barry Hacker's wife was two months pregnant at the time, and lingered in a coma for half a year before dying. It was a tragic loss for Barry Hacker. He hasn't been himself since. Barry Hacker's wife was a beautiful woman. She was also completely covered. Barry Hacker did not have to pay one dime. But his dead wife haunts him. She haunts all of us. We have seen her, reflected in the monitors of our computers, moving past our cubicles. We have seen the dim shadow of her face in our photocopies. She pencils herself in in the receptionist's appointment book, with the notation: To see Barry Hacker. She has left messages in the receptionist's Voicemail box, messages garbled by the electronic chirrups and buzzes in the phone line, her voice echoing from an immense distance within the ambient hum. But the voice is hers. And beneath her voice, beneath the tidal *whoosh* of static and hiss, the gurgling and crying of a baby can be heard.

In any case, if you bring a lunch, put a little something extra in the bag for Barry Hacker. We have four Barrys in this office. Isn't that a coincidence?

This is Matthew Payne's office. He is our Unit Manager, and his door is   20
always closed. We have never seen him, and you will never see him. But he is here. You can be sure of that. He is all around us.

This is the Custodian's Closet. You have no business in the Custodian's Closet.

And this, this is our Supplies Cabinet. If you need supplies, see Curtis Lance. He will log you in on the Supplies Cabinet Authorization Log, then give you a Supplies Authorization Slip. Present your pink copy of the Supplies Authorization Slip to Ellie Tapper. She will log you in on the Supplies Cabinet Key Log, then give you the key. Because the Supplies Cabinet is located outside the Unit Manager's office, you must be very quiet. Gather your supplies quietly. The Supplies Cabinet is divided into four sections. Section One contains letterhead stationery, blank paper and envelopes, memo and note pads, and so on. Section Two contains pens and pencils and typewriter and printer ribbons, and the like. In Section Three we have erasers, correction fluids, transparent tapes, glue sticks, et cetera. And in Section Four we have paper clips and push pins and scissors and razor blades. And here are the spare blades for the shredder. Do not touch the shredder, which is located over there. The shredder is of no concern to you.

Gwendolyn Stich sits in that office there. She is crazy about penguins, and collects penguin knickknacks: penguin posters and coffee mugs and stationery, penguin stuffed animals, penguin jewelry, penguin sweaters and T-shirts and socks. She has a pair of penguin fuzzy slippers she wears when working late at the office. She has a tape cassette of penguin sounds which she listens to for relaxation. Her favorite colors are black and white. She has personalized license plates that read PEN GWEN. Every morning, she passes through all the cubicles to wish each of us a *good* morning. She brings Danish on Wednesdays for Hump Day morning break, and doughnuts on Fridays for TGIF afternoon break. She organizes the Annual Christmas Potluck, and is in charge of the Birthday List. Gwendolyn Stich's door is always open to all of us. She will always lend an ear, and put in a good word for you; she will always give you a hand, or the shirt off her back, or a shoulder to cry on. Because her door is always open, she hides and cries in a stall in the women's room. And John LaFountaine — who, enthralled when a woman enters, sits quietly in his stall with his knees to his chest — John LaFountaine has heard her vomiting in there. We have come upon Gwendolyn Stich huddled in the stairwell, shivering in the updraft, sipping a Diet Mr. Pibb and hugging her knees. She does not let any of this interfere with her work. If it interfered with her work, she might have to be let go.

Kevin Howard sits in that cubicle over there. He is a serial killer, the one they call the Carpet Cutter, responsible for the mutilations across town. We're not supposed to know that, so do not let on. Don't worry. His compulsion inflicts itself on strangers only, and the routine established is elaborate and unwavering. The victim must be a white male, a young adult no older than thirty, heavyset, with dark hair and eyes, and the like. The victim must be chosen at random, before sunset, from a public place; the victim is followed home, and must put up a struggle; et cetera. The carnage inflicted is precise: the angle and direction of the incisions; the layering of skin and muscle tissue; the rearrangement of the visceral organs; and so on. Kevin Howard does not let any of this interfere with his work. He is, in fact, our fastest typist. He types as if he were on fire. He has a secret crush on Gwendolyn Stich, and leaves a red-foil-wrapped Hershey's Kiss on her desk every afternoon. But he hates Anika Bloom, and keeps well away from her. In his presence, she has uncontrollable fits of shaking and trembling. Her left palm does not stop bleeding.

In any case, when Kevin Howard gets caught, act surprised. Say that he seemed like a nice person, a bit of a loner, perhaps, but always quiet and polite.   25

This is the photocopier room. And this, this is our view. It faces southwest. West is down there, toward the water. North is back there. Because we are on the seventeenth floor, we are afforded a magnificent view. Isn't it beautiful? It overlooks the park, where the tops of those trees are. You can see a segment of the bay between those two buildings there. You can see the sun set in the gap between those two buildings over there. You can see this building reflected in the glass panels of that building across the way. There. See? That's you, waving. And look there. There's Anika Bloom in the kitchenette, waving back.

Enjoy this view while photocopying. If you have problems with the photocopier, see Russell Nash. If you have any questions, ask your supervisor. If you can't find your supervisor, ask Phillip Spiers. He sits over there. He'll check with Clarissa Nicks. She sits over there. If you can't find them, feel free to ask me. That's my cubicle. I sit in there.   *[1994]*

≡ THINKING ABOUT THE TEXT

1. Orozco reports that since his story was published, "it has even been included in an employee orientation manual, which is either very funny or very disturbing." What is *your* reaction to this news? Does this orientation resemble other orientations with which you are familiar? In what ways? Consider the kinds of advice given and language used.

2. Does the office described here resemble other offices with which you are familiar? In what ways? At what points in the story does this office seem unusual?

3. List at least three adjectives that describe Orozco's narrator. What influences your evaluation of this narrator? What would you say to someone who claims that the story is more about the narrator than about the office?

4. Which character or characters do you think would typically be fired for their behavior? Explain.

5. Which of the characters described seems the most plausible? Which the least? Explain. If you were the audience for this monologue, how would you tell your friends about it?

≡ MAKING COMPARISONS

1. It seems clear that neither author thinks highly of corporate culture. What specifically seem to be their complaints?

2. What specific incidents in "Orientation" seem the most satirical? The most obviously allegorical or metaphorical?

3. If you were to be frank about turning down these jobs, what reasons would you give?

≡ WRITING ABOUT THE ISSUES

1. Argue that "Orientation" is a dark satire of corporate culture. Be specific about what elements of that culture are being targeted.

2. Argue that "Exhortation" gets at the main problems of corporate/bureaucratic/organizational culture. Focus your essay on one organization, e.g., Congress, the military, universities, a specific company, a religious organization, prisons, or something else.

3. Argue that an actual moral dilemma a real business had to face was or was not handled ethically.

4. Assuming you have just taken over the company in "Exhortation," argue in a memorandum that new values will now be encouraged that differ from those in the past. Argue that this will be better for morale and profits.

≡ Resisting Stereotypes: Poems

CHRYSTOS, "Today Was a Bad Day like TB"

DWIGHT OKITA, "In Response to Executive Order 9066"

PAT MORA, "Legal Alien"

TOI DERRICOTTE, "Black Boys Play the Classics"

NAOMI SHIHAB NYE, "Blood"

DAVID HERNANDEZ, " 'Words without Thoughts Never to Heaven Go' "

UMA DWIVEDI, "I Conflate Shame and Desire and the Ocean Purses Her Lips"

When pressed, thoughtful people would agree that each of us has an individual personality and attributes that make us different from others. No one is an exact duplicate: even identical twins have both subtle and significant differences. Even so, cultures tend to lump together whole groups under dubious but convenient generalizations: used car dealers are dishonest, surfers are laid-back slackers, and computer geniuses are geeks. Usually based on limited, anecdotal, and often highly contextual historical and cultural evidence, these generalizations have a way of taking hold in a society long after the original context has disappeared (if there ever was one). Does anyone really think that dumb-blond jokes had any original validity? Is considering each person on his or her own merits too complicated?

When ethnic groups are stereotyped, their members may suffer consequences that are significantly more severe than those endured by, say, absentminded professors. Some stereotypes are benign: as children growing up in New York, we routinely heard about industrious Chinese or hardworking Germans. But we also heard many negative generalizations that went hand in hand with racial and sexual discrimination and psychological damage. Members of the dominant groups in America are often oblivious to the ways that members of minority groups internalize destructive and distorted images of themselves, often seeing themselves as inferior to the dominant group and irredeemably other. They become trapped in images rampant in the culture and struggle daily to overcome the limited reality these stereotypes portray. The following poems represent aspects of this struggle in various ways—some with anger, resentment, and despair, others with thoughtful reflection, but all with an awareness of the pain that thoughtless stereotypes have on millions of Americans.

≡ BEFORE YOU READ

Do you think of yourself as an ethnic American? Have you ever seen the term *English American* or *Dutch American*? What's the difference between those terms and *African American* or *Irish American*? Do you think ethnic traditions should be preserved, or should they be replaced with American traditions? Can these traditions coexist?

CHRYSTOS
Today Was a Bad Day like TB

Born in San Francisco of a Lithuanian/Alsace-Lorraine mother and a Native American father of the Menominee tribe, Chrystos (b. 1946) writes in the outsider traditions of her ancestry, her lesbian perspective, and her geographical position on Bainbridge Island off the coast of the Pacific Northwest. She is a women's and native rights advocate, a working artist, and a poet. Her poetry collections include Not Vanishing *(1988),* Dream On *(1991),* In Her I Am *(1993),* Fire Power *(1995), and the 1994 winner of the Audre Lorde International Poetry Competition,* Fugitive Colors. *In 2007, she published* Some Poems by People I Like. *She is a Lannan Foundation fellow and the 1995 recipient of the Sappho Award of Distinction. The poem reprinted here is from* Not Vanishing.

     For Amanda White

Saw whites clap during a sacred dance
Saw young blond hippie boy with a red stone pipe°
    My eyes burned him up
He smiled   *This is a Sioux pipe* he said from his sportscar
    Yes I hiss *I'm wondering how you got it*   5
    & the name is Lakota not Sioux
I'll tell you he said all friendly & liberal as only
    those with no pain can be
    I turned away Can't charm me can't bear to know
thinking of the medicine bundle I saw opened up in a glass case   10
    with a small white card beside it
    naming the rich whites who say they
    "own" it
Maybe they have an old Indian grandma back in time
    to excuse themselves   15
Today was a day I wanted to beat up the smirking man wearing
a pack with a Haida design from Moe's bookstore
Listen Moe's How many Indians do you have working there?
How much money are you sending the Haida people
to use their sacred Raven design?   20
    You probably have an Indian grandma too
    whose name you don't know
    Today was a day like TB
    you cough & cough trying to get it out
        all that comes   25
        is blood & spit   [1988]

---

2 red stone pipe: Traditionally, sacred peace pipes were made of red catlinite, a fine-grained stone.

≣ **THINKING ABOUT THE TEXT**

1. What argument about the ways whites relate to Native Americans is Chrystos making? What assumptions about whites does Chrystos seem to have? What stereotypes does she seem to harbor?

2. Might you have clapped during a Lakota dance? During a Catholic Mass? What is the "it" in line 24 that the poet is trying to get out? Do you think she is angry with her readers?

3. Is the ending too stark or perhaps too crude? Might the language have been more indirect and subtle, or is it appropriate to the theme?

4. Americans who are part of the "mainstream" — that is, white, male, middle class, or heterosexual — sometimes get annoyed when those who are not complain about bias, probably because the offense was inadvertent. (Think of Atlanta Braves fans doing "the tomahawk chop.") The young man in this poem, for example, seems quite oblivious of giving offense. Who determines who is right in these situations?

5. What other stereotypes can you think of that mainstream America harbors?

DWIGHT OKITA

In Response to Executive Order 9066

A third-generation Japanese American, poet and playwright Dwight Okita (b. 1958) won an Illinois Art Council Fellowship for poetry in 1988. Although Crossing with the Light *(1992), from which this poem is taken, is his first book of poetry, Okita has been more active in promoting the performance of poetry than the printing of it, and he is well known as a "slam" poet at open-mike readings in Chicago. A member of the large Japanese American community that developed in Chicago as a result of the migration from the West after the bitter experience of the internment camps during World War II, Okita expresses his family history in his poetry and plays. His dramas include* The Rainy Season *(1992) and* The Salad Bowl Dance *(1993). His book* The Prospect of My Arrival *(2008) was nominated for the Amazon Breakthrough Novel Award. His latest novel is* The Hope Store *(2017).*

> All Americans of Japanese Descent
> Must Report to Relocation Centers

Dear Sirs:
Of course I'll come. I've packed my galoshes
and three packets of tomato seeds. Denise calls them
love apples. My father says where we're going
they won't grow.   5

I am a fourteen-year-old girl with bad spelling
and a messy room. If it helps any, I will tell you
I have always felt funny using chopsticks
and my favorite food is hot dogs.
My best friend is a white girl named Denise—   10
we look at boys together. She sat in front of me
all through grade school because of our names:
O'Connor, Ozawa. I know the back of Denise's head very well.

I tell her she's going bald. She tells me I copy on tests.
We're best friends.   15

I saw Denise today in Geography class.
She was sitting on the other side of the room.
"You're trying to start a war," she said, "giving secrets
away to the Enemy. Why can't you keep your big
mouth shut?"   20

I didn't know what to say.
I gave her a packet of tomato seeds
and asked her to plant them for me, told her
when the first tomato ripened
she'd miss me.   *[1992]*   25

≡ THINKING ABOUT THE TEXT

1. What claim is Okita making in the last stanza? On what assumption
   about friendship is it based?

2. During the U.S. government's internment of Japanese American
   citizens, thousands were told to leave their homes to live in relocation
   centers for the duration of the war. To represent this complex
   historical event, why do you think it is effective to have a young girl
   writing a letter about being shunned by her best friend?

3. Explain Okita's use of the tomato seeds throughout the poem (lines
   3, 22). What about other concrete words: *galoshes* (line 2), *chopsticks*
   (line 8), *hot dogs* (line 9)?

4. Since there was no evidence that Japanese American citizens ever gave
   any "secrets / away to the Enemy" (lines 18–19) during World War II,
   why do you think Denise and millions of other Americans made that
   assumption?

5. What current situations seem comparable to the theme of this poem?

≡ MAKING COMPARISONS

1. Compare the tones of Okita's and Chrystos's poems. What emotions
   do you see in each?

2. Okita creates a young female narrator to speak for him. Does this make his poem less direct than Chrystos's?

3. Is the alienation described by Okita more or less painful than that described by Chrystos?

PAT MORA
Legal Alien

Pat Mora (b. 1942) was born in El Paso, Texas. She earned a B.A. from Texas Western College in 1963 and an M.A. from the University of Texas, El Paso, in 1967. She is a versatile writer of many children's books, essays, and poems. Her poems are, according to the New York Times, *"proudly bilingual." Her sixth collection,* Adobe Odes *(2006), was praised for turning its back on hopelessness, "finding a way to delight in the sensual world as well as its people," and a "must-have for libraries serving Latino communities." Her latest collection is* I Pledge Allegiance *(2014). Mora lives in Santa Fe, New Mexico. "Legal Alien" is from* Chants *(1984) and focuses on a common Chicana theme: the difficulties of living in two cultures simultaneously.*

Bi-lingual, Bi-cultural,
able to slip from "How's life?"
to *"Me'stan volviendo loca,"*°
able to sit in a paneled office
drafting memos in smooth English,   5
able to order in fluent Spanish
at a Mexican restaurant,
American but hyphenated,
viewed by Anglos as perhaps exotic,
perhaps inferior, definitely different,   10
viewed by Mexicans as alien,
(their eyes say, "You may speak
Spanish but you're not like me")
an American to Mexicans
a Mexican to Americans   15
a handy token
sliding back and forth
between the fringes of both worlds
by smiling
by masking the discomfort   20
of being pre-judged
Bi-laterally.

[1984]

3 *"Me'stan volviendo loca"*: They're driving me crazy (Spanish).

☰ THINKING ABOUT THE TEXT

1. Was your first response to the opening line to think that such a situation is an advantage? Is that Mora's intent?

2. What advantages does being bicultural have? What disadvantages?

3. What other Americans are referred to as "hyphenated"? Do you think the same pluses and minuses apply?

4. Is the title appropriate? Explain.

5. Explain the significance of the "token" metaphor in line 16.

☰ MAKING COMPARISONS

1. Mora sees some advantage to being bicultural. Do any of the other poets?

2. Compare Mora's tone with Chrystos's.

3. Which of the stereotypes in these poems seems the most psychologically damaging? Why?

TOI DERRICOTTE
Black Boys Play the Classics

Toi Derricotte (b. 1941) was born in Louisiana and was influenced as a child by her Creole and Catholic background. She graduated from Wayne State University in 1965. The first of her six books, The Empress of the Death House, *was published in 1978. Her latest collection of poems and stories,* The Undertaker's Daughter, *was published in 2011. Often compared to Sylvia Plath and Anne Sexton, Derricotte writes poems that, according to the poet and critic Marilyn Hacker, are "honest, fine-boned, deceptively simple . . . and deadly accurate." She is currently a professor of English at the University of Pittsburgh. The following poem is from* Tender *(1997).*

The most popular "act" in
Penn Station
is the three black kids in ratty
sneakers & T-shirts playing
two violins and a cello—Brahms.   5
White men in business suits
have already dug into their pockets
as they pass and they toss in
a dollar or two without stopping.
Brown men in work-soiled khakis   10
stand with their mouths open,
arms crossed on their bellies

as if they themselves have always
wanted to attempt those bars.
One white boy, three, sits   15
cross-legged in front of his
idols—in ecstasy—
their slick, dark faces,
their thin, wiry arms,
who must begin to look   20
like angels!
Why does this trembling
pull us?
A: *Beneath the surface we are one.*
B: *Amazing! I did not think that they could speak this tongue.*   [1997]   25

☰ THINKING ABOUT THE TEXT

1. Why do the "brown men" (line 10) respond as they do? Why do the "white men" (line 6)?

2. Why does the poet offer a description of the boys' clothes? Does it have to do with our stereotyped expectations?

3. What are some possible meanings for "pull us" (line 23)?

4. Explain what you think Derricotte means by the last line.

5. How would you state the theme of this poem? Do you agree with it? Who is the "we" in the next-to-last line?

☰ MAKING COMPARISONS

1. How does Derricotte's tone differ from Chrystos's tone?

2. How does the end of this poem differ from the ends of the other poems in this cluster? Is it more effective or less effective?

3. If you were to rewrite "Black Boys Play the Classics" as a first-person poem (as Okita's poem demonstrates), which character from this poem would you choose, and why? How would a different point of view change the poem?

NAOMI SHIHAB NYE
Blood

Naomi Shihab Nye (b. 1952) was born to a Lutheran German American mother and a Muslim Palestinian American father in St. Louis. Her parents moved to the Middle East near Jerusalem, where her father edited the Jerusalem Times, *for which Nye, at fourteen, wrote a weekly column. Eventually turmoil forced their return to the United States. They settled in Texas, and Nye graduated from*

Trinity University in San Antonio in 1974. She has published books for children and adolescents with subject matter she hopes will dispel stereotypes and foster an understanding of "difference." Her poetic focus is often on the Palestinian Diaspora and on themes of our common humanity. Her books include 19 Varieties of Gazelle *(2002) and* You and Yours: Poems *(2005). "Blood" is from* Yellow Glove *(1986).*

"A true Arab knows how to catch a fly in his hands,"
my father would say. And he'd prove it,
cupping the buzzer instantly
while the host with the swatter stared.

In the spring our palms peeled like snakes.   5
True Arabs believed watermelon could heal fifty ways.
I changed these to fit the occasion.

Years before, a girl knocked,
wanted to see the Arab.
I said we didn't have one.   10
After that, my father told me who he was,

"Shihab" — "shooting star" —
a good name, borrowed from the sky.
Once I said, "When we die, we give it back?"
He said that's what a true Arab would say.   15

Today the headlines clot in my blood.
A little Palestinian dangles a truck on the front page.
Homeless fig, this tragedy with a terrible root
is too big for us. What flag can we wave?
I wave the flag of stone and seed,   20
table mat stitched in blue.

I call my father, we talk around the news.
It is too much for him,
neither of his two languages can reach it.
I drive into the country to find sheep, cows,   25
to plead with the air:
Who calls anyone *civilized*?
Where can the crying heart graze?
What does a true Arab do now?   *[1986]*

≡ THINKING ABOUT THE TEXT

1. What is your response to the girl who comes looking "to see the Arab" (line 9)? What is the speaker's response?

2. What do you think the father means by "a true Arab"? Is there a true American? A true man? Woman? Texan?

3. What is the father's response to the news about the Middle East? What is the speaker's? What is yours?

4. What is the purpose of the speaker's drive into the country?

5. How would you answer the questions the speaker asks in the last stanza?

≡ MAKING COMPARISONS

1. Compare Nye's bicultural perspective to Mora's. Is Nye's status more precarious than Mora's in contemporary America?

2. Which of the speakers in all these poems seems angriest? Saddest? The most understanding?

3. What seems to be the most common theme among the poems?

DAVID HERNANDEZ
"Words without Thoughts Never to Heaven Go"°

David Hernandez (b. 1971) was born in Burbank, California, and received a B.A. at California State University, Long Beach. He is the author of several collections of poetry, including Hoodwinked *(2011) and* Always Danger *(2006). His most recent book is* Dear Sincerely *(2016). He teaches at California State University, Fullerton. The following poem was published in* The Southern Review *(Spring 2016).*

The n-word will never go, the k-word will never go.
My surname may allow me to say aloud
the slur beginning with *s*, but I won't, I won't,
it will never don a halo. Spoken, it is almost *speak*
and meant to make a person of my race   5
smaller, a speck inside his own skin. It is almost
speck. Earlier I typed "ethnic slurs" online,
scrolled through the list. At least a hundred words
will never rise, will never come within
earshot of divine clouds.   10
                    When I was a kid, timid
as a breeze, I rolled with this reckless boy
schooled in the art of aspersions.
Nothing in the alphabet could dodge his epithets
(the q-word will never go), but somehow   15
my flesh was pale enough to enter his home. Stark
differences, the two of us. We shared

Words without Thoughts Never to Heaven Go: from Shakespeare.

our given name. *David*, his father said
one summer afternoon, *remember when I*
rooted for that n-word at the race? He didn't say it   20
quite like that.
                    This is the story,
this is a racist cheering for an African American
speeding around a motocross track, the pack
droning behind him like angry hornets.   25
After he won, he said to me, *he took off*
his helmet. Had I known, he continued, dot
dot dot, then dropped again
                    the word from his lips.
Come December, he beat his wife, and David   30
grabbed an aluminum bat, attacked his house
all around the outside. I recall the damage
to the siding, open mouth after open mouth,
how each nested a hollow sound.

≣ THINKING ABOUT THE TEXT

1. Why does Hernandez say his surname allows him to use a slur? Why would you agree or disagree with this?

2. What effect does Hernandez say the "s-word" slur has? What seems to you to be the motivation for using ethnic slurs?

3. What does Hernandez mean by the poem's title?

4. Look up the title's quote from Claudius in *Hamlet*. How does the original meaning reinforce Hernandez's meaning in the poem?

5. What is the intended relationship between the last stanza and the rest of the poem?

≣ MAKING COMPARISONS

1. Hernandez writes about a racist. How might this term apply to Chrystos's and Okita's poems?

2. Which of the poetic devices in the preceding poems strikes you as the most effective? The least? Why?

3. Which ideas in these poems seem the most relevant today? Why?

≣ WRITING ABOUT ISSUES

1. Write a journal entry from either Chrystos's or Okita's perspective that comments on the writing of their respective poem, what you (as the author) were trying to do, how you feel about stereotyping, and what response you are hoping for from readers.

2. Write an essay that compares the stereotyping that occurs in "Black Boys Play the Classics" and "Legal Alien." Comment on its origins, consequences, and possible solutions.

3. Write an essay that explores the kind of stereotyping you were exposed to as a child and as an adolescent in your family, in your peer group, or in the larger culture.

4. After doing research on an ethnic group not represented here, locate a poet from that group and write a brief report on his or her work.

UMA DWIVEDI

I Conflate Shame and Desire and the Ocean Purses Her Lips

Uma Dwivedi (b. 2000) graduated from Lakeside High School in Seattle. Uma is a student at Yale University. Recent publications include Navigating the Maze *and* Winter Tangerine Review's *special issue,* Mouth Dreams. *Uma identifies as trans, nonbinary, and bigender and uses they/them pronouns. They have a chapbook,* They Named Her Goddess (we called her girl), *forthcoming from Dancing Girl Press.*

I dream of a self like her / rolling her hips
in waves / the edges of myself dissolved
saline / falling into something bigger something
realer something full of possibility. I move
and the movement keeps going   5

the self curling around the self / a helix
doubled/tripled/infinite / I am a thing that wants
and so I am all things / I am no thing I
just / want / to want a body like my own

is inevitable when the self covers so much ground.   10
A body like mine but not mine/ the gentle heft
of it the bound breasts of it the contracted
spine of it / gravity cannot touch desire because
desire dances into something green & growing
while gravity / grips the earth. I love.   15
I am a thing that loves I am the self and all

its downfalls / the self and all its glories / the open heart
and all its horrors / & is that not what the ocean
sings of, her voice lovely and treacherous & deep.
I am lovely and treacherous and deep & my hips   20
do not betray me / my rest does not betray me /
there is no edge to betray.

≣ THINIKING ABOUT THE TEXT

1. What qualities of the ocean seem appealing to the narrator?
2. Compare ideas about this poet's identify with Walt Whitman's "I am large, I contain multitudes."
3. The poet says that the poem is about "transgender desire." In what ways does this seem to be the case?
4. The poet seems somewhat ambivalent about identifying with the ocean: "her voice lovely and treacherous & deep." Comment on this idea.
5. How is the last line connected to the ideas expressed in their poem?

≣ MAKING COMPARISONS

1. Most of our poems in this cluster resist stereotyping. Explain how this is the case.
2. What conventional ideas about identity is Dwivedi resisting? What about Okita and Derricotte?
3. Dwivedi's poem about trans identity is the most recent. How are some of the stereotypes in the older poems still relevant?

≣ WRITING ABOUT ISSUES

1. Write an argument that one of these poems is relevant to a current issue of stereotyping.
2. Write an essay that argues that stereotyping of a racial, ethnic, gender, or sexual minority is prevalent in America today.
3. Do some research about America's historical attitudes toward a gay, lesbian, or transgender minority and argue that we have or have not made significant progress toward equality and understanding for that group.
4. Write an essay that argues that a particular minority group not mentioned in this cluster is stereotyped in America and reform needs to happen.

☰ A Creative Confinement: Poems by Emily Dickinson

EMILY DICKINSON, "Wild Nights—Wild Nights!"

EMILY DICKINSON, "Tell all the truth but tell it slant—"

EMILY DICKINSON, "Much Madness is divinest Sense—"

EMILY DICKINSON, "I'm Nobody! Who are you?"

Although Emily Dickinson was considered an eccentric recluse by many of her provincial neighbors, history has interpreted her life in various ways, changing with the thinking of the times. Once considered isolated, many critics now see her as vitally connected to the issues and literature of her age. Feminist and queer studies scholars now see the once-shy figure as an active champion who defied gender stereotypes. Although she has often been described as nunlike and passive, critics today see her as a nonconformist, mistrustful of power and dogma, and as someone who questioned any kind of received opinion, even popular views on religion and the afterlife. Although it may seem paradoxical to many, the artistic freedom necessary for a focused creative life is often achieved by isolation, by physically removing oneself from the temptation and distractions of social life. If ever there was an example of confinement nurturing the creative impulse, it is the life and poems of Emily Dickinson.

EMILY DICKINSON
Wild Nights—Wild Nights!

Emily Dickinson (1830–1886) spent most of her life in her father's house in Amherst, Massachusetts. Except for a year of college and several brief excursions to Philadelphia and Washington, D.C., Dickinson lived a quiet, reclusive life in a house she described as "pretty much all sobriety." Although a few poems were published during her lifetime, Dickinson wrote almost two thousand poems on love, death, immortality, and nature that are universally judged to be some of the most original, lyrical, and artistic works in American literature. Although the specific person to whom Dickinson wrote her love poems is unclear, many critics today believe her interests were both lesbian and heterosexual. As the four poems below suggest, Dickinson, although outwardly retiring and isolated, lived a lively, rich, and passionate life in her poetry.

> Wild Nights—Wild Nights!
> Were I with thee
> Wild Nights should be
> Our luxury!
> Futile—the Winds— 5

Wendy Maeda/Boston Globe/
Getty Images

To a Heart in port—
Done with the Compass—
Done with the Chart!

Rowing in Eden—
Ah, the Sea!   10
Might I but moor—Tonight—
In Thee   [c. 1861]

☰ THINKING ABOUT THE TEXT

1. Many critics see this poem as an erotic fantasy, perhaps a surprising
   subject for a reclusive spinster. Are there indications that this is not a
   poem about a real sexual encounter?

2. Comment on the imagery of the ocean and port. Could the port be
   Dickinson's isolation? The ocean, the actual consummation?

3. How do you read the speaker's claim that she is done with the
   compass and chart? Is she rejecting convention?

4. What are some ways to interpret "Eden" in line 9?

5. What does the image of "moor[ing] . . . In Thee" (lines 11–12) suggest
   about her erotic desire?

EMILY DICKINSON

Tell all the truth but tell it slant—

Tell all the truth but tell it slant—
Success in Circuit lies
Too bright for our infirm Delight
The Truth's superb surprise

As Lightning to the Children eased   5
With explanation kind
The Truth must dazzle gradually
Or every man be blind—   *[1868]*

≡ **THINKING ABOUT THE TEXT**

1. What is the primary dictionary definition of "slant"? What does Dickinson mean by it?
2. Why does Dickinson say we shouldn't be direct in telling the truth?
3. What similarity between the truth and lightning does Dickinson want us to make?
4. What is it about poetry that makes indirection a better path to truth?
5. How does this poem embody Dickinson's advice?

≡ **MAKING COMPARISONS**

1. How might both poems be about freedom and confinement?
2. Compare the images in both poems. Are they apt?
3. To whom is each poem addressed?

EMILY DICKINSON

Much Madness is divinest Sense—

Much Madness is divinest Sense—
To a discerning Eye—
Much Sense—the starkest Madness—
'Tis the Majority
In this, as all, prevail—   5
Assent—and you are sane—
Demur—you're straightway dangerous—
And handled with a Chain—   *[1871]*

≡ THINKING ABOUT THE TEXT

1. What does Dickinson suggest is one way to lose your freedom?
2. How might this poem be an example of Dickinson's own biography? (See also the introduction on p. 730.)
3. Why does Dickinson use "Demur" (line 7)? What synonyms might she have used?
4. Why does she use "divinest sense" (line 1)? Why does she say the majority is usually wrong? Why does she use the dramatic image of a chain? Is this an indication of her mood?
5. In your experience, how is Dickinson's idea that the majority is intolerant of dissent true?

≡ MAKING COMPARISONS

1. How might Dickinson be telling the truth in "Much Madness is divinest Sense" at a slant?
2. Why might Dickinson's "tell it slant" be necessary given the last two lines of "Much Madness is divinest Sense"?
3. Compare the idea that there is freedom in confinement with the themes of these poems.

EMILY DICKINSON
I'm Nobody! Who are you?

I'm Nobody! Who are you?
Are you — Nobody — too?
Then there's a pair of us!
Don't tell! they'd advertise — you know!

How dreary — to be — Somebody!   5
How public — like a Frog —
To tell one's name — the livelong June —
To an admiring Bog! —   *[1891]*

≡ THINKING ABOUT THE TEXT

1. How might this poem be about Dickinson's own life?
2. Why does Dickinson use "Bog" (line 8)? In what way is it an appropriate image for her theme? Why does she pick a frog and not something else — say, a robin or a horse?
3. Is this poem meant to be comical or satirical? Why does she invite the reader to identify with her?

4. How would you describe what the poet means by "Nobody" (line 1) and "Somebody" (line 5)?

5. How might this poem be applicable to fame in today's culture?

≣ MAKING COMPARISONS

1. How might the theme of "Much Madness is divinest Sense" be a reason for Dickinson's declaration, "I'm Nobody"?

2. Compare the intended audience for all four poems.

3. Compare the implications of "an admiring Bog" in "I'm Nobody! Who are you?" with "Majority" in "Much Madness is divinest Sense."

≣ WRITING ABOUT ISSUES

1. Write an analysis of these four poems as examples of the ideas mentioned in the introduction to this chapter and in the biographical note about Dickinson (p. 730).

2. Write an analysis of these four poems, focusing on the imagery Dickinson uses to support her themes.

3. Research Dickinson's poetry and choose two other poems that develop similar themes to those given here. Write an essay that demonstrates how freedom is developed in these two poems.

4. Argue that Dickinson's ideas about nonconformity and fame are relevant in today's culture.

■ Domestic Prisons: Plays

SUSAN GLASPELL, *Trifles*

LYNN NOTTAGE, *POOF!*

Marriage is, of course, an almost universal societal arrangement developed to serve the emotional, financial, and physical needs of men and women and transmit cultural mores and traditions. But its centuries-old heritage means that the traditions and laws governing marriage were almost exclusively written by men primarily to serve their interests. The emotional and financial needs of women were rarely considered. For hundreds of years, marriage offered little protection for emotionally and physically abused women. And in many societies, it was accepted behavior for husbands to discipline their wives for whatever behavior they saw as inappropriate. Even after significant reform in Western society over the past hundred years, vestiges of our sometimes cruel and unjust marital customs remain. As a result, domestic abuse is still an all-too-common cultural inheritance. The two plays that follow dramatize aspects of that vexed heritage.

Susan Glaspell's *Trifles* explores feelings of confinement in rural America and the gloomy, abandoned kitchen of Minnie Wright. Readers quickly get the feeling that the marriage of John and Minnie was one of emotional domination. As the details surrounding John's death are cleverly and subtly revealed to us, we also get the clear impression that we cannot look to the men in the play for insight and understanding of Minnie's situation. They are too concerned with a search for physical evidence to see the devastating emotional truth of this marriage that is in plain sight.

Written almost a hundred years after *Trifles*, *POOF!* deals with many of the same marriage problems of abuse and unequal status that were on Susan Glaspell's mind in 1916. That in itself should be cause for alarm, since we like to think we have made great strides in gender equality over the past century. And of course, in many significant ways that is the case. But because domestic abuse until the past twenty years or so was widely seen as a private matter, marriage is still a fertile ground for injustice. Verbal, physical, and emotional abuse is still a major issue in marriage, with women almost always the victims. And although the abuser in *POOF!* is punished for his crimes, that is more wishful thinking than a mirror of reality, as marriage for too many women is still a domestic prison.

■ BEFORE YOU READ

Do you think a woman is ever justified in leaving her children? Do you think absolute equality is necessary for love to exist in a marriage? Do you think an abused wife who takes revenge on her husband deserves punishment?

SUSAN GLASPELL
Trifles

Susan Glaspell (1876–1948) is best known for the frequently anthologized play
Trifles *and its short-story version, "A Jury of Her Peers." Surprisingly modern,*
Glaspell's work is in harmony with contemporary feminist concerns of identity,
the difficulty of female expression in a patriarchal culture, the disillusionment of
marriage for gifted women, and the necessity for female support and understanding.

Glaspell graduated from Drake University in 1899 and first worked as a jour-
nalist in Des Moines, Iowa. She soon began to publish short stories in prestigious
magazines like Harper's *and* The American. *After she married novelist and play-*
wright George Cram Cook, they moved to Greenwich Village, where they felt more
comfortable with its freethinking attitudes. Glaspell continued to publish both stories
and novels. She also began writing plays, and in 1916, she and her husband founded
the Provincetown Players, an important source for innovative American drama.
During the 1920s and 1930s, Glaspell published a number of best-selling novels,
including Brook Evans *(1928), which was turned into a successful movie. Her play*
Alison's House *won the Pulitzer Prize in 1931, and her novel* The Morning Is
Near *(1939) sold more than one hundred thousand copies. Today her significant*
successes in two genres, drama and fiction, are considered remarkable.

CHARACTERS

GEORGE HENDERSON, *county attorney*
HENRY PETERS, *sheriff*
LEWIS HALE, *a neighboring farmer*
MRS. PETERS
MRS. HALE

SCENE: *The kitchen in the now-abandoned farmhouse of John Wright, a gloomy*
kitchen, and left without having been put in order — the walls covered with a faded
wallpaper. Down right is a door leading to the parlor. On the right wall above this
door is a built-in kitchen cupboard with shelves in the upper portion and drawers
below. In the rear wall at right, up two steps is a door opening onto stairs leading to
the second floor. In the rear wall at left is a door to the shed and from there to the
outside. Between these two doors is an old-fashioned black iron stove. Running along
the left wall from the shed door is an old iron sink and sink shelf, in which is set a
hand pump. Downstage of the sink is an uncurtained window. Near the window is an
old wooden rocker. Center stage is an unpainted wooden kitchen table with straight
chairs on either side. There is a small chair down right. Unwashed pans under the
sink, a loaf of bread outside the breadbox, a dish towel on the table — other signs of
incomplete work. At the rear the shed door opens and the Sheriff comes in followed
by the County Attorney and Hale. The Sheriff and Hale are men in middle life, the
County Attorney is a young man; all are much bundled up and go at once to the
stove. They are followed by the two women — the Sheriff's wife, Mrs. Peters, first;

she is a slight wiry woman, a thin nervous face. Mrs. Hale is larger and would ordinarily be called more comfortable looking, but she is disturbed now and looks fearfully about as she enters. The women have come in slowly, and stand close together near the door.

COUNTY ATTORNEY *(at stove rubbing his hands)*:   This feels good. Come up to the fire, ladies.

MRS. PETERS *(after taking a step forward)*:   I'm not — cold.

SHERIFF *(unbuttoning his overcoat and stepping away from the stove to right of table as if to mark the beginning of official business)*:   Now, Mr. Hale, before we move things about, you explain to Mr. Henderson just what you saw when you came here yesterday morning.

COUNTY ATTORNEY *(crossing down to left of the table)*:   By the way, has anything been moved? Are things just as you left them yesterday?

SHERIFF *(looking about)*:   It's just about the same. When it dropped below zero last night I thought I'd better send Frank out this morning to make a fire for us — *(sits right of center table)* no use getting pneumonia with a big case on, but I told him not to touch anything except the stove — and you know Frank.

COUNTY ATTORNEY: Somebody should have been left here yesterday.

SHERIFF: Oh — yesterday. When I had to send Frank to Morris Center for that man who went crazy — I want you to know I had my hands full yesterday. I knew you could get back from Omaha by today and as long as I went over everything here myself — —

COUNTY ATTORNEY: Well, Mr. Hale, tell just what happened when you came here yesterday morning.

HALE *(crossing down to above table)*:   Harry and I had started to town with a load of potatoes. We came along the road from my place and as I got here I said, "I'm going to see if I can't get John Wright to go in with me on a party telephone." I spoke to Wright about it once before and he put me off, saying folks talked too much anyway, and all he asked was peace and quiet — I guess you know about how much he talked himself; but I thought maybe if I went to the house and talked about it before his wife, though I said to Harry that I didn't know as what his wife wanted made much difference to John — —

COUNTY ATTORNEY: Let's talk about that later, Mr. Hale. I do want to talk about that, but tell now just what happened when you got to the house.

HALE: I didn't hear or see anything; I knocked at the door, and still it was all quiet inside. I knew they must be up, it was past eight o'clock. So I knocked again, and I thought I heard somebody say, "Come in." I wasn't sure, I'm not sure yet, but I opened the door — this door *(indicating the door by which the two women are still standing)* and there in that rocker — *(pointing to it)* sat Mrs. Wright. *(They all look at the rocker down left.)*

COUNTY ATTORNEY: What — was she doing?

HALE: She was rockin' back and forth. She had her apron in her hand and was kind of — pleating it.

COUNTY ATTORNEY: And how did she—look?

HALE: Well, she looked queer.

COUNTY ATTORNEY: How do you mean—queer?

HALE: Well, as if she didn't know what she was going to do next. And kind of done up.

COUNTY ATTORNEY *(takes out notebook and pencil and sits left of center table)*:   How did she seem to feel about your coming?

HALE: Why, I don't think she minded—one way or other. She didn't pay much attention. I said, "How do, Mrs. Wright, it's cold, ain't it?" And she said, "Is it?"—and went on kind of pleating at her apron. Well, I was surprised; she didn't ask me to come up to the stove, or to set down, but just sat there, not even looking at me, so I said, "I want to see John." And then she—laughed. I guess you would call it a laugh. I thought of Harry and the team outside, so I said a little sharp: "Can't I see John?" "No," she says, kind o' dull like. "Ain't he home?" says I. "Yes," says she, "he's home." "Then why can't I see him?" I asked her, out of patience. " 'Cause he's dead," says she. "*Dead?*" says I. She just nodded her head, not getting a bit excited, but rockin' back and forth. "Why—where is he?" says I, not knowing what to say. She just pointed upstairs—like that. *(Himself pointing to the room above.)* I started for the stairs, with the idea of going up there. I walked from there to here—then I says, "Why, what did he die of?" "He died of a rope round his neck," says she, and just went on pleatin' at her apron. Well, I went out and called Harry. I thought I might—need help. We went upstairs and there he was lyin'——

COUNTY ATTORNEY: I think I'd rather have you go into that upstairs, where you can point it all out. Just go on now with the rest of the story.

HALE: Well, my first thought was to get that rope off. It looked . . . *(stops; his face twitches)* . . . but Harry, he went up to him, and he said, "No, he's dead all right, and we'd better not touch anything." So we went back downstairs. She was still sitting that same way. "Has anybody been notified?" I asked. "No," says she, unconcerned. "Who did this, Mrs. Wright?" said Harry. He said it businesslike—and she stopped pleatin' of her apron. "I don't know," she says. "You don't *know?*" says Harry. "No," says she. "Weren't you sleepin' in the bed with him?" says Harry. "Yes," says she, "but I was on the inside." "Somebody slipped a rope round his neck and strangled him and you didn't wake up?" says Harry. "I didn't wake up," she said after him. We must 'a' looked as if we didn't see how that could be, for after a minute she said, "I sleep sound." Harry was going to ask her more questions but I said maybe we ought to let her tell her story first to the coroner, or the sheriff, so Harry went fast as he could to Rivers's place, where there's a telephone.

COUNTY ATTORNEY: And what did Mrs. Wright do when she knew that you had gone for the coroner?

HALE: She moved from the rocker to that chair over there *(pointing to a small chair in the down right corner)* and just sat there with her hands held to-gether and looking down. I got a feeling that I ought to make some conversation, so I said I had come in to see if John wanted to put in a telephone, and at that she started to laugh, and then she stopped and looked at me—scared. *(The County Attorney, who has had his notebook out, makes a note.)* I dunno, maybe it wasn't scared. I wouldn't like to say it was. Soon Harry got back, and then Dr. Lloyd came and you, Mr. Peters, and so I guess that's all I know that you don't.

COUNTY ATTORNEY *(rising and looking around)*: I guess we'll go upstairs first—and then out to the barn and around there. *(To the Sheriff.)* You're convinced that there was nothing important here—nothing that would point to any motive?

SHERIFF: Nothing here but kitchen things. *(The County Attorney, after again looking around the kitchen, opens the door of a cupboard closet in right wall. He brings a small chair from right—gets on it and looks on a shelf. Pulls his hand away, sticky.)*

COUNTY ATTORNEY: Here's a nice mess. *(The women draw nearer up center.)*

MRS. PETERS *(to the other woman)*: Oh, her fruit; it did freeze. *(To the Lawyer.)* She worried about that when it turned so cold. She said the fire'd go out and her jars would break.

SHERIFF *(rises)*: Well, can you beat the woman! Held for murder and worryin' about her preserves.

COUNTY ATTORNEY *(getting down from chair)*: I guess before we're through she may have something more serious than preserves to worry about. *(Crosses down right center.)*

HALE: —Well, women are used to worrying over trifles. *(The two women move a little closer together.)*

COUNTY ATTORNEY *(with the gallantry of a young politician)*: And yet, for all their worries, what would we do without the ladies? *(The women do not unbend. He goes below the center table to the sink, takes a dipperful of water from the pail, and pouring it into a basin, washes his hands. While he is doing this the Sheriff and Hale cross to cupboard, which they inspect. The County Attorney starts to wipe his hands on the roller towel, turns it for a cleaner place.)* Dirty towels! *(Kicks his foot against the pans under the sink.)* Not much of a housekeeper, would you say, ladies?

MRS. HALE *(stiffly)*: There's a great deal of work to be done on a farm.

COUNTY ATTORNEY: To be sure. And yet *(with a little bow to her)* I know there are some Dickson County farmhouses which do not have such roller towels. *(He gives it a pull to expose its full-length again.)*

MRS. HALE: Those towels get dirty awful quick. Men's hands aren't always as clean as they might be.

COUNTY ATTORNEY: Ah, loyal to your sex, I see. But you and Mrs. Wright were neighbors. I suppose you were friends, too.

MRS. HALE *(shaking her head)*: I've not seen much of her of late years. I've not been in this house—it's more than a year.

COUNTY ATTORNEY *(crossing to women up center)*: And why was that? You didn't like her?

MRS. HALE: I liked her all well enough. Farmers' wives have their hands full, Mr. Henderson. And then ____

COUNTY ATTORNEY: Yes ____?

MRS. HALE *(looking about)*:   It never seemed a very cheerful place.

COUNTY ATTORNEY: No—it's not cheerful. I shouldn't say she had the home-making instinct.

MRS. HALE: Well, I don't know as Wright had, either.

COUNTY ATTORNEY: You mean that they didn't get on very well?

MRS. HALE: No, I don't mean anything. But I don't think a place'd be any cheerfuller for John Wright's being in it.

COUNTY ATTORNEY: I'd like to talk more of that a little later. I want to get the lay of things upstairs now. *(He goes past the women to up right where steps lead to a stair door.)*

SHERIFF: I suppose anything Mrs. Peters does'll be all right. She was to take in some clothes for her, you know, and a few little things. We left in such a hurry yesterday.

COUNTY ATTORNEY: Yes, but I would like to see what you take, Mrs. Peters, and keep an eye out for anything that might be of use to us.

MRS. PETERS: Yes, Mr. Henderson. *(The men leave by up right door to stairs. The women listen to the men's steps on the stairs, then look about the kitchen.)*

MRS. HALE *(crossing left to sink)*:   I'd hate to have men coming into my kitchen, snooping around and criticizing. *(She arranges the pans under sink which the lawyer had shoved out of place.)*

MRS. PETERS: Of course it's no more than their duty. *(Crosses to cupboard up right.)*

MRS. HALE: Duty's all right, but I guess that deputy sheriff that came out to make the fire might have got a little of this on. *(Gives the roller towel a pull.)* Wish I'd thought of that sooner. Seems mean to talk about her for not having things slicked up when she had to come away in such a hurry. *(Crosses right to Mrs. Peters at cupboard.)*

MRS. PETERS *(who has been looking through cupboard, lifts one end of towel that covers a pan)*:   She had bread set. *(Stands still.)*

MRS. HALE *(eyes fixed on a loaf of bread beside the breadbox, which is on a low shelf of the cupboard)*:   She was going to put this in there. *(Picks up loaf, abruptly drops it. In a manner of returning to familiar things.)* It's a shame about her fruit. I wonder if it's all gone. *(Gets up on the chair and looks.)* I think there's some here that's all right, Mrs. Peters. Yes—here; *(holding it toward the window)* this is cherries, too. *(Looking again.)* I declare I believe that's the only one. *(Gets down, jar in her hand. Goes to the sink and wipes it off on the outside.)* She'll feel awful bad after all her hard work in the hot weather. I remember the afternoon I put up my cherries last summer. *(She puts the jar on the big kitchen table, center of the room. With a sigh, is about to sit down in the rocking chair. Before she is seated realizes what chair it is; with a slow look at it, steps back. The chair which she has touched rocks back and forth. Mrs. Peters moves to center table and they both watch the chair rock for a moment or two.)*

MRS. PETERS *(shaking off the mood which the empty rocking chair has evoked. Now in a businesslike manner she speaks)*:   Well I must get those things from the front room closet. *(She goes to the door at the right but, after looking into the other room, steps back.)* You coming with me, Mrs. Hale? You could help me carry them. *(They go in the other room; reappear, Mrs. Peters carrying a dress, petticoat, and skirt, Mrs. Hale following with a pair of shoes.)* My, it's cold in there. *(She puts the clothes on the big table and hurries to the stove.)*

MRS. HALE *(right of center table examining the skirt)*:   Wright was close. I think maybe that's why she kept so much to herself. She didn't even belong to the Ladies' Aid. I suppose she felt she couldn't do her part, and then you don't enjoy things when you feel shabby. I heard she used to wear pretty clothes and be lively, when she was Minnie Foster, one of the town girls singing in the choir. But that—oh, that was thirty years ago. This all you want to take in?

MRS. PETERS: She said she wanted an apron. Funny thing to want, for there isn't much to get you dirty in jail, goodness knows. But I suppose just to make her feel more natural. *(Crosses to cupboard.)* She said they was in the top drawer in this cupboard. Yes, here. And then her little shawl that always hung behind the door. *(Opens stair door and looks.)* Yes, here it is. *(Quickly shuts door leading upstairs.)*

MRS. HALE *(abruptly moving toward her)*:   Mrs. Peters?

MRS. PETERS: Yes, Mrs. Hale? *(At up right door.)*

MRS. HALE: Do you think she did it?

MRS. PETERS *(in a frightened voice)*:   Oh, I don't know.

MRS. HALE: Well, I don't think she did. Asking for an apron and her little shawl. Worrying about her fruit.

MRS. PETERS *(starts to speak, glances up, where footsteps are heard in the room above. In a low voice)*:   Mr. Peters says it looks bad for her. Mr. Henderson is awful sarcastic in a speech and he'll make fun of her sayin' she didn't wake up.

MRS. HALE: Well, I guess John Wright didn't wake when they was slipping that rope under his neck.

MRS. PETERS *(crossing slowly to table and placing shawl and apron on table with other clothing)*:   No, it's strange. It must have been done awful crafty and still. They say it was such a—funny way to kill a man, rigging it all up like that.

MRS. HALE *(crossing to left of Mrs. Peters at table)*:   That's just what Mr. Hale said. There was a gun in the house. He says that's what he can't understand.

MRS. PETERS: Mr. Henderson said coming out that what was needed for the case was a motive; something to show anger, or—sudden feeling.

MRS. HALE *(who is standing by the table)*:   Well, I don't see any signs of anger around here. *(She puts her hand on the dish towel, which lies on the table, stands looking down at table, one-half of which is clean, the other half messy.)* It's wiped to here. *(Makes a move as if to finish work, then turns and looks at loaf of bread outside the breadbox. Drops towel. In that voice of coming back to familiar things.)* Wonder how they are finding things upstairs. *(Crossing below table to down right.)* I hope she had it a little more red-up° up there. You know, it seems kind of *sneaking.* Locking her up in town and then coming out here and trying to get her own house to turn against her!

red-up: To get ready or clean up.

MRS. PETERS: But, Mrs. Hale, the law is the law.

MRS. HALE: I s'pose 'tis. *(Unbuttoning her coat.)* Better loosen up your things, Mrs. Peters. You won't feel them when you go out. *(Mrs. Peters takes off her fur tippet, goes to hang it on chair back left of table, stands looking at the work basket on floor near down left window.)*

MRS. PETERS: She was piecing a quilt. *(She brings the large sewing basket to the center table and they look at the bright pieces, Mrs. Hale above the table and Mrs. Peters left of it.)*

MRS. HALE: It's a log cabin pattern. Pretty, isn't it? I wonder if she was goin' to quilt it or just knot it? *(Footsteps have been heard coming down the stairs. The Sheriff enters followed by Hale and the County Attorney.)*

SHERIFF: They wonder if she was going to quilt it or just knot it! *(The men laugh, the women look abashed.)*

COUNTY ATTORNEY *(rubbing his hands over the stove)*:   Frank's fire didn't do much up there, did it? Well, let's go out to the barn and get that cleared up. *(The men go outside by up left door.)*

MRS. HALE *(resentfully)*:   I don't know as there's anything so strange, our takin' up our time with little things while we're waiting for them to get the evidence. *(She sits in chair right of table smoothing out a block with decision.)* I don't see as it's anything to laugh about.

MRS. PETERS *(apologetically)*:   Of course they've got awful important things on their minds. *(Pulls up a chair and joins Mrs. Hale at the left of the table.)*

MRS. HALE *(examining another block)*:   Mrs. Peters, look at this one. Here, this is the one she was working on, and look at the sewing! All the rest of it has been so nice and even. And look at this! It's all over the place! Why, it looks as if she didn't know what she was about! *(After she has said this they look at each other, then start to glance back at the door. After an instant Mrs. Hale has pulled at a knot and ripped the sewing.)*

MRS. PETERS: Oh, what are you doing, Mrs. Hale?

MRS. HALE *(mildly)*:   Just pulling out a stitch or two that's not sewed very good. *(Threading a needle.)* Bad sewing always made me fidgety.

MRS. PETERS *(with a glance at door, nervously)*:   I don't think we ought to touch things.

MRS. HALE: I'll just finish up this end. *(Suddenly stopping and leaning forward.)* Mrs. Peters?

MRS. PETERS: Yes, Mrs. Hale?

MRS. HALE: What do you suppose she was so nervous about?

MRS. PETERS: Oh—I don't know. I don't know as she was nervous. I sometimes sew awful queer when I'm just tired. *(Mrs. Hale starts to say something, looks at Mrs. Peters, then goes on sewing.)* Well, I must get these things wrapped up. They may be through sooner than we think. *(Putting apron and other things together.)* I wonder where I can find a piece of paper, and string. *(Rises.)*

MRS. HALE: In that cupboard, maybe.

MRS. PETERS *(crosses right looking in cupboard)*:   Why, here's a bird-cage. *(Holds it up.)* Did she have a bird, Mrs. Hale?

MRS. HALE: Why, I don't know whether she did or not—I've not been here for so long. There was a man around last year selling canaries cheap, but I don't know as she took one; maybe she did. She used to sing real pretty herself.

MRS. PETERS *(glancing around)*: Seems funny to think of a bird here. But she must have had one, or why would she have a cage? I wonder what happened to it?

MRS. HALE: I s'pose maybe the cat got it.

MRS. PETERS: No, she didn't have a cat. She's got that feeling some people have about cats—being afraid of them. My cat got in her room and she was real upset and asked me to take it out.

MRS. HALE: My sister Bessie was like that. Queer, ain't it?

MRS. PETERS *(examining the cage)*: Why, look at this door. It's broke. One hinge is pulled apart. *(Takes a step down to Mrs. Hale's right.)*

MRS. HALE *(looking too)*: Looks as if someone must have been rough with it.

MRS. PETERS: Why, yes. *(She brings the cage forward and puts it on the table.)*

MRS. HALE *(glancing toward up left door)*: I wish if they're going to find any evidence they'd be about it. I don't like this place.

MRS. PETERS: But I'm awful glad you came with me, Mrs. Hale. It would be lonesome for me sitting here alone.

MRS. HALE: It would, wouldn't it? *(Dropping her sewing.)* But I tell you what I do wish, Mrs. Peters. I wish I had come over sometimes when *she* was here. I— *(looking around the room)*—wish I had.

MRS. PETERS: But of course you were awful busy, Mrs. Hale—your house and your children.

MRS. HALE *(rises and crosses left)*: I could've come. I stayed away because it weren't cheerful—and that's why I ought to have come. I— *(looking out left window)*—I've never liked this place. Maybe because it's down in a hollow and you don't see the road. I dunno what it is, but it's a lonesome place and always was. I wish I had come over to see Minnie Foster sometimes. I can see now— *(Shakes her head.)*

MRS. PETERS *(left of table and above it)*: Well, you mustn't reproach yourself, Mrs. Hale. Somehow we just don't see how it is with other folks until—something turns up.

MRS. HALE: Not having children makes less work—but it makes a quiet house, and Wright out to work all day, and no company when he did come in. *(Turning from window.)* Did you know John Wright, Mrs. Peters?

MRS. PETERS: Not to know him; I've seen him in town. They say he was a good man.

MRS. HALE: Yes—good; he didn't drink, and kept his word as well as most, I guess, and paid his debts. But he was a hard man, Mrs. Peters. Just to pass the time of day with him— *(Shivers.)* Like a raw wind that gets to the bone. *(Pauses, her eye falling on the cage.)* I should think she would 'a' wanted a bird. But what do you suppose went with it?

MRS. PETERS: I don't know, unless it got sick and died. *(She reaches over and swings the broken door, swings it again, both women watch it.)*

MRS. HALE: You weren't raised round here, were you? *(Mrs. Peters shakes her head.)* You didn't know—her?

MRS. PETERS: Not till they brought her yesterday.

MRS. HALE: She—come to think of it, she was kind of like a bird her-self—real sweet and pretty, but kind of timid and—fluttery. How—she—did—change. *(Silence: then as if struck by a happy thought and relieved to get back to everyday things. Crosses right above Mrs. Peters to cupboard, replaces small chair used to stand on to its original place down right.)* Tell you what, Mrs. Peters, why don't you take the quilt in with you? It might take up her mind.

MRS. PETERS: Why, I think that's a real nice idea, Mrs. Hale. There couldn't possibly be any objection to it could there? Now, just what would I take? I wonder if her patches are in here—and her things. *(They look in the sewing basket.)*

MRS. HALE *(crosses to right of table)*:   Here's some red. I expect this has got sewing things in it. *(Brings out a fancy box.)* What a pretty box. Looks like something somebody would give you. Maybe her scissors are in here. *(Opens box. Suddenly puts her hand to her nose.)* Why——*(Mrs. Peters bends nearer, then turns her face away.)* There's something wrapped up in this piece of silk.

MRS. PETERS: Why, this isn't her scissors.

MRS. HALE *(lifting the silk)*:   Oh, Mrs. Peters—it's——*(Mrs. Peters bends closer.)*

MRS. PETERS: It's the bird.

MRS. HALE: But, Mrs. Peters—look at it! Its neck! Look at its neck! It's all—other side *to.*

MRS. PETERS: Somebody—wrung—its—neck. *(Their eyes meet. A look of growing comprehension, of horror. Steps are heard outside. Mrs. Hale slips box under quilt pieces, and sinks into her chair. Enter Sheriff and County Attorney. Mrs. Peters steps down left and stands looking out of window.)*

COUNTY ATTORNEY *(as one turning from serious things to little pleasantries)*:   Well, ladies, have you decided whether she was going to quilt it or knot it? *(Crosses to center above table.)*

MRS. PETERS: We think she was going to—knot it. *(Sheriff crosses to right of stove, lifts stove lid, and glances at fire, then stands warming hands at stove.)*

COUNTY ATTORNEY: Well, that's interesting, I'm sure. *(Seeing the bird-cage.)* Has the bird flown?

MRS. HALE *(putting more quilt pieces over the box)*:   We think the—cat got it.

COUNTY ATTORNEY *(preoccupied)*:   Is there a cat? *(Mrs. Hale glances in a quick covert way at Mrs. Peters.)*

MRS. PETERS *(turning from window takes a step in)*:   Well, not *now.* They're superstitious, you know. They leave.

COUNTY ATTORNEY *(to Sheriff Peters, continuing an interrupted conversation)*:   No sign at all of anyone having come from the outside. Their own rope. Now let's go up again and go over it piece by piece. *(They start upstairs.)* It would have to have been someone who knew just the——*(Mrs. Peters sits down left of table. The two women sit there not looking at one another, but as if peering into something and at the same time holding back. When they talk now it is in the manner of feeling their way over strange ground, as if afraid of what they are saying, but as if they cannot help saying it.)*

MRS. HALE *(hesitatively and in hushed voice):* She liked the bird. She was going to bury it in that pretty box.

MRS. PETERS *(in a whisper):* When I was a girl — my kitten — there was a boy took a hatchet, and before my eyes — and before I could get there _____ *(Covers her face an instant.)* If they hadn't held me back I would have— *(catches herself, looks upstairs where steps are heard, falters weakly)* — hurt him.

MRS. HALE *(with a slow look around her):* I wonder how it would seem never to have had any children around. *(Pause.)* No, Wright wouldn't like the bird — a thing that sang. She used to sing. He killed that, too.

MRS. PETERS *(moving uneasily):* We don't know who killed the bird.

MRS. HALE: I knew John Wright.

MRS. PETERS: It was an awful thing was done in this house that night, Mrs. Hale. Killing a man while he slept, slipping a rope around his neck that choked the life out of him.

MRS. HALE: His neck. Choked the life out of him. *(Her hand goes out and rests on the bird-cage.)*

MRS. PETERS *(with rising voice):* We don't know who killed him. We don't *know.*

MRS. HALE *(her own feeling not interrupted):* If there'd been years and years of nothing, then a bird to sing to you, it would be awful — still, after the bird was still.

MRS. PETERS *(something within her speaking):* I know what stillness is. When we homesteaded in Dakota, and my first baby died — after he was two years old, and me with no other then——

MRS. HALE *(moving):* How soon do you suppose they'll be through looking for the evidence?

MRS. PETERS: I know what stillness is. *(Pulling herself back.)* The law has got to punish crime, Mrs. Hale.

MRS. HALE *(not as if answering that):* I wish you'd seen Minnie Foster when she wore a white dress with blue ribbons and stood up there in the choir and sang. *(A look around the room.)* Oh, I *wish* I'd come over here once in a while! That was a crime! That was a crime! Who's going to punish that?

MRS. PETERS *(looking upstairs):* We mustn't — take on.

MRS. HALE: I might have known she needed help! I know how things can be — for women. I tell you, it's queer, Mrs. Peters. We live close together and we live far apart. We all go through the same things — it's all just a different kind of the same thing. *(Brushes her eyes, noticing the jar of fruit, reaches out for it.)* If I was you I wouldn't tell her her fruit was gone. Tell her it *ain't.* Tell her it's all right. Take this in to prove it to her. She — she may never know whether it was broke or not.

MRS. PETERS *(takes the jar, looks about for something to wrap it in; takes petticoat from the clothes brought from the other room, very nervously begins winding this around the jar. In a false voice):* My, it's a good thing the men couldn't hear us. Wouldn't they just laugh! Getting all stirred up over a little thing like a — dead canary. As if that could have anything to do with — with — wouldn't they *laugh*! *(The men are heard coming downstairs.)*

MRS. HALE *(under her breath):*   Maybe they would — maybe they wouldn't.

COUNTY ATTORNEY: No, Peters, it's all perfectly clear except a reason for doing it. But you know juries when it comes to women. If there was some definite thing. *(Crosses slowly to above table. Sheriff crosses down right. Mrs. Hale and Mrs. Peters remain seated at either side of table.)* Something to show — something to make a story about — a thing that would connect up with this strange way of doing it —— *(The women's eyes meet for an instant. Enter Hale from outer door.)*

HALE *(remaining by door):*   Well, I've got the team around. Pretty cold out there.

COUNTY ATTORNEY: I'm going to stay awhile by myself. *(To the Sheriff.)* You can send Frank out for me, can't you? I want to go over everything. I'm not satisfied that we can't do better.

SHERIFF: Do you want to see what Mrs. Peters is going to take in? *(The Lawyer picks up the apron, laughs.)*

COUNTY ATTORNEY: Oh, I guess they're not very dangerous things the ladies have picked out. *(Moves a few things about, disturbing the quilt pieces which cover the box. Steps back.)* No, Mrs. Peters doesn't need supervising. For that matter a sheriff's wife is married to the law. Ever think of it that way, Mrs. Peters?

MRS. PETERS: Not — just that way.

SHERIFF *(chuckling):*   Married to the law. *(Moves to down right door to the other room.)* I just want you to come in here a minute, George. We ought to take a look at these windows.

COUNTY ATTORNEY *(scoffingly):*   Oh, windows!

SHERIFF: We'll be right out, Mr. Hale. *(Hale goes outside. The Sheriff follows the County Attorney into the room. Then Mrs. Hale rises, hands tight together, looking intensely at Mrs. Peters, whose eyes make a slow turn, finally meeting Mrs. Hale's. A moment Mrs. Hale holds her, then her own eyes point the way to where the box is concealed. Suddenly Mrs. Peters throws back quilt pieces and tries to put the box in the bag she is carrying. It is too big. She opens box, starts to take bird out, cannot touch it, goes to pieces, stands there helpless. Sound of a knob turning in the other room. Mrs. Hale snatches the box and puts it in the pocket of her big coat. Enter County Attorney and Sheriff, who remains down right.)*

COUNTY ATTORNEY *(crosses to up left door facetiously):*   Well, Henry, at least we found out that she was not going to quilt it. She was going to — what is it you call it, ladies?

MRS. HALE *(standing center below table facing front, her hand against her pocket):*   We call it — knot it, Mr. Henderson.

Curtain.   [1916]

≡ THINKING ABOUT THE TEXT

1. Although much of this play is about Minnie Wright, Glaspell keeps her offstage. Why, do you think?

2. What does Glaspell imply about differences between men and women? Support your inference with details from the text.

3. What do Mrs. Hale and Mrs. Peters realize about themselves during the course of the play? To what extent should they feel guilty about their own past behavior?

4. Ultimately, Mrs. Hale and Mrs. Peters cover up evidence to protect Minnie Wright. They seem to act out of loyalty to their gender. How sympathetic are you to their stand? Do you feel there are times when you should be someone's ally because that person is of the same gender as you?

5. Is this play about freedom and confinement? About the injustice of male domination? About the bonds that hold women together? Or something else? Explain your answer.

LYNN NOTTAGE

POOF!

Lynn Nottage (b. 1964) is an American playwright and an activist focused on preventing violence against women. She grew up in New York City and attended Brown University and the Yale School of Drama. She then worked for four years at Amnesty International. Ruined, *a play about Congolese women during civil war, was awarded the Pulitzer Prize for Drama in 2009. Nottage's plays have been performed in dozens of theaters. She has received a Guggenheim Fellowship and a MacArthur Grant. Her latest play is* By the Way, Meet Vera Stark *(2011).*

CHARACTERS

SAMUEL, *Loureen's husband*
LOUREEN, *a demure housewife, early thirties*
FLORENCE, *Loureen's best friend, early thirties*

TIME: *The present*

PLACE: *Kitchen*

A NOTE: *Nearly half the women on death row in the United States were convicted of killing abusive husbands. Spontaneous combustion is not recognized as a capital crime.*

Darkness.

SAMUEL (*In the darkness*):   WHEN I COUNT TO TEN I DON' WANT TO SEE YA! I
DON' WANT TO HEAR YA! ONE, TWO, THREE, FOUR—

LOUREEN (*In the darkness*):   DAMN YOU TO HELL, SAMUEL!

A bright flash.

*Lights rise. A huge pile of smoking ashes rests in the middle of the kitchen.
Loureen, a demure housewife in her early thirties, stares down at the ashes incredulously. She bends and lifts a pair of spectacles from the remains. She ever so slowly
backs away.*

Samuel? Uh! (*Places the spectacles on the kitchen table*) Uh! . . . Samuel?
(*Looks around*) Don't fool with me now. I'm not in the mood. (*Whispers*)
Samuel? I didn't mean it really. I'll be good if you come back . . . Come
on now, dinner's waiting. (*Chuckles, then stops abruptly*) Now stop your
foolishness . . . And let's sit down. (*Examines the spectacles*) Uh! (*Softly*)
Don't be cross with me. Sure I forgot to pick up your shirt for tomorrow.
I can wash another, I'll do it right now. Right now! Sam? . . . (*Cautiously*)
You hear me! (*Awaits a response*) Maybe I didn't ever intend to wash your
shirt. (*Pulls back as though about to receive a blow; a moment*) Uh! (*Sits down
and dials the telephone*) Florence, honey, could you come on down for a
moment. There's been a . . . little . . . accident . . . Quickly please. Uh!

*Loureen hangs up the phone. She gets a broom and a dust pan. She hesitantly
approaches the pile of ashes. She gets down on her hands and knees and takes a closer
look. A fatuous grin spreads across her face. She is startled by a sudden knock on the
door. She slowly walks across the room like a possessed child. Loureen lets in
Florence, her best friend and upstairs neighbor. Florence, also a housewife in her
early thirties, wears a floral housecoat and a pair of oversized slippers. Without
acknowledgment Loureen proceeds to saunter back across the room.*

FLORENCE: HEY!

LOUREEN (*Pointing at the ashes*):   Uh! . . . (*She struggles to formulate words, which
press at the inside of her mouth, not quite realized*) Uh! . . .

FLORENCE: You all right? What happened? (*Sniffs the air*) Smells like you burned
something? (*Stares at the huge pile of ashes*) What the devil is that?

LOUREEN (*Hushed*):   Samuel . . . It's Samuel, I think.

FLORENCE: What's he done now?

LOUREEN: It's him. It's him. (*Nods her head repeatedly*)

FLORENCE: Chile, what's wrong with you? Did he finally drive you out your
mind? I knew something was going to happen sooner or later.

LOUREEN: Dial 911, Florence!

FLORENCE: Why? You're scaring me!

LOUREEN: Dial 911!

Florence picks up the telephone and quickly dials.

I think I killed him.

Florence hangs up the telephone.

FLORENCE: What?

LOUREEN (*Whimpers*):   I killed him! I killed Samuel!

FLORENCE: Come again? . . . He's dead dead?

Loureen wrings her hands and nods her head twice, mouthing "dead dead." Florence backs away.

No, stop it, I don't have time for this. I'm going back upstairs. You know how Samuel hates to find me here when he gets home. You're not going to get me this time. (*Louder*) Y'all can have your little joke, I'm not part of it! (*A moment. She takes a hard look into Loureen's eyes; she squints*) Did you really do it this time?

LOUREEN (*Hushed*):   I don't know how or why it happened, it just did.

FLORENCE: Why are you whispering?

LOUREEN: I don't want to talk too loud—something else is liable to disappear.

FLORENCE: Where's his body?

LOUREEN (*Points to the pile of ashes*):   There! . . .

FLORENCE: You burned him?

LOUREEN: I DON'T KNOW! (*Covers her mouth as if to muffle her words; hushed*) I think so.

FLORENCE: Either you did or you didn't, what you mean you don't know? We're talking murder, Loureen, not oven settings.

LOUREEN: You think I'm playing?

FLORENCE: How many times have I heard you talk about being rid of him. How many times have we sat at this very table and laughed about the many ways we could do it and how many times have you done it? None.

LOUREEN (*Lifting the spectacles*):   A pair of cheap spectacles, that's all that's left. And you know how much I hate these. You ever seen him without them, no! . . . He counted to four and disappeared. I swear to God!

FLORENCE: Don't bring the Lord into this just yet! Sit down now . . . What you got to sip on?

LOUREEN: I don't know whether to have a stiff shot of scotch or a glass of champagne.

Florence takes a bottle of sherry out of the cupboard and pours them each a glass. Loureen downs hers, then holds out her glass for more.

He was . . .

FLORENCE: Take your time.

LOUREEN: Standing there.

FLORENCE: And?

LOUREEN: He exploded.

FLORENCE: Did that muthafucka hit you again?

LOUREEN: No . . . he exploded. Boom! Right in front of me. He was shouting like he does, being all colored, then he raised up that big crusty hand to hit me, and poof, he was gone . . . I barely got words out and I'm looking down at a pile of ash.

Florence belts back her sherry. She wipes her forehead and pours them both another.

FLORENCE: Chile, I'll give you this, in terms of color you've matched my husband Edgar, the story king. He came in at six Sunday morning, talking about he'd hit someone with his car, and had spent all night trying to outrun the police. I felt sorry for him. It turns out he was playing poker with his paycheck no less. You don't want to know how I found out . . . But I did.

LOUREEN: You think I'm lying?

FLORENCE: I certainly hope so, Loureen. For your sake and my heart's.

LOUREEN: Samuel always said if I raised my voice something horrible would happen. And it did. I'm a witch . . . the devil spawn!

FLORENCE: You've been watching too much television.

LOUREEN: Never seen anything like this on television. Wish I had, then I'd know what to do . . . There's no question, I'm a witch. (*Looks at her hands with disgust*)

FLORENCE: Chile, don't tell me you've been messing with them mojo women again? What did I tell ya.

Loureen, agitated, stands and sits back down.

LOUREEN: He's not coming back. Oh no, how could he? It would be a miracle! Two in one day . . . I could be canonized. Worse yet, he could be . . . All that needs to happen now is for my palms to bleed and I'll be eternally remembered as Saint Loureen, the patron of battered wives. Women from across the country will make pilgrimages to me, laying pies and pot roast at my feet and asking the good saint to make their husbands turn to dust. How often does a man like Samuel get damned to hell, and go?

She breaks down. Florence moves to console her friend, then realizes that Loureen is actually laughing hysterically.

FLORENCE: You smoking crack?

LOUREEN: Do I look like I am?

FLORENCE: Hell, I've seen old biddies creeping out of crack houses, talking about they were doing church work.

LOUREEN: Florence, please be helpful, I'm very close to the edge! . . . I don't know what to do next! Do I sweep him up? Do I call the police? Do I . . .

The phone rings.

Oh God.

FLORENCE: You gonna let it ring?

Loureen reaches for the telephone slowly.

LOUREEN: NO! (*Holds the receiver without picking it up, paralyzed*) What if it's his mother? . . . She knows!

The phone continues to ring. They sit until it stops. They both breathe a sigh of relief.

I should be mourning, I should be praying, I should be thinking of the burial, but all that keeps popping into my mind is what will I wear on television when I share my horrible and wonderful story with a studio audience . . . (*Whimpers*) He's made me a killer, Florence, and you remember what a gentle child I was. (*Whispers*) I'm a killer, I'm a killer, I'm a killer.

FLORENCE: I wouldn't throw that word about too lightly even in jest. Talk like that gets around.

LOUREEN: You think they'll lock me up? A few misplaced words and I'll probably get the death penalty, isn't that what they do with women like me, murderesses?

FLORENCE: Folks have done time for less.

LOUREEN: Thank you, just what I needed to hear!

FLORENCE: What did you expect, that I was going to throw up my arms and congratulate you? Why'd you have to go and lose your mind at this time of day, while I got a pot of rice on the stove and Edgar's about to walk in the door and wonder where his goddamn food is. (*Losing her cool*) And he's going to start in on me about all the nothing I've been doing during the day and why I can't work and then he'll mention how clean you keep your home. And I don't know how I'm going to look him in the eye without . . .

LOUREEN: I'm sorry, Florence. Really. It's out of my hands now.

She takes Florence's hand and squeezes it.

FLORENCE (*Regaining her composure*): You swear on your right tit?

LOUREEN (*Clutching both breasts*): I swear on both of them!

FLORENCE: Both your breasts, Loureen! You know what will happen if you're lying. (*Loureen nods; hushed*) Both your breasts Loureen?

LOUREEN: Yeah!

FLORENCE (*Examines the pile of ashes, then shakes her head*): Oh sweet, sweet Jesus. He must have done something truly terrible.

LOUREEN: No more than usual. I just couldn't take being hit one more time.

FLORENCE: You've taken a thousand blows from that man, couldn't you've turned the cheek and waited? I'd have helped you pack. Like we talked about.

A moment.

LOUREEN: Uh! . . . I could blow on him and he'd disappear across the linoleum. (*Snaps her fingers*) Just like that. Should I be feeling remorse or regret or some other "R" word? I'm strangely jubilant, like on prom night when Samuel and I first made love. That's the feeling! (*The women lock eyes*) Uh!

FLORENCE: Is it . . .

LOUREEN: Like a ton of bricks been lifted from my shoulders, yeah.

FLORENCE: Really?

LOUREEN: Yeah!

Florence walks to the other side of the room.

FLORENCE: You bitch!

LOUREEN: What?

FLORENCE: We made a pact.

LOUREEN: I know.

FLORENCE: You've broken it . . . We agreed that when things got real bad for both of us we'd . . . you know . . . together . . . Do I have to go back upstairs to that? . . . What next?

LOUREEN: I thought you'd tell me! . . . I don't know!

FLORENCE: I don't know!

LOUREEN: I don't know!

Florence begins to walk around the room, nervously touching objects. Loureen sits, wringing her hands and mumbling softly to herself.

FLORENCE: Now you got me, Loureen, I'm truly at a loss for words.

LOUREEN: Everybody always told me, "Keep your place, Loureen." My place, the silent spot on the couch with a wine cooler in my hand and a pleasant smile that warmed the heart. All this time I didn't know why he was so afraid for me to say anything, to speak up. Poof! . . . I've never been by myself, except for them two weeks when he won the office pool and went to Reno with his cousin Mitchell. He wouldn't tell me where he was going until I got that postcard with the cowboy smoking a hundred cigarettes . . . Didn't Sonny Larkin look good last week at Caroline's? He looked good, didn't he . . .

Florence nods. She nervously picks up Samuel's jacket, which is hanging on the back of the chair. She clutches it unconsciously.

NO! No! Don't wrinkle that, that's his favorite jacket. He'll kill me. Put it back!

Florence returns the jacket to its perch. Loureen begins to quiver.

I'm sorry. (*She grabs the jacket and wrinkles it up*) There! (*She then digs into the coat pockets and pulls out his wallet and a movie stub*) Look at that, he said he didn't go to the movies last night. Working late. (*Frantically thumbs through his wallet*) Picture of his motorcycle, Social Security card, driver's license, and look at that from our wedding. (*Smiling*) I looked good, didn't I? (*She puts the pictures back in the wallet and holds the jacket up to her face*) There were some good things. (*She then sweeps her hand over the jacket to remove the wrinkles, and folds it ever so carefully, and finally throws it in the garbage*) And out of my mouth those words made him disappear. All these years and just words, Florence. That's all they were.

FLORENCE: I'm afraid I won't ever get those words out. I'll start resenting you, honey. I'm afraid won't anything change for me.

LOUREEN: I been to that place.

FLORENCE: Yeah? But now I wish I could relax these old lines (*Touches her forehead*) for a minute maybe. Edgar has never done me the way Samuel did you, but he sure did take the better part of my life.

LOUREEN: Not yet, Florence.

FLORENCE (*Nods*): I have the children to think of . . . right?

LOUREEN: You can think up a hundred things before . . .

FLORENCE: Then come upstairs with me . . . we'll wait together for Edgar and then you can spit out your words and . . .

LOUREEN: I can't do that.

FLORENCE: Yes you can. Come on now.

Loureen shakes her head no.

Well, I guess my mornings are not going to be any different.

LOUREEN: If you can say for certain, then I guess they won't be. I couldn't say that.

FLORENCE: But you got a broom and a dust pan, you don't need anything more than that . . . He was a bastard and nobody will care that he's gone.

LOUREEN: Phone's gonna start ringing soon, people are gonna start asking soon, and they'll care.

FLORENCE: What's your crime? Speaking your mind?

LOUREEN: Maybe I should mail him to his mother. I owe her that. I feel bad for her, she didn't understand how it was. I can't just throw him away and pretend like it didn't happen. Can I?

FLORENCE: I didn't see anything but a pile of ash. As far as I know you got a little careless and burned a chicken.

LOUREEN: He was always threatening not to come back.

FLORENCE: I heard him.

LOUREEN: It would've been me eventually.

FLORENCE: Yes.

LOUREEN: I should call the police, or someone.

FLORENCE: Why? What are you gonna tell them? About all those times they refused to help, about all those nights you slept in my bed 'cause you were afraid to stay down here? About the time he nearly took out your eye 'cause you flipped the television channel?

LOUREEN: No.

FLORENCE: You've got it, girl!

LOUREEN: Good-bye to the fatty meats and the salty food. Good-bye to the bourbon and the bologna sandwiches. Good-bye to the smell of his feet, his breath and his bowel movements . . . (*A moment. She closes her eyes and, reliving a horrible memory, she shudders*) Good-bye. (*Walks over to the pile of ashes*) Samuel? . . . Just checking.

FLORENCE: Good-bye Samuel.

They both smile.

LOUREEN: I'll let the police know that he's missing tomorrow . . .

FLORENCE: Why not the next day?

LOUREEN: Chicken's warming in the oven, you're welcome to stay.

FLORENCE: Chile, I got a pot of rice on the stove, kids are probably acting out . . . and Edgar, well . . . Listen, I'll stop in tomorrow.

LOUREEN: For dinner?

FLORENCE: Edgar wouldn't stand for that. Cards maybe.

LOUREEN: Cards.

The women hug for a long moment. Florence exits. Loureen stands over the ashes for a few moments contemplating what to do. She finally decides to sweep them under the carpet, and then proceeds to set the table and sit down to eat her dinner.

END OF PLAY   [1993]

☰ WRITING ABOUT THE TEXT

1. How would you describe Loureen's relationship to her husband Samuel? What reasons can you suggest for Loureen staying in that relationship?

2. What specific offenses does Samuel commit? Which would be violations of wedding vows? Which would be legal issues?

3. Describe the progression of Loureen's response to Samuel's death.

4. What evidence might there be that Loureen could become a model for battered women? What do you think about Edgar's future?

5. Even though Samuel dies, the play doesn't seem tragic. Point out the comic element. How does Nottage get away with using humor in a play where someone loses his life?

☰ MAKING COMPARISONS

1. Compare the marital situations of Minnie and Loureen.

2. Explain the justification each woman has for her behavior. Which seems the most compelling? The least?

3. How would contemporary audiences judge John Wright and Samuel?

☰ WRITING ABOUT ISSUES

1. Write an essay that argues that justice was or was not served in either *Trifles* or *POOF!*

2. Based on these two plays, write an essay that argues that relationship problems in marriages have changed or remained the same since 1916.

3. One could argue that a mystical intervention killed Samuel. Argue that such a device would or would not be tolerated in Glaspell's in 1916. How do you account for these responses?

4. Write an argument that sets out your view of what a contemporary relationship between equals would be.

≡ Dreams of Escape: Stories

KATE CHOPIN, "The Story of an Hour"

KRISTEN VALDEZ QUADE, "The Manzanos"

Although the characters and setting for these two stories could hardly be more dissimilar, there are interesting comparisons. Ofelia is an eleven-year-old girl living with her grandfather in a small village in contemporary New Mexico, while Louise Mallard is a married woman living in Louisiana at the end of the nineteenth century. Both, however, are unhappy with their present lives and both dream of escape, although Ofelia seems more focused on a retrieved past and Louise on a future not meant to be. And both seem caught in a confining reality they long to escape.

≡ BEFORE YOU READ

Is it possible to love someone and at the same time want to be free?

KATE CHOPIN
The Story of an Hour

Kate Chopin (1851–1904) is known for her evocations of the unique, multiethnic Creole and Cajun societies of late-nineteenth-century Louisiana; however, her characters transcend the limitation of regional genre writing, striking a particularly resonant note among feminist readers. Born Katherine O'Flaherty in St. Louis, Missouri, she married Oscar Chopin in 1870 and went to live with him in New Orleans and on his plantation along the Mississippi River. Her short stories were collected in Bayou Folk *(1894) and* A Night in Acadie *(1897). Chopin's last novel,* The Awakening, *scandalized readers at the time of its publication in 1899 because of its frank portrayal of female sexuality in the context of an extramarital affair. Long ignored by readers and critics, her work was revived in the 1960s and continues to provoke heated discussion of her female characters: are they women who seek freedom in the only ways available to them, or are they willing participants in their own victimhood?*

The following story was first published in Bayou Folk *(1894). It is typical of her controversial writing and caused a sensation among the reading public.*

Knowing that Mrs. Mallard was afflicted with a heart trouble, great care was taken to break to her as gently as possible the news of her husband's death.

It was her sister Josephine who told her, in broken sentences; veiled hints that revealed in half concealing. Her husband's friend Richards was there, too, near her. It was he who had been in the newspaper office when intelligence of the railroad disaster was received, with Brently Mallard's name leading the list of "killed." He had only taken the time to assure himself of its truth by a second telegram, and had hastened to forestall any less careful, less tender friend in bearing the sad message.

She did not hear the story as many women have heard the same, with a paralyzed inability to accept its significance. She wept at once, with sudden, wild abandonment, in her sister's arms. When the storm of grief had spent itself she went away to her room alone. She would have no one follow her.

There stood, facing the open window, a comfortable, roomy armchair. Into this she sank, pressed down by a physical exhaustion that haunted her body and seemed to reach into her soul.

She could see in the open square before her house the tops of trees that   5
were all aquiver with the new spring life. The delicious breath of rain was in the air. In the street below a peddler was crying his wares. The notes of a distant song which some one was singing reached her faintly, and countless sparrows were twittering in the eaves.

There were patches of blue sky showing here and there through the clouds that had met and piled one above the other in the west facing her window.

She sat with her head thrown back upon the cushion of the chair, quite motionless, except when a sob came up into her throat and shook her, as a child who had cried itself to sleep continues to sob in its dreams.

She was young, with a fair, calm face, whose lines bespoke repression and even a certain strength. But now there was a dull stare in her eyes, whose gaze was fixed away off yonder on one of those patches of blue sky. It was not a glance of reflection, but rather indicated a suspension of intelligent thought.

There was something coming to her and she was waiting for it, fearfully. What was it? She did not know; it was too subtle and elusive to name. But she felt it, creeping out of the sky, reaching toward her through the sounds, the scents, the color that filled the air.

Now her bosom rose and fell tumultuously. She was beginning to recog-   10
nize this thing that was approaching to possess her, and she was striving to beat it back with her will—as powerless as her two white slender hands would have been.

When she abandoned herself a little whispered word escaped her slightly parted lips. She said it over and over under her breath: "free, free, free!" The vacant stare and the look of terror that had followed it went from her eyes. They stayed keen and bright. Her pulses beat fast, and the coursing blood warmed and relaxed every inch of her body.

She did not stop to ask if it were or were not a monstrous joy that held her. A clear and exalted perception enabled her to dismiss the suggestion as trivial.

She knew that she would weep again when she saw the kind, tender hands folded in death; the face that had never looked save with love upon her, fixed and gray and dead. But she saw beyond that bitter moment a long procession of years to come that would belong to her absolutely. And she opened and spread her arms out to them in welcome.

There would be no one to live for her during those coming years: she would live for herself. There would be no powerful will bending hers in that blind persistence with which men and women believe they have a right to impose a private will upon a fellow-creature. A kind intention or a cruel intention made the act seem no less a crime as she looked upon it in that brief moment of illumination.

And yet she had loved him—sometimes. Often she had not. What did it matter! What could love, the unsolved mystery, count for in face of this possession of self-assertion which she suddenly recognized as the strongest impulse of her being!

"Free! Body and soul free!" she kept whispering.

Josephine was kneeling before the closed door with her lips to the keyhole, imploring for admission. "Louise, open the door! I beg; open the door—you will make yourself ill. What are you doing, Louise? For heaven's sake open the door."

"Go away. I am not making myself ill." No; she was drinking in a very elixir of life through that open window.

Her fancy was running riot along those days ahead of her. Spring days, and summer days, and all sorts of days that would be her own. She breathed a quick prayer that life might be long. It was only yesterday she had thought with a shudder that life might be long.

She arose at length and opened the door to her sister's importunities. There was a feverish triumph in her eyes, and she carried herself unwittingly like a goddess of Victory. She clasped her sister's waist, and together they descended the stairs. Richards stood waiting for them at the bottom.

Some one was opening the front door with a latchkey. It was Brently Mallard who entered, a little travel-stained, composedly carrying his gripsack and umbrella. He had been far from the scene of accident, and did not even know there had been one. He stood amazed at Josephine's piercing cry; at Richards's quick motion to screen him from the view of his wife.

But Richards was too late.

When the doctors came they said she had died of heart disease—of joy that kills.

[1894]

≡ THINKING ABOUT THE TEXT

1. Chopin writes, "A kind intention or a cruel intention made the act seem no less a crime" (para. 14). Explain what Mrs. Mallard means by this thought.

2. Explain Louise Mallard's outlook on time before and after she hears of her husband's death.

3. Explain why you think Mrs. Mallard did or did not fantasize about escape during her marriage.

4. Describe the idea of ambiguity in the first and last sentence of this story.

5. Describe how happiness, loyalty, and love are problematic in the story.

KRISTEN VALDEZ QUADE

The Manzanos

Kristin Valdez Quade grew up in Albuquerque, New Mexico, and has lived in various places in the Southwest. She earned a B.A. from Stanford University and her M.F.A. in fiction from the University of Oregon in 2009. She has won numerous awards and has taught at Stanford and the University of Michigan. She is currently an assistant professor in creative writing at Princeton University. Most of Quade's stories focus on the dynamics of family life with "intensity and emotional precision." She has been compared to Annie Proulx, Alice Munro, and Flannery O'Connor. The following story is from Night at the Fiestas *(2016) which won the National Book Critics Circle John Leonard Prize.*

My name is my grandmother's: Ofelia Alma Zamora. I am eleven years old and too young to die, but I am dying nonetheless. I have been dying since the day my mother went away. I've been to doctors — to the clinic in Estancia, and all the way to Albuquerque — but they take my temperature, knead my stomach, check my throat, and tell my grandfather the same thing: perhaps it is a minor infection or virus, one of the usual brief illnesses of childhood, and they see nothing seriously wrong. They don't know about the ojo, the evil eye.

There is no one left in this town who can cure me, so for now I sit at the edge of the yard, my feet in the road, turning a piece of broken asphalt in my hands, in case a stranger passes. Are you a healer? I'll ask her. I think of how it will be when I find her, how when she lays her hands on my head I'll close my eyes and feel the blessing pass through me like fire.

I imagine this, knowing I can't be cured, knowing I couldn't bear to be.

I'm waiting for my grandfather, relieved because today, finally, he's gotten up and dressed for the city: plaid shirt buttoned all the way up his thin tortoise neck, bolo tie with the silver dollar set in a ring of turquoise. Face scrubbed, white hair combed in lines over the brown crown of his head. He is in the house rinsing our coffee cups and wiping toast crumbs from the oilcloth.

I am ready too, wearing my blue dress (though the sleeves no longer cover   5
my wrists), white tights (dingy and loose at the knees), and my sneakers. In my pocket is the address for the VA clinic, which I have copied from some papers in my grandfather's desk. This morning my grandfather braided my hair and fastened the ends with rubber bands from the newspaper. Because I'm tall I sat on the kitchen chair and he leaned over me, his trembling fingers slowly working the braid into shape. When I was younger he would tease me as he combed out the knots, pretend to find things in the tangled mass. "A jackrabbit!" he'd cry. "My pliers!" I'd laugh as the yank of the comb brought tears to my eyes.

Behind me the porch sags under the weight of the refrigerator and the gyrating washing machine on legs, which my grandparents bought during a good year in the fifties. There are places we cannot step because the boards are gray and fragile with rot. "I'll fix the porch," my grandfather says. "One day

I'll find the time and shore it up." But the truth is that for years he has been unable to do jobs that he once did without even thinking.

Every day for a week I have dressed for Albuquerque, and every day he has shivered and shaken his head. "Not today, mi hijita. Perhaps the weather will be better tomorrow."

He spent those mornings in his pajamas, blanket pulled tight around him. It's late spring, the sky above the swaying cottonwoods so blue it has a texture, but he wore his wool cap, sweating. He would not let me go to the neighbors or the priest.

But today he is up and dressed, preparing for our monthly trip to Albuquerque. We will shop for what we need, and we will have lunch in a restaurant, and my grandfather will see the doctor, though he doesn't know this yet.

I touch the slip of paper in my pocket. I catalog every detail of my grandfa-   10
ther as he is now, as if by leaving nothing out I can keep him safe. I catalog the smooth pink mole on his neck, the brown spots like smudged fingerprints on his temples. His eyebrows, gray and wiry and curled. Often a drop of clear fluid hangs from the end of his nose. My grandfather's nose is large now, almost a beak, but it wasn't always that way. In my cigar box I have a picture of him as a slight, handsome soldier in the army, his features delicate: serious mouth, light eyes, black lashes.

There are a few families still in our town — mostly old people, no other children — and those of us who are left are used to the high weeds, the crumbling houses of neighbors, the plaster that falls like puzzle pieces. The exposed mud bricks dissolve a little more each time it rains.

Across the road from where I sit is the dance hall that belonged to dead Uncle Fidel. It hasn't been a dance hall since long before I was born — hasn't been anything but empty and overgrown with prickly branches — but there is still the green silhouette of a bottle painted on the cracked wooden door. When he was young, my grandfather tells me, there were bailes° every Saturday night, and, if he'd had a drink and his shyness left him, he would dance until he was breathless and sweaty, twirling the girls, clapping and stomping with the rest of the town through cuadrillas and polcas.° In those days they sprinkled water on the ground to keep the dust down, and dirt clotted on the black toes of his shoes.

At night I imagine I can hear the accordions and fiddles and guitars across the street, but it takes effort, and soon I am weary and overcome with the sense that I have arrived too late. I long for that other Cuipas, for the families and the river. I want to have known my grandfather as he was then, to have been with him all those long years.

The sun stretches along the road and warms my legs in my tights. If I turn my face to its heat I must close my eyes, and in the drowsy redness behind my eyelids I remember what makes me uneasy. Last night I lay stiff in

bailes: Dance parties.
cuadrillas and polcas: Lit., quadrilles and polkas, lively dances.

my bed — which I used to share with my mother, which I imagine still smells of her — kept awake not by the ojo but by a sound I'd never heard before. Instead of my grandfather's steady sleeping breath from across the kitchen and through the open door of his bedroom, I could hear a rattling, chattering gurgle. The sound, so much like an animal — but an animal I have never heard and cannot picture — kept me tense and afraid until dawn, when my grandfather stirred, his bed creaked, and his slow footsteps assured me that he was okay.

Some days I go to school, some days I don't; like a fever the ojo comes   15
and goes in waves. I try not to bother my grandfather with it. When I am well enough I ride the bus into Estancia, listen to what they tell me. I buy my lunch in the cafeteria and sit with the younger children, who don't ask questions when I am silent.

My grades aren't good. I struggle to form letters on the page. Three times a week I'm called from the classroom by the resource teacher, a young woman — as young, perhaps, as my mother — whose skirt swishes against her hose when she walks. She and I sit together under a fluorescent light in a room that was intended to be a closet. She shows me flashcards, asks me to write sentences, tries to make me explain what I am thinking. I tilt my head. When she tires of waiting, she'll pat my hand and sigh and give me a chocolate wrapped in red foil. I learned this during my time at school: they want to replace the past with their rhymes and procedures, their *i before e* and *carry the one.*

When I was in kindergarten I used to beg my grandfather to move us to Estancia, because it is a town with a store and a school and a senior center, where he and I can have lunch for a dollar, dessert included. Now I understand what he has never told me, that we must watch over Cuipas until it shrinks to nothing, until the houses are mud once more, and dead Uncle Fidel's bar collapses to splinters.

Sometimes, when my grandfather is well and I skip school, we walk together, and he tells me again the history of this place: the original land grant, fifty thousand acres given years ago to my grandfather's great-great-great-grandfather, parceled smaller and smaller through the generations, until our piece, my grandfather's and mine, which he put in my name on my seventh birthday, became twenty-five acres, and not the best twenty-five but grassland. I wish it were in the mountains, with a spring and tall, fragrant piñon.° I would walk there in the fall and gather the dropped nuts, roast them to eat through the winter, sell the surplus in bags along the road. But my land is good only for cattle, which I do not have.

"When I was a boy," my grandfather said last time, as we stepped across the dry riverbed, "the water ran all the time. My cousins and me, we used to catch tadpoles and crayfish in glass jars."

"Where did the water go?" I asked.   20

---

piñon: A small pine tree that grows in the Southwest. Its nuts are widely eaten as a snack in New Mexican cuisine.

My grandfather squinted as if trying to remember. "Perhaps it was diverted into the bean fields. Perhaps it rains less now. Perhaps it all happened when I was at war."

My grandfather has told me that Cuipas was one place before he left and another when he returned. Though he was in the army for two years, the war had already ended, so he lived in Rome, an eighteen-month vacation, he said, on the government's dime. Each day he swam in Mussolini's pool. It was the first and best pool he'd ever seen, huge, lined with marble smooth under his feet. My grandfather was strong, glistening, brown muscle in blue water.

He almost married a girl there. Silvia Donati. As we walked along a furrow in the bean field—the plants no higher than my calf, leaves broad and soft and heart-shaped—I asked him to tell me about her again.

She had buckteeth, my grandfather said, and the palest, rosiest skin he had ever seen, and black-black hair. She lived with her mother above their hat shop, and she made ladies' hats.

Each afternoon after his swim — back in his uniform, wet hair combed — my grandfather sat across from her at the table by the open window, waiting as she finished her work. He listened to the sharp scissors pressing through wool felt, voices in the street below, watched her pale hands as she steamed and formed the pieces on faceless wooden heads. When my grandfather left Italy she gave him a hat for his mother in Cuipas: gray with pink velvet roses. For years my great-grandmother and Silvia Donati wrote each other — one in Spanish, the other in Italian — until my great-grandmother died. I often wonder if Silvia Donati heard about my grandfather's marriage, or my mother's birth, or my grandmother's death in one of those letters. I wonder if she heard about me, if she knows that these days we live alone. 25

She would be an old woman now. I like to think she does not dye her hair. I like to think she has kept a trim figure and pink cheeks, perhaps remained a virgin for my grandfather. (This is important, I know, from the romance novels my mother left behind.) I imagine they marry, raise me in Italy beside the sea. They hold hands and walk along the beach, and I trail behind, all of us wearing hats that were fashionable once.

My grandfather's uniform is folded in the cedar chest in the crowded back bedroom where I sleep, and which I once shared with my mother. This is my grandmother's wedding veil (netting torn), my grandfather's garrison cap. I don't know what became of my great-grandmother's gray hat, whether she wore it until it lost its shape and color, or it was trampled by a horse, or a gust of wind caught it and flung it across fields and mesas. Perhaps she left it on a bus in Albuquerque. Perhaps she gave it away.

There are some papers here too, records of business long since concluded. And here, the baptismal gowns of lost children, like limp little ghosts.

When the river does run, after the late-summer storms, I sometimes pull on a pair of my mother's old shorts and wade in the muddy water, thinking of Mussolini's pool. I cup the water in my hands and fling it in a sparkling arc around my head.

If the old women see me walking home, calves muddy, shorts wet, they   30
will shake their heads at my bare legs and call me a cabrasita. Bad little goat.
But they don't blame me too much for my wild ways; they tell each other I am
not at fault for being raised by a man alone. They don't know that I am at fault.

Our town is surrounded by grass. Yellow grass on land that shifts and dips
like waves. Distance is difficult to judge; the grass is deceptive. The Manzanos°
rise just beyond our town. I have tried to walk to the mountains, where a man
lived for weeks after killing his father-in-law with an iron poker. My grandfather's father was part of the posse that searched for him. My grandfather has
taken me in the car, pointed to the distant spot among the juniper and piñon
where they found the murderer's camp: fire burned down, dusty bedroll. They
never found him, though; I imagine him running from their excited voices and
the clomp of hooves in dry soil.

Once when I was seven I played a game that I was the murderer and
would be safe when I reached the mountains. The mountains loomed, and I
ran through the tall grass and into the sun, burrs catching on my socks and
pants. When my breath burned my throat and I could no longer run I walked,
my pursuers getting closer, and fear and guilt clogged my heart. At a barbed
fence I parted the wires and slid through, snaring my shirt above my shoulder blade. Long-horned cattle — black-and-white and mottled — backed away
from me, the calves close to their mothers. Two rattlesnakes slithered from my
footsteps, sounded a warning. Even the breeze knew what I'd done. When the
sun sank behind the Manzanos, Cuipas was small behind me under a depthless
violet sky, and the mountains were no closer.

Here are the places I've seen my mother: crossing the field behind the
courthouse, hair loose and tangled in the winter wind; through the front window of a bank, filling out a deposit slip; in the school library, glimpsed through
the stacks. When I see my mother it is always from afar or from behind or
through glass. Each time my heart flips like a fish in my chest, and each time
she is someone else.

My mother left us seven years ago to live in Albuquerque. Perhaps she is
there still; perhaps she has moved on to other places, Los Angeles or Chicago
or England. She would choose someplace big, I'm sure. She was too young, my
grandfather tells me. Never could take responsibility.

My grandfather knows the stories of every grave in the dirt churchyard: 35
This is a great-aunt, this a cousin, this a whole family killed by the Spanish
flu. The murdered man is here, here a woman who hung herself from a viga°
in her kitchen after her third stillborn child, but they buried her in sacred
ground nonetheless. *Profirio Narciso. Nacio Valentin. Maria Candelarita. Maria
Ascensión.* And this here, beside the plaster statue of the Blessed Mother, is my
name: my grandmother, whom I never met. When my mother was thirteen,
my grandmother left for Santa Fe, where she found work in the post office.
My grandfather went after her several times, but each time she refused to
return. She came home only to be buried — a heart attack.

Manzanos: A small mountain range in central New Mexico.
viga: Rafter, roof beam.

Once I asked my grandfather why she left, but he shook his head.

Some of the graves have iron fences around them, with little gates, as though for children. Some are decorated with plastic flowers, petals bleached from the sun. I imagine I know which spot will be mine in the churchyard: pressed between my grandfather and the boy whose neck was snapped so many years ago when he was thrown from a horse. Once we are gone, the memory of my mother will be extinguished as well. I wish I could reorder the graves in the yard, straighten the slanting stones, arrange them by date or name.

I can feel the ojo in my bones, which ache in the morning and at night, and in my skin, which is prickly and electric. Growing pains, the doctor at the clinic tells me. Still, I must put my affairs in order. First, there is the problem of the land. When I'm gone it will go to the distant offspring of a cousin of my grandfather's. My grandfather doesn't know I know this, doesn't know I won't have children of my own.

I have toys and books that must be disposed of too. A collection of stones.

The old women say the ojo is caused by a covetous glance, by looking over-long. The man who gave it did not admire me, however, and looked for only a moment. The one thing of mine he desired, he took.   40

These are the symptoms: At night heaviness crouches on my chest and I wake gasping for air. Occasionally my eyes blur for no reason and Cuipas slants and washes away. At my worst I shiver and burn, and my grandfather wraps my feet in cold rags.

My memories of my mother are insubstantial. I see her lying on her back on the living room floor, a beauty magazine held above her head as she reads, limp pages rustling. Holding me in the yard at night, bare feet, my hand gripping the flannel nightgown at her breast as I follow with my eyes her pointed finger to the moon. A dish of yogurt cracked on the board floors of the kitchen, my mother crying. I do not know if my grandfather remembers these moments, but he must remember others: my mother as a laughing tod-dler, perhaps; my mother at her first communion, my mother too young and pregnant with me. Possibly he remembers the sound of her voice.

Once a month we drive west to Albuquerque, once a week we drive east to Estancia. In Estancia we buy groceries and the newspaper. At home my grand-father prepares our favorite lunch: cheese and mustard sandwiches and a glass of milk. We wash our dishes, and then it is time for the paper. We turn to the back, to the comics, but we don't read them. Very carefully my grandfather tears out the puzzles, the spot-the-differences for me, the word-search for him.

We sit, working with our pencils.

"These are good for my eyes," he tells me. "They keep my mind sharp."   45

His favorites are the ones that match English and Spanish words. Some-times my grandfather disagrees with the paper's translation. "Moths are *palomitas*,"° he tells me, "not *polillas*,"° and I look up, try to remember. When I finish my puzzle I stand beside my grandfather's chair and point out words he's missed.

---

palomitas: Little doves.
polillas: Moths, grubs, any cause of progressive destruction.

At night, if I can't sleep I creep to the kitchen and take the paper from the crate by the woodstove. I spread it on the bedclothes. Somewhere north of here they are building a new casino. They are angry about the economy. In a country far away something has changed. I lie back on my pillow and try to imagine living in the world where these things matter. In the morning when my grandfather wakes me for my oatmeal he gathers the paper and replaces it beside the stove.

Sometimes my grandfather remembers church, and if it is Sunday he shakes me awake and braids my hair, and we walk to the chapel. We sit in the pews with our neighbors and try to listen. The priest talks about the soul, as beside me my grandfather's chin sinks to his chest. The soul is a ball of light or a jewel that must be treasured, given to Jesus.

"Christ calls for our souls though we are foul in body," says the priest.

Jesus looks down on us from the cross, mournful and distant and preoccu-   50
pied with his own story.

I feel my soul inside me, made of thin, pale paper, fragile as a Japanese lantern, resting above my heart. I move with care and take shallow breaths so as not to crush it.

Christ's frozen eyes gaze at the ground. He declines to see my sleeping grandfather; he declines to see what he has abandoned. Rage rises in my chest, threatening to crumple my soul. Christ has no time for Cuipas, no time for my grandfather.

"Peace be with you," the priest says, and my grandfather wakes, squeezes my hand.

I have never seen a Japanese lantern, only read about them in my mother's novels. Used chiefly at night parties they sway from strings above wide lawns, while music plays and women in backless gowns sip champagne.

My grandfather owns nine vehicles, several of which run, though none are   55
insured. When we go to Albuquerque he lets me choose the car. Usually I pick the old blue truck or the heavy brown ancient Mercedes with the rat's nest in the heating vent, which a man up north gave my grandfather as payment for a stone fireplace in his guesthouse. These are cars my mother will recognize.

Together my grandfather and I walk behind the house, where the vehicles sit, some with cracked tires, some parked on blocks. I hear him breathe beside me, even and smooth, familiar.

Today I pick the Mercedes.

In the car we roll down the stiff windows and trail our hands in the air outside. Along the road the yellow grass sifts the wind.

When my grandfather begins to talk, it isn't about the past but about a future in the world outside Cuipas.

"You must not be shy," he tells me.   60

"You must be happy and laugh."

"You must talk to strangers."

I nod and tell him, "I will, I'll try," and panic rises in me.

"This is no place for a young person," my grandfather says. I know he thinks of a day — a day that will never exist but that is as real to him as if it already did — when I shoulder a bag and climb up and over the Manzanos without turning back. He says again, "This is no place for a child."

I want to make him take it back. Instead I pull the slip of paper from my pocket. "I want to stop here," I say firmly. "I need to stop at this clinic."

He takes the slip from my hand and frowns at it. I nearly grab the steering wheel, but his one hand on it is steady and the road is straight. He lifts his foot from the pedal, and the car loses power. He turns to look at me for a moment, then turns back to the road. He folds the slip of paper, slips it into his breast pocket, and gives the car gas.

"So can we? Can we stop?"

"No," he says, in a voice he rarely uses with me, a voice that is harsh and foreign and final. The ojo stirs and my vision smears. I think of my mother. I'll never leave my grandfather, but it isn't even my loyalty that he wants.

The road twists and curves and begins to rise. When we are in the Manzanos I swallow the stone in my throat, look out over the piñon, imagine the murderer in these mountains, alone with the knowledge of his crime.

In the city the bright billboards flash along the highway, and white sun glints off the windows of the tall hospitals and hotels. As the fast cars pass I look for my mother. I don't think she will be in the driver's seat of one of the fancy cars, but I watch the faces anyway. Her hair could be different by now. Other things might be different for her too, I know, because in the world people's fortunes rise and fall.

If I find her, I think, then my grandfather will see the doctor. He will see the doctor and he will be cured and together we will bring my mother home.

I wonder if he is looking as well. He gives no indication, keeps both hands on the steering wheel. It's harder for him to drive now, and the traffic makes him nervous. "Look, hijita," he tells me before we shift lanes. His voice is familiar again. "Am I clear?" And I crane my neck, watch the cars coming at us, tell him yes.

At the Kmart we load our cart with things we will need for the next month: tubes of toothpaste, large packages of paper towels, cornflakes, sometimes new sneakers for me, undershirts for him. My grandfather buys me toys also, plastic dolls, characters from films and television shows I have never seen. He will ask me to open the toys in the car, and I will scatter the bright cardboard and plastic packaging on the floorboard. As he drops the toys into the cart I smile and exclaim, though I'm too old for them and wish he would save our money. At home I will line them on the windowsill in my room, leave a few scattered on the floor, so my grandfather, walking by, will think I have been playing.

When we've found all the things we need we continue to push the cart down aisles under fluorescent lights. We are both a little dazed by the colors of this place, the bustle, both of us unwilling, it seems, to leave and be alone together. We push the cart, turning our heads left and right.

The woman at the checkout is stout and middle-aged and wears braces on her teeth. She asks what we think should happen to the horses. When we look at her blankly, she asks if we're from here.

"Cuipas," my grandfather says.

The horses, the cashier explains, are wild, came down from the mountains because they were starving from the drought. They gather along the highway to eat chamisa° and grass and the corn tossed to them by concerned citizens.

"I can't believe you don't know," the cashier says. "It's all over the TV. They say the horses are the same ones brought by the Spanish hundreds of years ago."

The cashier scans each item as she talks. She moves too quickly. I'm afraid she will be done before she has told us everything about the horses.

"What will happen to them?" I ask.   80

"Who knows? People have to fight about it, like everything else. I saw on the news where some people are saying they'll have to be slaughtered because there just isn't enough grass, what with the drought."

My grandfather fingers the bills in his hand, ready to count them out when she gives us the total.

"Some people say the state should feed them until the rains come, some say they should be driven to Colorado or Wyoming." The cashier pauses, tongues her braces. "The one sure thing is no one's going to leave them alone. People will interfere."

When I look toward the doors I know it's for a reason. It takes a few moments for me to see her. My mother. She pushes a cart, the corner of a box of sugared cereal poking out of a bag. She is as young as I remember, her hair as straight and heavy. She squints up, her gaze brushing over my face.

When I turn to him, I know from the way he holds the bills in his trem-   85
bling hands that my grandfather has seen her too.

If it really were her I would run across the crowded store, throw myself against her. If it were her I would beat at her chest and belly with my fists. The cashier sighs and says that everything is expensive anymore. I want so much for the woman to be my mother, and suddenly I fear it too. If she returns my grandfather will get better, but he will also remember everything she put him through. If she returns she might leave again, and then he might get worse. But it isn't her, of course, and the woman passes through the automatic doors.

My grandfather is still looking toward the doors. His face is open and longing.

"Grandpa," I say, to draw his attention. "I'm hungry. I want my lunch."

Slowly he turns to me. He blinks, and then his face is shuttered.

In the car my grandfather asks where I want to eat.   90

"I want to go home. Let's eat at home. We'll have cheese and mustard sandwiches."

He nods, and we drive in silence until he begins to speak.

"Your mother never forgave me for the way I treated your grandma," he says, looking hard at the road.

"It wasn't her," I tell him. "It was just someone who looked like her."

chamisa: A flowering shrub.

My grandfather sits upright, close to the steering wheel, his gaze fixed on   95
the horizon. "Once I shook your grandma so hard the skin around her eyes
bruised," he says. "Your mother stood against the wall and watched."

"Grandpa, that lady didn't even look like her, not really."

He says, "Your grandma's head went back and forth."

I won't look at him. I won't.

"It took a week for the black to fade, and during those days I stayed away
from the house. One night I even slept at a jobsite. On the weekend I worked
on the cars. I changed the fluids in every single one, checked the pressure
on every tire, recorded the mileage. I couldn't go into the house where
they were."

The ojo begins to flare. I want his story to stop. My skin burns.   100

"It wasn't her," I say.

He clears his throat. "I never touched your grandma again. I wouldn't
have, even if she hadn't left. And I never touched your mother. But that didn't
matter because your mother never forgave me."

I can't stand it, but he keeps going. I hear him even over the hot throbbing
in my ears. I think of his voice earlier, that hard, hoarse severity, and think of
Ofelia Alma Zamora, my grandmother, being shaken so hard the fragile skin
around her eyes bruised. I've never heard this story, but now I understand that
I knew it all along. I need him to stop.

"She blamed me for her mother leaving her, and maybe she was right."

Usually as we leave the rush and concrete of Albuquerque, the vast beige   105
housing developments, my grandfather and I begin to relax and breathe.
Today, though, his terrible story remains packed around us, as thick and suffocating as cotton. I feel it would take great effort for me to move.

As we wind up and over the Manzanos, I thank him for the trip, say I'll be
glad to get home. My voice is stiff. He pats my hand, and behind his glasses his
eyes are rimmed red with age.

And because of what he has said, I remember the thing I nearly always
succeed in forgetting, the thing my grandfather believes I can't remember
because I was four: the day I last saw my mother.

She had been gone for three weeks, left without telling us. One day she
returned in a truck I'd never seen, driven by a man I'd never seen. She jumped
from the passenger's seat, and what I remember is being furious, but I ran
to her because I couldn't stop myself. When she opened her arms I backed
against the house and yelled at her to go away. She looked at me, lips parted in
hurt surprise, and I thought she'd come to me, but instead she walked into the
house.

The man in the truck — Anglo, cowboy hat tilted forward — looked
straight ahead, tapping his thumbs on the steering wheel.

My grandfather sat silently at the kitchen table, while in the tiny back   110
room she packed. I stood in the doorway, where by turning my head left or
right I could see them both, my grandfather sitting still, one palm pressed
against the table, and my mother working fast, shoving skirts and blouses into
my grandfather's canvas army duffle. Outside in the truck, the man waited.

My mother's back was to me and she cried as she packed. I looked at her with hate that burned her edges, until she browned and curled like a photograph cast into the stove. I looked at her and sliced through her with cuts so fine she hardly knew they were there until pieces of her began to drop away. I looked at her and she began to dry up and shrink from my gaze, until she was as cold and brittle as a marigold in November.

I wish now I had cried and flung myself at her and gripped the hem of her shirt. If I had, she might have stayed. Instead, I trailed her stiffly. Out on the porch she kneeled to hug me, and I remained rigid with hate, and over her shoulder I could see the man watching us. My mother was crying and murmuring in my ear, love or promises, but I couldn't listen. The man's eye caught mine, and that's when the ojo began to spread through me. My mother pulled away, jogged to the truck, where she swung her bag into the back. She didn't call to me when they drove away.

For a long time I watched the road that led to the Manzanos and beyond to Albuquerque. I watched until the sun dropped so low in the sky that it burned my eyes and I had to turn my head.

I don't remember what I did when I lost sight of the truck, but I imagine I went inside to where my grandfather was sitting in the kitchen. I imagine when he heard my step he looked up and saw me.

Now he says, "I told her to go, hijita."   115

Outside, the landscape blurs.

"I told her she couldn't come home. I didn't think she'd listen to me—when had she ever listened before?—but she did. She left you."

It wasn't the man's gaze at all, I realize now. It was my own eye that was evil, my own look that was covetous and overlong, my own furious, envious gaze that has made me sick. I wanted my mother and she'd gone to him.

We have begun our descent through the Manzanos—Cuipas is a meager cluster of buildings in the distance—when we see them, the wild horses. There are two, pulling at the dry grass. My grandfather slows the Mercedes in the middle of the road. The horses are thin. Ribs visible through dusty coats. The Mercedes thrums, diesel coursing, so he turns off the engine. It shudders and goes silent, and then we hear the wind in the grass, weeds scraping against the asphalt edges of the road, and, I'm sure of it, the sound of their mouths as they eat. One of them raises her head, cocks her ears, listening. The light is silver on her velvet muzzle. I'm certain she is aware of us, will raise the alarm, but she dips her head once more and tears at the grass with yellow teeth. I think about a relative long ago losing his horse, calling her name through the mountains, returning to the fort or mission on foot, perhaps never making it, his name lost to history. A third horse emerges from the piñon, swats at the air with her tail.

If I could time my death, I would time it thus: exactly fifteen seconds after   120
my grandfather. I would like to die in my sleep, but I must be certain I outlive him. I will lay my ear against his thin chest, listen to the silence beneath his humped sternum, and then, when I am sure, it will be my turn. Fifteen seconds is good: any longer and I might feel grief. Any longer and I might raise my head to the world opening up before me, wide and calling.

In a moment my grandfather will pat my hand again, and his hand will stay there, resting on mine. I'll look down, run a finger along the veins knotted and bruised under his thin brown skin. I wait for his touch. But now we watch the horses separately, sitting as still as we know how.

≣ THINKING ABOUT THE TEXT

1. What is the significance of Ofelia saying, "I long for that other Cuipas, for the families and the river" (para. 13)?

2. One way to see the theme of escape is that Ofelia wants to escape to the past, her mother to the future. Explain how this might be the case.

3. Explain how the setting is an important ingredient in understanding the story.

4. Explain how the two wild horses at the end of the story can be seen as symbolic.

5. Explain Ofelia's understanding of the ojo. What does she originally think about it, and what conclusion does she come to at the end?

≣ MAKING COMPARISONS

1. Compare the idea of loss in both stories.

2. Compare how Louise and Ofelia think about the present and the future.

3. Compare Ofelia's relationship to her grandfather and Louise Mallard's to her husband.

≣ WRITING ABOUT IDEAS

1. Write an essay that argues that loss and absence are major concerns of both stories.

2. Argue that the wild horses at the end of the story are meant metaphorically.

3. Argue that the dream of escape is the major thematic focus of both stories.

4. Argue that the setting of "The Manzanos" is crucial to understanding the story.

☰ Literature and Current Issues: Does Our Happiness Depend on Others' Misery?

URSULA K. LE GUIN, "The Ones Who Walk Away from Omelas"

ARGUMENTS ON THE ISSUE:
DAVID BROOKS, "The Child in the Basement"

JOHN R. EHRENFELD, "The Error of Trying to Measure Good and Bad"

College students are sometimes frustrated by discussion in their literature classes when the instructor isn't specific enough about a poem's meaning or the exact point of a story. Didn't the author have a clear intention in mind, they argue reasonably. Actually, it might be that writers do plan on saying something specific but often change their minds as they get deeper into their story. And like the rest of us, they sometimes intend one thing, but readers take it another way. And of course, writers have no control over the multiple ways the values and opinions of the world change over decades or centuries. Reading literature is more complicated than simply decoding. That skill is valuable in following recipes or assembling a swing set, but literature relies on the reader's input to complete the transaction between writer and audience. Shakespeare's audience responded enthusiastically to his plays, and four hundred years later, so do contemporary theater goers. These diverse audiences find the playwright's words powerful because they sense that they are relevant to their own lives, to the world they live in now, and to their fears, hopes, desires, and concerns.

The following classic story, written over forty years ago, resonates with contemporary readers because they seem to find in Le Guin's tale issues as fresh as this morning's news. We follow "The Ones Who Walk Away from Omelas" with a brief essay by the *New York Times* columnist David Brooks, titled "The Child in the Basement," and a direct response by John R. Ehrenfeld. Although one of the many possible topics for discussion in the story is the morality of exploitation, it remains for the reader to fill in the relevant details, perhaps focusing on the working conditions of young girls in Pakistan making Nike running shoes for a few dollars a day or ten-year-old migrant laborers harvesting lettuce in intolerable conditions in California. In their responses to Le Guin, Brooks wants to remind us of our conflicted values, while Ehrenfeld hopes to affirm absolute rights and duties. These two essays are challenging, focusing on philosophical ideas that demand but reward our attention. One simple but not reductive way to see their complex arguments is to think of the fairly common discussion in college classes between the relative and the absolute, between pragmatic compromise and moral absolutes, between who is morally good and who is not—and importantly, what standard or system of ethics is being used to judge our ethical choices. Whatever our perspective, reading and rereading their arguments can make us better thinkers and perhaps better people.

≡ **BEFORE YOU READ**

Who do you think about when the idea of an exploited worker is mentioned? If your professor said she would give A's to the whole class if they would designate one person to get an F, how would you react? How would others respond? Would there be a consensus? Are there rights that are inalienable? Is "the pursuit of happiness" one of them? Why?

URSULA K. LE GUIN

The Ones Who Walk Away from Omelas

Ursula K. Le Guin (1929–2018) was born and raised in Berkeley, California, where she began writing at age eleven, unsuccessfully submitting a story to Astounding Science Fiction. *She graduated from Radcliffe College (Phi Beta Kappa) in 1951 and received her M.A. from Columbia University a year later. She became famous with the publication of* The Left Hand of Darkness *(1969), an exploration of a hermaphroditic race that most critics see as a comment on contemporary gender politics. The novel won science fiction's highest awards: the Hugo and the Nebula.* The Farthest Shore *(1972) won the National Book Award, and* Tehanu: The Last Book of Earthsea *(1990) won the prestigious Nebula Award. More recently,* Powers *won the Nebula Award for 2008, and* Lavinia *won the 2009 Locus Award*

Dan Tuffs/Getty Images

for Best Fantasy Novel. Besides her twenty novels, Le Guin has also published scores of short stories, books for children, nonfiction, and six volumes of poems. In 2000, Le Guin received the Library of Congress Living Legends award for her "significant contribution to America's heritage." In 2014, she won the Medal for Distinguished Contributions to American Letters from the National Book Foundation.

With a clamor of bells that set the swallows soaring, the Festival of Summer came to the city Omelas, bright-towered by the sea. The rigging of the boats in harbor sparkled with flags. In the streets between houses with red roofs and painted walls, between old moss-grown gardens and under avenues of trees, past great parks and public buildings, processions moved. Some were decorous: old people in long stiff robes of mauve and gray, grave master workmen, quiet, merry women carrying their babies and chatting as they walked. In other streets the music beat faster, a shimmering of gong and tambourine, and the people went dancing, the procession was a dance. Children dodged in and out, their high calls rising like the swallows' crossing flights over the music and the singing. All the processions wound towards the north side of the city, where on the great water-meadow called the Green Fields boys and girls, naked in the bright air, with mudstained feet and ankles and long, lithe arms, exercised their restive horses before the race. The horses wore no gear at all but a halter without bit. Their manes were braided with streamers of silver, gold, and green. They flared their nostrils and pranced and boasted to one another; they were vastly excited, the horse being the only animal who has adopted our ceremonies as his own. Far off to the north and west the mountains stood up half encircling Omelas on her bay. The air of morning was so clear that the snow still crowning the Eighteen Peaks burned with white-gold fire across the miles of sunlit air, under the dark blue of the sky. There was just enough wind to make the banners that marked the racecourse snap and flutter now and then. In the silence of the broad green meadows one could hear the music winding through the city streets, farther and nearer and ever approaching, a cheerful faint sweetness of the air that from time to time trembled and gathered together and broke out into the great joyous clanging of the bells.

Joyous! How is one to tell about joy? How describe the citizens of Omelas?

They were not simple folk, you see, though they were happy. But we do not say the words of cheer much any more. All smiles have become archaic. Given a description such as this one tends to make certain assumptions. Given a description such as this one tends to look next for the King, mounted on a splendid stallion and surrounded by his noble knights, or perhaps in a golden litter borne by great-muscled slaves. But there was no king. They did not use swords, or keep slaves. They were not barbarians. I do not know the rules and laws of their society, but I suspect that they were singularly few. As they did without monarchy and slavery, so they also got on without the stock exchange, the advertisement, the secret police, and the bomb. Yet I repeat that these were not simple folk, not dulcet shepherds, noble savages, bland utopians. They were not less complex than us. The trouble is that we have a bad habit, encouraged by pedants and sophisticates, of considering happiness as something rather stupid. Only pain is intellectual, only evil interesting. This is the treason of the artist: a refusal to admit the banality of evil and the terrible boredom of pain. If you can't lick 'em, join 'em. If it hurts, repeat it. But to praise despair is to condemn delight, to embrace violence is to lose hold of everything else. We have almost lost hold, we can no longer describe a happy man, nor make any celebration of joy. How can I tell you about the people of Omelas? They were not naive and happy children — though their children were, in fact, happy. They were mature, intelligent, passionate adults whose lives were not wretched. O miracle! But I wish I could describe it better. I wish I could convince you. Omelas sounds in my words like a city in a fairy tale, long ago and far away, once upon a time. Perhaps it would be best if you imagined it as your own fancy bids, assuming it will rise to the occasion, for certainly I cannot suit you all. For instance, how about technology? I think that there would be no cars or helicopters in and above the streets; this follows from the fact that the people of Omelas are happy people. Happiness is based on a just discrimination of what is necessary, what is neither necessary nor destructive, and what is destructive. In the middle category, however — that of the unnecessary but undestructive, that of comfort, luxury, exuberance, etc. — they could perfectly well have central heating, subway trains, washing machines, and all kinds of marvelous devices not yet invented here, floating light-sources, fuelless power, a cure for the common cold. Or they could have none of that: it doesn't matter. As you like it. I incline to think that people from towns up and down the coast have been coming in to Omelas during the last days before the Festival on very fast little trains and double-decked trams, and that the train station of Omelas is actually the handsomest building in town, though plainer than the magnificent Farmers' Market. But even granted trains, I fear that Omelas so far strikes some of you as goody-goody. Smiles, bells, parades, horses, bleh. If so, please add an orgy. If an orgy would help, don't hesitate. Let us not, however, have temples from which issue beautiful nude priests and priestesses already half in ecstasy and ready to copulate with any man or woman, lover or stranger, who desires union with the deep godhead of the blood, although that was my first idea. But really it would be better not to have any temples in Omelas — at least, not manned temples. Religion yes, clergy no. Surely the beautiful nudes can just wander about, offering themselves like divine soufflés to the hunger of the needy and the rapture of the flesh. Let them join the processions. Let tambourines be struck above the copulations, and the glory of desire be proclaimed upon the gongs, and (a not unimportant point) let the offspring of these delightful rituals be beloved and looked after by all. One thing I know there is none of in Omelas is guilt. But what else should there be? I thought that first there were no drugs, but that is puritanical. For those who like it, the faint insistent sweetness of *drooz* may perfume the ways of the city, *drooz* which first brings a great lightness and brilliance to the mind and limbs, and then after some hours a dreamy languor, and wonderful visions at last of the very arcana and inmost secrets of the Universe, as well as exciting the pleasure of sex beyond all belief; and it is not habit-forming. For more modest tastes

I think there ought to be beer. What else, what else belongs in the joyous city? The sense of victory, surely, the celebration of courage. But as we did without clergy, let us do without soldiers. The joy built upon successful slaughter is not the right kind of joy; it will not do; it is fearful and it is trivial. A boundless and generous contentment, a magnanimous triumph felt not against some outer enemy but in communion with the finest and fairest in the souls of all men everywhere and the splendor of the world's summer: this is what swells the hearts of the people of Omelas, and the victory they celebrate is that of life. I really don't think many of them need to take *drooz.*

Most of the processions have reached the Green Fields by now. A marvelous smell of cooking goes forth from the red and blue tents of the provisioners. The faces of small children are amiably sticky; in the benign grey beard of a man a couple of crumbs of rich pastry are entangled. The youths and girls have mounted their horses and are beginning to group around the starting line of the course. An old woman, small, fat, and laughing, is passing out flowers from a basket, and tall young men wear her flowers in their shining hair. A child of nine or ten sits at the edge of the crowd, alone, playing on a wooden flute. People pause to listen, and they smile, but they do not speak to him, for he never ceases playing and never sees them, his dark eyes wholly rapt in the sweet, thin magic of the tune.

He finishes, and slowly lowers his hands holding the wooden flute.   5

As if that little private silence were the signal, all at once a trumpet sounds from the pavilion near the starting line: imperious, melancholy, piercing. The horses rear on their slender legs, and some of them neigh in answer. Sober-faced, the young riders stroke the horses' necks and soothe them, whispering, "Quiet, quiet, there my beauty, my hope. . . ." They begin to form in rank along the starting line. The crowds along the racecourse are like a field of grass and flowers in the wind. The Festival of Summer has begun.

Do you believe? Do you accept the festival, the city, the joy? No? Then let me describe one more thing.

In a basement under one of the beautiful public buildings of Omelas, or perhaps in the cellar of one of its spacious private homes, there is a room. It has one locked door, and no window. A little light seeps in dustily between cracks in the boards, secondhand from a cobwebbed window somewhere across the cellar. In one corner of the little room a couple of mops, with stiff, clotted, foul-smelling heads, stand near a rusty bucket. The floor is dirt, a little damp to the touch, as cellar dirt usually is. The room is about three paces long and two wide: a mere broom closet or disused tool room. In the room a child is sitting. It could be a boy or a girl. It looks about six, but actually is nearly ten. It is feebleminded. Perhaps it was born defective, or perhaps it has become imbecile through fear, malnutrition, and neglect. It picks its nose and occasionally fumbles vaguely with its toes or genitals, as it sits hunched in the corner farthest from the bucket and the two mops. It is afraid of the mops. It finds them horrible. It shuts its eyes, but it knows the mops are still standing there; and the door is locked; and nobody will come. The door is always locked; and nobody ever comes, except that sometimes—the child has no understanding of time or interval — sometimes the door rattles terribly and opens, and a person, or several people, are there. One of them may come in and kick the child to make it stand up. The others never come close, but peer in at it with frightened, disgusted eyes. The food bowl and the water jug are hastily filled, the door is locked, the eyes disappear. The people at the door never say anything, but the child, who has not always lived in the tool room, and can remember sunlight and its mother's voice, sometimes speaks. "I will be good," it says. "Please let me out. I will be good!" They never answer. The child used to scream for help at night, and cry a good deal, but now it only makes a kind of whining, "eh-haa, eh-haa," and it speaks less and less often. It is so thin there are no calves to its legs; its belly protrudes; it lives on a half-bowl of corn meal and grease a day. It is naked. Its buttocks and thighs are a mass of festered sores, as it sits in its own excrement continually.

They all know it is there, all the people of Omelas. Some of them have come to see it, others are content merely to know it is there. They all know that it has to be there. Some of them understand why, and some do not, but they all understand that their happiness, the beauty of their city, the tenderness of their friendships, the health of their children, the wisdom of their scholars, the skill of their makers, even the abundance of their harvest and the kindly weathers of their skies, depend wholly on this child's abominable misery.

This is usually explained to children when they are between eight and   10
twelve, whenever they seem capable of understanding; and most of those who come to see the child are young people, though often enough an adult comes, or comes back, to see the child. No matter how well the matter has been explained to them, these young spectators are always shocked and sickened at the sight. They feel disgust, which they had thought themselves superior to. They feel anger, outrage, impotence, despite all the explanations. They would like to do something for the child. But there is nothing they can do. If the child were brought up into the sunlight out of that vile place, if it were cleaned and fed and comforted, that would be a good thing, indeed; but if it were done, in that day and hour all the prosperity and beauty and delight of Omelas would wither and be destroyed. Those are the terms. To exchange all the goodness and grace of every life in Omelas for that single, small improvement: to throw away the happiness of thousands for the chance of the happiness of one: that would be to let guilt within the walls indeed.

The terms are strict and absolute; there may not even be a kind word spoken to the child.

Often the young people go home in tears, or in a tearless rage, when they have seen the child and faced this terrible paradox. They may brood over it for weeks or years. But as time goes on they begin to realize that even if the child could be released, it would not get much good of its freedom: a little vague pleasure of warmth and food, no doubt, but little more. It is too degraded and imbecile to know any real joy. It has been afraid too long ever to be free of fear. Its habits are too uncouth for it to respond to humane treatment. Indeed, after so long it would probably be wretched without walls about it to protect it, and darkness for its eyes, and its own excrement to sit in. Their tears at the bitter injustice dry when they begin to perceive the terrible justice of reality, and to accept it. Yet it is their tears and anger, the trying of their generosity and the acceptance of their helplessness, which are perhaps the true source of the splendor of their lives. Theirs is no vapid, irresponsible happiness. They know that they, like the child, are not free. They know compassion. It is the existence of the child, and their knowledge of its existence, that makes possible the nobility of their architecture, the poignancy of their music, the profundity of their science. It is because of the child that they are so gentle with children. They know that if the wretched one were not there snivelling in the dark, the other one, the flute-player, could make no joyful music as the young riders line up in their beauty for the race in the sunlight of the first morning of summer.

Now do you believe in them? Are they not more credible? But there is one more thing to tell, and this is quite incredible.

At times one of the adolescent girls or boys who go to see the child does not go home to weep or rage, does not, in fact, go home at all. Sometimes also a man or woman much older falls silent for a day or two, and then leaves home. These people go out into the street, and walk down the street alone. They keep walking, and walk straight out of the city of Omelas, through the beautiful gates. They keep walking across the farmlands of Omelas. Each one goes alone, youth or girl, man or woman. Night falls; the traveler must pass down village streets, between the houses with yellow-lit windows, and on out into the darkness of the fields. Each alone, they go west or north, towards the mountains. They go on. They leave Omelas, they walk ahead into the darkness, and they do not come back. The place they go towards is a place even less imaginable to most of us than the city of happiness. I cannot describe it at all. It is possible that it does not exist. But they seem to know where they are going, the ones who walk away from Omelas.   *[1973]*

≡ THINKING ABOUT THE TEXT

1. The opening three paragraphs make Omelas sound idyllic. Why might most people think of it as a utopia? What would you add or subtract? How might some aspects of our world be possible in Omelas?

2. Critics suggest that although many stories are set in the future or in an imaginary world, they are really about the present. How might this be true for this story?

3. How might you respond to the suffering child? How would you respond if you knew the happiness of a community of thousands was based on the suffering of this one individual?

4. Speculate about why some walk away from Omelas. Where are they going? Why do they seem so resolute?

5. What part does tradition play in the story? For example, if the people of Omelas didn't have such a tradition and someone proposed it, why would they be more or less likely to adopt the proposal, assuming that it would somehow work?

DAVID BROOKS

The Child in the Basement

David Brooks (b. 1961) was born in Toronto and grew up in downtown Manhattan. He graduated from the University of Chicago in 1983 with a degree in history. He then worked as an intern at the conservative magazine National Review. *Later, he worked as a columnist for the* Wall Street Journal. *In 2000, Brooks published the well-received* Bobos in Paradise, *a witty satire on the "new upper class" consumerism. Since 2003, Brooks has been a regular columnist for the* New York Times. *He is sometimes described as a conservative, although he was an early admirer of President Obama. Recent books include* The Social Animal: The Hidden Sources of Love, Character and Achievement *(2011) and* The Road to Character *(2015). The following piece was written for his column in early 2015.*

Maybe you're familiar with Ursula Le Guin's short story, "The Ones Who Walk Away from Omelas." It's about a sweet and peaceful city with lovely parks and delightful music.

The people in the city are genuinely happy. They enjoy their handsome buildings and a "magnificent" farmers' market.

Le Guin describes a festival day with delicious beer and horse races: "An old woman, small, fat, and laughing, is passing out flowers from a basket, and tall young men wear her flowers in their shining hair. A child of nine or ten sits at the edge of the crowd, alone, playing on a wooden flute."

It is an idyllic, magical place.

But then Le Guin describes one more feature of Omelas. In the basement   5
of one of the buildings, there is a small broom-closet-sized room with a locked door and no windows. A small child is locked inside the room. It looks about 6, but, actually, the child is nearly 10. "It is feebleminded. Perhaps it was born defective, or perhaps it has become imbecile through fear, malnutrition and neglect."

Occasionally, the door opens and people look in. The child used to cry out, "Please let me out. I will be good!" But the people never answered and now the child just whimpers. It is terribly thin, lives on a half-bowl of cornmeal a day and must sit in its own excrement.

"They all know it is there, all the people of Omelas," Le Guin writes. "Some of them have come to see it; others are content merely to know it is there. They all know it has to be there. Some of them understand why, and some do not, but they all understand that their happiness, the beauty of their city, the tenderness of their friendships, the health of their children . . . depend wholly on this child's abominable misery."

That is the social contract in Omelas. One child suffers horribly so that the rest can be happy. If the child were let free or comforted, Omelas would be destroyed. Most people feel horrible for the child, and some parents hold their kids tighter, and then they return to their happiness.

But some go to see the child in the room and then keep walking. They don't want to be part of that social contract. "They leave Omelas; they walk ahead into the darkness and they do not come back."

In one reading this is a parable about exploitation. According to this reading, many of us live in societies whose prosperity depends on some faraway child in the basement. When we buy a cellphone or a piece of cheap clothing, there is some exploited worker — a child in the basement. We tolerate exploitation, telling each other that their misery is necessary for overall affluence, though maybe it's not.   10

In another reading, the story is a challenge to the utilitarian mind-set so prevalent today.

In theory, most of us subscribe to a set of values based on the idea that a human being is an end not a means. You can't justifiably use a human being as an object. It is wrong to enslave a person, even if that slavery might produce a large good. It is wrong to kill a person for his organs, even if many lives might be saved.

And yet we don't actually live according to that moral imperative. Life is filled with tragic trade-offs. In many different venues, the suffering of the few is justified by those trying to deliver the greatest good for the greatest number.

Companies succeed because they fire people, even if a whole family depends on them. Schools become prestigious because they reject people — even if they put a lifetime of work into their application. Leaders fighting a war on terror accidentally kill innocents. These are children in the basement of our survival and happiness.

The story compels readers to ask if they are willing to live according to those contracts. Some are not. They walk away from prosperity, and they make some radical commitment. They would rather work toward some inner purity.   15

The rest of us live with the trade-offs. The story reminds us of the inner numbing this creates. The people who stay in Omelas aren't bad; they just find it easier and easier to live with the misery they depend upon. I've found that this story rivets people because it confronts them with all the tragic compromises built into modern life — all the children in the basements — and, at the same time, it elicits some desire to struggle against bland acceptance of it all.

In another reading, the whole city of Omelas is just different pieces of one person's psychology, a person living in the busy modern world, and that person's idealism and moral sensitivity is the shriveling child locked in the basement.   *[2015]*

≡ THINKING ABOUT THE TEXT

1. Brooks claims that this parable is "a challenge to the utilitarian mind-set." What does this mean to you? Give some examples.

2. Brooks also thinks exploitation is a key idea in Le Guin's story. Explain how this might be the case, and give some examples from contemporary life.

3. Explain what Brooks means by "Life is filled with 'tragic trade-offs.'" Give some examples from recent events.

4. Give a brief summary of Brooks's next-to-last paragraph. Why do you think people are moved by this story? Do you know people who might "walk away" from Omelas? How would you describe them?

5. Explain Brooks's thought in the last paragraph. Give some concrete examples from your own life, your reading, or films you have seen.

≡ MAKING COMPARISONS

1. How does guilt figure in both texts? What is guilt, and where does it come from?

2. Compare the paragraph in the essay that begins, "the story compels readers . . ." with the last paragraph in the story. In what ways do you or don't you behave according to our current social contract?

3. How would you describe your response to both texts? Is there an emotional or intellectual difference?

JOHN R. EHRENFELD
The Error of Trying to Measure Good and Bad

John R. Ehrenfeld (b. 1931) is currently the executive director of the International Society of Industrial Ecology. He retired in 2000 as director of MIT's Program on Technology, Business and Environment. He received a doctorate in chemical engineering from MIT. He has published widely, focusing on sustainability and industrial ecology. Sustainability by Design *was published in 2009. His latest book is* Flourishing: A Frank Conversation about Sustainability *(with Andrew J. Hoffman, 2013). The following essay was posted on* Flourishing Design *on December 14, 2015.*

It's another David Brooks day. Today he is riffing on a story by Ursula Le Guin, "The Ones Who Walk Away from Omelas." In a nutshell, the tale is about a peaceful and happy city with an important open secret. Hidden away from the wandering eyes of the inhabitants is a closet containing a misfit. In Le Guin's words, "It is feebleminded. Perhaps it was born defective, or perhaps it has become imbecile through fear, malnutrition and neglect." On occasions this poor human being is revealed for all who wish to observe. Like many of her stories, this one is a parable on the way we love and should live. The misfit sops up all the ills of society so that everyone else can live a happy, uncluttered life. Most of the citizens, even knowing the plight of the misfit, ignore the unfairness and go back to life as usual. A few with a deeper moral sensitivity leave to face the unknown world beyond the walls.

Brooks makes the obvious comparison to our world today. The citizens of Omelas have made a social contract to single out someone to serve as the means of their prosperity. This is far from the theory of the social contract on which our society is based, as Brooks writes:

> In theory, most of us subscribe to a set of values based on the idea that a human being is an end not a means. You can't justifiably use a human being as an object. It is wrong to enslave a person, even if that slavery might produce a large good. It is wrong to kill a person for his organs, even if many lives might be saved.

I am not sure he is correct in assuming that "most of us subscribe to [such] a set of values." I suspect that a great majority of Americans have never heard of Kant's moral imperatives or keep the more familiar "golden rule" in reach of their consciousness. Given the practical rules of our society, these moral guiding principles may not even be present in their unconsciousness waiting to be invoked in problematic situations. Brooks notes that these practical rules are utilitarian in essence, replacing the inherent priceless nature of human life with a number that can fit an maximizing algorithm, like economists and technocrats use to make decisions. In his words:

> The story compels readers to ask if they are willing to live according to those contracts. Some are not. They walk away from prosperity, and they make some radical commitment. They would rather work toward some inner purity . . . The rest of us live with the trade-offs. The story reminds us of the inner numbing this creates. The people who stay in Omelas aren't bad; they just find it easier and easier to live with the misery they depend upon. I've found that this story rivets people because it confronts them with all the tragic compromises built into modern life — all the children in the basements — and, at the same time, it elicits some desire to struggle against bland acceptance of it all.

Whoa! I would say that those who stay in Omelas are, indeed, bad. It all depends on what standards of moral goodness is to be used. Brooks glosses over the distinctiveness of normative ethical theories, the different ways of morally justifying one's actions. As a result, he misses the main point of Le Guin's marvelous story. You can't have it both ways and live an uncluttered moral life. It's not the same as the utilitarian trade-offs that are part of that system of thought; it's the absolute choice between one moral system or another. I am certainly no moral philosopher, but I have come to know that consequentialism, where utilitarianism fits, is incompatible with deontology, where Kantianism sits. The first kind measures the goodness or badness of an act by the outcomes and permits the use of more or better as criteria to compare one act with another. Different theories use different sets of values as the basis for making comparative judgments.

Deontological theories are based on the idea of duties and rights and look at the rightness of the act, itself, not the outcome of the act. Kant says it is

5

wrong to treat a human as a means, instead of as an end, period. Rawls says we have a duty to do the right thing based on a process in which we are ignorant of the reality of the world out there. Simplistically, we might say, this class of theories deals with absolutes, the other with relative measures. When I discussed this editorial with my wife in midstream, she pointed out that Judaism is largely built on duty-based ethics, such as the one that has guided me for quite some time: acts of lovingkindness, often expressed as tikkun olam or healing the world.

In researching ethical theories today as I write this post, I noticed a third class of theories based on care. I suspect that much of my work to date on flourishing falls into this class since my concerns over care and interconnectedness fit into its framework that emphasizes interdependence and relationships. I will be looking at this in much more detail as I continue working on my current book.

Brooks's failure to see the moral problem faced by the citizens of Omelas as having to choose between categories of ethics is the same problem virtually all of us in the United States have. Our much revered founding fathers dumped us into a moral dilemma with the first public document we live by, The Declaration of Independence. The most well-known sentence is: "We hold these truths to be self-evident, that all men are created equal, that they are endowed by their Creator with certain unalienable Rights, that among these are Life, Liberty and the pursuit of Happiness."

The dilemma rests in the conflation of life, liberty, and happiness. The first two are clearly absolute rights, except that philosophers argue about the meaning of liberty. Both call for a system of right-based principles. But the last, happiness, is not absolute. In fact, earlier drafts of the document used "property" instead. Further, economists have co-opted psychologists, and measure happiness in material terms. This outcome necessitates a consequentialist system. The dilemma was obvious from the get-go when human slaves were classed as property. We have ignored this dilemma right down to the present, as do the citizens of Omelas.

It is too easy, as Brooks does (see the above block quote) to excuse both the people of Omelas and us as not being bad because we have to become utilitarians to exist in this world. As utilitarians, trade-offs are simply means to maximize values, but one cannot trade-off the two distinct moral categories. As long as consequentialism dominates, as it does, we are indeed bad, and are always somewhere on a slippery slope. One cannot be just a little bad. It's very important to accept that. We can live and perhaps must live with our dilemma, but we must not brush it away. We do admit, if pushed, that our motor of utilitarianism, the free market, produces unfairness; that is, it is amoral in the rights and duties domains. But we do little these days to correct its ills. As Brooks notes, we have lots of misfits hidden away in closets.

What I miss in this column is a call to action; a challenge to see the bads in all of us. Brooks ends with an enigmatic paragraph.   10

In another reading, the whole city of Omelas is just different pieces of one person's psychology, a person living in the busy modern world, and that person's idealism and moral sensitivity is the shriveling child locked in the basement.

The use of the word, "just," is puzzling, suggesting that it's OK to carry around two opposing ideas. It is, rather, both OK and not OK, but merely is a reflection of the values of our present society. Few people, in my estimate based on watching the world around me everyday, have such a mixed "psychology." The clarity of deontology has been badly blurred by our utilitarian norm. Bad is just another value to be weighed against other things. Unfortunately, it has fallen far down the ladder. This is the scandal of our use of torture and other inhumane treatment. The absolute badness was measured and lost. Part of the story of flourishing I have been writing is that humans are fundamentally deontologists. We have certain rights and duties that cannot be weighed and exchanged. The centrality of care fits here. I have not stressed its moral nature, but will be doing this as I continue to think and write. I thank David Brooks for his provoking me once again.   *[2015]*

≡ THINKING ABOUT THE TEXT

1. Why does Ehrenfeld claim that "those who stay in Omelas are, indeed, bad"? Why do you agree or disagree with him? What does he mean by "bad"?

2. Ehrenfeld seems to agree with Immanuel Kant's categorical imperative, a concept that asserts that we should behave as if our action were an absolute guide for all rational beings. Consequences are not considered; it is an absolute rule to be followed in all circumstances. How does Ehrenfeld agree with this idea? Do you? What might be some problems in following this principle?

3. According to Ehrenfeld, how does Brooks miss "the main point" of Le Guin's story?

4. Explain how Ehrenfeld's argument turns on the difference between the absolute and the relative. How does Ehrenfeld connect "torture and other inhumane treatment" with our current utilitarian norms?

5. What is the problem Ehrenfeld asserts that most of us have in America? What does it have to do with happiness?

≡ MAKING COMPARISONS

1. How do Brooks and Ehrenfeld differ in their use of "bad"?

2. What does Ehrenfeld think the main point of the story is? What does Brooks think it is? What do you think it is?

3. Brooks suggests that we carry around opposing ideas. How might this be true for you? How does Ehrenfeld respond to this?

☰ WRITING ABOUT THE ISSUES

1. Write an essay that argues that Le Guin's story is an apt allegory for a contemporary issue that needs to be changed. Include Ehrenfeld's idea about tikkun, or social justice.

2. Look up the connection between the idea for Le Guin's story and the American philosopher William James. Write a brief report commenting on the idea that in this tale, the narrator as well as the reader is on trial.

3. Write an essay that argues that one of the readings that Brooks suggests is a more fruitful way of seeing the story than the others. Give specific contemporary examples; include Ehrenfeld's perspective.

4. Brooks's piece elicited over five hundred responses from readers, some of whom remembered the story fondly from reading it in college forty years ago; others had not yet read it. Many saw Le Guin's parable in political terms, with Republicans believing that "we live in a world of terrible injustice," while Democrats believed that "injustice is terrible." One pessimistic observer thought the story suggested that many thousands of years from now, there will be two separate species of humanity so different from one another that they will be "incapable of breeding with each other." Find Brooks's essay and the readers' comments online. After reading through a few dozen, write a report of your observations. Assuming the comments are a fair sampling of the thinking of educated readers, what is your assessment of their responses to Le Guin's tale? Quote brief phrases from their letters in support of your judgment.

≡ Literature and Current Issues: What Aren't Students Free to Say?

YEVGENY YEVTUSHENKO, "Flowers & Bullets"

ARGUMENTS ON THE ISSUE:
DAVID COLE, "Trust the First Amendment"

MINOUCHE SHAFIK, "Should Universities Host Speakers Who Propound Offensive Ideas?"

LARA KISWANI, "Should Universities Host Speakers Who Propound Offensive Ideas?"

Nothing is more contentious than the definition of "free" in the debate over First Amendment rights. Is "free speech" really free? Can you say anything, however offensive, insulting, or hateful? Many countries believe that prohibiting "hate speech" is a "necessary evil" to protect minority and religious groups against emotional and psychological harm. This especially relevant at universities, where speech codes are enacted to foster productive learning environments that may be destroyed by verbal attacks against groups that historically have faced discrimination or subjugation. These students, it is argued, may not be able to compete fairly in academics, thereby justifying speech limitations. Further it is argued that the university should be an ideal forum where rational argument prevails, not the irrational hate speech of bigotry. The right of a student to an education is seen, then, as more important than the "free speech" rights of others.

Those who argue against university speech codes maintain that nothing should trump the fundamental human right of freedom of speech. Their thinking is that the First Amendment demands tolerance for the intolerant. For them, no laws should regulate what is permissible or not. From the point of view of free speech advocate David Cole, "the path to equality of the civil rights movement, the women's rights movement, and the gay rights movement was paved by more and more free speech, not by the suppression of racist, sexist, or homophobic comments."

Although both those arguments from the left and right, from liberals and conservatives, are fairly typical, recent events on college campuses have complicated the usual political boundaries. Speech codes that were widespread at universities and colleges twenty years ago are now being looked at carefully, not only by conservatives who initially opposed them but by administrators and civil liberties groups who were early advocates of what are sometimes called hate speech codes. There is certainly continued concern that all students should be able to live and study in a tolerant environment. And indeed some universities have recently adopted new principles against intolerance. The problem, as some see it, is that some students and administrators, in their effort to respond to violations of tolerance, have become, as one critic claims, "sanctimonious bullies." This is, of course, one perspective on a complex situation, but one we should add that is shared by a considerable number of journalists, faculty, and politicians on the right and the left.

The debate used to be between conservative opponents and liberal defenders of speech codes, but the waters have of late been considerably muddied by those in favor of diversity and tolerance being accused of lack of diversity and intolerance. Administrators have not clarified the situation by sometimes agreeing with students who, on the one hand, demand that invited speakers they disagree with be banned from campus, while on the other hand, assert a commitment to free speech and diversity.

The consequence of these often contradictory and shifting principles is that both students and faculty on college campuses are sometimes unsure of what they are able to say and are fearful of running afoul of one group of students or another. The administrations at many universities seem equally baffled, often acting arbitrarily and thereby pleasing no one.

Yevgeny Yevtushenko dedicates "Flowers & Bullets," the poem in this cluster, to Allison Krause, one of four students killed at Kent State by bullets fired by the National Guard during a student protest in May 1970. The Vietnam War was already bitterly opposed by millions of students when Richard Nixon ordered the bombing of Cambodia. Since this indicated that the war was escalating, not winding down, protest marches erupted on campus all over America and Europe. But Kent State became the focal point of rage when unarmed students exercising their free speech rights were shot down, with sixty-seven shots fired. Immediately after video and photographs from Kent State went public, millions of college and high school students went on strike. Hundreds of schools were closed and tens of thousands marched on Washington, D.C., in protest. Now, fifty years later, the deaths of these four students (and more who were wounded) remain a tragic reminder of what can happen when there is no official tolerance for free speech and peaceful protest.

The poem reprinted here was written in direct response to the Kent State shootings. The student to whom Yevtushenko dedicates the poem reportedly placed a flower in the barrel of a National Guardsman's rifle, saying, "Flowers are better than bullets." In December 1970, Yevtushenko donated the manuscript of the poem to Kent State University Libraries Department of Special Collections and Archives where it is currently joined by hundreds of poems and songs written in memory of the slain students.

≡ BEFORE YOU READ

What do you think "free" means in the First Amendment's right to freedom of speech? What exceptions do you think might be reasonable? Are you constrained to use your free speech rights responsibly by laws and regulations or by social norms and ethics? Are you aware of speech codes at your college? What issues are dealt with in the university's code of conduct for students?

YEVGENY YEVTUSHENKO
Flowers & Bullets

Translated by Anthony Kahn

Yevgeny Yevtushenko (1933–2017) was born in Siberia near Lake Baikal. He was for decades one of Russia's best known poets, attracting stadium-sized audiences (200,000 at a 1991 reading). A multitalented artist, Yevtushenko also wrote novels, plays, and movie scripts, as well as acting in and directing films. His work focused on denouncing war atrocities, anti-Semitism, and dictators. He achieved fame with his 1961 poem "Babi Yar" that told of the slaughter of 34,000 Jews by the Nazis and the refusal of anti-Semites in the Ukraine to place a monument at the sight of the massacre. He said his poetry was not political, preferring the term "human rights poetry," which asserted the need for "human conscience as the greatest spiritual value." He taught at the University of Tulsa and Queens College in New York City.

    Of course: Bullets don't like people
                    who love flowers.
    They're jealous ladies, bullets,
                    short on kindness.
    Allison Krause, nineteen years old,   5
                    you're dead,
    for loving flowers.
    When, thin and open as the pulse of conscience,
    you put a flower in a rifle's mouth
                    and said,   10
    "Flowers are better than bullets,"
                    that
    was pure hope speaking.
    Give no flowers to a state
                    that outlaws truth;   15
    such states reciprocate
                    with cynical, cruel gifts,
    and your gift, Allison Krause,
    was the bullet
                    that blasted the flower.   20
    Let every apple orchard blossom black,
                    black in mourning.
    Ah, how the lilac smells!
                    You're without feeling.
    Nothing, Nixon said it: 25
                    "You're a bum."
    All the dead are bums.
                    It's not their crime.

You lie in the grass,
                a melting candy in your mouth,   30
done with dressing in new clothes,
                done with books.
You used to be a student.
                You studied fine arts.
But other arts exist,   35
                of blood and terror,
and headsmen with a genius for the axe.
Who was Hitler?
                A cubist of gas chambers.
In the name of all flowers   40
                I curse your works,
you architects of lies,
                maestros of murder!
Mothers of the world whisper
                'O God, God'   45
and seers are afraid
                to look ahead.
Death dances rock-and-roll upon the bones
                of Vietnam, Cambodia—
On what stage is it booked to dance tomorrow?   50
Rise up, Tokyo girls,
                Roman boys,
take up your flowers
                against the common foe.
Blow the world's dandelions up   55
                into a blizzard!
Flowers, to war!
                Punish the punishers!
Tulip after tulip,
                carnation after carnation,   60
rip out of your tidy beds in anger,
choke every lying throat
                with earth and root!
You, jasmine, clog
                the spinning blades of mine-layers!   65
Boldly,
        block the cross-hair sights,
        drive your sting into the lenses,
                        nettles!
Rise up, lily of the Ganges,   70
                lotus of the Nile,
stop the roaring props
        of planes pregnant
                with the death of children!

Roses, don't be proud   75
    to find yourselves sold
    at higher prices.
Nice as it is to touch a tender cheek,
thrust a sharper thorn a little deeper
      into the fuel tanks of bombers.   80
Of course:
    Bullets are stronger than flowers.
Flowers aren't enough to overwhelm them.
Stems are too fragile,
    petals are poor armor.   85
But a Vietnam girl of Allison's age,
    taking a gun in her hands,
is the armed flower
    of the people's wrath!
If even flowers rise,   90
    then we've had enough
    of playing games with history.
Young America,
    tie up the killer's hands.
Let there be an escalation of truth   95
to overwhelm the escalating lie
    crushing people's lives!
Flowers, make war!
    Defend what's beautiful!
Drown the city streets and country roads   100
    like the flood of an army advancing
and in the ranks of people and flowers
    arise, murdered Allison Krause,
Immortal of the age,
    Thorn-Flower of protest!   105

[1970]

☰ THINKING ABOUT THE TEXT

1. Yevtushenko uses personification throughout his poem (e.g., "Bullets don't like people"). Find examples that seem relevant and explain their significance.

2. Yevtushenko was known as an international poet. How is this evident in the poem?

3. What is Yevtushenko urging when he implores the flowers "to war / Punish the punishers"?

4. Why does the penultimate stanza begin with "Of course:"?

5. Discuss the implications of the lines that begin with line 14: "Give no flowers to a state / that outlaws truth."

DAVID COLE
Trust the First Amendment

David Cole (b. 1958) is currently the National Legal Director of the American Civil Liberties Union. He graduated from Yale College in 1980 and the Yale Law School in 1984. He has taught at Georgetown University Law Center and NYU School of Law. He has written eight books, including The Torture Memos: Rationalizing the Unthinkable *(2009) and most recently* Engines of Liberty: The Power of Citizen Activists to Make Constitutional Law *(2016).*

HAVE conservatives hijacked the First Amendment?

Critics are increasingly making this claim, maintaining that under Chief Justice John G. Roberts Jr., the First Amendment, once an important safeguard for progressive speech, has become a boon to corporations, conservatives and the powerful.

But in most instances, the First Amendment doesn't favor speech of the right or the left; it simply takes the government out of the business of controlling speakers by virtue of what they say. It often empowers the powerless. And most important, it helps check official abuse.

To be sure, conservatives and corporations are invoking the First Amendment, and sometimes winning. In Citizens United v. Federal Election Commission, the Roberts court deployed the First Amendment to guarantee that corporations can engage in unlimited campaign spending. A recent study found that the Roberts court has more often protected conservative than liberal speakers.

In June, Justice Elena Kagan accused her conservative colleagues of "weaponizing the First Amendment" when they ruled that public sector unions cannot charge nonmembers "agency fees" because it amounts to compelled speech.

But these developments should not lead liberals or progressives to lose faith in the First Amendment. For starters, the amendment's core requirement is that the government must remain neutral regarding the content of speech. So generally, a decision protecting conservative speech will equally support liberal speech.

While the Roberts court ruled that the First Amendment gave adherents of the Westboro Baptist Church a right to display anti-gay signs outside a military funeral, its rationale would equally protect Revolutionary Communist Party members holding anti-Christian signs outside the Westboro Baptist Church.

Some argue that the First Amendment's very neutrality is problematic, because in an unequal society, the amendment will favor the haves over the have-nots. We all have a formally equal right to speak, but only George Soros, the Koch brothers, and a handful of others can spend hundreds of millions of dollars advancing their preferred candidates or positions.

But this argument proves too much. All rights are more valuable for the rich. The rights to have an abortion, to send your children to private school, to exclude others from your property, or to hire your own criminal defense lawyer are all more fully enjoyed by people with resources. Social inequality may be a reason to support progressive taxation or robust equal protection guarantees; it's not a reason to retreat from free speech principles.

In a more fundamental sense, the First Amendment favors people without   10
power and influence. In a democracy, the rich and those in the majority don't need constitutional protections; they can generally enact their desires through ordinary political processes. The targets of censorship are typically dissidents, outsiders, the marginalized.

History illustrates the point. The Constitution's speech protections did not emerge fully formed when the nation was founded. During World War I, for example, the Supreme Court upheld long prison sentences for merely criticizing the war. Over many years, anarchists, communists, labor unions, and civil rights activists fought for and earned the speech rights we know and take for granted today.

Nor is the First Amendment outmoded. The need for its protections are as urgent as ever. In just the last two years, my organization, the American Civil Liberties Union, has invoked the First Amendment to defend high school students disciplined for walking out from school to call for gun control, as well as other students penalized for posting pictures of guns on social media; a student newspaper denied funding after publishing a satire of "safe spaces," as well as fans of a hip-hop band labeled gang members; Milo Yiannopoulos and People for the Ethical Treatment of Animals, both of whom were denied permission to advertise on the Washington subway; and anti-Trump as well as pro-Trump demonstrators. We've defended flag desecraters, union organizers, and citizens blocked from their representatives' Facebook sites for their criticism. And that's just the beginning.

As even this very partial list shows, government officials continue to be tempted to silence people for their views. Some of our clients are liberal, others conservative, but all have been singled out because they have upset those in power.

Not every First Amendment argument is justified, of course. The A.C.L.U. supported the public sector union in the case that inspired Justice Kagan's dissent. We said charging workers for services that the union is required to provide to them is not a First Amendment violation, any more than requiring people to pay taxes for government policies they oppose. But even if conservatives sometimes win free speech cases they should lose, now is not the time for anyone to dismiss the First Amendment as a tool of conservatives.

Since Donald Trump's election, Americans have been exercising their   15
First Amendment rights to engage in resistance: demonstrating, calling their representatives, associating with like-minded citizens in defense of core values, shedding light on official abuse through the free press, and expressing themselves on social media.

When one party controls all three branches of government, the checks and balances have to come from the people. And the First Amendment gives us the tools to act—including the rights to speak, associate, petition the government, and enjoy a free press.

The fact that conservatives benefit from the First Amendment is not something to bemoan. It is part of the constitutional bargain. It simply means the First Amendment is operating as it should, neutrally preserving the lifeblood of democracy.

≡ THINKING ABOUT THE TEXT

1. Do you agree or disagree that members of the Westboro Baptist Church have the right to protest outside military funerals by carrying anti-gay signs?

2. Why do some people argue that the First Amendment's neutrality is problematic? How does Cole deal with this issue?

3. In the twelfth paragraph, Cole lists groups the ACLU has defended. Should they not have defended one or more of these groups? Why?

4. Cole doesn't mention the KKK or Nazi groups. Should the ACLU defend their right to march or speak at your university? Explain.

5. What ground rules would you use if you were the student in charge of inviting speakers to campus?

MINOUCHE SHAFIK
Should Universities Host Speakers Who Propound Offensive Ideas?

Minouche Shafik (b. 1962) is the director of the London School of Economics and former Deputy Governor of the Bank of England. She was born in Alexandria, Egypt. She studied at the University of Massachusetts, Amherst, and the London School of Economics and later received her Ph.D. from St. Antony's College, Oxford, in 1989. She taught at the University of Pennsylvania and Georgetown University. The following article was posted on debates.economist.com on April 19, 2018.

Freedom of expression is a fundamental human right. In universities, freedom of speech is closely intertwined with the core value of academic freedom, which protects the spirit of inquiry. It is rarely seen as an absolute right. Most people accept some curbs on free speech: laws outlawing libel and slander, for instance, or punishing direct calls to incitement. But open societies start with a presumption of wanting to protect freedom of speech to the maximum extent possible within the law.

Karl Popper, a philosopher at the London School of Economics (LSE), wrote "The Open Society and Its Enemies"—a passionate defense of freedom and reason informed by his experience of fascism and communism. Repressive regimes have long tried to silence free speech and thought. But today, calls to curb free speech often come from people on the left who want to deny, platforms to far right or racist groups or to protect vulnerable groups from exposure to offensive ideas. These challenges are heightened in the digital age, when extreme views provide "clickbait," anonymity reduces accountability, and social media gives platforms to all.

Some would argue that we need to preserve universities as "safe spaces" that shield young people from offensive ideas. But I believe that universities should provide spaces for the civilized contestation of ideas. Bubbles where the like-minded reinforce their prejudices are dangerous for open societies, which depend upon the clash of ideas. We need to provide a forum in which those clashes occur productively to advance human knowledge.

The dilemma for universities is how to maximize freedom of speech while not undermining other important values such as democracy, protection of minority rights and equality under the law. Popper himself recognized these tensions when he wrote, "We should therefore claim, in the name of tolerance, the right not to tolerate the intolerant."

That does not necessarily mean denying offensive speakers a platform — rather, universities should provide tolerant spaces where views are challenged. Of course, offensiveness is in the eye of the beholder — as the cliché goes, one person's terrorist is another's freedom fighter. But open debate in which different views are presented and evaluated using reason and evidence is the best way to find out which is which.   5

How can universities make this happen? By using the principles and processes that help them determine what is valued as an intellectual contribution. Among these principles are ensuring that subjects of enquiry are determined by academics, not politicians; rigorous peer review; independently funded and competitively awarded research funding; publishing data to let others replicate results; and being transparent about conflicts of interest.

Eventually these processes weed out ill-informed views from legitimate ones. They also help ensure that the ideas that come out of universities are independent and based on rigorous analysis — which is why trust in technical and academic experts is higher than any other group in the world, according to the latest Edelman Trust Barometer.

These same principles can inform the approach for managing offensive speakers at universities. At LSE, we run one of the largest public events programmes in the world, with over 350 events each year. All of them are open to the public and attract millions of listeners through our podcasts. We do not have a safe space or no-platforming policy. We protect freedom of speech through responsible and robust chairing by our academic staff, who ensure that all events allow a range of views to be heard. We encourage participants to challenge speakers based on evidence and critical thinking. We also require all participants to maintain good order. That means not shouting down speakers, protesting violently, or behaving in ways that deny others their right to speak.

Universities have a special role in defending free speech and in teaching students how to engage in responsible debate. Too much public discourse today is divided and shrill. Now more than ever, young people need to be given the tools to distinguish between truth and fiction, between worthwhile ideas and propaganda. If they do not learn these skills on university campuses, how will they be prepared for a world in which they will inevitably encounter ignorance and prejudice? Standing up for free speech can mean listening to people whose views we find unacceptable. But engaging in civilized debate with offensive ideas is a vital part of an open, democratic society.

≡ THINKING ABOUT THE TEXT

1. How can universities protect vulnerable groups from racist speech from, say, the KKK and Nazis who speak on campus?

2. What do you think of the Karl Popper quote, "We should therefore claim, in the name of tolerance, the right not to tolerate the intolerant"?

3. What do you think of "safe spaces" on campus? Who should decide whether or not to have them? Should the whole university be one?

4. Is responsible debate a university's highest goal? Should it be? Should the university prepare students for a world of "ignorance and prejudice"? What is the best way to do this?

5. Shafik doesn't address the limits of offensive speech. Are there boundaries? For example, some groups deny that certain school shootings ever happened. Some deny the Holocaust. Some accuse famous politicians of belonging to pedophilia rings. Are speakers from these groups allowable?

≡ MAKING COMPARISONS

1. Explain how Cole and Shafik are in agreement about offensive speech.

2. Point out places in these two essays where you disagree with the authors. Explain why.

3. How might the Nixon administration and the governor of Ohio in 1970 respond to Cole and Shafik?

LARA KISWANI

Should Universities Host Speakers Who Propound Offensive Ideas?

Lara Kiswani is the Executive Director of the Arab Resource and Organizing Centre, and was born in the Bay Area of California to Palestinian parents. She holds a masters degree in education with a focus on equity and social justice, and she is a lecturer at San Francisco State University in the college of Ethnic Studies. The following essay was posted at debates.economist.com on April 19, 2018.

Free speech, like any other right, is fundamentally linked to questions of equality, inequity, and access to representation and power. It is irresponsible to discuss free speech without acknowledging, that for the most disenfranchised among us, the exercise of any civil right can be a life or death struggle.

I am the executive director of the Arab Resource and Organising Centre, and work closely with American Arab and Muslim communities. They suffer from vigilante violence, hate-speech and state-sanctioned racism and xenophobia. Misguided efforts to protect the so-called free-speech rights of white supremacists have been weaponised against them. Those rights provide a platform for hate, and contribute to powerful institutional and governmental initiatives committed to doing away with civil and human rights for large segments of society (for instance, the current administration's "Muslim ban," its zeal to deport nonwhite immigrants, the dismantling of DACA, labeling immigrants as rapists and murders — the list could go on).

In a well-funded, well-coordinated effort to target minority and refugee communities, the extreme right uses their free-speech rights to attack the rights of migrants to move and live, of women over their bodies, of trans people to live in safety, of workers to unionize, as well as the rights of minorities to vote and practice their faith. It is not a question of whether bigots should be allowed to express their views, but a deeper question of whether government policies to systematically and institutionally undermine these rights should be tolerated, and of how universities should take the initiative in defending these rights.

In 1964, the Berkeley Free Speech Movement began when students demanded the right to engage in anti-racist organizing on campus. Ironically, free speech today has become a weapon of the far right. In 1969, the United States Supreme Court ruled that speech can be restricted when it is likely to produce imminent lawless action. Black, Brown, and immigrant communities experience violent, lawless action daily as a direct result of white supremacist speech. Murders by white supremacists have more than doubled since Trump took office. Take for instance the deadly result of the Unite the Right rally in Virginia, or the deadly stabbing of two people defending a Muslim woman from a white supremacist in Portland. These episodes of violence are a direct attack on the most fundamental civil and human rights of all people from the targeted communities.

In my daily work with the Arab and Muslim community, the families I see   5
are concerned about basic access to human, civil and political rights — to reunite with loved ones, work, and be free from ICE raids. They are concerned for their children's safety and the lives of their families suffering through war. In short, they struggle against inhumane government policies and practices, and deeply embedded racist and xenophobic social attitudes.

In theory government policy protects their free-speech rights, but in practice, when my constituents are vocal about issues they care about, they are often censored, suppressed, and even criminalised. For example, consider the attack on Palestinian human rights activism and the suppression of the Boycott, Divestment and Sanctions (BDS) movement opposing Israel's human-rights violations, and what many consider to be policies of apartheid.

In December 2016, Fordham University refused to give a Palestinian human rights student organization status, claiming that such an organization creates "polarization" on campus and "run contrary to the mission and values." In September 2016, UC Berkeley suspended a course on Palestine a week after it began after complaints by Israeli advocacy organizations. Students and faculty from the refugee Palestinian communities are regularly suspended, lose careers, are smeared, and have their lives threatened for simply *vocalizing* their support of BDS activism.

For our communities, this is not a debate. It is a matter of life and death. For the most disenfranchised among us, the consequences are extreme. When it comes to struggles over free speech, I wish the question was simply about whether we can tolerate offensive ideas. But it is neither that simple, nor purely an academic argument. Our struggles for political rights, political speech, assembly, activity, and dissent, must account for the rights and liberties of marginalised peoples to not just speak freely, but to live, move and gather freely; and to call for and win increased social justice. Yes, we can explore questions of free speech while we fight for equity of other rights. But if we don't address the fundamental inequities that shape how we participate in these discussions, we will be trapped in a false narrative. In this moment, the last thing we can afford is to be is stuck. We must move forward to protect the lives of targeted communities, their right to exist, and their right to participate equally in the public sphere.

≡ THINKING ABOUT THE TEXT

1. When Kiswani speaks of "misguided efforts to protect the so-called free-speech rights of white supremacists," what exactly does she mean? Do these fringe groups have rights?

2. Why does she mention the "Unite the Right" rally and the "deadly stabbing"? What are these instances evidence of?

3. What is the problem she sees in the government policies about free speech when "constituents are vocal about issues they care about"?

4. Where is the evidence that Kiswani would not invite to campus those who propound offensive speech? And what, in short, are her reasons?

5. What does she mean that the debate over free speech is not "purely an academic argument"?

≡ MAKING COMPARISONS

1. Would Kiswani agree with Cole that the first amendment is neutral, "operating as it should"? Explain.

2. Does Kiswani seem less concerned with the rights of offensive speakers than Shafik? Why might this be the case?

3. Which of the three articles seems the most persuasive? The least? Explain.

≡ WRITING ABOUT THE ISSUES

1. Write an argument that agrees or disagrees with Oliver Wendell Holmes's comment: "The very aim and end of our institutions is just this: That we may think what we like and say what we think."

2. One of the most respected defenders of prohibitions on hate speech is Jeremy Waldron, whose book, *The Harm of Hate Speech* (2012), was reviewed by Justice John Paul Stevens in the *New York Review of Books*. Locate and read this review and summarize Stevens's points of agreement and disagreement with Waldron's position. Then write an argument setting forth your own points of agreement and disagreement with Stevens and Waldron. On balance, is your position closer to Stevens's or Waldron's? Explain your position and why it matters.

3. Look up the lyrics to the song "Ohio" by Crosby, Stills, Nash, and Young, and compare the argument made there to Yevtushenko's poem.

4. Pick one of the articles in this cluster and argue that it is or isn't relevant to an issue on your campus about free speech.

■ Contexts for Research: Domesticity, Women's Rights, and *A Doll's House*

HENRIK IBSEN, *A Doll's House*

CONTEXTS FOR RESEARCH:
AUGUST STRINDBERG, "Woman in *A Doll's House*"

EMMA GOLDMAN, Review of *A Doll's House*

JOAN TEMPLETON, From "*The* Doll House *Backlash: Criticism, Feminism, and Ibsen*"

SUSANNA RUSTIN, "Why *A Doll's House* by Henrik Ibsen Is More Relevant than Ever"

The writer and scientist Loren Eiseley notes that "to grow is a gain, an enlargement of life. . . . Yet it is also a departure." Eiseley's seems a more sophisticated idea than one portraying personal and social progress as only positive. Life is more complicated than that. Most of us eagerly anticipate becoming adults and embracing adult responsibilities and privileges. But our literature is filled with nostalgia for the innocence and wonder of childhood. We have a sense that we have lost something as our culture, technology, and lifestyles have advanced. There is no going back, but to some the old ways sometimes seem simpler. Our grandparents longed to leave the limitations of small-town life, but fifty years later their urban grandchildren idealize small communities. Women agonized over the legal and personal restrictions of Victorian marriages, but contemporary women understand that divorce is often painful and difficult. No reasonable thinker would want women to return to the childlike position that wives were expected to inhabit a hundred years ago, but that does not mean we cannot acknowledge that divorce often comes with a steep emotional and practical price.

It appears that Henrik Ibsen understood this when he wrote *A Doll's House* in 1879. It was an era of great political and social change, and Ibsen believed that writers could be instrumental in affecting the way people thought about the great issues of the day. His realistic problem plays confronted topical and controversial issues. Among the most debated was the status of women in society, especially their legal and emotional subjugation within marriage. To a contemporary audience, Nora, the main character of *A Doll's House*, is treated like a child. Although that disturbs most women today, Ibsen's female audience tended not to sympathize with Nora. The play's unsettling conclusion outraged most men. Changes in accepted thinking are always contested. But although most critics today see Ibsen as a social visionary who championed equality in marriage, he was not naive enough to think that great sacrifice and pain would not also accompany freedom and equality. The solution of one problem often creates new problems. When Nora begins to question the old ways, her future starts to grow uncertain. Knowing what she knows, can she really remain in a marriage that seems to her a cruel and unjust trap?

We have included several works that provide context for the play, but we have selected ones that focus especially on Nora. Over the past hundred years or so, Nora has been seen as either a villain or a hero, depending on the cultural context. If you support feminist ideals, you will probably see Nora in a positive light and support her dramatic departure as necessary and liberating. If you are not particularly sympathetic to feminist principles, you will most likely see Nora negatively and condemn her as vain, cruel, and self-centered. It would be unusual for a present-day critic not to empathize with Nora's plight, but that was clearly not always the case.

Many critics early in the twentieth century and into the fifties and sixties were not at all sympathetic. Some were even hostile. Nora's situation may seem clearly unjust to a progressive twenty-first-century consciousness, but that was certainly not obvious to those in the past who saw her marriage as perfectly acceptable, normal, and desirable and her behavior as deceitful, abnormal, and neurotic. In many ways, we are all children of our time, subject to the prevailing thinking about relationships, marriage, gender equality, parental responsibility, and so on. In Ibsen's day, audiences were upset by *A Doll's House*. And if there is currently a consensus about the necessity of Nora's actions, that shift in perspective happened exceedingly slowly and incrementally.

≣ BEFORE YOU READ

When do you think a woman can be justified in leaving her children? Why do you think equality is or is not necessary for love to exist in a marriage?

HENRIK IBSEN
A Doll's House

Translated by B. Farquharson Sharp

Henrik Ibsen (1828–1906) was born into a family with money in a small town in Norway, but his father soon went bankrupt. Ibsen later remembered this genteel poverty by writing about issues of social injustice that he experienced firsthand. At fifteen Ibsen was apprenticed to a pharmacist, a profession he had no interest in. He soon was drawn to the theater, working to establish a Norwegian national theater. But this led to frustration, and Ibsen spent almost thirty years in a self-imposed exile in Italy and Germany, where he wrote some of his most famous plays. Ibsen's plays are often performed today and still provoke controversy. They include Ghosts (1881), An Enemy of the People (1882), Hedda Gabler (1890), *and* When We Dead Awaken (1899).

DRAMATIS PERSONAE

TORVALD HELMER
NORA, *his wife*

DOCTOR RANK
MRS. LINDE
NILS KROGSTAD
Helmer's three young children
ANNE, *their nurse*
A Housemaid
A Porter

SCENE: *The action takes place in Helmer's house.*

ACT I

SCENE: *A room furnished comfortably and tastefully, but not extravagantly. At the back, a door to the right leads to the entrance-hall, another to the left leads to Helmer's study. Between the doors stands a piano. In the middle of the left-hand wall is a door, and beyond it a window. Near the window are a round table, arm-chairs, and a small sofa. In the right-hand wall, at the farther end, another door; and on the same side, nearer the footlights, a stove, two easy chairs, and a rocking-chair; between the stove and the door, a small table. Engravings on the walls; a cabinet with china and other small objects; a small book-case with well-bound books. The floors are carpeted, and a fire burns in the stove. It is winter.*

A bell rings in the hall; shortly afterwards the door is heard to open. Enter Nora, humming a tune and in high spirits. She is in outdoor dress and carries a number of parcels; these she lays on the table to the right. She leaves the outer door open after her, and through it is seen a Porter who is carrying a Christmas Tree and a basket, which he gives to the Maid who has opened the door.

NORA: Hide the Christmas Tree carefully, Helen. Be sure the children do not see it until this evening, when it is dressed. (*To the Porter, taking out her purse.*) How much?

PORTER: Sixpence.

NORA: There is a shilling. No, keep the change. (*The Porter thanks her, and goes out. Nora shuts the door. She is laughing to herself, as she takes off her hat and coat. She takes a packet of macaroons from her pocket and eats one or two; then goes cautiously to her husband's door and listens.*) Yes, he is in. (*Still humming, she goes to the table on the right.*)

HELMER (*calls out from his room*):   Is that my little lark twittering out there?

NORA (*busy opening some of the parcels*):   Yes, it is!

HELMER: Is it my little squirrel bustling about?

NORA: Yes!

HELMER: When did my squirrel come home?

NORA: Just now. (*Puts the bag of macaroons into her pocket and wipes her mouth.*) Come in here, Torvald, and see what I have bought.

HELMER: Don't disturb me. (*A little later, he opens the door and looks into the room, pen in hand.*) Bought, did you say? All these things? Has my little spendthrift been wasting money again?

NORA: Yes but, Torvald, this year we really can let ourselves go a little. This is the first Christmas that we have not needed to economize.

HELMER: Still, you know, we can't spend money recklessly.

NORA: Yes, Torvald, we may be a wee bit more reckless now, mayn't we? Just a tiny wee bit! You are going to have a big salary and earn lots and lots of money.

HELMER: Yes, after the New Year; but then it will be a whole quarter before the salary is due.

NORA: Pooh! we can borrow until then.

HELMER: Nora! (*Goes up to her and takes her playfully by the ear.*) The same little featherhead! Suppose, now, that I borrowed fifty pounds to-day, and you spent it all in the Christmas week, and then on New Year's Eve a slate fell on my head and killed me, and—

NORA (*putting her hands over his mouth*):   Oh! don't say such horrid things.

HELMER: Still, suppose that happened, — what then?

NORA: If that were to happen, I don't suppose I should care whether I owed money or not.

HELMER: Yes, but what about the people who had lent it?

NORA: They? Who would bother about them? I should not know who they were.

HELMER: That is like a woman! But seriously, Nora, you know what I think about that. No debt, no borrowing. There can be no freedom or beauty about a home life that depends on borrowing and debt. We two have kept bravely on the straight road so far, and we will go on the same way for the short time longer that there need be any struggle.

NORA (*moving towards the stove*):   As you please, Torvald.

HELMER (*following her*):   Come, come, my little skylark must not droop her wings. What is this! Is my little squirrel out of temper? (*Taking out his purse.*) Nora, what do you think I have got here?

NORA (*turning round quickly*):   Money!

HELMER: There you are. (*Gives her some money.*) Do you think I don't know what a lot is wanted for housekeeping at Christmas-time?

NORA (*counting*):   Ten shillings—a pound—two pounds! Thank you, thank you, Torvald; that will keep me going for a long time.

HELMER: Indeed it must.

NORA: Yes, yes, it will. But come here and let me show you what I have bought. And all so cheap! Look, here is a new suit for Ivar, and a sword; and a horse and a trumpet for Bob; and a doll and dolly's bedstead for Emmy,—they are very plain, but anyway she will soon break them in pieces. And here are dress-lengths and handkerchiefs for the maids; old Anne ought really to have something better.

HELMER: And what is in this parcel?

NORA (*crying out*):   No, no! you mustn't see that until this evening.

HELMER: Very well. But now tell me, you extravagant little person, what would you like for yourself?

NORA: For myself? Oh, I am sure I don't want anything.

HELMER: Yes, but you must. Tell me something reasonable that you would particularly like to have.

NORA: No, I really can't think of anything—unless, Torvald—

HELMER: Well?

NORA (*playing with his coat buttons, and without raising her eyes to his*):   If you really want to give me something, you might—you might—

HELMER: Well, out with it!

NORA (*speaking quickly*):   You might give me money, Torvald. Only just as much as you can afford; and then one of these days I will buy something with it.

HELMER: But, Nora—

NORA: Oh, do! dear Torvald; please, please do! Then I will wrap it up in beautiful gilt paper and hang it on the Christmas Tree. Wouldn't that be fun?

HELMER: What are little people called that are always wasting money?

NORA: Spendthrifts—I know. Let us do as you suggest, Torvald, and then I shall have time to think what I am most in want of. That is a very sensible plan, isn't it?

HELMER (*smiling*):   Indeed it is—that is to say, if you were really to save out of the money I give you, and then really buy something for yourself. But if you spend it all on the housekeeping and any number of unnecessary things, then I merely have to pay up again.

NORA: Oh but, Torvald—

HELMER: You can't deny it, my dear little Nora. (*Puts his arm round her waist.*) It's a sweet little spendthrift, but she uses up a deal of money. One would hardly believe how expensive such little persons are!

NORA: It's a shame to say that. I do really save all I can.

HELMER (*laughing*):   That's very true, — all you can. But you can't save anything!

NORA (*smiling quietly and happily*):   You haven't any idea how many expenses we skylarks and squirrels have, Torvald.

HELMER: You are an odd little soul. Very like your father. You always find some new way of wheedling money out of me, and, as soon as you have got it, it seems to melt in your hands. You never know where it has gone. Still, one must take you as you are. It is in the blood; for indeed it is true that you can inherit these things, Nora.

NORA: Ah, I wish I had inherited many of papa's qualities.

HELMER: And I would not wish you to be anything but just what you are, my sweet little skylark. But, do you know, it strikes me that you are looking rather — what shall I say — rather uneasy today?

NORA: Do I?

HELMER: You do, really. Look straight at me.

NORA (*looks at him*):   Well?

HELMER (*wagging his finger at her*):   Hasn't Miss Sweet Tooth been breaking rules in town today?

NORA: No; what makes you think that?

HELMER: Hasn't she paid a visit to the confectioner's?

NORA: No, I assure you, Torvald —

HELMER: Not been nibbling sweets?

NORA: No, certainly not.

HELMER: Not even taken a bite at a macaroon or two?

NORA: No, Torvald, I assure you really —

HELMER: There, there, of course I was only joking.

NORA (*going to the table on the right*):   I should not think of going against your wishes.

HELMER: No, I am sure of that; besides, you gave me your word — (*Going up to her.*) Keep your little Christmas secrets to yourself, my darling. They will all be revealed to-night when the Christmas Tree is lit, no doubt.

NORA: Did you remember to invite Doctor Rank?

HELMER: No. But there is no need; as a matter of course he will come to dinner with us. However, I will ask him when he comes in this morning. I have ordered some good wine. Nora, you can't think how I am looking forward to this evening.

NORA: So am I! And how the children will enjoy themselves, Torvald!

HELMER: It is splendid to feel that one has a perfectly safe appointment, and a big enough income. It's delightful to think of, isn't it?

NORA: It's wonderful!

HELMER: Do you remember last Christmas? For a full three weeks beforehand you shut yourself up every evening until long after midnight, making ornaments for the Christmas Tree, and all the other fine things that were to be a surprise to us. It was the dullest three weeks I ever spent!

NORA: I didn't find it dull.

HELMER (*smiling*):   But there was precious little result, Nora.

NORA: Oh, you shouldn't tease me about that again. How could I help the cat's going in and tearing everything to pieces?

HELMER: Of course you couldn't, poor little girl. You had the best of intentions to please us all, and that's the main thing. But it is a good thing that our hard times are over.

NORA: Yes, it is really wonderful.

HELMER: This time I needn't sit here and be dull all alone, and you needn't ruin your dear eyes and your pretty little hands—

NORA (*clapping her hands*):   No, Torvald, I needn't any longer, need I! It's wonderfully lovely to hear you say so! (*Taking his arm.*) Now I will tell you how I have been thinking we ought to arrange things, Torvald. As soon as Christmas is over—(*A bell rings in the hall.*) There's the bell. (*She tidies the room a little.*) There's some one at the door. What a nuisance!

HELMER: If it is a caller, remember I am not at home.

MAID (*in the doorway*):   A lady to see you, ma'am,—a stranger.

NORA: Ask her to come in.

MAID (*to Helmer*):   The doctor came at the same time, sir.

HELMER: Did he go straight into my room?

MAID: Yes, sir.

Helmer goes into his room. The Maid ushers in Mrs. Linde, who is in travelling dress, and shuts the door.

MRS. LINDE (*in a dejected and timid voice*):   How do you do, Nora?

NORA (*doubtfully*):   How do you do—

MRS. LINDE: You don't recognise me, I suppose.

NORA: No, I don't know—yes, to be sure, I seem to—(*Suddenly.*) Yes! Christine! Is it really you?

MRS. LINDE: Yes, it is I.

NORA: Christine! To think of my not recognising you! And yet how could I—(*In a gentle voice.*) How you have altered, Christine!

MRS. LINDE: Yes, I have indeed. In nine, ten long years—

NORA: Is it so long since we met? I suppose it is. The last eight years have been a happy time for me, I can tell you. And so now you have come into the town, and have taken this long journey in winter—that was plucky of you.

MRS. LINDE: I arrived by steamer this morning.

NORA: To have some fun at Christmas-time, of course. How delightful! We will have such fun together! But take off your things. You are not cold, I hope. (*Helps her.*) Now we will sit down by the stove, and be cosy. No, take this armchair; I will sit here in the rocking-chair. (*Takes her hands.*) Now you look like your old self again; it was only the first moment—You are a little paler, Christine, and perhaps a little thinner.

MRS. LINDE: And much, much older, Nora.

NORA: Perhaps a little older; very, very little; certainly not much. (*Stops suddenly and speaks seriously.*) What a thoughtless creature I am, chattering away like this. My poor, dear Christine, do forgive me.

MRS. LINDE: What do you mean, Nora?

NORA (*gently*):   Poor Christine, you are a widow.

MRS. LINDE: Yes; it is three years ago now.

NORA: Yes, I knew; I saw it in the papers. I assure you, Christine, I meant ever so often to write to you at the time, but I always put it off and something always prevented me.

MRS. LINDE: I quite understand, dear.

NORA: It was very bad of me, Christine. Poor thing, how you must have suffered. And he left you nothing?

MRS. LINDE: No.

NORA: And no children?

MRS. LINDE: No.

NORA: Nothing at all, then.

MRS. LINDE: Not even any sorrow or grief to live upon.

NORA (*looking incredulously at her*):   But, Christine, is that possible?

MRS. LINDE (*smiles sadly and strokes her hair*):   It sometimes happens, Nora.

NORA: So you are quite alone. How dreadfully sad that must be. I have three lovely children. You can't see them just now, for they are out with their nurse. But now you must tell me all about it.

MRS. LINDE: No, no; I want to hear about you.

NORA: No, you must begin. I mustn't be selfish today; today I must only think of your affairs. But there is one thing I must tell you. Do you know we have just had a great piece of good luck?

MRS. LINDE: No, what is it?

NORA: Just fancy, my husband has been made manager of the Bank!

MRS. LINDE: Your husband? What good luck!

NORA: Yes, tremendous! A barrister's profession is such an uncertain thing, especially if he won't undertake unsavoury cases; and naturally Torvald has never been willing to do that, and I quite agree with him. You may imagine how pleased we are! He is to take up his work in the Bank at the New Year, and then he will have a big salary and lots of commissions. For the future we can live quite differently — we can do just as we like. I feel so relieved and so happy, Christine! It will be splendid to have heaps of money and not need to have any anxiety, won't it?

MRS. LINDE: Yes, anyhow I think it would be delightful to have what one needs.

NORA: No, not only what one needs, but heaps and heaps of money.

MRS. LINDE (*smiling*):   Nora, Nora, haven't you learned sense yet? In our schooldays you were a great spendthrift.

NORA (*laughing*):   Yes, that is what Torvald says now. (*Wags her finger at her.*) But "Nora, Nora" is not so silly as you think. We have not been in a position for me to waste money. We have both had to work.

MRS. LINDE: You too?

NORA: Yes; odds and ends, needlework, crotchet-work, embroidery, and that kind of thing. (*Dropping her voice.*) And other things as well. You know

Torvald left his office when we were married? There was no prospect of promotion there, and he had to try and earn more than before. But during the first year he over-worked himself dreadfully. You see, he had to make money every way he could, and he worked early and late; but he couldn't stand it, and fell dreadfully ill, and the doctors said it was necessary for him to go south.

MRS. LINDE: You spent a whole year in Italy, didn't you?

NORA: Yes. It was no easy matter to get away, I can tell you. It was just after Ivar was born; but naturally we had to go. It was a wonderfully beautiful journey, and it saved Torvald's life. But it cost a tremendous lot of money, Christine.

MRS. LINDE: So I should think.

NORA: It cost about two hundred and fifty pounds. That's a lot, isn't it?

MRS. LINDE: Yes, and in emergencies like that it is lucky to have the money.

NORA: I ought to tell you that we had it from papa.

MRS. LINDE: Oh, I see. It was just about that time that he died, wasn't it?

NORA: Yes; and, just think of it, I couldn't go and nurse him. I was expecting little Ivar's birth every day and I had my poor sick Torvald to look after. My dear, kind father—I never saw him again, Christine. That was the saddest time I have known since our marriage.

MRS. LINDE: I know how fond you were of him. And then you went off to Italy?

NORA: Yes; you see we had money then, and the doctors insisted on our going, so we started a month later.

MRS. LINDE: And your husband came back quite well?

NORA: As sound as a bell!

MRS. LINDE: But—the doctor?

NORA: What doctor?

MRS. LINDE: I thought your maid said the gentleman who arrived here just as I did, was the doctor?

NORA: Yes, that was Doctor Rank, but he doesn't come here professionally. He is our greatest friend, and comes in at least once everyday. No, Torvald has not had an hour's illness since then, and our children are strong and healthy and so am I. (*Jumps up and claps her hands.*) Christine! Christine! it's good to be alive and happy!—But how horrid of me; I am talking of nothing but my own affairs. (*Sits on a stool near her, and rests her arms on her knees.*) You mustn't be angry with me. Tell me, is it really true that you did not love your husband? Why did you marry him?

MRS. LINDE: My mother was alive then, and was bedridden and helpless, and I had to provide for my two younger brothers; so I did not think I was justified in refusing his offer.

NORA: No, perhaps you were quite right. He was rich at that time, then?

MRS. LINDE: I believe he was quite well off. But his business was a precarious one; and, when he died, it all went to pieces and there was nothing left.

NORA: And then?—

MRS. LINDE: Well, I had to turn my hand to anything I could find—first a small shop, then a small school, and so on. The last three years have seemed like one long working-day, with no rest. Now it is at an end, Nora. My poor mother needs me no more, for she is gone; and the boys do not need me either; they have got situations and can shift for themselves.

NORA: What a relief you must feel it —

MRS. LINDE: No, indeed; I only feel my life unspeakably empty. No one to live for anymore. (*Gets up restlessly.*) That was why I could not stand the life in my little backwater any longer. I hope it may be easier here to find something which will busy me and occupy my thoughts. If only I could have the good luck to get some regular work — office work of some kind —

NORA: But, Christine, that is so frightfully tiring, and you look tired out now. You had far better go away to some watering-place.

MRS. LINDE (*walking to the window*):   I have no father to give me money for a journey, Nora.

NORA (*rising*):   Oh, don't be angry with me!

MRS. LINDE (*going up to her*):   It is you that must not be angry with me, dear. The worst of a position like mine is that it makes one so bitter. No one to work for, and yet obliged to be always on the lookout for chances. One must live, and so one becomes selfish. When you told me of the happy turn your fortunes have taken — you will hardly believe it — I was delighted not so much on your account as on my own.

NORA: How do you mean? — Oh, I understand. You mean that perhaps Torvald could get you something to do.

MRS. LINDE: Yes, that was what I was thinking of.

NORA: He must, Christine. Just leave it to me; I will broach the subject very cleverly — I will think of something that will please him very much. It will make me so happy to be of some use to you.

MRS. LINDE: How kind you are, Nora, to be so anxious to help me! It is doubly kind in you, for you know so little of the burdens and troubles of life.

NORA: I — ? I know so little of them?

MRS. LINDE (*smiling*):   My dear! Small household cares and that sort of thing! — You are a child, Nora.

NORA (*tosses her head and crosses the stage*):   You ought not to be so superior.

MRS. LINDE: No?

NORA: You are just like the others. They all think that I am incapable of anything really serious —

MRS. LINDE: Come, come —

NORA: — that I have gone through nothing in this world of cares.

MRS. LINDE: But, my dear Nora, you have just told me all your troubles.

NORA: Pooh! — those were trifles. (*Lowering her voice.*) I have not told you the important thing.

MRS. LINDE: The important thing? What do you mean?

NORA: You look down upon me altogether, Christine — but you ought not to. You are proud, aren't you, of having worked so hard and so long for your mother?

MRS. LINDE: Indeed, I don't look down on anyone. But it is true that I am both proud and glad to think that I was privileged to make the end of my mother's life almost free from care.

NORA: And you are proud to think of what you have done for your brothers?

MRS. LINDE: I think I have the right to be.

NORA: I think so, too. But now, listen to this; I too have something to be proud and glad of.

MRS. LINDE: I have no doubt you have. But what do you refer to?

NORA: Speak low. Suppose Torvald were to hear! He mustn't on any account—no one in the world must know, Christine, except you.

MRS. LINDE: But what is it?

NORA: Come here. (*Pulls her down on the sofa beside her.*) Now I will show you that I too have something to be proud and glad of. It was I who saved Torvald's life.

MRS. LINDE: "Saved"? How?

NORA: I told you about our trip to Italy. Torvald would never have recovered if he had not gone there—

MRS. LINDE: Yes, but your father gave you the necessary funds.

NORA (*smiling*):   Yes, that is what Torvald and all the others think, but—

MRS. LINDE: But—

NORA: Papa didn't give us a shilling. It was I who procured the money.

MRS. LINDE: You? All that large sum?

NORA: Two hundred and fifty pounds. What do you think of that?

MRS. LINDE: But, Nora, how could you possibly do it? Did you win a prize in the Lottery?

NORA (*contemptuously*):   In the Lottery? There would have been no credit in that.

MRS. LINDE: But where did you get it from, then?

NORA (*humming and smiling with an air of mystery*):   Hm, hm! Aha!

MRS. LINDE: Because you couldn't have borrowed it.

NORA: Couldn't I? Why not?

MRS. LINDE: No, a wife cannot borrow without her husband's consent.

NORA (*tossing her head*):   Oh, if it is a wife who has any head for business—a wife who has the wit to be a little bit clever—

MRS. LINDE: I don't understand it at all, Nora.

NORA: There is no need you should. I never said I had borrowed the money. I may have got it some other way. (*Lies back on the sofa.*) Perhaps I got it from some other admirer. When anyone is as attractive as I am—

MRS. LINDE: You are a mad creature.

NORA: Now, you know you're full of curiosity, Christine.

MRS. LINDE: Listen to me, Nora dear. Haven't you been a little bit imprudent?

NORA (*sits up straight*):   Is it imprudent to save your husband's life?

MRS. LINDE: It seems to me imprudent, without his knowledge, to—

NORA: But it was absolutely necessary that he should not know! My goodness, can't you understand that? It was necessary he should have no idea what a dangerous condition he was in. It was to me that the doctors came and said that his life was in danger, and that the only thing to save him was to live in the south. Do you suppose I didn't try, first of all, to get what I wanted as if it were for myself? I told him how much I should love to travel abroad like other young wives; I tried tears and entreaties with him; I told him that he ought to remember the condition I was in, and that he ought to be kind and indulgent to me; I even hinted that he might raise a loan. That nearly made him angry, Christine. He said I was thoughtless, and that it was his duty as my husband not to indulge me in my whims and caprices—as I believe he called them. Very well, I thought, you must be saved—and that was how I came to devise a way out of the difficulty—

MRS. LINDE: And did your husband never get to know from your father that the money had not come from him?

NORA: No, never. Papa died just at that time. I had meant to let him into the secret and beg him never to reveal it. But he was so ill then—alas, there never was any need to tell him.

MRS. LINDE: And since then have you never told your secret to your husband?

NORA: Good Heavens, no! How could you think so? A man who has such strong opinions about these things! And besides, how painful and humiliating it would be for Torvald, with his manly independence, to know that he owed me anything! It would upset our mutual relations altogether; our beautiful happy home would no longer be what it is now.

MRS. LINDE: Do you mean never to tell him about it?

NORA (*meditatively, and with a half smile*):   Yes—someday, perhaps, after many years, when I am no longer as nice-looking as I now. Don't laugh at me! I mean, of course, when Torvald is no longer as devoted to me as he is now; when my dancing and dressing-up and reciting have palled on him; then it may be a good thing to have something in reserve—(*Breaking off.*) What nonsense! That time will never come. Now, what do you think of my great secret, Christine? Do you still think I am of no use? I can tell you, too, that this affair has caused me a lot of worry. It has been by no means easy for me to meet my engagements punctually. I may tell you that there is something that is called, in business, quarterly interest, and another thing called payment in installments, and it is always so dreadfully difficult to manage them. I have had to save a little here and there, where I could, you understand. I have not been able to put aside much from my housekeeping money, for Torvald must have a good table. I couldn't let my children be shabbily dressed; I have felt obliged to use up all he gave me for them, the sweet little darlings!

MRS. LINDE: So it has all had to come out of your own necessaries of life, poor Nora?

NORA: Of course. Besides, I was the one responsible for it. Whenever Torvald has given me money for new dresses and such things, I have never spent more than half of it; I have always bought the simplest and cheapest things. Thank Heaven, any clothes look well on me, and so Torvald has never noticed it. But it was often very hard on me, Christine—because it is delightful to be really well dressed, isn't it?

MRS. LINDE: Quite so.

NORA: Well, then I have found other ways of earning money. Last winter I was lucky enough to get a lot of copying to do; so I locked myself up and sat writing every evening until quite late at night. Many a time I was desperately tired; but all the same it was a tremendous pleasure to sit there working and earning money. It was like being a man.

MRS. LINDE: How much have you been able to pay off in that way?

NORA: I can't tell you exactly. You see, it is very difficult to keep an account of a business matter of that kind. I only know that I have paid every penny that I could scrape together. Many a time I was at my wits' end. (*Smiles.*) Then I used to sit here and imagine that a rich old gentleman had fallen in love with me—

MRS. LINDE: What! Who was it?

NORA: Be quiet!—that he had died; and that when his will was opened it contained, written in big letters, the instruction: "The lovely Mrs. Nora Helmer is to have all I possess paid over to her at once in cash."

MRS. LINDE: But, my dear Nora—who could the man be?

NORA: Good gracious, can't you understand? There was no old gentleman at all; it was only something that I used to sit here and imagine, when I couldn't think of any way of procuring money. But it's all the same now; the tiresome old person can stay where he is, as far as I am concerned; I don't care about him or his will either, for I am free from care now. (*Jumps up.*) My goodness, it's delightful to think of, Christine! Free from care! To be able to be free from care, quite free from care; to be able to play and romp with the children; to be able to keep the house beautifully and have everything just as Torvald likes it! And, think of it, soon the spring will come and the big blue sky! Perhaps we shall be able to take a little trip—perhaps I shall see the sea again! Oh, it's a wonderful thing to be alive and be happy. (*A bell is heard in the hall.*)

MRS. LINDE (*rising*): There is the bell; perhaps I had better go.

NORA: No, don't go; no one will come in here; it is sure to be for Torvald.

SERVANT (*at the hall door*): Excuse me, ma'am—there is a gentleman to see the master, and as the doctor is with him—

NORA: Who is it?

KROGSTAD (*at the door*): It is I, Mrs. Helmer (*Mrs. Linde starts, trembles, and turns to the window.*)

NORA (*takes a step towards him, and speaks in a strained, low voice*): You? What is it? What do you want to see my husband about?

KROGSTAD: Bank business—in a way. I have a small post in the Bank, and I hear your husband is to be our chief now—

NORA: Then it is—

KROGSTAD: Nothing but dry business matters, Mrs. Helmer; absolutely nothing else.

NORA: Be so good as to go into the study, then. (*She bows indifferently to him and shuts the door into the hall; then comes back and makes up the fire in the stove.*)

MRS. LINDE: Nora—who was that man?

NORA: A lawyer, of the name of Krogstad.

MRS. LINDE: Then it really was he.

NORA: Do you know the man?

MRS. LINDE: I used to—many years ago. At one time he was a solicitor's clerk in our town.

NORA: Yes, he was.

MRS. LINDE: He is greatly altered.

NORA: He made a very unhappy marriage.

MRS. LINDE: He is a widower now, isn't he?

NORA: With several children. There now, it is burning up. (*Shuts the door of the stove and moves the rocking-chair aside.*)

MRS. LINDE: They say he carries on various kinds of business.

NORA: Really! Perhaps he does; I don't know anything about it. But don't let us think of business; it is so tiresome.

DOCTOR RANK (*comes out of Helmer's study. Before he shuts the door he calls to him*):   No, my dear fellow, I won't disturb you; I would rather go in to your wife for a little while. (*Shuts the door and sees Mrs. Linde.*) I beg your pardon; I am afraid I am disturbing you too.

NORA: No, not at all. (*Introducing him.*) Doctor Rank, Mrs. Linde.

RANK: I have often heard Mrs. Linde's name mentioned here. I think I passed you on the stairs when I arrived, Mrs. Linde?

MRS. LINDE: Yes, I go up very slowly; I can't manage stairs well.

RANK: Ah! some slight internal weakness?

MRS. LINDE: No, the fact is I have been overworking myself.

RANK: Nothing more than that? Then I suppose you have come to town to amuse yourself with our entertainments?

MRS. LINDE: I have come to look for work.

RANK: Is that a good cure for overwork?

MRS. LINDE: One must live, Doctor Rank.

RANK: Yes, the general opinion seems to be that it is necessary.

NORA: Look here, Doctor Rank — you know you want to live.

RANK: Certainly. However wretched I may feel, I want to prolong the agony as long as possible. All my patients are like that. And so are those who are morally diseased; one of them, and a bad case too, is at this very moment with Helmer—

MRS. LINDE (*sadly*):   Ah!

NORA: Whom do you mean?

RANK: A lawyer of the name of Krogstad, a fellow you don't know at all. He suffers from a diseased moral character, Mrs. Helmer; but even he began talking of its being highly important that he should live.

NORA: Did he? What did he want to speak to Torvald about?

RANK: I have no idea; I only heard that it was something about the Bank.

NORA: I didn't know this — what's his name — Krogstad had anything to do with the Bank.

RANK: Yes, he has some sort of appointment there. (*To Mrs. Linde.*) I don't know whether you find also in your part of the world that there are certain people who go zealously snuffing about to smell out moral corruption, and, as soon as they have found some, put the person concerned into some lucrative position where they can keep their eye on him. Healthy natures are left out in the cold.

MRS. LINDE: Still I think the sick are those who most need taking care of.

RANK (*shrugging his shoulders*):   Yes, there you are. That is the sentiment that is turning Society into a sick-house.

Nora, who has been absorbed in her thoughts, breaks out into smothered laughter and claps her hands.

RANK: Why do you laugh at that? Have you any notion what Society really is?

NORA: What do I care about tiresome Society? I am laughing at something quite different, something extremely amusing. Tell me, Doctor Rank, are all the people who are employed in the Bank dependent on Torvald now?

RANK: Is that what you find so extremely amusing?

NORA (*smiling and humming*):   That's my affair! (*Walking about the room.*) It's perfectly glorious to think that we have — that Torvald has so much power over so many people. (*Takes the packet from her pocket.*) Doctor Rank, what do you say to a macaroon?

RANK: What, macaroons? I thought they were forbidden here.

NORA: Yes, but these are some Christine gave me.

MRS. LINDE: What! I? —

NORA: Oh, well, don't be alarmed! You couldn't know that Torvald had forbidden them. I must tell you that he is afraid they will spoil my teeth. But, bah! — once in a way — That's so, isn't it, Doctor Rank? By your leave! (*Puts a macaroon into his mouth.*) You must have one too, Christine. And I shall have one, just a little one — or at most two. (*Walking about.*) I am tremendously happy. There is just one thing in the world now that I should dearly love to do.

RANK: Well, what is that?

NORA: It's something I should dearly love to say, if Torvald could hear me.

RANK: Well, why can't you say it?

NORA: No, I daren't; it's so shocking.

MRS. LINDE: Shocking?

RANK: Well, I should not advise you to say it. Still, with us you might. What is it you would so much like to say if Torvald could hear you?

NORA: I should just love to say — Well, I'm damned!

RANK: Are you mad?

MRS. LINDE: Nora, dear —!

RANK: Say it, here he is!

NORA (*hiding the packet*):   Hush! Hush! Hush! (*Helmer comes out of his room, with his coat over his arm and his hat in his hand.*)

NORA: Well, Torvald dear, have you got rid of him?

HELMER: Yes, he has just gone.

NORA: Let me introduce you — this is Christine, who has come to town.

HELMER: Christine —? Excuse me, but I don't know —

NORA: Mrs. Linde, dear; Christine Linde.

HELMER: Of course. A school friend of my wife's, I presume?

MRS. LINDE: Yes, we have known each other since then.

NORA: And just think, she has taken a long journey in order to see you.

HELMER: What do you mean?

MRS. LINDE: No, really, I —

NORA: Christine is tremendously clever at book-keeping, and she is frightfully anxious to work under some clever man, so as to perfect herself —

HELMER: Very sensible, Mrs. Linde.

NORA: And when she heard you had been appointed manager of the Bank — the news was telegraphed, you know — she travelled here as quick as she could. Torvald, I am sure you will be able to do something for Christine, for my sake, won't you?

HELMER: Well, it is not altogether impossible. I presume you are a widow, Mrs. Linde?

MRS. LINDE: Yes.

HELMER: And have had some experience of book-keeping?

MRS. LINDE: Yes, a fair amount.

HELMER: Ah! well, it's very likely I may be able to find something for you —

NORA (*clapping her hands*):   What did I tell you? What did I tell you?

HELMER: You have just come at a fortunate moment, Mrs. Linde.

MRS. LINDE: How am I to thank you?

HELMER: There is no need. (*Puts on his coat.*) But to-day you must excuse me —

RANK: Wait a minute; I will come with you. (*Brings his fur coat from the hall and warms it at the fire.*)

NORA: Don't be long away, Torvald dear.

HELMER: About an hour, not more.

NORA: Are you going too, Christine?

MRS. LINDE (*putting on her cloak*):   Yes, I must go and look for a room.

HELMER: Oh, well then, we can walk down the street together.

NORA (*helping her*):   What a pity it is we are so short of space here; I am afraid it is impossible for us —

MRS. LINDE: Please don't think of it! Good-bye, Nora dear, and many thanks.

NORA: Good-bye for the present. Of course you will come back this evening. And you too, Dr. Rank. What do you say? If you are well enough? Oh, you must be! Wrap yourself up well. (*They go to the door all talking together. Children's voices are heard on the staircase.*)

NORA: There they are! There they are! (*She runs to open the door. The Nurse comes in with the children.*) Come in! Come in! (*Stoops and kisses them.*) Oh, you sweet blessings! Look at them, Christine! Aren't they darlings?

RANK: Don't let us stand here in the draught.

HELMER: Come along, Mrs. Linde; the place will only be bearable for a mother now!

Rank, Helmer, and Mrs. Linde go downstairs. The Nurse comes forward with the children; Nora shuts the hall door.

NORA: How fresh and well you look! Such red cheeks like apples and roses. (*The children all talk at once while she speaks to them.*) Have you had great fun? That's splendid! What, you pulled both Emmy and Bob along on the sledge? — both at once? — that was good. You are a clever boy, Ivar. Let me take her for a little, Anne. My sweet little baby doll! (*Takes the baby from the Maid and dances it up and down.*) Yes, yes, mother will dance with Bob too. What! Have you been snowballing? I wish I had been there too! No, no, I will take their things off, Anne; please let me do it, it is such fun. Go in now, you look half frozen. There is some hot coffee for you on the stove.

The Nurse goes into the room on the left. Nora takes off the children's things and throws them about, while they all talk to her at once.

NORA: Really! Did a big dog run after you? But it didn't bite you? No, dogs don't bite nice little dolly children. You mustn't look at the parcels, Ivar. What are they? Ah, I daresay you would like to know. No, no—it's something nasty! Come, let us have a game! What shall we play at? Hide and Seek? Yes, we'll play Hide and Seek. Bob shall hide first. Must I hide? Very well, I'll hide first. (*She and the children laugh and shout, and romp in and out of the room; at last Nora hides under the table, the children rush in and out for her, but do not see her; they hear her smothered laughter, run to the table, lift up the cloth and find her. Shouts of laughter. She crawls forward and pretends to frighten them. Fresh laughter. Meanwhile there has been a knock at the hall door, but none of them has noticed it. The door is half opened, and Krogstad appears. He waits a little; the game goes on.*)

KROGSTAD: Excuse me, Mrs. Helmer.

NORA (*with a stifled cry, turns round and gets up on to her knees*): Ah! what do you want?

KROGSTAD: Excuse me, the outer door was ajar; I suppose someone forgot to shut it.

NORA (*rising*): My husband is out, Mr. Krogstad.

KROGSTAD: I know that.

NORA: What do you want here, then?

KROGSTAD: A word with you.

NORA: With me?—(*To the children, gently.*) Go in to nurse. What? No, the strange man won't do mother any harm. When he has gone we will have another game. (*She takes the children into the room on the left, and shuts the door after them.*) You want to speak to me?

KROGSTAD: Yes, I do.

NORA: To-day? It is not the first of the month yet.

KROGSTAD: No, it is Christmas Eve, and it will depend on yourself what sort of a Christmas you will spend.

NORA: What do you mean? To-day it is absolutely impossible for me—

KROGSTAD: We won't talk about that until later on. This is something different. I presume you can give me a moment?

NORA: Yes—yes, I can—although—

KROGSTAD: Good. I was in Olsen's Restaurant and saw your husband going down the street—

NORA: Yes?

KROGSTAD: With a lady.

NORA: What then?

KROGSTAD: May I make so bold as to ask if it was a Mrs. Linde?

NORA: It was.

KROGSTAD: Just arrived in town?

NORA: Yes, to-day.

KROGSTAD: She is a great friend of yours, isn't she?

NORA: She is. But I don't see—

KROGSTAD: I knew her too, once upon a time.

NORA: I am aware of that.

KROGSTAD: Are you? So you know all about it; I thought as much. Then I can ask you, without beating about the bush — is Mrs. Linde to have an appointment in the Bank?

NORA: What right have you to question me, Mr. Krogstad? — You, one of my husband's subordinates! But since you ask, you shall know. Yes, Mrs. Linde *is* to have an appointment. And it was I who pleaded her cause, Mr. Krogstad, let me tell you that.

KROGSTAD: I was right in what I thought, then.

NORA (*walking up and down the stage*):   Sometimes one has a tiny little bit of influence, I should hope. Because one is a woman, it does not necessarily follow that —. When anyone is in a subordinate position, Mr. Krogstad, they should really be careful to avoid offending anyone who — who —

KROGSTAD: Who has influence?

NORA: Exactly.

KROGSTAD (*changing his tone*):   Mrs. Helmer, you will be so good as to use your influence on my behalf.

NORA: What? What do you mean?

KROGSTAD: You will be so kind as to see that I am allowed to keep my subordinate position in the Bank.

NORA: What do you mean by that? Who proposes to take your post away from you?

KROGSTAD: Oh, there is no necessity to keep up the pretence of ignorance. I can quite understand that your friend is not very anxious to expose herself to the chance of rubbing shoulders with me; and I quite understand, too, whom I have to thank for being turned off.

NORA: But I assure you —

KROGSTAD: Very likely; but, to come to the point, the time has come when I should advise you to use your influence to prevent that.

NORA: But, Mr. Krogstad, I *have* no influence.

KROGSTAD: Haven't you? I thought you said yourself just now —

NORA: Naturally I did not mean you to put that construction on it. What should make you think I have any influence of that kind with my husband?

KROGSTAD: Oh, I have known your husband from our student days. I don't suppose he is any more unassailable than other husbands.

NORA: If you speak slightingly of my husband, I shall turn you out of the house.

KROGSTAD: You are bold, Mrs. Helmer.

NORA: I am not afraid of you any longer. As soon as the New Year comes, I shall in a very short time be free of the whole thing.

KROGSTAD (*controlling himself*):   Listen to me, Mrs. Helmer. If necessary, I am prepared to fight for my small post in the Bank as if I were fighting for my life.

NORA: So it seems.

KROGSTAD: It is not only for the sake of the money; indeed, that weighs least with me in the matter. There is another reason — well, I may as well tell you. My position is this. I daresay you know, like everybody else, that once, many years ago, I was guilty of an indiscretion.

NORA: I think I have heard something of the kind.

KROGSTAD: The matter never came into court; but every way seemed to be closed to me after that. So I took to the business that you know of. I had to do something; and, honestly, I don't think I've been one of the worst. But now I must cut myself free from all that. My sons are growing up; for their sake I must try and win back as much respect as I can in the town. This post in the Bank was like the first step up for me—and now your husband is going to kick me downstairs again into the mud.

NORA: But you must believe me, Mr. Krogstad; it is not in my power to help you at all.

KROGSTAD: Then it is because you haven't the will; but I have means to compel you.

NORA: You don't mean that you will tell my husband that I owe you money?

KROGSTAD: Hm!—suppose I were to tell him?

NORA: It would be perfectly infamous of you. (*Sobbing.*) To think of his learning my secret, which has been my joy and pride, in such an ugly, clumsy way—that he should learn it from you! And it would put me in a horribly disagreeable position—

KROGSTAD: Only disagreeable?

NORA (*impetuously*):   Well, do it, then!—and it will be the worse for you. My husband will see for himself what a blackguard you are, and you certainly won't keep your post then.

KROGSTAD: I asked you if it was only a disagreeable scene at home that you were afraid of?

NORA: If my husband does get to know of it, of course he will at once pay you what is still owing, and we shall have nothing more to do with you.

KROGSTAD (*coming a step nearer*):   Listen to me, Mrs. Helmer. Either you have a very bad memory or you know very little of business. I shall be obliged to remind you of a few details.

NORA: What do you mean?

KROGSTAD: When your husband was ill, you came to me to borrow two hundred and fifty pounds.

NORA: I didn't know anyone else to go to.

KROGSTAD: I promised to get you that amount—

NORA: Yes, and you did so.

KROGSTAD: I promised to get you that amount, on certain conditions. Your mind was so taken up with your husband's illness, and you were so anxious to get the money for your journey, that you seem to have paid no attention to the conditions of our bargain. Therefore it will not be amiss if I remind you of them. Now, I promised to get the money on the security of a bond which I drew up.

NORA: Yes, and which I signed.

KROGSTAD: Good. But below your signature there were a few lines constituting your father a surety for the money; those lines your father should have signed.

NORA: Should? He did sign them.

KROGSTAD: I had left the date blank; that is to say, your father should himself have inserted the date on which he signed the paper. Do you remember that?

NORA: Yes, I think I remember —

KROGSTAD: Then I gave you the bond to send by post to your father. Is that not so?

NORA: Yes.

KROGSTAD: And you naturally did so at once, because five or six days afterwards you brought me the bond with your father's signature. And then I gave you the money.

NORA: Well, haven't I been paying it off regularly?

KROGSTAD: Fairly so, yes. But — to come back to the matter in hand — that must have been a very trying time for you, Mrs. Helmer.

NORA: It was, indeed.

KROGSTAD: Your father was very ill, wasn't he?

NORA: He was very near his end.

KROGSTAD: And he died soon afterwards?

NORA: Yes.

KROGSTAD: Tell me, Mrs. Helmer, can you by any chance remember what day your father died? — on what day of the month, I mean.

NORA: Papa died on the 29th of September.

KROGSTAD: That is correct; I have ascertained it for myself. And, as that is so, there is a discrepancy (*taking a paper from his pocket*) which I cannot account for.

NORA: What discrepancy? I don't know —

KROGSTAD: The discrepancy consists, Mrs. Helmer, in the fact that your father signed this bond three days after his death.

NORA: What do you mean? I don't understand —

KROGSTAD: Your father died on the 29th of September. But, look here; your father has dated his signature the 2nd of October. It is a discrepancy, isn't it? (*Nora is silent.*) Can you explain it to me? (*Nora is still silent.*) It is a remarkable thing, too, that the words "2nd of October," as well as the year, are not written in your father's handwriting but in one that I think I know. Well, of course it can be explained; your father may have forgotten to date his signature, and someone else may have dated it haphazard before they knew of his death. There is no harm in that. It all depends on the signature of the name; and *that* is genuine, I suppose, Mrs. Helmer? It was your father himself who signed his name here?

NORA (*after a short pause, throws her head up and looks defiantly at him*):   No, it was not. It was I that wrote papa's name.

KROGSTAD: Are you aware that is a dangerous confession?

NORA: In what way? You shall have your money soon.

KROGSTAD: Let me ask you a question; why did you not send the paper to your father?

NORA: It was impossible; papa was so ill. If I had asked him for his signature, I should have had to tell him what the money was to be used for; and when he was so ill himself I couldn't tell him that my husband's life was in danger — it was impossible.

KROGSTAD: It would have been better for you if you had given up your trip abroad.

NORA: No, that was impossible. That trip was to save my husband's life; I couldn't give that up.

KROGSTAD: But did it never occur to you that you were committing a fraud on me?

NORA: I couldn't take that into account; I didn't trouble myself about you at all. I couldn't bear you, because you put so many heartless difficulties in my way, although you knew what a dangerous condition my husband was in.

KROGSTAD: Mrs. Helmer, you evidently do not realise clearly what it is that you have been guilty of. But I can assure you that my one false step, which lost me all my reputation, was nothing more or nothing worse than what you have done.

NORA: You? Do you ask me to believe that you were brave enough to run a risk to save your wife's life?

KROGSTAD: The law cares nothing about motives.

NORA: Then it must be a very foolish law.

KROGSTAD: Foolish or not, it is the law by which you will be judged, if I produce this paper in court.

NORA: I don't believe it. Is a daughter not to be allowed to spare her dying father anxiety and care? Is a wife not to be allowed to save her husband's life? I don't know much about law; but I am certain that there must be laws permitting such things as that. Have you no knowledge of such laws — you who are a lawyer? You must be a very poor lawyer, Mr. Krogstad.

KROGSTAD: Maybe. But matters of business — such business as you and I have had together — do you think I don't understand that? Very well. Do as you please. But let me tell you this — if I lose my position a second time, you shall lose yours with me. (*He bows, and goes out through the hall.*)

NORA (*appears buried in thought for a short time, then tosses her head*):   Nonsense! Trying to frighten me like that! — I am not so silly as he thinks. (*Begins to busy herself putting the children's things in order.*) And yet — ? No, it's impossible! I did it for love's sake.

CHILDREN (*in the doorway on the left*):   Mother, the stranger man has gone out through the gate.

NORA: Yes, dears, I know. But, don't tell anyone about the stranger man. Do you hear? Not even papa.

CHILDREN: No, mother; but will you come and play again?

NORA: No, no, — not now.

CHILDREN: But, mother, you promised us.

NORA: Yes, but I can't now. Run away in; I have such a lot to do. Run away in, my sweet little darlings. (*She gets them into the room by degrees and shuts the door on them; then sits down on the sofa, takes up a piece of needlework and sews a few stitches, but soon stops.*) No! (*Throws down the work, gets up, goes to the hall door and calls out.*) Helen! bring the Tree in. (*Goes to the table on the left, opens a drawer, and stops again.*) No, no! it is quite impossible!

MAID (*coming in with the Tree*):   Where shall I put it, ma'am?

NORA: Here, in the middle of the floor.

MAID: Shall I get you anything else?

NORA: No, thank you. I have all I want.   (*Exit Maid.*)

NORA (*begins dressing the tree*):   A candle here — and flowers here — . The horrible man! It's all nonsense — there's nothing wrong. The Tree shall be splendid! I will do everything I can think of to please you, Torvald! — I will sing for you, dance for you — (*Helmer comes in with some papers under his arm.*) Oh! are you back already?

HELMER: Yes. Has anyone been here?

NORA: Here? No.

HELMER: That is strange. I saw Krogstad going out of the gate.

NORA: Did you? Oh yes, I forgot, Krogstad was here for a moment.

HELMER: Nora, I can see from your manner that he has been here begging you to say a good word for him.

NORA: Yes.

HELMER: And you were to appear to do it of your own accord; you were to conceal from me the fact of his having been here; didn't he beg that of you too?

NORA: Yes, Torvald, but —

HELMER: Nora, Nora, and you would be a party to that sort of thing? To have any talk with a man like that, and give him any sort of promise? And to tell me a lie into the bargain?

NORA: A lie — ?

HELMER: Didn't you tell me no one had been here? (*Shakes his finger at her.*) My little song-bird must never do that again. A song-bird must have a clean beak to chirp with — no false notes! (*Puts his arm around her waist.*) That is so, isn't it? Yes, I am sure it is. (*Lets her go.*) We will say no more about it. (*Sits down by the stove.*) How warm and snug it is here! (*Turns over his papers.*)

NORA (*after a short pause, during which she busies herself with the Christmas Tree*):   Torvald!

HELMER: Yes.

NORA: I am looking forward tremendously to the fancy-dress ball at the Stenborgs' the day after to-morrow.

HELMER: And I am tremendously curious to see what you are going to surprise me with.

NORA: It was very silly of me to want to do that.

HELMER: What do you mean?

NORA: I can't hit upon anything that will do; everything I think of seems so silly and insignificant.

HELMER: Does my little Nora acknowledge that at last?

NORA (*standing behind his chair with her arms on the back of it*):   Are you very busy, Torvald?

HELMER: Well —

NORA: What are all those papers?

HELMER: Bank business.

NORA: Already?

HELMER: I have got authority from the retiring manager to undertake the necessary changes in the staff and in the rearrangement of the work; and I
must make use of the Christmas week for that, so as to have everything in
order for the new year.

NORA: Then that was why this poor Krogstad—

HELMER: Hm!

NORA (*leans against the back of his chair and strokes his hair*):   If you hadn't been
so busy I should have asked you a tremendously big favor, Torvald.

HELMER: What is that? Tell me.

NORA: There is no one has such good taste as you. And I do so want to look
nice at the fancy-dress ball. Torvald, couldn't you take me in hand and
decide what I shall go as, and what sort of a dress I shall wear?

HELMER: Aha! so my obstinate little woman is obliged to get someone to come
to her rescue?

NORA: Yes, Torvald, I can't get along a bit without your help.

HELMER: Very well, I will think it over, we shall manage to hit upon something.

NORA: That is nice of you. (*Goes to the Christmas Tree. A short pause.*) How
pretty the red flowers look—. But, tell me, was it really something very
bad that this Krogstad was guilty of?

HELMER: He forged someone's name. Have you any idea what that means?

NORA: Isn't it possible that he was driven to do it by necessity?

HELMER: Yes; or, as in so many cases, by imprudence. I am not so heartless as
to condemn a man altogether because of a single false step of that kind.

NORA: No, you wouldn't, would you, Torvald?

HELMER: Many a man has been able to retrieve his character, if he has openly
confessed his fault and taken his punishment.

NORA: Punishment—?

HELMER: But Krogstad did nothing of that sort; he got himself out of it by a
cunning trick, and that is why he has gone under altogether.

NORA: But do you think it would—?

HELMER: Just think how a guilty man like that has to lie and play the hypocrite
with every one, how he has to wear a mask in the presence of those near
and dear to him, even before his own wife and children. And about the
children—that is the most terrible part of it all, Nora.

NORA: How?

HELMER: Because such an atmosphere of lies infects and poisons the whole life
of a home. Each breath the children take in such a house is full of the
germs of evil.

NORA (*coming nearer him*):   Are you sure of that?

HELMER: My dear, I have often seen it in the course of my life as a lawyer.
Almost everyone who has gone to the bad early in life has had a deceitful
mother.

NORA: Why do you only say—mother?

HELMER: It seems most commonly to be the mother's influence, though
naturally a bad father's would have the same result. Every lawyer is
familiar with the fact. This Krogstad, now, has been persistently poisoning
his own children with lies and dissimulation; that is why I say he has lost

all moral character. (*Holds out his hands to her.*) That is why my sweet little Nora must promise me not to plead his cause. Give me your hand on it. Come, come, what is this? Give me your hand. There now, that's settled. I assure you it would be quite impossible for me to work with him; I literally feel physically ill when I am in the company of such people.

NORA (*takes her hand out of his and goes to the opposite side of the Christmas Tree*): How hot it is in here; and I have such a lot to do.

HELMER (*getting up and putting his papers in order*): Yes, and I must try and read through some of these before dinner; and I must think about your costume, too. And it is just possible I may have something ready in gold paper to hang up on the Tree. (*Puts his hand on her head.*) My precious little singing-bird! (*He goes into his room and shuts the door after him.*)

NORA (*after a pause, whispers*): No, no—it isn't true. It's impossible; it must be impossible.

The Nurse opens the door on the left.

NURSE: The little ones are begging so hard to be allowed to come in to mamma.

NORA: No, no, no! Don't let them come in to me! You stay with them, Anne.

NURSE: Very well, ma'am. (*Shuts the door.*)

NORA (*pale with terror*): Deprave my little children? Poison my home? (*A short pause. Then she tosses her head.*) It's not true. It can't possibly be true.

ACT II

THE SAME SCENE: *The Christmas Tree is in the corner by the piano, stripped of its ornaments and with burnt-down candle-ends on its dishevelled branches. Nora's cloak and hat are lying on the sofa. She is alone in the room, walking about uneasily. She stops by the sofa and takes up her cloak.*

NORA (*drops her cloak*): Someone is coming now! (*Goes to the door and listens.*) No—it is no one. Of course, no one will come to-day, Christmas Day—nor to-morrow either. But, perhaps—(*opens the door and looks out*). No, nothing in the letter-box; it is quite empty. (*Comes forward.*) What rubbish! of course he can't be in earnest about it. Such a thing couldn't happen; it is impossible—I have three little children.

Enter the Nurse from the room on the left, carrying a big cardboard box.

NURSE: At last I have found the box with the fancy dress.

NORA: Thanks; put it on the table.

NURSE (*doing so*): But it is very much in want of mending.

NORA: I should like to tear it into a hundred thousand pieces.

NURSE: What an idea! It can easily be put in order—just a little patience.

NORA: Yes, I will go and get Mrs. Linde to come and help me with it.

NURSE: What, out again? In this horrible weather? You will catch cold, ma'am, and make yourself ill.

NORA: Well, worse than that might happen. How are the children?

NURSE: The poor little souls are playing with their Christmas presents, but—

NORA: Do they ask much for me?

NURSE: You see, they are so accustomed to have their mamma with them.

NORA: Yes, but, nurse, I shall not be able to be so much with them now as I was before.

NURSE: Oh well, young children easily get accustomed to anything.

NORA: Do you think so? Do you think they would forget their mother if she went away altogether?

NURSE: Good heavens!—went away altogether?

NORA: Nurse, I want you to tell me something I have often wondered about—how could you have the heart to put your own child out among strangers?

NURSE: I was obliged to, if I wanted to be little Nora's nurse.

NORA: Yes, but how could you be willing to do it?

NURSE: What, when I was going to get such a good place by it? A poor girl who has got into trouble should be glad to. Besides, that wicked man didn't do a single thing for me.

NORA: But I suppose your daughter has quite forgotten you.

NURSE: No, indeed she hasn't. She wrote to me when she was confirmed, and when she was married.

NORA (*putting her arms round her neck*): Dear old Anne, you were a good mother to me when I was little.

NURSE: Little Nora, poor dear, had no other mother but me.

NORA: And if my little ones had no other mother, I am sure you would—What nonsense I am talking! (*Opens the box.*) Go in to them. Now I must—. You will see to-morrow how charming I shall look.

NURSE: I am sure there will be no one at the ball so charming as you, ma'am. (*Goes into the room on the left.*)

NORA (*begins to unpack the box, but soon pushes it away from her*): If only I dared go out. If only no one would come. If only I could be sure nothing would happen here in the meantime. Stuff and nonsense! No one will come. Only I mustn't think about it. I will brush my muff. What lovely, lovely gloves! Out of my thoughts, out of my thoughts! One, two, three, four, five, six—(*Screams.*) Ah! there is someone coming—. (*Makes a movement towards the door, but stands irresolute.*)

Enter Mrs. Linde from the hall, where she has taken off her cloak and hat.

NORA: Oh, it's you, Christine. There is no one else out there, is there? How good of you to come!

MRS. LINDE: I heard you were up asking for me.

NORA: Yes, I was passing by. As a matter of fact, it is something you could help me with. Let us sit down here on the sofa. Look here. To-morrow evening there is to be a fancy-dress ball at the Stenborgs', who live above us; and Torvald wants me to go as a Neapolitan fisher-girl, and dance the Tarantella that I learned at Capri.

MRS. LINDE: I see; you are going to keep up the character.

NORA: Yes, Torvald wants me to. Look, here is the dress; Torvald had it made for me there, but now it is all so torn, and I haven't any idea—

MRS. LINDE: We will easily put that right. It is only some of the trimming come unsewn here and there. Needle and thread? Now then, that's all we want.

NORA: It *is* nice of you.

MRS. LINDE (*sewing*):   So you are going to be dressed up to-morrow, Nora. I will tell you what — I shall come in for a moment and see you in your fine feathers. But I have completely forgotten to thank you for a delightful evening yesterday.

NORA (*gets up, and crosses the stage*):   Well, I don't think yesterday was as pleasant as usual. You ought to have come to town a little earlier, Christine. Certainly Torvald does understand how to make a house dainty and attractive.

MRS. LINDE: And so do you, it seems to me; you are not your father's daughter for nothing. But tell me, is Doctor Rank always as depressed as he was yesterday?

NORA: No; yesterday it was very noticeable. I must tell you that he suffers from a very dangerous disease. He has consumption of the spine, poor creature. His father was a horrible man who committed all sorts of excesses; and that is why his son was sickly from childhood, do you understand?

MRS. LINDE (*dropping her sewing*):   But, my dearest Nora, how do you know anything about such things?

NORA (*walking about*):   Pooh! When you have three children, you get visits now and then from — from married women, who know something of medical matters, and they talk about one thing and another.

MRS. LINDE: (*goes on sewing. A short silence*) Does Doctor Rank come here everyday?

NORA: Everyday regularly. He is Torvald's most intimate friend, and a great friend of mine too. He is just like one of the family.

MRS. LINDE: But tell me this — is he perfectly sincere? I mean, isn't he the kind of man that is very anxious to make himself agreeable?

NORA: Not in the least. What makes you think that?

MRS. LINDE: When you introduced him to me yesterday, he declared he had often heard my name mentioned in this house; but afterwards I noticed that your husband hadn't the slightest idea who I was. So how could Doctor Rank — ?

NORA: That is quite right, Christine. Torvald is so absurdly fond of me that he wants me absolutely to himself, as he says. At first he used to seem almost jealous if I mentioned any of the dear folk at home, so naturally I gave up doing so. But I often talk about such things with Doctor Rank, because he likes hearing about them.

MRS. LINDE: Listen to me, Nora. You are still very like a child in many things, and I am older than you in many ways and have a little more experience. Let me tell you this — you ought to make an end of it with Doctor Rank.

NORA: What ought I to make an end of?

MRS. LINDE: Of two things, I think. Yesterday you talked some nonsense about a rich admirer who was to leave you money —

NORA: An admirer who doesn't exist, unfortunately! But what then?

MRS. LINDE: Is Doctor Rank a man of means?

NORA: Yes, he is.

MRS. LINDE: And has no one to provide for?

NORA: No, no one; but—

MRS. LINDE: And comes here everyday?

NORA: Yes, I told you so.

MRS. LINDE: But how can this well-bred man be so tactless?

NORA: I don't understand you at all.

MRS. LINDE: Don't prevaricate, Nora. Do you suppose I don't guess who lent you the two hundred and fifty pounds?

NORA: Are you out of your senses? How can you think of such a thing! A friend of ours, who comes here everyday! Do you realise what a horribly painful position that would be?

MRS. LINDE: Then it really isn't he?

NORA: No, certainly not. It would never have entered into my head for a moment. Besides, he had no money to lend then; he came into his money afterwards.

MRS. LINDE: Well, I think that was lucky for you, my dear Nora.

NORA: No, it would never have come into my head to ask Doctor Rank. Although I am quite sure that if I had asked him—

MRS. LINDE: But of course you won't.

NORA: Of course not. I have no reason to think it could possibly be necessary. But I am quite sure that if I told Doctor Rank—

MRS. LINDE: Behind your husband's back?

NORA: I must make an end of it with the other one, and that will be behind his back too. I *must* make an end of it with him.

MRS. LINDE: Yes, that is what I told you yesterday, but—

NORA (*walking up and down*):   A man can put a thing like that straight much easier than a woman—

MRS. LINDE: One's husband, yes.

NORA: Nonsense! (*Standing still.*) When you pay off a debt you get your bond back, don't you?

MRS. LINDE: Yes, as a matter of course.

NORA: And can tear it into a hundred thousand pieces, and burn it up—the nasty dirty paper!

MRS. LINDE (*looks hard at her, lays down her sewing and gets up slowly*):   Nora, you are concealing something from me.

NORA: Do I look as if I were?

MRS. LINDE: Something has happened to you since yesterday morning. Nora, what is it?

NORA (*going nearer to her*):   Christine! (*Listens.*) Hush! there's Torvald come home. Do you mind going in to the children for the present? Torvald can't bear to see dressmaking going on. Let Anne help you.

MRS. LINDE (*gathering some of the things together*):   Certainly—but I am not going away from here until we have had it out with one another. (*She goes into the room on the left, as Helmer comes in from the hall.*)

NORA (*going up to Helmer*):   I have wanted you so much, Torvald dear.

HELMER: Was that the dressmaker?

NORA: No, it was Christine; she is helping me to put my dress in order. You will see I shall look quite smart.

HELMER: Wasn't that a happy thought of mine, now?

NORA: Splendid! But don't you think it is nice of me, too, to do as you wish?

HELMER: Nice?—because you do as your husband wishes? Well, well, you little rogue, I am sure you did not mean it in that way. But I am not going to disturb you; you will want to be trying on your dress, I expect.

NORA: I suppose you are going to work.

HELMER: Yes. (*Shows her a bundle of papers.*) Look at that. I have just been into the bank. (*Turns to go into his room.*)

NORA: Torvald.

HELMER: Yes.

NORA: If your little squirrel were to ask you for something very, very prettily—?

HELMER: What then?

NORA: Would you do it?

HELMER: I should like to hear what it is, first.

NORA: Your squirrel would run about and do all her tricks if you would be nice, and do what she wants.

HELMER: Speak plainly.

NORA: Your skylark would chirp about in every room, with her song rising and falling—

HELMER: Well, my skylark does that anyhow.

NORA: I would play the fairy and dance for you in the moonlight, Torvald.

HELMER: Nora—you surely don't mean that request you made to me this morning?

NORA (*going near him*):   Yes, Torvald, I beg you so earnestly—

HELMER: Have you really the courage to open up that question again?

NORA: Yes, dear, you *must* do as I ask; you *must* let Krogstad keep his post in the bank.

HELMER: My dear Nora, it is his post that I have arranged Mrs. Linde shall have.

NORA: Yes, you have been awfully kind about that; but you could just as well dismiss some other clerk instead of Krogstad.

HELMER: This is simply incredible obstinacy! Because you chose to give him a thoughtless promise that you would speak for him, I am expected to—

NORA: That isn't the reason, Torvald. It is for your own sake. This fellow writes in the most scurrilous newspapers; you have told me so yourself. He can do you an unspeakable amount of harm. I am frightened to death of him—

HELMER: Ah, I understand; it is recollections of the past that scare you.

NORA: What do you mean?

HELMER: Naturally you are thinking of your father.

NORA: Yes—yes, of course. Just recall to your mind what these malicious creatures wrote in the papers about papa, and how horribly they slandered him. I believe they would have procured his dismissal if the Department had not sent you over to inquire into it, and if you had not been so kindly disposed and helpful to him.

HELMER: My little Nora, there is an important difference between your father and me. Your father's reputation as a public official was not above suspicion. Mine is, and I hope it will continue to be so, as long as I hold my office.

NORA: You never can tell what mischief these men may contrive. We ought to be so well off, so snug and happy here in our peaceful home, and have no cares—you and I and the children, Torvald! That is why I beg you so earnestly—

HELMER: And it is just by interceding for him that you make it impossible for me to keep him. It is already known at the Bank that I mean to dismiss Krogstad. Is it to get about now that the new manager has changed his mind at his wife's bidding—

NORA: And what if it did?

HELMER: Of course!—if only this obstinate little person can get her way! Do you suppose I am going to make myself ridiculous before my whole staff, to let people think that I am a man to be swayed by all sorts of outside influence? I should very soon feel the consequences of it, I can tell you! And besides, there is one thing that makes it quite impossible for me to have Krogstad in the Bank as long as I am manager.

NORA: Whatever is that?

HELMER: His moral failings I might perhaps have overlooked, if necessary—

NORA: Yes, you could—couldn't you?

HELMER: And I hear he is a good worker, too. But I knew him when we were boys. It was one of those rash friendships that so often prove an incubus in afterlife. I may as well tell you plainly, we were once on very intimate terms with one another. But this tactless fellow lays no restraint on himself when other people are present. On the contrary, he thinks it gives him the right to adopt a familiar tone with me, and every minute it is "I say, Helmer, old fellow!" and that sort of thing. I assure you it is extremely painful for me. He would make my position in the Bank intolerable.

NORA: Torvald, I don't believe you mean that.

HELMER: Don't you? Why not?

NORA: Because it is such a narrow-minded way of looking at things.

HELMER: What are you saying? Narrow-minded? Do you think I am narrow-minded?

NORA: No, just the opposite, dear—and it is exactly for that reason.

HELMER: It's the same thing. You say my point of view is narrow-minded, so I must be so too. Narrow-minded! Very well—I must put an end to this. (*Goes to the hall door and calls.*) Helen!

NORA: What are you going to do?

HELMER (*looking among his papers*):   Settle it. (*Enter Maid.*) Look here; take this letter and go downstairs with it at once. Find a messenger and tell him to deliver it, and be quick. The address is on it, and here is the money.

MAID: Very well, sir. (*Exit with the letter.*)

HELMER (*putting his papers together*):   Now then, little Miss Obstinate.

NORA (*breathlessly*):   Torvald — what was that letter?

HELMER: Krogstad's dismissal.

NORA: Call her back, Torvald! There is still time. Oh Torvald, call her back! Do it for my sake — for your own sake — for the children's sake! Do you hear me, Torvald? Call her back! You don't know what that letter can bring upon us.

HELMER: It's too late.

NORA: Yes, it's too late.

HELMER: My dear Nora, I can forgive the anxiety you are in, although really it is an insult to me. It is, indeed. Isn't it an insult to think that I should be afraid of a starving quill-driver's vengeance? But I forgive you neverthe-less, because it is such eloquent witness to your great love for me. (*Takes her in his arms.*) And that is as it should be, my own darling Nora. Come what will, you may be sure I shall have both courage and strength if they be needed. You will see I am man enough to take everything upon myself.

NORA (*in a horror-stricken voice*):   What do you mean by that?

HELMER: Everything, I say —

NORA (*recovering herself*):   You will never have to do that.

HELMER: That's right. Well, we will share it, Nora, as man and wife should. That is how it shall be. (*Caressing her.*) Are you content now? There! there! — not these frightened dove's eyes! The whole thing is only the wildest fancy! — Now, you must go and play through the Tarantella and practise with your tambourine. I shall go into the inner office and shut the door, and I shall hear nothing; you can make as much noise as you please. (*Turns back at the door.*) And when Rank comes, tell him where he will find me. (*Nods to her, takes his papers and goes into his room, and shuts the door after him.*)

NORA (*bewildered with anxiety, stands as if rooted to the spot, and whispers*):   He was capable of doing it. He will do it. He will do it in spite of every-thing. — No, not that! Never, never! Anything rather than that! Oh, for some help, some way out of it! (*The door-bell rings.*) Doctor Rank! Anything rather than that — anything, whatever it is! (*She puts her hands over her face, pulls herself together, goes to the door and opens it. Rank is standing with-out, hanging up his coat. During the following dialogue it begins to grow dark.*)

NORA: Good-day, Doctor Rank. I knew your ring. But you mustn't go in to Tor-vald now; I think he is busy with something.

RANK: And you?

NORA (*brings him in and shuts the door after him*):   Oh, you know very well I always have time for you.

RANK: Thank you. I shall make use of as much of it as I can.

NORA: What do you mean by that? As much of it as you can?

RANK: Well, does that alarm you?

NORA: It was such a strange way of putting it. Is anything likely to happen?

RANK: Nothing but what I have long been prepared for. But I certainly didn't expect it to happen so soon.

NORA (*gripping him by the arm*):   What have you found out? Doctor Rank, you must tell me.

RANK (*sitting down by the stove*):   It is all up with me. And it can't be helped.

NORA (*with a sigh of relief*):   Is it about yourself?

RANK: Who else? It is no use lying to one's self. I am the most wretched of all my patients, Mrs. Helmer. Lately I have been taking stock of my internal economy. Bankrupt! Probably within a month I shall lie rotting in the churchyard.

NORA: What an ugly thing to say!

RANK: The thing itself is cursedly ugly, and the worst of it is that I shall have to face so much more that is ugly before that. I shall only make one more examination of myself; when I have done that, I shall know pretty certainly when it will be that the horrors of dissolution will begin. There is something I want to tell you. Helmer's refined nature gives him an un-conquerable disgust at everything that is ugly; I won't have him in my sick-room.

NORA: Oh, but, Doctor Rank—

RANK: I won't have him there. Not on any account. I bar my door to him. As soon as I am quite certain that the worst has come, I shall send you my card with a black cross on it, and then you will know that the loathsome end has begun.

NORA: You are quite absurd to-day. And I wanted you so much to be in a really good humour.

RANK: With death stalking beside me?—To have to pay this penalty for another man's sin? Is there any justice in that? And in every single family, in one way or another, some such inexorable retribution is being exacted—

NORA (*putting her hands over her ears*):   Rubbish! Do talk of something cheerful.

RANK: Oh, it's a mere laughing matter, the whole thing. My poor innocent spine has to suffer for my father's youthful amusements.

NORA (*sitting at the table on the left*):   I suppose you mean that he was too partial to asparagus and pâté de foie gras, don't you?

RANK: Yes, and to truffles.

NORA: Truffles, yes. And oysters too, I suppose?

RANK: Oysters, of course, that goes without saying.

NORA: And heaps of port and champagne. It is sad that all these nice things should take their revenge on our bones.

RANK: Especially that they should revenge themselves on the unlucky bones of those who have not had the satisfaction of enjoying them.

NORA: Yes, that's the saddest part of it all.

RANK (*with a searching look at her*):   Hm!—

NORA (*after a short pause*):   Why did you smile?

RANK: No, it was you that laughed.

NORA: No, it was you that smiled, Doctor Rank!

RANK (*rising*):   You are a greater rascal than I thought.

NORA: I am in a silly mood to-day.

RANK: So it seems.

NORA (*putting her hands on his shoulders*):   Dear, dear Doctor Rank, death mustn't take you away from Torvald and me.

RANK: It is a loss you would easily recover from. Those who are gone are soon forgotten.

NORA (*looking at him anxiously*):   Do you believe that?

RANK: People form new ties, and then—

NORA: Who will form new ties?

RANK: Both you and Helmer, when I am gone. You yourself are already on the high road to it, I think. What did that Mrs. Linde want here last night?

NORA: Oho!—you don't mean to say you are jealous of poor Christine?

RANK: Yes, I am. She will be my successor in this house. When I am done for, this woman will—

NORA: Hush! don't speak so loud. She is in that room.

RANK: To-day again. There, you see.

NORA: She has only come to sew my dress for me. Bless my soul, how unreasonable you are! (*Sits down on the sofa.*) Be nice now, Doctor Rank, and to-morrow you will see how beautifully I shall dance, and you can imagine I am doing it all for you—and for Torvald too, of course. (*Takes various things out of the box.*) Doctor Rank, come and sit down here, and I will show you something.

RANK (*sitting down*):   What is it?

NORA: Just look at those!

RANK: Silk stockings.

NORA: Flesh-coloured. Aren't they lovely? It is so dark here now, but tomorrow—. No, no, no! you must only look at the feet. Oh well, you may have leave to look at the legs too.

RANK: Hm!—

NORA: Why are you looking so critical? Don't you think they will fit me?

RANK: I have no means of forming an opinion about that.

NORA (*looks at him for a moment*):   For shame! (*Hits him lightly on the ear with the stockings.*) That's to punish you. (*Folds them up again.*)

RANK: And what other nice things am I to be allowed to see?

NORA: Not a single thing more, for being so naughty. (*She looks among the things, humming to herself.*)

RANK (*after a short silence*):   When I am sitting here, talking to you as intimately as this, I cannot imagine for a moment what would have become of me if I had never come into this house.

NORA (*smiling*):   I believe you do feel thoroughly at home with us.

RANK (*in a lower voice, looking straight in front of him*):   And to be obliged to leave it all—

NORA: Nonsense, you are not going to leave it.

RANK (*as before*):   And not be able to leave behind one the slightest token of one's gratitude, scarcely even a fleeting regret — nothing but an empty place which the first comer can fill as well as any other.

NORA: And if I asked you now for a — ? No!

RANK: For what?

NORA: For a big proof of your friendship —

RANK: Yes, yes!

NORA: I mean a tremendously big favour.

RANK: Would you really make me so happy for once?

NORA: Ah, but you don't know what it is yet.

RANK: No — but tell me.

NORA: I really can't, Doctor Rank. It is something out of all reason; it means advice, and help, and a favour —

RANK: The bigger a thing it is the better. I can't conceive what it is you mean. Do tell me. Haven't I your confidence?

NORA: More than anyone else. I know you are my truest and best friend, and so I will tell you what it is. Well, Doctor Rank, it is something you must help me to prevent. You know how devotedly, how inexpressibly deeply Torvald loves me; he would never for a moment hesitate to give his life for me.

RANK (*leaning towards her*):   Nora — do you think he is the only one — ?

NORA (*with a slight start*):   The only one — ?

RANK: The only one who would gladly give his life for your sake.

NORA (*sadly*):   Is that it?

RANK: I was determined you should know it before I went away, and there will never be a better opportunity than this. Now you know it, Nora. And now you know, too, that you can trust me as you would trust no one else.

NORA (*rises, deliberately and quietly*):   Let me pass.

RANK (*makes room for her to pass him, but sits still*):   Nora!

NORA (*at the hall door*):   Helen, bring in the lamp. (*Goes over to the stove.*) Dear Doctor Rank, that was really horrid of you.

RANK: To have loved you as much as anyone else does? Was that horrid?

NORA: No, but to go and tell me so. There was really no need —

RANK: What do you mean? Did you know — ? (*Maid enters with lamp, puts it down on the table, and goes out.*) Nora — Mrs. Helmer — tell me, had you any idea of this?

NORA: Oh, how do I know whether I had or whether I hadn't? I really can't tell you — To think you could be so clumsy, Doctor Rank! We were getting on so nicely.

RANK: Well, at all events you know now that you can command me, body and soul. So won't you speak out?

NORA (*looking at him*):   After what happened?

RANK: I beg you to let me know what it is.

NORA: I can't tell you anything now.

RANK: Yes, yes. You mustn't punish me in that way. Let me have permission to do for you whatever a man may do.

NORA: You can do nothing for me now. Besides, I really don't need any help at all. You will find that the whole thing is merely fancy on my part. It really is so — of course it is! (*Sits down in the rocking-chair, and looks at him with a smile.*) You are a nice sort of man, Doctor Rank! — don't you feel ashamed of yourself, now the lamp has come?

RANK: Not a bit. But perhaps I had better go — for ever?

NORA: No, indeed, you shall not. Of course you must come here just as before. You know very well Torvald can't do without you.

RANK: Yes, but you?

NORA: Oh, I am always tremendously pleased when you come.

RANK: It is just that, that put me on the wrong track. You are a riddle to me. I have often thought that you would almost as soon be in my company as in Helmer's.

NORA: Yes — you see there are some people one loves best, and others whom one would almost always rather have as companions.

RANK: Yes, there is something in that.

NORA: When I was at home, of course I loved papa best. But I always thought it tremendous fun if I could steal down into the maids' room, because they never moralised at all, and talked to each other about such entertaining things.

RANK: I see — it is *their* place I have taken.

NORA (*jumping up and going to him*):   Oh, dear, nice Doctor Rank, I never meant that at all. But surely you can understand that being with Torvald is a little like being with papa —

Enter Maid from the hall.

MAID: If you please, ma'am. (*Whispers and hands her a card.*)

NORA (*glancing at the card*):   Oh! (*Puts it in her pocket.*)

RANK: Is there anything wrong?

NORA: No, no, not in the least. It is only something — it is my new dress —

RANK: What? Your dress is lying there.

NORA: Oh, yes, that one; but this is another. I ordered it. Torvald mustn't know about it —

RANK: Oho! Then that was the great secret.

NORA: Of course. Just go in to him; he is sitting in the inner room. Keep him as long as —

RANK: Make your mind easy; I won't let him escape. (*Goes into Helmer's room.*)

NORA (*to the Maid*):   And he is standing waiting in the kitchen?

MAID: Yes; he came up the back stairs.

NORA: But didn't you tell him no one was in?

MAID: Yes, but it was no good.

NORA: He won't go away?

MAID: No; he says he won't until he has seen you, ma'am.

NORA: Well, let him come in — but quietly. Helen, you mustn't say anything about it to anyone. It is a surprise for my husband.

MAID: Yes, ma'am, I quite understand. (*Exit.*)

NORA: This dreadful thing is going to happen! It will happen in spite of me! No, no, no, it can't happen — it shan't happen! (*She bolts the door of Helmer's room. The Maid opens the hall door for Krogstad and shuts it after him. He is wearing a fur coat, high boots and a fur cap.*)

NORA (*advancing towards him*):   Speak low — my husband is at home.

KROGSTAD: No matter about that.

NORA: What do you want of me?

KROGSTAD: An explanation of something.

NORA: Make haste then. What is it?

KROGSTAD: You know, I suppose, that I have got my dismissal.

NORA: I couldn't prevent it, Mr. Krogstad. I fought as hard as I could on your side, but it was no good.

KROGSTAD: Does your husband love you so little, then? He knows what I can expose you to, and yet he ventures —

NORA: How can you suppose that he has any knowledge of the sort?

KROGSTAD: I didn't suppose so at all. It would not be the least like our dear Torvald Helmer to show so much courage —

NORA: Mr. Krogstad, a little respect for my husband, please.

KROGSTAD: Certainly — all the respect he deserves. But since you have kept the matter so carefully to yourself, I make bold to suppose that you have a little clearer idea, than you had yesterday, of what it actually is that you have done?

NORA: More than you could ever teach me.

KROGSTAD: Yes, such a bad lawyer as I am.

NORA: What is it you want of me?

KROGSTAD: Only to see how you were, Mrs. Helmer. I have been thinking about you all day long. A mere cashier, a quill-driver, a — well, a man like me — even he has a little of what is called feeling, you know.

NORA: Show it, then; think of my little children.

KROGSTAD: Have you and your husband thought of mine? But never mind about that. I only wanted to tell you that you need not take this matter too seriously. In the first place there will be no accusation made on my part.

NORA: No, of course not; I was sure of that.

KROGSTAD: The whole thing can be arranged amicably; there is no reason why anyone should know anything about it. It will remain a secret between us three.

NORA: My husband must never get to know anything about it.

KROGSTAD: How will you be able to prevent it? Am I to understand that you can pay the balance that is owing?

NORA: No, not just at present.

KROGSTAD: Or perhaps that you have some expedient for raising the money soon?

NORA: No expedient that I mean to make use of.

KROGSTAD: Well, in any case, it would have been of no use to you now. If you stood there with ever so much money in your hand, I would never part with your bond.

NORA: Tell me what purpose you mean to put it to.

KROGSTAD: I shall only preserve it — keep it in my possession. No one who is not concerned in the matter shall have the slightest hint of it. So that if the thought of it has driven you to any desperate resolution —

NORA: It has.

KROGSTAD: If you had it in your mind to run away from your home —

NORA: I had.

KROGSTAD: Or even something worse —

NORA: How could you know that?

KROGSTAD: Give up the idea.

NORA: How did you know I had thought of *that*?

KROGSTAD: Most of us think of that at first. I did, too — but I hadn't the courage.

NORA (*faintly*):   No more had I.

KROGSTAD (*in a tone of relief*):   No, that's it, isn't it — you hadn't the courage either?

NORA: No, I haven't — I haven't.

KROGSTAD: Besides, it would have been a great piece of folly. Once the first storm at home is over —. I have a letter for your husband in my pocket.

NORA: Telling him everything?

KROGSTAD: In as lenient a manner as I possibly could.

NORA (*quickly*):   He mustn't get the letter. Tear it up. I will find some means of getting money.

KROGSTAD: Excuse me, Mrs. Helmer, but I think I told you just now —

NORA: I am not speaking of what I owe you. Tell me what sum you are asking my husband for, and I will get the money.

KROGSTAD: I am not asking your husband for a penny.

NORA: What do you want, then?

KROGSTAD: I will tell you. I want to rehabilitate myself, Mrs. Helmer; I want to get on; and in that your husband must help me. For the last year and a half I have not had a hand in anything dishonourable, and all that time I have been struggling in most restricted circumstances. I was content to work my way up step by step. Now I am turned out, and I am not going to be satisfied with merely being taken into favour again. I want to get on, I tell you. I want to get into the Bank again, in a higher position. Your husband must make a place for me —

NORA: That he will never do!

KROGSTAD: He will; I know him; he dare not protest. And as soon as I am in there again with him, then you will see! Within a year I shall be the manager's right hand. It will be Nils Krogstad and not Torvald Helmer who manages the Bank.

NORA: That's a thing you will never see!

KROGSTAD: Do you mean that you will — ?

NORA: I have courage enough for it now.

KROGSTAD: Oh, you can't frighten me. A fine, spoilt lady like you —

NORA: You will see, you will see.

KROGSTAD: Under the ice, perhaps? Down into the cold, coal-black water? And then, in the spring, to float up to the surface, all horrible and unrecognisable, with your hair fallen out—

NORA: You can't frighten me.

KROGSTAD: Nor you me. People don't do such things, Mrs. Helmer. Besides, what use would it be? I should have him completely in my power all the same.

NORA: Afterwards? When I am no longer—

KROGSTAD: Have you forgotten that it is I who have the keeping of your reputation? (*Nora stands speechlessly looking at him.*) Well, now, I have warned you. Do not do anything foolish. When Helmer has had my letter, I shall expect a message from him. And be sure you remember that it is your husband himself who has forced me into such ways as this again. I will never forgive him for that. Good-bye, Mrs. Helmer. (*Exit through the hall.*)

NORA (*goes to the hall door, opens it slightly and listens*):   He is going. He is not putting the letter in the box. Oh no, no! that's impossible! (*Opens the door by degrees.*) What is that? He is standing outside. He is not going downstairs. Is he hesitating? Can he—? (*A letter drops into the box; then Krogstad's footsteps are heard, till they die away as he goes downstairs. Nora utters a stifled cry, and runs across the room to the table by the sofa. A short pause.*)

NORA: In the letter-box. (*Steals across to the hall door.*) There it lies—Torvald, Torvald, there is no hope for us now!

Mrs. Linde comes in from the room on the left, carrying the dress.

MRS. LINDE: There, I can't see anything more to mend now. Would you like to try it on—?

NORA (*in a hoarse whisper*):   Christine, come here.

MRS. LINDE (*throwing the dress down on the sofa*):   What is the matter with you? You look so agitated!

NORA: Come here. Do you see that letter? There, look—you can see it through the glass in the letter-box.

MRS. LINDE: Yes, I see it.

NORA: That letter is from Krogstad.

MRS. LINDE: Nora—it was Krogstad who lent you the money!

NORA: Yes, and now Torvald will know all about it.

MRS. LINDE: Believe me, Nora, that's the best thing for both of you.

NORA: You don't know all. I forged a name.

MRS. LINDE: Good heavens—!

NORA: I only want to say this to you, Christine—you must be my witness.

MRS. LINDE: Your witness? What do you mean? What am I to—?

NORA: If I should go out of my mind—and it might easily happen—

MRS. LINDE: Nora!

NORA: Or if anything else should happen to me—anything, for instance, that might prevent my being here—

MRS. LINDE: Nora! Nora! you are quite out of your mind.

NORA: And if it should happen that there were some one who wanted to take all the responsibility, all the blame, you understand—

MRS. LINDE: Yes, yes — but how can you suppose — ?

NORA: Then you must be my witness, that it is not true, Christine. I am not out of my mind at all! I am in my right senses now, and I tell you no one else has known anything about it; I, and I alone, did the whole thing. Remember that.

MRS. LINDE: I will, indeed. But I don't understand all this.

NORA: How should you understand it? A wonderful thing is going to happen!

MRS. LINDE: A wonderful thing?

NORA: Yes, a wonderful thing! — But it is so terrible, Christine; it *mustn't* happen, not for all the world.

MRS. LINDE: I will go at once and see Krogstad.

NORA: Don't go to him; he will do you some harm.

MRS. LINDE: There was a time when he would gladly do anything for my sake.

NORA: He?

MRS. LINDE: Where does he live?

NORA: How should I know — ? Yes (*feeling in her pocket*), here is his card. But the letter, the letter — !

HELMER (*calls from his room, knocking at the door*):   Nora!

NORA (*cries out anxiously*):   Oh, what's that? What do you want?

HELMER: Don't be so frightened. We are not coming in; you have locked the door. Are you trying on your dress?

NORA: Yes, that's it. I look so nice, Torvald.

MRS. LINDE (*who has read the card*):   I see he lives at the corner here.

NORA: Yes, but it's no use. It is hopeless. The letter is lying there in the box.

MRS. LINDE: And your husband keeps the key?

NORA: Yes, always.

MRS. LINDE: Krogstad must ask for his letter back unread, he must find some pretence —

NORA: But it is just at this time that Torvald generally —

MRS. LINDE: You must delay him. Go in to him in the meantime. I will come back as soon as I can. (*She goes out hurriedly through the hall door.*)

NORA (*goes to Helmer's door, opens it and peeps in*):   Torvald!

HELMER (*from the inner room*):   Well? May I venture at last to come into my own room again? Come along, Rank, now you will see — (*Halting in the doorway.*) But what is this?

NORA: What is what, dear?

HELMER: Rank led me to expect a splendid transformation.

RANK (*in the doorway*):   I understood so, but evidently I was mistaken.

NORA: Yes, nobody is to have the chance of admiring me in my dress until tomorrow.

HELMER: But, my dear Nora, you look so worn out. Have you been practising too much?

NORA: No, I have not practised at all.

HELMER: But you will need to —

NORA: Yes, indeed I shall, Torvald. But I can't get on a bit without you to help me; I have absolutely forgotten the whole thing.

HELMER: Oh, we will soon work it up again.

NORA: Yes, help me, Torvald. Promise that you will! I am so nervous about it — all the people — . You must give yourself up to me entirely this evening. Not the tiniest bit of business — you mustn't even take a pen in your hand. Will you promise, Torvald dear?

HELMER: I promise. This evening I will be wholly and absolutely at your service, you helpless little mortal. Ah, by the way, first of all I will just — (*Goes towards the hall door.*)

NORA: What are you going to do there?

HELMER: Only see if any letters have come.

NORA: No, no! don't do that, Torvald!

HELMER: Why not?

NORA: Torvald, please don't. There is nothing there.

HELMER: Well, let me look. (*Turns to go to the letter-box. Nora, at the piano, plays the first bars of the Tarantella. Helmer stops in the doorway.*) Aha!

NORA: I can't dance tomorrow if I don't practice with you.

HELMER (*going up to her*):   Are you really so afraid of it, dear?

NORA: Yes, so dreadfully afraid of it. Let me practice at once; there is time now, before we go to dinner. Sit down and play for me, Torvald dear; criticise me, and correct me as you play.

HELMER: With great pleasure, if you wish me to. (*Sits down at the piano.*)

NORA (*takes out of the box a tambourine and a long variegated shawl. She hastily drapes the shawl round her. Then she springs to the front of the stage and calls out*):   Now play for me! I am going to dance!

Helmer plays and Nora dances. Rank stands by the piano behind Helmer, and looks on.

HELMER (*as he plays*):   Slower, slower!

NORA: I can't do it any other way.

HELMER: Not so violently, Nora!

NORA: This is the way.

HELMER (*stops playing*):   No, no — that is not a bit right.

NORA (*laughing and swinging the tambourine*):   Didn't I tell you so?

RANK: Let me play for her.

HELMER (*getting up*):   Yes, do. I can correct her better then.

Rank sits down at the piano and plays. Nora dances more and more wildly. Helmer has taken up a position beside the stove, and during her dance gives her frequent instructions. She does not seem to hear him; her hair comes down and falls over her shoulders; she pays no attention to it, but goes on dancing. Enter Mrs. Linde.

MRS. LINDE (*standing as if spell-bound in the doorway*):   Oh! —

NORA (*as she dances*):   Such fun, Christine!

HELMER: My dear darling Nora, you are dancing as if your life depended on it.

NORA: So it does.

HELMER: Stop, Rank; this is sheer madness. Stop, I tell you! (*Rank stops playing, and Nora suddenly stands still. Helmer goes up to her.*) I could never have believed it. You have forgotten everything I taught you.

NORA (*throwing away the tambourine*):   There, you see.

HELMER: You will want a lot of coaching.

NORA: Yes, you see how much I need it. You must coach me up to the last minute. Promise me that, Torvald!

HELMER: You can depend on me.

NORA: You must not think of anything but me, either to-day or to-morrow; you mustn't open a single letter—not even open the letter-box—

HELMER: Ah, you are still afraid of that fellow—

NORA: Yes, indeed I am.

HELMER: Nora, I can tell from your looks that there is a letter from him lying there.

NORA: I don't know; I think there is; but you must not read anything of that kind now. Nothing horrid must come between us until this is all over.

RANK (*whispers to Helmer*):   You mustn't contradict her.

HELMER (*taking her in his arms*):   The child shall have her way. But to-morrow night, after you have danced—

NORA: Then you will be free. (*The Maid appears in the doorway to the right.*)

MAID: Dinner is served, ma'am.

NORA: We will have champagne, Helen.

MAID: Very good, ma'am.   [*Exit.*]

HELMER: Hullo!—are we going to have a banquet?

NORA: Yes, a champagne banquet until the small hours. (*Calls out.*) And a few macaroons, Helen—lots, just for once!

HELMER: Come, come, don't be so wild and nervous. Be my own little skylark, as you used.

NORA: Yes, dear, I will. But go in now and you too, Doctor Rank. Christine, you must help me to do up my hair.

RANK (*whispers to Helmer as they go out*):   I suppose there is nothing—she is not expecting anything?

HELMER: Far from it, my dear fellow; it is simply nothing more than this childish nervousness I was telling you of. (*They go into the right-hand room.*)

NORA: Well!

MRS. LINDE: Gone out of town.

NORA: I could tell from your face.

MRS. LINDE: He is coming home to-morrow evening. I wrote a note for him.

NORA: You should have let it alone; you must prevent nothing. After all, it is splendid to be waiting for a wonderful thing to happen.

MRS. LINDE: What is it that you are waiting for?

NORA: Oh, you wouldn't understand. Go in to them, I will come in a moment. (*Mrs. Linde goes into the dining-room. Nora stands still for a little while, as if to compose herself. Then she looks at her watch.*) Five o'clock. Seven hours until midnight; and then four-and-twenty hours until the next midnight. Then the Tarantella will be over. Twenty-four and seven? Thirty-one hours to live.

HELMER (*from the doorway on the right*):   Where's my little skylark?

NORA (*going to him with her arms outstretched*):   Here she is!

ACT III

THE SAME SCENE: *The table has been placed in the middle of the stage, with chairs round it. A lamp is burning on the table. The door into the hall stands open. Dance music is heard in the room above. Mrs. Linde is sitting at the table idly turning over the leaves of a book; she tries to read, but does not seem able to collect her thoughts. Every now and then she listens intently for a sound at the outer door.*

MRS. LINDE (*looking at her watch*):   Not yet—and the time is nearly up. If only he does not—. (*Listens again.*) Ah, there he is. (*Goes into the hall and opens the outer door carefully. Light footsteps are heard on the stairs. She whispers.*) Come in. There is no one here.

KROGSTAD (*in the doorway*):   I found a note from you at home. What does this mean?

MRS. LINDE: It is absolutely necessary that I should have a talk with you.

KROGSTAD: Really? And is it absolutely necessary that it should be here?

MRS. LINDE: It is impossible where I live; there is no private entrance to my rooms. Come in; we are quite alone. The maid is asleep, and the Helmers are at the dance upstairs.

KROGSTAD (*coming into the room*):   Are the Helmers really at a dance to-night?

MRS. LINDE: Yes, why not?

KROGSTAD: Certainly—why not?

MRS. LINDE: Now, Nils, let us have a talk.

KROGSTAD: Can we two have anything to talk about?

MRS. LINDE: We have a great deal to talk about.

KROGSTAD: I shouldn't have thought so.

MRS. LINDE: No, you have never properly understood me.

KROGSTAD: Was there anything else to understand except what was obvious to all the world—a heartless woman jilts a man when a more lucrative chance turns up?

MRS. LINDE: Do you believe I am as absolutely heartless as all that? And do you believe that I did it with a light heart?

KROGSTAD: Didn't you?

MRS. LINDE: Nils, did you really think that?

KROGSTAD: If it were as you say, why did you write to me as you did at the time?

MRS. LINDE: I could do nothing else. As I had to break with you, it was my duty also to put an end to all that you felt for me.

KROGSTAD (*wringing his hands*):   So that was it. And all this—only for the sake of money!

MRS. LINDE: You must not forget that I had a helpless mother and two little brothers. We couldn't wait for you, Nils; your prospects seemed hopeless then.

KROGSTAD: That may be so, but you had no right to throw me over for anyone else's sake.

MRS. LINDE: Indeed I don't know. Many a time did I ask myself if I had the right to do it.

KROGSTAD (*more gently*):   When I lost you, it was as if all the solid ground went from under my feet. Look at me now — I am a shipwrecked man clinging to a bit of wreckage.

MRS. LINDE: But help may be near.

KROGSTAD: It *was* near; but then you came and stood in my way.

MRS. LINDE: Unintentionally, Nils. It was only to-day that I learned it was your place I was going to take in the Bank.

KROGSTAD: I believe you, if you say so. But now that you know it, are you not going to give it up to me?

MRS. LINDE: No, because that would not benefit you in the least.

KROGSTAD: Oh, benefit, benefit — I would have done it whether or no.

MRS. LINDE: I have learned to act prudently. Life, and hard, bitter necessity have taught me that.

KROGSTAD: And life has taught me not to believe in fine speeches.

MRS. LINDE: Then life has taught you something very reasonable. But deeds you must believe in?

KROGSTAD: What do you mean by that?

MRS. LINDE: You said you were like a shipwrecked man clinging to some wreckage.

KROGSTAD: I had good reason to say so.

MRS. LINDE: Well, I am like a shipwrecked woman clinging to some wreckage — no one to mourn for, no one to care for.

KROGSTAD: It was your own choice.

MRS. LINDE: There was no other choice — then.

KROGSTAD: Well, what now?

MRS. LINDE: Nils, how would it be if we two shipwrecked people could join forces?

KROGSTAD: What are you saying?

MRS. LINDE: Two on the same piece of wreckage would stand a better chance than each on their own.

KROGSTAD: Christine!

MRS. LINDE: What do you suppose brought me to town?

KROGSTAD: Do you mean that you gave me a thought?

MRS. LINDE: I could not endure life without work. All my life, as long as I can remember, I have worked, and it has been my greatest and only pleasure. But now I am quite alone in the world — my life is so dreadfully empty and I feel so forsaken. There is not the least pleasure in working for one's self. Nils, give me someone and something to work for.

KROGSTAD: I don't trust that. It is nothing but a woman's overstrained sense of generosity that prompts you to make such an offer of yourself.

MRS. LINDE: Have you ever noticed anything of the sort in me?

KROGSTAD: Could you really do it? Tell me — do you know all about my past life?

MRS. LINDE: Yes.

KROGSTAD: And do you know what they think of me here?

MRS. LINDE: You seemed to me to imply that with me you might have been quite another man.

KROGSTAD: I am certain of it.

MRS. LINDE: Is it too late now?

KROGSTAD: Christine, are you saying this deliberately? Yes, I am sure you are. I see it in your face. Have you really the courage, then — ?

MRS. LINDE: I want to be a mother to someone, and your children need a mother. We two need each other. Nils, I have faith in your real character — I can dare anything together with you.

KROGSTAD (*grasps her hands*):   Thanks, thanks, Christine! Now I shall find a way to clear myself in the eyes of the world. Ah, but I forgot —

MRS. LINDE (*listening*):   Hush! The Tarantella! Go, go!

KROGSTAD: Why? What is it?

MRS. LINDE: Do you hear them up there? When that is over, we may expect them back.

KROGSTAD: Yes, yes — I will go. But it is all no use. Of course you are not aware what steps I have taken in the matter of the Helmers.

MRS. LINDE: Yes, I know all about that.

KROGSTAD: And in spite of that have you the courage to — ?

MRS. LINDE: I understand very well to what lengths a man like you might be driven by despair.

KROGSTAD: If I could only undo what I have done!

MRS. LINDE: You cannot. Your letter is lying in the letter-box now.

KROGSTAD: Are you sure of that?

MRS. LINDE: Quite sure, but —

KROGSTAD (*with a searching look at her*):   Is that what it all means? — that you want to save your friend at any cost? Tell me frankly. Is that it?

MRS. LINDE: Nils, a woman who has once sold herself for another's sake, doesn't do it a second time.

KROGSTAD: I will ask for my letter back.

MRS. LINDE: No, no.

KROGSTAD: Yes, of course I will. I will wait here until Helmer comes; I will tell him he must give me my letter back — that it only concerns my dismissal — that he is not to read it —

MRS. LINDE: No, Nils, you must not recall your letter.

KROGSTAD: But, tell me, wasn't it for that very purpose that you asked me to meet you here?

MRS. LINDE: In my first moment of fright, it was. But twenty-four hours have elapsed since then, and in that time I have witnessed incredible things in this house. Helmer must know all about it. This unhappy secret must be disclosed; they must have a complete understanding between them, which is impossible with all this concealment and falsehood going on.

KROGSTAD: Very well, if you will take the responsibility. But there is one thing I can do in any case, and I shall do it at once.

MRS. LINDE (*listening*):   You must be quick and go! The dance is over; we are not safe a moment longer.

KROGSTAD: I will wait for you below.

MRS. LINDE: Yes, do. You must see me back to my door.

KROGSTAD: I have never had such an amazing piece of good fortune in my life! (*Goes out through the outer door. The door between the room and the hall remains open.*)

MRS. LINDE (*tidying up the room and laying her hat and cloak ready*):   What a difference! what a difference! Some-one to work for and live for — a home to bring comfort into. That I will do, indeed. I wish they would be quick and come — (*Listens.*) Ah, there they are now. I must put on my things. (*Takes up her hat and cloak. Helmer's and Nora's voices are heard outside; a key is turned, and Helmer brings Nora almost by force into the hall. She is in an Italian costume with a large black shawl around her; he is in evening dress, and a black domino° which is flying open.*)

NORA (*hanging back in the doorway, and struggling with him*):   No, no, no! — don't take me in. I want to go upstairs again; I don't want to leave so early.

HELMER: But, my dearest Nora —

NORA: Please, Torvald dear — please, *please* — only an hour more.

HELMER: Not a single minute, my sweet Nora. You know that was our agreement. Come along into the room; you are catching cold standing there. (*He brings her gently into the room, in spite of her resistance.*)

MRS. LINDE: Good-evening.

NORA: Christine!

HELMER: You here, so late, Mrs. Linde?

MRS. LINDE: Yes, you must excuse me; I was so anxious to see Nora in her dress.

NORA: Have you been sitting here waiting for me?

MRS. LINDE: Yes, unfortunately I came too late, you had already gone upstairs; and I thought I couldn't go away again without having seen you.

HELMER (*taking off Nora's shawl*):   Yes, take a good look at her. I think she is worth looking at. Isn't she charming, Mrs. Linde?

MRS. LINDE: Yes, indeed she is.

HELMER: Doesn't she look remarkably pretty? Everyone thought so at the dance. But she is terribly self-willed, this sweet little person. What are we to do with her? You will hardly believe that I had almost to bring her away by force.

NORA: Torvald, you will repent not having let me stay, even if it were only for half an hour.

HELMER: Listen to her, Mrs. Linde! She had danced her Tarantella, and it had been a tremendous success, as it deserved — although possibly the performance was a trifle too realistic — a little more so, I mean, than was strictly compatible with the limitations of art. But never mind about that! The chief thing is, she had made a success — she had made a tremendous success. Do you think I was going to let her remain there after that, and spoil the effect? No, indeed! I took my charming little Capri maiden — my capricious little Capri maiden, I should say — on my arm; took one quick turn round the room; a curtsey on either side, and, as they say in novels, the beautiful apparition disappeared. An exit ought always to be effective,

---

domino: A loose cloak, worn with a mask for the upper part of the face at masquerades.

Mrs. Linde; but that is what I cannot make Nora understand. Pooh! this room is hot. (*Throws his domino on a chair, and opens the door of his room.*) Hullo! it's all dark in here. Oh, of course — excuse me — . (*He goes in, and lights some candles.*)

NORA (*in a hurried and breathless whisper*):   Well?

MRS. LINDE (*in a low voice*):   I have had a talk with him.

NORA: Yes, and —

MRS. LINDE: Nora, you must tell your husband all about it.

NORA (*in an expressionless voice*):   I knew it.

MRS. LINDE: You have nothing to be afraid of as far as Krogstad is concerned; but you must tell him.

NORA: I won't tell him.

MRS. LINDE: Then the letter will.

NORA: Thank you, Christine. Now I know what I must do. Hush —!

HELMER (*coming in again*):   Well, Mrs. Linde, have you admired her?

MRS. LINDE: Yes, and now I will say good-night.

HELMER: What, already? Is this yours, this knitting?

MRS. LINDE (*taking it*):   Yes, thank you, I had very nearly forgotten it.

HELMER: So you knit?

MRS. LINDE: Of course.

HELMER: Do you know, you ought to embroider.

MRS. LINDE: Really? Why?

HELMER: Yes, it's far more becoming. Let me show you. You hold the embroidery thus in your left hand, and use the needle with the right — like this — with a long, easy sweep. Do you see?

MRS. LINDE: Yes, perhaps —

HELMER: But in the case of knitting — that can never be anything but un-graceful; look here — the arms close together, the knitting-needles going up and down — it has a sort of Chinese effect — . That was really excellent champagne they gave us.

MRS. LINDE: Well, — good-night, Nora, and don't be self-willed any more.

HELMER: That's right, Mrs. Linde.

MRS. LINDE: Good-night, Mr. Helmer.

HELMER (*accompanying her to the door*):   Good-night, good-night. I hope you will get home all right. I should be very happy to — but you haven't any great distance to go. Good-night, good-night. (*She goes out; he shuts the door after her, and comes in again.*) Ah! — at last we have got rid of her. She is a frightful bore, that woman.

NORA: Aren't you very tired, Torvald?

HELMER: No, not in the least.

NORA: Nor sleepy?

HELMER: Not a bit. On the contrary, I feel extraordinarily lively. And you? — you really look both tired and sleepy.

NORA: Yes, I am very tired. I want to go to sleep at once.

HELMER: There, you see it was quite right of me not to let you stay there any longer.

NORA: Everything you do is quite right, Torvald.

HELMER (*kissing her on the forehead*):   Now my little skylark is speaking reasonably. Did you notice what good spirits Rank was in this evening?

NORA: Really? Was he? I didn't speak to him at all.

HELMER: And I very little, but I have not for a long time seen him in such good form. (*Looks for a while at her and then goes nearer to her.*) It is delightful to be at home by ourselves again, to be all alone with you — you fascinating, charming little darling!

NORA: Don't look at me like that, Torvald.

HELMER: Why shouldn't I look at my dearest treasure? — at all the beauty that is mine, all my very own?

NORA (*going to the other side of the table*):   You mustn't say things like that to me to-night.

HELMER (*following her*):   You have still got the Tarantella in your blood, I see. And it makes you more captivating than ever. Listen — the guests are beginning to go now. (*In a lower voice.*) Nora — soon the whole house will be quiet.

NORA: Yes, I hope so.

HELMER: Yes, my own darling Nora. Do you know, when I am out at a party with you like this, why I speak so little to you, keep away from you, and only send a stolen glance in your direction now and then? — do you know why I do that? It is because I make believe to myself that we are secretly in love, and you are my secretly promised bride, and that no one suspects there is anything between us.

NORA: Yes, yes — I know very well your thoughts are with me all the time.

HELMER: And when we are leaving, and I am putting the shawl over your beautiful young shoulders — on your lovely neck — then I imagine that you are my young bride and that we have just come from the wedding, and I am bringing you for the first time into our home — to be alone with you for the first time — quite alone with my shy little darling! All this evening I have longed for nothing but you. When I watched the seductive figures of the Tarantella, my blood was on fire; I could endure it no longer, and that was why I brought you down so early —

NORA: Go away, Torvald! You must let me go. I won't —

HELMER: What's that? You're joking, my little Nora! You won't — you won't? Am I not your husband — ? (*A knock is heard at the outer door.*)

NORA (*starting*):   Did you hear — ?

HELMER (*going into the hall*):   Who is it?

RANK (*outside*):   It is I. May I come in for a moment?

HELMER (*in a fretful whisper*):   Oh, what does he want now? (*Aloud.*) Wait a minute! (*Unlocks the door.*) Come, that's kind of you not to pass by our door.

RANK: I thought I heard your voice, and felt as if I should like to look in. (*With a swift glance round.*) Ah, yes! — these dear familiar rooms. You are very happy and cosy in here, you two.

HELMER: It seems to me that you looked after yourself pretty well upstairs too.

RANK: Excellently. Why shouldn't I? Why shouldn't one enjoy everything in this world?—at any rate as much as one can, and as long as one can. The wine was capital—

HELMER: Especially the champagne.

RANK: So you noticed that too? It is almost incredible how much I managed to put away!

NORA: Torvald drank a great deal of champagne to-night too.

RANK: Did he?

NORA: Yes, and he is always in such good spirits afterwards.

RANK: Well, why should one not enjoy a merry evening after a well-spent day?

HELMER: Well spent? I am afraid I can't take credit for that.

RANK (*clapping him on the back*):   But I can, you know!

NORA: Doctor Rank, you must have been occupied with some scientific investigation to-day.

RANK: Exactly.

HELMER: Just listen!—little Nora talking about scientific investigations!

NORA: And may I congratulate you on the result?

RANK: Indeed you may.

NORA: Was it favourable, then?

RANK: The best possible, for both doctor and patient—certainty.

NORA (*quickly and searchingly*):   Certainty?

RANK: Absolute certainty. So wasn't I entitled to make a merry evening of it after that?

NORA: Yes, you certainly were, Doctor Rank.

HELMER: I think so too, so long as you don't have to pay for it in the morning.

RANK: Oh well, one can't have anything in this life without paying for it.

NORA: Doctor Rank—are you fond of fancy-dress balls?

RANK: Yes, if there is a fine lot of pretty costumes.

NORA: Tell me—what shall we two wear at the next?

HELMER: Little featherbrain!—are you thinking of the next already?

RANK: We two? Yes, I can tell you. You shall go as a good fairy—

HELMER: Yes, but what do you suggest as an appropriate costume for that?

RANK: Let your wife go dressed just as she is in everyday life.

HELMER: That was really very prettily turned. But can't you tell us what you will be?

RANK: Yes, my dear friend, I have quite made up my mind about that.

HELMER: Well?

RANK: At the next fancy-dress ball I shall be invisible.

HELMER: That's a good joke!

RANK: There is a big black hat—have you never heard of hats that make you invisible? If you put one on, no one can see you.

HELMER (*suppressing a smile*):   Yes, you are quite right.

RANK: But I am clean forgetting what I came for. Helmer, give me a cigar—one of the dark Havanas.

HELMER: With the greatest pleasure. (*Offers him his case.*)

RANK (*takes a cigar and cuts off the end*):   Thanks.

NORA (*striking a match*):   Let me give you a light.

RANK: Thank you. (*She holds the match for him to light his cigar.*) And now good-bye!

HELMER: Good-bye, good-bye, dear old man!

NORA: Sleep well, Doctor Rank.

RANK: Thank you for that wish.

NORA: Wish me the same.

RANK: You? Well, if you want me to sleep well! And thanks for the light. (*He nods to them both and goes out.*)

HELMER (*in a subdued voice*):   He has drunk more than he ought.

NORA (*absently*):   Maybe. (*Helmer takes a bunch of keys out of his pocket and goes into the hall.*) Torvald! what are you going to do there?

HELMER: Empty the letter-box; it is quite full; there will be no room to put the newspaper in to-morrow morning.

NORA: Are you going to work to-night?

HELMER: You know quite well I'm not. What is this? Someone has been at the lock.

NORA: At the lock—?

HELMER: Yes, someone has. What can it mean? I should never have thought the maid—. Here is a broken hairpin. Nora, it is one of yours.

NORA (*quickly*):   Then it must have been the children—

HELMER: Then you must get them out of those ways. There, at last I have got it open. (*Takes out the contents of the letter-box, and calls to the kitchen.*) Helen!—Helen, put out the light over the front door. (*Goes back into the room and shuts the door into the hall. He holds out his hand full of letters.*) Look at that—look what a heap of them there are. (*Turning them over.*) What on earth is that?

NORA (*at the window*):   The letter—No! Torvald, no!

HELMER: Two cards—of Rank's.

NORA: Of Doctor Rank's?

HELMER (*looking at them*):   Doctor Rank. They were on the top. He must have put them in when he went out.

NORA: Is there anything written on them?

HELMER: There is a black cross over the name. Look there—what an uncomfortable idea! It looks as if he were announcing his own death.

NORA: It is just what he is doing.

HELMER: What? Do you know anything about it? Has he said anything to you?

NORA: Yes. He told me that when the cards came it would be his leave-taking from us. He means to shut himself up and die.

HELMER: My poor old friend! Certainly I knew we should not have him very long with us. But so soon! And so he hides himself away like a wounded animal.

NORA: If it has to happen, it is best it should be without a word—don't you think so, Torvald?

HELMER (*walking up and down*):   He had so grown into our lives. I can't think of him as having gone out of them. He, with his sufferings and his loneliness, was like a cloudy background to our sunlit happiness. Well, perhaps it is best so. For him, anyway. (*Standing still.*) And perhaps for us too, Nora. We two are thrown quite upon each other now. (*Puts his arms round her.*) My darling wife, I don't feel as if I could hold you tight enough. Do you know, Nora, I have often wished that you might be threatened by some great danger, so that I might risk my life's blood, and everything, for your sake.

NORA (*disengages herself, and says firmly and decidedly*): Now you must read your letters, Torvald.

HELMER: No, no; not to-night. I want to be with you, my darling wife.

NORA: With the thought of your friend's death—

HELMER: You are right, it has affected us both. Something ugly has come between us—the thought of the horrors of death. We must try and rid our minds of that. Until then—we will each go to our own room.

NORA (*hanging on his neck*): Good-night, Torvald—Good-night!

HELMER (*kissing her on the forehead*): Good-night, my little singing-bird. Sleep sound, Nora. Now I will read my letters through. (*He takes his letters and goes into his room, shutting the door after him.*)

NORA (*gropes distractedly about, seizes Helmer's domino, throws it round her, while she says in quick, hoarse, spasmodic whispers*): Never to see him again. Never! Never! (*Puts her shawl over her head.*) Never to see my children again either—never again. Never! Never!—Ah! the icy, black water—the unfathomable depths—If only it were over! He has got it now—now he is reading it. Good-bye, Torvald and my children! (*She is about to rush out through the hall, when Helmer opens his door hurriedly and stands with an open letter in his hand.*)

HELMER: Nora!

NORA: Ah!—

HELMER: What is this? Do you know what is in this letter?

NORA: Yes, I know. Let me go! Let me get out!

HELMER (*holding her back*): Where are you going?

NORA (*trying to get free*): You shan't save me, Torvald!

HELMER (*reeling*): True? Is this true, that I read here? Horrible! No, no—it is impossible that it can be true.

NORA: It is true. I have loved you above everything else in the world.

HELMER: Oh, don't let us have any silly excuses.

NORA (*taking a step towards him*): Torvald—!

HELMER: Miserable creature—what have you done?

NORA: Let me go. You shall not suffer for my sake. You shall not take it upon yourself.

HELMER: No tragedy airs, please. (*Locks the hall door.*) Here you shall stay and give me an explanation. Do you understand what you have done? Answer me! Do you understand what you have done?

NORA (*looks steadily at him and says with a growing look of coldness in her face*): Yes, now I am beginning to understand thoroughly.

HELMER (*walking about the room*): What a horrible awakening! All these eight years—she who was my joy and pride—a hypocrite, a liar—worse, worse—a criminal! The unutterable ugliness of it all!—For shame!

For shame! (*Nora is silent and looks steadily at him. He stops in front of her.*) I ought to have suspected that something of the sort would happen. I ought to have foreseen it. All your father's want of principle — be silent! — all your father's want of principle has come out in you. No religion, no morality, no sense of duty —. How I am punished for having winked at what he did! I did it for your sake, and this is how you repay me.

NORA: Yes, that's just it.

HELMER: Now you have destroyed all my happiness. You have ruined all my future. It is horrible to think of! I am in the power of an unscrupulous man; he can do what he likes with me, ask anything he likes of me, give me any orders he pleases — I dare not refuse. And I must sink to such miserable depths because of a thoughtless woman!

NORA: When I am out of the way, you will be free.

HELMER: No fine speeches, please. Your father had always plenty of those ready, too. What good would it be to me if you were out of the way, as you say? Not the slightest. He can make the affair known everywhere; and if he does, I may be falsely suspected of having been a party to your criminal action. Very likely people will think I was behind it all — that it was I who prompted you! And I have to thank you for all this — you whom I have cherished during the whole of our married life. Do you understand now what it is you have done for me?

NORA (*coldly and quietly*):   Yes.

HELMER: It is so incredible that I can't take it in. But we must come to some understanding. Take off that shawl. Take it off, I tell you. I must try and appease him some way or another. The matter must be hushed up at any cost. And as for you and me, it must appear as if everything between us were just as before — but naturally only in the eyes of the world. You will still remain in my house, that is a matter of course. But I shall not allow you to bring up the children; I dare not trust them to you. To think that I should be obliged to say so to one whom I have loved so dearly, and whom I still —. No, that is all over. From this moment happiness is not the question; all that concerns us is to save the remains, the fragments, the appearance —

A ring is heard at the front-door bell.

HELMER (*with a start*):   What is that? So late! Can the worst —? Can he —? Hide yourself, Nora. Say you are ill.

Nora stands motionless. Helmer goes and unlocks the hall door.

MAID (*half-dressed, comes to the door*):   A letter for the mistress.

HELMER: Give it to me. (*Takes the letter, and shuts the door.*) Yes, it is from him. You shall not have it; I will read it myself.

NORA: Yes, read it.

HELMER (*standing by the lamp*):   I scarcely have the courage to do it. It may mean ruin for both of us. No, I must know. (*Tears open the letter, runs his eye over a few lines, looks at a paper enclosed, and gives a shout of joy.*) Nora! (*She looks at him questioningly.*) Nora! — No, I must read it once again —. Yes, it is true! I am saved! Nora, I am saved!

NORA: And I?

HELMER: You too, of course; we are both saved, both you and I. Look, he
sends you your bond back. He says he regrets and repents—that a happy
change in his life—never mind what he says! We are saved, Nora! No one
can do anything to you. Oh, Nora, Nora!—no, first I must destroy these
hateful things. Let me see—. (*Takes a look at the bond.*) No, no, I won't look
at it. The whole thing shall be nothing but a bad dream to me. (*Tears up the
bond and both letters, throws them all into the stove, and watches them burn.*)
There—now it doesn't exist any longer. He says that since Christmas Eve
you—. These must have been three dreadful days for you, Nora.

NORA: I have fought a hard fight these three days.

HELMER: And suffered agonies, and seen no way out but—. No, we won't call
any of the horrors to mind. We will only shout with joy, and keep saying,
"It's all over! It's all over!" Listen to me, Nora. You don't seem to realise
that it is all over. What is this?—such a cold, set face! My poor little Nora, I
quite understand; you don't feel as if you could believe that I have forgiven
you. But it is true, Nora, I swear it; I have forgiven you everything. I know
that what you did, you did out of love for me.

NORA: That is true.

HELMER: You have loved me as a wife ought to love her husband. Only you had
not sufficient knowledge to judge of the means you used. But do you suppose you are any the less dear to me, because you don't understand how
to act on your own responsibility? No, no; only lean on me; I will advise
you and direct you. I should not be a man if this womanly helplessness did
not just give you a double attractiveness in my eyes. You must not think
anymore about the hard things I said in my first moment of consterna-
tion, when I thought everything was going to overwhelm me. I have forgiven you, Nora; I swear to you I have forgiven you.

NORA: Thank you for your forgiveness. (*She goes out through the door to the
right.*)

HELMER: No, don't go—. (*Looks in.*) What are you doing in there?

NORA (*from within*):   Taking off my fancy dress.

HELMER (*standing at the open door*):   Yes, do. Try and calm yourself, and make
your mind easy again, my frightened little singing-bird. Be at rest, and feel
secure; I have broad wings to shelter you under. (*Walks up and down by the
door.*) How warm and cosy our home is, Nora. Here is shelter for you; here
I will protect you like a hunted dove that I have saved from a hawk's claws;
I will bring peace to your poor beating heart. It will come, little by little,
Nora, believe me. To-morrow morning you will look upon it all quite differently; soon everything will be just as it was before. Very soon you won't
need me to assure you that I have forgiven you; you will yourself feel the
certainty that I have done so. Can you suppose I should ever think of such
a thing as repudiating you, or even reproaching you? You have no idea
what a true man's heart is like, Nora. There is something so indescribably
sweet and satisfying, to a man, in the knowledge that he has forgiven his
wife—forgiven her freely, and with all his heart. It seems as if that had

made her, as it were, doubly his own; he has given her a new life, so to speak; and she has in a way become both wife and child to him. So you shall be for me after this, my little scared, helpless darling. Have no anxiety about anything, Nora; only be frank and open with me, and I will serve as will and conscience both to you—. What is this? Not gone to bed? Have you changed your things?

NORA (*in everyday dress*):   Yes, Torvald, I have changed my things now.

HELMER: But what for?—so late as this.

NORA: I shall not sleep to-night.

HELMER: But, my dear Nora—

NORA (*looking at her watch*):   It is not so very late. Sit down here, Torvald. You and I have much to say to one another. (*She sits down at one side of the table.*)

HELMER: Nora—what is this?—this cold, set face?

NORA: Sit down. It will take some time; I have a lot to talk over with you.

HELMER (*sits down at the opposite side of the table*):   You alarm me, Nora!—and I don't understand you.

NORA: No, that is just it. You don't understand me, and I have never understood you either—before to-night. No, you mustn't interrupt me. You must simply listen to what I say. Torvald, this is a settling of accounts.

HELMER: What do you mean by that?

NORA (*after a short silence*):   Isn't there one thing that strikes you as strange in our sitting here like this?

HELMER: What is that?

NORA: We have been married now eight years. Does it not occur to you that this is the first time we two, you and I, husband and wife, have had a serious conversation?

HELMER: What do you mean by serious?

NORA: In all these eight years—longer than that—from the very beginning of our acquaintance, we have never exchanged a word on any serious subject.

HELMER: Was it likely that I would be continually and forever telling you about worries that you could not help me to bear?

NORA: I am not speaking about business matters. I say that we have never sat down in earnest together to try and get at the bottom of anything.

HELMER: But, dearest Nora, would it have been any good to you?

NORA: That is just it; you have never understood me. I have been greatly wronged, Torvald—first by papa and then by you.

HELMER: What! By us two—by us two, who have loved you better than anyone else in the world?

NORA (*shaking her head*):   You have never loved me. You have only thought it pleasant to be in love with me.

HELMER: Nora, what do I hear you saying?

NORA: It is perfectly true, Torvald. When I was at home with papa, he told me his opinion about everything, and so I had the same opinions; and if I differed from him I concealed the fact, because he would not have liked it.

He called me his doll-child, and he played with me just as I used to play with my dolls. And when I came to live with you—

HELMER: What sort of an expression is that to use about our marriage?

NORA (*undisturbed*):   I mean that I was simply transferred from papa's hands into yours. You arranged everything according to your own taste, and so I got the same tastes as you—or else I pretended to, I am really not quite sure which—I think sometimes the one and sometimes the other. When I look back on it, it seems to me as if I had been living here like a poor woman—just from hand to mouth. I have existed merely to perform tricks for you, Torvald. But you would have it so. You and papa have committed a great sin against me. It is your fault that I have made nothing of my life.

HELMER: How unreasonable and how ungrateful you are, Nora! Have you not been happy here?

NORA: No, I have never been happy. I thought I was, but it has never really been so.

HELMER: Not—not happy!

NORA: No, only merry. And you have always been so kind to me. But our home has been nothing but a playroom. I have been your doll-wife, just as at home I was papa's doll-child; and here the children have been my dolls. I thought it great fun when you played with me, just as they thought it great fun when I played with them. That is what our marriage has been, Torvald.

HELMER: There is some truth in what you say—exaggerated and strained as your view of it is. But for the future it shall be different. Playtime shall be over, and lesson-time shall begin.

NORA: Whose lessons? Mine, or the children's?

HELMER: Both yours and the children's, my darling Nora.

NORA: Alas, Torvald, you are not the man to educate me into being a proper wife for you.

HELMER: And you can say that!

NORA: And I—how am I fitted to bring up the children?

HELMER: Nora!

NORA: Didn't you say so yourself a little while ago—that you dare not trust me to bring them up?

HELMER: In a moment of anger! Why do you pay any heed to that?

NORA: Indeed, you were perfectly right. I am not fit for the task. There is another task I must undertake first. I must try and educate myself—you are not the man to help me in that. I must do that for myself. And that is why I am going to leave you now.

HELMER (*springing up*):   What do you say?

NORA: I must stand quite alone, if I am to understand myself and everything about me. It is for that reason that I cannot remain with you any longer.

HELMER: Nora, Nora!

NORA: I am going away from here now, at once. I am sure Christine will take me in for the night—

HELMER: You are out of your mind! I won't allow it! I forbid you!

NORA: It is no use forbidding me anything any longer. I will take with me what belongs to myself. I will take nothing from you, either now or later.

HELMER: What sort of madness is this!

NORA: To-morrow I shall go home — I mean, to my old home. It will be easiest for me to find something to do there.

HELMER: You blind, foolish woman!

NORA: I must try and get some sense, Torvald.

HELMER: To desert your home, your husband and your children! And you don't consider what people will say!

NORA: I cannot consider that at all. I only know that it is necessary for me.

HELMER: It's shocking. This is how you would neglect your most sacred duties.

NORA: What do you consider my most sacred duties?

HELMER: Do I need to tell you that? Are they not your duties to your husband and your children?

NORA: I have other duties just as sacred.

HELMER: That you have not. What duties could those be?

NORA: Duties to myself.

HELMER: Before all else, you are a wife and a mother.

NORA: I don't believe that any longer. I believe that before all else I am a reasonable human being, just as you are — or, at all events, that I must try and become one. I know quite well, Torvald, that most people would think you right, and that views of that kind are to be found in books; but I can no longer content myself with what most people say, or with what is found in books. I must think over things for myself and get to understand them.

HELMER: Can you not understand your place in your own home? Have you not a reliable guide in such matters as that? — have you no religion?

NORA: I am afraid, Torvald, I do not exactly know what religion is.

HELMER: What are you saying?

NORA: I know nothing but what the clergyman said, when I went to be confirmed. He told us that religion was this, and that, and the other. When I am away from all this, and am alone, I will look into that matter too. I will see if what the clergyman said is true, or at all events if it is true for me.

HELMER: This is unheard of in a girl of your age! But if religion cannot lead you aright, let me try and awaken your conscience. I suppose you have some moral sense? Or — answer me — am I to think you have none?

NORA: I assure you, Torvald, that is not an easy question to answer. I really don't know. The thing perplexes me altogether. I only know that you and I look at it in quite a different light. I am learning, too, that the law is quite another thing from what I supposed; but I find it impossible to convince myself that the law is right. According to it a woman has no right to spare her old dying father, or to save her husband's life. I can't believe that.

HELMER: You talk like a child. You don't understand the conditions of the world in which you live.

NORA: No, I don't. But now I am going to try. I am going to see if I can make out who is right, the world or I.

HELMER: You are ill, Nora; you are delirious; I almost think you are out of your mind.

NORA: I have never felt my mind so clear and certain as to-night.

HELMER: And is it with a clear and certain mind that you forsake your husband and your children?

NORA: Yes, it is.

HELMER: Then there is only one possible explanation.

NORA: What is that?

HELMER: You do not love me anymore.

NORA: No, that is just it.

HELMER: Nora!—and you can say that?

NORA: It gives me great pain, Torvald, for you have always been so kind to me, but I cannot help it. I do not love you any more.

HELMER (*regaining his composure*):   Is that a clear and certain conviction too?

NORA: Yes, absolutely clear and certain. That is the reason why I will not stay here any longer.

HELMER: And can you tell me what I have done to forfeit your love?

NORA: Yes, indeed I can. It was to-night, when the wonderful thing did not happen; then I saw you were not the man I had thought you.

HELMER: Explain yourself better. I don't understand you.

NORA: I have waited so patiently for eight years; for, goodness knows, I knew very well that wonderful things don't happen every day. Then this horrible misfortune came upon me; and then I felt quite certain that the wonderful thing was going to happen at last. When Krogstad's letter was lying out there, never for a moment did I imagine that you would consent to accept this man's conditions. I was so absolutely certain that you would say to him: Publish the thing to the whole world. And when that was done—

HELMER: Yes, what then?—when I had exposed my wife to shame and disgrace?

NORA: When that was done, I was so absolutely certain, you would come forward and take everything upon yourself, and say: I am the guilty one.

HELMER: Nora—!

NORA: You mean that I would never have accepted such a sacrifice on your part? No, of course not. But what would my assurances have been worth against yours? That was the wonderful thing which I hoped for and feared; and it was to prevent that, that I wanted to kill myself.

HELMER: I would gladly work night and day for you, Nora—bear sorrow and want for your sake. But no man would sacrifice his honour for the one he loves.

NORA: It is a thing hundreds of thousands of women have done.

HELMER: Oh, you think and talk like a heedless child.

NORA: Maybe. But you neither think nor talk like the man I could bind myself to. As soon as your fear was over—and it was not fear for what threatened me, but for what might happen to you—when the whole thing was past, as far as you were concerned it was exactly as if nothing at all had happened. Exactly as before, I was your little skylark, your doll, which you would in future treat with doubly gentle care, because it was so brittle and fragile. (*Getting up.*) Torvald—it was then it dawned upon me that for eight years I had been living here with a strange man, and had borne him three children—. Oh, I can't bear to think of it! I could tear myself into little bits!

HELMER (*sadly*):   I see, I see. An abyss has opened between us—there is no denying it. But, Nora, would it not be possible to fill it up?

NORA: As I am now, I am no wife for you.

HELMER: I have it in me to become a different man.

NORA: Perhaps—if your doll is taken away from you.

HELMER: But to part!—to part from you! No, no, Nora, I can't understand that idea.

NORA (*going out to the right*):   That makes it all the more certain that it must be done. (*She comes back with her cloak and hat and a small bag which she puts on a chair by the table.*)

HELMER: Nora, Nora, not now! Wait until to-morrow.

NORA (*putting on her cloak*):   I cannot spend the night in a strange man's room.

HELMER: But can't we live here like brother and sister—?

NORA (*putting on her hat*):   You know very well that would not last long. (*Puts the shawl round her.*) Good-bye, Torvald. I won't see the little ones. I know they are in better hands than mine. As I am now, I can be of no use to them.

HELMER: But some day, Nora—some day?

NORA: How can I tell? I have no idea what is going to become of me.

HELMER: But you are my wife, whatever becomes of you.

NORA: Listen, Torvald. I have heard that when a wife deserts her husband's house, as I am doing now, he is legally freed from all obligations towards her. In any case, I set you free from all your obligations. You are not to feel yourself bound in the slightest way, any more than I shall. There must be perfect freedom on both sides. See, here is your ring back. Give me mine.

HELMER: That too?

NORA: That too.

HELMER: Here it is.

NORA: That's right. Now it is all over. I have put the keys here. The maids know all about everything in the house—better than I do. To-morrow, after I have left her, Christine will come here and pack up my own things that I brought with me from home. I will have them sent after me.

HELMER: All over! All over!—Nora, shall you never think of me again?

NORA: I know I shall often think of you, the children, and this house.

HELMER: May I write to you, Nora?

NORA: No—never. You must not do that.

HELMER: But at least let me send you—

NORA: Nothing—nothing—

HELMER: Let me help you if you are in want.

NORA: No. I can receive nothing from a stranger.

HELMER: Nora—can I never be anything more than a stranger to you?

NORA (*taking her bag*):   Ah, Torvald, the most wonderful thing of all would have to happen.

HELMER: Tell me what that would be!

NORA: Both you and I would have to be so changed that — . Oh, Torvald, I don't believe any longer in wonderful things happening.

HELMER: But I will believe in it. Tell me! So changed that —?

NORA: That our life together would be a real wedlock. Good-bye. (*She goes out through the hall.*)

HELMER (*sinks down on a chair at the door and buries his face in his hands*):   Nora! Nora! (*Looks round, and rises.*) Empty. She is gone. (*A hope flashes across his mind.*) The most wonderful thing of all —?

The sound of a door shutting is heard from below.   [1879]

≣ THINKING ABOUT THE TEXT

1. Critics disagree about the necessity for Nora's leaving. How would you advise her? One critic thinks she has to leave because Torvald is impossible. What do you think?

2. Do you find the change in Nora's character from the first scene to the last credible? Do you know people who have been transformed?

3. Is Torvald in love with Nora in the first act? Explain. Is Nora in love with him in the first act? What is your idea of love in a marriage?

4. An early critic of the play claims that it is a comedy. Is this possible? How would you characterize it? Is it an optimistic or a pessimistic play? Is it tragic?

5. A few critics think Nora will return. Do you think this is possible? Under what conditions would you counsel her to do so? Do you think the "door heard 'round the world" had a positive or a negative effect on marriage?

AUGUST STRINDBERG
Woman in *A Doll's House*

August Strindberg (1849–1912), one of the most celebrated writers in Swedish literature, was born in Stockholm and described his childhood as subject to "emotional insecurity, poverty, religious fanaticism and neglect." Strindberg is known primarily as a naturalist playwright. Miss Julie *(1888) and* The Stronger *(1889) are his most famous dramas. Eugene O'Neill, in his Nobel Prize acceptance speech, said Strindberg was "that greatest genius of all modern dramatists." Strindberg had a troubled relationship with women, and some critics see him as misogynistic. The following essay was written as a preface to* Getting Married *(1884), a collection of stories. Some critics believe Strindberg was furious with Ibsen for encouraging "the new woman of the nineteenth century to focus on the injustices of marriage in a male-dominant society."*

Let us now take a look at how, for some unknown and incomprehensible reason, Ibsen has caricatured the cultured man and woman in his play *A Doll's House*, which has become the gospel of all the zealots for the Woman Question.

A Doll's House is a play. Perhaps it was written for a great actress whose performance of a sphinx-like part could be guaranteed to be a success. The author has done the husband a great injustice. He has done nothing to help him by making excuses for him on the grounds of inherited characteristics, as he has for his wife, and the excuses he makes for her he presses home over and over again when he talks about her father. But let us carefully examine this Nora, whom all our depraved cultured women have adopted as their ideal.

In the first act she lies to her husband. She conceals her forgery, she smuggles away some cakes, she behaves shiftily over all kinds of simple matters, apparently because she has a taste for lying. Her husband, on the other hand, openly confides everything to her, even the affairs of his Bank, which shows that he treats her as his true wife. She, not he, is the one who never tells anything. It is consequently a lie to say that he treats her like a doll, but true to say that she treats him like one. Surely no one believes that Nora did not know what she was doing when she committed forgery? Perhaps when they sit in the stalls and see an appealing actress in the footlights. I do not believe myself that she committed forgery *exclusively* for her husband's sake, for she tells us herself how tremendously she enjoyed their journey to Italy. No law, and no lawyer would accept that as an excuse. Thus we see that Nora is no saint; at best she is an accomplice who has also enjoyed the fruits of the theft. She incriminates herself. The author unintentionally gives her husband a further opportunity of showing how much he trusts and respects his wife when he lets him discuss with Nora the question of filling a vacancy at the Bank. But what a tyrant he is when he refuses to engage a forger as Head Clerk! What would Nora have said if Mr. Helmer had wanted to dismiss a maid? That would have been a very different story.

Then comes the scene in which she wants to borrow money from the syphilitic Dr. Rank. Nora really is sweet in this scene. As a prelude to her negotiations about the money she shows him her flesh-colored stockings.

> *Nora:* "Aren't they pretty? Of course it's dark in here now, but tomorrow. — No no, no, you're only allowed to see the feet. Oh well, I'll let you see the upper part too!"
>
> *Rank:* "Hm!"
>
> *Nora:* "Why are you looking so disapproving? Don't you think they'll suit me?"
>
> *Rank:* "I'm not qualified to express an opinion on that subject."
>
> *Nora:* (looks at him for a moment) "Shame on you!" (strikes him lightly on the ear with the stockings). "Take this then!" (Packs up the stockings.)
>
> *Rank:* "What are the other delights I'm to be allowed to see?"
>
> *Nora:* "You're so naughty I shan't let you see another thing." (She hums a little and looks for something in the box.)

As far as I can see Nora is offering herself — in return for hard cash. That   5
is idealistic and charming, of course. All done out of love for her husband.

To save him! But go to her husband and confess her dilemma, oh no, that would be too much for her pride! In Nora's language: she was not yet quite certain that he would respond by showing her the miracle of miracles.

Then comes the tarantella scene, which is introduced in order to throw a distorting light upon Helmer. The audience forgets that Nora is a hussy whom Helmer treats as a sensible woman, and is only allowed to see Helmer treating her *merely* as a doll. This is a dishonest scene, but it is very effective. In a word: it is good *theatre*.

That Helmer woos his wife that night simply shows that he is young, and that she is young. But the author makes it show that Helmer — who has not the least suspicion of the dirty game that Nora is playing — is nothing more than a sensual creature, sensual through and through, who has no appreciation whatever of his excellent wife's spiritual qualities, which she has not deigned to reveal, and this gives Nora a false halo of martyrdom. This is the most dishonest scene that Ibsen has ever written. After it comes the dénouement, which is a fine muddle, with a great deal of misrepresentation and many lies. Mr. Helmer wakes up, and finds that the wife to whom he is bound is a liar and a hypocrite. But the audience has been so impregnated with compassion for Nora that it thinks Helmer is wrong. If Helmer had witnessed the scene with the stockings he would not have begged Nora to stay, but of course he had not. Helmer learns that he, his wife, and his children have escaped social death and ruin. This makes him happy. Put your hand on your heart, you father of a family, and ask yourself if you would not be happy if you heard that your beloved wife, the mother of your children, was not going to be put into prison after all. But these feelings are too mundane. You must reach higher. Right up to the idealist's heaven of lies. Helmer must be chastised. He is the criminal. Yet all the same he speaks kindly to his deceitful wife. — "Oh," he says, "these must have been three dreadful days for you, Nora." But then the author regrets having been fair to the poor fellow, and puts some untrue words into his mouth. Of course it is clumsy of Helmer to tell Nora that he forgives her. And for her to accept forgiveness from one who has always trusted her, while she has lied to him would be far too simple-minded. No, Nora has grander ideas. She is so magnanimous about forgetting the past that she forgets everything that happened in the first act. This is what she now says, and the stalls have forgotten the first act too, for their handkerchiefs are out.

> *Nora:* "Doesn't it occur to you that this is the first time that we two, husband and wife, have talked seriously to one another?"

Helmer is so taken aback by this mendacious question that he (or the author!) answers: "Seriously — what do you mean by seriously?" — The author has achieved his object, Helmer has been made to look a fool. He should have answered: "No, my little pet, it doesn't occur to me at all. We talked very seriously together when our children were born, for we talked about their future. We talked very seriously when you wanted to install the forger, Krogstad, as head clerk in the Bank. We talked very seriously when my life was in danger, and about giving Mrs. Linde a job, and about running the house, and about your dead father, and our syphilitic friend Dr. Rank. We have talked seriously for eight long years, but we have joked too, and we were right to do so, for life isn't only a serious business. We could indeed have had more serious talk if you'd been kind enough to tell me of your worries, but you were too proud, for you preferred to be my doll rather than my friend." But Mr. Ibsen does not allow Helmer to say these sensible things, for he must be shown to be a fool, and Nora must be allowed her most brilliant answer, which will be quoted for twenty-five years. This is her reply:

> *Nora:* "For eight (8!) long years — why longer — from the very first time we met, we have never exchanged a serious word on a serious matter."

—But now, true to his unfortunate role of fool, Mr. Helmer answers: "Would you have liked me to be forever telling you of problems that you wouldn't have been able to help me with?" It is kind of Helmer to say this, but it is not honest, for he should have turned on her for not confiding in him. This scene is absurdly false. After it Nora has some very fine (French) replies, which consist of such hollow wisdom that they vanish when you blow at them.

> *Nora:* "You have never loved me. You have only thought it amusing to be in love with me!"

What is the difference? She also says: "You have never understood me!"   10
Not an easy thing for Helmer to do as she has always deceived him. Then poor Helmer is made to say some very stupid things, like: "I'm going to edu-cate you." That is surely the last thing a man should say to a woman. But Mr. Helmer must be stupid, for the end is drawing near, and Nora is going to "turn the screw." At that Helmer weakens. He begs for forgiveness; forgiveness because she has committed forgery, because she has lied, for all her faults.

Then Nora says a few sensible things. She wants to give up her marriage in order to find herself. The question is whether she could not do that just as well in the same house as her children, in contact with the realities of life, and while struggling with her love for Helmer, for her love will not die instanta-neously any more than any other love. But this is a question of taste. When she says that she is unfit to bring up her children she is lying, for not long before she had put herself on a pretty high pedestal when castigating the innocent Helmer. To be logical she ought to have stayed with her children if she really thought her husband was such a dolt that he would not be able to grasp the "miracle." For how could she leave the education of her children to such a poor specimen? All her babbling about the "miracle" that would have happened if Helmer had taken the blame for her crime upon himself is such romantic nonsense that it does not deserve discussion. That "hundreds of thousands of women" have sacrificed themselves for their husbands is a compliment to the ladies that Ibsen should be too old to pay. Nora rambles on pell-mell: she has loved him, he has loved her, and yet she can say that for eight years she has been a stranger to him, and borne three children to a man who has been a stranger to her. Helmer agrees that he has not been perfect, and promises to reform. This is handsome of him and there seems to be every guarantee that things will be better in the future than they have been in the past. But of course this will not do in a play. The curtain must come down on a Bang. So Nora proves (?) that she has been a doll. Had it not been Helmer who decided where the furniture should stand? Maybe. But if only the mistress of the house had deigned to make her wishes known there would have been no doubt about who was the master.

Why did she not do so? Probably because she thought it did not matter, and she may have been right. If Nora was a doll, then upon my word it was not Helmer's fault, for he had always shown that he trusted her as a man should trust his wife. But this was not what Ibsen wanted to prove, he wanted to prove the opposite, but he was not strong enough to do so, for he did not believe in his task, and his sense of justice broke through from time to time.

What its author himself really meant by *A Doll's House* we shall never know. The fact that it gave the impression of being, and was generally accepted as a manifesto for the oppressed woman, immediately raised a storm in which the steadiest people lost their heads. For the play proves the direct opposite of what it is intended to prove. Or is it that the whole play is a proof of the danger of writing plays on serious subjects? Or, to take another point of view altogether: is it in fact *not* a defense of the oppressed woman, but simply an illustration of the effect of heredity upon character? If this is the case then the author should have been honorable enough to give Helmer's heredity as an excuse for his behavior. Or is it Nora's bad upbringing? She herself places a lot of the blame on this. Why then cannot Helmer blame his bad upbringing? Or is it nothing more than a play, pure and simple, an example of our modern courtship of the ladies? If so it should be put among the plays classed as "Public Entertainments," and not be regarded as a matter for serious discussion, still less have the honor of setting the two halves of humanity against each other.   *[1884]*

≣ THINKING ABOUT THE TEXT

1. What specific evidence is there that Strindberg might be a misogynist?

2. Point out instances of Strindberg's sarcasm and irony.

3. What are some specific complaints Strindberg has against Nora? Do you think they are valid?

EMMA GOLDMAN
Review of *A Doll's House*

Emma Goldman (1869–1940), a leading radical activist, thinker, and writer in the first half of the twentieth century, was born in Russia and immigrated to the United States in 1885. She agitated passionately for women's and workers' rights. She was deported to Russia in 1919 for being an anarchist but left, eventually becoming a British citizen. She began the radical journal Mother Earth *and wrote influential books such as* Anarchism and Other Essays *(1910) and* The Social Significance of the Modern Drama *(1914), from which the following selection is taken.*

In *A Doll's House*, Ibsen returns to the subject so vital to him — the Social Lie and Duty — this time as manifesting themselves in the sacred institution of the home and in the position of woman in her gilded cage.

Nora is the beloved, adored wife of *Torvald Helmer*. He is an admirable man, rigidly honest, of high moral ideals, and passionately devoted to his wife and children. In short, a good man and an enviable husband. Almost every mother would be proud of such a match for her daughter, and the latter would consider herself fortunate to become the wife of such a man.

Nora, too, considers herself fortunate. Indeed, she worships her husband, believes in him implicitly, and is sure that if ever her safety should be menaced, *Torvald*, her idol, her god, would perform the miracle.

When a woman loves as *Nora* does, nothing else matters; least of all, social, legal, or moral considerations. Therefore, when her husband's life is threatened, it is no effort, it is joy for *Nora* to forge her father's name to a note and borrow 800 cronen on it, in order to take her sick husband to Italy.

In her eagerness to serve her husband, and in perfect innocence of the legal aspect of her act, she does not give the matter much thought, except for her anxiety to shield him from any emergency that may call upon him to perform the miracle in her behalf. She works hard, and saves every penny of her pin-money to pay back the amount she borrowed on the forged check.   5

Nora is light-hearted and gay, apparently without depth. Who, indeed, would expect depth of a doll, a "squirrel," a song-bird? Her purpose in life is to be happy for her husband's sake, for the sake of the children; to sing, dance, and play with them. Besides, is she not shielded, protected, and cared for? Who, then, would suspect *Nora* of depth? But already in the opening scene, when *Torvald* inquires what his precious "squirrel" wants for a Christmas present, *Nora* quickly asks him for money. Is it to buy macaroons or finery? In her talk with *Mrs. Linde*, *Nora* reveals her inner self, and forecasts the inevitable debacle of her doll's house.

After telling her friend how she had saved her husband, Nora says: "When Torvald gave me money for clothes and so on, I never used more than half of it; I always bought the simplest things. . . . Torvald never noticed anything. But it was often very hard, Christina dear. For it's nice to be beautifully dressed. Now, isn't it? . . . Well, and besides that, I made money in other ways. Last winter I was so lucky — I got a heap of copying to do. I shut myself up every evening and wrote far into the night. Oh, sometimes I was so tired, so tired. And yet it was splendid to work in that way and earn money. I almost felt as if I was a man."

Down deep in the consciousness of *Nora* there evidently slumbers personality and character, which could come into full bloom only through a great miracle — not the kind *Nora* hopes for, but a miracle just the same.

Nora had borrowed the money from *Nils Krogstad*, a man with a shady past in the eyes of the community and of the righteous moralist, *Torvald Helmer*. So long as *Krogstad* is allowed the little breathing space a Christian people grants to him who has once broken its laws, he is reasonably human. He does not molest *Nora*. But when *Helmer* becomes director of the bank in which *Krogstad* is employed, and threatens the man with dismissal, *Krogstad* naturally fights back. For as he says to *Nora*: "If need be, I shall fight as though for my life to keep my little place in the bank. . . . It's not only for the money: that matters least to me. It's something else. Well, I'd better make a clean breast of it. Of course you know, like every one else, that some years ago I — got into trouble. . . . The matter never came into court; but from that moment all paths were barred to me. Then I took up the business you know about. I was obliged to grasp at something; and I don't think I've been one of the worst. But now I must clear out of it all. My sons are growing up; for their sake I must try to win back as much respectability as I can. This place in the bank was the first step, and now your husband wants to kick me off the ladder, back into the mire. Mrs. Helmer, you evidently have no idea what you have really done. But I can assure you that it was nothing more and nothing worse that made me an outcast from society. . . . But this I may tell you, that if I'm flung into the gutter a second time, you shall keep me company."

Even when *Nora* is confronted with this awful threat, she does not fear   10
for herself, only for *Torvald* — so good, so true, who has such an aversion to debts, but who loves her so devotedly that for her sake he would take the blame upon himself. But this must never be. *Nora*, too, begins a fight for life, for her husband's life and that of her children. Did not *Helmer* tell her that the very presence of a criminal like *Krogstad* poisons the children? And is she not a criminal?

Torvald Helmer assures her, in his male conceit, that "early corruption generally comes from the mother's side, but of course the father's influence may act in the same way. And this Krogstad has been poisoning his own children for years past by a life of lies and hypocrisy — that's why I call him morally ruined."

Poor *Nora*, who cannot understand why a daughter has no right to spare her dying father anxiety, or why a wife has no right to save her husband's life, is surely not aware of the true character of her idol. But gradually the veil is lifted. At first, when in reply to her desperate pleading for *Krogstad*, her husband discloses the true reason for wanting to get rid of him: "The fact is, he was a college chum of mine — there was one of those rash friendships between us that one so often repents later. I don't mind confessing it — he calls me by my Christian name; and he insists on doing it even when others are present. He delights in putting on airs of familiarity — Torvald here, Torvald there! I assure you it's most painful to me. He would make my position at the bank perfectly unendurable."

And then again when the final blow comes. For forty-eight hours *Nora* battles for her ideal, never doubting *Torvald* for a moment. Indeed, so absolutely sure is she of her strong oak, her lord, her god, that she would rather kill herself than have him take the blame for her act. The end comes, and with it the doll's house tumbles down, and *Nora* discards her doll's dress — she sheds her skin, as it were. *Torvald Helmer* proves himself a petty Philistine, a bully and a coward, as so many good husbands when they throw off their respectable cloak.

Helmer's rage over *Nora*'s crime subsides the moment the danger of publicity is averted — proving that *Helmer*, like many a moralist, is not so much incensed at *Nora*'s offense as by the fear of being found out. Not so *Nora*. Finding out is her salvation. It is then that she realizes how much she has been wronged, that she is only a plaything, a doll to *Helmer*. In her disillusionment she says, "You have never loved me. You only thought it amusing to be in love with me. [. . .] I think that before all else I am a human being, just as much as you are—or, at least, I will try to become one. I know that most people agree with you, Torvald, and that they say so in books. But henceforth I can't be satisfied with what most people say, and what is in books. I must think things out for myself and try to get clear about them. . . . I had been living here these eight years with a strange man, and had borne him three children—Oh! I can't bear to think of it—I could tear myself to pieces!. . . . I can't spend the night in a strange man's house."

Is there anything more degrading to woman than to live with a stranger, and bear him children? Yet, the lie of the marriage institution decrees that she shall continue to do so, and the social conception of duty insists that for the sake of that lie she need be nothing else than a plaything, a doll, a nonentity.

When *Nora* closes behind her the door of her doll's house, she opens wide the gate of life for woman, and proclaims the revolutionary message that only perfect freedom and communion make a true bond between man and woman, meeting in the open, without lies, without shame, free from the bondage of duty.   *[1914]*

15

≣ THINKING ABOUT THE TEXT

1. What idea of Nora's does Goldman seem most impressed by?
2. What is Goldman's view of moralists? What does Nora mean by "a strange man"?
3. What specifically do you think Goldman meant in 1914 when referring to "the bondage of duty" (para. 16)?

JOAN TEMPLETON
From *"The* Doll House *Backlash: Criticism, Feminism, and Ibsen"*

Joan Templeton (b. 1942) received her undergraduate degree at Centenary College and her Ph.D. from the University of Oregon. She is a noted Ibsen scholar who has published widely on the dramatist and others. Her books include Ibsen's Women *(1997) and* Munch's Ibsen *(2008). She taught for many years at Long Island University, where she was professor of English and comparative literature. The following selection is from "The* Doll House *Backlash: Criticism, Feminism, and Ibsen," published in* PMLA *in 1989. Interestingly, most of the critics she cites as attacking Nora are men who wrote in an era when feminist thinking was largely disparaged.*

For over a hundred years, Nora has been under direct siege as exhibiting the most perfidious characteristics of her sex; the original outcry of the 1880s is swollen now to a mighty chorus of blame. She is denounced as an irrational and frivolous narcissist; an "abnormal" woman, a "hysteric"; a vain, unloving egoist who abandons her family in a paroxysm of selfishness. The proponents of the last view would seem to think Ibsen had in mind a housewife Medea, whose cruelty to husband and children he tailored down to fit the framed, domestic world of realist drama.

The first attacks were launched against Nora on moral grounds and against Ibsen, ostensibly, on "literary" ones. The outraged reviewers of the premiere claimed that *A Doll House* did not have to be taken as a serious statement about women's rights because the heroine of act 3 is an incomprehensible transformation of the heroine of acts 1 and 2. This reasoning provided an ideal way to dismiss Nora altogether; nothing she said needed to be taken seriously, and her door slamming could be written off as silly theatrics (Marker and Marker 85–87).

The argument for the two Noras, which still remains popular,[1] has had its most determined defender in the Norwegian scholar Else Høst, who argues that Ibsen's carefree, charming "lark" could never have become the "newly fledged feminist." In any case it is the "childish, expectant, ecstatic, broken-hearted Nora" who makes A Doll House immortal (28; my trans.); the other one, the unfeeling woman of act 3 who coldly analyzes the flaws in her marriage, is psychologically unconvincing and wholly unsympathetic.

The most unrelenting attempt on record to trivialize Ibsen's protagonist, and a favorite source for Nora's later detractors, is Hermann Weigand's.[2] In a classic 1925 study, Weigand labors through forty-nine pages to demonstrate that Ibsen conceived of Nora as a silly, lovable female. At the beginning, Weigand confesses, he was, like all men, momentarily shaken by the play: "Having had the misfortune to be born of the male sex, we slink away in shame, vowing to mend our ways." The chastened critic's remorse is short-lived, however, as a "clear male voice, irreverently breaking the silence," stuns with its critical acumen: " 'The meaning of the final scene,' the voice says, 'is epitomized by Nora's remark: "Yes, Torvald. Now I have changed my dress." ' " With this epiphany as guide, Weigand spends the night poring over the "little volume." Dawn arrives, bringing with it the return of "masculine self-respect" (26–27). For there is only one explanation for the revolt of "this winsome little woman" (52) and her childish door slamming: Ibsen meant *A Doll House* as comedy. Nora's erratic behavior at the curtain's fall leaves us laughing heartily, for there is no doubt that she will return home to "revert, imperceptibly, to her role of song-bird and charmer" (68). After all, since Nora is

---

[1] See, for example, Robert Brustein (49) and Marvin Rosenberg, whose article is a rehash of Høst's points, although Rosenberg seems unacquainted with her well-known essay.
[2] For a thoroughgoing defense of Weigand by a much later critic who understands that "A Doll House is not a feminist play," see R. F. Dietrich.

an irresistibly bewitching piece of femininity, an extravagant poet and romancer, utterly lacking in sense of fact, and endowed with a natural gift for play-acting which makes her instinctively dramatize her experiences: how can the settlement fail of a fundamentally comic appeal? (64)

The most popular way to render Nora inconsequential has been to attack   5
her morality; whatever the vocabulary used, the arguments have remained much the same for over a century. Oswald Crawford, writing in the *Fortnightly Review* in 1891, scolded that while Nora may be "charming as doll-women may be charming," she is "unprincipled" (732). A half century later, after Freudianism had produced a widely accepted "clinical" language of disapproval, Nora could be called "abnormal." Mary McCarthy lists Nora as one of the "neurotic" women whom Ibsen, she curiously claims, was the first playwright to put on stage (80). For Maurice Valency, Nora is a case study of female hysteria, a willful, unwomanly woman: "Nora is a carefully studied example of what we have come to know as the hysterical personality — bright, unstable, impulsive, romantic, quite immune from feelings of guilt, and, at bottom, not especially feminine" (151–52).

More recent assaults on Nora have argued that her forgery to obtain the money to save her husband's life proves her irresponsibility and egotism. Brian Johnston condemns Nora's love as "unintelligent" and her crime as "a trivial act which nevertheless turns to evil because it refused to take the universal ethical realm into consideration at all" (97); Ibsen uses Torvald's famous pet names for Nora — lark, squirrel — to give her a "strong 'animal' identity" and to underscore her inability to understand the ethical issues faced by human beings (97). Evert Sprinchorn argues that Nora had only to ask her husband's kindly friends (entirely missing from the play) for the necessary money: ". . . any other woman would have done so. But Nora knew that if she turned to one of Torvald's friends for help, she would have had to share her role of savior with someone else" (124).

Even Nora's sweet tooth is evidence of her unworthiness, as we see her "surreptitiously devouring the forbidden [by her husband] macaroons," even "brazenly offer[ing] macaroons to Doctor Rank, and finally lying in her denial that the macaroons are hers"; eating macaroons in secret suggests that "Nora is deceitful and manipulative from the start" and that her exit thus "reflects only a petulant woman's irresponsibility" (Schlueter 64–65). As she eats the cookies, Nora adds insult to injury by declaring her hidden wish to say "death and damnation" in front of her husband, thus revealing, according to Brian Downs, of Christ's College, Cambridge, "something a trifle febrile and morbid" in her nature (Downs 130).

Much has been made of Nora's relationship with Doctor Rank, the surest proof, it is argued, of her dishonesty. Nora is revealed as *la belle dame sans merci* when she "suggestively queries Rank whether a pair of silk stockings will fit her" (Schlueter 65); she "flirts cruelly with [him] and toys with his affection for her, drawing him on to find out how strong her hold over him actually is" (Sprinchorn 124).

Nora's detractors have often been, from the first, her husband's defenders. In an argument that claims to rescue Nora and Torvald from "the campaign for the liberation of women" so that they "become vivid and disturbingly real," Evert Sprinchorn pleads that Torvald "has given Nora all the material things and all the sexual attention that any young wife could reasonably desire. He loves beautiful things, and not least his pretty wife" (121). Nora is incapable of appreciating her husband because she "is not a normal woman. She is compulsive, highly imaginative, and very much inclined to go to extremes." Since it is she who has acquired the money to save his life, Torvald, and not Nora, is really the "wife in the family," although he "has regarded himself as the breadwinner . . . the main support of his wife and children, as any decent husband would like to regard himself" (122). In another defense, John Chamberlain argues that Torvald deserves our sympathy because he is no "mere common or garden chauvinist." If Nora were less the actress Weigand has proved her to be, "the woman in her might observe what the embarrassingly naive feminist overlooks or ignores, namely, the indications that Torvald, for all his faults, is taking her at least as seriously as he can — and perhaps even as seriously as she deserves" (85).

All female, or no woman at all, Nora loses either way. Frivolous, deceitful, or unwomanly, she qualifies neither as a heroine nor as a spokeswoman for feminism. Her famous exit embodies only "the latest and shallowest notion of emancipated womanhood, abandoning her family to go out into the world in search of 'her true identity' " (Freedman 4). And in any case, it is only naive Nora who believes she might make a life for herself; "the audience," argues an essayist in *College English*, "can see most clearly how Nora is exchanging a practical doll's role for an impractical one" (Pearce 343). We are back to the high condescension of the Victorians and Edward Dowden: 10

> Inquires should be set on foot to ascertain whether a manuscript may not lurk in some house in Christiania [Oslo] entitled *Nora Helmer's Reflections in Solitude*; it would be a document of singular interest, and probably would conclude with the words, "Tomorrow I return to Torvald; have been exactly one week away; shall insist on a free woman's right to unlimited macaroons as test of his reform."   (248)

In the first heady days of *A Doll House* Nora was rendered powerless by substituted denouements and sequels that sent her home to her husband. Now Nora's critics take the high-handed position that all the fuss was unnecessary, since Nora is not a feminist heroine. And yet in the twentieth-century case against her, whether Nora is judged childish, "neurotic," or unprincipled and whether her accuser's tone is one of witty derision, clinical sobriety, or moral earnestness, the purpose behind the verdict remains that of Nora's frightened contemporaries: to destroy her credibility and power as a representative of women. The demon in the house, the modern "half-woman," as Strindberg called her in the preface to *Miss Julie*, who, "now that she has been discovered has begun to make a noise" (65), must be silenced, her heretical forces destroyed, so that *A Doll House* can emerge a safe classic, rescued from feminism, and Ibsen can assume his place in the pantheon of true artists, unsullied by the "woman question" and the topical taint of history.   *[1989]*

Works Cited

Brustein, Robert. *The Theatre of Revolt*. Little Brown, 1962.

Chamberlain, John. *Ibsen: The Open Vision*. Athlone, 1982.

Crawfurd, Oswald. "The Ibsen Question." *Fortnightly Review*, vol. 55, 1891, pp. 727–40.

Dietrich, R. F. "Nora's Change of Dress: Weigand Revisited." *Theatre Annual*, no. 36, 1981, pp. 20–40.

Dowden, Edward. "Henrik Ibsen." *The Works of Henrik Ibsen*, vol. 13, Scribner's, 1912, pp. 218–58.

Downs, Brian. *A Study of Six Plays by Ibsen*. 1959. Octagon, 1978.

Freedman, Morris. *The Moral Impulse: Modern Drama from Ibsen to the Present*. Southern Illinois UP, 1967.

Høst, Else. "Nora." *Edda*, no. 46, 1946, pp. 13–48.

Ibsen, Henrik. *Ibsens Samlede Verker*. Vol. 3, Gyldendal, 1978.

———. *The Works of Henrik Ibsen*. Edited and translated by William Archer, Scribner's, 1912.

Johnston, Brian. *The Ibsen Cycle*. G.K. Hall, 1975.

Marker, Frederick, and Lisa-Lone Marker. "The First Nora: Notes on the World Premiere of *A Doll's House*." *Ibsenårboken*, vol 11, 1970–71, pp. 84–100.

McCarthy, Mary. "The Will and Testament of Ibsen." *Partisan Review*, vol 23, 1956, pp. 74–80.

Pearce, Richard. "The Limits of Realism." *College English*, vol. 31, 1970, pp. 335–43.

Rosenberg, Marvin. "Ibsen versus Ibsen: Or, Two Versions of *A Doll House*." *Modern Drama*, vol. 12, 1969, pp. 187–96.

Schlueter, June. "How to Get into *A Doll House*: Ibsen's Play as an Introduction to Drama." *Approaches to Teaching Ibsen's* A Doll House, edited by Yvonne Shafer, Modern Language Association, 1985, pp. 63–68.

Sprinchorn, Evert. "Ibsen and the Actors." *Ibsen and the Theatre*. Edited by Errol Durbach, New York UP, 1980, pp. 118–30.

Strindberg, August. "Author's Foreword to *Miss Julie*." *Six Plays of Strindberg*, translated by Elizabeth Sprigge, Doubleday, 1955, pp. 61–73.

Valency, Maurice. *The Flower and the Castle: An Introduction to Modern Drama*. (1963), Schocken, 1982.

Weigand, Hermann. *The Modern Ibsen: A Reconsideration*. Holt, 1925.

≡ THINKING ABOUT THE TEXT

1. What is your response to the Weigand block quote (para. 4)?

2. Templeton argues that critics, mostly men, wanted to make the play "a safe classic" (para. 10). How might our selection support the claim?

3. Explain why one of these critics seems to you to be misguided.

SUSANNA RUSTIN

Why *A Doll's House* by Henrik Ibsen Is More Relevant than Ever

Susanna Rustin (b. 1971) is a feature writer and editor for the Guardian. *She grew up in London and studied at York University. She is active in local politics, having run for the Green Party ticket.*

When, next Wednesday evening, Hattie Morahan picks up an armful of Christmas shopping and steps on stage to open a run of Ibsen's *A Doll's House*, it will be for the third time in just over a year. Morahan first starred as Nora, the 1870s Norwegian wife and mother who realizes her life is a sham, at the Young Vic last July, but such is the production's popularity that this is its second revival. Moreover, two other, brand new productions have been seen in recent months: in May an adaptation by Bryony Lavery received rave reviews at the Royal Exchange in Manchester, and in April Zinnie Harris's version, set in Edwardian London and first seen at the Donmar Warehouse in London with Gillian Anderson in the lead role, was staged by the National Theatre of Scotland in Edinburgh.

Three such high-profile productions in the space of a few months is unusual. Morahan has already won the *Evening Standard* and Critics' Circle awards for her performance and was unlucky to miss out to Helen Mirren at the Oliviers. But the combination of the play's brisk and thriller-like plotting, and the sense shared by everyone involved that the play still speaks to audiences in ways that feel fresh and interesting, means there is no fear of overkill.

In fact, Morahan, speaking to me just before Thursday's dress rehearsal, says she feels "liberated" to be occupying the role again, while director Carrie Cracknell says that even the last few days of rehearsals have thrown up new insights into Ibsen's endlessly complex characters. "There is something timeless about it," Morahan says, "which is what's so shocking. You try to keep it in its box of 19th-century Scandinavia, but the things Ibsen writes mean it ceases to be about a particular milieu and becomes about marriage (or partnership) and money. These are universal anxieties, and it seems from talking to people that it resonates in the most visceral way, especially if they are or have been in a difficult relationship. Someone said to me the other night, 'That's the play that broke my parents' marriage up.' It shines a very harsh light on the messy heart of relationships, and how difficult it can be to be honest with another human being even if you love them."

The play, hugely controversial when first published and performed in Copenhagen in 1879, is about the unravelling of a family. Nora and Torvald Helmer believe they are happily married and on the brink of a blissful new phase of life: Torvald has been promoted to bank manager and their money worries are over. But Nora has a secret debt, incurred with good intentions and a forged signature, and with her husband's new power comes the threat of blackmail.

Over three acts the illusion of bourgeois contentment unravels, and the   5
play culminates in a spectacular scene between the couple as Nora's lie is
exposed and Torvald first blames, then forgives her—and is finally abandoned
as Nora recognizes the truth of her situation. She accuses her husband, and
her father before him, of having used her as a doll, and declares herself unfit to
be a wife or mother until she has learned to be herself. Ibsen's final stage direction, of the door closing behind her, is one of the most famous ever written.

Unsurprisingly, feminist contemporaries of Ibsen welcomed the play,
although, as theatre critic Caroline McGinn points out, when he was invited
to speak at a women's congress, he told them he wasn't a feminist himself. The
first German production notoriously altered the ending so that Nora did not
leave home, when leading woman Hedwig Niemann-Raabe refused to act the
part as written, an amendment Ibsen later described as "a barbaric outrage."
In the century and more since, the play and the role of Nora have taken on
iconic status; Unesco's Memory of the World register calls Nora "a symbol
throughout the world, for women fighting for liberation and equality."

She is also a symbol for female actors, both of what is possible and of how
much they still have to fight for, when most plays and films still feature more
male than female characters and work famously dries up for older women
unless they are among a lucky handful of national treasures. Cush Jumbo,
star of the Royal Exchange's production, says "it's a role a lot of actresses have
on their list—if they have a wish list—because it's a very challenging part.
It's Ibsen's Rosalind [the heroine of Shakespeare's *As You Like It*], I suppose.
You never leave the stage and the journey she goes on is epic."

"I would compare it to *Hamlet*," says Morahan, whose interpretation has
been described as a career-changing breakthrough. Janet McTeer experienced a
similar effect two decades ago when her tempestuous, 6ft Nora, deeply in love with
her husband and completely broken by his betrayal, won plaudits in London and
then on Broadway, where the *New York Times* theatre critic Ben Brantley called
McTeer's "the single most compelling performance I have ever seen."

McTeer's take on the play was to sweep away some of the feminist baggage it carried—it doesn't work for Torvald's "sweet little skylark" to suddenly
turn into Emily Pankhurst,° she decided—and to treat it as the story not of a
woman, but of a marriage. Anthony Page, who directed, says "she was very
unexpected casting, being tall and strong-looking, but it heightened the idiocy
of the false identity she was living under. She had a wonderful way of playing
it very naturalistically, and she and Owen Teale [as Torvald] were playing off
each other. Sometimes it got a bit out of hand. They were throwing chairs at
each other, which had to be stopped, but they were remarkable."

But it is hard to ignore the play's strong feminist resonances in a culture   10
where it is blindingly obvious that any woman who puts herself in the public eye will become a target for abuse. Some complain that social media have
given misogynists—such as those who have been in the news this week
after threatening the MP Stella Creasy, or sending death threats to female

Emily Pankhurst: Militant Victorian activist.

journalists — a platform they don't deserve. Others argue they have simply revealed a woman-hating streak that has always been with us. Either way, it seems difficult to deny that virulent prejudice against women and the pressure on them to behave in certain ways still exist. Ibsen himself wrote in a note on his work-in-progress that women can't be themselves in an "exclusively male society, with laws made by men and with prosecutors and judges who assess feminine conduct from a masculine standpoint" — which felt startlingly pertinent when I read it shortly after learning of the male prosecutor and judge who this week labeled a 13-year-old child a sexual predator and suspended the prison sentence of the 41-year-old man convicted of abusing her.

Which is why some of the current generation of women acting, directing, and adapting *A Doll's House* have sought to reassert its feminist credentials. Director Carrie Cracknell made a short film that imagined Nora as an overstretched modern mother, her life a nightmare of spilled porridge, missed appointments, and hurriedly applied makeup. She says working on the play made her acutely aware of the ideas about gender that shaped her parenting of her two young children. "We live in a culture in which the way we represent women is becoming narrower. I think we have a generation of women growing up who understand that power is linked to how we look."

But all those I spoke to agree that the central dilemma the play presents, of how to be yourself and true to yourself, while being married and being a parent, is not exclusive to women. "In a sense," says Caroline McGinn, "Nora's famous dramatic exit [leaving home and children to work and pursue self-fulfilment] is something many parents do five days a week."

And perhaps this is the play's most radical aspect: that it presents a woman's dilemma as a human dilemma, relevant to both sexes, when so often women's stories are treated as a special subject of concern only to women (evidence of which can be seen everywhere in culture, from the small number of men who read books by and about women to the girl-heavy audience for the RSC's smash-hit musical *Matilda*, when there is no equivalent gender bias at *Charlie and the Chocolate Factory* down the road).

"I feel really strongly that we still obsess around male protagonists," Cracknell says. "There's a thousands-of-years-long legacy of storytelling in which men have been the protagonists — we go back to telling their stories over and over." McGinn says *A Doll's House* remains thrilling as a critic because "you go to new plays all the time where the ratio of men to women is 80/20."

Jumbo, who is currently starring in her own play about the singer Josephine Baker at the Bush Theatre in London, also acted in Phyllida Lloyd's all-female production of Julius Caesar earlier this year and found "it opened people's minds to the idea that it's not that there aren't any roles for us, it's that plays aren't produced in that way. Quite a lot of the time you are the minority sex in a cast, because most stories that are told are male-driven. So it's a case of telling more women-driven stories, or being open to casting things in different ways."

Or, as Zinnie Harris puts it: "Nora's departure started a journey, and it's incumbent on us to keep going." *[2013]*

15

≡ THINKING ABOUT THE TEXT

1. What does Rustin think the most radical aspect of the play is? What do you think of her evidence? Can you give other examples?

2. In your experience, is the Cracknell quote (para. 14) right about the ratio of men to women being 80/20 in films and TV shows?

3. Why do you think this play is so enduringly popular?

≡ WRITING ABOUT ISSUES

1. The feminist thinker and activist Gloria Steinem writes about the "big click," a kind of epiphany, a moment when a woman realizes her true position in a patriarchal society. Write an essay that uses Steinem's idea to argue that Nora's transformation in act 3 is realistic or not.

2. In her review, Rustin claims that the most radical aspect of the play is that a woman's dilemma is treated as a human dilemma rather than as an exclusively women's concern. She claims that this is not usually the case. Write an essay that agrees or disagrees with this position, offering support from popular culture, including films and TV shows.

3. Argue that Nora will or will not return.

4. Write an essay that argues that *A Doll's House* is or is not still relevant today.

≡ RESEARCHING THE ISSUES

1. Research the reviews of the 1973 film adaptation of *A Doll's House* (Jane Fonda as Nora) and argue that Ibsen would or would not be pleased by them.

2. Research the status of women in marriage in the 1870s in Norway and America, including acceptable gender roles, and argue that Ibsen's play is realistic or an exaggeration of the situation.

3. Read the complete *PMLA* essay by Joan Templeton and argue that most of the men cited are misguided or not.

CHAPTER 12

Crime and Justice

Thinking about literature involves people making judgments about other people's views. Throughout your course, you have been making judgments as you interpret and evaluate written works, including the texts in this book and those produced by your class. You have been deciding also how you feel about positions expressed by your teacher and classmates. In all these acts of judgment, you have considered where you stand on general issues of aesthetics, ethics, politics, religion, and law.

Outside school, you judge things all the time, though you may not always be aware that you are doing so. You may be more conscious of your judgments when other people disagree with you, when you face multiple options, when you are trying to understand something complex, when your decisions will have significant consequences, or when you must review an act you have already committed. Some people are quite conscious that they make judgments because they have the political, professional, or institutional authority to enforce their will. Of course, these people may wind up being judged by whomever they dominate, and they may even face active revolt.

A term closely related to *judgment* is *justice*, which many people associate with judgments that are wise, fair, and sensitive to the parties involved. In this sense, justice is an ideal, which may not always be achieved in real life. Indeed, though communities hope their police departments and courts will act soundly, sometimes representatives of our legal institutions are accused of violating justice instead of upholding it. Much, of course, depends on how *justice* is defined in any particular case, and equally crucial is who defines it. The same is true of the word *crime*. Many works of literature have challenged laws of the society in which they were written, while others have questioned or complicated the notions of justice prevailing in their culture. Often, literature has probed the complexities of situations that in real life are resolved as clear victories for one particular party. In this respect, literature draws attention to issues that we may normally oversimplify or overlook.

This chapter begins by juxtaposing Nathaniel Hawthorne's famous tale, "Young Goodman Brown," with modern-day stories by Toni Cade Bambara and Ha Jin that focus on the psychological effects of people confronting injustice. Poems of racial injustice, both titled "Incident," by Countee Cullen and Natasha Trethewey follow. How to define *justice* — especially with respect to conditions for workers — is a dominant question in the subsequent cluster: a pair of poems by William Blake and Deborah Garrison. Then we present two stories that remind us that secret crimes often involve guilt that is its own punishment. The next cluster features the poems of Langston Hughes, who repeatedly asked his society to treat African Americans more justly. Two plays about resisting injustice, Sophocles' *Antigone* and Ida Fink's *The Table*, are paired. Our Literature and Current Issues cluster focuses on Hafizah Geter's poem "Testimony," with three arguments on the issue of racial injustice. The last two clusters focus on criminal activities that seem to go unpunished. The first features Flannery O'Connor's story "A Good Man Is Hard to Find," along with critical commentaries on it; the second highlights Joyce Carol Oates's well-known story "Where Are You Going, Where Have You Been?," along with texts that help situate the work in cultural context.

NATHANIEL HAWTHORNE, "Young Goodman Brown"

TONI CADE BAMBARA, "The Lesson"

HA JIN, "Saboteur"

Much fiction depicts characters learning about injustice they had not been aware of before. They move from relative innocence to knowledge of corruption. Moreover, they must now figure out what to do about the wrongdoing they have found. They must also decide how, in general, they will live in a world where virtue mixes with vice. The title character of Nathaniel Hawthorne's classic tale "Young Goodman Brown" comes to believe that his New England community is satanic, and therefore he grows alienated from it. But does he thereby become excessively self-righteous? In Toni Cade Bambara's modern-day story "The Lesson," the narrator is an African American girl who must decide what to think when a woman of her race tries to teach her that whites monopolize society's wealth. In our third story, "Saboteur," the main character, Mr. Chiu, is the victim of police injustice. He finds himself helpless, frustrated, and angry. But injustice often has unintended consequences for the perpetrators. And at the story's end, the title of Jin's tale demonstrates just such an ironic consequence.

≡ BEFORE YOU READ

In his memoir *Fatheralong* (1994), John Edgar Wideman notes that his father's attitude toward society differs from that of his late mother. "The first rule of my father's world," Wideman writes, "is that you stand alone. Alone, alone, alone. . . . Accept the bottom line, icy clarity, of the one thing you can rely on: nothing" (50). On the other hand, "My mother's first rule was love. She refused to believe she was alone. *Be not dismayed, what e'er betides / God will take care of you*" (51). What were you taught about society as you were growing up? What specific messages were you given about it by your parents or the people who raised you? How did they convey these messages to you?

NATHANIEL HAWTHORNE
Young Goodman Brown

Nathaniel Hawthorne (1804–1864) was born in Salem, Massachusetts, into a family that was founded by New England's Puritan colonists. This lineage troubled Hawthorne, especially because his ancestor John Hathorne was involved as a judge in the Salem witch trials. After graduating from Maine's Bowdoin College in 1825, Hawthorne returned to Salem and began his career as a writer. In 1832, he self-published his first novel, Fanshawe, *but considered it an artistic as well as a commercial failure and tried to destroy all unsold copies of it. He was more successful with his 1832 short-story collection* Twice-Told Tales *(reprinted and enlarged in 1842). In the early 1840s, Hawthorne worked as a surveyor in the Boston Custom House, briefly joined the utopian community of Brook Farm, and then moved to Concord, Massachusetts. There he published several children's books and lived with his wife, Sophia, in writer Ralph Waldo Emerson's former home, the Old Manse. In 1846, he produced a second collection of short stories,* Mosses from an Old Manse. *For the next three years, Hawthorne worked in a custom house in his hometown of Salem before publishing his most famous analysis of Puritan culture,* The Scarlet Letter *(1850). Later novels included* The House of the Seven Gables *(1851),* The Blithedale Romance *(an 1852 satire on Brook Farm), and* The Marble Faun *(1860). When his friend Franklin Pierce became president of the United States, Hawthorne served as American consul in Liverpool, England, for four years and then traveled in Italy for two more. At his death in 1864, he was already highly respected as a writer. Much of his fiction deals with conflicted characters whose hearts and souls are torn by sin, guilt, pride, and isolation. Indeed, his good friend Herman Melville, author of* Moby-Dick, *praised "the power of blackness" he found in Hawthorne's works. The allegorical story "Young Goodman Brown" is an especially memorable example of this power. Hawthorne wrote the tale in 1835 and later included it in* Mosses from an Old Manse.

Young Goodman Brown came forth at sunset into the street at Salem village; but put his head back, after crossing the threshold, to exchange a parting kiss with his young wife. And Faith, as the wife was aptly named, thrust her own pretty head into the street, letting the wind play with the pink ribbons of her cap while she called to Goodman Brown.

"Dearest heart," whispered she, softly and rather sadly, when her lips were close to his ear, "prithee put off your journey until sunrise and sleep in your own bed to-night. A lone woman is troubled with such dreams and such thoughts that she's afeared of herself sometimes. Pray tarry with me this night, dear husband, of all nights in the year."

"My love and my Faith," replied young Goodman Brown, "of all nights in the year, this one night must I tarry away from thee. My journey, as thou callest it, forth and back again, must needs be done 'twixt now and sunrise. What, my sweet, pretty wife, dost thou doubt me already, and we but three months married?"

"Then God bless you!" said Faith, with the pink ribbons; "and may you find all well when you come back."

"Amen!" cried Goodman Brown. "Say thy prayers, dear Faith, and go to   5
bed at dusk, and no harm will come to thee."

So they parted; and the young man pursued his way until, being about to turn the corner by the meeting-house, he looked back and saw the head of Faith still peeping after him with a melancholy air, in spite of her pink ribbons.

"Poor little Faith!" thought he, for his heart smote him. "What a wretch am I to leave her on such an errand! She talks of dreams, too. Methought as she spoke there was trouble in her face, as if a dream had warned her what work is to be done to-night. But no, no; 't would kill her to think it. Well, she's a blessed angel on earth, and after this one night I'll cling to her skirts and follow her to heaven."

With this excellent resolve for the future, Goodman Brown felt himself justified in making more haste on his present evil purpose. He had taken a dreary road, darkened by all the gloomiest trees of the forest, which barely stood aside to let the narrow path creep through, and closed immediately behind. It was all as lonely as could be; and there is this peculiarity in such a solitude, that the traveller knows not who may be concealed by the innumerable trunks and the thick boughs overhead; so that with lonely footsteps he may yet be passing through an unseen multitude.

"There may be a devilish Indian behind every tree," said Goodman Brown to himself; and he glanced fearfully behind him as he added, "What if the devil himself should be at my very elbow!"

His head being turned back, he passed a crook of the road, and, looking forward again, beheld the figure of a man, in grave and decent attire, seated   10 at the foot of an old tree. He arose at Goodman Brown's approach and walked onward side by side with him.

"You are late, Goodman Brown," said he. "The clock of the Old South was striking as I came through Boston, and that is full fifteen minutes agone."

"Faith kept me back a while," replied the young man, with a tremor in his voice, caused by the sudden appearance of his companion, though not wholly unexpected.

It was now deep dusk in the forest, and deepest in that part of it where these two were journeying. As nearly as could be discerned, the second traveller was about fifty years old, apparently in the same rank of life as Goodman Brown, and bearing a considerable resemblance to him, though perhaps more in expression than features. Still they might have been taken for father and son. And yet, though the elder person was as simply clad as the younger, and as simple in manner too, he had an indescribable air of one who knew the world, and who would not have felt abashed at the governor's dinner table or in King William's court, were it possible that his affairs should call him thither. But the only thing about him that could be fixed upon as remarkable was his staff, which bore the likeness of a great black snake, so curiously wrought that it might almost be seen to twist and wriggle itself like a living serpent. This, of course, must have been an ocular deception, assisted by the uncertain light.

"Come, Goodman Brown," cried his fellow-traveller, "this is a dull pace for the beginning of a journey. Take my staff, if you are so soon weary."

"Friend," said the other, exchanging his slow pace for a full stop, "having   15 kept covenant by meeting thee here, it is my purpose now to return whence I came. I have scruples touching the matter thou wot'st of."

"Sayest thou so?" replied he of the serpent, smiling apart. "Let us walk on, nevertheless, reasoning as we go; and if I convince thee not thou shalt turn back. We are but a little way in the forest yet."

"Too far! too far!" exclaimed the goodman, unconsciously resuming his walk. "My father never went into the woods on such an errand, nor his father before him. We have been a race of honest men and good Christians since the days of the martyrs; and shall I be the first of the name of Brown that ever took this path and kept" —

"Such company, thou wouldst say," observed the elder person, interpreting his pause. "Well said, Goodman Brown! I have been as well acquainted with your family as with ever a one among the Puritans; and that's no trifle to say. I helped your grandfather, the constable, when he lashed the Quaker woman so smartly through the streets of Salem; and it was I that brought your father a pitch-pine knot, kindled at my own hearth, to set fire to an Indian village, in King Philip's war.° They were my good friends, both; and many a pleasant walk have we had along this path, and returned merrily after midnight. I would fain be friends with you for their sake."

"If it be as thou sayest," replied Goodman Brown, "I marvel they never spoke of these matters; or, verily, I marvel not, seeing that the least rumor of the sort would have driven them from New England. We are a people of prayer, and good works to boot, and abide no such wickedness."

"Wickedness or not," said the traveller with the twisted staff, "I have a very   20
general acquaintance here in New England. The deacons of many a church have drunk the communion wine with me; the selectmen of divers towns make me their chairman; and a majority of the Great and General Court are firm sup-porters of my interest. The governor and I, too—But these are state secrets."

"Can this be so?" cried Goodman Brown, with a stare of amazement at his undisturbed companion. "Howbeit, I have nothing to do with the governor and council; they have their own ways, and are no rule for a simple husband-man like me. But, were I to go on with thee, how should I meet the eye of that good old man, our minister, at Salem village? Oh, his voice would make me tremble both Sabbath day and lecture day."

Thus far the elder traveller had listened with due gravity; but now burst into a fit of irrepressible mirth, shaking himself so violently that his snake-like staff actually seemed to wriggle in sympathy.

"Ha! ha! ha!" shouted he again and again; then composing himself, "Well, go on, Goodman Brown, go on; but, prithee, don't kill me with laughing."

"Well, then, to end the matter at once," said Goodman Brown, consider-ably nettled, "there is my wife, Faith. It would break her dear little heart; and I'd rather break my own."

"Nay, if that be the case," answered the other, "e'en go thy ways, Goodman   25
Brown. I would not for twenty old women like the one hobbling before us that Faith should come to any harm."

As he spoke he pointed his staff at a female figure on the path, in whom Goodman Brown recognized a very pious and exemplary dame, who had taught him his catechism in youth, and was still his moral and spiritual adviser, jointly with the minister and Deacon Gookin.

King Philip's war: King Philip, a Wampanoag chief, waged a bloody war against the New England colonists from 1675 to 1676.

"A marvel, truly that Goody Cloyse should be so far in the wilderness at nightfall," said he. "But with your leave, friend, I shall take a cut through the woods until we have left this Christian woman behind. Being a stranger to you, she might ask whom I was consorting with and whither I was going."

"Be it so," said his fellow-traveller. "Betake you to the woods, and let me keep the path."

Accordingly the young man turned aside, but took care to watch his companion, who advanced softly along the road until he had come within a staff's length of the old dame. She, meanwhile, was making the best of her way, with singular speed for so aged a woman, and mumbling some indistinct words — a prayer, doubtless — as she went. The traveller put forth his staff and touched her withered neck with what seemed the serpent's tail.

"The devil!" screamed the pious old lady.   30

"Then Goody Cloyse knows her old friend?" observed the traveller, confronting her and leaning on his writhing stick.

"Ah, forsooth, and is it your worship indeed?" cried the good dame. "Yea, truly is it, and in the very image of my old gossip, Goodman Brown, the grandfather of the silly fellow that now is. But — would your worship believe it? — my broomstick hath strangely disappeared, stolen, as I suspect, by that unhanged witch, Goody Cory, and that, too, when I was all anointed with the juice of smallage, and cinquefoil, and wolf's bane" —

"Mingled with fine wheat and the fat of a new-born babe," said the shape of old Goodman Brown.

"Ah, your worship knows the recipe," cried the old lady, cackling aloud. "So, as I was saying, being all ready for the meeting, and no horse to ride on, I made up my mind to foot it; for they tell me there is a nice young man to be taken into communion to-night. But now your good worship will lend me your arm, and we shall be there in a twinkling."

"That can hardly be," answered her friend. "I may not spare you my arm,   35
Goody Cloyse; but here is my staff, if you will."

So saying, he threw it down at her feet, where, perhaps, it assumed life, being one of the rods which its owner had formerly lent to the Egyptian magi. Of this fact, however, Goodman Brown could not take cognizance. He had cast up his eyes in astonishment, and, looking down again, beheld neither Goody Cloyse nor the serpentine staff, but his fellow-traveller alone, who waited for him as calmly as if nothing had happened.

"That old woman taught me my catechism," said the young man; and there was a world of meaning in this simple comment.

They continued to walk onward, while the elder traveller exhorted his companion to make good speed and persevere in the path, discoursing so aptly that his arguments seemed rather to spring up in the bosom of his auditor than to be suggested by himself. As they went, he plucked a branch of maple to serve for a walking stick, and began to strip it of the twigs and little boughs, which were wet with evening dew. The moment his fingers touched them they became strangely withered and dried up as with a week's sunshine. Thus the pair proceeded, at a good free pace, until suddenly, in a gloomy hollow of the road, Goodman Brown sat himself down on the stump of a tree and refused to go any farther.

"Friend," he said, stubbornly, "my mind is made up. Not another step will I budge on this errand. What if a wretched old woman do choose to go to the devil when I thought she was going to heaven: is that any reason why I should quit my dear Faith and go after her?"

"You will think better of this by and by," said his acquaintance, composedly. "Sit here and rest yourself a while; and when you feel like moving again, there is my staff to help you along."   40

Without more words, he threw his companion the maple stick, and was as speedily out of sight as if he had vanished into the deepening gloom. The young man sat a few moments by the roadside, applauding himself greatly, and thinking with how clear a conscience he should meet the minister in his morning walk, nor shrink from the eye of good old Deacon Gookin. And what calm sleep would be his that very night, which was to have been spent so wickedly, but so purely and sweetly now, in the arms of Faith! Amidst these pleasant and praiseworthy meditations, Goodman Brown heard the tramp of horses along the road, and deemed it advisable to conceal himself within the verge of the forest, conscious of the guilty purpose that had brought him thither, though now so happily turned from it.

On came the hoof tramps and the voices of the riders, two grave old voices, conversing soberly as they drew near. These mingled sounds appeared to pass along the road, within a few yards of the young man's hiding-place; but, owing doubtless to the depth of the gloom at that particular spot, neither the travellers nor their steeds were visible. Though their figures brushed the small boughs by the wayside, it could not be seen that they intercepted, even for a moment, the faint gleam from the strip of bright sky athwart which they must have passed. Goodman Brown alternately crouched and stood on tiptoe, pulling aside the branches and thrusting forth his head as far as he durst without discerning so much as a shadow. It vexed him the more, because he could have sworn, were such a thing possible, that he recognized the voices of the minister and Deacon Gookin, jogging along quietly, as they were wont to do, when bound to some ordination or ecclesiastical council. While yet within hearing, one of the riders stopped to pluck a switch.

"Of the two, reverend sir," said the voice like the deacon's, "I had rather miss an ordination dinner than to-night's meeting. They tell me that some of our community are to be here from Falmouth and beyond, and others from Connecticut and Rhode Island, besides several of the Indian powwows, who, after their fashion, know almost as much deviltry as the best of us. Moreover, there is a goodly young woman to be taken into communion."

"Mighty well, Deacon Gookin!" replied the solemn old tones of the minister. "Spur up, or we shall be late. Nothing can be done, you know, until I get on the ground."

The hoofs clattered again; and the voices, talking so strangely in the empty   45
air, passed on through the forest, where no church had ever been gathered or solitary Christian prayed. Whither, then, could these holy men be journeying

so deep into the heathen wilderness? Young Goodman Brown caught hold of a tree for support, being ready to sink down on the ground, faint and overburdened with the heavy sickness of his heart. He looked up to the sky, doubting whether there really was a heaven above him. Yet there was the blue arch, and the stars brightening in it.

"With heaven above and Faith below, I will yet stand firm against the devil!" cried Goodman Brown.

While he still gazed upward into the deep arch of the firmament and had lifted his hands to pray, a cloud, though no wind was stirring, hurried across the zenith and hid the brightening stars. The blue sky was still visible, except directly overhead, where this black mass of cloud was sweeping swiftly northward. Aloft in the air, as if from the depths of the cloud, came a confused and doubtful sound of voices. Once the listener fancied that he could distinguish the accents of towns-people of his own, men and women, both pious and ungodly, many of whom he had met at the communion table, and had seen others rioting at the tavern. The next moment, so indistinct were the sounds, he doubted whether he had heard aught but the murmur of the old forest, whispering without a wind. Then came a stronger swell of those familiar tones, heard daily in the sunshine at Salem village, but never until now from a cloud of night. There was one voice, of a young woman, uttering lamentations, yet with an uncertain sorrow, and entreating for some favor, which, perhaps, it would grieve her to obtain; and all the unseen multitude, both saints and sinners, seemed to encourage her onward.

"Faith!" shouted Goodman Brown, in a voice of agony and desperation; and the echoes of the forest mocked him, crying, "Faith! Faith!" as if bewildered wretches were seeking her all through the wilderness.

The cry of grief, rage, and terror was yet piercing the night, when the unhappy husband held his breath for a response. There was a scream, drowned immediately in a louder murmur of voices, fading into far-off laughter, as the dark cloud swept away, leaving the clear and silent sky above Goodman Brown. But something fluttered lightly down through the air and caught on the branch of a tree. The young man seized it, and beheld a pink ribbon.

"My Faith is gone!" cried he after one stupefied moment. "There is no good   50
on earth; and sin is but a name. Come, devil; for to thee is this world given."

And, maddened with despair, so that he laughed loud and long, did Goodman Brown grasp his staff and set forth again, at such a rate that he seemed to fly along the forest path rather than to walk or run. The road grew wilder and drearier and more faintly traced, and vanished at length, leaving him in the heart of the dark wilderness, still rushing onward with the instinct that guides mortal man to evil. The whole forest was peopled with frightful sounds — the creaking of the trees, the howling of wild beasts, and the yell of Indians; while sometimes the wind tolled like a distant church bell, and sometimes gave a broad roar around the traveller, as if all Nature were laughing him to scorn. But he was himself the chief horror of the scene, and shrank not from its other horrors.

"Ha! ha! ha!" roared Goodman Brown when the wind laughed at him. "Let us hear which will laugh loudest. Think not to frighten me with your deviltry.

Come witch, come wizard, come Indian powwow, come devil himself, and here comes Goodman Brown. You may as well fear him as he fear you."

In truth, all through the haunted forest there could be nothing more frightful than the figure of Goodman Brown. On he flew among the black pines, brandishing his staff with frenzied gestures, now giving vent to an inspiration of horrid blasphemy, and now shouting forth such laughter as set all the echoes of the forest laughing like demons around him. The fiend in his own shape is less hideous than when he rages in the breast of man. Thus sped the demoniac on his course, until, quivering among the trees, he saw a red light before him, as when the felled trunks and branches of a clearing have been set on fire, and throw up their lurid blaze against the sky, at the hour of midnight. He paused, in a lull of the tempest that had driven him onward, and heard the swell of what seemed a hymn, rolling solemnly from a distance with the weight of many voices. He knew the tune; it was a familiar one in the choir of the village meeting-house. The verse died heavily away, and was lengthened by a chorus, not of human voices, but of all the sounds of the benighted wilderness pealing in awful harmony together. Goodman Brown cried out, and his cry was lost to his own ear by its unison with the cry of the desert.

In the interval of silence he stole forward until the light glared full upon his eyes. At one extremity of an open space, hemmed in by the dark wall of the forest, arose a rock, bearing some rude, natural resemblance either to an altar or a pulpit, and surrounded by four blazing pines, their tops aflame, their stems untouched, like candles at an evening meeting. The mass of foliage that had overgrown the summit of the rock was all on fire, blazing high into the night and fitfully illuminating the whole field. Each pendent twig and leafy festoon was in a blaze. As the red light arose and fell, a numerous congregation alternately shone forth, then disappeared in shadow, and again grew, as it were, out of the darkness, peopling the heart of the solitary woods at once.

"A grave and dark-clad company," quoth Goodman Brown.

55

In truth they were such. Among them, quivering to and fro between gloom and splendor, appeared faces that would be seen next day at the council board of the province, and others which, Sabbath after Sabbath, looked devoutly heavenward, and benignantly over the crowded pews, from the holiest pulpits in the land. Some affirm that the lady of the governor was there. At least there were high dames well known to her, and wives of honored husbands, and widows, a great multitude, and ancient maidens, all of excellent repute, and fair young girls, who trembled lest their mothers should espy them. Either the sudden gleams of light flashing over the obscure field bedazzled Goodman Brown, or he recognized a score of the church members of Salem village famous for their especial sanctity. Good old Deacon Gookin had arrived, and waited at the skirts of that venerable saint, his revered pastor. But, irreverently consorting with these grave, reputable, and pious people, these elders of the church, these chaste dames and dewy virgins, there were men of dissolute lives and women of spotted fame, wretches given over to all mean and filthy vice, and suspected even of horrid crimes. It was strange to see that the good shrank not from the wicked, nor were the sinners abashed by the saints. Scattered also among their pale-faced enemies were the Indian priests, or powwows, who had often scared their native forest with more hideous incantations than any known to English witchcraft.

"But where is Faith?" thought Goodman Brown; and, as hope came into his heart, he trembled.

Another verse of the hymn arose, a slow and mournful strain, such as the pious love, but joined to words which expressed all that our nature can conceive of sin, and darkly hinted at far more. Unfathomable to mere mortals is the lore of fiends. Verse after verse was sung; and still the chorus of the desert swelled between like the deepest tone of a mighty organ; and with the final peal of that dreadful anthem there came a sound, as if the roaring wind, the rushing streams, the howling beasts, and every other voice of the unconcerted wilderness were mingling and according with the voice of guilty man in homage to the prince of all. The four blazing pines threw up a loftier flame, and obscurely discovered shapes and visages of horror on the smoke wreaths above the impious assembly. At the same moment the fire on the rock shot redly forth and formed a flowing arch above its base, where now appeared a figure. With reverence be it spoken, the figure bore no slight similitude, both in garb and manner, to some grave divine of the New England churches.

"Bring forth the converts!" cried a voice that echoed through the field and rolled into the forest.

At the word, Goodman Brown stepped forth from the shadow of the trees 60 and approached the congregation, with whom he felt a loathful brotherhood by the sympathy of all that was wicked in his heart. He could have well-nigh sworn that the shape of his own dead father beckoned him to advance, looking downward from a smoke wreath, while a woman, with dim features of despair, threw out her hand to warn him back. Was it his mother? But he had no power to retreat one step, nor to resist, even in thought, when the minister and good old Deacon Gookin seized his arms and led him to the blazing rock. Thither came also the slender form of a veiled female, led between Goody Cloyse, that pious teacher of the catechism, and Martha Carrier, who had received the devil's promise to be queen of hell. A rampant hag was she. And there stood the proselytes beneath the canopy of fire.

"Welcome, my children," said the dark figure, "to the communion of your race. Ye have found thus young your nature and your destiny. My children, look behind you!"

They turned; and flashing forth, as it were, in a sheet of flame, the fiend worshippers were seen; the smile of welcome gleamed darkly on every visage.

"There," resumed the sable form, "are all whom ye have reverenced from youth. Ye deemed them holier than yourselves and shrank from your own sin, contrasting it with their lives of righteousness and prayerful aspirations heavenward. Yet here are they all in my worshipping assembly. This night it shall be granted you to know their secret deeds: how hoary-bearded elders of the church have whispered wanton words to the young maids of their households; how many a woman, eager for widows' weeds, has given her husband a drink at bedtime and let him sleep his last sleep in her bosom; how beardless youths have made haste to inherit their fathers' wealth; and how fair damsels—blush not, sweet ones—have dug little graves in the garden, and bidden me, the sole guest, to an infant's funeral. By the sympathy of your human hearts for sin ye shall scent out all the places—whether in church, bedchamber, street, field, or forest—where crime has been committed, and shall exult to behold the whole earth one stain of guilt, one mighty blood spot. Far more than this. It shall be yours to penetrate, in every bosom, the deep mystery of sin, the fountain of all wicked arts, and which inexhaustibly supplies more evil impulses than human power—than my power at its utmost—can make manifest in deeds. And now, my children, look upon each other."

They did so; and, by the blaze of the hell-kindled torches, the wretched man beheld his Faith, and the wife her husband, trembling before that unhallowed altar.

"Lo, there ye stand, my children," said the figure, in a deep and solemn   65
tone, almost sad with its despairing awfulness, as if his once angelic nature could yet mourn for our miserable race. "Depending upon one another's hearts, ye had still hoped that virtue were not all a dream. Now are ye undeceived. Evil is the nature of mankind. Evil must be your only happiness. Welcome again, my children, to the communion of your race."

"Welcome," repeated the fiend worshippers, in one cry of despair and triumph.

And there they stood, the only pair, as it seemed, who were yet hesitating on the verge of wickedness in this dark world. A basin was hallowed, naturally, in the rock. Did it contain water, reddened by the lurid light? or was it blood? or, perchance, a liquid flame? Herein did the shape of evil dip his hand and prepare to lay the mark of baptism upon their foreheads, that they might be partakers of the mystery of sin, more conscious of the secret guilt of others, both in deed and thought, than they could now be of their own. The husband cast one look at his pale wife, and Faith at him. What polluted wretches would the next glance show them to each other, shuddering alike at what they disclosed and what they saw!

"Faith! Faith!" cried the husband, "look up to heaven, and resist the wicked one."

Whether Faith obeyed he knew not. Hardly had he spoken when he found himself amid calm night and solitude, listening to a roar of the wind which died heavily away through the forest. He staggered against the rock, and felt it chill and damp; while a hanging twig, that had been all on fire, besprinkled his cheek with the coldest dew.

The next morning young Goodman Brown came slowly into the street of   70
Salem village, staring around him like a bewildered man. The good old minister was taking a walk along the graveyard to get an appetite for breakfast and meditate his sermon, and bestowed a blessing, as he passed, on Goodman Brown. He shrank from the venerable saint as if to avoid an anathema. Old Deacon Gookin was at domestic worship, and the holy words of his prayer were heard through the open window. "What God doth the wizard pray to?" quoth Goodman Brown. Goody Cloyse, that excellent old Christian, stood in the early

sunshine at her own lattice, catechizing a little girl who had brought her a pint of morning's milk. Goodman Brown snatched away the child as from the grasp of the fiend himself. Turning the corner by the meeting-house, he spied the head of Faith, with the pink ribbons, gazing anxiously forth, and bursting into such joy at sight of him that she skipped along the street and almost kissed her husband before the whole village. But Goodman Brown looked sternly and sadly into her face, and passed on without a greeting.

Had Goodman Brown fallen asleep in the forest and only dreamed a wild dream of a witch-meeting?

Be it so if you will; but, alas! it was a dream of evil omen for young Goodman Brown. A stern, a sad, a darkly meditative, a distrustful, if not a desperate man did he become from the night of that fearful dream. On the Sabbath day, when the congregation were singing a holy psalm, he could not listen because an anthem of sin rushed loudly upon his ear and drowned all the blessed strain. When the minister spoke from the pulpit with power and fervid eloquence, and, with his hand on the open Bible, of the sacred truths of our religion, and of saint-like lives and triumphant deaths, and of future bliss or misery unutterable, then did Goodman Brown turn pale, dreading lest the roof should thunder down upon the gray blasphemer and his hearers. Often, awaking suddenly at midnight, he shrank from the bosom of Faith; and at morning or eventide, when the family knelt down at prayer, he scowled and muttered to himself, and gazed sternly at his wife, and turned away. And when he had lived long, and was borne to his grave a hoary corpse, followed by Faith, an aged woman, and children and grandchildren, a goodly procession, besides neighbors not a few, they carved no hopeful verse upon his tombstone, for his dying hour was gloom.   *[1835]*

☰ THINKING ABOUT THE TEXT

1. "Young Goodman Brown" seems quite allegorical, with journeys in the night woods and statements like "My Faith is gone!" (para. 50). How would you explain this allegorical story? What is Brown looking for? What does he find out? How does he deal with his discoveries?

2. If you were a good friend of Brown's, what might you tell him to try to save him from a life of gloom?

3. The devil suggests that there is more evil in the human heart "than my power at its utmost" (para. 63). Do you agree? If so, is this a message to despair about?

4. The devil says he is well acquainted with Brown's family. What has his family done? Is Brown innocent and naive, or is he stubborn and arrogant, in his refusal to admit that evil exists all around us?

5. Do you suspect that Brown merely dreamed or imagined his experience in the woods? Or do you think it really took place? Refer to specific details of the text.

TONI CADE BAMBARA

The Lesson

Toni Cade Bambara (1939–1995) taught at various colleges and worked as a community activist. She edited The Black Woman *(1970), a collection of essays that became a landmark of contemporary black feminism. Bambara wrote two novels:* The Salt Eaters *(1980), which won the American Book Award, and* These Bones Are Not My Child *(2000), a posthumously published work about the murders of several African American children in Atlanta in the late 1970s. She also produced several collections of short stories. "The Lesson" comes from her first,* Gorilla, My Love *(1972).*

Back in the days when everyone was old and stupid or young and foolish and me and Sugar were the only ones just right, this lady moved on our block with nappy hair and proper speech and no makeup. And quite naturally we laughed at her, laughed the way we did at the junk man who went about his business like he was some big-time president and his sorry-ass horse his secretary. And we kinda hated her too, hated the way we did the winos who cluttered up our parks and pissed on our handball walls and stank up our hallways and stairs so you couldn't halfway play hide-and-seek without a goddamn gas mask. Miss Moore was her name. The only woman on the block with no first name. And she was black as hell, cept for her feet, which were fish-white and spooky. And she was always planning these boring-ass things for us to do, us being my cousin, mostly, who lived on the block cause we all moved North the same time and to the same apartment then spread out gradual to breathe. And our parents would yank our heads into some kinda shape and crisp up our clothes so we'd be presentable for travel with Miss Moore, who always looked like she was going to church, though she never did. Which is just one of the things the grownups talked about when they talked behind her back like a dog. But when she came calling with some sachet she'd sewed up or some gingerbread she'd made or some book, why then they'd all be too embarrassed to turn her down and we'd get handed over all spruced up. She'd been to college and said it was only right that she should take responsibility for the young ones' education, and she not even related by marriage or blood. So they'd go for it. Specially Aunt Gretchen. She was the main gofer in the family. You got some ole dumb shit foolishness you want somebody to go for, you send for Aunt Gretchen. She been screwed into the go-along for so long, it's a blood-deep natural thing with her. Which is how she got saddled with me and Sugar and Junior in the first place while our mothers were in a la-de-da apartment up the block having a good ole time.

So this one day, Miss Moore rounds us all up at the mailbox and it's pure-dee hot and she's knockin herself out about arithmetic. And school suppose to let up in summer I heard, but she don't never let up. And the starch in my pinafore scratching the shit outta me and I'm really hating this nappy-head bitch and her goddamn college degree. I'd much rather go to the pool or to the show where it's cool. So me and Sugar leaning on the mailbox being surly, which is a Miss Moore word. And Flyboy checking out what everybody brought for lunch. And Fat Butt already wasting his peanut-butter-and-jelly sandwich like the pig he is. And Junebug punchin on Q.T.'s arm for potato chips. And Rosie Giraffe shifting from one hip to the other waiting for somebody to step on her foot or ask her if she from Georgia so she can kick ass, preferably Mercedes's. And Miss Moore asking us do we know what money is, like we a bunch of retards. I mean real money, she say, like it's only poker chips or monopoly papers we lay on the grocer. So right away I'm tired of this and say so. And would much rather snatch Sugar and go to the Sunset and terrorize the West Indian kids and take their hair ribbons and their money too. And Miss Moore files that remark away for next week's lesson on brotherhood, I can tell. And finally I say we oughta get to the subway cause it's cooler and besides we might meet some cute boys. Sugar done swiped her mama's lipstick, so we ready.

So we heading down the street and she's boring us silly about what things cost and what our parents make and how much goes for rent and how money ain't divided up right in this country. And then she gets to the part about we all poor and live in the slums, which I don't feature. And I'm ready to speak on that, but she steps out in the street and hails two cabs just like that. Then she hustles half the crew in with her and hands me a five-dollar bill and tells me to calculate 10 percent tip for the driver. And we're off. Me and Sugar and Junebug and Flyboy hangin out the window and hollering to everybody, putting lipstick on each other cause Flyboy a faggot anyway, and making farts with our sweaty armpits. But I'm mostly trying to figure how to spend this money. But they all fascinated with the meter ticking and Junebug starts laying bets as to how much it'll read when Flyboy can't hold his breath no more. Then Sugar lays bets as to how much it'll be when we get there. So I'm stuck. Don't nobody want to go for my plan, which is to jump out at the next light and run off to the first bar-b-que we can find. Then the driver tells us to get the hell out cause we there already. And the meter reads eighty-five cents. And I'm stalling to figure out the tip and Sugar say give him a dime. And I decide he don't need it bad as I do, so later for him. But then he tries to take off with Junebug foot still in the door so we talk about his mama something ferocious. Then we check out that we on Fifth Avenue and everybody dressed up in stockings. One lady in a fur coat, hot as it is. White folks crazy.

"This is the place," Miss Moore say, presenting it to us in the voice she uses at the museum. "Let's look in the windows before we go in."

"Can we steal?" Sugar asks very serious like she's getting the ground rules squared away before she plays. "I beg your pardon," say Miss Moore, and we fall out. So she leads us around the windows of the toy store and me and Sugar screamin, "This is mine, that's mine, I gotta have that, that was made for me, I was born for that," till Big Butt drowns us out.

"Hey, I'm goin to buy that there."

"That there? You don't even know what it is, stupid."

"I do so," he say punchin on Rosie Giraffe. "It's a microscope."

"Whatcha gonna do with a microscope, fool?"

5

"Look at things."   10

"Like what, Ronald?" ask Miss Moore. And Big Butt ain't got the first notion. So here go Miss Moore gabbing about the thousands of bacteria in a drop of water and the somethinorother in a speck of blood and the million and one living things in the air around us is invisible to the naked eye. And what she say that for? Junebug go to town on that "naked" and we rolling. Then Miss Moore ask what it cost. So we all jam into the window smudgin it up and the price tag say $300. So then she ask how long'd take for Big Butt and Junebug to save up their allowances. "Too long," I say. "Yeh," adds Sugar, "outgrown it by that time." And Miss Moore say no, you never outgrow learning instruments. "Why, even medical students and interns and," blah, blah, blah. And we ready to choke Big Butt for bringing it up in the first damn place.

"This here costs four hundred eighty dollars," says Rosie Giraffe. So we pile up all over her to see what she pointin out. My eyes tell me it's a chunk of glass cracked with something heavy, and different-color inks dripped into the splits, then the whole thing put into a oven or something. But for $480 it don't make sense.

"That's a paperweight made of semi-precious stones fused together under tremendous pressure," she explains slowly, with her hands doing the mining and all the factory work.

"So what's a paperweight?" asks Rosie Giraffe.

"To weigh paper with, dumbbell," say Flyboy, the wise man from the East.   15

"Not exactly," say Miss Moore, which is what she say when you warm or way off too. "It's to weigh paper down so it won't scatter and make your desk untidy." So right away me and Sugar curtsy to each other and then to Mercedes who is more the tidy type.

"We don't keep paper on top of the desk in my class," say Junebug, figuring Miss Moore crazy or lyin one.

"At home, then," she say. "Don't you have a calendar and pencil case and a blotter and a letter-opener on your desk at home where you do your homework?" And she know damn well what our homes look like cause she nosys around in them every chance she gets.

"I don't even have a desk," say Junebug. "Do we?"

"No. And I don't get no homework neither," says Big Butt.   20

"And I don't even have a home," say Flyboy like he do at school to keep the white folks off his back and sorry for him. Send this poor kid to camp posters, is his specialty.

"I do," says Mercedes. "I have a box of stationery on my desk and a picture of my cat. My godmother bought the stationery and the desk. There's a big rose on each sheet and the envelopes smell like roses."

"Who wants to know about your smelly-ass stationery," say Rosie Giraffe fore I can get my two cents in.

"It's important to have a work area all your own so that . . ."

"Will you look at this sailboat, please," say Flyboy, cuttin her off and   25
pointin to the thing like it was his. So once again we tumble all over each other to gaze at this magnificent thing in the toy store which is just big enough to

maybe sail two kittens across the pond if you strap them to the posts tight. We all start reciting the price tag like we in assembly. "Handcrafted sailboat of fiberglass at one thousand one hundred ninety-five dollars."

"Unbelievable," I hear myself say and am really stunned. I read it again for myself just in case the group recitation put me in a trance. Same thing. For some reason this pisses me off. We look at Miss Moore and she lookin at us, waiting for I dunno what.

"Who'd pay all that when you can buy a sailboat set for a quarter at Pop's, a tube of glue for a dime, and a ball of string for eight cents? It must have a motor and a whole lot else besides," I say. "My sailboat cost me about fifty cents."

"But will it take water?" say Mercedes with her smart ass.

"Took mine to Alley Pond Park once," say Flyboy. "String broke. Lost it. Pity."

"Sailed mine in Central Park and it keeled over and sank. Had to ask my   30 father for another dollar."

"And you got the strap," laugh Big Butt. "The jerk didn't even have a string on it. My old man wailed on his behind."

Little Q.T. was staring hard at the sailboat and you could see he wanted it bad. But he too little and somebody'd just take it from him. So what the hell. "This boat for kids, Miss Moore?"

"Parents silly to buy something like that just to get all broke up," say Rosie Giraffe.

"That much money it should last forever," I figure.

"My father'd buy it for me if I wanted it."   35

"Your father, my ass," say Rosie Giraffe getting a chance to finally push Mercedes.

"Must be rich people shop here," say Q.T.

"You are a very bright boy," say Flyboy. "What was your first clue?" And he rap him on the head with the back of his knuckles, since Q.T. the only one he could get away with. Though Q.T. liable to come up behind you years later and get his licks in when you half expect it.

"What I want to know is," I says to Miss Moore though I never talk to her, I wouldn't give the bitch that satisfaction, "is how much a real boat costs? I figure a thousand'd get you a yacht any day."

"Why don't you check that out," she says, "and report back to the group?"   40 Which really pains my ass. If you gonna mess up a perfectly good swim day least you could do is have some answers. "Let's go in," she say like she got something up her sleeve. Only she don't lead the way. So me and Sugar turn the corner to where the entrance is, but when we get there I kinda hang back. Not that I'm scared, what's there to be afraid of, just a toy store. But I feel funny, shame. But what I got to be shamed about? Got as much right to go in as anybody. But somehow I can't seem to get hold of the door, so I step away from Sugar to lead. But she hangs back too. And I look at her and she looks at me and this is ridiculous. I mean, damn, I have never ever been shy about doing nothing or going nowhere. But then Mercedes steps up and then Rosie Giraffe and Big Butt crowd in behind and shove, and next thing we all stuffed into the doorway with only Mercedes squeezing past us, smoothing out her jumper and walking right down the aisle. Then the rest of us tumble in like a glued-together jigsaw done all wrong. And people lookin at us. And it's like the time me and Sugar crashed into the Catholic church on a dare. But once we got in there and everything so hushed and holy and the candles and the bowin and the handkerchiefs on all the drooping heads, I just couldn't go through with the plan. Which was for me to run up to the altar and do a tap dance while Sugar played the nose flute and messed around in the holy water. And Sugar kept givin me the elbow. Then later teased me so bad I tied her up in the shower and turned it on and locked her in. And she'd be there till this day if Aunt Gretchen hadn't finally figured I was lying about the boarder takin a shower.

Same thing in the store. We all walkin on tiptoe and hardly touchin the games and puzzles and things. And I watched Miss Moore who is steady watchin us like she waitin for a sign. Like Mama Drewery watches the sky and sniffs the air and takes note of just how much slant is in the bird formation. Then me and Sugar bump smack into each other, so busy gazing at the toys, 'specially the sailboat. But we don't laugh and go into our fat-lady bump-stomach routine. We just stare at that price tag. Then Sugar run a finger over the whole boat. And I'm jealous and want to hit her. Maybe not her, but I sure want to punch somebody in the mouth.

"Watcha bring us here for, Miss Moore?"

"You sound angry, Sylvia. Are you mad about something?" Givin me one of them grins like she tellin a grown-up joke that never turns out to be funny. And she's lookin very closely at me like maybe she plannin to do my portrait from memory. I'm mad, but I won't give her that satisfaction. So I slouch around the store bein very bored and say, "Let's go."

Me and Sugar at the back of the train watchin the tracks whizzin by large then small then getting gobbled up in the dark. I'm thinkin about this tricky toy I saw in the store. A clown that somersaults on a bar then does chin-ups just cause you yank lightly at his leg. Cost $35. I could see me askin my mother for a $35 birthday clown. "You wanna who that costs what?" she'd say, cocking her head to the side to get a better view of the hole in my head. Thirty-five dollars could buy new bunk beds for Junior and Gretchen's boy. Thirty-five dollars and the whole household could go visit Grand-daddy Nelson in the country. Thirty-five dollars would pay for the rent and the piano bill too. Who are these people that spend that much for performing clowns and $1000 for toy sailboats? What kinda work they do and how they live and how come we ain't in on it? Where we are is who we are, Miss Moore always pointin out. But it don't necessarily have to be that way, she always adds then waits for somebody to say that poor people have to wake up and demand their share of the pie and don't none of us know what kind of pie she talking about in the first damn place. But she ain't so smart cause I still got her four dollars from the taxi and she sure ain't gettin it. Messin up my day with this shit. Sugar nudges me in my pocket and winks.

Miss Moore lines us up in front of the mailbox where we started from, seem like years ago, and I got a headache for thinkin so hard. And we lean all over   45 each other so we can hold up under the draggy-ass lecture she always finishes us off with at the end before we thank her for borin us to tears. But she just looks at us like she readin tea leaves. Finally she say, "Well, what did you think of F. A. O. Schwarz?"

Rosie Giraffe mumbles, "White folks crazy."

"I'd like to go there again when I get my birthday money," says Mercedes, and we shove her out the pack so she has to lean on the mailbox by herself.

"I'd like a shower. Tiring day," say Flyboy.

Then Sugar surprises me by sayin, "You know, Miss Moore, I don't think all of us here put together eat in a year what that sailboat costs." And Miss Moore lights up like somebody goosed her. "And?" she say, urging Sugar on. Only I'm standin on her foot so she don't continue.

"Imagine for a minute what kind of society it is in which some people can spend on a toy what it would cost to feed a family of six or seven. What do you think?"

"I think," say Sugar pushing me off her feet like she never done before, cause I whip her ass in a minute, "that this is not much of a democracy if you ask me. Equal chance to pursue happiness means an equal crack at the dough, don't it?" Miss Moore is beside herself and I am disgusted with Sugar's treachery. So I stand on her foot one more time to see if she'll shove me. She shuts up, and Miss Moore looks at me, sorrowfully I'm thinkin. And somethin weird is goin on, I can feel it in my chest.

"Anybody else learn anything today?" lookin dead at me. I walk away and Sugar has to run to catch up and don't even seem to notice when I shrug her arm off my shoulder.

"Well, we got four dollars anyway," she says.

"Uh hunh."

"We could go to Hascombs and get half a chocolate layer and then go to the Sunset and still have plenty money for potato chips and ice cream sodas."

"Un hunh."

"Race you to Hascombs," she say.

We start down the block and she gets ahead which is O.K. by me cause I'm going to the West End and then over to the Drive to think this day through. She can run if she want to and even run faster. But ain't nobody gonna beat me at nuthin.   *[1972]*

≡ **THINKING ABOUT THE TEXT**

1. Bambara's story begins with "Back in the days," which suggests that Sylvia is significantly older now than she was then. How much time do you think has passed since the events she recalls? Does it matter to you how old she is now? Why, or why not?

2. Miss Moore is not officially a teacher. Nor is she a relative of the children she instructs. Is it right, then, for her to "take responsibility for the young ones' education" (para. 1)? Make an argument for and against her doing so.

3. Consider Miss Moore as making an argument. What are her claims? Which of her strategies, if any, seem effective in persuading her audience? Which, if any, seem ineffective?

4. What statements by the children articulate the lesson that Miss Moore teaches? Are all these statements saying pretty much the same thing? At the end of the story, is Sylvia ready to agree with all of them? Explain.

5. Do class and race seem equally important in this story, or does one seem more important than the other? Elaborate your reasoning.

≡ MAKING COMPARISONS

1. "The Lesson" is more humorous than "Young Goodman Brown." Does its humor lead you to take Bambara's story of injustice less seriously than you do Hawthorne's? Why, or why not?

2. "Young Goodman Brown" has an omniscient narrator, and Sylvia is the first-person narrator of "The Lesson." To what extent does this difference matter as you read the two stories together?

3. Sylvia is younger in age than Goodman Brown is. How significant is this difference to you as you consider their responses to injustice?

HA JIN

Saboteur

Although originally from China, Ha Jin (b. 1956) writes fiction in English. He served in the People's Liberation Army during his native country's Cultural Revolution, a period during the 1960s and 1970s when militant followers of leader Mao Zedong brutalized China's intellectuals and other segments of its population. After undergraduate and graduate education in China, Ha Jin was studying at Brandeis University in Massachusetts when in 1989, the Chinese government attacked protesters in Tiananmen Square. He has written about this event in his novel The Crazed *(2002), and it played a role in his deciding to settle in the United States. Currently a professor at Boston University, he is the author of several books. His other novels include* A Free Life *(2007),* War Trash *(2004), and* Waiting *(1999), for which he won the National Book Award. His latest novel is* A Map of Betrayal *(2014). The following story first appeared in a 1996 issue of* The Antioch Review *and was then reprinted in his 2001 collection* The Bridegroom: Stories.*

Mr. Chiu and his bride were having lunch in the square before Muji Train Station. On the table between them were two bottles of soda spewing out brown foam and two paper boxes of rice and sautéed cucumber and pork. "Let's eat," he said to her, and broke the connected ends of the chopsticks. He picked up a slice of streaky pork and put it into his mouth. As he was chewing, a few crinkles appeared on his thin jaw.

To his right, at another table, two railroad policemen were drinking tea and laughing; it seemed that the stout, middle-aged man was telling a joke to his young comrade, who was tall and of athletic build. Now and again they would steal a glance at Mr. Chiu's table.

The air smelled of rotten melon. A few flies kept buzzing above the couple's lunch. Hundreds of people were rushing around to get on the platform or to catch buses to downtown. Food and fruit vendors were crying for customers in lazy voices. About a dozen young women, representing the local hotels, held up placards which displayed the daily prices and words as large as a palm, like FREE MEALS, AIR-CONDITIONING, and ON THE RIVER. In the center of the square stood a concrete statue of Chairman Mao, at whose feet peasants were napping, their backs on the warm granite and their faces toward the sunny sky. A flock of pigeons perched on the Chairman's raised hand and forearm.

The rice and cucumber tasted good, and Mr. Chiu was eating unhurriedly. His sallow face showed exhaustion. He was glad that the honeymoon was finally over and that he and his bride were heading back for Harbin. During the two weeks' vacation, he had been worried about his liver, because three months ago he had suffered from acute hepatitis; he was afraid he might have a relapse. But he had had no severe symptoms, despite his liver being still big and tender. On the whole he was pleased with his health, which could endure even the strain of a honeymoon; indeed, he was on the course of recovery. He looked at his bride, who took off her wire glasses, kneading the root of her nose with her fingertips. Beads of sweat coated her pale cheeks.

"Are you all right, sweetheart?" he asked.   5

"I have a headache. I didn't sleep well last night."

"Take an aspirin, will you?"

"It's not that serious. Tomorrow is Sunday and I can sleep in. Don't worry."

As they were talking, the stout policeman at the next table stood up and threw a bowl of tea in their direction. Both Mr. Chiu's and his bride's sandals were wet instantly.

"Hooligan!" she said in a low voice.   10

Mr. Chiu got to his feet and said out loud, "Comrade Policeman, why did you do this?" He stretched out his right foot to show the wet sandal.

"Do what?" the stout man asked huskily, glaring at Mr. Chiu while the young fellow was whistling.

"See, you dumped tea on our feet."

"You're lying. You wet your shoes yourself."

"Comrade Policemen, your duty is to keep order, but you purposely tor-   15
tured us common citizens. Why violate the law you are supposed to enforce?" As Mr. Chiu was speaking, dozens of people began gathering around.

With a wave of his hand, the man said to the young fellow, "Let's get hold of him!"

They grabbed Mr. Chiu and clamped handcuffs around his wrists. He cried, "You can't do this to me. This is utterly unreasonable."

"Shut up!" The man pulled out his pistol. "You can use your tongue at our headquarters."

The young fellow added, "You're a saboteur, you know that? You're disrupting public order."

The bride was too petrified to say anything coherent. She was a recent college graduate, had majored in fine arts, and had never seen the police make an arrest. All she could say was, "Oh, please, please!"   20

The policemen were pulling Mr. Chiu, but he refused to go with them, holding the corner of the table and shouting, "We have a train to catch. We already bought the tickets."

The stout man punched him in the chest. "Shut up. Let your ticket expire." With the pistol butt he chopped Mr. Chiu's hands, which at once released the table. Together the two men were dragging him away to the police station.

Realizing he had to go with them, Mr. Chiu turned his head and shouted to his bride, "Don't wait for me here. Take the train. If I'm not back by tomorrow morning, send someone over to get me out."

She nodded, covering her sobbing mouth with her palm.

After removing his belt, they locked Mr. Chiu into a cell in the back of the Railroad Police Station. The single window in the room was blocked by six steel bars; it faced a spacious yard, in which stood a few pines. Beyond the trees, two swings hung from an iron frame, swaying gently in the breeze. Somewhere in the building a cleaver was chopping rhythmically. There must be a kitchen upstairs, Mr. Chiu thought.   25

He was too exhausted to worry about what they would do to him, so he lay down on the narrow bed and shut his eyes. He wasn't afraid. The Cultural Revolution was over already, and recently the Party had been propagating the idea that all citizens were equal before the law. The police ought to be a law-abiding model for common people. As long as he remained coolheaded and reasoned with them, they probably wouldn't harm him.

Late in the afternoon he was taken to the Interrogation Bureau on the second floor. On his way there, in the stairwell, he ran into the middle-aged policeman who had manhandled him. The man grinned, rolling his bulgy eyes and pointing his fingers at him as if firing a pistol. Egg of a tortoise! Mr. Chiu cursed mentally.

The moment he sat down in the office, he burped, his palm shielding his mouth. In front of him, across a long desk, sat the chief of the bureau and a donkey-faced man. On the glass desktop was a folder containing information on his case. He felt it bizarre that in just a matter of hours they had accumulated a small pile of writing about him. On second thought he began to wonder whether they had kept a file on him all the time. How could this have happened? He lived and worked in Harbin, more than three hundred miles away, and this was his first time in Muji City.

The chief of the bureau was a thin, bald man who looked serene and intelligent. His slim hands handled the written pages in the folder in the manner of a lecturing scholar. To Mr. Chiu's left sat a young scribe, with a clipboard on his knee and a black fountain pen in his hand.

"Your name?" the chief asked, apparently reading out the question from a form.   30

"Chiu Maguang."

"Age?"

"Thirty-four."

"Profession?"

"Lecturer."   35

"Work unit?"

"Harbin University."

"Political status?"

"Communist Party member."

The chief put down the paper and began to speak. "Your crime is sabo-   40
tage, although it hasn't induced serious consequences yet. Because you are a
Party member, you should be punished more. You have failed to be a model for
the masses and you —"

"Excuse me, sir," Mr. Chiu cut him off.

"What?"

"I didn't do anything. Your men are the saboteurs of our social order. They
threw hot tea on my feet and on my wife's feet. Logically speaking, you should
criticize them, if not punish them."

"That statement is groundless. You have no witness. Why should I believe
you?" the chief said matter-of-factly.

"This is my evidence." He raised his right hand. "Your man hit my fingers   45
with a pistol."

"That doesn't prove how your feet got wet. Besides, you could have hurt
your fingers yourself."

"But I am telling the truth!" Anger flared up in Mr. Chiu. "Your police
station owes me an apology. My train ticket has expired, my new leather
sandals are ruined, and I am late for a conference in the provincial capital. You
must compensate me for the damage and losses. Don't mistake me for a common citizen who would tremble when you sneeze. I'm a scholar, a philosopher,
and an expert in dialectical materialism. If necessary, we will argue about
this in *The Northeastern Daily*, or we will go to the highest People's Court in
Beijing. Tell me, what's your name?" He got carried away with his harangue,
which was by no means trivial and had worked to his advantage on numerous
occasions.

"Stop bluffing us," the donkey-faced man broke in. "We have seen a lot of
your kind. We can easily prove you are guilty. Here are some of the statements
given by eyewitnesses." He pushed a few sheets of paper toward Mr. Chiu.

Mr. Chiu was dazed to see the different handwritings, which all stated
that he had shouted in the square to attract attention and refused to obey the
police. One of the witnesses had identified herself as a purchasing agent from
a shipyard in Shanghai. Something stirred in Mr. Chiu's stomach, a pain rising
to his rib. He gave out a faint moan.

"Now you have to admit you are guilty," the chief said. "Although   50
it's a serious crime, we won't punish you severely, provided you write out a
self-criticism and promise that you won't disrupt the public order again. In
other words, your release will depend on your attitude toward this crime."

"You're daydreaming!" Mr. Chiu cried. "I won't write a word, because I'm innocent. I demand that you provide me with a letter of apology so I can explain to my university why I'm late."

Both the interrogators smiled contemptuously. "Well, we've never done that," said the chief, taking a puff of his cigarette.

"Then make this a precedent."

"That's unnecessary. We are pretty certain that you will comply with our wishes." The chief blew a column of smoke toward Mr. Chiu's face.

At the tilt of the chief's head, two guards stepped forward and grabbed the criminal by the arms. Mr. Chiu meanwhile went on saying, "I shall report you to the Provincial Administration. You'll have to pay for this! You are worse than the Japanese military police."

They dragged him out of the room.

After dinner, which consisted of a bowl of millet porridge, a corn bun, and a piece of pickled turnip, Mr. Chiu began to have a fever, shaking with a chill and sweating profusely. He knew that the fire of anger had gotten into his liver and that he was probably having a relapse. No medicine was available, because his briefcase had been left with his bride. At home it would have been time for him to sit in front of their color TV, drinking jasmine tea and watching the evening news. It was so lonesome in here. The orange bulb above the single bed was the only source of light, which enabled the guards to keep him under surveillance at night. A moment ago he had asked them for a newspaper or a magazine to read, but they turned him down.

Through the small opening on the door noises came in. It seemed that the police on duty were playing cards or chess in a nearby office; shouts and laughter could be heard now and then. Meanwhile, an accordion kept coughing from a remote corner in the building. Looking at the ballpoint and the letter paper left for him by the guards when they took him back from the Interrogation Bureau, Mr. Chiu remembered the old saying, "When a scholar runs into soldiers, the more he argues, the muddier his point becomes." How ridiculous this whole thing was. He ruffled his thick hair with his fingers.

He felt miserable, massaging his stomach continually. To tell the truth, he was more upset than frightened, because he would have to catch up with his work once he was back home — a paper that was due at the printers next week, and two dozen books he ought to read for the courses he was going to teach in the fall.

A human shadow flitted across the opening. Mr. Chiu rushed to the door   60
and shouted through the hole, "Comrade Guard, Comrade Guard!"

"What do you want?" a voice rasped.

"I want you to inform your leaders that I'm very sick. I have heart disease and hepatitis. I may die here if you keep me like this without medication."

"No leader is on duty on the weekend. You have to wait till Monday."

"What? You mean I'll stay in here tomorrow?"

"Yes."   65

"Your station will be held responsible if anything happens to me."

"We know that. Take it easy, you won't die."

It seemed illogical that Mr. Chiu slept quite well that night, though the light above his head had been on all the time and the straw mattress was hard and infested with fleas. He was afraid of ticks, mosquitoes, cockroaches — any kind of insect but fleas and bedbugs. Once, in the countryside, where his school's faculty and staff had helped the peasants harvest crops for a week, his colleagues had joked about his flesh, which they said must have tasted non-human to fleas. Except for him, they were all afflicted with hundreds of bites.

More amazing now, he didn't miss his bride a lot. He even enjoyed sleeping alone, perhaps because the honeymoon had tired him out and he needed more rest.

The backyard was quiet on Sunday morning. Pale sunlight streamed through the pine branches. A few sparrows were jumping on the ground, catching caterpillars and ladybugs. Holding the steel bars, Mr. Chiu inhaled the morning air, which smelled meaty. There must have been an eatery or a cooked-meat stand nearby. He reminded himself that he should take this detention with ease. A sentence that Chairman Mao had written to a hospitalized friend rose in his mind: "Since you are already in here, you may as well stay and make the best of it."

His desire for peace of mind originated in his fear that this hepatitis might get worse. He tried to remain unperturbed. However, he was sure that his liver was swelling up, since the fever still persisted. For a whole day he lay in bed, thinking about his paper on the nature of contradictions. Time and again he was overwhelmed by anger, cursing aloud. "A bunch of thugs!" He swore that once he was out, he would write an article about this experience. He had better find out some of the policemen's names.

It turned out to be a restful day for the most part; he was certain that his university would send somebody to his rescue. All he should do now was remain calm and wait patiently. Sooner or later the police would have to release him, although they had no idea that he might refuse to leave unless they wrote him an apology. Damn those hoodlums, they had ordered more than they could eat!

When he woke up on Monday morning, it was already light. Somewhere a man was moaning; the sound came from the backyard. After a long yawn, and kicking off the tattered blanket, Mr. Chiu climbed out of bed and went to the window. In the middle of the yard, a young man was fastened to a pine, his wrists handcuffed around the trunk from behind. He was wriggling and swearing loudly, but there was no sight of anyone else in the yard. He looked familiar to Mr. Chiu.

Mr. Chiu squinted his eyes to see who it was. To his astonishment, he recognized the man, who was Fenjin, a recent graduate from the Law Department at Harbin University. Two years ago Mr. Chiu had taught a course in Marxist materialism, in which Fenjin had enrolled. Now, how on earth had this young devil landed here?

Then it dawned on him that Fenjin must have been sent over by his bride. What a stupid woman! A bookworm, who only knew how to read foreign novels! He had expected that she would contact the school's Security Section,

70

75

which would for sure send a cadre here. Fenjin held no official position; he merely worked in a private law firm that had just two lawyers; in fact, they had little business except for some detective work for men and women who suspected their spouses of having extramarital affairs. Mr. Chiu was overcome with a wave of nausea.

Should he call out to let his student know he was nearby? He decided not to because he didn't know what had happened. Fenjin must have quarreled with the police to incur such a punishment. Yet this could never have occurred if Fenjin hadn't come to his rescue. So no matter what, Mr. Chiu had to do something. But what could he do?

It was going to be a scorcher. He could see purple steam shimmering and rising from the ground among the pines. Poor devil, he thought, as he raised a bowl of corn glue to his mouth, sipped, and took a bite of a piece of salted celery.

When a guard came to collect the bowl and the chopsticks, Mr. Chiu asked him what had happened to the man in the backyard. "He called our boss 'bandit,' " the guard said. "He claimed he was a lawyer or something. An arrogant son of a rabbit."

Now it was obvious to Mr. Chiu that he had to do something to help his rescuer. Before he could figure out a way, a scream broke out in the backyard. He rushed to the window and saw a tall policeman standing before Fenjin, an iron bucket on the ground. It was the same young fellow who had arrested Mr. Chiu in the square two days before. The man pinched Fenjin's nose, then raised his hand, which stayed in the air for a few seconds, then slapped the lawyer across the face. As Fenjin was groaning, the man lifted up the bucket and poured water on his head.

"This will keep you from getting sunstroke, boy. I'll give you some more every hour," the man said loudly.   80

Fenjin kept his eyes shut, yet his wry face showed that he was struggling to hold back from cursing the policeman, or, more likely, that he was sobbing in silence. He sneezed, then raised his face and shouted, "Let me go take a piss."

"Oh, yeah?" the man bawled. "Pee in your pants."

Still Mr. Chiu didn't make any noise, gripping the steel bars with both hands, his fingers white. The policeman turned and glanced at the cell's window; his pistol, partly holstered, glittered in the sun. With a snort he spat his cigarette butt to the ground and stamped it into the dust.

Then the door opened and the guards motioned Mr. Chiu to come out. Again they took him upstairs to the Interrogation Bureau.

The same men were in the office, though this time the scribe was sitting   85
there empty-handed. At the sight of Mr. Chiu the chief said, "Ah, here you are. Please be seated."

After Mr. Chiu sat down, the chief waved a white silk fan and said to him, "You may have seen your lawyer. He's a young man without manners, so our director had him taught a crash course in the backyard."

"It's illegal to do that. Aren't you afraid to appear in a newspaper?"

"No, we are not, not even on TV. What else can you do? We are not afraid of any story you make up. We call it fiction. What we do care about is that you cooperate with us. That is to say, you must admit your crime."

"What if I refuse to cooperate?"

"Then your lawyer will continue his education in the sunshine." 90

A swoon swayed Mr. Chiu, and he held the arms of the chair to steady himself. A numb pain stung him in the upper stomach and nauseated him, and his head was throbbing. He was sure that the hepatitis was finally attacking him. Anger was flaming up in his chest; his throat was tight and clogged.

The chief resumed, "As a matter of fact, you don't even have to write out your self-criticism. We have your crime described clearly here. All we need is your signature."

Holding back his rage, Mr. Chiu said, "Let me look at that."

With a smirk the donkey-faced man handed him a sheet which carried these words:

> I hereby admit that on July 13 I disrupted public order at Muji Train Station, and that I refused to listen to reason when the railroad police issued their warning. Thus I myself am responsible for my arrest. After two days' detention, I have realized the reactionary nature of my crime. From now on, I shall continue to educate myself with all my effort and shall never commit this kind of crime again.

A voice started screaming in Mr. Chiu's ears, "Lie, lie!" But he shook his 95 head and forced the voice away. He asked the chief, "If I sign this, will you release both my lawyer and me?"

"Of course, we'll do that." The chief was drumming his fingers on the blue folder—their file on him.

Mr. Chiu signed his name and put his thumbprint under his signature.

"Now you are free to go," the chief said with a smile, and handed him a piece of paper to wipe his thumb with.

Mr. Chiu was so sick that he couldn't stand up from the chair at first try. Then he doubled his effort and rose to his feet. He staggered out of the building to meet his lawyer in the backyard, having forgotten to ask for his belt back. In his chest he felt as though there were a bomb. If he were able to, he would have razed the entire police station and eliminated all their families. Though he knew he could do nothing like that, he made up his mind to do something.

"I'm sorry about this torture, Fenjin," Mr. Chiu said when they met. 100

"It doesn't matter. They are savages." The lawyer brushed a patch of dirt off his jacket with trembling fingers. Water was still dribbling from the bottoms of his trouser legs.

"Let's go now," the teacher said.

The moment they came out of the police station, Mr. Chiu caught sight of a tea stand. He grabbed Fenjin's arm and walked over to the old woman at the table. "Two bowls of black tea," he said and handed her a one-yuan note.

After the first bowl, they each had another one. Then they set out for the train station. But before they walked fifty yards, Mr. Chiu insisted on eating a bowl of tree-ear soup at a food stand. Fenjin agreed. He told his teacher, "You mustn't treat me like a guest."

"No, I want to eat something myself." 105

As if dying of hunger, Mr. Chiu dragged his lawyer from restaurant to restaurant near the police station, but at each place he ordered no more than two bowls of food. Fenjin wondered why his teacher wouldn't stay at one place and eat his fill.

Mr. Chiu bought noodles, wonton, eight-grain porridge, and chicken soup, respectively, at four restaurants. While eating, he kept saying through his teeth. "If only I could kill all the bastards!" At the last place he merely took a few sips of the soup without tasting the chicken cubes and mushrooms.

Fenjin was baffled by his teacher, who looked ferocious and muttered to himself mysteriously, and whose jaundiced face was covered with dark puckets. For the first time Fenjin thought of Mr. Chiu as an ugly man.

Within a month over eight hundred people contracted acute hepatitis in Muji. Six died of the disease, including two children. Nobody knew how the epidemic had started.   [2000]

≡ THINKING ABOUT THE TEXT

1. In what places in the story is its title especially relevant? Who can be considered a saboteur, and what acts of sabotage does the story deal with? Define what these terms mean to you.

2. What evidence is there that Mr. Chiu is not used to being treated the way that the police treat him? Identify specific passages. Do you find him unreasonably naive? Why, or why not?

3. Why, apparently, do the police arrest Mr. Chiu and demand a confession from him before they are willing to release him? How might the author be using their behavior to comment on Chinese authorities in general?

4. In his fiction, Ha Jin typically mentions small physical details that may appear trivial at first but can eventually be thought of as significant. Identify some moments in "Saboteur" when he uses such details, and explain what their actual importance might be.

5. How sympathetic are you toward Mr. Chiu until the story's end? Is your degree of sympathy affected by what he ultimately did? What do you conclude about him from his final action?

≡ MAKING COMPARISONS

1. Revenge is often a factor in stories of injustice. Compare this idea in our three stories.

2. Compare the different kinds of injustice depicted in our three stories.

3. Compare the growth of Young Goodman Brown, Sylvia, and Mr. Chiu. How does your opinion of them change from the beginning to the end of the story?

≡ WRITING ABOUT ISSUES

1. Write an essay that argues that given the circumstances of our stories, Mr. Chiu's response is or is not the most understandable of the three.

2. Argue that there is or is not (or should be) a commitment to social justice at your college.

3. Research a major religion's view on redress for social injustice and argue that this view is or is not compatible with today's difficulties with terrorists.

4. Read another revenge story. Some possibilities include Andre Dubus's "Killings," Poe's "The Cask of Amontillado" or "The Tell-Tale Heart," or Susan Glaspell's "A Jury of Her Peers." Using "Saboteur" and one of these stories, argue that the authors are making a similar or different point about revenge.

≡ Racial Injustice: Poems

COUNTEE CULLEN, "Incident"

NATASHA TRETHEWEY, "Incident"

Throughout literary history, writers have called attention to the injustices of racial oppression. The following pair of poems, both titled "Incident," remind us that racial prejudice could be blatant and vicious both early in the twentieth century and toward its end. Indeed, the subject is not likely to die out even now, when laws blatantly permitting slavery or segregation have ceased to exist. Racism continues in various forms, though perhaps subtler ones. As you read these poems, consider what recent "incidents" might be topics of similar texts.

≡ BEFORE YOU READ

How do you define *racism*? What, for you, are possible signs of it?

COUNTEE CULLEN
Incident

Countee Cullen (1903–1946) was one of the leading writers of the Harlem Renaissance, a New York–based movement of African American authors, artists, and intellectuals that flourished from World War I to the Great Depression. Cullen's place of birth may have been Baltimore, Louisville, or New York, but by 1918, he was living in New York as the adopted son of a Methodist minister. Cullen wrote poetry and received prizes for it even as he attended New York University. In 1925, while pursuing a master's degree from Harvard, he published his first book of poems, Color, *which contained "Incident." His later books include* Copper Sun *(1927),* The Black Christ and Other Poems *(1929), a translation of Euripides's play* Medea *(1935), and a children's book,* The Lost Zoo *(1940). Cullen gained much attention when in 1928, he wed the daughter of famed African American writer and scholar W. E. B. Du Bois, but their marriage ended just two years later. During the 1930s, Cullen's writing did not earn him enough to live on, so he taught English and French at Frederick Douglass High School. At the time of his death in 1946, he was collaborating on the Broadway musical* St. Louis Woman. *In part because he died relatively young, Cullen's reputation faded. Langston Hughes became much better known as a Harlem Renaissance figure. "Incident," however, has been consistently anthologized, and today Cullen is being rediscovered along with other contributors to African American literature.*

Once riding in old Baltimore
    Heart-filled, head-filled with glee,
I saw a Baltimorean
    Keep looking straight at me.

Now I was eight and very small,   5
    And he was no whit bigger,
And so I smiled, but he poked out
    His tongue and called me, "Nigger."

I saw the whole of Baltimore
    From May until December: 10
Of all the things that happened there
    That's all that I remember.   *[1925]*

≡ THINKING ABOUT THE TEXT

1. Why do you think the speaker calls attention to his heart *and* his head in the second line? Might referring to just one of these things have been enough?

2. "Baltimorean" (line 3) seems a rather unusual and abstract term for the boy that the speaker encountered. How do you explain its presence in the poem? How important is it that the speaker name the city where the incident occurred?

3. Although the incident that the speaker recalls must have been painful for him, why do you think he does not state his feelings about it more explicitly? What is the effect of his relative reticence about it?

4. The rhythm of this poem is rather singsongy. Why do you think Cullen made it so?

5. The speaker states that he was eight at the time of the incident. How old might he be now? How important is his age?

NATASHA TRETHEWEY
Incident

The child of an interracial marriage, Natasha Trethewey (b. 1966) graduated from the University of Georgia and earned a master's degree at Hollins College in Virginia. She was the U.S. poet laureate in 2012 and 2014, and teaches creative writing at Emory University in Atlanta, Georgia. She is the author of four volumes of poetry: Domestic Work *(2000);* Bellocq's Ophelia *(2002);* Native Guard *(2006), which won the Pulitzer Prize and includes the following poem; and* Thrall *(2012).* Beyond Katrina: A Meditation on the Mississippi Gulf Coast *(2010) is a combination of memoir and reportage that also mixes prose with verse.*

We tell the story every year—
how we peered from the windows, shades drawn—
though nothing really happened,
the charred grass now green again.

We peered from the windows, shade drawn,   5
at the cross trussed like a Christmas tree,
the charred grass still green. Then
we darkened our rooms, lit the hurricane lamps.

At the cross trussed like a Christmas tree,
a few men gathered, white as angels in their gowns.   10
We darkened our room and lit hurricane lamps,
the wicks trembling in their fonts of oil.

It seemed the angels had gathered, white men in their gowns.
When they were done, they left quietly. No one came.
The wicks trembled all night in their fonts of oil;   15
by morning the flames had all dimmed.

When they were done, the men left quietly. No one came.
Nothing really happened.
By morning all the flames had dimmed.
We tell the story every year.   [2006]   20

≡ THINKING ABOUT THE TEXT

1. Trethewey has acknowledged that this poem is a *pantoum*. This form of verse consists of *quatrains* (stanzas of four lines each); also, the second and fourth lines of a quatrain are repeated as the first and third lines of the following quatrain, with the final line of the entire poem repeating its very first line. It's a difficult type of poem to write. Why do you think Trethewey attempted it here?

2. How does the poem use religious imagery?

3. What information does the poet leave out? Why do you think she omits it?

4. Why do you think the "we" of the poem "tell[s] the story every year"? Why tell the story at all? Why not tell it more often?

5. Twice, the speaker claims that "nothing really happened." Do you agree with her? Why, or why not?

≡ MAKING COMPARISONS

1. In giving her poem the title "Incident," Trethewey is surely aware of Cullen's poem. What other connections between these two texts do you feel encouraged by her to make?

2. Which of the two poems, Cullen's or Trethewey's, strikes you as more abstract? Does this difference lead to a difference in effect? Why, or why not?

3. Do the speakers in these two poems strike you as using pretty much the same tone? Refer to specific lines in each work.

≡ WRITING ABOUT ISSUES

1. Choose either Cullen's poem or Trethewey's, and write an essay in which you examine what the poem suggests about the act of *remembering* an incident of race-related injustice.

2. Cullen's poem is famous; does Trethewey's deserve to be equally well known? Write an essay addressing this question for your audience, making clear your criteria for artistic success.

3. Take a line from either Cullen's poem or Trethewey's, and write an essay showing how the line is applicable to an "incident" that you recently witnessed or saw being reported in the media.

4. Find and read at least three articles on racial discrimination in early twentieth-century Baltimore or on American laws against interracial marriage. Then write an essay explaining how these articles illuminate the "incident" described in Cullen's or Trethewey's poem.

WILLIAM BLAKE, "The Chimney Sweeper"

DEBORAH GARRISON, "Worked Late on a Tuesday Night"

Since the dawn of industrialization, Western nations have been roiled by continual struggles between labor and capital for economic justice. Industrialization brought wealth and power to some and great poverty to many others. Labor movements of the nineteenth and twentieth centuries sought to halt the exploitation of workers, including women and children, and redress imbalances by giving workers a greater share of the economic pie as well as safer and more humane working conditions. The struggles often took a turn toward violence, particularly during the nadirs of boom-and-bust economic cycles.

During the 1930s, the world suffered a great economic depression, when millions who wanted employment couldn't find it. Today, many agree that conditions under the so-called Great Recession that began in 2008 never approached the economic depths of the 1930s. Still, not everyone thrives. To compete in the new global economy, corporations cut budgets, relocate plants, outsource services, and automate facilities. As a result, large numbers of people have lost their jobs, others work for low wages, and even college graduates worry about their prospects for careers.

Though defenses of capitalism continue to be voiced, protests against it, like Occupy Wall Street, burst forth. Whatever their political stances, social activists and average citizens ponder how to define *justice* for workers and argue about what policies would promote it. In effect, the following poems also raise these issues by depicting conditions of work at various times in modern economic history.

■ BEFORE YOU READ

What are the characteristics of your ideal job? In what ways, if any, have your real jobs fallen short?

WILLIAM BLAKE
The Chimney Sweeper

In his own time, considered eccentric or even mad, William Blake (1757–1827) is today considered a major poet, painter, and printmaker in Western culture. As a printer and engraver, he lavishly illustrated his own editions of his poems, including his 1789 collection Songs of Innocence, *in which "The Chimney Sweeper" appeared; in 1794, he produced a companion volume,* Songs of Experience. *Blake is often cited as a forerunner of contemporary secular liberalism, feminism, and even birth control and divorce. Through both his verbal and visual art, Blake promoted his own self-devised religion that incorporated stories and characters from the Bible, often in unorthodox and subversive ways.*

When my mother died I was very young,
And my father sold me while yet my tongue
Could scarcely cry " 'weep! 'weep! 'weep! 'weep!"
So your chimneys I sweep & in soot I sleep.

There's little Tom Dacre, who cried when his head   5
That curled like a lamb's back, was shaved, so I said,
"Hush, Tom! never mind it, for when your head's bare,
You know that the soot cannot spoil your white hair."

And so he was quiet, & that very night,
As Tom was a-sleeping he had such a sight!   10
That thousands of sweepers, Dick, Joe, Ned, & Jack,
Were all of them locked up in coffins of black;

And by came an Angel who had a bright key,
And he opened the coffins & set them all free;
Then down a green plain, leaping, laughing they run,   15
And wash in a river and shine in the Sun.

Then naked & white, all their bags left behind,
They rise upon clouds, and sport in the wind.
And the Angel told Tom, if he'd be a good boy,
He'd have God for his father & never want joy.   20

And so Tom awoke; and we rose in the dark
And got with our bags & our brushes to work.
Though the morning was cold, Tom was happy & warm;
So if all do their duty, they need not fear harm.   *[1789]*

≡ THINKING ABOUT THE TEXT

1. How do colors matter in this poem?

2. What is the effect of the poem's obvious rhyming?

3. Why do you think that Blake made the dream Tom's rather than the speaker's?

4. Do you assume that the author agrees with the last line?

5. Blake wrote his poem at a time when many children in London indeed labored in filth as chimney sweepers and were even sold by family members for this service. What are the possible counterparts to such child workers today?

DEBORAH GARRISON
Worked Late on a Tuesday Night

*Deborah Garrison (b. 1965) was born in Ann Arbor, Michigan. She graduated
from Brown University in 1986 and received an M.A. from New York University.
Garrison worked at* The New Yorker *for fifteen years, where she was the senior
nonfiction editor. She is currently the poetry editor at Alfred A. Knopf as well as an
editor at Pantheon Books. A* Working Girl Can't Win *(1998), her first poetry collection, sold 30,000 copies. John Updike wrote that her poems have "a Dickinsonian
intensity." Her latest collection is* The Second Child *(2007).*

Again.
Midtown is blasted out and silent,
drained of the crowd and its doggy day.
I trample the scraps of deli lunches
some ate outdoors as they stared dumbly   5
or hooted at us career girls — the haggard
beauties, the vivid can-dos, open raincoats aflap
in the March wind as we crossed to and fro
in front of the Public Library.

Never thought you'd be one of them,   10
did you, little Lady?
Little Miss Phi Beta Kappa,
with your closetful of pleated
skirts, twenty-nine till death do us
part! Don't you see?   15
The good schoolgirl turns thirty,
forty, singing the song of time management
all day long, lugging the briefcase

home. So at 10:00 PM
you're standing here   20
with your hand in the air,
cold but too stubborn to reach
into your pocket for a glove, cursing
the freezing rain as though it were
your difficulty. It's pathetic,   25
and nobody's fault but
your own. Now

the tears,
down into the collar.
Cabs, cabs, but none for hire.   30
I haven't had dinner; I'm not half

of what I meant to be.
Among other things, the mother
of three. Too tired, tonight,
to seduce the father.   *[2000]*   35

≡ THINKING ABOUT THE TEXT

1. What specific words convey the speaker's mood? How would you describe her attitude toward work?

2. Describe what you think the speaker means by "singing the song of time management/all day long."

3. What does the speaker mean by "and nobody's fault but/your own"? What might be an alternative explanation for her plight? Do you think a man would write such a poem? Why, or why not?

4. Do you think the speaker is talking just about her situation or a group of people?

5. What is the effect of beginning the poem with "Again"? Why might readers be surprised that she was in a prestigious honor society? How might success in college be linked to success after? How might it not?

≡ MAKING COMPARISONS

1. What is the attitude toward work in these two poems? Which is the most pessimistic? Which is the most troubling?

2. Compare the ending of both poems. What thought does each conclusion leave you with?

≡ WRITING ABOUT ISSUES

1. Choose one of the two poems in this cluster, and write an essay explaining how it seems to define *justice* for workers. Make clear your own understanding of this concept.

2. Write an essay comparing the attention the two poems give to the speaker's self. To what extent do these poems' speakers look beyond themselves to offer insights into the larger world?

3. Recall an occasion when you or someone you know suffered unjust working conditions and yet failed to challenge them right away. Then write an essay in which you analyze the sufferer's state of mind — the thoughts and feelings that this person had at the time, including any psychological changes that he or she went through. If you wish, refer to one or both poems in this cluster.

4. Write an essay in which you apply the title of one of this cluster's poems to a recent news report. What major aspects of the report does the poem's title fit? What major aspects, if any, does the title not cover?

≡ Secret Crimes: Stories

EDGAR ALLAN POE, "The Tell-Tale Heart"

EDWARD J. DELANEY, "Clean"

If we are to believe commercial television, all crimes are solved and all criminals are caught and suitably punished. We would like to think so, but, of course, that is not always the case. Many crimes are never solved; and many criminals manage to avoid all official punishment. In such cases, the perpetrators are left to their own thoughts, which may be tranquil, remorseful, or a blend of satisfaction and guilt. For the sociopath or professional criminal perhaps there are no internal consequences. For many, however, socialized into a society where right and wrong are stressed, guilt and shame might be a form of punishment more severe than the consequence of public disclosure. Secret crimes are hardly foolproof.

The consequences for the killers in these two stories are complicated. In Poe's "The Tell-Tale Heart," guilt and paranoia overwhelm the narrator. Troubled by a crime that shapes his very identity. A secret crime might avoid the light of public disclosure, but the real consequences are often hidden in the hearts and minds of those undone by guilt.

EDGAR ALLAN POE
The Tell-Tale Heart

The life of Edgar Allan Poe (1809–1849) was relatively brief, its end tragically hastened by his alcohol and drug abuse, but his contributions to literature are unique. As a book reviewer, he produced pieces of literary criticism and theory that are still widely respected. As a poet, he wrote such classics as "The Raven" (1845), "The Bells" (1849), and "Annabel Lee" (1849). Moreover, his short fiction was groundbreaking and continues to be popular, a source for many films and television shows. With works such as "The Murders in the Rue Morgue" (1841), "The Gold Bug" (1843), and "The Purloined Letter" (1844), he pioneered the modern detective story. Other Poe tales are masterpieces of horror, including "The Fall of the House of Usher" (1842) and "The Pit and the Pendulum" (1842). The following tale, also one of Poe's best known, appeared in an 1843 issue of the periodical The Pioneer *and an 1845 issue of* The Broadway Journal *before being included in the 1850 collection of Poe's writings published after his death. The story has been adapted for film, television, and radio numerous times.*

True! — nervous — very, very dreadfully nervous I had been and am; but why *will* you say that I am mad? The disease had sharpened my senses — not destroyed — not dulled them. Above all was the sense of hearing acute. I heard all things in the heaven and in the earth. I heard many things in hell.

How, then, am I mad? Hearken! and observe how healthily — how calmly I can tell you the whole story.

It is impossible to say how first the idea entered my brain; but once conceived, it haunted me day and night. Object there was none. Passion there was none. I loved the old man. He had never wronged me. He had never given me insult. For his gold I had no desire. I think it was his eye! yes, it was this! One of his eyes resembled that of a vulture — a pale blue eye, with a film over it. Whenever it fell upon me, my blood ran cold; and so by degrees — very gradually — I made up my mind to take the life of the old man, and thus rid myself of the eye for ever.

Now this is the point. You fancy me mad. Madmen know nothing. But you should have seen *me*. You should have seen how wisely I proceeded — with what caution — with what foresight — with what dissimulation I went to work! I was never kinder to the old man than during the whole week before I killed him. And every night, about midnight, I turned the latch of his door and opened it — oh, so gently! And then, when I had made an opening sufficient for my head, I put in a dark lantern, all closed, closed, so that no light shone out, and then I thrust in my head. Oh, you would have laughed to see how cunningly I thrust it in! I moved it slowly — very, very slowly, so that I might not disturb the old man's sleep. It took me an hour to place my whole head within the opening so far that I could see him as he lay upon his bed. Ha — would a madman have been so wise as this? And then, when my head was well in the room, I undid the lantern cautiously — oh, so cautiously — cautiously (for the hinges creaked) — I undid it just so much that a single thin ray fell upon the vulture eye. And this I did for seven long nights — every night just after midnight — but I found the eye always closed; and so it was impossible to do the work; for it was not the old man who vexed me, but his Evil Eye. And every morning, when the day broke, I went boldly into the chamber, and spoke courageously to him, calling him by name in a hearty tone, and inquiring how he had passed the night. So you see he would have been a very profound old man, indeed, to suspect that every night, just at twelve, I looked in upon him while he slept.

Upon the eighth night I was more than usually cautious in opening the door. A watch's minute hand moves more quickly than did mine. Never before that night had I *felt* the extent of my own powers — of my sagacity. I could scarcely contain my feelings of triumph. To think that there I was, opening the door, little by little, and he not even to dream of my secret deeds or thoughts. I fairly chuckled at the idea; and perhaps he heard me; for he moved on the bed suddenly, as if startled. Now you may think that I drew back — but no. His room was as black as pitch with the thick darkness (for the shutters were close fastened, through fear of robbers), and so I knew that he could not see the opening of the door, and I kept pushing it on steadily, steadily.

I had my head in, and was about to open the lantern, when my thumb slipped upon the tin fastening, and the old man sprang up in the bed, crying out — "Who's there?"

I kept quite still and said nothing. For a whole hour I did not move a muscle, and in the meantime I did not hear him lie down. He was still sitting

5

up in the bed listening; — just as I have done, night after night, hearkening to the death watches in the wall.

Presently I heard a slight groan, and I knew it was the groan of mortal terror. It was not a groan of pain or of grief — oh, no! — it was the low stifled sound that arises from the bottom of the soul when overcharged with awe. I knew the sound well. Many a night, just at midnight, when all the world slept, it has welled up from my own bosom, deepening with its dreadful echo, the terrors that distracted me. I say I knew it well. I knew what the old man felt, and pitied him, although I chuckled at heart. I knew that he had been lying awake ever since the first slight noise, when he had turned in the bed. His fears had been ever since growing upon him. He had been trying to fancy them causeless, but could not. He had been saying to himself — "It is nothing but the wind in the chimney — it is only a mouse crossing the floor," or "it is merely a cricket which has made a single chirp." Yes, he has been trying to comfort himself with these suppositions; but he had found all in vain. *All in vain*; because Death, in approaching him, had stalked with his black shadow before him, and enveloped the victim. And it was the mournful influence of the unperceived shadow that caused him to feel — although he neither saw nor heard — to *feel* the presence of my head within the room.

When I had waited a long time, very patiently, without hearing him lie down, I resolved to open a little — a very, very little crevice in the lantern. So I opened it — you cannot imagine how stealthily, stealthily — until, at length, a single dim ray, like the thread of the spider, shot from out the crevice and full upon the vulture eye.

It was open — wide, wide open — and I grew furious as I gazed upon it. I saw it with perfect distinctness — all a dull blue, with a hideous veil over it that chilled the very marrow in my bones, but I could see nothing else of the old man's face or person: for I had directed the ray as if by instinct, precisely upon the damned spot.

And now have I not told you that what you mistake for madness is but over-acuteness of the senses? — now, I say, there came to my ears a low, dull, quick sound, such as a watch makes when enveloped in cotton. I knew *that* sound well too. It was the beating of the old man's heart. It increased my fury, as the beating of a drum stimulates the soldier into courage.   10

But even yet I refrained and kept still. I scarcely breathed. I held the lantern motionless. I tried how steadily I could maintain the ray upon the eye. Meantime the hellish tattoo of the heart increased. It grew quicker and quicker, and louder and louder every instant. The old man's terror *must* have been extreme! It grew louder, I say, louder every moment — do you mark me well? I have told you that I am nervous: so I am. And now at the dead hour of the night, amid the dreadful silence of that old house, so strange a noise as this excited me to uncontrollable terror. Yet, for some minutes longer I refrained and stood still. But the beating grew louder, louder! I thought the heart must burst. And now a new anxiety seized me — the sound would be heard by a neighbor! The old man's hour had come! With a loud yell, I threw open the lantern and leaped into the room. He shrieked once — once only. In an instant I dragged him to the floor, and pulled the heavy bed over him. I then smiled gaily, to find the deed so far done. But, for many minutes, the heart beat on with a muffled sound. This, however, did not vex me; it would not be heard through the wall. At length it ceased. The old man was dead. I removed the bed and examined the corpse. Yes, he was stone, stone dead. I placed my hand upon the heart and held it there many minutes. There was no pulsation. He was stone dead. His eye would trouble me no more.

If still you think me mad, you will think so no longer when I describe the wise precautions I took for the concealment of the body. The night waned, and I worked hastily, but in silence. First of all I dismembered the corpse. I cut off the head and the arms and the legs.

I then took up three planks from the flooring of the chamber, and deposited all between the scantlings. I then replaced the boards so cleverly, so cunningly, that no human eye — not even *his* — could have detected anything wrong. There was nothing to wash out — no stain of any kind — no blood-spot whatever. I had been too wary for that. A tub had caught all — ha! ha!

When I had made an end of these labors, it was four o'clock — still dark as midnight. As the bell sounded the hour, there came a knocking at the street door. I went down to open it with a light heart — for what had I *now* to fear? There entered three men, who introduced themselves, with perfect suavity, as officers of the police. A shriek had been heard by a neighbor during the night; suspicion of foul play had been aroused; information had been lodged at the police office, and they (the officers) had been deputed to search the premises.

I smiled — for *what* had I to fear? I bade the gentlemen welcome. The shriek, I said, was my own in a dream. The old man, I mentioned, was absent in the country. I took my visitors all over the house. I bade them search — search well. I led them, at length, to *his* chamber. I showed them his treasures, secure, undisturbed. In the enthusiasm of my confidence, I brought chairs into the room, and desired them *here* to rest from their fatigues, while I myself, in the wild audacity of my perfect triumph, placed my own seat upon the very spot beneath which reposed the corpse of the victim.

The officers were satisfied. My *manner* had convinced them. I was singularly at ease. They sat, and while I answered cheerily, they chatted familiar things. But, ere long, I felt myself getting pale and wished them gone. My head ached, and I fancied a ringing in my ears: but still they sat and still chatted. The ringing became more distinct: — it continued and became more distinct: I talked more freely to get rid of the feeling: but it continued and gained definitiveness — until, at length, I found that the noise was *not* within my ears.

No doubt I now grew *very* pale; — but I talked more fluently, and with a heightened voice. Yet the sound increased — and what could I do? It was a *low, dull, quick sound — much such a sound as a watch makes when enveloped in cotton.* I gasped for breath — and yet the officers heard it not. I talked more quickly — more vehemently; but the noise steadily increased. I arose and argued about trifles, in a high key and with violent gesticulations, but the noise steadily increased. Why *would* they not be gone? I paced the floor to and fro with heavy strides, as if excited to fury by the observation of the men — but the noise steadily increased. Oh God! what *could* I do? I foamed — I raved — I swore! I swung the chair upon which I had been sitting, and grated it upon

15

the boards, but the noise arose over all and continually increased. It grew louder — louder — *louder*! And still the men chatted pleasantly, and smiled. Was it possible they heard not? Almighty God! — no, no! They heard! — they suspected! — they *knew*! — they were making a mockery of my horror! — this I thought, and this I think. But any thing was better than this agony! Any thing was more tolerable than this derision! I could bear those hypocritical smiles no longer! I felt that I must scream or die! — and now — again! — hark! louder! louder! louder! *louder*! —

"Villains!" I shrieked, "dissemble no more! I admit the deed! — tear up the planks! — here, here! — it is the beating of his hideous heart!"   *[1843]*

≡ THINKING ABOUT THE TEXT

1. Why do you think the narrator killed the old man? Was he simply "mad," or do you gather that he had a particular reason? Explain.

2. Why do you think Poe spends as much time as he does on the narrator's observations of the old man prior to the killing?

3. Of the various senses, hearing seems to be the one emphasized in this story. Where does it come up in the text? Why do you think Poe chose to focus his tale on this particular sense? What other senses are also referred to here?

4. Other than his hearing, what features of the narrator's behavior and thinking shape your view of him?

5. If the police didn't arrive, do you think the narrator would have been able to keep the secret? For how long? Explain.

EDWARD J. DELANEY

Clean

Edward J. Delaney (b. 1957) is a journalist and a producer of documentaries as well as a writer of fiction. Newspapers he has worked for include the Denver Post *and the* Chicago Tribune. *With Dustin Pedroia of the Boston Red Sox, he wrote the nonfiction book* Born to Play *(2009). One of his films,* The Times Were Never So Bad *(2007), is about Andre Dubus, author of the short story "Killings" that precedes this story. Delaney's works of fiction include the novels* Broken Irish *(2011) and* Warp & Weft *(2004), along with a short story collection,* The Drowning: And Other Stories *(1999). He teaches creative writing at Roger Williams University in Providence, Rhode Island. The following story appeared in the November 2012 issue of* The Atlantic *magazine.*

You think of that night endlessly from your imprisonment, the decisions made, the chain of mistakes. It had begun with your two buddies, a fifth of cheap vodka, and half a gallon of orange juice; one of these friends had suggested the confrontation. He said this kid, Barry, was cutting in on your girl—well, she wasn't even really your girl yet, the flirtation was just in its formative moments—something that you, at sixteen, had no intention of allowing.

He'd been walking home, at night. He worked at a burger place in town and, even drunk, you'd known a spot to intercept him. Again, at the suggestion of your friends. There he was, his backpack slung over his shoulder, looking at you as if not even sure who you were. You'd decided you would rough him up, and he'd decided to fight back, and you'd picked up a rock, and you'd swung it at his head. A minute later he was on the ground, dead.

You think of how, as drunk as you had been, you instantly sobered. The discussion was quick, and its determinations would last a lifetime. You waited for him to somehow come to; soon enough he was irredeemably cold. But you three had decided by then. No one would tell. No one would try to explain that the moment was one of passion and mistakes. In your long memory, telling wasn't even part of that shaky conversation, your voices all gone weepy and scared.

You took the rock, with its rime of blood, and threw it in a pond. You filled Barry's backpack with other rocks and into the pond that went, too. You were driving your old Pontiac, and the first odd decision was to drive home, go in your bedroom, and strip the top sheet off your bed, to bring it back to the scene as your buddies waited, hidden in the nearby woods with Barry, the body dragged in by the feet. You got your mother's gardening trowel from the nail in the garage. Then her garden claw.

By the time you drove up, watching for headlights, you had calmed a bit. You were thinking now, your head clicking with logic and forethought that were a revelation in themselves. Your buddies had kicked the blood under dirt, and you wondered as you came back if they had been talking of turning you in. Apparently they had not.   5

You wrapped the body in the sheet and drove to a place you thought would work. Again, the choices made: A place close to your house, less than half a mile. But a place far enough away from other houses, and with somewhat yielding ground. The three of you, all high-school athletes, did not tire that night, rotating through the clawing and digging, going deeper, no sloppy shallow grave here. When his sheet-wrapped body went into the groundwater that had gathered at the bottom, you felt for that glorious instant as if the problem was now solved. You all filled the hole with dirt and stomped it down, then drove to the ocean at dawn and walked into the surf, fully clothed, emerging salty and bloodless.

This was '72. You think of forty years gone past, and the girl. For days after, you did the calculus, of risk and probability. You realized in that panicky first day that his wallet had gone into the ground with him; everything had not been fully considered. You and the other two never spoke of it directly again, and you weighed the human factors you could not control. You sensed, by the light of day, some shrill and growing prospect of being caught. Then you got lucky. Barry, the aspiring hippie, had been trying to get her to take off with him, hitchhiking with backpacks, cross-country. He did not get along with his parents; he craved adventure and escape. She told the police she guessed he must have gone, then she keened at her presumed abandonment. You heard about that at school and felt a surge of both relief and fury, that Barry had made the plan and that she had apparently considered it. You hated her for choosing him.

The conclusion was simple. Barry was deemed just another wandering soul, a longhair, a dreamer. He'd return in due time. The only thing was that your mother could not stop going on about the missing bedsheet. Where did it go? How do you lose a bedsheet? "Now you've broken up the set," she said. You heard her telling the neighbor about her son's mysteriously losing a sheet, and you wanted to make her stop.

The girl: Barry gone, you dated her for a few months, but found you had nothing to talk about. She turned out, in fact, to be mildly irritating, and that was that.

Senior year: Thinking back over the decades, you are appalled to consider   10
how little you worried about what had happened. In fact, you barely thought about it at all. In your mind, It (you could not bring yourself to use the more specific word) wasn't even your fault. You'd been egged on, drunk, by the other two. You met other girls, and you played your games, and you avoided the vicinity of the grave. You were an adolescent; you did not dwell on things that might ruin your fun.

Your buddies: you realized that they would not talk, even when drunk. Besides, the three of you were no longer that friendly. Typical teenagers, you all had found other interests, other friends.

College: those were the years when you needed to tell yourself what you were, and what you were not. So: You were a good person. You were not violent. Indeed, in those years you became milder and milder, almost as if shedding the ill-thought fashions of your youth like a bad sweater. Changing times. You held that memory in your stomach, but you functioned, actually, *well.* It had been three years then, and no one was going to find out. Then you went home for Thanksgiving and you saw bulldozers edged up toward that place. A new housing tract. You spent the weekend sleepless, telling yourself that even when the body emerged, the police would have no suspects, no motive. But the soft ground in which your secret lay was wetland. New environmental laws had been passed, and the housing tract stopped fewer than a hundred yards from where the body lay buried. The next spring, you told your parents you were going to stay on at your distant school, do summer classes, accelerate, and when you were done with that, you stayed on as a grad student. When those unbidden memories occurred, those predawn panics, you pushed deeper into your studies, forcing the ghosts away. You graduated with your parents and sisters smiling at your side for the picture, and then you moved farther west still.

In love, you married. Some nights you felt so intimate with her that you wanted to tell her, felt you had to. Felt she would hold your secret and love you still. But then one odd night, an awkward dinner, and you weren't so sure you two were always in tune. The marriage evened into something mellow and a bit more distant, and the impulse passed. When you had children, you tried to be good. The business flourished, and the money came in without much struggle.

Why, in your thirties, did you begin to obsess about the hidden crime? When you read the articles about DNA, and how it could tell of a long-past crime, did you begin to see a story that hadn't been completely written? You became an insomniac. You played that one minute of your life in an endless loop on the pale wall of your skull. The phone suddenly felt as if it would go off. You would see a police car thousands of miles from your hometown and feel on edge. You worried in those years that your unmasking was imminent, but then nothing happened. During the holidays, you had your parents out for a visit to a warmer climate. Sometimes, your mother would start in about the missing sheet. You'd all laugh in reminiscence.

Your father died, and you flew back to take care of things. You went 15 through his desk, sorting out his papers, tending to your mother. At the bottom of a drawer was a yellowed bit of newspaper, clipped down to a tiny headline and one- paragraph item. *Local boy reported missing.* Strangely, the photo in the paper, though blurred, didn't match the memory in your head, of that face on the side of the road, turning to meet the judgment of your headlights.

Why had your father kept this? What did he guess? Did you make noise that night as you came and went? At the funeral, a Navy ensign played taps, and your mother got the triangled flag. Your father went into that neat, nearly surgically cut hole with his own secrets. You burned the newspaper in his kettle grill on the back deck, igniting some charcoal and then making a steak.

That evening, you left your mother's house near dark and went walking in those woods. Twenty years had passed, more. You'd built a life now. In this cold ground was what would always threaten to change it. You had an exact memory of the spot he was buried, but that memory failed you, too. You could find no place that was at all like the place you remembered.

Flying home, you realized someone had to have been following all this. Were the police so sure of the hitchhiking story, even in 1972? Could they not have tried to look into it? Who was assigned to the case, and could he have known of you? But you saw no signs of any investigation. Maybe when Barry eventually did not return home, too much time had passed. Maybe they just didn't care that much. But you knew a file must have been kept at the police station, and your desire to open that file and see what was written became instantly unbearable. You were 35,000 feet in the air, over the arrayed pivot-circles of Kansas, heading toward the sun. By the time you landed, you felt the anxiety was finally over. In long-term parking, you slipped into the leather seat of your German car as if it were a glove that fit you perfectly.

In your forties, you thought of the boy less, but when the memory came to you, it gave you an unremitting ache. You could barely remember who you were then, what urges drove you, or what aspirations you'd had. The indisputable irony was that the aftermath of it all had given you focus, and direction. Who would you have become instead, if It had not happened? You also felt a welling anger at Barry himself. If he was going to leave, why didn't he just leave? Was this talk of hitchhiking just something to woo his wanted girl, or was he really going to do it? You thought about how, if he'd decamped a day sooner, or if you three had not drunk that plastic jug of orange juice and that bottle of vodka, that night would just be something forgotten, rather than a specific date on the calendar you suffered through each year, and from which you could count, to the very minute, your growing remove. The colors faded like a washed-out Kodachrome.

In the eleventh year of your marriage, you found out your wife had been   20 having an affair. She confessed; you were shocked. Boredom, she told you tearfully. Someone else had offered escape, she said.

"I love you," she said, "but you're a dull, passionless person. You have no fire."

She was right, but now wrong. You knew who the man was. For the first time in thirty years, the familiar urge came back to you, for the same reasons. The careful decades of telling yourself you were different now crumbled, in an instant. You could have done it again, right then, had you decided to. But you did not.

Instead you got up from the couch and went out on your deck with a drink (good wine, never the hard stuff) and looked at the sky and thought about the careful, boring man you had sculpted yourself into. No passion at all. Later, your tearstained wife came out and sat with you in the wind of sunset and said she wanted to try to work things out, for your daughters. Her love of your daughters made her want to stay with you and find the middle ground. You wanted badly to offer your forgiveness, as you badly wanted forgiveness for yourself.

Yes, you'd had chances for affairs, but you always held back. Your reason wasn't strict morality, more the fear of the weight of yet another secret. The thought of that was just too heavy. You accepted life as it was, and you walked in the evening, to get air.

One night, a few years later, the phone rang and your wife held it in front   25 of you, saying "It's Dennis." Dennis who? You heard the voice and you were back to that night. Dennis, your long-ago buddy, was not well. Lymphoma. Three or four months. He had the urge to tell, to unburden. He had thought about that night every day of his life, he said into the phone. He'd spoken of it many times over the years, he said, in the darkness of the confessional. Father Shea had told him his soul was now clean, even as it felt not.

"Dennis, I can't tell you what to do," you said to him. "We're all different people now. Do what you feel you must. I would understand."

"Thank you for that," he said. "I guess telling would be easy for me now. I'll be dead before I have to face the consequences. But I think we all should have." You had the phone to your ear, listening to him. He was a stranger. As Barry had been. Someone about whom you knew nothing.

Dennis asked about your family then, and you told him. He said he had not heard from Jeff in years, no idea where he'd gone. When you hung up, you were giddy that the secret might come out. You were surprised, and gratified, at the relief you felt. For weeks you sat at your desk and prepared things, just in case. You slept straight through each night. You got on the computer and read about juvenile law. You were all sixteen when It happened. Had the three of you gone to the police that night, explained you'd been in a fight that went out of control, you probably would have been out by the age of eighteen. Now you quietly imagined the neat rectangle of a cell, with a thin mattress. The thought didn't seem as foreboding as it had when you were young and felt the possibilities of life. This future now seemed orderly, calm. You had forgiven your wife, and you imagined and craved her own understanding. You had never given her the opportunity, never shared the secret. You concluded that this was why, in your entire life, you'd never felt true intimacy.

That night, you Googled Barry's name, and found nothing. So many years had passed; who'd remember? Where would Barry's name have been preserved? He seemed to have never existed. You remembered back in '75, when word had quietly come that his parents had moved away, some new job, or escape from worries. But now, so long after, people would remember him. You lay down in bed against your sleeping wife and felt the powerful promise of the simplicity, and the real facts of your life.

But your conversation had apparently given Dennis the peace not to speak, or perhaps he had simply died before he had a chance. No one told you anything. After a long stretch of months in which a tap did not come on your door, you went to the online obituaries and saw that he was gone. You checked on Father Shea, and he too had passed, years before. Your younger daughter walked in the room, said you looked weird, and walked out. By dinner, you were who you were again.

Later that year, your mother succumbed, the story of the missing bedsheet forever silenced. Back in town to close the house, you now did not venture into the dark woods. You and your sisters sorted things out and renewed bonds. You promised to stay in touch, knowing you probably would not.

That evening, at a hotel by the airport, you watched local TV. To your shock, you saw a vaguely familiar face. A woman, real estate. She was the girl, from all those years before. You'd nearly forgotten her name. She was, like you, an aging person. Now she sold high-end real estate, and seemed to have had some ineffectual cosmetic surgery. She had a horsey, drawn face, and wore a giant rock on her left ring finger. Did she ever think of Barry? He'd only been a boy who made her promises then went off hitchhiking, leaving her out of his adventure. You wondered about it as you tried to sleep.

You flew home and idly considered the third of you, Jeff, somewhere out there with the other half of your secret. You sat on your deck and drank some wine and watched the sun set over the Pacific. Another day had elapsed between you and that night. You had come to this place, imprisoned by what you were, what you had done, never able fully to be inside the life you made. You imagined how you would feel to just live.

The irony of getting away with something was that you were your own keeper. You were the executioner: in a pang of remorse, you could just open your mouth and change your life. You felt almost as if you would. But, greedy,

30

you always wanted to savor one more day, even as that day turned leaden with a memory that no longer went away. It could not be put aside as it was your senior year of high school, when something that had happened the year before may as well have never happened at all. Who were you? How did you find the way to make it just not be? Now, an older man, you decided that if the time came to tell, you would edit Dennis and Jeff from the story, a small act of charity.

The vast ocean shimmered below you, endless expanses in which things   35 could be effortlessly hidden, even as what you looked at was only a knife's edge along greater stretches past the distant horizon. Even as the silver surface only whispered of the dark depths, the things you could not see. This was your life now, orderly, calm. This was how things were now. Clean. You knew you would sleep as well as one might be expected to, all of us with our own given histories.   *[2012]*

≡ THINKING ABOUT THE TEXT

1. It is fairly unusual for a story to be narrated in the second person ("you"). Why do you think Delaney uses this technique?

2. The story is entitled "Clean," and that word appears in the final paragraph. But how helpful is it as a guide to the story? Other than the ending, what specific passages does it connect to?

3. What, specifically, are the effects on the protagonist of his murder and of his failure to confess? How guilty does he seem to feel about the murder he has committed? Use specific passages to support your answer. How well does he seem to understand himself?

4. With the last words of the story — "all of us with our own given histories" — the protagonist seems to imply that many people go through comparable experiences. How typical a person does he strike you as being? Is he unusually bad? To what extent can you sympathize with him?

5. Did you think that after the phone conversation with Dennis the protagonist's secret would go public and his guilt would be revealed? Why, or why not?

≡ MAKING COMPARISONS

1. Describe the effect of secrecy on the two killers.

2. Describe what you think the relationship between truth and intimacy is for the narrators of these two stories. Are secrets an impediment to relationships? Explain.

☰ WRITING ABOUT ISSUES

1. Write an essay agreeing or disagreeing with the statement from the penultimate paragraph of "Clean": "The irony of getting away with something was that you were your own keeper." You might use the three stories here as support, your own experience, or other stories of films.

2. Recall an occasion when you agreed to keep a secret, though you felt guilty about doing so. (Choose a secret that you are willing to reveal now.) Then, write an essay in which you identify the issues that arose for you at the time. If you wish, refer to one or both of the stories in this cluster.

3. Research a real-life criminal case that is as yet unsolved—perhaps one in your local community. Then, write an essay in which you speculate about how the perpetrator(s) of this crime thinks. If you wish, refer to one or both of the stories in this cluster.

≡ A Dream of Justice: Poems by Langston Hughes

LANGSTON HUGHES, "Open Letter to the South"

LANGSTON HUGHES, "Theme for English B"

LANGSTON HUGHES, "Harlem"

Inspired by two of the great poetic voices of American life, Walt Whitman and Carl Sandburg, Langston Hughes is often thought of as the African American poet laureate, a writer who is able to sing eloquently about the reality and idealism of democracy in America. He was committed to telling the truth about the lives of black people. In the introduction to *The Collected Poems of Langston Hughes*, it is noted that Hughes wrote of "the joys and sorrows, the trials and triumphs, of ordinary black folk, in the language of their typical speech and composed out of a genuine love of these people."

In response to the Depression of the 1930s, Hughes became radicalized by the poverty and injustice he saw everywhere in black America. His poems from this period are radical, indeed. "Open Letter to the South" calls for a socialist solidarity against oppression. Although he later became less radical in his poetry, "Theme for English B" and "Harlem" still reflect his belief that poetry is a form of social action. At the heart of all Hughes's poetry was the deferred dream of African Americans to achieve the freedom and equality promised to all in America.

≡ BEFORE YOU READ

Can you imagine what would have happened to your personality if a dream of yours (perhaps going to college, playing a sport, or marrying someone you loved deeply) were denied? What would you do if America was not living up to its stated ideals or if those ideals were suddenly altered significantly? Would you express your disappointment publicly or only privately?

LANGSTON HUGHES
Open Letter to the South

Langston Hughes (1902–1967) has long been regarded as a major African American writer and is increasingly seen as an important contributor to American literature in general. Like Countee Cullen, Hughes was actively involved in the 1920s movement called the Harlem Renaissance. Then and later, he worked in various genres, including fiction, drama, and autobiography. Nevertheless, he is primarily known for his poems. This poem was originally published in New Masses *in 1932 as "Red Flag over Tuskegee." It clearly reflected the feeling among many working-class intellectuals and artists in the 1930s that solidarity among the workers of the world was the only sure path toward freedom and equality.*

914

Corbis Historical/
Getty Images

White workers of the South
    Miners,
    Farmers,
    Mechanics,
    Mill hands,   5
    Shop girls,
    Railway men,
    Servants,
    Tobacco workers,
    Sharecroppers,   10
    GREETINGS!

I am the black worker,
    Listen:
That the land might be ours,
And the mines and the factories and the office towers   15
At Harlan, Richmond, Gastonia, Atlanta, New Orleans;
That the plants and the roads and the tools of power
Be ours:

Let us forget what Booker T. said,
"Separate as the fingers."   20

Let us become instead, you and I,
One single hand
That can united rise
To smash the old dead dogmas of the past—
To kill the lies of color   25
That keep the rich enthroned
And drive us to the time-clock and the plow
Helpless, stupid, scattered, and alone — as now—
Race against race,
Because one is black,   30
Another white of face.

Let us new lessons learn,
All workers,
New life-ways make,
One union form: 35
Until the future burns out
Every past mistake
Let us together, say:
"You are my brother, black or white,
You my sister—now—today!"   40
For me, no more, the great migration to the North.

Instead: migration into force and power—
Tuskegee with a new flag on the tower!
On every lynching tree, a poster crying FREE
Because, O poor white workers,   45
You have linked your hands with me.

We did not know that we were brothers.
Now we know!
Out of that brotherhood
Let power grow!   50
We did not know
That we were strong.
Now we see
In union lies our strength.
Let union be   55
The force that breaks the time-clock,
Smashes misery,
Takes land,
Takes factories,
Takes office towers,   60
Takes tools and banks and mines.
Railroads, ships and dams,
Until the forces of the world
Are ours!

White worker,
Here is my hand.   65

Today,
We're Man to Man.   *[1932]*

≡ **THINKING ABOUT THE TEXT**

1. Who does Hughes blame for "the lies of color" (line 25) that divide black from white? Do you agree?

2. Booker T. Washington (1856–1915), the most prominent African American of his day, is now often seen as an accommodationist who urged only gradual progress toward equality between blacks and whites. Why do you think Hughes tells his readers to "forget what Booker T. said" (line 19)?

3. If you think of this poem as an argument, what is Hughes's claim? Who is his audience, and what is his evidence? Do you think he makes the right choices for his argument?

4. What do you think Hughes means by the following lines: "We did not know that we were brothers. / Now we know!" (lines 47–48)?

5. Hughes is hoping that class solidarity is stronger than racial divisions. Was this the case in 1932? Is it the case today?

LANGSTON HUGHES
Theme for English B

Langston Hughes wrote "Theme for English B" in 1949, when he was twenty-five years older than the poem's speaker. As a young man, he had attended a "college on the hill above Harlem": Columbia University.

The instructor said,
    Go home and write
    a page tonight.
    And let that page come out of you—
    Then, it will be true.   5

I wonder if it's that simple?
I am twenty-two, colored, born in Winston-Salem.
I went to school there, then Durham, then here
to this college on the hill above Harlem.
I am the only colored student in my class.   10
The steps from the hill lead down into Harlem,
through a park, then I cross St. Nicholas,

Eighth Avenue, Seventh, and I come to the Y,
the Harlem Branch Y, where I take the elevator
up to my room, sit down, and write this page: 15

It's not easy to know what is true for you or me
at twenty-two, my age. But I guess I'm what
I feel and see and hear, Harlem, I hear you:
hear you, hear me — we two — you, me, talk on this page.
(I hear New York, too.) Me — who?   20
Well, I like to eat, sleep, drink, and be in love.
I like to work, read, learn, and understand life.
I like a pipe for a Christmas present,
or records — Bessie,° bop, or Bach.
I guess being colored doesn't make me *not* like   25
the same things other folks like who are other races.
So will my page be colored that I write?
Being me, it will not be white.
But it will be
a part of you, instructor.   30
You are white —
yet a part of me, as I am part of you.
That's American.
Sometimes perhaps you don't want to be a part of me.
Nor do I often want to be a part of you.   35
But we are, that's true!
As I learn from you,
I guess you learn from me —
although you're older — and white —
and somewhat more free.   40
This is my page for English B.   [1949]

≡ THINKING ABOUT THE TEXT

1. What do you think the instructor's response to "my page" (line 41)
   would be? What would yours be?

2. What do you think the instructor was hoping for? On what basis does
   the narrator seem to critique the assignment?

3. What do you think the narrator means by "American" in line 33? After
   more than sixty years, does it mean something different?

4. What do you think he means by the line "It's not easy to know what is
   true for you or me / at twenty-two" (lines 16–17)? Do you agree?

Bessie: Bessie Smith (1898?–1937), the famous American blues singer.

≡ MAKING COMPARISONS

1. Although this poem, like the previous one, seems written to a white audience, its tone seems less aggressive. Is this your reading? What lines seem particularly diplomatic in contrast to "Open Letter to the South"?

2. The emphasis on freedom here seems more indirect than in the previous poem. What do you think Hughes means by "free" in the next-to-last line? Would you agree with him then (1949)? Now?

3. Is "Today, / We're Man to Man" (lines 67–68) from "Open Letter to the South" the most hopeful (or naive) line in the three poems?

LANGSTON HUGHES

Harlem

Sometimes called "A Dream Deferred," "Harlem" is Hughes's most anthologized poem and has become synonymous with African Americans' long struggle for freedom and equality.

What happens to a dream deferred?

    Does it dry up
    like a raisin in the sun?
    Or fester like a sore —
    And then run?
    Does it stink like rotten meat?   5
    Or crust and sugar over —
    like a syrupy sweet?

    Maybe it just sags
    like a heavy load.   10

    Or does it explode?   [1951]

≡ THINKING ABOUT THE TEXT

1. The inspiration for Lorraine Hansberry's famous play, *A Raisin in the Sun*, Hughes's brief poem asks a question and then answers it with more questions. Is this effective? Should he have been more explicit?

2. What is the "dream deferred" (line 1)?

3. The alternatives given are specific and concrete metaphors presumably embodied in people. What kind of person would be "like a raisin in the sun" (line 3)?

4. How would you imagine a person who stank "like rotten meat" (line 6) would behave? One who "sags / like a heavy load" (lines 9–10)? One who is "like a syrupy sweet" (line 8)?

5. How do you read the last line?

≡ MAKING COMPARISONS

1. Why do you think "Harlem" is the most popular of the three poems presented here?

2. Are there hints in the previous poems of the ideas developed in "Harlem"?

3. Which poem would you recommend to someone from another country who is trying to understand our racial history? Why?

≡ WRITING ABOUT ISSUES

1. Several arguments are made in "Open Letter to the South." Choose one to analyze in terms of issue, claim, evidence, audience, and persuasion. (See the section on "Looking at Literature as Argument," p. 63.)

2. Write an essay that agrees or disagrees with Hughes's suggestion in "Open Letter to the South."

3. Write an essay about your personal responses to these poems. Include what you think the poems mean, whether you agree or not with the writer's points, and what emotions the poems provoked.

4. "Open Letter to the South" was written in the 1930s, and we know that the civil rights movement didn't gain serious national attention until the mid-1960s. Since many other voices besides Hughes's were addressing the lack of freedom among America's minorities, especially African Americans, how can you account for the length of time it took for freedom and equality to become serious issues among white voters? Write an essay that addresses this issue.

SOPHOCLES, *Antigone*

IDA FINK, *The Table*

Civil disobedience is nonviolent dissent that assumes that moral law can require violation of human law. For recent examples, consider Myanmar, Iran, and China, where advocates of democracy dare to resist dictators. For most Americans, these are distant places. By studying the protests in them, however, you can better understand how literature has depicted similar acts. The reverse is true as well: literary works about such defiance can shed light on its current role in these nations. So, here we connect Sophocles' ancient tragedy *Antigone* with Ida Fink's account of the limits and strengths of recollecting the Holocaust.

Think in particular about how the following plays show different forms of carrying out—or attempting to carry out—justice, and how those efforts are resisted.

≡ BEFORE YOU READ

Around the world today, many protesters claim to be working on behalf of "human rights," a term that was the subject of a United Nations declaration in 1948. What does this term mean to you? What specific rights do you associate with it?

SOPHOCLES

Antigone

Translated by Robert Fagles

Along with Aeschylus and Euripides, Sophocles (496? B.C.E. – 406? B.C.E.) is considered one of the greatest writers of tragedy in ancient Athens. During his lifetime, he was much respected in the city, often winning its dramatic competitions. Evidently, he wrote over one hundred plays, but only seven survive complete. As a practitioner of tragedy, Sophocles was innovative. Among other things, he increased the number of actors on stage from two to three, while reducing the chorus from fifty to fifteen. Productions of his plays did remain traditional in that the performers wore masks and were exclusively male. Oedipus the King *and* Antigone *continue to be much performed today; through the centuries, there have been numerous adaptations of them, such as Jean Anouilh's 1944 version of* Antigone, *a challenge to the Nazi occupiers of Paris.* Antigone *was first produced in 441 B.C.E., more than a decade before* Oedipus the King *was first produced. Just before the action of* Antigone *begins, the heroine's two brothers have killed each other in battle. One, Eteocles, was defending Thebes; the other, Polynices, was leading an army against it. The current*

*ruler of Thebes, Antigone's uncle Creon, now forbids burial of Polynices — a com-
mand that Antigone will defy.*

CHARACTERS

ANTIGONE, *daughter of Oedipus and Jocasta*
ISMENE, *sister of Antigone*
A CHORUS *of old Theban citizens and their* LEADER
CREON, *king of Thebes, uncle of Antigone and Ismene*
A SENTRY
HAEMON, *son of Creon and Eurydice*
TIRESIAS, *a blind prophet*
A MESSENGER
EURYDICE, *wife of Creon*
GUARDS, ATTENDANTS, AND A BOY

TIME AND SCENE: *The royal house of Thebes. It is still night, and the invading armies
of Argos have just been driven from the city. Fighting on opposite sides, the sons
of Oedipus, Eteocles and Polynices, have killed each other in combat. Their uncle,
Creon, is now king of Thebes.*

   Enter Antigone, slipping through the central doors of the palace. She
motions to her sister, Ismene, who follows her cautiously toward an altar at
the center of the stage.

ANTIGONE:	My own flesh and blood — dear sister, dear Ismene,	
	how many griefs our father Oedipus handed down!	
	Do you know one, I ask you, one grief	
	that Zeus° will not perfect for the two of us	
	while we still live and breathe? There's nothing,	5
	no pain — our lives are pain — no private shame,	
	no public disgrace, nothing I haven't seen	
	in your griefs and mine. And now this:	
	an emergency decree, they say, the Commander	
	has just declared for all of Thebes.	10
	What, haven't you heard? Don't you see?	
	The doom reserved for enemies	
	marches on the ones we love the most.	
ISMENE:	Not I, I haven't heard a word, Antigone.	
	Nothing of loved ones,	15
	no joy or pain has come my way, not since	
	the two of us were robbed of our two brothers,	
	both gone in a day, a double blow —	
	not since the armies of Argos vanished,	
	just this very night. I know nothing more,	20

4 Zeus: The highest Olympian deity.

whether our luck's improved or ruin's still to come.
ANTIGONE: I thought so. That's why I brought you out here,
      past the gates, so you could hear in private.
ISMENE: What's the matter? Trouble, clearly . . .
      you sound so dark, so grim.   25
ANTIGONE: Why not? Our own brothers' burial!
      Hasn't Creon graced one with all the rites,
      disgraced the other? Eteocles, they say,
      has been given full military honors,
      rightly so — Creon's laid him in the earth   30
      and he goes with glory down among the dead.
      But the body of Polynices, who died miserably —
      why, a city-wide proclamation, rumor has it,
      forbids anyone to bury him, even mourn him.
      He's to be left unwept, unburied, a lovely treasure   35
      for birds that scan the field and feast to their heart's content.

      Such, I hear, is the martial law our good Creon
      lays down for you and me — yes, me, I tell you —
      and he's coming here to alert the uninformed
      in no uncertain terms,   40
      and he won't treat the matter lightly. Whoever
      disobeys in the least will die, his doom is sealed:
      stoning to death inside the city walls!

      There you have it. You'll soon show what you are,
      worth your breeding, Ismene, or a coward —   45
      for all your royal blood.
ISMENE: My poor sister, if things have come to this,
      who am I to make or mend them, tell me,
      what good am I to you?
ANTIGONE: Decide.
      Will you share the labor, share the work?   50
ISMENE: What work, what's the risk? What do you mean?
ANTIGONE:

Raising her hands.

      Will you lift up his body with these bare hands
      and lower it with me?
ISMENE: What? You'd bury him —
      when a law forbids the city?
ANTIGONE: Yes!
      He is my brother and — deny it as you will —   55
      your brother too.
      No one will ever convict me for a traitor.
ISMENE: So desperate, and Creon has expressly —
ANTIGONE: No,
      he has no right to keep me from my own.

ISMENE: Oh my sister, think—   60
    think how our own father died, hated,
    his reputation in ruins, driven on
    by the crimes he brought to light himself
    to gouge out his eyes with his own hands—
    then mother . . . his mother and wife, both in one,   65
    mutilating her life in the twisted noose—
    and last, our two brothers dead in a single day,
    both shedding their own blood, poor suffering boys,
    battling out their common destiny hand-to-hand.
    Now look at the two of us, left so alone . . .   70
    think what a death we'll die, the worst of all
    if we violate the laws and override
    the fixed decree of the throne, its power—
    we must be sensible. Remember we are women,
    we're not born to contend with men. Then too,   75
    we're underlings, ruled by much stronger hands,
    so we must submit in this, and things still worse.

    I, for one, I'll beg the dead to forgive me—
    I'm forced, I have no choice—I must obey
    the ones who stand in power. Why rush to extremes?   80
    It's madness, madness.
ANTIGONE: I won't insist,
    no, even if you should have a change of heart,
    I'd never welcome you in the labor, not with me.
    So, do as you like, whatever suits you best—
    I'll bury him myself.   85
    And even if I die in the act, that death will be a glory.
    I'll lie with the one I love and loved by him—
    an outrage sacred to the gods! I have longer
    to please the dead than please the living here:
    in the kingdom down below I'll lie forever.   90
    Do as you like, dishonor the laws
    the gods hold in honor.
ISMENE: I'd do them no dishonor . . .
    but defy the city? I have no strength for that.
ANTIGONE: You have your excuses. I am on my way,
    I'll raise a mound for him, for my dear brother.   95
ISMENE: Oh Antigone, you're so rash—I'm so afraid for you!
ANTIGONE: Don't fear for me. Set your own life in order.
ISMENE: Then don't, at least, blurt this out to anyone.
    Keep it a secret. I'll join you in that, I promise.
ANTIGONE: Dear god, shout it from the rooftops. I'll hate you   100
    all the more for silence—tell the world!
ISMENE: So fiery—and it ought to chill your heart.

ANTIGONE: I know I please where I must please the most.

ISMENE: Yes, if you can, but you're in love with impossibility.

ANTIGONE: Very well then, once my strength gives out   105
    I will be done at last.

ISMENE: You're wrong from the start,
    you're off on a hopeless quest.

ANTIGONE: If you say so, you will make me hate you,
    and the hatred of the dead, by all rights,
    will haunt you night and day.   110
    But leave me to my own absurdity, leave me
    to suffer this—dreadful thing. I'll suffer
    nothing as great as death without glory.

Exit to the side.

ISMENE: Then go if you must, but rest assured,
    wild, irrational as you are, my sister,   115
    you are truly dear to the ones who love you.

*Withdrawing to the palace. Enter a Chorus, the old citizens of Thebes, chanting as
the sun begins to rise.*

CHORUS: Glory!—great beam of sun, brightest of all
    that ever rose on the seven gates of Thebes,
        you burn through night at last!
                Great eye of the golden day,   120
    mounting the Dirce's° banks you throw him back—
    the enemy out of Argos, the white shield, the man of bronze—
    he's flying headlong now
                the bridle of fate stampeding him with pain!

    And he had driven against our borders,   125
    launched by the warring claims of Polynices—
    like an eagle screaming, winging havoc
    over the land, wings of armor
    shielded white as snow,
    a huge army massing,   130
    crested helmets bristling for assault.

He hovered above our roofs, his vast maw gaping
closing down around our seven gates,
        his spears thirsting for the kill
                but now he's gone, look,   135
before he could glut his jaws with Theban blood
or the god of fire put our crown of towers to the torch.

He grappled the Dragon none can master—Thebes—
        the clang of our arms like thunder at his back!

121 the Dirce: A river near Thebes.

Zeus hates with a vengeance all bravado,   140
the mighty boasts of men. He watched them
coming on in a rising flood, the pride
of their golden armor ringing shrill—
and brandishing his lightning
blasted the fighter just at the goal,   145
rushing to shout his triumph from our walls.

Down from the heights he crashed, pounding down on the earth!
And a moment ago, blazing torch in hand—
         mad for attack, ecstatic
he breathed his rage, the storm   150
      of his fury hurling at our heads!
But now his high hopes have laid him low
and down the enemy ranks the iron god of war
         deals his rewards, his stunning blows—Ares°
         rapture of battle, our right arm in the crisis.   155

Seven captains marshaled at seven gates
seven against their equals, gave
their brazen trophies up to Zeus,
god of the breaking rout of battle,
all but two: those blood brothers,   160
one father, one mother—matched in rage,
spears matched for the twin conquest—
clashed and won the common prize of death.

But now for Victory! Glorious in the morning,
joy in her eyes to meet our joy   165
      she is winging down to Thebes,
our fleets of chariots wheeling in her wake—
      Now let us win oblivion from the wars,
thronging the temples of the gods
in singing, dancing choirs through the night!   170
      Lord Dionysus,° god of the dance
      that shakes the land of Thebes, now lead the way!

Enter Creon from the palace, attended by his guard.

But look, the king of the realm is coming,
Creon, the new man for the new day,
whatever the gods are sending now . . .   175
what new plan will he launch?
Why this, this special session?
Why this sudden call to the old men
summoned at one command?

154 Ares: God of war.   **171 Dionysus:** God of fertility and wine.

CREON: My countrymen,
 the ship of state is safe. The gods who rocked her,   180
 after a long, merciless pounding in the storm,
 have righted her once more.
        Out of the whole city
 I have called you here alone. Well I know,
 first, your undeviating respect
 for the throne and royal power of King Laius.   185
 Next, while Oedipus steered the land of Thebes,
 and even after he died, your loyalty was unshakable,
 you still stood by their children. Now then,
 since the two sons are dead—two blows of fate
 in the same day, cut down by each other's hands,   190
 both killers, both brothers stained with blood—
 as I am next in kin to the dead,
 I now possess the throne and all its powers.

 Of course you cannot know a man completely,
 his character, his principles, sense of judgment,   195
 not till he's shown his colors, ruling the people,
 making laws. Experience, there's the test.
 As I see it, whoever assumes the task,
 the awesome task of setting the city's course,
 and refuses to adopt the soundest policies   200
 but fearing someone, keeps his lips locked tight,
 he's utterly worthless. So I rate him now,
 I always have. And whoever places a friend
 above the good of his own country, he is nothing:
 I have no use for him. Zeus my witness,   205
 Zeus who sees all things, always—
 I could never stand by silent, watching destruction
 march against our city, putting safety to rout,
 nor could I ever make that man a friend of mine
 who menaces our country. Remember this: 210
 our country *is* our safety.
 Only while she voyages true on course
 can we establish friendships, truer than blood itself.
 Such are my standards. They make our city great.

 Closely akin to them I have proclaimed,   215
 just now, the following decree to our people
 concerning the two sons of Oedipus.
 Eteocles, who died fighting for Thebes,
 excelling all in arms: he shall be buried,
 crowned with a hero's honors, the cups we pour   220
 to soak the earth and reach the famous dead.

But as for his blood brother, Polynices,
who returned from exile, home to his father-city
and the gods of his race, consumed with one desire—
to burn them roof to roots—who thirsted to drink   225
his kinsmen's blood and sell the rest to slavery:
that man—a proclamation has forbidden the city
to dignify him with burial, mourn him at all.
No, he must be left unburied, his corpse
carrion for the birds and dogs to tear,   230
an obscenity for the citizens to behold!
These are my principles. Never at my hands
will the traitor be honored above the patriot.
But whoever proves his loyalty to the state:
I'll prize that man in death as well as life.   235

LEADER: If this is your pleasure, Creon, treating
our city's enemy and our friend this way . . .
The power is yours, I suppose, to enforce it
with the laws, both for the dead and all of us,
the living.

CREON: Follow my orders closely then,   240
be on your guard.

LEADER: We're too old.
Lay that burden on younger shoulders.

CREON: No, no,
I don't mean the body—I've posted guards already.

LEADER: What commands for us then? What other service?

CREON: See that you never side with those who break my orders.   245

LEADER: Never. Only a fool could be in love with death.

CREON: Death is the price—you're right. But all too often
the mere hope of money has ruined many men.

A Sentry enters from the side.

SENTRY: My lord,
I can't say I'm winded from running, or set out
with any spring in my legs either—no sir,   250
I was lost in thought, and it made me stop, often,
dead in my tracks, wheeling, turning back,
and all the time a voice inside me muttering,
"Idiot, why? You're going straight to your death."
Then muttering, "Stopped again, poor fool?   255
If somebody gets the news to Creon first,
what's to save your neck?"
                                    And so,
mulling it over, on I trudged, dragging my feet,
you can make a short road take forever . . .
but at last, look, common sense won out,   260

I'm here, and I'm all yours,
and even though I come empty-handed
I'll tell my story just the same, because
I've come with a good grip on one hope,
what will come will come, whatever fate —   265
CREON: Come to the point!
    What's wrong — why so afraid?
SENTRY: First, myself, I've got to tell you,
    I didn't do it, didn't see who did —
    Be fair, don't take it out on me.   270
CREON: You're playing it safe, soldier,
    barricading yourself from any trouble.
    It's obvious, you've something strange to tell.
SENTRY: Dangerous too, and danger makes you delay
    for all you're worth.   275
CREON: Out with it — then dismiss!
SENTRY: All right, here it comes. The body —
    someone's just buried it, then run off . . .
    sprinkled some dry dust on the flesh,
    given it proper rites.
CREON: What?   280
    What man alive would dare —
SENTRY: I've no idea, I swear it.
    There was no mark of a spade, no pickaxe there,
    no earth turned up, the ground packed hard and dry,
    unbroken, no tracks, no wheelruts, nothing,
    the workman left no trace. Just at sunup   285
    the first watch of the day points it out —
    it was a wonder! We were stunned . . .
    a terrific burden too, for all of us, listen:
    you can't see the corpse, not that it's buried,
    really, just a light cover of road-dust on it,   290
    as if someone meant to lay the dead to rest
    and keep from getting cursed.
    Not a sign in sight that dogs or wild beasts
    had worried the body, even torn the skin.

But what came next! Rough talk flew thick and fast,   295
    guard grilling guard — we'd have come to blows
    at last, nothing to stop it; each man for himself
    and each the culprit, no one caught red-handed,
    all of us pleading ignorance, dodging the charges,
    ready to take up red-hot iron in our fists,   300
    go through fire, swear oaths to the gods —
    "I didn't do it, I had no hand in it either,
    not in the plotting, not in the work itself!"

Finally, after all this wrangling came to nothing,
one man spoke out and made us stare at the ground,   305
hanging our heads in fear. No way to counter him,
no way to take his advice and come through
safe and sound. Here's what he said:
"Look, we've got to report the facts to Creon,
we can't keep this hidden." Well, that won out,   310
and the lot fell on me, condemned me,
unlucky as ever, I got the prize. So here I am,
against my will and yours too, well I know—
no one wants the man who brings bad news.

LEADER: My king,
ever since he began I've been debating in my mind,   315
could this possibly be the work of the gods?

CREON: Stop—
before you make me choke with anger—the gods!
You, you're senile, must you be insane?
You say—why it's intolerable—say the gods
could have the slightest concern for that corpse?   320
Tell me, was it for meritorious service
they proceeded to bury him, prized him so? The hero
who came to burn their temples ringed with pillars,
their golden treasures—scorch their hallowed earth
and fling their laws to the winds.   325
Exactly when did you last see the gods
celebrating traitors? Inconceivable!

No, from the first there were certain citizens
who could hardly stand the spirit of my regime,
grumbling against me in the dark, heads together,   330
tossing wildly, never keeping their necks beneath
the yoke, loyally submitting to their king.
These are the instigators, I'm convinced—
they've perverted my own guard, bribed them
to do their work.
                        Money! Nothing worse   335
in our lives, so current, rampant, so corrupting.
Money—you demolish cities, root men from their homes,
you train and twist good minds and set them on
to the most atrocious schemes. No limit,
you make them adept at every kind of outrage,   340
every godless crime—money!
                        Everyone—
the whole crew bribed to commit this crime,
they've made one thing sure at least:
sooner or later they will pay the price.

Wheeling on the Sentry.

You—   345
I swear to Zeus as I still believe in Zeus,
if you don't find the man who buried that corpse,
the very man, and produce him before my eyes,
simple death won't be enough for you,
not till we string you up alive   350
and wring the immorality out of you.
Then you can steal the rest of your days,
better informed about where to make a killing.
You'll have learned, at last, it doesn't pay
to itch for rewards from every hand that beckons.   355
Filthy profits wreck most men, you'll see—
they'll never save your life.
SENTRY: Please,
        may I say a word or two, or just turn and go?
CREON: Can't you tell? Everything you say offends me.
SENTRY: Where does it hurt you, in the ears or in the heart?   360
CREON: And who are you to pinpoint my displeasure?
SENTRY: The culprit grates on your feelings,
        I just annoy your ears.
CREON: Still talking?
        You talk too much! A born nuisance—
SENTRY: Maybe so,
        but I never did this thing, so help me!
CREON: Yes you did—   365
        what's more, you squandered your life for silver!
SENTRY: Oh it's terrible when the one who does the judging
        judges things all wrong.
CREON: Well now,
        you just be clever about your judgments—
        if you fail to produce the criminals for me,   370
        you'll swear your dirty money brought you pain.

Turning sharply, reentering the palace.

SENTRY: I hope he's found. Best thing by far.
        But caught or not, that's in the lap of fortune;
        I'll never come back, you've seen the last of me.
        I'm saved, even now, and I never thought,   375
        I never hoped—
        dear gods, I owe you all my thanks!

Rushing out.

CHORUS: Numberless wonders
        terrible wonders walk the world but none the match for man—
        that great wonder crossing the heaving gray sea,
                driven on by the blasts of winter   380

on through breakers crashing left and right,
    holds his steady course
and the oldest of the gods he wears away—
the Earth, the immortal, the inexhaustible—
as his plows go back and forth, year in, year out   385
with the breed of stallions turning up the furrows.
And the blithe, lightheaded race of birds he snares,
the tribes of savage beasts, the life that swarms the depths—
        with one fling of his nets
woven and coiled tight, he takes them all,   390
    man the skilled, the brilliant!
He conquers all, taming with his techniques
the prey that roams the cliffs and wild lairs,
training the stallion, clamping the yoke across
    his shaggy neck, and the tireless mountain bull.   395
And speech and thought, quick as the wind
and the mood and mind for law that rules the city—
    all these he has taught himself
and shelter from the arrows of the frost
when there's rough lodging under the cold clear sky   400
and the shafts of lashing rain—
      ready, resourceful man!
        Never without resources
never an impasse as he marches on the future—
only Death, from Death alone he will find no rescue   405
but from desperate plagues he has plotted his escapes.

Man the master, ingenious past all measure
past all dreams, the skills within his grasp—
    he forges on, now to destruction
now again to greatness. When he weaves in   410
the laws of the land, and the justice of the gods
that binds his oaths together
      he and his city rise high—
        but the city casts out
that man who weds himself to inhumanity   415
thanks to reckless daring. Never share my hearth
never think my thoughts, whoever does such things.

Enter Antigone from the side, accompanied by the Sentry.

    Here is a dark sign from the gods—
    what to make of this? I know her,
    how can I deny it? That young girl's Antigone!   420
    Wretched, child of a wretched father,
    Oedipus. Look, is it possible?
    They bring you in like a prisoner—

why? did you break the king's laws?
Did they take you in some act of mad defiance?   425
SENTRY: She's the one, she did it single-handed—
we caught her burying the body. Where's Creon?

Enter Creon from the palace.

LEADER: Back again, just in time when you need him.
CREON: In time for what? What is it?
SENTRY: My king,
there's nothing you can swear you'll never do—   430
second thoughts make liars of us all.
I could have sworn I wouldn't hurry back
(what with your threats, the buffeting I just took),
but a stroke of luck beyond our wildest hopes,
what a joy, there's nothing like it. So,   435
back I've come, breaking my oath, who cares?
I'm bringing in our prisoner—this young girl—
we took her giving the dead the last rites.
But no casting lots this time; this is *my* luck,
my prize, no one else's.
                                Now, my lord,   440
here she is. Take her, question her,
cross-examine her to your heart's content.
But set me free, it's only right—
I'm rid of this dreadful business once for all.
CREON: Prisoner! Her? You took her—where, doing what?   445
SENTRY: Burying the man. That's the whole story.
CREON: What?
You mean what you say, you're telling me the truth?
SENTRY: She's the one. With my own eyes I saw her
bury the body, just what you've forbidden.
There. Is that plain and clear?   450
CREON: What did you see? Did you catch her in the act?
SENTRY: Here's what happened. We went back to our post,
those threats of yours breathing down our necks—
we brushed the corpse clean of the dust that covered it,
stripped it bare . . . it was slimy, going soft,   455
and we took to high ground, backs to the wind
so the stink of him couldn't hit us;
jostling, baiting each other to keep awake,
shouting back and forth—no napping on the job,
not this time. And so the hours dragged by   460
until the sun stood dead above our heads,
a huge white ball in the noon sky, beating,
blazing down, and then it happened—
suddenly, a whirlwind!

Twisting a great dust-storm up from the earth,   465
a black plague of the heavens, filling the plain,
ripping the leaves off every tree in sight,
choking the air and sky. We squinted hard
and took our whipping from the gods.

And after the storm passed—it seemed endless—   470
there, we saw the girl!
And she cried out a sharp, piercing cry,
like a bird come back to an empty nest,
peering into its bed, and all the babies gone . . .
Just so, when she sees the corpse bare   475
she bursts into a long, shattering wail
and calls down withering curses on the heads
of all who did the work. And she scoops up dry dust,
handfuls, quickly, and lifting a fine bronze urn,
lifting it high and pouring, she crowns the dead   480
with three full libations.
                      Soon as we saw
we rushed her, closed on the kill like hunters,
and she, she didn't flinch. We interrogated her,
charging her with offenses past and present—
she stood up to it all, denied nothing. I tell you,   485
it made me ache and laugh in the same breath.
It's pure joy to escape the worst yourself,
it hurts a man to bring down his friends.
But all that, I'm afraid, means less to me
than my own skin. That's the way I'm made.
CREON:

Wheeling on Antigone.

                                           You,   490
with your eyes fixed on the ground—speak up.
Do you deny you did this, yes or no?
ANTIGONE: I did it. I don't deny a thing.
CREON:

To the Sentry.

You, get out, wherever you please—
you're clear of a very heavy charge.   495

He leaves; Creon turns back to Antigone.

You, tell me briefly, no long speeches—
were you aware a decree had forbidden this?
ANTIGONE: Well aware. How could I avoid it? It was public.
CREON: And still you had the gall to break this law?

ANTIGONE: Of course I did. It wasn't Zeus, not in the least,   500
    who made this proclamation—not to me.
    Nor did that Justice, dwelling with the gods
    beneath the earth, ordain such laws for men.
    Nor did I think your edict had such force
    that you, a mere mortal, could override the gods,   505
    the great unwritten, unshakable traditions.
    They are alive, not just today or yesterday:
    they live forever, from the first of time,
    and no one knows when they first saw the light.

    These laws—I was not about to break them,   510
    not out of fear of some man's wounded pride,
    and face the retribution of the gods.
    Die I must, I've known it all my life—
    how could I keep from knowing?—even without
    your death-sentence ringing in my ears.   515
    And if I am to die before my time
    I consider that a gain. Who on earth,
    alive in the midst of so much grief as I,
    could fail to find his death a rich reward?
    So for me, at least, to meet this doom of yours   520
    is precious little pain. But if I had allowed
    my own mother's son to rot, an unburied corpse—
    that would have been an agony! This is nothing.
    And if my present actions strike you as foolish,
    let's just say I've been accused of folly   525
    by a fool.
LEADER: Like father like daughter,
    passionate, wild . . .
    she hasn't learned to bend before adversity.
CREON: No? Believe me, the stiffest stubborn wills
    fall the hardest; the toughest iron,   530
    tempered strong in the white-hot fire,
    you'll see it crack and shatter first of all.
    And I've known spirited horses you can break
    with a light bit—proud, rebellious horses.
    There's no room for pride, not in a slave,   535
    not with the lord and master standing by.

    This girl was an old hand at insolence
    when she overrode the edicts we made public.
    But once she'd done it—the insolence,
    twice over—to glory in it, laughing,   540
    mocking us to our face with what she'd done.

I'm not the man, not now: she is the man
if this victory goes to her and she goes free.

Never! Sister's child or closer in blood
than all my family clustered at my altar   545
worshiping Guardian Zeus—she'll never escape,
she and her blood sister, the most barbaric death.
Yes, I accuse her sister of an equal part
in scheming this, this burial.

To his attendants.

                              Bring her here!
I just saw her inside, hysterical, gone to pieces.   550
It never fails: the mind convicts itself
in advance, when scoundrels are up to no good,
plotting in the dark. Oh but I hate it more
when a traitor, caught red-handed,
tries to glorify his crimes.   555
ANTIGONE: Creon, what more do you want
    than my arrest and execution?
CREON: Nothing. Then I have it all.
ANTIGONE: Then why delay? Your moralizing repels me,
    every word you say—pray god it always will.   560
    So naturally all I say repels you too.
                              Enough.
    Give me glory! What greater glory could I win
    than to give my own brother decent burial?
    These citizens here would all agree,

To the Chorus.

    they'd praise me too   565
    if their lips weren't locked in fear.

Pointing to Creon.

    Lucky tyrants—the perquisites of power!
    Ruthless power to do and say whatever pleases *them*.
CREON: You alone, of all the people in Thebes,
    see things that way.
ANTIGONE: They see it just that way   570
    but defer to you and keep their tongues in leash.
CREON: And you, aren't you ashamed to differ so from them?
    So disloyal!
ANTIGONE: Not ashamed for a moment,
    not to honor my brother, my own flesh and blood.
CREON: Wasn't Eteocles a brother too—cut down, facing him?   575
ANTIGONE: Brother, yes, by the same mother, the same father.

CREON: Then how can you render his enemy such honors,
  such impieties in his eyes?
ANTIGONE: He'll never testify to that,
  Eteocles dead and buried.
CREON: He will—   580
  if you honor the traitor just as much as him.
ANTIGONE: But it was his brother, not some slave that died—
CREON: Ravaging our country!—
  but Eteocles died fighting in our behalf.
ANTIGONE: No matter—Death longs for the same rites for all.   585
CREON: Never the same for the patriot and the traitor.
ANTIGONE: Who, Creon, who on earth can say the ones below
  don't find this pure and uncorrupt?
CREON: Never. Once an enemy, never a friend,
  not even after death.   590
ANTIGONE: I was born to join in love, not hate—
  that is my nature.
CREON: Go down below and love,
  if love you must—love the dead! While I'm alive,
  no woman is going to lord it over me.

Enter Ismene from the palace, under guard.

CHORUS: Look,
  Ismene's coming, weeping a sister's tears,   595
  loving sister, under a cloud . . .
  her face is flushed, her cheeks streaming.
  Sorrow puts her lovely radiance in the dark.
CREON: You—
  in my house, you viper, slinking undetected,
  sucking my life-blood! I never knew   600
  I was breeding twin disasters, the two of you
  rising up against my throne. Come, tell me,
  will you confess your part in the crime or not?
  Answer me. Swear to me.
ISMENE: I did it, yes—
  if only she consents—I share the guilt,   605
  the consequences too.
ANTIGONE: No,
  Justice will never suffer that—not you,
  you were unwilling. I never brought you in.
ISMENE: But now you face such dangers . . . I'm not ashamed
  to sail through trouble with you,   610
  make your troubles mine.
ANTIGONE: Who did the work?
  Let the dead and the god of death bear witness!
  I've no love for a friend who loves in words alone.

ISMENE: Oh no, my sister, don't reject me, please,
    let me die beside you, consecrating   615
    the dead together.
ANTIGONE: Never share my dying,
    don't lay claim to what you never touched.
    My death will be enough.
ISMENE: What do I care for life, cut off from you?
ANTIGONE: Ask Creon. Your concern is all for him.   620
ISMENE: Why abuse me so? It doesn't help you now.
ANTIGONE: You're right—
    if I mock you, I get no pleasure from it,
    only pain.
ISMENE: Tell me, dear one,
    what can I do to help you, even now?
ANTIGONE: Save yourself. I don't grudge you your survival.   625
ISMENE: Oh no, no, denied my portion in your death?
ANTIGONE: You chose to live, I chose to die.
ISMENE: Not, at least,
    without every kind of caution I could voice.
ANTIGONE: Your wisdom appealed to one world—mine, another.
ISMENE: But look, we're both guilty, both condemned to death.   630
ANTIGONE: Courage! Live your life. I gave myself to death,
    long ago, so I might serve the dead.
CREON: They're both mad, I tell you, the two of them.
    One's just shown it, the other's been that way
    since she was born.
ISMENE: True, my king,   635
    the sense we were born with cannot last forever . . .
    commit cruelty on a person long enough
    and the mind begins to go.
CREON: Yours did,
    when you chose to commit your crimes with her.
ISMENE: How can I live alone, without her?
CREON: Her?   640
    Don't even mention her—she no longer exists.
ISMENE: What? You'd kill your own son's bride?
CREON: Absolutely:
    there are other fields for him to plow.
ISMENE: Perhaps,
    but never as true, as close a bond as theirs.
CREON: A worthless woman for my son? It repels me.   645
ISMENE: Dearest Haemon, your father wrongs you so!
CREON: Enough, enough—you and your talk of marriage!
ISMENE: Creon—you're really going to rob your son of Antigone?
CREON: Death will do it for me—break their marriage off.
LEADER: So, it's settled then? Antigone must die?   650

CREON: Settled, yes—we both know that.

To the guards.

    Stop wasting time. Take them in.
    From now on they'll act like women.
    Tie them up, no more running loose;
    even the bravest will cut and run,   655
    once they see Death coming for their lives.

The guards escort Antigone and Ismene into the palace. Creon remains while the old citizens form their chorus.

CHORUS: Blest, they are the truly blest who all their lives
    have never tasted devastation. For others, once
    the gods have rocked a house to its foundations
        the ruin will never cease, cresting on and on   660
    from one generation on throughout the race—
    like a great mounting tide
    driven on by savage northern gales,
        surging over the dead black depths
    roiling up from the bottom dark heaves of sand   665
    and the headlands, taking the storm's onslaught full-force,
    roar, and the low moaning
            echoes on and on
                and now
    as in ancient times I see the sorrows of the house,
    the living heirs of the old ancestral kings,
    piling on the sorrows of the dead   670
        and one generation cannot free the next—
    some god will bring them crashing down,
    the race finds no release.
    And now the light, the hope
        springing up from the late last root   675
    in the house of Oedipus, that hope's cut down in turn
    by the long, bloody knife swung by the gods of death
    by a senseless word
        by fury at the heart.
                  Zeus,
    yours is the power, Zeus, what man on earth
    can override it, who can hold it back?   680
    Power that neither Sleep, the all-ensnaring
        no, nor the tireless months of heaven
    can ever overmaster—young through all time,
    mighty lord of power, you hold fast
        the dazzling crystal mansions of Olympus.   685
    And throughout the future, late and soon
    as through the past, your law prevails:

no towering form of greatness
enters into the lives of mortals
free and clear of ruin.

True,   690
our dreams, our high hopes voyaging far and wide
bring sheer delight to many, to many others
    delusion, blithe, mindless lusts
and the fraud steals on one slowly . . . unaware
till he trips and puts his foot into the fire.   695
    He was a wise old man who coined
the famous saying: "Sooner or later
foul is fair, fair is foul
to the man the gods will ruin"—
    He goes his way for a moment only   700
    free of blinding ruin.

Enter Haemon from the palace.

Here's Haemon now, the last of all your sons.
Does he come in tears for his bride,
his doomed bride, Antigone—
bitter at being cheated of their marriage?   705
CREON: We'll soon know, better than seers could tell us.

Turning to Haemon.

Son, you've heard the final verdict on your bride?
Are you coming now, raving against your father?
Or do you love me, no matter what I do?
HAEMON: Father, I'm your *son* . . . you in your wisdom   710
set my bearings for me—I obey you.
No marriage could ever mean more to me than you,
whatever good direction you may offer.
CREON: Fine, Haemon.
That's how you ought to feel within your heart,
subordinate to your father's will in every way.   715
That's what a man prays for: to produce good sons—
households full of them, dutiful and attentive,
so they can pay his enemy back with interest
and match the respect their father shows his friend.
But the man who rears a brood of useless children,   720
what has he brought into the world, I ask you?
Nothing but trouble for himself, and mockery
from his enemies laughing in his face.
                        Oh Haemon,
never lose your sense of judgment over a woman.
The warmth, the rush of pleasure, it all goes cold   725
in your arms, I warn you . . . a worthless woman

in your house, a misery in your bed.
What wound cuts deeper than a loved one
turned against you? Spit her out,
like a mortal enemy—let the girl go.   730
Let her find a husband down among the dead.

Imagine it: I caught her in naked rebellion,
the traitor, the only one in the whole city.
I'm not about to prove myself a liar,
not to my people, no, I'm going to kill her!   735
That's right—so let her cry for mercy, sing her hymns
to Zeus who defends all bonds of kindred blood.
Why, if I bring up my own kin to be rebels,
think what I'd suffer from the world at large.
Show me the man who rules his household well: 740
I'll show you someone fit to rule the state.
That good man, my son,
I have every confidence he and he alone
can give commands and take them too. Staunch
in the storm of spears he'll stand his ground,   745
a loyal, unflinching comrade at your side.

But whoever steps out of line, violates the laws
or presumes to hand out orders to his superiors,
he'll win no praise from me. But that man
the city places in authority, his orders   750
must be obeyed, large and small,
right and wrong.
                    Anarchy—
show me a greater crime in all the earth!
She, she destroys cities, rips up houses,
breaks the ranks of spearmen into headlong rout.   755
But the ones who last it out, the great mass of them
owe their lives to discipline. Therefore
we must defend the men who live by law,
never let some woman triumph over us.
Better to fall from power, if fall we must,   760
at the hands of a man—never be rated
inferior to a woman, never.

LEADER: To us,
unless old age has robbed us of our wits,
you seem to say what you have to say with sense.

HAEMON: Father, only the gods endow a man with reason,   765
the finest of all their gifts, a treasure.
Far be it from me—I haven't the skill,
and certainly no desire, to tell you when,
if ever, you make a slip in speech . . . though

someone else might have a good suggestion.   770
Of course it's not for you,
in the normal run of things, to watch
whatever men say or do, or find to criticize.
The man in the street, you know, dreads your glance,
he'd never say anything displeasing to your face.   775
But it's for me to catch the murmurs in the dark,
the way the city mourns for this young girl.
"No woman," they say, "ever deserved death less,
and such a brutal death for such a glorious action.
She, with her own dear brother lying in his blood—   780
she couldn't bear to leave him dead, unburied,
food for the wild dogs or wheeling vultures.
Death? She deserves a glowing crown of gold!"
So they say, and the rumor spreads in secret,
darkly . . .
         I rejoice in your success, father—   785
nothing more precious to me in the world.
What medal of honor brighter to his children
than a father's growing glory? Or a child's
to his proud father? Now don't, please,
be quite so single-minded, self-involved,   790
or assume the world is wrong and you are right.
Whoever thinks that he alone possesses intelligence,
the gift of eloquence, he and no one else,
and character too . . . such men, I tell you,
spread them open—you will find them empty.
                      No,   795
it's no disgrace for a man, even a wise man,
to learn many things and not to be too rigid.
You've seen trees by a raging winter torrent,
how many sway with the flood and salvage every twig,
but not the stubborn—they're ripped out, roots and all.   800
Bend or break. The same when a man is sailing:
haul your sheets too taut, never give an inch,
you'll capsize, go the rest of the voyage
keel up and the rowing-benches under.

Oh give way. Relax your anger—change!   805
I'm young, I know, but let me offer this:
it would be best by far, I admit,
if a man were born infallible, right by nature.
If not—and things don't often go that way,
it's best to learn from those with good advice.   810
LEADER: You'd do well, my lord, if he's speaking to the point,
    to learn from him,

Turning to Haemon.

and you, my boy, from him.
You both are talking sense.

CREON: So,
men our age, we're to be lectured, are we?—
schooled by a boy his age?   815

HAEMON: Only in what is right. But if I seem young,
look less to my years and more to what I do.

CREON: Do? Is admiring rebels an achievement?

HAEMON: I'd never suggest that you admire treason.

CREON: Oh?—
isn't that just the sickness that's attacked her?   820

HAEMON: The whole city of Thebes denies it, to a man.

CREON: And is Thebes about to tell me how to rule?

HAEMON: Now, you see? Who's talking like a child?

CREON: Am I to rule this land for others—or myself?

HAEMON: It's no city at all, owned by one man alone.   825

CREON: What? The city *is* the king's—that's the law!

HAEMON: What a splendid king you'd make of a desert island—
you and you alone.

CREON:

To the Chorus.

This boy, I do believe,
is fighting on her side, the woman's side.

HAEMON: If you are a woman, yes;   830
my concern is all for you.

CREON: Why, you degenerate—bandying accusations,
threatening me with justice, your own father!

HAEMON: I see my father offending justice—wrong.

CREON: Wrong?
To protect my royal rights?

HAEMON: Protect your rights?   835
When you trample down the honors of the gods?

CREON: You, you soul of corruption, rotten through—
woman's accomplice!

HAEMON: That may be,
but you'll never find me accomplice to a criminal.

CREON: That's what *she* is,   840
and every word you say is a blatant appeal for her—

HAEMON: And you, and me, and the gods beneath the earth.

CREON: You'll never marry her, not while she's alive.

HAEMON: Then she'll die . . . but her death will kill another.

CREON: What, brazen threats? You go too far!

HAEMON: What threat?   845
Combating your empty, mindless judgments with a word?

CREON: You'll suffer for your sermons, you and your empty wisdom!

HAEMON: If you weren't my father, I'd say you were insane.

CREON: Don't flatter me with Father—you woman's slave!

HAEMON: You really expect to fling abuse at me   850
and not receive the same?

CREON: Is that so!
Now, by heaven, I promise you, you'll pay—
taunting, insulting me! Bring her out,
that hateful—she'll die now, here,
in front of his eyes, beside her groom!   855

HAEMON: No, no, she will never die beside me—
don't delude yourself. And you will never
see me, never set eyes on my face again.
Rage your heart out, rage with friends
who can stand the sight of you.   860

Rushing out.

LEADER: Gone, my king, in a burst of anger.
A temper young as his . . . hurt him once,
he may do something violent.

CREON: Let him do—
dream up something desperate, past all human limit!
Good riddance. Rest assured,   865
he'll never save those two young girls from death.

LEADER: Both of them, you really intend to kill them both?

CREON: No, not her, the one whose hands are clean;
you're quite right.

LEADER: But Antigone—
what sort of death do you have in mind for her?   870

CREON: I'll take her down some wild, desolate path
never trod by men, and wall her up alive
in a rocky vault, and set out short rations,
just a gesture of piety
to keep the entire city free of defilement.   875
There let her pray to the one god she worships:
Death—who knows?—may just reprieve her from death.
Or she may learn at last, better late than never,
what a waste of breath it is to worship Death.

Exit to the palace.

CHORUS: Love, never conquered in battle   880
Love the plunderer laying waste the rich!
Love standing the night-watch
                    guarding a girl's soft cheek,
you range the seas, the shepherds' steadings off in the wilds—
not even the deathless gods can flee your onset,   885
nothing human born for a day—

whoever feels your grip is driven mad.
                        Love
you wrench the minds of the righteous into outrage,
swerve them to their ruin—you have ignited this,
this kindred strife, father and son at war   890
                        and Love alone the victor—
warm glance of the bride triumphant, burning with desire!
Throned in power, side-by-side with the mighty laws!
Irresistible Aphrodite,° never conquered—
Love, you mock us for your sport.   895

Antigone is brought from the palace under guard.

            But now, even I'd rebel against the king,
            I'd break all bounds when I see this—
            I fill with tears, can't hold them back,
            not any more . . . I see Antigone make her way
            to the bridal vault where all are laid to rest.   900
ANTIGONE: Look at me, men of my fatherland,
            setting out on the last road
        looking into the last light of day
        the last I'll ever see . . .
        the god of death who puts us all to bed   905
        takes me down to the banks of Acheron° alive—
            denied my part in the wedding-songs,
        no wedding-song in the dusk has crowned my marriage—
        I go to wed the lord of the dark waters.
CHORUS: Not crowned with glory, crowned with a dirge,   910
            you leave for the deep pit of the dead.
            No withering illness laid you low,
            no strokes of the sword—a law to yourself,
            alone, no mortal like you, ever, you go down
            to the halls of Death alive and breathing.   915
ANTIGONE: But think of Niobe°—well I know her story—
            think what a living death she died,
        Tantalus's daughter, stranger queen from the east:
        there on the mountain heights, growing stone
        binding as ivy, slowly walled her round   920
        and the rains will never cease, the legends say
        the snows will never leave her . . .
            wasting away, under her brows the tears
        showering down her breasting ridge and slopes—
        a rocky death like hers puts me to sleep.   925

894 Aphrodite: Goddess of love.   **906 Acheron:** A river in the underworld, to which the dead go.   **916 Niobe:** A queen of Thebes who was punished by the gods for her pride and was turned into stone.

CHORUS: But she was a god, born of gods,
            and we are only mortals born to die.
            And yet, of course, it's a great thing
            for a dying girl to hear, just hear
            she shares a destiny equal to the gods,   930
            during life and later, once she's dead.
ANTIGONE: O you mock me!
        Why, in the name of all my fathers' gods
        why can't you wait till I am gone —
            must you abuse me to my face?
        O my city, all your fine rich sons!   935
        And you, you springs of the Dirce,
        holy grove of Thebes where the chariots gather,
                you at least, you'll bear me witness, look,
        unmourned by friends and forced by such crude laws
        I go to my rockbound prison, strange new tomb —   940
            always a stranger, O dear god,
            I have no home on earth and none below,
                not with the living, not with the breathless dead.
CHORUS: You went too far, the last limits of daring —
            smashing against the high throne of Justice!   945
                Your life's in ruins, child — I wonder . . .
            do you pay for your father's terrible ordeal?
ANTIGONE: There — at last you've touched it, the worst pain
        the worst anguish! Raking up the grief for father
            three times over, for all the doom   950
        that's struck us down, the brilliant house of Laius.
        O mother, your marriage-bed
        the coiling horrors, the coupling there —
            you with your own son, my father — doomstruck mother!
        Such, such were my parents, and I their wretched child.   955
        I go to them now, cursed, unwed, to share their home —
            I am a stranger! O dear brother, doomed
            in your marriage — your marriage murders mine,
                your dying drags me down to death alive!

Enter Creon.

CHORUS: Reverence asks some reverence in return —   960
                but attacks on power never go unchecked,
                    not by the man who holds the reins of power.
                Your own blind will, your passion has destroyed you.
ANTIGONE: No one to weep for me, my friends,
            no wedding-song — they take me away   965
            in all my pain . . . the road lies open, waiting.
            Never again, the law forbids me to see
            the sacred eye of day. I am agony!

No tears for the destiny that's mine,
no loved one mourns my death.
CREON: Can't you see?   970
If a man could wail his own dirge *before* he dies,
he'd never finish.

To the guards.

Take her away, quickly!
Wall her up in the tomb, you have your orders.
Abandon her there, alone, and let her choose—
death or a buried life with a good roof for shelter.   975
As for myself, my hands are clean. This young girl—
dead or alive, she will be stripped of her rights,
her stranger's rights, here in the world above.
ANTIGONE: O tomb, my bridal-bed—my house, my prison
cut in the hollow rock, my everlasting watch!   980
I'll soon be there, soon embrace my own,
the great growing family of our dead
Persephone° has received among her ghosts.
                                                        I,
the last of them all, the most reviled by far,
go down before my destined time's run out.   985
But still I go, cherishing one good hope:
my arrival may be dear to father,
dear to you, my mother,
dear to you, my loving brother, Eteocles—
When you died I washed you with my hands,   990
I dressed you all, I poured the cups
across your tombs. But now, Polynices,
because I laid your body out as well,
this, this is my reward. Nevertheless
I honored you—the decent will admit it—   995
well and wisely too.
                        Never, I tell you,
if I had been the mother of children
or if my husband died, exposed and rotting—
I'd never have taken this ordeal upon myself,
never defied our people's will. What law,   1000
you ask, do I satisfy with what I say?
A husband dead, there might have been another.
A child by another too, if I had lost the first.
But mother and father both lost in the halls of Death,
no brother could ever spring to light again.   1005
For this law alone I held you first in honor.
For this, Creon, the king, judges me a criminal

983 Persephone: Queen of the underworld.

guilty of dreadful outrage, my dear brother!
And now he leads me off, a captive in his hands,
with no part in the bridal-song, the bridal-bed,   1010
denied all joy of marriage, raising children—
deserted so by loved ones, struck by fate,
I descend alive to the caverns of the dead.
What law of the mighty gods have I transgressed?
Why look to the heavens any more, tormented as I am?   1015
Whom to call, what comrades now? Just think,
my reverence only brands me for irreverence!
Very well: if this is the pleasure of the gods,
once I suffer I will know that I was wrong.
But if these men are wrong, let them suffer   1020
nothing worse than they mete out to me—
these masters of injustice!

LEADER: Still the same rough winds, the wild passion
raging through the girl.

CREON:

To the guards.

                          Take her away.
You're wasting time—you'll pay for it too.   1025

ANTIGONE: Oh god, the voice of death. It's come, it's here.

CREON: True. Not a word of hope—your doom is sealed.

ANTIGONE: Land of Thebes, city of all my fathers—
O you gods, the first gods of the race!
They drag me away, now, no more delay.   1030
Look on me, you noble sons of Thebes—
the last of a great line of kings,
I alone, see what I suffer now
at the hands of what breed of men—
all for reverence, my reverence for the gods!   1035

She leaves under guard; the Chorus gathers.

CHORUS: Danaë, Danaë°—
even she endured a fate like yours,
    in all her lovely strength she traded
the light of day for the bolted brazen vault—
buried within her tomb, her bridal-chamber,   1040
wed to the yoke and broken.
        But she was of glorious birth
                    my child, my child
and treasured the seed of Zeus within her womb,
the cloudburst streaming gold!   1045

1036 Danaë: Locked in a cell by her father because it was prophesied that her son would
kill him, but visited by Zeus in the form of a shower of gold. Their son was Perseus.

The power of fate is a wonder,
dark, terrible wonder —
neither wealth nor armies
towered walls nor ships
black hulls lashed by the salt   1050
can save us from that force.
The yoke tamed him too
    young Lycurgus° flaming in anger
king of Edonia, all for his mad taunts
Dionysus clamped him down, encased   1055
in the chain-mail of rock
    and there his rage
                his terrible flowering rage burst —
sobbing, dying away . . . at last that madman
came to know his god —   1060
    the power he mocked, the power
    he taunted in all his frenzy
    trying to stamp out
    the women strong with the god —
    the torch, the raving sacred cries —   1065
    enraging the Muses° who adore the flute.

And far north where the Black Rocks
    cut the sea in half
and murderous straits
split the coast of Thrace   1070
    a forbidding city stands
where once, hard by the walls
the savage Ares thrilled to watch
a king's new queen, a Fury rearing in rage
    against his two royal sons —   1075
    her bloody hands, her dagger-shuttle
stabbing out their eyes — cursed, blinding wounds —
their eyes blind sockets screaming for revenge!

They wailed in agony, cries echoing cries
    the princes doomed at birth . . .   1080
and their mother doomed to chains,
walled off in a tomb of stone —
    but she traced her own birth back
to a proud Athenian line and the high gods
and off in caverns half the world away,   1085
born of the wild North Wind
    she sprang on her father's gales,

1053 Lycurgus: Punished by Dionysus because he would not worship him.   **1066
Muses:** Goddesses of the arts.

racing stallions up the leaping cliffs—
child of the heavens. But even on her the Fates
the gray everlasting Fates rode hard   1090
my child, my child.

Enter Tiresias, the blind prophet, led by a boy.

TIRESIAS: Lords of Thebes,
   I and the boy have come together,
   hand in hand. Two see with the eyes of one . . .
   so the blind must go, with a guide to lead the way.
CREON: What is it, old Tiresias? What news now?   1095
TIRESIAS: I will teach you. And you obey the seer.
CREON: I will,
   I've never wavered from your advice before.
TIRESIAS: And so you kept the city straight on course.
CREON: I owe you a great deal, I swear to that.
TIRESIAS: Then reflect, my son: you are poised,   1100
   once more, on the razor-edge of fate.
CREON: What is it? I shudder to hear you.
TIRESIAS: You will learn
   when you listen to the warnings of my craft.
   As I sat on the ancient seat of augury,°
   in the sanctuary where every bird I know   1105
   will hover at my hands—suddenly I heard it,
   a strange voice in the wingbeats, unintelligible,
   barbaric, a mad scream! Talons flashing, ripping,
   they were killing each other—that much I knew—
   the murderous fury whirring in those wings   1110
   made that much clear!
                          I was afraid,
   I turned quickly, tested the burnt-sacrifice,
   ignited the altar at all points—but no fire,
   the god in the fire never blazed.
   Not from those offerings . . . over the embers   1115
   slid a heavy ooze from the long thighbones,
   smoking, sputtering out, and the bladder
   puffed and burst—spraying gall into the air—
   and the fat wrapping the bones slithered off
   and left them glistening white. No fire!   1120
   The rites failed that might have blazed the future
   with a sign. So I learned from the boy here;
   he is my guide, as I am guide to others.
                          And it's you—
   your high resolve that sets this plague on Thebes.
   The public altars and sacred hearths are fouled,   1125

1104 seat of augury: Where Tiresias looked for omens among birds.

one and all, by the birds and dogs with carrion
torn from the corpse, the doomstruck son of Oedipus!
And so the gods are deaf to our prayers, they spurn
the offerings in our hands, the flame of holy flesh.
No birds cry out an omen clear and true—   1130
they're gorged with the murdered victim's blood and fat.
Take these things to heart, my son, I warn you.
All men make mistakes, it is only human.
But once the wrong is done, a man
can turn his back on folly, misfortune too,   1135
if he tries to make amends, however low he's fallen,
and stops his bullnecked ways. Stubbornness
brands you for stupidity—pride is a crime.
No, yield to the dead!
Never stab the fighter when he's down.   1140
Where's the glory, killing the dead twice over?

I mean you well. I give you sound advice.
It's best to learn from a good adviser
when he speaks for your own good:
it's pure gain.
CREON: Old man—all of you! So,   1145
you shoot your arrows at my head like archers at the target—
I even have *him* loosed on me, this fortune-teller.
Oh his ilk has tried to sell me short
and ship me off for years. Well,
drive your bargains, traffic—much as you like—   1150
in the gold of India, silver-gold of Sardis.
You'll never bury that body in the grave,
not even if Zeus's eagles rip the corpse
and wing their rotten pickings off to the throne of god!
Never, not even in fear of such defilement   1155
will I tolerate his burial, that traitor.
Well I know, we can't defile the gods—
no mortal has the power.
                              No,
reverend old Tiresias, all men fall,
it's only human, but the wisest fall obscenely   1160
when they glorify obscene advice with rhetoric—
all for their own gain.
TIRESIAS: Oh god, is there a man alive
who knows, who actually believes . . .
CREON: What now?
What earth-shattering truth are you about to utter?   1165
TIRESIAS: . . . just how much a sense of judgment, wisdom
is the greatest gift we have?

CREON: Just as much, I'd say,
    as a twisted mind is the worst affliction going.
TIRESIAS: You are the one who's sick, Creon, sick to death.
CREON: I am in no mood to trade insults with a seer.   1170
TIRESIAS: You have already, calling my prophecies a lie.
CREON: Why not?
    You and the whole breed of seers are mad for money!
TIRESIAS: And the whole race of tyrants lusts to rake it in.
CREON: This slander of yours —
    are you aware you're speaking to the king?   1175
TIRESIAS: Well aware. Who helped you save the city?
CREON: You —
    you have your skills, old seer, but you lust for injustice!
TIRESIAS: You will drive me to utter the dreadful secret in my heart.
CREON: Spit it out! Just don't speak it out for profit.
TIRESIAS: Profit? No, not a bit of profit, not for you.   1180
CREON: Know full well, you'll never buy off my resolve.
TIRESIAS: Then know this too, learn this by heart!
    The chariot of the sun will not race through
    so many circuits more, before you have surrendered
    one born of your own loins, your own flesh and blood,   1185
    a corpse for corpses given in return, since you have thrust
    to the world below a child sprung for the world above,
    ruthlessly lodged a living soul within the grave —
    then you've robbed the gods below the earth,
    keeping a dead body here in the bright air,   1190
    unburied, unsung, unhallowed by the rites.

    You, you have no business with the dead,
    nor do the gods above — this is violence
    you have forced upon the heavens.
    And so the avengers, the dark destroyers late   1195
    but true to the mark, now lie in wait for you,
    the Furies sent by the gods and the god of death
    to strike you down with the pains that you perfected!

    There. Reflect on that, tell me I've been bribed.
    The day comes soon, no long test of time, not now,   1200
    that wakes the wails for men and women in your halls.
    Great hatred rises against you —
    cities in tumult, all whose mutilated sons
    the dogs have graced with burial, or the wild beasts,
    some wheeling crow that wings the ungodly stench of carrion   1205
    back to each city, each warrior's hearth and home.

    These arrows for your heart! Since you've raked me
    I loose them like an archer in my anger,

arrows deadly true. You'll never escape
their burning, searing force. 1210

Motioning to his escort.

Come, boy, take me home.
So he can vent his rage on younger men,
and learn to keep a gentler tongue in his head
and better sense than what he carries now.

Exit to the side.

LEADER: The old man's gone, my king — 1215
terrible prophecies. Well I know,
since the hair on this old head went gray,
he's never lied to Thebes.
CREON: I know it myself — I'm shaken, torn.
It's a dreadful thing to yield . . . but resist now? 1220
Lay my pride bare to the blows of ruin?
That's dreadful too.
LEADER: But good advice,
Creon, take it now, you must.
CREON: What should I do? Tell me . . . I'll obey.
LEADER: Go! Free the girl from the rocky vault 1225
and raise a mound for the body you exposed.
CREON: That's your advice? You think I should give in?
LEADER: Yes, my king, quickly. Disasters sent by the gods
cut short our follies in a flash.
CREON: Oh it's hard.
giving up the heart's desire . . . but I will do it — 1230
no more fighting a losing battle with necessity.
LEADER: Do it now, go, don't leave it to others.
CREON: Now — I'm on my way! Come, each of you,
take up axes, make for the high ground,
over there, quickly! I and my better judgment 1235
have come round to this — I shackled her,
I'll set her free myself. I am afraid . . .
it's best to keep the established laws
to the very day we die.

Rushing out, followed by his entourage. The Chorus clusters around the altar.

CHORUS: God of a hundred names!
                              Great Dionysus — 1240
              Son and glory of Semele! Pride of Thebes —
Child of Zeus whose thunder rocks the clouds —
Lord of the famous lands of evening —
King of the Mysteries!
                    King of Eleusis, Demeter's plain°

1244 Demeter's plain: The goddess of grain was worshipped at Eleusis, near Athens.

her breasting hills that welcome in the world—   1245
Great Dionysus!
                   Bacchus,° living in Thebes
the mother-city of all your frenzied women—
                                 Bacchus
         living along the Ismenus's° rippling waters
standing over the field sown with the Dragon's teeth!

You—we have seen you through the flaring smoky fires,   1250
    your torches blazing over the twin peaks
where nymphs of the hallowed cave climb onward
                   fired with you, your sacred rage—
we have seen you at Castalia's running spring°
and down from the heights of Nysa° crowned with ivy   1255
the greening shore rioting vines and grapes
        down you come in your storm of wild women
            ecstatic, mystic cries—
                    Dionysus—
down to watch and ward the roads of Thebes!

First of all cities, Thebes you honor first   1260
you and your mother, bride of the lightning—
come, Dionysus! now your people lie
in the iron grip of plague,
come in your racing, healing stride
             down Parnassus's° slopes   1265
or across the moaning straits.
               Lord of the dancing—
dance, dance the constellations breathing fire!
Great master of the voices of the night!
Child of Zeus, God's offspring, come, come forth!
Lord, king, dance with your nymphs, swirling, raving   1270
arm-in-arm in frenzy through the night
       they dance you, Iacchus°—
               Dance, Dionysus
giver of all good things!

Enter a Messenger from the side.

MESSENGER: Neighbors,
friends of the house of Cadmus° and the kings,
there's not a thing in this life of ours   1275

1246 Bacchus: Another name for Dionysus.   **1248 Ismenus:** A river near Thebes
where the founders of the city were said to have sprung from a dragon's teeth.
1254 Castalia's running spring: The sacred spring of Apollo's oracle at Delphi.
1255 Nysa: A mountain where Dionysus was worshipped.   **1265 Parnassus:** A
mountain in Greece that was sacred to Dionysus as well as other gods and goddesses.
1272 Iacchus: Dionysus.   **1274 Cadmus:** The legendary founder of Thebes.

I'd praise or blame as settled once for all.
Fortune lifts and Fortune fells the lucky
and unlucky every day. No prophet on earth
can tell a man his fate. Take Creon:
there was a man to rouse your envy once,   1280
as I see it. He saved the realm from enemies;
taking power, he alone, the lord of the fatherland,
he set us true on course — flourished like a tree
with the noble line of sons he bred and reared . . .
and now it's lost, all gone.
                    Believe me,   1285
when a man has squandered his true joys,
he's good as dead, I tell you, a living corpse.
Pile up riches in your house, as much as you like —
live like a king with a huge show of pomp,
but if real delight is missing from the lot,   1290
I wouldn't give you a wisp of smoke for it,
not compared with joy.

LEADER: What now?
What new grief do you bring the house of kings?

MESSENGER: Dead, dead — and the living are guilty of their death!

LEADER: Who's the murderer? Who is dead? Tell us.   1295

MESSENGER: Haemon's gone, his blood spilled by the very hand —

LEADER: His father's or his own?

MESSENGER: His own . . .
raging mad with his father for the death —

LEADER: Oh great seer,
you saw it all, you brought your word to birth!

MESSENGER: Those are the facts. Deal with them as you will.   1300

As he turns to go, Eurydice enters from the palace.

LEADER: Look, Eurydice. Poor woman, Creon's wife,
so close at hand. By chance perhaps,
unless she's heard the news about her son.

EURYDICE: My countrymen,
all of you — I caught the sound of your words
as I was leaving to do my part,   1305
to appeal to queen Athena° with my prayers.
I was just loosing the bolts, opening the doors,
when a voice filled with sorrow, family sorrow,
struck my ears, and I fell back, terrified,
into the women's arms — everything went black.   1310
Tell me the news, again, whatever it is . . .
sorrow and I are hardly strangers;
I can bear the worst.

1306 Athena: Goddess of wisdom and protector of Greek cities.

MESSENGER: I—dear lady,
    I'll speak as an eye-witness. I was there.
    And I won't pass over one word of the truth.   1315
    Why should I try to soothe you with a story,
    only to prove a liar in a moment?
    Truth is always best.
                  So,
    I escorted your lord, I guided him
    to the edge of the plain where the body lay,   1320
    Polynices, torn by the dogs and still unmourned.
    And saying a prayer to Hecate of the Crossroads,
    Pluto° too, to hold their anger and be kind,
    we washed the dead in a bath of holy water
    and plucking some fresh branches, gathering . . .   1325
    what was left of him, we burned them all together
    and raised a high mound of native earth, and then
    we turned and made for that rocky vault of hers,
    the hollow, empty bed of the bride of Death.
    And far off, one of us heard a voice,   1330
    a long wail rising, echoing
    out of that unhallowed wedding-chamber;
    he ran to alert the master and Creon pressed on,
    closer—the strange, inscrutable cry came sharper,
    throbbing around him now, and he let loose   1335
    a cry of his own, enough to wrench the heart,
    "Oh god, am I the prophet now? going down
    the darkest road I've ever gone? My son—
    it's *his* dear voice, he greets me! Go, men,
    closer, quickly! Go through the gap,   1340
    the rocks are dragged back—
    right to the tomb's very mouth—and look,
    see if it's Haemon's voice I think I hear,
    or the gods have robbed me of my senses."

    The king was shattered. We took his orders,   1345
    went and searched, and there in the deepest,
    dark recesses of the tomb we found her . . .
    hanged by the neck in a fine linen noose,
    strangled in her veils—and the boy,
    his arms flung around her waist,   1350
    clinging to her, wailing for his bride,
    dead and down below, for his father's crimes
    and the bed of his marriage blighted by misfortune.
    When Creon saw him, he gave a deep sob,

1322–23 Hecate, Pluto: Gods of the underworld.

he ran in, shouting, crying out to him,   1355
"Oh my child—what have you done? what seized you,
what insanity? what disaster drove you mad?
Come out, my son! I beg you on my knees!"
But the boy gave him a wild burning glance,
spat in his face, not a word in reply,   1360
he drew his sword—his father rushed out,
running as Haemon lunged and missed!—
and then, doomed, desperate with himself,
suddenly leaning his full weight on the blade,
he buried it in his body, halfway to the hilt.   1365
And still in his senses, pouring his arms around her,
he embraced the girl and breathing hard,
released a quick rush of blood,
bright red on her cheek glistening white.
And there he lies, body enfolding body . . .   1370
he has won his bride at last, poor boy,
not here but in the houses of the dead.

Creon shows the world that of all the ills
afflicting men the worst is lack of judgment.

Eurydice turns and reenters the palace.

LEADER: What do you make of that? The lady's gone,   1375
      without a word, good or bad.
MESSENGER: I'm alarmed too
      but here's my hope—faced with her son's death,
      she finds it unbecoming to mourn in public.
      Inside, under her roof, she'll set her women
      to the task and wail the sorrow of the house.   1380
      She's too discreet. She won't do something rash.
LEADER: I'm not so sure. To me, at least,
      a long heavy silence promises danger,
      just as much as a lot of empty outcries.
MESSENGER: We'll see if she's holding something back,   1385
      hiding some passion in her heart.
      I'm going in. You may be right—who knows?
      Even too much silence has its dangers.

Exit to the palace. Enter Creon from the side, escorted by attendants carrying
Haemon's body on a bier.

LEADER: The king himself! Coming toward us,
            look, holding the boy's head in his hands.   1390
            Clear, damning proof, if it's right to say so—
            proof of his own madness, no one else's,
                  no, his own blind wrongs.
CREON: Ohhh,

so senseless, so insane . . . my crimes,
my stubborn, deadly—   1395
Look at us, the killer, the killed,
father and son, the same blood—the misery!
My plans, my mad fanatic heart,
my son, cut off so young!
Ai, dead, lost to the world,   1400
not through your stupidity, no, my own.

LEADER: Too late,
too late, you see what justice means.

CREON: Oh I've learned
through blood and tears! Then, it was then,
when the god came down and struck me—a great weight
shattering, driving me down that wild savage path,   1405
ruining, trampling down my joy. Oh the agony,
the heartbreaking agonies of our lives.

Enter the Messenger from the palace.

MESSENGER: Master,
what a hoard of grief you have, and you'll have more.
The grief that lies to hand you've brought yourself—

Pointing to Haemon's body.

the rest, in the house, you'll see it all too soon.   1410

CREON: What now? What's worse than this?

MESSENGER: The queen is dead.
The mother of this dead boy . . . mother to the end—
poor thing, her wounds are fresh.

CREON: No, no,
harbor of Death, so choked, so hard to cleanse!—
why me? why are you killing me?   1415
Herald of pain, more words, more grief?
I died once, you kill me again and again!
What's the report, boy . . . some news for me?
My wife dead? O dear god!
Slaughter heaped on slaughter?

The doors open; the body of Eurydice is brought out on her bier.

MESSENGER: See for yourself: 1420
now they bring her body from the palace.

CREON: Oh no,
another, a second loss to break the heart.
What next, what fate still waits for me?
I just held my son in my arms and now,
look, a new corpse rising before my eyes—   1425
wretched, helpless mother—O my son!

MESSENGER: She stabbed herself at the altar,
 then her eyes went dark, after she'd raised
 a cry for the noble fate of Megareus,° the hero
 killed in the first assault, then for Haemon,   1430
 then with her dying breath she called down
 torments on your head — you killed her sons.

CREON: Oh the dread,
 I shudder with dread! Why not kill me too? —
 run me through with a good sharp sword?
 Oh god, the misery, anguish —   1435
 I, I'm churning with it, going under.

MESSENGER: Yes, and the dead, the woman lying there,
 piles the guilt of all their deaths on you.

CREON: How did she end her life, what bloody stroke?

MESSENGER: She drove home to the heart with her own hand, 1440
 once she learned her son was dead . . . that agony.

CREON: And the guilt is all mine —
 can never be fixed on another man,
 no escape for me. I killed you,
 I, god help me, I admit it all!   1445

To his attendants.

 Take me away, quickly, out of sight.
 I don't even exist — I'm no one. Nothing.

LEADER: Good advice, if there's any good in suffering.
 Quickest is best when troubles block the way.

CREON:

Kneeling in prayer.

 Come, let it come! — that best of fates for me   1450
 that brings the final day, best fate of all.
 Oh quickly, now —
 so I never have to see another sunrise.

LEADER: That will come when it comes;
 we must deal with all that lies before us.   1455
 The future rests with the ones who tend the future.

CREON: That prayer — I poured my heart into that prayer!

LEADER: No more prayers now. For mortal men
 there is no escape from the doom we must endure.

CREON: Take me away, I beg you, out of sight.   1460
 A rash, indiscriminate fool!
 I murdered you, my son, against my will —
 you too, my wife . . .

1429 Megareus: A son of Creon and Eurydice; he died when Thebes was attacked.

Wailing wreck of a man,
whom to look to? where to lean for support?

Desperately turning from Haemon to Eurydice on their biers.

Whatever I touch goes wrong—once more   1465
a crushing fate's come down upon my head.

The Messenger and attendants lead Creon into the palace.

CHORUS: Wisdom is by far the greatest part of joy,
and reverence toward the gods must be safeguarded.
The mighty words of the proud are paid in full
with mighty blows of fate, and at long last   1470
those blows will teach us wisdom.

The old citizens exit to the side.   [c. 441 B.C.E.]

≡ THINKING ABOUT THE TEXT

1. Describe Antigone with at least three adjectives. How much do you sympathize with her? Do you consider her morally superior to Creon? Identify specific places that influence your view of her. Do your feelings about her shift during the course of the play? If so, when and how?

2. Do you feel any sympathy for Creon? For Ismene? Explain your reasoning. What values seem to be in conflict as Antigone argues with each?

3. Do you see the chorus as expressing wisdom? Do the members of the chorus strike you as imperfect people?

4. Here is an issue of genre: Ever since the ancient Greek philosopher Aristotle analyzed tragedy in his *Poetics*, a common definition of this kind of play is that its central character has a fatal flaw. How well does this definition fit *Antigone*? Must it be altered to accommodate Sophocles' play? Explain. Here is another issue of genre: In the *Poetics*, Aristotle also argued that a tragedy ends in catharsis. After arousing pity and fear in the audience, a tragedy relieves the audience of these feelings. How well do Aristotle's observations apply in the case of *Antigone*?

5. As was customary in Greek tragedy, the violent events in this play occur offstage and are merely reported. Had they occurred onstage, how might the audience's reaction have been different? Today, many films and television shows directly confront their audience with violence. Do you prefer this directness to Greek tragedy's way of dealing with violence? Support your answer by comparing some contemporary presentations of violence with *Antigone*'s.

IDA FINK
The Table

A Play for Four Voices and Basso Ostinato
Translated by Francine Prose and Madeline G. Levine

Originally from Zbaraz, Poland (now part of the Ukraine), Ida Fink (1921–2011)
wrote in Polish about the Holocaust. During the Nazi occupation of her country, she
was confined along with other Jews to a ghetto in her hometown but then escaped
to its "Aryan" section and hid there using false identity papers. In 1957, she moved
to Israel, where she lived until her death at the age of ninety. Her works of fiction
include a novel, The Journey *(1990), as well as the short-story collections* Traces
(1997) and A Scrap of Time *(1987), a book that also contains the following play.*
Fink wrote The Table *for Israeli radio in 1970. "At that time," she reported, "I was*
working as an interpreter and a clerk of the court during hearings of witnesses at
the trials of Nazi criminals." Eleven years later, the play was performed on German
television. Fink identified it as being "for four voices and basso ostinato," a term that
literally means "obstinate bass" and that in music refers to a continuously repeating
bass line. Here, Fink evidently associated the term with the prosecutor's voice.

CHARACTERS:

FIRST MAN, *50 years old*
FIRST WOMAN, *45 years old*
SECOND MAN, *60 years old*
SECOND WOMAN, *38 years old*
PROSECUTOR, *35–40 years old*

The stage is empty and dark. Spotlights only on the witness, seated in a chair, and the
prosecutor, seated at a desk.

PROSECUTOR: Have you recovered, Mr. Grumbach? Can we go on? Where did we
stop? . . . Oh, yes. So you remember precisely that there was a table there.
FIRST MAN: Yes. A small table.
PROSECUTOR: A *small* table? How small? How many people could sit at a table
that size?
FIRST MAN: Do I know? It's hard for me to say now.
PROSECUTOR: How long was it? A meter? Eight centimeters? Fifty centimeters?
FIRST MAN: A table. A regular table — not too small, not too big. It's been so
many years . . . And at a time like that, who was thinking about a table?
PROSECUTOR: Yes, of course, I understand. But you have to understand me, too,
Mr. Grumbach: every detail is crucial. You must understand that it's for a
good purpose that I'm tormenting you with such details.
FIRST MAN: *(resigned)* All right, let it be eighty centimeters. Maybe ninety.
PROSECUTOR: Where did that table — that small table — stand? On the right
side or the left side of the marketplace as you face the town hall?
FIRST MAN: On the left. Yes.
PROSECUTOR: Are you certain?

FIRST MAN: Yes . . . I saw them carry it out.

PROSECUTOR: That means that at the moment you arrived at the marketplace the table was not there yet.

FIRST MAN: No . . . Or maybe it was. You know, I don't remember. Maybe I saw them carrying it from one place to another. But is it so important if they were bringing it out or just moving it?

PROSECUTOR: Please concentrate.

FIRST MAN: How many years has it been? Twenty-five? And you want me to remember such details? I haven't thought about that table once in twenty-five years.

PROSECUTOR: And yet today, while you were telling your story, on your own, without prompting, you said, "He was sitting at a table." Please concentrate and tell me what you saw as you entered the square.

FIRST MAN: What did I see? I was coming from Rozana Street, from the opposite direction, because Rozana is on the other side of the market. I was struck by the silence. That was my first thought: so many people, and so quiet. I noticed a group of people I knew; among them was the druggist, Mr. Weidel, and I asked Weidel, "What do you think, Doctor, what will they do with us?" And he answered me, "My dear Mr. Grumbach . . ."

PROSECUTOR: You already mentioned that, please stick to the point. What did you see in the square?

FIRST MAN: The square was black with people.

PROSECUTOR: Earlier you said that the people assembled in the marketplace were standing at the rear of the square, facing the town hall, and that there was an empty space between the people and the town hall.

FIRST MAN: That's right.

PROSECUTOR: In other words, to say, "The square was black with people," is not completely accurate. That empty space was, shall we say, white — especially since, as you've mentioned, fresh snow had fallen during the night.

FIRST MAN: Yes, that's right.

PROSECUTOR: Now please think, Mr. Grumbach. Did you notice anything or anyone in that empty white space?

FIRST MAN: Kiper was sitting in a chair and striking his boots with a riding crop.

PROSECUTOR: I would like to call your attention to the fact that none of the witnesses until now has mentioned that Kiper was walking around with a riding crop. Are you certain that Kiper was striking his boots with a riding crop?

FIRST MAN: Maybe it was a stick or a branch. In any case, he was striking his boots — *that* I remember. Sometimes you remember such tiny details. Hamke and Bondke were standing next to him, smoking cigarettes. There were policemen and Ukrainians standing all around the square — a lot of them, one next to the other.

PROSECUTOR: Yes, we know that already. So, you remember that Kiper was sitting in a chair.

FIRST MAN: Absolutely.

PROSECUTOR: So if there was a chair in the marketplace, wouldn't there have been a table as well?

FIRST MAN: A table . . . just a minute . . . a table . . . no. Because that chair seemed so . . . wait a minute . . . No, there wasn't any table there. But they carried out a small table later. Now I remember exactly. Two policemen brought a small table out from the town hall.

PROSECUTOR: *(relieved)* Well, something concrete at last. What time would that have been?

FIRST MAN: *(reproachfully)* Really, I . . .

PROSECUTOR: Please, think about it.

FIRST MAN: The time? . . . God knows, I have no idea. I left the house at 6:15, that I know. I stopped in at my aunt's on Poprzeczna Street, that took ten minutes, then I walked down Miodna, Krotka, Okolna, and Mickiewicza streets. On Mickiewicza I hid for a few minutes inside the gate of one of the houses because I heard shots. It must have taken me about half an hour to walk there.

PROSECUTOR: How much time elapsed from the moment you arrived in the square to the moment when you noticed the policemen carrying the table out from the town hall?

FIRST MAN: Not a long time. Let's say half an hour.

PROSECUTOR: In other words, the policemen carried a table into the market-place around 7:15. A small table.

FIRST MAN: That's right. Now I recall that Kiper pointed with his riding crop to the place where they were supposed to set the table down.

PROSECUTOR: Please indicate on the map you drew for us the exact place where the policemen set the table down. With a cross or a circle. Thank you. *(satisfied)* Excellent. Kiper is sitting in a chair, the policemen carry in the table, the length of the table is about eighty centimeters. How was the table placed? I mean, in front of Kiper? Next to him?

FIRST MAN: I don't know. That I couldn't see.

PROSECUTOR: If you could see them carrying in the table you could see that, too — perhaps you just don't remember. But maybe you can remember where Kiper sat? At the table? Beside it? In front of it?

FIRST MAN: Obviously, at the table. When someone waits for a table, it's so he can sit at it. He was sitting at the table. Of course. That's what people do.

PROSECUTOR: Alone?

FIRST MAN: In the beginning? I don't know. I wasn't looking that way the whole time. But later — this I know — they were all there: Kiper, Hamke, Bondke, Rossel, Kuntz, and Wittelmann.

PROSECUTOR: *(slowly)* Kiper, Hamke, Bondke, Rossel, Kuntz, and Wittelmann. When you testified a year ago you didn't mention either Rossel or Wittelmann.

FIRST MAN: I must have forgotten about them then. Now I remember that they were there, too.

PROSECUTOR: Were they all sitting at the table?

FIRST MAN: No. Not all of them. Some of them were standing next to it.

PROSECUTOR: Who was sitting?

FIRST MAN: What I saw was that Kiper, Hamke, Bondke, and Kuntz were sitting. The rest were standing. There were more than a dozen of them, I don't remember all the names.

PROSECUTOR: How were they seated, one beside the other?

FIRST MAN: Yes.

PROSECUTOR: Is it possible that four grown men could sit one beside the other at a table that is eighty centimeters long?

FIRST MAN: I don't know. Maybe the table was longer than that; or maybe it wasn't big enough for all of them. In any event, they were sitting in a row.

PROSECUTOR: Who read the names from the list?

FIRST MAN: Hamke or Bondke.

PROSECUTOR: How did they do it?

FIRST MAN: People walked up to the table, showed their *Arbeitskarten,*° and Kiper looked them over and pointed either to the right or to the left. The people who had good *Arbeitskarten* went to the right, and those whose work wasn't considered important, or who didn't have any *Arbeitskarten,* they went to the left.

PROSECUTOR: Was Kiper the one who conducted the selection?

FIRST MAN: Yes, I'm positive about that.

PROSECUTOR: Did Kiper stay in that spot during the whole time the names were read? Or did he get up from the table?

FIRST MAN: I don't know. Maybe he got up. I wasn't looking at him every minute. It took a very long time. And anyway, is it that important?

PROSECUTOR: I'm sorry to be tormenting you with these seemingly unimportant details . . . In other words, is it possible that Kiper got up and walked away from the table, or even left the square?

FIRST MAN: I can't give a definite answer. I wasn't watching Kiper every minute. It's possible that he did get up from the table. That's not out of the question. Still, he was the one in charge at the marketplace. Kiper — and no one else. And he was the one who shot the mother and child.

PROSECUTOR: Did you see this with your own eyes?

FIRST MAN: Yes.

PROSECUTOR: Please describe the incident.

FIRST MAN: The woman wasn't from our town, so I don't know her name. She was young, she worked in the brickworks. She had a ten-year-old daughter, Mala. I remember the child's name; she was a pretty little girl. When this woman's name was called she walked up to the table with her daughter. She was holding the child by the hand. Kiper gave her back her *Arbeitskarte* and ordered her to go to the right. But he ordered the child to go to the left. The mother started begging him to leave the child with her, but he wouldn't agree. Then she placed her *Arbeitskarte* on the table and walked to the left side with the child. Kiper called her back and asked her if she knew the penalty for disobeying an order, and then he shot them — first the girl, and then the mother.

Arbeitskarten: Identity cards.

PROSECUTOR: Did you actually see Kiper shoot?

FIRST MAN: I saw the woman approach the table with the child. I saw them standing in front of Kiper. A moment later I heard two shots.

PROSECUTOR: Where were you standing at that moment? Please mark it on the map. With a cross or a circle. Thank you. So, you were standing near the pharmacy. How far was it from the table to the pharmacy?

FIRST MAN: Thirty meters, maybe fifty.

PROSECUTOR: Then you couldn't have heard the conversation between Kiper and the mother.

FIRST MAN: No, obviously. I didn't hear what they said, but I saw that the mother exchanged several sentences with Kiper. It was perfectly clear what they were talking about. Everyone understood what the mother was asking. Then I saw the mother place her *Arbeitskarte* on the table and go to the left with the child. I heard Kiper call her back. They went back.

PROSECUTOR: They went back and stood in front of the table, correct?

FIRST MAN: That's correct.

PROSECUTOR: In other words, they were blocking your view of the men who were sitting at the table, or at least of some of the men sitting at the table.

FIRST MAN: It's possible. I don't remember exactly. In any case, I saw them come back to the table, and a moment later there were two shots, and then I saw them lying on the ground. People who stood closer to them clearly heard Kiper ask her if she knew the penalty for disobeying an order.

PROSECUTOR: Was Kiper standing or sitting at that moment?

FIRST MAN: I don't remember.

PROSECUTOR: So, you didn't see him at the exact moment you heard the shots. Did you see a gun in his hand? What kind of gun? A pistol? A machine gun?

FIRST MAN: He must have shot them with a pistol. Those were pistol shots.

PROSECUTOR: Did you see a pistol in Kiper's hand?

FIRST MAN: No . . . perhaps the mother and child were blocking my view; or maybe I was looking at the victims and not at the murderer. I don't know. But in any case, I did see something that told me it was Kiper who shot them, and no one else.

PROSECUTOR: Namely?

FIRST MAN: Namely . . . immediately after the shots, when the mother and child were lying on the ground, I saw with my own eyes how Kiper rubbed his hands together with a disgusted gesture, as if to cleanse them of filth. I won't forget that gesture.

PROSECUTOR: *(summarizing)* And so, Mr. Grumbach, you saw Kiper sitting at a table in the company of Hamke, Bondke, Rossel, and Kuntz. Then you saw Kiper carrying out the selection and Kiper brushing off his hands immediately after you heard the shots that killed the mother and child. But you didn't see a gun in Kiper's hand nor the shooting itself. Is that correct?

FIRST MAN: Still, I assert with absolute confidence that the murderer of the mother and child was Kiper.

PROSECUTOR: Was Kiper sitting behind the table when your name was called?

FIRST MAN: *(hesitating)* I was one of the last to be called. My *Arbeitskarte* was taken and returned by Bondke. I don't remember if Kiper was present or not. By then I was already half dead.

PROSECUTOR: Of course. What time would it have been when your name was called?

FIRST MAN: What time? My God, I don't know, it was already past noon.

PROSECUTOR: Did you witness any other murders committed that day?

FIRST MAN: That day more than four hundred people were shot in the town. Another eight hundred at the cemetery.

PROSECUTOR: Did you see any member of the Gestapo shoot someone?

FIRST MAN: No.

PROSECUTOR: Were you one of the group that buried the victims in the cemetery?

FIRST MAN: No.

PROSECUTOR: Is there anything else that you would like to say in connection with that day?

FIRST MAN: Yes.

PROSECUTOR: Please, go ahead.

FIRST MAN: It was a sunny, cold day. There was snow in the streets. The snow was red.

FIRST WOMAN: It was a Sunday. I remember it perfectly. As I was walking to the square, the church bells were ringing. It was a Sunday. Black Sunday.

PROSECUTOR: Is that what the day was called afterwards?

FIRST WOMAN: Yes.

PROSECUTOR: Some of the witnesses have testified that the day was called Bloody Sunday.

FIRST WOMAN: *(dryly)* I should think the name would be unimportant. It was certainly bloody. Four hundred corpses on the streets of the town.

PROSECUTOR: How do you know the exact figure?

FIRST WOMAN: From those who buried the victims. The *Ordnungsdienst°* did that. Later they told us, four hundred murdered in the town alone. A hard, packed snow lay on the streets; it was red with blood. The worst one was Kiper.

PROSECUTOR: Slow down. Please describe the events in the square as they occurred.

FIRST WOMAN: At six they ordered us to leave our houses and go to the market-place. First I decided not to go, and I ran up to the attic. There was a window there, so I looked out. I saw people pouring down Rozana, Kwiatowa, Piekna, and Mickiewicza streets towards the square. Suddenly I noticed two SS entering the house next door. They stayed inside for a moment, then came out leading an elderly couple, the Weintals. Mrs. Weintal was crying. I saw that. They were elderly people. They owned a paper goods store. The SS-men ordered them to stand facing the wall of the house, and then they shot them.

Ordnungsdienst: Jewish police forces controlled by the Nazis.

PROSECUTOR: Do you know the names of the two SS-men?

FIRST WOMAN: No. One was tall and thin. He had a terrifying face. I might be able to recognize him in a photograph. You don't forget such a face. But they were local SS, because there were no outside SS in town that day. *They* did it, the locals. Four hundred murdered on the spot, twice that number in the cemetery.

PROSECUTOR: Let's take it slowly now. So, you saw two SS leading the Weintal couple out of the building and putting them against the wall. You lived on Kwiatowa Street. Was their house also located on Kwiatowa?

FIRST WOMAN: I lived on Kwiatowa at number 1; it was the corner building. The Weintals lived in a building on Rozana.

PROSECUTOR: What number?

FIRST WOMAN: I don't know, I don't remember . . .

PROSECUTOR: Did you see which of the two SS shot them? The tall one or the other one?

FIRST WOMAN: That I didn't see, because when they ordered them to stand facing the wall, I knew what would happen next and I couldn't watch. I was afraid. I moved away from the window. I was terribly afraid.

PROSECUTOR: Afterwards, did you see the Weintal couple lying on the ground dead?

FIRST WOMAN: They shot them from a distance of two meters; I assume they knew how to aim.

PROSECUTOR: Did you see the bodies afterwards?

FIRST WOMAN: No, I ran downstairs from the attic, I was afraid — with good reason — I was afraid that they would search the houses for people who were trying to hide, but I didn't go out into the street, I took the back exit to the garden and made my way to the marketplace by a roundabout route.

PROSECUTOR: Would you recognize those two SS in photos?

FIRST WOMAN: Perhaps. I'm fairly certain I could recognize the tall thin one. You don't forget such a face.

PROSECUTOR: Please look through this album. It contains photographs of members of the Gestapo who were in your town; but there are also photographs here of people who were never there.

FIRST WOMAN: *(she turns the pages; a pause)* Oh, that's him.

PROSECUTOR: Is that one of the men you saw from the window?

FIRST WOMAN: No, it's that awful murderer. It's Kiper. Yes, I remember, it's definitely him.

PROSECUTOR: Please look through all the photographs.

FIRST WOMAN: *(a pause)* No, I can't find that face. Unfortunately.

PROSECUTOR: You said "awful murderer." Did you ever witness a murder committed by Kiper?

FIRST WOMAN: *(laughs)* Witness? You're joking. The witnesses to his murders aren't alive.

PROSECUTOR: But there are people who saw him shoot.

FIRST WOMAN: I did, too. Sure — in the square, he fired into the crowd. Just like that.

PROSECUTOR: Do you know who he killed then?

FIRST WOMAN: I don't know. There were fifteen hundred of us in the square. But I saw him rushing around like a wild man and shooting. Not just him, others, too. Bendke, for example.

PROSECUTOR: When was that?

FIRST WOMAN: In the morning. Before the selection. But it's possible it also went on during the selection. I don't remember. I know that they fired into the crowd. Just like that.

PROSECUTOR: Who read the names from the list?

FIRST WOMAN: An SS-man. I don't know his name.

PROSECUTOR: How did they do it?

FIRST WOMAN: Very simply. Names were called out, some people went to the right and others to the left. The left meant death.

PROSECUTOR: Who conducted the selection?

FIRST WOMAN: They were all there: Kiper, Bendke, Hamm, Rosse.

PROSECUTOR: Which one of them reviewed the *Arbeitskarten*?

FIRST WOMAN: I don't remember.

PROSECUTOR: Who ordered you to go to the right? Kiper? Bendke? Hamm? Rosse?

FIRST WOMAN: I don't remember. At such a time, you know . . . at such a time, when you don't know . . . life or death . . . I didn't look at their faces. To me, they all had the same face. All of them! What difference does it make whether it was Kiper or Bendke or Hamm or Rosse? They were all there. There were ten or maybe fifteen of those murderers. They stood in a semi-circle, with their machine guns across their chests. What difference does it make which one? They all gave orders, they all shot! All of them!

PROSECUTOR: Please calm yourself. I am terribly sorry that I have to provoke you with such questions. But you see, we can only convict people if we can *prove* that they committed murder. You say that all the members of the local Gestapo were there. But it could be that one of them was on leave, or possibly on duty in the *Dienststelle*.° And didn't shoot.

FIRST WOMAN: Every one of them shot. If not that day, then another. During the second or third action, during the liquidation.

PROSECUTOR: The law requires proof. And I, as the prosecuting attorney, am asking you for proof. I am asking for the names of the murderers, the names of the victims, the circumstances in which they were murdered. Otherwise, I can do nothing.

FIRST WOMAN: *(quietly)* My God . . .

PROSECUTOR: Excuse me?

FIRST WOMAN: Nothing, nothing.

PROSECUTOR: Please think: which one of them was in charge of the selection in the square?

FIRST WOMAN: They all participated in the selection. Kiper, Bendke, Hamm, Rosse. They were standing in a semicircle.

Dienststelle: Police station.

PROSECUTOR: Standing? Were all of them standing? Or perhaps some of them were seated?

FIRST WOMAN: No, they were standing. Is it that important?

PROSECUTOR: It's very important. Do you remember seeing a table in the marketplace at which several Gestapo men were seated? The others were standing near the table.

FIRST WOMAN: A table? I don't remember. There was no table there.

SECOND MAN: Here's the map. The marketplace was shaped like a trapezoid. At the top was the town hall, a beautiful old building that had been built by a Polish nobleman in the seventeenth century. The jewel of the town. The square sloped down towards the actual market where the stores were, as if the town hall reigned over the place. On the left, by the ruins of the old ramparts, stood those whose *Arbeitskarten* were taken away and also those who did not have *Arbeitskarten*. Note that the streets radiate out like a star. Here's Rozana, then Sienkiewicza, then Piekna, then Male Targi, then Nadrzeczna. There was no river in the town, but maybe once upon a time there was one, and that's why it was called Nadrzeczna — Riverside. Then came Zamkowa Street. All the streets I've named were later included in the ghetto, with the exception of Piekna. Beyond Male Targi there was a cemetery. Yes. That's where they were shot. Nadrzeczna was adjacent to the cemetery. Most of the people who lived on Nadrzeczna were Poles, but it was incorporated into the ghetto nonetheless, because of the cemetery. Because the cemetery played a major role in our life then. Between Rozana and Sienkiewicza there were shops. First, Weidel's pharmacy — he was killed in the camp; then Rosenzweig's iron shop — he was shot during the second action. Then Kreitz's dry goods store, the Haubers' restaurant and hotel — they were the wealthiest people among us, their daughter lives in Canada — and then two groceries, one beside the other, Blumenthal's and Hochwald's. They were rivals all their lives, and now they're lying in the same grave. Oh yes, I can draw every single stone for you, describe every single person. Do you know how many of us survived?

PROSECUTOR: Forty.

SECOND MAN: How do you know?

PROSECUTOR: They are my witnesses.

SECOND MAN: And have you found all of them? And taken their testimony?

PROSECUTOR: I have found almost all of them, but I still haven't taken testimony from everyone. Several witnesses live in America; they will be questioned by our consular officials, and if necessary, subpoenaed for the trial. Two live in Australia, one in Venezuela. Now I would like to ask you about the details of the selection that took place during the first action. When was it, do you remember?

SECOND MAN: Of course. It was a Sunday, in December, towards the end of the month. It was a sunny, cold day. Nature, you see, was also against us. She was mocking us. Yes, indeed. If it had rained, or if there had been a storm, who knows, perhaps they wouldn't have kept shooting from morning till night. Darkness was already falling when they led those people to the cemetery. Oh, you want proof, don't you? The snow on the town's streets was red. Red! Does that satisfy you?

PROSECUTOR: Unfortunately, Mr. Zachwacki, snow doesn't constitute proof for judges, especially snow that melted twenty-five years ago.

SECOND MAN: The snow was red. Bloody Sunday. Four hundred fifty corpses on the streets. That's not proof? Then go there and dig up the mass graves.

PROSECUTOR: I'm interested in the selection. Who was in charge of it?

SECOND MAN: Kiper. A thug, a murderer. The worst sort. I can't talk about this calmly. No. Do you mind if I smoke? These are things . . . I'm sixty, my blood pressure shoots right up. A cutthroat like that . . .

PROSECUTOR: How do you know that Kiper was in charge of the selection?

SECOND MAN: What do you mean, how? I gave him my *Arbeitskarte* myself. He peered at me from under his brows and snarled, *"Rechts!"* I went to the right. Saved. Saved until the next time.

PROSECUTOR: Please describe the scene in more detail.

SECOND MAN: I was standing some distance away. We all tried to stand as far away from them as possible, as if that could have helped. I was standing near the Haubers' hotel. It was one in the afternoon. The church bell struck one, and since it was quiet in the square, you could hear the bell clearly even though the church was in a different part of town, near Waly Ksiazece. By then they had been calling out names for about an hour. Suddenly I hear, "Zachwacki!"

PROSECUTOR: Who called your name?

SECOND MAN: One of the Gestapo, but I don't know which one.

PROSECUTOR: Didn't you notice which of them was holding the list?

SECOND MAN: No, you're asking too much. There was a list, because they read the names from a list, but I didn't see it. If a person saw a scene like that in the theater, maybe he could describe it in detail. This here, that there, and so on. But when a tragedy like this is being played in real life? You expect me to look at a list when my life is hanging by a thread? I was standing there with my wife. She had an *Arbeitskarte* from the sawmill—that was a good place to work—and I had one from the cement works. Also a good place. When they called my name, my wife grabbed my arm. "Let's stay together!" she cried. Dr. Gluck was standing nearby, a kind old doctor. He told my wife, "Mrs. Zachwacki, calm down, your husband has a good *Arbeitskarte*, you have a good *Arbeitskarte*, get a grip on yourself." But she kept saying, "I want to stay together, if we don't we won't see each other ever again. Albert," she said, "I'm afraid." I literally had to tear myself away, she was holding on to me so tight. There, you see, so much for instinct, intuition . . . I never saw her again. All the women who worked in the sawmill were sent to the left. *(he clears his throat)*

PROSECUTOR: *(a short pause)* Then what happened?

SECOND MAN: I dashed through the crowd. There was an empty space between us and them, you had to walk about thirty meters to cross the empty square. First—I remember this—someone kicked me, who I don't know.

I took a deep breath and ran as hard as I could to get to the town hall as fast as possible. When I handed them my *Arbeitskarte* my hand was trembling like an aspen leaf, although I'm not a coward. Not at all!

PROSECUTOR: To whom did you hand your *Arbeitskarte?*

SECOND MAN: I already told you, to Kiper. He opened it, read it, handed it back to me and snarled, "*Rechts!*" I was young, tall, strong. He gave me a reprieve.

PROSECUTOR: At the moment that you handed him your *Arbeitskarte*, was Kiper standing or sitting?

SECOND MAN: He was standing with his legs apart, his machine gun across his chest. His face was swollen, red.

PROSECUTOR: And the rest of the Gestapo?

SECOND MAN: I didn't see. I don't remember if any of them were standing next to Kiper.

PROSECUTOR: Did you see a table?

SECOND MAN: Yes, there was a table, but it was further to the right, as if it had nothing to do with what was happening there.

PROSECUTOR: A small table?

SECOND MAN: No, not at all. It was a big, long oak table, like one of those trestle tables you see in monasteries. It was probably one of those antique tables from the old town hall.

PROSECUTOR: Long, you say. What were its dimensions, more or less?

SECOND MAN: How should I know? Two, three meters. The Gestapo sat in a row on one side of the table; and there was quite a large group of them sitting there. Bondke was sitting, Rossel was sitting — them I remember. And there were at least six others.

PROSECUTOR: Did you by any chance notice whether Kiper was sitting at the table earlier and whether the reviewing of the *Arbeitskarten* took place at the table?

SECOND MAN: I didn't notice. When I was called, Kiper was standing several meters from the table.

PROSECUTOR: Who do you think was in charge of the action?

SECOND MAN: Kuntze. He had the highest rank.

PROSECUTOR: Did you see him in the square?

SECOND MAN: I don't remember if I saw Kuntze. Presumably he was sitting at the table. But I only remember Bondke and Rossel.

PROSECUTOR: Was the table already there when you got to the square?

SECOND MAN: Yes.

PROSECUTOR: Who was seated at it?

SECOND MAN: No one.

PROSECUTOR: Some people claim that Kiper was sitting in a chair even before the table was brought out and that afterwards he sat at the head of the table. That he took the *Arbeitskarten* while he was sitting.

SECOND MAN: It's possible. Everything is possible. When I was called, Kiper was standing.

PROSECUTOR: Mr. Zachwacki, do you recall an incident with a mother and child who were shot in the square?

SECOND MAN: Yes, I do. It was Rosa Rubinstein and her daughter Ala. They were from another town and had lived in our town only since the beginning of the war. I knew them.

PROSECUTOR: Who shot them, and under what circumstances?

SECOND MAN: I was standing in the group of workers on the right side of the square, beside the well.

PROSECUTOR: Please indicate the place on the map. With a circle or a cross. Thank you. There was a well there, you say. No one has yet mentioned that well.

SECOND MAN: It was an old well, wooden, with a wooden fence around it. All around it, in a semicircle, there were trees, poplars. At one moment I heard a shot, and people who were standing somewhat closer said that Rosa Rubinstein and her daughter had been shot. It seems that both of them had been sent to the left, but they went to the right. People said that Kiper ran after them and shot them.

PROSECUTOR: You said, "I heard a shot." Do you mean you heard a single shot?

SECOND MAN: Those were my words, but it's hard for me to say if I heard one shot, or two, or three. No doubt he fired at least twice.

PROSECUTOR: Did you see the shooting with your own eyes?

SECOND MAN: No. I saw the bodies lying on the ground. They were lying next to each other. Then the *Ordnungsdienst* picked them up. A red stain was left on the snow.

PROSECUTOR: You were part of the group that helped to bury the victims afterwards?

SECOND MAN: That's correct. There were so many victims that the *Ordnungsdienst* had to take twenty men to help. Four hundred and fifty people were killed in the town — in the square and in the house searches — and eight hundred and forty were shot in the cemetery. My wife was one of them.

PROSECUTOR: *(pause)* But you didn't see any murders with your own eyes? Can you say, "I saw with my own eyes that this one or that one shot so-and-so or so-and-so?"

SECOND MAN: I saw thirteen hundred victims. The mass grave was thirty meters long, three meters wide, five meters deep.

SECOND WOMAN: No, I wasn't in the square. Because I worked as a cleaning woman for the Gestapo, and in the morning, when everyone was going to the marketplace, Mama said to me, "See if they'll let you stay at work." I took my pail and a rag and a brush and said goodbye to my parents on the corner of Mickiewicza and Rozana. We lived on Mickiewicza Street. My parents kept going straight, and I turned onto Rozana. I had gone a few steps when suddenly I caught sight of Rossel and Hamke; they were walking towards me and I got terribly frightened, so I ran into the first gate, and they passed by, they didn't notice me. Later I saw them entering the building at number 13. I kept going.

PROSECUTOR: Who lived in the house?

SECOND WOMAN: I don't know, I was young, I was thirteen years old, but I said I was sixteen because children, you know, were killed. I was well developed, so I said I was sixteen and they let me work for them. That was good luck. That day the Gestapo were going around to all the houses looking for people who hadn't gone to the square, and if they found someone, they shot him either in his apartment or on the street.

PROSECUTOR: Was there a family named Weintal in the house at number 13?

SECOND WOMAN: Weintal? No, I never heard of anyone with that name. I stayed at the Gestapo all day long, hiding. I knew the building, I knew where I could hide. Well, I must say, I certainly was lucky.

PROSECUTOR: Which Gestapo members were in the building that day?

SECOND WOMAN: I don't know. I was hiding in an alcove next to the stairway to the cellar, at the very end of the corridor. Once I thought I heard Wittelmann's voice; he seemed to be on the telephone and was yelling something awful.

PROSECUTOR: Did you ever witness an execution while you worked there?

SECOND WOMAN: I know that they took place, and I know where. But I never saw them shoot anyone. I was afraid, and as soon as they brought someone in, I would hide, get out of their way. I was afraid that they might shoot me, too. They killed them against the fence.

PROSECUTOR: Which fence?

SECOND WOMAN: There was a courtyard at the back surrounded by a fence, and behind the fence there was a trench. That's where they were shot. I know, because afterwards the *Ordnungsdienst* would come and collect the bodies. Once I saw them carrying a doctor whom they had killed. His name was Gluck. But that was after the first action, in the spring. Another time I saw a group of Gestapo men walk out into the courtyard and immediately afterwards I heard a burst of machine-gun fire.

PROSECUTOR: Who did you see then?

SECOND WOMAN: Bondke, Rossel, Hamke, and Wittelmann.

PROSECUTOR: All together?

SECOND WOMAN: Yes. All together. I was washing the stairs to the cellar then.

PROSECUTOR: Were they all armed? Did each of them have a weapon?

SECOND WOMAN: Yes.

PROSECUTOR: Those shots you heard then, were they from a single machine gun or from several?

SECOND WOMAN: I don't know. I didn't pay attention. I wasn't thinking that someday someone would ask me about that. Maybe one of them shot, maybe two. Maybe they took turns. How should I know?

PROSECUTOR: When was that?

SECOND WOMAN: That was even before the first action, probably in the fall.

PROSECUTOR: Do you know how many people were shot then? Do you know their names?

SECOND WOMAN: I don't. I didn't see their bodies being taken away. I saw them collect the dead only once or twice. I don't know who was killed then.

PROSECUTOR: And you never saw a Gestapo man fire a gun?

SECOND WOMAN: No. I only worked there until the second action. I couldn't stand it any longer, I preferred to go to a camp. In general they were nice to me and never did anything bad. Once Bondke gave me cigarettes. The best-mannered was Kiper. He was an educated man, like Kuntze. But the others, no. Kiper had a lot of books in his room. He wanted fresh flowers in a vase every day. Once, when I didn't bring flowers, he yelled at me. Once he broke the vase because the flowers were wilted. On the desk in his room was a photograph of an elegant woman with a dog. But it was Hamke who had a dog. I used to prepare food for the dog. His name was Roosevelt. A wolfhound, very well trained. He tore the druggist Weidel's child to pieces. I heard Hamke boasting about him: *"Roosevelt hat heute ein Jüdlein zum Frühstück bekommen"* — Roosevelt had a little Jew for breakfast today. He said that to Kiper, and Kiper screwed up his face in disgust. Kiper couldn't stand Hamke and used to quarrel with Bondke. In general, he kept to himself. He didn't drink. That Sunday he was the first to come back from the marketplace.

PROSECUTOR: How do you know it was Kiper? Did you see him?

SECOND WOMAN: I heard his voice.

PROSECUTOR: Who was he talking to?

SECOND WOMAN: He was talking to himself. I thought he was reciting a poem. Anyway, that's what it sounded like. Then he went to his room and played his violin — I forgot to say that he was a trained musician. Bondke used to make fun of him and call him *Gestapogeiger* — Gestapo-fiddler. I don't know much about music, but I think he played very well. I heard him play several times. Always the same thing. I don't know what melody it was, I don't know much about music.

PROSECUTOR: Did you see him that day?

SECOND WOMAN: No, I only heard him playing.

PROSECUTOR: What time would that have been?

SECOND WOMAN: I don't know. It was growing dark.

PROSECUTOR: Could you hear the shots from the cemetery inside the Gestapo building?

SECOND WOMAN: I don't know. Maybe not. The cemetery is on Male Targi, and the Gestapo headquarters was on St. Jerzy Square. That's quite a distance. But maybe in the silence, in the clear air . . .

PROSECUTOR: Did you hear any shots when Kiper returned?

SECOND WOMAN: I can't say. Because the way I felt that Sunday and for several days afterwards, I was hearing shots all the time, and my parents thought I had lost my mind. I kept saying, "Listen, they're shooting . . . ," and I'd run and hide. Mama took me to Gluck, who gave me a powder, but it didn't help. I kept on hearing shots for a week. It was my nerves.

PROSECUTOR: When did the other Gestapo men come back?

SECOND WOMAN: I don't know. When it got dark, I sneaked out through the courtyard and returned home. The city was empty, as if no one was left alive. I was astonished: the snow was black. That was the blood. The most blood was on Sienkiewicza Street, and on Rozana. I didn't meet anyone in the marketplace either. It was empty. In the center of the square, lying on its back with its legs in the air, was a small, broken table.   *[1970]*

▤ THINKING ABOUT THE TEXT

1. Is the prosecutor being reasonable when he seeks to know facts about the table? In general, how fair is he in his questioning of the witnesses? Why do you think Fink decided to focus on a prosecutor as the interrogator rather than confronting them with the defense attorney for the person or persons they are testifying against?

2. What sorts of details do the witnesses recall?

3. How much does the order of the witnesses matter in this play? Would the play have the same effect if their testimonies appeared in a different order? Why, or why not?

4. This play was originally written for radio, which is evidently the reason that Fink does not provide any description of the set. Describe the kind of set you would use if you were staging the play in a theater. What props and pieces of furniture, if any, would you employ?

5. Fink herself has stated that this play "is a protest against the law which tries genocide according to the code intended for trivial crimes." What do you think she means? Refer to specific lines in the script.

▤ MAKING COMPARISONS

1. Both Creon and Fink's prosecutor represent a system of laws. Do both men behave in ways that make that system seem unjust? Explain by referring to their specific words and acts.

2. In their exchanges with the prosecutor, do the witnesses in Fink's play seem much more passive than Antigone is? Or do they, too, engage in active resistance? Explain what *active* and *passive* mean to you.

3. *The Table* is concerned with attempts to remember. In what ways, if any, is *Antigone* also about memory?

▤ WRITING ABOUT ISSUES

1. Write an essay in which you imagine that one of Sophocles' or Fink's characters is transported to a particular place in today's world where the government persecutes its critics. How would the character behave in this contemporary context? Let your answer be a claim that you develop and support, in part by doing research on the place you select.

2. Do research on a present-day person or group that uses an unconventional strategy to fight injustice. Then write an essay in which you argue for taking a certain view of this strategy. Do you see it as productive? Ethical?

3. Various countries have a history of mass violence or discrimination. Some are trying to atone for the past by establishing what's been called *restorative justice*. In this arrangement, perpetrators of injustice meet with

their victims, apologize to them, and seek their forgiveness. Do you think a procedure like this can serve the public good? Write an argument that examines restorative justice in a particular country that you have researched. Feel free to refer to *Antigone* or *The Table*.

4. Various countries have built memorials that recall an act of injustice. What kind of monument would you propose for memorializing Antigone's execution or the massacre that *The Table* focuses on? Choose one of these plays and write an essay arguing for a particular design. In your proposal, refer to at least one existing memorial you have discovered through research.

HAFIZAH GETER, "Testimony"

ARGUMENTS ON THE ISSUE:
BARBARA RANSBY, "Black Lives Matter Is Democracy in Action"

BARBARA REYNOLDS, "I was a civil rights activist in the 1960s . . ."

THE ECONOMIST, "The Misplaced Arguments Against Black Lives Matter"

In recent years, much public attention and debate has focused on police killings of young black men. In 2014, for example, white policeman Darren Wilson's fatal shooting of an eighteen-year-old African American Michael Brown led to wide press coverage and mass protests. It's the subject of this cluster's poem, Hafizah Geter's "Testimony." Yet Brown's death is one in a series of such shootings — forming what looks to many people like a deadly *pattern* of racial injustice. Notable among the resisters is the Black Lives Matter movement (BLM). As you may know, this group has not been universally praised. They've gained a lot of praise, but they've also been strongly criticized. No matter what, BLM has raised important issues. The question that serves as this cluster's title is one; what constitutes racial injustice is another. The three arguments that follow Geter's poem invite you to consider your own answers.

HAFIZAH GETER

Testimony

Though now residing in Brooklyn, New York, Hafizah Geter (b. 1984) was born in Nigeria and grew up in South Carolina. She majored in English and Economics at Clemson University, then earned an M.F.A. degree in Poetry Writing at Columbia College Chicago. In addition to her work as a poet, she is a board member for VIDA: Women in the Literary Arts and serves as an editor for Amazon Publishing. Geter has published her poetry in several major journals, including Boston Review, Narrative Magazine, *and* The New Yorker. *The following poem appeared in the Summer 2017 issue of* Tin House, *which focused on the topic of "True Crime." Geter's piece was part of a quartet of poems she contributed to this issue. Each is entitled "Testimony," and each centers on a real-life African American who died at the hands of police. Many people denounced these deaths as racist killings, a view that Geter clearly shares. The speaker of this particular poem is Michael Brown. On August 9, 2014, he was shot to death on a street in Ferguson, Missouri by white police officer Darren Wilson. The killing of Brown sparked several days of mass protest in Ferguson, with Black Lives Matter playing a prominent role. Officially, Wilson was cleared of wrongdoing, but BLM and other activist groups continue to call Brown's death a prime case of racial injustice.*

for Michael Brown (1996–2014)

Officer, for hours I lay there.
The sun at my back.
My blood running a country

mile between the pavement
and the crown of my head.   5
No ambulance ever came.

It took a long time to cover my body.
There are politics to death
and here politics performs

its own autopsies. My aunties   10
say things like, *Boy big and black as you.*
Then, the prosecution rests.

My neighbors never do. They lose
sleep as the National Guard parades
down Canfield. I heard my blood   15

was barely dry. I heard there were soldiers
beating their shields like war cries,
my boys holding hands to hold on

through your tear gas. Heard my mother
wandered the streets,   20
her body trembling

between a sign of a cross
and a fist. I heard a rumor
about riots got started.

Officer, I heard that after so much blood,   25
the ground develops
a taste for it.

                                                    [2017]

≡ THINKING ABOUT THE TEXT

1. Geter writes that this poem is "for Michael Brown (1996–2014)."
   What might "for" mean here? Think of the multiple ways this little
   word can be defined. Evidently Brown himself is the poem's speaker.
   Why, conceivably, does Geter have him address an officer? What's the
   significance of *this* person's being his audience?

2. What might Geter be attempting to explain? What notions might she
   be challenging?

3. In the last five stanzas (the second half of the poem), the speaker
   uses the word "heard" five times. Why do you think Geter has him

emphasizing this particular word? What's the effect on you when it's repeated so much?

4. In four places, the poem features enjambment: that is, a sentence spills over from one stanza to the next. In four other places, a stanza ends more definitely, with a period. Why do you think Geter employs these patterns?

5. Note the last stanza. Someone might argue that, in a literal sense, "the ground" *can't* acquire "a taste for" blood. What idea might Geter be expressing metaphorically?

BARBARA RANSBY
Black Lives Matter Is Democracy in Action

Barbara Ransby (b. 1957) earned a B.A. in History from Columbia University, then an M.A. and Ph.D. in the same field at the University of Michigan. Currently she is a Distinguished Professor of African American Studies, Gender and Women's Studies, and History at the University of Illinois at Chicago. She also directs that institution's Social Justice Initiative. Ransby's 2003 biography of civil rights advocate Ella Baker won multiple awards. She has also written Eslanda: The Large and Unconventional Life of Mrs. Paul Robeson *(2013) and* Making All Black Lives Matter: Reimagining Freedom in the Twenty-First Century, *in addition to publishing many articles in scholarly journals and the mainstream press. As a political activist, she has played a leading role in major initiatives, including the African American Women in Defense of Ourselves campaign, The Black Radical Congress, and Ella's Daughters, a women's network. Ransby's op-ed column on Black Lives Matter appeared in the October 21, 2017 issue of* The New York Times.

Why has this generation of black activists failed to produce a Rev. Dr. Martin Luther King Jr. or a Malcolm X — a charismatic, messiah-like figure who can lead a major movement?

The answer is a choice, not a deficiency. The suggestion that the organizations that have emerged from the Black Lives Matter protests are somehow lacking because they have rejected the old style of leadership misses what makes this movement most powerful: its cultivation of skilled local organizers who take up many issues beyond police violence.

This is radical democracy in action. The Movement for Black Lives, a coalition that includes the Black Lives Matter Global Network and other groups, coalesced in response to high-profile police shootings of black people from 2014 to 2016. It is reinvigorating the 21st-century racial-justice movement, and by extension the anti-racist left, by offering a better model for social movements.

The idea behind that model is that when people on the ground make decisions, articulate problems and come up with answers, the results are more likely to meet real needs. And that's more sustainable in the long run: People are better prepared to carry out solutions they themselves created, instead of ones handed down by national leaders unfamiliar with realities in local communities. Such local work allows people to take ownership of the political struggles that affect their lives.

Ella Baker, a N.A.A.C.P. field secretary, executive of the Southern Christian Leadership Conference and midwife of the Student Non-Violent Coordinating Committee, once said, "Strong people don't need strong leaders." Today's black organizers have taken that message to heart.   5

Ms. Baker considered the top-down, male-centered, charismatic model of leadership a political dead end. It disempowered ordinary people, especially women and low-income and working-class people, because it told them that they need a savior. If that person is assassinated or co-opted, the movement founders.

At the same time, local leadership is not a magic solution, since local leaders can also be dominant, hierarchical and self-aggrandizing. Group-centered leadership practices, where even celebrities in the movement are responsible to the will of rank-and-file members, help to keep organizations honest.

The lead organizers of the Movement for Black Lives have been influenced by 40 years of work by black feminist and L.G.B.T. scholars and activists. Their writings and practice emphasize collective models of leadership instead of hierarchical ones, center on society's most marginalized people and focus on how multiple systems of oppression intersect and reinforce one another.

This year, the Movement for Black Lives, with support from a team of strategists called Blackbird, coordinated three major days of action: two to commemorate Dr. King's "Beyond Vietnam" speech and a day of national protests against symbols of white supremacy after the racist attacks in Charlottesville, Va. In each case, national coordinators kept a low profile, offering support while encouraging local groups to set their own agendas.

Critics argue that the Movement for Black Lives needs to tighten control of its messaging, discipline its local affiliates and shore up its "brand." It's too bad they can't see the momentum happening at the grass-roots level. To paraphrase Ms. Baker, leaders who teach following as the only way of fighting weaken the movement in the long run.   10

Local organizers are not passive followers. They are leading creative campaigns in major cities. For example, the Black Youth Project 100, along with other local groups, is working to overturn the New York City Housing Authority's "permanent exclusion" policy, under which people convicted of a crime can be barred from living in or visiting public housing.

Seshat Mack, a student at the Icahn School of Medicine at Mount Sinai and a leader of the Black Youth Project 100's New York chapter, explained to me that the campaign, called Housing Over Monitoring and Eviction, has relied heavily on local leadership — in particular, black New Yorkers who live in public housing.

In Chicago, one of the most segregated cities in the country, an "expanded sanctuary" campaign has brought together black people and Latino immigrants to demand an end to punitive practices like the city's gang database. Activists have argued that the criteria for inclusion is vague and that people often don't know they're on the list. A lead organizer in that campaign, Maxx Boykin, underscores the importance of "building trust between people and organizations," which can happen only on the local level.

The fight to end cash bail was bolstered by Mama's Bail Out Day, a campaign that is the brainchild of the Atlanta organizer Mary Hooks, a director of Southerners on New Ground, a queer social-justice organization. The organizers raised over $1 million to bail out more than 100 low-income black women on Mother's Day this year. The Movement for Black Lives umbrella group oversaw the effort by pulling in local bail-reform groups.

One of the most intense efforts within the Movement for Black Lives has been to develop an electoral strategy that can be applied locally. Recently, activists started a project to lay the groundwork for creating local black political power. According to Kayla Reed, a St. Louis organizer who helped develop the project, the goal is to transfer the clarity and radical vision brought to the protest lines to electoral campaigns. The organizers of the project are drawing lessons from the successful progressive mayoral campaigns of Chokwe Lumumba in Jackson, Miss., and Randall Woodfin in Birmingham, Ala., as well as the narrow defeat of Tishaura O. Jones in St. Louis.   15

Despite progress on many fronts, there is still work to do. The movement does need an easier way for people to get involved and more transparent collective decision-making, as well as space for broader ideological and policy debates.

The Movement for Black Lives is distinctive because it defers to the local wisdom of its members and affiliates, rather than trying to dictate from above. In fact, the local organizers have insisted upon it. This democratic inflection will pay off if they persevere. Brick by brick, relationship by relationship, decision by decision, the edifices of resistance are being built. The national organizations are the mortar between the bricks. That fortified space will be a necessary training ground and refuge for the political battles that lay ahead, as white supremacists inside and outside of our government seek to undermine racial and economic justice.

≡ THINKING ABOUT THE TEXT

1. What is Ransby's main claim? What notions does she aim to counter? What's her answer to the question she starts off with?

2. What possible imperfections does Ransby associate with the model of activism she prefers?

3. What do you think of Ransby's suggestions to do away with gang databases and cash bail? If some people don't agree with these suggestions, can they still be persuaded to join her in basically approving of Black Lives Matter? Explain your reasoning.

4. Ransby is a noted biographer of civil rights activist Ella Baker. It's no surprise, then, that she decides to quote her here. But does the quotation strike you as an effective rhetorical move? Why, or why not?

5. In her last sentence, Ransby refers to white supremacists. How big a threat do you think they are? What are some recent events or developments that influence your answer?

BARBARA REYNOLDS

I Was a Civil Rights Activist in the 1960s.
But It's Hard for Me to Get Behind Black Lives Matter.

Besides being an ordained minister, Reverend Dr. Barbara Reynolds (b. 1942) has flourished as a reporter, as a columnist, as a talk show host, as a poet, and as an author of nonfiction books. She is an alumnus of The Ohio State University *(where she majored in Journalism),* Howard University Divinity School, *and* United Theological Seminary. *Media outlets she has written for include* The Cleveland Press, Ebony, The Chicago Tribune, *and* USA Today. *Her books include* Jesse Jackson: The Man, The Movement, The Myth *(1975),* No, I Won't Shut Up! *(1998),* Out of Hell & Living Well *(2004), and* My Life, My Love, My Legacy *(2017), an autobiography of Coretta Scott King constructed from Reynolds's interviews with her. Reynolds herself is a veteran activist for civil rights and women's equality, receiving such honors as the Southern Christian Leadership Conference's Martin Luther King, Jr. Drum Major for Justice Award. She contributed her thoughts on Black Lives Matter to the August 24, 2015 issue of* The Washington Post.

As the rapper Tef Poe sharply pointed out at a St. Louis rally in October protesting the death of unarmed teenager Michael Brown in Ferguson, Mo.: "This ain't your grandparents' civil rights movement."

He's right. It looks, sounds and feels different. Black Lives Matter is a motley-looking group to this septuagenarian grandmother, an activist in the civil rights movement of the 1960s. Many in my crowd admire the cause and courage of these young activists but fundamentally disagree with their approach. Trained in the tradition of Martin Luther King Jr., we were nonviolent activists who won hearts by conveying respectability and changed laws by delivering a message of love and unity. BLM seems intent on rejecting our proven methods. This movement is ignoring what our history has taught.

The baby boomers who drove the success of the civil rights movement want to get behind Black Lives Matter, but the group's confrontational and divisive tactics make it difficult. In the 1960s, activists confronted white mobs and police with dignity and decorum, sometimes dressing in church clothes and kneeling in prayer during protests to make a clear distinction between who was evil and who was good.

But at protests today, it is difficult to distinguish legitimate activists from the mob actors who burn and loot. The demonstrations are peppered with hate speech, profanity, and guys with sagging pants that show their underwear. Even if the BLM activists aren't the ones participating in the boorish language and dress, neither are they condemning it.

The 1960s movement also had an innate respectability because our leaders   5
often were heads of the black church, as well. Unfortunately, church and spirituality are not high priorities for Black Lives Matter, and the ethics of love, forgiveness and reconciliation that empowered black leaders such as King and Nelson Mandela in their successful quests to win over their oppressors are missing from this movement. The power of the spiritual approach was evident recently in the way relatives of the nine victims in the Charleston church shooting responded at the bond hearing for Dylann Roof, the young white man who reportedly confessed to killing the church members "to start a race war." One by one, the relatives stood in the courtroom, forgave the accused racist killer and prayed for mercy on his soul. As a result, in the wake of that horrific tragedy, not a single building was burned down. There was no riot or looting.

"Their response was solidly spiritual, one of forgiveness and mercy for the perpetrator," the Rev. Andrew Young, a top King aide, told me in a recent telephone interview.

"White supremacy is a sickness," said Young, who also has served as a U.S. congressman, ambassador to the United Nations, and mayor of Atlanta. "You don't get angry with sick people; you work to heal the system. If you get angry, it is contagious, and you end up acting as bad as the perpetrators."

The loving, nonviolent approach is what wins allies and mollifies enemies. But what we have seen come out of Black Lives Matter is rage and anger — justifiable emotions, but questionable strategy. For months, it seemed that BLM hadn't thought beyond that raw emotion, hadn't questioned where it would all lead. I and other elders openly worried that, without a clear strategy and well-defined goals, BLM could soon crash and burn out. Oprah Winfrey voiced that concern earlier this year, saying, "What I'm looking for is some kind of leadership to come out of this to say, 'This is what we want. This is what has to change, and these are the steps that we need to take to make these changes, and this is what we're willing to do to get it.'"

For her wise counsel, Oprah became the target of a deluge of tweets from young activists, who denounced her as elitist and "out of touch," which caused some well-meaning older sages to grit their teeth in silence. Now, nearly 10 months later, BLM has finally come around, releasing a list of policy demands last week. If this young movement had embraced the well-meaning advice of its elders earlier, instead of responding with disdain, it could have spent recent months making headway with political leaders, instead of battling the disheartening images of violence and destruction that have followed its protests against police brutality in black neighborhoods.

This opportunity for mentorship is fleeting, evidenced by the recent deaths   10
of civil rights movement giants Maya Angelou, Julian Bond and Louis Stokes. Seizing the wisdom of veteran civil rights activists will only help Black Lives Matter achieve its goals. The Revs. Jesse Jackson and Al Sharpton would be the most obvious assets to BLM, as civil rights leaders who have run for president

and led political campaigns — but BLM has welcomed neither. Long before they targeted Sen. Bernie Sanders, a Democratic presidential candidate, young activists stormed the stage and stole the microphone at Sharpton's "Justice for All" march against police brutality in Washington in December.

Some have defended the young activists. Speaking at a conference at Boston University's Social Justice Institute in April, Pamela Lightsey, a noted theologian and lecturer on queer theology at Boston University's Theological Seminary who chronicled the Ferguson protests, explained the disconnect between Black Lives Matter and the older civil rights cohort: BLM activists "respect the leaders of another day, but they are not going to bow down to them. They can't come into a protest march and demand a front seat or to jump on the front lines when the cameras are on."

She added that, while there are clergy participating in the BLM protests, "the movement is not a black church initiative."

Young doesn't take BLM's dismissive attitude toward preachers and the movement's lack of discipline lightly.

"In our movement, we were not only spiritual, we were thoughtful," he said. "The reason our campaigns for change were successful in Montgomery and Birmingham was because they were undergirded by boycotts. We didn't burn any businesses down. I don't see that discipline here. We also trained people not to get angry because we knew our minds, not our emotions, were our most powerful weapons. We knew — to lose your wits was to lose your life."

What Young is selling — discipline, respect for elders, restraint — is badly   15
needed in the movement. But right now, BLM isn't buying.

"BLM rejects the usual hierarchical style of leadership, with the straight black male at the top giving orders," Lightsey said. The BLM also gives special "attention to the needs of black queers, the black transgendered, the black undocumented, black incarcerated and others who are hardly a speck on today's political agenda."

In this way, BLM has improved on the previous generation. The new movement has embraced black women as leaders and was, in fact, founded by three black women. King's model, by contrast, was sexist to the core, imitating the tone of the country at that time. Civil rights heroines such as Fannie Lou Hamer, Ella Baker and even Rosa Parks — whose refusal to move to the back of the bus in Montgomery launched the 1960s movement — were not allowed to speak or march with the male leaders at the 1963 March on Washington.

In social movements of the past, "black" meant male and "women" meant white, but BLM is unapologetically refusing to let the plight of black women go unnoticed. Black women are incarcerated at three times the rate of white women. Recent deaths of black women in police custody generally haven't received the widespread news coverage that black men killed by officers have. The names of these black women are hardly known: Raynette Turner; Joyce Curnell; Ralkina Jones and Kindra Chapman. But with the backing of BLM, the case of Sandra Bland, a black woman who died in a Texas jail cell after she was aggressively arrested in a minor traffic violation, was given nationwide coverage last month.

Still, the movement has remained too narrow in its focus. I understand why, as a new movement, BLM has focused on black pain and suffering. But to win broader appeal, it must work harder to acknowledge the humanity in the lives of others. The movement loses sympathy when it shouts down those who dare to utter "all lives matter." Activists insist that this slogan diverts attention from their cause of racial justice, saying it puts the spotlight on people whose lives have always mattered.

But we should remember the words of King: "Injustice anywhere is a   20
threat to justice everywhere." The civil rights movement was not exclusively a black movement for black people. It valued all human lives, even those of people who worked against us. I can't believe that the life of a murdered white police officer, or an Asian child sold into sex slavery, or a hungry family in Appalachia are lives that don't matter. In a sense, even the slogan "Black Lives Matter" is too broad because the movement overlooks black-on-black homicides, the leading cause of death for black males between the ages of 15 and 34. That horrific fact remains off the movement's radar, for fear that it puts black men in a negative light. So which black lives really matter?

In an attempt to unify the different groups, some organizations are hosting interracial and intergenerational events. Black Women for Positive Change has established Oct. 17–25 as the Week of Non-Violence in 10 cities, where officials, faith institutions and youth groups will come together. Keith Magee, director of Boston's Social Justice Institute, is organizing a rally and all-day talk-a-thon on Oct. 10 with similar goals.

"The older generation can no more retire to the sidelines than the BLM can isolate itself just focusing on black lives mattering," Magee said. "We must create a space for people to come together and listen to each other."

Admittedly, baby boomers like myself can be too judgmental, expecting a certain reverence for our past journey. But it is critical that these two generations find a middle ground. Among Americans killed by police, blacks are more than twice as likely to be unarmed than whites. To reach their common goal of ending this unequal treatment, baby boomers and millennials must overcome their differences and pair the experience of the old with the energy of the young to change a criminal justice system that has historically abused both.

Xavier Johnson, a 32-year-old pastor in Dayton who monitors the movement for his doctoral dissertation, argues that boomers should do more to fix the generational misunderstanding. "When you look at this group [BLM] from the bottom up, you see young people who are grieving from the pain inflicted on black bodies," he told me. "They saw Michael Brown, someone their age, uncovered in the street for four hours baking in the hot sun. There were unarmed Eric Garner in New York, and Tamir Rice, a little kid police killed who was playing with a toy gun. They see churches on mostly every corner, but not where they are. They see a black president who they feel ignores them. They are showing righteous indignation for a system that does not value their humanity."

Johnson encouraged me, and others in my cohort, to spend more time   25
trying to understand BLM activists, instead of judging them. To help me
gain insight, he referred me to a popular song. "Every movement has its own
soundtrack," he told me. "One of ours is by rapper Kendrick Lamar, who sings
'Alright.'"

So I listened to the song, expecting it would be as uplifting as "We Shall
Overcome." I was terribly disappointed. The beat was too harsh; the lyrics
were nasty and misogynistic.

"Let me tell you about my life / Painkillers only put me in the twilight /
Where pretty pussy and Benjamin is the highlight."

Instead of imparting understanding, the song was a staunch reminder of
the generation gap that afflicts civil rights activism, and the struggle it is going
to take to overcome it.

≡ THINKING ABOUT THE TEXT

1. Reynolds acknowledges that she writes about Black Lives Matter from
   the perspective of an older generation of civil rights activists. What
   are the main differences she draws between her generation and the
   younger one she analyzes?

2. Where does Reynolds make concessions, finding virtues in the
   movement she mainly criticizes? Do you think she should have made
   more, and made them earlier? Why, or why not?

3. Reynolds is a minister. What aspects of her argument seem to reflect
   this fact? Can her argument persuade someone who isn't as religious
   as she is? Explain your reasoning.

4. What are Reynolds's specific values? What principles does she hold in
   high regard and want other people to follow?

5. Reynolds criticizes the slogan "Black Lives Matter" itself. Why does
   she object to it? To what extent do you find her logic sound?

THE ECONOMIST
The Misplaced Arguments Against Black Lives Matter

A weekly magazine established in 1843, The Economist *is based in London but has
an international reach. Though especially of interest to people in business and specialists in financial policy, it also addresses issues of politics and culture. At its Web
site, the magazine points out that it has advocated for "a variety of liberal causes."
For example, it has long opposed capital punishment and lately favored gun control
as well as same-sex marriage. Nevertheless,* The Economist *is more known for
expressing conservative views. This reputation makes its August 18, 2017, defense
of* Black Lives Matter *noteworthy.*

On August 15, 2017, Donald Trump repeated his belief that "both sides" were to blame for the violence on August 12 at a white-supremacist rally in Charlottesville, Virginia, that left one woman dead. David Duke, a former leader of the Ku Klux Klan, thanked him for "condemn[ing] the leftist terrorists in BLM," referring to the Black Lives Matter movement. David Clarke, the sheriff of Milwaukee County and a supporter of Mr. Trump, has also called Black Lives Matter "purveyors of hate," and urged the Southern Poverty Law Centre (SPLC), to include it among the hate groups it monitors. Many on the right share this belief. It is mistaken.

To be sure, some protestors who claim affiliation with BLM have said hateful things. A group outside the Minnesota State Fair chanted, "Pigs in a blanket; fry 'em like bacon." The previous night, a sheriff's deputy had been shot in Houston, for which some BLM opponents blame the movement—without evidence. Some have blamed BLM for the fatal car crash in Charlottesville, saying that it happened because BLM supporters were throwing bricks at the car. The movement may have begun with honorable intentions, one argument runs, but it has been "hijacked by a group that hates white people and looks to burn down cities and towns." And some seem to object to the name, hearing in the phrase "Black lives matter" the implication that other lives do not matter.

That argument is easily dismissed. Affirming one thing does not negate all else. Donating money to support, say, cancer research does not make one a cheerleader for tuberculosis. Someone who says that black lives matter does not imply that other lives do not—they are simply reminding people that for most of American history, black lives have been valued less than white ones. The days of slavery and de jure segregation have mercifully passed, but black Americans remain poorer, less healthy, and more likely to be killed by police than whites. You can agree or disagree with BLM's platform, but nothing in it promotes hatred of any race or group.

Richard Cohen, who heads the SPLC, defines hate groups as "those that vilify entire groups of people based on immutable characteristics such as race or ethnicity." BLM does not fit the bill: it welcomes white supporters, has condemned violence, and addresses structural racial inequities. Jacob Levy, a political philosopher, argues that BLM is "one of the most significant political mobilizations in defense of freedom" in decades. Its supporters oppose police brutality, mass incarceration, America's drug war, police militarization, and civil-forfeiture abuses. All of those are causes that liberals, libertarians, and conservatives—anyone who fears unchecked state power—ought to cheer.

≡ THINKING ABOUT THE TEXT

1. Many people who post arguments online don't disclose their identities. They choose to remain anonymous. But an increasing number of people, it seems, object to this practice. They contend that anonymous arguments are sneaky and ethically irresponsible if

they aren't attached to a specific name. The editorial board of *The Economist* doesn't sign its opinions, such as the one you've just read. Does the absence of an author's name matter to you as you evaluate the magazine's defense of Black Lives Matter? Why, or why not?

2. What claims does the editorial staff refute? What issue of definition does it address?

3. Note the cancer analogy in the third paragraph. How effective is this as an argumentative move?

4. In the age of Twitter, many arguments are brief. The opinion piece here is longer than a tweet, but not by much. What would you want to see in an additional paragraph or two?

5. What would you say to someone who argues that because *The Economist* is based in London, it has no right or authority to comment on a political movement in the United States?

≡ MAKING COMPARISONS

1. When you read all of the text in this cluster, what kinds of "testimony" do you see? You might want to look up definitions of the word.

2. Does each of these texts call the reader to action, or do they focus on influencing the reader's beliefs?

3. To what extent does each of these texts assume the reader already has some knowledge of its subject?

≡ WRITING ABOUT ISSUES

1. Write an essay in which you explain how one of the opinion pieces in this cluster could have made use of Geter's poems. What specific lines of hers might the opinion writer have quoted, and for what purpose?

2. Research the shooting death of Michael Brown or another case that involved protests by Black Lives Matter. Then, write an essay in which you argue for a position of your own on the movement's practices in this case. Refer to at least one of the texts in the cluster.

3. At a March 2015 public presentation, white poet Kenneth Goldsmith sparked protest when he read aloud "The Body of Michael Brown," a poem he constructed mostly from Brown's autopsy report. Many people denounced Goldsmith for being insensitive — indeed, racist — appropriation of Brown's tragic death. You can find more information online here: https://hyperallergic.com/190954/kenneth-goldsmith-remixes-michael-brown-autopsy-report-as-poetry/

Drawing on details of this controversy, write an essay in which you identify and defend principles that *you* think a poet should bear in mind if tempted to compose a poem about an African American shot to death by police. In the course of your argument, you might find it useful to bring up Geter's poem and/or another text in this cluster.

4. After he was shot to death on August 9, 2014, various media outlets published the picture of Michael Brown that appears on the left (below).

Many people criticized the press's use of this image. The implication, they claimed, was that Brown's gesture in the photo indicated that he belonged to a gang. Indeed, much of the press seemed uninterested in positive images of him, such as the one on the right. In response to such selectivity, a protest campaign emerged with the Twitter hashtag "IfTheyGunnedMeDown." Each entry featured two images of an African-American man: a negative one that the media might seize upon, and a positive one that the media might ignore.

Research another campaign that uses visual images to protest racial injustice. Then, write an essay in which you not only identify the campaign's techniques but also develop a claim about the impact they might have. Feel free to refer to one or more of the texts in this cluster.

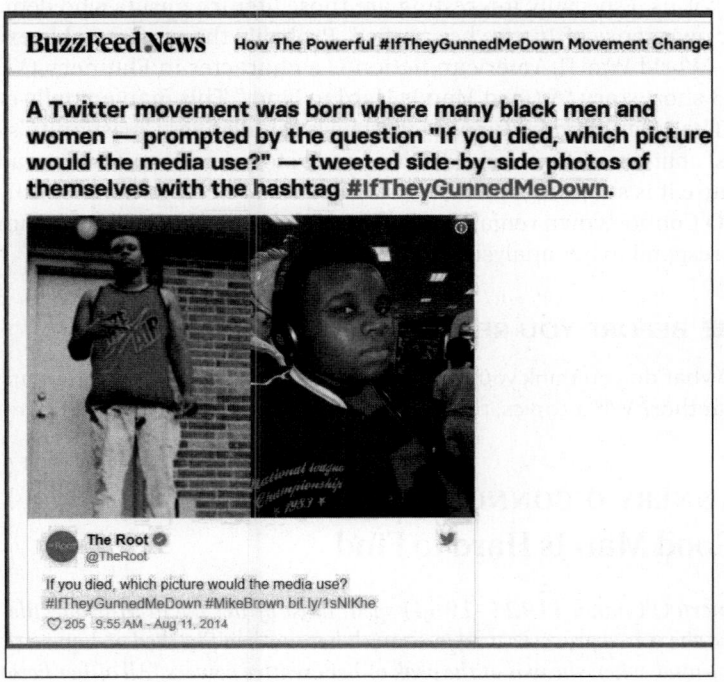

BuzzFeed News   How The Powerful #IfTheyGunnedMeDown Movement Change

A Twitter movement was born where many black men and women — prompted by the question "If you died, which picture would the media use?" — tweeted side-by-side photos of themselves with the hashtag #IfTheyGunnedMeDown.

The Root ✓
@TheRoot

If you died, which picture would the media use?
#IfTheyGunnedMeDown #MikeBrown bit.ly/1sNIKhe

♡ 205 9:55 AM - Aug 11, 2014

▤ Arguments about a Story: "A Good Man Is Hard to Find"

FLANNERY O'CONNOR, "A Good Man Is Hard to Find"

ARGUMENTS ABOUT THE STORY:
FLANNERY O'CONNOR, From *Mystery and Manners*

MARTHA STEPHENS, From *The Question of Flannery O'Connor*

STEPHEN BANDY, From *" 'One of My Babies': The Misfit and the Grandmother"*

JOHN DESMOND, From *"Flannery O'Connor's Misfit and the Mystery of Evil"*

Most of us are social beings; we long to fit in. The communities we form sustain us, giving us our moral compasses and our psychological bearings. But sometimes people voluntarily remove themselves from all traditional communities. Indeed, literature is filled with misfits. Their decisions may intrigue us but also perplex and trouble us, perhaps because they represent antisocial impulses in all of us. Especially interesting are those literary misfits who demand that their own sense of justice be satisfied. Probably the most notable example in post–World War II American fiction is a character in Flannery O'Connor's 1953 short story "A Good Man Is Hard to Find." This man actually calls himself The Misfit, and he turns violent as he challenges Christianity's belief in Jesus' ability to raise the dead. O'Connor's story has been widely read, in part because it is subject to various interpretations. Here, in addition to the story and O'Connor's own remarks about it, we present three critical commentaries that respond to her analysis.

▤ BEFORE YOU READ

What do you think you might find in a story by a practicing Roman Catholic author? What topics, themes, characters, and events might she write about?

FLANNERY O'CONNOR
A Good Man Is Hard to Find

Flannery O'Connor (1925–1964) spent most of her life in Milledgeville, Georgia, where she raised peacocks on a farm with her mother. She died of lupus at the age of thirty-nine, when she was at the peak of her creative powers. All of her fiction reflects her Roman Catholic faith and Southern heritage, as do her nonfiction writings, which were collected after her death in Mystery and Manners *(1969). Critics have often seen in her work Christian parables of grace and redemption in the face of random violence. Like other Southern writers such as William Faulkner and Carson McCullers,*

Apic/Getty Images

she uses grotesque characters to suggest our own morally flawed humanity. O'Connor's early stories won her a scholarship to the University of Iowa, where she received an M.F.A. She went on to produce two novels, Wise Blood *(1952) and* The Violent Bear It Away *(1960), but she is known and admired mostly for her short fiction. The following story was first published in the volume* Modern Writing 1 *in 1953. O'Connor then included it in her 1955 collection titled* A Good Man Is Hard to Find and Other Stories. *The book won her national acclaim, as did a later collection, the posthumously published* Everything That Rises Must Converge *(1965). These two volumes were combined in 1979 as* The Complete Stories of Flannery O'Connor, *which won the National Book Award for fiction.*

> The dragon is by the side of the road, watching those who pass. Beware lest he devour you. We go to the Father of Souls, but it is necessary to pass by the dragon.
> —St. Cyril of Jerusalem

The grandmother didn't want to go to Florida. She wanted to visit some of her connections in east Tennessee and she was seizing at every chance to change Bailey's mind. Bailey was the son she lived with, her only boy. He was sitting on the edge of his chair at the table, bent over the orange sports section of the *Journal.* "Now look here, Bailey," she said, "see here, read this," and she stood with one hand on her thin hip and the other rattling the newspaper at his bald head. "Here this fellow that calls himself The Misfit is aloose from the Federal Pen and headed toward Florida and you read here what it says he did to these people. Just you read it. I wouldn't take my children in any direction with a criminal like that aloose in it. I couldn't answer to my conscience if I did."

Bailey didn't look up from his reading so she wheeled around then and faced the children's mother, a young woman in slacks, whose face was as broad and innocent as a cabbage and was tied around with a green head-kerchief that had two points on the top like rabbit's ears. She was sitting on the sofa, feeding the baby his apricots out of a jar. "The children have been to Florida before," the old lady said. "You all ought to take them somewhere else for a change so they would see different parts of the world and be broad. They never have been to east Tennessee."

The children's mother didn't seem to hear her but the eight-year-old boy, John Wesley, a stocky child with glasses, said, "If you don't want to go to Florida, why dontcha stay at home?" He and the little girl, June Star, were reading the funny papers on the floor.

"She wouldn't stay at home to be queen for a day," June Star said without raising her yellow head.

"Yes and what would you do if this fellow, The Misfit, caught you?" the grandmother asked.   5

"I'd smack his face," John Wesley said.

"She wouldn't stay at home for a million bucks," June Star said. "Afraid she'd miss something. She has to go everywhere we go."

"All right, Miss," the grandmother said. "Just remember that the next time you want me to curl your hair."

June Star said her hair was naturally curly.

The next morning the grandmother was the first one in the car, ready to go. She had her big black valise that looked like the head of a hippopotamus in one corner, and underneath it she was hiding a basket with Pitty Sing, the cat, in it. She didn't intend for the cat to be left alone in the house for three days because he would miss her too much and she was afraid he might brush against one of the gas burners and accidentally asphyxiate himself. Her son, Bailey, didn't like to arrive at a motel with a cat.   10

She sat in the middle of the back seat with John Wesley and June Star on either side of her. Bailey and the children's mother and the baby sat in front and they left Atlanta at eight forty-five with the mileage on the car at 55890. The grandmother wrote this down because she thought it would be interesting to say how many miles they had been when they got back. It took them twenty minutes to reach the outskirts of the city.

The old lady settled herself comfortably, removing her white cotton gloves and putting them up with her purse on the shelf in front of the back window. The children's mother still had on slacks and still had her head tied up in a green kerchief, but the grandmother had on a navy blue straw sailor hat with a bunch of white violets on the brim and a navy blue dress with a small white dot in the print. Her collars and cuffs were white organdy trimmed with lace and at her neckline she had pinned a purple spray of cloth violets containing a sachet. In case of an accident, anyone seeing her dead on the highway would know at once that she was a lady.

She said she thought it was going to be a good day for driving, neither too hot nor too cold, and she cautioned Bailey that the speed limit was fifty-five miles an hour and that the patrolmen hid themselves behind billboards and small clumps of trees and sped out after you before you had a chance to slow down. She pointed out interesting details of the scenery: Stone Mountain; the blue granite that in some places came up to both sides of the highway; the brilliant red clay banks slightly streaked with purple; and the various crops that made rows of green lace-work on the ground. The trees were full of silver-white sunlight and the meanest of them sparkled. The children were reading comic magazines and their mother had gone back to sleep.

"Let's go through Georgia fast so we won't have to look at it much," John Wesley said.

"If I were a little boy," said the grandmother, "I wouldn't talk about my native state that way. Tennessee has the mountains and Georgia has the hills." 15

"Tennessee is just a hillbilly dumping ground," John Wesley said, "and Georgia is a lousy state too."

"You said it," June Star said.

"In my time," said the grandmother, folding her thin veined fingers, "children were more respectful of their native states and their parents and everything else. People did right then. Oh look at the cute little pickaninny!" she said and pointed to a Negro child standing in the door of a shack. "Wouldn't that make a picture, now?" she asked and they all turned and looked at the little Negro out of the back window. He waved.

"He didn't have any britches on," June Star said.

"He probably didn't have any," the grandmother explained. "Little nig- gers in the country don't have things like we do. If I could paint, I'd paint that picture," she said. 20

The children exchanged comic books.

The grandmother offered to hold the baby and the children's mother passed him over the front seat to her. She set him on her knee and bounced him and told him about the things they were passing. She rolled her eyes and screwed up her mouth and stuck her leathery thin face into his smooth bland one. Occasionally he gave her a faraway smile. They passed a large cotton field with five or six graves fenced in the middle of it, like a small island. "Look at the graveyard!" the grandmother said, pointing it out. "That was the old fam- ily burying ground. That belonged to the plantation."

"Where's the plantation?" John Wesley asked.

"Gone with the Wind," said the grandmother. "Ha. Ha."

When the children finished all the comic books they had brought, they opened the lunch and ate it. The grandmother ate a peanut butter sandwich and an olive and would not let the children throw the box and the paper nap- kins out the window. When there was nothing else to do they played a game by choosing a cloud and making the other two guess what shape it suggested. John Wesley took one the shape of a cow and June Star guessed a cow and 25

John Wesley said, no, an automobile, and June Star said he didn't play fair, and they began to slap each other over the grandmother.

The grandmother said she would tell them a story if they would keep quiet. When she told a story, she rolled her eyes and waved her head and was very dramatic. She said once when she was a maiden lady she had been courted by a Mr. Edgar Atkins Teagarden from Jasper, Georgia. She said he was a very good-looking man and a gentleman and that he brought her a watermelon every Saturday afternoon with his initials cut in it, E. A. T. Well, one Saturday, she said, Mr. Teagarden brought the watermelon and there was nobody at home and he left it on the front porch and returned in his buggy to Jasper, but she never got the watermelon, she said, because a nigger boy ate it when he saw the initials, E. A. T.! This story tickled John Wesley's funny bone and he giggled and giggled but June Star didn't think it was any good. She said she wouldn't marry a man that just brought her a watermelon on Saturday. The grandmother said she would have done well to marry Mr. Teagarden because he was a gentleman and had bought Coca-Cola stock when it first came out and that he had died only a few years ago, a very wealthy man.

They stopped at The Tower for barbecued sandwiches. The Tower was a part stucco and part wood filling station and dance hall set in a clearing outside of Timothy. A fat man named Red Sammy Butts ran it and there were signs stuck here and there on the building and for miles up and down the highway saying, TRY RED SAMMY'S FAMOUS BARBECUE. NONE LIKE FAMOUS RED SAMMY'S! RED SAM! THE FAT BOY WITH THE HAPPY LAUGH. A VETERAN! RED SAMMY'S YOUR MAN!

Red Sammy was lying on the bare ground outside The Tower with his head under a truck while a gray monkey about a foot high, chained to a small chinaberry tree, chattered nearby. The monkey sprang back into the tree and got on the highest limb as soon as he saw the children jump out of the car and run toward him.

Inside, The Tower was a long dark room with a counter at one end and tables at the other and dancing space in the middle. They all sat down at a board table next to the nickelodeon and Red Sam's wife, a tall burnt-brown woman with hair and eyes lighter than her skin, came and took their order. The children's mother put a dime in the machine and played "The Tennessee Waltz," and the grandmother said that tune always made her want to dance. She asked Bailey if he would like to dance but he only glared at her. He didn't have a naturally sunny disposition like she did and trips made him nervous. The grandmother's brown eyes were very bright. She swayed her head from side to side and pretended she was dancing in her chair. June Star said play something she could tap to so the children's mother put in another dime and played a fast number and June Star stepped out onto the dance floor and did her tap routine.

"Ain't she cute?" Red Sam's wife said, leaning over the counter. "Would you like to come be my little girl?"   30

"No I certainly wouldn't," June Star said. "I wouldn't live in a broken-down place like this for a million bucks!" and she ran back to the table.

"Ain't she cute?" the woman repeated, stretching her mouth politely.

"Aren't you ashamed?" hissed the grandmother.

Red Sam came in and told his wife to quit lounging on the counter and hurry up with these people's order. His khaki trousers reached just to his hip bones and his stomach hung over them like a sack of meal swaying under his shirt. He came over and sat down at a table nearby and let out a combination sigh and yodel. "You can't win," he said. "You can't win," and he wiped his sweating red face off with a gray handkerchief. "These days you don't know who to trust," he said. "Ain't that the truth?"

"People are certainly not nice like they used to be," said the grandmother.   35

"Two fellers come in here last week," Red Sammy said, "driving a Chrysler. It was a old beat-up car but it was a good one and these boys looked all right to me. Said they worked at the mill and you know I let them fellers charge the gas they bought? Now why did I do that?"

"Because you're a good man!" the grandmother said at once.

"Yes'm, I suppose so," Red Sam said as if he were struck with this answer.

His wife brought the orders, carrying the five plates all at once without a tray, two in each hand and one balanced on her arm. "It isn't a soul in this green world of God's that you can trust," she said. "And I don't count nobody out of that, not nobody," she repeated, looking at Red Sammy.

"Did you read about that criminal, The Misfit, that's escaped?" asked the   40
grandmother.

"I wouldn't be a bit surprised if he didn't attack this place right here," said the woman. "If he hears about it being here, I wouldn't be none surprised to see him. If he hears it's two cent in the cash register, I wouldn't be a tall surprised if he . . ."

"That'll do," Red Sam said. "Go bring these people their Co'-Colas," and the woman went off to get the rest of the order.

"A good man is hard to find," Red Sammy said. "Everything is getting terrible. I remember the day you could go off and leave your screen door unlatched. Not no more."

He and the grandmother discussed better times. The old lady said that in her opinion Europe was entirely to blame for the way things were now. She said the way Europe acted you would think we were made of money and Red Sam said it was no use talking about it, she was exactly right. The children ran outside into the white sunlight and looked at the monkey in the lacy china-berry tree. He was busy catching fleas on himself and biting each one carefully between his teeth as if it were a delicacy.

They drove off again into the hot afternoon. The grandmother took   45
cat naps and woke up every few minutes with her own snoring. Outside of Toombsboro she woke up and recalled an old plantation that she had visited in this neighborhood once when she was a young lady. She said the house had six white columns across the front and that there was an avenue of oaks leading up to it and two little wooden trellis arbors on either side in front where you sat down with your suitor after a stroll in the garden. She recalled exactly which road to turn off to get to it. She knew that Bailey would not be willing to lose

any time looking at an old house, but the more she talked about it, the more she wanted to see it once again and find out if the little twin arbors were still standing. "There was a secret panel in this house," she said craftily, not telling the truth but wishing that she were, "and the story went that all the family silver was hidden in it when Sherman came through but it was never found . . ."

"Hey!" John Wesley said. "Let's go see it! We'll find it! We'll poke all the woodwork and find it! Who lives there? Where do you turn off at? Hey Pop, can't we turn off there?"

"We never have seen a house with a secret panel!" June Star shrieked. "Let's go to the house with the secret panel! Hey Pop, can't we go see the house with the secret panel!"

"It's not far from here, I know," the grandmother said. "It wouldn't take over twenty minutes."

Bailey was looking straight ahead. His jaw was as rigid as a horseshoe. "No," he said.

The children began to yell and scream that they wanted to see the house   50
with the secret panel. John Wesley kicked the back of the front seat and June Star hung over her mother's shoulder and whined desperately into her ear that they never had any fun even on their vacation, that they could never do what THEY wanted to do. The baby began to scream and John Wesley kicked the back of the seat so hard that his father could feel the blows in his kidney.

"All right!" he shouted and drew the car to a stop at the side of the road. "Will you all shut up? Will you all just shut up for one second? If you don't shut up, we won't go anywhere."

"It would be very educational for them," the grandmother murmured.

"All right," Bailey said, "but get this: this is the only time we're going to stop for anything like this. This is the one and only time."

"The dirt road that you have to turn down is about a mile back," the grandmother directed. "I marked it when we passed."

"A dirt road," Bailey groaned.   55

After they had turned around and were headed toward the dirt road, the grandmother recalled other points about the house, the beautiful glass over the front doorway and the candle-lamp in the hall. John Wesley said that the secret panel was probably in the fireplace.

"You can't go inside this house," Bailey said. "You don't know who lives there."

"While you all talk to the people in front, I'll run around behind and get in a window," John Wesley suggested.

"We'll all stay in the car," his mother said.

They turned onto the dirt road and the car raced roughly along in a swirl   60
of pink dust. The grandmother recalled the times when there were no paved roads and thirty miles was a day's journey. The dirt road was hilly and there were sudden washes in it and sharp curves on dangerous embankments. All at once they would be on a hill, looking down over the blue tops of trees for miles around, then the next minute, they would be in a red depression with the dust-coated trees looking down on them.

"This place had better turn up in a minute," Bailey said, "or I'm going to turn around."

The road looked as if no one had traveled on it in months.

"It's not much farther," the grandmother said and just as she said it, a horrible thought came to her. The thought was so embarrassing that she turned red in the face and her eyes dilated and her feet jumped up, upsetting her valise in the corner. The instant the valise moved, the newspaper top she had over the basket under it rose with a snarl and Pitty Sing, the cat, sprang onto Bailey's shoulder.

The children were thrown to the floor and their mother, clutching the baby, was thrown out the door onto the ground; the old lady was thrown into the front seat. The car turned over once and landed right-side-up in a gulch off the side of the road. Bailey remained in the driver's seat with the cat — gray-striped with a broad white face and an orange nose — clinging to his neck like a caterpillar.

As soon as the children saw they could move their arms and legs, they scrambled out of the car, shouting, "We've had an ACCIDENT!" The grandmother was curled up under the dashboard, hoping she was injured so that Bailey's wrath would not come down on her all at once. The horrible thought she had had before the accident was that the house she had remembered so vividly was not in Georgia but in Tennessee. 65

Bailey removed the cat from his neck with both hands and flung it out the window against the side of a pine tree. Then he got out of the car and started looking for the children's mother. She was sitting against the side of the red gutted ditch, holding the screaming baby, but she only had a cut down her face and a broken shoulder. "We've had an ACCIDENT!" the children screamed in a frenzy of delight.

"But nobody's killed," June Star said with disappointment as the grandmother limped out of the car, her hat still pinned to her head but the broken front brim standing up at a jaunty angle and the violet spray hanging off the side. They all sat down in the ditch, except the children, to recover from the shock. They were all shaking.

"Maybe a car will come along," said the children's mother hoarsely.

"I believe I have injured an organ," said the grandmother, pressing her side, but no one answered her. Bailey's teeth were clattering. He had on a yellow sport shirt with bright blue parrots designed in it and his face was as yellow as the shirt. The grandmother decided that she would not mention that the house was in Tennessee.

The road was about ten feet above and they could only see the tops of the trees on the other side of it. Behind the ditch they were sitting in there were more woods, tall and dark and deep. In a few minutes they saw a car some distance away on top of a hill, coming slowly as if the occupants were watching them. The grandmother stood up and waved both arms dramatically to attract their attention. The car continued to come on slowly, disappeared around a bend and appeared again, moving even slower, on top of the hill they had gone over. It was a big black battered hearse-like automobile. There were three men in it. 70

It came to a stop just over them and for some minutes, the driver looked down with a steady expressionless gaze to where they were sitting, and didn't speak. Then he turned his head and muttered something to the other two and they got out. One was a fat boy in black trousers and a red sweat shirt with a silver stallion embossed on the front of it. He moved around on the right side of them and stood staring, his mouth partly open in a kind of loose grin. The other had on khaki pants and a blue striped coat and a gray hat pulled very low, hiding most of his face. He came around slowly on the left side. Neither spoke.

The driver got out of the car and stood by the side of it, looking down at them. He was an older man than the other two. His hair was just beginning to gray and he wore silver-rimmed spectacles that gave him a scholarly look. He had a long creased face and didn't have on any shirt or undershirt. He had on blue jeans that were too tight for him and was holding a black hat and a gun. The two boys also had guns.

"We've had an ACCIDENT!" the children screamed.

The grandmother had the peculiar feeling that the bespectacled man was someone she knew. His face was as familiar to her as if she had known him all her life but she could not recall who he was. He moved away from the car and began to come down the embankment, placing his feet carefully so that he wouldn't slip. He had on tan and white shoes and no socks, and his ankles were red and thin. "Good afternoon," he said. "I see you all had you a little spill."

"We turned over twice!" said the grandmother.   75

"Oncet," he corrected. "We seen it happen. Try their car and see will it run, Hiram," he said quietly to the boy with the gray hat.

"What you got that gun for?" John Wesley asked. "Whatcha gonna do with that gun?"

"Lady," the man said to the children's mother, "would you mind calling them children to sit down by you? Children make me nervous. I want all you all to sit down right together there where you're at."

"What are you telling US what to do for?" June Star asked.

Behind them the line of woods gaped like a dark open mouth. "Come   80
here," said the mother.

"Look here now," Bailey began suddenly, "we're in a predicament! We're in . . ."

The grandmother shrieked. She scrambled to her feet and stood staring. "You're The Misfit!" she said. "I recognized you at once!"

"Yes'm," the man said, smiling slightly as if he were pleased in spite of himself to be known, "but it would have been better for all of you, lady, if you hadn't of reckernized me."

Bailey turned his head sharply and said something to his mother that shocked even the children. The old lady began to cry and The Misfit reddened.

"Lady," he said, "don't you get upset. Sometimes a man says things he   85
don't mean. I don't reckon he meant to talk to you thataway."

"You wouldn't shoot a lady, would you?" the grandmother said and removed a clean handkerchief from her cuff and began to slap at her eyes with it.

The Misfit pointed the toe of his shoe into the ground and made a little hole and then covered it up again. "I would hate to have to," he said.

"Listen," the grandmother almost screamed, "I know you're a good man. You don't look a bit like you have common blood. I know you must come from nice people!"

"Yes mam," he said, "finest people in the world." When he smiled he showed a row of strong white teeth. "God never made a finer woman than my mother and my daddy's heart was pure gold," he said. The boy with the red sweat shirt had come around behind them and was standing with his gun at his hip. The Misfit squatted down on the ground. "Watch them children, Bobby Lee," he said. "You know they make me nervous." He looked at the six of them huddled together in front of him and he seemed to be embarrassed as if he couldn't think of anything to say. "Ain't a cloud in the sky," he remarked, looking up at it. "Don't see no sun but don't see no cloud neither."

"Yes, it's a beautiful day," said the grandmother. "Listen," she said, "you shouldn't call yourself The Misfit because I know you're a good man at heart. I can just look at you and tell." 90

"Hush!" Bailey yelled. "Hush! Everybody shut up and let me handle this!" He was squatting in the position of a runner about to sprint forward but he didn't move.

"I pre-chate that, lady," The Misfit said and drew a little circle in the ground with the butt of his gun.

"It'll take a half a hour to fix this here car," Hiram called, looking over the raised hood of it.

"Well, first you and Bobby Lee get him and that little boy to step over yonder with you," The Misfit said, pointing to Bailey and John Wesley. "The boys want to ast you something," he said to Bailey. "Would you mind stepping back in them woods there with them?"

"Listen," Bailey began, "we're in a terrible predicament! Nobody realizes what this is," and his voice cracked. His eyes were as blue and intense as the parrots in his shirt and he remained perfectly still. 95

The grandmother reached up to adjust her hat brim as if she were going to the woods with him but it came off in her hand. She stood staring at it and after a second she let it fall on the ground. Hiram pulled Bailey up by the arm as if he were assisting an old man. John Wesley caught hold of his father's hand and Bobby Lee followed. They went off toward the woods and just as they reached the dark edge, Bailey turned and supporting himself against a gray naked pine trunk, he shouted, "I'll be back in a minute, Mamma, wait on me!"

"Come back this instant!" his mother shrilled but they all disappeared into the woods.

"Bailey Boy!" the grandmother called in a tragic voice but she found she was looking at The Misfit squatting on the ground in front of her. "I just know you're a good man," she said desperately. "You're not a bit common!"

"Nome, I ain't a good man," The Misfit said after a second as if he had considered her statement carefully, "but I ain't the worst in the world neither. My daddy said I was a different breed of dog from my brothers and sisters.

'You know,' Daddy said, 'it's some that can live their whole life out without asking about it and it's others has to know why it is, and this boy is one of the latters. He's going to be into everything!' " He put on his black hat and looked up suddenly and then away deep into the woods as if he were embarrassed again. "I'm sorry I don't have on a shirt before you ladies," he said, hunching his shoulders slightly. "We buried our clothes that we had on when we escaped and we're just making do until we can get better. We borrowed these from some folks we met," he explained.

"That's perfectly all right," the grandmother said. "Maybe Bailey has an extra shirt in his suitcase."   100

"I'll look and see terrectly," The Misfit said.

"Where are they taking him?" the children's mother screamed.

"Daddy was a card himself," The Misfit said. "You couldn't put anything over on him. He never got in trouble with the Authorities though. Just had the knack of handling them."

"You could be honest too if you'd only try," said the grandmother. "Think how wonderful it would be to settle down and live a comfortable life and not have to think about somebody chasing you all the time."

The Misfit kept scratching in the ground with the butt of his gun as if he were thinking about it. "Yes'm, somebody is always after you," he murmured.   105

The grandmother noticed how thin his shoulder blades were just behind his hat because she was standing up looking down at him. "Do you ever pray?" she asked.

He shook his head. All she saw was the black hat wiggle between his shoulder blades. "Nome," he said.

There was a pistol shot from the woods, followed closely by another. Then silence. The old lady's head jerked around. She could hear the wind move through the tree tops like a long satisfied insuck of breath. "Bailey Boy!" she called.

"I was a gospel singer for a while," The Misfit said. "I been most everything. Been in the arm service, both land and sea, at home and abroad, been twict married, been an undertaker, been with the railroads, plowed Mother Earth, been in a tornado, seen a man burnt alive oncet," and he looked up at the children's mother and the little girl who were sitting close together, their faces white and their eyes glassy; "I even seen a woman flogged," he said.

"Pray, pray," the grandmother began, "pray, pray . . ."   110

"I never was a bad boy that I remember of," The Misfit said in an almost dreamy voice, "but somewheres along the line I done something wrong and got sent to the penitentiary. I was buried alive," and he looked up and held her attention to him by a steady stare.

"That's when you should have started to pray," she said. "What did you do to get sent to the penitentiary, that first time?"

"Turn to the right, it was a wall," The Misfit said, looking up again at the cloudless sky. "Turn to the left, it was a wall. Look up it was a ceiling, look down it was a floor. I forgot what I done, lady. I set there and set there, trying to remember what it was I done and I ain't recalled it to this day. Oncet in a while, I would think it was coming to me, but it never come."

"Maybe they put you in by mistake," the old lady said vaguely.

"Nome," he said. "It wasn't no mistake. They had the papers on me." 115

"You must have stolen something," she said.

The Misfit sneered slightly. "Nobody had nothing I wanted," he said. "It was a head-doctor at the penitentiary said what I had done was kill my daddy but I known that for a lie. My daddy died in nineteen ought nineteen of the epidemic flu and I never had a thing to do with it. He was buried in the Mount Hopewell Baptist churchyard and you can go there and see for yourself."

"If you would pray," the old lady said, "Jesus would help you."

"That's right," The Misfit said.

"Well then, why don't you pray?" she asked trembling with delight 120 suddenly.

"I don't want no hep," he said. "I'm doing all right by myself."

Bobby Lee and Hiram came ambling back from the woods. Bobby Lee was dragging a yellow shirt with bright blue parrots in it.

"Thow me that shirt, Bobby Lee," The Misfit said. The shirt came flying at him and landed on his shoulder and he put it on. The grandmother couldn't name what the shirt reminded her of. "No, lady," The Misfit said while he was buttoning it up, "I found out the crime don't matter. You can do one thing or you can do another, kill a man or take a tire off his car, because sooner or later you're going to forget what it was you done and just be punished for it."

The children's mother had begun to make heaving noises as if she couldn't get her breath. "Lady," he asked, "would you and that little girl like to step off yonder with Bobby Lee and Hiram and join your husband?"

"Yes, thank you," the mother said faintly. Her left arm dangled helplessly 125 and she was holding the baby, who had gone to sleep, in the other. "Hep that lady up, Hiram," The Misfit said as she struggled to climb out of the ditch, "and Bobby Lee, you hold onto that little girl's hand."

"I don't want to hold hands with him," June Star said. "He reminds me of a pig."

The fat boy blushed and laughed and caught her by the arm and pulled her off into the woods after Hiram and her mother.

Alone with The Misfit, the grandmother found that she had lost her voice. There was not a cloud in the sky nor any sun. There was nothing around her but woods. She wanted to tell him that he must pray. She opened and closed her mouth several times before anything came out. Finally she found herself saying, "Jesus. Jesus," meaning, Jesus will help you, but the way she was saying it, it sounded as if she might be cursing.

"Yes'm," The Misfit said as if he agreed. "Jesus thown everything off balance. It was the same case with Him as with me except He hadn't committed any crime and they could prove I had committed one because they had the papers on me. Of course," he said, "they never shown me my papers. That's why I sign myself now. I said long ago, you get you a signature and sign everything you do and keep a copy of it. Then you'll know what you done and you can hold up the crime to the punishment and see do they match and in the end you'll have something to prove you ain't been treated right. I call myself The Misfit," he said, "because I can't make what all I done wrong fit what all I gone through in punishment."

There was a piercing scream from the woods, followed closely by a pistol   130
report. "Does it seem right to you, lady, that one is punished a heap and another ain't punished at all?"

"Jesus!" the old lady cried. "You've got good blood! I know you wouldn't shoot a lady! I know you come from nice people! Pray! Jesus, you ought not to shoot a lady. I'll give you all the money I've got!"

"Lady," The Misfit said, looking beyond her far into the woods, "there never was a body that give the undertaker a tip."

There were two more pistol reports and the grandmother raised her head like a parched old turkey hen crying for water and called, "Bailey Boy, Bailey Boy!" as if her heart would break.

"Jesus was the only One that ever raised the dead," The Misfit continued, "and He shouldn't have done it. He thown everything off balance. If He did what He said, then it's nothing for you to do but thow away everything and follow Him, and if He didn't, then it's nothing for you to do but enjoy the few minutes you got left the best you can—by killing somebody or burning down his house or doing some other meanness to him. No pleasure but meanness," he said and his voice had become almost a snarl.

"Maybe He didn't raise the dead," the old lady mumbled, not knowing   135
what she was saying and feeling so dizzy that she sank down in the ditch with her legs twisted under her.

"I wasn't there so I can't say He didn't," The Misfit said. "I wisht I had of been there," he said, hitting the ground with his fist. "It ain't right I wasn't there because if I had of been there I would of known. Listen lady," he said in a high voice, "if I had of been there I would of known and I wouldn't be like I am now." His voice seemed about to crack and the grandmother's head cleared for an instant. She saw the man's face twisted close to her own as if he were going to cry and she murmured, "Why you're one of my babies. You're one of my own children!" She reached out and touched him on the shoulder. The Misfit sprang back as if a snake had bitten him and shot her three times through the chest. Then he put his gun down on the ground and took off his glasses and began to clean them.

Hiram and Bobby Lee returned from the woods and stood over the ditch, looking down at the grandmother who half sat and half lay in a puddle of blood with her legs crossed under her like a child's and her face smiling up at the cloudless sky.

Without his glasses, The Misfit's eyes were red-rimmed and pale and defenseless-looking. "Take her off and thow her where you thown the others," he said, picking up the cat that was rubbing itself against his leg.

"She was a talker, wasn't she?" Bobby Lee said, sliding down the ditch with a yodel.

"She would of been a good woman," The Misfit said, "if it had been some-   140
body there to shoot her every minute of her life."

"Some fun!" Bobby Lee said.

"Shut up, Bobby Lee," The Misfit said. "It's no real pleasure in life." *[1955]*

≡ THINKING ABOUT THE TEXT

1. Although this story begins with comedy, ultimately it shocks many readers. Did it shock you? Why, or why not? What would you say to someone who argues that the shift in tone is a flaw in the story?

2. Note places where the word *good* comes up in this story. How is it defined? Do the definitions change? Do you think the author has in mind a definition that does not occur to the characters? If so, what might that definition be?

3. What in his life history is The Misfit unsure about? Why do you think he is hazy about these matters? Should O'Connor have resolved for us all the issues of fact that bother him? Why, or why not?

4. Does The Misfit have any redeeming qualities? Does the grandmother? Explain. What do you think the grandmother means when she murmurs, "Why you're one of my babies. You're one of my own children!" (para. 136)? Why do you think The Misfit responds as he does?

5. There is much talk about Jesus and Christianity in this story. Should O'Connor have done more to help non-Christian readers see the story as relevant to them? Explain your reasoning.

FLANNERY O'CONNOR
From *Mystery and Manners*

For public presentations at colleges and other places, Flannery O'Connor often chose to read and comment on "A Good Man Is Hard to Find." The following remarks come from her introduction to the story when she read it at Hollins College in Virginia in 1963. After her death, the introduction was published as "On Her Own Work" in Mystery and Manners, *a 1969 collection of O'Connor's nonfiction pieces. Her comments on "A Good Man Is Hard to Find" encourage a religious analysis of it. How helpful, though, is her interpretation? Many critics who have subsequently written about the story have raised and addressed this issue.*

It is true that the old lady is a hypocritical old soul; her wits are no match for the Misfit's, nor is her capacity for grace equal to his; yet I think the unpreju-diced reader will feel that the Grandmother has a special kind of triumph in this story which instinctively we do not allow to someone altogether bad.

I often ask myself what makes a story work and what makes it hold up as a story, and I have decided that it is probably some action, some gesture of a character that is unlike any other in the story, one which indicates where the real heart of the story lies. This would have to be an action or a gesture which was both totally right and totally unexpected; it would have to be one that was both in character and beyond character; it would have to suggest both the world and eternity. The action or gesture I'm talking about would have to be on the anagogical level, that is, the level which has to do with the Divine life and our participation in it. It would be a gesture that transcended any neat allegory that might have been intended or any pat moral categories a reader could make. It would be a gesture which somehow made contact with mystery.

There is a point in this story where such a gesture occurs. The Grandmother is at last alone, facing the Misfit. Her head clears for an instant and she realizes, even in her limited way, that she is responsible for the man before her and joined to him by ties of kinship which have their roots deep in the mystery she has been merely prattling about so far. And at this point, she does the right thing, she makes the right gesture.

I find that students are often puzzled by what she says and does here, but I think myself that if I took out this gesture and what she says with it, I would have no story. What was left would not be worth your attention. Our age not only does not have a very sharp eye for the almost imperceptible intrusions of grace, it no longer has much feeling for the nature of the violences which precede and follow them. The devil's greatest wile, Baudelaire has said, is to convince us that he does not exist.

I suppose the reasons for the use of so much violence in modern fiction will differ with each writer who uses it, but in my own stories I have found that violence is strangely capable of returning my characters to reality and preparing them to accept their moment of grace. Their heads are so hard that almost nothing else will do the work. This idea, that reality is something to which we must be returned at considerable cost, is one which is seldom understood by the casual reader, but it is one which is implicit in the Christian view of the world.

I don't want to equate the Misfit with the devil. I prefer to think that, however unlikely this may seem, the old lady's gesture, like the mustard-seed, will grow to be a great crow-filled tree in the Misfit's heart and will be enough of a pain to him there to turn him into the prophet he was meant to become. But that's another story.

This story has been called grotesque, but I prefer to call it literal. A good story is literal in the same sense that a child's drawing is literal. When a child draws, he doesn't intend to distort but to set down exactly what he sees, and as his gaze is direct, he sees the lines that create motion. Now the lines of motion that interest the writer are usually invisible. They are lines of spiritual motion. And in this story you should be on the lookout for such things as the action of grace in the Grandmother's soul, and not for the dead bodies.

[1963]

MARTHA STEPHENS

From *The Question of Flannery O'Connor*

Martha Stephens is professor emeritus of English and comparative literature at the University of Cincinnati. After Flannery O'Connor's religious explanation of "A Good Man Is Hard to Find" was published in the 1969 volume Mystery and Manners, *other readers of the story began responding to her comments. Stephens's 1973 book* The Question of Flannery O'Connor *includes one of the earliest attempts to gauge the helpfulness of O'Connor's analysis. Stephens is disturbed by the story's apparent shift of tone as it moves from farce to violent tragedy. O'Connor's remarks clarify this shift, Stephens thinks, but the religious doctrine reflected in them is severe.*

An ordinary and undistinguished family, a family even comical in its dullness, ill-naturedness, and triviality, sets out on a trip to Florida and on an ordinary summer day meets with a terrible fate. In what would the interest of such a story normally lie? Perhaps, one might think, in something that is revealed about the family in the way it meets its death, in some ironical or interesting truth about the nature of those people or those relationships—something we had been prepared unbeknownst to see, at the end plainly dramatized by their final common travail and death. But obviously, as regards the family as a whole, no such thing happens. The family is shown to be in death just as ordinary and ridiculous as before. With the possible exception of the grandmother, we know them no better; nothing about them of particular significance is brought forth.

The grandmother, being as we have seen the last to die, suffers the deaths of all her family while carrying on the intermittent conversation with the Misfit, and any reader will have some dim sense that it is through this encounter that the story is trying to transform and justify itself. One senses that this conversation—even though our attention is in reality fastened upon the horrible acts that are taking place in the background (and apparently against the thrust of the story)—is meant to be the real center of the story and the part in which the "point," as it were, of the whole tale lies.

But what is the burden of that queer conversation between the Misfit and the grandmother; what power does it have, even when we retrospectively sift and weigh it line by line, to transform our attitude towards the seemingly gratuitous—in terms of the art of the tale—horror of the massacre? The uninitiated reader will not, most likely, be able to unravel the strange complaint of the killer without some difficulty, but when we see the convict's peculiar dilemma in the context of O'Connor's whole work and what is known of her religious thought, it is not difficult to explain.

The Misfit's most intriguing statement—the line that seemingly the reader must ponder, set as it is as the final pronouncement on the grandmother after her death—is from the final passage . . . . : "She would of been a good woman if it had been somebody there to shoot her every minute of her life." Certainly we know from the first half of the story that the grandmother has seen herself as a good woman—and a good woman in a day when good men and women are hard to find, when people are disrespectful and dishonest, when they are not nice like they used to be. The grandmother is not common but a lady; and at the end of the story we know that she will be found dead just as we know she wanted to be — in the costume of a lady. She was not common, and the Misfit, with his "scholarly spectacles," his courtly apology for not wearing a shirt, his yes ma'ams and no ma'ams, was not common either — she had believed, wanted to believe, or pretended to believe. "Why I can see you come from good people," she said, "not common at all." Yet the Misfit says of her that she *would* have been a good woman if somebody had been there to shoot her all her life. And if we take the Misfit's statement as the right one about the grandmother, how was she a good woman in her death?

A good woman, perhaps we are given to believe, is one who understands   5
the worthlessness and emptiness of being or not being a "lady," of having or not having Coca-Cola stock, of "being broad" and seeing the world, of good manners and genteel attire. "Woe to them," said Isaiah, "that are wise in their own eyes, and prudent in their own sight." The futility of all the grandmother's values, the story strives to encapsulate in this image of her disarray after the car has overturned and she has recognized the Misfit: "The grandmother reached up to adjust her hat brim as if she were going to the woods with him but it came off in her hand. She stood staring at it and after a second she let it fall on the ground."

The Misfit is a figure that seems, one must say to the story's credit, to have fascinated more readers than any other single O'Connor character, and it is by contrast with the tormented spiritual state of this seeming monster that the nature of the grandmother's futile values becomes evident. We learn that the center of the Misfit's thought has always been Jesus Christ, and what becomes clear as we study over the final scene is that the Misfit has, in the eyes of the author, the enormous distinction of having at least faced up to the problem of Christian belief. And everything he has done — everything he so monstrously does here — proceeds from his inability to accept Christ, to truly believe. This is the speech which opens the narrow and emotionally difficult route into the meaning of the story:

> "Jesus was the only One that ever raised the dead," The Misfit continued, "and He shouldn't have done it. He thown everything off balance. If He did what He said, then it's nothing for you to do but thow away everything and follow Him, and if He didn't, then it's nothing for you to do but enjoy the few minutes you got left the best way you can — by killing somebody or burning down his house or doing some other meanness to him. No pleasure but meanness," he said and his voice had become almost a snarl.

The Misfit has chosen, at least, whom he would serve — has followed the injunction of the prophet in I Kings 18:21: "And Elijah came unto all the people, and said, How long halt ye between two opinions? if the Lord be God, follow him: but if Baal, then follow him." The crucial modern text for the authorial view here, which belongs to a tradition in religio-literary thought sometimes referred to as the sanctification of the sinner, is T. S. Eliot's essay on Baudelaire, in which he states: "So far as we are human, what we do must be either evil or good; so far as we do evil or good, we are human; and it is better, in a paradoxical way, to do evil than to do nothing; at least, we exist. It is true that the glory of man is his capacity for salvation; it is also true to say that his glory is his capacity for damnation."

Thus observe how, in the context of these statements, "A Good Man Is Hard to Find" begins to yield its meaning. What O'Connor has done is to take, in effect, Eliot's maxim — "It is better, in a paradoxical way, to do evil than to do nothing" — and to stretch our tolerance of this idea to its limits. The conclusion that one cannot avoid is that the story depends, for its final effect, on our being able to appreciate — even to be startled by, to be pleasurably struck with — the notion of the essential moral superiority of the Misfit over his victims, who have lived without choice or commitment of any kind, who have in effect not "lived" at all.

But again, in what sense is the grandmother a "good woman" in her death, as the Misfit claims? Here even exegesis falters. Because in her terror she calls on the name of Jesus, because she exhorts the Misfit to pray? Is she "good" because as the old lady sinks fainting into the ditch, after the Misfit's Jesus speech recorded above, she mumbles, "Maybe he didn't raise the dead"? Are we to see her as at last beginning to face the central question of human existence: did God send his son to save the world? Perhaps there is a clue in the dead grandmother's final image: she is said to half lie and half sit "in a puddle of blood with her legs crossed under her like a child's and her face smiling up at the cloudless sky." For Christ said, after all, that "whosoever shall not receive the kingdom of God as a little child shall in no wise enter herein."

To see that the Misfit is really the one courageous and admirable figure in the story; that the grandmother was perhaps — even as he said — a better woman in her death than she had ever been; to see that the pain of the other members of the family, that any godless pain or pleasure that human beings may experience is, beside the one great question of existence, *unimportant* — to see all these things is to enter fully into the experience of the story. Not to see them is to find oneself pitted not only against the forces that torture and destroy the wretched subjects of the story, but against the story itself and its attitude of indifference to and contempt for human pain.

Now as it happens, "A Good Man Is Hard to Find" was a favorite story of   10
O'Connor's. It was the story she chose to read whenever she was asked to read from her work, and clearly it held a meaning for her that was particularly important. Whenever she read the story, she closed by reading a statement giving her own explanation of it. (One version of that statement can now be read in the collection of O'Connor's incidental prose edited by Robert and Sally Fitzgerald titled *Mystery and Manners*.) She had come to realize that it was a story that readers found difficult, and she said in her statement that she felt that the reason the story was misunderstood was that the present age "not only does not have a very sharp eye for the almost imperceptible intrusions of grace, it no longer has much feeling for the nature of the violences which precede and follow them." The intrusion of grace in "A Good Man Is Hard to Find" comes, Miss O'Connor said, in that much-discussed passage in which the

grandmother, her head suddenly clearing for a moment, murmurs to the Misfit, "Why, you're one of my babies. You're one of my own children!" and is shot just as she reaches out to touch him. The grandmother's gesture here is what, according to O'Connor, makes the story work; it shows that the grandmother realizes that "she is responsible for the man before her and joined to him by ties of kinship which have their roots deep in the mystery she has been merely prattling about so far," and it affords the grandmother "a special kind of triumph . . . which we instinctively do not allow to someone altogether bad."

This explanation does solve, in a sense, one of the riddles of this odd story — although, of course, one must say that while it is interesting to know the intent of the author, speaking outside the story and after the fact, such knowledge does not change the fact that the intent of the narrator manifested strictly within the story is damagingly unclear on this important point. And what is even more important here is that O'Connor's statement about the story, taken as a whole, only further confirms the fact that the only problem in this tale is really a function of our difficulty with O'Connor's formidable doctrine. About the Misfit, O'Connor says that while he is not to be seen as the hero of the story, yet his capacity for grace is far greater than the grandmother's and that the author herself prefers to think "that the old lady's gesture, like the mustard-seed, will grow to be a great crow-filled tree in the Misfit's heart, and will be enough of a pain to him there to turn him into the prophet he was meant to become." The capacity for grace of the other members of the family is apparently zero, and hence — Christian grace in O'Connor, one cannot help noting, is rather an expensive process — it is proper that their deaths should have no spiritual context whatever.   [1973]

STEPHEN BANDY

From " 'One of My Babies': The Misfit and the Grandmother"

In an article published in a 1996 issue of Studies in Short Fiction, *Stephen Bandy strongly disagrees with O'Connor's interpretation of "A Good Man Is Hard to Find." In particular, he thinks that the grandmother is sentimental and vindictive, whereas O'Connor is sympathetic to the character and believes that she manifests grace. Following are excerpts from Bandy's analysis.*

Grasping at any appeal, and hardly aware of what she is saying, the Grandmother declares to the Misfit: " 'Why you're one of my babies. You're one of my own children!' " As she utters these shocking words, "She reached out and touched him on the shoulder. The Misfit sprang back as if a snake had bitten him and shot her three times through the chest".

Noting that some squeamish readers had found this ending too strong, O'Connor defended the scene in this way: "If I took out this gesture and what she says with it, I would have no story. What was left would not be worth your attention" (*Mystery and Manners* 112).[1] Certainly the scene is crucial to the story, and most readers, I think, grant its dramatic "rightness" as a conclusion. What is arguable is the meaning to the Grandmother's final words to the Misfit, as well as her "gesture," which seemed equally important to O'Connor. One's interpretation depends on one's opinion of the Grandmother.

What *are* we to think of this woman? At the story's beginning, she seems a harmless busybody, utterly self-absorbed but also amusing, in her way. And, in her way, she provides a sort of human Rorschach test of her readers. We readily forgive her so much, including her mindless racism — she points at the "cute little pickaninny" by the roadside, and entertains her grandchildren with a story in which a watermelon is devoured by "a nigger boy." She is filled with the prejudices of her class and her time. And so, some readers conclude, she is in spite of it all a "good" person. Somewhat more ominously, the Misfit — after he has fired three bullets into her chest — pronounces that she might have been " 'a good woman . . . if it had been somebody there to shoot her every minute of her life' ". We surmise that in the universe of this story, the quality of what is "good" (which is after all the key word of the story's title) depends greatly on who is using the term. I do not think the Misfit is capable of irony — he truly means what he says about her, even though he finds it necessary to kill her. Indeed, the opposing categories of "good" and "evil" are very much in the air throughout this story. But like most supposed opposites, they have an alarming tendency to merge. It is probably worth noting that the second line of the once-popular song that gave O'Connor her title is "You always get the other kind."

Much criticism of the story appears to take a sentimental view of the Grandmother largely because she *is* a grandmother. Flannery O'Connor herself, as we shall see shortly, found little to blame in this woman, choosing to wrap her in the comfortable mantle of elderly Southern womanhood. O'Connor applies this generalization so uncritically that we half suspect she is pulling our leg. In any case, we can be sure that such sentimentality (in the mind of either the writer or her character) is fatal to clear thinking. If the Grandmother is old (although she does not seem to be *that* old), grey-haired, and "respectable," it follows that she must be weak, gentle, and benevolent — precisely the Grandmother's opinion of herself, and she is not shy of letting others know it. Intentionally or not, O'Connor has etched the Grandmother's character with wicked irony, which makes it all the more surprising to read the author's response to a frustrated teacher whose (Southern) students persisted in favoring the Grandmother, despite his strenuous efforts to point out her flaws. O'Connor said,

> I had to tell him that they resisted . . . because they all had grand-
> mothers or great-aunts just like her at home, and they knew, from

---

[1] Flannery O'Connor, *Mystery and Manners: Occasional Prose*. Selected and Edited by Sally and Robert Fitzgerald (New York: Farrar, Straus, and Giroux, 1969).

personal experience, that the old lady lacked comprehension, but that she had a good heart.

O'Connor continued,

> The Southerner is usually tolerant of those weaknesses that proceed from innocence, and he knows that a taste for self-preservation can be readily combined with the missionary spirit. (*Mystery and Manners* 110)

What is most disappointing in this moral summary of the Grandmother, and her ilk, is its disservice to the spiky, vindictive woman of the story. There may be a purpose to O'Connor's betrayal of her own character: her phrase "missionary spirit" gives the game away. O'Connor is determined that the Grandmother shall be the Misfit's savior, even though she may not seem so in the story.

The Grandmother's role as grace-bringer is by now a received idea, largely because the author said it is so. But one must question the propriety of such tinkering with the character, after the fact. It reduces the fire-breathing woman who animates this story to nothing much more than a cranky maiden aunt. On the contrary, the Grandmother is a fierce fighter, never more so than in her final moments, nose-to-nose with the Misfit.

Granted, the Grandmother is not a homicidal monster like the Misfit, and she certainly does not deserve to die for her minor sins. And yet, does she quite earn absolution from any moral weakness beyond that of "a hypocritical old soul"? For every reader who sees the image of his or her own grandmother printed on this character's cold face, as O'Connor suggested we might do, there are surely many others who can only be appalled by a calculating opportunist who is capable of embracing her family's murderer, to save her own skin. Where indeed is the "good heart" which unites this unprincipled woman with all those "grandmothers or great-aunts just like her at home"? The answer to that question can only be an affirmation of the "banality of evil," to use Hannah Arendt's well-known phrase. . . .

What does in fact happen in this part of the story is quite straightforward: the Grandmother, having exhausted all other appeals to the Misfit, resorts to her only remaining (though certainly imperfect) weapon: motherhood. Declaring to the Misfit that he is one of her babies, she sets out to conquer him. Perhaps she hopes that this ultimate flattery will melt his heart, and he will collapse in her comforting motherly embrace. Such are the stratagems of sentimentality. The moral shoddiness of her action is almost beyond description. If we had not already guessed the depths to which the Grandmother might sink, now we know. It is not easy to say who is the more evil, the Misfit or the Grandmother, and indeed that is the point. Her behavior is the manifest of her character.

It has been said that no action is without its redeeming aspect. Could this unspeakable act of selfishness carry within it the seeds of grace, acting, as it were, above the Grandmother? So Flannery O'Connor believed. But what is the precise movement of grace in this scene? It is surely straining the text to propose that the Grandmother has in this moment "seen the light." Are we to regard her as the unwitting agent of divine grace whose selfish intentions are somehow transfigured into a blessing? Such seems to have been O'Connor's opinion:

> . . . however unlikely this may seem, the old lady's gesture, like the mustard-seed, will grow to be a great crow-filled tree in the Misfit's heart, and will be enough of a pain to him there to turn him into the prophet he was meant to become. (*Mystery and Manners* 113)

We are almost persuaded to forget that none of this happens in the story itself. If this can be so, then we can just as easily attribute any interpretation we like to the scene. But in fact he is in no way changed. There is no "later on" in fiction. We do not, and will not, see "created grace" in the spirit of the Misfit.

But more important, this is not the way grace works. As we read in the   10
New Catholic Encyclopedia:

> . . . the spiritual creature must respond to this divine self-donation freely. Hence, the doctrine of grace supposes a creature already constituted in its own being in such wise that it has the possibility of entering into a free and personal relationship with the Divine Persons or of rejecting that relationship. (6:661)

If grace was extended to the Misfit, he refused it and that is the end. There can be no crow-filled tree, nor can there be the "lines of spiritual motion" leading to that tree, however attractive the image may be. Prudently, O'Connor added, "But that's another story" (*Mystery and Manners* 113)   [1996]

JOHN DESMOND

From "Flannery O'Connor's Misfit and the Mystery of Evil"

In an article published in a 2004 issue of Renascence, *a journal that examines religious issues in literature, John Desmond tends to support O'Connor's interpretation of "A Good Man Is Hard to Find." For help in understanding the climactic scene between The Misfit and the grandmother, he turns to the late French Catholic philosopher Simone Weil. The following is an excerpt from his analysis.*

This climactic scene, full of ambiguity, has occasioned a wealth of critical comment. O'Connor herself argued that the grandmother's final words and actions represent the mysterious action of grace. Some readers have viewed it more skeptically, even arguing that the grandmother's gesture may be a final desperate attempt to save her own life. Other critics have argued a middle ground, granting O'Connor's right to her theological view, while judging the scene as satisfactory or not on the basis of strictly literary criteria. My focus here is on what this climactic scene suggests about the mysterious interpenetration of good and evil.

What initially strikes the reader about the scene is the enormous gap or lacuna between the grandmother's statement of doubt — "Maybe He didn't raise the dead. . ." — and her reaching out fatally to touch the Misfit and embrace him as "one of my babies. . . ," one of "my own children." O'Connor explains nothing of what happens in the grandmother's mind and heart to bring her to this touch of kinship with the criminal, except to say that "her head cleared for an instant." The gap is mysterious, perhaps supernatural, yet also exactly right in the human sense. Such acts of meta-noia,° while inexplicable, are totally within the range of human behavior. What is significant about her calling him "one of my babies. . . ," one of "my own children," and "touching him" is that her actions threaten to under-mine his self-designation of himself as the Misfit, the name he chose to sig-nify his difference from ordinary humanity. The Misfit rejects the communal world, just as his sense of "justice" is individualistic rather than communal. Significantly, he remarked earlier in that story that "children make me ner-vous." The grandmother's claim of kinship rejects his solitary identity, and instead places him within the community as a child of man, like any other. So also, her touching him threatens his proud, isolated self-created role as the Misfit, a threat he cannot tolerate. After all, if he is not the Misfit, what is he? An ordinary, frail, suffering creature. So what we view from the grand-mother's perspective as a good act — her recognition of her own bond with an evil man, her complicity, yet also her compassion for his suffering — is viewed by the Misfit as evil: he springs back from her touch "as if a snake had bitten him. . . ."

Why does the Misfit regard the touch as evil, and then answer it with evil? We recall Simone Weil's maxim: "Evil is to love, what mystery is to the intelligence." The grandmother's touch brings the Misfit into direct contact with the good of charity. The touch of charity measures the gap between him and the good. He cannot abide such threatening contact because it would mean opening himself to an admission of failure, and more importantly, to the possibility of good within the human community. Instead, he chooses the "hell" of isolation and despair. The truth of compassion, and being named a child of the human community, is for the Misfit an "evil" he must escape. Once again, Weil's comments are insightful:

> The sin against the Spirit consists of knowing a thing to be good, and hat-ing it because it is good. We experience the equivalent of it in the form of resistance every time we set our faces in the direction of good. For every contact with good leads to a knowledge of the distance between good and evil and the commencement of a painful effort of assimilation. It is some-thing which hurts and we are afraid. This fear is perhaps the sign of the reality of the contact. The corresponding sin cannot come about unless a lack of hope makes the consciousness of the distance intolerable and changes the pain into hatred. (*Gravity and Grace* 67)

---

metanoia: A Greek term meaning repentance or spiritual conversion.

The Misfit's pain at the grandmother's touch is instantly transformed into a hatred of the gratuitous act of charity, which he then answers with a brutal execution. What the Misfit fears is the mystery of love, the demands of love which the grandmother mysteriously responded to when faced with the criminal's suffering, and her own impending death. In her case, evil issued finally in good, or as Weil expressed it, evil exposed the good. But if the encounter with evil exposed the good in the grandmother, the final predicament of the Misfit is more complicated, more mysterious.

As I noted earlier, the Misfit acts under the delusion that his actions are   5
somehow good, i.e., good for him. Since he cannot make sense of his spiritual condition, he now tries to reduce ethical mystery to a perverse pleasure-pain principle. Initially he told the grandmother: "No pleasure but meanness." Yet his encounter with her touch has exposed his need, his human vulnerability. In his crucial final remark, he shifts from the earlier "No pleasure but meanness" to "It's no real pleasure in life." He has again failed to liberate himself from his predicament through violence, failed to "balance out" his deeds and find the meaning of his life. He himself is his own deepest mystery, a profoundly human condition which he can neither fathom nor abide. His last statement, that there is no "real pleasure" in life, shows that what he thought might bring pleasure, i.e., acts of meanness, has also proven to be bankrupt, a hollow illusion.

In the end, the Misfit's spiritual and mental suffering continues and intensifies, for with the failure of his code, his awareness of the gap between good and evil has widened. His violence is projected back onto himself as self-hatred. Perhaps at some future time his knowledge of this interior chasm will bring about the collapse of his self-begotten identity as a "Misfit," and an acceptance of his broken humanity. O'Connor suggested the possibility that he might ultimately be brought to such a conversion. She called the Misfit a "prophet gone wrong," and referred to the grandmother's touching him as "like the mustard-seed," which "will grow to be a great crow-filled tree in the Misfit's heart, and will be enough of a pain to him there to turn him into the prophet he was meant to become" (*Mystery and Manners* 110, 112–13). The grandmother's touch may bring him to the point where the mystery of good and evil is finally subsumed in the mystery of love. For the Misfit, evil may, in the end, through the grace of charity, bring about his ultimate good.   *[2004]*

≡ MAKING COMPARISONS

1. Stephens believes that her interpretation of "A Good Man Is Hard to Find" is compatible with O'Connor's. Do you accept both? Why, or why not?

2. In what ways, if any, does Desmond's use of Simone Weil go beyond O'Connor's view of her story or complicate it? Do the two critics, Stephens and Bandy, make you hesitate to accept O'Connor's account? In general, do you think readers should accept an author's interpretation of his or her work? Explain your reasoning.

3. All of these commentaries on the story focus on religious aspects of it, though not all of them agree on how much of a role and what kind of a role religion plays in it. Are you similarly inclined to put the story in a religious framework? Why, or why not?

≡ WRITING ABOUT ISSUES

1. The Misfit says that the grandmother "would of been a good woman . . . if it had been somebody there to shoot her every minute of her life" (para. 140). Write an essay in which you argue for your own understanding of this claim. Is The Misfit right or just cruel? How should we define *good* in this context?

2. Choose one of the critics' interpretations featured in this cluster and write an essay in which you imagine how O'Connor would respond to its points. Feel free to express and support your own views, too.

3. The man in O'Connor's story calls himself The Misfit " 'because I can't make what all I done wrong fit what all I gone through in punishment' " (para. 129). But plainly he is also a misfit in the sense that he has become alienated from society. Write an essay recalling someone you knew who seemed to be a misfit in this sense. More specifically, speculate on and try to describe this person's own perspective — what the person believed, how the person viewed the world, why he or she acted in certain ways. If you wish, your essay can be in the form of a letter to this person.

4. O'Connor promoted her version of Christianity in "A Good Man Is Hard to Find" and in her commentary on the story. On the basis of both texts, list various principles and concepts that she associates with her religion. Then do research on another religion, perhaps by reading two or three articles on it. Write an essay in which you compare O'Connor's theology with the religion you have researched. If you wish, you can focus your comparison by imagining what adherents to the other religion would say about "A Good Man Is Hard to Find."

≡ Contexts for Research: Innocence, Evil, and "Where Are You Going, Where Have You Been?"

JOYCE CAROL OATES, "Where Are You Going, Where Have You Been?"

CONTEXTS FOR RESEARCH:
DON MOSER, "The Pied Piper of Tucson: He Cruised in a Golden Car, Looking for the Action"

JOYCE CAROL OATES, "*Smooth Talk*: Short Story into Film"

MEGHAN DAUM, "Jaycee Dugard and the Feel-Good Imperative"

The harrowing ending of Joyce Carol Oates's much-anthologized initiation tale of innocence versus evil may shock you. The fifteen-year-old Connie, focused on boys and pop music, seems defenseless against her menacing stalker. This 1966 story uses the prospect of violent crime to remind readers, in its own chilling way, that adolescence may be fraught with anxieties, challenges, and risks. Often, however, a literary text reflects and responds to specific cultural contexts. Such is the case with this one. Therefore, we include with Oates's story three other texts: the *Life* magazine article that evidently led Oates to conceive her work of fiction, a *New York Times* article she wrote when her story became the movie *Smooth Talk*, and an essay from the *Los Angeles Times* by Meghan Daum, "Jaycee Dugard and the Feel-Good Imperative."

≡ BEFORE YOU READ

Many historians of literature and culture have pointed out that as far back as colonial times, Americans have been fascinated with narratives of female captivity. Why do you think this kind of story has engaged them?

JOYCE CAROL OATES
Where Are You Going, Where Have You Been?

Joyce Carol Oates (b. 1938) is perhaps the most prolific of major American writers, publishing about two books a year for more than forty years. Oates has won numerous awards, including a National Book Award for fiction (1970). Oates grew up in the countryside of upstate New York. She started writing early and won a scholarship to Syracuse University, where she was valedictorian in 1960. She received her M.A. from the University of Wisconsin a year later. She taught at the University of Detroit and the University of Windsor before joining the faculty at Princeton, where she has taught since 1978. Like Flannery O'Connor's and William Faulkner's work, Oates's is usually referred to as gothic, probably because of her

Jeremy Sutton-Hibbert/
Getty Images

violent characters, many of whom are filled with enigmatic malice and tormented emotions. Working in the realistic tradition, the "Dark Lady of American Literature" writes compelling narratives about seemingly ordinary people who beneath the surface live in a nightmare world of unconscious forces and sometimes sensational events.

Oates claims the story printed here was written after listening to Bob Dylan's "It's All Over Now, Baby Blue." The serial killer Charles Schmid, also known as "The Pied Piper of Tucson," inspired the story. Her latest work includes two novels from 2018: Hazards of Time Travel *and* A Book of American Martyrs *and the short story collection,* Night-Gaunts and Other Tales of Suspense, *also from 2018.*

For Bob Dylan

Her name was Connie. She was fifteen and she had a quick nervous giggling habit of craning her neck to glance into mirrors, or checking other people's faces to make sure her own was all right. Her mother, who noticed everything and knew everything and who hadn't much reason any longer to look at her own face, always scolded Connie about it. "Stop gawking at yourself, who are you? You think you're so pretty?" she would say. Connie would raise her eyebrows at these familiar complaints and look right through her mother, into a shadowy vision of herself as she was right at that moment: she knew she was pretty and that was everything. Her mother had been pretty once too, if you could believe those old snapshots in the album, but now her looks were gone and that was why she was always after Connie.

"Why don't you keep your room clean like your sister? How've you got your hair fixed — what the hell stinks? Hair spray? You don't see your sister using that junk."

Her sister June was twenty-four and still lived at home. She was a secretary in the high school Connie attended, and if that wasn't bad enough — with her in the same building — she was so plain and chunky and steady that Connie had to hear her praised all the time by her mother and her mother's sisters. June did this, June did that, she saved money and helped clean the house and cooked and Connie couldn't do a thing, her mind was all filled with trashy daydreams. Their father was away at work most of the time and when he came home he wanted supper and he read the newspaper at supper and after supper he went to bed. He didn't bother talking much to them, but around his bent head Connie's mother kept picking at her until Connie wished her mother was dead and she herself was dead and it was all over. "She makes me want to throw up sometimes," she complained to her friends. She had a high, breathless, amused voice which made everything she said a little forced, whether it was sincere or not.

There was one good thing: June went places with girl friends of hers, girls who were just as plain and steady as she, and so when Connie wanted to do that her mother had no objections. The father of Connie's best girl friend drove the girls the three miles to town and left them off at a shopping plaza, so that they could walk through the stores or go to a movie, and when he came to pick them up again at eleven he never bothered to ask what they had done.

They must have been familiar sights, walking around that shopping plaza in their shorts and flat ballerina slippers that always scuffed the sidewalk, with charm bracelets jingling on their thin wrists; they would lean together to whisper and laugh secretly if someone passed by who amused or interested them. Connie had long dark blond hair that drew anyone's eye to it, and she wore part of it pulled up on her head and puffed out and the rest of it she let fall down her back. She wore a pullover jersey blouse that looked one way when she was at home and another way when she was away from home. Everything about her had two sides to it, one for home and one for anywhere that was not home: her walk that could be childlike and bobbing, or languid enough to make anyone think she was hearing music in her head, her mouth which was pale and smirking most of the time, but bright and pink on these evenings out, her laugh which was cynical and drawling at home — "Ha, ha, very funny" — but high-pitched and nervous anywhere else, like the jingling of the charms on her bracelet.

Sometimes they did go shopping or to a movie, but sometimes they went across the highway, ducking fast across the busy road, to a drive-in restaurant where older kids hung out. The restaurant was shaped like a big bottle, though squatter than a real bottle, and on its cap was a revolving figure of a grinning boy who held a hamburger aloft. One night in midsummer they ran across,

5

breathless with daring, and right away someone leaned out a car window and invited them over, but it was just a boy from high school they didn't like. It made them feel good to be able to ignore him. They went up through the maze of parked and cruising cars to the bright-lit, fly-infested restaurant, their faces pleased and expectant as if they were entering a sacred building that loomed out of the night to give them what haven and what blessing they yearned for. They sat at the counter and crossed their legs at the ankles, their thin shoulders rigid with excitement and listened to the music that made everything so good: the music was always in the background like music at a church service, it was something to depend upon.

A boy named Eddie came in to talk with them. He sat backwards on his stool, turning himself jerkily around in semi-circles and then stopping and turning again, and after a while he asked Connie if she would like something to eat. She said she did and so she tapped her friend's arm on her way out—her friend pulled her face up into a brave droll look—and Connie said she would meet her at eleven, across the way. "I just hate to leave her like that," Connie said earnestly, but the boy said that she wouldn't be alone for long. So they went out to his car and on the way Connie couldn't help but let her eyes wander over the windshields and faces all around her, her face gleaming with the joy that had nothing to do with Eddie or even this place; it might have been the music. She drew her shoulders up and sucked in her breath with the pure pleasure of being alive, and just at that moment she happened to glance at a face just a few feet from hers. It was a boy with shaggy black hair, in a convertible jalopy painted gold. He stared at her and then his lips widened into a grin. Connie slit her eyes at him and turned away, but she couldn't help glancing back and there he was still watching her. He wagged a finger and laughed and said, "Gonna get you, baby," and Connie turned away again without Eddie noticing anything.

She spent three hours with him, at the restaurant where they ate hamburgers and drank Cokes in wax cups that were always sweating, and then down an alley a mile or so away, and when he left her off at five to eleven only the movie house was still open at the plaza. Her girl friend was there, talking with a boy. When Connie came up the two girls smiled at each other and Connie said, "How was the movie?" and the girl said, "*You* should know." They rode off with the girl's father, sleepy and pleased, and Connie couldn't help but look at the darkened shopping plaza with its big empty parking lot and its signs that were faded and ghostly now, and over at the drive-in restaurant where cars were still circling tirelessly. She couldn't hear the music at this distance.

Next morning June asked her how the movie was and Connie said, "So-so."

She and that girl and occasionally another girl went out several times a week that way, and the rest of the time Connie spent around the house—it was summer vacation—getting in her mother's way and thinking, dreaming, about the boys she met. But all the boys fell back and dissolved into a single face that was not even a face, but an idea, a feeling, mixed up with the urgent insistent pounding of the music and the humid night air of July. Connie's

10

mother kept dragging her back to the daylight by finding things for her to do or saying suddenly, "What's this about the Pettinger girl?"

And Connie would say nervously, "Oh, her. That dope." She always drew thick clear lines between herself and such girls, and her mother was simple and kindly enough to believe her. Her mother was so simple, Connie thought, that it was maybe cruel to fool her so much. Her mother went scuffling around the house in old bedroom slippers and complained over the telephone to one sister about the other, then the other called up and the two of them complained about the third one. If June's name was mentioned her mother's tone was approving, and if Connie's name was mentioned it was disapproving. This did not really mean she disliked Connie and actually Connie thought that her mother preferred her to June because she was prettier, but the two of them kept up a pretense of exasperation, a sense that they were tugging and struggling over something of little value to either of them. Sometimes, over coffee, they were almost friends, but something would come up—some vexation that was like a fly buzzing suddenly around their heads—and their faces went hard with contempt.

One Sunday Connie got up at eleven—none of them bothered with church—and washed her hair so that it could dry all day long, in the sun. Her parents and sister were going to a barbecue at an aunt's house and Connie said no, she wasn't interested, rolling her eyes, to let mother know just what she thought of it. "Stay home alone then," her mother said sharply. Connie sat out back in a lawn chair and watched them drive away, her father quiet and bald, hunched around so that he could back the car out, her mother with a look that was still angry and not at all softened through the windshield, and in the back seat poor old June all dressed up as if she didn't know what a barbecue was, with all the running yelling kids and the flies. Connie sat with her eyes closed in the sun, dreaming and dazed with the warmth about her as if this were a kind of love, the caresses of love, and her mind slipped over onto thoughts of the boy she had been with the night before and how nice he had been, how sweet it always was, not the way someone like June would suppose but sweet, gentle, the way it was in movies and promised in songs; and when she opened her eyes she hardly knew where she was, the back yard ran off into weeds and a fenceline of trees and behind it the sky was perfectly blue and still. The asbestos "ranch house" that was now three years old startled her—it looked small. She shook her head as if to get awake.

It was too hot. She went inside the house and turned on the radio to drown out the quiet. She sat on the edge of her bed, barefoot, and listened for an hour and a half to a program called XYZ Sunday Jamboree, record after record of hard, fast, shrieking songs she sang along with, interspersed by exclamations from "Bobby King": "An' look here you girls at Napoleon's—Son and Charley want you to pay real close attention to this song coming up!"

And Connie paid close attention herself, bathed in a glow of slow-pulsed joy that seemed to rise mysteriously out of the music itself and lay languidly about the airless little room, breathed in and breathed out with each gentle rise and fall of her chest.

After a while she heard a car coming up the drive. She sat up at once, star-   15
tled, because it couldn't be her father so soon. The gravel kept crunching all
the way in from the road—the driveway was long—and Connie ran to the
window. It was a car she didn't know. It was an open jalopy, painted a bright
gold that caught the sun opaquely. Her heart began to pound and her fingers
snatched at her hair, checking it, and she whispered "Christ. Christ," wondering how bad she looked. The car came to a stop at the side door and the horn
sounded four short taps as if this were a signal Connie knew.

She went into the kitchen and approached the door slowly, then hung out
the screen door, her bare toes curling down off the step. There were two boys
in the car and now she recognized the driver: he had shaggy, shabby black hair
that looked crazy as a wig and he was grinning at her.

"I ain't late, am I?" he said.

"Who the hell do you think you are?" Connie said.

"Toldja I'd be out, didn't I?"

"I don't even know who you are."   20

She spoke sullenly, careful to show no interest or pleasure, and he spoke
in a fast bright monotone. Connie looked past him to the other boy, taking her
time. He had fair brown hair, with a lock that fell onto his forehead. His side-
burns gave him a fierce, embarrassed look, but so far he hadn't even bothered
to glance at her. Both boys wore sunglasses. The driver's glasses were metallic
and mirrored everything in miniature.

"You wanta come for a ride?" he said.

Connie smirked and let her hair fall loose over one shoulder.

"Don'tcha like my car? New paint job," he said. "Hey."

"What?"   25

"You're cute."

She pretended to fidget, chasing flies away from the door.

"Don'tcha believe me, or what?" he said.

"Look, I don't even know who you are," Connie said in disgust.

"Hey, Ellie's got a radio, see. Mine's broke down." He lifted his friend's arm   30
and showed her the little transistor the boy was holding, and now Connie began
to hear the music. It was the same program that was playing inside the house.

"Bobby King?" she said.

"I listen to him all the time. I think he's great."

"He's kind of great," Connie said reluctantly.

"Listen, that guy's *great*. He knows where the action is."

Connie blushed a little, because the glasses made it impossible for her to   35
see just what this boy was looking at. She couldn't decide if she liked him or
if he was just a jerk, and so she dawdled in the doorway and wouldn't come
down or go back inside. She said, "What's all that stuff painted on your car?"

"Can'tcha read it?" He opened the door very carefully, as if he was afraid
it might fall off. He slid out just as carefully, planting his feet firmly on the
ground, the tiny metallic world in his glasses slowing down like gelatine hard-
ening and in the midst of it Connie's bright green blouse. "This here is my
name, to begin with," he said. ARNOLD FRIEND was written in tar-like black letters

on the side, with a drawing of a round grinning face that reminded Connie of a pumpkin, except it wore sunglasses. "I wanta introduce myself, I'm Arnold Friend and that's my real name and I'm gonna be your friend, honey, and inside the car's Ellie Oscar, he's kinda shy." Ellie brought his transistor up to his shoulder and balanced it there. "Now these numbers are a secret code, honey," Arnold Friend explained. He read off the numbers 33, 19, 17 and raised his eyebrows at her to see what she thought of that, but she didn't think much of it. The left rear fender had been smashed and around it was written, on the gleaming gold background: DONE BY CRAZY WOMAN DRIVER. Connie had to laugh at that. Arnold Friend was pleased at her laughter and looked up at her. "Around the other side's a lot more—you wanta come and see them?"

"No."

"Why not?"

"Why should I?"

"Don'tcha wanta see what's on the car? Don'tcha wanta go for a ride?"   40

"I don't know."

"Why not?"

"I got things to do."

"Like what?"

"Things."   45

He laughed as if she had said something funny. He slapped his thighs. He was standing in a strange way, leaning back against the car as if he were balancing himself. He wasn't tall, only an inch or so taller than she would be if she came down to him. Connie liked the way he was dressed, which was the way all of them dressed: tight faded jeans stuffed into black, scuffed boots, a belt that pulled his waist in and showed how lean he was, and a white pullover shirt that was a little soiled and showed the hard small muscles of his arms and shoulders. He looked as if he probably did hard work, lifting and carrying things. Even his neck looked muscular. And his face was a familiar face, somehow: the jaw and chin and cheeks slightly darkened, because he hadn't shaved for a day or two, and the nose long and hawk-like, sniffing as if she were a treat he was going to gobble up and it was all a joke.

"Connie, you ain't telling the truth. This is your day set aside for a ride with me and you know it," he said, still laughing. The way he straightened and recovered from his fit of laughing showed that it had been all fake.

"How do you know what my name is?" she said suspiciously.

"It's Connie."

"Maybe and maybe not."   50

"I know my Connie," he said, wagging his finger. Now she remembered him even better, back at the restaurant, and her cheeks warmed at the thought of how she sucked in her breath just at the moment she passed him—how she must have looked to him. And he had remembered her. "Ellie and I come out here especially for you," he said. "Ellie can sit in back. How about it?"

"Where?"

"Where what?"

"Where're we going?"

He looked at her. He took off the sunglasses and she saw how pale the skin   55
around his eyes was, like holes that were not in shadow but instead in light.
His eyes were like chips of broken glass that catch the light in an amiable way.
He smiled. It was as if the idea of going for a ride somewhere, to some place,
was a new idea to him.

"Just for a ride, Connie sweetheart."

"I never said my name was Connie," she said.

"But I know what it is. I know your name and all about you, lots of
things," Arnold Friend said. He had not moved yet but stood still leaning back
against the side of his jalopy. "I took a special interest in you, such a pretty girl,
and found out all about you like I know your parents and sister are gone some-
wheres and I know where and how long they're going to be gone, and I know
who you were with last night, and your best friend's name is Betty. Right?"

He spoke in a simple lilting voice, exactly as if he were reciting the words to
a song. His smile assured her that everything was fine. In the car Ellie turned
up the volume on his radio and did not bother to look around at them.

"Ellie can sit in the back seat," Arnold Friend said. He indicated his friend   60
with a casual jerk of his chin, as if Ellie did not count and she could not bother
with him.

"How'd you find out all that stuff?" Connie said.

"Listen: Betty Schultz and Tony Fitch and Jimmy Pettinger and Nancy
Pettinger," he said, in a chant. "Raymond Stanley and Bob Hutter—"

"Do you know all those kids?"

"I know everybody."

"Look, you're kidding. You're not from around here."   65

"Sure."

"But—how come we never saw you before?"

"Sure you saw me before," he said. He looked down at his boots, as if he
were a little offended. "You just don't remember."

"I guess I'd remember you," Connie said.

"Yeah?" He looked up at this, beaming. He was pleased. He began to mark   70
time with the music from Ellie's radio, tapping his fists lightly together. Connie
looked away from his smile to the car, which was painted so bright it almost
hurt her eyes to look at it. She looked at that name, ARNOLD FRIEND. And up at
the front fender was an expression that was familiar—MAN THE FLYING SAUCERS.
It was an expression kids had used the year before, but didn't use this year. She
looked at it for a while as if the words meant something to her that she did not
yet know.

"What're you thinking about? Huh?" Arnold Friend demanded. "Not
worried about your hair blowing around in the car, are you?"

"No."

"Think I maybe can't drive good?"

"How do I know?"

"You're a hard girl to handle. How come?" he said. "Don't you know I'm   75
your friend? Didn't you see me put my sign in the air when you walked by?"

"What sign?"

"My sign." And he drew an X in the air, leaning out toward her. They were maybe ten feet apart. After his hand fell back to his side the X was still in the air, almost visible. Connie let the screen door close and stood perfectly still inside it, listening to the music from her radio and the boy's blend together. She stared at Arnold Friend. He stood there so stiffly relaxed, pretending to be relaxed, with one hand idly on the door handle as if he were keeping himself up that way and had no intention of ever moving again. She recognized most things about him, the tight jeans that showed his thighs and buttocks and the greasy leather boots and the tight shirt, and even that slippery friendly smile of his, that sleepy dreamy smile that all the boys used to get across ideas they didn't want to put into words. She recognized all this and also the singsong way he talked, slightly mocking, kidding, but serious and a little melancholy, and she recognized the way he tapped one fist against the other in homage to the perpetual music behind him. But all these things did not come together.

She said suddenly, "Hey, how old are you?"

His smile faded. She could see then that he wasn't a kid, he was much older — thirty, maybe more. At this knowledge her heart began to pound faster.

"That's a crazy thing to ask. Can'tcha see I'm your own age?"   80

"Like hell you are."

"Or maybe a coupla years older, I'm eighteen."

"Eighteen?" she said doubtfully.

He grinned to reassure her and lines appeared at the corners of his mouth. His teeth were big and white. He grinned so broadly his eyes became slits and she saw how thick the lashes were, thick and black as if painted with a black tar-like material. Then he seemed to become embarrassed, abruptly, and looked over his shoulder at Ellie. "*Him,* he's crazy," he said. "Ain't he a riot, he's a nut, a real character." Ellie was still listening to the music. His sunglasses told nothing about what he was thinking. He wore a bright orange shirt unbuttoned halfway to show his chest, which was a pale, bluish chest and not muscular like Arnold Friend's. His shirt collar was turned up all around and the very tips of the collar pointed out past his chin as if they were protecting him. He was pressing the transistor radio up against his ear and sat there in a kind of daze, right in the sun.

"He's kinda strange," Connie said.   85

"Hey, she says you're kinda strange! Kinda strange!" Arnold Friend cried. He pounded on the car to get Ellie's attention. Ellie turned for the first time and Connie saw with shock that he wasn't a kid either — he had a fair, hairless face, cheeks reddened slightly as if the veins grew too close to the surface of his skin, the face of a forty-year-old baby. Connie felt a wave of dizziness rise in her at this sight and she stared at him as if waiting for something to change the shock of the moment, make it all right again. Ellie's lips kept shaping words, mumbling along with the words blasting his ear.

"Maybe you two better go away," Connie said faintly.

"What? How come?" Arnold Friend cried. "We come out here to take you for a ride. It's Sunday." He had the voice of the man on the radio now. It was the same voice, Connie thought. "Don'tcha know it's Sunday all day and honey, no matter who you were with last night today you're with Arnold Friend and don't you forget it!—Maybe you better step out here," he said, and this last was in a different voice. It was a little flatter, as if the heat was finally getting to him.

"No. I got things to do."

"Hey." 90

"You two better leave."

"We ain't leaving until you come with us."

"Like hell I am—"

"Connie, don't fool around with me. I mean—I mean, don't fool *around*," he said, shaking his head. He laughed incredulously. He placed his sunglasses on top of his head, carefully, as if he were indeed wearing a wig, and brought the stems down behind his ears. Connie stared at him, another wave of dizziness and fear rising in her so that for a moment he wasn't even in focus but was just a blur; standing there against his gold car, and she had the idea that he had driven up the driveway all right but had come from nowhere before that and belonged nowhere and that everything about him and even the music that was so familiar to her was only half real.

"If my father comes and sees you—" 95

"He ain't coming. He's at a barbecue."

"How do you know that?"

"Aunt Tillie's. Right now they're—uh—they're drinking. Sitting around," he said vaguely, squinting as if he were staring all the way to town and over to Aunt Tillie's back yard. Then the vision seemed to clear and he nodded energetically. "Yeah. Sitting around. There's your sister in a blue dress, huh? And high heels, the poor sad bitch—nothing like you, sweetheart! And your mother's helping some fat woman with the corn, they're cleaning the corn—husking the corn—"

"What fat woman?" Connie cried.

"How do I know what fat woman. I don't know every goddamn fat woman 100 in the world!" Arnold Friend laughed.

"Oh, that's Mrs. Hornby. . . . Who invited her?" Connie said. She felt a little light-headed. Her breath was coming quickly.

"She's too fat. I don't like them fat. I like them the way you are, honey," he said, smiling sleepily at her. They stared at each other for a while, through the screen door. He said softly, "Now what you're going to do is this: you're going to come out that door. You're going to sit up front with me and Ellie's going to sit in the back, the hell with Ellie, right? This isn't Ellie's date. You're my date. I'm your lover, honey."

"What? You're crazy—"

"Yes, I'm your lover. You don't know what that is but you will," he said. "I know that too. I know all about you. But look: it's real nice and you couldn't ask for nobody better than me, or more polite. I always keep my word. I'll tell you how it is, I'm always nice at first, the first time. I'll hold you so tight you won't think you have to try to get away or pretend anything because you'll know you can't. And I'll come inside you where it's all secret and you'll give in to me and you'll love me—"

"Shut up! You're crazy!" Connie said. She backed away from the door. She   105
put her hands against her ears as if she'd heard something terrible, something
not meant for her. "People don't talk like that, you're crazy," she muttered. Her
heart was almost too big now for her chest and its pumping made sweat break
out all over her. She looked out to see Arnold Friend pause and then take a step
toward the porch lurching. He almost fell. But, like a clever drunken man, he
managed to catch his balance. He wobbled in his high boots and grabbed hold
of one of the porch posts.

"Honey?" he said. "You still listening?"

"Get the hell out of here!"

"Be nice, honey. Listen."

"I'm going to call the police—"

He wobbled again and out of the side of his mouth came a fast spat curse,   110
an aside not meant for her to hear. But even this "Christ!" sounded forced.
Then he began to smile again. She watched this smile come, awkward as if
he were smiling from inside a mask. His whole face was a mask, she thought
wildly, tanned down onto his throat but then running out as if he had plastered make-up on his face but had forgotten about his throat.

"Honey—? Listen, here's how it is. I always tell the truth and I promise
you this: I ain't coming in that house after you."

"You better not! I'm going to call the police if you—if you don't—"

"Honey," he said, talking right through her voice, "honey, I'm not coming
in there but you are coming out here. You know why?"

She was panting. The kitchen looked like a place she had never seen
before, some room she had run inside but which wasn't good enough, wasn't
going to help her. The kitchen window had never had a curtain, after three
years, and there were dishes in the sink for her to do—probably—and if you
ran your hand across the table you'd probably feel something sticky there.

"You listening, honey? Hey?"   115

"—going to call the police—"

"Soon as you touch the phone I don't need to keep my promise and can
come inside. You won't want that."

She rushed forward and tried to lock the door. Her fingers were shaking.
"But why lock it," Arnold Friend said gently, talking right into her face. "It's
just a screen door. It's just nothing." One of his boots was at a strange angle,
as if his foot wasn't in it. It pointed out to the left, bent at the ankle. "I mean,
anybody can break through a screen door and glass and wood and iron or
anything else if he needs to, anybody at all and specially Arnold Friend. If the
place got lit up with a fire, honey, you'd come runnin' out into my arms, right
into my arms an' safe at home—like you knew I was your lover and'd stopped
fooling around, I don't mind a nice shy girl but I don't like no fooling around."
Part of those words were spoken with a slight rhythmic lilt, and Connie somehow recognized them—the echo of a song from last year, about a girl rushing
into her boy friend's arms and coming home again—

Connie stood barefoot on the linoleum floor, staring at him. "What do you
want?" she whispered.

"I want you," he said.   120

"What?"

"Seen you that night and thought, that's the one, yes sir. I never needed to look any more."

"But my father's coming back. He's coming to get me. I had to wash my hair first—" She spoke in a dry, rapid voice, hardly raising it for him to hear.

"No, your daddy is not coming and yes, you had to wash your hair and you washed it for me. It's nice and shining and all for me. I thank you, sweetheart," he said, with a mock bow, but again he almost lost his balance. He had to bend and adjust his boots. Evidently his feet did not go all the way down; the boots must have been stuffed with something so that he would seem taller. Connie stared out at him and behind him at Ellie in the car, who seemed to be looking off toward Connie's right, into nothing. Then Ellie said, pulling the words out of the air one after another as if he were just discovering them, "You want me to pull out the phone?"

"Shut your mouth and keep it shut," Arnold Friend said, his face red from   125
bending over or maybe from embarrassment because Connie had seen his boots. "This ain't none of your business."

"What—what are you doing? What do you want?" Connie said. "If I call the police they'll get you, they'll arrest you—"

"Promise was not to come in unless you touch that phone, and I'll keep that promise," he said. He resumed his erect position and tried to force his shoulders back. He sounded like a hero in a movie, declaring something important. He spoke too loudly and it was as if he were speaking to someone behind Connie. "I ain't made plans for coming in that house where I don't belong but just for you to come out to me, the way you should. Don't you know who I am?"

"You're crazy," she whispered. She backed away from the door but did not want to go into another part of the house, as if this would give him permission to come through the door. "What do you . . . You're crazy, you. . . ."

"Huh? What're you saying, honey?"

Her eyes darted everywhere in the kitchen. She could not remember what   130
it was, this room.

"This is how it is, honey: you come out and we'll drive away, have a nice ride. But if you don't come out we're gonna wait till your people come home and then they're all going to get it."

"You want that telephone pulled out?" Ellie said. He held the radio away from his ear and grimaced, as if without the radio the air was too much for him.

"I toldja shut up, Ellie," Arnold Friend said, "you're deaf, get a hearing aid, right? Fix yourself up. This little girl's no trouble and's gonna be nice to me, so Ellie keep to yourself, this ain't your date—right? Don't hem in on me, don't hog, don't crush, don't bird dog, don't trail me," he said in a rapid, meaning-less voice, as if he were running through all the expressions he'd learned but was no longer sure which one of them was in style, then rushing on to new ones, making them up with his eyes closed. "Don't crawl under my fence, don't squeeze in my chipmunk hole, don't sniff my glue, suck my popsicle, keep your own greasy fingers on yourself!" He shaded his eyes and peered in at Connie, who was backed against the kitchen table. "Don't mind him, honey, he's just a creep. He's a dope. Right? I'm the boy for you and like I said, you come out here nice like a lady and give me your hand, and nobody else gets hurt, I mean, your nice old bald-headed daddy and your mummy and your sister in her high heels. Because listen: why bring them in this?"

"Leave me alone," Connie whispered.

"Hey, you know that old woman down the road, the one with the chickens and stuff — you know her?"   135

"She's dead!"

"Dead? What? You know her?" Arnold Friend said.

"She's dead —"

"Don't you like her?"

"She's dead — she's — she isn't here any more —"   140

"But don't you like her, I mean, you got something against her? Some grudge or something?" Then his voice dipped as if he were conscious of rudeness. He touched the sunglasses on top of his head as if to make sure they were still there. "Now you be a good girl."

"What are you going to do?"

"Just two things, or maybe three," Arnold Friend said. "But I promise it won't last long and you'll like me that way you get to like people you're close to. You will. It's all over for you here, so come on out. You don't want your people in any trouble, do you?"

She turned and bumped against a chair or something, hurting her leg, but she ran into the back room and picked up the telephone. Something roared in her ear, a tiny roaring, and she was so sick with fear that she could do nothing but listen to it — the telephone was clammy and very heavy and her fingers groped down to the dial but were too weak to touch it. She began to scream into the phone, into the roaring. She cried out, she cried for her mother, she felt her breath start jerking back and forth in her lungs as if it were something Arnold Friend was stabbing her with again and again with no tenderness. A noisy sorrowful wailing rose all about her and she was locked inside it the way she was locked inside this house.

After a while she could hear again. She was sitting on the floor, with her wet back against the wall.   145

Arnold Friend was saying from the door, "That's a good girl. Put the phone back."

She kicked the phone away from her.

"No, honey. Pick it up. Put it back right."

She picked it up and put it back. The dial tone stopped.

"That's a good girl. Now you come outside."   150

She was hollow with what had been fear but what was now just an emptiness. All that screaming had blasted it out of her. She sat, one leg cramped under her, and deep inside her brain was something like a pinpoint of light that kept going and would not let her relax. She thought, I'm not going to see my mother again. She thought, I'm not going to sleep in my bed again. Her bright green blouse was all wet.

Arnold Friend said, in a gentle-loud voice that was like a stage voice, "The place where you came from ain't there any more, and where you had in mind to go is cancelled out. This place you are now — inside your daddy's house — is nothing but a cardboard box I can knock down any time. You know that and always did know it. You hear me?"

She thought, I have got to think. I have got to know what to do.

"We'll go out to a nice field, out in the country here where it smells so nice and it's sunny," Arnold Friend said. "I'll have my arms tight around you so you won't need to try to get away and I'll show you what love is like, what it does. The hell with this house! It looks solid all right," he said. He ran a fingernail down the screen and the noise did not make Connie shiver, as it would have the day before. "Now put your hand on your heart, honey. Feel that? That feels solid too but we know better. Be nice to me, be sweet like you can because what else is there for a girl like you but to be sweet and pretty and give in? — and get away before her people get back?"

She felt her pounding heart. Her hand seemed to enclose it. She thought   155 for the first time in her life that it was nothing that was hers, that belonged to her, but just a pounding, living thing inside this body that wasn't really hers either.

"You don't want them to get hurt," Arnold Friend went on. "Now get up, honey. Get up all by yourself."

She stood.

"Now turn this way. That's right. Come over to me — Ellie, put that away, didn't I tell you? You dope. You miserable creepy dope," Arnold Friend said. His words were not angry but only part of an incantation. The incantation was kindly. "Now come out through the kitchen to me honey and let's see a smile, try it, you're a brave sweet little girl and now they're eating corn and hotdogs cooked to bursting over an outdoor fire, and they don't know one thing about you and never did and honey you're better than them because not a one of them would have done this for you."

Connie felt the linoleum under her feet; it was cool. She brushed her hair back out of her eyes. Arnold Friend let go of the post tentatively and opened his arms for her, his elbows pointing in toward each other and his wrists limp, to show that this was an embarrassed embrace and a little mocking, he didn't want to make her self-conscious.

She put out her hand against the screen. She watched herself push the   160 door slowly open as if she were back safe somewhere in the other doorway, watching this body and this head of long hair moving out into the sunlight where Arnold Friend waited.

"My sweet little blue-eyed girl," he said in a half-sung sigh that had nothing to do with her brown eyes but was taken up just the same by the vast sunlit reaches of the land behind him and on all sides of him — so much land that Connie had never seen before and did not recognize except to know that she was going to it.   *[1966]*

≡ THINKING ABOUT THE TEXT

1. This story was first published in 1966. What still seems typical of fifteen-year-old Connie's behavior? What seems dated about her?

2. Is Oates making a comment about the effect music has on Connie? Should popular music be accountable for the behavior of its listeners? Can popular culture make us oblivious to the real dangers of the world? Can it make us suspicious and cynical?

3. The suggestions about what will happen to Connie when she leaves the protection of her home are not so subtle. What is your view of her future? What does Connie mean when she says, " 'People don't talk like that, you're crazy' " (para. 105)? What is your reading of her response? Is Arnold Friend crazy?

4. A common response to this story is frustration with Connie's hesitation and her inability to take appropriate action in the face of serious danger. Was this your response? Why isn't she more assertive?

5. Could Connie have been better prepared for this encounter with evil? What evidence does the author give to show how prepared she is or isn't? What is her relationship with her parents? Is her social awareness primarily her parents' responsibility? If not, whose is it?

DON MOSER
The Pied Piper of Tucson: He Cruised in a Golden Car, Looking for the Action

Published in the March 4, 1966, issue of Life *magazine, this article by Don Moser (1932–2013) focuses on a real-life murderer who in major ways resembled Joyce Carol Oates's character Arnold Friend. Indeed, in the essay by Oates that follows, she indicates some familiarity with Moser's piece, although she claims that she didn't read it fully. However much his article inspired Oates to write her story, he illuminates American youth culture of the mid-1960s — including the role that deadly crime could play in it.*

> *Hey, c 'mon babe, follow me,*
> *I'm the Pied Piper, follow me,*
> *I'm the Pied Piper,*
> *And I'll show you where it's at.*
> —Popular song
> Tucson, winter 1965

At dusk in Tucson, as the stark, yellow-flared mountains begin to blur against the sky, the golden car slowly cruises Speedway. Smoothly it rolls down the long divided avenue, past the supermarkets, the gas stations, and the motels; past the twist joints, the sprawling drive-in restaurants. The car slows for an intersection, stops, then pulls away again. The exhaust mutters against the pavement as the young man driving takes the machine swiftly, expertly through the gears. A car pulls even with him; the teen-age girls in the front seat laugh, wave, and call his name. The young man glances toward the rearview mirror, turned always so he can look at his own reflection, and he appraises himself.

The face is his own creation; the hair dyed raven black, the skin darkened to a deep tan with pancake make-up, the lips whitened, the whole effect heightened by a mole he has painted on one cheek. But the deep-set blue eyes are all his own. Beautiful eyes, the girls say.

Approaching the Hi-Ho, the teen-agers' nightclub, he backs off on the accelerator, then slowly cruises on past Johnie's Drive-in. The cars are beginning to orbit and accumulate in the parking lot—near sharp cars with deep-throated mufflers and Maltese-cross decals on the windows. But it's early yet. Not much going on. The driver shifts up again through the gears, and the golden car slides away along the glitter and gimcrack of Speedway. Smitty keeps looking for the action.

Whether the juries in the two trials decide that Charles Howard Schmid Jr. did or did not brutally murder Alleen Rowe, Gretchen Fritz, and Wendy Fritz has from the beginning seemed of almost secondary importance to the people of Tucson. They are not indifferent. But what disturbs them far beyond the question of Smitty's guilt or innocence are the revelations about Tucson itself that have followed on the disclosure of the crimes. Starting from the bizarre circumstances of the killings and on through the ugly fragments of the plot—which in turn hint at other murders as yet undiscovered, at teen-age sex, blackmail, even connections with the Cosa Nostra—they have had to view their city in a new and unpleasant light. The fact is that Charles Schmid—who cannot be dismissed as a freak, an aberrant of no consequence—had for years functioned successfully as a member, even a leader, of the yeastiest stratum of Tucson's teen-age society.

As a high school student Smitty had been, as classmates remember, an outsider—but not that far outside. He was small but he was a fine athlete, and in his last year—1960—he was a state gymnastics champion. His grades were poor, but he was in no trouble to speak of until his senior year, when he was suspended for stealing tools from a welding class.

But Smitty never really left the school. After his suspension he hung around waiting to pick up kids in a succession of sharp cars which he drove fast and well. He haunted all the teen-age hangouts along Speedway, including the bowling alleys and the public swimming pool—and he put on spectacular driving exhibitions for girls far younger than he.

5

At the time of his arrest last November, Charles Schmid was 23 years old. He wore face make-up and dyed his hair. He habitually stuffed three or four inches of old rags and tin cans into the bottoms of his high-topped boots to make himself taller than his five-foot-three and stumbled about so awkwardly while walking that some people thought he had wooden feet. He pursed his lips and let his eyelids droop in order to emulate his idol, Elvis Presley. He bragged to girls that he knew 100 ways to make love, and that he ran dope, that he was a Hell's Angel. He talked about being a rough customer in a fight (he was, though he was rarely in one), and he always carried in his pocket tiny bottles of salt and pepper, which he said he used to blind his opponents. He liked to use highfalutin language and had a favorite saying, "I can manifest my neurotical emotions, emancipate an epicureal instinct, and elaborate on my heterosexual tendencies."

He occasionally shocked even those who thought they knew him well. A friend says that he once saw Smitty tie a string to the tail of his pet cat, swing it around his head and beat it bloody against a wall. Then he turned calmly and asked, "You feel compassion—why?"

Yet even while Smitty tried to create an exalted, heroic image of himself, he had worked on a pitiable one. "He thrived on feeling sorry for himself," recalls a friend, "and making others feel sorry for him." At various times Smitty told inmates that he had leukemia and didn't have long to live. He claimed that he was adopted, that his real name was Angel Rodriguez, that his father was a "bean" (local slang for Mexican, an inferior race in Smitty's view), and that his mother was a famous lawyer who would have nothing to do with him.

What made Smitty a hero to Tucson's youth?   10

Isn't Tucson—out there in the Golden West, in the grand setting where the skies are not cloudy all day—supposed to be a flowering of the American Dream? One envisions teen-agers who drink milk, wear crewcuts, go to bed at half past 9, say "Sir" and "Ma'am," and like to go fishing with Dad. Part of Tucson is like this—but the city is not yet Utopia. It is glass and chrome and well-weathered stucco; it is also gimcrack, ersatz, and urban sprawl at its worst. Its suburbs stretch for mile after mile—a level sea of bungalows, broken only by mammoth shopping centers, that ultimately peters out among the cholla and saguaro. The city has grown from 85,000 to 300,000 since World War II. Few who live there were born there, and a lot are just passing through. Its superb climate attracts the old and the infirm, many of whom, as one citizen put it, "have come here to retire from their responsibilities to life." Jobs are hard to find and there is little industry to stabilize employment. ("What do people do in Tucson?" the visitor asks. Answer: "They do each other's laundry.")

As for the youngsters, they must compete with the army of semi-retired who are willing to take on part-time work for the minimum wage. Schools are beautiful but overcrowded; and at those with split sessions, the kids are on the loose from noon on, or from 6 p.m. till noon the next day. When they get into trouble, Tucson teenagers are capable of getting into trouble in style: a couple of years ago they shocked the city fathers by throwing a series of beer-drinking parties in the desert, attended by scores of kids. The fests were called "boondockers" and if they were no more sinful than any other kid's drinking parties, they were at least on a magnificent scale. One statistic seems relevant: 50 runaways are reported to the Tucson police department each month.

Of an evening kids with nothing to do wind up on Speedway, looking for action. There is the teen-age nightclub ("Pickup Palace," the kids call it). There are the rock'n'roll beer joints (the owners check ages meticulously, but young girls can enter if they don't drink; besides, anyone can buy a phony I.D. card for $2.50 around the high schools) where they can Jerk, Swim, and Frug away the evening to the room-shaking electronic blare of *Hang on Sloopy*, *The Pied Piper*, and a number called *The Bo Diddley Rock*. At the drive-in hamburger and pizza stands their cars circle endlessly, mufflers rumbling, as they check each other over.

Here on Speedway you find Ritchie and Ronny, out of work and bored and with nothing to do. Here you find Debby and Jabron, from the wrong side of the tracks, aimlessly cruising in their battered old car looking for something — anything — to relieve the tedium of their lives, looking for somebody neat. ("Well if the boys look bitchin' you pull up next to them in your car and you roll down the window and say 'Hey, how about a dollar for gas?' and if they give you the dollar then maybe you let them take you to Johnie's for a coke.") Here you find Gretchen, pretty and rich and with problems, bad problems. Of a Saturday night, all of them cruising the long, bright street that seems endlessly in motion with the young. Smitty's people.

He had a nice car. He had plenty of money from his parents, who ran a nursing home, and he was always glad to spend it on anyone who'd listen to him. He had a pad of his own where he threw parties and he had impeccable manners. He was always willing to help a friend and he would send flowers to girls who were ill. He was older and more mature than most of his friends. He knew where the action was, and if he wore make-up — well, at least he was *different*.

15

Some of the older kids — those who worked, who had something else to do — thought Smitty was a creep. But to the youngsters — to the bored and the lonely, to the dropout and the delinquent, to the young girls with beehive hairdos and tight pants they didn't quite fill out, and to the boys with acne and no jobs — to these people, Smitty was a kind of folk hero. Nutty maybe, but at least more dramatic, more theatrical, more *interesting* than anyone else in their lives: a semi-ludicrous, sexy-eyed pied piper who, stumbling along in his rag-stuffed boots, led them up and down Speedway.

On the evening of May 31, 1964, Alleen Rowe prepared to go to bed early. She had to be in class by 6 a.m., and she had an examination the next day. Alleen was a pretty girl of 15, a better-than-average student who talked about going to college and becoming an oceanographer. She was also a sensitive child — given to reading romantic novels and taking long walks in the desert at night. Recently she had been going through a period of adolescent melancholia, often talking with her mother, a nurse, about death. She would, she hoped, be some day reincarnated as a cat.

On this evening, dressed in a black bathing suit and thongs, her usual costume around the house, she had watched the Beatles on TV and had tried to teach her mother to dance the Frug. Then she took her bath, washed her hair, and came out to kiss her mother good night. Norma Rowe, an attractive, womanly divorcee, was somehow moved by the girl's clean fragrance and said, "You smell so good — are you wearing perfume?"

"No, Mom," the girl answered, laughing, "it's just me."

A little later Mrs. Rowe looked in on her daughter, found her apparently   20
sleeping peacefully, and then left for her job as a night nurse in a Tucson hospital. She had no premonition of danger, but she had lately been concerned about Alleen's friendship with a neighbor girl named Mary French.

Mary and Alleen had been spending a good deal of time together, smoking and giggling and talking girl talk in the Rowe backyard. Norma Rowe did not approve. She particularly did not approve of Mary French's friends, a tall, gangling boy of 19 named John Saunders and another named Charles Schmid. She had seen Smitty racing up and down the street in his car and once, when he came to call on Alleen and found her not at home, he had looked at Norma so menacingly with his "pinpoint eyes" that she had been frightened.

Her daughter, on the other hand, seemed to have mixed feelings about Smitty. "He's creepy," she once told her mother, "he just makes me crawl. But he can be nice when he wants to."

At any rate, later that night — according to Mary French's sworn testimony — three friends arrived at Alleen Rowe's house: Smitty, Mary French and Saunders. Smitty had frequently talked with Mary French about killing the Rowe girl by hitting her over the head with a rock. Mary French tapped on Alleen's window and asked her to come out and drink beer with them. Wearing a shift over her bathing suit, she came willingly enough.

Schmid's accomplices were strange and pitiable creatures. Each of them was afraid of Smitty, yet each was drawn to him. As a baby, John Saunders had been so afflicted with allergies that scabs encrusted his entire body. To keep him from scratching himself his parents had tied his hands and feet to the crib each night, and when eventually he was cured he was so conditioned that he could not go to sleep without being bound hand and foot.

Later, a scrawny boy with poor eyesight ("Just a skinny little body with   25
a big head on it"), he was taunted and bullied by larger children; in turn he bullied those who were smaller. He also suffered badly from asthma and he had few friends. In high school he was a poor student and constantly in minor trouble.

Mary French, 19, was — to put it straight — a frump. Her face, which might have been pretty, seemed somehow lumpy, her body shapeless. She was not dull but she was always a poor student, and she finally had simply stopped going to high school. She was, a friend remembers, "fantastically in love with Smitty. She just sat home and waited while he went out with other girls."

Now, with Smitty at the wheel, the four teen-agers headed for the desert, which begins out Golf Links Road. It is spooky country, dry and empty, the yellow sand clotted with cholla and mesquite and stunted, strangely green palo verde trees, and the great humanoid saguaro that hulk against the sky. Out there at night you can hear the yip and ki-yi of coyotes, the piercing screams of wild creatures—cats, perhaps.

According to Mary French, they got out of the car and walked down into a wash, where they sat on the sand and talked for a while, the four of them. Schmid and Mary then started back to the car. Before they got there, they heard a cry and Schmid turned back toward the wash. Mary went on to the car and sat in it alone. After 45 minutes, Saunders appeared and said Smitty wanted her to come back down. She refused, and Saunders went away. Five or 10 minutes later, Smitty showed up. "He got into the car," says Mary, "and he said 'We killed her. I love you very much.' He kissed me. He was breathing real hard and seemed excited." Then Schmid got a shovel from the trunk of the car and they returned to the wash. "She was lying on her back and there was blood on her face and head," Mary French testified. Then the three of them dug a shallow grave and put the body in it and covered it up. Afterwards, they wiped Schmid's car clean of Alleen's fingerprints.

More than a year passed. Norma Rowe had reported her daughter missing and the police searched for her—after a fashion. At Mrs. Rowe's insistence they picked up Schmid, but they had no reason to hold him. The police, in fact, assumed that Alleen was just one more of Tucson's runaways.

Norma Rowe, however, had become convinced that Alleen had been killed   30 by Schmid, although she left her kitchen light on every night just in case Alleen did come home. She badgered the police and she badgered the sheriff until the authorities began to dismiss her as a crank. She began to imagine a high-level conspiracy against her. She wrote the state attorney general, the FBI, the U.S. Department of Health, Education and Welfare. She even contacted a New Jersey mystic, who said she could see Alleen's body out in the desert under a big tree.

Ultimately Norma Rowe started her own investigation, questioning Alleen's friends, poking around, dictating her findings to a tape recorder; she even tailed Smitty at night, following him in her car, scared stiff that he might spot her.

Schmid, during this time, acquired a little house of his own. There he held frequent parties, where people sat around amid his stacks of *Playboy* magazines, playing Elvis Presley records and drinking beer.

He read Jules Feiffer's novel, *Harry, the Rat with Women*, and said that his ambition was to be like Harry and have a girl commit suicide over him. Once, according to a friend, he went to see a minister, who gave him a Bible and told him to read the first three chapters of John. Instead Schmid tore the pages out and burned them in the street. "Religion is a farce," he announced. He started an upholstery business with some friends, called himself "founder and president," but then failed to put up the money he'd promised and the venture was short-lived.

He decided he liked blondes best, and took to dyeing the hair of various teen-age girls he went around with. He went out and bought two imitation diamond rings for about $13 apiece and then engaged himself, on the same day, both to Mary French and to a 15-year-old girl named Kathy Morath. His plan, he confided to a friend, was to put each of the girls to work and have them deposit their salaries in a bank account held jointly with him. Mary French did indeed go to work in the convalescent home Smitty's parents operated. When their bank account was fat enough, Smitty withdrew the money and bought a tape recorder.

By this time Smitty also had a girl from a higher social stratum than he usually was involved with. She was Gretchen Fritz, daughter of a prominent Tucson heart surgeon. Gretchen was a pretty, thin, nervous girl of 17 with a knack for trouble. A teacher described her as "erratic, subversive, a psychopathic liar."

At the horsy private school she attended for a time she was a misfit. She not only didn't care about horses, but she shocked her classmates by telling them they were foolish for going out with boys without getting paid for it. Once she even committed the unpardonable social sin of turning up at a formal dance accompanied by boys wearing what was described as beatnik dress. She cut classes, she was suspected of stealing and when, in the summer before her senior year, she got into trouble with juvenile authorities for her role in an attempted theft at a liquor store, the headmaster suggested she not return and then recommended she get psychiatric treatment.

Charles Schmid saw Gretchen for the first time at a public swimming pool in the summer of 1964. He met her by the simple expedient of following her home, knocking on the door and, when she answered, saying, "Don't I know you?" They talked for an hour. Thus began a fierce and stormy relationship. A good deal of what authorities know of the development of this relationship comes from the statements of a spindly scarecrow of a young man who wears pipestem trousers and Beatle boots: Richard Bruns. At the time Smitty was becoming involved with Gretchen, Bruns was 18 years old. He had served two terms in the reformatory at Fort Grant. He had been in and out of trouble his whole life, had never fit in anywhere. Yet, although he never went beyond the tenth grade in school and his credibility on many counts is suspect, he is clearly intelligent and even sensitive. He was, for a time, Smitty's closest friend and confidant, and he is today one of the mainstays of the state's case against Smitty. His story:

"He and Gretchen were always fighting," says Bruns. "She didn't want him to drink or go out with the guys or go out with other girls. She wanted him to stay home, call her on the phone, be punctual. First she would get suspicious of him, then he'd get suspicious of her. They were made for each other."

35

Their mutual jealousy led to sharp and continual arguments. Once she infuriated him by throwing a bottle of shoe polish on his car. Another time she was driving past Smitty's house and saw him there with some other girls. She jumped out of her car and began screaming. Smitty took off into the house, out the back, and climbed a tree in his backyard.

His feelings for her were an odd mixture of hate and adoration. He said he was   40
madly in love with her, but he called her a whore. She would let Smitty in her bedroom window at night. Yet he wrote an anonymous letter to the Tucson Health Department accusing her of having venereal disease and spreading it about town. But Smitty also went to enormous lengths to impress Gretchen, once shooting holes through the windows of his car and telling her that thugs, from whom he was protecting her, had fired at him. So Bruns described the relationship.

On the evening of Aug. 16, 1965, Gretchen Fritz left the house with her little sister Wendy, a friendly, lively 13-year-old, to go to a drive-in movie. Neither girl ever came home again. Gretchen's father, like Alleen Rowe's mother, felt sure that Charles Schmid had something to do with his daughters' disappearance, and eventually he hired Bill Heilig, a private detective, to handle the case. One of Heilig's men soon found Gretchen's red compact car parked behind a motel, but the police continued to assume that the girls had joined the ranks of Tucson's runaways.

About a week after Gretchen disappeared, Bruns was at Smitty's house. "We were sitting in the living room," Bruns recalls. "He was sitting on the sofa and I was in the chair by the window and we got on the subject of Gretchen. He said, 'You know I killed her?' I said I didn't, and he said 'You know where?' I said no. He said, 'I did it here in the living room. First I killed Gretchen, then Wendy was still going "*huh, huh, huh,*" so I . . . [Here Bruns showed how Smitty made a garroting gesture.] Then I took the bodies and I put them in the trunk of the car. I put the bodies in the most obvious place I could think of because I just didn't care anymore. Then I ditched the car and wiped it clean.' "

Bruns was not particularly upset by Smitty's story. Months before, Smitty had told him of the murder of Alleen Rowe, and nothing had come of that. So he was not certain Smitty was telling the truth about the Fritz girls. Besides, Bruns detested Gretchen himself. But what happened next, still according to Bruns's story, did shake him up.

One night not long after, a couple of tough-looking characters, wearing sharp suits and smoking cigars, came by with Smitty and picked up Bruns. Smitty said they were Mafia, and that someone had hired them to look for Gretchen. Smitty and Bruns were taken to an apartment where several men were present whom Smitty later claimed to have recognized as local Cosa Nostra figures.

They wanted to know what had happened to the girls. They made no   45
threats, but the message, Bruns remembers, came across loud and clear. These were no street-corner punks: these were the real boys. In spite of the intimidating company, Schmid lost none of his insouciance. He said he didn't

know where Gretchen was, but if she turned up hurt he wanted these men to help him get whoever was responsible. He added that she might have gone to California.

By the time Smitty and Bruns got back to Smitty's house, they were both a little shaky. Later that night, says Bruns, Smitty did the most unlikely thing imaginable: he called the FBI. First he tried the Tucson office and couldn't raise anyone. Then he called Phoenix and couldn't get an agent there either. Finally he put in a person-to-person call to J. Edgar Hoover in Washington. He didn't get Hoover, of course, but he got someone and told him that the Mafia was harassing him over the disappearance of a girl. The FBI promised to have someone in touch with him soon.

Bruns was scared and said so. It occurred to him now that if Smitty really had killed the Fritz girls and left their bodies in an obvious place, they were in very bad trouble indeed — with the Mafia on one hand and the FBI on the other. "Let's go bury them," Bruns said.

"Smitty stole the keys to his old man's station wagon," says Bruns, "and then we got a flat shovel — the only one we could find. We went to Johnie's and got a hamburger, and then we drove out to the old drinking spot [in the desert] — that's what Smitty meant when he said the most obvious place. It's where we used to drink beer and make out with girls.

"So we parked the car and got the shovel and walked down there, and we couldn't find anything. Then Smitty said, 'Wait, I smell something.' We went in opposite directions looking, and then I heard Smitty say, 'Come here.' I found him kneeling over Gretchen. There was a white rag tied around her legs. Her blouse was pulled up and she was wearing a white bra and Capris.

"Then he said, 'Wendy's up this way.' I sat there for a minute. Then I followed Smitty to where Wendy was. He'd had the decency to cover her — except for one leg, which was sticking up out of the ground.

"We tried to dig with the flat shovel. We each took turns. He'd dig for a while and then I'd dig for a while, but the ground was hard and we couldn't get anywhere with that flat shovel. We dug for twenty minutes and finally Smitty said we'd better do something because it's going to get light. So he grabbed the rag that was around Gretchen's legs and dragged her down in the wash. It made a noise like dragging a hollow shell. It stunk like hell. Then Smitty said wipe off her shoes, there might be fingerprints, so I wiped them off with my handkerchief and threw it away.

"We went back to Wendy. Her leg was sticking up with a shoe on it. He said take off her tennis shoe and throw it over there. I did, I threw it. Then he said, 'Now you're in this as deep as I am.'" By then, the sisters had been missing for about two weeks.

Early next morning Smitty did see the FBI. Nevertheless — here Bruns's story grows even wilder — that same day Smitty left for California, accompanied by a couple of Mafia types, to look for Gretchen Fritz. While there, he was picked up by the San Diego police on a complaint the he was impersonating an FBI officer. He was detained briefly, released and returned to Tucson.

50

But now, it seemed to Richard Bruns, Smitty began acting very strangely. He startled Bruns by saying, "I've killed — not three times, but four. Now it's your turn, Ritchie." He went berserk in his little house, smashing his fist through a wall, slamming doors, then rushing out into the backyard in nothing but his undershorts, where he ran through the night screaming, "God is going to punish me!" He also decided, suddenly, to get married — to a 15-year-old girl who was a stranger to most of his friends.

If Smitty seemed to Bruns to be losing his grip, Ritchie Bruns himself was not   55
in much better shape. His particular quirk revolved around Kathy Morath, the thin, pretty, 16-year-old daughter of a Tucson postman. Kathy had once been attracted to Smitty. He had given her one of his two cut-glass engagement rings. But Smitty never really took her seriously, and one day, in a fit of pique and jealousy, she threw the ring back in his face. Ritchie Bruns comforted her and then started dating her himself. He was soon utterly and irrevocably smitten with goofy adoration.

Kathy accepted Bruns as a suitor, but halfheartedly. She thought him weird (oddly enough, she did not think Smitty in the least weird) and their romance was short-lived. After she broke up with him last July, Bruns went into a blue funk, a nosedive into romantic melancholy, and then, like some love-swacked Elizabethan poet, he started pouring out his heart to her on paper. He sent her poems, short stories, letters 24 pages long. ("My God, you should have read the stuff," says her perplexed father. "His letters were so romantic it was like 'Next week, East Lynne.' ") Bruns even began writing a novel dedicated to "My Darling Kathy."

If Bruns had confined himself to literary catharsis, the murders of the Rowe and Fritz girls might never have been disclosed. But Ritchie went a little bit around the bend. He became obsessed with the notion that Kathy Morath was the next victim on Smitty's list. Someone had cut the Moraths' screen door, there had been a prowler around her house, and Bruns was sure that it was Smitty. (Kathy and her father, meantime, were sure it was Bruns.)

"I started having this dream," Bruns says. "It was the same dream every night. Smitty would have Kathy out in the desert and he'd be doing all those things to her, and strangling her, and I'd be running across the desert with a gun in my hand, but I could never get there."

If Bruns couldn't save Kathy in his dreams, he could, he figured, stop a walking, breathing Smitty. His scheme for doing so was so wild and so simple that it put the whole Morath family into a state of panic and very nearly landed Bruns in jail.

Bruns undertook to stand guard over Kathy Morath. He kept watch in   60
front of her house, in the alley, and in the street. He patrolled the sidewalk from early in the morning till late at night, seven days a week. If Kathy was home he would be there. If she went out, he would follow her. Kathy's father called the police, and when they told Bruns he couldn't loiter around like that, Bruns fetched his dog and walked the animal up and down the block, hour after hour.

Bruns by now was wallowing in feelings of sacrifice and nobility—all of it unappreciated by Kathy Morath and her parents. At the end of October, he was finally arrested for harassing the Morath family. The judge, facing the obviously woebegone and smitten young man, told Bruns that he wouldn't be jailed if he'd agree to get out of town until he got over his infatuation.

Bruns agreed and a few days later went to Ohio to stay with his grandmother and try to get a job. It was hopeless. He couldn't sleep at night, and if he did doze off he had his old nightmare again.

One night he blurted out the whole story to his grandmother in their kitchen. She thought he had had too many beers and didn't believe him. "I hear beer does strange things to a person," she said comfortingly. At her words Bruns exploded, knocked over a chair and shouted, "The one time in my life when I need advice and what do I get?" A few minutes later he was on the phone to the Tucson police.

Things happened swiftly. At Bruns's frantic insistence, the police picked up Kathy Morath and put her in protective custody. They went into the desert and discovered—precisely as Bruns had described them—the grisly, skeletal remains of Gretchen and Wendy Fritz. They started the machinery that resulted in the arrest a week later of John Saunders and Mary French. They found Charles Schmid working in the yard of his little house, his face layered with make-up, his nose covered by a patch of adhesive plaster which he had worn for five months, boasting that his nose was broken in a fight, and his boots packed full of old rags and tin cans. He put up no resistance.

John Saunders and Mary French confessed immediately to their roles in the slaying of Alleen Rowe and were quickly sentenced, Mary French to four to five years, Saunders to life. When Smitty goes on trial for this crime, on March 15, they will be principal witnesses against him.   65

Meanwhile Ritchie Bruns, the perpetual misfit, waits apprehensively for the end of the Fritz trial, desperately afraid that Schmid will go free. "If he does," Bruns says glumly, "I'll be the first one he'll kill."

As for Charles Schmid, he has adjusted well to his period of waiting. He is polite and agreeable with all, though at the preliminary hearings he glared menacingly at Ritchie Bruns. Dressed tastefully, tie neatly knotted, hair carefully combed, his face scrubbed clean of make-up, he is a short, compact, darkly handsome young man with a wide, engaging smile and those deepset eyes.

The people of Tucson wait uneasily for what fresh scandal the two trials may develop. Civic leaders publicly cry that a slur has been cast on their community by an isolated crime. High school students have held rallies and written vehement editorials in the school papers, protesting that they all are being judged by the actions of a few oddballs and misfits. But the city reverberates with stories of organized teen-age crime and vice, in which Smitty is cast in the role of a minor-league underworld boss. None of these later stories has been substantiated.

One disclosure, however, has most disturbing implications: Smitty's boasts may have been heard not just by Bruns and his other intimates, but by other teen-agers as well. How many — and precisely how much they knew — it remains impossible to say. One authoritative source, however, having listened to the admissions of six high school students, says they unquestionably knew enough so that they should have gone to the police — but were either afraid to talk, or didn't want to rock the boat.

As for Smitty's friends, the thought of telling the police never entered their minds.   70

"I didn't know he killed her," said one, "and even if I had, I wouldn't have said anything. I wouldn't want to be a fink."

Out in the respectable Tucson suburbs parents have started to crack down on the youngsters and have declared Speedway hangouts off limits. "I thought my folks were bad before," laments one grounded 16-year-old, "but now they're just impossible."

As for the others — Smitty's people — most don't care very much. Things are duller without Smitty around, but things have always been dull.

"There's nothing to do in this town," says one of his girls, shaking her dyed blond hair. "The only other town I know is Las Vegas and there's nothing to do there either." For her, and for her friends, there's nothing to do in any town.

They are down on Speedway again tonight, cruising, orbiting the drive-   75
ins, stopping by the joints, where the words of *The Bo Diddley Rock* cut through the smoke and the electronic dissonance like some macabre reminder of their fallen hero:

> *All you women stand in line,*
> *And I'll love you all in an hour's time. . . .*
> *I got a cobra snake for a necktie,*
> *I got a brand-new house on the roadside*
> *Covered with rattlesnake hide,*
> *I got a brand-new chimney made on top,*
> *Made out of human skulls.*
> *Come on baby, take a walk with me,*
> *And tell me, who do you love?*
> *Who do you love?*
> *Who do you love?*
> *Who do you love?*   [1966]

≡ THINKING ABOUT THE TEXT

1. As his title implies, Moser analyzes Tucson at least as much as he analyzes Charles Schmid. What main points does he make about the city, especially about its youth? To what extent is setting similarly important in Oates's story?

2. Moser himself gave the name "the pied piper" to Charles Schmid. Why does Moser call Schmid this? How helpful is it to think of Arnold

Friend as a "pied piper," too? (You may wish to look up details of the classic tale "The Pied Piper of Hamelin.")

3. After Moser's article was published, Charles Schmid pled guilty to second-degree murder of Alleen Rowe. For murdering the Fritz sisters, he received the death penalty, but he was spared execution when the state of Arizona abandoned capital punishment in 1971. Schmid remained in prison, where in 1975 two other inmates stabbed him to death. Does Oates's story leave you with the impression that Arnold Friend will meet a similar fate? Why, or why not?

JOYCE CAROL OATES
Smooth Talk: Short Story into Film

Joyce Carol Oates published the following article in the March 23, 1986, issue of the New York Times. *She wrote it upon the release of* Smooth Talk, *a film adaptation of "Where Are You Going, Where Have You Been?"*

Some years ago in the American Southwest there surfaced a tabloid psychopath known as "The Pied Piper of Tucson." I have forgotten his name, but his specialty was the seduction and occasional murder of teen-aged girls. He may or may not have had actual accomplices, but his bizarre activities were known among a circle of teenagers in the Tucson area; for some reason they kept his secret, deliberately did not inform parents or police. It was this fact, not the fact of the mass murderer himself, that struck me at the time. And this was a pre-Manson time, early or mid-1960s.

The Pied Piper mimicked teenagers in talk, dress, and behavior, but he was not a teenager — he was a man in his early thirties. Rather short, he stuffed rags in his leather boots to give himself height. (And sometimes walked unsteadily as a consequence: did none among his admiring constituency notice?) He charmed his victims as charismatic psychopaths have always charmed their victims, to the bewilderment of others who fancy themselves free of all lunatic attractions. The Pied Piper of Tucson: a trashy dream, a tabloid archetype, sheer artifice, comedy, cartoon — surrounded, however improbably, and finally tragically, by real people. You think that, if you look twice, he won't be there. But there he is.

I don't remember any longer where I first read about this Pied Piper — very likely in *Life* Magazine. I do recall deliberately not reading the full article because I didn't want to be distracted by too much detail. It was not after all the mass murderer himself who intrigued me, but the disturbing fact that a number of teenagers — from "good" families — aided and abetted his crimes. This is the sort of thing authorities and responsible citizens invariably call "inexplicable" because they can't find explanations for it. They would not have fallen under this maniac's spell, after all.

An early draft of my short story "Where Are You Going, Where Have You Been?"—from which the film *Smooth Talk* was adapted by Joyce Chopra and Tom Cole—had the rather too explicit title "Death and the Maiden." It was cast in a mode of fiction to which I am still partial—indeed, every third or fourth story of mine is probably in this mode—"realistic allegory," it might be called. It is Hawthornean, romantic, shading into parable. Like the medieval German engraving from which my title was taken, the story was minutely detailed yet clearly an allegory of the fatal attractions of death (or the devil). An innocent young girl is seduced by way of her own vanity; she mistakes death for erotic romance of a particularly American/trashy sort.

In subsequent drafts the story changed its tone, its focus, its language, its title. It became "Where Are You Going, Where Have You Been?" Written at a time when the author was intrigued by the music of Bob Dylan, particularly the hauntingly elegiac song "It's All Over Now, Baby Blue," it was dedicated to Bob Dylan. The charismatic mass murderer drops into the background and his innocent victim, a fifteen-year-old, moves into the foreground. She becomes the true protagonist of the tale, courting and being courted by her fate, a self-styled 1950s pop figure, alternately absurd and winning. There is no suggestion in the published story that "Arnold Friend" has seduced and murdered other young girls, or even that he necessarily intends to murder Connie. Is his interest "merely" sexual? (Nor is there anything about the complicity of other teenagers. I saved that yet more provocative note for a current story, "Testimony.") Connie is shallow, vain, silly, hopeful, doomed—but capable nonetheless of an unexpected gesture of heroism at the story's end. Her smooth-talking seducer, who cannot lie, promises her that her family will be unharmed if she gives herself to him; and so she does. The story ends abruptly at the point of her "crossing over." We don't know the nature of her sacrifice, only that she is generous enough to make it.

In adapting a narrative so spare and thematically foreshortened as "Where Are You Going, Where Have You Been?" film director Joyce Chopra and screenwriter Tom Cole were required to do a good deal of filling in, expanding, inventing. Connie's story becomes lavishly, and lovingly, textured; she is not an allegorical figure so much as a "typical" teenaged girl (if Laura Dern, spectacularly good-looking, can be so defined). Joyce Chopra, who has done documentary films on contemporary teenage culture and, yet more authoritatively, has an adolescent daughter of her own, creates in *Smooth Talk* a vivid and absolutely believable world for Connie to inhabit. Or worlds: as in the original story there is Connie-at-home, and there is Connie-with-her-friends. Two fifteen-year-old girls, two finely honed styles, two voices, sometimes but not often overlapping. It is one of the marvelous visual features of the film that we *see* Connie and her friends transform themselves, once they are safely free of parental observation. The girls claim their true identities in the neighborhood shopping mall. What freedom, what joy!

Smooth Talk is, in a way, as much Connie's mother's story as it is Connie's; its center of gravity, its emotional nexus, is frequently with the mother—warmly and convincingly played by Mary Kay Place. (Though the mother's sexual jealousy of her daughter is slighted in the film.) Connie's ambiguous relationship with her affable, somewhat mysterious father (well played by Levon Helm) is an excellent touch: I had thought, subsequent to the story's publication, that I should have built up the father, suggesting, as subtly as I could, an attraction there paralleling the attraction Connie feels for her seducer, Arnold Friend. And Arnold Friend himself — "A. Friend" as he says — is played with appropriately overdone sexual swagger by Treat Williams, who is perfect for the part; and just the right age. We see that Arnold Friend isn't a teenager even as Connie, mesmerized by his presumed charm, does not seem to see him at all. What is so difficult to accomplish in prose — nudging the reader to look over the protagonist's shoulder, so to speak — is accomplished with enviable ease in film.

Treat Williams as Arnold Friend is supreme in his very awfulness, as, surely, the original Pied Piper of Tucson must have been. (Though no one involved in the film knew about the original source.) Mr. Williams flawlessly impersonates Arnold Friend as Arnold Friend impersonates — is it James Dean? James Dean regarding himself in mirrors, doing James Dean imperson-ations? That Connie's fate is so trashy is in fact her fate.

What is outstanding in Joyce Chopra's *Smooth Talk* is its visual freshness, its sense of motion and life; the attentive intelligence the director has brought to the semi-secret world of the American adolescent — shopping mall flirta-tions, drive-in restaurant romances, highway hitchhiking, the fascination of rock music played very, very loud. (James Taylor's music for the film is won-derfully appropriate. We hear it as Connie hears it; it is the music of her spiri-tual being.) Also outstanding, as I have indicated, and numerous critics have noted, are the acting performances. Laura Dern is so dazzlingly right as "my" Connie that I may come to think I modeled the fictitious girl on her, in the way that writers frequently delude themselves about notions of causality.

My difficulties with *Smooth Talk* have primarily to do with my chronic hes- 10 itation — about seeing/hearing work of mine abstracted from its contexture of language. All writers know that Language is their subject; quirky word choices, patterns of rhythm, enigmatic pauses, punctuation marks. Where the quick scanner sees "quick" writing, the writer conceals nine tenths of the iceberg. Of course we all have "real" subjects, and we will fight to the death to defend those subjects, but beneath the tale-telling it is the tale-telling that grips us so very fiercely. The writer works in a single dimension, the director works in three. I assume they are professionals to their fingertips; authorities in their medium as I am an authority (if I am) in mine. I would fiercely defend the placement of a semicolon in one of my novels but I would probably have deferred in the end to Joyce Chopra's decision to reverse the story's conclusion, turn it upside down, in a sense, so that the film ends not with death, not with a sleepwalker's crossing over to her fate, but upon a scene of reconciliation, rejuvenation.

A girl's loss of virginity, bittersweet but not necessarily tragic. Not today. A girl's coming-of-age that involves her succumbing to, but then rejecting, the "trashy dreams" of her pop teenage culture. "Where Are You Going, Where Have You Been?" defines itself as allegorical in its conclusion: Death and

Death's chariot (a funky souped-up convertible) have come for the Maiden. Awakening is, in the story's final lines, moving out into the sunlight where Arnold Friend waits:

> "My sweet little blue-eyed girl," he said in a half-sung sigh that had nothing to do with [Connie's] brown eyes but was taken up just the same by the vast sunlit reaches of the land behind him and on all sides of him—so much land that Connie had never seen before and did not recognize except to know that she was going to it.

—a conclusion impossible to transfigure into film.   [1986]

≡ THINKING ABOUT THE TEXT

1. In discussing Moser's article and Joyce Chopra's film, Oates specifies various elements that she put into "Where Are You Going, Where Have You Been?" How accurate do you find her description of her story? Do you think she distorts or ignores any aspects of her text?

2. At the end of the film *Smooth Talk*, Connie is alive. She returns home from her outing with Arnold Friend, and she dances with her sister to James Taylor's song "Handy Man." What does Oates seem to think of this ending? Do you object to it? Why, or why not?

3. To what extent should readers of a short story be guided by the author's explanation of it? Explain your reasoning, and refer to Oates's story as well as her article about it.

MEGHAN DAUM
Jaycee Dugard and the Feel-Good Imperative

Meghan Daum (b. 1970) was born in California but grew up in Texas and New Jersey. An author, essayist, and journalist, she has a B.A. from Vassar College and an M.F.A. from Columbia University. Her work includes a novel, The Quality of Life Report *(2003), and essay collections that include* My Misspent Youth: Essays *(2001) and* The Unspeakable: And Other Subjects of Discussion *(2014). In 2015, she published* Selfish, Shallow, and Self-Absorbed: Sixteen Writers on the Decision Not to Have Kids. *She is a Guggenheim fellow and has been contributing columnist to the* Los Angeles Times, *where her essay on Jaycee Dugard appeared on July 14, 2011.*

[Los Angeles Times, July 14, 2011]

To watch Diane Sawyer's interview Sunday night with Jaycee Dugard was to wonder at times if that was Dugard herself on screen or an actress hired to play the role of the quintessential survivor. Dugard was so serene and lacking in rancor that it was hard to believe she had been kidnapped at age 11 and held prisoner for 18 years, during which she was repeatedly raped and bore two children, the first when she was just 14.

But there she was, saying things like "there is life after something tragic" and joking about how being locked indoors for so many years was her secret to smooth skin.

The interview, tied to Dugard's just-published memoir, scored big in the ratings. As with the 2002 abduction of Elizabeth Smart, Dugard's story has generated pity, anger and prurient fascination. It's a story that's horrifying in pretty much every imaginable way. Dugard was kept in handcuffs, forced to give birth in a backyard shed and so psychologically damaged that she passed up several opportunities to escape over the years. What's more, parole officers checking on her captor, convicted sex offender Phillip Garrido, managed to miss Dugard 60 times.

These revelations, stunning and grotesque as they are, haven't kept the events from being framed as the kind of tale Americans love best: a redemption story. Although we're not being asked to forget what Dugard endured or to forgive law enforcement's unconscionable negligence, it's clear that just about everyone involved in revealing what happened—from Sawyer to People magazine (which, shortly after Dugard was found, reported on her "sense of comfort and optimism") to Dugard herself — is invested in the notion that this ultimately is a feel-good story. As Sawyer listened to Dugard read from the journal she kept during her captivity—"I am so lucky and blessed for all the wonderful things that I do have" — you can almost see your great-aunt typing them into an email and forwarding them to 100 people under the heading "Words to Live By."

It's interesting (and perhaps not entirely coincidental) that the Dugard   5 special aired around the same time as ABC's announcement that Smart, now 23, would be joining the network as a commentator on missing-persons cases and child abductions. It's an appointment that generates a certain queasiness. Doesn't Smart, who was kidnapped at 14 and raped repeatedly over nine months, want to move on with her life? In fairness, she's already established as a victims rights advocate, but as with Dugard, I detect a need on the part of the media to wrap her story up in a bow, to assure the public that she's OK, to reinforce the central narrative of just about everything we see on TV: Change is possible, maybe even easy; that adversity can be overcome; and that, as Dr. Phil likes to say, there are no victims, only volunteers.

The trouble is, that's simply not true. Dugard and Smart seem to have successfully made the transition to survivor, but to turn them into generic symbols of hope or, worse, to saddle them with the job of being publicly loving, forgiving and grateful despite what they endured minimizes their trauma and panders to audiences by creating a false sense of closure.

The redemption narrative (along with its corollary, the recovery narrative) is dependent on closure—especially on TV. We watch the addict, the obese person and the villainous reality show contestant in the sure and certain hope that sobriety, fitness and a trip off the island are right around the corner. Part of the reason the Casey Anthony verdict touched such a nerve was that it didn't conform to the redemption narrative. The survivor was anything but a hero. No lessons were learned.

None of this is to say that Dugard's grace isn't genuine or that Smart won't do just fine as a talking head. When Sawyer introduced Dugard as "a woman who endured the unimaginable and emerged with powerful lessons on love and life," she certainly wasn't wrong. But Dugard undoubtedly emerged with a lot more than that. All's well that ends well is more spin than reality. That's why we'd do well to recognize Dugard's courage not just in the face of the story she's telling but the one she's living.

≡ THINKING ABOUT THE TEXT

1. From your experience, what evidence is there that Americans love "feel-good" stories? What might be an objection to these tales?

2. What exactly is Daum's objection to the redemptive story? What does Daum mean by "pandering to audiences"?

3. What is Daum's view of trauma and closure, and how does the expression "all's well that ends well" contradict her position?

≡ WRITING ABOUT ISSUES

1. Write an essay in which you explain how the title of Oates's story applies to it. Consider how Connie *thinks*, not just what she does. Where, psychologically, is Connie going? Where, psychologically, has she been?

2. To what extent does present-day American culture prepare its young women for the dangers of the world? Write an essay that addresses this question by referring to Oates's story and another text in this cluster.

3. Write an essay about the Casey Anthony case that Daum mentions. How does this case fit into the redemptive story or the feel-good narrative? What seems to be the difference between this case and the others Daum mentions?

4. Research an actual case of female captivity: for example, the kidnapping of Patty Hearst, Jaycee Dugard, Elizabeth Smart, or the group of women who escaped from their abductor's Cleveland house in 2013. Then write an essay in which you develop and support a claim about the media's coverage of your chosen case. Make reference to the Meghan Daum piece.

≡ RESEARCHING THE ISSUES

1. Watch *Smooth Talk*, the film version of this story, and, after reading several reviews, argue that the film version does or does not conform to the ideas in Daum's essay.

2. Although the story was published in 1966 and draws on a serial killer case of that time, Oates implies that the setting is the late 1950s. Research youth culture in the 1950s and argue whether Oates's representation is or is not accurate.

3. Research several critical essays on the symbolism of this story and argue that certain interpretations are or are not more reasonable than others.

CHAPTER 13

Journeys

Perhaps no impulse is as ancient and as natural as the desire to leave one's home, to journey out of the village to unknown lands. Ancient epics like the *Iliad* and the *Odyssey* and more modern tales like Mark Twain's *Adventures of Huckleberry Finn* and Jack Kerouac's *On the Road* are narratives of wandering, encountering the strange and the wondrous. Sometimes the journey has a specific goal: a quest for riches, for fame, or for adventure. Sometimes the journey is simply for escape, for curiosity's sake, for an understanding of the wider world. Of course the idea of the journey easily lends itself to both the literal and the metaphorical, to quests external and internal. We all take journeys of self-discovery from childhood to adolescence to adulthood and eventually to death. Life as a journey is a notion deeply woven into our cultural understanding from Greek mythology, epics, novels, religious beliefs, and popular culture.

It is no surprise then that writers for thousands of years have written about their perilous journeys to dangerous places, their contemplative journeys to self-reflection and wisdom, as well as their imaginative treks to dystopic futures. Our selections in this chapter work with an expansive idea of the journey.

For some the journey is quite literal; for others the path is decidedly metaphorical. Like the dancers in the Eagles' song "Hotel California," some writers journey to remember, others to forget. Whether the journey is the writer's own or a fictional one a character takes, the creative leap is thoughtful, illuminating, and moving.

The chapter begins with a trio of stories that present different versions of the fairy tale now commonly titled "Little Red Riding Hood." Then the protagonists of Tim O'Brien's "The Things They Carried" and Ambrose Beirce's "An Occurrence at Owl Creek Bridge" undertake harrowing wartime journeys. Three famous journey poems by Robert Frost are gathered in the next cluster. Death is the destination for the four poems that follow. And then we present three science fiction stories focusing on journeys through time by three masters of the genre. The Literature and Current Issues cluster tackles the controversial topic of immigration first with a poem by Juan Felipe Herrera and then with three essays with varying perspectives. Our last cluster uses Ralph Ellison's classic tale of coming of age in pre-civil rights America and three related essays to provide a context for research into race and social equality.

CHARLES PERRAULT, "Little Red Riding Hood"

JACOB AND WILHELM GRIMM, "Little Red Cap"

ANGELA CARTER, "The Company of Wolves"

The story of Little Red Riding Hood is still told to children throughout the world. Her adventure in facing mortal danger is part of their education. What, though, do they learn from this narrative? Scholars have suggested various interpretations, many of which hold that the tale helps its young readers face their own childhood fears. Among the best known and most provocative interpreters of the story is the psychoanalyst Bruno Bettelheim, who sees it as a symbolic treatment of a girl's effort to understand her sexual development. In this view, the story teaches girls to work through adolescent anxieties. But whatever decoding the tale receives, some aspects of it remain important. It depicts a child's journey from innocence to experience, however these terms are defined. Little Red Riding Hood learns something from her encounters with the murderous wolf, and she does so largely on her own. Several versions of her story exist. Because this tale of a perilous journey is so popular and has circulated in various forms, we invite you to compare three versions of it: Charles Perrault's from the seventeenth century, the Brothers Grimm's from the nineteenth century, and Angela Carter's modern variation. Note that the Grimms' tale does not stray too far from Perrault's, at least not in representing Little Red Riding Hood as an innocent in need of male protection. Under the influence of contemporary feminism, however, Carter feels no need to conform to the fairy-tale tradition. As a result, Little Red Riding Hood is freed not only from genre conventions but also from a centuries-old stereotype about passive females.

≡ BEFORE YOU READ

Write down what you remember about the story of Little Red Riding Hood, and then compare your version with those of your classmates. What elements of the story do your class's various renditions of it have in common? What differences, if any, emerge? Why do you think the story has been so popular?

CHARLES PERRAULT
Little Red Riding Hood

Along with the Brothers Grimm, Charles Perrault (1628–1703) was the most influential teller of the fairy tales many of us learned as children. Born in Paris to a fairly wealthy family, Perrault was trained as a lawyer. For his literary and philosophical achievements, however, Perrault was elected to the prestigious Académie Française in 1671. During his lifetime, he and others were involved in a major cultural dispute over the relative merits of ancient authors and modern ones, with Perrault favoring the more up-to-date group. Later generations remember him best, though, for his 1697 book Stories or Tales from Times Past, with Morals: Tales of Mother Goose. *This collection included "Le Petit Chaperon Rouge," which English-speaking readers have come to know as "Little Red Riding Hood." This story did not completely originate with Perrault; probably he had heard folktales containing some of its narrative elements. Nevertheless, his version became popular on publication and has remained so ever since.*

Once upon a time there lived in a certain village a little country girl, the prettiest creature who was ever seen. Her mother was excessively fond of her, and her grandmother doted on her still more. This good woman had a little red riding hood made for her. It suited the girl so extremely well that everybody called her Little Red Riding Hood.

One day her mother, having made some cakes, said to her, "Go, my dear, and see how your grandmother is doing, for I hear she has been very ill. Take her a cake, and this little pot of butter."

Little Red Riding Hood set out immediately to go to her grandmother, who lived in another village.

As she was going through the wood, she met with a wolf, who had a very great mind to eat her up, but he dared not, because of some woodcutters working nearby in the forest. He asked her where she was going. The poor child, who did not know that it was dangerous to stay and talk to a wolf, said to him, "I am going to see my grandmother and carry her a cake and a little pot of butter from my mother."

"Does she live far off?" said the wolf.   5

"Oh I say," answered Little Red Riding Hood. "It is beyond that mill you see there, at the first house in the village."

"Well," said the wolf, "and I'll go and see her too. I'll go this way and go you that, and we shall see who will be there first."

The wolf ran as fast as he could, taking the shortest path, and the little girl took a roundabout way, entertaining herself by gathering nuts, running after butterflies, and gathering bouquets of little flowers. It was not long before the wolf arrived at the old woman's house. He knocked at the door: tap, tap.

"Who's there?"

"Your grandchild, Little Red Riding Hood," replied the wolf, counterfeiting   10
her voice, "who has brought you a cake and a little pot of butter sent you by Mother."

The good grandmother, who was in bed because she was somewhat ill, cried out, "Pull the bobbin, and the latch will go up."

The wolf pulled the bobbin, and the door opened, and then he immediately fell upon the good woman and ate her up in a moment, for it had been more than three days since he had eaten. He then shut the door and got into the grandmother's bed, expecting Little Red Riding Hood, who came some time afterwards and knocked at the door: tap, tap.

"Who's there?"

Little Red Riding Hood, hearing the big voice of the wolf, was at first afraid but, believing her grandmother had a cold and was hoarse, answered, "It is your grandchild Little Red Riding Hood, who has brought you a cake and a little pot of butter Mother sends you."

The wolf cried out to her, softening his voice as much as he could, "Pull   15
the bobbin, and the latch will go up."

Little Red Riding Hood pulled the bobbin, and the door opened.

The wolf, seeing her come in, said to her, hiding himself under the bedclothes, "Put the cake and the little pot of butter upon the stool, and come get into bed with me."

Little Red Riding Hood took off her clothes and got into bed. She was greatly amazed to see how her grandmother looked in her nightclothes and said to her, "Grandmother, what big arms you have!"

"All the better to hug you with, my dear."

"Grandmother, what big legs you have!"   20

"All the better to run with, my child."

"Grandmother, what big ears you have!"

"All the better to hear with, my child."

"Grandmother, what big eyes you have!"

"All the better to see with, my child."   25

"Grandmother, what big teeth you have got!"

"All the better to eat you up with."

And saying these words, this wicked wolf fell upon Little Red Riding Hood, and ate her all up.

Moral: Children, especially attractive, well bred young ladies, should never talk to strangers, for if they should do so, they may well provide dinner for a wolf. I say "wolf," but there are various kinds of wolves. There are also those who are charming, quiet, polite, unassuming, complacent, and sweet, who pursue young women at home and in the streets. And unfortunately, it is these gentle wolves who are the most dangerous ones of all.   *[1697]*

≡ THINKING ABOUT THE TEXT

1. To what extent does it matter to the story that Little Red Riding Hood is pretty? Would your reaction be the same if you learned she was homely, or if you did not know how she looked? Explain.

2. The two main female characters are Little Red Riding Hood and her grandmother. Although the girl's mother appears briefly at the start, she then disappears from the narrative. What are Perrault's purposes by leaving her out?

3. How would you describe Little Red Riding Hood as Perrault depicts her? Refer to specific details of the text.

4. In this version, Little Red Riding Hood dies. Would you draw different ideas from the text if she had lived? If so, what?

5. Does Perrault's moral seem well connected to the preceding story? Why, or why not? What metaphoric wolves might this moral apply to?

JACOB AND WILHELM GRIMM
Little Red Cap

Jacob Grimm (1785–1863) and Wilhelm Grimm (1786–1859) were born in Hanau, Germany, and studied law at Marburg University. They served as linguistics professors at Göttingen University and made major contributions to the historical study of language. The Grimms began to collect folktales from various oral European traditions for their friends but later published their efforts for both children and adults. Their methods became a model for the scientific collection of folktales and folk songs. Today they are known best for their volume Children's and Household Tales, *which was first published in 1812 and went through six more editions, the last in 1857. Their book included their version of the Little Red Riding Hood story, although their title in English translation for it was "Little Red Cap."*

Once upon a time there was a sweet little girl. Everyone who saw her liked her, but most of all her grandmother, who did not know what to give the child next. Once she gave her a little cap made of red velvet. Because it suited her so well, and she wanted to wear it all the time, she came to be known as Little Red Cap.

One day her mother said to her, "Come Little Red Cap. Here is a piece of cake and a bottle of wine. Take them to your grandmother. She is sick and weak, and they will do her well. Mind your manners, and give her my greetings. Behave yourself on the way, and do not leave the path, or you might fall down and break the glass, and then there will be nothing for your grandmother. And when you enter her parlor, don't forget to say 'Good morning,' and don't peer into all the corners first."

"I'll do everything just right," said Little Red Cap, shaking her mother's hand.

The grandmother lived out in the woods, a half hour from the village. When Little Red Cap entered the woods, a wolf came up to her. She did not know what a wicked animal he was and was not afraid of him.

"Good day to you, Little Red Cap."

"Thank you, wolf."

"Where are you going so early, Little Red Cap?"

"To Grandmother's."

"And what are you carrying under your apron?"

5

"Grandmother is sick and weak, and I am taking her some cake and wine. 10
We baked yesterday, and they should be good for her and give her strength."

"Little Red Cap, just where does your grandmother live?"

"Her house is a good quarter hour from here in the woods, under the three
large oak trees. There's a hedge of hazel bushes there. You must know the
place," said Little Red Cap.

The wolf thought to himself, "Now that sweet young thing is a tasty bite
for me. She will taste even better than the old woman. You must be sly, and you
can catch them both."

He walked along a little while with Little Red Cap. Then he said, "Little Red
Cap, just look at the beautiful flowers that are all around us. Why don't you go
and take a look? And I don't believe you can hear how beautifully the birds are
singing. You are walking along as though you were on your way to school. It is
very beautiful in the woods."

Little Red Cap opened her eyes, and when she saw the sunbeams dancing 15
to and fro through the trees and how the ground was covered with beautiful
flowers, she thought, "If I take a fresh bouquet to Grandmother, she will be
very pleased. Anyway, it is still early, and I'll be home on time." And she ran
off the path into the woods looking for flowers. Each time she picked one, she
thought that she could see an even more beautiful one a little way off, and she
ran after it, going farther and farther into the woods. But the wolf ran straight
to the grandmother's house and knocked on the door.

"Who's there?"

"Little Red Cap. I'm bringing you some cake and wine. Open the door."

"Just press the latch," called out the grandmother. "I'm too weak to get up."

The wolf pressed the latch, and the door opened. He stepped inside, went
straight to the grandmother's bed, and ate her up. Then he put on her clothes,
put her cap on his head, got into her bed, and pulled the curtains shut.

Little Red Cap had run after the flowers. After she had gathered so 20
many that she could not carry any more, she remembered her grandmother
and then continued on her way to her house. She found, to her surprise,
that the door was open. She walked into the parlor, and everything looked so
strange that she thought, "Oh, my God, why am I so afraid? I usually like it at
Grandmother's."

She called out, "Good morning!" but received no answer.

Then she went to the bed and pulled back the curtains. Grandmother was
lying there with her cap pulled down over her face and looking very strange.

"Oh, Grandmother, what big ears you have!"

"All the better to hear you with."

"Oh, Grandmother, what big eyes you have!" 25

"All the better to see you with."

"Oh, Grandmother, what big hands you have!"

"All the better to grab you with!"

"Oh, Grandmother, what a horribly big mouth you have!"

"All the better to eat you with!" 30

The wolf had scarcely finished speaking when he jumped from the bed with a single leap and ate up poor Little Red Cap. As soon as the wolf had satisfied his desires, he climbed back into bed, fell asleep, and began to snore very loudly.

A huntsman was just passing by. He thought, "The old woman is snoring so loudly. You had better see if something is wrong with her."

He stepped into the parlor, and when he approached the bed, he saw the wolf lying there. "So here I find you, you old sinner," he said. "I have been hunting for you a long time."

He was about to aim his rifle when it occurred to him that the wolf might have eaten the grandmother and that she still might be rescued. So instead of shooting, he took a pair of scissors and began to cut open the wolf's belly. After a few cuts he saw the red cap shining through, and after a few more cuts the girl jumped out, crying, "Oh, I was so frightened! It was so dark inside the wolf's body!"

And then the grandmother came out as well, alive but hardly able to   35
breathe. Then Little Red Cap fetched some large stones. She filled the wolf's body with them, and when he woke up and tried to run away, the stones were so heavy that he immediately fell down dead.

The three of them were happy. The huntsman skinned the wolf and went home with the pelt. The grandmother ate the cake and drank the wine that Little Red Cap had brought. And Little Red Cap thought, "As long as I live, I will never leave the path and run off into the woods by myself if Mother tells me not to."

They also tell how Little Red Cap was taking some baked things to her grandmother another time, when another wolf spoke to her and wanted her to leave the path. But Little Red Cap took care and went straight to Grandmother's. She told her that she had seen the wolf and that he had wished her a good day but had stared at her in a wicked manner. "If we hadn't been on a public road, he would have eaten me up," she said.

"Come," said the grandmother. "Let's lock the door, so he can't get in."

Soon afterward the wolf knocked on the door and called out, "Open up, Grandmother. It's Little Red Cap, and I'm bringing you some baked things."

They remained silent and did not open the door. Gray-Head crept around   40
the house several times and finally jumped onto the roof. He wanted to wait until Little Red Cap went home that evening and then follow her and eat her up in the darkness. But the grandmother saw what he was up to. There was a large stone trough in front of the house.

"Fetch a bucket, Little Red Cap," she said to the child. "Yesterday I cooked some sausage. Carry the water that I boiled them with to the trough." Little Red Cap carried water until the large, large trough was clear full. The smell of sausage arose into the wolf's nose. He sniffed and looked down, stretching his neck so long that he could no longer hold himself, and he began to slide. He slid off the roof, fell into the trough, and drowned. And Little Red Cap returned home happily, and no one harmed her.   *[1857]*

≡ **THINKING ABOUT THE TEXT**

1. At the beginning of the tale, why do you think that the Grimms emphasize how sweet and likable Little Red Cap is?

2. To what extent do you blame Little Red Cap for being distracted by the beauty of nature? Explain your reasoning.

3. The Grimms have Little Red Cap and her grandmother rescued by a hunter. What would you say to someone who sees the Grimms as implying that women always need help from a man?

4. The wolf dies because Little Red Cap has filled his body with stones. Why do you think the Grimms did not have the huntsman simply shoot the wolf after freeing Little Red Cap and her grandmother?

5. Why do you think the Grimms added the second story? What is its effect?

≡ **MAKING COMPARISONS**

1. Does Little Red Riding Hood seem basically the same in both Perrault's version and the Grimms' version? Refer to specific details from both texts.

2. In Perrault's tale, the wolf persuades Little Red Riding Hood to take off her clothes and get into bed with him. In the Grimms' account, the wolf jumps up from the bed and eats her. How significant is this difference between the two versions?

3. In Perrault's version, Little Red Riding Hood and her grandmother die. In the Grimms' tale, on the other hand, they are rescued. Do you therefore see these two versions as putting forth different views of life? Explain.

ANGELA CARTER
The Company of Wolves

A native of Sussex, England, Angela Carter (1940–1991) worked in various genres, writing novels, short stories, screenplays, essays, and newspaper articles. Her fiction is most known for imaginatively refashioning classic tales of fantasy, including supernatural and gothic thrillers as well as fairy tales. Often, Carter rewrote these narratives from a distinctly female point of view, challenging what she saw as their patriarchal values and using them to explore the psychology of both genders. "The Company of Wolves," her version of the Little Red Riding Hood tale, was first published in the journal Bananas *in 1977. It then appeared in Carter's short-story volume* The Bloody Chamber *(1979) and was reprinted in* Burning Our Boats *(1995), a posthumous collection of all her stories. This tale also served as the basis for a 1984 film of the same title, which Carter wrote with director Neil Jordan.*

One beast and only one howls in the woods by night.

The wolf is carnivore incarnate, and he's as cunning as he is ferocious; once he's had a taste of flesh then nothing else will do.

At night, the eyes of wolves shine like candle flames, yellowish, reddish, but that is because the pupils of their eyes fatten on darkness and catch the light from your lantern to flash it back to you — red for danger; if a wolf's eyes reflect only moonlight, then they gleam a cold and unnatural green, a mineral, a piercing color. If the benighted traveler spies those luminous, terrible sequins stitched suddenly on the black thickets, then he knows he must run, if fear has not struck him stock-still.

But those eyes are all you will be able to glimpse of the forest assassins as they cluster invisibly round your smell of meat as you go through the wood unwisely late. They will be like shadows, they will be like wraiths, gray members of a congregation of nightmare; hark! his long, wavering howl . . . an aria of fear made audible.

The wolfsong is the sound of the rending you will suffer, in itself a   5
murdering.

It is winter and cold weather. In this region of mountain and forest, there is now nothing for the wolves to eat. Goats and sheep are locked up in the byre,° the deer departed for the remaining pasturage on the southern slopes — wolves grow lean and famished. There is so little flesh on them that you could count the starveling ribs through their pelts, if they gave you time before they pounced. Those slavering jaws; the lolling tongue; the rime of saliva on the grizzled chops — of all the teeming perils of the night and the forest, ghosts, hobgoblins, ogres that grill babies upon gridirons, witches that fatten their captives in cages for cannibal tables, the wolf is worst for he cannot listen to reason.

You are always in danger in the forest, where no people are. Step between the portals of the great pines where the shaggy branches tangle about you, trapping the unwary traveler in nets as if the vegetation itself were in a plot with the wolves who live there, as though the wicked trees go fishing on behalf of their friends — step between the gateposts of the forest with the greatest trepidation and infinite precautions, for if you stray from the path for one instant, the wolves will eat you. They are gray as famine, they are as unkind as plague.

The grave-eyed children of the sparse villages always carry knives with them when they go out to tend the little flocks of goats that provide the homesteads with acrid milk and rank, maggoty cheeses. Their knives are half as big as they are, the blades are sharpened daily.

But the wolves have ways of arriving at your own hearthside. We try and try but sometimes we cannot keep them out. There is no winter's night the cottager does not fear to see a lean, gray, famished snout questing under the door, and there was a woman once bitten in her own kitchen as she was straining the macaroni.

---

byre: Barn or shed.

Fear and flee the wolf; for, worst of all, the wolf may be more than   10
he seems.

There was a hunter once, near here, that trapped a wolf in a pit. This wolf had massacred the sheep and goats; eaten up a mad old man who used to live by himself in a hut halfway up the mountain and sing to Jesus all day; pounced on a girl looking after the sheep, but she made such a commotion that men came with rifles and scared him away and tried to track him into the forest but he was cunning and easily gave them the slip. So this hunter dug a pit and put a duck in it, for bait, all alive-oh; and he covered the pit with straw smeared with wolf dung. Quack, quack! went the duck and a wolf came slinking out of the forest, a big one, a heavy one, he weighed as much as a grown man, and the straw gave way beneath him — into the pit he tumbled. The hunter jumped down after him, slit his throat, cut off all his paws for a trophy.

And then no wolf at all lay in front of the hunter but the bloody trunk of a man, headless, footless, dying, dead.

A witch from up the valley once turned an entire wedding party into wolves because the groom had settled on another girl. She used to order them to visit her, at night, from spite, and they would sit and howl around her cottage for her, serenading her with their misery.

Not so very long ago, a young woman in our village married a man who vanished clean away on her wedding night. The bed was made with new sheets and the bride lay down in it; the groom said, he was going out to relieve himself, insisted on it, for the sake of decency, and she drew the coverlet up to her chin and she lay there. And she waited and she waited and then she waited again — surely he's been gone a long time? Until she jumps up in bed and shrieks to hear a howling, coming on the wind from the forest.

That long-drawn, wavering howl has, for all its fearful resonance, some   15
inherent sadness in it, as if the beasts would love to be less beastly if only they knew how and never cease to mourn their own condition. There is a vast melancholy in the canticles° of the wolves, melancholy infinite as the forest, endless as these long nights of winter and yet that ghastly sadness, that mourning for their own, irremediable appetites, can never move the heart for not one phrase in it hints at the possibility of redemption; grace could not come to the wolf from its own despair, only through some external mediator, so that, sometimes, the beast will look as if he half welcomes the knife that dispatches him.

The young woman's brothers searched the outhouses and the haystacks but never found any remains, so the sensible girl dried her eyes and found herself another husband not too shy to piss into a pot who spent the nights indoors. She gave him a pair of bonny babies and all went right as a trivet until, one freezing night, the night of the solstice, the hinge of the year when things do not fit together as well as they should, the longest night, her first good man came home again.

A great thump on the door announced him as she was stirring the soup for the father of her children, and she knew him the moment she lifted the

canticles: Songs or chants.

latch to him although it was years since she'd worn black for him and now he was in rags and his hair hung down his back and never saw a comb, alive with lice.

"Here I am again, missus," he said. "Get me my bowl of cabbage and be quick about it."

Then her second husband came in with wood for the fire and when the first one saw she'd slept with another man and, worse, clapped his red eyes on her little children who'd crept into the kitchen to see what all the din was about, he shouted: "I wish I were a wolf again, to teach this whore a lesson!" So a wolf he instantly became and tore off the eldest boy's left foot before he was chopped up with the hatchet they used for chopping logs. But when the wolf lay bleeding and gasping its last, the pelt peeled off again and he was just as he had been, years ago, when he ran away from his marriage bed, so that she wept and her second husband beat her.

They say there's an ointment the Devil gives you that turns you into a wolf   20
the minute you rub it on. Or that he was born feet first and had a wolf for his father and his torso is a man's but his legs and genitals are a wolf's. And he has a wolf's heart.

Seven years is a werewolf's natural span but if you burn his human clothing you condemn him to wolfishness for the rest of his life, so old wives hereabouts think it some protection to throw a hat or an apron at the werewolf, as if clothes made the man. Yet by the eyes, those phosphorescent eyes, you know him in all his shapes; the eyes alone unchanged by metamorphosis.

Before he can become a wolf, the lycanthrope° strips stark naked. If you spy a naked man among the pines, you must run as if the Devil were after you.

It is midwinter and the robin, the friend of man, sits on the handle of the gardener's spade and sings. It is the worst time in all the year for wolves, but this strong-minded child insists she will go off through the wood. She is quite sure the wild beasts cannot harm her although, well-warned, she lays a carving knife in the basket her mother has packed with cheeses. There is a bottle of harsh liquor distilled from brambles; a batch of flat oatcakes baked on the hearthstone; a pot or two of jam. The flaxen-haired girl will take these delicious gifts to a reclusive grandmother so old the burden of her years is crushing her to death. Granny lives two hours' trudge through the winter woods; the child wraps herself up in her thick shawl, draws it over her head. She steps into her stout wooden shoes; she is dressed and ready and it is Christmas Eve. The malign door of the solstice still swings upon its hinges, but she has been too much loved ever to feel scared.

Children do not stay young for long in this savage country. There are no toys for them to play with, so they work hard and grow wise, but this one, so pretty and the youngest of her family, a little late-comer, had been indulged by her mother and the grandmother who'd knitted her the red shawl that, today, has the ominous if brilliant look of blood on snow. Her breasts have just begun to swell; her

lycanthrope: Werewolf.

hair is like lint, so fair it hardly makes a shadow on her pale forehead; her cheeks are an emblematic scarlet and white and she has just started her woman's bleeding, the clock inside her that will strike, henceforward, once a month.

She stands and moves within the invisible pentacle° of her own virginity.   25
She is an unbroken egg; she is a sealed vessel; she has inside her a magic space the entrance to which is shut tight with a plug of membrane; she is a closed system; she does not know how to shiver. She has her knife and she is afraid of nothing.

Her father might forbid her, if he were home, but he is away in the forest, gathering wood, and her mother cannot deny her.

The forest closed upon her like a pair of jaws.

There is always something to look at in the forest, even in the middle of winter — the huddled mounds of birds, succumbed to the lethargy of the season, heaped on the creaking boughs and too forlorn to sing; the bright frills of the winter fungi on the blotched trunks of the trees; the cuneiform° slots of rabbits and deer, the herringbone tracks of the birds, a hare as lean as a rasher of bacon streaking across the path where the thin sunlight dapples the russet brakes of last year's bracken.

When she heard the freezing howl of a distant wolf, her practiced hand sprang to the handle of her knife, but she saw no sign of a wolf at all, nor of a naked man, neither, but then she heard a clattering among the brushwood and there sprang on to the path a fully clothed one, a very handsome young one, in the green coat and wide-awake hat of a hunter, laden with carcasses of game birds. She had her hand on her knife at the first rustle of twigs, but he laughed with a flash of white teeth when he saw her and made her a comic yet flattering little bow; she'd never seen such a fine fellow before, not among the rustic clowns of her native village. So on they went together, through the thickening light of the afternoon.

Soon they were laughing and joking like old friends. When he offered to   30
carry her basket, she gave it to him although her knife was in it because he told her his rifle would protect them. As the day darkened, it began to snow again; she felt the first flakes settle on her eyelashes, but now there was only half a mile to go and there would be a fire, and hot tea, and a welcome, a warm one, surely, for the dashing huntsman as well as for herself.

This young man had a remarkable object in his pocket. It was a compass. She looked at the little round glass face in the palm of his hand and watched the wavering needle with a vague wonder. He assured her this compass had taken him safely through the wood on his hunting trip because the needle always told him with perfect accuracy where the north was. She did not believe it; she knew she should never leave the path on the way through the wood or else she would be lost instantly. He laughed at her again; gleaming trails of spittle clung to his teeth. He said, if he plunged off the path into the forest that surrounded them, he could guarantee to arrive at her grandmother's house a good quarter of an hour before she did, plotting his way

pentacle: Five-pointed star; also called a pentagram.   **cuneiform:** Wedge-shaped.

through the undergrowth with his compass, while she trudged the long way, along the winding path.

I don't believe you. Besides, aren't you afraid of the wolves?

He only tapped the gleaming butt of his rifle and grinned.

Is it a bet? he asked her. Shall we make a game of it? What will you give me if I get to your grandmother's house before you?

What would you like? she asked disingenuously.   35

A kiss.

Commonplaces of a rustic seduction; she lowered her eyes and blushed.

He went through the undergrowth and took her basket with him but she forgot to be afraid of the beasts, although now the moon was rising, for she wanted to dawdle on her way to make sure the handsome gentleman would win his wager.

Grandmother's house stood by itself a little way out of the village. The freshly falling snow blew in eddies about the kitchen garden, and the young man stepped delicately up the snowy path to the door as if he were reluctant to get his feet wet, swinging his bundle of game and the girl's basket and humming a little tune to himself.

There is a faint trace of blood on his chin; he has been snacking on his catch.   40

He rapped upon the panels with his knuckles.

Aged and frail, granny is three-quarters succumbed to the mortality the ache in her bones promises her and almost ready to give in entirely. A boy came out from the village to build up her hearth for the night an hour ago and the kitchen crackles with busy firelight. She has her Bible for company, she is a pious old woman. She is propped up on several pillows in the bed set into the wall peasant-fashion, wrapped up in the patchwork quilt she made before she was married, more years ago than she cares to remember. Two china spaniels with liver-colored blotches on their coats and black noses sit on either side of the fireplace. There is a bright rug of woven rags on the pantiles. The grandfather clock ticks away her eroding time.

We keep the wolves outside by living well.

He rapped upon the panels with his hairy knuckles.

It is your granddaughter, he mimicked in a high soprano.   45

Lift up the latch and walk in, my darling.

You can tell them by their eyes, eyes of a beast of prey, nocturnal, devastating eyes as red as a wound; you can hurl your Bible at him and your apron after, granny, you thought that was a sure prophylactic against these infernal vermin . . . now call on Christ and his mother and all the angels in heaven to protect you but it won't do you any good.

His feral muzzle is sharp as a knife; he drops his golden burden of gnawed pheasant on the table and puts down your dear girl's basket, too. Oh, my God, what have you done with her?

Off with his disguise, that coat of forest-colored cloth, the hat with the feather tucked into the ribbon; his matted hair streams down his white shirt and she can see the lice moving in it. The sticks in the hearth shift and hiss; night and the forest has come into the kitchen with darkness tangled in its hair.

He strips off his shirt. His skin is the color and texture of vellum. A crisp   50
stripe of hair runs down his belly, his nipples are ripe and dark as poison fruit,
but he's so thin you could count the ribs under his skin if only he gave you
the time. He strips off his trousers and she can see how hairy his legs are. His
genitals, huge. Ah! huge.

The last thing the old lady saw in all this world was a young man, eyes like
cinders, naked as a stone, approaching her bed.

The wolf is carnivore incarnate.

When he had finished with her, he licked his chops and quickly dressed
himself again, until he was just as he had been when he came through her
door. He burned the inedible hair in the fireplace and wrapped the bones up
in a napkin that he hid away under the bed in the wooden chest in which
he found a clean pair of sheets. These he carefully put on the bed instead of
the tell-tale stained ones he stowed away in the laundry basket. He plumped
up the pillows and shook out the patchwork quilt, he picked up the Bible
from the floor, closed it and laid it on the table. All was as it had been before
except that grandmother was gone. The sticks twitched in the grate, the
clock ticked and the young man sat patiently, deceitfully beside the bed in
granny's nightcap.

Rat-a-tap-tap.

Who's there, he quavers in granny's antique falsetto.   55

Only your granddaughter.

So she came in, bringing with her a flurry of snow that melted in tears on
the tiles, and perhaps she was a little disappointed to see only her grandmother
sitting beside the fire. But then he flung off the blanket and sprang to the door,
pressing his back against it so that she could not get out again.

The girl looked round the room and saw there was not even the indentation of a head on the smooth cheek of the pillow and how, for the first time
she'd seen it so, the Bible lay closed on the table. The tick of the clock cracked
like a whip. She wanted her knife from her basket, but she did not dare reach
for it because his eyes were fixed upon her — huge eyes that now seemed to
shine with a unique, interior light, eyes the size of saucers, saucers full of
Greek fire, diabolic phosphorescence.

What big eyes you have.

All the better to see you with.   60

No trace at all of the old woman except for a tuft of white hair that had
caught in the bark of an unburned log. When the girl saw that, she knew she
was in danger of death.

Where is my grandmother?

There's nobody here but we two, my darling.

Now a great howling rose up all around them, near, very near, as close as
the kitchen garden, the howling of a multitude of wolves; she knew the worst
wolves are hairy on the inside and she shivered, in spite of the scarlet shawl
she pulled more closely round herself as if it could protect her although it was
as red as the blood she must spill.

Who has come to sing us carols, she said.   65

Those are the voices of my brothers, darling; I love the company of wolves. Look out of the window and you'll see them.

Snow half-caked the lattice and she opened it to look into the garden. It was a white night of moon and snow; the blizzard whirled round the gaunt, grey beasts who squatted on their haunches among the rows of winter cabbage, pointing their sharp snouts to the moon and howling as if their hearts would break. Ten wolves; twenty wolves—so many wolves she could not count them, howling in concert as if demented or deranged. Their eyes reflected the light from the kitchen and shone like a hundred candles.

It is very cold, poor things, she said; no wonder they howl so.

She closed the window on the wolves' threnody° and took off her scarlet shawl, the color of poppies, the color of sacrifices, the color of her menses, and, since her fear did her no good, she ceased to be afraid.

What shall I do with my shawl?   70

Throw it on the fire, dear one. You won't need it again.

She bundled up her shawl and threw it on the blaze, which instantly consumed it. Then she drew her blouse over her head; her small breasts gleamed as if the snow had invaded the room.

What shall I do with my blouse?

Into the fire with it, too, my pet.

The thin muslin went flaring up the chimney like a magic bird and now off   75
came her skirt, her woolen stockings, her shoes, and on to the fire they went, too, and were gone for good. The firelight shone through the edges of her skin; now she was clothed only in her untouched integument° of flesh. This dazzling, naked she combed out her hair with her fingers; her hair looked white as the snow outside. Then went directly to the man with red eyes in whose unkempt mane the lice moved; she stood up on tiptoe and unbuttoned the collar of his shirt.

What big arms you have.

All the better to hug you with.

Every wolf in the world now howled a prothalamion° outside the window as she freely gave the kiss she owed him.

What big teeth you have!

She saw how his jaw began to slaver and the room was full of the clamor   80
of the forest's Liebestod° but the wise child never flinched, even when he answered:

All the better to eat you with.

The girl burst out laughing; she knew she was nobody's meat. She laughed at him full in the face, she ripped off his shirt for him and flung it into the fire, in the fiery wake of her own discarded clothing. The flames danced like dead souls on Walpurgisnacht,° and the old bones under the bed set up a terrible clattering, but she did not pay them any heed.

---

threnody: Lament or dirge.   **integument:** Outer covering, such as animal skin or seed coat.   **prothalamion:** Wedding song.   **Liebestod:** Final aria in Richard Wagner's opera *Tristan und Isolde,* in which Isolde sings over Tristan's dead body and ultimately dies herself.   **Walpurgisnacht:** May Day eve, the medieval witches' sabbath.

Carnivore incarnate, only immaculate flesh appeases him.

She will lay his fearful head on her lap and she will pick out the lice from his pelt and perhaps she will put the lice into her mouth and eat them, as he will bid her, as she would do in a savage marriage ceremony.

The blizzard will die down.   85

The blizzard died down, leaving the mountains as randomly covered with snow as if a blind woman had thrown a sheet over them, the upper branches of the forest pines limed, creaking, swollen with the fall.

Snowlight, moonlight, a confusion of paw-prints.

All silent, all still.

Midnight; and the clock strikes. It is Christmas Day, the werewolves' birthday, the door of the solstice stands wide open; let them all sink through.

See! sweet and sound she sleeps in granny's bed, between the paws of the   90
tender wolf.   *[1977]*

≣ THINKING ABOUT THE TEXT

1. The story begins with a section about wolves before it gets to the Little Red Riding Hood narrative. What image of wolves does this prologue convey? What in particular seems the purpose of the extended anecdote about the wife with two husbands?

2. Point out various places where Carter diverges from the conventions of the fairy tale.

3. Do you find it surprising that the girl does not get to her grandmother's house first? Do you suspect that the girl is not so innocent?

4. Obviously this is not a story for children. What traditional ideas about females and sexuality is Carter revising?

5. What do you conclude about the girl from her behavior at the end of the story? To what extent is "savage marriage ceremony" (para. 84) indeed an apt term for what occurs?

≣ MAKING COMPARISONS

1. To what extent is Carter's image of wolves different from Perrault's and the Grimms'? Refer to details from all three texts.

2. Several critics have described Carter's versions of fairy tales as feminist. To what extent can this term be applied to Perrault's and the Grimms' narratives as well as to hers? Define what you mean by *feminist*.

3. Would you say Carter's writing style is more realistic than that of Perrault and the Grimms? Or is the term *realism* completely irrelevant in the case of fairy tales? Explain.

≡ WRITING ABOUT ISSUES

1. Choose one of these versions of the Little Red Riding Hood story, and write an essay in which you elaborate a moral that modern *adults* might learn from. Or write an essay in which you explain what an adolescent might learn from Carter's version.

2. Does Carter's version radically depart from Perrault's and the Grimms', or does it basically resemble them? Write an essay that addresses this question by focusing on Carter's story and one of the other two.

3. Write an essay explaining what you think you learned from a fairy tale or other fictional story that you heard as a child. If you want to contrast your thinking about the story now with your thinking about it then, do so. Feel free to compare the story you focus on with any of the versions of Little Red Riding Hood in this cluster.

4. Write your own version of the story of Little Red Riding Hood, and on a separate piece of paper write the moral you think should be drawn from your text. Then give your version to a classmate, and see if he or she can guess your moral.

TIM O'BRIEN, "The Things They Carried"

AMBROSE BIERCE, "An Occurrence at Owl Creek Bridge"

Perhaps no transition is as psychologically traumatic as the one soldiers endure as they move from home to the battlefield, from the familiar and comfortable to the strange and disturbingly dangerous environment of war. Traditional values must be suppressed to survive in a brutal and unforgiving landscape. It is not surprising that soldiers desperately want to hold onto memories of home, part real, part fantasy. To escape the terrors of war, they imagine their previous home life through rose-colored lenses. The transition is often slow, painful, and psychologically scarring. Tim O'Brien's classic war story focuses on the psychological journey Jimmy Cross undergoes from imagination and escape to reality and commitment. Peyton Farquhar, in Bierce's story, is deep in the horrors of war as the story opens. His only recourse is to lovingly remember his idyllic home and family. But will this be enough?

≡ BEFORE YOU READ

When under the stress of deadlines for papers and exams, do you sometimes daydream, fantasizing of adventure, romance, and escape? Is this an effective strategy? Explain. Do you feel guilty about such psychological maneuvers?

TIM O'BRIEN

The Things They Carried

A native of Minnesota, Tim O'Brien (b. 1946) was drafted after he graduated from Macalester College. Subsequently, he served in the Vietnam War, during which he received a Purple Heart. In one way or another, practically all of his fiction deals with the war, although he has been repeatedly ambiguous about how and when his work incorporates his own Vietnam experiences. O'Brien's novels include If I Die in a Combat Zone *(1973),* Going After Cacciato *(which won the National Book Award in 1978),* In the Lake of the Woods *(a 1994 book that touches on the massacre at My Lai),* Tomcat in Love *(1998), and* July, July *(2002). Originally published in* Esquire *magazine, the following story was reprinted in* The Best American Short Stories 1987. *It then appeared along with related stories by O'Brien in a 1990 book also titled* The Things They Carried.

First Lieutenant Jimmy Cross carried letters from a girl named Martha, a junior at Mount Sebastian College in New Jersey. They were not love letters, but Lieutenant Cross was hoping, so he kept them folded in plastic at the bottom of his rucksack. In the late afternoon, after a day's march, he would dig his fox-hole, wash his hands under a canteen, unwrap the letters, hold them with the tips of his fingers, and spend the last hour of light pretending. He would imagine romantic camping trips into the White Mountains in New Hampshire. He would sometimes taste the envelope flaps, knowing her tongue had been there. More than anything, he wanted Martha to love him as he loved her, but the letters were mostly chatty, elusive on the matter of love. She was a virgin, he was almost sure. She was an English major at Mount Sebastian, and she wrote beautifully about her professors and roommates and midterm exams, about her respect for Chaucer and her great affection for Virginia Woolf. She often quoted lines of poetry; she never mentioned the war, except to say, Jimmy, take care of yourself. The letters weighed ten ounces. They were signed "Love, Martha," but Lieutenant Cross understood that "Love" was only a way of signing and did not mean what he sometimes pretended it meant. At dusk, he would carefully return the letters to his rucksack. Slowly, a bit distracted, he would get up and move among his men, checking the perimeter, then at full dark he would return to his hole and watch the night and wonder if Martha was a virgin.

The things they carried were largely determined by necessity. Among the necessities or near necessities were P-38 can openers, pocket knives, heat tabs, wrist watches, dog tags, mosquito repellant, chewing gum, candy, cigarettes, salt tablets, packets of Kool-Aid, lighters, matches, sewing kits, Military Payment Certificates, C rations, and two or three canteens of water. Together, these items weighed between fifteen and twenty pounds, depending upon a man's habits or rate of metabolism. Henry Dobbins, who was a big man, carried extra rations; he was especially fond of canned peaches in heavy syrup over pound cake. Dave Jensen, who practiced field hygiene, carried a tooth-brush, dental floss, and several hotel-size bars of soap he'd stolen on R&R in Sydney, Australia. Ted Lavender, who was scared, carried tranquilizers until he was shot in the head outside the village of Than Khe in mid-April. By necessity and because it was SOP,° they all carried steel helmets that weighed five pounds including the liner and camouflage cover. They carried the standard fatigue jackets and trousers. Very few carried underwear. On their feet they carried jungle boots — 2.1 pounds — and Dave Jensen carried three pairs of socks and a can of Dr. Scholl's foot powder as a precaution against trench foot. Until he was shot, Ted Lavender carried six or seven ounces of premium dope, which for him was a necessity. Mitchell Sanders, the RTO,° carried condoms. Norman Bowker carried a diary. Rat Kiley carried comic books. Kiowa, a devout Baptist, carried an illustrated New Testament that had been presented to him by his father, who taught Sunday school in Oklahoma City, Oklahoma. As a hedge against bad times, however, Kiowa also carried his grandmother's distrust of the white man, his grandfather's old hunting hatchet. Necessity dictated. Because the land was mined and booby-trapped, it was SOP for each man to

---

SOP: Standard operating procedure.   **RTO:** Radiotelephone operator.

carry a steel-centered, nylon-covered flak jacket, which weighed 6.7 pounds, but which on hot days seemed much heavier. Because you could die so quickly, each man carried at least one large compress bandage, usually in the helmet band for easy access. Because the nights were cold, and because the monsoons were wet, each carried a green plastic poncho that could be used as a raincoat or ground sheet or makeshift tent. With its quilted liner, the poncho weighed almost two pounds, but it was worth every ounce. In April, for instance, when Ted Lavender was shot, they used his poncho to wrap him up, then to carry him across the paddy, then to lift him into the chopper that took him away.

They were called legs or grunts.

To carry something was to "hump" it, as when Lieutenant Jimmy Cross humped his love for Martha up the hills and through the swamps. In its intransitive form, "to hump" meant "to walk," or "to march," but it implied burdens far beyond the intransitive.

Almost everyone humped photographs. In his wallet, Lieutenant Cross   5
carried two photographs of Martha. The first was a Kodachrome snapshot signed "Love," though he knew better. She stood against a brick wall. Her eyes were gray and neutral, her lips slightly open as she stared straight-on at the camera. At night, sometimes, Lieutenant Cross wondered who had taken the picture, because he knew she had boyfriends, because he loved her so much, and because he could see the shadow of the picture taker spreading out against the brick wall. The second photograph had been clipped from the 1968 Mount Sebastian yearbook. It was an action shot — women's volleyball — and Martha was bent horizontal to the floor, reaching, the palms of her hands in sharp focus, the tongue taut, the expression frank and competitive. There was no visible sweat. She wore white gym shorts. Her legs, he thought, were almost certainly the legs of a virgin, dry and without hair, the left knee cocked and carrying her entire weight, which was just over one hundred pounds. Lieutenant Cross remembered touching that left knee. A dark theater, he remembered, and the movie was *Bonnie and Clyde*, and Martha wore a tweed skirt, and during the final scene, when he touched her knee, she turned and looked at him in a sad, sober way that made him pull his hand back, but he would always remember the feel of the tweed skirt and the knee beneath it and the sound of the gunfire that killed Bonnie and Clyde, how embarrassing it was, how slow and oppressive. He remembered kissing her good night at the dorm door. Right then, he thought, he should've done something brave. He should've carried her up the stairs to her room and tied her to the bed and touched that left knee all night long. He should've risked it. Whenever he looked at the photographs, he thought of new things he should've done.

What they carried was partly a function of rank, partly of field specialty.

As a first lieutenant and platoon leader, Jimmy Cross carried a compass, maps, code books, binoculars, and a .45-caliber pistol that weighed 2.9 pounds fully loaded. He carried a strobe light and the responsibility for the lives of his men.

As an RTO, Mitchell Sanders carried the PRC-25 radio, a killer, twenty-six pounds with its battery.

As a medic, Rat Kiley carried a canvas satchel filled with morphine and plasma and malaria tablets and surgical tape and comic books and all the things a medic must carry, including M&M's for especially bad wounds, for a total weight of nearly twenty pounds.

As a big man, therefore a machine gunner, Henry Dobbins carried the   10
M-60, which weighed twenty-three pounds unloaded, but which was almost always loaded. In addition, Dobbins carried between ten and fifteen pounds of ammunition draped in belts across his chest and shoulders.

As PFCs or Spec 4s, most of them were common grunts and carried the standard M-16 gas-operated assault rifle. The weapon weighed 7.5 pounds unloaded, 8.2 pounds with its full twenty-round magazine. Depending on numerous factors, such as topography and psychology, the riflemen carried anywhere from twelve to twenty magazines, usually in cloth bandoliers, adding on another 8.4 pounds at minimum, fourteen pounds at maximum. When it was available, they also carried M-16 maintenance gear — rods and steel brushes and swabs and tubes of LSA on — all of which weighed about a pound. Among the grunts, some carried the M-79 grenade launcher, 5.9 pounds unloaded, a reasonably light weapon except for the ammunition, which was heavy. A single round weighed ten ounces. The typical load was twenty-five rounds. But Ted Lavender, who was scared, carried thirty-four rounds when he was shot and killed outside Than Khe, and he went down under an exceptional burden, more than twenty pounds of ammunition, plus the flak jacket and helmet and rations and water and toilet paper and tranquilizers and all the rest, plus the unweighed fear. He was dead weight. There was no twitching or flopping. Kiowa, who saw it happen, said it was like watching a rock fall, or a big sandbag or something — just boom, then down — not like the movies where the dead guy rolls around and does fancy spins and goes ass over teakettle — not like that, Kiowa said, the poor bastard just flat-fuck fell Boom. Down. Nothing else. It was a bright morning in mid-April. Lieutenant Cross felt the pain. He blamed himself. They stripped off Lavender's canteens and ammo, all the heavy things, and Rat Kiley said the obvious, the guy's dead, and Mitchell Sanders used his radio to report one U.S. KIA° and to request a chopper. Then they wrapped Lavender in his poncho. They carried him out to a dry paddy, established security, and sat smoking the dead man's dope until the chopper came. Lieutenant Cross kept to himself. He pictured Martha's smooth young face, thinking he loved her more than anything, more than his men, and now Ted Lavender was dead because he loved her so much and could not stop thinking about her. When the dust-off arrived, they carried Lavender aboard. Afterward they burned Than Khe. They marched until dusk, then dug their holes, and that night Kiowa kept explaining how you had to be there, how fast it was, how the poor guy just dropped like so much concrete. Boom-down, he said. Like cement.

KIA: Killed in action.

*   *   *

In addition to the three standard weapons — the M-60, M-16, and M-79 — they carried whatever presented itself, or whatever seemed appropriate as a means of killing or staying alive. They carried catch-as-catch-can. At various times, in various situations, they carried M-14s and CAR-15s and Swedish Ks and grease guns and captured AK-47s and Chi-Coms and RPGs and Simonov carbines and black-market Uzis and .38-caliber Smith & Wesson handguns and 66 mm LAWs and shotguns and silencers and blackjacks and bayonets and C-4 plastic explosives. Lee Strunk carried a slingshot; a weapon of last resort, he called it. Mitchell Sanders carried brass knuckles. Kiowa carried his grandfather's feathered hatchet. Every third or fourth man carried a Claymore antipersonnel mine — 3.5 pounds with its firing device. They all carried fragmentation grenades — fourteen ounces each. They all carried at least one M-18 colored smoke grenade — twenty-four ounces. Some carried CS or tear-gas grenades. Some carried white-phosphorus grenades. They carried all they could bear, and then some, including a silent awe for the terrible power of the things they carried.

In the first week of April, before Lavender died, Lieutenant Jimmy Cross received a good-luck charm from Martha. It was a simple pebble, an ounce at most. Smooth to the touch, it was a milky-white color with flecks of orange and violet, oval-shaped, like a miniature egg. In the accompanying letter, Martha wrote that she had found the pebble on the Jersey shoreline, precisely where the land touched water at high tide, where things came together but also separated. It was this separate-but-together quality, she wrote, that had inspired her to pick up the pebble and to carry it in her breast pocket for several days, where it seemed weightless, and then to send it through the mail, by air, as a token of her truest feelings for him. Lieutenant Cross found this romantic. But he wondered what her truest feelings were, exactly, and what she meant by separate-but-together. He wondered how the tides and waves had come into play on that afternoon along the Jersey shoreline when Martha saw the pebble and bent down to rescue it from geology. He imagined bare feet. Martha was a poet, with the poet's sensibilities, and her feet would be brown and bare, the toenails unpainted, the eyes chilly and somber like the ocean in March, and though it was painful, he wondered who had been with her that afternoon. He imagined a pair of shadows moving along the strip of sand where things came together but also separated. It was phantom jealousy, he knew, but he couldn't help himself. He loved her so much. On the march, through the hot days of early April, he carried the pebble in his mouth, turning it with his tongue, tasting sea salts and moisture. His mind wandered. He had difficulty keeping his attention on the war. On occasion he would yell at his men to spread out the column, to keep their eyes open, but then he would slip away into daydreams, just pretending, walking barefoot along the Jersey shore, with Martha, carrying nothing. He would feel himself rising. Sun and waves and gentle winds, all love and lightness.

What they carried varied by mission.

When a mission took them to the mountains, they carried mosquito netting, machetes, canvas tarps, and extra bug juice.   15

If a mission seemed especially hazardous, or if it involved a place they knew to be bad, they carried everything they could. In certain heavily mined AOs,° where the land was dense with Toe Poppers and Bouncing Betties, they took turns humping a twenty-eight-pound mine detector. With its headphones and big sensing plate, the equipment was a stress on the lower back and shoulders, awkward to handle, often useless because of the shrapnel in the earth, but they carried it anyway, partly for safety, partly for the illusion of safety.

On ambush, or other night missions, they carried peculiar little odds and ends. Kiowa always took along his New Testament and a pair of moccasins for silence. Dave Jensen carried night-sight vitamins high in carotin. Lee Strunk carried his slingshot; ammo, he claimed, would never be a problem. Rat Kiley carried brandy and M&M's. Until he was shot, Ted Lavender carried the star-light scope, which weighed 6.3 pounds with its aluminum carrying case. Henry Dobbins carried his girlfriend's pantyhose wrapped around his neck as a comforter. They all carried ghosts. When dark came, they would move out single file across the meadows and paddies to their ambush coordinates, where they would quietly set up the Claymores and lie down and spend the night waiting.

Other missions were more complicated and required special equipment. In mid-April, it was their mission to search out and destroy the elaborate tunnel complexes in the Than Khe area south of Chu Lai. To blow the tunnels, they carried one-pound blocks of pentrite high explosives, four blocks to a man, sixty-eight pounds in all. They carried wiring, detonators, and battery-powered clackers. Dave Jensen carried earplugs. Most often, before blowing the tunnels, they were ordered by higher command to search them, which was considered bad news, but by and large they just shrugged and carried out orders. Because he was a big man, Henry Dobbins was excused from tunnel duty. The others would draw numbers. Before Lavender died there were seventeen men in the platoon, and whoever drew the number seventeen would strip off his gear and crawl in head first with a flashlight and Lieutenant Cross's .45-caliber pistol. The rest of them would fan out as security. They would sit down or kneel, not facing the hole, listening to the ground beneath them, imagining cobwebs and ghosts, whatever was down there — the tunnel walls squeezing in — how the flashlight seemed impossibly heavy in the hand and how it was tunnel vision in the very strictest sense, compression in all ways, even time, and how you had to wiggle in — ass and elbows — a swallowed-up feeling — and how you found yourself worrying about odd things — will your flashlight go dead? Do rats carry rabies? If you screamed, how far would the sound carry? Would your buddies hear it? Would they have the courage to drag you out? In some respects, though not many, the waiting was worse than the tunnel itself. Imagination was a killer.

On April 16, when Lee Strunk drew the number seventeen, he laughed and muttered something and went down quickly. The morning was hot and very still. Not good, Kiowa said. He looked at the tunnel opening, then out across a dry paddy toward the village of Than Khe. Nothing moved. No clouds

AOs: Areas of operations.

or birds or people. As they waited, the men smoked and drank Kool-Aid, not talking much, feeling sympathy for Lee Strunk but also feeling the luck of the draw. You win some, you lose some, said Mitchell Sanders, and sometimes you settle for a rain check. It was a tired line and no one laughed.

Henry Dobbins ate a tropical chocolate bar. Ted Lavender popped a tranquilizer and went off to pee.   20

After five minutes, Lieutenant Jimmy Cross moved to the tunnel, leaned down, and examined the darkness. Trouble, he thought—a cave-in maybe. And then suddenly, without willing it, he was thinking about Martha. The stresses and fractures, the quick collapse, the two of them buried alive under all that weight. Dense, crushing love. Kneeling, watching the hole, he tried to concentrate on Lee Strunk and the war, all the dangers, but his love was too much for him, he felt paralyzed, he wanted to sleep inside her lungs and breathe her blood and be smothered. He wanted her to be a virgin and not a virgin, all at once. He wanted to know her. Intimate secrets—why poetry? Why so sad? Why the grayness in her eyes? Why so alone? Not lonely, just alone—riding her bike across campus or sitting off by herself in the cafeteria. Even dancing, she danced alone—and it was the aloneness that filled him with love. He remembered telling her that one evening. How she nodded and looked away. And how, later, when he kissed her, she received the kiss without returning it, her eyes wide open, not afraid, not a virgin's eyes, just flat and uninvolved.

Lieutenant Cross gazed at the tunnel. But he was not there. He was buried with Martha under the white sand at the Jersey shore. They were pressed together, and the pebble in his mouth was her tongue. He was smiling. Vaguely, he was aware of how quiet the day was, the sullen paddies, yet he could not bring himself to worry about matters of security. He was beyond that. He was just a kid at war, in love. He was twenty-two years old. He couldn't help it.

A few moments later Lee Strunk crawled out of the tunnel. He came up grinning, filthy but alive. Lieutenant Cross nodded and closed his eyes while the others clapped Strunk on the back and made jokes about rising from the dead.

Worms, Rat Kiley said. Right out of the grave. Fuckin' zombie.

The men laughed. They all felt great relief.   25

Spook City, said Mitchell Sanders.

Lee Strunk made a funny ghost sound, a kind of moaning, yet very happy, and right then, when Strunk made that high happy moaning sound, when he went *Ahhooooo*, right then Ted Lavender was shot in the head on his way back from peeing. He lay with his mouth open. The teeth were broken. There was a swollen black bruise under his left eye. The cheekbone was gone. Oh shit, Rat Kiley said, the guy's dead. The guy's dead, he kept saying, which seemed profound—the guy's dead. I mean really.

The things they carried were determined to some extent by superstition. Lieutenant Cross carried his good-luck pebble. Dave Jensen carried a rabbit's foot. Norman Bowker, otherwise a very gentle person, carried a thumb that had been presented to him as a gift by Mitchell Sanders. The thumb was dark brown, rubbery to the touch, and weighed four ounces at most. It had been cut from a VC corpse, a boy of fifteen or sixteen. They'd found him at the bottom of an irrigation ditch, badly burned, flies in his mouth and eyes. The boy wore black shorts and sandals. At the time of his death he had been carrying a pouch of rice, a rifle, and three magazines of ammunition.

You want my opinion, Mitchell Sanders said, there's a definite moral here.

He put his hand on the dead boy's wrist. He was quiet for a time, as if   30
counting a pulse, then he patted the stomach, almost affectionately, and used Kiowa's hunting hatchet to remove the thumb.

Henry Dobbins asked what the moral was.

Moral?

You know. *Moral.*

Sanders wrapped the thumb in toilet paper and handed it across to Norman Bowker. There was no blood. Smiling, he kicked the boy's head, watched the flies scatter, and said, It's like with that old TV show — Paladin. Have gun, will travel.

Henry Dobbins thought about it.   35

Yeah, well, he finally said. I don't see no moral.

There it *is*, man.

Fuck off.

They carried USO stationery and pencils and pens. They carried Sterno, safety pins, trip flares, signal flares, spools of wire, razor blades, chewing tobacco, liberated joss sticks and statuettes of the smiling Buddha, candles, grease pencils, *The Stars and Stripes*, fingernail clippers, Psy Ops° leaflets, bush hats, bolos, and much more. Twice a week, when the resupply choppers came in, they carried hot chow in green Mermite cans and large canvas bags filled with iced beer and soda pop. They carried plastic water containers, each with a two-gallon capacity. Mitchell Sanders carried a set of starched tiger fatigues for special occasions. Henry Dobbins carried Black Flag insecticide. Dave Jensen carried empty sandbags that could be filled at night for added protection. Lee Strunk carried tanning lotion. Some things they carried in common. Taking turns, they carried the big PRC-77 scrambler radio, which weighed thirty pounds with its battery. They shared the weight of memory. They took up what others could no longer bear. Often, they carried each other, the wounded or weak. They carried infections. They carried chess sets, basketballs, Vietnamese-English dictionaries, insignia of rank, Bronze Stars and Purple Hearts, plastic cards imprinted with the Code of Conduct. They carried diseases, among them malaria and dysentery. They carried lice and ringworm and leeches and paddy algae and various rots and molds. They carried the land itself — Vietnam, the place, the soil — a powdery orange-red dust that covered their boots and fatigues and faces. They carried the sky. The whole atmosphere, they carried it, the humidity, the monsoons, the stink of fungus and decay, all of it, they carried gravity. They moved like mules. By daylight

Psy Ops: Psychological operations.

they took sniper fire, at night they were mortared, but it was not battle, it was just the endless march, village to village, without purpose, nothing won or lost. They marched for the sake of the march. They plodded along slowly, dumbly, leaning forward against the heat, unthinking, all blood and bone, simple grunts, soldiering with their legs, toiling up the hills and down into the paddies and across the rivers and up again and down, just humping, one step and then the next and then another, but no volition, no will, because it was automatic, it was anatomy, and the war was entirely a matter of posture and carriage, the hump was everything, a kind of inertia, a kind of emptiness, a dullness of desire and intellect and conscience and hope and human sensibility. Their principles were in their feet. Their calculations were biological. They had no sense of strategy or mission. They searched the villages without knowing what to look for, not caring, kicking over jars of rice, frisking children and old men, blowing tunnels, sometimes setting fires and sometimes not, then forming up and moving on to the next village, then other villages, where it would always be the same. They carried their own lives. The pressures were enormous. In the heat of early afternoon, they would remove their helmets and flak jackets, walking bare, which was dangerous but which helped ease the strain. They would often discard things along the route of march. Purely for comfort, they would throw away rations, blow their Claymores and grenades, no matter, because by nightfall the resupply choppers would arrive with more of the same, then a day or two later still more, fresh watermelons and crates of ammunition and sunglasses and woolen sweaters — the resources were stunning — sparklers for the Fourth of July, colored eggs for Easter. It was the great American war chest — the fruits of science, the smokestacks, the canneries, the arsenals at Hartford, the Minnesota forests, the machine shops, the vast fields of corn and wheat — they carried like freight trains, they carried it on their backs and shoulders — and for all the ambiguities of Vietnam, all the mysteries and unknowns, there was at least the single abiding certainty that they would never be at a loss for things to carry.

After the chopper took Lavender away, Lieutenant Jimmy Cross led his men   40
into the village of Than Khe. They burned everything. They shot chickens and dogs, they trashed the village well, they called in artillery and watched the wreckage, then they marched for several hours through the hot afternoon, and then at dusk, while Kiowa explained how Lavender died, Lieutenant Cross found himself trembling.

He tried not to cry. With his entrenching tool, which weighed five pounds, he began digging a hole in the earth.

He felt shame. He hated himself. He had loved Martha more than his men, and as a consequence Lavender was now dead, and this was something he would have to carry like a stone in his stomach for the rest of the war.

All he could do was dig. He used his entrenching tool like an ax, slashing, feeling both love and hate, and then later, when it was full dark, he sat at the bottom of his foxhole and wept. It went on for a long while. In part, he was grieving for Ted Lavender, but mostly it was for Martha, and for himself, because she belonged to another world, which was not quite real, and because she was a junior at Mount Sebastian College in New Jersey, a poet and a virgin and uninvolved, and because he realized she did not love him and never would.

Like cement, Kiowa whispered in the dark. I swear to God—boom-down. Not a word.

I've heard this, said Norman Bowker.   45

A pisser, you know? Still zipping himself up. Zapped while zipping.

All right, fine. That's enough.

Yeah, but you had to see it, the guy just—

I *heard*, man. Cement. So why not shut the fuck *up?*

Kiowa shook his head sadly and glanced over at the hole where Lieutenant   50
Jimmy Cross sat watching the night. The air was thick and wet. A warm, dense fog had settled over the paddies and there was the stillness that precedes rain.

After a time Kiowa sighed.

One thing for sure, he said. The Lieutenant's in some deep hurt. I mean that crying jag—the way he was carrying on—it wasn't fake or anything, it was real heavy-duty hurt. The man cares.

Sure, Norman Bowker said.

Say what you want, the man does care.

We all got problems.   55

Not Lavender.

No, I guess not, Bowker said. Do me a favor, though.

Shut up?

That's a smart Indian. Shut up.

Shrugging, Kiowa pulled off his boots. He wanted to say more, just to   60
lighten up his sleep, but instead he opened his New Testament and arranged it beneath his head as a pillow. The fog made things seem hollow and unattached. He tried not to think about Ted Lavender, but then he was thinking how fast it was, no drama, down and dead, and how it was hard to feel anything except surprise. It seemed un-Christian. He wished he could find some great sadness, or even anger, but the emotion wasn't there and he couldn't make it happen. Mostly he felt pleased to be alive. He liked the smell of the New Testament under his cheek, the leather and ink and paper and glue, whatever the chemicals were. He liked hearing the sounds of night. Even his fatigue, it felt fine, the stiff muscles and the prickly awareness of his own body, a floating feeling. He enjoyed not being dead. Lying there, Kiowa admired Lieutenant Jimmy Cross's capacity for grief. He wanted to share the man's pain, he wanted to care as Jimmy Cross cared. And yet when he closed his eyes, all he could think was Boom-down, and all he could feel was the pleasure of having his boots off and the fog curling in around him and the damp soil and the Bible smells and the plush comfort of night.

After a moment Norman Bowker sat up in the dark.

What the hell, he said. You want to talk, *talk*. Tell it to me.

Forget it.

No, man, go on. One thing I hate, it's a silent Indian.

For the most part they carried themselves with poise, a kind of dignity. Now 65
and then, however, there were times of panic, when they squealed or wanted
to squeal but couldn't, when they twitched and made moaning sounds and
covered their heads and said Dear Jesus and flopped around on the earth and
fired their weapons blindly and cringed and sobbed and begged for the noise
to stop and went wild and made stupid promises to themselves and to God
and to their mothers and fathers, hoping not to die. In different ways, it happened to all of them. Afterward, when the firing ended, they would blink and
peek up. They would touch their bodies, feeling shame, then quickly hiding it.
They would force themselves to stand. As if in slow motion, frame by frame,
the world would take on the old logic — absolute silence, then the wind, then
sunlight, then voices. It was the burden of being alive. Awkwardly, the men
would reassemble themselves, first in private, then in groups, becoming soldiers again. They would repair the leaks in their eyes. They would check for
casualties, call in dust-offs, light cigarettes, try to smile, clear their throats and
spit and begin cleaning their weapons. After a time someone would shake his
head and say, No lie, I almost shit my pants, and someone else would laugh,
which meant it was bad, yes, but the guy had obviously not shit his pants, it
wasn't that bad, and in any case nobody would ever do such a thing and then
go ahead and talk about it. They would squint into the dense, oppressive sunlight. For a few moments, perhaps, they would fall silent, lighting a joint and
tracking its passage from man to man, inhaling, holding in the humiliation.
Scary stuff, one of them might say. But then someone else would grin or flick
his eyebrows and say, Roger-dodger, almost cut me a new asshole, *almost.*

There were numerous such poses. Some carried themselves with a sort of
wistful resignation, others with pride or stiff soldierly discipline or good humor
or macho zeal. They were afraid of dying but they were even more afraid to
show it.

They found jokes to tell.

They used a hard vocabulary to contain the terrible softness. *Greased,* they'd
say. *Offed, lit up, zapped while zipping.* It wasn't cruelty, just stage presence. They
were actors and the war came at them in 3-D. When someone died, it wasn't
quite dying, because in a curious way it seemed scripted, and because they had
their lines mostly memorized, irony mixed with tragedy, and because they called
it by other names, as if to encyst and destroy the reality of death itself. They
kicked corpses. They cut off thumbs. They talked grunt lingo. They told stories
about Ted Lavender's supply of tranquilizers, how the poor guy didn't feel a
thing, how incredibly tranquil he was.

There's a moral here, said Mitchell Sanders.

They were waiting for Lavender's chopper, smoking the dead man's dope. 70

The moral's pretty obvious, Sanders said, and winked. Stay away from
drugs. No joke, they'll ruin your day every time.

Cute, said Henry Dobbins.

Mind-blower, get it? Talk about wiggy — nothing left, just blood and brains. They made themselves laugh.

There it is, they'd say, over and over, as if the repetition itself were an act   75 of poise, a balance between crazy and almost crazy, knowing without going. There it is, which meant be cool, let it ride, because oh yeah, man, you can't change what can't be changed, there it is, there it absolutely and positively and fucking well *is*.

They were tough.

They carried all the emotional baggage of men who might die. Grief, terror, love, longing — these were intangibles, but the intangibles had their own mass and specific gravity, they had tangible weight. They carried shameful memories. They carried the common secret of cowardice barely restrained, the instinct to run or freeze or hide, and in many respects this was the heaviest burden of all, for it could never be put down, it required perfect balance and perfect posture. They carried their reputations. They carried the soldier's greatest fear, which was the fear of blushing. Men killed, and died, because they were embarrassed not to. It was what had brought them to the war in the first place, nothing positive, no dreams of glory or honor, just to avoid the blush of dishonor. They died so as not to die of embarrassment. They crawled into tunnels and walked point and advanced under fire. Each morning, despite the unknowns, they made their legs move. They endured. They kept humping. They did not submit to the obvious alternative, which was simply to close the eyes and fall. So easy, really. Go limp and tumble to the ground and let the muscles unwind and not speak and not budge until your buddies picked you up and lifted you into the chopper that would roar and dip its nose and carry you off to the world. A mere matter of falling, yet no one ever fell. It was not courage, exactly; the object was not valor. Rather, they were too frightened to be cowards.

By and large they carried these things inside, maintaining the masks of composure. They sneered at sick call. They spoke bitterly about guys who had found release by shooting off their own toes or fingers. Pussies, they'd say. Candyasses. It was fierce, mocking talk, with only a trace of envy or awe, but even so, the image played itself out behind their eyes.

They imagined the muzzle against flesh. They imagined the quick, sweet pain, then the evacuation to Japan, then a hospital with warm beds and cute geisha nurses.

They dreamed of freedom birds.   80

At night, on guard, staring into the dark, they were carried away by jumbo jets. They felt the rush of takeoff. *Gone!* they yelled. And then velocity, wings and engines, a smiling stewardess — but it was more than a plane, it was a real bird, a big sleek silver bird with feathers and talons and high screeching. They were flying. The weights fell off, there was nothing to bear. They laughed and held on tight, feeling the cold slap of wind and altitude, soaring, thinking *It's over, I'm gone!* — they were naked, they were light and free — it was all lightness, bright and fast and buoyant, light as light, a helium buzz in the brain, a giddy bubbling in the lungs as they were taken up over the clouds and the war, beyond duty, beyond gravity and mortification and global entanglements—*Sin loi!°* they yelled, *I'm sorry, motherfuckers, but I'm out of it. I'm goofed, I'm on a space cruise, I'm gone!*—and it was a restful, disencumbered sensation, just riding the light waves, sailing that big silver freedom bird over the mountains and oceans, over America, over the farms and great sleeping cities and cemeteries and highways and the golden arches of McDonald's. It was flight, a kind of fleeing, a kind of falling, falling higher and higher, spinning off the edge of the earth and beyond the sun and through the vast, silent vacuum where there were no burdens and where everything weighed exactly nothing. *Gone!* they screamed, *I'm sorry but I'm gone!* And so at night, not quite dreaming, they gave themselves over to lightness, they were carried, they were purely borne.

On the morning after Ted Lavender died, First Lieutenant Jimmy Cross crouched at the bottom of his foxhole and burned Martha's letters. Then he burned the two photographs. There was a steady rain falling, which made it difficult, but he used heat tabs and Sterno to build a small fire, screening it with his body, holding the photographs over the tight blue flame with the tips of his fingers.

He realized it was only a gesture. Stupid, he thought. Sentimental, too, but mostly just stupid.

Lavender was dead. You couldn't burn the blame.

Besides, the letters were in his head. And even now, without photographs,   85
Lieutenant Cross could see Martha playing volleyball in her white gym shorts and yellow T-shirt. He could see her moving in the rain.

When the fire died out, Lieutenant Cross pulled his poncho over his shoulders and ate breakfast from a can.

There was no great mystery, he decided.

In those burned letters Martha had never mentioned the war, except to say, Jimmy, take care of yourself. She wasn't involved. She signed the letters "Love," but it wasn't love, and all the fine lines and technicalities did not matter.

The morning came up wet and blurry. Everything seemed part of everything else, the fog and Martha and the deepening rain.

It was a war, after all.   90

Half smiling, Lieutenant Jimmy Cross took out his maps. He shook his head hard, as if to clear it, then bent forward and began planning the day's march. In ten minutes, or maybe twenty, he would rouse the men and they would pack up and head west, where the maps showed the country to be green and inviting. They would do what they had always done. The rain might add some weight, but otherwise it would be one more day layered upon all the other days.

He was realistic about it. There was that new hardness in his stomach.

No more fantasies, he told himself.

Henceforth, when he thought about Martha, it would be only to think that she belonged elsewhere. He would shut down the day dreams. This was

---

Sin loi!: "Sorry about that."

not Mount Sebastian, it was another world, where there were no pretty poems or midterm exams, a place where men died because of carelessness and gross stupidity. Kiowa was right. Boom-down, and you were dead, never partly dead.

Briefly, in the rain, Lieutenant Cross saw Martha's gray eyes gazing back   95
at him.

He understood.

It was very sad, he thought. The things men carried inside. The things men did or felt they had to do.

He almost nodded at her, but didn't.

Instead he went back to his maps. He was now determined to perform his duties firmly and without negligence. It wouldn't help Lavender, he knew that, but from this point on he would comport himself as a soldier. He would dispose of his good-luck pebble. Swallow it, maybe, or use Lee Strunk's slingshot, or just drop it along the trail. On the march he would impose strict field discipline. He would be careful to send out flank security, to prevent straggling or bunching up, to keep his troops moving at the proper pace and at the proper interval. He would insist on clean weapons. He would confiscate the remainder of Lavender's dope. Later in the day, perhaps, he would call the men together and speak to them plainly. He would accept the blame for what had happened to Ted Lavender. He would be a man about it. He would look them in the eyes, keeping his chin level, and he would issue the new SOPs in a calm, impersonal tone of voice, an officer's voice, leaving no room for argument or discussion. Commencing immediately, he'd tell them, they would no longer abandon equipment along the route of march. They would police up their acts. They would get their shit together, and keep it together, and maintain it neatly and in good working order.

He would not tolerate laxity. He would show strength, distancing himself.   100

Among the men there would be grumbling, of course, and maybe worse, because their days would seem longer and their loads heavier, but Lieutenant Cross reminded himself that his obligation was not to be loved but to lead. He would dispense with love; it was not now a factor. And if anyone quarreled or complained, he would simply tighten his lips and arrange his shoulders in the correct command posture. He might give a curt little nod. Or he might not. He might just shrug and say Carry on, then they would saddle up and form into a column and move out toward the villages of Than Khe.   *[1986]*

≣ THINKING ABOUT THE TEXT

1. What specific psychological and emotional "things" do the soldiers carry into battle? Did any of these surprise you? Explain.

2. In three or four sentences, how would you describe the experience of war, using this story as a basis?

3. What are some significant differences, if any, among the soldiers under Jimmy Cross's command?

4. What is your attitude toward Jimmy Cross's apparent obsession with Martha?

5. Jimmy Cross seems to feel guilty about Ted Lavender's death. To
what extent does his feeling seem rational? *Should* he feel guilty, in
your view? Why, or why not? In the final two paragraphs, he makes a
number of resolutions. Which, if any, do you think that he is capable
of keeping?

AMBROSE BIERCE

An Occurrence at Owl Creek Bridge

*Ambrose Bierce (1842–1914) was a journalist, short story writer, and satirist.
He was born into a large family in Ohio, leaving home at fifteen to work at an Ohio
newspaper. He fought in the Civil War, an experience that deeply affected his fiction,
including the story printed here. He worked as a journalist in San Francisco, where
he became a prominent and influential editor and writer, known for his distinctive
style and biting wit. One of his most famous works is* The Devil's Dictionary, *a
satire of cant and political double talk. Around 1914, he vanished in Mexico while
reporting on Pancho Villa's army. This story was originally published in the* San
Francisco Examiner *in 1890. Kurt Vonnegut thought the story "the greatest
American short story."*

I

A man stood upon a railroad bridge in Northern Alabama, looking down into
the swift waters twenty feet below. The man's hands were behind his back, the
wrists bound with a cord. A rope loosely encircled his neck. It was attached to
a stout cross-timber above his head, and the slack fell to the level of his knees.
Some loose boards laid upon the sleepers supporting the metals of the railway
supplied a footing for him and his executioners — two private soldiers of the
Federal army, directed by a sergeant, who in civil life may have been a deputy
sheriff. At a short remove upon the same temporary platform was an officer
in the uniform of his rank, armed. He was a captain. A sentinel at each end
of the bridge stood with his rifle in the position known as "support," that is to
say, vertical in front of the left shoulder, the hammer resting on the forearm
thrown straight across the chest — a formal and unnatural position, enforcing
an erect carriage of the body. It did not appear to be the duty of these two men
to know what was occurring at the centre of the bridge; they merely block-
aded the two ends of the foot plank which traversed it.

Beyond one of the sentinels nobody was in sight; the railroad ran straight
away into a forest for a hundred yards, then, curving, was lost to view. Doubtless there was an outpost further along. The other bank of the stream was
open ground — a gentle acclivity crowned with a stockade of vertical tree
trunks, loop-holed for rifles, with a single embrasure through which protruded
the muzzle of a brass cannon commanding the bridge. Midway of the slope

between bridge and fort were the spectators — a single company of infantry in line, at "parade rest," the butts of the rifles on the ground, the barrels inclining slightly backward against the right shoulder, the hands crossed upon the stock. A lieutenant stood at the right of the line, the point of his sword upon the ground, his left hand resting upon his right. Excepting the group of four at the centre of the bridge not a man moved. The company faced the bridge, staring stonily, motionless. The sentinels, facing the banks of the stream, might have been statues to adorn the bridge. The captain stood with folded arms, silent, observing the work of his subordinates but making no sign. Death is a dignitary who, when he comes announced, is to be received with formal manifestations of respect, even by those most familiar with him. In the code of military etiquette silence and fixity are forms of deference.

The man who was engaged in being hanged was apparently about thirty-five years of age. He was a civilian, if one might judge from his dress, which was that of a planter. His features were good — a straight nose, firm mouth, broad forehead, from which his long, dark hair was combed straight back, falling behind his ears to the collar of his well-fitted frock coat. He wore a moustache and pointed beard, but no whiskers; his eyes were large and dark grey and had a kindly expression which one would hardly have expected in one whose neck was in the hemp. Evidently this was no vulgar assassin. The liberal military code makes provision for hanging many kinds of people, and gentlemen are not excluded.

The preparations being complete, the two private soldiers stepped aside and each drew away the plank upon which he had been standing. The sergeant turned to the captain, saluted and placed himself immediately behind that officer, who in turn moved apart one pace. These movements left the condemned man and the sergeant standing on the two ends of the same plank, which spanned three of the cross-ties of the bridge. The end upon which the civilian stood almost, but not quite, reached a fourth. This plank had been held in place by the weight of the captain; it was now held by that of the sergeant. At a signal from the former, the latter would step aside, the plank would tilt and the condemned man go down between two ties. The arrangement commended itself to his judgment as simple and effective. His face had not been covered nor his eyes bandaged. He looked a moment at his "unsteadfast footing," then let his gaze wander to the swirling water of the stream racing madly beneath his feet. A piece of dancing driftwood caught his attention and his eyes followed it down the current. How slowly it appeared to move! What a sluggish stream!

He closed his eyes in order to fix his last thoughts upon his wife and children. The water, touched to gold by the early sun, the brooding mists under the banks at some distance down the stream, the fort, the soldiers, the piece of driftwood — all had distracted him. And now he became conscious of a new disturbance. Striking through the thought of his dear ones was a sound which he could neither ignore nor understand, a sharp, distinct, metallic percussion like the stroke of a blacksmith's hammer upon the anvil; it had the same ringing quality. He wondered what it was, and whether immeasurably distant or near by — it seemed both. Its recurrence was regular, but as slow as the tolling

5

of a death knell. He awaited each stroke with impatience and — he knew not why — apprehension. The intervals of silence grew progressively longer; the delays became maddening. With their greater infrequency the sounds increased in strength and sharpness. They hurt his ear like the thrust of a knife; he feared he would shriek. What he heard was the ticking of his watch.

He unclosed his eyes and saw again the water below him. "If I could free my hands," he thought, "I might throw off the noose and spring into the stream. By diving I could evade the bullets, and, swimming vigorously, reach the bank, take to the woods, and get away home. My home, thank God, is as yet outside their lines; my wife and little ones are still beyond the invader's farthest advance."

As these thoughts, which have here to be set down in words, were flashed into the doomed man's brain rather than evolved from it, the captain nodded to the sergeant. The sergeant stepped aside.

II

Peyton Farquhar was a well-to-do planter, of an old and highly respected Alabama family. Being a slave owner, and, like other slave owners, a politician, he was naturally an original secessionist and ardently devoted to the Southern cause. Circumstances of an imperious nature which it is unnecessary to relate here, had prevented him from taking service with the gallant army which had fought the disastrous campaigns ending with the fall of Corinth, and he chafed under the inglorious restraint, longing for the release of his energies, the larger life of the soldier, the opportunity for distinction. That opportunity, he felt, would come, as it comes to all in war time. Meanwhile he did what he could. No service was too humble for him to perform in aid of the South, no adventure too perilous for him to undertake if consistent with the character of a civilian who was at heart a soldier, and who in good faith and without too much qualification assented to at least a part of the frankly villainous dictum that all is fair in love and war.

One evening while Farquhar and his wife were sitting on a rustic bench near the entrance to his grounds, a grey-clad soldier rode up to the gate and asked for a drink of water. Mrs. Farquhar was only too happy to serve him with her own white hands. While she was gone to fetch the water, her husband approached the dusty horseman and inquired eagerly for news from the front.

"The Yanks are repairing the railroads," said the man, "and are getting ready for another advance. They have reached the Owl Creek bridge, put it in order, and built a stockade on the other bank. The commandant has issued an order, which is posted everywhere, declaring that any civilian caught interfering with the railroad, its bridges, tunnels, or trains, will be summarily hanged. I saw the order." 10

"How far is it to the Owl Creek bridge?" Farquhar asked.

"About thirty miles."

"Is there no force on this side the creek?"

"Only a picket post half a mile out, on the railroad, and a single sentinel at this end of the bridge."

"Suppose a man — a civilian and student of hanging — should elude the picket post and perhaps get the better of the sentinel," said Farquhar, smiling, "what could he accomplish?"   15

The soldier reflected. "I was there a month ago," he replied. "I observed that the flood of last winter had lodged a great quantity of driftwood against the wooden pier at this end of the bridge. It is now dry and would burn like tow."

The lady had now brought the water, which the soldier drank. He thanked her ceremoniously, bowed to her husband, and rode away. An hour later, after nightfall, he repassed the plantation, going northward in the direction from which he had come. He was a Federal scout.

III

As Peyton Farquhar fell straight downward through the bridge, he lost consciousness and was as one already dead. From this state he was awakened — ages later, it seemed to him — by the pain of a sharp pressure upon his throat, followed by a sense of suffocation. Keen, poignant agonies seemed to shoot from his neck downward through every fibre of his body and limbs. These pains appeared to flash along well-defined lines of ramification, and to beat with an inconceivably rapid periodicity. They seemed like streams of pulsating fire heating him to an intolerable temperature. As to his head, he was conscious of nothing but a feeling of fullness — of congestion. These sensations were unaccompanied by thought. The intellectual part of his nature was already effaced; he had power only to feel, and feeling was torment. He was conscious of motion. Encompassed in a luminous cloud, of which he was now merely the fiery heart, without material substance, he swung through unthinkable arcs of oscillation, like a vast pendulum. Then all at once, with terrible suddenness, the light about him shot upward with the noise of a loud splash; a frightful roaring was in his ears, and all was cold and dark. The power of thought was restored; he knew that the rope had broken and he had fallen into the stream. There was no additional strangulation; the noose about his neck was already suffocating him, and kept the water from his lungs. To die of hanging at the bottom of a river — the idea seemed to him ludicrous. He opened his eyes in the blackness and saw above him a gleam of light, but how distant, how inaccessible! He was still sinking, for the light became fainter and fainter until it was a mere glimmer. Then it began to grow and brighten, and he knew that he was rising toward the surface — knew it with reluctance, for he was now very comfortable. "To be hanged and drowned," he thought, "that is not so bad; but I do not wish to be shot. No; I will not be shot; that is not fair."

He was not conscious of an effort, but a sharp pain in his wrist apprised him that he was trying to free his hands. He gave the struggle his attention, as an idler might observe the feat of a juggler, without interest in the outcome. What splendid effort! — what magnificent, what superhuman strength! Ah, that was a fine endeavor! Bravo! The cord fell away; his arms parted and floated upward, the hands dimly seen on each side in the growing light. He watched them with a new interest as first one and then the other pounced upon the noose at his neck. They tore it away and thrust it fiercely aside, its undulations resembling those of a water-snake. "Put it back, put it back!" He thought he shouted these words to his hands, for the undoing of the noose had been succeeded by the direst pang which he had yet experienced. His neck ached horribly; his brain was on fire; his heart, which had been fluttering faintly, gave a great leap, trying to force itself out at his mouth. His whole body was racked and wrenched with an insupportable anguish! But his disobedient hands gave no heed to the command. They beat the water vigorously with quick, downward strokes, forcing him to the surface. He felt his head emerge; his eyes were blinded by the sunlight; his chest expanded convulsively, and with a supreme and crowning agony his lungs engulfed a great draught of air, which instantly he expelled in a shriek!

He was now in full possession of his physical senses. They were, indeed,   20
preternaturally keen and alert. Something in the awful disturbance of his organic system had so exalted and refined them that they made record of things never before perceived. He felt the ripples upon his face and heard their separate sounds as they struck. He looked at the forest on the bank of the stream, saw the individual trees, the leaves and the veining of each leaf — saw the very insects upon them, the locusts, the brilliant-bodied flies, the grey spiders stretching their webs from twig to twig. He noted the prismatic colors in all the dewdrops upon a million blades of grass. The humming of the gnats that danced above the eddies of the stream, the beating of the dragon flies' wings, the strokes of the water spiders' legs, like oars which had lifted their boat — all these made audible music. A fish slid along beneath his eyes and he heard the rush of its body parting the water.

He had come to the surface facing down the stream; in a moment the visible world seemed to wheel slowly round, himself the pivotal point, and he saw the bridge, the fort, the soldiers upon the bridge, the captain, the sergeant, the two privates, his executioners. They were in silhouette against the blue sky. They shouted and gesticulated, pointing at him; the captain had drawn his pistol, but did not fire; the others were unarmed. Their movements were grotesque and horrible, their forms gigantic.

Suddenly he heard a sharp report and something struck the water smartly within a few inches of his head, spattering his face with spray. He heard a second report, and saw one of the sentinels with his rifle at his shoulder, a light cloud of blue smoke rising from the muzzle. The man in the water saw the eye of the man on the bridge gazing into his own through the sights of the rifle. He observed that it was a grey eye, and remembered having read that grey eyes were keenest and that all famous marksmen had them. Nevertheless, this one had missed.

A counter swirl had caught Farquhar and turned him half round; he was again looking into the forest on the bank opposite the fort. The sound of a clear, high voice in a monotonous singsong now rang out behind him and came across the water with a distinctness that pierced and subdued all other sounds, even the beating of the ripples in his ears. Although no soldier, he had frequented camps enough to know the dread significance of that deliberate, drawling, aspirated chant; the lieutenant on shore was taking a part in the morning's work. How coldly and pitilessly — with what an even, calm intonation, presaging and enforcing tranquility in the men — with what accurately-measured intervals fell those cruel words:

"Attention, company. . . . Shoulder arms. . . . Ready. . . . Aim. . . . Fire."

Farquhar dived — dived as deeply as he could. The water roared in his ears   25
like the voice of Niagara, yet he heard the dulled thunder of the volley, and rising again toward the surface, met shining bits of metal, singularly flattened, oscillating slowly downward. Some of them touched him on the face and hands, then fell away, continuing their descent. One lodged between his collar and neck; it was uncomfortably warm, and he snatched it out.

As he rose to the surface, gasping for breath, he saw that he had been a long time under water; he was perceptibly farther down stream — nearer to safety. The soldiers had almost finished reloading; the metal ramrods flashed all at once in the sunshine as they were drawn from the barrels, turned in the air, and thrust into their sockets. The two sentinels fired again, independently and ineffectually.

The hunted man saw all this over his shoulder; he was now swimming vigorously with the current. His brain was as energetic as his arms and legs; he thought with the rapidity of lightning.

"The officer," he reasoned, "will not make the martinet's error a second time. It is as easy to dodge a volley as a single shot. He has probably already given the command to fire at will. God help me, I cannot dodge them all!"

An appalling plash within two yards of him, followed by a loud rushing sound, *diminuendo*, which seemed to travel back through the air to the fort and died in an explosion which stirred the very river to its deeps! A rising sheet of water, which curved over him, fell down upon him, blinded him, strangled him! The cannon had taken a hand in the game. As he shook his head free from the commotion of the smitten water, he heard the deflected shot humming through the air ahead, and in an instant it was cracking and smashing the branches in the forest beyond.

"They will not do that again," he thought; "the next time they will use   30
a charge of grape. I must keep my eye upon the gun; the smoke will apprise me — the report arrives too late; it lags behind the missile. It is a good gun."

Suddenly he felt himself whirled round and round — spinning like a top. The water, the banks, the forest, the now distant bridge, fort, and men — all were commingled and blurred. Objects were represented by their colors only; circular horizontal streaks of color — that was all he saw. He had been caught in a vortex and was being whirled on with a velocity of advance and gyration which made him giddy and sick. In a few moments he was flung upon the gravel at the foot of the left bank of the stream — the southern bank — and behind a projecting point which concealed him from his enemies. The sudden arrest of his motion, the abrasion of one of his hands on the gravel, restored him and he wept with delight. He dug his fingers into the sand, threw it over himself in handfuls and audibly blessed it. It looked like gold, like diamonds, rubies, emeralds; he could think of nothing beautiful which it did not resemble. The trees upon the bank were giant garden plants; he noted a definite order in their arrangement, inhaled the fragrance of their blooms. A strange, roseate light shone through the spaces among their trunks, and the wind made in their branches the music of æolian harps. He had no wish to perfect his escape, was content to remain in that enchanting spot until retaken.

A whizz and rattle of grapeshot among the branches high above his head roused him from his dream. The baffled cannoneer had fired him a random farewell. He sprang to his feet, rushed up the sloping bank, and plunged into the forest.

All that day he travelled, laying his course by the rounding sun. The forest seemed interminable; nowhere did he discover a break in it, not even a woodman's road. He had not known that he lived in so wild a region. There was something uncanny in the revelation.

By nightfall he was fatigued, footsore, famishing. The thought of his wife and children urged him on. At last he found a road which led him in what he knew to be the right direction. It was as wide and straight as a city street, yet it seemed untravelled. No fields bordered it, no dwelling anywhere. Not so much as the barking of a dog suggested human habitation. The black bodies of the great trees formed a straight wall on both sides, terminating on the horizon in a point, like a diagram in a lesson in perspective. Overhead, as he looked up through this rift in the wood, shone great golden stars looking unfamiliar and grouped in strange constellations. He was sure they were arranged in some order which had a secret and malign significance. The wood on either side was full of singular noises, among which—once, twice, and again—he distinctly heard whispers in an unknown tongue.

His neck was in pain, and, lifting his hand to it, he found it horribly swol-   35
len. He knew that it had a circle of black where the rope had bruised it. His eyes felt congested; he could no longer close them. His tongue was swollen with thirst; he relieved its fever by thrusting it forward from between his teeth into the cool air. How softly the turf had carpeted the untravelled avenue! He could no longer feel the roadway beneath his feet!

Doubtless, despite his suffering, he fell asleep while walking, for now he sees another scene—perhaps he has merely recovered from a delirium. He stands at the gate of his own home. All is as he left it, and all bright and beautiful in the morning sunshine. He must have travelled the entire night. As he pushes open the gate and passes up the wide white walk, he sees a flutter of female garments; his wife, looking fresh and cool and sweet, steps down from the verandah to meet him. At the bottom of the steps she stands waiting, with a smile of ineffable joy, an attitude of matchless grace and dignity. Ah, how beautiful she is! He springs forward with extended arms. As he is about to clasp her, he feels a stunning blow upon the back of the neck; a blinding white light blazes all about him, with a sound like the shock of a cannon—then all is darkness and silence!

Peyton Farquhar was dead; his body, with a broken neck, swung gently from side to side beneath the timbers of the Owl Creek bridge.   *[1891]*

≡ THINKING ABOUT THE TEXT

1. One of the most popular themes in literature is the tension between reality and illusion. How does Bierce play with these ideas?

2. Comment on Bierce's use of time. What indications suggest it is either objective or subjective?

3. What was the first time in the story when you suspected that something about Farquhar's journey was unreal? What specific details and words then confirmed your suspicion?

4. Note Bierce's recurring use of the color gray. What significance does it seem to have? How does he also use driftwood as a symbol?

5. What significance does Bierce's description of Farquhar have? What is he trying to do?

≡ MAKING COMPARISONS

1. What are some of the authentic details from both stories that suggest the authors had firsthand observations of war?

2. Compare Cross's and Farquhar's thoughts about home, especially Farquhar's wife and Martha.

3. How do both Cross and Farquhar escape from the reality of war?

≡ WRITING ABOUT ISSUES

1. Write an essay that argues that an attempt to escape from war's trauma is or is not an illusion. Use O'Brien and Bierce and any other writer or filmmaker as evidence.

2. Watch a film adaptation of "An Occurrence at Owl Creek Bridge" and write an argument that one is more effective, realistic, or artistic than the other.

3. Read O'Brien's story "The Sweetheart of the Song Tra Bong," and write an essay that argues that the themes are or are not similar to "The Things They Carried." Or read Bierce's "Chickamauga" and argue that Bierce's themes are or are not comparable to his story here.

4. Write an essay that argues that Jimmy and Martha are or are not in love with each other.

≡ Roads Taken: Poems by Robert Frost

ROBERT FROST, "Stopping by Woods on a Snowy Evening"

ROBERT FROST, "The Road Not Taken"

ROBERT FROST, "Acquainted with the Night"

Critic Randall Jarrell saw Robert Frost as "the subtlest and saddest of poets." Although many readers thought of this esteemed, pastoral poet as the optimistic voice of the common man, his lyrical vision is actually quite tragic, a quality President Kennedy thought helped strengthen his own presidential character. Alert readers should be careful about equating Frost's simple language and rural settings with lack of depth. The three poems assembled here (and "Mending Wall," p. 65) use the common motif of an external journey to comment on the internal burdens of adult responsibility, the anxiety inherent in making choices, and the loneliness of the human heart. The language of these journeys is beautifully crafted and evocative, able to be read profitably by both schoolchildren and sophisticated critics.

≡ BEFORE YOU READ

Do you remember reading a Frost poem in high school? What is your memory of that reading and discussion in class?

ROBERT FROST

Stopping by Woods on a Snowy Evening

Robert Frost (1874–1963) was perhaps the best-known poet of the twentieth century: winning four Pulitzer Prizes, garnering more than forty honorary degrees, and being widely anthologized throughout the world. His popular image, perhaps forever fixed by his reading at John Kennedy's inauguration, is of a white-haired New Englander fond of simple, homey descriptions of nature. Actually, Frost was born in San Francisco, and most critics think his poetry is anything but simple.

Frost spent his childhood in California and later moved with his mother to eastern Massachusetts, where he grew up in the small city of Lawrence. He briefly attended Dartmouth College and married in 1895. Frost and his wife taught school together, but they soon moved to a farm in New Hampshire, where he worked and wrote poetry. In 1912, he moved to a town outside London and soon published his first book of poetry, A Boy's Will, in 1913. The book was well received, and a few years later Frost moved to Franconia, New Hampshire, and began a lifelong career of writing and teaching. For more than twenty years, he was a professor at Amherst College and for decades taught summers at the Bread Loaf School in Vermont.

Bettmann/Getty Images

*Frost's most popular poems — "Mending Wall," "After Apple-Picking,"
"Birches," and "Fire and Ice" — and those printed here deal with complex social
issues in a seemingly natural manner. But even a casual search of essays interpreting "Mending Wall," for example, demonstrates that critics see in Frost's poems a
sophisticated, searching, and often dark commentary on the human condition.*

Whose woods these are I think I know.
His house is in the village, though;
He will not see me stopping here
To watch his woods fill up with snow.

My little horse must think it queer   5
To stop without a farmhouse near
Between the woods and frozen lake
The darkest evening of the year.

He gives his harness bells a shake
To ask if there is some mistake.   10

The only other sound's the sweep
Of easy wind and downy flake.

The woods are lovely, dark and deep,
But I have promises to keep,
And miles to go before I sleep,   15
And miles to go before I sleep.   *[1923]*

≡ THINKING ABOUT THE TEXT

1. Why does the narrator seem so concerned that someone will notice him watching "woods fill up with snow" (line 4)?

2. Is the "darkest evening" (line 8) meant literally, metaphorically, or both?

3. Notice the alliteration in lines 11–12. What effect is Frost trying to achieve with this poetic device?

4. Some critics see the narrator's pause and the lure of woods that "are lovely, dark and deep" (line 13) as something like a death wish. Do you agree?

5. How do you interpret the last lines? Are they a literal or a figurative statement? Why the repetition?

ROBERT FROST
The Road Not Taken

Two roads diverged in a yellow wood,
And sorry I could not travel both
And be one traveler, long I stood
And looked down one as far as I could
To where it bent in the undergrowth;   5

Then took the other, as just as fair,
And having perhaps the better claim,
Because it was grassy and wanted wear;
Though as for that the passing there
Had worn them really about the same,   10

And both that morning equally lay
In leaves no step had trodden black.
Oh, I kept the first for another day!
Yet knowing how way leads on to way,
I doubted if I should ever come back.   15

I shall be telling this with a sigh
Somewhere ages and ages hence:

Two roads diverged in a wood, and I—
I took the one less traveled by,
And that has made all the difference.   *[1916]*   20

≡ THINKING ABOUT THE TEXT

1. Is it odd that the title would refer to a road *not* taken?

2. This is clearly a poem about a journey. Did you ever think of your life as a journey on a particular path? How far can you see your future on this path?

3. Critics have noticed that although the narrator says he has taken the path less traveled, he also says the paths were worn about the same. How might you account for this?

4. The conventional interpretation of this poem is that it is about nonconformity. Does this make sense? Why? Given the issue in the previous question, might there be other interpretations?

5. Why does the narrator "sigh" in the last stanza? Is it due to boredom? Regret? Resignation? Nostalgia?

≡ MAKING COMPARISONS

1. Compare the moods of the speakers in both poems.

2. Both poems touch on the future. In what ways?

3. Is the focus of "Stopping by Woods on a Snowy Evening" more pessimistic than that of "The Road Not Taken"?

ROBERT FROST
Acquainted with the Night

I have been one acquainted with the night.
I have walked out in rain—and back in rain.
I have outwalked the furthest city light.

I have looked down the saddest city lane.
I have passed by the watchman on his beat   5
And dropped my eyes, unwilling to explain.

I have stood still and stopped the sound of feet
When far away an interrupted cry
Came over houses from another street,

But not to call me back or say good-by;   10
And further still at an unearthly height

One luminary clock against the sky
Proclaimed the time was neither wrong nor right.
I have been one acquainted with the night.   [1928]

☰ THINKING ABOUT THE TEXT

1. When the narrator passes the watchman, he drops his eyes (lines 5–6). Why?

2. It seems that the cry (line 8) has nothing to do with the narrator. Is this detail a key to his psychological and emotional state?

3. The narrator says the "time was neither wrong nor right" (line 13). What is he trying to suggest? What might the "time was right" suggest?

4. Why does the narrator choose the night for his walks? Why not walk during the day?

5. Although the first and last lines are identical, do you sense a difference in meaning?

☰ MAKING COMPARISONS

1. Which of these three journeys in Frost's poems seems the most hopeful?

2. Is the speaker in "Acquainted with the Night" more honest than the other speakers? Why, or why not?

3. Which line in the three poems seems the most enigmatic? Why?

☰ WRITING ABOUT ISSUES

1. Write an essay about a decision you made that you assumed would make a difference in your life.

2. All three poems involve journeys. Write an essay that compares the three journeys in terms of purpose, mood, and meaning.

3. Write an essay about a significant and recent journey that you have taken. Did you learn something about yourself? Did you change?

4. Another Frost poem, "Mending Wall," appears in the first part of this book (p. 65). Write an essay that compares the attitude of that speaker with the three speakers in this cluster.

≡ Final Journeys: Poems

JOHN DONNE, "Death Be Not Proud"

DYLAN THOMAS, "Do Not Go Gentle into That Good Night"

EMILY DICKINSON, "Because I could not stop for Death"

E. A. ROBINSON, "Richard Cory"

For many cultures, death seems more than a metaphorical journey. This is especially true of the Greeks, in whose mythology Charon, the ferryman of the underworld, is literally charged with taking the dead across the river Styx, where they will continue their trek for better or worse. Contemporary poets tend to see death's journey differently than the ancient poets did, but their appreciation of the mysteries and power of death is enduring. Poets reflect on death's presence in our lives in lyrical and illuminating ways.

John Donne sneers at death, perhaps to demonstrate its power, and Dylan Thomas wants to resist that power. Reducing the significance of death was probably on Emily Dickinson's mind when she describes Death as a civil carriage driver who kindly stops for her on the way to eternity. E. A. Robinson's famous poem is so memorable because it works dramatically against our most cherished stereotypes about the advantages of popularity and wealth. Death has intrigued and puzzled poets for centuries, perhaps because, as Shakespeare reminds us, it is a country from which no traveler returns.

≡ BEFORE YOU READ

Do you think our society has a particular attitude toward death? Can you point to films that might reveal such a cultural inclination? If you practice a religion, does it have a specific way of seeing death? What is your general attitude toward death, and where does it come from?

JOHN DONNE
Death Be Not Proud

Long regarded as a major English writer, John Donne (1572–1631) was also trained as a lawyer and clergyman. Around 1594, he converted from Catholicism to Anglicanism; in 1615, he was ordained; and in 1621, he was appointed to the prestigious position of dean of St. Paul's Cathedral in London. Today, his sermons continue to be studied as literature, yet he is more known for his poetry. When he was a young man, he often wrote about love, but later he focused on religious themes. The following poem, one of Donne's "holy sonnets," is from 1611.

Death be not proud, though some have callèd thee
Mighty and dreadful, for thou art not so;
For those whom thou think'st thou dost overthrow
Die not, poor Death, nor yet canst thou kill me.
From rest and sleep, which but thy pictures° be,   *images*   5
Much pleasure; then from thee much more must flow,
And soonest our best men with thee do go,
Rest of their bones, and soul's delivery.°   *deliverance*
Thou art slave to Fate, Chance, kings, and desperate men,
And dost with Poison, War, and Sickness dwell;   10
And poppy or charms can make us sleep as well,
And better than thy stroke; why swell'st° thou then?   *swell with pride*
One short sleep past, we wake eternally
And death shall be no more; Death, thou shalt die.   *[1611]*

≡ THINKING ABOUT THE TEXT

1. In a sense, Death is the speaker's audience. But presumably Donne expected the living to read his poem. What reaction might he have wanted from this audience?

2. Is the speaker proud? Define what you mean by the term.

3. Evidently the speaker believes in an afterlife. What would you say to people who consider the speaker naive and the poem irrelevant because they don't believe that "we wake eternally" (line 13)? How significant is this warrant or assumption? Do you share it?

4. What are the arguments the narrator uses to diminish Death?

5. Imagine Death writing a sonnet in response to the speaker. Perhaps it would be titled "Life Be Not Proud." What might Death say in it?

DYLAN THOMAS

Do Not Go Gentle into That Good Night

Dylan Thomas (1914–1953) was a Welsh poet, short story writer, and playwright. Among his most enduring works are his radio dramas Under Milk Wood *(1954) and* A Child's Christmas in Wales *(1955). A frequent visitor to the United States, Thomas built a devoted audience in this country through his electrifying public readings. Unfortunately, he was also well known for his alcoholism, which killed him at a relatively young age. He wrote the following poem in 1952, not long before his own death. It takes the form of a villanelle, which consists of nineteen lines: five tercets (three-line stanzas) followed by a quatrain (four-line stanza). The first and third lines of the opening tercet are used alternately to conclude each succeeding tercet, and they are joined to form a rhyme at the poem's end.*

Do not go gentle into that good night,
Old age should burn and rave at close of day;
Rage, rage against the dying of the light.

Though wise men at their end know dark is right,
Because their words had forked no lightning they   5
Do not go gentle into that good night.

Good men, the last wave by, crying how bright
Their frail deeds might have danced in a green bay,
Rage, rage against the dying of the light.

Wild men who caught and sang the sun in flight,   10
And learn, too late, they grieved it on its way,
Do not go gentle into that good night.

Grave men, near death, who see with blinding sight
Blind eyes could blaze like meteors and be gay,
Rage, rage against the dying of the light.   15

And you, my father, there on the sad height,
Curse, bless, me now with your fierce tears, I pray.
Do not go gentle into that good night.
Rage, rage against the dying of the light.   *[1952]*

≡ THINKING ABOUT THE TEXT

1. In what sense could the night possibly be "good," given that people are supposed to "rage" at it?

2. Why do you think Thomas has his speaker refer to "the dying of the light" instead of simply to "dying"? What other parts of the poem relate to the word *light*?

3. The speaker refers to four kinds of men. Restate in your own words the description given of each. Should Thomas's language about them have been less abstract? Why, or why not?

4. What is the effect of climaxing the poem with a reference to "you, my father" (line 16)? If the father had been introduced in the first or second stanzas, would the effect have been different? If so, how?

5. What is the effect of the villanelle form? Judging by Thomas's poem, do you think it is worthwhile for a poet to write in this way, despite the technical challenges of the form? Should teachers of poetry writing encourage their students to write a villanelle? Explain your reasoning.

≡ MAKING COMPARISONS

1. Is this poem an affirmation of life? Could Donne's poem be considered as such?
2. Compare the speaker's attitude in this poem to that in Donne's.
3. Which poet seems most at peace with death?

EMILY DICKINSON
Because I could not stop for Death

Although Emily Dickinson (1830–1886) was considered an eccentric recluse by many of her provincial neighbors, history has interpreted Emily Dickinson's life in various ways, according to the thinking of the times. Although she was once considered isolated, she is now seen by many critics as connected to the issues and literature of her age. Feminist and queer studies scholars now see the once-shy figure as an active champion of defying gender stereotypes. Although she has often been described as a nunlike, passive figure, critics today see her as a nonconformist, mistrustful of power and dogma, and as someone who questioned any kind of received opinion, even popular views on religion and the afterlife.

The following much-discussed poem has intrigued and puzzled critics for generations. Its elusive meaning and its combination of Christian promises and Gothic imagery has allowed critics to see the poem as everything from an acceptance of New England Protestant dogma to a rejection of religion in favor of the immortality of art. The poem was originally published in 1890 as "The Chariot."

> Because I could not stop for Death —
> He kindly stopped for me —
> The Carriage held but just Ourselves —
> And Immortality.
>
> We slowly drove — He knew no haste   5
> And I had put away
> My labor and my leisure too,
> For His Civility —
>
> We passed the School, where Children strove
> At Recess — in the Ring —   10
> We passed the Fields of Gazing Grain —
> We passed the Setting Sun —
>
> Or rather — He passed us —
> The Dews drew quivering and chill —
> For only Gossamer, my Gown —   15
> My Tippet — only Tulle —

We paused before a House that seemed
A Swelling of the Ground—
The Roof was scarcely visible—
The Cornice—in the Ground—   20

Since then—'tis Centuries—and yet
Feels shorter than the Day
I first surmised the Horses' Heads
Were toward Eternity—   *[1890]*

≡ **THINKING ABOUT THE TEXT**

1. Who are the passengers in the carriage? What is the effect of "kindly" in line 2? How might we imagine "Immortality"? Fear of death was a common theme in nineteenth-century sermons. How might this poem be a rejection of that fear?

2. How might the second stanza be an acceptance of death? Why does Death drive slowly?

3. What might the three images in the third stanza stand for?

4. Critics have debated the reference for "He" in stanza 4. What do you think she means? What do "gossamer," "tippet," and "tulle" mean?

5. What suggests that the narrator might already be dead? What might "House" in the fifth stanza refer to?

≡ **MAKING COMPARISONS**

1. Using just a phrase or a word, how would you characterize the attitude of these three poems toward death?

2. What do you assume Donne's response to Dickinson's poem would be?

3. Explain which of the three poems seem the most religious and which seem the most secular.

EDWIN ARLINGTON ROBINSON
Richard Cory

E. A. Robinson (1869–1935) eventually gained fame through poems such as "Richard Cory," but he spent much of his life in relative obscurity. Robinson was born in Head Tide, Maine, and educated at Harvard. While he was living in the Maine town of Gardner, he began writing poems based on his community. The following poem was probably inspired by the shotgun suicide of a Gardner man. It appeared in his 1897 book The Children of the Night. *After years of being unable to make a living as a poet, he eventually came back to the town of Gardner, where his reputation grew over the years. He won the Pulitzer Prize for poetry three times.*

Whenever Richard Cory went down town,
We people on the pavement looked at him:
He was a gentleman from sole to crown,
Clean favored, and imperially slim.

And he was always quietly arrayed,   5
And he was always human when he talked;
But still he fluttered pulses when he said,
"Good-morning," and he glittered when he walked.

And he was rich — yes, richer than a king —
And admirably schooled in every grace: 10
In fine, we thought that he was everything
To make us wish that we were in his place.

So on we worked, and waited for the light,
And went without the meat, and cursed the bread;
And Richard Cory, one calm summer night,   15
Went home and put a bullet through his head.

≡ THINKING ABOUT THE TEXT

1. Why does the poem's ending surprise readers?

2. On a second reading, do you get any sense of why Richard Cory kills himself?

3. From your experience, your reading, or watching films, why do people commit suicide? Suicide is often characterized as a selfish and/or cowardly act. Is this necessarily so? Explain.

4. What are some plausible theses for this poem? Is "Money can't buy happiness" too simple?

5. In 1966, Paul Simon wrote a song called "Richard Cory" subtitled "with apologies to Edwin Arlington Robinson." Even after the narrator, who works in Cory's factory, finds out that Richard Cory has killed himself, he still sings, "Oh I wish that I could be Richard Cory." How are we meant to understand this line?

≡ MAKING COMPARISONS

1. Do you think Richard Cory would have liked the attitude toward death expressed in any of these poems? Explain.

2. Which narrator of our three poems would have disliked the ending of "Richard Cory" the most? Explain.

3. If the narrator of Thomas's poem met Richard Cory on that fateful night, what advice might he give him?

≡ WRITING ABOUT ISSUES

1. Choose one of our four poems, analyzing it as making an argument for a certain position on death. Specify the main claim and the evidence given in support.

2. Imagine you are on the staff of a nursing home. The chief administrator asks you to choose one of our poems for a group discussion with the elderly residents. Write a brief argument that one of these poems would be appropriate. Mention briefly why the others would not.

3. Write an argument that one of these poems is the most reflective of our culture's view of death.

RAY BRADBURY, "Mars Is Heaven!"

OCTAVIA BUTLER, "Human Evolution"

T. C. BOYLE, "The Relive Box"

Time has been a central concern of science fiction ever since H.G. Wells's 1895 classic, *The Time Machine*. Our culture's most significant ways of thinking, from religious, historical, philosophical to scientific and literary are greatly influenced by our concept of time. Is it linear or cyclical, fixed or changeable? Is there a coherent narrative to time's passing or simply random events? The playwright Arthur Miller stated that "everything we are is at every moment alive in us," highlighting that time is multidimensional. And the novelist William Faulkner noted, "The past is never dead. It's not even past."

Although much of science fiction is set in an imaginary future like that in Octavia Butler's "Human Evolution," many writers also travel back in time. In fact, Butler's famous novel *Kindred* (1979) focuses on a young African American writer who goes back in time to a pre-Civil War plantation. In Ray Bradbury's story, printed here, the truth of Faulkner's notion is incorporated into a chilling tale of memory and danger. And in T. C. Boyle's tale, people are able to relive moments from their past with troubling consequences for their present lives.

≡ BEFORE YOU READ

If time travel were possible, would you go to the future or the past? What if such a journey were permanent? If you could watch events from your past, which ones would you choose? What would you hope to learn?

RAY BRADBURY
Mars Is Heaven!

Ray Bradbury (1920–2012), perhaps the most well-known American science fiction writer, was born in Waukegan, Illinois, a beloved town often represented in his fiction as a comforting metaphor for safety, especially in his dangerous fictional dystopias. Although he did not go to college, Bradbury was well read. His professional career began in 1941 with the publication of "Pendulum" in Super Science Stories. *In 1945, his first collection of stories,* Dark Carnival, *appeared. His reputation as a literary science fiction writer was assured in 1950 with the publication of* The Martian Chronicles. *This masterpiece uses a fictional attempt to colonize Mars to comment on American society and its racial, political, and psychological struggles in the 1950s.* Fahrenheit 451 *(1953), another widely praised novel, is set in a dystopic future where books are burned by a totalitarian regime. His best work is characterized by a vivid imagination and the psychological complexity and depth of his characters. He won numerous awards, including the Nebula Grand Master Award in 1989. The haunting story printed here, from* The Martian Chronicles, *builds its suspense from a masterful blend of hope and suspicion. We want the nostalgic and sentimental vision of the astronauts to be true, but we wisely fear the worst.*

The ship came down from space. It came from the stars and the black velocities, and the shining movements, and the silent gulfs of space. It was a new ship; it had fire in its body and men in its metal cells, and it moved with a clean silence, fiery and warm. In it were seventeen men, including a captain. The crowd at the Ohio field had shouted and waved their hands up into the sunlight, and the rocket had bloomed out great flowers of heat and color and run away into space on the *third* voyage to Mars!

Now it was decelerating with metal efficiency in the upper Martian atmospheres. It was still a thing of beauty and strength. It had moved in the midnight waters of space like a pale sea leviathan; it had passed the ancient moon and thrown itself onward into one nothingness following another. The men within it had been battered, thrown about, sickened, made well again, each in his turn. One man had died, but now the remaining sixteen, with their eyes clear in their heads and their faces pressed to the thick glass ports, watched Mars swing up under them.

"Mars! Mars! Good old Mars, here we are!" cried Navigator Lustig.

"Good old Mars!" said Samuel Hinkston, archaeologist.

"Well," said Captain John Black.   5

The ship landed softly on a lawn of green grass. Outside, upon the lawn, stood an iron deer. Further up the lawn, a tall brown Victorian house sat in the quiet sunlight, all covered with scrolls and rococo, its windows made of blue and pink and yellow and green colored glass. Upon the porch were hairy geraniums and an old swing which was hooked into the porch ceiling and which now swung back and forth, back and forth, in a little breeze. At the top of the house was a cupola with diamond, leaded-glass windows, and a dunce-cap roof! Through the front window you could see an ancient piano with yellow keys and a piece of music titled *Beautiful Ohio* sitting on the music rest.

Around the rocket in four directions spread the little town, green and motionless in the Martian spring. There were white houses and red brick ones, and tall elm trees blowing in the wind, and tall maples and horse chestnuts. And church steeples with golden bells silent in them.

The men in the rocket looked out and saw this. Then they looked at one another and then they looked out again. They held on to each other's elbows, suddenly unable to breathe, it seemed. Their faces grew pale and they blinked constantly, running from glass port to glass port of the ship.

"I'll be damned," whispered Lustig, rubbing his face with his numb fingers, his eyes wet. "I'll be damned, damned, damned."

"It can't be, it just can't be," said Samuel Hinkston.   10

"Lord," said Captain John Black.

There was a call from the chemist. "Sir, the atmosphere is fine for breathing, sir."

Black turned slowly. "Are you sure?"

"No doubt of it, sir."

"Then we'll go out," said Lustig.   15

"Lord, yes," said Samuel Hinkston.

"Hold on," said Captain John Black. "Just a moment. Nobody gave any orders."

"But, sir —"

"Sir, nothing. How do we know what this is?"

"We know what it is, sir," said the chemist. "It's a small town with good   20
air in it, sir."

"And it's a small town the like of Earth towns," said Samuel Hinkston, the archaeologist. "Incredible. It can't be, but it is."

Captain John Black looked at him, idly. "Do you think that the civilizations of two planets can progress at the same rate and evolve in the same way, Hinkston?"

"I wouldn't have thought so, sir."

Captain Black stood by the port. "Look out there. The geraniums. A specialized plant. That specific variety has only been known on Earth for fifty years. Think of the thousands of years of time it takes to evolve plants. Then tell me if it is logical that the Martians should have: one, leaded glass windows; two, cupolas; three, porch swings; four, an instrument that looks like a piano and probably is a piano; and, five, if you look closely, if a Martian composer would have published a piece of music titled, strangely enough, *Beautiful Ohio*. All of which means that we have an Ohio River here on Mars!"

"It is quite strange, sir."   25

"Strange, hell, it's absolutely impossible, and I suspect the whole bloody shooting setup. Something's wrong here, and I'm not leaving the ship until I know what it is."

"Oh, sir," said Lustig.

"Darn it," said Samuel Hinkston. "Sir, I want to investigate this at first hand. It may be that there are similar patterns of thought, movement, civilization on *every* planet in our system. We may be on the threshold of the great psychological and metaphysical discovery in our time, sir, don't you think?"

"I'm willing to wait a moment," said Captain John Black.

"It may be, sir, that we are looking upon a phenomenon that, for the first   30
time, would absolutely prove the existence of a God, sir."

"There are many people who are of good faith without such proof, Mr. Hinkston."

"I'm one myself, sir. But certainly a thing like this, out there," said Hinkston, "could not occur without divine intervention, sir. It fills me with such terror and elation I don't know whether to laugh or cry, sir."

"Do neither, then, until we know what we're up against."

"Up against, sir?" inquired Lustig. "I see that we're up against nothing. It's a good quiet, green town, much like the one I was born in, and I like the looks of it."

"When were you born, Lustig?"   35

"In 1910, sir."

"That makes you fifty years old, now, doesn't it?"

"This being 1960, yes, sir."

"And you, Hinkston?"

"1920, sir. In Illinois. And this looks swell to me, sir."   40

"This couldn't be Heaven," said the captain, ironically. "Though, I must admit, it looks peaceful and cool, and pretty much like Green Bluff, where I was born, in 1915." He looked at the chemist. "The air's all right, is it?"

"Yes, sir."

"Well, then, tell you what we'll do. Lustig, you and Hinkston and I will fetch ourselves out to look this town over. The other 14 men will stay aboard ship. If anything untoward happens, lift the ship and get the hell out, do you hear what I say, Craner?"

"Yes, sir. The hell out we'll go, sir. Leaving *you*?"

"A loss of three men's better than a whole ship. If something bad hap-   45
pens get back to Earth and warn the next Rocket, that's Lingle's Rocket, I think, which will be completed and ready to take off some time around next Christmas, what he has to meet up with. If there's something hostile about Mars we certainly want the next expedition to be well armed."

"So are we, sir. We've got a regular arsenal with us."

"Tell the men to stand by the guns, then, as Lustig and Hinkston and I go out."

"Right, sir."

"Come along, Lustig, Hinkston."

The three men walked together, down through the levels of the ship.   50

It was a beautiful spring day. A robin sat on a blossoming apple tree and sang continuously. Showers of petal snow sifted down when the wind touched the apple tree, and the blossom smell drifted upon the air. Somewhere in the town, somebody was playing the piano and the music came and went, came and went, softly, drowsily. The song was *Beautiful Dreamer*. Somewhere else, a phonograph, scratchy and faded, was hissing out a record of *Roamin' in the Gloamin'*, sung by Harry Lauder.

The three men stood outside the ship. The port closed behind them. At every window, a face pressed, looking out. The large metal guns pointed this way and that, ready.

Now the phonograph record being played was:

> "Oh give me a June night
> The moonlight and you—"

Lustig began to tremble. Samuel Hinkston did likewise.

Hinkston's voice was so feeble and uneven that the captain had to ask him to   55
repeat what he had said. "I said, sir, that I think I have solved this, all of this, sir!"

"And what is the solution, Hinkston?"

The soft wind blew. The sky was serene and quiet and somewhere a stream of water ran through the cool caverns and tree-shadings of a ravine. Somewhere a horse and wagon trotted and rolled by, bumping.

"Sir, it must be, it has to be, this is the *only* solution! Rocket travel began to Mars in the years before the first World War, sir!"

The captain stared at his archaeologist. "No!"

"But, yes, sir! You must admit, look at all of this! How else to explain it, the houses, the lawns, the iron deer, the flowers, the pianos, the music!"

"Hinkston, Hinkston, oh," and the captain put his hand to his face, shaking his head, his hand shaking now, his lips blue.

"Sir, listen to me." Hinkston took his elbow persuasively and looked up into the captain's face, pleading. "Say that there were some people in the year 1905, perhaps, who hated wars and wanted to get away from Earth and they got together, some scientists, in secret, and built a rocket and came out here to Mars."

"No, no, Hinkston."

"Why not? The world was a different place in 1905, they could have kept it a secret much more easily."

"But the work, Hinkston, the work of building a complex thing like a rocket, oh, no, no." The captain looked at his shoes, looked at his hands, looked at the houses, and then at Hinkston.

"And they came up here, and naturally the houses they built were similar to Earth houses because they brought the cultural architecture with them, and here it is!"

"And they've lived here all these years?" said the captain.

"In peace and quiet, sir, yes. Maybe they made a few trips, to bring enough people here for one small town, and then stopped, for fear of being discovered. That's why the town seems so old-fashioned. I don't see a thing, myself, that is older than the year 1927, do you?"

"No frankly, I don't, Hinkston."

"These are *our* people, sir. This is an American city; it's definitely not European!"

"That—that's right, too, Hinkston."

"Or maybe, just maybe, sir, rocket travel is older than we think. Perhaps it started in some part of the world hundreds of years ago, was discovered and kept secret by a small number of men, and they came to Mars, with only occasional visits to Earth over the centuries."

"You make it sound almost reasonable."

"It is, sir. It has to be. We have the proof here before us, all we have to do now, is find some people and verify it!"

"You're right there, of course. We can't just stand here and talk. Did you bring your gun?"

"Yes, but we won't need it."

"We'll see about it. Come along, we'll ring that doorbell and see if anyone is home."

Their boots were deadened of all sound in the thick green grass. It smelled from a fresh mowing. In spite of himself, Captain John Black felt a great peace come over him. It had been thirty years since he had been in a small town, and the buzzing of spring bees on the air lulled and quieted him, and the fresh look of things was a balm to the soul.

Hollow echoes sounded from under the boards as they walked across the porch and stood before the screen door. Inside, they could see a bead curtain hung across the hall entry, and a crystal chandelier and a Maxfield Parrish painting framed on one wall over a comfortable Morris Chair. The house smelled old, and of the attic, and infinitely comfortable. You could hear the tinkle of ice rattling in a lemonade pitcher. In a distant kitchen, because of the heat of the day, someone was preparing a soft, lemon drink.

Captain John Black rang the bell.   80

Footsteps, dainty and thin, came along the hall and a kind faced lady of some forty years, dressed in the sort of dress you might expect in the year 1909, peered out at them.

"Can I help you?" she asked.

"Beg your pardon," said Captain Black, uncertainly. "But we're looking for, that is, could you help us, I mean." He stopped. She looked out at him with dark wondering eyes.

"If you're selling something," she said, "I'm much too busy and I haven't time." She turned to go.

"No, *wait*," he cried, bewilderedly. "What town is this?"   85

She looked him up and down as if he were crazy. "What do you mean, what town is it? How could you be in a town and not know what town it was?"

The captain looked as if he wanted to go sit under a shady apple tree. "I beg your pardon," he said. "But we're strangers here. We're from Earth, and we want to know how this town got here and you got here."

"Are you census takers?" she asked.

"No," he said.

"What do you want then?" she demanded.   90

"Well," said the captain.

"Well?" she asked.

"How long has this town been here?" he wondered.

"It was built in 1868," she snapped at them. "Is this a game?"

"No, not a game," cried the captain. "Oh, God," he said. "Look here. We're   95
from Earth!"

"From *where*?" she said.

"From Earth!" he said.

"Where's that?" she said.

"From Earth," he cried.

"Out of the ground, do you mean?"   100

"No, from the planet Earth!" he almost shouted. "Here," he insisted, "come out on the porch and I'll show you."

"No," she said. "I won't come out there, you are all evidently quite mad from the sun."

Lustig and Hinkston stood behind the captain. Hinkston now spoke up. "Mrs.," he said. "We came in a flying ship across space, among the stars. We came from the third planet from the sun, Earth, to this planet, which is Mars. *Now* do you understand, Mrs.?"

"Mad from the sun," she said, taking hold of the door. "Go away now, before I call my husband who's upstairs taking a nap, and he'll beat you all with his fists."

"But —" said Hinkston. "This is Mars, is it not?"   105

"This," explained the woman, as if she were addressing a child, "is Green Lake, Wisconsin, on the continent of America, surrounded by the Pacific and Atlantic Oceans, on a place called the world, or sometimes, the Earth. Go away now. Good-bye!"

She slammed the door.

The three men stood before the door with their hands up in the air toward it, as if pleading with her to open it once more.

They looked at one another.

"Let's knock the door down," said Lustig.   110

"We can't," sighed the captain.

"Why not?"

"She didn't do anything bad, did she? We're the strangers here. This is private property. Good God, Hinkston!" He went and sat down on the porchstep.

"What, sir?"

"Did it ever strike you, that maybe we got ourselves, somehow, some way,   115
fouled up. And, by accident, came back and landed on Earth!"

"Oh, sir, oh, sir, oh oh, sir." And Hinkston sat down numbly and thought about it.

Lustig stood up in the sunlight. "How could we have done that?"

"I don't know, just let me think."

Hinkston said, "But we checked every mile of the way, and we saw Mars and our chronometers said so many miles gone, and we went past the moon and out into space and here we are, on Mars. I'm sure we're on Mars, sir."

Lustig said, "But, suppose, just suppose that, by accident, in space, in time,   120
or something, we landed on a planet in space, in another time. Suppose this is Earth, thirty or fifty years ago? Maybe we got lost in the dimensions, do you think?"

"Oh, go away, Lustig."

"Are the men in the ship keeping an eye on us, Hinkston?"

"At their guns, sir."

Lustig went to the door, rang the bell. When the door opened again, he asked, "What year is this?"

"1926, of course!" cried the woman, furiously, and slammed the door   125
again.

"Did you hear that?" Lustig ran back to them, wildly. "She said 1926! We *have* gone back in time! This *is* Earth!"

Lustig sat down and the three men let the wonder and terror of the thought afflict them. Their hands stirred fitfully on their knees. The wind blew, nodding the locks of hair on their heads.

The captain stood up, brushing off his pants. "I never thought it would be like this. It scares the hell out of me. How can a thing like this happen?"

"Will anybody in the whole town believe us?" wondered Hinkston. "Are we playing around with something dangerous? Time, I mean. Shouldn't we just take off and go home?"

"No. We'll try another house."   130

They walked three houses down to a little white cottage under an oak tree. "I like to be as logical as I can get," said the captain. He nodded at the town. "How does this sound to you, Hinkston? Suppose, as you said originally, that rocket travel occurred years ago. And when the Earth people had lived here a number of years they began to get homesick for Earth. First a mild neurosis about it, then a full fledged psychosis. Then, threatened insanity. What would you do, as a psychiatrist, if faced with such a problem?"

Hinkston thought. "Well, I think I'd re-arrange the civilization on Mars so it resembled Earth more and more each day. If there was any way of reproducing every plant, every road and every lake, and even an ocean, I would do so. Then I would, by some vast crowd hypnosis, theoretically anyway, convince everyone in a town this size that this really *was* Earth, not Mars at all."

"Good enough, Hinkston. I think we're on the right track now. That woman in that house back there, just *thinks* she's living on Earth. It protects her sanity. She and all the others in this town are the patients of the greatest experiment in migration and hypnosis you will ever lay your eyes on in your life."

"That's it, sir!" cried Lustig.

"Well," the captain sighed. "Now we're getting somewhere. I feel better.   135 It all sounds a bit more logical now. This talk about time and going back and forth and traveling in time turns my stomach upside down. But, *this* way — " He actually smiled for the first time in a month. "Well. It looks as if we'll be fairly welcome here."

"Or, will we, sir?" said Lustig. "After all, like the Pilgrims, these people came here to escape Earth. Maybe they won't be too happy to see us, sir. Maybe they'll try to drive us out or kill us?"

"We have superior weapons if that should happen. Anyway, all we can do is try. This next house now. Up we go."

But they had hardly crossed the lawn when Lustig stopped and looked off across the town, down the quiet, dreaming afternoon street. "Sir," he said.

"What is it, Lustig?" asked the captain.

"Oh, sir, *sir*, what I see, what I do see now before me, oh, oh — " said   140 Lustig, and he began to cry. His fingers came up, twisting and trembling, and his face was all wonder and joy and incredulity. He sounded as if any moment he might go quite insane with happiness. He looked down the street and he began to run, stumbling, awkwardly, falling, picking himself up, and running on. "Oh, God, God, thank you, God! Thank you!"

"Don't let him get away!" The captain broke into a run.

Now Lustig was running at full speed, shouting. He turned into a yard half way down the little shady side street and leaped up upon the porch of a large green house with an iron rooster on the roof.

He was beating upon the door, shouting and hollering and crying when Hinkston and the captain ran up and stood in the yard.

The door opened. Lustig yanked the screen wide and in a high wail of discovery and happiness, cried out, "Grandma! Grandpa!"

Two old people stood in the doorway, their faces lighting up.   145

"Albert!" Their voices piped and they rushed out to embrace and pat him on the back and move around him. "Albert, oh, Albert, it's been so many years! How you've grown, boy, how big you are, boy, oh, Albert boy, how are you!"

"Grandma, Grandpa!" sobbed Albert Lustig. "Good to see you! You look fine, fine! Oh, fine!" He held them, turned them, kissed them, hugged them, cried on them, held them out again, blinked at the little old people. The sun was in the sky, the wind blew, the grass was green, the screen door stood open.

"Come in, lad, come in, there's lemonade for you, fresh, lots of it!"

"Grandma, Grandpa, good to see you! I've got friends down here! Here!" Lustig turned and waved wildly at the captain and Hinkston, who, all during the adventure on the porch, had stood in the shade of a tree, holding onto each other. "Captain, captain, come up, come up, I want you to meet my grandfolks!"

"Howdy," said the folks. "Any friend of Albert's is ours, too! Don't stand   150
there with your mouths open! Come on!"

In the living room of the old house it was cool and a grandfather clock ticked high and long and bronzed in one corner. There were soft pillows on large couches and walls filled with books and a rug cut in a thick rose pattern and antimacassars pinned to furniture, and lemonade in the hand, sweating, and cool on the thirsty tongue.

"Here's to our health." Grandma tipped her glass to her porcelain teeth.

"How long have you *been* here, Grandma?" said Lustig.

"A good many years," she said, tartly. "Ever since we died."

"Ever since you what?" asked Captain John Black, putting his drink down.   155

"Oh, yes," Lustig looked at his captain. "They've been dead thirty years."

"And you *sit* there, calmly!" cried the captain.

"Tush," said the old woman, and winked glitteringly at John Black. "Who are we to question what happens? Here we are. What's life, anyways? Who does what for why and where? All we know is here we are, alive again, and no questions asked. A second chance." She toddled over and held out her thin wrist to Captain John Black. "Feel." He felt. "Solid, ain't I?" she asked. He nodded. "You hear my voice don't you?" she inquired. Yes, he did. "Well, then," she said in triumph, "why go around questioning?"

"Well," said the captain, "it's simply that we never thought we'd find a thing like this on Mars."

"And now you've found it. I dare say there's lots on every planet that'll   160
show you God's infinite ways."

"Is this Heaven?" asked Hinkston.

"Nonsense, no. It's a world and we get a second chance. Nobody told us why. But then nobody told us why we were on Earth, either. That *other* Earth, I mean. The one you came from. How do we know there wasn't *another* before *that* one?"

"A good question," said the captain.

The captain stood up and slapped his hand on his leg in an off-hand fashion. "We've got to be going. It's been nice. Thank you for the drinks."

He stopped. He turned and looked toward the door, startled.   165

Far away, in the sunlight, there was a sound of voices, a crowd, a shouting and a great hello.

"What's that?" asked Hinkston.

"We'll soon find out!" And Captain John Black was out the front door abruptly, jolting across the green lawn and into the street of the Martian town.

He stood looking at the ship. The ports were open and his crew were streaming out, waving their hands. A crowd of people had gathered and in and through and among these people the members of the crew were running, talking, laughing, shaking hands. People did little dances. People swarmed. The rocket lay empty and abandoned.

A brass band exploded in the sunlight, flinging off a gay tune from   170
upraised tubas and trumpets. There was a bang of drums and a shrill of fifes. Little girls with golden hair jumped up and down. Little boys shouted, "Hooray!" And fat men passed around ten-cent cigars. The mayor of the town made a speech. Then, each member of the crew with a mother on one arm, a father or sister on the other, was spirited off down the street, into little cottages or big mansions and doors slammed shut.

The wind rose in the clear spring sky and all was silent. The brass band had banged off around a corner leaving the rocket to shine and dazzle alone in the sunlight.

"Abandoned!" cried the captain. "Abandoned the ship, they did! I'll have their skins, by God! They had orders!"

"Sir," said Lustig. "Don't be too hard on them. Those were all old relatives and friends."

"That's no excuse!"

"Think how they felt, captain, seeing familiar faces outside the ship!"   175

"I would have obeyed orders! I would have —" The captain's mouth remained open.

Striding along the sidewalk under the Martian sun, tall, smiling, eyes blue, face tan, came a young man of some twenty-six years.

"John!" the man cried, and broke into a run.

"What?" said Captain John Black. He swayed.

"John, you old beggar, you!"   180

The man ran up and gripped his hand and slapped him on the back.

"It's you," said John Black.

"Of course, who'd you *think* it was!"

"Edward!" The captain appealed now to Lustig and Hinkston, holding the stranger's hand. "This is my brother Edward. Ed, meet my men, Lustig, Hinkston! My brother!"

They tugged at each other's hands and arms and then finally embraced.   185
"Ed!" "John, you old bum, you!" "You're looking fine, Ed, but, Ed, what is this? You haven't changed over the years. You died, I remember, when you were twenty-six, and I was nineteen, oh God, so many years ago, and here you are, and, Lord, what goes on, what goes on?"

Edward Black gave him a brotherly knock on the chin. "Mom's waiting," he said.

"Mom?"

"And Dad, too."

"And Dad?" The captain almost fell to earth as if hit upon the chest with a mighty weapon. He walked stiffly and awkwardly, out of coordination. He stuttered and whispered and talked only one or two words at a time. "Mom alive? Dad? Where?"

"At the old house on Oak Knoll Avenue."   190

"The old house." The captain stared in delighted amazement. "Did you *hear* that, Lustig, Hinkston?"

"I know it's hard for you to believe."

"But alive. Real."

"Don't I *feel* real?" The strong aim, the firm grip, the white smile. The light, curling hair.

Hinkston was gone. He had seen his own house down the street and was   195
running for it. Lustig was grinning. "Now you understand, sir, what happened to everybody on the ship. They couldn't help themselves."

"Yes. Yes," said the captain, eyes shut. "Yes." He put out his hand. "When I open my eyes, you'll be gone." He opened his eyes. "You're still here. God, Edward, you look fine!"

"Come along, lunch is waiting for you. I told Mom."

Lustig said, "Sir, I'll be with my grandfolks if you want me."

"What? Oh, fine, Lustig. Later, then."

Edward grabbed his arm and marched him. "You need support."   200

"I do. My knees, all funny. My stomach, loose. God."

"There's the house. Remember it?"

"Remember it? Hell! I can beat you to the front porch!"

They ran. The wind roared over Captain John Black's ears. The earth roared under his feet. He saw the golden figure of Edward Black pull ahead of him in the amazing dream of reality. He saw the house rush forward, the door open, the screen swing back. "Beat you!" cried Edward, bounding up the steps. "I'm an old man," panted the captain, "and you're still young. But, then, you *always* beat me, I remember!"

In the doorway, Mom, pink and plump and bright. And behind her, pepper   205
grey, Dad, with his pipe in his hand.

"Mom, Dad!"

He ran up the steps like a child, to meet them.

It was a fine long afternoon. They finished lunch and they sat in the living room and he told them all about his rocket and his being captain and they nodded and smiled upon him and Mother was just the same, and Dad bit the end off a cigar and lighted it in his old fashion. Mom brought in some iced tea in the middle of the afternoon. Then, there was a big turkey dinner at night and time flowing on. When the drumsticks were sucked clean and lay brittle upon the plates, the captain leaned back in his chair and exhaled his deep contentment. Dad poured him a small glass of dry sherry. It was seven-thirty in the evening. Night was in all the trees and coloring the sky, and the lamps were halos of dim light in the gentle house. From all the other houses down the streets came sounds of music, pianos playing, laughter.

Mom put a record on the victrola and she and Captain John Black had a dance. She was wearing the same perfume he remembered from the summer when she and Dad had been killed in the train accident. She was very real in his arms as they danced lightly to the music.

"I'll wake in the morning," said the captain. "And I'll be in my rocket in   210 space, and all this will be gone."

"No, no, don't think that," she cried, softly, pleadingly. "We're here. Don't question. God is good to us. Let's be happy."

The record ended with a circular hissing.

"You're tired, son," said Dad. He waved his pipe. "You and Ed go on upstairs. Your old bedroom is waiting for you."

"The old one?"

"The brass bed and all," laughed Edward.   215

"But I should report my men in."

"Why?" Mother was logical.

"Why? Well, I don't know. No reason, I guess. No, none at all. What's the difference?" He shook his head. "I'm not being very logical these days."

"Good night, son." She kissed his cheek.

"'Night, Mom."   220

"Sleep tight, son." Dad shook his hand.

"Same to you, Pop."

"It's good to have you home."

"It's good to *be* home."

He left the land of cigar smoke and perfume and books and gentle light   225 and ascended the stairs, talking, talking with Edward. Edward pushed a door open and there was the yellow brass bed and the old semaphore banners from college days and a very musty raccoon coat which he petted with strange, muted affection. "It's too much," he said faintly. "Like being in a thunder shower without an umbrella. I'm soaked to the skin with emotion. I'm numb. I'm tired."

"A night's sleep between cool clean sheets for you, my bucko." Edward slapped wide the snowy linens and flounced the pillows. Then he put up a window and let the night blooming jasmine float in. There was moonlight and the sound of distant dancing and whispering.

"So this is Mars," said the captain undressing.

"So this is Mars," Edward undressed in idle, leisurely moves, drawing his shirt off over his head, revealing golden shoulders and the good muscular neck.

The lights were out, they were into bed, side by side, as in the days, how many decades ago? The captain lolled and was nourished by the night wind pushing the lace curtains out upon the dark room air. Among the trees, upon a lawn, someone had cranked up a portable phonograph and now it was playing softly. "I'll be loving you, always, with a love that's true, always."

The thought of Anna came to his mind. "Is Anna here?"   230

His brother, lying straight out in the moonlight from the window, waited and then said, "Yes. She's out of town. But she'll be here in the morning."

The captain shut his eyes. "I want to see Anna very much."

The room was square and quiet except for their breathing. "Good night, Ed." A pause. "Good night, John."

He lay peacefully, letting his thoughts float. For the first time the stress of the day was moved aside, all of the excitement was calmed. He could think logically now. It had all been emotion. The bands playing, the sight of familiar faces, the sick pounding of your heart. But — now . . .

How? He thought. How was all this made? And why? For what purpose? Out of the goodness of some kind God? Was God, then, really that fine and thoughtful of his children? How and why and what for?

He thought of the various theories advanced in the first heat of the afternoon by Hinkston and Lustig. He let all kinds of new theories drop in lazy pebbles down through his mind, as through a dark water, now, turning, throwing out dull flashes of white light. Mars. Earth. Mom. Dad. Edward. Mars. Martians.

Who had lived here a thousand years ago on Mars? Martians? Or had this always been like this? Martians. He repeated the word quietly, inwardly.

He laughed out loud, almost. He had the most ridiculous theory, all of a sudden. It gave him a kind of chilled feeling. It was really nothing to think of, of course. Highly improbable. Silly. Forget it. Ridiculous.

But, he thought, just suppose. Just *suppose* now, that there were Martians living on Mars and they saw our ship coming and saw us inside our ship and hated us. Suppose, now, just for the hell of it, that they wanted to destroy us, as invaders, as unwanted ones, and they wanted to do it in a very clever way, so that we would be taken off guard. Well, what would the best weapon be that a Martian could use against Earth-men with atom weapons?

The answer was interesting. Telepathy, hypnosis, memory, and imagination.

Suppose all these houses weren't real at all, this bed not real, but only figments of my own imagination, given substance by telepathy and hypnosis by the Martians.

Suppose these houses are really some other shape, a Martian shape, but, by playing on my desires and wants, these Martians have made this seem like my old home town, my old house, to lull me out of my suspicions? What better way to fool a man, by his own emotions.

And suppose those two people in the next room, asleep, are not my mother and father at all. But two Martians, incredibly brilliant, with the ability to keep me under this dreaming hypnosis all of the time?

And that brass band, today? What a clever plan it would be. First, fool Lustig, then fool Hinkston, then gather a crowd around the rocket ship and wave. And all the men in the ship, seeing mothers, aunts, uncles, sweethearts dead ten, twenty years ago, naturally, disregarding orders, would rush out and abandon the ship. What more natural? What more unsuspecting? What more simple? A man doesn't ask too many questions when his mother is suddenly brought back to life; he's much too happy. And the brass band played and everybody was taken off to private homes. And here we all are, tonight, in various houses, in various beds, with no weapons to protect us, and the rocket lies in the moonlight, empty. And wouldn't it be horrible and terrifying to discover that all of this was part of some great clever plan by the Martians to divide and conquer us, and kill us. Some time during the night, perhaps, my brother on this bed, will change form, melt, shift, and become a one-eyed, green and yellow-toothed Martian. It would be very simple for him just to turn over in bed and put a knife into my heart. And in all those other houses down the street a dozen other brothers or fathers suddenly melting away and taking out knives and doing things to the unsuspecting, sleeping men of Earth.

His hands were shaking under the covers. His body was cold. Suddenly it was not a theory. Suddenly he was very afraid. He lifted himself in bed and listened. The night was very quiet. The music had stopped. The wind had died. His brother (?) lay sleeping beside him.

Very carefully he lifted the sheets, rolled them back. He slipped from bed and was walking softly across the room when his brother's voice said, "Where are you going?"

"What?"

His brother's voice was quite cold. "I said, where do you think you're going?"

"For a drink of water." 250

"But you're not thirsty."

"Yes, yes, I am."

"No, you're not."

Captain John Black broke and ran across the room. He screamed. He screamed twice.

He never reached the door. 255

In the morning, the brass band played a mournful dirge. From every house in the street came little solemn processions bearing long boxes and along the sun-filled street, weeping and changing, came the grandmas and grandfathers and mothers and sisters and brothers, walking to the churchyard, where there were open holes dug freshly and new tombstones installed. Seventeen holes in all, and seventeen tombstones. Three of the tombstones said, CAPTAIN JOHN BLACK, ALBERT LUSTIG, and SAMUEL HINKSTON.

The mayor made a little sad speech, his face sometimes looking like the mayor, sometimes looking like something else.

Mother and Father Black were there, with Brother Edward, and they cried, their faces melting now from a familiar face into something else.

Grandpa and Grandma Lustig were there, weeping, their faces also shifting like wax, shivering as a thing does in waves of heat on a summer day.

The coffins were lowered. Somebody murmured about "the unexpected 260 and sudden deaths of seventeen fine men during the night—"

Earth was shoveled in on the coffin tops.

After the funeral the brass band slammed and banged back into town and the crowd stood around and waved and shouted as the rocket was torn to pieces and strewn about and blown up.   *[1948]*

≡ THINKING ABOUT THE TEXT

1. What was your first response to the Victorian town? The captain says that "it's absolutely impossible" (para. 26). Did you think he is right?

2. What was your response to the attempted explanations for the town's appearance? Isn't seeing believing? Did you think that perhaps time travel is involved?

3. Comment on the thematic significance of the line "the buzzing of spring bees on the air lulled and quieted him, and the fresh look of things was a balm to the soul" (para. 78).

4. After Captain Black recovers from being "soaked to the skin with emotion" (para. 225), he begins thinking logically. At this point, as you sense the ending is near, what logical explanation did you suspect was coming — something about illusion, or perhaps delusion? What is ironic about the astronauts' coming armed with atomic weapons?

5. Readers are often puzzled by the ending. Indeed, it is strange that the Martians would hold a human funeral. After all, if the men are dead, why continue the charade? Why do you think they perform the ritual?

OCTAVIA BUTLER

Human Evolution

Octavia Butler (1947–2006), one of the few female African American science fiction writers, won numerous prizes for her work, including the prestigious Hugo and Nebula Awards. In 1995, she became the first science fiction writer to receive a MacArthur Foundation "genius" grant. Butler was born in Pasadena, California, where, as an introspective child, she began reading and writing science fiction at a young age. Her first novel, Master Pattern, *was published in 1976. Her most popular novel,* Kindred *(1979), transports an African American antagonist from the present to the time of slavery in the antebellum South. It has sold well over two hundred thousand copies. The story printed here is from* Imago *(1989), a popular novel in her alien-human hybrid world of the Xenogenesis Trilogy, a narrative about a handful of survivors from a missile war that destroys most of Earth. Themes of intolerance, racial and sexual ambiguity, and environmentalism are common in her work. The second edition of* Bloodchild and Other Stories *was published posthumously in 2006.*

I

I slipped into my first metamorphosis so quietly that no one noticed. Metamorphoses were not supposed to begin that way. Most people begin with small, obvious, physical changes — the loss of fingers and toes, for instance, or the budding of new fingers and toes of a different design.

I wish my experience had been that normal, that safe.

For several days, I changed without attracting attention. Early stages of metamorphosis didn't normally last for days without bringing on deep sleep, but mine did. My first changes were sensory. Tastes, scents, all sensations suddenly became complex, confusing, yet unexpectedly seductive.

I had to relearn everything. River water, for instance: when I swam in it, I noticed that it had two distinctive major flavors — hydrogen and oxygen? — and many minor flavors. I could separate out and savor each one individually. In fact, I couldn't help separating them. But I learned them quickly and accepted them in their new complexity so that only occasional changes in minor flavors demanded my attention.

Our river water at Lo always came to us clouded with sediment. "Rich," the Oankali called it. "Muddy," the Humans said, and filtered it or let the silt settle to the bottom before they drank it. "Just water," we constructs said, and shrugged. We had never known any other water.   5

As quickly as I could, I learned again to understand and accept my sensory impressions of the people and things around me. The experience absorbed so much of my attention that I didn't understand how my family could fail to see that something unusual was happening to me. But beyond mentioning that I was daydreaming too much, even my parents missed the signs.

They were, after all, the wrong signs. No one was expecting them, so no one noticed when they appeared.

All five of my parents were old when I was born. They didn't look any older than my adult sisters and brothers, but they had helped with the founding of Lo. They had grandchildren who were old. I don't think I had ever surprised them before. I wasn't sure I liked surprising them now, I didn't want to tell them. I especially didn't want to tell Tino, my Human father. He was supposed to stay with me through my metamorphosis — since he was my same-sex Human parent. But I did not feel drawn to him as I should have. Nor did I feel drawn to Lilith, my birth mother. She was Human, too, and what was happening to me was definitely not a Human thing. Strangely I didn't want to go to my Oankali father, Dichaan, either, and he was my logical choice after Tino. My Oankali mother, Ahajas, would have talked to one of my fathers for me. She had done that for two of my brothers who had been afraid of metamorphosis — afraid they would change too much, lose all signs of their Humanity. That could happen to me, though I had never worried about it. Ahajas would have talked to me and for me, no matter what my problem was. Of all my parents, she was the easiest to talk to. I would have gone to her if the thought of doing so had been more appealing — or if I had understood why it was so unappealing. What was wrong with me? I wasn't shy or afraid, but when I thought of going to her, I felt first drawn, then . . . almost repelled.

Finally there was my ooloi parent, Nikanj.

It would tell me to go to one of my same-sex parents — one of my fathers.   10
What else could it say? I knew well enough that I was in metamorphosis, and that that was one of the few things ooloi parents could not help with.

There were still some Humans who insisted on seeing the ooloi as some kind of male-female combination, but the ooloi were no such thing. They were themselves — a different sex altogether.

So I went to Nikanj only hoping to enjoy its company for a while. Eventually it would notice what was happening to me and send me to my fathers. Until it did, I would rest near it. I was tired, sleepy. Metamorphosis was mostly sleep.

I found Nikanj inside the family house, talking to a pair of Human strangers. The Humans were standing back from Nikanj. The female was almost sheltering behind the male, and the male was making a painful effort to appear courageous. Both looked alarmed when they saw me open a wall and step through into the room. Then, as they got a look at me, they seemed to relax a little. I looked very Human — especially if they compared me to Nikanj, who wasn't Human at all.

The Humans smelled most obviously of sweat and adrenaline, food and sex. I sat down on the floor and let myself work out the complex combinations of scents. My new awareness wouldn't allow me to do anything else. By the time I was finished, I thought I would be able to track those two Humans through anything.

Nikanj paid no attention to me except to notice me when I came in. It was used to its children coming and going as they chose, used to all of us spending time with it, learning whatever it was willing to teach us.

It has an incredibly complex scent because it was ooloi. It had collected within itself not only the reproductive material of other members of the family but cells of other plant and animal species that it had dealt with recently. These it would study, memorize, then either consume or store. It consumed the ones it knew it could re-create from memory, using its own DNA. It kept the others alive in a kind of stasis until they were needed.

Its most noticeable underscent was Kaal, the kin group it was born into. I had never met its parents, but I knew the Kaal scent from other members of the Kaal kin group. Somehow, though, I had never noticed that scent on Nikanj, never separated it out this way.

The main scent was Lo, of course. It had mated with Oankali of the Lo kin group, and on mating, it had altered its own scent as an ooloi must. The word *ooloi* could not be translated directly into English because its meaning was as complex as Nikanj's scent. "Treasured stranger." "Bridge." "Life trader." "Weaver." "Magnet."

Magnet, my birth mother says. People are drawn to ooloi and can't escape. She couldn't, certainly. But then, neither could Nikanj escape her or any of its mates. The Oankali said the chemical bonds of mating were as difficult to break as the habit of breathing.

Scents . . . The two visiting Humans were longtime mates and smelled of each other.

"We don't know yet whether we want to emigrate," the female was saying. "We've come to see for ourselves and for our people."

"You'll be shown everything," Nikanj told them. "There are no secrets about the Mars colony or travel to it. But right now the shuttles allotted to emigration are all in use. We have a guest area where Humans can wait."

The two Humans looked at one another. They still smelled frightened, but now both were making an effort to look brave. Their faces were almost expressionless.

"We don't want to stay here," the male said. "We'll come back when there's a ship."

Nikanj stood up—unfolded, as Humans say. "I can't tell you when there'll be a ship," it said. "They arrive when they arrive. Let me show you the guest area. It isn't like this house. Humans built it of cut wood."

The pair stumbled back from Nikanj.   25

Nikanj's sensory tentacles flattened against its body in amusement. It sat down again. "There are other Humans waiting in the guest area," it told them gently. "They're like you. They want their own all-Human world. They'll be traveling with you when you go." It paused, looked at me. "Eka, why don't you show them?"

I wanted to stay with it now more than ever, but I could see that the two Humans were relieved to be turned over to someone who at least looked Human. I stood up and faced them.

"This is Jodahs," Nikanj told them, "one of my younger children."

The female gave me a look that I had seen too often not to recognize. She said, "But I thought . . ."

"No," I said to her, and smiled. "I'm not Human. I'm a Human-born con-   30
struct. Come out this way. The guest area isn't far."

They did not want to follow me through the wall I opened until it was fully open—as though they thought the wall might close on them, as though it would hurt them if it did.

"It would be like being grasped gently by a big hand," I told them when we were all outside.

"What?" the male asked.

"If the wall shut on you. It couldn't hurt you because you're alive. It might eat your clothing, though."

"No, thanks!"   35

I laughed. "I've never seen that happen, but I've heard it can."

"What's your name?" the female asked.

"All of it?" She looked interested in me—smelled sexually attracted, which made her interesting to me. Human females did tend to like me as long as I kept my few body tentacles covered by clothing and my few head tentacles hidden in my hair. The sensory spots on my face and arms looked like ordinary skin, though they didn't feel ordinary.

"Your Human name," the female said. "I already know . . . Eka and Jodahs, but I'm not sure which to call you."

"Eka is just a term of endearment for young children," I told her, "like lelka   40
for married children and Chka between mates. Jodahs is my personal name. The Human version of my whole name is Jodahs Iyapo Leal Kaalnikanjlo.

My name, the surnames of my birth mother and Human father, and Nikanj's name beginning with the kin group it was born into and ending with the kin group of its Oankali mates. If I were Oankali-born or if I gave you the Oankali version of my name, it would be a lot longer and more complicated."

"I've heard some of them," the female said. "You'll probably drop them eventually."

"No. We'll change them to suit our needs, but we won't drop them. They give very useful information, especially when people are looking for mates."

"Jodahs doesn't sound like any name I've heard before," the male said.

"Oankali name. An Oankali named Jodahs died helping with the emigration. My birth mother said he should be remembered. The Oankali don't have a tradition of remembering people by naming kids after them, but my birth mother insisted. She does that sometimes — insists on keeping Human customs."

"You look very Human," the female said softly.   45

I smiled. "I'm a child. I just look unfinished."

"How old are you?"

"Twenty-nine."

"Good God! When will you be considered an adult?"

"After metamorphosis." I smiled to myself. Soon. "I have a brother   50
who went through it at twenty-one, and a sister who didn't reach it until she was thirty-three. People change when their bodies are ready, not at some specific age."

She was silent for some time. We reached the last of the true houses of Lo — the houses that had been grown from the living substance of the Lo entity. Humans without Oankali mates could not open walls or raise table, bed, or chair platforms in such houses. Left alone in our houses, these Humans were prisoners until some construct, Oankali, or mated Human freed them. Thus, they had been given first a guest house, then a guest area. In that area they had built their dead houses of cut wood and woven thatch. They used fire for light and cooking and occasionally they burned down one of their houses. Houses that did not burn became infested with rodents and insects which ate the Human's food and bit or stung the Humans themselves. Periodically Oankali went in and drove the non-Human life out. It always came back. It had been feeding on Humans, eating their food, and living in their buildings since long before the Oankali arrived. Still the guest area was reasonably comfortable. Guests ate from trees and plants that were not what they appeared to be. They were extensions of the Lo entity. They had been induced to synthesize fruits and vegetables in shapes, flowers, and textures that Humans recognized. The foods grew from what appeared to be their proper trees and plants. Lo took care of the Humans' wastes, keeping their area clean, though they tended to be careless about where they threw or dumped things in this temporary place.

"There's an empty house there," I said, pointing.

The female stared at my hand rather than at where I pointed. I had, from a Human point of view, too many fingers and toes. Seven per. Since they were part of distinctly Human-looking hands and feet, Humans didn't usually notice them at once.

I held my hand open, palm up so that she could see it, and her expression flickered from curiosity and surprise through embarrassment back to curiosity.

"Will you change much in metamorphosis?" she asked.   55

"Probably. The Human-born get more Oankali and the Oankali-born get more Human. I'm first-generation. If you want to see the future, take a look at some of the third- and fourth-generations constructs. They're a lot more uniform from start to finish."

"That's not our future," the male said.

"Your choice," I said.

The male walked away toward the empty house. The female hesitated. "What do you think of our emigration?" she asked.

I looked at her, liking her, not wanting to answer. But such questions   60 should be answered. Why, though, were the Human females who insisted on asking them so often small, weak people? The Martian environment they were headed for was harsher than any they had known. We would see that they had the best possible chance to survive. Many would live to bear children on their new world. But they would suffer so. And in the end, it would all be for nothing. Their own genetic conflict had betrayed and destroyed them once. It would do so again.

"You should stay," I told the female. "You should join us."

"Why?"

I wanted very much not to look at her, to go away from her. Instead I continued to face her. "I understand that Humans must be free to go," I said softly. "I'm Human enough for my body to understand that. But I'm Oankali enough to know that you will eventually destroy yourselves again."

She frowned, marring her smooth forehead. "You mean another war?"

"Perhaps. Or maybe you'll find some other way to do it. You were working   65 on several ways before your war."

"You don't know anything about it. You're too young."

"You should stay and mate with constructs or with Oankali," I said. "The children we construct are free of inherent flaws. What we build will last."

"You're just a child, repeating what you've been told!"

I shook my head. "I perceive what I perceive. No one had to tell me how to use my senses any more than they had to tell you how to see or hear. There is a lethal genetic conflict in Humanity, and you know it."

"All we know is what the Oankali have told us." The male had come back.   70 He put his arm around the female, drawing her away from me as though I had offered some threat. "They could be lying for their own reasons."

I shifted my attention to him. "You know they're not," I said softly. "Your own history tells you. Your people are intelligent, and that's good. The Oankali say you're potentially one of the most intelligent species they've found. But you're also hierarchical — you and your nearest animal relatives and your most distant animal ancestors. Intelligence is relatively new to life on Earth, but your hierarchical tendencies are ancient. The new was too often put at the service of the old. It will be again. You're bright enough to learn to live in your new world, but you're so hierarchical you'll destroy yourselves trying to dominate it and each other. You might last a long time, but in the end, you'll destroy yourselves."

"We could last a thousand years," the male said. "We did all right on Earth until the war."

"You could. Your new world will be difficult. It will demand most of your attention, perhaps occupy your hierarchical tendencies safely for a while."

"We'll be free—us, our children, their children."

"Perhaps."   75

"We'll be fully Human and free. That's enough. We might even get into space again on our own someday. Your people might be dead wrong about us."

"No." He couldn't read the gene combinations as I could. It was as though he were about to walk off a cliff simply because he could not see it—or because he, or rather his descendants, would not hit the rocks below for a long time. And what were we doing, we who knew the truth? Helping him reach the cliff. Ferrying him to it.

"We might outlast your people here on Earth," he said.

"I hope so," I told him. His expression said he didn't believe me, but I meant it. We would not be here—the Earth he knew would not be here—for more than a few centuries. We, Oankali and construct, were space-going people, as curious about other life and as acquisitive of it as Humans were hierarchical. Eventually we would have to begin the long, long search for a new species to combine with to construct new life-forms. Much of Oankali existence was spent in such searches. We would leave this solar system in perhaps three centuries. I would live to see the leave-taking myself. And when we broke and scattered, we would leave behind a lump of stripped rock more like the moon than like his blue Earth. He did not know that. He would never know it. To tell him would be a cruelty.

"Do you ever think of yourself or your kind as Human?" the female asked.   80
"Some of you look so Human."

"We feel our Humanity. It helps us to understand both you and the Oankali. Oankali alone could never have let you have your Mars colony."

"I heard they were helping!" the male said. "Your . . . your parent said they were helping!"

"They help because of what we constructs tell them: that you should be allowed to go even though you'll eventually destroy yourselves. The Oankali believe . . . the Oankali *know to the bone* that it's wrong to help the Human species regenerate unchanged because it *will* destroy itself again. To them it's like deliberately causing the conception of a child who is so defective that it must die in infancy."

"They're wrong. Someday we'll show them how wrong."

It was a threat. It was meaningless, but it gave him some slight satisfac- 85
tion. "The other Humans here will show you where to gather food," I said. "If
you need anything else, ask one of us." I turned to go.

"So goddamn patronizing," the male muttered.

I turned back without thinking. "Am I really?"

The male frowned, muttered a curse, and went back into the house.
I understood then that he was just angry. It bothered me that I sometimes
made them angry. I never intended to.

The female stepped to me, touched my face, examined a little of my hair.
Humans who hadn't mated among us never really learned to touch us. At
best, they annoyed us by rubbing their hands over sensory spots, and once
their hands found the spots they never liked them.

The female jerked her hand back when her fingers discovered the one 90
below my left ear.

"They're a little like eyes that can't close to protect themselves," I said. "It
doesn't exactly hurt us when you touch them, but we don't like you to."

"So what? You have to teach people how to touch you?"

I smiled and took her hand between my own. "Hands are always safe,"
I said. I left her standing there, watching me. I could see her through sensory
tentacles in my hair. She stood there until the male came out and drew her
inside.   *[1989]*

≡ THINKING ABOUT THE TEXT

1. Butler wastes no time getting the reader into an alien world. Comment
   on some of the "otherness" of this future.

2. Discuss Butler's characterization of the human male in this story.
   What is Butler concerned with? Comment on the story's last line.

3. What scientific aspects of contemporary life is extended with Butler's
   story's constructs?

4. Some critics believe that much of serious science fiction is meant as a
   warning. Is this true here? Can humans change? How might we know
   our destruction was near?

5. Butler's narrative focus seems to revolve around basic flaws in the
   human makeup. What are some of them? Do you agree? Might these
   flaws be learned or a product of specific contexts?

≡ MAKING COMPARISONS

1. Compare the flaws in human nature that both stories focus on.

2. Explain how one of these stories is relevant to your present concerns.

3. Explain the authors' attitudes toward men in these stories.

T. C. BOYLE
The Relive Box

T. C. Boyle (b. 1948) graduated from the State University of New York, Potsdam, with a B.A. in English and history. Boyle taught high school for several years in his hometown, then attended the Iowa Writers' Workshop, and later received a Ph.D. in nineteenth-century British literature from the University of Iowa in 1977. He has published more than twenty books of fiction and has received numerous awards, including many O. Henry Awards and Best American story selections. He is a Distinguished Professor of English at the University of Southern California. Some of his recent work includes the novels, The Harder They Come *(2015),* The Terranauts *(2016), and* Outside Looking In *(2019); and the collection* The Relive Box and Other Stories *(2017), from which the following story is taken.*

Katie wanted to relive Katie at nine, before her mother left, and I could appreciate that, but we had only one console at the time, and I really didn't want to go there. It was coming up on the holidays, absolutely grim outside, nine-thirty at night—on a school night—and she had to be up at six to catch the bus in the dark. She'd already missed too much school, staying home on any pretext and reliving all day, while I was at work, so there really were no limits, and who was being a bad father here? A single father unable to discipline his fifteen-year-old daughter, let alone inculcate a work ethic in her?

Me. I was. And I felt bad about it. I wanted to put my foot down and at the same time give her something, make a concession, a peace offering. But, even more, I wanted the box myself, wanted it so baldly it was showing in my face, I'm sure, and she needed to get ready for school, needed sleep, needed to stop reliving and worry about the now, the now and the future. "Why don't you wait till the weekend?" I said.

She was wearing those tights which all the girls wear like painted-on skin, standing in the doorway to the living room, perching on one foot the way she did when she was doing her dance exercises. Her face belonged to her mother, my ex, Christine, who hadn't been there for her for six years and counting. "I want to relive now," she said, diminishing her voice to a shaky, hesitant plaint that was calculated to make me give in to whatever she wanted, but it wasn't going to work this time, no way. She was going to bed, and I was going back to a rainy February night in 1982, a sold-out show at the Roxy, a band I loved then, and the girl I was mad crazy for before she broke my heart and Christine came along to break it all over again.

"Why don't you go upstairs and text your friends or something?" I said.

"I don't want to text my friends. I want to be with my mom."   5

This was a plaint, too, and it cut even deeper. She was deprived, that was the theme here, and my behavior, as any impartial observer could have seen in a heartbeat, verged on child abuse. "I know, honey, I know. But it's not healthy. You're spending too much time there."

"You're just selfish, that's all," she said, and here was the shift to a new tone, a tone of animus and opposition, the subtext being that I never thought of anybody but myself. "You want to, what, relive when you were, like, my age or something? Let me guess: you're going to go back and relive yourself doing homework, right? As an example for your daughter?"

The room was a mess. The next day was the day the maid came, so I was standing amid the debris of the past week, a healthy percentage of it — abandoned sweat socks, energy-drink cans, crumpled foil pouches that had once contained biscotti, popcorn, or Salami Bites — generated by the child standing there before me. "I don't like your sarcasm," I said.

Her face was pinched so that her lips were reduced to the smallest little O-ring of disgust. "What *do* you like?"

"A clean house. A little peace and quiet. Some privacy, for Christ's sake — is that too much to ask?"   10

"I want to be with Mom."

"Go text your friends."

"I don't have any friends."

"Make some."

And this, thrown over her shoulder, preparatory to the furious pounding   15
retreat up the stairs and the slamming of her bedroom door: "You're a pig!"

And my response, which had been ritualized ever since I'd sprung for the five-thousand-dollar, second-generation Halcom X1520 Relive Box with the In-Flesh Retinal Projection Stream and altered forever the dynamic between me and my only child: "I know."

Most people, when they got their first Relive Box, went straight for sex, which was only natural. In fact, it was a selling point in the TV ads, which featured shimmering adolescents walking hand in hand along a generic strip of beach or leaning in for a tender kiss over the ball return at the bowling alley. Who wouldn't want to go back there? Who wouldn't want to relive innocence, the nascent stirrings of love and desire, or the first time you removed her clothes and she removed yours? What of girlfriends (or boyfriends, as the case may be), wives, ex-wives, one-night stands, the casual encounter that got you halfway there, then flitted out of reach on the wings of an unfulfilled promise? I was no different. The sex part of it obsessed me through those first couple of months, and if I drifted into work each morning feeling drained (and not just figuratively) at least I knew that it was a problem, that it was adversely affecting my job performance, and, if I didn't cut back, threatening my job itself. Still, to relive Christine when we first met, to relive her in bed, in candlelight, clinging fast to me and whispering my name in the throes of her passion, was too great a temptation. Or even just sitting there across from me in the Moroccan restaurant where I took her for our first date, her eyes like portals, as she leaned into the table and drank up every word and witticism that came out of my mouth. Or to go farther back, before my wife entered the picture, to Rennie Porter, the girl I took to the senior prom and spent two delicious hours rubbing up against in the back seat of my father's Buick Regal — every second of which I'd relived six or seven times now. And to Lisa, Lisa Denardo, the girl I met that night at the Roxy, hoping I was going to score.

I started coming in late to work. Giving everybody, even my boss, the zombie stare. I got my first warning. Then my second. And my boss — Kevin Moos, a decent enough guy, five years younger than me, who didn't have an X1520, or not that he was letting on — sat me down in his office and told me, in no uncertain terms, that there wouldn't be a third.

But it was a miserable night, and I was depressed. And bored. So bored you could have drilled holes in the back of my head and taken core samples and I wouldn't have known the difference. I'd already denied my daughter, who was thumping around upstairs with the cumulative weight of ten daughters, and the next day was Friday, T.G.I.F., end of the week, the slimmest of workdays, when just about everybody alive thinks about slipping out early. I figured that even if I did relive for more than the two hours I was going to strictly limit myself to, even if I woke up exhausted, I could always find a way to make it to lunch and just let things coast after that. So I went into the kitchen and fixed myself a gin-and-tonic, because that was what I'd been drinking that night at the Roxy, and carried it into the room at the end of the hall that had once been a bedroom and was now (Katie's joke, not mine) the reliving room.

The console sat squarely on the low table that was the only piece of furniture in the room, aside from the straight-backed chair I'd set in front of it the day I brought the thing home. It wasn't much bigger than the gaming consoles I'd had to make do with in the old days, a slick black metal cube with a single recessed glass slit running across the face of it from one side to the other. It activated the minute I took my seat. "Hello, Wes," it said, in the voice I'd selected, male, with the slightest bump of an accent to make it seem less synthetic. "Welcome back."   20

I lifted the drink to my lips to steady myself — think of a conductor raising his baton — and cleared my throat. "February 28, 1982," I said. "9:45 P.M. Play."

The box flashed the date and time and then suddenly I was there, the club exploding into life like a comet touching down, light and noise and movement obliterating the now, the house gone, my daughter gone, the world of getting and doing and bosses and work vanished in an instant. I was standing at the bar with my best friend, Zach Ronalds, who turned up his shirt collars and wore his hair in a Joe Strummer pompadour just like me, only his hair was black and mine choirboy blond (I'd dye it within the week), and I was trying to get the bartender's attention so I could order us G.-and-T.s with my fake I.D. The band, more New Wave than punk, hadn't started yet, and the only thing to look at onstage was the opening band, whose members were packing up their equipment while hypervigilant girls in vampire makeup and torn fishnet stockings washed around them in a human tide that ebbed and flowed on the waves of music crashing through the speakers. It was bliss. Bliss because I knew now that this night alone, out of all the long succession of dull, nugatory nights building up to it, would be special, that this was the night I'd meet Lisa and take her home with me. To my parents' house in Pasadena, where I had a room of my own above the detached garage and could come and go as I pleased. My room. The place where I greased up my hair and stared at myself in the mirror and waited for something to happen, something like this, like what was coming in seven and a half real-time minutes.

Zach said what sounded like "Look at that skank," but since he had his face turned away from me and the music was cranked to the sonic level of a rocket launch (give credit to the X1520's parametric speaker/audio-beam technology, which is infinitely more refined than the first generation's), I wasn't quite sure, though I must have heard him that night, my ears younger then, less damaged by scenes like this one, because I took hold of his arm and said, "Who? Her?"

What I said now, though, was "Reset, reverse ten seconds," and everything stalled, vanished, and started up once more, and here I was trying all over again to get the bartender's attention and listening hard when Zach, leaning casually against the bar on two splayed elbows, opened his mouth to speak. "Look at that skank," he said, undeniably, and there it was, coloring everything in the moment, because he was snap-judging Lisa, with her coathanger shoulders, Kabuki makeup, and shining black lips, and I said, "Who? Her?," already attracted, because in my eyes she wasn't a skank at all, or, if she was, she was a skank from some other realm altogether, and I couldn't from that moment on think of anything but getting her to talk to me.

Now, the frustrating thing about the current relive technology is that you can't be an actor in the scene, only an observer, like Scrooge reliving his boarding-school agonies with the Ghost of Christmas Past at his elbow, so whatever howlers your adolescent self might have uttered are right there, hanging in the air, unedited. You can fast-forward, and I suppose most people do — skip the chatter; get to the sex — but, personally, after going straight to the carnal moments the first five or six times I relived a scene, I liked to go back and hear what I'd had to say, what she'd had to say, no matter how banal it might sound now. What I did that night — and I'd already relived this moment twice that week — was catch hold of the bartender and order not two but three G.-and-T.s, though I only had something like eighteen dollars in my wallet, set one on the bar for Zach, and cross the floor to where she was standing, just beneath the stage, in what would be the mosh pit half an hour later. She saw me coming, saw the drinks — two drinks — and looked away, covering herself, because she was sure I was toting that extra drink for somebody else, a girlfriend or a best bud, lurking in the drift of shadow that the stage lights drew up out of the murky walls.

I tapped her shoulder. She turned her face to me.

"Pause," I said.

Everything stopped. I was in a 3-D painting now, and so was she, and for the longest time I just kept things there, studying her face. She was eighteen years old, like me, beautiful enough underneath the paint and gel and eyeliner and all the rest to make me feel faint even now, and her eyes weren't wary, weren't *used*, but candid, ready, rich with expectation. I held my drink just under my nose, inhaling the smell of juniper berries to tweak the memory, and said, "Play."

"You look thirsty," I said.

The music boomed. Behind me, at the bar, Zach was giving me a look of disbelief, like *What the?*, because this was a violation of our club-going protocol.

25

30

We didn't talk to the girls, and especially not the skanks, because we were there for the *music*, at least that was what we told ourselves. (Second time around I did pause this part, just for the expression on his face—Zach, poor Zach, who never did find himself a girlfriend, as far as I know, and who's probably someplace reliving every club he's ever been in and every date he's ever had, just to feel sorry for himself.)

She levelled her eyes on me, gave it a beat, then took the cold glass from my hand. "How did you guess?" she said.

What followed was the usual exchange of information about bands, books, neighborhood, high school, college, and then I was bragging about the bands I'd seen lately and she was countering with the band members she knew personally—like John Doe and the drummer for the Germs—and letting her eyes reveal just how personal that was, which only managed to inflame me till I wanted nothing more on this earth than to pin her in a corner and kiss the black lipstick right off her. What I said then, unaware that my carefully sculpted pompadour was collapsing across my brow in something very much like a bowl cut (or worse—*anathema*—a Beatles shag), was "You want to dance?"

She gave me a look. Shot her eyes to the stage and back, then around the room. A few people were dancing to the canned music, most of them jerking and gyrating to their own drugged-out beat, and there was no sign—yet—of the band we'd come to hear.

"To this?"

"Yeah," I said, and I looked so—what was it?—*needy*, though at the time   35
I must have thought I was chiselled out of a block of pure cool. "Come on," I said, and I reached out a hand to her.

I watched the decision firm up in her eyes, deep in this moment which would give rise to all the rest, to the part I was about to fast-forward to because I had to get up in the morning. For work. And no excuses. But watch, watch what comes next . . .

She took my hand, the soft friction of her touch alive still somewhere in my cell memory, and then she was leading me out onto the dance floor.

She was leading. And I was following.

Will it surprise you to know that I exceeded my self-imposed two-hour limit? That after the sex I fast-forwarded to our first date, which was really just an agreed-upon meeting at Tower Records (March 2, 1982, 4:30 P.M.), and then up to Barney's Beanery for cheeseburgers and beers and shots of peppermint schnapps (!), which she paid for, because her father was a rich executive at Warner Bros.? Or that that made me feel so good I couldn't resist skipping ahead three months, to when she was as integral to my life as the Black Flag T-shirt that never left my back except in the shower? Lisa. Lisa Denardo. With her cat's tongue and her tight, torquing body that was a girl's and a woman's at the same time and her perfect, evenly spaced set of glistening white teeth (perfect, that is, but for the incisor she'd had a dentist in Tijuana remove, in the spirit of punk solidarity). The scene I hit on was early the following summer, summer break of my sophomore year in college, when I gave up on my parents' garage and Lisa and I moved into an off-campus apartment on Vermont and decided to paint the walls, ceiling, and floors the color of midnight in the Carlsbad Caverns. June 6, 1982, 2:44 P.M. The glisten of black paint, a too bright sun caught in the windows, and Lisa saying, "Think we should paint the glass, too?" I was oblivious of anything but her and me and the way I looked and the way she looked, a streak of paint on her left forearm and another, scimitar-shaped, just over one eyebrow, when suddenly everything went neutral and I was back in the reliving room, staring into the furious face of my daughter.

But let me explain the technology here a moment, for those of you who   40
don't already know. This isn't a computer screen or a TV or a hologram or anything anybody else can see — we're talking retinal projection, two laser beams fixed on two eyeballs. Anybody coming into the room (daughter, wife, boss) will simply see you sitting there silently in a chair with your retinas lit like furnaces. Step in front of the projector — as my daughter had done now — and the image vanishes.

"Stop," I said, and I wasn't talking to her.

But there she was, her hair brushed out for school and her jaw clenched, looking hate at me. "I can't believe you," she said. "Do you have any idea what time it is?"

Bleary, depleted — and guilty, deeply guilty — I just gawked at her, the light she'd flicked on when she came into the room transfixing me in the chair. I shook my head.

"It's 6:45 A.M. In the morning. The *morning*, Dad."

I started to say something, but the words were tangled up inside me,   45
because Lisa was saying — had just said — "You're not going to make me stay here and watch the paint dry, are you? Because I'm thinking maybe we could drive out to the beach or something, just to cool down," and I said, or was going to say, "There's, like, maybe half a pint of gas in the car."

"What?" Katie demanded. "Were you with Mom again? Is that it? Like you can be with her and I can't?"

"No," I said, "no, that wasn't it. It wasn't your mom at all . . ."

A tremor ran through her. "Yeah, right. So what was it, then? Some girlfriend, somebody you were gaga over when you were in college? Or high school? Or, what, *junior* high?"

"I must have fallen asleep," I said. "Really. I just zoned out."

She knew I was lying. She'd come looking for me, dutiful child, motherless   50
child, and found me not up and about and bustling around the kitchen, preparing to fuss over her and see her off to school, the way I used to, but pinned here in this chair, like an exhibit in a museum, blind to anything but the past, my past and nobody else's, not hers or her mother's, or the country's or the world's, just mine.

I heard the door slam. Heard the thump of her angry feet in the hallway, the distant muffled crash of the front door, and then the house was quiet. I looked at the slit in the box. "Play," I said.

By the time I got to work, I was an hour and a half late, but on this day — miracle of miracles — Kevin was even later, and when he did show up I was ensconced in my cubicle, dutifully rattling keys on my keyboard. He didn't say anything, just brushed by me and buried himself in his office, but I could see that he was wearing the same vacant pre-now look I was, and it didn't take much of an intuitive leap to guess the reason. In fact, since the new model had come on the market, I'd noticed that randy, faraway gaze in the eyes of half a dozen of my fellow-employees, including Linda Blanco, the receptionist, who'd stopped buttoning the top three buttons of her blouse and wore shorter and shorter skirts every day. Instead of breathing "Moos and Associates, how may I help you?" into the receiver, now she just said, "Reset."

Was this a recipe for disaster? Was our whole society on the verge of breaking down? Was the N.S.A. going to step in? Were they going to pass laws? Ban the box? I didn't know. I didn't care. I had a daughter to worry about. Thing was, all I could think of was getting home to relive, straight home, and if the image of a carton of milk or a loaf of bread flitted into my head I batted it away. Takeout. We could always get takeout. I was in a crucial phase with Lisa, heading inexorably for the grimmer scenes, the disagreements — petty at first, then monumental, unbridgeable, like the day I got home from my makeup class in calculus and found her sitting at the kitchen table with a stoner whose name I never did catch and didn't want to know, not then or now — and I needed to get through it, not to analyze whether it hurt or not but because it was there and I had to relive it. I couldn't help myself. I just kept picking at it like a scab.

Ultimately, this was all about Christine, of course, about when I began to fail instead of succeed, to lose instead of win. I needed Lisa to remind me of a time before that, to help me trace my missteps and assign blame, because, as intoxicating as it was to relive the birds-atwitter moments with Christine, there was always something nagging at me in any given scene, some twitch of her face or a comment she threw out that should have raised flags at the time but never did. All right. Fine. I was going to go there, I was, and relive the minutiae of our relationship, the ecstasy and the agony both, the moments of mindless contentment and the swelling tide of antipathy that drove us apart, but first things first, and, as I fought my way home on the freeway that afternoon, all I could think about was Lisa.

In the old days, before we got the box, my daughter and I had a Friday-afternoon ritual whereby I would stop in at the Italian place down the street from the house, have a drink and chat up whoever was there, then call Katie and have her come join me for a father-daughter dinner, so that I could have some face time with her, read into her, and suss out her thoughts and feelings as she grew into a young woman herself, but we didn't do that anymore. There wasn't time. The best I could offer — lately, especially — was takeout or a microwave pizza and a limp salad, choked down in the cold confines of the kitchen, while we separately calculated how long we had to put up with the pretense before slipping off to relive.

55

There were no lights on in the house as I pulled into the driveway, and that was odd, because Katie should have been home from school by now — and she hadn't texted me or phoned to say she'd be staying late. I climbed out of the car feeling stiff all over — I needed to get more exercise, I knew that, and I resolved to do it, too, as soon as I got my head above water — and as I came up the walk I saw the sad, frosted artificial wreath hanging crookedly there in the center panel of the front door. Katie must have dug it out of the box of ornaments in the garage on her own initiative, to do something by way of Christmas, and that gave me pause, that stopped me right there, the thought of it, of my daughter having to make the effort all by herself. That crushed me. It did. And as I put the key in the lock and pushed the door open I knew things were going to have to change. Dinner. I'd take her out to dinner and forget about Lisa. At least for now.

"Katie?" I called. "You home?"

No response. I shrugged out of my coat and went on into the kitchen, thinking to make myself a drink. There were traces of her there, her backpack flung down on the floor, an open bag of Doritos spilling across the counter, a Diet Sprite, half-full, on the breadboard. I called her name again, standing stock-still in the middle of the room and listening for the slightest hint of sound or movement as my voice echoed through the house. I was about to pull out my phone and call her when I thought of the reliving room, and it was a sinking thought, not a selfish one, because if she was in there, reliving — and she was, I knew she was — what did that say about her social life? Didn't teenage girls go out anymore? Didn't they gather in packs at the mall or go to movies or post things on Facebook, or, forgive me, go out on dates? Group dates, even? How else were they going to experience the inchoate beginnings of what the Relive Box people were pushing in the first place?

I shoved into the room, which was dark but for the lights of her eyes, and just stood there watching her for a long moment as I adjusted to the gloom. She sat riveted, her body present but her mind elsewhere, and if I was embarrassed — for her, and for me, too, her father, invading her privacy when she was most vulnerable — the embarrassment gave way to a sorrow so oceanic I thought I would drown in it. I studied her face. Watched her smile and grimace and go cold and smile again. What could she possibly be reliving when she'd lived so little? Family vacations? Christmases past? Her biannual trips to Hong Kong to be with her mother and stepfather? I couldn't fathom it. I didn't like it. It had to stop. I turned on the overhead light and stepped in front of the projector.

She blinked at me and she didn't recognize me, didn't know me at all, because I was in the now and she was in the past. "Katie," I said, "that's enough, now. Come on." I held out my arms to her, even as recognition came back into her eyes and she made a vague gesture of irritation, of pushing away.

"Katie," I said, "let's go out to dinner. Just the two of us. Like we used to."

"I'm not hungry," she said. "And it's not fair. You can use it all you want, like, day and night, but whenever I want it —" And she broke off, tears starting in her eyes.

60

"Come on," I said. "It'll be fun."

The look she gave me was unsparing. I was trying to deflect it, trying to think of something to say, when she got up out of the chair so suddenly it startled me, and, though I tried to take hold of her arm, she was too quick. Before I could react, she was at the door, pausing only to scorch me with another glare. "I don't believe you," she spat, before vanishing down the hall.

I should have followed her, should have tried to make things right — or better, anyway — but I didn't. The box was right there. It had shut down when she leaped up from the chair, and whatever she'd been reliving was buried back inside it, accessible to no one, though you can bet there are hackers out there right now trying to subvert the retinal-recognition feature. For a long moment, I stared at the open door, fighting myself, then I went over and softly shut it. I realized I didn't need a drink or dinner, either. I sat down in the chair. "Hello, Wes," the box said. "Welcome back."

65

We didn't have a Christmas tree that year, and neither of us really cared all that much, I think — if we wanted to look at spangle-draped trees, we could relive holidays past, happier ones, or, in my case, I could go back to my childhood and relive my father's whiskey in a glass and my mother's long-suffering face blossoming over the greedy joy of her golden boy, her only child, tearing open his presents as a weak, bleached-out California sun haunted the windows and the turkey crackled in the oven. Katie went off (reluctantly, I thought) on a skiing vacation to Mammoth with the family of her best friend, Allison, whom she hardly saw anymore, not outside of school, not in the now, and I went back to Lisa, because if I was going to get to Christine in any serious way — beyond the sex, that is, beyond the holiday greetings and picture-postcard moments — Lisa was my bridge.

As soon as I'd dropped Katie at Allison's house and exchanged a few previously scripted salutations with Allison's grinning parents and her grinning twin brothers, I stopped at a convenience store for a case of eight-ounce bottles of spring water and the biggest box of PowerBars I could find and went straight home to the reliving room. The night before, I'd been close to the crucial scene with Lisa, one that was as fixed in my memory as the blow-up with Christine a quarter century later, but elusive as to the date and time. I'd been up all night — again — fast-forwarding, reversing, jumping locales and facial expressions, Lisa's first piercing, the evolution of my haircut, but I hadn't been able to pinpoint the exact moment, not yet. I set the water on the floor on my left side, the PowerBars on my right. "May 9, 1983," I said. "4 A.M."

The numbers flashed and then I was in darkness, zero visibility, confused as to where I was until the illuminated dial of a clock radio began to bleed through and I could make out the dim outline of myself lying in bed in the back room of that apartment with the black walls and the black ceiling and the black floor. Lisa was there beside me, an irregular hump in the darkness, snoring with a harsh gag and stutter. She was stoned. And drunk. Half an hour earlier, she'd been in the bathroom, heaving over the toilet, and I realized I'd come too far. "Reset," I said. "Reverse ninety minutes."

Sudden light, blinding after the darkness, and I was alone in the living room of the apartment, studying, or trying to. My hair hung limp, my muscles were barely there, but I was young and reasonably good-looking, even excusing any bias. I saw that my Black Flag T-shirt had faded to gray from too much sun and too many washings, and the book in my lap looked as familiar as something I might have been buried with in a previous life, but then this *was* my previous life. I watched myself turn a page, crane my neck toward the door, get up to flip over the album that was providing the soundtrack. "Reset," I said. "Fast-forward ten minutes." And here it was, what I'd been searching for: a sudden crash, the front door flinging back, Lisa and the stoner whose name I didn't want to know fumbling their way in, both of them as slow as syrup with the cumulative effect of downers and alcohol, and though the box didn't have an olfactory feature, I swear I could smell the tequila on them. I jumped up out of my chair, spilling the book, and shouted something I couldn't quite make out, so I said, "Reset, reverse five seconds."

"You fucker!" was what I'd shouted, and now I shouted it again, prior to   70
slapping something out of the guy's hand, a beer bottle, and all at once I had him in a hammerlock and Lisa was beating at my back with her bird-claw fists and I was wrestling the guy out the door, cursing over the soundtrack ("Should I Stay or Should I Go" — one of those flatline ironies which almost make you believe everything in this life's been programmed). I saw now that he was bigger than I was, probably stronger, too, but the drugs had taken the volition out of him, and in the next moment he was outside the door and the three bolts were hammered home. By me. Who now turned in a rage to Lisa.

"Stop," I said. "Freeze." Lisa hung there, defiant and guilty at the same time, pretty, breath takingly pretty, despite the slack mouth and the drugged-out eyes. I should have left it there and gone on to those first cornucopian weeks and months and even years with Christine, but I couldn't help myself. "Play," I said, and Lisa raised a hand to swat at me, but she was too unsteady and knocked the lamp over instead.

"Did you fuck him?" I demanded.

There was a long pause, so long I almost fast-forwarded, and then she said, "Yeah. Yeah, I fucked him. And I'll tell you something" — her words glutinous, the syllables coalescing on her tongue — "you're no punk. And he is. He's the real deal. And you? You're, you're — "

I should have stopped it right there.

" — you're *prissy.*"   75

"Prissy?" I couldn't believe it. Not then and not now.

She made a broad stoned gesture, weaving on her feet. "Anal-retentive. Like, who left the dishes in the sink or who didn't take out the garbage or what about the cockroaches — "

"Stop," I said. "Reset. June 19, 1994, 11:02 P.M."

I was in another bedroom now, one with walls the color of cream, and I was in another bed, this time with Christine, and I'd timed the memory to the very minute, postcoital, in the afterglow, and Christine, with her soft aspirated whisper of a voice, was saying, "I love you, Wes, you know that, don't you?"

"Stop," I said. "Reverse five seconds." 80

She said it again. And I stopped again. And reversed again. And she said it again. And again.

Time has no meaning when you're reliving. I don't know how long I kept it up, how long I kept surfing through those moments with Christine — not the sexual ones but the loving ones, the companionable ones, the ordinary day-to-day moments when I could see in her eyes that she loved me more than anybody alive and was never going to stop loving me, never. Dinner at the kitchen table, any dinner, any night. Just to be there. My wife. My daughter. The way the light poured liquid gold over the hardwood floors of our starter house, in Canoga Park. Katie's first birthday. Her first word ("Cake!"). The look on Christine's face as she curled up with Katie in bed and read her "Where the Wild Things Are." Her voice as she hoarsened it for Max: "I'll eat you up!"

Enough analysis, enough hurt. I was no masochist.

At some point, I had to get up from that chair in the now and evacuate a living bladder, the house silent, spectral, unreal. I didn't live here. I didn't live in the now with its deadening nine-to-five job I was in danger of losing and the daughter I was failing and a wife who'd left me — and her own daughter — for Winston Chen, a choreographer of martial-arts movies in Hong Kong, who was loving and kind and funny and not the control freak I was. (*Prissy*, anyone? *Anal-retentive?*) The house echoed with my footsteps, a stage set and nothing more. I went to the kitchen and dug the biggest pot I could find out from under the sink, brought it back to the reliving room, and set it on the floor between my legs to save me the trouble of getting up next time around.

Time passed. Relived time and lived time, too. There were two windows 85 in the room, shades drawn so as not to interfere with the business of the moment, and sometimes a faint glow appeared around the margins of them, an effect I noticed when I was searching for a particular scene and couldn't quite pin it down. Sometimes the glow was gone. Sometimes it wasn't. What happened then, and I may have been two days in or three or five, I couldn't really say, was that things began to cloy. I'd relived an exclusive diet of the transcendent, the joyful, the insouciant, the best of Christine, the best of Lisa, and all the key moments of the women who came between and after, and I'd gone back to the Intermediate Algebra test, the very instant, pencil to paper, when I knew I'd scored a perfect one hundred per cent, and to the time I'd squirted a ball to right field with two outs, two strikes, ninth inning and my Little League team (the Condors, yellow Ts, white lettering) down by three, and watched it rise majestically over the glove of the spastic red-haired kid sucking back allergic snot and roll all the way to the wall. Triumph after triumph, goodness abounding — till it stuck in my throat.

"Reset," I said. "January 2, 2009, 4:30 P.M."

I found myself in the kitchen of our second house, this house, the one we'd moved to because it was outside the L.A. city limits and had schools we felt comfortable sending Katie to. That was what mattered: the schools. And, if it lengthened our commutes, so be it. This house. The one I was reliving in now. Everything gleamed around me, counters polished, the glass of the cabinets as transparent as air, because details mattered then, everything in its place whether Christine was there or not — especially if she wasn't there, and where was she? Or where had she been? To China. With her boss. On film business. Her bags were just inside the front door, where she'd dropped them forty-five minutes ago, after I'd picked her up at the airport and we'd had our talk in the car, the talk I was going to relive when I got done here, because it was all about pain now, about reality, and this scene was the capper, the coup de grâce. You want wounds? You want to take a razor blade to the meat of your inner thigh just to see if you can still feel? Well, here it was.

Christine entered the scene now, coming down the stairs from Katie's room, her eyes wet, or damp, anyway, and her face composed. I pushed myself up from the table, my beginner's bald spot a glint of exposed flesh under the glare of the overhead light. I spoke first. "You tell her?"

Christine was dressed in her business attire, black stockings, heels, skirt to the knee, tailored jacket. She looked exhausted, and not simply from the fifteen-hour flight but from what she'd had to tell me. And our daughter. (How I'd like to be able to relive *that*, to hear how she'd even broached the subject, let alone how she'd smoke-screened her own selfishness and betrayal with some specious concern for Katie's well-being — let's not rock the boat and you'll be better off here with your father and your school and your teachers and it's not the end but just the beginning, buck up, you'll see.)

Christine's voice was barely audible. "I don't like this any better than you do."   90

"Then why do it?"

A long pause. Too long. "Stop," I said.

I couldn't do this. My heart was hammering. My eyes felt as if they were being squeezed in a vise. I could barely swallow. I reached down for a bottle of water and a PowerBar, drank, chewed. She was going to say, "This isn't working," and I was going to say, "*Working?* What the fuck are you talking about? What does work have to do with it? I thought this was about love. I thought it was about commitment." I knew I wasn't going to get violent, though I should have, should have chased her out to the cab that was even then waiting at the curb and slammed my way in and flown all the way to Hong Kong to confront Winston Chen, the martial-arts genius, who could have crippled me with his bare feet.

"Reset," I said. "August, 1975, any day, any time."

There was a hum from the box. "Incomplete command. Please select date   95
and time."

I was twelve years old, the summer we went to Vermont, to a lake there, where the mist came up off the water like the fumes of a dream and deer mice lived under the refrigerator, and I didn't have a date or time fixed in my mind — I just needed to get away from Christine, that was all. I picked the first thing that came into my head.

"August 19th," I said. "11:30 A.M. Play."

A blacktop road. Sun like a nuclear blast. A kid, running. I recognized myself — I'd been to this summer before, one I remembered as idyllic, messing around in boats, fishing, swimming, wandering the woods with one of the local kids, Billy Scharf, everything neutral, copacetic. But why was I running? And why did I have that look on my face, a look that fused determination and helplessness both? Up the drive now, up the steps to the house, shouting for my parents: "Mom! Dad!"

I began to have a bad feeling.

I saw my father get up off the wicker sofa on the porch, my vigorous   100
young father, who was dressed in a T-shirt and jeans and didn't have even a trace of gray in his hair, my father, who always made everything right. But not this time. "What's the matter?" he said. "What is it?"

And my mother coming through the screen door to the porch, a towel in one hand and her hair snarled wet from the lake. And me. I was fighting back tears, my legs and arms like sticks, striped polo shirt, faded shorts. "It's," I said, "it's—"

"Stop," I said. "Reset." It was my dog, Queenie, that was what it was, dead on the road that morning, and who'd left the gate ajar so she could get out in the first place? Even though he'd been warned about it a hundred times?

I was in a dark room. There was a pot between my legs, and it was giving off a fierce odor. I needed to go deeper, needed out of this. I spouted random dates, saw myself driving to work, stuck in traffic with ten thousand other fools who could only wish they had a fast-forward app, saw myself in my thirties, post-Lisa, pre-Christine, obsessing over Halo, and I stayed there through all the toppling hours, reliving myself in the game, boxes within boxes, until finally I thought of God, or what passes for God in my life, the mystery beyond words, beyond lasers and silicon chips. I gave a date nine months before I was born, "December 30, 1962, 6 A.M.," when I was, what — a zygote? — but the box gave me nothing, neither visual nor audio. And that was wrong, deeply wrong. There should have been a heartbeat. My mother's heartbeat, the first thing we hear — or feel, feel before we even have ears.

"Stop," I said. "Reset." A wave of rising exhilaration swept over me even as the words came to my lips, "September 30, 1963, 2:35 A.M.," and the drumbeat started up, *ba-boom*, *ba-boom*, but no visual, not yet, the minutes ticking by, *ba-boom*, *ba-boom*, and then I was there, in the light of this world, and my mother in her stained hospital gown and the man with the monobrow and the flashing glasses, the stranger, the doctor, saying what he was going to say by way of congratulations and relief. A boy. It's a boy.

Then it all went dead, and there was somebody standing in front of me,   105
and I didn't recognize her, not at first, how could I? "Dad," she was saying. "Dad, are you there?"

I blinked. Tried to focus.

"No," I said finally, shaking my head in slow emphasis, the word itself, the denial, heavy as a stone in my mouth. "I'm not here. I'm not. I'm not."

≡ THINKING ABOUT THE TEXT

1. Why are the relive boxes so popular with Wes and his daughter? Do you think they are typical users? Is Wes's use of the box particularly male? Katie's female? Explain.

2. What is Wes hoping to achieve by going back to the same scenes over and over again? What might be some positive effects? What are the obvious negative consequences?

3. What is ironic about Katie's use of the box? What might be the ethical issues in using the box to relive the past?

4. While Wes is watching Katie on the relive box, he says "the embarrassment gave way to a sorrow so oceanic I thought I would drown in it." Comment on the emotions he experiences. Why does he then want her to stop?

5. Why does Wes finally go back to the very beginning of his life? Comment on the last scene in the story. Is Wes now a hopeless addict?

≡ MAKING COMPARISONS

1. What contemporary concerns do each of our three stories bring to mind?

2. Which of the story's endings was the most satisfying? Why? Which the least?

3. What does each of these stories warn us against?

≡ WRITING ABOUT ISSUES

1. Argue that the relive box is a metaphor for concerns in contemporary culture.

2. Argue that "Mars Is Heaven!" and "The Relive Box" have common themes.

3. Argue that the societal concerns that "Human Evolution," published in 1995, deals with are still relevant.

4. Read Butler's story "Bloodchild" and argue that its concerns are or are not still relevant.

≡ Literature and Current Issues: How Should the United States Handle Immigration?

JUAN FELIPE HERRERA, "Borderbus"

ARGUMENTS ON THE ISSUE:
DOUGLAS RAND, "Want to Get Rich? Let in More Immigrants"

DAN CRENSHAW, "The U.S. Should Work with Mexico to Stem Central American Migration"

FRANCIA RAISA, "I Can't (and Won't) Stop Talking about the Dangerous Decision to End DACA"

In the context of American history, the recent heated debate over Mexican and Central American immigration is, unfortunately, not a new development. In the middle of the nineteenth century, a devastating potato famine in Ireland sent hundreds of thousands of refugees to America. These desperate farmers and their families were among the poorest in Europe. Most were unskilled and uneducated and long used to brutal treatment by the British. They were met with authorized discrimination and overt hostility, often accused of being rapists and murderers and thought to be incapable of being educated or assimilated. Their churches were burned and a common sign in stores and factories was "No Irish need apply." At the same time, Chinese immigrants met with even worse, facing legal discrimination and exploitation.

Xenophobia has been an element of American immigration policy for over two hundred years. Fortunately, there has also been an even stronger, more ethical impulse that has welcomed immigrants. After all, the sonnet on the Statue of Liberty reads in part: "Give me your tired, your poor / Your huddled masses yearning to breathe free." All of the familiar fears of recent immigration have been heard over and over again: the stranger will dilute the national character and take jobs away from Americans. But a majority of Americans realize that what immigrants want has remained largely unchanged for hundreds of years: they come here in pursuit of a better life. And in fleeing economic disasters and political injustice, immigrants have believed that the better angels of American citizens will welcome them on their journey toward freedom.

Clearly, the Honduran couple in Herrera's poem, "Borderbus" is on the same quest that the Irish, the Chinese, and countless other immigrants from Europe, Africa, and elsewhere were and are on: a chance to be fully human.

≡ BEFORE YOU READ

Where did your ancestors emigrate from? What was their reception by those already living in America? What are your reasons for supporting or opposing immigration?

JUAN FELIPE HERRERA
Borderbus

Juan Felipe Herrera (b. 1948) was born in Fowler, California, the son of immigrant farmers. He graduated from San Diego High School in 1967 and received a B.A. in Social Anthropology from UCLA and an M.A. from Stanford in the same subject. He also received an M.F.A. in Creative Writing from the University of Iowa Writers' Workshop in 1990. He was named California's Poet Laureate in 2012, and in 2015, he became Poet Laureate of the United States. His most recent work includes Notes on the Assemblage *(2015), from which the following poem is taken;* Senegal Taxi *(2013) and* Half of the World in Light *(2008). He is Professor Emeritus at California State University, Fresno. Called "exuberant and socially engaged, reflective and healing," Herrera also has, as* National Public Radio (NPR) *noted, the "unusual capacity to write convincing political poems that are as personally felt as poems can be."*

A dónde vamos where are we going
Speak in English or the guard is going to come
A dónde vamos where are we going
Speak in English or the guard is gonna get us hermana
Pero qué hicimos but what did we do   5
Speak in English come on
Nomás sé unas pocas palabras I just know a few words

You better figure it out hermana the guard is right there
See the bus driver

Tantos días y ni sabíamos para donde íbamos   10
So many days and we didn't even know where we were headed

I know where we're going
Where we always go
To some detention center to some fingerprinting hall or cube
Some warehouse warehouse after warehouse   15

Pero ya nos investigaron ya cruzamos ya nos cacharon
Los federates del bordo qué más quieren
But they already questioned us we already crossed over they
already grabbed us the Border Patrol what more do they want

We are on the bus now   20
that is all

A dónde vamos te digo salí desde Honduras
No hemos comido nada y dónde vamos a dormir

Where are we going I am telling you I came from Honduras
We haven't eaten anything and where are we going to sleep   25

I don't want to talk about it just tell them
That you came from nowhere
I came from nowhere

And we crossed the border from nowhere
And now you and me and everybody else here is   30
On a bus to nowehere you got it?

Pero por eso nos venimos para salir de la nada
But that's why we came to leave all that nothing behind

When the bus stops there will be more nothing
We're here hermana   35

Y esas gentes quiénes son
no quieren que siga el camión
No quieren que sigamos
Están bloqueando el bus
A dónde vamos ahora   40
Those people there who are they
they don't want the bus to keep going
they don't want us to keep going
now they are blocking the bus
so where do we go   45

What?

He tardado 47 días para llegar acá no fue fácil hermana
45 días desde Honduras con los coyotes los que se — bueno
ya sabes lo que les hicieron a las chicas allí mero en frente
de nosotros pero qué íbamos a hacer y los trenes los trenes   50
cómo diré hermana cientos de
nosotros como gallinas como topos en jaulas y verduras
pudriendóse en los trenes de miles me oyes de miles y se resbalaban
de los techos y los desiertos de Arizona de Tajas sed y hambre
sed y hambre dos cosas sed y hambre día tras día hermana   55
y ahora aquí en este camión y quién sabe a dónde
vamos hermana fijate vengo desde Brownsville dónde nos amarraron
y ahora en California pero todavía no entramos y todavía el bordo
está por delante
It took me 47 days to get here it wasn't easy hermana   60
45 days from Honduras with the coyotes the ones that — well
you know what they did to las chicas
right there in front of us so what were we supposed
to do and the trains the trains how can I tell you hermana hundreds
of us like chickens like gophers in cages and vegetables   65
rotting on trains of thousands you hear me of thousands and they slid
from the rooftops and the deserts of Arizona and Texas thirst and hunger
thirst and hunger two things thirst and hunger day after day hermana

and now here on this bus of who-knows-where we are going
hermana listen I come from Brownsville where they tied us up   70
and now in California but still we're not inside and still the border
lies ahead of us

I told you to speak in English even un poquito
the guard is going to think we are doing something
people are screaming outside   75
they want to push the bus back

Pero para dónde le damos hermana
por eso me vine
le quebraron las piernas a mi padre
las pandillas mataron a mi hijo   80
solo quiero que estemos juntos
tantos años hermana
separados
But where do we go hermana
that's why I came here   85
they broke my father's legs
gangs killed my son
I just want us to be together
so many years hermana
pulled apart   90

What?

Mi madre me dijo que lo más importante
es la libertad la bondad y la buenas acciones
con el prójimo
My mother told me that the most important thing   95
is freedom kindness and doing good
for others

What are you talking about?
I told you to be quiet

La libertad viene desde muy adentro   100
allí reside todo el dolor de todo el mundo
el momento en que purguemos ese dolor de nuestras entrañas
seremos libres y en ese momento tenemos que
llenarnos de todo el dolor de todos los seres
para liberarlos a ellos mismos   105
Freedom comes from deep inside
all the pain of the world lives there
the second we cleanse that pain from our guts
we shall be free and in that moment we have to
fill ourselves up with all the pain of all beings   110
to free them — all of them

The guard is coming well
now what   maybe they'll take us
to another detention center we'll eat we'll have a floor
a blanket toilets water and each other   115
for a while

No somos nada y venimos de la nada
pero esa nada lo es todo si la nutres de amor
por eso venceremos
We are nothing and we come from nothing   120
but that nothing is everything, if you feed it with love
that is why we will triumph

We are everything hermana
Because we come from everything

≡ THINKING ABOUT THE TEXT

1. Hermana seems to be the narrator's sister. How would you describe
   their relationship?
2. Even though this is a specific journey of two people, there are
   references to more universal experiences. Cite two of these and explain
   what they mean.
3. Why do the narrator and the sister have an ambivalent feeling toward
   the detention centers? What does this tell us about their journey?
   How would you describe what seems to motivate them to continue
   their journey?
4. Describe the effect of having half the text in Spanish. What do you
   think Herrera hopes to accomplish with this technique? Do you think
   he is successful?
5. What does Herrera mean by the paradoxical, "we come from nothing /
   but that nothing is everything, if you feed it with love"?

DOUGLAS RAND

Want to Get Rich? Let in More Immigrants

*Douglas Rand (b. 1977?) graduated from Harvard in 1998 and its Graduate School of
the Arts in 2001. He holds a degree from Yale Law School (2010) and an M.A. from
the School of Management (2010). He is the co-founder and president of Boundless,
a technology company that helps families affordably navigate the immigration system. He formerly worked at the White House Office of Science and Technology.*

Underneath the latest headlines about DACA and sanctuary cities, the Trump
administration is quietly implementing major changes throughout the legal

system, making it much harder to obtain visas to live and work in the United States. Yet immigrants as a whole — from housekeepers to biochemists — are net job creators, grow the economy and pay into the public treasury far more than they take out. To make the average American richer, we should encourage immigration across the board.

Some background is in order. President Trump said in his first address to Congress, "According to the National Academy of Sciences, our current immigration system costs American taxpayers many billions of dollars a year." That's true, in the sense that our current education system costs American taxpayers many billions of dollars a year, too. Are all those schoolkids also moochers?

As every small business owner in America knows, you don't measure failure just by how much money is going out the door, any more than you measure success just by how much money is coming in. It's the *net* amount that tells you if you're succeeding. And when it comes to immigration, the net benefits are extraordinary.

There are a few more conclusions from that National Academy study that the President didn't mention: On average, during our working years, *everyone* pays more in taxes than they receive in public resources. Immigrants don't replenish the national treasury quite as much as the native-born do . . . until retirement age, when the native-born consume far more public benefits than do immigrants. Then the children of immigrants pay in much more than they take out, compared with their parents *and* their native-born peers, largely because of their greater educational attainment and earnings.

Bottom line: Today's immigrant families are projected to deliver as much as $259 billion in net present value as taxpayers, including federal, state and local taxes combined. That works out to $800 in avoided taxes (or deficits) for every man, woman and child in the United States.   5

Texas is no exception. Immigrants in the state employ over 420,000 people, pay nearly $10 billion in taxes to Texas state and local government coffers, and pay another $22.5 billion in federal taxes.

Yet the Trump administration is reportedly considering a policy that would punish immigrants for taking advantage of public benefits that they and their U.S.-citizen children are legally entitled to, such as food stamps and earned income tax credits. Such a policy doesn't account for the taxes that immigrants pay into the system.

Consider Abosede Akingbade Thomas, a Nigerian immigrant who took advantage of government nutrition programs for a few months while she was pregnant with her first child. Over the course of her career in the United States as a tax-paying nurse, she did her part to improve the nation's fiscal health — and that's before factoring in the career of her child, Omolara, who is now a pediatrician after earning her medical degree at age 22. Or consider Ukrainian immigrant Jan Koum, who received food stamps and housing support as a teenager before going on to create WhatsApp, which now employs 100 people and enables 1.2 billion people to communicate with their friends and loved ones for free.

Given immigrants' return on investment for the average American, we shouldn't just be pocketing the economic benefits of our current immigration system—we should be doubling down. Just five years ago, it looked like comprehensive immigration reform was finally coming to fruition (even Sean Hannity endorsed the idea). The Senate passed a bipartisan overhaul that would have increased legal immigration across the board, including a path to citizenship for Dreamers. The nonpartisan Congressional Budget Office projected that it would reduce the federal budget deficit by nearly $850 billion over 20 years. That's another $2,600 of avoided fiscal burden for every American.

The House of Representatives failed to even debate this bill, effectively turning its back on a gigantic windfall. (Did I mention that these reforms would have also increased GDP by $1.4 trillion over the same period? That's dramatically more economic growth than even the rosiest estimates of what the recent tax bill will deliver.)   10

Perhaps there is one glimmer of hope: The Trump administration recently announced (via tweet) that immigrants can now apply for U.S. citizenship online, skipping the mass of paper documents that was previously required. This isn't just good news for individual immigrants, who tend to increase their earning power after becoming Americans. It's good news for the average *current* American. More citizenship means more tax revenue for the U.S. Treasury, more funds to prop up Social Security and more economic growth. If half of the nearly nine million eligible immigrants in the United States became citizens, their increased earnings and demand could boost GDP by up to $52 billion per year.

As any business owner will tell you, growth is hard. It requires smart investments and a clear-eyed understanding of what will ultimately boost the bottom line. When the best evidence indicates that taking a certain action will generate revenue far in excess of costs, you do it. For the benefit of all Americans, we must encourage immigrants' continued contributions to our nation's fiscal health and economic growth.

≡ THINKING ABOUT THE TEXT

1. What is Rand's straightforward claim?

2. What economic reason does Rand offer to counter Trump's proposal to punish immigrants for taking advantage of public benefits?

3. What are Rand's anecdotes about Abosede Akingbade Thomas and Jan Koum evidence of?

4. How effective is Rand's almost exclusive use of logos to persuade? How could he have used ethos or pathos?

5. Is Rand's conclusion about the overall benefit to "all Americans" effective? Why?

DAN CRENSHAW

The U.S. Should Work with Mexico to Stem Central American Migration

Dan Crenshaw (b. 1985) was born in Houston, Texas, and graduated from Tufts University in 2006. He also received an M.A. from Harvard's Kennedy School of Government. He was Lieutenant Commander in the US Navy SEALS and is currently a politician in Texas.

Earlier this week, Mexican president-elect Andrés Manuel López Obrador announced that border security and regional development along Mexico's southern border will be a priority for his new administration. Obrador's future chief of public security told reporters that a new "border police force" would be created to deal with the increasing immigrant inflows, drugs, and guns from Central America.

The United States, and especially Texans, should applaud such efforts and seize this opportunity to partner with Mexico to increase security cooperation and socioeconomic development efforts in Central America.

For those of us living in Texas and other border states, the reality of an open and unsecured border is a part of everyday life. Despite the claim that illegal crossings are the lowest in decades, the numbers are still astronomical—nearly half a million, versus the 2000 high of 1.6 million. Over 400,000 illegal crossings per year is an unsustainable situation that strains our law-enforcement and judicial institutions to the point of breaking. Without greatly increased resources, our legal system will always be ill-equipped to deal with these kinds of numbers. Even if we were able to agree on an ideal set of immigration laws, enforcing such laws in the face of hundreds of thousands of cases is impossible in practice. The current crisis with separated families on the border is certainly proof of that.

The need for physical border security is a very real one. But equally important is the need to focus on the source of the problem: mass emigration from Central America. With the Mexican president-elect showing a clear willingness to tackle this problem, the U.S. should show equal and enthusiastic willingness to be a strong partner in such efforts.

Such partnerships are not entirely new, but they could use a political reboot. The Merida Initiative, established in 2007, enshrines U.S.–Mexico security cooperation, according to the U.S. State Department, by "supporting Mexico's efforts to improve security, enhance criminal prosecution and rule of law, build public confidence in the justice sector, improve border security and reduce irregular migration, and promote greater respect for human rights." U.S. Border Patrol agents regularly partner with Mexican federal law enforcement along the Guatemalan border to help train and advise their Mexican counterparts along chokepoints where illicit trafficking is most prevalent.

5

The U.S. military and intelligence communities regularly work with Mexican authorities to thwart transnational criminal organizations (i.e., the drug cartels) and help the Mexican navy interdict illicit goods, such as fentanyl shipments from China. Given the heroin- and fentanyl-fueled crisis here in the United States, which is responsible for over 40,000 deaths in 2016 alone, these efforts are a crucial pillar of U.S. national security.

With a persistent media focus on more glaring global threats, such as North Korean nuclear weapons and Russian threats to democracy, it is easy to forget that our neighbors south of the border are equally deserving of America's attention. Violence in Mexico is at an all-time high, with 25,340 homicides occurring last year alone. Gang violence and the breakdown of civil society in Central America are causing mass emigration through Mexico and across our southern border. Immigration reform and border security here in the U.S. are necessary and urgent parts of the solution, but so is recognizing that Mexico is a partner on this issue, not an enemy.

While U.S.-Mexico security cooperation has remained strong at the operational level, political relations have clearly been strained by a rhetorically heated debate on border security and NAFTA negotiations. Some Mexican officials have demonstrated a willingness to forgo security cooperation as negotiating leverage to keep favorable NAFTA terms intact. Such setbacks will only make our situation on the border more difficult. It is time for a reset in relations, and if we are willing to look, we may find a willing partner in Obrador as he seeks to decrease corruption and tackle uncontrolled immigration across Mexico's southern border.

The interests of the U.S. and Mexico in Central America are clearly aligned, and our role should be one of supporting Mexican leadership in the region, a far preferable solution to tackling the issue ourselves with potentially endless U.S. resources. The Merida Initiative should be kept in place and even expanded to support a new Mexican border-police force. The U.S. and Mexico should work together to support and expand existing socioeconomic development programs in Central America, such as the Plan of the Alliance for Prosperity in the Northern Triangle. Rebuilding the civic fabric of Central American countries is the only long-term solution to stemming the flow of illegal migration, and without Mexico as a willing partner, the U.S. will continue to fight an impossibly uphill battle.

≡ THINKING ABOUT THE TEXT

1. Crenshaw's claim seems straightforward. What is it?

2. Crenshaw is a politician. What kind of persona is he trying to project? What are some examples? Often politicians resort to pathos when dealing with immigration issues. Can you give any examples of Crenshaw doing that?

3. What specific evidence does Crenshaw give to support the need for greater cooperation between the United States and Mexico?

4. What solutions does Crenshaw offer for his assertions about violence and the breakdown of civil society in Central America? What solutions would you propose?

5. As far as you know, have any of Crenshaw's beliefs about the situation in immigration come to pass?

≡ MAKING COMPARISONS

1. Describe the different perspectives Rand and Crenshaw have about immigration.

2. Which perspective on immigration is closest to your own? Explain why.

3. Which essay do you think immigrants would favor? Explain why.

FRANCIA RAISA

I Can't (and Won't) Stop Talking about the Dangerous Decision to End DACA

Francia Raisa (b. 1988) is an American actress who was born in Los Angeles, California. She is of Mexican and Honduran descent. She began modeling and acting in high school. She appeared in a lead role in Bring It On: All or Nothing *(2006) and* Shredderman Rules *(2007). She played the role of Adrian Lee in the hit ABC family drama,* The Secret Life of the American Teenager *from 2008 to 2013. Her latest project is the TV series* Grown-ish *(2018 – present). The following essay appeared in* Marie Claire *on February 22, 2018.*

I was 5 years old, walking next to my mom and wearing a new dress as we stepped into the school office to sign up for kindergarten. While most people don't remember kindergarten, this day stands out in my mind because my mom was so frustrated. At the time I didn't understand what was happening — mostly because I didn't speak English.

I remember standing there watching my mom and trying to comprehend why she was so upset. Before I knew it, she grabbed my hand and we stormed out. Later that evening, when I heard her tell my dad that the school wouldn't accept me because I only spoke Spanish, it all made sense. They were heartbroken.

My mom came to America with her mom and a few siblings in 1981, when she was just 16. They were escaping my mom's abusive father, and traveled to Los Angeles with hopes of having a better life. My dad arrived in 1982 — just after his parents died — with the dream of building a career for himself in Hollywood. It was a dream he worked on tirelessly to make a reality, and a dream that ended up coming true.

When both my parents arrived in America, Ronald Reagan was President. It was in 1986 that President Reagan passed the Immigration Reform and

Control Act, which allowed undocumented immigrants who had arrived *before* 1982 a pathway towards citizenship. Luckily, my mom was eligible and safe. She applied and obtained her temporary green card while waiting for her background check, medical history, and proof of employment to be cleared. My dad barely missed the cut, but later was able to obtain a green card through his employer.

Six years later, I was born. We only spoke Spanish in the house, and once my parents found a school that would finally accept us, my sisters and I eventually learned English. I grew up deeply immersed in our culture and surrounded by our traditions. I watched everyone around me work hard to achieve their dreams while providing a good life that was full of opportunity for my sisters and me.

We went from only being able to afford beans and rice to living in a beautiful two-story home. My parents worked hard and raised a family in America, while barely speaking English. My father, whose English primarily consists of the phrase "Hello my friend," hustled every day to achieve his dreams of being a successful radio personality in Los Angeles.

At the peak of his career, he averaged about 35 million listeners and used his platform to be an advocate for the Latino community. He told jokes, provided commentary on current events, gave life advice, and, in 2006, launched a national voter registration drive called "Votos por America." He encouraged Latinos to take part in activism against anti-immigration legislation. Throughout his career he helped millions of people. All of which was possible because he was given the opportunity to stay in America while he worked hard to receive his citizenship.

I grew up very aware of where my family came from and how lucky we were to have all the opportunities America had to offer. When President Obama announced Deferred Action for Childhood Arrivals (DACA) on June 2012, I was both relieved and excited. The policy allows some undocumented immigrants who entered the country as minors (also known as Dreamers) to receive a renewable two-year period of deferred action from deportation. It also means they are eligible for a work permit. Though it isn't the same opportunity that my parents received, it felt like a small victory and reminded me that we need to keep fighting for the bigger goal — a pathway to citizenship.

So it's no surprise that when the news of DACA being rescinded by the current administration hit, I immediately panicked. I was at home when the phone notifications started flooding in. Instantly I turned on the news, started my online search for additional information, and then called my mom. *Is anyone in our family in this program? Was anyone going to be in trouble? Are you okay?* Fear rushed through me as the horrors of losing everything we'd worked so hard for played in my mind.

These fears are rippling through our communities, being lived out at this very moment by thousands of people. What most people may not realize is that not only does it take tons of paperwork *and* multiple background checks to apply for DACA, once you finally get it, you're then asked to go through *more* paperwork and background checks. Needless to say, the entire process of getting a green card and/or being granted citizenship is both mentally and emotionally stressful.

In today's world, there are programs that my parents didn't have access to in 1982. Programs like TPS for Central Americans and the Dreamer Program, through which employment is obtained, families are formed, homes are bought, and children are raised. Through these programs, our vulnerable communities have access to the resources our country provides — or rather, resources our country used to provide.

It's 2018 and the President of the United States of America is trying to revoke these programs. Parents who have had children in America and were once allowed to stay and raise them here are being forced out. Families who rely on programs that have allowed for them to call America home for years are being threatened with deportation and injustice. Vulnerable populations are now at a higher risk for exploitation through human trafficking — and at a higher risk of being taken advantage of by a fraudulent attorney. This is not an isolated situation. This is something that will impact people we know in our very own neighborhoods.

Dreamers built their lives here, were educated here, and have been raised with all the opportunities that America has to offer. And now — if Congress doesn't act to extend DACA — anyone whose permit expires after March 5, 2018, will no longer have Deferred Action or employment authorization. It's not just stripping away a policy, it's stripping away lives.

The statue of liberty stands tall today as a reminder of the open arms this country once had. It is a beacon of light to those — like my mom, grandmother, and aunts — whom escaped their countries, and it's the ultimate symbol of opportunity to those — like my father — who are chasing after their dreams. Our country fought hard to be the land of the free and the home of the brave, and by revoking existing programs we're eradicating what we stand for. By spreading fear and increasing vulnerability within our communities, we're doing an injustice to those who need us most. Freedom is what makes America great, and I pray we go back to welcoming those who want to join us here.

≡ THINKING ABOUT THE TEXT

1. Is the author's reliance mainly on ethos and pathos to make her claim effective?

2. Where are the instances of the author relying on logic to advance her argument?

3. What consequences does Raisa suggest will occur if DACA is rescinded?

4. Is Raisa's last paragraph effective in making her case for welcoming immigrants?

5. What could Raisa have done to be more persuasive in this essay? What would you suggest she leave out or change? What is the single most effective aspect in her essay?

▤ MAKING COMPARISONS

1. If you were undecided, which essay makes the best case for welcoming immigrants?
2. What might Herrera's response to these essays be?
3. Since immigration is such an emotional issue for many Americans, is the use of logos, pathos, or ethos the most effective?

▤ WRITING ABOUT THE ISSUES

1. Write an argument that much of current immigration policy is based more on emotion than logic.
2. Argue for your interpretation of the last several stanzas of Herrera's poem.
3. Write an argument essay in which you disagree with the claims made by one of our three essays.
4. Write an argument essay in which you answer the question posed by this cluster: how should the United States handle immigration?

☰ Contexts for Research: Race, Social Equality, and "Battle Royal"

RALPH ELLISON, "Battle Royal"

CONTEXTS FOR RESEARCH:

BOOKER T. WASHINGTON, "Atlanta Exposition Address (The Atlanta Compromise)"

W. E. B. DU BOIS, "Of Mr. Booker T. Washington"

GUNNAR MYRDAL, "Social Equality"

More than forty years after the civil rights movement of the 1960s, our national awareness of how brutal discrimination was against African Americans is diminished. Although educational and economic equality has not been completely attained, progress has been made, especially in eliminating official policies and gestures of bias. Before World War II, however, overt discrimination was common, especially in the small towns of the segregated South and the rural Midwest. African Americans were rarely allowed to hold anything other than menial jobs in small towns, and most middle-class whites knew African Americans only as maids, gardeners, and servants. African Americans were completely outside the established power structure and rarely able to complain about or obtain justice for their many grievances. Public protest was out of the question.

Many African Americans even avoided private protest against their outsider status because they feared that it would worsen their situation. Among African American intellectuals and ordinary citizens, debates raged about which strategy to pursue: to cooperate with the white establishment, hoping to modify hostility, or to agitate for change. Generations of blacks followed the first course until the 1960s, when the nonviolent sit-ins of the civil rights movement ushered in the public protests that ended state-sanctioned segregation. Ralph Ellison's story takes place in the era of segregation and graphically portrays how marginalized African Americans were and how difficult they found it to decide on an effective strategy for progress. At the story's end, the main character, like Ellison himself, begins a lifelong journey from racism toward social justice.

☰ BEFORE YOU READ

Have you ever been in a situation in which you felt discriminated against because of your race, religion, gender, sexual orientation, or age? Did you ever see someone else suffer discrimination? Did you feel powerless? What was your strategy for dealing with this feeling?

National Archives and
Records Administration

RALPH ELLISON
Battle Royal

*Born in Oklahoma to an activist mother and an intellectual father, Ralph Ellison
(1914–1994) was well grounded in literary and social matters by the time he
entered Tuskegee Institute to study music in 1933. Finding the conservatism and
accommodationism of Tuskegee limiting, Ellison read modernist poets like T. S.
Eliot and in 1936, moved to New York, where he met writers Langston Hughes
and Richard Wright. Inspired by Wright and by the works of Conrad, Dostoyevsky,
and other writers of fiction, Ellison began drafting his novel* Invisible Man *(1952)
while he was serving in the merchant marine during World War II. Published as a
short story in 1947, "Battle Royal" became the first chapter of this National Book
Award–winning novel.*

It goes a long way back, some twenty years. All my life I had been looking for
something, and everywhere I turned someone tried to tell me what it was.
I accepted their answers too, though they were often in contradiction and
even self-contradictory. I was naive. I was looking for myself and asking everyone except myself questions which I, and only I, could answer. It took me a
long time and much painful boomeranging of my expectations to achieve a

realization everyone else appears to have been born with: that I am nobody but myself. But first I had to discover that I am an invisible man!

And yet I am no freak of nature, not of history. I was in the cards, other things having been equal (or unequal) eighty-five years ago. I am not ashamed of my grandparents for having been slaves. I am only ashamed of myself for having at one time been ashamed. About eighty-five years ago they were told that they were free, united with others of our country in everything pertaining to the common good, and, in everything social, separate like the fingers of the hand. And they believed it. They exulted in it. They stayed in their place, worked hard, and brought up my father to do the same. But my grandfather is the one. He was an odd old guy, my grandfather, and I am told I take after him. It was he who caused the trouble. On his deathbed he called my father to him and said, "Son, after I'm gone I want you to keep up the good fight. I never told you, but our life is a war and I have been a traitor all my born days, a spy in the enemy's country ever since I give up my gun back in the Reconstruction. Live with your head in the lion's mouth. I want you to overcome 'em with yeses, undermine 'em with grins, agree 'em to death and destruction, let 'em swoller you till they vomit or bust wide open." They thought the old man had gone out of his mind. He had been the meekest of men. The younger children were rushed from the room, the shades drawn and the flame of the lamp turned so low that it sputtered on the wick like the old man's breathing. "Learn it to the younguns," he whispered fiercely; then he died.

But my folks were more alarmed over his last words than over his dying. It was as though he had not died at all, his words caused so much anxiety. I was warned emphatically to forget what he had said and, indeed, this is the first time it has been mentioned outside the family circle. It had a tremendous effect upon me, however. I could never be sure of what he meant. Grandfather had been a quiet old man who never made any trouble, yet on his deathbed he had called himself a traitor and a spy, and he had spoken of his meekness as a dangerous activity. It became a constant puzzle which lay unanswered in the back of my mind. And whenever things went well for me I remembered my grandfather and felt guilty and uncomfortable. It was as though I was carrying out his advice in spite of myself. And to make it worse, everyone loved me for it. I was praised by the most lily-white men of the town. I was considered an example of desirable conduct — just as my grandfather had been. And what puzzled me was that the old man had defined it as *treachery*. When I was praised for my conduct I felt a guilt that in some way I was doing something that was really against the wishes of the white folks, that if they had understood they would have desired me to act just the opposite, that I should have been sulky and mean, and that that really would have been what they wanted, even though they were fooled and thought they wanted me to act as I did. It made me afraid that some day they would look upon me as a traitor and I would be lost. Still I was more afraid to act any other way because they didn't like that at all. The old man's words were like a curse. On my graduation day I delivered an oration in which I showed that humility was the secret, indeed, the very essence of progress. (Not that I believed this — how could I, remembering my grandfather? — I only believed that it worked.) It was a great success. Everyone praised me and I was invited to give the speech at a gathering of the town's leading white citizens. It was a triumph for our whole community.

It was in the main ballroom of the leading hotel. When I got there I discovered that it was on the occasion of a smoker, and I was told that since I was to be there anyway I might as well take part in the battle royal to be fought by some of my schoolmates as part of the entertainment. The battle royal came first.

All of the town's big shots were there in their tuxedoes, wolfing down the buffet foods, drinking beer and whiskey and smoking black cigars. It was a large room with a high ceiling. Chairs were arranged in neat rows around three sides of a portable boxing ring. The fourth side was clear, revealing a gleaming space of polished floor. I had some misgivings over the battle royal, by the way. Not from a distaste for fighting, but because I didn't care too much for the other fellows who were to take part. They were tough guys who seemed to have no grandfather's curse worrying their minds. No one could mistake their toughness. And besides, I suspected that fighting a battle royal might detract from the dignity of my speech. In those pre-invisible days I visualized myself as a potential Booker T. Washington. But the other fellows didn't care too much for me either, and there were nine of them. I felt superior to them in my way, and I didn't like the manner in which we were all crowded together into the servants' elevator. Nor did they like my being there. In fact, as the warmly lighted floors flashed past the elevator we had words over the fact that I, by taking part in the fight, had knocked one of their friends out of a night's work.

We were led out of the elevator through a rococo hall into an anteroom and told to get into our fighting togs. Each of us was issued a pair of boxing gloves and ushered out into the big mirrored hall, which we entered looking cautiously about us and whispering, lest we might accidentally be heard above the noise of the room. It was foggy with cigar smoke. And already the whiskey was taking effect. I was shocked to see some of the most important men of the town quite tipsy. They were all there — bankers, lawyers, judges, doctors, fire chiefs, teachers, merchants. Even one of the more fashionable pastors. Something we could not see was going on up front. A clarinet was vibrating sensuously and the men were standing up and moving eagerly forward. We were a small tight group, clustered together, our bare upper bodies touching and shining with anticipatory sweat; while up front the big shots were becoming increasingly excited over something we still could not see. Suddenly I heard the school superintendent, who had told me to come, yell, "Bring up the shines, gentlemen! Bring up the little shines!"

We were rushed up to the front of the ballroom, where it smelled even more strongly of tobacco and whiskey. Then we were pushed into place. I almost wet my pants. A sea of faces, some hostile, some amused, ringed around us, and in the center, facing us, stood a magnificent blonde — stark naked. There was dead silence. I felt a blast of cold air chill me. I tried to back away, but they were behind me and around me. Some of the boys stood with lowered

5

heads, trembling. I felt a wave of irrational guilt and fear. My teeth chattered, my skin turned to goose flesh, my knees knocked. Yet I was strongly attracted and looked in spite of myself. Had the price of looking been blindness, I would have looked. The hair was yellow like that of a circus kewpie doll, the face heavily powdered and rouged, as though to form an abstract mask, the eyes hollow and smeared a cool blue, the color of a baboon's butt. I felt a desire to spit upon her as my eyes brushed slowly over her body. Her breasts were firm and round as the domes of East Indian temples, and I stood so close as to see the fine skin texture and beads of pearly perspiration glistening like dew around the pink and erected buds of her nipples. I wanted at one and the same time to run from the room, to sink through the floor, or go to her and cover her from my eyes and the eyes of the others with my body; to feel the soft thighs, to caress her and destroy her, to love her and murder her, to hide from her, and yet to stroke where below the small American flag tattooed upon her belly her thighs formed a capital V. I had a notion that of all in the room she saw only me with her impersonal eyes.

And then she began to dance, a slow sensuous movement; the smoke of a hundred cigars clinging to her like the thinnest of veils. She seemed like a fair bird-girl girdled in veils calling to me from the angry surface of some gray and threatening sea. I was transported. Then I became aware of the clarinet playing and the big shots yelling at us. Some threatened us if we looked and others if we did not. On my right I saw one boy faint. And now a man grabbed a silver pitcher from a table and stepped close as he dashed ice water upon him and stood him up and forced two of us to support him as his head hung and moans issued from his thick bluish lips. Another boy began to plead to go home. He was the largest of the group, wearing dark red fighting trunks much too small to conceal the erection which projected from him as though in answer to the insinuating low-registered moaning of the clarinet. He tried to hide himself with his boxing gloves.

And all the while the blonde continued dancing, smiling faintly at the big shots who watched her with fascination, and faintly smiling at our fear. I noticed a certain merchant who followed her hungrily, his lips loose and drooling. He was a large man who wore diamond studs in a shirtfront which swelled with the ample paunch underneath, and each time the blonde swayed her undulating hips he ran his hand through the thin hair of his bald head and, with his arms upheld, his posture clumsy like that of an intoxicated panda, wound his belly in a slow and obscene grind. This creature was completely hypnotized. The music had quickened. As the dancer flung herself about with a detached expression on her face, the men began reaching out to touch her. I could see their beefy fingers sink into the soft flesh. Some of the others tried to stop them as she began to move around the floor in graceful circles, as they gave chase, slipping and sliding over the polished floor. It was mad. Chairs went crashing, drinks were spilt, as they ran laughing and howling after her. They caught her just as she reached a door, raised her from the floor, and tossed her as college boys are tossed at a hazing, and above her red, fixed-smiling lips I saw the terror and disgust in her eyes, almost like my own terror and that which I saw in some of the other boys. As I watched, they tossed her twice and her soft breasts seemed to flatten against the air and her legs flung wildly as she spun. Some of the more sober ones helped her to escape. And I started off the floor, heading for the anteroom with the rest of the boys.

Some were still crying in hysteria. But as we tried to leave we were stopped and ordered to get into the ring. There was nothing to do but what we were told. All ten of us climbed under the ropes and allowed ourselves to be blindfolded with broad bands of white cloth. One of the men seemed to feel a bit sympathetic and tried to cheer us up as we stood with our backs against the ropes. Some of us tried to grin. "See that boy over there?" one of the men said. "I want you to run across at the bell and give it to him right in the belly. If you don't get him, I'm going to get you. I don't like his looks." Each of us was told the same. The blindfolds were put on. Yet even then I had been going over my speech. In my mind each word was as bright as flame. I felt the cloth pressed into place, and frowned so that it would be loosened when I relaxed.

But now I felt a sudden fit of blind terror. I was unused to darkness. It was as though I had suddenly found myself in a dark room filled with poisonous cotton-mouths. I could hear the bleary voices yelling insistently for the battle royal to begin.

"Get going in there!"

"Let me at that big nigger!"

I strained to pick up the school superintendent's voice, as though to squeeze some security out of that slightly more familiar sound.

"Let me at those black sonsabitches!" someone yelled.

"No, Jackson, no!" another voice yelled. "Here, somebody, help me hold Jack."

"I want to get at that ginger-colored nigger. Tear him limb from limb," the first voice yelled.

I stood against the ropes trembling. For in those days I was what they called ginger-colored, and he sounded as though he might crunch me between his teeth like a crisp ginger cookie.

Quite a struggle was going on. Chairs were being kicked about and I could hear voices grunting as with a terrific effort. I wanted to see, to see more desperately than ever before. But the blindfold was tight as a thick skin-puckering scab and when I raised my gloved hands to push the layers of white aside a voice yelled, "Oh, no you don't, black bastard! Leave that alone!"

"Ring the bell before Jackson kills him a coon!" someone boomed in the sudden silence. And I heard the bell clang and the sound of the feet scuffling forward.

A glove smacked against my head. I pivoted, striking out stiffly as someone went past, and felt the jar ripple along the length of my arm to my shoulder. Then it seemed as though all nine of the boys had turned upon me at once. Blows pounded me from all sides while I struck out as best I could. So many blows landed upon me that I wondered if I were not the only blindfolded fighter in the ring, or if the man called Jackson hadn't succeeded in getting me after all.

Blindfolded, I could no longer control my motions. I had no dignity. I stumbled about like a baby or a drunken man. The smoke had become thicker and with each new blow it seemed to sear and further restrict my lungs. My saliva became like hot bitter glue. A glove connected with my head, filling my mouth with warm blood. It was everywhere. I could not tell if the moisture I felt upon my body was sweat or blood. A blow landed hard against the nape of my neck. I felt myself going over, my head hitting the floor. Streaks of blue light filled the black world behind the blindfold. I lay prone, pretending that I was knocked out, but felt myself seized by hands and yanked to my feet. "Get going, black boy! Mix it up!" My arms were like lead, my head smarting from blows. I managed to feel my way to the ropes and held on, trying to catch my breath. A glove landed in my mid-section and I went over again, feeling as though the smoke had become a knife jabbed into my guts. Pushed this way and that by the legs milling around me, I finally pulled erect and discovered that I could see the black, sweat-washed forms weaving in the smoky-blue atmosphere like drunken dancers weaving to the rapid drumlike thuds of blows.

Everyone fought hysterically. It was complete anarchy. Everybody fought everybody else. No group fought together for long. Two, three, four, fought one, then turned to fight each other, were themselves attacked. Blows landed below the belt and in the kidney, with the gloves open as well as closed, and with my eye partly opened now there was not so much terror. I moved carefully, avoiding blows, although not too many to attract attention, fighting from group to group. The boys groped about like blind, cautious crabs crouching to protect their mid-sections, their heads pulled in short against their shoulders, their arms stretched nervously before them, with their fists testing the smoke-filled air like the knobbed feelers of hypersensitive snails. In one corner I glimpsed a boy violently punching the air and heard him scream in pain as he smashed his hand against a ring post. For a second I saw him bent over holding his hand, then going down as a blow caught his unprotected head. I played one group against the other, slipping in and throwing a punch then stepping out of range while pushing the others into the melee to take the blows blindly aimed at me. The smoke was agonizing and there were no rounds, no bells at three minute intervals to relieve our exhaustion. The room spun round me, a swirl of lights, smoke, sweating bodies surrounded by tense white faces. I bled from both nose and mouth, the blood spattering upon my chest.

The men kept yelling, "Slug him, black boy! Knock his guts out!"

"Uppercut him! Kill him! Kill that big boy!"   25

Taking a fake fall, I saw a boy going down heavily beside me as though we were felled by a single blow, saw a sneaker-clad foot shoot into his groin as the two who had knocked him down stumbled upon him. I rolled out of range, feeling a twinge of nausea.

The harder we fought the more threatening the men became. And yet, I had begun to worry about my speech again. How would it go? Would they recognize my ability? What would they give me?

I was fighting automatically when suddenly I noticed that one after another of the boys was leaving the ring. I was surprised, filled with panic, as though I had been left alone with an unknown danger. Then I understood. The boys had arranged it among themselves. It was the custom for the two men left in the ring to slug it out for the winner's prize. I discovered this too late. When the bell sounded two men in tuxedoes leaped into the ring and removed the blindfold. I found myself facing Tatlock, the biggest of the gang. I felt sick at my stomach. Hardly had the bell stopped ringing in my ears than it clanged again and I saw him moving swiftly toward me. Thinking of nothing else to do I hit him smash on the nose. He kept coming, bringing the rank sharp violence of stale sweat. His face was a black blank of a face, only his eyes alive — with hate of me and aglow with a feverish terror from what had happened to us all. I became anxious. I wanted to deliver my speech and he came at me as though he meant to beat it out of me. I smashed him again and again, taking his blows as they came. Then on a sudden impulse I struck him lightly and as we clinched, I whispered, "Fake like I knocked you out, you can have the prize."

"I'll break your behind," he whispered hoarsely.

"For *them?*"

"For *me*, sonofabitch!"

They were yelling for us to break it up and Tatlock spun me half around with a blow, and as a joggled camera sweeps in a reeling scene, I saw the howling red faces crouching tense beneath the cloud of blue-gray smoke. For a moment the world wavered, unraveled, flowed, then my head cleared and Tatlock bounced before me. That fluttering shadow before my eyes was his jabbing left hand. Then falling forward, my head against his damp shoulder, I whispered,

"I'll make it five dollars more."

"Go to hell!"

But his muscles relaxed a trifle beneath my pressure and I breathed, "Seven?"

"Give it to your ma," he said, ripping me beneath the heart.

And while I still held him I butted him and moved away. I felt myself bombarded with punches. I fought back with hopeless desperation. I wanted to deliver my speech more than anything else in the world, because I felt that only these men could judge truly my ability, and now this stupid clown was ruining my chances. I began fighting carefully now, moving in to punch him and out again with my greater speed. A lucky blow to his chin and I had him going too — until I heard a loud voice yell, "I got my money on the big boy."

Hearing this, I almost dropped my guard. I was confused: Should I try to win against the voice out there? Would not this go against my speech, and was not this a moment for humility, for nonresistance? A blow to my head as I danced about sent my right eye popping like a jack-in-the-box and settled my dilemma. The room went red as I fell. It was a dream fall, my body languid and fastidious as to where to land, until the floor became impatient and smashed up to meet me. A moment later I came to. An hypnotic voice said FIVE, emphatically. And I lay there, hazily watching a dark red spot of my own blood shaping itself into a butterfly, glistening and soaking into the soiled gray world of the canvas.

When the voice drawled TEN I was lifted up and dragged to a chair. I sat dazed. My eye pained and swelled with each throb of my pounding heart and I wondered if now I would be allowed to speak, I was wringing wet, my mouth still bleeding. We were grouped along the wall now. The other boys ignored me as they congratulated Tatlock and speculated as to how much they would be paid. One boy whimpered over his smashed hand. Looking up front, I saw attendants in white jackets rolling the portable ring away and placing a small square rug in the vacant space surrounded by chairs. Perhaps, I thought, I will stand on the rug to deliver my speech.

Then the M.C. called to us, "Come on up here boys and get your money."   40 We ran forward to where the men laughed and talked in their chairs, waiting. Everyone seemed friendly now.

"There it is on the rug," the man said. I saw the rug covered with coins of all dimensions and a few crumpled bills. But what excited me, scattered here and there, were the gold pieces.

"Boys, it's all yours," the man said. "You get all you grab."

"That's right, Sambo," a blond man said, winking at me confidentially.

I trembled with excitement, forgetting my pain. I would get the gold and the bills, I thought. I would use both hands. I would throw my body against the boys nearest me to block them from the gold.

"Get down around the rug now," the man commanded, "and don't any-   45 one touch it until I give the signal."

"This ought to be good," I heard.

As told, we got around the square rug on our knees. Slowly the man raised his freckled hand as we followed it upward with our eyes.

I heard, "These niggers look like they're about to pray!"

Then, "Ready," the man said. "Go!"

I lunged for a yellow coin lying on the blue design of the carpet, touch-   50 ing it and sending a surprised shriek to join those rising around me. I tried frantically to remove my hand but could not let go. A hot, violent force tore through my body, shaking me like a wet rat. The rug was electrified. The hair bristled up on my head as I shook myself free. My muscles jumped, my nerves jangled, writhed. But I saw that this was not stopping the other boys. Laughing in fear and embarrassment, some were holding back and scooping up the coins knocked off by the painful contortions of the others. The men roared above us as we struggled.

"Pick it up, goddamnit, pick it up!" someone called like a bass-voiced parrot. "Go on, get it!"

I crawled rapidly around the floor, picking up the coins, trying to avoid the coppers and to get greenbacks and the gold. Ignoring the shock by laughing, as I brushed the coins off quickly, I discovered that I could contain the electricity—a contradiction, but it works. Then the men began to push us onto the rug. Laughing embarrassedly, we struggled out of their hands and kept after the coins. We were all wet and slippery and hard to hold. Suddenly I saw a boy lifted into the air, glistening with sweat like a circus seal, and dropped, his wet back landing flush upon the charged rug, heard him yell and saw him literally dance upon his back, his elbows beating a frenzied tattoo upon the floor, his muscles twitching like the flesh of a horse stung by many flies. When he finally rolled off, his face was gray and no one stopped him when he ran from the floor amid booming laughter.

"Get the money," the M.C. called. "That's good hard American cash!"

And we snatched and grabbed, snatched and grabbed. I was careful not to come too close to the rug now, and when I felt the hot whiskey breath descend upon me like a cloud of foul air I reached out and grabbed the leg of a chair. It was occupied and I held on desperately.

"Leggo, nigger! Leggo!"   55

The huge face wavered down to mine as he tried to push me free. But my body was slippery and he was too drunk. It was Mr. Colcord, who owned a chain of movie houses and "entertainment palaces." Each time he grabbed me I slipped out of his hands. It became a real struggle. I feared the rug more than I did the drunk, so I held on, surprising myself for a moment by trying to topple *him* upon the rug. It was such an enormous idea that I found myself actually carrying it out. I tried not to be obvious, yet when I grabbed his leg, trying to tumble him out of the chair, he raised up roaring with laughter, and, looking at me with soberness dead in the eye, kicked me viciously in the chest. The chair leg flew out of my hand and I felt myself going and rolled. It was as though I had rolled through a bed of hot coals. It seemed a whole century would pass before I would roll free, a century in which I was seared through the deepest levels of my body to the fearful breath within me and the breath seared and heated to the point of explosion. It'll all be over in a flash, I thought as I rolled clear. It'll all be over in a flash.

But not yet, the men on the other side were waiting, red faces swollen as though from apoplexy as they bent forward in their chairs. Seeing their fingers coming toward me I rolled away as a fumbled football rolls off the receiver's fingertips, back into the coals. That time I luckily sent the rug sliding out of place and heard the coins ringing against the floor and the boys scuffling to pick them up and the M.C. calling, "All right, boys, that's all. Go get dressed and get your money."

I was limp as a dish rag. My back felt as though it had been beaten with wires.

When we had dressed the M.C. came in and gave us each five dollars, except Tatlock, who got ten for being last in the ring. Then he told us to leave. I was not to get a chance to deliver my speech, I thought. I was going out into the dim alley in despair when I was stopped and told to go back. I returned to the ballroom, where the men were pushing back their chairs and gathering in groups to talk.

The M.C. knocked on a table for quiet. "Gentlemen," he said, "we almost   60
forgot an important part of the program. A most serious part, gentlemen. This boy was brought here to deliver a speech which he made at his graduation yesterday . . ."

"Bravo!"

"I'm told that he is the smartest boy we've got out there in Greenwood. I'm told that he knows more big words than a pocket-sized dictionary."

Much applause and laughter.

"So now, gentlemen, I want you to give him your attention."

There was still laughter as I faced them, my mouth dry, my eye throbbing. I began slowly, but evidently my throat was tense, because they began shouting, "Louder! Louder!"

"We of the younger generation extol the wisdom of that great leader and educator," I shouted, "who first spoke these flaming words of wisdom: 'A ship lost at sea for many days suddenly sighted a friendly vessel. From the mast of the unfortunate vessel was seen a signal: "Water, water; we die of thirst!" The answer from the friendly vessel came back: "Cast down your bucket where you are." The captain of the distressed vessel, at last heeding the injunction, cast down his bucket, and it came up full of fresh sparkling water from the mouth of the Amazon River.' And like him I say, and in his words, 'To those of my race who depend upon bettering their condition in a foreign land, or who underestimate the importance of cultivating friendly relations with the Southern white man, who is his next-door neighbor, I would say: "Cast down your bucket where you are" — cast it down in making friends in every manly way of the people of all races by whom we are surrounded . . .'"

I spoke automatically and with such fervor that I did not realize that the men were still talking and laughing until my dry mouth, filling up with blood from the cut, almost strangled me. I coughed, wanting to stop and go to one of the tall brass, sand-filled spittoons to relieve myself, but a few of the men, especially the superintendent, were listening and I was afraid. So I gulped it down, blood, saliva, and all, and continued. (What powers of endurance I had during those days! What enthusiasm! What a belief in the rightness of things!) I spoke even louder in spite of the pain. But still they talked and still they laughed, as though deaf with cotton in dirty ears. So I spoke with greater emotional emphasis. I closed my ears and swallowed blood until I was nauseated. The speech seemed a hundred times as long as before, but I could not leave out a single word. All had to be said, each memorized nuance considered, rendered. Nor was that all. Whenever I uttered a word of three or more syllables a group of voices would yell for me to repeat it. I used the phrase "social responsibility" and they yelled:

"What's that word you say, boy?"

"Social responsibility," I said.

"What?"

"Social . . ."

"Louder."

". . . responsibility."

"More!"

"Respon —"

"Repeat!"

" — sibility."

The room filled with the uproar of laughter until, no doubt, distracted by having to gulp down my blood, I made a mistake and yelled a phrase I had often seen denounced in newspaper editorials, heard debated in private.

"Social . . ."

"What?" they yelled.

". . . equality—"

The laughter hung smokelike in the sudden stillness. I opened my eyes, puzzled. Sounds of displeasure filled the room. The M.C. rushed forward. They shouted hostile phrases at me. But I did not understand.

A small dry mustached man in the front row blared out, "Say that slowly, son!"

"What, sir?"

"What you just said!"

"Social responsibility, sir," I said.

"You weren't being smart, were you, boy?" he said, not unkindly.

"No, sir!"

"You sure that about 'equality' was a mistake?"

"Oh, yes, sir," I said. "I was swallowing blood."

"Well, you had better speak more slowly so we can understand. We mean to do right by you, but you've got to know your place at all times. All right, now, go on with your speech."

I was afraid. I wanted to leave but I wanted also to speak and I was afraid they'd snatch me down.

"Thank you, sir," I said, beginning where I had left off, and having them ignore me as before.

Yet when I finished there was a thunderous applause. I was surprised to see the superintendent come forth with a package wrapped in white tissue paper, and, gesturing for quiet, address the men.

"Gentlemen, you see that I did not overpraise this boy. He makes a good speech and some day he'll lead his people in the proper paths. And I don't have to tell you that that is important in these days and times. This is a good, smart boy, and so to encourage him in the right direction, in the name of the Board of Education I wish to present him a prize in the form of this . . ."

He paused, removing the tissue paper and revealing a gleaming calfskin brief case.

". . . in the form of this first-class article from Shad Whitmore's shop."

"Boy," he said, addressing me, "take this prize and keep it well. Consider it a badge of office. Prize it. Keep developing as you are and some day it will be filled with important papers that will help shape the destiny of your people."

I was so moved that I could hardly express my thanks. A rope of bloody saliva forming a shape like an undiscovered continent drooled upon the leather and I wiped it quickly away. I felt an importance that I had never dreamed.

"Open it and see what's inside," I was told.

My fingers a-tremble, I complied, smelling the fresh leather and finding an official-looking document inside. It was a scholarship to the state college for Negroes. My eyes filled with tears and I ran awkwardly off the floor.

I was overjoyed; I did not even mind when I discovered that the gold pieces I had scrambled for were brass pocket tokens advertising a certain make of automobile.

When I reached home everyone was excited. Next day the neighbors came to congratulate me. I even felt safe from grandfather, whose deathbed curse usually spoiled my triumphs. I stood beneath his photograph with my brief case in hand and smiled triumphantly into his stolid black peasant's face. It was a face that fascinated me. The eyes seemed to follow everywhere I went.

That night I dreamed I was at a circus with him and that he refused to laugh at the clowns no matter what they did. Then later he told me to open my brief case and read what was inside and I did, finding an official envelope stamped with the state seal; and inside the envelope I found another and another, endlessly, and I thought I would fall of weariness. "Them's years," he said. "Now open that one." And I did and in it I found an engraved document containing a short message in letters of gold. "Read it," my grandfather said. "Out loud!"

"To Whom It May Concern," I intoned. "Keep This Nigger-Boy Running."   105
I awoke with the old man's laughter ringing in my ears.

(It was a dream I was to remember and dream again for many years after. But at that time I had no insight into its meaning. First I had to attend college.)   *[1947]*

≡ THINKING ABOUT THE TEXT

1. Some critics have seen the events at the smoker as symbolic or perhaps as an allegory of the plight of African Americans in the segregated South. Pick at least two specific events from the story. How are they meant to explain certain aspects of the African American experience before the civil rights movement of the 1960s?

2. Some readers are surprised by the bizarre and cruel behavior of the town's leaders. Are you? How do you explain what goes on there?

3. How do you interpret the narrator's dream (paras. 104–06)? Why would his grandfather be laughing?

4. Reread paragraphs 1 through 3. How is this opening section connected to the story? To the last paragraph? What might Ellison's narrator mean when he says in paragraph 1 that he is "an invisible man"?

5. The grandfather's deathbed advice in paragraph 2 causes quite a stir. In your own words, what is his advice? Why are his relatives surprised? What might be some alternatives for dealing with oppression? Which "solution" sounds like the one you would have promoted for our society during Ellison's boyhood?

BOOKER T. WASHINGTON
Atlanta Exposition Address (The Atlanta Compromise)

Recognized in his time as the major spokesman for his race, Booker T. Washington (1856–1915) is often seen today as an accommodationist whose insistence on gradual progress and vocational rather than intellectual education played into the hands of the white power structure, delaying racial equality. He founded and served as president of Tuskegee Institute, wrote twelve books (including the autobiographical Up from Slavery in 1901), controlled much of the Negro press, and spoke in cities throughout the nation. His speech at the Atlanta Cotton States and International Exposition in 1895, in which he praised the South, condoned segregation and the glory of "common labor" for his race, and called for harmony and cooperation between the races, is often called "The Atlanta Compromise."

One-third of the population of the South is of the Negro race. No enterprise seeking the material, civil, or moral welfare of this section can disregard this element of our population and reach the highest success. I but convey to you, Mr. President and Directors, the sentiment of the masses of my race when I say that in no way have the value and manhood of the American Negro been more fittingly and generously recognized than by the managers of this magnificent Exposition at every stage of its progress. It is a recognition that will do more to cement the friendship of the two races than any occurrence since the dawn of our freedom.

Not only this, but the opportunity here afforded will awaken among us a new era of industrial progress. Ignorant and inexperienced, it is not strange that in the first years of our new life we began at the top instead of at the bottom; that a seat in Congress or the state legislature was more sought than real estate or industrial skill; that the political convention or stump speaking had more attractions than starting a dairy farm or truck garden.

A ship lost at sea for many days suddenly sighted a friendly vessel. From the mast of the unfortunate vessel was seen a signal, "Water, water; we die of thirst!" The answer from the friendly vessel at once came back, "Cast down your bucket where you are." A second time the signal, "Water, water, send us water!" ran up from the distressed vessel, and was answered, "Cast down your bucket where you are." And a third and fourth signal for water was answered, "Cast down your bucket where you are." The captain of the distressed vessel, at last heeding the injunction, cast down his bucket, and it came up full of fresh, sparkling water from the mouth of the Amazon River. To those of my race who depend on bettering their condition in a foreign land or who underestimate the importance of cultivating friendly relations with the Southern white man, who is their next-door neighbor, I would say: "Cast down your bucket where you are" — cast it down in making friends in every manly way of the people of all races by whom we are surrounded.

Cast it down in agriculture, mechanics, in commerce, in domestic service, and in the professions. And in this connection it is well to bear in mind that whatever other sins the South may be called to bear, when it comes to business, pure and simple, it is in the South that the Negro is given a man's chance in the commercial world, and in nothing is this Exposition more eloquent than in emphasizing this chance. Our greatest danger is that in the great leap from slavery to freedom we may overlook the fact that the masses of us are to live by the productions of our hands, and fail to keep in mind that we shall prosper in proportion as we learn to dignify and glorify common labor and put brains and skill into the common occupations of life; shall prosper in proportion as we learn to draw the line between the superficial and the substantial, the ornamental gewgaws of life and the useful. No race can prosper till it learns that there is as much dignity in tilling a field as in writing a poem. It is at the bottom of life we must begin, and not at the top. Nor should we permit our grievances to overshadow our opportunities.

To those of the white race who look to the incoming of those of foreign birth and strange tongue and habits for the prosperity of the South, were I permitted I would repeat what I say to my own race, "Cast down your bucket where you are." Cast it down among the eight millions of Negroes whose habits you know, whose fidelity and love you have tested in days when to have proved treacherous meant the ruin of your firesides. Cast down your bucket among these people who have, without strikes and labor wars, tilled your fields, cleared your forests, builded your railroads and cities, and brought forth treasures from the bowels of the earth, and helped make possible this magnificent representation of the progress of the South. Casting down your bucket among my people, helping and encouraging them as you are doing on these grounds, and to education of head, hand, and heart, you will find that they will buy your surplus land, make blossom the waste places in your fields, and run your factories. While doing this, you can be sure in the future, as in the past, that you and your families will be surrounded by the most patient, faithful, law-abiding, and unresentful people that the world has seen. As we have proved our loyalty to you in the past, in nursing your children, watching by the sick-bed of your mothers and fathers, and often following them with tear-dimmed eyes to their graves, so in the future, in our humble way, we shall stand by you with a devotion that no foreigner can approach, ready to lay down our lives, if need be, in defense of yours, interlacing our industrial, commercial, civil, and religious life with yours in a way that shall make the interests of both races one. In all things that are purely social we can be as separate as the fingers, yet one as the hand in all things essential to mutual progress.

There is no defense or security for any of us except in the highest intelligence and development of all. If anywhere there are efforts tending to curtail the fullest growth of the Negro, let these efforts be turned into stimulating, encouraging, and making him the most useful and intelligent citizen. Effort or

5

means so invested will pay a thousand per cent interest. These efforts will be twice blessed—"blessing him that gives and him that takes."

There is no escape through law of man or God from the inevitable:—

> The laws of changeless justice bind
> Oppressor with oppressed;
> And close as sin and suffering joined
> We march to fate abreast.

Nearly sixteen millions of hands will aid you in pulling the load upward, or they will pull against you the load downward. We shall constitute one-third and more of the ignorance and crime of the South, or one-third its intelligence and progress; we shall contribute one-third to the business and industrial prosperity of the South, or we shall prove a veritable body of death, stagnating, depressing, retarding every effort to advance the body politic.

Gentlemen of the Exposition, as we present to you our humble effort at an exhibition of our progress, you must not expect overmuch. Starting thirty years ago with ownership here and there in a few quilts and pumpkins and chickens (gathered from miscellaneous sources), remember the path that has led from these to the inventions and production of agricultural implements, buggies, steam-engines, newspapers, books, statuary, carving, paintings, the management of drug-stores and banks, has not been trodden without contact with thorns and thistles. While we take pride in what we exhibit as a result of our independent efforts, we do not for a moment forget that our part in this exhibition would fall far short of your expectations but for the constant help that has come to our educational life, not only from the Southern states, but especially from Northern philanthropists who have made their gifts a constant stream of blessing and encouragement.

The wisest among my race understand that the agitation of questions of social equality is the extremest folly, and that progress in the enjoyment of all the privileges that will come to us must be the result of severe and constant struggle rather than of artificial forcing. No race that has anything to contribute to the markets of the world is long in any degree ostracized. It is important and right that all privileges of the law be ours, but it is vastly more important that we be prepared for the exercises of these privileges. The opportunity to earn a dollar in a factory just now is worth infinitely more than the opportunity to spend a dollar in an opera-house. 10

In conclusion, may I repeat that nothing in thirty years has given us more hope and encouragement, and drawn us so near to you of the white race, as this opportunity offered by the Exposition; and here bending, as it were, over the altar that represents the results of the struggles of your race and mine, both starting practically empty-handed three decades ago, I pledge that in your effort to work out the great and intricate problem which God has laid at the doors of the South, you shall have at all times the patient, sympathetic help of my race; only let this be constantly in mind, that, while from representations in these buildings of the product of field, of forest, of mine, of factory, letters, and art, much good will come, yet far above and beyond material benefits will be that higher good, that, let us pray God, will come, in a blotting out of sectional differences and racial animosities and suspicions, in a determination to administer absolute justice, in a willing obedience among all classes to the mandates of law. This, this, coupled with our material prosperity, will bring into our beloved South a new heaven and a new earth.   [1895]

≡ THINKING ABOUT THE TEXT

1. Cite two passages from Washington's speech that would probably have had an impact on the African American characters in "Battle Royal."

2. Do you think Washington is right in saying, "No race can prosper till it learns that there is as much dignity in tilling a field as in writing a poem" (para. 4)?

3. Are you surprised that Washington pledges "the patient, sympathetic help of my race" as those whites in power "work out the great and intricate problem which God has laid at the doors of the South" (para. 11)? What might contemporary black leaders think of this attitude?

W. E. B. DU BOIS
Of Mr. Booker T. Washington

W. E. B. Du Bois (1868–1963) was a driving force in the movement for equality for people of color in America and throughout the world well into his nineties. He was born in Massachusetts soon after the Civil War, and his death in Africa coincided with the March on Washington in 1963. Du Bois was educated at Fisk, Berlin, and Harvard universities, receiving a Ph.D. from Harvard in 1895 for his dissertation on the history of the slave trade. He is best known for his work with the National Association for the Advancement of Colored People (NAACP), serving as editor of The Crisis *from 1910 to 1932. As a scholar, writer, and intellectual, Du Bois openly opposed policies such as those supported by Booker T. Washington that kept social, political, and educational opportunities from most African Americans.* The Souls of Black Folk *(1903), from which our reading is taken, is perhaps the most influential of his many writings.*

Easily the most striking thing in the history of the American Negro since 1876 is the ascendancy of Mr. Booker T. Washington. It began at the time when war memories and ideals were rapidly passing; a day of astonishing commercial development was dawning; a sense of doubt and hesitation overtook the freedmen's sons, — then it was that his leading began. Mr. Washington came, with a simple definite programme, at the psychological moment when the nation was a little ashamed of having bestowed so much sentiment on Negroes, and was concentrating its energies on Dollars. His programme of industrial education, conciliation of the South, and submission and silence as to civil and political rights, was not wholly original; the Free Negroes from 1830 up to wartime had striven to build industrial schools, and the American Missionary Association had from the first taught various trades; and Price° and others had sought a way of honorable alliance with the best of the Southerners. But Mr. Washington first indissolubly linked these things; he put enthusiasm, unlimited energy, and perfect faith into this programme, and changed it from a by-path into a veritable Way of Life. And the tale of the methods by which he did this is a fascinating study of human life.

It startled the nation to hear a Negro advocating such a programme after many decades of bitter complaint; it startled and won the applause of the South, it interested and won the admiration of the North; and after a confused murmur of protest, it silenced if it did not convert the Negroes themselves.

To gain the sympathy and cooperation of the various elements comprising the white South was Mr. Washington's first task; and this, at the time Tuskegee was founded, seemed, for a black man, well-nigh impossible. And yet ten years later it was done in the word spoken at Atlanta: "In all things purely social we can be as separate as the five fingers, and yet one as the hand in all things essential to mutual progress." This "Atlanta Compromise" is by all odds the most notable thing in Mr. Washington's career. The South interpreted it in different ways: the radicals received it as a complete surrender of the demand for civil and political equality; the conservatives, as a generously conceived working basis for mutual understanding. So both approved it, and today its author is certainly the most distinguished Southerner since Jefferson Davis, and the one with the largest personal following. . . .

Mr. Washington represents in Negro thought the old attitude of adjustment and submission; but adjustment at such a peculiar time as to make his programme unique. This is an age of unusual economic development, and Mr. Washington's programme naturally takes an economic cast, becoming a gospel of Work and Money to such an extent as apparently almost completely to over-shadow the higher aims of life. Moreover, this is an age when the more advanced races are coming in closer contact with the less developed races, and the race-feeling is therefore intensified; and Mr. Washington's programme practically accepts the alleged inferiority of the Negro races. Again, in our own land, the reaction from the sentiment of war time has given impetus to race-prejudice against Negroes, and Mr. Washington withdraws many of the high demands of Negroes as men and American citizens. In other periods of intensified prejudice all the Negro's tendency to self-assertion has been called forth; at this period a policy of submission is advocated. In the history of nearly all

Price: Joseph C. Price (1854–1893), founder of Zion Wesley College and Livingstone College, was a prominent African American educator and championed liberal-arts education.

other races and people the doctrine preached at such crises has been that manly self-respect is worth more than lands and houses, and that a people who voluntarily surrender such respect, or cease striving for it, are not worth civilizing.

In answer to this, it has been claimed that the Negro can survive only   5 through submission. Mr. Washington distinctly asks that black people give up, at least for the present, three things —

> First, political power,
> Second, insistence on civil rights,
> Third, higher education of Negro youth, —

and concentrate all their energies on industrial education, the accumulation of wealth, and the conciliation of the South. This policy has been courageously and insistently advocated for over fifteen years, and has been triumphant for perhaps ten years. As a result of this tender of the palm-branch, what has been the return? In these years there have occurred:

1. The disfranchisement of the Negro.
2. The legal creation of a distinct status of civil inferiority for the Negro.
3. The steady withdrawal of aid from institutions for the higher training of the Negro.

These movements are not, to be sure, direct results of Mr. Washington's teachings; but his propaganda has, without a shadow of doubt, helped their speedier accomplishment. The question then comes: Is it possible, and probable, that nine millions of men can make effective progress in economic lines if they are deprived of political rights, made a servile caste, and allowed only the most meager chance for developing their exceptional men? If history and reason give any distinct answer to these questions, it is an emphatic *No. . . .*

In failing thus to state plainly and unequivocally the legitimate demands of their people, even at the cost of opposing an honored leader the thinking classes of American Negroes would shirk a heavy responsibility, — a responsibility to themselves, a responsibility to struggling masses, a responsibility to the darker races of men whose future depends so largely on this American experiment, but especially a responsibility to this nation, — this common Fatherland. It is wrong to encourage a man or a people in evil-doing; it is wrong to aid and abet a national crime simply because it is unpopular not to do so. The growing spirit of kindliness and reconciliation between the North and South after the frightful differences of a generation ago ought to be a source of deep congratulation to all, and especially to those whose mistreatment caused the war; but if that reconciliation is to be marked by the industrial slavery and civic death of those same black men, with permanent legislation into a position of inferiority, then those black men, if they are really men, are called upon by every consideration of patriotism and loyalty to oppose such a course by all civilized methods, even though such opposition involves disagreement with Mr. Booker

T. Washington. We have no right to sit silently by while the inevitable seeds are sown for a harvest of disaster to our children, black and white.

First, it is the duty of black men to judge the South discriminatingly. The present generation of Southerners are not responsible for the past, and they should not be blindly hated or blamed for it. Furthermore, to no class is the indiscriminate endorsement of the recent course of the South toward Negroes more nauseating than to the best thought of the South. The South is not "solid"; it is a land in the ferment of social change, wherein forces of all kinds are fighting for supremacy; and to praise the ill the South is today perpetrating is just as wrong as to condemn the good. Discriminating and broad-minded criticism is what the South needs, — needs it for the sake of her own white sons and daughters, and for the insurance of robust, healthy mental and moral development.

Today even the attitude of the Southern whites toward the blacks is not, as so many assume, in all cases the same; the ignorant Southerner hates the Negro, the workingmen fear his competition, the money-makers wish to use him as a laborer, some of the educated see a menace in his upward development, while others, — usually the sons of the masters — wish to help him to rise. National opinion has enabled this last class to maintain the Negro common schools, and to protect the Negro partially in property, life, and limb. Through the pressure of the money-makers, the Negro is in danger of being reduced to semi-slavery, especially in the country districts; the workingmen, and those of the educated who fear the Negro, have united to disfranchise him, and some have urged his deportation; while the passions of the ignorant are easily aroused to lynch and abuse any black man. To praise this intricate whirl of thought and prejudice is nonsense, to inveigh indiscriminately against "the South" is unjust; but to use the same breath in praising Governor Aycock, exposing Senator Morgan, arguing with Mr. Thomas Nelson Page, and denouncing Senator Ben Tillman, is not only sane, but the imperative duty of thinking black men.

It would be unjust to Mr. Washington not to acknowledge that in several   10
instances he has opposed movements in the South which were unjust to the Negro; he sent memorials to the Louisiana and Alabama constitutional conventions, he has spoken against lynching, and in other ways has openly or silently set his influence against sinister schemes and unfortunate happenings. Notwithstanding this, it is equally true to assert that on the whole the distinct impression left by Mr. Washington's propaganda is, first, that the South is justified in its present attitude toward the Negro because of the Negro's degradation; secondly, that the prime cause of the Negro's failure to rise more quickly is his wrong education in the past; and, thirdly, that his future rise depends primarily on his own efforts. Each of these propositions is a dangerous half-truth. The supplementary truths must never be lost sight of: first, slavery and race-prejudice are potent if not sufficient causes of the Negro's position; second, industrial and common-school training were necessarily slow in planting because they had to await the black teachers trained by higher institutions, — it being extremely doubtful if any essentially different development was

possible, and certainly a Tuskegee was unthinkable before 1880; and, third, while it is a great truth to say that the Negro must strive and strive mightily to help himself, it is equally true that unless his striving be not simply seconded, but rather aroused and encouraged, by the initiative of the richer and wiser environing group, he cannot hope for great success.

In his failure to realize and impress this last point, Mr. Washington is especially to be criticized. His doctrine has tended to make the whites, North and South, shift the burden of the Negro problem to the Negro's shoulders and stand aside as critical and rather pessimistic spectators; when in fact the burden belongs to the nation, and the hands of none of us are clean if we bend not our energies to righting these great wrongs.

The South ought to be led, by candid and honest criticism, to assert her better self and do her full duty to the race she has cruelly wronged and is still wronging. The North — her copartner in guilt — cannot salve her conscience by plastering it with gold. We cannot settle this problem by diplomacy and suaveness, by "policy" alone. If worse come to worst, can the moral fiber of this country survive the slow throttling and murder of nine millions of men?

The black men of America have a duty to perform, a duty stern and delicate, — a forward movement to oppose a part of the work of their greatest leader. So far as Mr. Washington preaches Thrift, Patience, and Industrial Training for the masses, we must hold up his hands and strive with him, rejoicing in his honors and glorying in the strength of this Joshua called of God and of man to lead the headless host. But so far as Mr. Washington apologizes for injustice, North or South, does not rightly value the privilege and duty of voting, belittles the emasculating effects of caste distinctions, and opposes the higher training and ambition of our brighter minds, — so far as he, the South, or the Nation, does this, — we must unceasingly and firmly oppose them. By every civilized and peaceful method we must strive for the rights which the world accords to men, clinging unwaveringly to those great words which the sons of the Fathers would fain forget: "We hold these truths to be self-evident: that all men are created equal; that they are endowed by their Creator with certain unalienable rights; that among these are life, liberty, and the pursuit of happiness."

[1903]

≡ THINKING ABOUT THE TEXT

1. Du Bois is clearly upset with Washington. What is his main objection to the Atlanta Compromise? Do you agree with him?

2. Is the narrator of "Battle Royal" still under Washington's influence, or has the thinking of Du Bois made some inroads?

3. What might the grandfather in "Battle Royal" think of Du Bois's last paragraph?

GUNNAR MYRDAL
Social Equality

A Swedish economist who with his wife, Alva Myrdal (winner of the 1982 Nobel Peace Prize), established a model social-welfare system for Sweden in the 1930s, Gunnar Myrdal (1898–1987) was asked by the Carnegie Foundation in 1938 to study racism in the United States. "Social Equality" is an excerpt from the book that elaborated on the results of his study, An American Dilemma: The Negro Problem and Modern Democracy *(1944). In* Cultural Contexts for Ralph Ellison's Invisible Man, *historian Eric Sundquist points out that for the white men in "Battle Royal," the term social equality would have included sexual relations and marriage between black men and white women, which was then an important cultural taboo.*

In his first encounter with the American Negro problem, perhaps nothing perplexes the outside observer more than the popular term and the popular theory of "no social equality." He will be made to feel from the start that it has concrete implications and a central importance for the Negro problem in America. But, nevertheless, the term is kept vague and elusive, and the theory loose and ambiguous. One moment it will be stretched to cover and justify every form of social segregation and discrimination, and, in addition, all the inequalities in justice, politics, and breadwinning. The next moment it will be narrowed to express only the denial of close personal intimacies and intermarriage. The very lack of precision allows the notion of "no social equality" to rationalize the rather illogical and wavering system of color caste in America.

The kernel of the popular theory of "no social equality" will, when pursued, be presented as a firm determination on the part of the whites to block amalgamation and preserve "the purity of the white race." The white man identifies himself with "the white race" and feels that he has a stake in resisting the dissipation of its racial identity. Important in this identification is the notion of "the absolute and unchangeable superiority of the white race." From this racial dogma will often be drawn the *direct* inference that the white man shall dominate in all spheres. But when the logic of this inference is inquired about, the inference will be made *indirect* and will be made to lead over to the danger of amalgamation, or, as it is popularly expressed, "intermarriage."

It is further found that the ban on intermarriage is focused on white women. For them it covers both formal marriage and illicit intercourse. In regard to white men it is taken more or less for granted that they would not stoop to marry Negro women, and that illicit intercourse does not fall under the same intense taboo. Their offspring, under the popular doctrine that maternity is more certain than paternity, become Negroes anyway, and the white race easily avoids pollution with Negro blood. To prevent "intermarriage" in this specific sense of sex relations between white women and Negro men, it is not enough to apply legal and social sanctions against it — so the popular theory runs. In using the danger of intermarriage as a defense for the whole caste system, it is assumed both that Negro men have a strong desire for "intermarriage," and that white women would be open to proposals from Negro men, *if* they are not guarded from even meeting them on an equal plane. The latter assumption, of course, is never openly expressed, but is logically implicit in the popular theory. The conclusion follows that the whole system of segregation and discrimination is justified. Every single measure is defended as necessary to block "social equality" which in its turn is held necessary to prevent "intermarriage."

The basic role of the fear of amalgamation in white attitudes to the race problem is indicated by the popular magical concept of "blood." Educated white Southerners, who know everything about modern genetic and biological research, confess readily that they actually feel an irrational or "instinctive" repugnance in thinking of "intermarriage." These measures of segregation and discrimination are often of the type found in the true taboos, and in the notion "not to be touched" of primitive religion. The specific taboos are characterized, further, by a different degree of excitement which attends their violation and a different degree of punishment to the violator: the closer the act to sexual association, the more furious is the public reaction. Sexual association itself is punished by death and is accompanied by tremendous public excitement; the other social relations meet decreasing degrees of public fury. Sex becomes in this popular theory the principle around which the whole structure of segregation of the Negroes — down to disfranchisement and denial of equal opportunities on the labor market — is organized. The reasoning is this: "For, say what we will, may not all the equalities be ultimately based on potential social equality, and that in turn on intermarriage? Here we reach the real *crux* of the question." In cruder language, but with the same logic, the Southern man on the street responds to any plea for social equality: "Would you like to have your daughter marry a Negro?"

This theory of color caste centering around the aversion to amalgamation determines, as we have just observed, the white man's rather definite rank order of the various measures of segregation and discrimination against Negroes. The relative significance attached to each of those measures is dependent upon their degree of expediency or necessity — in the view of white people — as means of upholding the ban on "intermarriage." In this rank order, (1) the ban on intermarriage and other sex relations involving white women and colored men takes precedence before everything else. It is the end for which the other restrictions are arranged as means. Thereafter follow: (2) all sorts of taboos and etiquettes in personal contacts; (3) segregation in schools and churches; (4) segregation in hotels, restaurants, and theaters, and other public places where people meet socially; (5) segregation in public conveyances; (6) discrimination in public services; and, finally, inequality in (7) politics, (8) justice, and (9) breadwinning and relief.

The degree of liberalism on racial matters in the white South can be designated mainly by the point on this rank order where a man stops because he believes further segregation and discrimination are not necessary to prevent "intermarriage." We have seen that white liberals in the South of the present day, as a matter of principle, rather unanimously stand up against inequality in breadwinning, relief, justice, and politics. These fields of discrimination form

5

the chief battleground and considerable changes in them are, as we have seen, on the way. When we ascend to the higher ranks which concern social relations in the narrow sense, we find the Southern liberals less prepared to split off from the majority opinion of the region. Hardly anybody in the South is prepared to go the whole way and argue that even the ban on intermarriage should be lifted. Practically all agree, not only upon the high desirability of preventing "intermarriage," but also that a certain amount of separation between the two groups is expedient and necessary to prevent it. Even the one who has his philosophical doubts on the point must, if he is reasonable, abstain from ever voicing them. The social pressure is so strong that it would be foolish not to conform. Conformity is a political necessity for having any hope of influence; it is, in addition, a personal necessity for not meeting social ostracism. . . .

The fixation on the purity of white womanhood, and also part of the intensity of emotion surrounding the whole sphere of segregation and discrimination, are to be understood as the backwashes of the sore conscience on the part of white men for their own or their compeers' relations with, or desires for, Negro women. These psychological effects are greatly magnified because of the puritan *milieu* of America and especially of the South. The upper class men in a less puritanical people could probably have indulged in sex relations with, and sexual day-dreams of, lower caste women in a more matter-of-course way and without generating so much pathos about white womanhood. The Negro people have to carry the burden not only of the white men's sins but also of their virtues. The virtues of the honest, democratic, puritan white Americans in the South are great, and the burden upon the Negroes becomes ponderous.

Our practical conclusion is that it would have cleansing effects on race relations in America, and particularly in the South, to have an open and sober discussion in rational terms of this ever present popular theory of "intermarriage" and "social equality," giving matters their factual ground, true proportions and logical relations. Because it is, to a great extent, an opportunistic rationalization, and because it refers directly and indirectly to the most touchy spots in American life and American morals, tremendous inhibitions have been built up against a detached and critical discussion of this theory. But such inhibitions are gradually overcome when, in the course of secularized education, people become rational about their life problems. It must never be forgotten that in our increasingly intellectualized civilization even the plain citizen feels an urge for truth and objectivity, and that this rationalistic urge is increasingly competing with the opportunistic demands for rationalization and escape.

There are reasons to believe that a slow but steady cleansing of the American mind is proceeding as the cultural level is raised. The basic racial inferiority doctrine is being undermined by research and education. For a white man to have illicit relations with Negro women is increasingly meeting disapproval. Negroes themselves are more and more frowning upon such relations. This all must tend to dampen the emotional fires around "social equality." Sex and race fears are, however, even today the main defense for segregation and, in fact, for the whole caste order. The question shot at the interviewer touching any point of this order is still: "Would you like to have your daughter (sister) marry a Negro?"   *[1944]*

▤ THINKING ABOUT THE TEXT

1. Look back at the smoker section in "Battle Royal," especially when the narrator during his speech says "social equality" instead of "social responsibility." Why do you think there was a "sudden stillness" in the room?

2. Based on his ideas about white sexual fears, how might Myrdal read the part of the smoker dealing with the naked dancer?

3. Myrdal writes that "conformity is a political necessity for having any hope of influence; it is, in addition, a personal necessity for not meeting social ostracism" (para. 6). Does this insight help your understanding of the world of the smoker?

▤ WRITING ABOUT ISSUES

1. Argue that the episode at the smoker is or is not evidence that the grandfather's advice in "Battle Royal" to " 'overcome 'em with yeses, undermine 'em with grins, agree 'em to death and destruction' " (para. 2) will not work.

2. Analyze the arguments of Washington and Du Bois in terms of the claims they both make, the assumptions they base their claims on, the evidence they use as support for their assumptions, and the effectiveness of their claims with the intended audience. Which writer do you find more persuasive?

3. Write a personal narrative detailing an experience either when you were the victim of bias because of your race, sex, age, religion, ethnicity, sexual preference, or any other personal dynamic, or when you were part of a group that held biased views. Be specific about what happened, how you felt then, how you feel now, and what you learned from the experience.

▤ RESEARCHING THE ISSUES

1. Find a detailed plot summary of Ellison's *Invisible Man* and argue that the first chapter ("Battle Royal") anticipates what Ellison thought was a key theme of his novel: a clash of "innocence and human error, a struggle through illusion to reality."

2. Research the phenomenon of the battle royal in American history and argue that Ellison chose this type of fight because of its literal and symbolic significance.

3. Research race relations in the South (including Oklahoma) in the 1930s and write an argument that Ellison's story is or is not literally and symbolically accurate.

Writing with Critical Approaches to Literature

Exploring the topics of literary criticism can help readers understand the various ways literature can matter. One popular way to investigate critical approaches to literature is to group critics into schools. Critics who are concerned primarily with equality for women, for example, are often classified as feminist critics, and those concerned with the responses of readers are classified as reader-response critics. Likewise, critics who focus on the unconscious are said to belong to the psychoanalytic school, and those who analyze class conflicts belong to the Marxist school.

Classifying critics in this way is probably more convenient than precise. Few critics like to be pigeonholed or thought predictable, and many professional readers tend to be eclectic — that is, they use ideas from various schools to help them illuminate the text. Nevertheless, knowing something about contemporary schools of criticism can make you a more informed reader and help literature matter to you even more.

There is a commonsense belief that words mean just what they say — that to understand a certain passage in a text, a reader simply needs to know what the words mean. But meaning is rarely straightforward. Scholars have been arguing over the meaning of passages in the bible, in the Constitution, and in Shakespeare's plays for centuries without reaching agreement. Pinning down the exact meaning of words like *sin, justice,* and *love* is almost impossible, but even more daunting is the unacknowledged theory of reading that each person brings to any text, including literature. Some people who read the bible or the Constitution, for example, believe in the literal meaning of the words, and some think the real meaning lies in the original intention of the writer, while others believe that the only meaning we can be sure of is our own perspective. For these latter readers, there is no objective meaning, and no absolutely true meaning is possible.

Indeed, a good deal of what a text means depends on the perspective that readers bring with them. Passages can be read effectively from numerous points of view. A generation ago, most English professors taught their students to pay attention to the internal aspects of a poem and not to the poem's larger social and political contexts. So oppositions, irony, paradox, and coherence — not gender equality or social justice — were topics of discussion. Proponents of this approach were said to belong to the New Critical school. In the past twenty-five years or so, however, professors have put much more emphasis on the external aspects of interpretation, stressing social, political, cultural, sexual, and gender-based perspectives. Each one of these perspectives can give us a valuable window on a text, helping us see the rich possibilities of literature. Even though each approach can provide insights into a text, it can also be blind to other textual elements. When we read in too focused a way, we can sometimes miss the opportunity to see what others see.

In this chapter, however, we want to present our interpretation in a clear, logical, and reflective manner as we take a position and try to persuade others of its reasonableness. Since there are many possible lenses to see a text through, you can be sure your classmates will see things differently. Part of the excitement and challenge of making arguments that matter is your ability to analyze and clarify your ideas, gather and organize your evidence, and present your claim in carefully revised and edited prose.

Contemporary Schools of Criticism

The following nine approaches are just a few of the many different literary schools or perspectives a reader can use in engaging a text. Think of them as intellectual tools or informed lenses that you can employ to enhance your interpretation of a particular literary text:

- New Criticism
- Feminist criticism
- Psychoanalytic criticism
- Marxist criticism
- Deconstruction
- Reader-response criticism
- Postcolonial criticism
- New Historicism
- Queer theory

NEW CRITICISM

New Criticism was developed about seventy years ago as a way to focus on "the text itself." Although it is no longer as popular as it once was, some of its principles are still widely accepted, especially the use of specific examples from the text as evidence for a particular interpretation. Sometimes called *close reading*, this approach does not see either the writer's intention or the reader's personal response as relevant. It is also uninterested in the text's social context, the spirit of the age, or its relevance to issues of gender, social justice, or oppression. These critics are interested, for example, in a poem's internal structure, images, symbols, metaphors, point of view, plot, and characterizations. Emphasis is placed on literary language — on the ways connotation, ambiguity, irony, and paradox all reinforce the meaning. In fact, *how* a poem means is inseparable from *what* it means. The primary method for judging the worth of a piece of literature is its organic unity or the complex way all the elements of a text contribute to the poem's meaning.

Critics often argue that their interpretations are the most consistent with textual evidence. A popular approach is to note the oppositions in the text and to focus on tensions, ironies, and paradoxes. Typically, a paradox early in the text is shown at the end not to be that contradictory after all. The critic then argues that all the elements of the text can be seen as contributing to this resolution.

FEMINIST CRITICISM

Feminist criticism developed during the 1970s as an outgrowth of a resurgent women's movement. The goals of the feminist critic and the feminist political activist are similar — to contest the patriarchal point of view as the standard for all moral, aesthetic, political, and intellectual judgments and to assert that gender roles are primarily learned, not universal. They hope to uncover and challenge essentialist attitudes that hold it is normal for women to be kept in domestic, secondary, and subservient roles, and they affirm the value of a woman's experiences and perspectives in understanding the world. Recently, both female and male critics have become interested in gender studies, a branch of theory concerned with the ways cultural practices socialize us to act in certain ways because of our gender. Focused primarily on issues of identity, gender criticism looks at the ways characters in literary texts are represented or how they are constructed in a particular culture as feminine or masculine. Like the broader area of feminism, many gender specialists hope that studying the arbitrary ways we are expected to dress, walk, talk, and behave can help us widen the conventional notions of gender.

PSYCHOANALYTIC CRITICISM

Psychoanalytic criticism began with Sigmund Freud's theories of the unconscious, especially the numerous repressed wounds, fears, unresolved conflicts, and guilty desires from childhood that can significantly affect behavior and mental health in our adult lives. Freud developed the tripart division of the mind into the ego (the conscious self), the superego (the site of what our culture has taught us about good and bad), and the id (the primitive unconscious and source of our sexual drive). Psychoanalytic critics often see literature as a kind of dream, filled with symbolic elements that often mask their real meaning. Freud also theorized that young males were threatened by their fathers in the competition for the affection of their mothers. Critics are alert to the complex ways this Oedipal drama unfolds in literature.

MARXIST CRITICISM

Marxist criticism is based on the political and economic theories of Karl Marx. Marxists think that a society is propelled by its economy, which is manipulated by a class system. Most people, especially blue-collar workers (the proletariat), do not understand the complex ways their lives are subject to economic forces beyond their control. This false consciousness about history and material well-being prevents workers from seeing that their values have been socially constructed to keep them in their place. What most interests contemporary Marxists is the way ideology shapes our consciousness. And since literature both represents and projects ideology, Marxist critics see it as a way to unmask our limited view of society's structures.

DECONSTRUCTION

Deconstruction is really more a philosophical movement than a school of literary criticism, but many of its techniques have been used by Marxist and feminist literary critics to uncover important concepts they believe are hidden in texts. Made famous by the French philosopher Jacques Derrida, deconstruction's main tenet is that Western thought has divided the world into binary opposites. To gain a semblance of control over the complexity of human experience, we have constructed a worldview in which good is clearly at one end of a continuum and bad at the other. Additional examples of binary opposites include masculine and feminine, freedom and slavery, objective and subjective, mind and body, and presence and absence. According to Derrida, however, this arbitrary and illusory construct simply reflects the specific ideology of one culture. Far from being opposed to each other, masculinity and femininity, for example, are intimately interconnected, and traces of the feminine are to be found within the masculine. The concepts need each other for meaning to occur, an idea referred to as *différance.* Derrida also notes that language, far from being a neutral medium of communication, is infused with our biases, assumptions, and values — which leads some of us to refer to sexually active women as "sluts" and to sexually active men as "studs." One term ("sluts") is marginalized, and the other ("studs") is privileged because our culture grants men more power than women in shaping the language that benefits them.

Thus, language filters, distorts, and alters our perception of the world. For deconstructors or deconstructive critics, language is not stable or reliable, and when closely scrutinized, it becomes slippery and ambiguous, constantly overflowing with implications, associations, and contradictions. For Derrida, this endless free play of meaning suggests that language is always changing, always in flux — especially so when we understand that words can be viewed from almost endless points of view or contexts. That is why deconstructionists claim that texts (or individuals or systems of thought) have no fixed definition, no center, no absolute meaning. And so one way to deconstruct or lay bare the arbitrary construction of a text is to show that the oppositions in the text are not really absolutely opposed, that outsiders can be seen to be insiders, and that words that seem to mean one thing can mean many things.

READER-RESPONSE CRITICISM

Reader-response criticism is often misunderstood to be simply giving one's opinion about a text: "I liked it," "I hate happy endings," "I think the characters were unrealistic." But reader-response criticism is actually more interested in why readers have certain responses. The central assumption is that texts do not come alive and do not mean anything until active readers engage them with specific assumptions about what reading is. New Critics think a reader's response is irrelevant because a text's meaning is timeless. But response critics, including feminists and Marxists, maintain that what a text means cannot be separated from the reading process used by readers as they draw on personal and literary experiences to make meaning. In other words, the text is not an object but an event that occurs in readers over time.

Response criticism includes critics who think that the reader's contribution to the making of meaning is quite small as well as critics who think that readers play a primary role in the process. Louise Rosenblatt is a moderate response critic since she thinks the contributions are about equal. Her transactive theory claims that the text guides our response, like a printed musical score that we adjust as we move through the text. She allows for a range of acceptable meanings as long as she can find reasonable textual support in the writing.

Response critics like Stanley Fish downplay individual responses, focusing instead on how communities influence our responses to texts. We probably all belong to a number of these interpretive communities (such as churches, universities, neighborhoods, political parties, and social class) and have internalized their interpretive strategies, their discourse, or their way of reading texts of all kinds. Fish's point is that we all come to texts already predisposed to read them in a certain way: we do not interpret stories, but we create them by using the reading tools and cultural assumptions we bring with us. Our reading then reveals what is in us more than what is in the text. We find what we expect to see.

POSTCOLONIAL CRITICISM

Postcolonial criticism, like feminist criticism, has developed because of the dramatic shrinking of the world and the increasing multicultural cast of our own country. It is mainly interested in the ways nineteenth-century European political domination affects the lives of people living in former colonies, especially the way the dominant culture becomes the norm and those without power are portrayed as inferior. Postcolonial critics often look for stereotypes in texts as well as in characters whose self-image has been damaged by being forced to see themselves as Other, as less than. As oppressed people try to negotiate life in both the dominant and the oppressed cultures, they can develop a double consciousness that leads to feelings of alienation and deep conflicts.

Literary critics often argue that being caught between the demands of two cultures — one dominant and privileged, the other marginalized and scorned — causes a character to be "unhomed," a psychological refugee who is uncomfortable everywhere.

NEW HISTORICISM

New historicism was developed because critics were dissatisfied with the old historicism, a long-standing traditional approach that viewed history simply as a background for understanding the literary text. History was thought to be an accurate record of what happened because the professional historian used objective and proven methods. But most literary critics no longer hold to this view of history. Instead, history is now thought to be just one perspective among many possibilities, inevitably subjective and biased. Influenced by the theorist Michel Foucault, history is seen as one of many discourses that can shed light on the past. But the dominant view is that all of us, including historians, writers, and critics, live in a particular culture and cannot escape its influences. And since these social, cultural, literary, economic, and political influences are all interrelated, all texts can tell us something important. Stories, histories, diaries, laws, speeches, newspapers, and magazines are all relevant. Culture permeates all texts, influencing everyone to see society's view of reality, of what's right and wrong and which values, assumptions, and truths are acceptable. Critics and historians try to interpret a vast web of interconnected discourses and forces in order to understand an era. Naturally, since many of these forces are competing for power, critics are always looking for power struggles among discourses. Think of the present struggle over the amount of influence religion should have in politics or who has the right to marry. Literature is one of the texts in a culture that shapes our views and which critics investigate to unearth these competing ideas.

QUEER THEORY

Influenced by the social, cultural, and academic advances of feminist theory in the 1980s, gay and lesbian critics in the 1990s began to join the critical conversation taking place in universities. Besides uncovering the possible homosexuality or bisexuality of canonical authors (such as Christopher Marlowe, Willa Cather, Emily Dickinson, and Henry James), these critics sought to reveal and discredit long-held stereotypes of gay and lesbian fictional characters. By challenging the homophobic prejudice they found in literature and society, lesbian and gay critics hoped to raise awareness of the complex ways society privileges heterosexual behavior and marginalizes any deviation from its norms. Adrienne Rich, an influential lesbian theorist, popularized the term "compulsive heterosexuality" to suggest the subtle and explicit ways the dominant straight culture unthinkingly socializes us to see heterosexuality as a given, the taken-for-granted default sexual identity for all. As a result, same-sex relationships suffer the disempowering injustices allotted to those judged abnormal. Therefore, another concern of gay and lesbian critics has been to suggest that sexual identity is not a stable or an absolute given. Again, Adrienne Rich is helpful with her idea of a "lesbian continuum" where sexual identity is not absolute but is best seen as contextual and fluid, ranging from young girls holding hands (homosocial) to same-sex flirting and kissing (homoerotic) to genital sex (homosexual).

The idea of sexual identity as fluid and contingent can be seen as a bridge to queer theory, an umbrella term that became popular in the 1990s in the Lesbian-Gay-Bisexual-Transgender-Questioning-Intersex-Asexual (LGBTQIA) community. Although *queer* had been a term of homophobic abuse, it was rehabilitated to refer to whatever is at odds with the norm, the accepted, and the dominant. Practitioners of queer theory want to challenge the many institutions in which heteronormativity is so deeply embedded. Like deconstructionists, queer theorists do not believe in stable identities; consequently, they always debunk and question conventional gender identity and roles. Performance is more important than what you are; action counts, not biology.

Working with the Critical Approaches

Keep these brief descriptions of the critical approaches in mind as you read the following story by James Joyce, one of the most important writers of the twentieth century. Joyce (1882–1941) was born in Ireland, although he spent most of his life in self-imposed exile on the European continent. "Counterparts" is from *Dubliners* (1914), a collection of stories set in the Irish city of his childhood years.

JAMES JOYCE
Counterparts

The bell rang furiously and, when Miss Parker went to the tube, a furious voice called out in a piercing North of Ireland accent:

—Send Farrington here!

Miss Parker returned to her machine, saying to a man who was writing at a desk:

—Mr Alleyne wants you upstairs.

The man muttered *Blast him!* under his breath and pushed back his chair   5
to stand up. When he stood up he was tall and of great bulk. He had a hanging face, dark wine-coloured, with fair eyebrows and moustache: his eyes bulged forward slightly and the whites of them were dirty. He lifted up the counter and, passing by the clients, went out of the office with a heavy step.

He went heavily upstairs until he came to the second landing, where a door bore a brass plate with the inscription *Mr Alleyne.* Here he halted, puffing with labor and vexation, and knocked. The shrill voice cried:

—Come in!

The man entered Mr Alleyne's room. Simultaneously Mr Alleyne, a little man wearing gold-rimmed glasses on a cleanshaven face, shot his head up over a pile of documents. The head itself was so pink and hairless that it seemed like a large egg reposing on the papers. Mr Alleyne did not lose a moment:

—Farrington? What is the meaning of this? Why have I always to complain of you? May I ask you why you haven't made a copy of that contract between Bodley and Kirwan? I told you it must be ready by four o'clock.

—But Mr Shelley said, sir—   10

—*Mr Shelley said, sir.* . . . Kindly attend to what I say and not to what *Mr Shelley says, sir.* You have always some excuse or another for shirking work.

Let me tell you that if the contract is not copied before this evening I'll lay the matter before Mr Crosbie. . . . Do you hear me now?

—Yes, sir.

—Do you hear me now? . . . Ay and another little matter! I might as well be talking to the wall as talking to you. Understand once for all that you get a half an hour for your lunch and not an hour and a half. How many courses do you want, I'd like to know. . . . Do you mind me, now?

—Yes, sir.

Mr Alleyne bent his head again upon his pile of papers. The man stared   15
fixedly at the polished skull which directed the affairs of Crosbie & Alleyne, gauging its fragility. A spasm of rage gripped his throat for a few moments and then passed, leaving after it a sharp sensation of thirst. The man recognized the sensation and felt that he must have a good night's drinking. The middle of the month was passed and, if he could get the copy done in time, Mr Alleyne might give him an order on the cashier. He stood still, gazing fixedly at the head upon the pile of papers. Suddenly Mr Alleyne began to upset all the papers, searching for something. Then, as if he had been unaware of the man's presence till that moment, he shot up his head again, saying:

—Eh? Are you going to stand there all day? Upon my word, Farrington, you take things easy!

—I was waiting to see . . .

—Very good, you needn't wait to see. Go downstairs and do your work.

The man walked heavily towards the door and, as he went out of the room, he heard Mr Alleyne cry after him that if the contract was not copied by evening Mr Crosbie would hear of the matter.

He returned to his desk in the lower office and counted the sheets which   20
remained to be copied. He took up his pen and dipped it in the ink but he continued to stare stupidly at the last words he had written: *In no case shall the said Bernard Bodley be*. . . . The evening was falling and in a few minutes they would be lighting the gas: then he could write. He felt that he must slake the thirst in his throat. He stood up from his desk and, lifting the counter as before, passed out of the office. As he was passing out the chief clerk looked at him inquiringly.

—It's all right, Mr Shelley, said the man, pointing with his finger to indicate the objective of his journey.

The chief clerk glanced at the hat-rack but, seeing the row complete, offered no remark. As soon as he was on the landing the man pulled a shepherd's plaid cap out of his pocket, put it on his head and ran quickly down the rickety stairs. From the street door he walked on furtively on the inner side of the path towards the corner and all at once dived into a doorway. He was now safe in the dark snug of O'Neill's shop, and, filling up the little window that looked into the bar with his inflamed face, the color of dark wine or dark meat, he called out:

—Here, Pat, give us a g.p., like a good fellow.

The curate brought him a glass of plain porter. The man drank it at a gulp and asked for a caraway seed. He put his penny on the counter and, leaving the curate to grope for it in the gloom, retreated out of the snug as furtively as he had entered it.

Darkness, accompanied by a thick fog, was gaining upon the dusk of   25
February and the lamps in Eustace Street had been lit. The man went up by the
houses until he reached the door of the office, wondering whether he could
finish his copy in time. On the stairs a moist pungent odor of perfumes saluted
his nose: evidently Miss Delacour had come while he was out in O'Neill's. He
crammed his cap back again into his pocket and re-entered the office assuming
an air of absent-mindedness.

— Mr Alleyne has been calling for you, said the chief clerk severely. Where
were you?

The man glanced at the two clients who were standing at the counter as if
to intimate that their presence prevented him from answering. As the clients
were both male the chief clerk allowed himself a laugh.

— I know that game, he said. Five times in one day is a little bit. . . . Well,
you better look sharp and get a copy of our correspondence in the Delacour
case for Mr Alleyne.

This address in the presence of the public, his run upstairs, and the porter
he had gulped down so hastily confused the man and, as he sat down at his
desk to get what was required, he realized how hopeless was the task of finishing his copy of the contract before half past five. The dark damp night was
coming and he longed to spend it in the bars, drinking with his friends amid
the glare of gas and the clatter of glasses. He got out the Delacour correspondence and passed out of the office. He hoped Mr Alleyne would not discover
that the last two letters were missing.

The moist pungent perfume lay all the way up to Mr Alleyne's room.   30
Miss Delacour was a middle-aged woman of Jewish appearance. Mr Alleyne
was said to be sweet on her or on her money. She came to the office often and
stayed a long time when she came. She was sitting beside his desk now in an
aroma of perfumes, smoothing the handle of her umbrella, and nodding the
great black feather in her hat. Mr Alleyne had swivelled his chair round to face
her and thrown his right foot jauntily upon his left knee. The man put the correspondence on the desk and bowed respectfully but neither Mr Alleyne nor
Miss Delacour took any notice of his bow. Mr Alleyne tapped a finger on the
correspondence and then flicked it towards him as if to say: *That's all right: you
can go.*

The man returned to the lower office and sat down again at his desk. He
stared intently at the incomplete phrase: *In no case shall the said Bernard Bodley
be . . .* and thought how strange it was that the last three words began with
the same letter. The chief clerk began to hurry Miss Parker, saying she would
never have the letters typed in time for post. The man listened to the clicking of
the machine for a few minutes and then set to work to finish his copy. But his
head was not clear and his mind wandered away to the glare and rattle of the
public-house. It was a night for hot punches. He struggled on with his copy,
but when the clock struck five he had still fourteen pages to write. Blast it! He
couldn't finish it in time. He longed to execrate aloud, to bring his fist down on
something violently. He was so enraged that he wrote *Bernard Bernard* instead
of *Bernard Bodley* and had to begin again on a clean sheet.

He felt strong enough to clear out the whole office singlehanded. His body ached to do something, to rush out and revel in violence. All the indignities of his life enraged him. . . . Could he ask the cashier privately for an advance? No, the cashier was no good, no damn good: he wouldn't give an advance. . . . He knew where he would meet the boys: Leonard and O'Halloran and Nosey Flynn. The barometer of his emotional nature was set for a spell of riot.

His imagination had so abstracted him that his name was called twice before he answered. Mr Alleyne and Miss Delacour were standing outside the counter and all the clerks had turned round in anticipation of something. The man got up from his desk. Mr Alleyne began a tirade of abuse, saying that two letters were missing. The man answered that he knew nothing about them, that he had made a faithful copy. The tirade continued: it was so bitter and violent that the man could hardly restrain his fist from descending upon the head of the manikin before him.

— I know nothing about any other two letters, he said stupidly.

— *You — know — nothing.* Of course you know nothing, said Mr Alleyne.   35 Tell me, he added, glancing first for approval to the lady beside him, do you take me for a fool? Do you think me an utter fool?

The man glanced from the lady's face to the little egg-shaped head and back again; and, almost before he was aware of it, his tongue had found a felicitous moment:

— I don't think, sir, he said, that that's a fair question to put to me.

There was a pause in the very breathing of the clerks. Everyone was astounded (the author of the witticism no less than his neighbors) and Miss Delacour, who was a stout amiable person, began to smile broadly. Mr Alleyne flushed to the hue of a wild rose and his mouth twitched with a dwarf's passion. He shook his fist in the man's face till it seemed to vibrate like the knob of some electric machine:

— You impertinent ruffian! You impertinent ruffian! I'll make short work of you! Wait till you see! You'll apologize to me for your impertinence or you'll quit the office instanter! You'll quit this, I'm telling you, or you'll apologize to me!

He stood in a doorway opposite the office watching to see if the cashier would   40 come out alone. All the clerks passed out and finally the cashier came out with the chief clerk. It was no use trying to say a word to him when he was with the chief clerk. The man felt that his position was bad enough. He had been obliged to offer an abject apology to Mr Alleyne for his impertinence but he knew what a hornet's nest the office would be for him. He could remember the way in which Mr Alleyne had hounded little Peake out of the office in order to make room for his own nephew. He felt savage and thirsty and revengeful, annoyed with himself and with everyone else. Mr Alleyne would never give him an hour's rest; his life would be a hell to him. He had made a proper fool of himself this time. Could he not keep his tongue in his cheek? But they had never pulled together from the first, he and Mr Alleyne, ever since the day Mr Alleyne had overheard him mimicking his North of Ireland accent to amuse Higgins and

Miss Parker: that had been the beginning of it. He might have tried Higgins for the money, but sure Higgins never had anything for himself. A man with two establishments to keep up, of course he couldn't. . . .

He felt his great body again aching for the comfort of the public-house. The fog had begun to chill him and he wondered could he touch Pat in O'Neill's. He could not touch him for more than a bob — and a bob was no use. Yet he must get money somewhere or other: he had spent his last penny for the g.p. and soon it would be too late for getting money anywhere. Suddenly, as he was fingering his watch-chain, he thought of Terry Kelly's pawn-office in Fleet Street. That was the dart! Why didn't he think of it sooner?

He went through the narrow alley of Temple Bar quickly, muttering to himself that they could all go to hell because he was going to have a good night of it. The clerk in Terry Kelly's said *A crown!* but the consignor held out for six shillings; and in the end the six shillings was allowed him literally. He came out of the pawn-office joyfully, making a little cylinder of the coins between his thumb and fingers. In Westmoreland Street the footpaths were crowded with young men and women returning from business and ragged urchins ran here and there yelling out the names of the evening editions. The man passed through the crowd, looking on the spectacle generally with proud satisfaction and staring masterfully at the office-girls. His head was full of the noises of tram-gongs and swishing trolleys and his nose already sniffed the curling fumes of punch. As he walked on he preconsidered the terms in which he would narrate the incident to the boys:

— So, I just looked at him — coolly, you know, and looked at her. Then I looked back at him again — taking my time, you know. *I don't think that that's a fair question to put to me*, says I.

Nosey Flynn was sitting up in his usual corner of Davy Byrne's and, when he heard the story, he stood Farrington a half-one, saying it was as smart a thing as ever he heard. Farrington stood a drink in his turn. After a while O'Halloran and Paddy Leonard came in and the story was repeated to them. O'Halloran stood tailors of malt, hot, all round and told the story of the retort he had made to the chief clerk when he was in Callan's of Fownes's Street; but, as the retort was after the manner of the liberal shepherds in the eclogues, he had to admit that it was not so clever as Farrington's retort. At this Farrington told the boys to polish off that and have another.

Just as they were naming their poisons who should come in but Higgins! 45 Of course he had to join in with the others. The men asked him to give his version of it, and he did so with great vivacity for the sight of five small hot whiskies was very exhilarating. Everyone roared laughing when he showed the way in which Mr Alleyne shook his fist in Farrington's face. Then he imitated Farrington, saying, *And here was my nabs, as cool as you please,* while Farrington looked at the company out of his heavy dirty eyes, smiling and at times drawing forth stray drops of liquor from his moustache with the aid of his lower lip.

When that round was over there was a pause. O'Halloran had money but neither of the other two seemed to have any; so the whole party left the shop somewhat regretfully. At the corner of Duke Street Higgins and Nosey Flynn bevelled off to the left while the other three turned back towards the city. Rain was drizzling down on the cold streets and, when they reached the Ballast Office, Farrington suggested the Scotch House. The bar was full of men and loud with the noise of tongues and glasses. The three men pushed past the whining match-sellers at the door and formed a little party at the corner of the counter. They began to exchange stories. Leonard introduced them to a young fellow named Weathers who was performing at the Tivoli as an acrobat and knock-about *artiste*. Farrington stood a drink all round. Weathers said he would take a small Irish and Apollinaris. Farrington, who had definite notions of what was what, asked the boys would they have an Apollinaris too; but the boys told Tim to make theirs hot. The talk became theatrical. O'Halloran stood a round and then Farrington stood another round, Weathers protesting that the hospitality was too Irish. He promised to get them in behind the scenes and introduce them to some nice girls. O'Halloran said that he and Leonard would go but that Farrington wouldn't go because he was a married man; and Farrington's heavy dirty eyes leered at the company in token that he understood he was being chaffed. Weathers made them all have just one little tincture at his expense and promised to meet them later on at Mulligan's in Poolbeg Street.

When the Scotch House closed they went round to Mulligan's. They went into the parlor at the back and O'Halloran ordered small hot specials all round. They were all beginning to feel mellow. Farrington was just standing another round when Weathers came back. Much to Farrington's relief he drank a glass of bitter this time. Funds were running low but they had enough to keep them going. Presently two young women with big hats and a young man in a check suit came in and sat at a table close by. Weathers saluted them and told the company that they were out of the Tivoli. Farrington's eyes wandered at every moment in the direction of one of the young women. There was something striking in her appearance. An immense scarf of peacock-blue muslin was wound round her hat and knotted in a great bow under her chin; and she wore bright yellow gloves, reaching to the elbow. Farrington gazed admiringly at the plump arm which she moved very often and with much grace; and when, after a little time, she answered his gaze he admired still more her large dark brown eyes. The oblique staring expression in them fascinated him. She glanced at him once or twice and, when the party was leaving the room, she brushed against his chair and said O, pardon! in a London accent. He watched her leave the room in the hope that she would look back at him, but he was disappointed. He cursed his want of money and cursed all the rounds he had stood, particularly all the whiskies and Apollinaris which he had stood to Weathers. If there was one thing that he hated it was a sponge. He was so angry that he lost count of the conversation of his friends.

When Paddy Leonard called him he found that they were talking about feats of strength. Weathers was showing his biceps muscle to the company and boasting so much that the other two had called on Farrington to uphold the national honor. Farrington pulled up his sleeve accordingly and showed his biceps muscle to the company. The two arms were examined and compared and finally it was agreed to have a trial of strength. The table was cleared and the two men rested their elbows on it, clasping hands. When Paddy Leonard said *Go!* each was to try to bring down the other's hand on to the table. Farrington looked very serious and determined.

The trial began. After about thirty seconds Weathers brought his opponent's hand slowly down on to the table. Farrington's dark wine-coloured face flushed darker still with anger and humiliation at having been defeated by such a stripling.

—You're not to put the weight of your body behind it. Play fair, he said.   50

—Who's not playing fair? said the other.

—Come on again. The two best out of three.

The trial began again. The veins stood out on Farrington's forehead, and the pallor of Weathers' complexion changed to peony. Their hands and arms trembled under the stress. After a long struggle Weathers again brought his opponent's hand slowly on to the table. There was a murmur of applause from the spectators. The curate, who was standing beside the table, nodded his red head towards the victor and said with loutish familiarity:

—Ah! that's the knack!

—What the hell do you know about it? said Farrington fiercely, turning   55
on the man. What do you put in your gab for?

—Sh, sh! said O'Halloran, observing the violent expression of Farrington's face. Pony up, boys. We'll have just one little smahan more and then we'll be off.

A very sullen-faced man stood at the corner of O'Connell Bridge waiting for the little Sandymount tram to take him home. He was full of smouldering anger and revengefulness. He felt humiliated and discontented; he did not even feel drunk; and he had only twopence in his pocket. He cursed everything. He had done for himself in the office, pawned his watch, spent all his money; and he had not even got drunk. He began to feel thirsty again and he longed to be back again in the hot reeking public-house. He had lost his reputation as a strong man, having been defeated twice by a mere boy. His heart swelled with fury and, when he thought of the woman in the big hat who had brushed against him and said *Pardon!* his fury nearly choked him.

His tram let him down at Shelbourne Road and he steered his great body along in the shadow of the wall of the barracks. He loathed returning to his home. When he went in by the side-door he found the kitchen empty and the kitchen fire nearly out. He bawled upstairs:

—Ada! Ada!

His wife was a little sharp-faced woman who bullied her husband when he   60
was sober and was bullied by him when he was drunk. They had five children. A little boy came running down the stairs.

—Who is that? said the man, peering through the darkness.

—Me, pa.

—Who are you? Charlie?

—No, pa. Tom.

—Where's your mother?   65

—She's out at the chapel.

—That's right. . . . Did she think of leaving any dinner for me?

—Yes, pa. I—

—Light the lamp. What do you mean by having the place in darkness? Are the other children in bed?

The man sat down heavily on one of the chairs while the little boy lit the   70
lamp. He began to mimic his son's flat accent, saying half to himself: *At the chapel. At the chapel, if you please!* When the lamp was lit he banged his fist on the table and shouted:

—What's for my dinner?

—I'm going . . . to cook it, pa, said the little boy.

The man jumped up furiously and pointed to the fire.

—On that fire! You let the fire out! By God, I'll teach you to do that again!

He took a step to the door and seized the walking-stick which was stand-   75
ing behind it.

—I'll teach you to let the fire out! he said, rolling up his sleeve in order to give his arm free play.

The little boy cried *O, pa!* and ran whimpering round the table, but the man followed him and caught him by the coat. The little boy looked about him wildly but, seeing no way of escape fell upon his knees.

—Now, you'll let the fire out the next time! said the man, striking at him viciously with the stick. Take that, you little whelp!

The boy uttered a squeal of pain as the stick cut his thigh. He clasped his hands together in the air and his voice shook with fright.

—O, pa! he cried. Don't beat me, pa! And I'll . . . I'll say a *Hail Mary* for   80
you. . . . I'll say a *Hail Mary* for you, pa, if you don't beat me. . . . I'll say a *Hail Mary*. . . .   [1914]

A thorough critical analysis of "Counterparts" using any one of these approaches would take dozens of pages. The following are brief suggestions for how such a reading might proceed.

NEW CRITICISM

A New Critic might want to demonstrate the multiple ways the title holds the narrative together, giving it unity and coherence — for example, Farrington and his son Tom are counterparts since Tom is the victim of his father's bullying just as Farrington is bullied by Mr. Alleyne at work. You can also probably spot other counterparts: Farrington and his wife, for example, trade off bullying each other, and their means of escaping from the drudgery of their lives, the bar and the church, are also parallel. And naturally when Weathers, the acrobat, defeats the much larger Farrington in arm wrestling, we are reminded of the verbal beating Farrington must endure from his equally diminutive boss, Mr. Alleyne. New Critics are fond of finding the ways all the elements of a text reinforce one another.

A New Critic might argue that these counterparts or oppositions introduce tensions into the story from the first few lines when the "bell rang furiously" for Farrington to report to Mr. Alleyne for a dressing down. The irony is that Farrington is big and Alleyne is small, that Farrington is powerful and Alleyne is fragile as an egg. But it is Mr. Alleyne who breaks Farrington; it is Farrington who is weak. Throughout the story, tensions, oppositions, and ironies continue, for example, when Farrington is defeated by the smaller Weathers. In the last scene, the tension is finally resolved when the larger Farrington beats his small son, making him a counterpart to both Alleyne and Weathers in oppressing the weak. The final evidence that Farrington is ethically powerless is cruelly obvious as the son promises to pray for his abusing father.

FEMINIST CRITICISM

Feminist critics and their first cousins, gender critics, would naturally be struck by the violent masculinity of Farrington, his fantasies of riot and abuse, his savage feelings of revenge, and his "smouldering anger" (para. 57). Farrington is depicted not only as crude and brutish but also as a kind of perverse stereotype of male vanity, self-centeredness, and irresponsibility. His obsession with obtaining money for drinking completely disregards his role as the provider for a large family, and, of course, the beatings of his son are a cruel parody of his role as paternal protector. And if he had not wasted his money on drink, Farrington would also be a womanizer ("Farrington's eyes wandered at every moment in the direction of one of the young women," para. 47). Gender critics would be interested in the social and cultural mechanisms that could construct such primitive masculinity.

A reasonable argument might focus on the representation of women in the story. Miss Parker, Miss Delacour, Farrington's wife, and the performer Farrington sees in the bar are marginal characters. One student made the following claim: "The women in Farrington's world, and Irish society in general, have no agency: they are prevented from taking an active part in determining their lives and futures." Another student argued differently, saying, "While women in general are oppressed by the raw and brutal masculinity represented by Farrington, the women in this story do hold a degree of power over men." Based on their own analysis and interpretations, these students demonstrated that there was reasonable textual evidence to support their claims.

PSYCHOANALYTIC CRITICISM

A psychoanalytic critic would first notice the extreme pattern of behavior Farrington exhibits, as he repeatedly withdraws from his adult work responsibilities and as he fantasizes about being physically violent against his supervisors. Critics would argue that such behavior is typical of Farrington's repressed wounds and his unresolved conflicts with his own father. Farrington seems to be playing out painful childhood experiences. Given the violent displacement (taking it out on someone else) visited on Tom, we can imagine that Farrington is beating not only his boss, Mr. Alleyne, but also perhaps his own abusive father. The fantasies at work in Farrington also suggest the psychological defense of projection, since Farrington is blaming his problems on Mr. Alleyne and his job. Although his tasks do seem to be tedious, they certainly cannot account for his "spasm of rage" (para. 15) or his desire "to clear out the whole office singlehanded" (para. 32). When Farrington feels "humiliated and discontented" (para. 57), it is only in part because of his immediate context. It is the return of the repressed that plagues Farrington, a resurfacing of a buried pain. These ideas should also be tied to Farrington's death wish, especially his stunningly self-destructive behavior at work. Freudian critics would also argue that these specific actions are related to other core issues that would include intense loss of self-esteem, fear of intimacy, and betrayal.

MARXIST CRITICISM

A Marxist critic would be interested in focusing on the specific historical moment of "Counterparts" and not on Farrington's individual psyche, which can only distract us from the real force that affects human experience — the economic system in which Farrington is trapped. Economic power — not the Oedipal drama or gender — is the crucial human motivator. Farrington's material circumstances and not timeless values are the key to understanding his behavior. The real battle lines are drawn between Crosbie and Alleyne (the "haves") and Farrington (a "have-not") — that is, between the bourgeoisie and the proletariat, between those who control economic resources and those who perform the labor that fills the coffers of the rich. In a Marxist analysis, critics would argue that Farrington is a victim of class warfare. His desperation, his humiliation, his rage, his cruel violence are all traceable to classism — an ideology that determines people's worth according to their economic class. Although Farrington does appear shiftless and irresponsible, it is not because of his class; it is because of the meaninglessness of his work and the demeaning hierarchy that keeps him at the bottom. In his alienation, he reverts to a primitive physical masculinity, a false consciousness that only further diminishes his sense of his worth.

Marxists are often interested in what lies beneath the text in its political unconscious. To get at the unconscious, Marxists, like psychoanalytic critics, look for symptoms on the surface that suggest problems beneath. Typically, such symptomatic readings reveal class conflicts that authors are sometimes unaware of themselves. Marxist critics might debate whether Joyce himself understood that the root cause of Farrington's aberrant behavior was economic and not psychological. This makes sense since for Marxists both reader and writer are under the sway of the same ideological system that they see as natural.

One student made the following claim: "Farrington's role as proletarian results in his feelings of inferiority, resentment over lack of entitlement, and an expectation of disappointment." This same student, like many Marxist critics who see the function of literature through a pragmatic lens, concluded her essay with an appeal toward change, arguing that "The remedy does not lie in changing Farrington's consciousness, but rather in changing the economic and political discourse of power that has constituted him."

DECONSTRUCTION

One of many possible deconstructions of "Counterparts" would involve focusing on a troubling or puzzling point called an *aporia*. Some deconstructive critics have looked at the incomplete phrase that Farrington copies, "*In no case shall the said Bernard Bodley be . . .*" as an aporia, an ambiguous and not completely understandable textual puzzle that might nonetheless offer a way into the story's meaning. The oppositions that are being deconstructed or laid bare here are *presence* and *absence, word* and *reality.* Working off the implications of the title "Counterparts," Bernard Bodley can be seen as a double or counterpart for Farrington, a character like Bodley whose existence is in doubt. Although Farrington's size suggests that he is very much physically present, his behavior might suggest otherwise. He spends his time copying other people's words and has a compelling need to repeat the narrative of his encounter with Mr. Alleyne, as if he must demonstrate his own existence through repetition. He does not have a viable inner life, an authentic identity. Farrington's essence is not present but absent. His identity is insubstantial. He tries to fill the emptiness at the center of his being with camaraderie and potency, but his efforts produce the opposite — escape, loneliness, and weakness. In other words, the said Farrington does not really exist and cannot be. In this way, we can deconstruct "Counterparts" as a story in which presence is absence, strength is weakness, Farrington's actions lead only to paralysis and repetition, and Farrington's frustration with his impotence makes his oppressors more powerful.

One student working with similar interpretations of "Counterparts" noted other oppositions, especially between male and female, escape and confinement. She argued that Farrington spends most of his time trying to avoid being thought of as stereotypically feminine. However, the more exaggerated his masculine aggression, drinking, violence, and irresponsibility become, the weaker, the more stereotypically feminine he becomes. Similarly, the more Farrington tries to escape, the more ensnared he is. In this way, the student argued, our conventional understandings of these opposing terms are deconstructed, so that we are no longer confident about the meaning of escape, masculinity, or strength.

READER-RESPONSE CRITICISM

Willa Ervinman, a student, was asked to respond to the story by using Stanley Fish's ideas and noting the conflicts between the interpretive or discourse communities Willa belonged to and those depicted in the story. The following are excerpts from her response journal:

> I was upset by Farrington's lack of responsibility at work. He is completely unreliable and demonstrates very little self-esteem. He must know that the people he works with consider him a slacker and a fake. I was raised in a middle-class home where both my parents worked hard in a bank from 9 to 5. Just the idea that they would sneak out of work to drink in dark bars is absurd. My belief in the

discourse of middle-class responsibility or perhaps the Protestant work ethic makes it almost impossible for me to see Farrington with sympathy even though I can see that his work is probably completely mechanical and unfulfilling. . . .

Farrington's domestic violence against his son is such a violation of the discourse of domesticity that it is hard to understand any other response. Someone in my response group thought that Farrington was a victim of his working-class discourse of masculinity. I can see how he was humiliated by the smaller men, Mr. Alleyne and Weathers, but beating his innocent son as a kind of revenge cannot be forgiven. My grandmother tells me that it was common for children to be physically punished in her day, but in the interpretive community I was raised in, there is no excuse for domestic violence. It is more than a character flaw; it is criminal behavior, and I judge Farrington to be a social menace, beyond compassion.

Willa went on to argue that Farrington's violent behavior is inexcusable, interpreting our current understandings of domestic violence and responsible masculinity as evidence. She blended this personal view with textual support. Her warrant for her claim was that historical circumstances and norms should not be used to excuse reprehensible behavior.

POSTCOLONIAL CRITICISM

"Counterparts" was written in the early twentieth century at a time when the Ireland Joyce writes about was still a colony of the British Empire. Farrington is, then, a colonial subject and subject to political domination. At the story's opening, Farrington, a Catholic from the south of Ireland, is summoned by a "furious voice" from Northern Ireland, a stronghold of British sympathy and Protestant domination. The tension is announced early because it is crucial to Farrington's behavior and his internalized and colonized mindset. Many colonials have a negative self-image because they are alienated from their own indigenous culture. Indeed, Farrington seems completely ill suited to the office copying task he is relegated to. He seems more suited to some physical endeavor, but given the difficult economics of Dublin, he probably has few career options.

Farrington is the Other in the discourse of colonialism, and he is made to seem inferior at every turn, from the verbal lashing of Mr. Alleyne to the physical defeat by Weathers, who is probably British. Symbolically, Farrington tries to resist his subjugation by the British establishment but fails. He is what postcolonial theorists refer to as *unhomed* or *displaced*. He is uncomfortable at work, in the bars where he seeks solace, and finally in his ultimate refuge, a place unprepared even to feed him. Indeed, in an act likely to perpetuate abuse upon future generations, Farrington turns on his own family, becoming, through his enraged attack on his child Tom, a metaphor for the conflicted, tormented, and defeated Ireland. When a colonial is not "at home" even in his own home, he is truly in psychological agony and exile. Joyce represents the trauma of British domination through one subject's self-destructive and self-hating journey, a journey made even more cruelly ironic by Farrington's attack—in a mimicry of British aggression and injustice—on his own subjected son.

NEW HISTORICISM

A critic influenced by Foucault and New Historicism might argue that Farrington is a victim of an inflexible discourse of masculinity, that he has been socialized by working-class norms of how a man should behave to such an extent that he cannot change. Growing up in a working-class culture, Farrington would have received high marks among his peers for his size and strength, just as Mr. Alleyne would be diminished in status for his. And in another context, say, on a construction site, Farrington's sense of masculinity might be a plus. But in an office, his aggressive masculinity is a liability. In all cultures, people are subject to multiple discourses that pull them one way then another. Farrington's sarcasm, his drinking, his longing for camaraderie, and his resorting to violence to solve problems are the results of being too enmeshed in a discourse of masculinity from working-class Dublin and not enough in the middle-class business assumptions about discipline, responsibility, and concentration. Farrington is defeated at work, in the pubs, and at home because he is unable to move from one discourse to another. He is stuck in a subject position that only reinforces his powerlessness. His self-esteem is so damaged by the end of the story that he even violates his own code of masculinity by beating a defenseless child.

QUEER THEORY

Because queer theorists are as concerned with gender identities as they are with sexuality, they would be interested in the asymmetrical power relationship between Farrington's "great bulk" (para. 5) and Mr. Alleyne's "little man" with a "pink and hairless" head (para. 8). Farrington is surely performing as a queer character when he betrays his traditional masculine role by being thoroughly emasculated at work; he is incompetent at simple tasks, and his status in the hierarchy is diminishing. And the reader knows that Farrington's occupation as a copier will soon be obsolete, replaced by legions of female typists. He is a queer figure in a queer job. However, his sexuality is less of an issue than the idea that heterosexuality as a pervasive and rigid institution causes Farrington intense humiliation and anguish as he fails at every traditional (albeit arbitrary) masculine standard.

Farrington seeks solace and escape from his newfound queerness in the male homosocial pubs of Dublin. Here, he does seem to perform masterfully with the retelling of his witty put-down of his boss. But the reader is well aware that Farrington has queered the real narrative of his confrontation with Mr. Alleyne. In actuality, he was forced to apologize abjectly for his remarks and will pay dearly for not knowing his place. It is also here in his beloved pub space that he receives the greatest blow to what remains of his masculinity. He is humiliated in a contest of strength by an "artiste," "a mere boy" (para. 57).

When as an alienated outcast he returns home in rage and anger, and "viciously" (para. 78) beats his own son in a traditionally female space, the kitchen, his impotence is complete. In a good example of fluid gender roles, his wife, Ada, "who bullied [Farrington] when he was sober and was bullied by him when he was drunk" (para. 60), temporarily abandons her traditional role of caring for him. Their relationship is indeed queer. Farrington's performative queerness is never clearer than in his final violent undoing of the conventional role of the protective father, making a mockery of masculine decency, compassion, and fairness.

Alert to the inconsistencies, contradictions, and ambiguities of conventional gender behaviors, protocols, and values, queer theorists offer provocative and enriching readings that remind readers how easy it is to oversimplify the bewildering complexities of being men and women.

Sample Student Essay

The following essay was written by a first-year student using a postcolonial perspective.

Molly Frye
Prof. Christine Hardee
English 102
10 May - - - -

A Refugee at Home

It is difficult to argue that Farrington, the main character in James Joyce's "Counterparts," should be seen in a sympathetic light. After all, he seems an extreme stereotype of an aggressive, irresponsible drinker. Although his character traits certainly do not conform to our modern standards of mature masculinity, I want to argue that although we do not want to condone Farrington's brutal behavior, we can find it understandable. As an Irish subject in the British Empire, Farrington is more sinned against than sinner, more victim than victimizer. Farrington is not simply an obnoxious male since his actions can be understood as stemming from his colonial consciousness in struggling vainly against his powerlessness. His frustrations are especially clear in the three spaces Farrington inhabits: his office, the bars, and his home.

After setting up a context, states her claim supported by three examples.

Farrington's first appearance is telling. Because of his poor job performance, his boss demands to see him: "Send Farrington here!" Farrington, who most often is referred to as "the man," mutters his first words, "Blast him!" This typical antagonistic relationship in a colonial context foreshadows the rest of the story. Farrington is the working-class subject caught in a menial and unsatisfying job he can never complete under a boss who has social and cultural power. This counterpart relationship is similar to the positions of Ireland and England where the colony is disparaged and oppressed by the empire. In his office run by Protestants loyal to the British, Farrington is ironically "tall and of great bulk," while his boss, Mr. Alleyne, is "a little man" whose head, "pink and hairless," resembles a "large egg." Farrington's only asset, his size and strength, is irrelevant because he is so economically and socially weak. This disparity only increases Farrington's frustration and precipitates fantasies of violence against his oppressor. When Mr. Alleyne rebukes him, "Do you mind me now," Farrington is sent into a "spasm of rage." He cannot, of course, act on his aggressive urges, so he represses these feelings by rationalizing that he must have a "good night's drinking." Thus begins a pattern of self-destructive behavior that only increases Farrington's marginal position in society.

First concrete example of Farrington as frustrated colonial subject.

Transition to explanation of Farrington's failures at work.

Farrington is so uncomfortable at work, a postcolonial condition known as being unhomed, that he cannot concentrate on anything but drinking. He seems quite unsuited for the tedious task of copying legal documents, staring "stupidly at the last words he has written," knowing he will never finish his task, never advance, never get anywhere. Farrington is paralyzed by his alienation. He feels his only recourse is sneaking out to drink, which only exacerbates his poverty and powerlessness. When he attempts to cover up his inability to concentrate and finish copying letters for Mr. Alleyne, he is caught and confronted. Instead of acknowledging his underling position, he attempts a witticism which, of course, backfires. Even though he is forced to apologize, his job now seems in jeopardy. Mr. Alleyne humiliates him by calling him an "impertinent ruffian," a status that seems to him the most he can hope for. As a colonial subject, Farrington is plagued by a double consciousness. He longs for the masculine status his physical strength should give him in his working-class culture, but he must suffer indignities at the hands of Mr. Alleyne because of his inability to perform a simple task a competent child could do. Farrington should probably be working in construction as a laborer, not an office worker where discipline, patience, and mental concentration are necessary.

Uses postcolonial ideas to explain Farrington's behavior.

When Farrington finally leaves work, he expects to find some solace in the Dublin pubs. He has hocked his watch for

Transition to second example of Farrington as colonized.

drinking money, a clear indication of how desperate he is to escape the confines of regimented office work. The camaraderie of Paddy Leonard and Nosey Flynn is temporary, and Farrington is not at home in these public spaces either. He runs out of money he would have spent drinking and womanizing, and he is finally humiliated by another small British man. Called on to "uphold the national honor," Farrington's loss in an arm-wrestling contest with Weathers leaves him "full of smouldering anger and revengefulness. He is humiliated and discontented . . . His heart swelled with fury. . . ." His longing for escape from the confinement and disappointment of work has taken a disastrous turn. Farrington's already damaged self-esteem is degraded, and his repressed anger at his oppressor is near the breaking point. Perhaps his self-destructive behavior can be redirected at his home, his last possibility for comfort and acceptance.

Transition to last example.

For the unhomed colonized, however, this is not to be. Farrington enters the kitchen to find it symbolically empty, "the fire nearly out." His wife is at chapel, his five children in bed, and his dinner is cold. His agonies continue. Having internalized the humiliations suffered at work and in the pubs, Farrington has no resources left. And so in a bitter irony, he beats his son for not attending to the fire, "striking at him viciously with a stick. 'Take that, you little whelp!' " Farrington the oppressed becomes Farrington the oppressor. His role as provider and protector is cruelly turned upside-down. Farrington compensates for his defeats at the hands of Mr. Alleyne and Weathers by beating his son, and in doing so, mimics the cycle of oppression prevalent in countries dominated by the empire. Farrington is not only a cog in the bureaucratic wheel at work; he is also a pathetic, but understandable cog crushed by the wheel of power even in his own home.

Uses all three examples in concluding.

≡ FOR THINKING AND WRITING

1. Using a feminist critique of Joyce, one student claimed that "Joyce's text indulges dominance over submission." Do you think there is textual evidence to support this assertion?

2. How might various critics (postcolonial, feminist, Marxist, psychoanalytical) interpret these lines from "Counterparts":

   • "The man passed through the crowd, looking on the spectacle generally with proud satisfaction and staring masterfully at the office-girls" (para. 42).

- "His heart swelled with fury and, when he thought of the woman in the big hat who had brushed against him and said *Pardon!* his fury nearly choked him" (para. 57).
  - "What's for my dinner?" (para. 71).

3. Influenced by New Critical ideas, one student wrote, "'Counterparts' is filled with parallel scenes and emotions that reflect one another." What textual evidence would help support this notion?

4. Engaging in a Marxist critique, one student wrote, "His unfair work conditions so distract him that he does not even know the names of his children." What is the warrant behind such an assertion? What work conditions might the student think "fair"?

5. Using a New Historicist approach, what might you learn about this story from doing research on the elementary-school curriculum in Dublin, the pay scale in a law office, the legal rights of women, the laws on domestic violence, the unemployment rate? What other practices and texts do you think would illuminate the story?

≡ A WRITING EXERCISE

Now you try. After reading the following story, construct an argument influenced by one or more of the following critical approaches: postcolonial, Marxist, reader-response, or feminist.

JAMES JOYCE
Eveline

Like "Counterparts," "Eveline" is from Dubliners *(1914).*

She sat at the window watching the evening invade the avenue. Her head was leaned against the window curtains and in her nostrils was the odor of dusty cretonne. She was tired.

Few people passed. The man out of the last house passed on his way home; she heard his footsteps clacking along the concrete pavement and afterwards crunching on the cinder path before the new red houses. One time there used to be a field there in which they used to play every evening with other people's children. Then a man from Belfast bought the field and built houses in it — not like their little brown houses but bright brick houses with shining roofs. The children of the avenue used to play together in that field — the Devines, the Waters, the Dunns, little Keogh the cripple, she and her brothers and sisters. Ernest, however, never played: he was too grown up. Her father used often to hunt them in out of the field with his blackthorn stick; but usually little Keogh

used to keep *nix* and call out when he saw her father coming. Still they seemed
to have been rather happy then. Her father was not so bad then; and besides,
her mother was alive. That was a long time ago; she and her brothers and sisters were all grown up; her mother was dead. Tizzie Dunn was dead, too, and
the Waters had gone back to England. Everything changes. Now she was going
to go away like the others, to leave her home.

Home! She looked round the room, reviewing all its familiar objects which
she had dusted once a week for so many years, wondering where on earth all
the dust came from. Perhaps she would never see again those familiar objects
from which she had never dreamed of being divided. And yet during all those
years she had never found out the name of the priest whose yellowing photograph hung on the wall above the broken harmonium beside the colored
print of the promises made to Blessed Margaret Mary Alacoque. He had been
a school friend of her father. Whenever he showed the photograph to a visitor
her father used to pass it with a casual word:

—He is in Melbourne now.

She had consented to go away, to leave her home. Was that wise? She tried   5
to weigh each side of the question. In her home anyway she had shelter and
food; she had those whom she had known all her life about her. Of course she
had to work hard both in the house and at business. What would they say of
her in the Stores when they found out that she had run away with a fellow? Say
she was a fool, perhaps; and her place would be filled up by advertisement. Miss
Gavan would be glad. She had always had an edge on her, especially whenever
there were people listening.

—Miss Hill, don't you see these ladies are waiting?

—Look lively, Miss Hill, please.

She would not cry many tears at leaving the Stores.

But in her new home, in a distant unknown country, it would not be like
that. Then she would be married—she, Eveline. People would treat her with
respect then. She would not be treated as her mother had been. Even now,
though she was over nineteen, she sometimes felt herself in danger of her
father's violence. She knew it was that that had given her the palpitations.
When they were growing up he had never gone for her, like he used to go for
Harry and Ernest, because she was a girl; but latterly he had begun to threaten
her and say what he would do to her only for her dead mother's sake. And now
she had nobody to protect her. Ernest was dead and Harry, who was in the
church decorating business, was nearly always down somewhere in the country. Besides, the invariable squabble for money on Saturday nights had begun to
weary her unspeakably. She always gave her entire wages—seven shillings—
and Harry always sent up what he could but the trouble was to get any money
from her father. He said she used to squander the money, that she had no head,
that he wasn't going to give her his hard-earned money to throw about the
streets, and much more, for he was usually fairly bad of a Saturday night. In the
end he would give her the money and ask her had she any intention of buying
Sunday's dinner. Then she had to rush out as quickly as she could and do her
marketing, holding her black leather purse tightly in her hand as she elbowed

her way through the crowds and returning home late under her load of provisions. She had hard work to keep the house together and to see that the two young children who had been left to her charge went to school regularly and got their meals regularly. It was hard work—a hard life—but now that she was about to leave it she did not find it a wholly undesirable life.

She was about to explore another life with Frank. Frank was very kind, manly, open-hearted. She was to go away with him by the night-boat to be his wife and to live with him in Buenos Aires where he had a home waiting for her. How well she remembered the first time she had seen him; he was lodging in a house on the main road where she used to visit. It seemed a few weeks ago. He was standing at the gate, his peaked cap pushed back on his head and his hair tumbled forward over a face of bronze. Then they had come to know each other. He used to meet her outside the Stores every evening and see her home. He took her to see *The Bohemian Girl* and she felt elated as she sat in an unaccustomed part of the theater with him. He was awfully fond of music and sang a little. People knew that they were courting and, when he sang about the lass that loves a sailor, she always felt pleasantly confused. He used to call her Poppens out of fun. First of all it had been an excitement for her to have a fellow and then she had begun to like him. He had tales of distant countries. He had started as a deck boy at a pound a month on a ship of the Allan Line going out to Canada. He told her the names of the ships he had been on and the names of the different services. He had sailed through the Straits of Magellan and he told her stories of the terrible Patagonians. He had fallen on his feet in Buenos Aires, he said, and had come over to the old country just for a holiday. Of course, her father had found out the affair and had forbidden her to have anything to say to him.

—I know these sailor chaps, he said.

One day he had quarreled with Frank and after that she had to meet her lover secretly.

The evening deepened in the avenue. The white of two letters in her lap grew indistinct. One was to Harry; the other was to her father. Ernest had been her favorite but she liked Harry too. Her father was becoming old lately, she noticed; he would miss her. Sometimes he could be very nice. Not long before, when she had been laid up for a day, he had read her out a ghost story and made toast for her at the fire. Another day, when their mother was alive, they had all gone for a picnic to the Hill of Howth. She remembered her father putting on her mother's bonnet to make the children laugh.

Her time was running out but she continued to sit by the window, leaning her head against the window curtain, inhaling the odor of dusty cretonne. Down far in the avenue she could hear a street organ playing. She knew the air. Strange that it should come that very night to remind her of the promise to her mother, her promise to keep the home together as long as she could. She remembered the last night of her mother's illness; she was again in the close dark room at the other side of the hall and outside she heard a melancholy air of Italy. The organ-player had been ordered to go away and given sixpence. She remembered her father strutting back into the sickroom saying:

10

—Damned Italians! coming over here!   15

As she mused the pitiful vision of her mother's life laid its spell on the very quick of her being — that life of commonplace sacrifices closing in final craziness. She trembled as she heard again her mother's voice saying constantly with foolish insistence:

—Derevaun Seraun! Derevaun Seraun!°

She stood up in a sudden impulse of terror. Escape! She must escape! Frank would save her. He would give her life, perhaps love, too. But she wanted to live. Why should she be unhappy? She had a right to happiness. Frank would take her in his arms, fold her in his arms. He would save her.

She stood among the swaying crowd in the station at the North Wall. He held her hand and she knew that he was speaking to her, saying something about the passage over and over again. The station was full of soldiers with brown baggages. Through the wide doors of the sheds she caught a glimpse of the black mass of the boat, lying in beside the quay wall, with illumined portholes. She answered nothing. She felt her cheek pale and cold and, out of a maze of distress, she prayed to God to direct her, to show her what was her duty. The boat blew a long mournful whistle into the mist. If she went, tomorrow she would be on the sea with Frank, steaming toward Buenos Aires. Their passage had been booked. Could she still draw back after all he had done for her? Her distress awoke a nausea in her body and she kept moving her lips in silent fervent prayer.

A bell clanged upon her heart. She felt him seize her hand: 20

—Come!

All the seas of the world tumbled about her heart. He was drawing her into them: he would drown her. She gripped with both hands at the iron railing.

—Come!

No! No! No! It was impossible. Her hands clutched the iron in frenzy. Amid the seas she sent a cry of anguish!

—Eveline! Evvy!   25

He rushed beyond the barrier and called to her to follow. He was shouted at to go on but he still called to her. She set her white face to him, passive, like a helpless animal. Her eyes gave him no sign of love or farewell or recognition.

[1914]

≡ FOR THINKING AND WRITING

1. There is a French expression that says to understand all is to forgive all. Given the ending of "Eveline," argue for or against this idea.

2. Compare "Counterparts" and "Eveline" (see "Strategies for Writing a Comparative Paper," p. 130), arguing that Joyce has or has not prepared us for the endings.

Derevaun Seraun!: Gaelic for "The end of pleasure is pain."

Acknowledgments *(continued from page iv)*

James Eli Adams, "Narrating Nature: Darwin," From *A History of Victorian Literature*. Republished with permission of John Wiley & Sons; permission conveyed through Copyright Clearance Center, Inc.

Isaac Asimov, "Liar!," from *The Complete Robot* by Isaac Asimov, copyright © 1982 by Nightfall, Inc. Used by permission of Doubleday, an imprint of the Knopf Doubleday Publishing Group, a division of Penguin Random House LLC. All rights reserved.

Steven Gould Axelrod. *Sylvia Plath: The Wound and the Cure of Words*. pp. 1–8. © 1990 The Johns Hopkins University Press. Reprinted with permission of The Johns Hopkins University Press.

James Baldwin. "Sonny's Blues," © 1957 by James Baldwin, was originally published in *Partisan Review*. Copyright renewed. Collected in *Going to Meet the Man*, published by Vintage Books. Used by arrangement with the James Baldwin Estate.

Toni Cade Bambara. "The Lesson," copyright © 1972 by Toni Cade Bambara; from *Gorilla, My Love* by Toni Cade Bambara. Used by permission of Random House, an imprint and division of Penguin Random House LLC. All rights reserved.

Stephen Bandy. Excerpt from "One of My Babies": The Misfit and the Grandmother. Originally published in *Studies in Short Fiction*. Copyright 1996 by Stephen Bandy. Reprinted with permission.

David Barno. "A New Moral Compact," *Foreign Policy*, November 9, 2012. Copyright © 2012 by Foreign Policy. Used with permission.

Robin Becker, "Morning Poem," from *Backtalk*. Copyright © 1982 by Robin Becker. Reprinted with the permission of The Permissions Company, Inc., on behalf of Alice James Books, www .alicejamesbooks.org

Aimee Bender, "The Devourings," from *The Color Master: Stories* by Aimee Bender, copyright © 2013 by Aimee Bender. Used by permission of Doubleday, an imprint of the Knopf Doubleday Publishing Group, a division of Penguin Random House LLC. All rights reserved.

Katie Bickham, "The Ferryman," *Rattle*, October 5, 2017. Copyright © 2017 by Katie Bickham. Used with permission.

Richard Blanco, "Queer Theory: According to My Grandmother," from *Looking for the Gulf Motel* by Richard Blanco, © 2012. Reprinted by permission of the University of Pittsburgh Press.

T. C. Boyle, "The Relive Box," by T. Coraghessan Boyle. Copyright © 2014 by T. Coraghessan Boyle. Originally published in the March 17, 2014 issue of *The New Yorker*. Reprinted by permission of Georges Borchardt, Inc., on behalf of the author.

Ray Bradbury, "Mars Is Heaven," Originally published in *Planet Stories* (1948). Copyright © 1948 by Love Romances, Inc., renewed 1975 by Ray Bradbury. Reprinted by permission of Don Congdon Associates, Inc.

Wendy Brenner, "Prayer for Gluten," *The Sun*, September 2014. Copyright © 2014 by The Sun. Used with permission.

David Brooks, "The Child in the Basement," *New York Times*, January 13, 2015. Copyright © 2015 The New York Times. All rights reserved. Used under license.

Lynda K. Bundtzen. From *Plath's Incarnations: Woman and the Creative Process* by Lynda K. Bundtzen, published by The University of Michigan Press in 1989. Reprinted by permission of The University of Michigan Press.

Octavia Butler, From *Imago*, pp. 3–12. Copyright © 1989 by Octavia E. Butler. Reprinted by permission of Grand Central Publishing.

Angela Carter, "The Company of Wolves," from *The Bloody Chamber* by Angela Carter. Published by Vintage, 2006. Copyright © Angela Carter. Reproduced by permission of the Estate of Angela Carter c/o Rogers, Coleridge & White Ltd., 20 Powis Mews, London W11 1JN.

Raymond Carver, "What We Talk About When We Talk About Love," from *What We Talk About When We Talk About Love: Stories by Raymond Carver*, copyright © 1974, 1976, 1978, 1980,

1981 by Raymond Carver. Used by permission of Alfred A. Knopf, an imprint of the Knopf Doubleday Publishing Group, a division of Random House LLC. All rights reserved.

Chrystos, "Today Was a Bad Day Like TB," Used by permission of the author, Chrystos © 1993.

Amy Chua, "How America's Identity Politics Went from Inclusion to Division," Introduction from *Political Tribes: Group Instinct and The Fate of Nations* by Amy Chua, copyright © 2018 by Amy Chua. Used by permission of Penguin Press, an imprint of Penguin Publishing Group, a division of Penguin Random House LLC. All rights reserved.

Lucille Clifton, "Forgiving My Father," copyright © 1980 by Lucille Clifton. First appeared in *two-headed woman*, published by University of Massachusetts Press. Now appears in *good woman: poems and a memoir 1969–1980*, published by BOA Editions. Reprinted by permission of Curtis Brown, Ltd.

Judith Ortiz Cofer, "Claims," by Judith Ortiz Cofer, from *Reaching for the Mainland and Selected New Poems* by Judith Ortiz, copyright © 1987. Reprinted by permission of Bilingual Press/Editorial Bilingue, Arizona State University, Tempe, AZ.

David Cole, "Don't Lose Faith in the First Amendment." *New York Times*, August 1, 2018. Copyright © 2018 The New York Times. All rights reserved. Used under license.

Dan Crenshaw, "The US Should Work with Mexico to Stem Central American Migration," from *The National Review*, 7/30/2018. Copyright © 2018 by The National Review. Used with permission.

Countee Cullen, "Incident." Copyrights held by Amnistad Research Center, Tulane University. Administered by Thompson and Thompson, Brooklyn, NY.

E. E. Cummings, "Somewhere I Have Never Traveled, Gladly Beyond," copyright 1931, © 1959, 1991 by the Trustees for the E. E. Cummings Trust. Copyright © 1979 by George James Firmage, from *Complete Poems: 1904–1962* by E. E. Cummings, edited by George J. Firmage. Used by Permission of Liveright Publishing Corporation.

Meghan Daum, "Jaycee Dugard and the Feel-Good Imperative," originally appeared in *Los Angeles Times*, July 4, 2011. Copyright © 2011 by Megham Daum. Used by permission of William Morris Endeavor Entertainment, LLC.

Edward J. Delaney, "Clean," originally appeared in *The Atlantic*, November 2012 issue. Copyright © 2012 by Edward J. Delaney. Used with permission.

Toi Derricotte, "Black Boys Play the Classics," from *Tender* by Toi Derricotte, © 1997. Reprinted by permission of the University of Pittsburgh Press.

John Desmond. From "Flannery O'Connor's Misfit and the Mystery of Evil," Reprinted by permission of Renascence.

Emily Dickinson. Reprinted by permission of the publishers and the Trustees of Amherst College from *The Poems of Emily Dickinson: Reading Edition* by Ralph W. Franklin, Cambridge, Mass.: The Belknap Press of Harvard University Press, Copyright © 1998, 1999 by the President and Fellows of Harvard College. Copyright © 1951, 1955 by the President and Fellows of Harvard College. Copyright © renewed 1979, 1983 by the President and Fellows of Harvard College. Copyright © 1914, 1918, 1919, 1924, 1929, 1930, 1932, 1935, 1937, 1942 by Martha Dickinson Bianchi. Copyright © 1952, 1957, 1958, 1963, 1965 by Mary L. Hampson.

Maureen Dowd, "Silicon Valley Sharknado," *New York Times*, July 8, 2014. Copyright © 2014 The New York Times. All rights reserved. Used under license.

The Economist, "The Misplaced Arguments Against Black Lives Matter," *The Economist*, August 18, 2017. Copyright © 2017 by The Economist. Republished with permission of The Economist; permission conveyed through Copyright Clearance Center, Inc.

John R. Ehrenfeld, "The Error of Trying to Measure Good and Bad," *Flourishing by Design*, January 13, 2015. Copyright © 2015 by Flourishing by Design. Used with permission.

Janet Ellerby, excerpts from *Choice*, eds Karen Bender & Nina de Gramont, (Mac Adam Cage 2007). Used with permission from the author.

Index of Authors, Titles, First Lines, and Key Terms